Lecture Notes of the Institute for Computer Sciences, Social Informatics and Telecommunications Engineering 294

More information about this series at http://www.springer.com/series/8197

Xiangping Bryce Zhai · Bing Chen · Kun Zhu (Eds.)

Machine Learning and Intelligent Communications

4th International Conference, MLICOM 2019
Nanjing, China, August 24–25, 2019
Proceedings

 Springer

Editors
Xiangping Bryce Zhai ⓘ
Aeronautics and Astronautics
of Nanjing University
Nanjing, China

Bing Chen
Aeronautics and Astronautics
of Nanjing University
Nanjing, China

Kun Zhu
Aeronautics and Astronautics
of Nanjing University
Nanjing, China

ISSN 1867-8211   ISSN 1867-822X   (electronic)
Lecture Notes of the Institute for Computer Sciences, Social Informatics
and Telecommunications Engineering
ISBN 978-3-030-32387-5   ISBN 978-3-030-32388-2   (eBook)
https://doi.org/10.1007/978-3-030-32388-2

This Springer imprint is published by the registered company Springer Nature Switzerland AG
The registered company address is: Gewerbestrasse 11, 6330 Cham, Switzerland

Preface

We are delighted to introduce the proceedings of the fourth edition of the 2019 European Alliance for Innovation (EAI) International Conference on Machine Learning and Intelligent Communications (MLICOM), held in Nanjing, China, in August 2019. This conference has brought together researchers, developers, and practitioners from around the world who are leveraging and developing smart green communications.

The 64 revised full papers were carefully selected from 115 submissions. The papers are organized thematically in machine learning, intelligent positioning and navigation, intelligent multimedia processing and security, wireless mobile network and security, cognitive radio and intelligent networking, IoT, intelligent satellite communications and networking, green communication and intelligent networking, ad-hoc and sensor networks, resource allocation in wireless and cloud networks, signal processing in wireless and optical communications, and intelligent cooperative communications and networking. Aside from the high-quality, technical paper presentations, the technical program also featured three keynote speeches, i.e., invited talks. The three keynote speeches were given by Prof. Jiannong Cao from Hong Kong Polytechnic University, SAR China, Prof. Rui Zhang from National University of Singapore, Singapore, and Prof. Chee Wei Tan from City University of Hong Kong, SAR China.

Coordination with the steering chairs, Imrich Chlamtac, Xin Liu, and Xin-lin Huang was essential for the success of the conference. We sincerely appreciate their constant support and guidance. It was also a great pleasure to work with such an excellent Organizing Committee team and we thank them for their hard work in organizing and supporting the conference. We are also grateful to conference manager, Karolina Marcinova, for her support and all the authors who submitted their papers to the MLICOM 2019 conference.

We strongly believe that the MLICOM conference provides a good forum for all researcher, developers, and practitioners to discuss all science and technology aspects that are relevant to smart communications. We also expect that the future MLICOM conference will be as successful and stimulating, as indicated by the contributions presented in this volume.

August 2019

Xiangping Bryce Zhai
Bing Chen
Kun Zhu

Conference Organization

Steering Committee

Imrich Chlamtac	Bruno Kessler Professor, University of Trento, Italy
Xin Liu	Dalian University of Technology, China
Xin-Lin Huang	Tongji University, China

Organizing Committee

General Chairs

Bing Chen	Nanjing University of Aeronautics and Astronautics, China
Qihui Wu	Nanjing University of Aeronautics and Astronautics, China
Ekram Hossain	University of Manitoba, Canada

Program Chairs

Kun Zhu	Nanjing University of Aeronautics and Astronautics, China
Xu Chen	Sun Yat-sen University, China

Sponsorship and Exhibit Chairs

Bo Li	Harbin Institute of Technology (Weihai), China
Xin Li	Nanjing University of Aeronautics and Astronautics, China
Jian Xie	Nanjing University of Aeronautics and Astronautics, China

Local Chair

Xiangping Bryce Zhai	Nanjing University of Aeronautics and Astronautics, China

Workshops Chair

Xin Liu	Dalian University of Technology, China

Publicity and Social Media Chairs

Sheng Zhou	Tsinghua University, China
Yanchao Zhao	Nanjing University of Aeronautics and Astronautics, China
Xiaodong Li	Hohai University, China

Publications Chairs

Weijie Xia	Nanjing University of Aeronautics and Astronautics, China
Chunsheng Zhu	University of British Columbia, Canada

Web Chairs

Xiaojun Zhu   Nanjing University of Aeronautics and Astronautics, China
Kai Liu   Chongqing University, China

Co-organizers

Collaborative Innovation Center of Novel Software Technology and Industrialization, China
Jiangsu Computer Society, China

Conference Manager

Karolina Marcinova   EAI – European Alliance for Innovation, Slovakia

Technical Program Committee

Cloud-support Communications

Lin Cui   Jinan University, China
Xiangmao Chang   Nanjing University of Aeronautics and Astronautics, China
Jin Wang   Soochow University, China

Cognitive Radio and Networking

Mu Zhou   Chongqing University of Posts
                    and Telecommunications, China
Weidang Lu   Zhejiang University of Technology, China
Yongliang Sun   Nanjing Tech University, China

Deep Learning in Wireless Networking

Shimin Gong   Shenzhen Institutes of Advanced Technology,
                    Chinese Academy of Sciences, China
Nan Zhao   Dalian University of Technology, China
Yuan Liu   South China University of Technology, China

Machine Learning

Xin-Lin Huang   Tongji University, China
Lin Mei   Harbin Institute of Technology, China
Shui Yu   Deakin University, Australia

Security in Intelligent Communication and Information Systems

Yuhua Xu   PLA Army Engineering University, China
Jiajia Liu   Xidian University, China
Bin Li   Beijing University of Post and Telecommunications, China

Smart Internet of Things

Siyuan Zhou	Hohai University, China
Shu Shen	Nanjing University of Posts and Telecommunications, China
Cunlai Pu	Nanjing University of Science and Technology, China

Smart Multimedia Communications

Guanyu Gao	Nanyang Technological University, Singapore
Xujie Li	Hohai University, China
Ran Wang	Nanjing University of Aeronautics and Astronautics, China

Smart Network Estimation

Honggui Han	Beijing University of Technology, China
Cuili Yang	Beijing University of Technology, China
Qiang Jia	Jiangsu University, China

Smart Unmanned Vehicle Technology

Weiwei Wu	Southeast University, China
Xinye Cai	Nanjing University of Aeronautics and Astronautics, China
Jingjing Gu	Nanjing University of Aeronautics and Astronautics, China

Contents

Smart Internet of Things

Machine Learning I

Machine Learning II

Applications of Machine Learning I

Applications of Machine Learning II

Wireless Networks

High-Dimensional Data Anomaly Detection Framework Based on Feature Extraction of Elastic Network

Yang Shen[1], Jue Bo[1], KeXin Li[2(✉)], Shuo Chen[1], Lin Qiao[1], and Jing Li[2]

[1] State Grid Liaoning Electric Power Supply Co., Ltd., Shenyang 110004, Liaoning, China
[2] College of Computer Science and Technology, Nanjing University of Aeronautics and Astronautics, Nanjing 210016, Jiangsu, China
kexinli@nuaa.edu.cn

Abstract. Although appropriate feature extraction can improve the performance of anomaly detection, it is a challenging task due to the complex interaction between features, the mixture of irrelevant features and relevant features, and the unavailability of data tags. When conventional anomaly detection methods deal with the problem of anomaly detection of high dimensional data, the performance of anomaly detection will be degraded due to the existence of irrelevant features. This paper proposed a method of feature extraction and anomaly detection for high dimensional data based on elastic network, which can filter irrelevant features and improve the accuracy and efficiency of anomaly detection. In this paper, an outlier scoring method was used to score the outliers of the original data, and then outliers and the original data were input into the elastic network for sparse regression. After feature extraction of elastic network, those irrelevant features to abnormal data are ignored, thus reducing the dimension of data. Finally, high-dimensional data are detected efficiently according to extracted features. In the experimental stage, we used the high-dimensional anomaly dataset provided by ODDS to detect the performance of the proposed method based on AUC detection accuracy, ROC curve, feature number, convergence speed and other indicators. The results show that the proposed method not only can effectively extract the features related to high-dimensional anomaly data, but also the detection accuracy of outliers has been greatly improved.

Keywords: Elastic network · Feature extraction · Anomaly detection · High-dimensional data · Data mining

1 Introduction

An outlier is a data point that is significantly different from the remaining data. Hawkins defined [1] an outlier as "An outlier is an observation which deviates so much from the other observations as to arouse suspicions that it was generated by a different

X. B. Zhai et al. (Eds.): MLICOM 2019, LNICST 294, pp. 3–17, 2019.
https://doi.org/10.1007/978-3-030-32388-2_1

mechanism." Outliers are also referred to as abnormalities, discordant, deviants, or anomalies in the data mining and statistics literature. In most applications, the data is created by one or more generating process, which could either reflect behaves unusually, it results in the creation of outliers. Therefore, an outlier often contains useful information about abnormal characteristics of the systems and entities that impact the data generation process. The recognition of such unusual characteristics provides useful application-specific insights. Some examples are as follows:

Intrusion detection systems [2]: In many computer systems, different types of data were collected about the operation system calls, network traffic, or other user actions. This data may show unusual behavior because of malicious activity. The recognition of such activity was referred to as intrusion detection.

Credit-card fraud [3]: Credit-card fraud had become increasingly prevalent because of greater ease with which sensitive information such as a credit-card number can be compromised. In many cased, unauthorized use of a credit card may show different patterns, such as buying sprees from particular locations or very larger transactions. Such patterns can be used to detect outliers in credit-card transaction data.

Power equipment failure: the effective analysis of distribution network data can not only meet the needs of planning and design, production scheduling, load forecasting, power quality and power decision-making, but also solve the problems faced by the future distribution network, such as accurate energy supply, power demand side management and decentralized energy storage. With the deep integration of sensor measurement, information communication, analysis and decision-making technology and modern distribution network data, massive heterogeneous, polymorphic and high-dimensional load data are produced. Abnormal data in these data can often reflect the operation status of power equipment. If abnormal data can be detected in time, the status of power equipment can be timely diagnosed, thus avoiding unnecessary losses.

The so-called high-dimensional data refers to the data with a high number of dimensions, which can reach hundreds of thousands or even higher. There are two main difficulties in analyzing and processing high-dimensional data. First, the problem that Euclidean distance cannot be used. In low dimensional space, Euclidean distance can be used to measure the similarity between data, but in high dimensional space, distance does not make much sense. The second is the disaster of dimensionality. With the increasing dimensionality, many of the conventional outlier detection methods do not work very effectively. This is an artifact of the well-known curse of dimensionality. In high-dimensional space, the data becomes sparse, and the true outliers become masked by the noise effects of multiple irrelevant dimensions, when analyzed in full dimensionality. Besides, the amount of calculations for analyzing and processing these data will increase rapidly, and the cost of calculation will increase exponentially. Therefore, in the process of abnormal data detection for high-dimensional data, the following challenges are encountered: (i) High-dimensional data usually contain features unrelated to abnormal data. These extraneous features will affect the anomaly detection of high-dimensional data. (ii) As the increase of data dimension, relevant concepts in low-dimensional space such as neighbor, distance and nearest neighbor will be unusable, resulting in the inability to use conventional abnormal data detection methods based on distance, density and so on. Conventional abnormal data detection methods tend to use all the features of the data in the process of abnormal data detection, but these data often contained many useless features, which will lead to a large deviation in the results of abnormal data detection. In addition, there may be redundancy between different features to reduce the efficiency of anomaly detection. At present, there are many methods for detecting abnormal data, such as probabilistic statistical model-based method [4, 5], linear model-based method [6–8], and nearest-neighbor based method [9–11]. However, due to the computational complexity and efficiency of these methods, it will take a lot of cost to carry out anomaly detection on high-dimensional data, and they do not perform particularly well in the aspect of anomaly detection effect of high-dimensional data. Therefore, these methods cannot be simply applied to the anomaly detection of high-dimensional data, which needs to be processed and then detected by these methods.

Filtering irrelevant features can significantly improve the detection effect and performance of abnormal data detection, but it is more difficult to extract and remove irrelevant features when there is a complex interaction between features. At present, there is little work on feature extraction in abnormal data detection. Most feature extractions were devoted to classification, regression and clustering [12–14]. In terms of outlier feature extraction, most of the existing work focuses on unbalanced classification [15] and data categories, without considering how to filter the data used in the abnormal data detection process. Elastic network [16] is a sparse regression model. In the process of sparse regression, the purpose of feature extraction is achieved by continuously shrinking the coefficients of the relevant features. If there is a correlation between features, elastic network will select two or more features from them, so as to ensure that the selected features are the most representative and correct. In this paper, elastic network was used to extract features from high-dimensional data so as to filter irrelevant features to reduce the impact of irrelevant features on abnormal data detection. A high-dimensional anomaly data detection model based on multi-level feature extraction is constructed by elastic network. The model firstly used the existing anomaly detection approach score the original data, and then the abnormal scores and the original data were input to the elastic network so as to extract the features which were most related to the abnormal data. Then the extracted features were used to score the abnormal data again, and the above steps are continuously cycled until the loss function of elastic network will no longer reduced. Finally, the abnormal score obtained by the above process is integrated to obtain the final detection result. According to the work done in this paper, the main contributions are as follows:

(i)   A feature extraction method of high-dimensional data based on elastic network was proposed. In the process of extracting features of abnormal data by elastic network, the outlier score was used as target feature and the original data was used as predictors to filter irrelevant features of high-dimensional data.

(ii) A cyclic feature extraction and anomaly data detection model was constructed. In the process of detection abnormal data, we use isolated forest algorithm [17] to achieve outlier scoring of data, and then use elastic network and outlier score to extract features of high-dimensional data. According to the loss function of elastic network, the above process is looped until the loss function of elastic network is no longer reduced, so as to realize the loop feature extraction and anomaly detection of abnormal data.

(iii)   A multi-level detection method for anomaly data based on elastic network was proposed. At each level, different thresholds were set for the abnormal score calculated by the isolated forest method, so as to select different data input into the elastic network, and then extract more feature related to abnormal data. Finally, the extracted features and detection results of each level are integrated.

2 Related Work

Abnormal data detection [18] is a very popular research direction in the field of data mining. The general problem of identifying outliers has been addressed by very different methods that can be roughly classified as global versus local outlier models. A global outlier model [5] leads to a binary decision of whether or not a given object is an outlier. A local outlier method rather assigns a degree of outlierness to each object. Such an "outlier factor" is a value characterizing each object in "how much" this object is an outlier. Many classical approaches for abnormal data detection, such as probabilistic and statistical models [2] for outlier detection, linear models for outlier detection [6], proximity-based outlier detection [8], etc. were used to process low dimensional data. The earliest methods for outlier detection were rooted in probabilistic and statistical models and data back to the nineteenth century. These methods were proposed well before the advent and popularization of computer technology and were therefore designed without much focus on practical issues such as data representation or computational efficiency. Nevertheless, the underlying mathematical models are extremely useful and have eventually been adapted to a variety of computational scenarios. The main assumption in linear models is that the normal data is embedded in a lower-dimensional subspace. Data points that do not naturally fit this embedding model are, therefore regarded as outlier. In the case of proximity-based methods, the goal is to determine specific regions of the space in which outlier points behave very differently from other points. On the other hand, in linear methods, the goal is to find lower-dimensional subspaces, in which the outlier points behave very differently from other points. This can be viewed as an orthogonal points of view to clustering- or nearest-neighbor methods, which try to summarize the data horizontally (i.e., on the rows or data values) rather than vertically (i.e., on the columns or dimensions). Proximity-based techniques define a data point as an outlier when its locality (or proximity) is sparsely populated. The proximity of a data point may be defined in a variety of ways, which are subtly different from one another but are similar enough. The most common ways of defining proximity for outlier analysis are as follows:

Distance-Based [7]: The distance of a data point to its k-nearest neighbor (or other variant) is used in order to define proximity. Data points with large k-nearest neighbor distance are defined as outliers. Distance-based algorithms typically perform the analysis at a much more detailed granularity that the other two methods. On the other hand, this greater granularity often comes at a significant computational cost.

Density-Based [8]: The number of other points within a specified local region (grid region or distance-based region) of a data point, is used in order to define local density.

These local density values may be converted into outlier scores. On kernel-based methods or statistical methods for density estimation may also be used. The major difference between clustering and density-based methods is that clustering methods partition the data points, whereas density-based methods partition the data space.

Cluster-Based [9]: The non-membership of a data point in any of the clusters, its distance from other clusters, the size of the closest, or a combination of these factors are used to quantify the outlier score. The clustering problem has a complementary relationship to outlier detection problem in which points either belong to cluster or they should be considered outliers.

Clearly, all these techniques are closely related because they are based on some notion of proximity (or similarity). The major difference is at the detailed level of how this proximity is defined. These different ways of defining outliers may have different advantages and disadvantages. In many cases, the distinctions between these different classes of methods become blurred when the outlier scores are defined using more than one of these concepts. Many real data sets are very high dimensional. In some scenarios, real data sets may contain hundreds of thousands of dimensions. With increasing dimensionality, many of the conventional outlier detection methods do not work very effectively. This is an artifact of the well-known curse of dimensionality. In high-dimensional space, the data becomes sparse, and the true outliers become masked by the noise effects of multiple irrelevant dimensions, when analyzed in full dimensionality. A main cause of the dimensionality curse is the difficulty in defining the relevant locality of a point in the high-dimensional case. For example, proximity-based methods define locality with the use of distance functions on all the dimensions. On the other hand, all the dimensions may not be relevant for a specific test point, which also affects the quality of the underlying distance functions. For example, all pairs of points are almost equidistant in high-dimensional space. The challenges arising from the dimensionality curse are not specific to outlier detection. It is well known that many problems such as clustering and similarity search experience qualitative challenges with increasing dimensionality. The subspace-based outlier detection method can process high-dimensional data. The more successful method [19] is to identify multiple related subspaces for candidate anomaly data, and then combine the results from different subspaces to create a more robust collection-based ranking. While many collection methods for subspace analysis have achieved great success, the particularly difficult case is that a large number of dimensions are weakly related (but not very relevant), and even more dimensions are not locally relevant.

3 The Proposed Approach

Aiming at the problem that the abnormal data detection of high-dimensional is faced with hundreds of thousands dimensions and irrelevant features, this paper proposed a cyclic feature extraction method based on elastic network to filter irrelevant features, so as to reduce the dimension of data and realize the detection of abnormal data in a lower data space. The method included three parts: isolated forest anomaly score calculation function, anomaly selection function based on Chebyshev theorem and elastic network feature extraction. In step t of the method, for a given data set $X = \{X_1, X_1, \cdots, X_N\}$, each data has M features, namely $X_i = (x_1, x_2, \cdots, x_M)$ and their abnormal score vector $S^{t-1} \in R^N$. The abnormal selection function $H(S^t)$ is used to select a part of the data as the possible abnormal data C^t, and then the selected abnormal data and abnormal scores S^t are input into the elastic network feature selection module ElN^t to obtain the mean square error (mse^t for short) and the features F^t which are most relevant to the abnormal score. Then, the selected features were used to perform the abnormal score by the isolated forest abnormal score calculation function G. Repeat the above steps until the mean square error of the current elastic network is greater than the previous mean square error, i.e. $mse^{t+1} > mse^t$ or the current detection accuracy is less than the initial detection accuracy, i.e. $AUC(S^t) < AUC(S^0)$. The overall framework of the method is shown in Fig. 1.

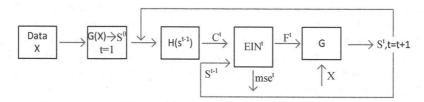

Fig. 1. The framework of feature extraction and anomaly detection by elastic network

Among them, the G is a kind of abnormal scoring function, we used isolated forest to calculate the abnormal score in this paper. H is a selection function, and some possible abnormal data is selected according to the abnormal score S^t. ElN^t is elastic network, which mainly performs feature extraction of high-dimensional data. When the above loop is completed, we integrate the sequence of abnormal score to obtain the final abnormal scores, so as to realize the anomaly detection of high-dimensional data.

3.1   The Isolated Forest Abnormal Score Calculation Function G

Isolated forest uses the idea of random sampling to randomly sample the original data set and then constructs the isolated tree on the sub-samples. This method considers that the data close to the root node is more likely to be abnormal data. The process of constructing the isolation tree, calculating the path length and calculating the abnormal score is as follows:

iTree: The construction method of isolation tree is similar to the construction process of binary tree. Suppose T is a node of the isolation tree, then T is either an external node with no child nodes or an internal node with two children nodes. On each sub-sample randomly select a data attribute as separate property, and put all the data in the root node, and then randomly selected a data as the segmentation value (the value between maximum and the minimum) from the selected attribute. The value about selected attribute of the data less than the segmentation value was divided into left child node, otherwise was divided into right child node. Do the same for the left child and right child until all the data is on the external node or at the height specified in the isolation tree.

Path Length: The path length $h(x)$ of the data record x refers to the number of edges x traverses an iTree from the root node until the traversal is terminated at an external node.

Outlier Score: After constructing the isolation tree, calculate the path length of the data x in different isolation trees, then obtain the average value and normalize the abnormal score by the normalization factor. The specific calculation method is:

$$E(h(x)) = \sum_{i=1}^{n} h_i(x)/n \tag{1}$$

$$s(x, \varphi) = 2^{-\frac{E(h(x))}{c(\varphi)}} \tag{2}$$

Where, $s(x, \varphi)$ represent the outlier score; $h_i(x)$ represents the path length of the data x in the i-th iTree; $E(h(x))$ represents the average path length of the data x in all the iTree; $c(\varphi)$ denotes the normalization factor, which means the maximum path length in the corresponding iTree, and $c(\varphi)$ is calculated as:

$$c(\varphi) = \begin{cases} 2H(\varphi - 1) - \frac{2(\varphi-1)}{\varphi}, & \text{if } \varphi > 2 \\ 1, & \varphi = 2 \\ 0, & \text{otherwise.} \end{cases} \tag{3}$$

Where, φ is sample size, $H(\varphi)$ is the harmonic function that can be calculated by $ln(\varphi) + 0.5772156649$ (Euler constant).

3.2 Anomaly Selection Function Based on Chebyshev's Theorem $H(S^t)$

After getting the abnormal score of the data, we think that the abnormal score is a random variable X, and then we calculate the expectation and variance of X. Suppose the expectation of X is $E(X) = \mu$ and the variance is $D(X) = \sigma^2$. According to Chebyshev's inequality, we can get:

$$P(X - \mu \geq \varepsilon) = \begin{cases} \leq \frac{\sigma^2}{\sigma^2 + \varepsilon^2}, & \text{if } \varepsilon > 0 \\ \geq 1 - \frac{\sigma^2}{\sigma^2 + \varepsilon^2}, & \text{else} \end{cases} \tag{4}$$

In the above formula, taking $\varepsilon = \alpha\sigma$, we can get:

$$P(X \geq \mu + \alpha\sigma) = \begin{cases} \leq \frac{1}{1+\alpha^2}, & \text{if } \varepsilon > 0 \\ \geq 1 - \frac{1}{1+\alpha^2}, & \text{else} \end{cases} \tag{5}$$

Through the above formula, we obtain the range of values corresponding to the event $|X \geq \mu + \alpha\sigma|$. In this paper we considered that the X corresponding to the event $|X \geq \mu + \alpha\sigma|$ is a possible abnormal data. The anomaly data is usually different from the distribution of most data or data that is significantly deviated from most data objects, and is only a small part of the entire data set. Therefore, we control the number of elements in the candidate set of outliers by the value of α. After obtaining the outlier scores S^t at different stages, the average value μ and the variance of the abnormal scores are calculated as σ^2, and the outliers are composed of data satisfying the following conditions:

$$C = \{(X_i, S_i)|H(S_i, \alpha) \geq 0\}, \forall X_i \in X, S_i \in S \tag{6}$$

Where $H(S_i, \alpha) = S_i - \mu - \alpha\sigma$, the value of α is 1.732 in the loop (i.e., the upper bound for false positive in η is 25%).

3.3 Elastic Network Feature Extraction Function ELN^t

Elastic network is a linear regression model that combines lasso regression and ridge regression and uses L_1 and L_2 norm as prior regular terms for training. The combination of lasso and ridge regression allows the learning of a sparse model with a small number of non-zero parameters, thereby ignoring those features with zero parameters to realize feature selection. Elastic network can realize automatic selection of variables and continuous contraction at the same time. When there is a high correlation between multiple variables or features, elastic network will select two or more of them, so as to preserve as many features as possible while selecting features. In addition, based on the lasso regression, the elastic network draws on the idea of ridge regression to achieve the double contraction of the correlation coefficient, which makes the elastic network inherit the stability of the ridge regression. In this paper, the process of feature extraction of high-dimensional data using elastic network is based on the possible anomaly data C^t. The process takes the abnormal score as the target feature and the original feature of the data as predictor, so as to find those relevant feature about the abnormal score. The sparse regression principle of elastic network for high-dimensional data is:

$$EIN(C, \lambda) = argmin_\omega \left(\frac{1}{2N} \sum_{i=1}^{N} \left(S_i - X_i^T \omega \right)^2 + \lambda * a\|\omega\|_1 + \frac{a(1-\lambda)}{2}\|\omega\|_2 \right) \tag{7}$$

Among them, N is the number of possible abnormal data records, ω is the regression coefficient, λ is a non-negative regularization parameter, and the value of a determines the relationship between elastic network and lasso regression and ridge regression. With the gradual increase of the parameter λ, the number of non-zero coefficients in the regression coefficient obtained by the Eq. (7) will gradually decrease, thus achieving the purpose of feature extraction. After obtaining the coefficient of regression, we can get the feature most relevant to the outlier score by (8), and realize the feature extraction:

$$F = \{X_i|\omega_i \neq 0, 1 < i < M\} \tag{8}$$

The selection of the parameter λ in an elastic network is crucial, and an inappropriate λ can lead to over-fitting or under-fitting. For this problem, we use 10 cross-validation methods on the possible outlier C^t to select the optimal λ to minimize the mean square error.

When the loop elastic network execution ends, it is assumed that a total of T times are performed. In this process, a series of abnormal scores $S^t \in R^N, 1 \leq t \leq T$ and mean square error $mse^t, 1 \leq t \leq T$ are generated.

(1) Firstly sum the mean square error mse^t, and get $SUM = \sum_{i=1}^{T} mse^i$;
(2) Subtract SUM from each mean square error mse^t to get a new error term $MSE^t, 1 \leq t \leq T$ i.e. $MSE^t = SUM - mse^t$;
(3) Normalizing the MSE^t to obtain a series of weights $\omega^t, 1 \leq t \leq T$, i.e.

$$\omega^t = \frac{MSE^t}{\sum_{i=1}^{T} MSE^i}, 1 \leq t \leq T \tag{9}$$

(4) Unitize the outlier score S^t, i.e.

$$\tau^t = \frac{S^t}{||S^t||}, 1 \leq t \leq T \tag{10}$$

(5) Calculate the final outlier score.

$$S\_L = \frac{1}{T} \sum_{t=1}^{T} \omega^t \tau^t \tag{11}$$

4 Multi-level Feature Extraction and Outlier Detection Model Based on Elastic Network

In the process of feature extraction and anomaly detection of high-dimensional data using elastic network, the value of α in the anomaly data selection function $H(S^t)$ based on Chebyshev's theorem is fixed. The fixed value of α limited the range of feature extraction and the effect of anomaly detection to a certain extent. Here, we extend the above high-dimensional data anomaly detection method based on elastic network loop feature extraction to build a multi-level feature extraction and anomaly detection model. In each layer, the value of α can be adjusted according to the detection results of the previous level. If the detection result is too small of upper level, adjusting the value of α in this layer appropriately, and then using elastic network for feature extraction and anomaly detection again. The specific framework is shown in the Fig. 2:

In the above model, the α value of the lower layer is appropriately adjusted according to the detection result of the upper layer, thereby adjusting the feature extraction and abnormality detection of the layer. After obtaining the detection result of each level $S\_L_i, 1 \leq i \leq n$, the results of each level are combined and averaged to obtain the final abnormality detection result.

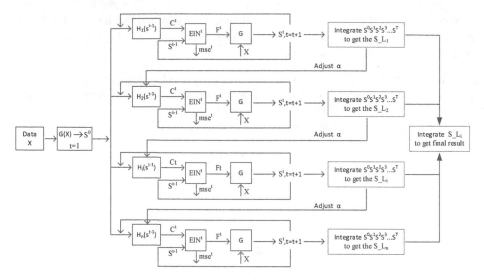

Fig. 2. The framework of multi-level elastic network feature extraction and outlier detection

5 Experiment

In order to verify the effectiveness of the proposed method, we selected 12 of the detection data sets of high-dimensional abnormal data provided by ODDS and built the experimental environment based on MATLAB 2018b, 64-bit Win7 operate system, Inter (R) Core (TM) i5-4460 3.20 GHz and etc. The method in this paper is compared with the methods of LOF, CARE and iForest by using ROC curve, detection accuracy AUC, extracted feature number, elastic network convergence speed and other indicators. In the LOF algorithm, the number of nearest neighbors K is set to 6. The number of isolated trees in the iForest method is set to 100, and the sampling size φ is set to 256. The specific information of the data set used in the experiment is as follows (Table 1):

(1) Extracting feature numbers
Noise or extraneous features are usually included in high-dimensional data, which are often ignored by conventional outlier detection methods. The high-dimensional abnormal data detection model based on elastic network firstly extracted the features of high-dimensional data in the process of anomaly detection. The characteristics of elastic network sparse regression were used to filter the noise irrelevant to the abnormal score, so as to screen out the features most related to the abnormal score, and then the high-dimensional data was abnormal detected by using these selected features. The feature extraction of the elastic network in this paper is to establish the correlation between the original data features and the anomaly scores, and then carry out sparse regression for the corresponding coefficients. In the procedure of regression, while keeping the objective function unchanged, the coefficients of corresponding features are constantly reduced until the coefficient of some features is 0, so as to achieve the filtering of irrelevant features. When there is a correlation between the original features,

Table 1. The information of experiment dataset

Dataset	Instance	Dimension	Outlier (%)
AID362	4279	117	60 (1.4%)
aPascal	12695	64	176 (1.3%)
Annthyroid	6832	6	534 (7.42%)
Arrhythmia	452	274	66 (15%)
Pima	768	8	268 (35%)
Cardio	1831	21	176 (9.6%)
L-Recognition	1600	32	100 (6.25)
Mnist	7603	100	700 (9.2%)
Musk	3062	166	97 (3.2%)
Optdigits	5216	64	150 (3%)
Satellite	6435	36	2036 (32%)
Sateimage-2	5803	36	71 (1.2%)

Table 2. Extracted feature number

Dataset	Original feature number	Extract feature number
AID362	117	64
aPascal	64	46
Annthyroid	6	3
Arrhythmia	274	131
Pima	8	4
Cardio	21	9
L Recognition	32	18
Mnist	100	58
Musk	166	48
Optdigits	64	28
Satellite	36	23
Sateimage-2	36	22

the elastic network will select two or more of them to retain the features related to the abnormal score as much as possible. In addition, elastic networks retain the stability of ridge regression and can always produce effective solutions. In this paper, elastic network is used to extract the feature number of different data sets, as shown in Table 2:

Elastic network realizes feature extraction of high dimension data by shrinking the relevant regression coefficient while keeping the training error as small as possible. When the parameter λ in the elastic network is increasing, the coefficient of the feature will gradually decrease until it reaches 0, thus achieving the purpose of feature extraction. Here we show the contraction process of different feature coefficients in the process of feature extraction by elastic network. Each curve in the graph represents trajectory of each independent variable (feature), where the abscissa is the value of λ,

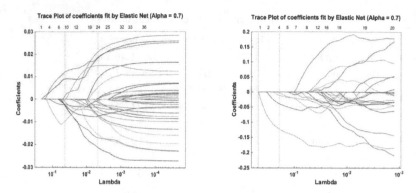

Fig. 3. The contraction process of coefficients during feature extraction

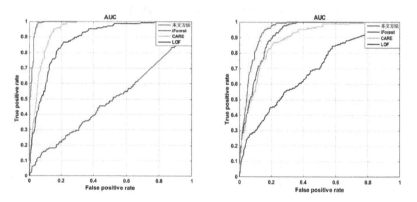

Fig. 4. The ROC curve on Cardio and Mnist dataset

and the ordinate is the size of the coefficient. We can see that the coefficient of the independent variable is decreasing to zero with the increase of the λ (Fig. 3).

(2) Detection accuracy

The ROC curve and the value of AUC can well reflect the detection accuracy. Generally, the larger of the area under the ROC curve (i.e., AUC), the higher the detection accuracy will be. Intuitively speaking, if one ROC curve can completely cover another ROC curve, the detection accuracy of the covered curve will be lower than the other one. We compared the detection accuracy of different abnormal data detection algorithm by the ROC curves and AUC values in the experimental data set. For the ROC curve, we selected the Cardio and Mnist datasets as representatives, and the results from the other datasets were compared by the area under the ROC curve (AUC) (Fig. 4).

It can be seen from the above ROC curve that the ROC curve of the proposed method in the data set Cardio and Mnist can completely cover the ROC curve of other methods, which indicates that the proposed method is superior to other methods in terms of detection accuracy. In order to fully demonstrate that the effect of the method

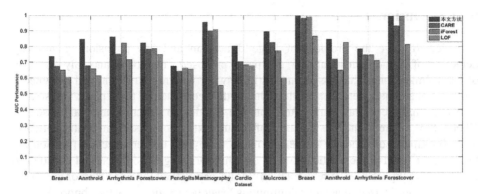

Fig. 5. The comparison of AUC of different outlier detection methods

is better than other methods compared with the method in this paper, we have compared it on other data sets. The results are shown in the Fig. 5. We use AUC as an indicator to measure the accuracy of detection. It can be seen from the AUC histogram that the detection accuracy of the proposed method is improved on several other data sets.

(3) Convergence rate of elastic network
In this paper, the anomaly detection of high-dimensional data is realized through the looping execution of isolated forest anomaly scoring function, the anomaly selection function based on Chebyshev theorem and the feature extraction of elastic network. In the feature extraction process of the elastic network, the value of λ was selected by cross validation because the improper selection of λ would lead to over-fitting or under-fitting of the elastic network. The green circle and dotted line locate the λ with minimum cross-validation error. The blue circle and dotted line locate the point with minimum cross-validation error plus one standard deviation. In the selection of the elastic network parameter λ, we select the green circle and dotted line located λ to ensure the minimum cross-validation dislocation. The change of training error of elastic network with λ is shown in the Fig. 6:

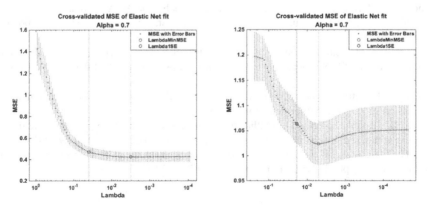

Fig. 6. The training error of the elastic network varies with lambda

6   Conclusion

In order to solve the problem of large dimension and low precision in anomaly detection of high-dimensional data, this paper proposed a method of anomaly detection of high-dimensional data based on elastic network feature extraction, and designed a multi-level anomaly detection model. The method consisted of three parts: the isolated forest anomaly score calculation function, the function to select the anomaly based on Chebyshev theorem and the function of feature extraction based on elastic network. The abnormal score and the outlier data selected by the outlier selection function are taken as the input of the elastic network, and the sparse regression is carried out so as to achieve the purpose of feature extraction. In this paper, the loop execution of the above three functions is used to achieve continuous feature extraction, and the abnormal score generated in the above process is integrated to obtain the final abnormal score, so as to realize the anomaly detection of high-dimensional data. The experimental results show that the proposed method can effectively realize feature extraction in the process of anomaly detection of high-dimensional data, and the accuracy and efficiency of anomaly detection were improved.

Acknowledgement. The research was supported by the State Grid Liaoning Electric Power Supply CO., LTD, and we are grateful for the financial support for the "Key Technology and Application Research of the Self-Service Grid Big Data Governance (SGLNXT00YJJS1 800110)".

References

1. Hawkins, D.M.: Identification of Outliers, 1st edn, pp. 11–12. Springer, Berlin (1980). https://doi.org/10.1007/978-94-015-3994-4
2. Li, L., Hao, Z., Peng, H., et al.: Nearest neighbors based density peaks approach to intrusion detection. Chaos Solitons Fractals **110**, 33–40 (2018)
3. Wang, C., Dong, H.: Credit card fraud forecasting model based on clustering analysis and integrated support vector machine. Cluster Comput. **16**, 1–6 (2018)
4. Gao, X., Fang, Y.: Penalized weighted least squares for outlier detection and robust regression (2016)
5. Chen, T., Martin, E., Montague, G.: Robust probabilistic PCA with missing data and contribution analysis for outlier detection. Comput. Stat. Data Anal. **53**(10), 3706–3716 (2009)
6. Aggarwal, C.C.: Linear models for outlier detection. In: Aggarwal, C.C. (ed.) Outlier Analysis, pp. 75–99. Springer, New York (2013). https://doi.org/10.1007/978-1-4614-6396-2_3
7. Dalatu, P.I., Fitrianto, A., Mustapha, A.: A comparative study of linear and nonlinear regression models for outlier detection (2016)
8. Pérez, B., Molina, I., Peña, D.: Outlier detection and robust estimation in linear regression models with fixed group effects. J. Stat. Comput. Simul. **84**(12), 2652–2669 (2014)
9. Xu, H., Mao, R., Liao, H., et al.: Closest neighbors excluded outlier detection. In: Online Analysis & Computing Science, pp. 105–110. IEEE (2016)

10. Liu, J., Wang, G.: Outlier detection based on local minima density. In: IEEE Information Technology, Networking, Electronic & Automation Control Conference, pp. 718–723. IEEE (2016)
11. Vwema, P., Yadava, R.D.S.: Fuzzy c-means clustering based outlier detection for SAW electronic nose. In: Convergence in Technology, pp. 513–519. IEEE (2017)
12. Bolón-Canedo, V., Sánchez-Maro, N., Alonso-Betanzos, A.: Recent advances and emerging challenges of feature selection in the context of big data. Knowl.-Based Syst. **86**, 33–45 (2015)
13. Du, L., Shen, Y.D.: Unsupervised feature selection with adaptive structure learning (2015)
14. Yu, K., Wu, X., Ding, W., et al.: Scalable and accurate online feature selection for big data. ACM Trans. Knowl. Discovery Data **11**, 16 (2015)
15. Zhang, C., Wang, G., Zhou, Y., et al.: Feature selection for high dimensional imbalanced class data based on F-measure optimization. In: International Conference on Security. IEEE (2018)
16. Feng, S., Sen, P.N.: Percolation on elastic networks: new exponent and threshold. Phys. Rev. Lett. **52**(3), 216–219 (1984)
17. Liu, F., Ting, K.M., Zhou, Z.H.: Isolation-based anomaly detection. ACM Trans. Knowl. Discovery Data **6**(1), 1556–4681 (2012)
18. Yang, Z., Zheng, Y., Gao, Y., et al.: Abnormal data detection for an e-business using object-oriented approach. In: Integration and Innovation Orient to E-Society, vol. 1 (2007)
19. Zimek, A., Gaudet, M., Campello, R.J.G.B., et al.: Subsampling for efficient and effective unsupervised outlier detection ensembles. In: Proceedings of the 19th ACM SIGKDD International Conference on Knowledge Discovery and Data Mining. ACM (2013)

A Drone Formation Transformation Approach

Chenghao Jin, Bing Chen$^{(\boxtimes)}$, and Feng Hu

College of Computer Science and Technology,
Nanjing University of Aeronautics and Astronautics, Nanjing, China
{jinchenghao,cb_china,huf}@nuaa.edu.cn

Abstract. In the process of performing fixed-wing drone formations, it is usually necessary to perform a variety of formations according to mission requirements or environmental changes. However, performing such formation transformation during formation flight will face many technical challenges. In this paper, we first present a Six-Tuple State Coherence (STSC) model for fixed-wing drone formations, and based on this model, the definition of drone formation transformation is given. Moreover, a drone formation change algorithm (DFCA) is proposed. When a new formation is needed, the master node first adopts the centralized Hungarian algorithm to determine the location allocation scheme of the new formation, and then each node calculates and executes dubins paths distributedly to maintain the consistency of the formation yaw angle, and finally adjusts the speed of the nodes to ensure the formation of STSC. The prototype system conforming to DFCA algorithm is implemented on OMNET++ platform, and numerous simulation experiments are carried out. The experimental results show the feasibility of the DFCA algorithm and show that it can control the drone formation transformation at a lower cost.

Keywords: Drone formation · Formation transformation · Consistent state · OMNET++ platform

1 Introduction

Recently, enormous progress has been made in the field of cooperative control for multi-drone system. A formation composed of inexpensive small drones can replace expensive multi-functional large drones and be more efficient and reliable when executing missions. Formation in multi-drone system is critical to efficient execution of coordinated tasks such as surveillance [2,8], investigation [14], search and rescue [11], measuring [12], aerial photography [15]. When the number of drones is limited, the formation control can cover a larger continuous areas or shorten the time to execute the task. However, in the process of executing the above tasks, the drones often need to change the formation to adapt to the battlefield environment and mission requirements. [1] proposed a method to

© ICST Institute for Computer Sciences, Social Informatics and Telecommunications Engineering 2019
Published by Springer Nature Switzerland AG 2019. All Rights Reserved
X. B. Zhai et al. (Eds.): MLICOM 2019, LNICST 294, pp. 18–31, 2019.
https://doi.org/10.1007/978-3-030-32388-2_2

avoid obstacles by changing formation. [19] proposed a method of switching attack or defensive formations according to the battlefield environment.

The coordinated control of multi-drone formation has always been a hot issue for industry and academia. Master-follower is currently the most common method of formation control, but since it is a centralized method, once the master fails, the entire formation system will be paralyzed [5,10,18]. In [7], a distributed formation control method based on the master-follower model is proposed, in which each drone can respond to emergencies by switching the following, leading, and accelerating modes. [4,6] proposed a behavior-based formation control method. Each drone in formation divides its actions into collision avoidance, obstacle avoidance, target search and formation maintenance based on its perception of the external environment. The output of each drone is weighted by various behaviors. In fact, the above method must require that each drone in the formation be consistent in speed, heading, position, etc. In some studies, to simplify computation, the drone is abstracted into a freely moving particle [3,13,16,17], but this model is too idealistic, especially for fixed-wing drones. In the real world, the drone needs to move along a smooth trajectory of suitable curvature and cannot turn at any angle. Therefore, this is also a problem that must be considered when the formation changes. In [9], a novel distributed cascade robust feedback control approach is proposed for formation and reconfiguration control of a team of vertical takeoff and landing (VTOL) unmanned air vehicles (drones). But this method assumes that the drone can move and hover freely, so it is only suitable for quadrotor. But this method assumes that the drone can move and hover freely, so it is not suitable for fixed-wing drones. In [17], a B-spline-based formation control method is proposed to maintain the formation by ensuring that the spline parameters of each drone are consistent. This method supports the formation change. However this method ignore the constraints on the heading and speed of each drone in the formation. Although these drones can reach the formation at the current moment, if their headings and speeds are different, the formation will not be maintained at the next moment.

To address the above mentioned challenges, we propose a Six-Tuple State Coherence (STSC) model for the fixed-wing drone formation transformation problem, and based on the STSC model, the drone formation transformation problem is formulated as a two-process problem: the first process completes the location assignment from the old formation to the new formation; the second process is to program the route with time, speed and heading constraints for each drone during formation transformation. In addition, we propose a Drone formation change algorithm (DFCA) for this two-process problem. Firstly, Hungarian algorithm is used to solve the optimization problem of position allocation in formation transformation, which minimizes the cost of formation transformation. Then each drone independently solves the formation change route based on the dubins model. Our salient contributions are summarized as follows:

– We propose an STSC model to define the state of each drone in the formation after the formation transformation, and then formulates the drone formation transformation as a two-process problem.
– Based on the STSC model, the DFCA algorithm is proposed. When changing to the new formation, the master drone firstly uses the Hungarian algorithm to determine the location assignment scheme of the old formation to the new formation, and then the drones distributedly calculate and execute the dubins path to make the yaw angle of each drone consistent, next, adjust the speed of each drone to ensure the STSC.
– We validate our proposed algorithm with a drone formation and evaluate its performance by extensive simulation in OMNeT++ simulation environment. Moreover, our proposed DFCA algorithm was compared with an existing deterministic programming approach. Simulation results show that our proposed algorithm performs significantly better than the existing works on both formation transformation cost and communication cost.

The rest of paper is organized as follows. We present the system model and some related solution concepts in Sect. 2. The DFCA algorithm for drone formation is detailed in Sect. 3. Section 4 reports our performance evaluation results in which we compare our approach to an existing approach. Finally, we draw a conclusion in Sect. 5.

2   System Model

2.1   STSC Model

The drone is an autonomous agent, whose state can be defined as a six-tuple, $P(t, X, Y, Z, \theta, v)$, which is located at position $[X, Y, Z]^T$ at a time t, the yaw angle is θ (the angle between the fuselage and north) and the speed is v. For a drone that flies from the starting point $P_s(t_s, X_s, Y_s, Z_s, \theta_s, v_s)$ to the end point $P_t(t_t, X_t, Y_t, Z_t, \theta_t, v_t)$, the path plan will produce one or more path r connection points P_s and P_t, which can be expressed as follows:

$$P_s(t_1, X_s, Y_s, Z_s, \theta_s, v_s) \xrightarrow{r} P_t(t_2, X_t, Y_t, Z_t, \theta_t, v_t) \tag{1}$$

Extend multiple drones into a formation consisting of N drones, which is a collection of agents. One of the drones is the master, which is the logical center of the formation, mastering and controlling the formation and route; others are slaver, which can communicate with the master, receive the instructions of master and control themselves according to the instruction and their own situation. The starting point P_{si} and the target point P_{ti} of each drone in the formation are connected by a path r_i, and the formation track is a set satisfying the form of (2):

$$\bigcup_{i \in N} P_{si}(t_1, X_{si}, Y_{si}, Z_{si}, \theta_{si}, v_{si}) \xrightarrow{r} P_{ti}(t_2, X_{ti}, Y_{ti}, Z_{ti}, \theta_{ti}i, v_{ti}) \tag{2}$$

STSC is a necessary condition for multiple drones to form a formation. It means that the six-tuple $P(t, X, Y, Z, \theta, v)$ of each drone in the formation should be consistent, that is, at the same time t, the headings are the same, the speeds v are equal, and the relative positions of each drone are unchanged.

2.2 Definition of Formation

Assume that a reference path is planned for the formation before the mission, which is denoted by $R^{ref}(t)$. The reference path $R^{ref}(t)$ is a curve in the global coordinate system that is changed with time t. $R^{ref}(t_0) = [x(t_0), y(t_0), z(t_0)]^T \in R_G^3$ represents a way point in the route at t_0. We use the tangent coordinate system of the reference path $R^{ref}(t)$ to describe the relative position between the drones and the formation of the drones [17]. In particular, we define a tangent coordinate system using coordinate axes parallel to the following vectors:

$$
\begin{aligned}
T(t) &= \frac{dR^{ref}}{dt}, \\
N(t) &= T(t) \times (-g), \\
B(t) &= N(t) \times T(t),
\end{aligned} \tag{3}
$$

where, $T(t)$ is the tangent to the reference trajectory, g is the acceleration due to gravity, $N(t)$ is the normal to the plane containing the tangent and the vertical direction, and (t) is the bi-normal vector. We define the orthogonal rotation matrix $M(t) \in R^{(33)}$

$$
M(t) = [\frac{T(t)}{\|T(t)\|}, \frac{N(t)}{\|N(t)\|}, \frac{B(t)}{\|B(t)\|}], \tag{4}
$$

So that the transformation between the local tangent frame and the global frame is given by,

$$
\begin{bmatrix} X \\ Y \\ Z \end{bmatrix} = f_t \left(\begin{bmatrix} X \\ Y \\ Z \end{bmatrix} \right) = M(t) \begin{bmatrix} X \\ Y \\ Z \end{bmatrix} + R^{ref}(t), \tag{5}
$$

then the drone formation can be defined as $F_i = \{t, \theta, v_i, r_{i\_1}, r_{i\_2}, ..., r_{i\_n}\}$, where $r_{i\_j} = [x_{i\_j}, y_{i\_j}, z_{i\_j}]^T$ is the relative position of drone j in formation F_i (indicated by the tangent coordinate system F). θ_i and v_i are the formation heading and formation speed respectively, and the heading of the formation is the tangential direction of the current position, $dR^{ref}(t)/dt$.

Since the necessary condition for the configuration of the drone formation is the STSC, the heading and speed of each drone in the formation are the same as the formation course and formation speed, and the relative position remains unchanged. Therefore, according to the formation model F_i, the six-tuple of each drone in the formation can be obtained by:

$$
P_{i\_j}(t_{i\_j}, X_{i\_j}, Y_{i\_j}, Z_{i\_j}, \theta_{i\_j}, v_{i\_j}), j = 1, 2, ..., N
$$

$$t_{i\_j} = t_i;$$

$$\theta_{i\_j} = \theta_i = \frac{dR^{ref}(t_i)}{dt_i};$$

$$v_{i\_j} = v_i; \tag{6}$$

$$\begin{bmatrix} X \\ Y \\ Z \end{bmatrix} = f_{t\_i}\left(\begin{bmatrix} X_{i\_j} \\ Y_{i\_j} \\ Z_{i\_j} \end{bmatrix}\right)$$

(6) describes the conversion process, $F_i = \{P_{i\_1}, ..., P_{i\_n}\}$, from formation model to six-tuple set of all drones under STSC conditions.

2.3   Definition of Formation Transformation

During the execution of the mission, the drone formation may need to transform a variety of formations, and the STSC must be satisfied when the formation transformation is completed, as shown in Fig. 1. Assume that the transformation of the formation $F_1 \rightarrow F_2$ needs to be completed. The old formation is $F_1 = \{t_1, \theta_1, v_1, r_{1\_1}, r_{1\_2}, ..., r_{1\_n}\}$, and the new formation is $F_2 = \{t_2, \theta_2, v_2, r_{2\_1}, r_{2\_2}, ..., r_{2\_n}\}$. Through the Eq. (6), the six-tuple $f1$ from the old formation $F1$, $F1 = \{P_{1\_1}, P_{1\_2}, ..., P_{1\_n}\}$ and the six-tuple from the target formation $F2$, $F2 = \{P_{2\_1}, P_{2\_2}, ..., P_{2\_n}\}$ can be obtained. Therefore, the formation transformation of the drone formation can be modeled as follows,

$$P_{1\_i}(t_1, X_{1\_i}, Y_{1\_i}, Z_{1\_i}, \theta_1, v_1) \overset{r_i, \phi_{ij}}{\rightarrow} P_{2\_i}(t_{2\_j}, X_{2\_j}, Y_{2\_j}, Z_{2\_j}, \theta_2, v_2) \tag{7}$$

ϕ is a position distribution matrix, $\phi_{ij} = 1$ indicates $P_{1\_i} \rightarrow P_{2\_j}$ (P_{1_i} is assigned to P_{2_j}), and r_i is a flight path from P_{1_i} to P_{2_j}. Therefore, the solution to Eq. 7 can be divided into the following two processes:

Step 1. Location assignment from old formation to new formation, i.e. solving assignment matrix ϕ;

Step 2. Calculation of flight path r_i for each drone.

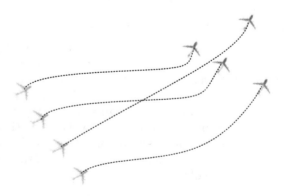

Fig. 1. An example of formation transformation.

3   Our Proposed Formation Transformation Algorithm for Drone Formation

Based on the above definition of drone formation, we propose a DFCA algorithm to calculate the distribution matrix ϕ and flight path r_i. The algorithm first solves the optimization problem to obtain the distribution matrix ϕ through the Hungarian algorithm, and then solves the route r_i of each drone that satisfies the STSC constraint based on the dubins model.

3.1   Location Assignment

According to the definition of the formation transformation, we need to solve the distribution matrix ϕ and the route r_i of each drone. Suppose the formation needs to be transformed from the formation $F1 = \{P_{1\_1}, P_{1\_2}, ..., P_{1\_n}\}$ to the formation $F2 = \{P_{2\_1}, P_{2\_2}, ..., P_{2\_n}\}$. Then, the first step of the formation transformation is to assign a position in $F2$ for each drone in $F1$, that is, to solve the distribution matrix ϕ. Before we solve the distribution matrix ϕ, a cost function is constructed.

$$C\left(P_i, P_j\right) = w_d \left\|\left[X_i, Y_i, Z_i\right]^T - \left[X_j, Y_j, Z_j\right]^T\right\|^2 + w_h \left\|\theta_i - \theta_j\right\|^2 + w_v \left\|v_i - v_j\right\|^2 \tag{8}$$

$C\left(P_i, P_j\right)$ represents the cost of the transformation of the six-tuple from P_i to P_j, which is the weighted sum of the squared differences, and w_d, w_h, w_v are the weights of the items. Our goal is to minimize the total cost of building an initial formation, which is an optimization issue as follows,

$$\min_{\phi} \sum_{i=1}^{n} \sum_{j=1}^{n} \phi_{ij} C\left(P_i, P_{init\_j}\right) \tag{9}$$

This optimization problem is solved using the Hungarian algorithm. The Hungarian algorithm employs a reduction process on the distance matrix, $D_{ij} = C\left(P_{1\_i}, P_{2\_j}\right)$. This reduction process involves minimizing each element of the distance matrix, D_{ij}, through row and column operations. These row and column operations involve adding and subtracting minimum row and column elements, resulting in entries where $D_{ij} = 1$. When this occurs in non-conflicting rows/columns (i.e. unique j for each i), the algorithm terminates, and the assignment matrix, ϕ_{ij}, can be determined. This is done by searching the reduced distance matrix for $D_{ij} = 0$, such that for each i there is a unique j. When this is the case, $\phi_{ij} = 1$, otherwise, $\phi_{ij} = 0$. It is a centralized algorithm that needs to be calculated on the master. The detailed solution process for ϕ is illustrated in Algorithm 1.

3.2   Path Programming

This section describes how to solve the flight path r_i for each drone formation transformation. This method is a distributed algorithm, and each drone is

---

Algorithm 1. Location Assignment

Input: Old formation F1, new formation F2.
Output: ϕ_{ij}.
1: **Get the Six-tuple of each drone in old formation $F1$:**
2: **for** $P_{1\_i} \in F1$ **do**
3: 　　$\theta_{1\_i} = \theta_1$,
4: 　　$v_{1\_i} = v_1$,
5: 　　$[X_{1\_i}, Y_{1\_i}, Z_{1\_i}] = M(t_1)[X_{1\_j}, Y_{1\_j}, Z_{1\_j}] + R^{ref}(t_1)$,
6: 　　$P_{1\_i} \leftarrow [t_1, X_{1\_i}, Y_{1\_i}, Z_{1\_i}, \theta_{1\_i}, v_{1\_i}]$.
7: **end for**
8: 　**Get the Six-tuple of each drone in new formation $F2$:**
9: **for** $P_{2\_i} \in F2$ **do**
10: 　　$\theta_{2\_i} = \theta_2$,
11: 　　$v_{2\_i} = v_2$,
12: 　　$[X_{2\_i}, Y_{2\_i}, Z_{2\_i}] = M(t_2)[X_{2\_j}, Y_{2\_j}, Z_{2\_j}] + R^{ref}(t_2)$,
13: 　　$P_{2\_i} \leftarrow [t_2, X_{2\_i}, Y_{2\_i}, Z_{2\_i}, \theta_{2\_i}, v_{2\_i}]$.
14: **end for**
15: **for** $P_{1\_i} \in F1$ **do**
16: 　　**for** $P_{2\_i} \in F2$ **do**
17: 　　　　Get $C(P_{1\_i}, P_{2\_j})$ by (9).
18: 　　**end for**
19: **end for**
20: $\phi^* = arg\min_\phi \sum_{i=1}^n \sum_{j=1}^n \phi_{ij} C(P_{1\_i}, P_{2\_j})$.
21: **return** ϕ^*.

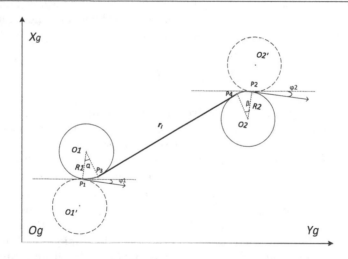

Fig. 2. An example of formation transformation.

executed independently. Assuming $\phi_{ij} = 1$, we will calculate the smoothing of a connection P_{1_i} and P_{2_j} for the drone using the dubins model as shown in Fig. 2. In order to ensure that the route is the shortest to reduce the cost of flight, we make the radius of the two turning circles $R_1 = R_2 = r_{min}$. r_{min} is the minimum turning radius of the drone, which is related to the flying speed and rolling angle of the drone:

$$r_{min} = \frac{v^2}{g * \tan \gamma_{max}} \tag{10}$$

where v is the flight speed of the drone, and γ_{max} is the maximum roll angle of the drone.

Since the transformation of $P_{1\_i} \rightarrow P_{2\_j}$ needs to satisfy the STSC constraint, the dubins model can only satisfy the transformation constraints of the four-tuple of position and velocity (ie, X, Y, Z, θ). Therefore, it is necessary to apply a speed control method based on the dubins model to ensure that each drone can reach the target state at the same time and at the same speed. In order to ensure the same speed before and after formation transformation of drone, that is $v_1 = v_2 = v$. The velocity of each drone needs to converge to V at the same time after the formation transformation process is completed along r_i. Since the formation transformation time $T = t_2 - t_1$, the drone completes the entire formation conversion process at a fixed speed v, and the time required is:

$$T_i = \frac{L_{r_i}}{v} \tag{11}$$

where L_{r_i} is the length of the path r_i. If $T_i < T$, the drone must decelerate to consume redundant time, and if $T_i > T$, the drone must accelerate the flight to compensate for this time difference, besides $T_i - T$ then the drone continues to maintain a uniform speed with v. Figure 3 shows the speed adjustment process of $T_i > T$, that is, the drone needs to accelerate the flight. Assuming that the acceleration during the acceleration of the drone is α_1, and the deceleration is α_2, then the relationship of the speed change is as follows.

$$\frac{1}{2}\left(t'' - t' + T\right) \cdot (v_{max} - v) + vT = L_{r_i},$$
$$v_{max} = v + \alpha_1 \cdot t', \tag{12}$$
$$v = v_{max} + \alpha_2 \cdot \left(T - t''\right)$$

Through (12), the acceleration phase $\left[t_1, t_1 + t'\right]$ and the deceleration phase $\left[t_1 + t', t_2\right]$ can be solved. The case of $T_i < T$ is similar here. The detailed process of solving the route r_i is in Algorithm 2.

4   Simulation

To verify the feasibility of our proposed DFCA algorithm, we first carry out the simulation experiment design, then carry out the simulation experiment, and finally analyze the experimental results.

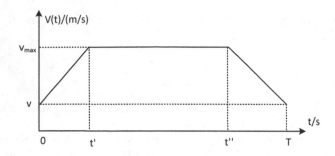

Fig. 3. An example of drone speed adjustment.

Algorithm 2. Path Programming

Input: Six-tuple $P_{1\_i}(t_1, X_{1\_i}, Y_{1\_i}, Z_{1\_i}, \theta_1, v_1)$, $P_{2\_i}(t_{2\_j}, X_{2\_j}, Y_{2\_j}, Z_{2\_j}, \theta_2, v_2)$, initialize time T.

Output: Dubins path r_i, two time for adjusting velocity t' and t''.

1: **Get the dubins route r_i and L_{r_i}:**
2: r_i=dubins.shortest_path(P_{1_i}, P_{2_j}),
3: $L_{r_i} = r_i.length()$.
4: **Velocity adjustment:**
5: $T_i = L_{r_i}/v_i$.
6: **Slow down to consume redundant time:**
7: **if** $T_i < T$ **then**
8:     Get t' and t'' by solving the formula.
9: **end if**
10: **Acceleration to compensate time:**
11: **if** $T_i > T$ **then**
12:     Get t' and t'' by solving the formula.
13: **end if**
14: **No need to adjust the speed:**
15: **if** $T_i = T$ **then**
16:     $t' = 0, t'' = T$.
17: **end if**
18: **return** r_i, t' and t''.

4.1 Simulation Platform

In the process of drone formation flight and formation transformation, the drones need to exchange information continuously, so the communication process between drones must be incorporated into the simulation platform to make the simulation more realistic. In view of the fact that there is no mature drone simulation platform, we choose OMNET++ as the basic environment of the simulation platform. OMNET++ is an open source discrete event simulator with modular, component-based C++ simulation library and framework. In view of the fact that there is no mature drone group simulation platform, we choose OMNET++ as the basic environment of the simulation platform. OMNET++

is an open source discrete event simulator with modular, component-based C++ simulation library and framework. In particular, the link layer model of the INET framework includes PPP, the Internet, and 802.11, as well as wireless and mobile emulation. At the same time, various types of mobile models are integrated in the INET framework, including deterministic movement models and random movement models. Users can build their own mobile models by expanding these mobile models. Based on the INET framework, we built the drone simulation platform shown in Fig. 4. The drone simulation platform includes three modules: communication module, processor module, and mobile module, in which the communication module utilizes the INET framework, and the physical layer mainly adopts the Radio model and the Medium model, the MAC layer uses the Ad hoc-based 802.11 model, the network layer uses the OLSR model, and the transport layer uses the UDP model. The processor module is abstracted as an embedded computer, which mainly runs the DFCA algorithm. Since the Assignment algorithm is a centralized algorithm, it runs only on the master, while the route planning algorithm is a distributed algorithm that runs on all drones. The mobile module is an extension and redesign module based on INET mobile model, which can simulate drone's point flight mode. The interaction between modules during the formation transformation includes:

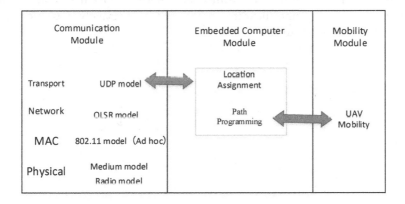

Fig. 4. Drone simulation platform.

Step 1. The processor module of the master sends the location allocation result obtained by the Assignment algorithm to each of the drones in the form of UDP datagram through communication module;

Step 2. The processor module of follower obtains the location allocation result sent by master through communication module, runs Route planning algorithm according to the result, and finally transmits the output result of route planning algorithm to mobile module to control drone movement.

Table 1. Formation parameters.

Parameter	Formation	
	Abreast	Diamond
t	0	35
θ	$\pi/3$	0
v	$20\,\text{m/s}$	0
r_1	$(0, 25)$	$(0, 25)$
r_2	$(0, 75)$	$(0, -25)$
r_3	$(0, -25)$	$(-40, 0)$
r_4	$(0, -75)$	$(40, 0)$

4.2   Simulation Results and Analysis

We designed a simulation experiment to verify the feasibility and performance of the DFCA algorithm. We designed a simulation experiment to verify the feasibility and performance of the DFCA algorithm. The formation consisting of four drones was transformed from the formation 'Abreast' to the formation 'Diamond' (See Fig. 5), and the detailed parameters of each formation are in the Table 1, t, θ, v are time, heading, and speed, respectively, besides r_i is the relative position of each drone.

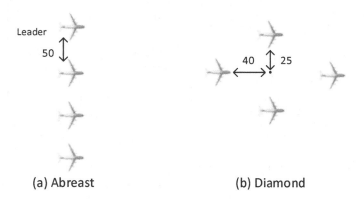

(a) Abreast   (b) Diamond

Fig. 5. Formation definitions of drone position offsets.

In the process of the drone formation changing from Abreast formation to Diamond formation, a path point is collected every 1 s, which forms the path map of drone formation transformation shown in Fig. 6. It can be seen from Fig. 6 that the final drone has reached the target formation and the heading has been adjusted to be consistent. Compared with the method in [17], the DFCA algorithm can complete the formation transformation in a shorter distance to

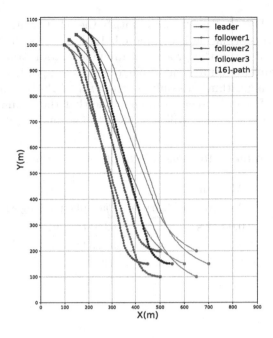

Fig. 6. Path map of drone formation.

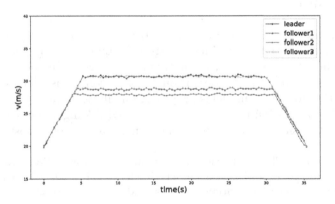

Fig. 7. Speed changing of drone formation.

save resources. Figure 7 shows the speed change diagram of the formation transformation process. In order to ensure that the speed of the formation before and after the formation transformation is constant, each drone has a process of first accelerating and then decelerating. It can be seen from Fig. 7 that the final drone speed converges to 20 m/s. The velocity transformation process can also be seen in Fig. 6, where the points are denser at the initial and end stages and sparse at the intermediate process points because the flight speeds are slower and the intermediate process speeds are faster in the initial and final phases. It can be concluded that the DFCA algorithm can satisfy the STSC constraint when each drone formation transformation is completed. Table 2 shows the time consumed to run DFCA algorithm in the process of drone formation transformation. All our DFCA algorithms are implemented based on C/C++, so they have high efficiency. Assignment algorithm runs only on master, and Path planning algorithm runs on all drones. It can be seen from the table that the running time of each algorithm is in milliseconds and will not affect the normal flight of drone.

Table 2. Running time of DFCA algorithm.

ID	Algorithm	
	Assignment algorithm	Path planning algorithm
Master	0.00098 s	0.0044 s
Follower 1	NULL	0.0033 s
Follower 2	NULL	0.0035 s
Follower 3	NULL	0.0036 s

5   Conclusion

In the process of performing missions, a drone formation usually change from one formation to another according to mission requirements or environmental changes. Aiming at this problem, we firstly presents a STSC model of fixed-wing drone formation, and gives the definition of formation transformation. Then a DFCA algorithm for STSC model is proposed. Finally, the simulation platform is presented. The simulation results show that the DFCA algorithm can complete the formation transformation of the drone formation at a lower cost.

Acknowledgments. This work was supported in part by the National Key Research and Development Program of China, under Grant 2017YFB0802303, in part by the National Natural Science Foundation of China, under Grant 61672283.

References

1. Alonso-Mora, J., Baker, S., Rus, D.: Multi-robot formation control and object transport in dynamic environments via constrained optimization. Int. J. Rob. Res. **36**(9), 1000–1021 (2017)
2. Beard, R.W., Lawton, J., Hadaegh, F.Y.: A coordination architecture for spacecraft formation control. IEEE Trans. Control Syst. Technol. **9**(6), 777–790 (2001)
3. Bogdanowicz, Z.R.: Flying swarm of drones over circulant digraph. IEEE Trans. Aerosp. Electron. Syst. **53**(6), 2662–2670 (2017)
4. Chen, J., Gan, M., Huang, J., Dou, L., Fang, H.: Formation control of multiple euler-lagrange systems via null-space-based behavioral control. Sci. China Inf. Sci. **59**(1), 1–11 (2016)

5. Defoort, M., Polyakov, A., Demesure, G., Djemai, M., Veluvolu, K.: Leader-follower
   fixed-time consensus for multi-agent systems with unknown non-linear inherent
   dynamics. IET Control Theory Appl. **9**(14), 2165–2170 (2015)
6. Dong, X., Yu, B., Shi, Z., Zhong, Y.: Time-varying formation control for unmanned
   aerial vehicles: theories and applications. IEEE Trans. Control Syst. Technol.
   23(1), 340–348 (2015)
7. Duan, H., Qiu, H.: Unmanned aerial vehicle distributed formation rotation control
   inspired by leader-follower reciprocation of migrant birds. IEEE Access **6**, 23431–
   23443 (2018)
8. Jaimes, A., Kota, S., Gomez, J.: An approach to surveillance an area using swarm
   of fixed wing and quad-rotor unmanned aerial vehicles UAV(s). In: Proceedings of
   IEEE International Conference on System of Systems Engineering, pp. 1–6, June
   2008
9. Liao, F., Teo, R., Wang, J.L., Dong, X., Lin, F., Peng, K.: Distributed formation
   and reconfiguration control of VTOL UAVs. IEEE Trans. Control Syst. Technol.
   25(1), 270–277 (2017)
10. Loria, A., Dasdemir, J., Alvarez Jarquin, N.: Leader-follower formation and track-
    ing control of mobile robots along straight paths. IEEE Trans. Control Syst. Tech-
    nol. **24**(2), 727–732 (2016)
11. Mcgee, T.G.: Autonomous search and surveillance with small fixed wing aircraft.
    Ph.D. thesis, Berkeley, CA, USA (2006)
12. Paull, L., Thibault, C., Nagaty, A., Seto, M., Li, H.: Sensor-driven area coverage for
    an autonomous fixed-wing unmanned aerial vehicle. IEEE Trans. Cybern. **44**(9),
    1605–1618 (2014)
13. Pinciroli, C., Beltrame, G.: Swarm-oriented programming of distributed robot net-
    works. Computer **49**(12), 32–41 (2016)
14. Rafi, F., Khan, S., Shafiq, K., Shah, M.: Autonomous target following by unmanned
    aerial vehicles. In: Proceedings of SPIE 6230, Unmanned Systems Technology VIII,
    vol. 6230, May 2006
15. Tokekar, P., Vander Hook, J., Mulla, D., Isler, V.: Sensor planning for a symbiotic
    UAV and UGV system for precision agriculture. In: Proceedings of IEEE/RSJ
    International Conference on Intelligent Robots and Systems, pp. 5321–5326,
    November 2013
16. Wang, Y., Sun, T., Rao, G., Li, D.: Formation tracking in sparse airborne networks.
    IEEE J. Sel. Areas Commun. **36**(9), 2000–2014 (2018)
17. Whitzer, M., et al.: In-flight formation control for a team of fixed-wing aerial vehi-
    cles. In: Proceedings of International Conference on Unmanned Aircraft Systems
    (ICUAS), pp. 372–380, June 2016
18. Xianfu, Z., Liu, L., Feng, G.: Leader–follower consensus of time-varying nonlinear
    multi-agent systems. Automatica **52**, 8–14 (2014)
19. Yu, D., Chen, C.L.P.: Automatic leader-follower persistent formation generation
    with minimum agent-movement in various switching topologies. IEEE Trans.
    Cybern. 1–13 (2018)

The Principle and Design of Separate Fingerprint Identification System

Meng-meng Liu$^{(\boxtimes)}$

School of Teacher Education, Anqing Normal University, Anqing, China
Liumm@aqnu.edu.cn

Abstract. Separate fingerprint identification system (SFIS) is composed of high-speed DSP (digital signal processor), SRAM and Flash chip, whose modules include fingerprint entry, image processing, fingerprint contrasting, fingerprint searching and module storing. SFIS can be an integrated outer equipment with the help of corresponding fingerprint sensor.

Keywords: Separate fingerprint identification system (SFIS) · Upper computer · DSP (digital signal processor)

1 Introduction

1.1 Working Principle

As shown in Fig. 1, Fingerprint processing basically includes two parts: fingerprint logging process and fingerprint matching process. Fingerprint matching includes fingerprint contrasting (1:1) and fingerprint searching (1:N).

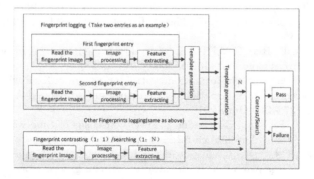

Fig. 1. Working principle diagram.

In the course of fingerprint logging, via fingerprint sensor, the module will record every fingerprint several times. Three times by default, but can be modified into two times at command mode by the corresponding instruction. The

X. B. Zhai et al. (Eds.): MLICOM 2019, LNICST 294, pp. 32–41, 2019.
https://doi.org/10.1007/978-3-030-32388-2_3

following step are processing the recorded image and extracting the features of the image. The distinctive data extracted from the image every time will be first temporarily put in the buffer and then processed. As a result, a group of data representing fingerprint features, which is the template of the fingerprint, can be attained. These data are the basis of fingerprint matching and are stored in the buffer. Finally, the template is stored in the Flash ROM of the module.

In the course of fingerprint matching, module records fingerprint image which requires testing via fingerprint sensor. The feature of the fingerprint image will be extracted. The distinctive data are stored in the buffer, and then will be contrasted with the template generated in the course of fingerprint logging, which will be called 1:1 fingerprint contrasting if the distinctive data are contrasted with one template, or 1:N fingerprint searching if contrasted with several templates.

There are two contrasting results: passing and failure. When the contrasting result is passing, the corresponding template storing serial numbers will be obtained (ID number).

1.2 Main Characters

DSP is the processing center of the fingerprint identifying module. It basically integrates all aspects of fingerprint processing. The advantages are as follows:

(1) Independence: the function of fingerprint entry, image processing, feature extracting, template generating, template storing, fingerprint contracting and fingerprint searching will be finished separately without the control of the upper computer.

(2) Widespread applications: providing two working modes (i.e. Command and Separate) and two module control ports. Four combination states, which are command, contrast, record and delete, appear when the module control ports are powered up. There exist two modes of application scope separate mode application scope, including simple safe box and door lock, and command mode application scope, including more complicated door control, fingerprint IC card terminal, PC online fingerprint recognition and authentication system.

(3) High security: The storage area of fingerprint template in different modes is separated physically and logically. Separate mode is protected by super fingerprint, and command mode by verifying equipment password.

2 Working Mode

There are two working modes of fingerprint identification module: separate mode and command mode. Which mode will be chosen depends on working environment.

2.1 Separate Mode

Separate mode refers to a separate working style of the modules, by which the simple operations, such as fingerprint logging, deleting and contrasting, can be finished. There are three states in separate working mode: logging, fingerprint searching and template deleting.

Fingerprint Logging

Fingerprint logging refers to the process of recording the same fingerprint image several times, generating fingerprint template and storing into module sequentially. If you want to enter one template, you should input fingerprint image three times by default, which means you have to press your finger for three times. But under command mode, you can use system setting command to modify it into two times. As a security measure, the earliest four module logging fingerprints are set as super fingerprints. If there is at least one super fingerprint in the module, fingerprint logging again requires verifying super fingerprint before following fingerprints are entered. The capacity of fingerprint database is 64 fingerprints in separate working mode. When the database is full, new fingerprint will cover the last template and the next direction is given.

Fingerprint Searching

Fingerprint searching refers to recording a fingerprint image that will then be processed and contrasted with all fingerprint templates stored in the module, after which two contrasting results (passing and failure) will be generated. At the fingerprint searching state, the module has dormancy function: if waiting time exceeds 14 s, the module will go into hibernation state. Users can wake up the module by pressing the waking-up pin in the users interface.

Template Deleting

Template deleting refers to deleting thoroughly all fingerprint templates, including super fingerprints in the module. Under the separate working mode, deleting template requires verifying the super fingerprint. After that, the module deletes template and gives direction.

2.2 Command Mode

In the relatively complicated application system, separate working mode can't meet the requirement already. Fingerprint identification modules can work in command working mode. When there is a upper computer (single chip or PC) or network, fingerprint identification and identity authentication management can be finished. Command mode refers to module linking with a upper computer via communication ports, and can finish relatively complicated and complete fingerprint identification management under the control of the upper computers command. Fingerprint identification integrates 28 basic instructions. Combining these basic instructions can satisfy all fingerprint management function in practical applications. The database capacity in command working mode is 512 fingerprints, which are divided into high-end and low-end, with each 256 fingerprints. In the command mode, upper computer should first send a command to the module to verify the equipment password. The module will accept the following command only if the verification is passed.

The differences of the two working modes are shown in Table 1.

Table 1. Differences between two working mode

Project	Separate module	Command module
Working method	Separate	Receive and execute upper computer commands
Fingerprint database capacity	64 pieces	512 pieces
Fingerprint section	Not segmented	High and low two sections (256 pieces each)
OUT2	Pulse width	1800 ms
Automatic power saving management	Yes (contrasting state)	No

3   Communication Protocols

Communication protocols define the exchanging rules between the fingerprint identification module and the upper computer. The communication protocols of the fingerprint identification module include four levels, which are in Table 2.

Table 2. Communication protocol in fingerprint identification module

Level	Content and Role of?protocol
Application layer	Top level. Specifying rules for specific applications. Application oriented. Mainly providing standard interface for application system
Representation layer	Expression of module working status and execution results of instructions
Transport layer	Specifying convention of data structure rules, response and instruction process
Physical layer	Communication medium and connection of module and upper computer. Mechanical, electrical functions and regulation

3.1   Physical Layer

Module provides two kinds of electrical level Serial communication interfaces: 0 communication interface meeting RS-232C electrical level standard and 1 communication interface adopting standard 5 V logical electrical level (TXD, RXD pin).

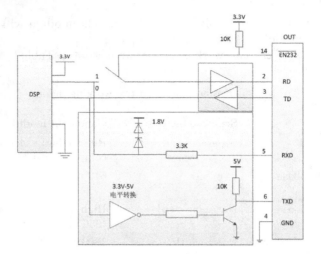

Fig. 2. Serial communication section hardware equivalent diagram.

Auxiliary pin has communication port choosing pin (EN232) and ground (GND). Equivalent Diagram of module inner Serial communication hardware is shown in Fig. 2.

Operating Principle

DSP communicates data with external through serial interfaces. One of them is converted to electrical level fitting for RS232C through 3.3V-RS232C logical level, then linked to the 0 communication port of user interface (that is TD, RD pin). The other is converted to logical electrical level of 3.3 V–5 V, and linked to 1 communication port of user interface (that is TXD, RXD pin).

To prevent interference to the 0 communication port and the 1 communication port, a control pin EN232 is added. When the pin hangs in the air, high level is available, by which the data import of the 0 communication interface is shielded, with only the 1 communication interface available.

When the pin short connects with ground (GND), 0 communication interface is available.

The external links of using serial port are shown in Fig. 3.

Interface Communication Protocols

When the data communicates, the protocol is in semi-duplex asynchronous communication. Porter rate is 57600 bit/s by default.

The porter rate can be set to 115200 bit/s through command. The transferred frame format is 10 bits. One bit 0 is level start bit. 8 bits consist of data and one stop bit and there is no check bit. Frame format is shown in Fig. 4.

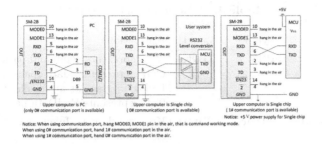

Fig. 3. External connection of serial port diagram.

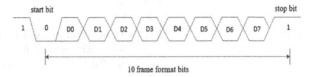

Fig. 4. Frame format.

3.2 Transport Layer

This layer protocol stipulates data structure, sending mechanism and process and convention of directions corresponding to ensure the correctness and reliability of data communication.

Data Flow
The process of data transferring from the module to the upper computer is called upload. The opposite process is called download.

Package Format and Definition
Data transferring adopts the data package of unified structure, whether it is uploaded or downloaded. Data package format is shown in Table 3.

Table 3. Packet format

Packet ID	Address code	Packet length	Packet content	Checksum
	Reserved word		(Instruction/data/parameter)	

The detailed definition of data package is as shown in Table 4.

Table 4. Definition of data packet

Name	Symbol	Length	Instructions
Package ID	PID	1Byte	01H represents command packet 02 H represents data packet and Follow-up packets are available 03 H represents EndData packet
Address code	ADDER	2Bytes	Keep words now, functional extensions later. (0000H)
Packet length	LENGTH	1Byte	Length of packet contents (byte) decided by maximum received buffer size of module, maximum 128 bytes
Packet content			Instructions, data or instruction parameters. Fingerprint feature value and fingerprint template are all data
Checksum	SUJM	2Bytes	Arithmetic cumulative sum from packet ID to the last byte of Packet content. High byte is in front and low byte is in the back, carry more than 2 bytes is ignored

Answer Word

In the course of data communication, module and upper computer check the data transmitted from the other side respectively. In order to confirm the correctness of data transmitted or enable the other side to take remedial measure, verification results to the other side have to be responded. The definition of the answer words are as follows:

(a) The module responds the upper computer

The answer word content package of module responding to upper computer data is 2 bytes, including the answer word and its check. Answer word checking is the original code of answer word. The detailed rules are shown in Table 5.

Table 5. The meaning of module response words

Sequence number	Meaning	Code	Featuring
1	Package received correctly	81H	ACK
2	Package received error, upper computer reissuing packet is required	82H	REIN
3	Package received error, terminate the current packet	83H	EOT
4	Module is busy	84H	BUSY

(b) Upper computer responding module

The answer word content package of upper computer data responding to module is 2 bytes, including answer word and answer word checking. Answer word checking is original code of answer word. The detailed rules are shown in Table 6.

Table 6. The meaning of upper computer response word

Sequence number	Meaning	Code	Featuring
1	Package received correctly	81H	ACK
2	Package received error, upper computer reissuing packet is required	82H	REIN
3	Package received error, terminate the current packet	83H	EOT

Rules of Direction Process

Typical direction process is as shown in Fig. 5.

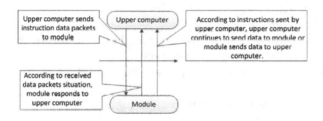

Fig. 5. Typical instruction flow.

3.3   Representation Layer

Representation Layer protocol is the formulation about module working states and direction implementation results. Layers below representation layer only care about transmitting bit stream, while the representation layer cares about grammar and semantics of transmitted information.

Representation Layer protocol divides feedback information into four parts:

(1) States of command completion (success, failure, in progress, await orders etc);
(2) directions types (fingerprint entry, operation, contrasting, searching etc);
(3) results obtained (authentication approved, authentication denied, security level etc);

(4) ID number searched.

This layer protocol stipulates that the application layer obtains module states of implementation and processing results through the states direction.

Module feedback information is through states words (2 bytes).

The first byte was recorded as Ack States (state indication words). The feedback information is mentioned in (1) and (2) above.

The last byte is recorded as Rst States (result indication words). Feedback information is mentioned in (3) above.

4   Module Instruction System

Fingerprint identification module integrates 28 basic instructions, therefore it fits all the fingerprint management functions in practical applications, and can be combined with these basic instructions:

Fingerprint local login (store inside module);
Fingerprint remote login (upload to upper computer through module);
Fingerprint deleting;
Templates download (upper computer download fingerprint templates to module);
Fingerprint searching on site (fingerprint on site for searching and contrasting is recorded through sensor);
Remote fingerprint contrasting (contrasting between fingerprints of recorded on site and specified by upper computer);
Access fingerprint image on site (access fingerprint image on site through upper computer);
Provide storage accessing space to remote users;
Different security level;
Set equipment address code (used for mobile communication) etc.

According to the approach of implementation, instructions are divided into One-way execution and Interactive execution. One-way execution means that the module executes immediately after upper computer commanding and the feedback on implementation results is not necessary.

Fingerprint login, generating feature value, fingerprint contrasting, feature value searching, generating fingerprint image, setting password and verifying password are interactive execution instruction. Interactive execution instruction means that the module must feedback the states and results of this instructions execution after the command from the upper computer is received. Upper computer decides the next operation according to the feedback results.

Data flow control instructions are shown in Fig. 6.

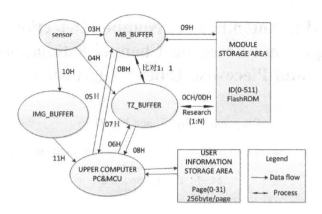

Fig. 6. Data flow control instruction.

5 Conclusion

The principle mentioned in this paper can make up a separate fingerprint identification system or an integrated outer equipment with the help of corresponding fingerprint sensor.

References

1. Jomaa, D., Dougherty, M., Fleyeh, H.: Segmentation of low quality fingerprint images. In: International Conference on Multimedia Computing and Information Technology (MCIT), Sharjah, 2–4 March 2010
2. Iwai, R., Yoshimura, H.: Matching accuracy analysis of fingerprint templates generated by data processing method using the fractional fourier transform. Int. J. Commun. Netw. Syst. Sci. **4**, 24–32 (2011)
3. Perichappan, K.A.P., Sasubilli, S.: Accurate fingerprint enhancement and identification using minutiae extraction. J. Comput. Commun. **5**, 28–38 (2017)
4. Dakhil, I.G., Ibrahim, A.A.: Design and implementation of fingerprint identification system based on KNN neural network. J. Comput. Commun. **6**, 1–18 (2018)
5. Kouamo, S., Tangha, C.: Fingerprint recognition with artificial neural networks: application to e-learning. J. Intell. Learn. Syst. Appl. **08**, 39–49 (2016)
6. Althobaiti, O.S., Aboalsamh, H.A.: An enhanced elliptic curve cryptography for biometric. In: Proceedings of the 7th International Conference on Computing and Convergence Technology, Seoul, 3–5 December, pp. 1048–1055 (2012)
7. Scheirer, W., Bishop, B., Boult, T.: The biocryptographic key infrastructure. In: Proceedings of the IEEE International Workshop on Information Forensics and Security, Seattle, 12–15 December, pp. 1–6 (2010)
8. Maltoni, D., Maio, D., Jain, A.K., Prabhakar, S.: Handbook of Fingerprint Recognition, 2nd edn. Springer, London (2009). https://doi.org/10.1007/978-1-84882-254-2
9. Maio, D., Maltoni, D., Cappelli, R., Wayman, J.L.: Second fingerprint verification competition. In: Proceedings of the 16th International Conference on Pattern Recognition, vol. 3, pp. 811–814 (2002)
10. Schaad, J.: Internet X.509 Public Key Infrastructure Certificate Request Message Format (CRMF). 10.RFC 4211 (Proposed Standard) (2005)

LTE Antenna Port Number Detection Algorithm Based on Channel Estimation and Piecewise Linear Regression

Pengchun Jiang[✉] and Mu Zhou

Chongqing University of Posts and Telecommunications,
Chongqing 400065, China
13368124190@163.com

Abstract. In LTE system, blind detection of traditional antenna port number detection generated a lot of computational redundancy and delay. To solve this problem, an improved detection algorithm based on channel estimation and piecewise linear regression is proposed. This algorithm fits the phase information of channel state and determines the number of antenna ports. The problem of decision error caused by phase jump is solved by piecewise. The theoretical analysis and simulation results show that the proposed algorithm has the advantages of low complexity and delay.

Keywords: LTE system · Antenna port number detection · Cell reference signal · Channel state information · Piecewise linear regression

1 Introduction

Long Term Evolution (LTE), compared with the previous generation communication system, it has the significant increase of data transmission rate and system capacity is largely due to the adoption of Multiple Input Multiple Output (MIMO) technology [1]. The transmitting end can choose to use 1, 2, or 4 antennas to send Physical Broadcast Channel (PBCH) system messages. The User Equipment (UE) performs the PBCH message decoding after the cell search and downlink synchronization operations are conducted [2]. The PBCH system message can be successfully decoded only if the correct antenna port number configuration information is obtained.

The traditional antenna port number blind detection algorithm repeats PBCH decoding by traversing all possible antenna ports. This method requires up to three complete decoding, so the calculation amount is large and the delay is high. In [3], the authors propose a power detection algorithm that estimates the signal-to-noise ratio of possible antenna ports using the antenna reference signal and secondary synchronization code power of each antenna port, and then uses the signal-to-noise ratio to perform threshold decision to obtain the number of antenna ports. However, when the channel signal-to-noise ratio is relatively poor, the performance of the algorithm drops sharply. The correlation detection algorithm proposed by the authors in [4] is based on the repeatable correlation properties of cell reference signals of different antenna ports and extract the data related to the reference signal position corresponding to the antenna

X. B. Zhai et al. (Eds.): MLICOM 2019, LNICST 294, pp. 42–48, 2019.
https://doi.org/10.1007/978-3-030-32388-2_4

port, then determining whether to use the antenna port to transmit data according to the size of the correlation value.

This paper presents an antenna port number detection algorithm based on channel estimation and piecewise linear regression. This algorithm obtains the possible channel state information (CSI) for sending PBCH messages using different antenna ports based on the reference signal. The phase diagram of CSI is fitted by piecewise linear regression algorithm, and then the number of antenna ports used at the sending end is determined.

2 Channel Status Information Extraction

CRS maps the time-frequency resource map according to the antenna port number used to transmit data [5]. When the antenna port $p = 0$ or 1, CRS is located on the first or penultimate OFDM symbol of each slot; when the antenna port $p = 2$ or 3, CRS is located on the second OFDM symbol of each slot.

Channel estimation by comparing the locally generated reference signal with the received reference signal [6]. We assume that the frequency domain information of transmitting end which are not undergone OFDM modulation is $S(j\omega)$ and the baseband signal information is $s(t)$. After $s(t)$ transmitted by the transmitting end, and receiving by the receiving end, the received signal $r(t)$ is obtained as

$$r(t) = A \cdot s(t + \Delta t)e^{j\Delta \omega t} + n \tag{1}$$

where A is the amplitude gain during channel transmission, Δt is transmission delay, $\Delta \omega$ is frequency offset, n is Gaussian white noise, which is ignored for simplicity. By the OFDM demodulation [7], $r(t)$ can be transformed into

$$R(j\omega) = A \cdot e^{j(\omega - \Delta \omega)\Delta t}S[j(\omega - \Delta \omega)] \tag{2}$$

Then, the channel estimation [8] is obtained as

$$H(j\omega) = R(j\omega)/S(j\omega) = \frac{A \cdot e^{j(\omega - \Delta \omega)\Delta t}S[j(\omega - \Delta \omega)]}{S(j\omega)} \tag{3}$$

3 Piecewise Linear Regression Algorithm

The theoretical regression model [9] of the linear regression equation is:

$$Y_i = \beta_0 + \beta_1 X_i + \varepsilon_i \tag{4}$$

where i is the sample point sequence, Y_i is the explained variable, X_i is the explanatory variable, ε_i is the random error term, β_0 and β_1 are the regression coefficients.

Define N as the number of sample points, $\bar{X}$ as the average of X_i and $\bar{Y}$ as the average of Y_i. Obtain the regression coefficient solution expression as:

$$\beta_1 = \frac{\sum\limits_{i=1}^{N} (X_i - \bar{X})(Y_i - \bar{Y})}{\sum\limits_{i=1}^{N} (X_i - \bar{X})^2} = \frac{\sum\limits_{i=1}^{N} X_i Y_i - N\overline{XY}}{\sum\limits_{i=1}^{N} X_i^2 - n\bar{X}^2} \tag{5}$$

$$\beta_0 = \bar{Y} - \beta_1 \bar{X} \tag{6}$$

The absolute average error is:

$$\bar{\varepsilon} = \frac{\sum\limits_{i=1}^{N} |\varepsilon_i|}{N} = \frac{\sum\limits_{i=1}^{N} |\beta_0 + \beta_1 X_i - Y_i|}{N} \tag{7}$$

According to the linear regression equation, the random error ε_i can be calculated, and the mean of the absolute error $\bar{\varepsilon}$ can be obtained. After threshold γ decision, whether the antenna port is equipped with CRS or not can be determined, and finally the number of antenna ports can be determined.

$Y(k)$ represents the estimated phase value of the channel at sampling point k. In this paper, by comparing the average error $\bar{\varepsilon}$ of different antenna ports with the size of the preset threshold γ, we determine whether the current antenna ports are equipped with CRS. The four antenna ports are judged in the order given in Fig. 1, and finally the number of antenna ports used at the transmitter is determined. The specific processing steps of the whole decision process are as Fig. 1.

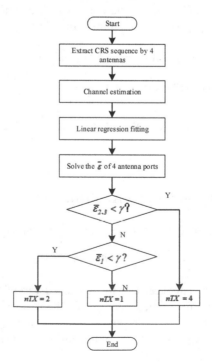

Fig. 1. Flow chart of antenna port number decision

4 Piecewise Linear Regression Algorithm

4.1 Verify Piecewise Linear Regression Fit Performance

This section simulates the generation of LTE downlink signals according to specific signal parameters. The specific parameters are shown in Table 1:

Table 1. Simulation parameter settings.

System parameters	Parameter value
Number of transmit antenna ports	1/2/4
Number of receiving antenna ports	1
bandwidth/MHz	20
Frequency offset/Hz	100
Delay/Ts	0.5
Signal to noise ratio/dB	0
Channel model	AWGN

In the process of simulation verification, a decision error occurs due to a large phase jump of the discrete point, as shown in the left subgraph of Fig. 2. It is necessary to add a mutation decision, when the different of phase value which between the current sampling point and the next sampling point reaches a certain threshold, the second stage of fitting is performed, as shown in the right subgraph of Fig. 2.

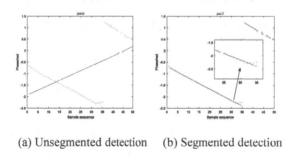

(a) Unsegmented detection   (b) Segmented detection

Fig. 2. Unsegmented/segmented detection comparison chart

Figures 3, 4 and 5 shows the case where the sender uses single antenna and two antennas and four antennas to transmit data. When channel estimation is performed using the correct antenna port, the phase value of the channel estimation will form a relatively concentrated arc under the action of frequency offset and phase offset, as shown in the port 0 subgraph of Fig. 4(a). In Fig. 4(b), the red discrete point represents the phase value of the received signal, and the blue line represents the fitted line of the discrete point phase after piecewise linear filter. The phase dispersion point can be well matched when the phase changes regularly. After the simulation test, the threshold γ is generally in the range of 0.2 to 0.6. In this paper, the value of γ is 0.4.

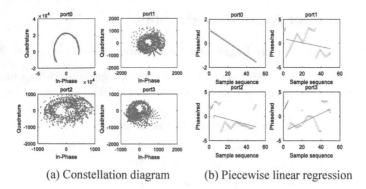

(a) Constellation diagram   (b) Piecewise linear regression

Fig. 3. Single antenna constellation and phase fitting diagram

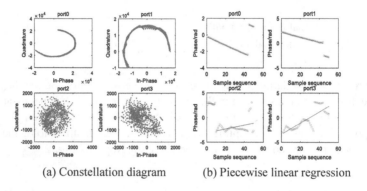

(a) Constellation diagram   (b) Piecewise linear regression

Fig. 4. Two antenna constellation and phase fitting diagram (Color figure online)

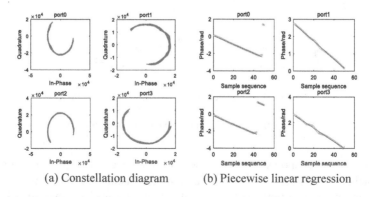

(a) Constellation diagram   (b) Piecewise linear regression

Fig. 5. Four antenna constellation and phase fitting diagram

According to the measured data sent by two antenna ports, verification can be obtained that $\bar{\varepsilon}_0 = 0.0624$, $\bar{\varepsilon}_1 = 0.0763$, $\bar{\varepsilon}_2 = 0.6445$, $\bar{\varepsilon}_3 = 0.7247$. According to the process of Fig. 1, the threshold decision is made, and the number of antenna ports can be correctly solved as two.

4.2 Algorithm Detection Performance Comparison

Section 4.1 has verified the availability of the algorithm when the frequency offset is 100 Hz. This section adds the power detection algorithm and the correlation detection algorithm to the comparison, and adds the frequency offset to 500 Hz and 1000 Hz. If the PBCH message can pass the CRC check, it is determined that the antenna port detection is successful. The detection success rate is shown in Fig. 6.

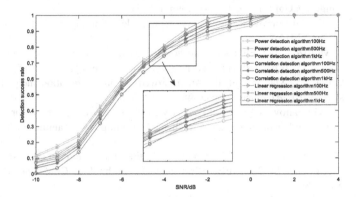

Fig. 6. Comparison of success rates under different frequency offsets

Taking the case of SNR of −3 dB as an example, after the frequency offset is increased from 100 Hz to 500 Hz, the detection success rate of this algorithm is reduced by 1.1%, and the correlation and power detection are reduced by 1.78% and 1.81%, respectively. So the proposed algorithm is more robust. Success rate of piecewise linear regression algorithm detection is always higher than the others. Therefore, the piecewise linear regression algorithm in this paper has more resistance to frequency deviation, better robustness and higher detection success rate than the other two algorithms.

5 Piecewise Linear Regression Algorithm

This paper proposes an antenna port number detection algorithm based on linear regression of channel estimation values. The algorithm uses the channel estimation value through the linear regression equation matching method to determine the number of antenna ports, which solves the problem of the antenna port number decision error caused by the phase mutation of the sampling point of the channel estimation value for fitting. Theoretical and simulation results prove the detection algorithm based on channel estimation has lower complexity performance and better anti-frequency offset performance. The detection of antenna port number directly affects channel estimation and channel decoding, so it is of great significance to study it in detail.

References

1. Liu, K., Tao, C., Liu, L., et al.: Asymptotic analysis for low-resolution massive MIMO systems with MMSE receiver. China Commun. **15**(9), 189–199 (2018)
2. Nassralla, M.H., Mansour, M.M., Jalloul, L.M.A.: A low-complexity detection algorithm for the primary synchronization signal in LTE. IEEE Trans. Veh. Technol. **65**(10), 8751–8757 (2016)
3. Chen, F., Chen, B., Wang, D.: Design and realization on the number of antennas in LTE system. J. Chongqing Univ. Posts Telecommun. (2013)
4. Jiang, Q., Wei, S.: An improved antenna port number detection algorithm for LTE system. Telecommun. Eng. (2016)
5. Davysov, A., Morozov, G.: Enhanced interference cancellation of cell-specific reference signals for LTE-A. In: IEEE Vehicular Technology Conference, pp. 1–5 (2015)
6. Wang, Y., Zhang, X., Xiao, L., et al.: An improved channel estimation method for LTE downlink system. IEEE Antennas Propag. 480–484 (2016)
7. Bochkov, G.N., Gorokhov, K.V., Kolobkov, A.V.: Demodulation algorithms for the OFDM signals in the time- and frequency-scattering channels. Radiophys. Quantum Electron. **59**(1), 1–21 (2016)
8. Baghaki, A., Champagne, B.: Joint frequency offset, time offset, and channel estimation for OFDM/OQAM systems. In: 2015 IEEE 82nd Vehicular Technology Conference (VTC2015-Fall), pp. 1–5 (2018)
9. Ennouri, K., Ayed, R.B., Triki, M.A., et al.: Multiple linear regression and artificial neural networks for delta-endotoxin and protease yields modelling of Bacillus thuringiensis. Biotech **7**(3), 187 (2017)

Topology Sensing in Wireless Networks by Leveraging Symmetrical Connectivity

Zitong Liu[1], Jiachen Sun[2], Feng Shen[1], Guoru Ding[2(✉)], and Qihui Wu[1]

[1] Key Laboratory of Dynamic Cognitive System of Electromagnetic Spectrum Space, Ministry of Industry and Information Technology, College of Electronics and Information Engineering, Nanjing University of Aeronautics and Astronautics, Nanjing 211106, China
zt_liu@126.com, sfjx_nuaa@163.com, qihuiwu2014@sina.com
[2] College of Communications Engineering, Army Engineering University, Nanjing 210007, China
sun_jiachen@outlook.com, dr.guoru.ding@ieee.org

Abstract. With the popularization of wireless networks, the role of machine intelligence is becoming more and more important, where the core is that the network needs to make its own decisions through learning. Topology sensing is a fundamental issue in the field of network intellectualization, but most of the related existing studies have focused on wired networks, while the characteristics of wireless networks are relatively few investigated. In this paper, a wireless channel-oriented topology sensing method based on Hawkes process modeling is proposed for the wireless network with symmetrical connectivity. Simulation are carried out to demonstrate that how to combine wireless channel with Hawkes process and how to further process the results to improve performance.

Keywords: Topology sensing · Symmetrical connectivity · Hawkes process · Wireless channel

1 Introduction

Research on intelligent analysis of network behavior, dynamic analysis of network topology and real-time analysis of key nodes/links can realize automatic identification of network nodes, dynamic analysis of network connectivity and automatic generation of network topology. Traditional network topology sensing usually requires a lot of prior information, such as operating mode and network protocol. However, considering reconnaissance on the wireless network of adversary Unmanned Aerial Vehicle (UAV), we are more concerned about the information inside the network, which is difficult to obtain for an observer outside the network. Therefore, topology sensing with limited information is what we need to do next.

In [1], it introduces the background, methods and applications of graph topology sensing from a macro perspective and points out that learning-based approach is the

© ICST Institute for Computer Sciences, Social Informatics and Telecommunications Engineering 2019
Published by Springer Nature Switzerland AG 2019. All Rights Reserved
X. B. Zhai et al. (Eds.): MLICOM 2019, LNICST 294, pp. 49–57, 2019.
https://doi.org/10.1007/978-3-030-32388-2_5

development trend of topology sensing. Reference [2] aims at identifying network connections by modelling the information transmission process as Granger Causality (GC) and puts forward the method of time window to solve the problem of data fusion. Dynamic Causality Models (DCMs) is proposed in [3] to model interactions among neuronal populations, which can be extended to the field of communication. Hawkes process has only recently been applied to topology sensing, [4, 5] use it to recognition connection and present a method named Low Cost Paths for Acyclic Graphs (LCPAG) to discover event chains. However, the above works have their limitations: First, a clear physical model considering wireless channel has not been formulated. Second, the application conditions are so harsh that they unable to adapt to complex real scenarios.

Thus, improvement and extension on the Hawkes are made in response to the above problems. The main contributions of this paper are summarized as follows:

- We formulated a physical model for external topology sensing considering wireless channels.
- Using threshold setting and symmetry, we proposed a wireless channel-oriented topology sensing method based on Hawkes process.
- We not only presented topology sensing simulation of virtual data, but also proved performance by actual database.

The rest of this paper is organized as follows. Section 2 introduces the system model. In Sect. 3, a wireless channel-oriented topology sensing method based on Hawkes process is proposed by using threshold and symmetry. Then, in Sect. 4, we give the simulation results to prove the effectiveness of the algorithm. In addition, the conclusions and future prospects are mentioned in Sect. 5.

2 System Model

2.1 Network Physical Model

As shown in the Fig. 1, we formulate the physical model of the whole process as follows:

Target. As an external observer of the network, how to restore the network topology through effective algorithm under the condition of limited data, so as to get the key node information of the network.

Assumptions for Simplifying the Problem. There are only two kinds of information available to external observer: the node that transmits the data and the time when the transmission takes place. The information transmission channel within the network is an ideal channel, i.e. channel fading is not considered. The information transmission channel outside the network is AWGN channel without considering the influence of distance. For a long enough period of time, all links are used several times.

Process Description. The network S is an unknown wireless network, and the sensor O is an external observer. It monitors the transmission of information in the network S from $t = 0$. Once the information transmission is monitored, the corresponding event n_i and time t_i are automatically recorded. In the end, we can get two one-to-one corresponding sequences. The sequence of the originator is called the set of events, and the sequence of the recording time is called the set of times. Through the corresponding calculation of these initial data, we can get the interconnection of the network nodes.

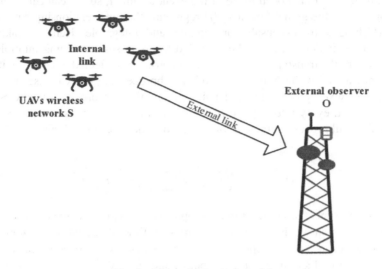

Fig. 1. Network physical model

2.2 Wireless Channel Model

There are two wireless channels in this problem, as shown in Fig. 1: One is the transmission channel of information within the network, and the other is the channel through which information is monitored by external observers outside of the network. For the first channel, because the target network we want to know is mostly used in military, such as UAV group communication network, we have reason to believe the high reliability of the network link. In order to simplify the problem, we do not consider the fading of this channel, as we said in the hypothesis. For the second channel, since the external observer listens in private without the permission of the internal network, it is likely to be subject to various external interference, so the fading of this channel cannot be ignored. As an exploration, we complete the simulation of AWGN channel without considering the distance.

2.3 Network Mathematical Model

Hawkes process is a point process which depends on autoregressive past events. Its main idea is that the transmission rate of an event at any time is a function of the recent events in the process [5].

For an event, in a case which has given t_k, the transmission rate of the event is

$$\lambda(t) = \mu(t) + A \sum_{k=1}^{K} \gamma(t - t_k), \tag{1}$$

which can also be called Conditional Intensity Function (CIF) [5]. The parameter $\mu(t) \geq 0$ is the basic rate of the event, or the rate of innovation; the parameter $A \geq 0$ indicates the degree of self-motivation of the event, that is, how much influence the event at time t_k has on the occurrence of the event at time t, so we can call it the self-motivation matrix; the kernel function $\gamma(t)$ represents the time relationship between the events, which is known, causal, non-negative and integrable. Here we take it as $\gamma(t) = e^{-t}$. This model can easily be extended to processes containing multiple sub-processes, where the transmission rate of one subprocess is affected not only by its own behavior, but also by the behavior of other subprocesses. We can use the multi-dimensional Hawkes process to model the communication process in wireless networks, and regard every information transmission in the network as a subprocess. For process with N subprocesses, the CIF of the ith subprocess can be obtained by formula (1) as

$$\lambda_i(t) = \mu_i + \sum_{j=1}^{N} A_{ij} \sum_{k \in K_j} \gamma(t - t_k), \tag{2}$$

in which K_j represents the event set in jth subprocess, μ_i represents the basic rate of the ith subprocess, which we think is not changing with time, A_{ij} quantifies how much the ith subprocess reacts to jth subprocess, $A_{ij} = 0$ represents the occurrence of the jth subprocess has no effect on the ith subprocess, and $A_{ij} > 0$ represents that the occurrence of the jth subprocess will lead to the temporary increase of the occurrence probability of the ith subprocess. We call it the influence matrix [5].

3 Topology Sensing Methods in Wireless Channels

3.1 Determination of Hawkes Process Parameters

In many cases, parameters μ_i and A_{ij} cannot be known beforehand, so we need to use mathematical tools to reasonably infer the parameters according to the observed values in a certain period of time to find the most realistic parameters. Here we use the maximum likelihood estimation method to determine μ_i and A_{ij} in $t \in [0, T]$, the negative log-likelihood function of the ith subprocess [5] is

$$L_i(\mu, A) = \int_0^T \lambda_i(t) dt - \sum_{K \in K_i} log \lambda_i(t_k). \tag{3}$$

Maximum likelihood function requires us to minimize this convex function. There are many ways to choose. Through practice, we find that the quasi-Newton method is simple and effective, so we finally use quasi-Newton method in the program.

3.2 Threshold and Symmetry

Using the influence matrix A obtained by Hawkes process and maximum log-likelihood function, redundant links can easily be generated due to a little interference. At this time, we can set a threshold to reduce redundant links, which can achieve self-adaptation by analyzing the preliminary simulation results. However, we must admit that it is contradictory to find real links and reduce redundant links. We need to find a balance between the two things according to different application scenarios and requirements.

Considering the cooperative communication in the scenario of UAVs, links usually have no direction. Therefore, the influence matrix should be symmetrical, using which we can simply optimize the results. When A_{ij} & $A_{ji} > 0$, we think there is a connection, which we call the "and" rule; when $A_{ij} | A_{ji} > 0$, we think there is a connection, which we call the "or" rule. Selecting the "and" rule will cause some real links not to be found, while the "or" rule will cause link redundancy.

4 Performance Evaluation

4.1 Basic Simulation Setup

In the simulation, we first set up a simple tree network topology. The network has 25 nodes, including 5 root nodes and 20 leaf nodes. We do not consider the communication between the nodes and themselves. The true physical topology is shown in Fig. 2.

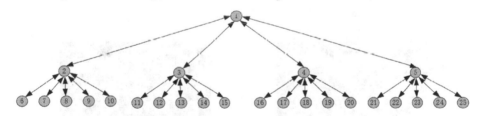

Fig. 2. True physical topology

Because the simulation tool we use is MATLAB, we cannot really restore the transmission of network node information. Firstly, we use the true CIF to weigh the sub-processes, so as to generate the ideal set of times and the ideal set of events. In order to explore the influence of AWGN channels on the performance of Hawkes process, we first simulate the channel and calculate its correct detection probability P_d and false alarm probability P_f. Then we filter the original data by P_d, and supplement the original data by P_d. Finally, we can get the initial data under the channel.

4.2 Simulation Result

As shown in Fig. 3, the simulation results are given when SNR = 10, $\lambda = 20$ (decision threshold of AWGN channel), $P_d = 0.9862$, $P_f = 0.4561$. It can be seen that the performance of the system is satisfying when SNR is relatively large. Figure 3(a) shows the true influence matrix, in which yellow represents connected, blue represents disconnected. Comparing the results of Fig. 3(b) and (c), we can find that all redundant links can be removed by setting threshold and utilizing symmetry. Finally, Fig. 3(d) can be got by binarizing the Fig. 3(c). For a binary classification problem, there are four kinds of discriminant situations. If a sample is true and the prediction is true, we call it true positive; if a sample is false but the prediction is true, we call it false positive. The Receiver Operating Characteristic (ROC) curve can well reflect the performance of the algorithm, which represents the relationship between the true positive weight and the false positive weight. The ROC curve at this point is shown in Fig. 4, in which the red dotted line represents the ROC when nothing is known, and the blue solid line represents the simulation results.

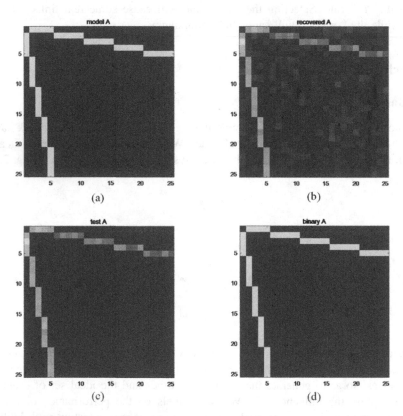

Fig. 3. Comparison of simulation results (a) True influence matrix (b) Reductive influence matrix (c) Reductive influence matrix with threshold (d) Influence matrix after binarization (Color figure online)

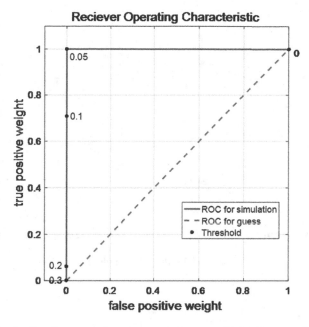

Fig. 4. Receiver operating characteristic curve (Color figure online)

4.3 Real Data Simulation

Table 1 is the part of the initial data in actual database, from left to right is the Index, Source ID, Destination ID, Start Time, Receive Time, Destination Abscissa, Destination Ordinate respectively. Our specific approach is to extract the first 10,000 data from the database as raw data, assuming that we only know srcID and starttime. And input the two sequences into the Hawkes process, we will eventually get the influence matrix, then compare with the real influence matrix, so that the conclusion will be drawn.

Table 1. Partial initial data

idx	srcID	dstID	starttime	receivetime	DstxPos	DstyPos
1	93	24	7.234305	17.234356	0.067886	−0.04369
2	24	93	17.23461	17.234668	0.05631	−0.04242
3	93	24	17.234822	17.23488	0.067886	−0.04369
4	93	24	17.234999	17.235057	0.067886	−0.04369
5	93	24	17.235491	17.235549	0.067886	−0.04369
6	93	24	17.235768	17.235826	0.067886	−0.04369
7	86	24	17.235945	17.236003	0.067886	−0.04369

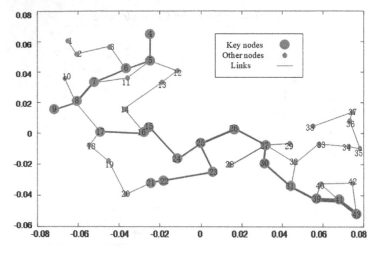

Fig. 5. True physical topology

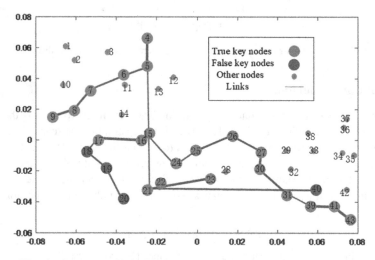

Fig. 6. Strong topological links under "or" rule with threshold of 0.3

Figure 5 is a true physical topology, in which the horizontal and vertical coordinates represent the physical location of nodes, and the thickness between nodes represents the strength of links. For convenience, we renumber the nodes, and if two nodes communicate more than 200 times, we consider these two nodes as key nodes. Since we want to find all key nodes, we choose "or" rule to symmetry the influence matrix. At this time, a large number of redundant links will be generated. In order to remove the redundant links, we set corresponding thresholds and get the final results, as shown in Fig. 6.

From the results, we can see that after symmetry and threshold setting, most redundant links have been eliminated, and all key nodes and strong links have been found. But what we have to see is that there is a case of error detection, i.e. redundant links that cannot be eliminated even if a higher threshold is set. Therefore, there is room for further performance improvement.

5   Conclusion and Outlook

Topology sensing is an important research direction. This paper has carried out exploratory research from three aspects: system model, method improvement and data simulation. Firstly, we combine topology sensing with wireless channel characteristics for the first time and formulate a clear physical model of topology sensing over wireless channel. Then, we propose a wireless channel-oriented topology sensing method based on Hawkes process using threshold and symmetry. Finally, we verify the reliability of the algorithm by real communication database. The expected research results have been achieved and the predetermined technical requirements have been fulfilled. Through the simulation results, we can see that the Hawkes process can still maintain good performance in AWGN channel, which is related to the threshold in the channel. How to set the threshold is also a very worthwhile problem. However, in real data simulation, the performance of Hawkes process is not ideal, but after symmetry and threshold processing, it can identify key nodes in the topology. We still have a long way to go to adapt the Hawkes process to the real situation.

At present, the work of topology sensing using Hawkes process is still in the immature stage. There are still many improvements in the future. This paper has also stimulated many new and interesting research directions, which is worth further research and exploration. such as the impact of distance on the channel, data preprocessing and so on. In addition to the Hawkes process, the use of machine learning for topology sensing is also a very challenging task, which we will leave to future work.

References

1. Giannakis, G.B., Shen, Y., Karanikolas, G.V.: Topology identification and learning over graphs: accounting for nonlinearities and dynamics. Proc. IEEE **106**(5), 787–807 (2018)
2. Tilghman, P., Rosenbluth, D.: Inferring wireless communications links and network topology from externals using granger causality. In: 2013 IEEE Military Communications Conference, MILCOM 2013, San Diego, CA, pp. 1284–1289 (2013)
3. Friston, K.J., Harrison, L., Penny, W.: Dynamic causal modelling. Neuroimage **19**(4), 1273–1302 (2003)
4. Moore, M.G., Davenport, M.A.: Analysis of wireless networks using Hawkes processes. In: 17th International Workshop on Signal Processing Advances in Wireless Communications, pp. 1–5. IEEE, Edinburgh (2016)
5. Moore, M.G., Davenport, M.A.: A Hawkes' eye view of network information flow. In: IEEE Statistical Signal Processing Workshop (SSP), Palma de Mallorca, pp. 1–5 (2016)

Multi-destination Two-Hop Untrusted AF Relay Networks with Destination-Aided Cooperative Jamming

Hui Shi[✉], Weiwei Yang, Yueming Cai, Yongxing Jia, and Wendong Yang

College of Communication Engineering, Army Engineering University of PLA,
Nanjing 210007, China
lgdhpkry@aliyun.com

Abstract. We consider a multi-destination two-hop untrusted amplify-and-forward (AF) relay networks, where each node is equipped with a single antenna and the confidential information communication needs the aid of the untrusted relay over the Nakagami-m channel. Because the relay is energy-constrained, the relay needs to harvest energy from the received information and the jamming signals by applying the power splitting relaying (PSR) protocol. The confidential information can be protected from the untrusted relay eavesdropping with destination-aided cooperative jamming. We focus on the secure and reliable performance of the presented system. The secrecy outage probability (SOP) and the connection outage probability (COP) are specially examined, which mainly show in the closed-form expressions of SOP and COP. In addition, the effective secrecy throughput (EST) performance is also investigated to comprehensively measure the secure and reliable performance. Moreover, we also present the asymptotic analysis of EST at the high signal-to-noise ratio (SNR). The Monte Carlo simulation is applied to validate the accuracy of the derived expressions and reveals the effects of different parameters, such as the transmit SNR, the power allocation factor, the fading factor and other parameters on the EST.

Keywords: Multi-destination · Untrusted relay · Energy harvesting · Performance analysis · Power splitting relaying · Nakagami-m fading

1 Introduction

The relaying technique has been applied to improve the throughput and coverage area of wireless communication systems [1–6]. The two main protocols applied in relay systems are amplify-and-forward (AF) and decode-and-forward (DF), respectively [7]. However, due to the constrained energy, the application of the relay is limited. The energy harvesting (EH) has been particularly noticed to prolong the lifetime of the relay [8–11]. The power splitting and time switching methods are the two main energy harvesting methods [12–14]. The power splitting relaying (PSR) protocol is one of the two relaying protocols. The energy

© ICST Institute for Computer Sciences, Social Informatics and Telecommunications Engineering 2019
Published by Springer Nature Switzerland AG 2019. All Rights Reserved
X. B. Zhai et al. (Eds.): MLICOM 2019, LNICST 294, pp. 58–71, 2019.
https://doi.org/10.1007/978-3-030-32388-2_6

harvesting technique has been applied with the relaying technique. In [15], the authors applied the PSR protocol to divide the harvested energy at the relay.

It is well known that the Nakagami-m fading channel is more practical and general when characterizing the fading effect over wireless channels. The literatures in [15–20], the transmissions were Nakagami-m fading channels. In [15, 16], all nodes were equipped with a single antenna and the relay was trusted. The authors in [15] focused on a two-way AF communication system, where consisted the source, the destination, and the relay. With harvesting energy from the surrounding radio frequency environment, the relay assisted the transmission between the source and the destination. In [16], the source node transmitted the information to the destination node via the DF relay, where the average symbol error rate was analyzed under two relaying scenarios, i.e., the existence or non-existence of direct link between the source and the destination.

In [17], Mahendra et al. analyzed the cellular multiuser two-way relay network, where consisted a multi-antenna base station, a single-antenna trusted relay and several single-antenna mobile stations. The overall outage probability expressions and optimal power allocation were investigated. In [18], the authors considered a dual-hop multiple-input multiple-output (MIMO) relay system, where each node was equipped with multiple antennas. The eavesdropper could intercept the transmission between the source and the destination, aided by the trusted relay under the DF protocol. The authors examined the secrecy outage probability and ergodic secrecy rate to evaluate the secrecy performance. Fan et al. [19] studied the system outage probability in the multiple AF relay network, where the best relay was chosen to maximize the received signal-to-noise ratio (SNR) at the destination. In [20], both antenna and relay selection were jointed to improve the system capacity, and the outage probability expression was examined.

However, when assisting the confidential information transmission, the relay may eavesdrop or decode the information at the same time. Utilizing the inherent nature of wireless channels, the secure communications could be realized with the physical-layer security (PLS) technology.

The works in [21], the authors investigated the secrecy outage probability (SOP) of the dual-hop AF untrusted relay networks with a single destination, besides the minimal SOP with optimal power allocation scheme. However, the authors just presented the tight closed-form and asymptotic expressions for the lower and upper bounds of SOP under Nakagami-m fading channels, rather than the closed-form expression of the SOP. The authors in [22] considered the secure communication in nonorthogonal multiple access (NOMA) networks with an untrusted AF relay, where the exact and asymptotic expressions for effective secrecy throughput (EST) over Nakagami-m fading was derived. In the first time slot, one of the two users were chosen to transmit the jamming signal to protect the information. Distinguished from the works in [22], our works considered all the destinations transmitted the jamming signals to the untrusted relay, without the user choice.

To the best of our knowledge, the connection outage probability (COP) and EST performance in the multi-destination two-hop untrusted AF relay networks have been relatively litter analyzed in the literatures. Motivated by this, the paper examines the multi-destination two-hop untrusted AF relay networks, where all nodes have a single antenna and the untrusted relay assists the confidential information communication between the source and the destinations over the Nakagami-m channel. In view of the untrusted relay may eavesdrop the confidential information when forwarding the information to the destinations, the destination-aided cooperative jamming technique is considered. The SOP, COP and EST performance are investigated to evaluate the secure transmission in the proposed system. The main contributions can be summarized as follows.

- We derive the closed-form expressions of SOP, COP, and EST in the multi-destination two-hop untrusted AF relay networks with destination-aided cooperative jamming over Nakagami-m fading channel. Moreover, we also derive the closed-form asymptotic expression for the EST at the high transmit SNR. The accuracy of these expressions are verified by the Monte Carlo simulations.
- The simulation results show that the EST increases with gradually increasing the transmit SNR and then tends to the constant, which can be validated by the asymptotic analysis of the EST. The number of the destinations can improve the EST to some extent. The simulations also demonstrate how the other parameters affect the EST.

The remainder of the paper is organized as follows. Section 2 describes the proposed system model and the secure communication process. Section 3 presents the analytical expressions for the SOP, COP, and EST, as well as the asymptotic analytical expression for the EST. In Sect. 4, we validate the derived expressions with the Monte Carlo simulation and illustrate the parameters impact on the EST. Finally, Sect. 5 summarizes the conclusions.

2 System Model

Consider a one-source multi-destination two-hop untrusted relay network depicted in Fig. 1. Each node is equipped with a single antenna and in a half-duplex mode. Assuming that the direct links between the source S and the destinations D_n ($n \in \{1, ..., N\}$) are unavailable [10], thus all the communications are aided by the untrusted relay R, which is assumed to be honest but curious. The channels between the source and the relay, the relay and the destinations are subject to the Nakagami-m fading, distributed independently and identically, denoted by h_{SR} and $\mathbf{h_{RD}} \in \mathbb{C}^{1 \times N}$ with parameters $\bar{\gamma}_{SR}$ and $\bar{\gamma}_{RD}$, respectively ($\mathbf{h_{RD}} = \mathbf{h_{DR}}$ [23,24]). The N destinations are close to each other and subject to the same Nakagami-m fading.

Applying PSR protocol, the total transmitted power P of the system is divided into two parts with the power allocation factor $\beta \in (0, 1)$. The information communication between the S and the D_n is divided into two equal hops. In the first hop $T/2$, the S transmits the confidential information to R with power βP, meanwhile, all the destinations D_n apply the maximal ratio transmission (MRT) technique to send the jamming signals to R with power $(1 - \beta) P$, making it impossible for the R to eavesdrop the confidential information. The R splits the received signal power into two parts with the power splitting factor $\rho \in (0,1)$. The ρ part of the received signal power is applied to harvest energy and the remaining part is utilized to transmit the information.

Then the received instantaneous signal-to-interference-plus-noise ratio (SINR) at the R is given by

$$\gamma_R = \frac{(1 - \rho)\beta\lambda X}{(1 - \rho)(1 - \beta)\lambda Y + 1}, \tag{1}$$

where $X = |h_{SR}|^2$, $Y = \|\mathbf{h_{DR}}\|^2$, $\lambda = P/N_0$. λ is the transmit SNR, and the N_0 denotes the zero mean additive white Gaussian noise (AWGN) power at the relay. $\|\bullet\|$ represents the Frobenius Norm.

Therefore, the transmit power at the R can be expressed as

$$P_R = \omega\eta\rho P G, \tag{2}$$

where $G = \beta X + (1 - \beta) Y$. The parameters ω and η denote the allocation factor of the harvested energy and the energy conversion efficiency factor of the harvested energy at the R, respectively. Both ω and η range from 0 to 1.

The harvested energy at the R is divided into ω and $(1 - \omega)$ parts. The ω proportion is applied for forwarding the confidential information to D_n and the other proportion is utilized to eavesdrop and decode consumption.

In the second hop, the R amplifies and forwards the information to D_n with the normalization factor $1/\sqrt{PG + N_0}$, and the D_n receive the information with

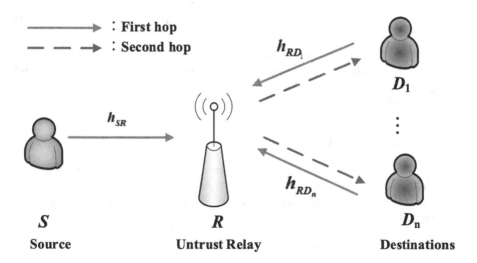

Fig. 1. System model.

maximal ratio combining (MRC) technique. Then the received instantaneous SINR of D_n is given by

$$\gamma_D \approx \frac{\omega\eta\rho(1-\rho)\beta\lambda XY}{\omega\eta\rho Y + 1 - \rho}. \tag{3}$$

where the approximation bases on the fact that 1 item could be neglected compared with $((\omega\eta\rho Y + 1 - \rho)\lambda G)$, when the SNR is high compared with the transmit power and channel gains [10,23,25].

3 Performance Analysis

Firstly, we derive the closed-form expressions for the SOP and the COP to evaluate the secure and the reliable performance. Then the closed-form expression and the asymptotic analysis at high transmit SNR of EST are also applied to evaluate the comprehensive performance of the system.

3.1 Preliminaries

Notations: Both $X = |h_{SR}|^2$ and $Y = \|\mathbf{h_{DR}}\|^2$ undergo the Nakagami-m fading distribution, therefore, the probability density function (PDF) of X and Y can be therefore given by

$$f(x) = \left(\frac{m_1}{\bar{\gamma}_{SR}}\right)^{m_1} \frac{x^{m_1-1}e^{-\frac{m_1 x}{\bar{\gamma}_{SR}}}}{\Gamma(m_1)} \tag{4}$$

and

$$f_N(y) = \left(\frac{m_2}{\bar{\gamma}_{RD}}\right)^{m_2 N} \frac{y^{m_2 N-1}e^{-\frac{m_2 y}{\bar{\gamma}_{RD}}}}{\Gamma(m_2 N)}, \tag{5}$$

where $\Gamma(\bullet)$ is the Gamma function, m_1 and m_2 are the Nakagami-m fading parameters for the channel between S and R, between R and D_n. Both m_1 and m_2 range from $1/2$ to ∞. Obviously, when $m_1 = 1$, the Nakagami-m distribution is Rayleigh fading distribution.

3.2 Secrecy Outage Probability

The secrecy outage event may occur when the channel capacity of the untrusted relay is higher than the positive difference between the codeword transmission rate R_{ct} and the confidential information rate R_{ci}, which is the definition of the SOP. Therefore, the SOP is given by

$$P_{SOP} = \mathbf{Pr}\{C_R > R_{dif}\}, \tag{6}$$

where $C_R = 1/(2\log_2(1 + \gamma_R))$, $R_{dif} = R_{ct} - R_{ci}$.

Plugging (1) into (6), (6) can rewritten as

$$P_{SOP} = \mathbf{Pr}\left\{X > \frac{(1-\beta)\vartheta_1 Y}{\beta} + \frac{\vartheta_1}{(1-\rho)\beta\lambda}\right\}$$

$$= \int_0^\infty \int_{X_1}^\infty f(x)f_N(y)\mathrm{d}x\mathrm{d}y, \tag{7}$$

where $X_1 = \frac{(1-\beta)\vartheta_1 Y}{\beta} + \frac{\vartheta_1}{(1-\rho)\beta\lambda}$, $\vartheta_1 = 2^{2R_{dif}} - 1$.

Substituting (4) and (5) into (7), the close-form expression of the SOP can be calculated as

$$P_{SOP} = \sum_{i=0}^{m_1-1}\sum_{k=0}^{i}\binom{i}{k}\frac{1}{i!}(m_2)^{m_2 N}(m_1\vartheta_1)^i e^{-\frac{m_1\vartheta_1}{(1-\rho)\beta\lambda\bar{\gamma}_{SR}}}$$

$$\times \frac{\Gamma(m_2 N + k)(\beta\bar{\gamma}_{SR})^{m_2 N + k - i}((1-\rho)\lambda)^{k-i}((1-\beta)\bar{\gamma}_{RD})^k}{\Gamma(m_2 N)((1-\beta)m_1\vartheta_1\bar{\gamma}_{RD} + m_2\beta\bar{\gamma}_{SR})^{m_2 N + k}}. \tag{8}$$

The Eq. (8) shows that the SOP is associated with the fading factors m_1 and m_2, the number of the destinations N, the power allocation factor β, the power splitting factor ρ and other parameters.

3.3   Connection Outage Probability

The connection outage event would occur when the channel capacity of the destinations is less than the R_{ct}, which is the definition of the COP. Thus, the COP is given by [26].

$$P_{COP} = \mathbf{Pr}\left\{C_D < R_{ct}\right\}, \tag{9}$$

where $C_D = \log_2(1 + \gamma_D)/2$.

Substituting (3) into (9), the expression of the COP can be rewritten as

$$P_{COP} = \mathbf{Pr}\left\{X < \frac{\vartheta_2}{(1-\rho)\beta\lambda} + \frac{\vartheta_2}{\omega\eta\rho\beta\lambda Y}\right\}$$

$$= \int_0^\infty \int_0^{X_2} f(x)f_N(y)\mathrm{d}x\mathrm{d}y, \tag{10}$$

where $X_2 = \frac{\vartheta_2}{(1-\rho)\beta\lambda} + \frac{\vartheta_2}{\omega\eta\rho\beta\lambda Y}$, $\vartheta_2 = 2^{2R_{ct}} - 1$.

Substituting (4) and (5) into (10), the closed-form expression of the COP can be obtained as

$$P_{COP} = 1 - \sum_{i=0}^{m_1-1}\sum_{k=0}^{i}\binom{i}{k}\frac{1}{i!}\frac{2e^{\frac{-m_1\vartheta_2}{(1-\rho)\beta\lambda\bar{\gamma}_{SR}}}(m_1\vartheta_2)^{\frac{m_2 N + 2i - k}{2}}}{\Gamma(m_2 N)(1-\rho)^{i-k}}$$

$$\times \frac{(m_2)^{\frac{k+m_2 N}{2}}\mathrm{K}_{(m_2 N - k)}\left(\sqrt{\frac{4m_1 m_2\vartheta_2}{\omega\eta\rho\beta\lambda\bar{\gamma}_{SR}\bar{\gamma}_{RD}}}\right)}{(\beta\lambda\bar{\gamma}_{SR})^{\frac{m_2 N + 2i - k}{2}}(\omega\eta\rho\bar{\gamma}_{RD})^{\frac{m_2 N + k}{2}}}, \tag{11}$$

where $K_z(\bullet)$ represents the zth order modified Bessel functions of second kind.

Equation (11) indicates that the COP is related to the fading factors, the number of the destinations, the allocation factor of the harvested energy ω, the energy conversion efficiency factor η and other parameters.

3.4 Effective Secrecy Throughput

The confidential information needs to be secure and reliable when transmitted between the S and the D_n, aided by the untrusted relay. To measure the secure and reliable performance of the transmission information, the EST is defined as follows.

$$
\begin{aligned}
\zeta &= \frac{R_{ci}}{2} \mathbf{Pr} \left\{ C_R < R_{dif}, C_D > R_{ct} \right\} \\
&= \frac{R_{ci}}{2} \left\{ X < \frac{(1-\beta)\vartheta_1 Y}{\beta} + \frac{\vartheta_1}{(1-\rho)\beta\lambda}, \ X > \frac{\vartheta_2}{(1-\rho)\beta\lambda} + \frac{\vartheta_2}{\omega\eta\rho\beta\lambda Y} \right\} \\
&= \frac{R_{ci}}{2} \int_u^\infty \int_{X_2}^{X_1} f(x)dx f_N(y)dy,
\end{aligned}
\tag{12}
$$

where $u = \left(b + \sqrt{b^2 + 4ac} \right)/2a$, $a = \omega\eta\rho\lambda(1-\rho)(1-\beta)\vartheta_1$, $b = \omega\eta\rho(\vartheta_2 - \vartheta_1)$, and $c = (1-\rho)\vartheta_2$.

Based on (4) and (5), and after some manipulations, the closed-form expression of EST is calculated as

$$
\zeta^{PSR} = \frac{R_{ci}}{2} \left\{ \Xi_1 - \Xi_2 \right\},
\tag{13}
$$

where Ξ_1 and Ξ_2 are given by

$$
\begin{aligned}
\Xi_1 &= \sum_{i=0}^{m_1-1} \sum_{k=0}^{i} \sum_{j=0}^{\infty} \binom{i}{k}(-1)^j \frac{1}{i!j!} e^{\frac{-m_1\vartheta_2}{(1-\rho)\beta\lambda\bar{\gamma}_{SR}}} \left(\frac{m_1\vartheta_2}{\beta\lambda\bar{\gamma}_{SR}} \right)^{i+j} \left(\frac{m_2}{\omega\eta\rho\bar{\gamma}_{RD}} \right)^{k+j} \\
&\times \frac{\Gamma\left(m_2N - j - k, \frac{m_2 u}{\bar{\gamma}_{RD}} \right)}{\Gamma(m_2N)(1-\rho)^{i-k}}
\end{aligned}
\tag{14}
$$

and

$$
\begin{aligned}
\Xi_2 &= \sum_{i=0}^{m_1-1} \sum_{k=0}^{i} \binom{i}{k} \frac{1}{i!} \frac{e^{-\frac{m_1\vartheta_1}{(1-\rho)\beta\lambda\bar{\gamma}_{SR}}} (m_1\vartheta_1)^i (m_2)^{m_2N} ((1-\beta)\bar{\gamma}_{RD})^k (\beta\bar{\gamma}_{SR})^{m_2N+k-i}}{\Gamma(m_2N)((1-\rho)\lambda)^{i-k}((1-\beta)m_1\vartheta_1\bar{\gamma}_{RD} + m_2\beta\bar{\gamma}_{SR})^{m_2N+k}} \\
&\times \Gamma\left(m_2N + k, \frac{((1-\beta)m_1\vartheta_1\bar{\gamma}_{RD} + m_2\beta\bar{\gamma}_{SR})u}{\beta\bar{\gamma}_{SR}\bar{\gamma}_{RD}} \right).
\end{aligned}
\tag{15}
$$

When $\lambda \to \infty$, the asymptotical expression of EST can be given by

$$\lim_{\lambda \to \infty} \zeta = \frac{\mathrm{R}_{ci}}{2} \left\{ 1 - \sum_{i=0}^{m_1-1} \frac{1}{i!} \frac{\Gamma\left(m_2 N + i\right) \left(m_2 \beta \bar{\gamma}_{SR}\right)^{m_2 N} \left((1-\beta) m_1 \vartheta_1 \bar{\gamma}_{RD}\right)^i}{\Gamma\left(m_2 N\right) \left((1-\beta) m_1 \vartheta_1 \bar{\gamma}_{RD} + m_2 \beta \bar{\gamma}_{SR}\right)^{m_2 N + i}} \right\}.$$

(16)

4 Numerical Results

In this section, we present the numerical results of the SOP, COP, and EST under different parameters to demonstrate the secure and reliable performance of the proposed system. Without loss of generality, the parameters in each figure are set as $N = 3$, $\beta = 0.5$, $\rho = 0.5$, $\omega = 0.9$, $\eta = 0.5$, $R_{ct} = 2\mathrm{bit/s/Hz}$, $R_{ci} = 1\mathrm{bit/s/Hz}$. It is assumed that the fading factors are the same, i.e., $m_1 = m_2$. The solid curves denote the numerical analysis, and the symbols '□', 'o' and '∇' represent the figures under the fading factors $m = 1$, $m = 2$, $m = 4$, successively.

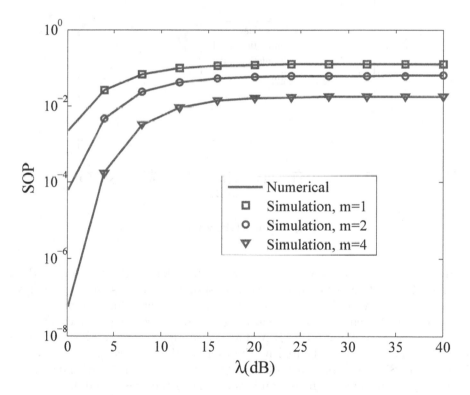

Fig. 2. The SOPs versus λ.

Figures 2 and 3 show the SOPs and COPs of the proposed system with various values of the transmit SNR λ, respectively. It is observed that: (1) When the transmit SNR λ increases, the SOPs increase and then approaches the constant. The reason is that the untrusted relay R can acquire more confidential information with λ increase at first. However, when λ is high, the destinations send the jamming signals to protect the information from eavesdropping. (2) The COPs decrease with increasing λ. It is due to that the destinations can receive more confidential information in the higher the transmit SNR regime. (3) With increasing the value of the fading factor, the channel fading gradually becomes smaller, which leads to decrease the SOP and the COP.

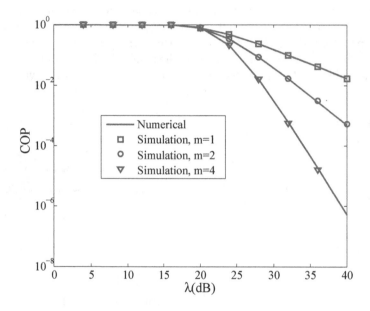

Fig. 3. The COPs versus λ.

In Fig. 4, the ESTs are presented as the function of the transmit SNR λ for the different fading factor m. The corresponding EST asymptotic analysis curves are demonstrated with the dashed lines. Two observations can be obtained as follows. (1) When the fading factors are fixed, the ESTs gradually increase with increasing the transmit SNR λ. The net result is that the EST tends to a constant, which can be validated by the asymptotic analysis curves. (2) When the transmit SNR λ is fixed, it is obvious that the ESTs increase with increasing the fading factor values. The reason is the same as the Figs. 2 and 3.

Figure 5 plots the impact of the number of the destinations on the ESTs. We observe that the ESTs become larger by increasing the number of the destinations N firstly. However, when the number N is larger than 20, the ESTs increase slowly, at this moment, it does not make much sense to increase the number N of the destinations anymore.

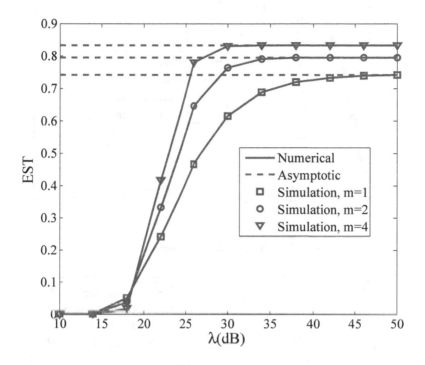

Fig. 4. The ESTs versus λ.

Figures 6 and 7 show the ESTs under different values of the power splitting factor ρ and the power allocation factor β, respectively. It is observed that the ESTs increase firstly and then turn to decrease along with increasing the parameters ρ and β. Therefore, there are the optimal values ρ and β, which could maximize the ESTs. The larger power splitting factor ρ demonstrates that the received signal power at R applied to harvest energy is larger, on the contrary, the received signal power at R utilized to transmit the information is smaller. The power allocation factor β is bigger, the power applied to transmit the confidential information to R is larger. Conversely, the power utilized to transmit the jamming signals to R is smaller. Figure 8 describes the EST versus both the parameters ρ and β in detail.

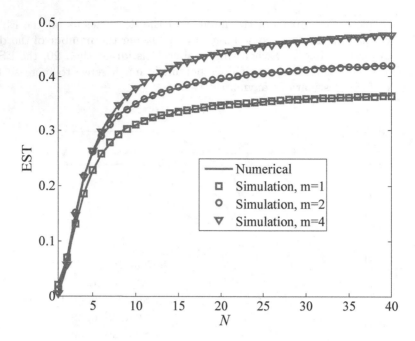

Fig. 5. The ESTs versus N.

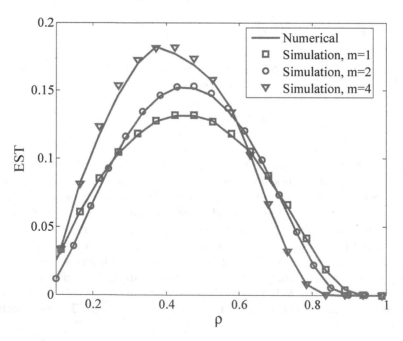

Fig. 6. The ESTs versus ρ.

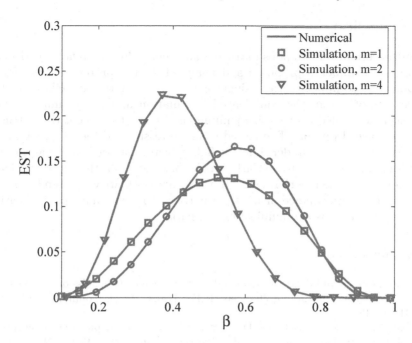

Fig. 7. The ESTs versus β.

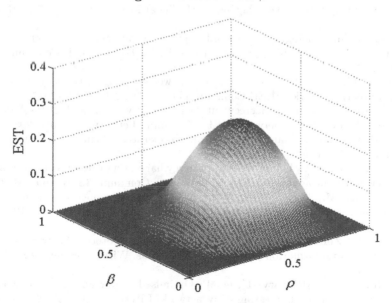

Fig. 8. The EST versus ρ and β with $m = 2$.

5   Conclusion

The multi-destination two hops untrusted and energy-limited relay network over Nakagami-m channel is proposed and analyzed. In the proposed networks, all the nodes are equipped with a single antenna, the untrusted relay can harvest energy both from the confidential information and the jamming signals. The destination-aided cooperative jamming is utilized to prevent the untrusted relay from eavesdropping. The closed-form expressions of the SOP, COP, and EST have been derived under different fading factors, as well as the asymptotic expressions of EST. The Monte Carlo simulations show that the effect of different parameters on the EST performance. In the future work, we will extend this work to analyze the performance of multiple untrusted relays, multiple destinations and multiple antennas communications scenario.

References

1. Hasna, M.O., Alouini, M.: End-to-end performance of transmission systems with relays over Rayleigh-fading channels. IEEE Trans. Wirel. Commun. **2**(6), 1126–1131 (2003)
2. Pabst, R., Walke, B., Schultz, D.C., et al.: Relay-based deployment concepts for wireless and mobile broadband radio. IEEE Commun. Mag. **42**(9), 80–89 (2004)
3. Ye, Y., Li, Y., et al.: Dynamic asymmetric power splitting scheme for SWIPT-based two-way multiplicative AF relaying. IEEE Signal Process. Lett. **25**(7), 1014–1018 (2018)
4. Zhang, Z., Ma, Z., Ding, Z., et al.: Full-duplex two-way and one-way relaying: average rate, outage probability, and tradeoffs. IEEE Trans. Wirel. Commun. **15**(6), 3920–3933 (2016)
5. Peng, C., Li, F., Liu, H., et al.: Optimal power splitting in two-way decode-and-forward relay networks. IEEE Commun. Lett. **21**(9), 2009–2012 (2017)
6. Van Nguyen, B., Kim, K.: Secrecy outage probability of optimal relay selection for secure AnF cooperative networks. IEEE Commun. Lett. **19**(12), 2086–2089 (2015)
7. Peter Hong, Y.-W., Huang, W.-J., et al.: Cooperative Communications and Networking. Springer, New York (2014)
8. Ulukus, S., Yener, A., Erkip, E., et al.: Energy harvesting wireless communications: a review of recent advances. IEEE J. Sel. Areas Commun. **33**(3), 360–381 (2015)
9. Qi, N., Xiao, M., Tsiftsis, T.A., et al.: Efficient coded cooperative networks with energy harvesting and transferring. IEEE Trans. Wirel. Commun. **16**(10), 6335–6349 (2017)
10. Nasir, A.A., Zhou, X., Durrani, S., et al.: Relaying protocols for wireless energy harvesting and information processing. IEEE Trans. Wirel. Commun. **12**(7), 3622–3636 (2013)
11. Yao, R., Xu, F., Mekkawy, T., et al.: Optimised power allocation to maximise secure rate in energy harvesting relay network. Electron. Lett. **52**(22), 1879–1881 (2016)
12. Liu, L., Zhang, R., Chua, K.C., et al.: Wireless information and power transfer: a dynamic power splitting approach. IEEE Trans. Commun. **61**(9), 3990–4001 (2013)
13. Zhou, X., Zhang, R., Ho, C.K., et al.: Wireless information and power transfer: architecture design and rate-energy tradeoff. IEEE Trans. Commun. **61**(11), 4754–4767 (2013)

14. Liu, L., Zhang, R., Chua, K.C., et al.: Wireless information transfer with opportunistic energy harvesting. IEEE Trans. Wirel. Commun. **12**(1), 288–300 (2013)
15. Bao, V.N., Van Toan, H., Le, K.N., et al.: Performance of two-way AF relaying with energy harvesting over Nakagami-m fading channels. IET Commun. **12**(20), 2592–2599 (2018)
16. Kumar, P., Dhaka, K.: Performance analysis of wireless powered DF relay system under Nakagami-m fading. IEEE Trans. Veh. Technol. **67**(8), 7073–7085 (2018)
17. Shukla, M.K., Yadav, S., Purohit, N., et al.: Performance evaluation and optimization of traffic-aware cellular multiuser two-way relay networks over Nakagami-m fading. IEEE Syst. J. **12**(2), 1933–1944 (2018)
18. Zhao, R., Lin, H., He, Y., et al.: Secrecy performance of transmit antenna selection for MIMO relay systems with outdated CSI. IEEE Trans. Commun. **66**(2), 546–559 (2018)
19. Fan, L., Zhao, N., Lei, X., et al.: Outage probability and optimal cache placement for multiple amplify-and-forward relay networks. IEEE Trans. Veh. Technol. **67**(12), 12373–12378 (2018)
20. Zhang, Y., Ge, J.: Joint antenna-and-relay selection in MIMO decode-and-forward relaying networks over Nakagami-m fading channels. IEEE Signal Process. Lett. **24**(4), 456–460 (2017)
21. Ding, F., Wang, H., Zhou, Y., et al.: Impact of relays eavesdropping on untrusted amplify-and-forward networks over Nakagami-m fading. IEEE Wirel. Commun. Lett. **7**(1), 102–105 (2018)
22. Xiang, Z., Yang, W., Pan, G., et al.: Secure transmission in non-orthogonal multiple access networks with an untrusted relay. IEEE Wirel. Commun. Lett. 1 (2019)
23. Kalamkar, S.S., Banerjee, A.: Secure communication via a wireless energy harvesting untrusted relay. IEEE Trans. Veh. Technol. **00**(3), 2199–2213 (2017)
24. Huang, J., Mukherjee, A., Swindlehurst, A.L., et al.: Secure communication via an untrusted non-regenerative relay in fading channels. IEEE Trans. Signal Process. **61**(10), 2536–2550 (2013)
25. Wang, Z., Chen, Z., Xia, B., et al.: Cognitive relay networks with energy harvesting and information transfer: design, analysis, and optimization. IEEE Trans. Wirel. Commun. **15**(4), 2562–2576 (2016)
26. Chen, D., Cheng, Y., Yang, W., et al.: Physical layer security in cognitive untrusted relay networks. IEEE Access **6**, 7055–7065 (2018)

Secrecy Sum Rate for Two-Way
Untrusted Relay in SCMA Networks

Yiteng Huang[1], Shuai Han[1(✉)], Shizeng Guo[1], Ming Li[2], and Zhiqiang Li[1]

[1] Communication Research Center, Harbin Institute of Technology, Harbin, China
hanshuai@hit.edu.cn
[2] China Academy of Space Technology, Beijing, China

Abstract. Sparse code multiple access (SCMA) is a novel non-orthogonal multiple access technology that combines the concepts of CDMA and OFDMA. The advantages of SCMA include high capacity, low time delay and high transfer rate. The information security is also very important in 5G network. Relay is essential to be used for long distance cooperative transmission. In this paper, we consider a two-way relay system that each user pair can only communicate through an untrusted intermediate relay. We regard the intermediate relay as an eavesdropper and the confidential information must be kept secret to it. In order to maximize the sum security capacity, a subcarrier assignment algorithm based on matching theory is proposed in this paper. Finally, the theoretical analysis is verified by simulation. Simulation results show that security performance is improved significantly.

Keywords: Amplify-and-forward · Two-way communication ·
Untrusted relay · Sparse code multiple access

1 Introduction

In future 5G networks, the data flow rate of the system will be greatly improved and will occupy an increased range of bandwidth compared with 4G networks [1]. Sparse code multiple access (SCMA) is a multidimensional codebook-based technique to increase connectivity and multiuser capacity. SCMA combines the concepts of CDMA and OFDMA [2,3] to achieve non-orthogonal multiple access in the frequency domain. Information theoretic security was proposed by Shannon [4]. Wyner, in [2], pointed out that the eavesdropper only has a noisy copy of the signal transmitted from the source, and building a useful secure communication system per Shannons notion is possible [5,6].

Recent progress in physical layer security area has been extended. Examples include using multiple antennas to steer the transmitted signal away from an eavesdropper [7] or taking advantage of variations in channel state to provide secrecy [8]. According to the information theoretic security, if the wiretap

This work is supported by the National Natural Science Foundation of China (No. 41861134010 and No. 61831002).

channel is less noisy than the main channel the secrecy capacity will be zero. Cooperative relaying is utilized to overcome secrecy capacity limitation respectively in [9]. Decode-and-Forward (DF)- and Amplify-and-Forward (AF)-based cooperative relaying protocols are proposed to improve physical layer security. In [10], cooperative jamming is regarded as a promising approach to improve the secrecy capacity by confusing the eavesdropper with cooperative interference. Different cooperative jamming schemes were researched for different communication scenarios in related research work.

The focus of this paper differs from all above models, which is on a class of relay networks where the source and the destination have no direct link and thus can only communicate utilizing an intermediate relay node. It is a communication network whose nodes have different levels of security clearance. In SCMA system, it is inefficiency and costly for two long physical distance communication node to communicate directly without relaying. Thus, in this case, it will uses relay nodes to participate in cooperative communication. In this model, different nodes in the communication network has different levels of security clearance. Examples like this exist in real life. In a government intelligence network or the network of a financial institution, not every node in the network is supposed to have the same level of access to information, despite operating with agreed protocols and serving as relay nodes in the network [11]. The relay node are vulnerable to eavesdropping because of its low level of security clearance. Thus, the relay node is considered to be untrusted. Untrusted relay channels were first studied in [12] and [13], where the intermediate relay acts as both an eavesdropper and a helper.

In this paper, we consider a two-way relay system that each user pair can only communicate through an untrusted intermediate relay. This does not mean that the relay node is malicious. On the contrary, it may be part of the network. We will assume that it is willing to faithfully implement the relay scheme. However, the relay only has low security clearance in the network, so we can't trust the confidential messages that it is relaying [11]. It assumes that the confidential messages are used to identify source nodes for authentication [12]. In order not to be attacked illegally by eavesdroppers, the message should never be leaked to relay nodes. In this case it supposes that there is a eavesdropper on the relay node when designing the relay system. In [14], a relay channel is considered, in which the relay helps to transmit messages from the sender to the receiver. Relays are not only regarded as senders to assist the message transmission, but also as eavesdroppers to obtain some information about the transmission message [15]. The sender wants to send two different types of messages. One is called the public message, which is sent to the receiver and relay. The other is called the private message, which is only sent to the receiver and keep confidential to the relay. Even if there are no external eavesdroppers in the system, security is still a problem. That's because although relays help to forward information to destination, designers still hope the source signal itself keep secret from the relay [14].

The main contributions of this work are as follows:

- This paper studies the physical layer security in relay cooperative SCMA multiple access communication system. The physical layer security model of two-way relay cooperative SCMA network is also established in this paper.
- The untrusted relay works on the amplify-and-forward mode. This paper formulates the subcarrier allocation as a non-convex optimization problem to maximize the total security capacity.
- This paper proposes a subcarrier allocation algorithm based on two-side matching game to enhance the security performance without compromising the communication quality of the system. This paper formulates the subcarrier allocation as a non-convex optimization problem to maximize the total security capacity.

The remainder of this paper is organized as follows. Section 2 presents the two-way relay cooperative SCMA network model, the basic principles of SCMA and physical layer security. The proposed subcarrier allocation algorithm based on user-subchannel swap-matching is introduced in Sect. 3. Next, the security performance of the proposed two-way relay system is verified through simulations presented in Sect. 4, and the numerical results are discussed in this section. Finally, the conclusions are described in Sect. 5.

2 System Model

2.1 SCMA Link-Level Model

The structure of the SCMA transmitter is shown in Fig. 1. The data streams from multiple users are first processed by an FEC encoder module; subsequently, the encoded data are interleaved to prevent burst errors. The processed data streams are sent to an SCMA encoder and directly mapped to several orthogonal subcarriers according to predesigned codebooks. Finally, the full data stream outputs from the SCMA encoder are transmitted through the channel.

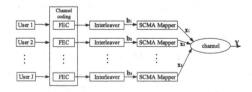

Fig. 1. SCMA transmitter structure

The transmitted signal is superimposed onto the data of other users carried by the same subcarrier, which introduces noise in the transmission process. Then, the transmitted signal is sent to the receiver. At the receiver, the received symbol can be expressed as

$$y = \sum_{j=1}^{J} \text{diag}(\mathbf{h}_j)\mathbf{x}_j + \mathbf{n}, \tag{1}$$

where $\mathbf{h}_j = (h_{1j}, h_{2j}, ..., h_{Kj})^T$ is the channel transmission vector of user j, indicating signal attenuation during transmission; $\mathbf{x}_j = (x_{1j}, x_{2j}, ..., x_{Kj})^T$ is the SCMA codeword of user j; and $\mathbf{n}$ is Gaussian white noise in the complex domain.

The SCMA receiver structure is shown in Fig. 2. The SCMA decoder detects the user data streams that have interference by channel noise and other user data streams according to known codebook and subcarrier allocation information. Subsequently, the convolution code is decoded, and the data bits are restored with hard decisions.

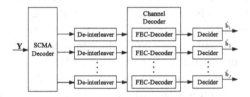

Fig. 2. SCMA receiver structure

2.2 Two-Way Untrusted Relay in SCMA System

A two-way untrusted relay SCMA system is shown in Fig. 3. We consider a two-way relay scenario, which exists many user pair in the system. Each user pair consists two sources, which communicate with each other with the help of an untrusted intermediate relay. Each source is equipped with a single omnidirectional antenna and operates in a half-duplex manner. The intermediate relay works in Amplify-and-Forward (AF) mode in this study.

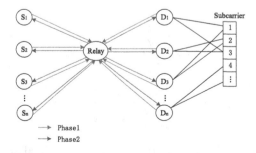

Fig. 3. System model of two-way untrusted relaying

Suppose that there is an untrusted intermediate relay and N user pairs in an SCMA cell. Denote the set of indices $\{1, 2, \cdots, N\}$ by $\mathcal{N}$. Let S_i and $D_i, i = 1, 2, ..., N$ denote the two sources in the same user pair. We denote the user pair as U_i. The intermediate relay divides the available bandwidth of the system into a set of subcarriers, denoted by $\mathcal{K}_{SC} = \{1, 2, \cdots, K\}$. The signals transmitted from the N user pairs are multiplexed to K orthogonal subcarriers. Then, the communication process can be divided into two stages. In the first stage, all the source nodes in user pairs send their message to the intermediate relay. The user signals are nonorthogonally superimposed on the subcarriers based on multiple access using SCMA. The signal received by malicious relay consists of the superposition of the signals sent by all the source nodes in the system. In the second stage, the intermediate relay amplifies the superposition of received signal and broadcasts it to all the source nodes. There is only one intermediate relay in the system model and no direct link between the two sources of any user pair. Thus, the signal can only be transmitted through the malicious relay to the destination node. We consider a block fading channel, for which the channel remains constant within a certain time-slot, but varies independently from one to another. For subcarrier SC_k, the channel transfer function between source node S_m and intermediate relay is denoted by $h_{k,m} = g_{k,m}/(d_m)^a$, where d_m means the distance between relay and source node S_m, $g_{k,m}$ is the Rayleigh fading channel gain between source node S_m and relay and a is the path loss coefficient. At the relay node, the attenuation signals of different users after channel transmission are superimposed onto each other. Then, the received symbol on the subcarrier SC_k can be expressed as

$$y_{r,i,k} = n_{r,k} + \sqrt{p_{k,s_i}}s_{i,k}h_{k,s_i} + \sqrt{p_{k,d_i}}d_{i,k}h_{k,d_i} + I_{i,k} \tag{2}$$

$$I_{i,k} = \sum_{S_n \in \{S \setminus S_i\}} \left(\sqrt{p_{k,s_n}}s_{n,k}h_{k,s_n} + \sqrt{p_{k,d_n}}d_{n,k}h_{k,d_n}\right), \tag{3}$$

where $n_{r,k}$ denotes the thermal noise at the relay node, $I_{i,k}$ denotes the interference caused by other user signals multiplexing the same subcarrier with the selected user.

Then, the untrusted intermediate relay has the signal-to-noise ratios on the subcarrier SC_k with respect to signals transmitted from user S_i and D_i are as follows

$$\gamma_{s_i}^r = \frac{p_{k,s_i}|h_{k,s_i}|^2}{\delta^2 + p_{k,d_i}\left|h_{k,d_i}\right|^2 + \sum\limits_{S_n \in \{S \setminus S_i\}}\left(p_{k,s_n}s_{n,k}|h_{k,s_n}|^2 + p_{k,d_n}d_{n,k}|h_{k,d_i}|^2\right)} \tag{4}$$

$$\gamma_{d_i}^r = \frac{p_{k,d_i}|h_{k,d_i}|^2}{\delta^2 + p_{k,s_i}|h_{k,s_i}|^2 + \sum\limits_{S_n \in \{S \setminus S_i\}}\left(p_{k,s_n}s_{n,k}|h_{k,s_n}|^2 + p_{k,d_n}d_{n,k}|h_{k,d_i}|^2\right)} \tag{5}$$

The relay works in AF mode and broadcasts amplified signals to each user node in the downlink. The corresponding signal received by S_i at subcarrier SC_k

can be written as

$$
\begin{aligned}
y_{s_i,k} &= h_{k,s_i} G_{R,k} y_{r,i,k} + n_{s_i} \\
&= h_{k,s_i} G_{R,k} \left(n_{r,k} + \sqrt{p_{k,s_i}} s_{i,k} h_{k,s_i} + \sqrt{p_{k,d_i}} d_{i,k} h_{k,d_i} + I_{i,k} \right) + n_{s_i}
\end{aligned}
\tag{6}
$$

Similarly, the signal received by D_i at subcarrier SC_k can be written as

$$
\begin{aligned}
y_{d_i,k} &= h_{k,d_i} G_{R,k} y_{r,i,k} + n_{d_i} \\
&= h_{k,d_i} G_{R,k} \left(n_{r,k} + \sqrt{p_{k,s_i}} s_{i,k} h_{k,d_i} + \sqrt{p_{k,d_i}} d_{i,k} h_{k,d_i} + I_{i,k} \right) + n_{d_i}
\end{aligned}
\tag{7}
$$

As for node S_i, the security capacity at subcarrier SC_k can be expressed as

$$
\begin{aligned}
C^S_{k,s_i} &= \left(C_{k,s_i} - C^r_{k,s_i} \right)^+ \\
&= \frac{1}{2} \log_2 \left(1 + \frac{G_{R,k}^2 h_{k,d_i}^2 h_{k,s_i}^2 p_{k,s_i}}{\left(1 + h_{k,d_i}^2\right) \delta^2 + h_{k,d_i}^2 G_{R,k}^2 \left[\sum_{S_n \in \{S \setminus S_i\}} \left(p_{k,s_n} |h_{k,s_n}|^2 + p_{k,d_n} |h_{k,d_n}|^2 \right) \right]} \right) \\
&\quad - \frac{1}{2} \log_2 \left(1 + \frac{p_{k,s_i} |h_{k,s_i}|^2}{\delta^2 + p_{k,d_i} h_{k,d_i}^2 + \sum_{S_n \in \{S \setminus S_i\}} \left(p_{k,s_n} s_{n,k} |h_{k,s_n}|^2 + p_{k,d_n} d_{n,k} |h_{k,d_i}|^2 \right)} \right)
\end{aligned}
\tag{8}
$$

Similarly, the security capacity that D_i obtains at subcarrier SC_k can be expressed as

$$
\begin{aligned}
C^S_{k,d_i} &= \left(C_{k,d_i} - C^r_{k,d_i} \right)^+ \\
&= \frac{1}{2} \log_2 \left(1 + \frac{G_{R,k}^2 h_{k,d_i}^2 h_{k,s_i}^2 p_{k,d_i}}{\left(1 + h_{k,s_i}^2\right) \delta^2 + h_{k,s_i}^2 G_{R,k}^2 \left[\sum_{S_n \in \{S \setminus S_i\}} \left(p_{k,s_n} |h_{k,s_n}|^2 + p_{k,d_n} |h_{k,d_n}|^2 \right) \right]} \right) \\
&\quad - \frac{1}{2} \log_2 \left(1 + \frac{p_{k,d_i} |h_{k,d_i}|^2}{\delta^2 + p_{k,s_i} |h_{k,s_i}|^2 + \sum_{S_n \in \{S \setminus S_i\}} \left(p_{k,s_n} s_{n,k} |h_{k,s_n}|^2 + p_{k,d_n} d_{n,k} |h_{k,d_i}|^2 \right)} \right)
\end{aligned}
\tag{9}
$$

Then the system sum security capacity can be expressed as:

$$
C^S = \sum_{k=1}^{K} \left(C^S_{k,s_i} + C^S_{k,d_i} \right)
\tag{10}
$$

3 Secrecy Rate of Two-Way Relay Channel in SCMA System

In order to improve the secrecy performance of relay system, we should design a resource allocation scheme to make more system users get positive security capacity. In the relay system, power amplification and subcarrier allocations are performed by intermediate relay. As for subcarrier allocations, it can be formulated as a many-to-many two-sided matching problem, which can be solved by utilizing the matching theory [16]. The subcarrier allocations scheme will be introduced in this section.

3.1   Subcarrier Allocation Based on Two-Sided Matching Game

We formulate the optimization subcarrier allocation problem into a two-sided matching problem. Then, an optimized subcarrier allocation algorithm is proposed in this section to improve system security performance.

To describe the subcarrier allocation problem, this paper introduces a binary $N \times K$ user pair and subcarrier mapping matrix $F = [f_1, f_2, \cdots, f_N]$. If the subcarrier SC_k is occupied by the mth user pair, $f_{m,k} = 1$, otherwise $f_{m,k} = 0$. Assuming that there are N user pairs and K subcarriers in the system. To evaluate the total security capacity of all users, and then the optimization problem is formulated as:

$$\underset{\mathbf{F}}{\text{maximize}} \quad \sum_{k=1}^{K} \sum_{n=1}^{N} R_{k,n}(p,G) f_{k,n},$$

$$\text{subject to} \quad \sum_{n \in N_{user}} f_{k,n} \leq d_f, \forall k \in K_{sc},$$

$$\sum_{k \in K_{sc}} f_{k,n} \leq d_v, \forall n \in N_{user}, \tag{11}$$

$$f_{k,n} \in \{0,1\}, \forall k \in K_{sc}, \forall n \in N_{user},$$

$$\sum_{k \in K_{sc}} p_{k,n} \leq P_s, \forall n \in N_{user},$$

$$p_{k,n} \geq 0, \forall k \in K_{sc}, \forall n \in N_{user},$$

One subcarrier can be allocated to at most d_f users and one user can access to the system through at most d_v subcarriers. It is a non-convex optimization problem. Thus the complexity of finding the optimal solutions is prohibitive. To solve the problem with low complexity, this paper solve the problem by utilizing the matching theory.

We first make each source node allocate its power equally over all its occupied subcarriers. Subcarrier allocation is considered by intermediate relay. The subcarrier set and the user pair set are two disjoint sets which aim at matching with each other. The element in both sets are selfish and intelligent which aims to maximize their own interests. If subcarrier SC_k is occupied by user pair N_m, we consider the user pair N_m and the subcarrier SC_k are already paired. It is denoted as (N_m, SC_k). The conflict of interests between elements in the same set and the game between elements in different sets to maximize their own interests have a great impact on the result of the matching game. This paper use $\succ$ denote the preference relation for both subcarriers and user pairs. The preference for user pair $N_j \in N_{user}$ over the set of subcarriers is denoted as $\succ_{N_j}$. For any two subcarriers SC_k and $SC_{K'}$, $k \neq k'$, there exists two different mapping relationship ψ and ψ', satisfies $SC_k \in \psi(N_j), SC_{k'} \notin \psi(N_j), SC_{k'} \in \psi'(N_j), SC_k \notin \psi'(N_j)$. Thus, the preference for user pair over the set of subcarriers $\succ_{N_j}$ can be described as follows

$$(SC_k, \psi) \succ_{N_j} (SC_{k'}, \psi') \Leftrightarrow R_{kj}(\psi) > R_{k'j}(\psi'), \tag{12}$$

which means that user pair N_j chooses to occupy SC_k in ψ rather than $SC_{K'}$ in ψ' because N_j can obtain higher security capacity over SC_k than over $SC_{K'}$.

Similarly, for any two subcarrier $SC_k, SC_{k'} \in K_{SC}$, $k \neq k'$, the preference for subcarriers over the subsets of users is denoted as $\succ_{SC_k}$. For two different user pair subsets U and U', $U, U' \subseteq N_{user}, U \neq U'$, there exists two different mapping relationship ψ and ψ', satisfies $U = \psi(SC_k), U' = \psi'(SC_k)$. Thus, the preference for subcarrier over the subsets of user pairs $\succ_{SC_k}$ can be described as follows

$$(U, \psi) \succ_{SC_k} (U', \psi') \Leftrightarrow R_{SC_k}(\psi) > R_{SC_k}(\psi'), \tag{13}$$

which means that subcarrier SC_k chooses to match with subset U in ψ rather than subset U' in ψ' because it can obtain higher security capacity from U'.

In the whole matching process, the user pair's preferences for subcarriers are interactional, so does the selection of subcarriers to user pairs. The algorithm procedures that update the mapping relationship between two sets depend on the structure of current matching. Every two user pairs have rights to exchange their matches in the algorithm. Therefore, this paper introduces swap matching and swap matching pairs to maximize the system security capacity.

Swap Matching. It is assume that there exists a mapping relation ψ satisfies $SC_p \in \psi(N_i), SC_q \in \psi(N_j) \&\& SC_p \notin \psi(N_j), SC_q \notin \psi(N_i)$. A swap matching is denoted as ψ_{jq}^{ip}. It is a swap operation which makes $SC_q \in \psi_{jq}^{ip}(N_i), SC_p \in \psi_{jq}^{ip}(N_j) \&\& SC_q \notin \psi_{jq}^{ip}(N_j), SC_p \notin \psi_{jq}^{ip}(N_i)$. In general, a swap matching is a operation that makes two of user pairs in the set exchange one of their occupying subcarriers and keep all other mapping relation the same.

Swap Matching Pairs. Assuming that there is a mapping relation ψ and exists a block pair (N_i, N_j) in ψ which satisfies $SC_p \in \psi(N_i), SC_q \in \psi(N_j)$. If the block pair (N_i, N_j) meet the following two conditions, then (N_i, N_j) is a swap matching pair in ψ.

(i) $\forall t \in \{N_i, N_j, SC_p, SC_q\}, \left(\psi_{jq}^{ip}(t), \psi_{jq}^{ip} \right) \geq_t (\psi(t), \psi)$

(ii) $\exists t \in \{N_i, N_j, SC_p, SC_q\}, \left(\psi_{jq}^{ip}(t), \psi_{jq}^{ip} \right) \succ_t (\psi(t), \psi)$

Each user pair should find another user pair to form a swap matching pair and then swap their occupying subcarrier of the set in above inequality. For the elements in swap matching pair, they can benefit each other by swap their subcarrier without hurting the benefits of corresponding subcarriers. Then, the algorithm can obtain the optimal mapping result after multiple swap operations.

The specific details of our proposed algorithm are showed in Algorithm 1. The algorithm is divided into two parts: One is initialization and another is swap matching. First, initial mapping relation via random subcarrier allocation and each source node construct its preference matching list. Then source node keep searching its partner to form swap matching pair and change their occupying subcarrier to update matching relation ψ. The algorithm finishes until no

source node can form new swap matching pair and the optimal matching will be
obtained.

Algorithm 1. Matching Subcarrier Allocation Algorithm

1: **Input: h,** σ_n, G_k, α, N, K
2: **Initialization**
3:      **Obtain initial mapping result based on random subcarrier allocation**
4:         i $L(N_i)$, $N_i \in N_{user}$
5:         ii $L(SC_k)$, $SC_k \in K_{sc}$
6:         iii **Each source node construct its preference list** $P(N_i)$, $N_i \in N_{user}$
7: **Swap Matching**
8: **while** $\exists P(N_i) \neq \emptyset$, $N_i \in N_{user}$ **do**
9:      **for** $i = 1 : n$ **do**
10:         **if** $P(N_i)$ is not empty **then**
11:            **Current source node proposes itself to the most-preferred** SC_k
         and give up SC_l
12:            **Remove** SC_k **from** $P(N_i)$
13:            **for** $j = 1 : |L(SC_k)|$ **do**
14:               **if** It's a swap matching pair **then**
15:                  SC_k **accept the proposal**
16:                  **Update** $L(N_i)$, $N_i \in N_{user}$ **and** $L(SC_k)$, $SC_k \in K_{sc}$
17:               **else**
18:                  **Refuse the proposal**
19:               **end if**
20:            **end for**
21:         **end if**
22:      **end for**
23: **end while**
24: **Matching Finish**

3.2   Stability and Convergence

Assuming that the optimal matching mapping result ψ^* is not a stable matching. Then there exists a matching pair (N_i, SC_k), so that both N_i and SC_k
can achieve higher secure transmission rates and $(N_i, SC_k) \notin \psi^*$. According to the algorithm details, N_i will propose itself to SC_k and SC_k will
agree to this application, then matching switching operation will be implemented. (N_i, SC_k) is a candidate match in the iterative updating process.
We assume that in the t round, SC_k discover a preferable user and delete
N_i from the list, that is $\psi^t(SC_k) \succ_{SC_k} L, L \subseteq \{N_i\} \cup \psi^t(SC_k), L \subseteq \{N_i\} \cup$
$\psi^t(SC_k)$, $N_i \in L$. Now, a new matching relationship $\psi^t(SC_k)$ is obtained. How-
ever, $\psi^t(SC_k)$ did not survive and was replaced by the new matching relationship in the end. As for SC_k, its final matching list is $\psi(SC_k)$. Finally, we get
$L \succ_{SC_k} \psi(SC_k)$, $\psi^t(SC_k) \succ_{SC_k} L, \psi(SC_k) \succ_{SC_k} \psi^t(SC_k)$. It is contradictory to
the transitive property, therefore, the hypothesis is not valid. So the matching

mapping result ψ^* is the optimal matching, the two-side matching algorithm is stable.

In each iteration process, every user node will propose itself to its favorite subcarrier. Whether the application is accepted or rejected by the subchannel, the user node will not propose itself to the same subcarrier anymore. As the iteration continues the potential choices of each user node are decreasing. For each iteration the corresponding subchannel will be removed from its preference list. The preference list of each user source node will be empty after no more than K iterations. Then the matching phase of the algorithm is over and get the optimal matching result. It proves the algorithm is convergent.

4   System Simulation

The security performance with different subcarrier allocations is shown in this section. The transmission signal is over Block Fading Channel. Users are randomly distributed in the cell. In the simulation, the peak power of each source node is 20 dBm, the path loss factor is set as 2, the cell radius is 200 m, overload coefficient in SCMA system is 2, noise variance is -174 dBm/Hz. The simulation results is obtained based on over 10000 instances of the algorithms.

We evaluate the performance of the proposed subcarrier allocation algorithm, and compare it with random subcarrier allocation and OFDMA scheme. We set the relay magnification factor as 15 dB. Figure 4 shows the relation between the total security capacity with the number of users with $d_v = 3$, and $d_f = 6$. The proposed algorithm significantly outperforms random allocation and OFDMA scheme. For optimize scheme, the total security capacity increases with the number of users, but the growth becomes slower as user number increases. That's because as the number of users increases, the candidate matching solutions go up accordingly. The proposed algorithm can converge to the optimal matching solution. Thus the security capacity continue to rise as the number of users increase. However this kind of subcarrier allocation scheme always provide services to users with better security performance. Therefore the fairness of the algorithm is poor. For OFDMA scheme, the total security capacity increases at first and then remains constant when all subcarriers are fully loaded. For random allocation scheme, its security performance is better than OFDMA scheme when the number of user is small. As the number of users increases, the total security capacity decreases even smaller than OFDMA scheme, and then remains constant when all subcarriers are fully loaded. That's because the subcarriers is not fully loaded and the interference to users is relatively small while there is few users. Compared with OFDMA users, each SCMA user can occupy more subcarriers to access to system. Therefore, the security performance of random allocation is better than OFDMA scheme when the number of users in the system is small. As the number of users becomes larger, the multiplexing users on each subcarrier increase, and then each user will suffer more severe Multi-Use interference. Since random allocation algorithm generate the result in a random way, it can't find an optimal matching solution, no security performance gains will be obtained, even if the number of users increases. Besides the severe Multi-Use interference degrades the system security performance. Therefore, for random allocation scheme, the total security capacity decreases even smaller than OFDMA scheme as the number of users increases. If the number of system users continues to increase, all subcarriers has been fully loaded, the security performance of both schemes remain constant.

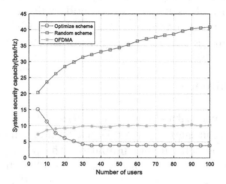

Fig. 4. Sum security capacity v.s. the number of users

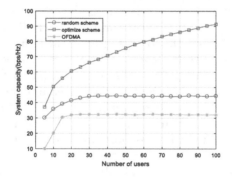

Fig. 5. Sum capacity v.s. the number of users

Figure 5 simulates the system capacity performance with three different subcarrier allocations. Simulation results indicate that the proposed subcarrier allocation scheme won't deteriorate the communication quality. It can improve both system capacity and security performance.

5 Conclusion

In this paper, we investigated the physical layer security for two-way communications with an untrusted intermediate relay in the SCMA networks. This paper researches the subcarrier allocation problem to improve system security performance by optimizing the subcarrier assignment. The proposed subcarrier allocation algorithm can converge to an optimal matching with a low complexity and it will improve the communication quality of the system.

References

1. Nikopour, H., Baligh, H.: Sparse code multiple access. In: Proceedings of the 2013 IEEE 24th Annual International Symposium on Personal, Indoor, and Mobile Radio Communications (PIMRC), London, U.K., pp. 332–336, September 2013
2. Renfors, M., et al.: On the use of filter bank based multicarrier modulation for professional mobile radio. In: Proceedings of the 2013 IEEE 77th Vehicular Technology Conference (VTC Spring), Dresden, DE, pp. 1–5, June 2013
3. Song, G., Wang, X., Cheng, J.: Signature design of sparsely spread code division multiple access based on superposed constellation distance analysis. IEEE Access 5, 23809–23821 (2017)
4. Shannon, C.E.: Communication theory of secrecy systems. Bell Syst. Tech. J. 28(4), 656–715 (1949)
5. Wyner, A.D.: The wire-tap channel. Bell Syst. Tech. J. 54(8), 1355–1387 (1975)
6. Csiszár, I., Korner, J.: Broadcast channels with confidential messages. IEEE Trans. Inf. Theory IT–24, 339–348 (1978)
7. Oggier, F., Hassibi, B.: The secrecy capacity of the MIMO wiretap channel. In: Proceedings IEEE International Symposium on Information Theory (ISIT 2008), Toronto, Canada, pp. 524–528, July 2008
8. Koyluoglu, O., El-Gamal, H., Lai, L., Poor, H.V.: Interference alignment for secrecy. IEEE Trans. Inf. Theory (2008, submitted). http://arxiv.org/abs/0810. 1187
9. Dong, L., Han, Z., Petropulu, A.P., Poor, H.V.: Secure wireless communications via cooperation. In: Proceedings of the 46th Annual Allerton Conference on Communication, Control, and Computing/UIUC, Monticello, IL, pp. 1132–1138, September 2008
10. Tekin, E., Yener, A.: The general Gaussian multiple-access and twoway wiretap channels: achievable rates and cooperative jamming. IEEE Trans. Inf. Theory 54(6), 2735–2751 (2008)
11. He, X., Yener, A.: Cooperation with an untrusted relay: a secrecy perspective. IEEE Trans. Inf. Theory 56(8), 3807–3827 (2010)
12. Oohama, Y.: Coding for relay channels with confidential messages. In: Proceedings of the IEEE Information Theory Workshop, Cairns, Australia, pp. 87–89, September 2001
13. Oohama, Y.: Capacity theorems for relay channels with confidential messages. In: Proceedings of the IEEE International Symposium on Information Theory, Nice, France, pp. 926–930, June 2007
14. Huang, J., Mukherjee, A., Swindlehurst, A.L.: Secure communication via an untrusted non-regenerative relay in fading channels. IEEE Trans. Signal Process. 61(10), 2536–2550 (2013)
15. He, X., Yener, A.: Two-hop secure communication using an untrusted relay. EURASIP J. Wirel. Commun. Netw. 2009(1), 305146 (2009)
16. Di, B., Song, L., Li, Y.: Radio resource allocation for uplink sparse code multiple access (SCMA) networks using matching game. In: 2016 IEEE International Conference on Communications (ICC), Kuala Lumpur, pp. 1–6 (2016)

Improving Complex Network Controllability via Link Prediction

Ran Wei[1,2], Weiwei Yuan[1,2](✉), Donghai Guan[1,2],
Asad Masood Khattak[3], and Muhammad Fahim[4]

[1] College of Computer Science and Technology,
Nanjing University of Aeronautics and Astronautics, Nanjing 211106, China
ran_dlml@163.com, {yuanweiwei, dhguan}@nuaa.edu.cn
[2] Collaborative Innovation Center of Novel Software Technology
and Industrialization, Nanjing 210016, China
[3] College of Technological Innovation, Zayed University, Dubai,
United Arab Emirates
Asad.Khattak@zu.ac.ae
[4] Institute of Information System, Innopolis University, Innopolis, Russia
m.fahim@innopolis.ru

Abstract. Complex network is a network structure composed of a large number of nodes and complex relationships between these nodes. Using complex network can model many systems in real life. The individual in the system corresponds to the node in the network and the relationship between these individuals corresponds to the edge in the network. The controllability of complex networks is to study how to enable the network to arrive at the desired state from any initial state by external input signals. The external input signals transmit to the whole network through some nodes in the network, and these nodes are called driver node. For the study of controllability of complex network, it is mainly to judge whether the network is controllable or not and how to select the appropriate driver nodes at present. If a network has a high controllability, the network will be easy to control. However, complex networks are vulnerable and will cause declining of controllability. Therefore, we propose in this paper a link prediction-based method to make the network more robust to different modes of attacking. Through experiments we have validated the effectiveness of the proposed method.

Keywords: Network controllability · Link prediction · Complex networks

1 Introduction

Social networking has brought convenience to our life but also brought some negative effects, for example, traffic congestion and large area blackouts. So controlling the state of a complex network is critical.

The research on the controllability [3] of complex networks focuses on controlling the state of the entire network by controlling a few nodes. Due to the large scale of complex networks and the vague information of individuals, traditional control theory can't be directly used to model. Liu et al. [1] put forward the theory of structural

© ICST Institute for Computer Sciences, Social Informatics and Telecommunications Engineering 2019
Published by Springer Nature Switzerland AG 2019. All Rights Reserved
X. B. Zhai et al. (Eds.): MLICOM 2019, LNICST 294, pp. 84–97, 2019.
https://doi.org/10.1007/978-3-030-32388-2_8

controllability [1], and define the concept of driver node which can control the state of other nodes. But structural controllability cannot solve the problem of controllability of networks with all known weights. Subsequently, Yuan et al. put forward the theory of strict controllability [2] and perfected the theory of controllability of complex networks.

Strict controllability has been verified that the controllability of a network is determined by its structure. In most cases, a change in the structure of the network manifests itself in the loss of some links. And usually the dense network structure is easy to control. Our experiments show that the loss of network links in most cases will increase the difficulty of control, that is, the controllability becomes worse. So the most direct way to improve network control is to add links. Due to a lack of purpose, the effect of improvement on controllability is not obvious by adding links randomly in most cases, we can only improve control by restoring the network as much as possible to the pre-lost link structure.

To solve the problems of poor network controllability, in this paper, a link prediction [13] method is proposed to improve the controllability of the network. In our method we extract node properties and local structural features [17] according to current network structure, using these properties and features to train a learning algorithm and then predict the lost edges. Compared to adding edges randomly, link prediction can restore the network as much as possible, and it is simple and the execution efficiency is high. In the case of lost network links, link prediction can effectively improve the controllability of most networks compared to other methods. Our experimental results show that the higher the accuracy of link prediction, the better the controllability improves. In order to improve the accuracy of link prediction, we put forward a Reverse-training method when we don't know the label of test data, this method can effectively adjust learning algorithm and improve accuracy.

The rest of paper is organized as follows. In Sect. 2, we review the related work. In Sect. 3, we introduce our link prediction model. The experimental results are provided and discussed in Sect. 4. Finally, we conclude the paper in Sect. 5.

2 Related Work

2.1 Network Controllability Theory

At present, there are two kinds of controllability theories for complex networks: structural controllability and strict controllability.

If the system matrix [15] A of the complex network system is determined, according to the Kalman controllability criterion, the key to completely control the whole system is to find the appropriate input matrix B and make the matrix C full rank. According to Kalman criterion, Liu et al. put forward the theory of structural controllability: A system is converted into a digraph, if the system is controllable, the directed graph must not contain unreachable nodes and expansion, or it is made of cactus.

The theory of structural controllability [20] can be used to determine whether a network is controllable in most cases, but the foundation of its establishment ignores the edge weight information in the network, and can not exclude that the side weight combination of the network structure matrix A and the input matrix B happens to be ill conditioned, which causes the network to be controllable theoretically but not controllable in reality. According to Kalman criterion, Liu et al. put forward the theory of structural controllability:

The minimum number of driver nodes required to achieve complete controllability is N_D equals to the largest geometric multiplicity of matrix A:

$$N_D = \max\{\mu(\lambda_i)\} \tag{1}$$

$$\mu(\lambda_i) = N - rank(\lambda_i I_N - A) \tag{2}$$

A is the system matrix, and λ_i is the eigenvalue of the matrix A.

To facilitate the measurement of the difficulty of controlling a network, we define controllable n_D to measure the difficulty of controlling the network:

$$n_D = 1 - \frac{N_D}{N} \tag{3}$$

N is the total node number of the network, and N_D is the minimum number of driving nodes needed to control the network. The less the number of drivers needed to control a network, the better the controllability of the network; the more the minimum number of drivers needed, the worse the controllability.

2.2   Network Attack

The attack modes [4] of complex networks are mainly divided into random attack and selective attack. The random attack is to destroy nodes or edges in a network with some probability. Holme [4] and others have done a more comprehensive study of complex network attacks, divided the attacks into node attacks and edge attacks, each of which contains 4 attack strategies.

① ID (initial degree) attack mode. The nodes (edges) are removed according to the order of their degree in initial network.
② IB (initial betweenness) attack mode. The nodes (edges) are removed according to the order of their betweenness in initial network.
③ RD (recalculated degree) attack mode. The nodes (edges) are removed according to the order of their degree.in current network.
④ RB (recalculated betweenness) attack mode. The nodes (edges) are removed according to the order of their betweenness in current network.

2.3   Link Prediction

Link prediction aims to predict the missing edges or possible links in the future based on the current network structure. The method is divided into local similarity-based approaches and global similarity-based approaches.

Local similarity-based [17] approaches use node neighborhood-related [5] structural information to compute the similarity of each node with other nodes in the network. These approaches have good results for link prediction and it is very efficient. The existing methods includes Common Neighbors (CN) [6], Jaccard's Coefficient (JC) [7], and Adamic Adar (AA) [8]. CN is represented as the number of common neighbors between two nodes. The more common neighbors two nodes have, the more likely there is a link between them. Compared with the CN coefficient, the JC coefficient takes into account the whole network structure. Adamic and Adar (AA) take into account the correlation when deciding the strong correlation between the two nodes.

3   Model

3.1   Link Prediction Framework

When a complex network is attacked, the network loses some edges. We now consider the problem of predicting the missing edges in the attack in our dataset. For undirected unweighted networks, the essence of link prediction is a classification problem, which can be solved by machine learning classification algorithm [16].

Local similarity-based approaches have good performance for link prediction [19]. In our model, we try to combine these approaches with some attributes of the network as feature for training learning algorithm. The features are divided into two classes. The first class is based on the attribute of the edge. The second class is based on the local approach of the network. For the edge (x, y), the first class we choose is the degree of x and y and the shortest path between x and y; the second class we choose is JC, AA and CN.

We use a logistic regression classifier to combine the evidence from these individual features into link prediction. Logistic regression learns a model of the form

$$P(+|x) = \frac{1}{1 + e^{-(b_0 + \sum_i^n b_i x_i)}} \qquad (4)$$

where x is a vector of features $(x1, \ldots, xn)$ and $(b0, \ldots, bn)$ are the coefficients we estimate based on the training data. For every edge (u, v) with label 1 we sample a random edge with label 0, which ensures that the number of the two labels edges in the data we consider for training and prediction is balanced. Moreover, we also consider two different evaluation measures: the classification accuracy and the area under the ROC curve (AUC). For ease of exposition we focus on classification accuracy on a balanced dataset.

3.2   Reverse-Training Method

The higher the accuracy of link prediction, the better the network recovery. So we now consider the problem of improving the accuracy of link prediction. If we know the labels of training data and test data, we can easily adjust to the best classifier. In addition to the parameters of learning algorithm, the training data which is used to train classifier also affects the accuracy of link prediction. We put forward a reverse-training method here. Compared to the traditional method, this method is more efficient and it shows a good effect in cases that we only know the labels of training data.

This method is divided into two steps, the first step is clearing interfering data and the second step is adjusting the parameters of learning algorithm.

To obtain good classifiers, good training data is required. Some sample features can't reflect the category labels it belongs to, these samples will affect the training of learning algorithms. So we call these samples as interfering data. In filtering the interfering data, we use the idea of data partition [11]. The algorithm is shown in Table 1.

Table 1. Interfering data filtering algorithm.

Algorithm 1 interfering data filtering algorithm
Input: T(training data), n(number of subset), m(division times), H(learning algorithm)
Output: A(detected interfering subset of E)
1: $A \leftarrow \varnothing$
2: **for** i = 1, ..., m **do**
3:    form n disjoint almost equally sized subset of E_i, where $\bigcup_i E_i = E$
4:    **for** j = 1, ..., n **do**
5:       form $E_t \leftarrow E \backslash E_i$
6:       **for** k = 1, ..., t **do**
7:          ues E_t train H to classify E_i
8:          **for** every $e \in E_i$ **do**
9:             **if** H incorrectly classifies e
10:                **then** $A \leftarrow A \cup e$
11:       **end for**
12:    **end for**
13:    **end for**
14: **end for**

After clearing up the interfering data [9, 20], the second step is adjusting classifier. The idea of dual-learning is used here [10]. Dual-learning has a good effect on Machine Translation and solves the shortage of parallel training data.

Table 2. Classifier adjustment algorithm.

Algorithm 2 classifier adjustment algorithm
1:**Input:** T_1(the training set after filtering interfering data), H(learning algorithm), T_2(the test data), n(the number of T_1)
2: max = 0
3: **repeat**
4:    count = 0
5:    use T_1 train H to classify T_2 and get labels of test data, L_1
6:    use T_2 and L train H to classify T_1 and get labels of training data, $L_{2\backslash}$
7:    **for** i = 1, ..., n **do**
8:       **if** $L_{1i} == L_{2i}$
9:          **then** count = count + 1
10:    **end for**
11:    max = count
12: **until** convergence

We use the training data to train the classifier, and classify the test data. Conversely, we use the test data and the results as labels for the test data to train the classifier. We get new labels of training data after classifying. By comparing the new labels and the original labels of the training set, we can evaluate the performance of the classifier. If most new labels and the original labels of the training data are identical, it can be proved that the classifier is good. Just like Machine Translation, we convert a message from language A to language B using a translation model. Then we convert the received message from language B back to language A using another translation model. If the message is consistent in language A, we can know whether the two translation model perform well or not. We can adjust the classifier to repeat this process. This process can be iterated for many rounds until the new label of the training set and the original label of the test set have the maximum similarity. We can think the classifier is the best at this time. The Algorithm of adjusting classifier is shown in Table 2.

4   Experiments

In this paper we use four real world networks: Airport, Ant, Jazz, Email, they are all undirected and unweighted. Their network topology properties are shown in Table 3.

Table 3. The information of Network topology.

Network	Node	Edge	Number of driver node
Airport	500	2980	132
Email-Enron	1133	5451	42
Ant	453	2040	27
Jazz	198	2742	7

We remove a certain proportion of edges in the network according to the attack mode, then calculate the controllability of the missing edge network. The ratio of edges removed is called the attack ratio. The attack modes we used in the experiment are: random attack mode, ID attack mode and IB attack mode. ID(IB) attack mode is divided into ID-max(IB-max) mode and ID-min(IB-min) mode, which is defined as removing the edge has the maximum degree (betweenness) in initial network and removing the edge has the minimum degree (betweenness) in initial network. For each network, we adopt different attack ratios and attack modes and analysis the maximal connected subgraph after attacking. Taking into account the randomness of random attack mode, we take the average of the results of the 10 experiments as a reference.

The controllability of each network varies little under random attack. Airport and email have a little decline. When the attack ratio is low, the controllability of Ant has an improvement, but has a decline when the attack ratio is over 15%. Jazz has an improvement in controllability and controllability gradually converges to 1. Even if the attack ratio reaches 40%, the controllability of Email changes very slightly compared to other networks because Email has good controllability initially. Based on the topology information of the network, the better the controllability of the network is, the smaller the range of variation suffered by random attacks. The experimental results are shown in Fig. 1.

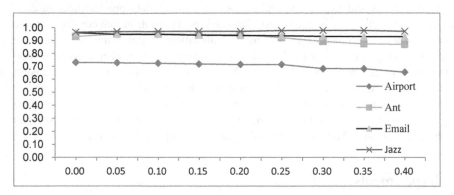

Fig. 1. Controllability of every network under random mode with different attack ratio, the horizontal axis is attack ratio and the vertical axis is controllability.

Depending on the degree of the edge being removed, ID mode is divided into ID-max and ID-min. The controllability of these real world networks has almost no change under ID-max and varies greatly under ID-min, the experimental results are shown in Fig. 2.

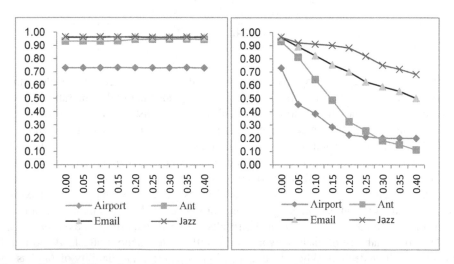

Fig. 2. Controllability of every network under ID mode with different attack ratio, the horizontal axis is attack ratio and the vertical axis is controllability. (a) is ID-max and (b) is ID-min.

There are some edges have no influence in the controllability of network, and these edges are called redundant edge. If a node has no influence on the controllability of the network, it is said to be a redundant node and the degree of redundant node is usually relatively large. Similarly, edges that have no effect on network controllability are called redundant edge. The experimental results show that the controllability of these networks has barely changed under ID-max mode, which prove that the degree of redundant edge is also relatively large. Removing the edges with small degree will have great influence on the network structure and the experimental results show that the controllability of these networks varies greatly even if the attack ratio is low under ID-min mode. It can be proved that the edges which have small degree are crucial for the controllability of network.

Betweenness is also an important topological feature of complex networks. Edge betweenness is defined as the proportion of the number of paths passing through the edge in all shortest paths in the network to the total number of shortest paths. The experimental results of IB mode are similar with which under ID mode, but the controllability of the network under IB-max is not as stable as ID-max. With the increase of attack proportion, the controllability of Airport even improves. It is possible that some edges with large betweenness have certain obstacles to the controllability of the network. Similar to the results under ID-min mode, the controllability of the network under IB-min mode becomes worse with the increase of attack proportion, but the decline rate is not as fast as that under ID-min mode. We can also infer that the small betweenness of edges have an important influence on the controllability of the network. The experimental results are shown in Fig. 3.

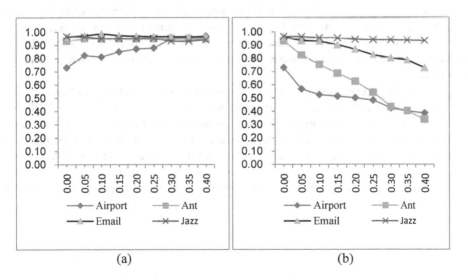

(a)   (b)

Fig. 3. Controllability of every network under IB mode with different attack ratio, the horizontal axis is attack ratio and the vertical axis is controllability. (a) is ID-max and (b) is ID-min.

The controllability of all networks has a decline under ID-min mode and some networks have a decline under random attack mode. Random addition of edges could not improve the network controllability, so we tried to restore the network structure as much as possible through link prediction. We use the model proposed in this paper to extract attribute features from the network, and take the calculated results of CN, AA and JC as local features. Finally, we use these features to train logistic regression learning algorithm. The link prediction problem can be solved as a binary classification problem. There is an edge between two nodes that belongs to category '1', while there is no edge that belongs to category '0'.

Our model is used to predict the restoration of three networks with reduced controllability through links, and the comparison of the controllability of the network before and after improvement is shown in Fig. 4.

We recorded the controllability curve of the network under different proportions before link prediction as CBLP, and the curve after link prediction as CALP. Experimental results are shown in Fig. 4. The experimental results show that the controllability of the three networks is improved significantly after link prediction under random attacks. When the attack proportion of Ant network is low, the effect does not improve, but decreases. When the attack proportion exceeds 20%, the controllability begins to improve greatly. Compared with random attack mode, the controllability of the network is not significantly improved after link prediction in ID-min mode, and only improves a little when the attack rate is high. From the experimental results we can infer that link prediction is helpful to improve the controllability of the network.

The prediction accuracy of each network through links under different attack modes is shown in Table 4. The structures of every network are seriously damaged under ID-min attack mode because this mode will generate many isolated nodes. So the accuracy of link prediction under this attack mode is low. The function of link prediction is to restore the structure of the network before the attack as much as possible. If the network structure is restored more, the controllability of the network should be improved.

We use the reverse-training method in this paper to improve the accuracy of link prediction. The accuracy after improvement of every network are shown in Table 5.

From the experimental results, we can see that the accuracy of network link prediction using our method has been improved to some extent. We recorded the controllability curve of the network before improving the accuracy rate as CBIA, and the curve after improving the accuracy rate as CAIA. Comparison results of network controllability before and after link prediction accuracy improvement are shown in Fig. 5.

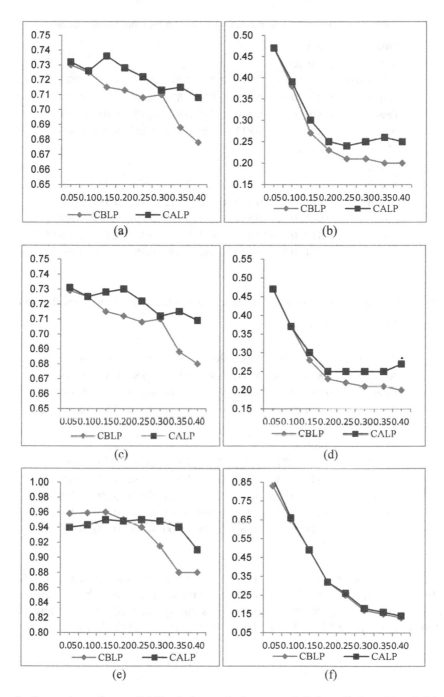

Fig. 4. Comparison of controllability before and after network link prediction. (a) and (b) are comparison of controllability of Airport before and after link prediction in random attack mode and ID-min mode respectively; (c) and (d) are comparison of controllability of Email before and after link prediction in random attack mode and ID-min mode respectively; (e) and (f) are comparison of controllability of Ant before and after link prediction in random attack mode and ID-min mode respectively.

Table 4. Accuracy of link prediction under random and ID-min mode

Mode	Random							
Metric	Accuracy							
Attack ratio	5%	10%	15%	20%	25%	30%	35%	40%
Airport	0.876	0.884	0.869	0.878	0.876	0.867	0.852	0.869
Email	0.810	0.812	0.796	0.801	0.813	0.800	0.800	0.781
Ant	0.831	0.823	0.812	0.825	0.828	0.783	0.803	0.805
Mode	ID-min							
Metric	Accuracy							
Attack ratio	5%	10%	15%	20%	25%	30%	35%	40%
Airport	0.445	0.439	0.445	0.492	0.512	0.512	0.550	0.539
Email	0.502	0.521	0.511	0.513	0.497	0.509	0.498	0.497
Ant	0.472	0.450	0.467	0.469	0.473	0.477	0.482	0.480
Jazz	0.524	0.579	0.550	0.486	0.480	0.485	0.496	0.497

Table 5. Accuracy of link prediction after improvement under random mode and ID-min mode

Mode	Random							
Metric	Accuracy							
Attack ratio	5%	10%	15%	20%	25%	30%	35%	40%
Airport	0.889	0.900	0.896	0.891	0.893	0.884	0.883	0.879
Email	0.842	0.842	0.835	0.828	0.814	0.799	0.800	0.781
Ant	0.896	0.878	0.858	0.855	0.851	0.842	0.838	0.836
Mode	ID-min							
Metric	Accuracy							
Attack ratio	5%	10%	15%	20%	25%	30%	35%	40%
Airport	0.454	0.446	0.447	0.544	0.579	0.582	0.627	0.620
Email	0.647	0.526	0.519	0.528	0.531	0.539	0.509	0.509
Ant	0.637	0.615	0.495	0.469	0.493	0.480	0.486	0.490
Jazz	0.544	0.605	0.562	0.525	0.500	0.506	0.496	0.505

The experimental results show that under random attack mode, the controllability of the three networks has been improved after the improvement of link prediction accuracy. The controllability of the three networks hardly changed when the attack proportion was low in the ID mode, also because the accuracy of the link prediction in the ID mode was low.

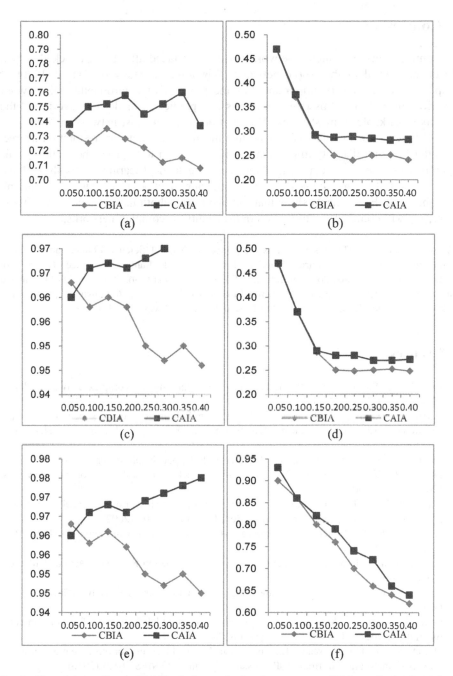

Fig. 5. Comparison of controllability before and after the accuracy of link prediction improved. (a) and (b) are comparison of controllability of Airport before and after improving in random attack mode and id-min mode respectively; (c) and (d) are comparison of controllability of Email before and after improving in random attack mode and id-min mode respectively; (e) and (f) are comparison of controllability of Ant before and after improving in random attack mode and id-min mode respectively.

5 Conclusion

The controllability of complex network is usually reduced after being attacked, which affects the control of the whole network. Therefore, the study of controllability of complex network is very important. For the problem of controllability of network reduction under attack, this paper proposes link prediction model to solve it and the effect is remarkable in most cases. The controllability of most networks is improved under different attack modes. We found that the higher the network restoration degree, the better the controllability improvement effect. In order to improve the accuracy, this paper proposes reverse-training method according to dual-learning algorithm. If the labels of test data are unknown, reverse-training method can adjust the learning algorithm well. Experiments show that the two models both have a good effect. In the future, we will continue to study the controllability of complex networks.

Acknowledgements. This research was supported by Natural Science Foundation of China (Grant no. 61672284), Natural Science Foundation of Jiangsu Province (Grant no. BK20171418), China Postdoctoral Science Foundation (Grant no. 2016M591841), Jiangsu Planned Projects for Postdoctoral Research Funds (No. 1601225C). Meanwhile, this research work was supported by Zayed University Research Cluster Award \# R18038.

References

1. Liu, Y.-Y., Slotine, J.J., Barabási, A.L.: Controllability of complex network. Nature **473**(7346), 167–173 (2011)
2. Yuan, Z., Zhao, C., Di, Z., et al.: Exact controllability of complex networks. Nature Commun. **4**, (2013). Conference 2016. LNCS, vol. 9999, pp. 1–13. Springer, Heidelberg (2016)
3. Rugh, W.J.: Linear System Theory. Prentice Hall, Upper Saddle River (1996)
4. Holme, P., Kim, B.J., Yoon, C.N., Han, S.K.: Attack vulnerability of complex networks. Phys. Rev. E (2002)
5. Davidsen, J., Ebel, H., Bornholdt, S.: Emergence of a small world from local interactions: modeling acquaintance networks. Phys. Rev. Lett. **88**, 128701 (2002)
6. Newman, M.E.J.: Clustering and preferential attachment in growing networks. Phys. Rev. Lett. E **64**, 025102 (2001)
7. Salton, G., McGill, M.J.: Introduction to Modern Information Retrieval. McGrawHill, New York (1983)
8. Adamic, L.A., Adar, E.: Friends and neighbors on the web. Soc. Netw. **25**(3), 211–230 (2003)
9. Guan, D., Yuan, W., Ma, T., Lee, S.: Detecting potential labeling errors for bioinformatics by multiple voting. Knowl.-Based Syst. **66**, 28–35 (2014)
10. He, D., Xia, Y., Qin, T., Wang, L., Yu, N., Liu, T.: Dual learning for machine translation. In: Advances in Neural Information Processing Systems 29 (NIPS 2016) (2016)
11. John, G.H.: Robust decision trees: removing outliers from databases. In: Proceeding of International Conference on Knowledge Discovery and Data Mining, pp. 174–179 (1995)
12. Wu, X., Zhu, X., Chen, Q.: Eliminating class noise in large datasets. In: Proceeding of International Conference on Machine Learning, pp. 920–927 (2003)

13. Hasan, M.A., Zaki, M.J.: A survey of link prediction in social networks. In: Aggarwal, C. (ed.) Social Network Data Analytics, pp. 243–275. Springer, Boston (2011). https://doi.org/10.1007/978-1-4419-8462-3_9

14. Bianchin, G., Pasqualetti, F., Zampieri, S.: The role of diameter in the controllability of complex networks. In: CDC 2015, pp. 980–985 (2015)

15. Benavides, P.T., Diwekar, U.M., Cabezas, H.: Controllability of complex networks for sustainable system dynamics. J. Complex Netw. 3(4), 566–583 (2015)

16. Curiskis, S.A., Osborn, T.R., Kennedy, P.J.: Link prediction and topological feature importance in social networks. In: AusDM 2015, pp. 39–50 (2015)

17. Yu, Z., Kening, G., Feng, L., Ge, Y.: A new method for link prediction using various features in social networks. In: IEEE WISA 2014, pp. 144–147 (2014)

18. Verbaeten, S., Van Assche, A.: Ensemble methods for noise elimination in classification problems. In: Windeatt, T., Roli, F. (eds.) MCS 2003. LNCS, vol. 2709, pp. 317–325. Springer, Heidelberg (2003). https://doi.org/10.1007/3-540-44938-8_32

19. Pasqualetti, F., Zampieri, S., Bullo, F.: Controllability metrics, limitations and algorithms for complex networks. IEEE Trans. Control. Netw. Syst. 1(1), 40–52 (2014)

20. Sun, P.G.: Controllability and modularity of complex networks. Inf. Sci. 325, 20–32 (2015)

Communications

Rectangular Waveguide Design Optimization by Sequential Nonlinear Programming and Genetic Algorithm

Meijiao Lin[1], Xin Zhang[1(✉)], Yang Li[1], and Zhou Wu[2]

[1] Tianjin Key Laboratory of Wireless Mobile Communications and Power
Transmission, Tianjin Normal University, Tianjin 300387, China
1648016529@qq.com, ecemark@tjnu.edu.cn,
liyang_tongxin@163.com
[2] School of Automation, Chongqing University, Chongqing 400044, China
zhouwu@cqu.edu.cn

Abstract. Rectangular waveguide is a common metal waveguide with simple fabrication, low loss and dual polarization. It is often used in antenna feeders requiring dual polarization mode, and also widely used in various resonators and wavelength meters. This paper attempts to design, simulate and optimize rectangular waveguide. By setting the length, width and height of rectangular waveguide, the required rectangular waveguide is designed. The resonant frequency of rectangular waveguide is setting to 9.25 GHz. Moreover, the input return loss is required to be as small as possible. After satisfying the requirements, sequential nonlinear programming and genetic algorithm are used to optimize both voltage standing wave ratio and normalized impedance matching. Simulation results show that the proposed method is able to accomplish the optimal design of rectangular waveguide.

Keywords: Rectangular waveguide · Optimal design · Sequential nonlinear programming · Genetic algorithm

1 Introduction

Rectangular waveguide is a kind of metal tube with rectangular cross section [1]. If the inner conductor of the coaxial line is removed, under certain conditions, electromagnetic energy can also be transmitted in the rectangular space surrounded by the outer conductor, which is the rectangular waveguide [2]. Rectangular waveguide has the advantages of simple fabrication, low loss and bipolarity [3]. They are usually used in antenna feeders requiring bipolar mode, and are also widely used in various resonators and wavelength meters. They are commonly used conventional metal waveguide [4]. Rectangular waveguide cannot propagate Transverse Electric and Magnetic Field, but can only propagate Transverse Electric or Transverse Magnetic waves [5].

As a global method, genetic algorithm [6] can use the idea of genetics to find the optimal value without considering the specific characteristics of the objective function to be optimized [7]. The objective function of antenna array optimization has the

© ICST Institute for Computer Sciences, Social Informatics and Telecommunications Engineering 2019
Published by Springer Nature Switzerland AG 2019. All Rights Reserved
X. B. Zhai et al. (Eds.): MLICOM 2019, LNICST 294, pp. 101–108, 2019.
https://doi.org/10.1007/978-3-030-32388-2_9

characteristics of complex shape and many peaks, so it is more appropriate to use genetic algorithm to optimize the antenna array [8].

Similar to quasi-Newton method, sequential nonlinear programming algorithm is suitable for solving low-noise problem of objective function. Noise filtering is introduced in sequential nonlinear programming, which can reduce the influence of noise appropriately. Sequential nonlinear programming uses response surface modeling technology to estimate the value of the objective function more accurately. Compared with quasi-Newton method, sequential nonlinear programming has faster convergence speed. In addition, sequential nonlinear programming allows the use of non-linear constraints, which is more widely used than Newton's method and pattern search method [9].

2   Waveguide Model and Optimization Model

2.1   Waveguide Model

The rectangular waveguide model consists of two cuboid models. One is used to simulate a rectangular waveguide with a cross-section size of 0.4 in. × 0.9 in., and the other is used to simulate a free space with a cross-section size of 0.5 in. × 1.0 in. The height of both the simulated rectangular waveguide and the cuboid in the free space is 1 in., as shown in Fig. 1.

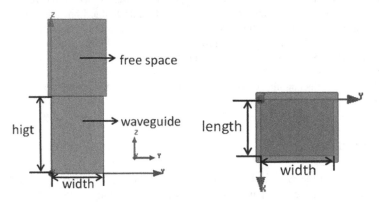

Fig. 1. Rectangular waveguide model.

2.2   Optimization Model

The parameter scanning analysis function is used to analyze the relationship between the resonant frequency points and the length, width and height of the rectangular waveguide. The design of rectangular waveguide is expressed as (1).

$$\begin{aligned}
\min \quad & InputReturnLoss(l, w, h) \\
s.t. \quad & Frequency(l, w, h) = 9.25 \text{ GHz} \\
& Impedance(l, w, h) = 50 \ \Omega \\
& 0.2 \le l \le 0.6 \\
& 0.7 \le w \le 1.1 \\
& 0.8 \le h \le 1.2
\end{aligned} \tag{1}$$

where variables l, w, and h are respectively the length, width and height of rectangular waveguide. The objective is to minimizing input return loss of waveguide under resonant frequency and impedance constraints. The ranges of variables l, w, and h are set based on empirical experience.

Then, the optimal design is carried out by Sequential Nonlinear Programming to optimize the length, width and height of the rectangular waveguide so that the resonant frequency of the antenna falls to 9.25 GHz.

3   Optimized Model Analysis and Discussion

3.1   Genetic Algorithm

S11 represents the echo loss, that is, how much energy is reflected back to the source, the smaller the value, the better. Length optimization ranges from 0.2 to 0.6 in., Width optimization ranges from 0.7 to 1.1 in. and High optimization ranges from 0.8 to 1.2 in.

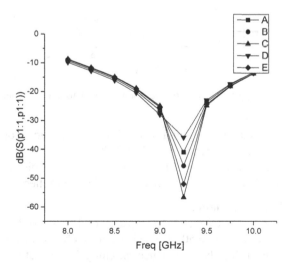

Fig. 2. Echo loss graphs of different variables found by genetic algorithm.

In Fig. 2, the five graphs labeled from A to E are as follows.

A: High = 0.903066 in., Length = 0.584262 in., Width = 0.782867 in.
B: High = 1.071951 in., Length = 0.584290 in., Width = 0.779443 in.
C: High = 1.124028 in., Length = 0.584294 in., Width = 0.777727 in.
D: High = 1.093114 in., Length = 0.584325 in., Width = 0.787910 in.
E: High = 0.998307 in., Length = 0.584334 in., Width = 0.778503 in.

From Fig. 2, when Length = 0.584294 in., Width = 0.777727 in. and High = 1.124028 in., the lowest point of S11 curve is above 9.25 GHz and the lowest point is −56.7140 dB. Therefore, the rectangular waveguide is set to change its size, and the voltage rejection ratio and the normalized matched impedance of the rectangular waveguide are analyzed.

Voltage Standing Wave Ratio (VSWR)

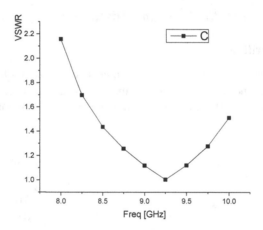

Fig. 3. Voltage standing wave ratio of the optimal result found by genetic algorithm.

Figure 3 is analyzed based on the optimal result found by genetic algorithm. As shown in Fig. 3, the voltage standing wave ratio is 1.002923, close to 1. At this time, the impedance of the feeder and antenna is highly matched. At this time, all the high frequency energy is radiated by the antenna, and there is no reflection loss of energy.

Normalized Matching Impedance
As shown in Fig. 4, normalized matching impedance [10] is 1.0013, close to 1. The number is normalized according to 50 Ω. The impedance obtained by genetic algorithm is 50.065 Ω. It is proved that the impedance matching is good at this time, which is consistent with the results of VSWR mentioned above.

3.2 Sequential Nonlinear Programming

Sequential nonlinear programming is used to solve rectangular waveguide model (1). The parameter settings and simulation environment are the same as Sect. 3.1.

In Fig. 5, the five graphs labeled from A to E are as follows.

A': High = 1.088738 in., Length = 0.586402 in., Width = 0.774999 in.
B': High = 1.080961 in., Length = 0.586469 in., Width = 0.775927 in.
C': High = 1.085099 in., Length = 0.586591 in., Width = 0.775738 in.
D': High = 1.084712 in., Length = 0.586621 in., Width = 0.775624 in.
E': High = 1.085877 in., Length = 0.586668 in., Width = 0.775699 in.

Name	Freq	Ang	Mag	RX
m1	9.2500	62.5288	0.0015	1.0013 + 0.0026i

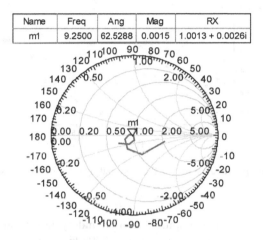

Fig. 4. Smith chart of the optimal result found by genetic algorithm.

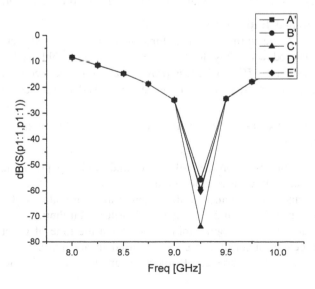

Fig. 5. Echo loss graphs of different variables found by sequential nonlinear programming.

From   Fig. 5,   when   Length = 0.586591 in.,   Width = 0.775738 in.,   High = 1.085099 in., the lowest point of the S11 curve is above 9.25 GHz and the lowest value is −74.0596 dB. Therefore, the rectangular waveguide is set to change its size, and the voltage rejection ratio and the normalized matched impedance of the rectangular waveguide are analyzed.

Voltage Standing Wave Ratio

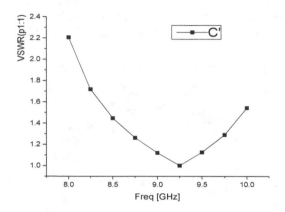

Fig. 6. Voltage standing wave ratio of the optimal result found by sequential nonlinear programming.

Figure 6 is analyzed based on the optimal result found by genetic algorithm. As shown in Fig. 6, the voltage standing wave ratio is 1.000396, close to 1. At this time, the impedance of the feeder and antenna is highly matched. At this time, all the high frequency energy is radiated by the antenna, and there is no reflection loss of energy.

Normalized Matched Impedance
As shown in Fig. 7, the normalized matching impedance is 1.0003, close to 1. The number is normalized according to 50 Ω. The impedance obtained by sequential nonlinear programming is 50.015 Ω. It is proved that the impedance matching is good at this time, which is consistent with the results of VSWR mentioned above.

3.3   Comparison of Genetic Algorithm and Sequential Nonlinear Programming

Comparing the two optimization methods, sequential nonlinear programming is better than genetic algorithm in terms of antenna impedance matching. Moreover, impedance of the solution found by sequential nonlinear programming matches 50 Ω better than impedance of the solution found by genetic algorithm. Furthermore, the simulation time of sequential nonlinear programming is less than the time of genetic algorithm. This is because genetic algorithm is generally used in antenna arrays with complex shape and multi-peak characteristics of objective function, which is not applicable to simple antenna model. Therefore, sequential nonlinear programming is more suitable to solve the rectangular waveguide model (1) than genetic algorithm.

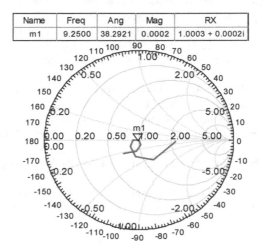

Name	Freq	Ang	Mag	RX
m1	9.2500	38.2921	0.0002	1.0003 + 0.0002i

Fig. 7. Smith chart of the optimal result found by sequential nonlinear programming.

4 Conclusion

This paper focuses on the optimization design of rectangular waveguide based on genetic algorithm and sequential nonlinear programming. By setting the length, width and height of rectangular waveguide as variables, a rectangular waveguide model is designed to minimize input return loss of radiation direction at 9.25 GHz frequency. Then two methods are used to solve the optimization model. Based on simulation results, sequential nonlinear programming attains better solution and costs less computational time than genetic algorithm.

Acknowledgment. This research was supported in part by the National Natural Science Foundation of China (Project No. 61603275, 61601329, 61803054), the Tianjin Higher Education Creative Team Funds Program, the Basic Research and Frontier Exploration Project (Project No. cstc2018jcyjAX0297), the Fundamental Research Funds for the Central Universities (Project No. 2019CDQYZDH030), and the Doctor Fund of Tianjin Normal University (Project No. 52XB1905).

References

1. Deslandes, D., Wu, K.: Integrated microstrip and rectangular waveguide in planar form. IEEE Microw. Wirel. Compon. Lett. **11**(2), 68–70 (2001)
2. Sun, D., Xu, J.: Rectangular waveguide coupler with adjustable coupling coefficient using gap waveguide technology. Electron. Lett. **53**(3), 167–169 (2017)

3. Sutthaweekul, R., Tian, G.Y.: Steel corrosion stages characterization using open-ended rectangular waveguide probe. IEEE Sens. J. **18**(3), 1054–1062 (2018)
4. Filins'kyy, L.A.: Microwave propagation in specimens of foam materials located in rectangular waveguide. In: 6th International Conference on Ultrawideband and Ultrashort Impulse Signals, pp. 108–110. IEEE, Sevastopol (2012)
5. Zhang, Y., Krasheninnikov, S.I.: Electron dynamics in the laser and quasi-static electric and magnetic fields. Phys. Lett. A **382**(27), 1801–1806 (2018)
6. Goldberg, D.: Genetic Algorithms in Search, Optimization, and Machine Learning. Addison-Wesley, Boston (1989)
7. Horton, P., Jaboyedoff, M., Obled, C.: Global optimization of an analog method by means of genetic algorithms. Mon. Weather Rev. **145**(4), 1275–1294 (2017)
8. Coccioli, R., Pelosi, G., Selleri, S.: Optimization of bends in rectangular waveguide by a finite-element genetic-algorithm procedure. Microw. Opt. Technol. Lett. **16**(5), 287–290 (1997)
9. Optimization Methods. http://blog.sina.com.cn/s/blog_4bc5db550100prev.html. Accessed 27 Feb 2019
10. Williams, D.F., Jargon, J., Arz, U.: Rectangular-waveguide impedance. In: 85th Microwave Measurement Conference (ARFTG), pp. 1–5. IEEE, Phoenix (2015)

Noise Reduction in Network Embedding

Cong Li[1,2], Donghai Guan[1,2(✉)], Zhiyuan Cui[1,2], Weiwei Yuan[1,2],
Asad Masood Khattak[3], and Muhammad Fahim[4]

[1] College of Computer Science and Technology,
Nanjing University of Aeronautics and Astronautics, Nanjing 211106, China
18851870127@163.com, {dhguan,yuanweiwei}@nuaa.edu.cn,
565508802@qq.com
[2] Collaborative Innovation Center of Novel Software Technology
and Industrialization, Nanjing 210016, China
[3] College of Technological Innovation, Zayed University, Dubai,
United Arab Emirates
Asad.Khattak@zu.ac.ae
[4] Institute of Information System, Innopolis University, Innopolis, Russia
m.fahim@innopolis.ru

Abstract. Network Embedding aims to learn latent representations and effectively preserves structure of network and information of vertices. Recently, networks with rich side information such as vertex's label and links between vertices have attracted significant interest due to its wide applications such as node classification and link prediction. It's well known that, in real world applications, network always contains mislabeled vertices and edges, which will cause the embedding preserves mistake information. However, current semi-supervised graph embedding algorithms assume the vertex label is ground-truth. Manually relabel all mislabeled vertices is always inapplicable, therefore, how to effective reduce noise so as to maximize the graph analysis task performance is extremely important. In this paper, we focus on reducing label noise ratio in dataset to obtain more reasonable embedding. We proposed two methods for any semi-supervised network embedding algorithm to tackle it: first approach uses a model to identify potential noise vertices and correct them, second approach uses two voting strategy to precisely relabel vertex. To the best of our knowledge, we are the first to tackle this issue in network embedding. Our experiments are conducted on three public data sets.

Keywords: Network embedding · Noise identification · Voting

1 Introduction

Networks naturally exist in a widely diversity of real world scenarios, e.g., citation paper in research areas, social network such as Face Book, Wei Bo. Directly analysis these networks may suffer the high computation and space cost [1]. One fundamental and effective solution is graph embedding. With such kind of vertex representations, the graph analytic tasks can be conducted efficiently in both time and space.

© ICST Institute for Computer Sciences, Social Informatics and Telecommunications Engineering 2019
Published by Springer Nature Switzerland AG 2019. All Rights Reserved
X. B. Zhai et al. (Eds.): MLICOM 2019, LNICST 294, pp. 109–120, 2019.
https://doi.org/10.1007/978-3-030-32388-2_10

A network can be regarded as a graph $G = (V_U, V_L, E)$. V_U represent unlabeled vertex set, and V_L represent labeled vertex set in a network, and E represent edge set, which is the relationship among the vertices.

Nowadays network embedding method can be divided into two categories based on whether the vertex's label is considered in the embedding procedure. In this paper, we focus on the networks containing labelled vertices. There are GCN [2], which proposes a multi-layer Graph Convolutional Network for semi-supervised node classification on graph and LANE [3] is also proposed to incorporate the label information into the attributed network embedding. However, all these methods based on a hypothesis that the labeled data is given ground-truth label, which is impossible in real word applications. Take user recommend system as an example, we recommend some users to a target user for they have same label, which can represent their age, gender, interest, and they are linked by n-hop. Obviously, mislabeled data impact the performance of a recommend system. Mislabeled data can be divided into two classes, mislabeled vertex and mislabeled edge [4].

In this work, we focus on mislabeled vertex, leaving the latter to future work. Given a network, our goal is to design a framework which can efficiently relabel mislabeled data to obtain more reasonable embedding. There are two main issues. First, we need to identify mislabeled vertex as candidates for relabel. Second, after we relabel the vertex, how do we use relabel data sets. In other words, how do we combine relabel methods with network embedding framework.

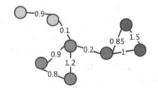

Fig. 1. Weight between vertices

In this paper, we proposed an effective framework tackles above mentioned issues. For identify and correct, we use the cost of misclassification to estimate potential noise vertex and correct. And, we consider a popular noise correct method, majority voting, to relabel vertex. Considered characteristic of network, after re-label process, we also propose a label propagation process [5, 6], to gain more labeled vertex. The intuition behind propagation process is the following: two vertices are more similar if they are connected by an edge with larger weight named first-order proximity. Same color circles belong to one class (see Fig. 1). In the context of our work, we use cosine similarity to represent weight of an edge. As the process progresses, our framework will gain more and more vertices with reasonable label. Meanwhile, with the more reasonable labeled vertices, the network embedding framework able to train more reasonable vertex embedding.

The chiefly contributions of this paper are follows:

(1) We are the first to tackle noise issue in network. Our framework can optimize the network embedding's performance by accurately identify and relabel mislabeled vertex.
(2) We study the impact of label noise and edge noise on network embedding's performance. Combing our method and network embedding, we effective eliminate the impact of label noise.
(3) We verify the effectiveness of our method by conducting experiments on three public citation datasets. And the results prove our method can improve embedding's performance in task node classification.

The rest of the paper is organized as follows: Sect. 2 introduces the related work of network embedding and noise relabel. Our proposed method will be introduced in Sect. 3. Section 4 introduce datasets and show experiments and results. Section 5 summarizes our paper, and we discuss our future work.

2   Related Works

In this paper, we focus on identifying mislabeled vertex and relabeling them so as to improve the network embedding's performance in task of node classification. In this section, we review the literature in two relevant areas: network embedding and noise reduction.

2.1   Network Embedding

Many complex applications take the form of networks. Most exist analysis methods for network embedding are high computation and space cost. Early study [7] aims to preserve the network's structure information, such as first-order, second-order and high-order proximities by matrix factorization. In series of matrix factorization models, Singular Value Decomposition (SVD) is commonly used in network embedding due to its optimality for low-rank approximation [8] These methods always have a poor performance when vertex's number grow up. Inspired by the recent success of natural language processing(NLP)some researchers [9, 10] start to embed network use a random walk or biased walk to sample paths from networks, and then apply skip-gram [11] on these walks to preserve network's information. Obviously, methods mentioned before only consider network topology. In nowadays networks always are accompanied rich side information [8], such as vertex label, signed link between vertices. With vertex label, network embedding can train in a semi-supervised manner. On the one hand, GCN [2], considers the problem of classifying nodes (such as documents) in a graph (such as a citation network), where labels are only available for a small subset of vertices. On the other hand, SNE [12, 16], which exploits the network structure and user attributes simultaneously for network representation learning. In this paper, we adopt GCN as an example embedding framework.

GCN considers a multi-layer Graph Convolutional Network (GCN) with the following layer-wise propagation rule:

$$f(H^{(l)}, A) = \sigma\left(\hat{D}^{-\frac{1}{2}}\hat{A}\hat{D}^{-\frac{1}{2}}H^{(l)}W^{(l)}\right) \tag{1}$$

Where W is a weight matrix for the l-th neural network layer and $\sigma(\cdot)$ is a non-linear activation function like the ReLU. And $\hat{A} = A + 1$, where I is the identity matrix and D is the diagonal node degree matrix of $\hat{A}$. A is symmetric adjacency matrix (binary or weighted). $H^0 = X$, which is a matrix of node feature vectors X_i. Then the forward of GCN take the simple form:

$$Z = f(X, A) = softmax\left(\hat{A}ReLU\left(\hat{A}XW^{(0)}\right)W^{(1)}\right) \tag{2}$$

For a semi-supervised multiclass classification, GCN evaluate the cross-entropy error over all labeled examples:

$$Loss = -\sum_{l \in y_L}\sum_{f=1}^{F} Y_{lf} \ln Z_{lf} \tag{3}$$

Where y_L is set of node indices that have labels.

2.2   Noise Reduction

Since ground-truth labelled data is often expensive to obtain and manually label all training data is inapplicable [13]. In real applications, labelled data always contains mislabeled data. A popular noise reduction method is that relabel vertex by its nearest neighbors which can calculate by similarity function such as cosine similarity:

$$similarity = \cos(\theta) = \frac{A \bullet B}{\|A\|\|B\|} \tag{4}$$

where A, B representative vector. $\bullet$ is dot product. Another noise data relabel framework aims to find and relabel mislabeled data, which usually consists of two primary processes: a classification system and voting system, and k-fold cross-validation [15]. For classification system, the majority work is build classifiers based on current features (embedding) and predict label for all labelled data. Then voting system votes a label for a target data. Based on the vote strategy, there are two voting strategies: majority vote and consensus vote [17]. Majority voting choose a label, which are predicted by more than half classifiers. Consensus voting choose label which are predicted by all the classifiers [15].

In network embedding scenario, our work is distinct different from the most noise relabel frameworks in two ways. First the features (embedding) trained by classifiers will be updated after iteration in our framework, which is constant in traditionally relabel framework. Second, as we mentioned before at Sect. 1, propagation process able to generate more reasonable labelled vertices. The detailed framework is discussed in next section.

3 Proposed Method

Given a network dataset with mislabeled vertices, we propose methods to identify and relabel vertex to optimize network embedding's performance. In our framework, we relabel the vertices after the training of GCN. The two processes, noise reduction and graph embedding, reinforce each other. Next, we introduce detailed of our proposed method in two subsections: relabel, propagate. The main algorithm's steps of our proposed method are illustrated as bellows.

Algorithm 1 : Noise Reduction In Network Embedding

Input: Network data with mislabeled vertices

Output: Cleaned label set and reasonable vertex's embedding

1: **for** i = 0 − > n

2:     **repeat**

3:         Obtain vertex embedding on current network data by GCN

4:         Relabel labelled vertex

5:         Propagate label to vertex's neighbor

6:     **until** node performance is steady or exit in step 4

7: **end for**

The detail of step 4, step 5: relabel labelled vertex and propagate label will discuss in next section. We proposed two ways to implement step 4.

Noted that our method can combine any semi-supervised network embedding framework.

3.1 Relabel

We propose two methods to implement relabel: Identify and Correct, Vote.

In this work, each labelled vertex v (y, x), where x is vertex's embedding and y is vertex's label in current iteration. We use $1 - P(y \mid x)$ to estimate potentially mislabeled vertex. The conditional probability $P(y \mid x)$ is probability that vertex is a sample of class 'y'. At each iteration, we only choose the most likely mislabeled vertex to relabel. Although in our framework more iterations mean more time consuming, we can reduce noise ratio and improve network embedding's performance.

The intuition behind using this strategy is the following: if there is a robust classifier, the conditional probability can successfully represent which class a vertex should be in current iteration. Generally speaking, on the one hand, if $P(y \mid x)$ is great than 0.9, it may be safe to label vertex as y, on the other hand, if $P(y \mid x)$ is less than 0.1, it may be safe to assume the vertex is mislabeled.

For example, let us consider a three classification problem. $\{1, -1, 0\}$ is class set. There is a vertex is labelled as '1'. And a trained classifier calculates the conditional probability for each class is $P(1 \mid x) = 0.1$, $P(-1 \mid x) = 0.2$, $P(0 \mid x) = 0.7$. As we mentioned above, this vertex is regarded as a mislabeled vertex (identify), and we can simple assume this vertex should be class '0' (correct). Algorithm 2 gives a detailed process of Identify and Correct.

Algorithm 2: Identify and Correct

Input: Vertex embedding set X with noise label set Y

Output: Cleaned label set

1: Train a base-classifier on X

2: Compute M, an ordered set of potentially mislabeled vertex

3: **if** $M \neq \{\ \}$

4:     a. Select top n vertex

5:     b. Correct label base on conditional probability $P(y \mid x)$

6: **exit**

There are two shortcomings about Identify and Correct. First, one classifier may not effective identify mislabeled vertex, especially as our method process. In on hand, it means we only identify portion of noise. In other hand, this method will only able to identify mislabeled vertices which are easy to identify. Second, considering we can't have enough absolutely clean labelled data to generate a robust classifier, which means in correct step the performance is not powerful as we expected.

As we mentioned above, in order to reduce noise effect in one classifier, we propose other method: Vote. For vote, we process majority vote process and consensus vote on labelled data set. The detailed showed in Algorithm 3.

We score all vertices for each class. The score can be defined as follows:

$$Score_{v,y} = \sum_i^n \theta_i \tag{5}$$

where $\theta_i = 1$ when $f_i(X_v) = y$, otherwise $\theta_i = 0$. X_v, y are embedding and label for vertex v. f_i is one of classifiers and n is number of classifiers. In majority vote, for each vertex, if there is a score of one class is not less than half of n, we relabel vertex by this class. In consensus vote, we only relabel vertex which score for a class is equal n.

We divide labelled data into n groups and select $n - 1$ groups data as the training samples and the rest as the test samples. We train a set of classifiers based on current training samples and predict label of vertex. But unlikely traditional process, we not only predict target vertex, we also predict its fist-order neighbors as references to help us decide a final label to relabel target vertex. Because they have a significant odds share same label. The detail is showed in Algorithm 3.

Using above methods, at a specific iteration, we gain some reasonable labelled vertex. Before retrain embedding we propagate the label to its neighbors, which will be discussed in next section.

Algorithm 3: Vote

Input: vertex embedding X with noise label Y

Output: Cleaned label

1: Divided data to train and test sample

2: Train a set of classifiers on train sample, named C

3: Initialize a vote pool, name P

4: **for** vertex in test sample:

5:      a. Predict vertex's label and add results to P

6:      b. Find vertex's neighbors, named N

7:      **for** neighbor in N:

8:          **if** neighbor labelled:

9:              Add neighbor's label to P

10:      **else**:

11:              Predict and add results to P

12:      **end for**

13:      Vote a label for vertex by P

14:**end for**

3.2   Propagate Label and Retrain Embedding

Propagating label is a trade-off between more labelled vertices and more noise labelled vertices. Generally speaking, in one hand, propagating label means labeled vertex set is enlarged. In other, there are odds we propagate wrong label to its neighbors. In order to reduce mislabeled vertex by propagating, two criterions are proposed. First-order neighbor and high similarity between vertices. Then propagation set of V_i can be defined as follows:

$$S = \{V_i, V_j \,|\, f(E_i, E_j) \geq \alpha\} \tag{6}$$

where V_j is first-order of V_i. f can be any similarity function, such as inner product or the cosine similarity. A larger similarity implies that the two vertices may have a higher propensity to be linked [7] in data set. In this paper, we use cosine similarity to estimate similarity between vertices. And α is a threshold, which will provide lower bound for similarity. At every iteration of label propagation, vertex adopts the label shared most by its first-hop neighbors T_i. Hence,

$$C_i = \arg\max_C \{j \in T_i \mid C_i = C\} \tag{7}$$

Then we obtain more reasonable embedding by network embedding framework to relabel more mislabeled vertex at next iteration.

4 Dataset and Experiments

4.1 Dataset

In this paper, we use three public citation networks dataset: Citeseer, Cora and Pumbed, and more detail network statistics showed in Table 1. Each of dataset contains sparse bag-of-words feature vectors for each document, which are linked by citation links. The unweight and undirected links are treated edges in a network.

Table 1. Data statistics

Dataset	Nodes	Edges	Classes	Features	Label rate
Cora	2,708	5,429	7	1,433	0.052
Citeseer	3,327	4,732	6	3,703	0.036
Pumbed	19,717	44,338	3	500	0.003

4.2 Experiments

The experiments are conducted on above mentioned datasets. First, we verify noise impact. Then we use our framework to identify and correct mislabeled vertex to improve network embedding's performance. All experiments are evaluated by reasonable metrics. More detail discussion and results in following section.

In this paper, we evaluate the network embedding by embedding's performance in node classification, and use accuracy to measure the classification performance.

4.2.1 Noise Impact

We verify noise impact on three different types noise: label noise, edge noise and label with edge noise.

We randomly add noise into dataset from noise rate 0 to 0.4. As we expected, no matter what type of noise, higher noise ratio produces lower performance in node classification task (see Fig. 2). Specially, because edge noise will change the structure of network, its impact is greater than label noise. When label noise ratio increase, the data set Pubmed still has acceptable performance in node classification (see Fig. 2). But, if there are label and edge noise exists in data set, its performance significant decline (see Figs. 3 and 4).

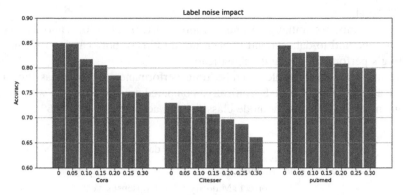

Fig. 2. Label noise impact

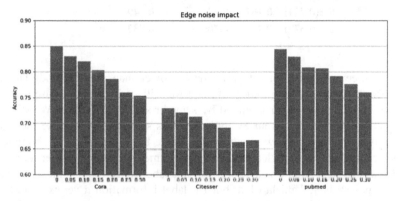

Fig. 3. Edge noise impact

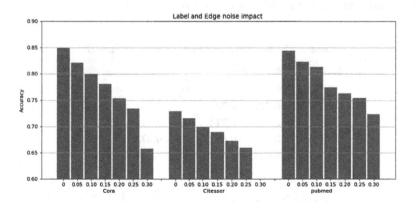

Fig. 4. Label and edge noise impact

4.2.2   Relabel

In our experiments, we initially add noise ratio of 0.1, 0.2, 0.3, 0.4, into dataset. We conduct our method to data set and in each noise ratio we both can improve network embedding's performance in node classification task.

As results showed in Table 2, embedding performance in node classification is improved at each noise ratio. Specifically, compared to the accuracy with specific noise, our method improves the node classification accuracy by 2% to 6%.

Table 2. Perform accuracy on dataset Cora

Noise ratio	Method		
	Correct	Majority vote	Consensus vote
0.1(0.803)	**0.815**	**0.822**	**0.826**
0.2(0.786)	**0.790**	**0.803**	**0.798**
0.3(0.724)	**0.767**	**0.745**	**0.749**
0.4(0.679)	**0.716**	**0.703**	**0.733**

Among three methods, correct performance lower than vote method. There is a straight forward understanding and guess and we will verify at our future work. In a citation networks dataset paper is linked by same or similar discipline. We still take a three classification problem as an example. A class set is {Computer Science, Mathematics, Physics}. As we know, mathematics is the basic discipline of computer science, especially in machine learning area. Assume a computer science paper is mislabeled as Physics. After a vote process, if it is labelled as Mathematics. For data set this vertex (paper) is still mislabeled, but for label information a vertex containing is become more reasonable, which leads to gaining a more robust classifier and a better performance in node classification. And this also explains why the noise ratio is not significant reduced and the performance is improved (Table 3).

Table 3. Performance accuracy on dataset Citeseer

Noise ratio	Method		
	Correct	Majority vote	Consensus vote
0.1(0.721)	**0.727**	**0.742**	**0.727**
0.2(0.707)	**0.711**	**0.714**	**0.710**
0.3(0.658)	**0.676**	**0.682**	**0.673**
0.4(0.602)	**0.628**	**0.687**	**0.627**

5   Summary and Future Work

In this paper we propose a framework to tackle noise label in network embedding area. Our framework incorporates network embedding and noise reduction, which reduces noise ratio of dataset to obtain more reasonable embedding by iterative relabeling vertex and retraining embedding. Unlike the traditional noise reduction algorithms, our method handles the data with rich side information: label, and edge learnt representations (vertex embedding), and it is carefully designed to exploit the usefulness brought by these two characteristics. First, to exploit the edge information, a label propagation process is considered in first-hop neighbors. Second, the noise reduction method and graph embedding process are run together in iteration manner. Relabeling the label and retraining embedding at each iteration process. For experiments, we first verify the noise impact with different noise ratio and noise type over three public citation networks. Then we have evaluated our proposed method over two public citation network dataset which performance is significant decline when label noise grows. Experiments show that our framework is effectiveness.

For future work, in one hand, we will focus on reducing networks structure's impact on network embedding. Further-more, we will also focus on tackle there are edge and label noise issue by combining the method for edge and label. In other hand, the guess we method at Sect. 4, we aim to give a mathematical proof and verify on more dataset.

Acknowledgements. This research was supported by Natural Science Foundation of China (Grant no. 61572252, 61672284). Meanwhile, this research work was supported by Zayed University Research Cluster Award \# R18038.

References

1. Cai, H.Y., Zheng, V.W., Chang, K.: A comprehensive survey of graph embedding: problems, techniques and applications. IEEE Trans. Knowl. Data Eng. **30**, 1616–1637 (2018)
2. Kipf, T.N., Welling, M.: Semi-supervised classification with graph convolutional network. In: 5th International Conference on Learning Representations (2017)
3. Huang, X., Li, J., Hu, X.: Label informed attributed network embedding. In: Tenth ACM International Conference on Web Search and Data Mining. ACM (2017)
4. Li, Z., Fang, X., Sheng, O.R.L.: A survey of link recommendation for social networks: methods, theoretical foundations, and future research directions. Social Science Electronic Publishing (2015)
5. Zhang, X.K., Ren, J., Song, C., et al.: Label propagation algorithm for community detection based on node importance and label influence. Phys. Lett. A **381**, 2691–2698 (2017). https://www.sciencedirect.com/science/article/abs/pii/S0375960117305868
6. Wang, F., Zhang, C.: Label propagation through linear neighborhoods. IEEE Trans. Knowl. Data Eng. **20**(1), 55–67 (2007)
7. Ahmed, A., Shervashidze, N., Narayanamurthy, S., et al.: Distributed large-scale natural graph factorization (2013)
8. Peng, C., Xiao, W., Jian, P., et al.: A survey on network embedding. IEEE Trans. Knowl. Data Eng. 1 (2018)
9. Perozzi, B., Al-Rfou, R., Skiena, S.: DeepWalk: online learning of social representations. In: ACM SIGKDD International Conference on Knowledge Discovery and Data Mining (2014)
10. Grover, A., Leskovec, J.: node2vec: scalable feature learning for networks. In: ACM SIGKDD International Conference on Knowledge Discovery and Data Mining (2016)

11. Mikolov, T., Chen, K., Corrado, G., et al.: Efficient estimation of word representations in vector space. Computer Science (2013)
12. Yuan, S., Wu, X., Xiang, Y.: SNE: signed network embedding. In: Kim, J., Shim, K., Cao, L., Lee, J.-G., Lin, X., Moon, Y.-S. (eds.) PAKDD 2017. LNCS (LNAI), vol. 10235, pp. 183–195. Springer, Cham (2017). https://doi.org/10.1007/978-3-319-57529-2_15
13. Cai, H., Zheng, V.W., Chang, C.C.: Active learning for graph embedding (2017)
14. Frenay, B., Verleysen, M.: Classification in the presence of label noise: a survey. IEEE Trans. Neural Netw. Learn. Syst. **25**(5), 845–869 (2014)
15. Chen, K., Guan, D., Yuan, W., et al.: A novel feature selection-based sequential ensemble learning method for class noise detection in high-dimensional data. In: International Conference on Advanced Data Mining and Applications (2018)
16. Wang, S., Aggarwal, C., Tang, J., et al.: Attributed signed network embedding. In: CIKM 2017 (2017)
17. Ruta, D., Gabrys, B.: Classifier selection for majority voting. Inf. Fusion **6**(1), 63–81 (2005)

Indoor Localization Based on Centroid Constraints of AP Quadrilateral Networks

Xinyue Li[(⊠)], Mu Zhou, Zhenya Zhang, and Zhu Liu

School of Communication and Information Engineering,
Chongqing University of Posts and Telecommunications,
Chongqing 400065, China
443126330@qq.com

Abstract. With the development of wireless communication technology at home and abroad, wireless indoor positioning technology has become an indispensable technology. In the current indoor scenes, due to the extensive deployment of Wireless Local Area Network (WLAN) infrastructure, indoor WLAN location method has become a research hotspot. There are a variety of WLAN Access Points (APs) in indoor environment, which can be used in indoor localization. While existing indoor positioning technology often works along with high cost and low system stability especially in complex indoor environment. To solve this problem, a centroid constraint indoor location method based on AP quadrilateral network is proposed. By collecting and processing the Received Signal Strength (RSS) of APs, this method exploits propagation models and trilateration method to get the target quadrilateral centroid set, which can be applied to obtain the ultimate estimate coordinates of pending points under the condition of geometric constraints. This method enhances the robustness of indoor localization system and implements low-cost indoor localization.

Keywords: Indoor localization · Centroid constraint · Quadrilateral network · WLAN

1 Introduction

Since the Federal Communications Commission (FCC) established the E-911 positioning standard [1], wireless positioning technology has attracted the attention of various companies due to its practicality. Many foreign universities, research institutes and major companies have increased their investment into the research of wireless positioning technology [2]. At the same time, many journals and related patents have been published gradually in various magazines and periodicals. Domestic research on indoor positioning technology starts late, but with the increase of domestic attention to indoor positioning technology, has also obtained a lot of achievements. Outdoor positioning technology such as GPS is basically mature [3]. However, due to the complexity of indoor environment, many indoor positioning algorithms are often not unfaithful in actual environment. For example, the traditional APIT algorithm is prone to misjudge whether the pending points are located in the triangle, which will lead to

X. B. Zhai et al. (Eds.): MLICOM 2019, LNICST 294, pp. 121–129, 2019.
https://doi.org/10.1007/978-3-030-32388-2_11

the reduction of positioning accuracy [4]. On the other hand, the location results of APIT location algorithm are excessively dependent on network connectivity and the density of APs deployment, which will lead to high volatility of location results [5]. Moreover, the general use of polygon centroid positioning algorithm requires the deployment of numerous AP, which will lead to excessive positioning system overhead. Therefore, it is very important to reduce the positioning cost while ensuring the stability of the positioning system. To the end, we propose a centroid constraint indoor location method based on AP quadrilateral network to obtain the ultimate estimate coordinates of pending points under complex indoor environment. In this way, it is dispensable to collect fingerprint and build fingerprint database in the offline phase. We simply deploy some known APs in the test area and combine them into a number of quadrangles. Then, the initial estimated coordinates are calculated by using the propagation model and tri-lateral measurement positioning method. Finally, all quadrangles containing the initial estimated coordinates are extracted to obtain the target quadrangle set, which will be utilized to obtain the ultimate estimate coordinates of pending points under the constraint of centroids. The structure of this paper is as follows. The related work is introduced in Sect. 2 and the proposed method is described in Sect. 3. The experimental results are presented in Sect. 4. Finally, we conclude this paper and provide an outlook of future work in Sect. 5.

2   Related Work

In the information era with the rapid development of the Internet, wireless users can enjoy the convenience anytime and anywhere by using intelligent portable devices. Therefore, people's demand for Location-Based Service (LBS) shows a significant growth trend. However, in the indoor environment, it is not easy to capture the satellite signals of the Global Positioning System (GPS) continuously and stably. Therefore GPS which is commonly used outdoor cannot meet the positioning accuracy requirements of most indoor LBS. We can see that indoor positioning technology has a good development prospect. Among numerous indoor positioning technologies, WLAN-based indoor positioning has the advantages of wide coverage, low deployment cost and it does not need special hardware equipment [6]. Therefore, WLAN location based on RSS has gradually become the mainstream of indoor positioning technology.

The indoor localization methods based on WLAN RSS can be roughly divided into propagation model method and location fingerprint method. The former establishes the mathematical relationship between the propagation distance and RSS through the signal propagation model, and then estimates the location of the pending points according to the known location of WLAN AP by using geometric positioning algorithms such as trilateral measurement positioning method. However, in this way, it is difficult to establish accurate signal propagation model in complex indoor environment, which will affect the positioning accuracy [7]. The latter mainly includes offline and online stages. In the offline stage, the location fingerprint database is built by collecting RSS from different APs at a certain number of pre-calibrated Reference Points (RP). Afterwards, in the online phase, the newly acquired RSS is matched with the location fingerprint database to obtain the estimated location of the pending points.

3   Approach Overview

3.1   Collecting and Processing RSS Sequences

Existing studies have shown that the indoor propagation model can better reflect the relationship between physical location and RSS data. Deploy n APs in the test area, whose communication range covers the entire test area. It is necessary to ensure that the APs can form at least one quadrilateral containing the test area, as shown in Fig. 3. APs are combined in the test area to get p ($p \leq C_n^4$, p is an integer) different initial quadrangles and the set of their centroid coordinates is obtained accordingly. RSS of APs was collected at the pending point, then the RSS set: can be represented as

$$\mathbf{RSS} = \begin{bmatrix} rss_1^1 & rss_1^2 & \cdots & rss_1^n \\ rss_2^1 & rss_2^2 & \cdots & rss_2^n \\ \vdots & \vdots & rss_j^l & \vdots \\ rss_k^1 & rss_k^2 & \cdots & rss_k^n \end{bmatrix} \tag{1}$$

where rss_j^l ($j = 1, 2, \cdots, k$; $l = 1, 2, \cdots, n$) is the RSS from the l-th AP, which is collected for the j-th time at the pending point. From this set, whole RSS data from the l-th AP can be easily represented as

$$\mathbf{RSS}^l = \left\{ rss_1^l, rss_2^l, \cdots, rss_k^l \right\} \tag{2}$$

In this way, we can get RSS data of all Aps. Finally, the mean value of each $\mathbf{RSS}^l$ ($l = 1, 2, \cdots, n$) is calculated to obtain the average received signal strength set $\overline{\mathbf{RSS}}$, which can be represented as

$$\overline{\mathbf{RSS}} = \left\{ \overline{RSS^1}, \cdots, \overline{RSS^l}, \cdots, \overline{RSS^n} \right\} \tag{3}$$

3.2   Calculation of Initial Estimated Coordinates

Based on $\overline{\mathbf{RSS}}$ and propagation model, the propagation distance from the pending point to each AP in the test area can be worked out accordingly by

$$d = d_0 10^{\frac{RSS_0 - \overline{RSS_i} + Z}{10\rho}} \tag{4}$$

where RSS_0 is the signal strength at reference distance d_0 and $\overline{RSS_l}$ is the average received signal strength from the l-th AP. ρ is path attenuation index and Z is Gaussian noise. we usually set ρ to 2, the mean value of Z to 2, and the variance of Z to 4 dBm.

We sort the propagation distance of the positioning point to each AP and extract the AP coordinates corresponding to the minimum three propagation distances. It is necessary to ensure that the three APs are not on the same line and the extracted AP coordinates are recorded as: (x_{min1}, y_{min1}), (x_{min2}, y_{min2}), (x_{min3}, y_{min3}). According to the

AP coordinates corresponding to the minimum three propagation distances and the distance from the pending points to these three APs (We can write them as d_1, d_2, d_3), then the equation set can be obtained as

$$
\begin{cases}
\sqrt{(\hat{x} - x_{min1})^2 + (\hat{y} - y_{min1})^2} = d_1 \\
\sqrt{(\hat{x} - x_{min2})^2 + (\hat{y} - y_{min2})^2} = d_2 \\
\sqrt{(\hat{x} - x_{min3})^2 + (\hat{y} - y_{min3})^2} = d_3
\end{cases}
\tag{5}
$$

Due to the influence of noise and multi-path effect, the initial estimated coordinates of the pending points can't be obtained accurately. Therefore, its estimated coordinates $(\hat{x}, \hat{y})$ are used to express the position. The above equations can be expressed by

$$
\mathbf{H}\hat{\mathbf{X}} = \hat{\mathbf{b}}
\tag{6}
$$

$$
\mathbf{H} = \begin{bmatrix} 2(x_{min2} - x_{min1}) \, 2(y_{min2} - y_{min1}) \\ 2(x_{min3} - x_{min1}) \, 2(y_{min3} - y_{min1}) \end{bmatrix}
\tag{7}
$$

$$
\hat{\mathbf{b}} = \begin{bmatrix} x_{min2}^2 - x_{min1}^2 + y_{min2}^2 - y_{min1}^2 + d_{min1}^2 - d_{min2}^2 \\ x_{min3}^2 - x_{min1}^2 + y_{min3}^2 - y_{min1}^2 + d_{min1}^2 - d_{min3}^2 \end{bmatrix}
\tag{8}
$$

where $\hat{\mathbf{X}} = \begin{bmatrix} \hat{x} \\ \hat{y} \end{bmatrix}$ is the preliminary estimated coordinate of the pending points, which can be calculated by

$$
\hat{\mathbf{X}} = (\mathbf{H}^T\mathbf{H})^{-1}\mathbf{H}^T\hat{\mathbf{b}}
\tag{9}
$$

3.3 Final Estimated Coordinates Under the Centroid Constraint

Based on the estimated coordinates of the pending points, the set of the target quadrilaterals can be obtained by extracting all the quadrilaterals containing the pending points with the method of inner angle sum method. We can assume that the four vertices of the quadrilateral are A, B, C, and D. If the pending points are on the line which connects any two adjacent vertices of the quadrilateral, it is determined that the pending points are outside the quadrilateral. At this time, this quadrilateral is not target quadrilateral. The decision diagram is shown in Fig. 1.

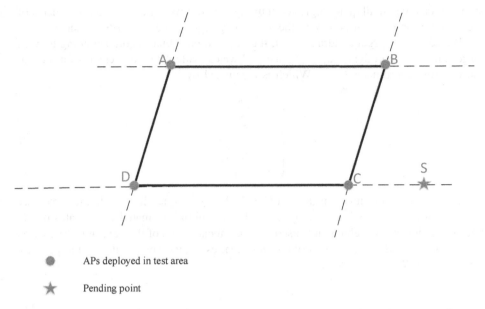

●   APs deployed in test area

★   Pending point

Fig. 1. Diagram of decision when the pending point is located on the line of any two adjacent vertices of the quadrilateral.

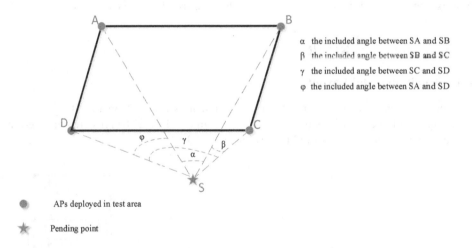

α   the included angle between SA and SB
β   the included angle between SB and SC
γ   the included angle between SC and SD
φ   the included angle between SA and SD

●   APs deployed in test area

★   Pending point

Fig. 2. Diagram of decision when the pending point is not located on the line of any two adjacent vertices of the quadrilateral.

When the pending points are not on the line of any two vertices of the quadrilateral, the pending points are connected with the four vertices of the quadrilateral, A, B, C and D. Then, the triangle cosine theorem is used to calculate the four included angles formed by connecting the pending points with the four vertices. If the sum of included angles is equal to 2π, the pending points are determined to be within the quadrilateral, that is to say, this quadrilateral is the target quadrilateral. Otherwise, the pending points are determined to be located outside the quadrilateral, that is to say, the quadrilateral is not the target quadrilateral. The decision diagram is shown in Fig. 2. Following this step, we can obtain all quadrangles containing the preliminary estimated coordinates of the pending points, that is to say, the set of target quadrangles can be obtained.

Based on the target quadrangle set, the centroid coordinates corresponding to each target quadrangle in the set are obtained and we can calculate the average values of all the centroid coordinates $(\bar{x}, \bar{y})$, Which is calculated by

$$\begin{cases} \bar{x} = \sum_{i=1}^{p} x_i/i \\ \bar{y} = \sum_{i=1}^{p} y_i/i \end{cases} \tag{10}$$

where x_i is the x-coordinate of the i-th $(i = 1, 2, \cdots, p)$ quadrilateral. In the same way and y_i can be calculated accordingly. Finally, the initial estimated coordinates of the pending points are weighted and fused with the mean value of the centroid coordinates of the target quadrilateral set to obtain the final estimated coordinates of the pending points (x, y), Which is calculated by

$$\begin{cases} x = \lambda_1 \hat{x} + \lambda_2 \bar{x} \\ y = \lambda_1 \hat{y} + \lambda_2 \bar{y} \end{cases} \tag{11}$$

among them, λ_1 and λ_2 are the fusion weights, we usually set $\lambda_1 = 0.8$ and $\lambda_2 = 0.2$.

4 Experimental Result

4.1 Environmental Layout

As shown in Fig. 3, the experimental environment is selected on the 5th floor in a building with the dimensions of 57 m × 25 m. Nine D-Link2310 APs are deployed in test area which includes a straight corridor and a lab.

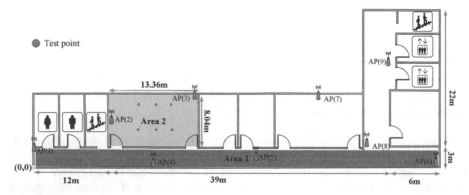

Fig. 3. Diagram of decision when the pending point is not located on the line of any two adjacent vertices of the quadrilateral.

4.2   Test Results

In order to perform the experiment conveniently, as shown in Fig. 3, we randomly selected 17 pending points for testing. The received signal strength from APs is then collected orderly at the pending points to calculate the initial estimated coordinates. Afterwards, the interior Angle sum method is used to extract all quadrangles which contain the initial estimated coordinates. That is to say, the target quadrangle set is obtained. Finally, the final estimated coordinates of the pending points are obtained by weighted fusion. The cumulative probability distribution diagram of positioning error of experimental results is shown in Fig. 4. It can be seen that compared with the least square method, our method improves the accuracy of positioning system in complex indoor environment.

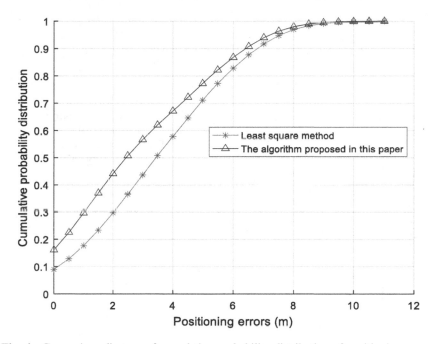

Fig. 4. Comparison diagram of cumulative probability distribution of positioning errors.

Based on Fig. 4, Table 1 can be obtained easily. It can be seen that, compared with the least square method, the average positioning error and the maximum positioning error of the algorithm proposed in this paper are both smaller than the least square method, which indicates that our method also enhances the stability of the positioning system under complex indoor environment.

Table 1. Positioning performance comparison.

Localization algorithm/Performance indicators	Error probability within 5 meters	Mean localization error	Maximum localization error
Least square method	67.87%	3.62 m	7.89 m
The algorithm proposed in this paper	77.26%	2.71 m	6.10 m

In addition, we also tested the influence of different fusion weights on the positioning performance of the experiment, and the results are shown in Fig. 5. Based on a large number of experimental data, $\lambda_1 = 0.8$ and $\lambda_2 = 0.2$ are selected as the fusion weight.

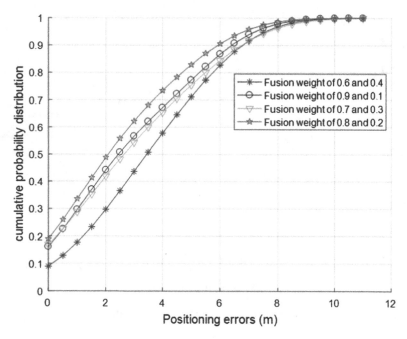

Fig. 5. Comparison diagram of cumulative probability distribution of positioning errors corresponding to different fusion weights.

5   Conclusion

In this paper, a new indoor localization method based on polygonal centroid is proposed. This method does not need to collect fingerprint and build fingerprint database in the off-line stage. We should only deploy a certain number of known APs in the test area and combine them to obtain the initial quadrilaterals which contain the test area. Then, the received signal strength from APs is collected at the pending points, and the preliminary estimated coordinates of the pending points are calculated by combining the propagation model formula and trilateral measurement positioning method. Based on the initial estimated coordinates, the target quadrilateral set containing the initial estimated coordinates is extracted by using the method of interior angle sum. Finally, the initial estimated coordinates of the pending points are weighted and fused with the mean value of the centroid coordinates of the target quadrilateral set to obtain the final estimated coordinates of pending points. The experiment results show that the proposed algorithm not only realizes the low-cost indoor positioning, but also effectively enhances the stability of the positioning system in complex indoor environment.

Acknowledgments. This work was supported in part by the National Natural Science Foundation of China (61771083, 61704015) and Fundamental and Frontier Research Project of Chongqing (cstc2017jcyjAX0380).

References

1. Coase, R.H.: The federal communications commission. J. Law Econ. **2**(1), 1–40 (1959)
2. Zhou, Q., Shen, C., Chen, X., Feng, G.: UWB wireless positioning technology in the application. In: Conference on Wireless Sensors, pp. 106–109. IEEE, Langkawi (2016)
3. Wang, X., Liang, M.: GPS positioning method based on Kalman filtering. In: International Conference on Robots and Intelligent System, pp. 77–80. IEEE, Changsha (2018)
4. Li, X., Gao, H., Lv, L., et al.: An improved APIT algorithm based on direction searching. In: International Conference on Wireless Communications, pp. 1–4. IEEE, Beijing (2009)
5. Wan, X., Shen, L., Chen, Z., Xu, H.: An efficient virtual nodes-based APIT localization algorithm with low computational cost. In: International Conference on Digital Signal Processing, pp. 1–4. IEEE, Shanghai (2018)
6. Ye, A., Shao, J., Li, X., et al.: Local HMM for indoor positioning based on fingerprinting and displacement ranging. IET Commun. **12**(10), 1163–1170 (2018)
7. Wong, S., Ni, X.: Signal propagation model calibration under metal noise factor for indoor localization by using RFID. In: International Conference on Industrial Engineering and Engineering Management, pp. 978–982. IEEE, Bandar Sunway (2014)

Partially Overlapping Channel Selection in Jamming Environment: A Hierarchical Learning Approach

Lei Zhao[1,2]([⊠]), Jincheng Ge[3], Kailing Yao[1,2], Yifan Xu[1,2], Xiaobo Zhang[1], and Menglan Fan[4]

[1] College of Communications Engineering, PLA Army Engineering University, Nanjing, China
leizhao365@163.com, kailing-yao@126.com, yifanxu@163.com, xb_zhang2008@126.com
[2] Key Embedded Technology and Intelligent System Laboratory, Guilin University of Technology, Guilin, China
[3] Unit 95965 of PLA, Hengshui, China
gejincheng@hotmail.com
[4] Unit 31102 of PLA, Nanjing, China
fanmenglan@126.com

Abstract. This paper solves the channel selection with anti-jamming problem using partially overlapping channel (POC) in limited spectrum environment. Since it is difficult for users to obtain global information of networks, this paper realizes the coordination of channel access by the local information interaction. The channel selection with anti-jamming problem is formulated as a Stackelberg game where the jammer acts as leader and users act as followers. We prove that the game model exists at least one Stackelberg equilibrium (SE) solution. To achieve the equilibrium, a hierarchical learning algorithm (HLA) is proposed. Based on the proposed method, the system can achieve the improvement of throughput performance by minimizing local interference. Simulation results show the proposed algorithm can achieve good performance under jamming environment, and the network throughput can maintain a stable state with the jamming intensity increasing.

Keywords: Intelligent anti-jamming · Stackelberg game · Channel selection · Partially overlapping channel

---

This work was supported by the National Natural Science Foundation of China under Grant No. 61771488, No. 61671473 and No. 61701533, in part by Natural Science Foundation for Distinguished Young Scholars of Jiangsu Province under Grant No. BK20160034, and the Guang Xi Universities Key Laboratory Fund of Embedded Technology and Intelligent System (Guilin University of Technology).

X. B. Zhai et al. (Eds.): MLICOM 2019, LNICST 294, pp. 130–144, 2019.
https://doi.org/10.1007/978-3-030-32388-2_12

1   Introduction

With the development of technology, the communication security has attracted great attention. Nowadays, there are mainly two challenges for this problem. For one thing, the internal interference of multi-node networks will become serious as the number of network nodes increases. For another, the malicious jammer has become more and more intelligent which is able to sense the strategy of users and select the optimal channel to maximize the damage to the network.

Studies on anti-jamming problems have been a hot topic these years which are discussed from the following aspects: power domain, spectrum domain, space domain and multi-domains. In power domain, users adjust the transmission power to combat with the smart jammer. In [1,2], authors studied the anti-jamming problem with one jammer and one user. They modeled the power control problem based on the Stackelberg game. Authors of [3] considered the observed errors in power control problems on basis of [1,2]. In [4], authors considered the power control problem in unmanned aerial vehicle networks. In spectrum domain, legitimate users selected proper channels to escape from attacks of the malicious jammer. Authors of [5] discussed non-overlapping channel (NOC) selection problem which considered outer jamming and internal interference at the same time. In [6], authors proposed an effective channel selection with anti-jamming problem in cognitive radio network. In space domain, the existing work mainly focused on beam forming, users attempted to deal with the smart jammer by changing the antenna direction. In [7], a muti-domains anti-jamming problem was studied. When strength of jamming was weak, users adjusted their transmission power to confront the smart jammer. While the strength was becoming stronger, users had to select proper channels to maximize their utility function. In [8,9], authors investigated the anti-jamming problems by considering joint channel selection and transmission rate. Analysing these studies above, we can easily find most papers consider anti-jamming problems based on NOCs, assuming spectrum resource is sufficient. However, as the number of users becomes larger, network bandwidth becomes scarce in practical environment. To tackle this problem, the technology of Partially overlapping channel (POC) is developed in this paper. POC, which is proposed by Mishra Arunesh of [10,11], has attracted great attention in wireless systems with limited spectrum resource. Based on POC, authors of [13] proposed a greedy algorithm to improve throughput compared with NOC. The existing work mentioned above shows that most studies about POC focused on interference elimination, rarely considering jamming communication environment.

It is of great significance to investigate the channel selection problems based on POCs in limited resource environment. In this paper, malicious jamming and mutual interference are both considered. We optimize the channel selection problem from the perspective of minimizing generalized interference. We formulate this problem as a Stackelberg game [5]. In this game, the jammer acts as the leader and the users act as the followers. The interference mitigation problem between users is modeled as a potential game [17]. After that, we propose a hierarchical learning framework to achieve the Stackelberg Equilibrium (SE).

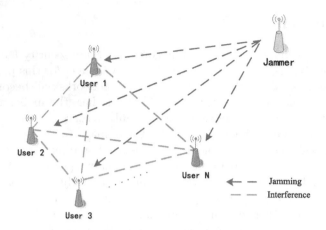

Fig. 1. Multi-user channel access model in jamming environment.

We assume that the jammer with learning ability uses Q learning to simulate the jammer's strategy. We propose the SAP-based algorithm to deal with the jamming impact as well as mutual interference between users. The contributions are summarized as follows:

(1) To study the anti-jaming problem in limited network bandwidth environment, the POC model is proposed and channel selection with anti-jamming problem is formulated as a Stackelberg game. We have proven the jammer's stationary action and users' policy consist a SE.

(2) We propose a hierarchical learning framework to deal with the proposed problem. Simulation results show that the proposed algorithm can achieve good performance in the jamming environment, and the network throughput can maintain a stable state when the jamming intensity increases.

The differences between [5] and our work are displayed as follows. Firstly, we study the channel selection problems based on POCs in limited resource environment while the channel selection problems are discussed in NOCs environment with abundant bandwidth resources. What's more, from the algorithm perspective, we formulate a SAP-based algorithm to deal with the channel selection problem while a Stochastic-learning-automata(SLA)-based algorithm is proposed in [5].

The rest of this paper is discussed as follows. In Sect. 2, the system model and the anti-jamming problem are introduced. In Sect. 3, we propose a Stackelberg game to model the anti-jamming problem. In Sect. 4, a hierarchical framework based on SAP is discussed. In Sects. 5 and 6, we present the simulation results and draw the conclusion.

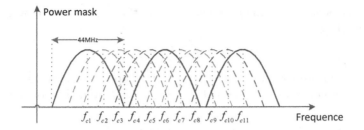

Fig. 2. The illustration of POC.

2 System Model and Problem Formulation

As shown in Fig. 1, there is a distributed mesh network consisting of N users. A smart jammer outside the network aims to block the communication of users. In this work, we take the IEEE 802.11b standard for example. Figure 2 shows the illustration of POC. In the limited spectrum environment, the bandwidth of each channel is 22 MHz and there are only 3 orthogonal channels. In POC situation, adjacent channels overlap partially and separation between two near channels is 5 MHz. As the imaginal lines show, there are 11 partially overlapping channels in the same bandwidth range of the 3 orthogonal channels mentioned above.

The user set is denoted by $\mathcal{N} = \{1, 2, ..., N\}$. Strategy profile of all users is denoted as $\mathbf{a} = \{a_1, ..., a_N\}$, where a_n is denoted as user n's action and $\mathbf{a}_{-n} = \{a_1, a_2, ..., a_{n-1}, a_{n+1}, ..., a_N\}$ is the action profile of other users except user n. The channel sets of users and the jammer are denoted as $\mathcal{M} = \{1, 2, ..., M\}$ and $\mathcal{C} = \{1, 2, ..., H\}$ and $\mathcal{M} = \mathcal{C}$. For simplicity, we assume that the jammer only selects one channel to jam each decision-making time. In this paper, as we study on the channel selection problem, we assume that the transmission power of each user is the same as each other.

The smart jammer can recognize users' actions and adjust its jamming strategy dynamically to maximize its damage. Having acknowledged the jammer's strategy, users adopt proper strategies to minimize the external jamming and interference from adjacent channels. However, as the scale of network becomes larger, network bandwidth becomes scarce in practical environment. To overcome this problem, the technology of POC is introduced in this paper.

In POC situation, interference between user n and m is affected by the physical distance d_{mn} and channel distance $\delta_{mn} = |a_m - a_n|$ [12]. For example, when the physical distance between two users are large, they could select the same channel without interfering with each other. To the opposite, when the physical distance is small, users have to choose different channels to decrease the interference. In this work, we have to consider two aspects. Firstly, due to the property of partially overlapping, interference from adjacent channels inevitably degrades the network performance. Secondly, the smart jammer could sense and recognize the users' channel selection strategy and destroy the information transmission.

As two users select channels independently, the overlapping power mask is expressed as [12]:

$$H(f) = \int p_m(f) \cdot p_n(f) df, \tag{1}$$

$p_m(f)$ and $p_n(f)$ are the power mask selected independently by user m and n. The central frequency of one channel is denoted as f_c and the power mask can be expressed as:

$$p(f) = \begin{cases} 0\text{dB}, & |f - f_c| \leq 11\text{MHz} \\ -30\text{dB}, & 11\text{MHz} \leq |f - f_c| \leq 22\text{MHz} \\ -50\text{dB}, & |f - f_c| \geq 22\text{MHz} \end{cases} \tag{2}$$

As is verified in [14], the overlapping power mask between user m and user n can be expressed as:

$$H(\delta_{mn}) = \begin{cases} 1, & \delta_{mn} = 0 \\ 0.605, & \delta_{mn} = 1 \\ 0.305, & \delta_{mn} = 2 \\ 0.108, & \delta_{mn} = 3 \\ 0.012, & \delta_{mn} = 4 \\ 0, & \delta_{mn} \geq 5 \end{cases} \tag{3}$$

where δ_{mn} denotes the channel distance between user m and n, $\delta_{mn} = |a_m - a_n|$. Users within the interference range of user n is denoted as neighbour set. It can be expressed as:

$$\xi_n = \{m \in \mathcal{N} : d_{mn} < d_\tau\}, \forall n \in \mathcal{N}, \tag{4}$$

where the interference range is denoted by d_τ. When the physical distance between user m and n is larger than d_τ, interference can be ignored and user m is not user n's neighbour. Oppositely, when d_{mn} is smaller than d_τ, user m is the neighbour of user n and interference can not be ignored. As a result, the interference which user n suffers is equal to the sum of interference which comes from all its neighbours. Mathematically, it is expressed as:

$$I_n = \sum_{m \in \xi_n} p_m H(\delta_{mn})(d_{mn})^{-\alpha_1} \varepsilon_{mn}^{a_n}, \forall m, n \in \mathcal{N}, \tag{5}$$

where α_1 and $\varepsilon_{mn}^{a_n}$ denote the pass-loss exponent and instantaneous fading coefficient between users, respectively. Similarly, the jamming caused by malicious jammer can be denoted by J_n. d_{jn} and $\delta_{jn} = |c_j - a_n|$ denote as the physical distance and channel distance between user n and the jammer. c_j and a_n are the selected channels of the jammer and user n, respectively. The overlapping power mask between the smart jammer and user n can be expressed as [14]:

$$H(\delta_{jn}) = \begin{cases} 1, & \delta_{jn} = 0 \\ 0.605, & \delta_{jn} = 1 \\ 0.305, & \delta_{jn} = 2 \\ 0.108, & \delta_{jn} = 3 \\ 0.012, & \delta_{jn} = 4 \\ 0, & \delta_{jn} \geq 5 \end{cases} \tag{6}$$

Then, the jamming is denoted as:

$$J_n = p_j H(\delta_{jn})(d_{jn})^{-\alpha_2} \varepsilon_{jn}^{c_j}, \forall n \in \mathcal{N}, \tag{7}$$

where d_{jn}, α_2 and $\varepsilon_{jn}^{c_j}$ are physical distance, pass-loss exponent and instantaneous fading coefficient, respectively. As a result, the user n's throughput should be expressed as:

$$R_n(a_n, \mathbf{a}_{-n}, c_j) = B \log(1 + \frac{p_n(d_{nn})^{-\alpha_1} \varepsilon_{nn}^{a_n}}{N_0 + I_n + J_n}), \forall n \in \mathcal{N}, \tag{8}$$

where B and N_0 are channel's bandwidth and background noise, respectively. I_n and J_n are denoted by the adjacent interference and external jamming. p_n is the transmission power of user n and d_{nn} is the physical distance between user n's transmitter and receiver. In a whole, the optimization goal is the maximization of network throughput. Mathematically, the network throughput is denoted as:

$$R = \sum_{n \in \mathcal{N}} R_n(a_n, \mathbf{a}_{-n}, c_j) = \sum_{n \in \mathcal{N}} B \log(1 + \frac{p_n(d_{nn})^{-\alpha_1} \varepsilon_{nn}^{a_n}}{N_0 + I_n + J_n}), \forall n \in \mathcal{N}. \tag{9}$$

Since it is hard to obtain the global information of the open and dense mesh network, we could not optimize this problem from the perspective of maximizing the throughput. Therefore, we view this problem from the perspective of minimizing generalized interference. The generalized jamming is denoted as D_n. It means the sum of adjacent interference and external jamming, that is:

$$D_n = I_n + J_n, \tag{10}$$

and the network generalized jamming is expressed as:

$$D = \sum_{n \in \mathcal{N}} D_n. \tag{11}$$

According to [12], the expected throughput of user n decreases monotonously while the generalized interference increases. Their relationship is displayed as followed:

$$R_n = f(D_n), \tag{12}$$

where the function $f(\cdot)$ is a monotone decreasing function equals to the minimization of the generalized interference of the network. The network throughput can be expressed as:

$$R = \sum_{n \in \mathcal{N}} R_n. \tag{13}$$

The optimization goal of the channel selection with anti-jamming problem is the maximization of the network which can be formulated as follows:

$$P1 : (a_1, a_2, ..., a_n, c_j) = \arg \max R. \tag{14}$$

3   Hierarchical Channel Selection Stackelberg Game

In this paper, we model the multi-users channel selection problem as a Stackelberg game. Firstly, the jammer learns the users' channel selection strategy and chooses the optimal strategy to degrade the network performance. After sensing the jammer's strategy, users adjust their strategies to minimize the generalized interference, so as to maximize the network throughput. Mathematically, the hierarchical channel selection Stackelberg game is denoted as $\mathcal{G} = \{\mathcal{N}, \mathcal{J}, \mathcal{M}, \mathcal{C}, u_n, u_j\}$. $\mathcal{N}$ and $\mathcal{J}$ denote user set and the smart jammer. $\mathcal{M}$ and $\mathcal{C}$ denote the channel sets of users and the smart jammer. We denote u_n and u_j as the utility function of user n and the jammer. Based on the game $\mathcal{G}$, there exists two sub-games, which is defined as leader sub-game $\mathcal{G}_l$ and follower sub-game $\mathcal{G}_f$. The leader sub-game can be expressed as:

$$\mathcal{G}_l = \{\mathcal{J}, \mathcal{C}, u_j(a_n, \mathbf{a}_{-n}, c_j)\}, \tag{15}$$

where $\mathcal{J}$ and $\mathcal{C}$ denote the smart jammer and available channel for the jammer. $u_j(a_n, a_{-n}, c_j)$ is the utility function of the smart jammer. From the perspective of jammer, it aims to select proper channel in order to maximize the damage to the network. Therefore, the jammer's utility function is:

$$u_j(a_n, \mathbf{a}_{-n}, c_j) = \sum_{n \in \mathcal{N}} J_n = \sum_{n \in \mathcal{N}} p_j H(\delta_{jn})(d_{jn})^{-\beta} \varepsilon_{jn}^{c_j}, \forall n \in \mathcal{N}. \tag{16}$$

The follower sub-game can be expressed as:

$$\mathcal{G}_f = \{\mathcal{N}, \mathcal{M}, u_n(a_n, \mathbf{a}_{-n}, c_j)\}, \tag{17}$$

where $\mathcal{N}$ and $\mathcal{M}$ denote the user set and available channel for these users. $u_n(a_n, a_{-n}, c_j)$ is user n's utility function. From the perspective of users, the optimization goal is to minimize the generalized interference. Mathematically, user n's utility function can be given as:

$$\begin{aligned} u_n(a_n, \mathbf{a}_{-n}, c_j) &= -D_n = -(I_n + J_n) \\ &= -(\sum_{m \in \mathcal{N}} p_m H(\delta_{mn})(d_{mn})^{-\alpha} \varepsilon_{mn}^{a_n} + p_j H(\delta_{jn})(d_{jn})^{-\beta} \varepsilon_{jn}^{c_j}), \forall m, n \in \mathcal{N}. \end{aligned} \tag{18}$$

Definition 1 (Exact Potential Game (EPG) [17]**).** $\mathcal{G}_f$ *is an exact potential game as long as there exists a potential function φ whose variation is equal to variation in the utility function caused by any player's unilateral deviation. Mathematically,*

$$\begin{aligned} \varphi(\overline{a}_n, \mathbf{a}_{-n}, c_j) - \varphi(a_n, \mathbf{a}_{-n}, c_j) &= u_n(\overline{a}_n, \mathbf{a}_{-n}, c_j) - u_n(a_n, \mathbf{a}_{-n}, c_j), \\ \forall n \in \mathcal{N}, \overline{a}_n, a_n &\subseteq \mathcal{M}, \overline{a}_n \neq a_n, \end{aligned} \tag{19}$$

where $\overline{a}_n$ denotes the changed action of user n after unilateral deviation.

Theorem 1. *When c_j is determined, the users' sub-game is an EPG and there exists at least one pure strategy NE.*

Proof: Motivated by [19], when the strategy of jammer is given as c_j, the potential function of the follower sub-game $\mathcal{G}_f$ is:

$$
\begin{aligned}
\varphi(a_n, \mathbf{a}_{-n}, c_j) &= \varphi_1(a_n, \mathbf{a}_{-n}, c_j) + \varphi_2(a_n, \mathbf{a}_{-n}, c_j) \\
&= -\tfrac{1}{2} \sum_{n \in \mathcal{N}} I_n(a_n, \mathbf{a}_{-n}, c_j) - \sum_{n \in \mathcal{N}} J_n(a_n, \mathbf{a}_{-n}, c_j)
\end{aligned}
\tag{20}
$$

We denote the function $\varphi_1(a_n, \mathbf{a}_{-n}, c_j)$ and $\varphi_2(a_n, \mathbf{a}_{-n}, c_j)$ with the following rules:

$$
\begin{aligned}
\varphi_1(a_n, \mathbf{a}_{-n}, c_j) &= -\tfrac{1}{2} \sum_{n \in \mathcal{N}} I_n(a_n, \mathbf{a}_{-n}, c_j), \\
\varphi_2(a_n, \mathbf{a}_{-n}, c_j) &= - \sum_{n \in \mathcal{N}} J_n(a_n, \mathbf{a}_{-n}, c_j).
\end{aligned}
\tag{21}
$$

In the POC situation, when the physical distance between two users is out of the interference range, they are not neighbour and there is no interference between them. For the function $\varphi_1(a_n, a_{-n}, c_j)$, as user n's action changes from a_n to $\overline{a}_n$, the interference of the non-neighbors does not change at all. Therefore, the variation of the function φ_1 can be expressed as:

$$
\begin{aligned}
&\varphi_1(\overline{a}_n, \mathbf{a}_{-n}, c_j) - \varphi_1(a_n, \mathbf{a}_{-n}, c_j) \\
&= -\tfrac{1}{2} \Big(\sum_{n \in \mathcal{N}} I_n(\overline{a}_n, \mathbf{a}_{-n}, c_j) - \sum_{n \in \mathcal{N}} I_n(a_n, \mathbf{a}_{-n}, c_j) \Big) \\
&= -\tfrac{1}{2} \Big(\sum_{m \in \zeta_n} I_m(\overline{a}_n, \mathbf{a}_{-n}, c_j) - \sum_{m \in \zeta_n} I_m(a_n, \mathbf{a}_{-n}, c_j) \\
&\quad + I_n(\overline{a}_n, \mathbf{a}_{-n}, c_j) - I_n(a_n, \mathbf{a}_{-n}, c_j) \Big)
\end{aligned}
\tag{22}
$$

where ζ_n denotes the user n's neighbour set.

For user n's neighbor m, the variation of the interference before and after user n unilaterally changes its action is shown as:

$$
I_m(\overline{a}_n, \mathbf{a}_{-n}, c_j) - I_m(a_n, \mathbf{a}_{-n}, c_j) = p_n(d_{mn})^{-\alpha} \varepsilon_{mn}^{a_n} [H(\overline{\delta}_{mn}) - H(\delta_{mn})].
\tag{23}
$$

And for user n, the change of interference can be expressed as:

$$
I_n(\overline{a}_n, \mathbf{a}_{-n}, c_j) - I_n(a_n, \mathbf{a}_{-n}, c_j) = \sum_{m \in \zeta_n} p_m(d_{mn})^{-\alpha} \varepsilon_{mn}^{a_n} [H(\overline{\delta}_{mn}) - H(\delta_{mn})].
\tag{24}
$$

In this work, we assume the transmission power of each user is the same as each other. Therefore, combining Eqs. (23) and (24), Eq. (22) can be expressed as:

$$
\begin{aligned}
&\varphi_1(\overline{a}_n, a_{-n}, c_j) - \varphi_1(a_n, a_{-n}, c_j) \\
&= -\tfrac{1}{2} \Big(\sum_{m \in \zeta_n} I_m(\overline{a}_n, a_{-n}, c_j) - \sum_{m \in \zeta_n} I_m(a_n, a_{-n}, c_j) + I_n(\overline{a}_n, a_{-n}, c_j) - I_n(a_n, a_{-n}, c_j) \Big) \\
&= -\tfrac{1}{2} \Big(\sum_{m \in \zeta_n} p_n(d_{mn})^{-\alpha} \varepsilon_{mn}^{a_n} [H(\overline{\delta}_{mn}) - H(\delta_{mn})] + \sum_{m \in \zeta_n} p_m(d_{mn})^{-\alpha} \varepsilon_{mn}^{a_n} [H(\overline{\delta}_{mn}) - H(\delta_{mn})] \Big) \\
&= - \sum_{m \in \zeta_n} p_m(d_{mn})^{-\alpha} \varepsilon_{mn}^{a_n} [H(\overline{\delta}_{mn}) - H(\delta_{mn})] \\
&= -(I_n(\overline{a}_n, a_{-n}, c_j) - I_n(a_n, a_{-n}, c_j)).
\end{aligned}
\tag{25}
$$

On the other hand, the strategy unilaterally changed by user n does not influence the jamming of user n's neighbor. Therefore, the variation of the function φ_2 is shown as:

$$
\begin{aligned}
&\varphi_2(\bar{a}_n, \mathbf{a}_{-n}, c_j) - \varphi_2(a_n, \mathbf{a}_{-n}, c_j) \\
&= -(\sum_{m \in \{\mathcal{N}/n\}} J_m(\bar{a}_n, \mathbf{a}_{-n}, c_j) + J_n(\bar{a}_n, \mathbf{a}_{-n}, c_j) \\
&\quad - \sum_{i \in \{\mathcal{N}/n\}} J_i(a_n, \mathbf{a}_{-n}, c_j) - J_n(a_n, \mathbf{a}_{-n}, c_j)) \\
&= -(\sum_{m \in \{\mathcal{N}/n\}} J_m(\bar{a}_n, \mathbf{a}_{-n}, c_j) - \sum_{i \in \{\mathcal{N}/n\}} J_i(a_n, \mathbf{a}_{-n}, c_j)) \\
&\quad -(J_n(\bar{a}_n, \mathbf{a}_{-n}, c_j) - J_n(a_n, \mathbf{a}_{-n}, c_j)) \\
&= -(J_n(\bar{a}_n, \mathbf{a}_{-n}, c_j) - J_n(a_n, \mathbf{a}_{-n}, c_j)).
\end{aligned}
\tag{26}
$$

As a result, the variation of the potential function φ is:

$$
\begin{aligned}
&\varphi(\bar{a}_n, \mathbf{a}_{-n}, c_j) - \varphi(a_n, \mathbf{a}_{-n}, c_j) \\
&= \varphi_1(\bar{a}_n, \mathbf{a}_{-n}, c_j) + \varphi_2(\bar{a}_n, \mathbf{a}_{-n}, c_j) - (\varphi_1(a_n, \mathbf{a}_{-n}, c_j) + \varphi_2(a_n, \mathbf{a}_{-n}, c_j)) \\
&= -(I_n(\bar{a}_n, \mathbf{a}_{-n}, c_j) - I_n(a_n, \mathbf{a}_{-n}, c_j)) + (-(J_n(\bar{a}_n, \mathbf{a}_{-n}, c_j) - J_n(a_n, \mathbf{a}_{-n}, c_j))) \\
&= -(I_n(\bar{a}_n, \mathbf{a}_{-n}, c_j) + J_n(\bar{a}_n, \mathbf{a}_{-n}, c_j)) - (-I_n(a_n, \mathbf{a}_{-n}, c_j) + J_n(a_n, \mathbf{a}_{-n}, c_j)) \\
&= u_n(\bar{a}_n, \mathbf{a}_{-n}, c_j) - u_n(a_n, \mathbf{a}_{-n}, c_j).
\end{aligned}
\tag{27}
$$

According to the proof above, when the jamming strategy is determined and user n changes its actions unilaterally, the variation of φ is equal to the variation of the user n's utility function. Therefore, the follower sub-game is an EPG and there exacts at least a pure strategy NE. As user n's throughput is in monotone decreasing relationship with generalized interference, $u_n' = f(D_n)$ [19], we formulate the throughput maximization game as:

$$
\mathcal{G}_f' : \max_{a_n \in \mathcal{M}} u_n'(a_n, \mathbf{a}_{-n}, c_j), \forall n \in \mathcal{N}.
\tag{28}
$$

Definition 2 (Ordinary Potential Game(OPG) [16]). *If there is a potential game which satisfies the following equation, this game is an OPG:*

$$
\begin{aligned}
&\mathrm{sgn}[u_n'(\bar{a}_n, \mathbf{a}_{-n}, c_j) - u_n'(a_n, \mathbf{a}_{-n}, c_j)] \\
&= \mathrm{sgn}[\varphi'(\bar{a}_n, \mathbf{a}_{-n}, c_j) - \varphi'(a_n, \mathbf{a}_{-n}, c_j)] \\
&\forall n \in \mathcal{N}, \bar{a}_n, a_n \subseteq \mathcal{M}, \bar{a}_n \neq a_n,
\end{aligned}
\tag{29}
$$

where $\mathrm{sgn}(\cdot)$ is expressed as:

$$
\mathrm{sgn}(n) = \begin{cases} 1, & n > 0 \\ 0, & n = 0 \\ -1, & n < 0. \end{cases}
\tag{30}
$$

Theorem 2. *The throughput maximization game is an OPG and there exists at least a pure strategy NE.*

Proof. The following proof follows the lines given in [19]. The utility function of the throughput maximization game is denoted as $u'_n(a_n, \mathbf{a}_{-n}, c_j) = R_n$ and the potential function is denoted as:

$$\varphi'(a_n, \mathbf{a}_{-n}, c_j) = -f[\varphi(a_n, \mathbf{a}_{-n}, c_j)]. \tag{31}$$

Assuming user n changes its action from a_n to $\bar{a}_n$, the variation of the utility function is expressed as:

$$\begin{aligned}
\Delta u'_n(a_n, \mathbf{a}_{-n}, c_j) &= u'_n(\bar{a}_n, \mathbf{a}_{-n}, c_j) - u'_n(a_n, \mathbf{a}_{-n}, c_j) \\
&= R_n(\bar{a}_n, \mathbf{a}_{-n}, c_j) - R_n(a_n, \mathbf{a}_{-n}, c_j) \\
&\approx f[D_n(\bar{a}_n, \mathbf{a}_{-n}, c_j)] - f[D_n(a_n, \mathbf{a}_{-n}, c_j)],
\end{aligned} \tag{32}$$

and the changes of φ is:

$$\begin{aligned}
\Delta\varphi'(a_n, \mathbf{a}_{-n}, c_j) &= \varphi'(\bar{a}_n, \mathbf{a}_{-n}, c_j) - \varphi'(a_n, \mathbf{a}_{-n}, c_j) \\
&= f[\varphi(a_n, \mathbf{a}_{-n}, c_j)] - f[\varphi(\bar{a}_n, \mathbf{a}_{-n}, c_j)].
\end{aligned} \tag{33}$$

Observing the equation above, we find that the variation of user n's utility function equals to that of the potential function, that is:

$$D_n(\bar{a}_n, \mathbf{a}_{-n}, c_j) - D_n(a_n, \mathbf{a}_{-n}, c_j) = \varphi(\bar{a}_n, \mathbf{a}_{-n}, c_j) - \varphi(a_n, \mathbf{a}_{-n}, c_j). \tag{34}$$

Due to the fact that $f(\cdot)$ is a monotone decreasing function, we can prove that:

$$\mathrm{sgn}[\Delta u'_n] = \mathrm{sgn}[\Delta\varphi'_n]. \tag{35}$$

Note that OPG has the same properties with EPG.

Theorem 3. *The jammer's strategy and users' NE policy constitute a SE in the hierarchical channel selection game.*

Proof. When jammer's strategy is given, the Stackelberg game becomes a non-cooperative game. It has been proven the follower sub-game is an EPG and there exacts at least a pure strategy NE. The stationary strategy of the jammer can be expressed as:

$$\vartheta_0^* = \arg\max_{\vartheta_0} u_j(\vartheta_0, NE(\vartheta_0)), \tag{39}$$

every finite strategic game has a mixed strategy equilibrium. As a result, $(\vartheta_0^*, NE(\vartheta_0^*))$ constitutes a SE in the sense of stationary strategy.

4   Hierarchical Learning Algorithm for Channel Selection Problem

To overcome the anti-jamming channel selection problem, we propose a hierarchical learning framework. We propose a Spatial Adaptive Play (SAP) [22] algorithm to select the channels in the follower sub-game and a Q-learning

Algorithm 1. Hierarchical learning algorithm for anti-jamming channel selection problem

1: **Initialzation:** Set $k=0$, $t = 0$ and initialize the mixed strategy of both users and smart jammer as $q_{nm}(t) = 1/|\mathcal{M}|$, $q_{oh}(k) = 1/|\mathcal{C}|$, $\forall m \in \mathcal{M}, \forall h \in \mathcal{C}$.

2: **loop** $k = 0, 1, 2, ..., K_{\max}$ ($K_{\max}$ is the preestablished iteration number of the smart jammer). In the kth epoch, the smart jammer randomly selects a channel $c_j(k)$ and records this channel.

3: For the epoch k, users update their strategies based on SAP.
   (1) **loop** $t = 0, 1, 2, ..., T_{\max}$ ($T_{\max}$ is the preestablished iteration number of users). In the time slot t, every user randomly selects one channel and calculates the reward value $u_n(t)$ based on equation (36).
   (2) Among all users, randomly select one user n to adjust its action while keeping other users' strategies unchanged.
   (3) For user n, exchange the information with neighbourhood and the surrounding environment. Traverse all available channels and calculate the corresponding utility functions.
   (4) Updating the channel selection probabilities of all channels based on the Boltzmann distribution:

$$q_n(t+1) = \frac{\exp\{\omega u_n(a_n(t), c_j(k))\}}{\sum\limits_{a_n \in \mathcal{M}} \exp\{\omega u_n(a_n(t), c_j(k))\}}, \tag{36}$$

where ω is the temperature parameter which controls the tradeoff of exploration-exploitation.
   (5) Based on the channel selection probability, the user n selects one of the channels.
   (6) **End loop**

4: The jammer calculates $u_j(k)$ and updates its Q values based on the following rule:

$$Q_0^{k+1}(c_j(k+1)) = (1-\alpha)Q_0^k(c_j(k)) + \alpha u_j(k), \tag{37}$$

where $\alpha = \lambda^k \in [0, 1)$ is the learning rate, and the jammer updates its strategy based on the same rule as users.

$$q_0(k) = \frac{\exp\{Q_0^k(c_j(k))/\tau_0\}}{\sum\limits_{c_j \in \mathcal{C}} \exp\{Q_0^k(c_j(k))/\tau_0\}}, \tag{38}$$

where τ_0 is the temperature coefficient with the same function as ω.

5: If epoch number reaches the stopping criterion, cycle stops running, otherwise updates $k = k + 1$ and switches to step 2.

6: **End loop**

---

algorithm for the jammer to update the jamming strategy in the leader sub-game. Both two algorithms update strategies based on the probabilities of the channels selected by players. We define the mixed strategy of user n as $q_n(t) = (q_{n1}(t), ..., q_{nm}(t), ..., q_{nM}(t))$, where $q_{nm}(t)$ is the probability of channel m selected by user n and $\sum\limits_{m \in \mathcal{M}} q_{nm}(t) = 1$. Similarly, the mixed strategy of the smart jammer is denoted as $q_0(k) = (q_{01}(k), ..., q_{oh}(k), ..., q_{0H}(k))$, where $q_{oh}(k)$

means the probability of channel h selected by the smart jammer at epoch k and $\sum_{h \in \mathcal{C}} q_{oh}(k) = 1$. They update their strategies based on different time scales.

As shown in Algorithm 1, a SAP algorithm is proposed for the legitimate users to overcome the channel selection problem. In each learning process, only one user can be selected to update actions while other users keep their actions unchanged. This process is repeated running once the probability achieve the convergence. The smart jammer achieves its optimal action based on Q-learning [23]. Q-learning is widely used in dynamic and unknown environment with great performance. In this algorithm, the jammer repeatedly interacts with the environment with error trial in order to achieve the higher reward value. In the process of reinforcing the reward value, the jammer updates its Q function and makes a new action.

In the hierarchical learning framework, each epoch consists of T time slots and when the smart jammer updates one time, the users update their strategies T times. For both jammer and users, the iteration stops when the channel section probabilities vector achieves the convergence or the iteration numbers reach the preestablished number.

5   Simulation Results and Discussion

In this section, we consider a $120\,\mathrm{m} \times 120\,\mathrm{m}$ scale network. The users exist in a region of $100\,\mathrm{m} \times 100\,\mathrm{m}$ and the smart jammer is located in the region of $[100,120\,\mathrm{m}]$. Parameters in this simulation are set as follows: the users' transmitting power $p_n = 2\,\mathrm{W}$ and the jammer's transmitting power $p_j = 15\,\mathrm{W}$, the path loss exponent $\alpha = \beta = 3$, the background noise $N_0 = -130\,\mathrm{dBm}$, the instantaneous fading coefficient $\varepsilon_{jn}^{cj} = \varepsilon_{mn}^{u_m} = \varepsilon_{nn}^{u_n} = 3$, the physical distance between user n's transmitter and receiver d_{nn} $-30\,\mathrm{m}$.

Figure 3 shows the influence of users' number on the network throughput. Assuming there are 11 available channels and the power of jammer is set as 15 W. When the number of users is 25, the network throughput is 110.4 Mbps, and when the number of user is 45, the network throughput decreases to 71.2 Mbps. We can find that the network throughput decreases with the number of users increasing. In the dense network with large number of users, influence between users would degrade the network throughput.

Figure 4 shows the effect of jammer's power on the network performance. We set the number of available channels and users as 11 and 35. Assuming jammer's power as 15 W, 25 W and 35 W. According to the figure, we can find that the network throughput would decrease with the jammer's power enhancing. The simulation result shows the network throughput can maintain a stable state when the jamming intensity increases, which coincides with the practical situations.

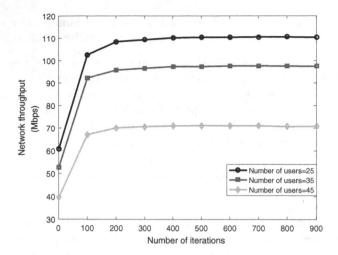

Fig. 3. The influence of users' number on the network throughput.

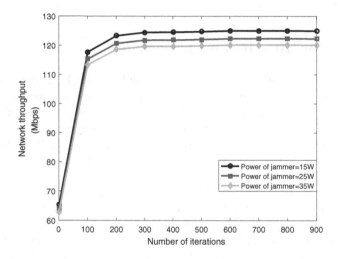

Fig. 4. The influence of jammer's power on the network throughput.

6   Conclusion

In this paper, we had investigated the intelligent anti-jamming problems with limited network bandwidth. Different from most papers focusing on orthogonal channels, this paper studied the channel selection problems in POC situation, where channels overlapped partially. The adversarial relationship between users and the samrt jammer was formulated as a hierarchical channel selection Stackelberg game. A hierarchical learning algorithm was proposed to reach the SE. Finally, simulation results showed that the network throughput can maintain a stable state when the jamming intensity increases, and it coincides with the practical situations.

References

1. Yang, D., Zhang, J., Fang, X., et al.: Optimal transmission power control in the presence of a smart jammer. In: Global Communications Conference, pp. 5506–5511 (2015)
2. Yang, D., Xue, G., Zhang, J., et al.: Coping with a smart jammer in wireless networks: a Stackelberg game approach. IEEE Trans. Wirel. Commun. 12(8), 4038–4047 (2013)
3. Xiao, L., Chen, T., Liu, J., et al.: Anti-jamming transmission Stackelberg game with observation errors. IEEE Commun. Lett. 19(6), 949–952 (2015)
4. Lv, S., Xiao, L., Hu, Q., Wang, X., Hu, C., Sun, L.: Anti-jamming power control game in unmanned aerial vehicle networks. In: IEEE GLOBECOM, pp. 1–6 (2017)
5. Yao, F., Jia, L., et al.: A hierarchical learning approach to anti-jamming channel selection strategies. Wirel. Netw. 25, 201–213 (2017). https://doi.org/10.1007/s11276-017-1551-9
6. Wu, Y., Wang, B., Liu, K., et al.: Anti-jamming games in multi-channel cognitive radio networks. IEEE J. Sel. Areas Commun. 30, 4–15 (2012)
7. Jia, L., et al.: A multi-domain anti-jamming defence scheme in heterogeneous wireless networks. IEEE Trans. Veh. Technol. (2018)
8. Hanawal, M.K., Abdel-Rahman, M.J., Krunz, M.: Joint adaptation of frequency hopping and transmission rate for anti-jamming wireless system. IEEE Trans. Mob. Comput. 15(9), 2247–2259 (2016)
9. Hanawal, M.K., Abdel-Rahman, M.J., Krunz, M.: Game theoretic anti-jamming dynamic frequency hopping and rate adaption in wireless system. In: IEEE WiOpt, pp. 247–254 (2014)
10. Mishra, A., Rozner, E., Banerjee, S., et al.: Exploiting partially overlapping channels in wireless networks: turning a peril into an advantage. In: Proceedings of the 5th ACM SIGCOMM Conference on Internet Measurement, Berkeley, United States, pp. 311–316 (2005)
11. Mishra, A., Rozner, E., Banerjee, S., et al.: Exploiting partially overlapping channels not considered harmful. SIGMetrics Performance, Saint Malo, France (2006)
12. Yao, K., et al.: Oriented partially overlapping channel access in wireless networks: a game-theoretic learning approach. Wirel. Netw. (to appear)
13. Ding, Y., Huang, Y., Zeng, G., et al.: Using partially overlapping channels to improve throughput in wireless mesh networks. IEEE Trans. Mob. Comput. 11(11), 1720–1733 (2012)
14. Tandjaoui, A., Kaddour, M., et al.: Refining the impact of partially overlapping channels in wireless mesh networks through a cross-layer optimization model. In: IEEE STWiMob, pp. 1–8 (2016)
15. Xu, Y., Wu, Q., Wang, J., et al.: Opportunistic spectrum access using partially overlapping channels: graphical game and uncoupled learning. IEEE Trans. Commun. 61(9), 3906–3918 (2013)
16. Myerson, R.: Game Theory: Analysis of Conflict. Harvard University Press, Cambridge (1991)
17. Monderer, D., Shapley, L.S.: Potential games. Games Econ. Behav. 14, 124–143 (1996)

18. Han, Z., Niyato, D., Saad, W., Basar, T., et al.: Game Theory in Wireless and Communication Networks. Cambridge University Press, Cambridge (2012)
19. Yao, K., Wu, Q., Xu, Y., Jing, J.: Distributed ABS-slot access in dense heterogeneous networks: a potential game approach with generalized interference model. IEEE Access **5**, 94–104 (2017)
20. Rad, A.H.M., Wong, V.W.S.: Joint optimal channel assignment and congestion control for multi-channel wireless mesh network. In: IEEE International Conference on Communications, Istanbul, Turkey, pp. 1984–1989 (2006)
21. Mohsenian, R.A.D.A.H., Wong, V.W.S.: Congestion-aware channel assignment for multi-cahnnel wireless mesh networks. Comput. Netw. **53**(14), 2502–2516 (2009)
22. Young, H.P.: Individual Strategy and Social Structure: An Evolutionary Theory of Institutions. Princeton University Press, Princeton (2001)
23. Watkins, C.J.C.H., Danyan, P.: Q-learning. Mach. Learn. **8**, 279–292 (1992)

A Q-Learning-Based Channel Selection and Data Scheduling Approach for High-Frequency Communications in Jamming Environment

Wen Li[1], Yuhua Xu[1(✉)], Qiuju Guo[2], Yuli Zhang[3], Dianxiong Liu[1],
Yangyang Li[1], and Wei Bai[1]

[1] College of Communications Engineering, Army Engineering University of PLA,
Nanjing 210000, China
wen-li13@outlook.com, yuhuaenator@gmail.com, dianxiongliu@163.com,
15651858962@163.com, baiweiaeu@163.com
[2] PLA 75836 Troops, Guangzhou 510000, China
dolly517@163.com
[3] National Innovation Institute of Defense Technology,
Academy of Military Sciences PLA China, Beijing 100000, China
yulipkueecs08@126.com

Abstract. The existence of jammer and the limited buffer space bring major challenge to data transmission efficiency in high-frequency (HF) commuication. The data transmission problem of how to select transmission strategy with multi-channel and different buffer states to maximize the system throughput is studied in this paper. We model the data transmission problem as a Makov decision process (MDP). Then, a modified Q-learning with additional value is proposed to help transmitter to learn the appropriate strategy and improve the system throughput. The simulation results show the proposed Q-learning algorithm can converge to the optimal Q value. Simultaneously, the QL algorithm compared with the sensing algorithm has better system throughput and less packet loss.

Keywords: Anti-jamming · Dynamic spectrum access · Q-learning ·
High-frequency(HF) communication · Markov decision process (MDP)

1 Introduction

The high-frequency (HF) (3–30 MHz) communication which is mainly used in transmitting important telegram and low bit-rate speech and image, plays a significant role in military, disaster relief and long voyage [1–3]. The main challenge

This work was supported by the National Natural Science Foundation of China under Grant No. 61771488, No. 61671473 and No. 61631020, in part by the Natural Science Foundation for Distinguished Young Scholars of Jiangsu Province under Grant No. BK20160034.

for data transmission in HF networks is to find appropriate channel selection strategy. This is for several reasons. First, the available HF spectrum resources are limited due to narrow bandwidth and multi-user accessing. Second, the time-varying characteristic which caused by the ionospheric variation makes the communication unstable. Third, there exists different kind of jamming including natural and malicious jamming with development cognitive radio [4,5] and the intelligent technologies [6,7], the jammer becomes more and more intelligent. In this paper, we mainly consider the data transmission problem in jamming environment.

The traditional anti-jamming methods in HF networks mainly include power control [8–10], frequency hopping (FH) [11,12] and automatic link establishment (ALE) [13,14]. The power control enhances communication performance by the game theory to find the optimal Nash Equilibrium(NE) point. The FH extensively used in real equipments switches in several frequencies to reduce the influence of fading and jamming. Now, the adaptive FH [11] and intelligent FH [12] technologies have attracted great attention. The power control and frequency hopping, however, are not able to deal with the intelligent jamming. The automatic link establishment (ALE) has been developed to the fourth generation, which aims to make link establishment more intelligent and faster. However, the ALE technology becomes weak, when the state of environment changes rapidly.

To cope with the complicated jamming environment, the reinforcement learning which can interact with environment and learns to get action by the reward, has attracted lots of attention [15–20]. [15] uses the Q-learning to fight against the sweep jamming considering the Markov channel model, and the simulation result shows that the agent can avoid jamming totally. [16,17] have settled the intelligent jamming by the reinforcement learning. However, the reinforcement learning is nor able to resist the complex and changeable jamming. The deep reinforcement learning (DRL) combining the deep learning and reinforcement learning is proposed to deal with above challenge [18–20]. In [18,19], the input of deep neural network uses the spectrum waterfall, and then acquires the optimal anti-jamming decision by training.

Most of existing anti-jamming studies only considered how to find the idle channels to avoid jamming and assume that the time of each data transmission is fixed. They ignored the transmission demand and the limited buffer space. In actual networks, the agent would send appropriate data packets according to the buffer and the environment state. The agent will send data packets as much as possible in the time gap between previous jamming and next jamming. Therefore, the agent should not only choose the idle channel, but also decide how many packets should send. Currently, many literatures [21,22] have studied data transmission problem in an unknown environment. However, they do not consider the existence of malicious jamming. Therefore, it is a meaningful task to solve the data transmission problem in jamming environment.

In this paper, we study the data transmission problem for high-frequency communication in the jamming environment using a modified Q-learning method. The problem is challenging due to following reasons: (1) the time-varying channels; (2)

the existence of malicious jamming; (3) the limited buffer space. The communication probability is proposed to deal with the time-varying characteristic in [23]. Motivated by [15,21], a modified Q-learning algorithm is proposed, which considers the balance of exploration and exploitation to optimize data transmission. Different from [15], the new system state is defined including the previous transmission channel, the current jamming channel, and the number of data packets in buffer. The state transmission is formulated as a markov decision process(MDP), which aims to maximize the throughput. Simulation results show that the modified Q-learning algorithm can avoid jamming effectively and data transmission compared with the sensing algorithm.

The main contributions of this paper are summarized as follow:

– The data buffer is considered and the time of each transmission is not fixed. The data transmission problem in HF jamming environment is formulated as a MDP, in which the new state contains the previous transmission channel, the current jamming channel, and the number of data packets in buffer is used.
– We proposed a modified Q-learning algorithm to solve data transmission problem. The modified Q-learning balances exploration and exploitation of action selection, which reduces the convergence time to optimal Q value.

The rest of the paper is organized as follows. In Sect. 2, the system model is introduced, and the data transmission problem is formulated as a MDP problem. The Q-Learning-based data transmission scheme which proves to converge to the optimal strategy is proposed in Sect. 3. Section 4 gives the simulation results and analysis. Finally, we draw a conclusion in Sect. 5.

2   System Model and Problem Formulation

2.1   System Model

As depicted in Fig. 1, we consider a high-frequency (HF) communication system which is composed of a transmitter, a receiver and a jammer. The point-to-point from the transmitter to receiver is considered and there are M available channels denoted by $\mathcal{M} = \{1, 2, \cdots, M\}$. The jammer intending to damage the point-to-point communication generates jamming signals in modes like comb, sweeping and intelligence. We assume that the transmitter and the jammer keep the transmitting power unchanged all the time. The data packets generated according to task demands are stored in the buffer. The maximum length of the buffer is L. We assume that the arriving data packets follow the Poisson distribution with the arrival rate λ. When the buffer is full, the packets arrive later will be lost. When one packet is jammed by the jammer, the receiver will not get this packet and then tell the transmitter to send it again. The transmission schedule is decided by the transmitter based on the channel and buffer state. The transmitter can get the current jamming channel by wide band spectrum sensing(WBSS). In each transmission, the transmitter selects a channel and sends several packets to the receiver. The transmitter must comprehensively consider the channel state and the number of packets in the buffer.

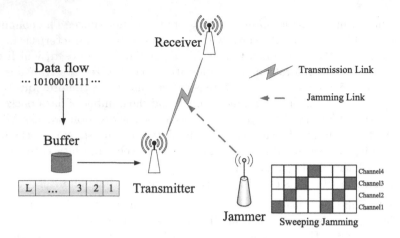

Fig. 1. System model.

Channel State. The HF communication achieves the long-distance depending on ionosphere to reflect signals. The ionosphere, however, is influenced by various factors like season, weather, location and solar activity [1]. The above factors make the HF channel time-varying and hard to predict. Therefore, the HF channel state is hard to be modeled as a Markov chain which is widely used in other literatures [24,25]. As shown in Fig. 2, the transmission will fail, when the channel is deep fading or jammed by jammer. For example, the channel 2 is unavailable in time-slot 5 with deep fading, 5 and 7 with jamming. Motivated by [23], the communication probability of channel is defined to describe the communication performance. It is a statistical concept, which can be calculated by long-time observation. The communication probability of the M available channels is denoted by $P = \{p_1, p_2, \cdots, p_M\}$, where p_i means that the data is transmitted successfully with p_i, when the transmitter chooses channel i.

Buffer State. The arriving packets follow the Poisson distribution with the arrival rate λ, which means that there are d_k arriving packets with probability $P(d_k) = e^{-\lambda T_k}(\lambda T_k)^{d_k}/d_k!$ in k-th transmission, where T_k is k-th transmission time. We assume the buffer length is l_k at the beginning of k-th transmission. If the number of transmitted packets is l_k^T, the number of arriving packets is l_k^A and the number of packets which are jammed or suffer deep fading is l_k^J, then the buffer length after k-th transmission is

$$l_{k+1} = \min(L, l_k + l_k^A + l_k^J - l_k^T), \tag{1}$$

where L is the maximum length of buffer. Since the buffer space is limited, if the number of packets is more than L, packet loss happens. It is noted that the buffer state of $k+1$-th transmission is only associated with the k-th buffer state. Thus, the buffer state is a Markov state and the transition probability is denoted by $p(l_{k+1}|l_k, b_k)$, where b_k is the of number of packets selected to transmit in k-th transmission.

2.2 Problem Formulation

In this section, we formulate the data transmission problem in HF networks as a Markov decision process(MDP) and give the explanation of the state, the action and the utility.

We consider the data transmission with limited buffer space in jamming environment. In Fig. 2, let the available channels $M = 3$, the buffer length $L = 6$ and the jammer generates the sweeping jamming. We assume the time-slot of jamming denoted by T_J and the time to transmit each packet are fixed. However, the transmitter can choose different number of packets to transmit in each transmission according to the buffer state. As shown in Fig. 2, there is a gap between adjacent interference in the same channel. For the transmitter, it would like to send all its packets in the buffer if it can find the gap. However, the gap it choose may not be enough for all packets transmission, and then the jamming happens which makes it has to retransmit these packets. Thus, in each transmission, the transmitter has to choose a better channel which can support more packets be transmitted without being jammed.

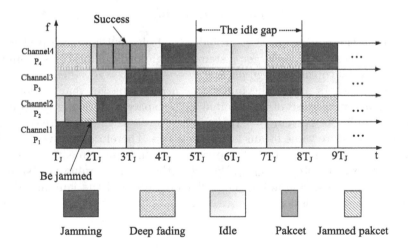

Fig. 2. The data transmission process in HF networks.

The system state in k-th transmission is defined as $s_k = (f_k^n, f_k^J, l_k)$, where f_k^n is the communication channel in last transmission, f_k^J is the jamming channel obtained by WBSS at the beginning of the transmission and l_k is the current buffer length. The process of data transmission in HF networks is actually a process of state transition. It is obvious that the next system state s_{k+1} is obtained, after the transmitter executes an action according the current state s_k. The next state is only associated with the current state and previous states have no effect on it, which can be expressed as

$$p(s_{k+1}|s_k, s_{k-1}, \cdots, s_1) = p(s_{k+1}|s_k), \tag{2}$$

where $p(\cdot)$ is the transition probability. Therefore, we can model the problem of data transmission as a Markov Decision Process (MDP) [26].

Action Set. The transmitter has to select an action which contains the channel and the number of packets at the beginning of k-th transmission. The channel selection is denoted by $c_k \in \{1, 2, \cdots, M\}$ and the packets to transmit is $b_k \in \{0, 1, 2, \cdots, l_k\}$, where l_k is current buffer length. For easy analysis, we map the two actions to a new action a_k, i.e., $f : (c_k, b_k) \rightarrow a_k$. The map f is expressed as $a_k = f(c_k, b_k) = b_k \cdot M + c_k$. Therefore, we denote the action set as $\mathcal{A} = \{1, 2, \cdots, (L+1)M\}$.

System Utility. In this paper, our goal is to maximize the system throughput. In the state s_k, we assume the number of packets which are not jammed is n_{succ} after taking action $a_k = f(c_k, b_k)$. Since the channel is unstable, the average packets transmitted successfully is denoted by

$$N(s_k, a_k) = p(c_k) \times n_{succ}, \tag{3}$$

where $p(c_k)$ is the communication probability of channel c_k. more packets are transmitted successfully, the larger system throughput is. Thus, the system utility is proportional to the average packets.

The more packets are in the buffer, the arriving packet may be lost with larger probability because of the limited buffer space. We define the pressure value of the buffer as $f(s_k, a_k) = \exp(\theta \times l_k)$, where θ is the pressure coefficient [21]. The less pressure value means less packets loss. Therefore, the system utility is inversely proportional to the buffer pressure. At the same time, the number of jammed packets is denoted by n_{Jam}. We define the jamming value as $J(s_k, a_k) = \exp(\beta \times n_{Jam})$. Thus, combining the buffer pressure and the jamming degree, the loss of data transmission is expressed as

$$H(s_k, a_k) = f(s_k, a_k) \times J(s_k, a_k). \tag{4}$$

The system utility, which is related to the packets transmitted successfully and the transmission loss, is described as

$$u_k = u(s_k, a_k) = N(s_k, a_k)/H(s_k, a_k). \tag{5}$$

In this paper, we want to maximize the throughput performance of the HF networks by online learning method. The action a_k is related to the history data transmission strategies $\{a_1, a_2, \cdots, a_{k-1}\}$ and history utility information

$(\{u_1, u_2, \cdots, u_{k-1}\})$. Our problem is to find the optimal data transmission strategy to maximize the cumulative expected throughput [15]

$$P : \max E[\sum_{i=1}^{k} u_i(a_i)], a_i \in \mathcal{A}. \tag{6}$$

According to previous analysis, the data transmission problem is modeled as a MDP problem. The reinforcement learning(RL) which interacts with the environment to find the optimal action is widely used for the MDP problem [15–19]. As the system state and the action are discrete, the Q-learning is suitable to solve the data transmission problem. In the next section, we will propose a modified Q-learning algorithm and prove the convergence of it.

3   Q-Learning-Based Data Transmission Scheme

The Q-learning algorithm interacts with the environment and learn to obtain the optimal action in a online-learning way. The Q-value table is used to evaluate the performance of the action. In the state s_k, the agent takes an action a_k according to the Q-value table, then, it obtains instantaneous reward r_k and switch to next state s_{k+1}. At the same time, it updates the Q-value table. The more detailed explanation about Q-learning can be found in [27].

In the learning process, the agent interacts with the environment to find the optimal actions, considering the immediate reward and the future rewards. The discounted future rewards under a policy π is defined as

$$V^{\pi}(s_k) = \sum_{j=k}^{+\infty} \gamma^{j-k} u_j, \tag{7}$$

where $0 < \gamma < 1$ is the discount factor. Then, the corresponding Q value can be formulated as

$$Q(s_k, a_k) \leftarrow r_k + \gamma V^{\pi}(s_{k+1}). \tag{8}$$

Our goal is to maximize the discounted utility. According to the Bellman equation [18], the Q value by replacing the r_k and $V^{\pi}(s_{k+1})$ can be expressed as

$$Q(s_k, a_k) \leftarrow u_k + \gamma \max_{a_{k+1}} Q(s_{k+1}, a_{k+1}). \tag{9}$$

Different from [15] and [18] in which the number of available actions is small, the number of the actions in this paper is calculated as $M(L+1)$. Since the action set is large, the normal Q-learning may converge to the optimal Q value with large steps. Motivated by [21], we proposed a modified Q-learning algorithm in jamming environment. It is important to balance the exploration and exploitation of the large action set for Q-learning algorithm. In order to choose the action effectively, a additional value is added to find the optimal action quickly [21]. The additional value can reduce the convergence time by taking advantage of history rewards and adjusting the explore range. The action a_k is selected by following equation,

$$a_k = \arg\max_a(Q(s_k, a) + Add(s_k, a)). \tag{10}$$

The additional value $Add(s_k, a)$ which can help to find the optimal with less learning steps is expressed as

$$Add(s_k, a) = C_p\sqrt{2\ln k \times \min\{1/4, V_a(k)\}/T_a(k)}, \tag{11}$$

where C_p is a greater than zero [28], and $T_a(k)$ is the number of times that action a has been executed after k transmissions. $V_a(k)$ is the bias factor, which is defined as

$$V_a(k) = \sigma_a^2(k) + \sqrt{2\ln k/T_a(k)}, \tag{12}$$

where $\sigma_a^2(k)$ is the utility variance. The variance can reflect the volatility of the action. It can be calculated by

$$\sigma_a^2(k) = \sum_{i=1}^{T_a(k)} u^2(s_i(a), a)/T_a(k) - (\sum_{i=1}^{T_a(k)} u(s_i(a), a)/T_a(k))^2, \tag{13}$$

where $s_i(a)$ is the i-th of states which have selected the action a. The above action selection method with the additional value makes the best of history rewards and chooses the action with larger reward, which is the exploitation characteristic of the system. Simultaneously, it will explore the action which is not selected or rarely selected, which reflects the exploration of the system.

When the transmitter chooses an action a_k according to the state s_k and the above method, it obtains the reward $r_k = u_k$, and then it updates the Q values as follow:

$$Q_{k+1}(s_k, a_k) = (1 - \alpha)Q_k(s_k, a_k) + \alpha(r_k + \gamma\max_a(Q_k(S_{k+1}, a)), \tag{14}$$

where $\alpha(0 < \alpha \leq 1)$ is the learning rate which is defined as $\alpha = 1/(1 + T_{a_k}(k))$, and γ is the discount factor.

In the jamming environment, the transmitter performs the modified algorithm to adjust the transmission strategy at the beginning of each transmission. The Fig. 3 shows the time-slot of the modified Q-learning algorithm. At the beginning of k-th transmission, the current state $s_k = (f_k^n, f_k^J, l_k)$ is obtained according the last transmitting channel, the jamming channel by WBSS and the buffer length. In the T_A period, the receiver feedbacks the jammed packets n_J to the transmitter by ACK. The current jamming channel f_{k+1}^J is obtained by WBSS in the T_W period. During the T_L, the transmitter observes the buffer length l_{k+1} and obtains the next state $s_{k+1} = (f_{k+1}^n, f_{k+1}^J, l_{k+1})$. At the same time, it updates the Q values according to (14). The detailed process of the modified QL algorithm is shown in Algorithm 1.

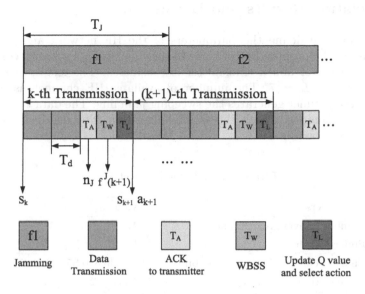

Fig. 3. The time-slot structure of the modified QL algorithm.

Algorithm 1. The modified Q-learning-based HF data transmission algorithm

1: Set parameter γ, simulation time K, and the time index $k = 0$.
2: Initialize the action recording vector $T_k = 0$ and the Q value $Q(s, a) = 0$.
3: Initialize the jamming channel f_0^J by WBSS and the buffer length $l_0 \leq L$, choose the initial transmitting channel f_0^n, and acquiring the initial state $s_0 = (f_0^n, f_0', l_0)$.
4: While $k < K$, do
5:     if $k < 1000$
6:         Select an action a_k randomly.
7:     else
8:         Calculate the additional value
$$Add(s_k, a) = C_p\sqrt{2\ln k \times \min\{1/4, V_a(k)\}/T_a(k)}.$$
9:         Select action according to (10)
$$a_k = \arg \max_a (Q(s_k, a) + Add(s_k, a)).$$
10:     end
11:     Upgrade the action recording vector $T_{a_k}(k) = T_{a_k}(k) + 1$.
12:     Execute a_k, and obtain the reward r_k based on (5).
13:     Receive the ACK from the receiver, calculate the buffer length l_{k+1}.
14:     Obtain f_{k+1}^n according to a_k and the f_{k+1}^J by WBSS, Then the next state is $s_{k+1} = (f_{k+1}^n, f_{k+1}^J, l_{k+1})$.
15:     Calculate $\alpha = 1/(1 + T_{a_k}(k))$.
16:     Update $Q_k(s_k, a_k)$
$$Q_{k+1}(s_k, a_k) = (1 - \alpha)Q_k(s_k, a_k) + \alpha(r_k + \gamma \max(Q_k(S_{k+1}, a_{k+1})).$$
17:     $k = k + 1$
18: End while

4   Simulation Results and Discussion

In this section, we define the parameters of the HF network and study the performance of the proposed algorithm. In the simulation, a network containing a jammer, a receiver and a transmitter is considered. The length of buffer in the transmitter is $L = 7$. The number of available HF channels is $M = 4$. We assume the jammer generates the sweeping jamming. The data transmission performance is compared with the sensing algorithm. The detailed simulation parameters are shown in Table 1.

Table 1. Simulation parameters.

Parameters	Value
Number of available channels	$M = 4$
Buffer length	$L = 7$
Channel communication probability	$P = [0.8, 0.85, 0.9, 0.95]$
Jammer time-slot /ms	$T_{jam} = 2$
Transmission time of each packet /ms	$T_d = 0.8$
ACK transmission time /ms	$T_{ACK} = 0.1$
WBSS time /ms	$T_{WBSS} = 0.2$
Simulation steps	$K = 25000$
Buffer pressure coefficient	$\theta = 0.5$
Jammed pakcet press coefficient	$\beta = 0.5$
Arrive rate	$\lambda = [0.6, 0.7, \cdots, 1.3]$
Learning rate	$\alpha = (0, 1]$
Discount factor	$\gamma = 0.8$
Index weight	$C_p = 1/\sqrt{2}$
Transmission power of each packet /mw	$P_{signle} = 0.3$

Figures 4 and 6 show the time-frequency diagram of the transmitter and the jammer at the initial and convergent stage, respectively, in which the red squares represent the sweeping jamming, the green squares are the data transmission and the blue squares are the WBSS and ACK transmission. As shown in Fig. 4, at the initial stage, there are mass of the overlapping squares which represent data transmission being jammed. At the same time, Figs. 5 and 7 show the buffer length after each transmission. It can be noted that the pressure of the buffer is large because of the jammed packets. However, it is noted that the transmitter can choose right transmission action to avoid the jamming after the Q-learning stage, which is depicted in Fig. 6. At the same time, The pressure of buffer is small after the learning phase which is shown in Fig. 7.

Figure 8 shows the Q value changing curve in the learning process at the state $s(1, 2, 4)$ for different actions. From the figure, we can see that the Q value

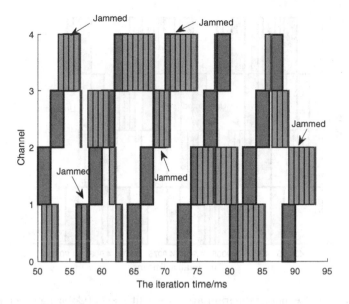

Fig. 4. Time-frequency diagram at initial stage. (Color figure online)

curve converges to a stable value. At the sate in which last transmission is in 1-th channel, the jammer is in 2-th channel and the buffer length is 4, the transmitter learns the jamming pattern and acquires the optimal action. As shown in figure, the transmitter will select the action $a = (4, 4)$ which sends 4 packets in the

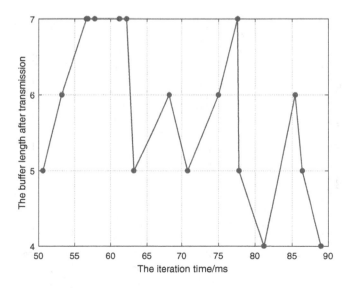

Fig. 5. The buffer state at initial stage.

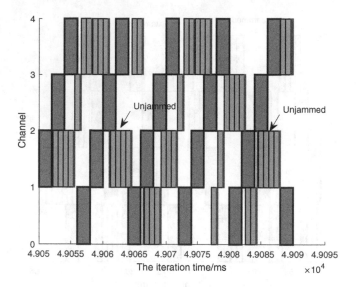

Fig. 6. Time-frequency diagram at convergent stage. (Color figure online)

channel 4. It finds the optimal action in the state $s(1,2,4)$. The convergence of the algorithm is verified.

Figure 9 shows the system throughput under two different algorithms containing the proposed QL algorithm and the sensing algorithm. The sensing algorithm is that each transmission randomly selects an action according to the

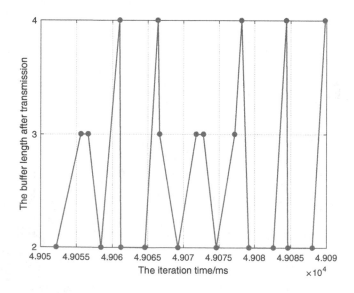

Fig. 7. The buffer state at convergent stage.

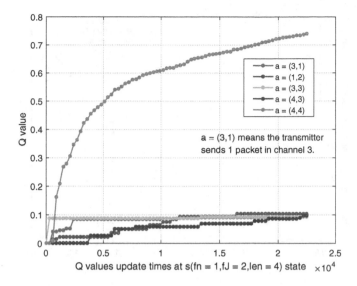

Fig. 8. Q value changing curve at the state $s = (1, 2, 4)$ with different actions.

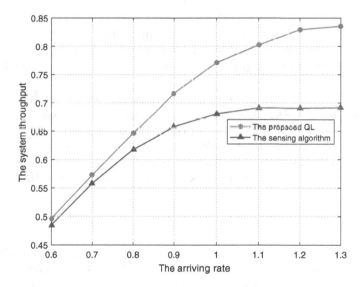

Fig. 9. Throughput comparison of different algorithms.

current sensing result. The throughput is calculated after each 100 transmissions, which is the ratio between sum of packets transmitted successfully and the total time. From the Fig. 9, we can find that the two algorithm have almost equivalent system throughput with small packet arriving rate. Because the pressure of the buffer is small, there are not enough packets to transmit. With the packet arriving rate increasing, the number of packets in the buffer gradually

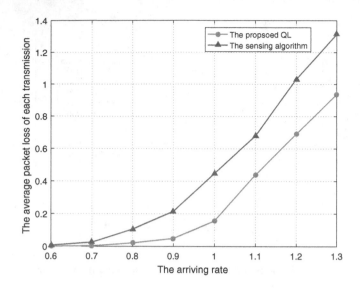

Fig. 10. Average packet loss of different algorithms.

increases which brings larger system throughput. Since the QL algorithm can learn to select appropriate action by interacting with the jamming environment, it has a better system throughput performance in the unknown and jamming environment.

Since the buffer space is limited, more packets will be lost, when the arriving rate of packet is large. As shown in Fig. 10, the average packet loss of each transmission is compared with different algorithms. With the arriving rate increasing, the packet loss is growing and it is almost linear. Because the sensing algorithm chooses the action randomly according to current sensing result, there are more jammed packets which make more packet loss than the QL algorithm.

5   Conclusion

In this paper, we considered the data transmission problem with jamming environment in the HF environment. To cope with the unstable characteristic of HF channel, the communication probability was used. A modified Q-learning algorithm has been proposed to optimize the strategy selection and achieve better communication performance. The data transmission problem in the jamming environment which was formulated as a MDP problem, was solved by the proposed algorithm. The proposed algorithm adding the additional value could balance the exploration and exploitation of action. The simulation results confirmed the convergence of the proposed QL algorithm and indicated that the QL had higher system throughput and less packet loss than the sensing algorithm. This paper only considered sweeping jamming. In the next step, the intelligent jammer will be further studied.

References

1. Wang, J.: Research and Development of HF Digital Communications. Science Press, Beijing, China (2013)
2. Hanson, R.: Military applications of HF communications. Mil. Technol. **10**, 70–77 (2010)
3. Xu, K., Jiang, B., Su, Z., et al.: High frequency communication network with diversity: system structure and key enabling techniques. China Commun. **15**(9), 46–59 (2018)
4. Haykin, S.: Cognitive radio: brain-empowered wireless communications. IEEE J. Sel. Areas Commun. **23**(2), 201–220 (2015)
5. Yucek, T., Arslan, H.: A survey of spectrum sensing algorithms for cognitive radio applications. IEEE Commun. Surv. Tutor. **11**(1), 116–130 (2009)
6. Bkassiny, M., Li, Y., Jayaweera, S.K.: A survey on machine learning techniques in cognitive radios. IEEE Commun. Surv. Tutor. **15**(3), 1136–1159 (2013)
7. Luong, N.C., Hoang, D.T., Gong, S., et al.: Applications of deep reinforcement learning in communications and networking: a survey. arXiv:1810.07862
8. Yang, D., Xue, G., Zhang, J., Richa, A., Fang, X.: Coping with a smart jammer in wireless networks: a Stackelberg game approach. IEEE Trans. Wirel. Commun. **12**(8), 4038–4047 (2013)
9. Jia, L., Xu, Y., Sun, Y., Feng, S., Anpalagan, A.: Stackelberg game approaches for anti-jamming defence in wireless networks. IEEE Trans. Wirel. Commun. **25**(6), 120–128 (2018)
10. Feng, Z., Ren, G., Chen, J.: Power control in relay-assisted anti-jamming systems: a Bayesian three-layer stackelberg game approach. IEEE Access **7**, 14623–14636 (2019)
11. Michael, R.M., et al.: Adaptive coding for frequency-Hop transmission over fading channels with partial-Band interference. IEEE Trans. Commun. **59**(3), 854–862 (2011)
12. Duan, R.J., et al.: Research on spectrum allocation of HF access network based on intelligent frequency hopping. In: 8th International Symposium on Computational Intelligence and Design (ISCID), Hangzhou, pp. 295–300 (2015)
13. Johnson, E., et al.: Third-Generation and Wideband HF Radio Communications. Artech House, Norwood (2013)
14. Wang, J., Ding, G., Wang, H.: HF communications: past, present, and future. China Commun. **15**(9), 1–9 (2018)
15. Kong, L., Xu, Y., Zhang, Y., et al.: A reinforcement learning approach for dynamic spectrum anti-jamming in fading environment. In: IEEE 18th International Conference on Communication Technology (ICCT), Chongqing, pp. 51–58 (2018)
16. Slimeni, F., Chtourou, Z., Schaeers, B., Nir, V.L., Attia, R.: Cooperative Q-learning based channel selection for cognitive radio. Wirel. Netw. **4**, 1–11 (2018)
17. Xiao, L., Lu, X., Xu, D., Tang, Y., Wang, L., Zhuang, W.: Uav relay in vanets against smart jamming with reinforcement learning. IEEE Trans. Veh. Technol. **67**(5), 4087–4097 (2018)
18. Liu, X., Xu, Y., Jia, L., et al.: Anti-jamming communications using spectrum waterfall: a deep reinforcement learning approach. IEEE Commun. Lett. **22**(5), 998–1001 (2018)
19. Liu, X., Xu, Y., Cheng, Y., et al.: A heterogeneous information fusion deep reinforcement learning for intelligent frequency selection of HF communication. China Commun. **15**(9), 73–84 (2018)

20. Chen, Y., Li, Y., Xu, D., Xiao, L.: DQN-based power control for IOT transmission against jamming. In: IEEE 87th Vehicular Technology Conference (VTC Spring), Porto, pp. 1–5 (2018)

21. Zhu, J., Song, Y., Jiang, D., Song, H.: A new deep-Q-learning-based transmission scheduling mechanism for the cognitive internet of things. IEEE Internet Things J. 5(4), 2375–2385 (2018)

22. Lin, X., Tan, Y., Zhang, J.: A MDP-based energy efficient policy for wireless transmission. Commun. Netw. 36(7), 1433–1438 (2014)

23. Li, W., Ruan, L., Xu, Y., et al.: Exploring channel diversity in HF communication systems: a matching-potential game approach. China Commun. 15(9), 60–72 (2018)

24. Wang, H.S., Moayeri, N.: Finite-state Markov channel-a useful model for radio communication channels. IEEE Trans. Veh. Technol. 44(1), 163–171 (1995)

25. Zhang, Q., Kassam, S.A.: Finite-state Markov model for Rayleigh fading channels. IEEE Trans. Commun. 47(11), 1688–1692 (1999)

26. Monahan, G.E.: State of the art-a survey of partially observable Markov decision processes: theory, models, and algorithms. Manag. Sci. 28(1), 1–16 (1982)

27. Luong, N.C., Hoang, D.T., Gong, S., et al.: Applications of deep reinforcement learning in communications and networking: a survey (2018). arXiv:1810.07862

28. Browne, C.B., Powley, E., Whitehouse, D., et al.: A survey of Monte Carlo tree search methods, 4(1), 1–43 (2012)

RFID Indoor Location Based on Optimized Generalized Regression Neural Network

Fangjin Chen[1,2], Xiangmao Chang[1,2(✉)], Xiaoxiang Xu[1,2], and Yanjun Lu[3]

[1] College of Computer Science and Technology,
Nanjing University of Aeronautics and Astronautics, Nanjing, China
xiangmaoch@nuaa.edu.cn
[2] Collaborative Innovation Center of Novel Software Technology
and Industrialization, Nanjing, China
[3] Urban Construction College, Wuchang University of Technology,
Wuhan, China

Abstract. Nowadays, location-based services are common in our daily lives. Traditional Global Positioning System (GPS) location can provide real-time location function in outdoor complex environments, but it is insufficient for indoor location. There are many indoor location technologies, such as ultrasound, Zigbee, RFID and WIFI. RFID location technology has attracted the attention of researchers due to its high precision and low cost. Most existing RFID location algorithms are based on RSSI (Received Signal Strength Indicator) measurement. When converting RSSI to distance, the inaccurate estimation of the path loss parameter may lead to large error. In order to reduce the deviation, this paper proposes a new RFID location algorithm. Specifically, the RSSI of the target tag is read in different directions of the antenna, and the position information is predicted by the general regression neural network, which is optimized by the optimization algorithm. The experimental results show the efficiency of our proposed algorithm.

Keywords: RFID · Generalized regression neural network · Indoor location

1 Introduction

In recent years, the development of the Internet of Things (IoT) has great facilitated our lives. Its device performance has grown rapidly and location-aware applications have proliferated [13]. Location awareness has played an increasingly important role. Providing location information continuously and reliably in both indoor and outdoor environments can provide users with a better user experience. Outdoor location and location-based services have matured, and location-based services based on GPS and maps are widely used and become one of the most used applications for mobile devices. However, due to the interference of building shielding and indoor environment, GPS cannot be used indoors well, such as searching for books in the library and looking for luggage at the airport. Researchers are more focused on how to perform high-precision indoor location.

X. B. Zhai et al. (Eds.): MLICOM 2019, LNICST 294, pp. 161–172, 2019.
https://doi.org/10.1007/978-3-030-32388-2_14

In order to meet the needs of indoor object location, the researchers proposed many indoor location technologies [9]. Ultrasonic, sensor, Bluetooth, WIFI and Zigbee technologies are used for location. The author [1] proposed an ultrasound-based indoor location system that calculates the position of the mobile platform by using only ultrasonic signals and the accuracy reaches the centimeter level. The position of the moving target is calculated from the receiver's time difference of arrival (TDOA), and the system has a relatively high cost. In [6], the authors propose a Bayesian inference-based localization algorithm for locating target objects in a 3D WLAN indoor environment, which uses fingerprint technology and the location error is about three meters.

Radio Frequency Identification (RFID) is the crucial technology required to implement the Internet of Thing (IOT), widely used in health detection, smart home, smart city, vehicle location and target tracking, etc. Compare with Sensor, WIFI and Bluetooth, RFID technology has attracted many researchers to deploy applications in indoor positioning environments due to its low cost, high efficiency and low power consumption [3]. There are two types of location algorithm based on Received Signal Strength indicator (RSSI): geometric and fingerprint tags. The geometric method uses the geometric relationship of a circle, sphere or triangle [7] to estimate the position of the target by calculating the distance, as well as the Time of Arrival (TOA) and Angle of Arrival (AOA) [2]. The author [5] proposed an algorithm for RFID location based on hyperbola, which is positioned by limiting the position of the antenna. The reference tag method needs to establish a database of known RFID tag's location information, then to estimate the location of the target tag. In [4, 14], the author proposes a KNN nearest neighbor algorithm to estimate the location information of the test tag, which need a large number of references tags. We hope to design a joint location method to reduce the error of indoor location and not be limited by the location relationship of the antenna.

This paper proposes an indoor location algorithm combining neural network and RFID, without reference tags. After conducting a series of experimental studies, we decided to use three different directions of the antenna to receive the RSSI of the tag, then construct the training data as the input vector of the neural network. The real coordinates of the test tag in the environment is the output vector of the neural network. At the same time, this paper proposes a new optimization algorithm improves the network parameter, and establish the corresponding fitting model to achieve different location in the room.

The main contributions of this paper are summarized as follows:

- We extensively analyze and compare the signal characteristics collected from RFID reader, indicating that RSSI is a stable characteristic of the tag location algorithm proposed in this paper. Not affected by the direction and period of the tag.
- We propose an RFID location method for general regression neural network optimized by mutation particle swarm, called MPSO-GRNN, with regrading to the size of training samples, and the convergence speed of the neural network.

- We design a prototype of MPSO-GRNN using ImpinJ Revolution R420 reader and EPC Gen2 tag. The experimental result shows that the average location error is 0.26 m, and the convergence speed of the optimized GRNN is increased by 61%.

The rest of the structure of this paper is as follows. We will present the background of the second part and conduct an empirical study. The main design of MPSO-GRNN is described in the third part. The fourth section gives the implementation and evaluation. Finally, the fifth section summarizes the paper.

2   Preliminaries

In this section, we will present the background of RFID technology and compare the RSSI and phase signal characteristics using the COTS reader-Impinj Revolution R420 RFID reader and EPC Gen2 tag [12].

2.1   RSSI (Received Signal Strength)

As one of the important characteristic values of RFID signals, RSSI can be received by RFID tags through reading by RFID antenna [8]. The RSSI has an inverse relationship with the distance between the RFID reader's antenna and the RFID tag [16]. The longer the signal propagation distance, the weaker the signal strength. For a better description of the influence of indoor complex environment on signal strength, the path loss signal propagation model is often used as the indoor signal propagation model [11]:

$$RSSI(d) = RSSI(d_0) - 10n \lg \frac{d}{d_0} \qquad (1)$$

where n is the path loss factor, d_0 is the known near ground reference distance, d is the distance from the target to the reader and $RSSI(d)$, $RSSI(d_0)$ are the tag signal strengths at distances d and d_0, respectively. When $d_0 = 1m$, $RSSI(d_0)$ is the average of the received signal strengths at 1 m from the signal transmission location, and the actual applied RSSI ranging formula is obtained:

$$RSSI(d) = RSSI(d_0) - 10n \lg d \qquad (2)$$

since each indoor environment is complex, the path loss factor in the equation is not a stable number. This article is mainly used in the location of static tags, we place the tag about 0.45 m in front of the reader antenna, at the same time, we record the RSSI value fed back by the tag, as shown in Fig. 1. When the static tag is within the reader's readable range, the RSSI value is in a small amplitude fluctuation, maintaining between −42 dBm positive and negative.

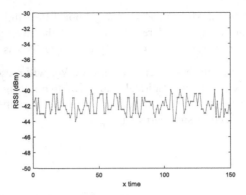

Fig. 1. The RSSI value in an interference environment.

2.2 Phase

Another important feature value of the RFID signal is the phase value, and it can be obtained from the signal fed back from the tag. Again, we place the tag at 0.45 m and record the value of the phase, as shown in Fig. 2. We can find that the phase value will fluctuate greatly and have periodicity. the relationship between RF carrier of frequency f (Hz) and wavelength λ is determined by $\lambda = c/f$, where c indicates that the velocity of the EM wave is equal to the velocity of light ($\approx 3 \times 10^8$ m/s). In addition to the RF phase rotating with distance, the reader's transmission circuit, the reflective characteristics of the tag, and the receiver's receiver circuit introduce some phase rotations called θ_T, θ_{TAG}, and θ_R [10, 15]. Therefore, the total phase rotation is calculated as follows:

$$\theta + 2k\pi = 2\pi\frac{2d}{\lambda} + \theta_T + \theta_{TAG} + \theta_R \tag{3}$$

where θ are the output parameters supported by the generic RFID reader and the number of period is k. Due to the periodicity and sensitivity of the phase, passive tag RFID is difficult to use for large-scale location in phase value characteristics.

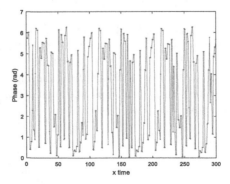

Fig. 2. The phase value in an interference environment.

Therefore, when we decide to use the RFID signals for indoor location, we need overcome the different path loss coefficients and phase cycling characteristics in complex indoor environments. In this paper, we mainly improve the adaptability of multiple environments and the location accuracy. Next, we will use the RSSI eigenvalues and filter to perform data preprocessing. At the same time, we optimize the neural network model to increase the location accuracy of the RFID location and speed up the network convergence.

3 MPSO-GRNN

In this part, we propose an algorithm for generalized regression neural network optimized by mutation particle swarm, called MPOS-GRNN, then gradually introduce our technical details.

3.1 Mean Filter

In order to make the measured value of RSSI approximately equal to the true values, we need to filter out the fluctuation of RSSI values caused by indoor environment or noise interference. Since the target object in this paper is a static tag. We choose the mean filter whose main idea is to average over the domain, the filter formula has the following representation:

$$RSSI_{average} = \frac{1}{n}\sum_{i=1}^{n} RSSI_i \tag{4}$$

where $RSSI_i$ is the i th RSSI value and the size of the sliding window of the filter is n. The average is then calculated, $RSSI_{average}$ is considered the target tag RSSI value.

3.2 GRNN

Generalized Regression Neural Network (GRNN) is a one of the radial basis function network (RBF). But GRNN has more powerful non-linear mapping capabilities and learning speed than RBF, which requires less modeling samples and better prediction results. After determining the number of training samples, the connection weight factor between the corresponding network structure and the neuron can be also determined. The purpose of network training is only to determine its unique parameter smoothing factor σ.

The GRNN structure is shown in Fig. 3. The input layer, mode layer, summation layer and output layer construct the feed forward neural network structure.

The neuron data of the pattern layer comes directly from the input vector of the input layer. Assume the input vector a is n-dimensional $A = [a_1, a_2, \cdots, a_n]^T$, the output layer vector Y is q-dimensional and the number of samples is n. The dimensions of the sample simultaneously determine the number of input layer neurons and the number of pattern layer neurons, and each neuron represents to a different sample.

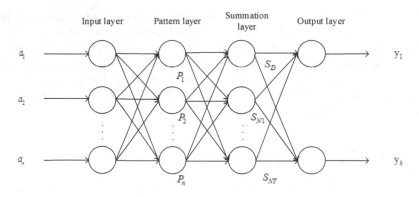

Fig. 3. General regression neural network structure.

The pattern layer is also called the implicit regression layer, and each neuron corresponds to a different learning sample. The number of neurons is the same as the size of training samples, and the neuron transfer function of the pattern layer is:

$$p_i = \exp\left[-\frac{(A - A_i)^T(A - A_i)}{2\sigma_i^2}\right], (i = 1, 2, \ldots, n) \tag{5}$$

Two types of neurons are summed at the summation layer, one of which is calculated as:

$$\sum_{i=1}^n \exp\left[-(A - A_i)^T(A - A_i)/2\sigma_i^2\right] \tag{6}$$

it performs arithmetic sum on the mode layer neuron's output, its mode layer and each neuron have a connection weight of 1, and the transfer function is $S_D = \sum_{i=1}^n P_i$. Another calculation method is

$$\sum_{i=1}^n Y_i \exp\left[-(A - A_i)^T(A - A_i)/2\sigma_i^2\right] \tag{7}$$

it weights the pattern layer's neurons, and the weight factor between the i th neuron in the pattern layer and the j th molecule in the summation layer is the first in the i th output sample, the Mapping relations is $S_{Nj} = \sum_{i=1}^n y_{ij}P_i(j = 1, 2, \cdots, k)$.

The number of the output layer's neurons is the dimension of the output vector, and the output layer's neurons represents to the j th element of the estimation result $\overline{Y}(X)$, which is $y_{ij} = S_{Nj}/S_D(j = 1, 2, \cdots, k)$.

3.3   MPSO

The PSO algorithm is derived from the discovery of behavioral characteristics of biological groups and is often used to find the best solution. Each particle in the algorithm represents a possible solution to the issue, and fitness function determines the fitness value of each particle. Particles have direction, distance and speed of motion. Each particle dynamically adjusts its own velocity by comparing it with the motion information of other particles, thereby realizing the optimization of the individual in the solution space.

Suppose $A = (A_1, A_2, \cdots, A_n)$ is the n particles in a M-dimensional search space, the i th particle is represented as a M-dimensional vector $A_i = [a_{i1}, a_{i2}, \cdots, a_{iM}]^T$, which represents the information of the i th particle in the M-dimensional search space and a possible solution to the issue. Then the fitness function can calculate the fitness value of each particle. The velocity of the ith particle is $V_i = [V_{i1}, V_{i2}, \cdots, V_{iM}]^T$, Its individual extremum is $Q_i = [Q_{i1}, Q_{i2}, \cdots, Q_{iM}]^T$, The global extremum of the population is $Q_g = [Q_{g1}, Q_{g2}, \cdots, Q_{gM}]^T$.

Each individual updates its own speed and position with reference to other individual extremum and global extrema during each iteration. The calculation is as follows:

$$V_{im}^{k+1} = \omega V_{im}^k + e_1 n_1 (Q_{im}^k - A_{im}^k) + e_2 n_2 (Q_{gm}^k - A_{im}^k) \tag{8}$$

$$A_{im}^{k+1} = A_{im}^k + V_{im}^{k+1} \tag{9}$$

where ω is the inertia weight, k is the number of iterations, V_{im} is the velocity of the particle, e_1 and e_2 are the acceleration factor and are non-negative, n_1 and n_2 are random numbers from 0 to 1. We find that the particle swarm optimization algorithm is easy to achieve local optimization and low iteration efficiency. Therefore, we use the variation idea in the genetic algorithm to reinitialize the particles with a certain probability after each update of the particles. We call MPSO (Mutation Particle Swarm Algorithm).

When the GRNN learning sample is established, which also determine the corresponding network structure and the weight coefficient between the neurons. The network training process is to determine the optimal solution of its unique parameter smoothing factor σ. We define the smoothing factor parameter σ of GRNN as the particle of MPSO. Therefore, this paper proposes to use MPSO to optimize GRNN.

According to the characteristics of the tag feedback signal, we set the actual measured RSSI to the input vector of the GRNN network, and the tags are read simultaneously by the antennas in three different directions. Therefore, the dimension of input layer neurons in GRNN is three dimensional, the size of neurons in the pattern layer is the same as the size of neurons in the input layer, and the output layer is defined as the 2D coordinates of the plane in which the tag is located.

4   Implementation and Evaluation

4.1   Experimental Settings

We used the ImpinJ Revolution R420 RFID antenna and the EPC Gen2 tags to lay out the experimental environment, the entire test area is 3.0 m × 4.2 m as shown in Fig. 4a. Since the antenna radiant energy is concentrated within the lobe width, we placed the antenna at 45° in three fixed positions. We place 30 sets of tags to acquire the RSSI values in three directions in the readable area of the RFID reader, then test 10 positions by moving the tags. The detail of position and area of each antenna are shown in Fig. 4b, where the rectangle and the shaded area represent the antenna and the tags, respectively.

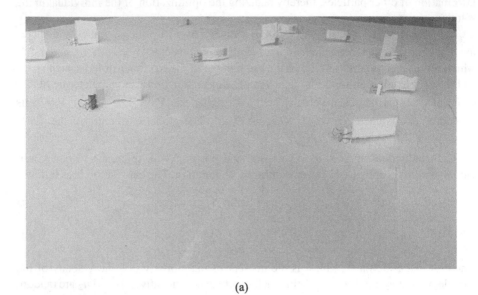

(a)

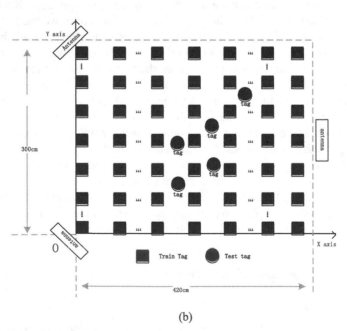

(b)

Fig. 4. Experimental environment. (a) Part of the readable area; (b) Position of each antenna and tag.

4.2   Preprocess for RSSI

We collect the RSSI values of 30 tags by the R420 reader. As shown by the blue curve in the Fig. 5, it shows that the data is unstable. We use the mean filter to handle the RSSI fluctuations. The orange curve in the figure shows the result of the filter processing, and it can be seen that there is stability and there is no large fluctuation.

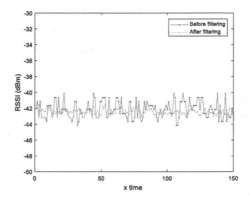

Fig. 5. The RSSI value of tag processed by the filter.

4.3   Average Location Error

First, the RSSI values of 30 sets of static training tags are read from antennas in three different directions of the experimental area. We repeat the process of acquiring the tag data 10 times and input it into the averaging filter with a sliding window of 10. After obtaining the preprocessed data, set the 5/6 of the sample as the input layer training data of the GRNN network, the remaining set is used as the verification set. We consider the network slip factor as the position of the particle, and the MSE of the actual result and the network prediction result is used as the particle fitness. At the same time, the number of particle population and the number of iteration is 50 and 100, respectively. The position of the particle is optimized by the MPSO. On the MATLAB platform, the experimental optimization results are shown in Fig. 6.

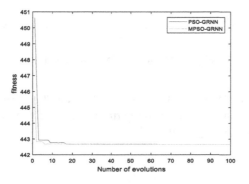

Fig. 6. Optimal fitness particle.

As the figure shows, our proposed optimization algorithm speeds up the convergence and finds the best fitness of particles. It is considered that the position parameter corresponding to the best adaptive particle is used as the optimal sliding factor, and then move the tag to different positions to test the model. At the same time, we will demonstrate the traditional fixed path loss model localization algorithm of RSSI. The results are shown in Figs. 7 and 8:

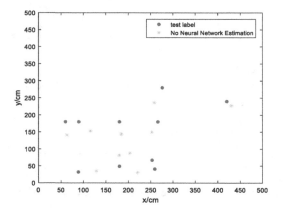

Fig. 7. No neural network localization.

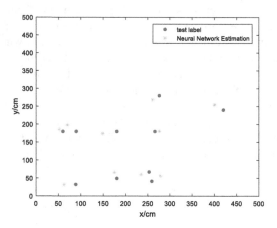

Fig. 8. MPSO-GRNN localization.

As can be seen from the Fig. 9, we also performed 20 repeated tests of different locations for statistical analysis of position error values to obtain the root mean square error curve of the location algorithm.

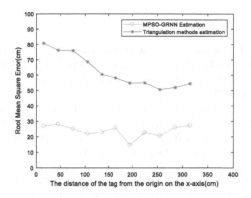

Fig. 9. Root mean square error curve.

The figure shows that the average error of the MPSO-GRNN algorithm is 0.26 m, and the error in the middle of the monitoring area can be reduced to 0.18 m, while the average error of the fixed path loss location algorithm(triangle location algorithm [7]) is 0.49 m, when the tag is located near the coordinate axis (The farthest distance from the antenna), the position error is about 1 m. According to the above analysis results, the traditional path loss location algorithm no well applied to complex indoor environment. This paper proposed the MPSO-GRNN location algorithm reduces the average error and speeds up the convergence. In a way, it overcomes environmental disturbances.

5   Conclusion

This paper proposes an RFID localization algorithm based on generalized regression neural network optimized by mutation particle swarm. This method uses the directional antenna to collect data in different directions in the indoor environment, and finds the optimal particle position information in training model. The more training position information, the higher the test accuracy. The algorithm uses "black box" to correlate the location information with the RSSI value of the tag, thus avoiding the influence of the environmental factor estimation, which improves the location accuracy to a certain extent. It can be applied to complex indoor environments such as factories, laboratories and warehouses.

Acknowledgement. This work is supported by the National Natural Science Foundation of China (Grant No. 61672282) and the Basic Research Program of Jiangsu Province (Grant No. BK20161491).

References

1. Yayan, U., Yucel, H., Yazici, A.: A low cost ultrasonic based positioning system for the indoor navigation of mobile robots. J. Intell. Robot. Syst. **78**(3–4), 541–552 (2015)
2. Qiu, L., Liang, X., Huang, Z.: PATL: a RFID tag localization based on phased array antenna. Sci. Rep. **7**(44183) (2017)
3. Xu, H., Ding, Y., Li, P., Wang, R., Li, Y.: An RFID indoor positioning algorithm based on Bayesian probability and K-nearest neighbor. Sensors **17**(8), 1806 (2017)
4. Xu, H., Wu, M., Li, P., Zhu, F., Wang, R.: An RFID indoor positioning algorithm based on support vector regression. Sensors **18**(5), 1504 (2018)
5. Liu, T., Yang, L., Lin, Q, Guo, Y., Liu, Y.: Anchor-free backscatter positioning for RFID tags with high accuracy. In: Liu, T., Yang, L., Lin, Q., Guo, Y., Liu, Y. (eds.) IEEE Conference on Computer Communications, pp. 379–387. IEEE INFOCOM, Toronto (2014)
6. Nascimento, H., Cavalcanti, F.R.P., Rodrigues, E.B., Paiva, A.R.: An algorithm for three-dimensional indoor location based on Bayesian inference, fingerprinting method and Wi-Fi technology. Int. J. Adv. Eng. Res. Sci. **4**(10), 166–175 (2017)
7. Wang, Y., Yang, X., Zhao, Y., Liu, Y., Cuthbert, L.: Bluetooth positioning using RSSI and triangulation methods. In: 10th Consumer Communications and Networking Conference, Las Vegas, NV, pp. 837–842 (2013)
8. Li, X., Zhang, Y., Marsic, I., Sarcevic, A., Burd, R.S.: Deep learning for RFID-based activity recognition. In: 14th ACM Conference on Embedded Network Sensor Systems CD-ROM, pp. 164–175. ACM, New York (2016)
9. Ma, Y., Selby, N., Singh, M., Adib, F.: Fine-grained RFID localization via ultra-wide band emulation. In: Proceedings of the SIGCOMM Posters and Demo, pp. 116–118. ACM, New York (2017)
10. Jiang, C., He, Y., Zheng, X., Liu, Y.: Orientation-aware RFID tracking with centimeter-level accuracy. In: 17th ACM/IEEE International Conference on Information Processing in Sensor Networks, pp. 290–301. IEEE Press, Piscataway (2018)
11. Wang, J., Wei, W., Wang, W., Li, R.: RFID hybrid positioning method of phased array antenna based on neural network. IEEE Access **6**, 74953–74960 (2018)
12. Motroni, A., Nepa, P., Buffi, A., Tripicchio, P., Unetti, M.: RFID tag localization with UGV in retail applications. In: 3rd International Conference on Smart and Sustainable Technologies, Split, pp. 1–5 (2018)
13. Buffi, A., D'Andrea, E., Lazzerini, B., Nepa, P.: UHF-RFID smart gate: tag action classifier by artificial neural networks, In: Buffi, A., D'Andrea, E., Lazzerini, B., Nepa, P. (eds.) IEEE International Conference on RFID Technology & Application, Warsaw, pp. 45–50 (2017)
14. Zhou-guo, H., Fang, L., Yi, Y.: An improved indoor UHF RFID localization method based on deviation correction. In: 4th International Conference on Information Science and Control Engineering, pp. 1401–1404. Changsha (2017)
15. Ding, H.: FEMO: a platform for free-weight exercise monitoring with RFIDs. In: 13th ACM Conference on Embedded Networked Sensor Systems, pp. 141–154. ACM, New York (2015)
16. Zhang, K., He, B., Xie, L., Bu, Y., Wang, C., Lu, S.: RF-iCare: an WRFID-based approach for infusion status monitoring. In: 24th Annual International Conference on Mobile Computing and Networking, pp. 814–816. ACM, New York (2018)

Beacon in the Air: Optimizing Data Delivery for Wireless Energy Powered UAVs

Huajian Jin[1], Jiangming Jin[2], and Yang Zhang[1]([✉])

[1] Wuhan University of Technology, Wuhan, China
{jinhuajian,yangzhang}@whut.edu.cn
[2] TuSimple, Beijing, China
jiangming.jin@tusimple.com

Abstract. UAV-aided Internet of Things (IoT) systems enable IoT devices to relay up-to-date information to base stations with UAVs, which extends the IoT network coverage and improves data transmission efficiency. To achieve a perpetual UAV data delivery system, simultaneous wireless data and power transfer (SWIPT) is employed for energy-constrained UAVs to harvest energy from wireless chargers to support data sensing and transmission from IoT devices (e.g., sensors) deployed at different locations. In this paper, the design objective is to pursue the optimal energy charging policy for each UAV considering the system states of location, the queue length and energy storage. We formulate and solve a Markov decision process for the UAV data delivery to optimally take the actions of energy charging, and data delivery to base stations. The performance evaluation shows that the proposed MDP scheme outperforms baseline schemes in terms of lower expected overall cost and high energy efficiency.

Keywords: Unmanned Aerial Vehicle · Wireless energy harvesting · Markov decision process

1 Introduction

Internet of Things (IoT) systems, e.g., wireless sensor networks (WSNs) [1], provide a spatially distributed cyber-physical approach to interconnect various components and enable efficient data transmission. To improve data transmission efficiency, using Unmanned Aerial Vehicle (UAV) as a relay in wireless sensor network introduced in this study. The UAV are deployed to assist the WSN and used to transfer data between sensors and base station. Unmanned aerial vehicle (UAV), also often knowns as drones, has been used in many areas ranging from agriculture, to military, and disaster scenarios [2], providing remote data collection and service providing. UAVs can be sent to different geographically

Supported by National Natural Science Foundation of China (Grant No. 61601336).

locations to deliver on-site data in a real time manner. With the agile mobility and communication capability of UAVs, IoT communications can be efficiently extended.

Meanwhile, UAV-aided wireless communications can also introduce many new challenges. In particular, the energy consumption by the communication equipment of the UAV is substantial and reduce useful flying time by more than one-fifth [3]. Besides, once a UAV has not enough energy to transfer data stored in its queue to a base station, it will introduces high packet delivery delay. Fortunately, simultaneous wireless information and power transfer (SWIPT) as a upsurge of recent research topic can be a cost-effective way to replenish the energy of a UAV by radio frequency (RF) transmission [4]. Moreover, an efficient energy charging policy is highly desirable. RF is employed as a source of backscatter transmission in the work [5].

In this paper, we propose an optimal wireless energy charging policy focusing on the UAV transmission energy consumption with SWIPT. To achieve this goal, we model a UAV-aided wireless sensor networks from the perspective of the UAV as a relay. The UAV equipped with wireless charging facility can move among the locations to collect the data produced from sensors and send a request for energy transferring when it is at the location with an energy source (e.g.,a wireless charger). The UAV transfers data to a base station will consume units of energy, and the UAV's battery need to replenish energy for transferring by charging energy from energy sources at a certain cost. We formulate a Markov decision process to minimize the cost of the UAV consisting of the delay of storing data, the payments to the energy sources and the penalty cost of energy insufficiency. We conduct extensive simulations, which shows that the proposed MDP scheme greatly outperforms other baseline schemes.

2   Related Work

Several previous studies employing UAV in wireless networks have been proposed. For example, [2] illustrated typical use cases of UAV-aided wireless communications and surveyed several future challenges, including the energy constraint issues. Experimental analysis in [3] confirmed that energy constraint and power consumption can be one of the key research concerns in UAV applications.

How to improve energy efficiency of the UAV has became one of major research issue. An energy-efficient relaying scheme was introduced in [6] by decoupling the processes of energy balancing and data rate adjustment. Designing the trajectory of drones has been used to reduce energy consumption in [7–9]. The literature [7] studied the scenario in which a UAV-mounted energy transmitter broadcasts energy to distributed IoT devices as energy receivers on the ground. The Pareto boundary of the energy region has been characterized by optimizing the UAV's trajectory. In [8], the authors determined the optimal ground terminal transmit power and UAV trajectory by analytically deriving the energy consumption expressions of the UAV and ground terminal in a UAV-enabled data collection system. Energy-efficient UAV communication with a

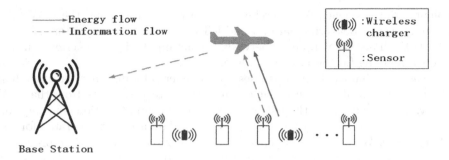

Fig. 1. System model.

ground terminal via trajectory optimization by considering the energy consumption of UAV has been studied in [9]. The authors in [10] maximized the spectrum efficiency and energy efficiency by jointly optimizing the UAV's relaying communication time allocation and the UAV trajectory in a UAV-enabled mobile relaying system. In [11] the authors proposed a novel design for energy-efficient data collection in UAV-enabled WSNs which jointly optimizes the wakeup schedules of the sensors and UAV's trajectory to minimize the maximum energy consumption of all sensors.

Instead of energy consumption management, wireless power transfer technique can be employed for perpetually replenishing energy in UAV-aided IoT systems. Using laser power as energy supply resource for UAV, the work in [12] maximized the UAV's communication throughput by jointly optimizing the UAV's trajectory and its transmit power allocation. The authors of [13] proposed an orthogonal frequency division multiplexing relaying based SWIPT protocol for energy-constrained UAV communication network. The authors of [14] solved the end-to-end cooperative throughput maximization problem by using UAV serves as an aerial mobile relay and its transmission capability powered with SWIPT.

To the best of our knowledge, employing wireless energy harvesting technology to replenish UAVs to provide perpetual wireless data collection and transmission has not been studied in recent literature. Moreover, wireless energy charging policy for UAV need to be studied for efficient data relaying.

3   System Model

We consider a UAV-aided IoT system which consists of four major components: End IoT devices, wireless chargers, UAVs, and an UAV base station, as shown in Fig. 1.

An IoT device sensor continues to sense and generate data to be potentially transmitted by the UAV to the UAV base station for further usage. The IoT devices are geographically distributed at different locations. A UAV is equipped with energy storage (e.g., a battery) and wireless communication components can charge energy from wireless energy charging sources (e.g., dedicated and ambient radio frequencies), and relay data between sensors and the UAV base station. However, delivering data for end IoT devices will consume stored energy of the UAV. There is a trade-off between the action of wireless energy charging and data relaying for the UAV to decide.

We assume that the UAV consumes units of energy for flighting per single-hop and the communication equipment has its own battery, separate from the UAV battery. We here consider the battery in charge of communication consumption for the model to be reasonable. In each location, data are kept generated for the UAV to sense. Without loss of generality, we assume the data update process is Poisson with rate λ, the UAV can receive several data from one sensor at a slot time. The data transition consumes certain units of energy stored in the battery of the UAV. The UAV can charge its battery from energy sources (i.e., wireless chargers) when it is in a location with wireless charging facility and pay a cost for charging.

The goal is that designing an optimal wireless charging policy for the drone to performs the mission of transferring data.

4 Optimization Problem Formation

To optimize the UAV-aided data delivery, we formulate the process that the UAV receives energy from wireless charger and relays data message to the UAV base station as a Markov decision process (MDP) [15]. We define the state and action spaces and derive the transition matrix.

4.1 State and Action Space

The state space of the UAV is defined as follows:

$$\mathbb{S} = \{\mathcal{L}, \mathcal{Q}, \mathcal{E}\} \tag{1}$$

where $\mathcal{S} \in \mathbb{S}$ is a composite state including all the system state variables $\mathcal{L}$, $\mathcal{Q}$, and $\mathcal{E}$. The state $\mathcal{L} \in \mathbb{L} = \{0, \cdots, L\}$ indicates the set of all the locations which the UAV can visit, the total number of locations is $L + 1$. $\mathcal{Q} \in \mathbb{Q} = \{0, \cdots, Q\}$ denotes the number of messages stored in the queue, respectively. The maximum capacity of the queue is Q, i.e., the UAV can store up to Q data messages. $\mathcal{E} \in \mathbb{E} = \{0, \cdots, E\}$ is the energy state (i.e., the current energy level of the battery) of the UAV, where E is the maximum capacity of the stored energy in the battery.

We divide the time into time slots. In each time slot when the system is in operation, the UAV takes and action defined as $\mathcal{A} \in \mathbb{A} = \{a_0, a_1, a_2\}$, where $\mathbb{A}$ is the action space. Action $\mathcal{A} = a_0$ denotes that the UAV is idle. $\mathcal{A} = a_1$ denotes that the UAV charges energy from energy charging devices. $\mathcal{A} = a_2$ is the action that the UAV deliveries the messages back to the base station.

4.2   Transition Matrix for Location States

With the dynamics of UAV and IoT systems, the system state in each time slot changes. For the ease of notations, we divide the locations into two regions (i.e., sets of locations) with respect to the existence of wireless energy charging facilities. At locations $\mathbb{L}_{es} \in \{1, \cdots, G\}$, there are wireless chargers for the UAV charging and at locations $\mathbb{L}_{node} \in \{G+1, \cdots, L\}$, there are no chargers. Therefore, $L = |\mathbb{L}_{es}| + |\mathbb{L}_{node}|$ where there are G locations in $\mathbb{L}_{es}$ region and $L - G$ locations in $\mathbb{L}_{node}$. The transition of the location state $\mathcal{L}$ of the UAV is as follows:

$$L = \begin{bmatrix} M_{es,es} & M_{es,node} \\ M_{node,es} & M_{node,node} \end{bmatrix} \tag{2}$$

In Eq. (2), $M_{l,l'}$ is a submatrix denoting the transition when the current location is in the region $\mathbb{L}_l$, and the next location is in the region $\mathbb{L}_{l'}$, where the footnotes l and l' denote notations es or $node$. Each element $m_{i,j}$ in $M_{l,l'}$ represents the probability that the location changes from location $i \in \mathbb{L}_l$ to location $j \in \mathbb{L}_{l'}$.

4.3   Transition Matrix for Queue States

Once the UAV arrives at a location $\mathcal{L}$, on-site data generated by the local IoT devices will be immediately transferred to the UAV for further process. The UAV can choose whether to carry the received data until returning to the UAV base station for relaying the data in a near field manner, or to directly relay the data back to the UAV base station using far field wireless transfer. Once the action $\mathcal{A} = a_2$ is taken, the UAV will remotely transfer the stored data. In this case, the queue state transitions can be be discussed in two conditions.

Increasing Queue State Case. As all the locations are equipped with IoT devices generating data messages for the UAV to help deliver, we assume that the update process is Poisson with rate λ. Intuitively, the queue state may increase when the UAV arrives at any location before the data messages are not delivered by the UAV, i.e., $\mathcal{A} = a_2$ is not taken. The transition matrix for such increasing queue state case is denoted as follows:

$$Q^+(\mathcal{Q}, \mathcal{Q}') = \begin{bmatrix} P_{0,0} & P_{0,1} & \cdots & P_{0,Q-1} & \sum_{k=Q}^{\infty} P_{0,k} \\ & P_{1,0} & \cdots & P_{1,Q-2} & \sum_{k=Q-1}^{\infty} P_{1,k} \\ & & \ddots & & \vdots \\ & & & & 1 \end{bmatrix} \tag{3}$$

Each row of the matrix $Q^+(\mathcal{Q}, \mathcal{Q}')$ in Eq. (3) represents the current queue state $\mathcal{Q}$ ranging from 0 to Q, and each column denotes the queue state of the next decision period $\mathcal{Q}'$. $P_{i,k}$, $k = 0, 1, \cdots, \infty$, denotes the transition probability that k data messages are generated from the local IoT devices in a decision period when the current queue state $\mathcal{Q} = i$. We can calculate the probability that the number of data messages received by the UAV during decision period according to Poisson distribution, i.e.,$P_{i,k} = \frac{\lambda^k e^{-\lambda}}{k!}$. The matrix $\boldsymbol{Q}^+(\mathcal{Q}, \mathcal{Q}')$ is a $(Q+1) \times (Q+1)$ upper triangular matrix.

Decreasing Queue State Case. The queue state can decrease by one message if the UAV takes the action $\mathcal{A} = a_2$ when there is at least one message in the queue. At the same time, there can still be new data messages generated in the current time slot. Without loss of generality, we assume that the delivering action is taken before the data messages are generated by the local IoT devices. The transition matrix for the decreasing queue state case is denoted as follows:

$$\boldsymbol{Q}^-(\mathcal{Q}, \mathcal{Q}') = \begin{bmatrix} P_{0,0} & P_{0,1} & \cdots & P_{0,Q-1} & \sum_{k=Q}^{\infty} P_{0,k} \\ P_{1,0} & P_{1,1} & \cdots & P_{1,Q-1} & \sum_{k=Q-1}^{\infty} P_{1,k} \\ & P_{2,0} & \cdots & P_{2,Q-2} & \sum_{k=Q-2}^{\infty} P_{2,k} \\ & & \ddots & \vdots & \vdots \\ & & & P_{Q,0} & \sum_{k=1}^{\infty} P_{Q,k} \end{bmatrix} \tag{4}$$

The first row of the matrix in Eq. (4) indicates that there is currently no message stored in the UAV data queue. The rest rows denote that the queue has at least one data message to be relayed. After the data message in the queue is transferred, there can be a message arrival. Note that here we assume that the message leaves the queue of the UAV if it takes the action of transferring the data back.

Overall Queue State Transition Matrix. As aforementioned, the queue state transition relies on the action taken at current state, as shown by $\boldsymbol{Q}^+$ and $\boldsymbol{Q}^-$. The overall transition matrix of the queue state $\mathcal{Q}$ is derived as follows:

$$\boldsymbol{W}(\mathcal{Q}|\mathcal{A}) = \begin{cases} \boldsymbol{Q}^+, & \mathcal{A} \in \{a_0, a_1\}, \\ \boldsymbol{Q}^-. & \mathcal{A} = a_2. \end{cases} \tag{5}$$

where the first condition in Eq. (5) is for the case that the UAV takes idle action $\mathcal{A} = a_0$ or charging action $\mathcal{A} = a_1$. The second condition is for the case that the UAV takes delivering back action $\mathcal{A} = a_2$, where the length of queue decreases.

4.4 Transition Matrix for Energy States

We derive the transition matrix of the energy state under different cases. We assume that the UAV increases and decreases energy after the action $\mathcal{A} = a_1$ and $\mathcal{A} = a_2$) taken. The energy state transition matrix can be divided into following three cases.

Increasing Energy State Case. The battery is able to store at most E units of energy. The transition matrix is expressed as follows:

$$E^+(\mathcal{E}, \mathcal{E}'|\mathcal{L}) = \begin{bmatrix} 1-\alpha & \alpha & & \\ & \ddots & \ddots & \\ & & 1-\alpha & \alpha \\ & & & 1 \end{bmatrix} \tag{6}$$

where each row of the matrix denotes the current energy sate $\mathcal{E}$, and each column represents the next energy state $\mathcal{E}'$. Let α denotes the successful probability of charging energy. The shape of $E^+(\mathcal{E}, \mathcal{E}'|\mathcal{L})$ is a $(E+1) \times (E+1)$.

Decreasing Energy State Case. When the UAV takes the delivering back action $\mathcal{A} = a_2$, one unit of energy stored in battery of the UAV will be consumed. The transition matrix is expressed as follows:

$$E^-(\mathcal{E}, \mathcal{E}'|\mathcal{L}) = \begin{bmatrix} 1 & & & \\ 1 & 0 & & \\ & \ddots & \ddots & \\ & & 1 & 0 \end{bmatrix} \tag{7}$$

Unchanged Energy State Case. The energy state may not change if the UAV neither charges energy nor transfers messages. Under such situation, the energy transition matrix is denoted as the case $E^0 = I_{E+1}$, where I is an $(E+1) \times (E+1)$ identity matrix.

Overall Energy State Transition Matrix. The energy state transition relies on the current location state $\mathcal{L}$ and the action $\mathcal{A}$ taken, as shown in E^+, E^+ and E^0. Therefore, when the current state takes action $\mathcal{A}$, we define the composite transition matrix of the location state $\mathcal{L}$ and the energy state E, i.e., $(\mathcal{L}, \mathcal{E})$, as $W(\mathcal{L}, \mathcal{E}|\mathcal{A})$. When action $\mathcal{A} = a_0$ is taken, $W(\mathcal{L}, \mathcal{E}|\mathcal{A} = a_0)$ is defined as follows:

$$W(\mathcal{L}, \mathcal{E}|\mathcal{A} = a_0) = L \bigotimes E^0. \tag{8}$$

since when the UAV takes idle, it does not charge any energy from energy provider. The energy state is not changed.

When action $\mathcal{A} = a_1$ is taken, the UAV charges energy. $W(\mathcal{L}, \mathcal{E}|\mathcal{A} = a_1)$ is defined as follows:

$$W(\mathcal{L}, \mathcal{E}|\mathcal{A} = a_1) = \begin{bmatrix} M_{es,es} \bigotimes E^+ & M_{es,node} \bigotimes E^+ \\ M_{node,es} \bigotimes E^0 & M_{node,node} \bigotimes E^0 \end{bmatrix} \tag{9}$$

In Eq. (9), when the UAV arrives at a location $\mathcal{L}$ belongs to region $\mathbb{L}_{node}$ without energy charging devices, it can't supplement energy for battery. Consequently,

E^0 is assigned to the second row respecting the current location in region $\mathbb{L}_{node}$. Besides, the UAV can charge energy, E^+ is assigned to the first row corresponding to the location in region $\mathbb{L}_{es}$.

When action $\mathcal{A} = a_2$ is taken, $W(\mathcal{L}, \mathcal{E}|\mathcal{A} = a_2)$ is defined as follows:

$$W(\mathcal{L}, \mathcal{E}|\mathcal{A} = a_2) = L \bigotimes E^-. \tag{10}$$

since when the UAV takes a_2 action, it consumes energy for transferring messages, the energy capacity level of battery will decrease.

4.5   Overall Transition Matrix

In summary, given that the action $\mathcal{A}$, we denote the transition matrix of the overall state state space as $W(\mathcal{S}, \mathcal{S}'|\mathcal{A})$ and combine the location state, queue state and energy state transition as follows:

$$W(\mathcal{S}, \mathcal{S}'|\mathcal{A}) = W(\mathcal{L}, \mathcal{E}|\mathcal{A}) \bigotimes W(\mathcal{Q}|\mathcal{A}) \tag{11}$$

where $\bigotimes$ is the Kronecker product.

5   Optimization Formulation

5.1   Immediate Cost Function

Immediate cost of the MDP model is defined as the myopic reward of the current state when the UAV takes any particular action. We define immediate cost as a function $I(\mathcal{S}|\mathcal{A})$ of the current state $\mathbb{S} = \{\mathcal{L}, \mathcal{Q}, \mathcal{E}\}$ and the action $\mathcal{A}$ taken by the UAV, as follows:

$$I(\mathcal{S}|\mathcal{A}) = \begin{cases} F(\mathcal{Q}) - \rho, & (\mathcal{A} = a_2) \text{ and } (\mathcal{E} \neq 0), \\ F(\mathcal{Q}) + \tau, & (\mathcal{A} = a_2) \text{ and } (\mathcal{E} = 0), \\ F(\mathcal{Q}) + \rho, & (\mathcal{A} = a_1) \text{ and } (\mathcal{L} \in \mathbb{L}_{es}), \\ F(\mathcal{Q}), & \text{otherwise.} \end{cases} \tag{12}$$

where $F(\mathcal{Q})$ is the cost of delay caused by the messages stored in the queue, i.e., $\mathcal{Q}$. When the UAV has enough energy to transfer messages (i.e., $\mathcal{E} > 0$), if the UAV takes the delivering back action, it incurs the reward denoted by ρ. When the UAV'battery is empty, it will incur not only the cost of delay but the insufficient energy cost τ if the UAV takes the delivering back action. Moreover, if the UAV takes the charge action from charger, it need pay ρ as cost to charger.

5.2   Solving the Optimization

Then we solve the optimization problem to find an optimal policy $\pi^*(\mathcal{S})$ of the UAV that minimizing the expected discounted long term cost of the UAV, i.e., $V_\pi^*(\mathcal{S})$. The Bellman equation [15] is employed as follows:

$$V_\pi^*(\mathcal{S}) = \min_{a \in \mathcal{A}} \left(I(\mathcal{S}|\mathcal{A}) + \gamma \sum_{\mathcal{S}' \in \mathbb{S}} (W(\mathcal{S}, \mathcal{S}'|\mathcal{A})) V_\pi^*(\mathcal{S}') \right) \tag{13}$$

$$\pi^*(\mathcal{S}) = \arg \min_{a \in \mathcal{A}} \left(I(\mathcal{S}|\mathcal{A}) + \gamma \sum_{\mathcal{S}' \in \mathbb{S}} (W(\mathcal{S}, \mathcal{S}'|\mathcal{A})) V_\pi^*(\mathcal{S}') \right) \tag{14}$$

Value iteration algorithm [15] is applied to solve the Bellman equation, where $I(\mathcal{S}|\mathcal{A})$ is the immediate cost function and $\sum_{\mathcal{S}' \in \mathbb{S}} (W(\mathcal{S}, \mathcal{S}'|\mathcal{A})) V(\mathcal{S}')$ is the expected future cost as defined in Sect. 5.1. $\gamma \in [0, 1)$ is a discount factor presenting value of expected future cost.

6   Numerical Results

6.1   Parameter Setting

We consider a UAV moving between 2 locations, where location $\mathcal{L} = 1$ belongs to the region $\mathbb{L}_{es}$, which can provides energy for the UAV charging energy. The transition matrix L with both rows of $[0.4, 0.6]$. The maximum capacity of the queue and the battery of the UAV are both set at 15 units. In the immediate cost function, the delay cost is set to be proportional to the number of messages stored in the queue, i.e., $F(\mathcal{Q}) = \omega \mathcal{Q}$, where $\omega = 0.8$. The charging energy cost $\rho = 0.5$ and the immediate insufficient energy cost τ when the UAV takes $\mathcal{A} = a_1$ is 1. The probability of successfully charging energy is $\alpha = 0.95$. The discount factor γ is 0.9. The data update rate λ is 1.

For evaluating the performance of the proposed MDP policy, we consider three baseline policies consisting of a greedy policy where the UAV only minimizes the current immediate cost function, an location-aware policy where the UAV always charges energy from chargers and delivers messages back to base station in the region $\mathbb{L}_{es}$ and $\mathbb{L}_{node}$ respectively, a random policy where the UAV randomly selects an action from action sets $\mathcal{A}$.

6.2   Performance Analysis

We define following performance metrics which are evaluated and compared between the propose MDP policy and the baseline policies:

- Expected cost: We know state cost C_s incurred to the UAV is measured from any arbitrary initial state $\mathcal{S}$. We derive the expected cost C_s^- as the average cost of all state cost, so $C_s^- = \mathbb{E}(\sum_{s \in \mathbb{S}} C_s^-)$, $\mathbb{E}$ denotes Expectation.
- Delay: The delay of messages at the UAV is equivalent to the queue length of the UAV.
- Energy inefficiency probability: The probability that the UAV is not able to transfer message owing to insufficient energy (i.e., $\mathcal{E} = 0$).

Impacts of Maximum Queue Capacity. We vary the maximum queue capacity Q from 0 to 20 and set the energy storage capacity of battery at 15 units. We then compare the results obtained from the MDP policy with the results from the baseline policies.

The expected cost of the UAV is shown in Fig. 2. As the maximum queue capacity Q increases, the costs of all policies tend to increase. The reason is that with a higher capacity Q, the UAV may accumulate more messages in its queue, causing large delay cost $F(Q)$. The results of MDP policy outperform other baseline policies in terms of lowest cost, since the UAV can optimally take charging and delivering action to minimize the expected cost.

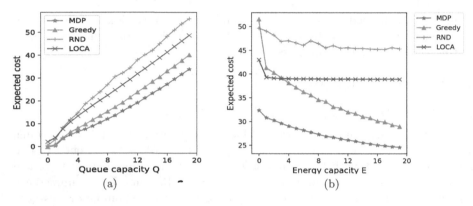

Fig. 2. Impacts to the expected cost by (a) the maximum queue capacity Q and (b) the maximum battery capacity Q.

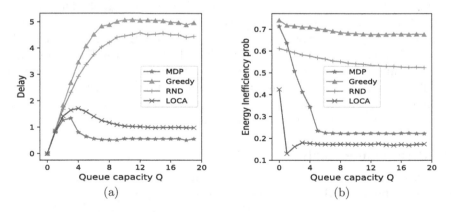

Fig. 3. Impacts of the maximum queue capacity Q to (a) delay and (b) energy insufficiency probability.

Figure 3(a) and (b) show the delay metric and the energy inefficiency probability of the steady states. Figure 3(b) shows that as Q increases, the delay of MDP policies tends to increases first. Because with a low capacity Q, the UAV tends to take idle action to reduce cost. However, after Q becomes large, e.g., $Q > 4$ for the MDP policy, the increasing delay cost make the UAV tend to take delivering back action. In contrast, the energy inefficiency probability of MDP policy tends to decreases first as Q increases, as show in Fig. 3(a). The reason is that the UAV optimally takes charging action to avoid frequent insufficient penalty. It is worth noting that the location-aware policy gets a better performance than MDP policy in terms of energy insufficient probability. Since adopting the location-aware policy, the UAV has enough energy supply by always charging energy from chargers. A trade-off exists between minimizing the delay and energy inefficiency probability.

From Figs. 3(a) and (b), we may obtain more meaningful parameter for the system. Figure 3(a) shows that when the value of Q increases to 10, the delay does not change. In addition, as shown in Fig. 3(b), increasing the queue capacity after $Q > 6$ does not increase the energy inefficiency probability. Therefore, we find that the best value of the queue capacity is 10.

Impacts of Energy Storage Capacity. We vary the maximum number of the energy storage capacity E of the battery in the UAV. When the maximum energy storage capacity from 0 to 20, as shows in Fig. 4(a), the expected cost of MDP policy decrease. The reason is that the increase battery capacity allows more energy units to be stored to support further messages transferring by the UAV. As the queue capacity is a constant, the expected cost of random policy and location-aware policy doesn't decrease after battery capacity increases to a large value.

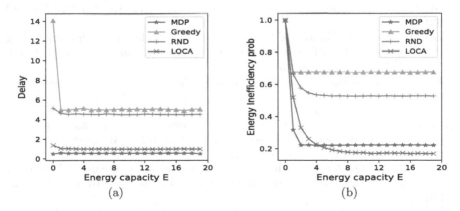

(a)   (b)

Fig. 4. Impacts of the maximum battery capacity E to (a) delay and (b) energy insufficiency probability.

As in Fig. 2(b) shows, the delay of the proposed MDP outperforms other policies, since the UAV optimally takes charging/delivering action to reduce the delay cost $F(\mathcal{Q})$, resulting in low delay. Figure 4(b) shows the energy insufficiency probability of all policies decrease first as battery capacity increases, this is because the UAV has more energy to transfer messages, the frequency of insufficient energy is getting lower. Similarly, the location-aware policy outperforms the MDP policies due to the UAV always charging when it meets chargers. From Figs. 4(a) and (b), it is the best that the energy storage capacity is set as $E = 3$.

7   Conclusion

In this work, a SWIPT assisted optimal wireless charging scheme for UAV data transmission and energy management has been studied by employing an MDP approach. In the optimization, the overall expected cost of UAV has been minimized, including the delay of data storage, the payment for energy charging, as well as the occasional penalty cost due to energy insufficiency. Extensive numerical studies have been conducted to show the fact that the proposed MDP outperforms the baseline schemes.

References

1. Abu Alsheikh, M., Hoang, D., Niyato, D., Tan, H.P., Lin, S.: Markov decision processes with applications in wireless sensor networks: a survey. IEEE Commun. Surv. Tutor. **17**(3), 1239–1267 (2015)
2. Zeng, Y., Zhang, R., Lim, T.J.: Wireless communications with unmanned aerial vehicles: opportunities and challenges. IEEE Commun. Mag. **54**(5), 36–42 (2016)
3. Gupta, L., Jain, R., Vaszkun, G.: Survey of important issues in UAV communication networks. IEEE Commun. Surv. Tutor. **18**(2), 1132–1152 (2015)
4. Lu, X., Wang, P., Niyato, D., Kim, D.I., Han, Z.: Wireless networks with RF energy harvesting: a contemporary survey. IEEE Commun. Surv. Tutor. **17**(2), 757–789 (2015)
5. Gao, X., Wang, P., Niyato, D., Yang, K., An, J.: Auction-based time scheduling for backscatter-aided RF-powered cognitive radio networks. IEEE Trans. Wirel. Commun. **18**(3), 1684–1697 (2019)
6. Li, K., Ni, W., Wang, X., Liu, R., Kanhere, S., Jha, S.: EPLA: energy-balancing packets scheduling for airborne relaying networks. In: IEEE International Conference on Communications (2015)
7. Xu, J., Zeng, Y., Zhang, R.: UAV-enabled wireless power transfer: Trajectory design and energy region characterization. In: 2017 IEEE Globecom Workshops (GC Wkshps), Singapore, pp. 1–7 (2017)
8. Yang, D., Wu, Q., Zeng, Y., Zhang, R.: Energy trade-off in ground-to-UAV communication via trajectory design. IEEE Trans. Veh. Technol. **67**(7), 6721–6726 (2018)
9. Zeng, Y., Zhang, R.: Energy-efficient UAV communication with trajectory optimization. IEEE Trans. Wirel. Commun. **16**(6), 3747–3760 (2017)
10. Zhang, J., Zeng, Y., Zhang, R.: Spectrum and energy efficiency maximization in UAV-enabled mobile relaying. In: IEEE International Conference on Communications (2017)

11. Zhan, C., Zeng, Y., Zhang, R.: Energy-efficient information collection in UAV enabled wireless sensor network. IEEE Wirel. Commun. Lett. **7**(93), 328–331 (2017)
12. Ouyang, J., Che, Y., Xu, J., Wu, K.: Throughput maximization for laser-powered UAV wireless communication systems. In: IEEE International Conference on Communications Workshops (ICC Workshops), Kansas City, MO, pp. 1–6 (2018)
13. Lu, W., Fang, S., Gong, Y., Qian, L., Liu, X., Hua, J.: Resource allocation for OFDM relaying wireless power transfer based energy-constrained UAV communication network. In: IEEE International Conference on Communications Workshops (ICC Workshops), Kansas City, MO, 2018, pp. 1–6 (2018)
14. Yin, S., Zhao, Y., Li, L.: UAV-assisted cooperative communications with time-sharing SWIPT. In: IEEE International Conference on Communications (ICC), Kansas City, MO, pp. 1–6 (2018)
15. Bellman, R.: A Markovian decision process (1957)

Power Optimization in Wireless Powered Based Mobile Edge Computing

Xiaohan Xu[1], Qibin Ye[1], Weidang Lu[1(✉)], Hong Peng[1], and Bo Li[2]

[1] College of Information Engineering, Zhejiang University of Technology,
Hangzhou 310023, China
{luweid, ph}@zjut.edu.cn
[2] School of Information and Electrical Engineering,
Harbin Institute of Technology, Weihai 264209, China
libo1983@hit.edu.cn

Abstract. Mobile edge computing (MEC) can meet the requirements of high-bandwidth and low delay commanded by the boost developing of mobile network and shorten the network load. This paper investigates a wireless powered MEC system consists a single antenna AP, and two single antenna mobile devices, which are powered by wireless power transmissions (WPT) from AP. In order to settle the users' near-far influence, the system will let the mobile devices closer from the AP mobile devices as a relay for unloading. The Objective of this paper is to minimize the transmission energy of the AP, taking into account the restraints of the computing task. Our solution is divided into two steps: first, the mathematical model of the problem is listed, and then the optimal solution of each feasible scheme is discussed in a classified manner, and the minimum transmission power of AP is obtained through comparison. Simulation results show that collaboration can reduce energy consumption and improve the user performance.

Keywords: Mobile edge computing · User cooperation · Wireless power transfer

1 Introduction

With the boost developing of communication technologies, a lot of smart mobile devices have been spread all over our life, gesture recognition, virtual reality (VR) and augment reality (AR), as well as smart home. These are computation-intensive applications, when they run, they require a lot of computing and storage resources and use electricity very fast. To solve these problems, MEC came into being, which mainly migrates heavy computing tasks to MEC servers at the wireless access points to improve mobile services capability [1]. MEC technology provides IT and cloud computing capabilities for mobile communication wireless access networks, enabling wireless networks with low latency and high bandwidth, thus solving the problem of heavy computing tasks [2].

MEC effectively integrates wireless network and Internet, and adds calculation, storage, processing and other features at the edge of wireless network. Computing

© ICST Institute for Computer Sciences, Social Informatics and Telecommunications Engineering 2019
Published by Springer Nature Switzerland AG 2019. All Rights Reserved
X. B. Zhai et al. (Eds.): MLICOM 2019, LNICST 294, pp. 186–195, 2019.
https://doi.org/10.1007/978-3-030-32388-2_16

offloading in MEC has the characteristics of ultralow latency and good network scalability. MEC can be studied from two different systems, single-user [3, 4] and multi-user [5–8]. In [3], the energy-optimal execution of mobile equipment and cloud computing is in random wireless channel by using Lagrange multiplier method, and the system is single-user. Computation offloading use a Markov decision process method to solve two-timescale stochastic optimization problem, and the system model is a multi-user in [5]. Later in [6], a MIMO system is studied, which several mobile users request computation unloading to a public cloud server grounded on a novel continuous convex approximation technology. The resource sharing problem was considered by proposing a framework in order to sustain mobile applications in a mobile cloud computing environment was addressed in [7]. Random joint wireless and computer resource governance were considered for multi-user MEC systems in [8].

There are some difficulties in making the best of the computing power at the edge. Lacking power provision is an important limitation for battery-based equipment that will stop when the battery uses up. So it is meaningful to use WPT technology to allow mobile equipment to be charged far, without having to deal with battery [4, 9–12]. In particular, WPT, represented by wireless powered communication networks (WPCN), has been recognized as a significant example of furnishing durative for mobile communications. The synergistic study of WPT and MEC was conducted in [4], which is a represent of a wireless powered system. In this paper, binary offloading is studied in order to improve the property.

However, WPCN is vulnerable to what is known as the "double near and far" effect, since users farther away from the AP obtain less energy and need to communicate over longer distances [9, 10]. User collaboration has been widely studied to improve the transmission rate under bad channel. Especially [11, 12] concentrate on the impact of collaboration among near-far users and manage to further the function of WPCNs.

In this paper, we investigate how MEC systems powered by wireless perform computation-intensive tasks between two near-far users, powered entirely by AP throughout the entire process. Therefore, our goal is to minimize the transmission energy of AP and combine the power distribution. Our contributions are summarized as follows:

Aiming at the double near-far influence in WPT-MEC system, a block-based time division protocol is raised. We proposed the problem of minimizing the transmitted energy of AP, and compared the transmitted power of two users by comparing two different situations. The total transfer energy of AP is minimized when the delay is satisfied. Simulation products prove the explanation of the designed program. The results show that the program can take the full advantage of the cooperation between near-far users to process intensive tasks.

2   System Model and Problem Formulation

2.1   System Model

As shown in Fig. 1, we are considering building a wireless powered MEC system with a single antenna AP, including two single antenna mobile devices, expressed as D_1 and D_2. They both work on the same frequency band and D_1 needs to complete computationally intensive latency critical tasks. A block-based TDMA structure is employed in which each block has a duration of T seconds. AP powers D_1 and D_2 in the downlink through the WPT during each block. The two devices use the harvested energy to complete the computing task of D_1 in a partially offloading manner [13].

Since local computing and WPT can be done at the same time, when considering that two users are transmitting in half-duplex mode, the wireless communication for offloading and the WPT are not overlapping. Therefore, the harvest-then-transmit protocol proposed in [9] is applied to our model, but we call it the harvest-then-offload protocol for wireless powered computation offloading.

Assuming the AP can obtain accurate data on all channels and task related parameters through feedback, then AP can make the best offload decision to optimally allocate radio and computational resources. And our goal is to minimize the transfer energy of the AP to complete the calculation tasks.

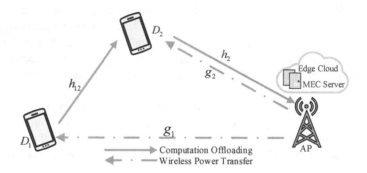

Fig. 1. The model for the two-user WPT-MEC system.

Computation Task Model
The user D_1 has a task in each block, which we can use a parameter tuple $\langle I, C, O, T \rangle$ to represent, where I indicates the size of the input computation data, C is the amount of computing resources needed to calculate 1-bit input data, O is the output data size and T is the maximum tolerable latency. In [14], we can obtain the information of I and C. In this article, we assume users D_2's and D_2's the maximum tolerable delay time T is the same.

User Collaboration Model for Calculate Offloading
Because of the double-near-far effects in WPCN, collaboration between near and far users can improve computing performance during offloading. Without loss of

generality, we assume d_1, d_2 and d_{12} are expressed as the distances between AP and D_1, AP and D_2, D_1 and D_2, respectively, with $d_2 \leq d_1$. Besides, we must have $d_{12} \leq d_1$. Only than the cooperative communications are useful. Table 1 shows the time division structure of a single block.

Table 1. The time division structure of the harvest-then-offload protocol.

$T/3$	$T/3$	$T/3$
$AP \rightarrow D_1, D_2$	$D_1 \rightarrow D_2$	$D_2(D_1) \rightarrow AP$
WPT	Computation Offloading	

In the first period $T/3$ (WPT), AP transmits wireless power to both D_1 and D_2 with power P_0, and thus the energy harvested by each device is given by

$$E_i = \frac{T}{3} v_i g_i P_0, i \in \{1, 2\} \tag{1}$$

where g_i is power gain from the AP to D_i and $0 < v_i \leq 1$ is the energy conversion efficiency of D_i.

After that, D_1 transmits its information with power p_1 by using the energy harvested in the second period $T/3$, and D_2 decodes received signals from D_1. During the last period $T/3$, D_2 will relay the D_1's data information with power p_2 to the AP by using its harvested energy. We define a power allocation vector as $\mathbf{p} = [p_1, p_2]$. With a given $\mathbf{p}$, at the AP and D_2, the smaller value between the decoded data sizes should be the offloaded data size of D_1 at the AP for remote computation, i.e.

$$L_1(\mathbf{p}) = \min\{L_{1,12}(p_1), L_{1,2}(p_2)\} \leq I \tag{2}$$

where $L_{1,12}(p_1)$ and $L_{1,2}(p_2)$ denote the D_1's offloaded data size from D_1 to D_2 and from D_2 to the AP, respectively, which are given by

$$L_{1,12}(p_1) = \frac{T}{3} r_{1,12}(p_1) = \frac{T}{3} B \log_2\left(1 + \frac{p_1 h_{12}}{N_2}\right) \tag{3}$$

$$L_{1,2}(p_2) = \frac{T}{3} r_{1,2}(p_2) = \frac{T}{3} B \log_2\left(1 + \frac{p_2 h_2}{N_0}\right) \tag{4}$$

where $r_{1,12}(p_1)$ and $r_{1,2}(p_2)$ are the transmission rates for offloading D_1's data information. In expressions, h_{12} and h_2 are the channel gains from D_1 to D_2 and from D_2 to AP, respectively. Also, the channel bandwidth denote B. At the AP and D_2, the receiver noise power are N_0 and N_2, respectively, and we assume that $N_0 = N_2$ without loss of generality.

The energy required to receive the calculations returned from the AP can be ignore. Therefore, D_1 and D_2 are used to calculate the energy consumption of the offloading, which can be regarded as the energy consumed for wireless transmissions, which can be given by

$$E_{\text{off},i}(\mathbf{p}) = \frac{T}{3} p_i, i \in \{1,2\} \tag{5}$$

Local Computing Model

Given a power allocation vector $\mathbf{p}$, we will know the offloaded data sizes $L_1(\mathbf{p})$, so the data $I - L_1(\mathbf{p})$ of tasks should be computed locally at D_1. We assume that the D_1's computing resources of the CPU is limited and the frequency is f. In order to meet the constraint $(I - L_1(\mathbf{p}))C/f \leq T$ of latency, so D_1's offloaded data should be a minimum size of $L_1(\mathbf{p}) \geq M^+$ with $M = I - fT/C$, $(x)^+ = \max\{x, 0\}$. At D_1, the energy consumption of the CPU for local calculation can be expressed as $Q = \kappa f^2$, where κ is the effective capacitance coefficient. Hence, the locally calculated energy consumption of D_1 can be denoted as

$$E_{\text{loc},1}(\mathbf{p}) = (I - L_1(\mathbf{p}))CQ \tag{6}$$

2.2 Problem Formulation

Based on the model, D_i's saving energy can be expressed as

$$E_{s,1}(P_0, \mathbf{p}) = E_1 - E_{\text{off},1}(\mathbf{p}) - E_{\text{loc},1}(\mathbf{p}) = \frac{T}{3} v_1 g_1 P_0 - \frac{T}{3} p_1 - (I - L_1(\mathbf{p}))CQ \tag{7}$$

$$E_{s,2}(P_0, \mathbf{p}) = E_2 - E_{\text{off},1}(\mathbf{p}) = \frac{T}{3} v_2 g_2 P_0 - \frac{T}{3} p_2 \tag{8}$$

Furthermore, the APTEM problem can be formulated below

$$\min_{P_0 > 0, \mathbf{p}} P_0 T$$
$$\text{s.t.} \quad M^+ \leq L_1(\mathbf{p}) \leq I, \ T \geq 0, \ p_1 \geq 0, p_2 \geq 0, \tag{9}$$
$$E_{s,1}(P_0, \mathbf{p}) \geq 0, \ E_{s,2}(P_0, \mathbf{p}) \geq 0.$$

3 Optimal Solution

Here, we can find that for the different value of $L_1(\mathbf{p})$ in (2), the APTEM problem for minimizing AP's transmit energy has different form. Thus, we should analyze the constraint of the APTEM problem as well as the different value of $L_1(\mathbf{p})$ to obtain the optimal solution.

3.1   Condition 1

If $L_{1,2}(p_2) < L_{1,12}(p_1)$, obviously, we have that $L_1(\mathbf{p}) = L_{1,2}(p_2)$. Furthermore, combining the constraints of the problem, we can rewrite the constraints as the follow:

$$N_0\left(2^{\frac{3}{B}\left(\frac{l}{T}-\frac{F}{C}\right)}-1\right) \le p_2h_2 \le N_0\left(2^{\frac{3l}{BT}}-1\right) \tag{10}$$

$$P_0 \ge \frac{1}{v_1g_1}\left(p_1 + \frac{3}{T}ICQ - BCQ\log_2\left(1+\frac{p_2h_2}{N_0}\right)\right) \tag{11}$$

$$P_0 \ge \frac{p_2}{v_2g_2} \tag{12}$$

Moreover, we also find $L_{1,12}(p_1) \le I$ from (2), then we have

$$p_2h_2 \le p_1h_{12} \le N_2\left(2^{\frac{3l}{BT}}-1\right) \tag{13}$$

In order to analysis in the inequality group, we define a function

$$f(\mathbf{p}) = p_1 - BCQ\log_2\left(1+\frac{p_2h_2}{N_0}\right) \tag{14}$$

Obviously, $f(\mathbf{p})$ is monotonically increasing when $p_1 \ge 0$, and it is also monotonically decreasing when $p_2 \ge 0$. Thus, the optimal P_0 is given by

$$P_0 = \max\left\{\frac{1}{v_1g_1}\left(\frac{N_2}{h_{12}}\left(2^{\frac{3l}{BT}}-1\right)+3Qf\right), \frac{N_0}{v_2g_2h_2}\left(2^{\frac{3l}{BT}}-1\right)\right\} \tag{15}$$

3.2   Condition 2

If $L_{1,2}(p_2) \ge L_{1,12}(p_1)$, obviously, we have that $L_1(\mathbf{p}) = L_{1,12}(p_1)$. With the similar analysis as above, we can rewrite the constraints of the problem as the follow:

$$N_2\left(2^{\frac{3}{B}\left(\frac{l}{T}-\frac{F}{C}\right)}-1\right) \le p_1h_{12} \le N_2\left(2^{\frac{3l}{BT}}-1\right) \tag{16}$$

$$P_0 \ge \frac{1}{v_1g_1}\left(p_1 + \frac{3}{T}ICQ - BCQ\log_2\left(1+\frac{p_1h_{12}}{N_2}\right)\right) \tag{17}$$

$$P_0 \ge \frac{p_2}{v_2g_2} \tag{18}$$

$$p_1h_{12} \le p_2h_2 \le N_0\left(2^{\frac{3l}{BT}}-1\right) \tag{19}$$

In this condition, for analyzing, we redefine the function

$$f(p_1) = p_1 - BCQ \log_2\left(1 + \frac{p_1 h_{12}}{N_2}\right) \tag{20}$$

By deriving the function $f(p_1)$ and making $f'(p_1) = 0$, we can find that $f(p_1)$ gets the minimum $f(p_1^*)$ when $p_1^* = BCQ/\ln 2 - N_2/h_{12}$. Besides that, $f(p_1)$ is an increasing function when $p_1 \in (BCQ/\ln 2 - N_2/h_{12}, \infty)$, and $f(p_1)$ is a decreasing function when $p_1 \in (0, BCQ/\ln 2 - N_2/h_{12})$. Thus, we should analyze the constraint of p_1^* to obtain the optimal value of P_0.

Condision 2.1

When $p_1^* \in \left[\frac{N_2}{h_{12}}\left(2^{\frac{3}{B}\left(\frac{L}{T} - \frac{f}{C}\right)} - 1\right), \frac{N_2}{h_{12}}\left(2^{\frac{3L}{BT}} - 1\right)\right]$, the optimal P_0 is given by

$$P_0 = \max\left\{\frac{N_2}{v_1 g_1 h_{12}}\left(2^{\frac{3L}{BT}} - 1\right), \frac{1}{v_1 g_1}\left(\frac{N_2}{h_{12}}\left(2^{\frac{3}{B}\left(\frac{L}{T} - \frac{f}{C}\right)} - 1\right) + 3fQ\right), \frac{N_0}{v_2 g_2 h_2}\left(2^{\frac{3L}{BT}} - 1\right)\right\} \tag{21}$$

Condision 2.2

When $p_1^* \in \left(\frac{N_2}{h_{12}}\left(2^{\frac{3L}{BT}} - 1\right), \infty\right)$, the optimal P_0 is given by

$$P_0 = \max\left\{\frac{1}{v_1 g_1}\left(\frac{N_2}{h_{12}}\left(2^{\frac{3}{B}\left(\frac{L}{T} - \frac{f}{C}\right)} - 1\right) + 3fQ\right), \frac{N_0}{v_2 g_2 h_2}\left(2^{\frac{3L}{BT}} - 1\right)\right\} \tag{22}$$

Condision 2.3

When $p_1^* \in \left(0, \frac{N_2}{h_{12}}\left(2^{\frac{3}{B}\left(\frac{L}{T} - \frac{f}{C}\right)} - 1\right)\right)$, the optimal P_0 is given by

$$P_0 = \max\left\{\frac{N_2}{v_1 g_1 h_{12}}\left(2^{\frac{3L}{BT}} - 1\right), \frac{N_0}{v_2 g_2 h_2}\left(2^{\frac{3L}{BT}} - 1\right)\right\} \tag{23}$$

4   Simulation Results and Discussion

Here, computer simulation is used to study the performance of the offloading scheme by combining user collaboration and optimizing the power allocation for wireless power.

Unless otherwise stated, the simulation parameters are set as follows. It is assumed that the uplink and downlink channels are reciprocal, and thus $g_1 = h_1, g_2 = h_2$. The power gain of the channel is modeled as $h_j = d_j^{-\alpha^2}, j \in \{1, 2, 12\}$. For distance d_i in meters with the same path-loss index $\alpha = 2$. At the AP and D_2, the noise power is assumed as $N_2 = N_0 = 10^{-9}$ W. The bandwidth $B = 10\,\text{MHz}$, the distance $d_1 = 10\,\text{m}$, $d_2 = 6\,\text{m}$. For D_1, the CPU frequency $f = 0.2\,\text{GHz}$ and the number of CPU cycles required per bit of data is 1500cycles/bit. Then we set $v_i = 0.8$ and $\kappa_i = 10^{-28}$, $i \in \{1, 2\}$. The figures by simulations are modeling the real heterogeneous computing scenarios.

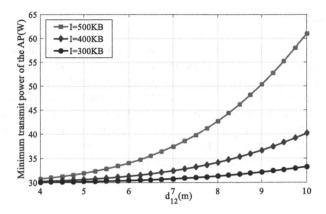

Fig. 2. Minimum transmit power of the AP versus d_{12}

Figure 2 shows the minimum transmit power P_0 of the AP versus d_{12}. We can easily find that P_0 increases with the farther distance between D_1 and D_2. Besides that, we can know that with I larger, the P_0 becomes larger. Further, when the d_{12} is increased from $d_{12} = 4$ m to 10 m, we can find that before $d_{12} = 7$ m, the P_0 grows slowly but rapidly increases after $d_{12} = 7$ m. And more, when the amount of tasks is small, the P_0 increases gently in the case of increasing d_{12}, but when the amount of tasks increases, the P_0's growth range becomes larger.

Figure 3 shows the minimum transmit power P_0 of the AP versus I. The distance between D_1 and D_2 remains unchanged, $d_{12} = 6$ m. The task quantity of D_1 is $I \in [100, 600]$KB. We can easily find that P_0 increases with the larger I. Besides that, we can know that with T smaller, the P_0 becomes larger. And more, the P_0 is small when $I \leq 350$ KB but then the growth rate of P_0 increasingly. Especially, when $T = 0.15$ s, the P_0 of AP increases more rapidly.

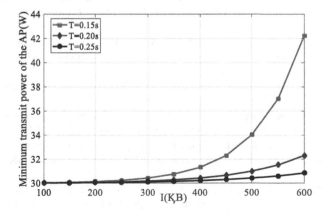

Fig. 3. Minimum transmit power of the AP versus I

5 Conclusion

In the article, we study the application of collaborative communication in computational offloading, where the AP acts as an energy source through the WPT and as a MEC server to help remote mobile terminal devices to complete their computationally intensive delay critical tasks. The block-based harvest-then-offload protocol is used to cooperatively calculate the power allocation of the offload, to achieve the purpose of minimizing the transmit energy of the AP for completing the computation task of the user. Simulation results revealed that utilizing cooperation can decrease the energy consumption and improve performance of users.

References

1. Yang, L., Cao, J., Yuan, Y., Li, T., Han, A., Chan, A.: A framework for partitioning and execution of data stream applications in mobile cloud computing. ACM SIGMETRICS Perform. Eval. Rev. **40**(4), 23–32 (2013)
2. Patel, M., Naughton, B., Chan, C., Sprecher, N., Abeta, S., Neal, A.: Mobile-edge computing introductory technical white paper. In: White Paper, Mobile-edge Computing (MEC) Industry Initiative, pp. 1089–7801(2014)
3. Zhang, W., Wen, Y., Guan, K., Kilper, D., Luo, H., Wu, D.O.: Energy-optimal mobile cloud computing under stochastic wireless channel. IEEE Trans. Wireless Commun. **12**(9), 4569–4581 (2013)
4. You, C., Huang, K., Chae, H.: Energy efficient mobile cloud computing powered by wireless energy transfer. IEEE J. Sel. Areas Commun. **34**(5), 1757–1771 (2016)
5. Liu, J., Mao, Y., Zhang, J., Letaief, K.B.: Delay-optimal computation task scheduling for mobile-edge computing systems. In: 2016 IEEE International Symposium on Information Theory (ISIT), pp. 1451–1455. IEEE (2016)
6. Sardellitti, S., Scutari, G., Barbarossa, S.: Joint optimization of radio and computational resources for multicell mobile-edge computing. IEEE Trans. Sig. Inf. Process. over Netw. **1**(2), 89–103 (2015)
7. Kaewpuang, R., Niyato, D., Wang, P., Hossain, E.: A framework for cooperative resource management in mobile cloud computing. IEEE J. Sel. Areas Commun. **31**(12), 2685–2700 (2013)
8. Mao, Y., Zhang, J., Song, S.H., Letaief, K.B.: Stochastic joint radio and computational resource management for multi-user mobile-edge computing systems. IEEE Trans. Wireless Commun. **16**(9), 5994–6009 (2017)
9. Ju, H., Zhang, R.: Throughput maximization in wireless powered communication networks. IEEE Trans. Wireless Commun. **13**(1), 418–428 (2014)
10. Ju, H., Zhang, R.: User cooperation in wireless powered communication networks. In: 2014 IEEE Global Communications Conference, pp. 1430–1435. IEEE (2014)
11. Chen, H., Li, Y., Rebelatto, J.L., Uchoa-Filho, B.F., Vucetic, B.: Harvest-then-cooperate: wireless-powered cooperative communications. IEEE Trans. Sig. Process. **63**(7), 1700–1711 (2015)
12. Liang, H., Zhong, C., Suraweera, H.A., Zheng, G., Zhang, Z.: Optimization and analysis of wireless powered multi-antenna cooperative systems. IEEE Trans. Wireless Commun. **16**(5), 3267–3281 (2017)

13. Mao, Y., You, C., Zhang, J., Huang, K., Letaief, K.B.: A survey on mobile edge computing: The communication perspective. IEEE Commun. Surv. Tutorials **19**(4), 2322–2358 (2017)
14. Cuervo, E., Balasubramanian, A., Cho, D.K., Wolman, A., Saroiu, S., Chandra, R., Bahl, P.: MAUI: making smartphones last longer with code offload. In: Proceedings of the 8th International Conference on Mobile Systems, Applications, and Services, pp. 49–62. ACM (2010)

Big Data and Internet of Things

Predicting Socio-Economic Levels of Individuals via App Usage Records

Yi Ren[1,2], Weimin Mai[1,2], Yong Li[3], and Xiang Chen[1,2(✉)]

[1] School of Electronics and Information Technology, Sun Yat-sen University,
Guangzhou 510006, China
`chenxiang@mail.sysu.edu.cn`
[2] Key Lab of EDA, Research Institute of Tsinghua University in Shenzhen (RITS),
Shenzhen 518075, China
[3] Department of Electronic Engineering, Tsinghua University, Beijing 100084, China

Abstract. The socio-economic level of an individual is an indicator of the education, purchasing power and housing. Accurate and proper prediction of the individuals is of great significance for market campaign. However, the previous approaches estimating the socio-economic status of an individual mainly rely on census data which demands a great quantity of money and manpower. In this paper, we analyse two datasets: App usage records and occupation data of individuals in a metropolis of China. We divide the individuals into 4 socio-economic levels according to their occupations. Then, we propose a low-cost socio-economic level classification model constructed with machine learning algorithm. Our predictive model achieves a high accuracy over 80%. Our results show that the features extracted from user's App usage records are valuable indicators to predict the socio-economics levels of individuals.

Keywords: Data mining · Mobile data · Socio-economics level

1 Introduction

The socio-economic level (SEL) is an important indicator used to characterize the social status of the individuals in sociology. With the information about people's social status, the company can estimate the consumer's purchasing power and implement precision marketing to different consumer groups. In addition, from a public perspective, socio-economics status of individuals is useful for making social proper policies. Some studies found that people with different socio-economics levels might have various scenarios in choosing health services [22] and the ways of transportation [13].

The current approaches of investigating the SELs of individuals usually depend on the economics survey constructed by National Statistical Institute (NSI). The data obtained from the survey is detailed and authoritative. However, this method has some limitations. For the government leading the economics survey, it would demand much money and manpower to obtain the data

© ICST Institute for Computer Sciences, Social Informatics and Telecommunications Engineering 2019
Published by Springer Nature Switzerland AG 2019. All Rights Reserved
X. B. Zhai et al. (Eds.): MLICOM 2019, LNICST 294, pp. 199–210, 2019.
https://doi.org/10.1007/978-3-030-32388-2_17

of all the residents. In addition, NSI holds the economics survey every 5 years in China, thus not being able to provide timely changes about human's economics status. Furthermore, for the areas in poor economic status, it might have no access to obtain the economics data. Therefore, a low-cost and timely method to estimate the SELs of individuals is needed.

Many researchers have been attempting to investigate the individual's SEL using novel data and methods [14,17,19]. Previous work has found that social network influents economic status [7]. Shaojun Luo et al. extracted social networks of users from their telecommunications [14]. Then, they inferred personal economic status from their social networks. However, with the ubiquitous usage of smart phones and applications (App), people gradually connect with others using chat Apps instead of callings. Therefore, the calling data used to generate users' social networks is being outdated. Some other studies [9,10,21] predicted SELs of individuals by using data collected from users' social media, such as Twitter and Sina Weibo. However, there exist some users just browsing Blogs instead of updating their own microblog. Therefore, it's difficult to characterise the users who are not active in social media.

In this paper, we analyse two datasets: the App usage records of users in Shanghai and their occupation information collected from Sina Weibo. We divide the users into 4 SELs based on their occupations. We extract users' App features and mobility features from their App usage records. Then we enter these features into machine learning algorithms to train the personal SEL predictive model. Our model achieves an accuracy over 80% when classifying the SELs of users.

2 Datasets

In this research, we investigate and predict the SELs of some individuals in Shanghai. Firstly, we obtain the App usage records of 1,200 users from China Telecom. Secondly, we crawl the Sina Weibo identifications of these users according to the user ID that corresponding to their App usage records. Then, we obtain 660 effective users whose Sina Weibo identifications contain their occupation information. At last, we divide the 660 users into 4 socio-economic levels and train a classification predictive model.

Data privacy has been protected through many measures. Firstly, we use reconstructed user ID instead of the actual identification in order to protect the privacy of the users. Secondly, all the datasets used in this research are stored in off-line server. People who are not related to this study were unable to access these datasets. Thirdly, all the researchers signed Non-disclosure agreement.

2.1 App Usage Records

The App usage records used in this research contain 1,200 users' information during a week from April 20th to April 26th, 2016. The dataset contains 2,000 applications and covers 9,858 base stations distributed in 15 districts of Shanghai. Each record consists of user ID, timestramp, base station ID and App ID as shown in Table 1. With the time and geographic information of users, we can discover their mobility behaviors. In addition, the records can reflect human's preferences and habits in using Apps.

Table 1. The examples of app usage records.

User ID	Timestramp	Base station ID	App ID
1001628504	20160421171508	3610000B2B02	2
1001628504	20160421171518	3610000B2B02	2
1001628504	20160421171535	3610000B2B03	2
1002143827	20160419192243	3610000C21A3	5
1002143827	20160419213052	3610000C21A3	5
1002143827	20160419213430	3610000C21A3	1120

2.2 Occupation Information

In order to validate the performance of our classification model, we crawl the occupation contained in the Sina Weibo identification of each user as ground truth. At last, 660 users with occupation are obtained and regarded as effective data. Usually, the sociology researchers stratify people into 5 levels according to their occupations [11]: upper socio-economic level, upper middle socio-economic level, middle socio-economics level, lower middle socio-economic level, lower socio-economic level. Qiang Li et al. surveyed 99 occupations in Beijing and computed their corresponding scores [23]. They also divided 99 occupations into 5 classes. A subset of the social stratification is shown as Table 2. Beijing is a metropolis which is similar to Shanghai in terms of social development, population and urbanization level. Therefore, we used the stratified standard in Qiang Li's research to define the SELs of the 660 users.

Table 2. Samples of socio-economic stratification.

Socio-economic stratification	Occupation examples
Upper SEL	Scientist, bank president, lawyer
Upper middle SEL	Writer, translator, police
Middle SEL	Nurse, purchasing agent
Lower middle SEL	Hairdresser, insurance salesman
Lower SEL	Rickshaw puller, junkman

The 660 users in our study cover 4 SELs except the lower SEL. This may be caused by the fact that people with lower SEL have no need to apply for

Sina Weibo identification, or they don't use Sina Weibo. Thus, we divide 660 user into 4 SELs (SEL A, SEL B, SEL C, SEL D), where SEL A represents the highest level, SEL D represents the lowest level. The 660 users are distributed as follows, 45 users in SEL A, 497 users in SEL B, 112 users in SEL C and 7 users in SEL D.

3   Feature Engineering

In this section, we overview and generate the features of 660 users used in the SEL classification model. The features contain 2 categories, including App features and mobility features.

3.1   App Features

Previous researchers [12,26,27] found that people's App usage behaviors could reflect their attributes and traits. Therefore, we expect that people's App usage behaviors have correlations with their economic status. We extract people's App features from App usage records as the following steps. (1) We classify 2,000 Apps into 18 categories based on their core functions as shown in Table 3. For the categories of $SYSTEM\ TOOL$ and $OTHERS$ can not reflect users' preference, we drop these 2 categories when extracting features. (2) Previous App usage work [25] has found that the App usage patterns have differences in different time periods. Thus, we divide a week into workdays and weekends. Then, we divide a day into four 6-hour ranges i.e. $T \in \{[0-6), [6-12), [12-18), [18-24)\}$. (3) For each user, the App feature is a vector of 2(weekdays and weekends) × 4(time periods) × 16(App categories). Each element of the vector represents the time that the user spends on every App category during a certain period.

Table 3. App categories

App Category	Apps	App Category	Apps
SOCIAL	QQ	BROWSER	UC Browser
FINANCE	TongHuaShun	TRAVEL	Qvnar
VIDEO	iQiYi	GAME	Xiaoxiaole
TRANSPORTATION	Didi Taxi	OFFICE	163Mail
AUDIO	QQ Music	HEALTH	Keep
NAVIGATION	GaoDe Map	STOCK	Eastmoney
NEWS	QQNews	SYSTEM TOOL	Wifi
LIFE	Clouds Weather	OTHERS	Androdasync

3.2 Mobility Features

Luca Pappalardo et al. [18] found that there exist links between human mobility and socio-economic development. With the App usage records with time and space information, we can extract the mobility features of users. The distribution of 9858 base stations in Shanghai is shown with red points in Fig. 1. According to the longitudes and latitudes, we aggregate all the base stations into 188 blocks as shown in Fig. 2.

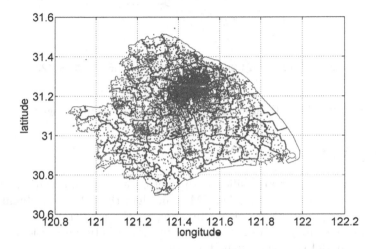

Fig. 1. The distribution of 9,858 base stations in Shanghai.

Table 4 introduces the 3 types of mobility features. m_1 represents the times of a user visiting 188 blocks in a week, respectively. The 188 blocks are in 3 socio-economic levels. m_2 represents the times of a user visiting rich, intermediate and poor blocks, respectively. In addition, we divide a day into 4 time periods as mentioned above. Then, we count the number of times a user visit blocks in 3 SELs during a certain period. m_3 is a tuple of 2(weekdays and weekends) × 3(3 SELs of blocks) × 4(time periods).

Table 4. Three types of mobility features.

m_1	Number of times a user visit 188 blocks in a week
m_2	Number of times a user visit rich, intermediate and poor blocks
m_3	Number of times a user visit blocks in 3 SEL during a certain period

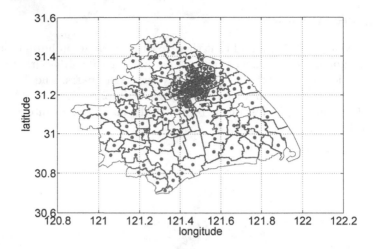

Fig. 2. The distribution of administrative blocks in Shanghai.

4   Classification with FM

In this section, we use the classification model based on Factorization Machine (FM) to train the predictive model. FM is an algorithm of solving binary classification predictive problem [24]. Comparing to the traditional linear model, FM concerns the impact brought by the interaction between the i-th and j-th features. FM model is shown as the following.

$$\hat{y}(x) := w_0 + \sum_{i=1}^{n} w_i x_i + \sum_{i=1}^{n} \sum_{j=i+1}^{n} w_{ij} x_i x_j \tag{1}$$

where w_0 is the global bias, w_i represents the weight of the feature x_i, w_{ij} is the interaction between feature x_i and x_j. For the convenience of estimating the w_{ij}, we set $w_{ij} := \boldsymbol{v}\boldsymbol{v}^T$, where $\boldsymbol{v}_i = (v_{i1}, v_{i2}, ..., v_{ik})^T, i = 1, 2, ..., n$.

In order to discover insight, we train a multi-class classification model based on FM instead of using multi-classification algorithms. For each class, we train a one-vs-all binary classification with FM. We apply Stochastic Gradient Descent (SGD) to learn the parameters of FM model. Finally, we select the level which has the highest probability to be the SEL of the user.

5   Results and Discussions

Class-imbalance is one of the most common but difficult problems in data mining. A large number of researchers have been studying how to train proper model from class-imbalance datasets. As revealed in Sect. 2, the samples distributed in 4 SELs are extremely unbalanced. Therefore, we train the classification model after applying SMOTE algorithm to datasets. SMOTE is an oversampling technique by synthetizing new samples from the minority [3].

Algorithm 3. SGD for training the FM model

1: input: training set $D = \{(\boldsymbol{x}_1, y_1), (\boldsymbol{x}_2, y_2), ..., (\boldsymbol{x}_m, y_m)\}$, learning rates η

2: output: the parameters of FM model, $\Theta = (w_0, \boldsymbol{w}, \boldsymbol{v})$

3: initialization: $w_0 := 0; \boldsymbol{w} := 0; \boldsymbol{v} \sim \mathcal{N}(0, \sigma)$

4: **for** $(x_i, y_i) \in D$ **do**

$\quad w_0 = w_0 - \eta(\frac{\partial loss(\hat{y}(x_i), y_i)}{\partial w_0} + 2\lambda^0 w_0)$

$\quad$ **for** $i \in \{1, 2, ..., n\}$ **do**

$\quad\quad$ **if** $\boldsymbol{x}_i \neq 0$

$\quad\quad\quad w_i = w_i - \eta(\frac{\partial loss(\hat{y}(x_i), y_i)}{\partial w_i} + 2\lambda^{w_{\pi(i)}} w_i)$

$\quad\quad\quad$ **for** $j \in \{1, 2, ..., k\}$ **do**

$\quad\quad\quad\quad v_{ij} = v_{ij} - \eta(\frac{\partial loss(\hat{y}(x_i), y_i)}{\partial v_{ij}} + 2\lambda^v_{\pi(i),j} v_{ij})$

stop until meeting criterion

There are 660 users distributing in 4 SELs in this research. We implement the FM-based classification through a 5-fold cross-validation over the training set. The normalized confusion matrix is shown as Fig. 3. The model achieves the accuracy over 85% when predicting the users in SEL B. However, it performs badly in identifying the users from other classes. Most users from SEL A and SEL C are mistakenly predicted as SEL B. This phenomenon is caused by the fact that the users from SEL B occupy over 75%. Thus, the model learns the features of users in SEL B better. For the classes with less users, the model is not able to learn enough information to predict them accurately. Therefore, the predictive model is inclined to regard users without obvious characteristics as SEL B.

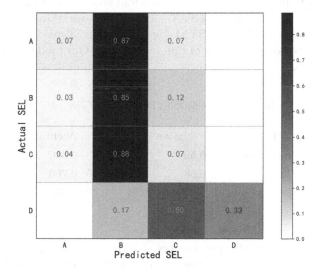

Fig. 3. Normalized confusion matrix.

In order to solve the class-imbalance problem, we apply the SMOTE algorithm to the row datasets. The number of users distributed in 4 classes is same after the SMOTE oversampling. The normalized confusion matrix based on SMOTE is shown as Fig. 4. The accuracies of predicting the users in SEL A, SEL C and SEL D are extremely improved.

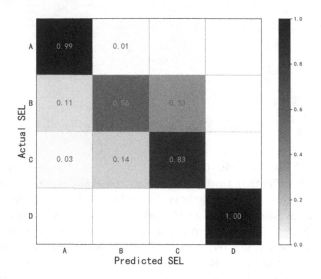

Fig. 4. Normalized confusion matrix based on SMOTE.

The FM-based model performs well on the datasets after oversampling. We implement the predictive model through a 5-fold cross-validation over the training set and achieve the accuracy of 84.3%. In addition, we train predictive models with Random Forests (RF) and SVM for comparison. Table 5 shows the precision, recall, F1 score and accuracy of different models. Our model performs better than RF and SVM.

Table 5. The examples of app usage records.

Model	Precision	Recall	F1	Accuracy
Random forests	0.59	0.68	0.63	0.680
SVM	0.58	0.76	0.65	0.756
FM-based model	0.84	0.84	0.84	0.843

SGD is used to learn the parameters of FM model. In order to investigate how the SGD influences the accuracy of our model, we compute the accuracy versus regularization coefficient λ as shown in Fig. 5. With the decrease of λ, the accuracy is significantly improved. The larger λ is, the more serious punishment to the model. Thus, the model is too simple to learn the features of samples. However, it is important to learn the information from each sample for classification model. Therefore, we set a relatively small λ.

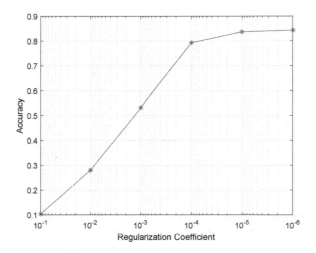

Fig. 5. Accuracy versus regularization coefficient λ.

In addition, we compute the accuracy versus learning rate α as shown in Fig. 6. With the increase of α, the accuracy increases gradually. While the accuracy becomes decreasing when α is over 0.8.

6   Related Work

Inferring the SELs of individuals is important for both policy makers and companies. The traditional approaches to predicting the individuals' economic status mainly rely on census. With the development of data mining technologies, many researchers attempt to predict SELs of individuals via novel datasets and algorithms.

Some researchers found that there exist correlations between social networks and the economic status of individuals [1,2,16]. Shaojun Luo et al. extracted social networks from user's calling data to infer individuals' SELs [14]. The majority of researchers focus on the research of using mobile phone data to estimate individuals' economic status. Luca Pappalardo et al. studied the links between human mobility extracted from calling data and economic development [18]. Other studies employed calling data to investigate consumer behaviors [4] and economic development [5,8].

Other researchers attempt to use data collected from Internet to discover indicators about society or economics. Michal Kosinski et al. [15] predicted users'

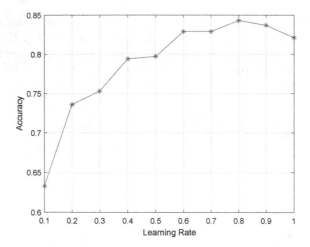

Fig. 6. Accuracy versus learning rate α.

personal attributes like intelligence, ethnicity from digital records of Facebook. Renato Miranda Filho et al. [6] took advantage of user data obtained from Foursquare and Twitter to propose a method of inferring user social class. Other researchers analysed user occupation class through the social content of Twitter [20].

7   Conclusions

This research proposes a method to predict SELs of individuals using their App usage records provided by China Telecom. We first define the SEL according to the social stratification method in sociology. With a dataset containing 660 users provided by the operator China Telecom, we divided 660 users into 4 classes. We then train the FM-based model from the datasets after SMOTE oversampling. The accuracy achieves 84.3%, which performs much better than the previous research using tweets [6].

Although this is a pioneering work using App usage records to predict socio-economic status, there are still some limitations. The samples in our study only cover 4 socio-economic classes except the lower socio-economic level. In addition, our method may not work in the environment where smart phones and Apps are not popular. However, this paper proved the correlations between users' App usage behaviors and their socio-economic status, which provides a promising method and idea for other researchers.

Acknowledgements. The work is supported in part by Science, Technology and Innovation Commission of Shenzhen Municipality (No. JCYJ20170816151823313), NSFC (No. U1711263, 61501527), States Key Project of Research and Development Plan (No. 2017YFE0121300-6), Fundamental Research Funds for the Central Universities,

MOE-CMCC Joint Research Fund of China (MCM20160101), Guangdong Science and Technology Project (No. 2016B010126003) and Guangdong Provincial Special Fund For Modern Agriculture Industry Technology Innovation Teams (No. 2019KJ122).

References

1. Arveson, W.: Methods and Applications (2002)
2. Caldarelli, G., Vespignani, A.: Large Scale Structure and Dynamics of Complex Networks: From Information Technology to Finance and Natural Science. World Scientific Publishing Co., Inc., River Edge (2007)
3. Chawla, N.V., Bowyer, K.W., Hall, L.O., Kegelmeyer, W.P.: Smote: synthetic minority over-sampling technique. J. Artif. Intell. Res. 16(1), 321–357 (2002)
4. Decuyper, A., et al.: Estimating food consumption and poverty indices with mobile phone data. CoRR, abs/1412.2595 (2014). http://arxiv.org/abs/1412.2595
5. Eagle, N., Macy, M., Claxton, R.: Network diversity and economic development. Science 328(5981), 1029–1031 (2010). https://doi.org/10.1126/science.1186605
6. Filho, R.M., Borges, G.R., Almeida, J.M., Pappa, G.L.: Inferring user social class in online social networks (2014)
7. Freeman, L.C.: Centrality in social networks conceptual clarification. Soc. Netw. 1(3), 215–239 (1978)
8. Gutierrez, T., Krings, G., Blondel, V.D.: Evaluating socio-economic state of a country analyzing airtime credit and mobile phone datasets. CoRR, abs/1309.4496 (2013). http://arxiv.org/abs/1309.4496
9. Huang, Y., Yu, L., Xiang, W., Cui, B.: A multi-source integration framework for user occupation inference in social media systems. World Wide Web-internet Web Inf. Syst. 18(5), 1247–1267 (2015)
10. Lampos, V., Aletras, N., Geyti, J.K., Zou, B., Cox, I.J.: Inferring the socioeconomic status of social media users based on behaviour and language. In: European Conference on Information Retrieval (2016)
11. Li, C.: Prestige stratification in contemporary chinese society. Sociol. Stud. 2, 74–102 (2005)
12. Li, H., et al.: Characterizing smartphone usage patterns from millions of android users. In: Internet Measurement Conference (2015)
13. Lindén, A.L.: Travel patterns and environmental effects now and in the future: implications of differences in energy consumption among socio-economic groups. Ecol. Econ. 30(3), 405–417 (1999)
14. Luo, S., Morone, F., Sarraute, C., Travizano, M., Makse, H.A.: Inferring personal economic status from social network location. Nature Commun. 8, 15227 (2017)
15. Michal, K., David, S., Thore, G.: Private traits and attributes are predictable from digital records of human behavior. PNAS 110(15), 5802–5805 (2013)
16. Newman, M.E.J.: The structure and function of complex networks. SIAM Rev. 45(2), 167–256 (2003)
17. Pan, W., Ghoshal, G., Krumme, C., Cebrian, M., Pentland, A.: Urban characteristics attributable to density-driven tie formation. Nature Commun. 4(3), 1961 (2012)
18. Pappalardo, L., Pedreschi, D., Smoreda, Z., Giannotti, F.: Using big data to study the link between human mobility and socio-economic development. In: IEEE International Conference on Big Data (2015)

19. Pappalardo, L., Vanhoof, M., Gabrielli, L., Smoreda, Z., Pedreschi, D., Giannotti, F.: An analytical framework to nowcast well-being using mobile phone data. Int. J. Data Sci. Anal. **2**(1–2), 1–18 (2016)
20. Preotiucpietro, D., Lampos, V., Aletras, N.: An analysis of the user occupational class through twitter content (2015)
21. Preot, D., Lampos, V., Aletras, N.: An analysis of the user occupational class through twitter content (2015)
22. Propper, C., Damiani, M., Leckie, G., Dixon, J.: Impact of patients' socioeconomic status on the distance travelled for hospital admission in the english national health service. J. Health Serv. Res. Policy **12**(3), 153–159 (2007)
23. Qiang Li, H.L.: Vocational prestige in transition. Acad. Res. **12**, 34–42 (2009)
24. Rendle, S.: Factorization machines. In: IEEE International Conference on Data Mining (2011)
25. Van Canneyt, S., Bron, M., Haines, A., Lalmas, M.: Describing patterns and disruptions in large scale mobile app usage data. In: Proceedings of the 26th International Conference on World Wide Web Companion, WWW 2017 Companion, pp. 1579–1584 (2017). https://doi.org/10.1145/3041021.3051113
26. Welke, P., Andone, I., Blaszkiewicz, K., Markowetz, A.: Differentiating smartphone users by app usage. In: ACM International Joint Conference on Pervasive & Ubiquitous Computing (2016)
27. Ye, X., et al.: Preference, context and communities:a multi-faceted approach to predicting smartphone app usage patterns. In: International Symposium on Wearable Computers (2013)

Multiple Tasks Assignment for Cooperating Homogeneous Unmanned Aerial Vehicles

Li Li[1,2]([✉]), Xiangping Bryce Zhai[1,2], Bing Chen[1,2], and Congduan Li[3]

[1] Nanjing University of Aeronautics and Astronautics, Nanjing 211106, China
li_li11@126.com, {blueicezhaixp,cb_china}@nuaa.edu.cn
[2] Collaborative Innovation Center of Novel Software Technology
and Industrialization, Nanjing 210032, China
[3] Sun Yat-Sen University, Guangzhou 510275, China
licongd@mail.sysu.edu.cn

Abstract. Using multiple unmanned aerial vehicles (UAVs) to perform some tasks cooperatively has received growing attention in recent years. Task assignment is a difficult problem in mission planning. Multiple tasks assignment problem for cooperating homogeneous UAVs is considered as a traditional combinatorial optimization problem. This paper addresses the problem of assigning multiple tasks to cooperative homogeneous UAVs, minimizing the total cost and balancing the cost of each UAV. We propose a centralized task assignment scheme which is based on minimum spanning tree. This scheme involves two phases. In the first phase, we use the Kruskal algorithm and the breadth first search algorithm to assign all tasks to UAVs and get a proper initial task assignment solution. The second phase involves the Pareto optimization improvement in the solution generated from the first phase. For a single UAV, we use the dynamic programming algorithm to calculate the total cost of completing all assigned tasks. The performance of the proposed scheme is compared to that of heuristic simulated annealing algorithm. The simulation results show that the proposed scheme can solve the homogeneous multi-UAV cooperative task assignment problem effectively.

Keywords: Unmanned aerial vehicle · Task assignment · Minimum spanning tree · Pareto optimization

1 Introduction

In recent years, the advantage of using UAV to perform various military and civilian missions in the air, sea, and on the ground has become more and more obvious. Compared with manned aircraft, UAV has the advantages of small size,

Supported in part by the National Natural Science Foundation of China under Grants No. 61701231, No. 61672283.

X. B. Zhai et al. (Eds.): MLICOM 2019, LNICST 294, pp. 211–221, 2019.
https://doi.org/10.1007/978-3-030-32388-2_18

light weight, low cost, no risk of casualties, good concealment, strong surviv-ability, strong self-control ability, and ability to fly in some high-risk areas. In the military field, UAV can be used to complete battlefield reconnaissance and surveillance, deceive enemy decoys, locate shots, strike against the ground, and also serve as targets for artillery and missiles. In the civilian sector, UAV can be used for search rescue, disaster monitoring, meteorological detection, communi-cation relay, pesticide spraying, etc. However, the role that a single UAV can play is very limited. Especially, it is often impossible to complete some compli-cated tasks. An effective method is to use multiple UAVs to accomplish some tasks collaboratively. It is expected that the capabilities of a joint system far exceeds the sum of its individual parts. Most tasks can be accomplished more effective by cooperation and coordination of multiple UAVs.

Multi-UAVs collaborative mission planning is usually divided into two major parts: task assignment and path planning. Due to the certain coupling between task assignment and path planning, the current research on multi-UAVs collab-orative mission planning usually has two methods. One is to research separately and the other is to research together. In this paper, we only concentrate on task assignment problem.

Multiple tasks assignment problem is an NP-hard problem. Numerous exact and heuristic methods have been proposed for solving this problem [2]. Exact methods include mixed integer linear programming (MILP) [3,10], branch and bound [9], network flow [7], iterative CTP algorithm [11], and so on. Nygard et al. [7] propose a network flow optimization model for solving task assign-ment. The network optimization problem is formulated as a linear programming problem. Mixed Integer Linear Programming (MILP) is an effective method for task assignment because it can use discrete decision variables to deal with dynamic system. Bellingham et al. [3] use MILP for task assignment to deal with waypoint visiting problem. However, the complexity of these exact algo-rithm rapidly grows as the number of UAVs and tasks increase. Therefore exact algorithm is often suitable for some small-size problems. Recently, several heuris-tic algorithms have been used to solve task assignment problem including ant colony optimization (ACO) [1,15,16], genetic algorithm (GA) [8,12], and par-ticle swarm optimization [4,6,13,14]. The ACO was introduced in early 90's and simulates the process of ants foraging. Zaza et al. [16] propose an enhanced version of ACO for solving UAV task allocation and route planning. The ACO adopts a multi-colony approach to incorporate variable loitering times. In com-parison with MILP, the method has been shown to offer near-optimal solutions in faster time and with better scalability with the number of tasks. The GA is a stochastic search method which is described in many papers. Shima et al. [12] use genetic algorithm for assigning the multiple agents to perform multiple tasks on multiple targets. Monte Carlo simulations demonstrate the viability of the genetic algorithm, providing good feasible solutions quickly. Heuristic algorithms can effectively solve some hard large-size optimization problems, but they have a large amount of calculation and their convergence is challenging in some cases.

This paper investigates the multi-objective multiple-UAV multiple tasks assignment problem, optimizing two objectives: the total cost of all UAVs and the workload among the UAVs. We propose a MST-based method to solve the above problem effectively. Firstly, we use Kruskal algorithm to obtain a minimum spanning tree (MST) for UAV and task point. Then, based on the MST, BFS algorithm is used to obtain a proper initial task assignment solution. Finally, Pareto optimization is used to improve the initial solution. On the one hand, we consider the multi-objective optimization problem. On the other hand, compared with heuristic algorithm, our method has good convergence.

The rest of the paper is organized as follows. Section 2 describes the system model. Section 3 presents the MST-based task assignment algorithm. Section 4 presents some experimental results to validate the proposed method. Finally, we conclude the paper in Sect. 5.

2   System Model

In this paper, we are interested in solving the multi-objective multiple-UAV multiple tasks assignment problem. We assume that each UAV has the same capabilities and can perform every task. Task can be defined as reconnaissance, attack, or assessment and so on. Without loss of generality, we define the task as visiting a waypoint. Also, each task must have at least one UAV to execute. The total environment is modeled as a two-dimensional (2D) Euclidean space. Our goal is to accomplish all tasks at the lowest cost. Since we use multiple UAVs to perform tasks, we usually don't let one UAV accomplish tasks too many or even tens of times that of other UAVs. In this case, UAV may not be able to accomplish all tasks due to its own energy constraints. Therefore, balancing the cost of UAVs is an important issue with practical significance in multiple tasks assignment. So the other objective is to balance the cost of each UAV.

The problem can be formulated as follows. Consider a set of m UAVs $\{r_1, \ldots, r_m\}$, initially located at different positions $\{p_1, \ldots, p_m\}$, which must visit a set of n $(m < n)$ task locations $\{t_1, \ldots, t_n\}$ and return to their initial positions after task completion. We define $tour_i$ as the tour of UAV r_i starting from and ending at its initial position p_i and going through the list of its all allocated tasks $\{t_{i_1}, \ldots, t_{i_k}\}$ in some order. The tour cost of the UAV r_i is defined as:

$$cost(tour_i) = cost(p_i, t_{i_1}) + \sum_{j=1}^{k} cost(t_{i_j}, t_{i_{j+1}}) + cost(t_{i_k}, p_i) \tag{1}$$

where k is the number of task assigned to UAV r_i. $cost(t_{i_j}, t_{i_{j+1}})$ represents the cost between task t_{i_j} and $t_{i_{j+1}}$. The tour cost of UAV r_i may be any of several things, including consumed energy, time, or distance. In this paper, we use Euclidean distance to represent the cost between tasks. t_{i_1} and t_{i_k} are the first and the last task locations for UAV r_i. $cost(p_i, t_{i_1})$ represents the cost between the initial position of UAV r_i and the first task location, and $cost(t_{i_k}, p_i)$

represents the cost between the last task location and the initial position of UAV r_i.

In the context of the multi-objectives optimization problem, the goal is to generate a solution that provides a good trade-off between the objectives. In this paper, we have two objectives. One is to minimize the cost of completing all tasks and the other is to balance the cost of each UAV. Because the cost of each UAV is not necessarily balanced when the total cost is the smallest, it is necessary to put forward some requirements for balancing. The objective function is defined as:

$$minimize \quad \sum_{i=1}^{m} cost(tour_i) \tag{2}$$

$$minimize \quad \max_{i \in 1 \cdots m} cost(tour_i) \tag{3}$$

3   Minimum Spanning Tree-Based Task Assignment

From the perspective of graph theory, our method abstracts UAVs and task points as vertices, and paths between points as edges in undirected graph. Moreover, the cost of the path is used as the weight of the edge in the graph. Since we have a goal to accomplish all tasks at the lowest cost, we associate the minimum spanning tree in graph theory. Using the minimum spanning tree, we can get the lower bound of the total cost, that is, the sum of the weights of the minimum spanning tree. Based on the MST, our method includes two steps: generating a proper initial task assignment solution and Pareto optimization improvement.

When task assignment problem is abstracted into graph theory problem, we can find that the final result of modeling is an undirected fully connected graph. Because when an obstacle is encountered in the process of connecting two points in a straight line, the two points can be connected in a curved manner around the obstacle. Therefore, the points can be interconnected to form an undirected fully connected graph. In this paper, the weight between points is represented by the distance between two points. Based on the graph generated above, we use the Kruskal algorithm which is one of the most popular methods used to generate MST [5]. Then we can calculate the sum of the weights of the edges of the minimum spanning tree which is taken as the lower bound of the total cost.

According to the lower bound and the number of UAVs, we can get the lower bound of the cost of each UAV. Starting with a UAV, we use the BFS algorithm to assign task to each UAV. The sum of the weights is calculated while assigning. When a task is assigned, the sum of the weights exceeds the lower bound of the UAV and the allocation is stopped. Each UAV repeats the above process until all UAVs are assigned. Finally, there may be some remaining tasks that are not assigned. We assign each remaining task to the UAV that is closest to the task. In the end, we will get a initial task assignment solution.

Algorithm 1 (Task Assignment)

---

1. **Inputs:** UAVs r_i ($1 < i < m$), Tasks t_j ($1 < j < n$), Minimum spanning tree T, Distance matrix G

2. Calculate the sum of the weights of the minimum spanning tree T

3. Divide the total weight by the number of UAVs to get the lower bound of each UAV

4. **For** each UAV r_i **do**

5.   **while** isEmpty(queue)==false&&sum¡lower bound **do**

6.   Assign a task to UAV r_i using breadth-first search algorithm

7.   Calculate the sum of weights

8.   **end**

9. **end**

10. **For** each task t_i **do**

11.   **If** t_i is not assigned **do**

12.   Assign it to the nearest UAV

13.   **end**

14. **end**

15. **Outputs:** Assignment(r_i, t_j) $1 < i < m$ $1 < j < n$

The Pareto optimization improvement step is to adjust tasks between UAVs in order to optimize our two objectives, as shown in Algorithm 2. Based on the initial task assignment solution obtained in the first step, for each UAV, we use the dynamic programming algorithm to calculate the cost for completing all assigned tasks. Further, the total cost can be obtained. From all UAVs, we first select the UAV with the largest and smallest cost which are denoted as UAV r_{max} and r_{min} respectively. Then, we select a task from the task assigned to the UAV r_{max}, which is farthest from the UAV r_{max} and closest to the UAV r_i, and assign it to the UAV r_i. If such a task can not be found, we look for a UAV closest to the UAV r_{max}, denoted r_j. The task closest to the UAV r_j in the task of UAV r_{max} is assigned to r_j. After the end of one adjustment, the above process is repeated for the UAV r_i or r_j, while it encounter a bad solution or UAV r_{min}. After the end of a round of cycles, a new task assignment solution is obtained. According to the total cost of completing all tasks and the maximum cost of all UAVs, we decide whether to add the new solution to the candidate set of Pareto solution. The above process is repeated until the Pareto candidate set remains unchanged regardless of which task in the UAV r_{max} is adjusted.

Algorithm 2 (Pareto Optimization Improvement)

---

1. **Inputs:** UAVs r_i $(1 < i < m)$, Tasks t_j $(1 < j < n)$, Assignment(r_i,t_j) $1 < i < m$ $1 < j < n$

2. Calculate the cost of each UAV r_i and total cost d_1 of the initial task assignment solution using dynamic programming algorithm

3. **Repeat** until r_{max} remains unchanged **do**

4.   Select r_{max} and r_{min}

5.   **while** $r_{max} \neq r_{min}$ **do**

6.   Select a task from UAV r_{max} and assign it to r_i

7.   Calculate the cost of each UAV r_i and total cost d_2 of the new task assignment solution

8.   Update the Pareto candidate set

9.   **If** the Pareto candidate set remains unchanged **do**

10.   break

11.   **end**

12. $r_{max} = r_i$

13.   **end**

14. **end**

15. **Outputs:** Assignment(r_i,t_j) $1 < i < m$ $1 < j < n$,total distance

---

4   Performance Evaluation

In this section, we evaluate the performance of the proposed approach to solve multiple tasks assignment problem for cooperating homogeneous UAVs. The UAVs are initially located at different positions and the number of UAVs is less than the number of tasks. We evaluate the total cost and the maximum cost. The proposed scheme has been implemented and tested in MATLAB. We set up two test scenarios in which the location of the UAVs and tasks are randomly placed in a predefined area.

In order to validate the effectiveness of the proposed scheme, we compare it with the simulated annealing algorithm. The first test scenario contains three UAVs and twenty tasks. The size of the predefined area is 800 m × 800 m. Figure 1 shows the experimental results of the MST-based and the simulated annealing algorithm. Another test scenario consists of five UAVs and thirty-five tasks. The size of the operational area is 3000 m × 3000 m. Figure 2 shows the experimental results of the two kinds of algorithms. Detailed task assignment results of the two algorithms in Figs. 1 and 2 are recorded in Table 1. From the data in Table 1, we can find that the total and maximum cost of the proposed algorithm is smaller than that of the simulated annealing algorithm. Therefore, the proposed MST-based algorithm can provide a better balance between two objectives, compared to simulated annealing algorithm.

Table 1. The task assignment results of the MST-based and the simulated annealing algorithm

Algorithm	The number of UAV	The number of task	Operation area	Total cost (m)	The cost of each UAV (m)		The maximum cost (m)
MST-based algorithm	3	20	800 m × 800 m	3904.2	1464.7 1087.8	1351.6	1464.7
Simulated annealing algorithm	3	20	800 m × 800 m	3930.3	1837.0 807.5	1285.8	1837.0
MST-based algorithm	5	35	3000 m × 3000 m	18075	4076.5 3591.9 3414.8	3564.4 3427.3	4076.5
Simulated annealing algorithm	5	35	3000 m × 3000 m	18278	5706.0 2636.4 2144.7	5690.1 2100.5	5706.0

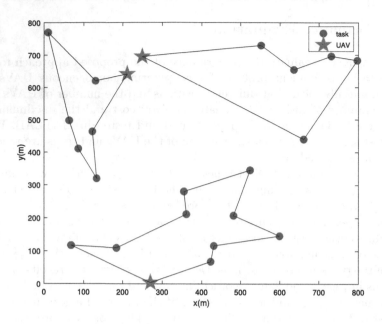

(a) MST-based algorithm

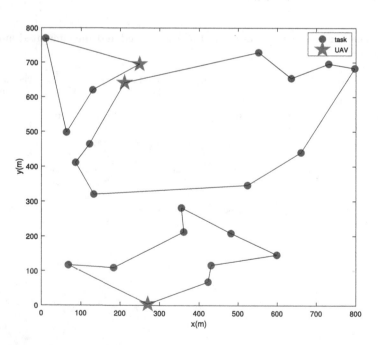

(b) Simulated annealing algorithm

Fig. 1. The task assignment result of 3 UAVs and 20 tasks of the MST-based and the simulated annealing algorithm

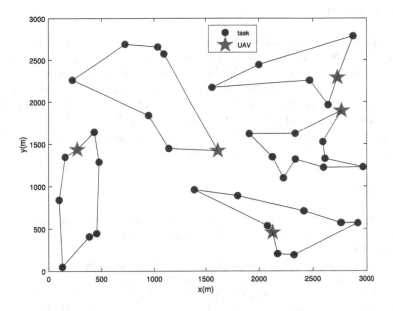

(a) MST-based algorithm

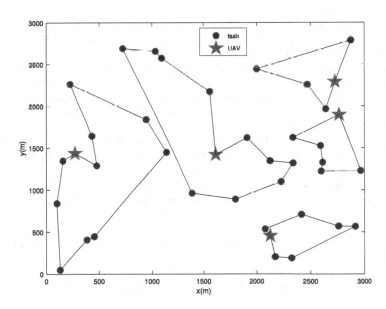

(b) Simulated annealing algorithm

Fig. 2. The task assignment result of 5 UAVs and 35 tasks of the MST-based and the simulated annealing algorithm

5 Conclusion

We decouple task assignment and path planning and only concentrate on task assignment problem. We consider multiple tasks assignment problem for multiple cooperating homogeneous UAV. In order to solve this problem, we propose a minimum spanning tree-based method. Our objective is to minimize the total cost and the maximum cost of all UAVs. In the performance evaluation part, our comparison of the MST-based method with existing simulated annealing algorithm shows that our method outperforms the simulated annealing algorithm, and provides a good trade-off between two objectives.

References

1. Adolf, F., Langer, A., Silva, L.D.M.P.E., Thielecke, F.: Probabilistic roadmaps and ant colony optimization for UAV mission planning. IFAC Proc. vol. **40**(15), 264–269 (2007)
2. Ahuja, R.K., Kumar, A., Jha, K.C., Orlin, J.B.: Exact and heuristic algorithms for the weapon-target assignment problem. Oper. Res. **55**(6), 1136–1146 (2007)
3. Bellingham, J., Tillerson, M., Richards, A., How, J.P.: Multi-task allocation and path planning for cooperating UAVs. In: Butenko, S., Murphey, R., Pardalos, P.M. (eds.) Cooperative Control: Models, Applications and Algorithms. Cooperative Systems, vol. 1, pp. 23–41. Springer, Boston (2003). https://doi.org/10.1007/978-1-4757-3758-5_2
4. Chen, K., Sun, Q., Zhou, A., Wang, S.: Adaptive multiple task assignments for UAVs using discrete particle swarm optimization. In: Internet of Vehicles. Technologies and Services Towards Smart City, pp. 220–229 (2018)
5. Joseph, B., Kruskal, J.: On the shortest spanning subtree of a graph and the traveling salesman problem. Proc. Am. Math. Soc. **7**(1), 48–50 (1956)
6. Na, G., et al.: On modeling and discrete particle swarm optimization for task assignment of cooperating UAVs. In: Chinese Control and Decision Conference (CCDC), pp. 1044–1049 (2011)
7. Nygard, K.E., Chandler, P.R., Pachter, M.: Dynamic network flow optimization models for air vehicle resource allocation. In: Proceedings of the 2001 American Control Conference, vol. 3, pp. 1853–1858 (2001)
8. Ramirez-Atencia, C., Bello-Orgaz, G., R-Moreno, M.D., Camacho, D.: Solving complex multi-UAV mission planning problems using multi-objective genetic algorithms. Soft. Comput. **21**(17), 4883–4900 (2017)
9. Rasmussen, S.J., Shima, T.: Branch and bound tree search for assigning cooperating UAVs to multiple tasks. In: 2006 American Control Conference, pp. 2171–2176 (2006)
10. Schumacher, C., Chandler, P., Pachter, M., Pachter, L.: Constrained optimization for UAV task assignment. In: AIAA Guidance, Navigation, and Control Conference and Exhibit, pp. 1–14 (2004)
11. Schumacher, C., Chandler, P.R., Rasmussen, S.R.: Task allocation for wide area search munitions. In: Proceedings of the 2002 American Control Conference, vol. 3, pp. 1917–1922 (2002)
12. Shima, T., Rasmussen, S.J., Sparks, A.G.: UAV cooperative multiple task assignments using genetic algorithms. In: American Control Conference, pp. 2989–2994 (2005)

13. Sujit, P., George, J., Beard, R.: Multiple UAV task allocation using particle swarm optimization. In: AIAA Guidance, Navigation and Control Conference and Exhibit, pp. 1–9 (2008)
14. Wang, X., Linlin, C., Li, J., Ning, Y.: Based on PSO algorithm multiple task assignments for cooperating UAVs. In: 2010 International Conference on Educational and Information Technology, vol. 2, pp. V2-25–V2-28 (2010)
15. Wang, Z., Zhang, W., Li, G.: UAVs task allocation using multiple colonies of ants. In: IEEE International Conference on Automation and Logistics, pp. 371–374 (2009)
16. Zaza, T., Richards, A.: Ant colony optimization for routing and tasking problems for teams of UAVs. In: UKACC International Conference on Control, pp. 652–655 (2014)

Design of Overall Framework of Self-Service Big Data Governance for Power Grid

Lin Qiao[1], Qiaoni Zhou[1], Chunhe Song[2,3]([⊠]), Hao Wu[1], Biqi Liu[1], and Shimao Yu[2,3]

[1] State Grid Liaoning Electric Power Co., Ltd.,
Shenyang 110000, People's Republic of China
[2] Key Laboratory of Networked Control Systems,
Shenyang Institute of Automation,
Chinese Academy of Sciences, Shenyang 110016, People's Republic of China
songchunhe@sia.cn
[3] Institutes for Robotics and Intelligent Manufacturing,
Chinese Academy of Sciences, Shenyang 110016, China

Abstract. At present, power grid companies have not formed a complete data quality control system and a comprehensive and effective data quality assurance mechanism, which restricts the deep mining of data value. In this paper, based on the full-service unified data center of power Grid Company, a general framework of self-service power grid big data governance is presented. Firstly, the related work of big data governance is reviewed; secondly, the architecture and characteristics of the grid company's full-service unified data center are analyzed; thirdly, the related requirements of self-service grid big data governance are analyzed; fourthly, the overall framework of self-service grid big data governance is proposed. Compared with other general big data governance framework, the proposed framework considers the specification of power grid as well as the features of self-service, making the framework more feasible.

Keywords: Data governance · Power grid · Self-service · Framework design

1 Introduction

In recent years, with the global energy problem becoming more and more serious, the research work of smart grid has been carried out all over the world. The ultimate goal of smart grid is to build a panoramic real-time system covering the whole production process of power system, including power generation, transmission, substation, distribution, power consumption and dispatch [1]. The basis of supporting the safe, self-healing, green, strong and reliable operation of smart grid is the panoramic real-time data acquisition, transmission and storage of power grid, and the rapid analysis of accumulated massive multi-source data [2]. With the development of smart grid construction, the amount of data generated by grid operation and equipment inspection/monitoring increases exponentially, which gradually constitutes the big data concerned by today's information academia, which needs corresponding storage and fast processing technology as support [3].

© ICST Institute for Computer Sciences, Social Informatics and Telecommunications Engineering 2019
Published by Springer Nature Switzerland AG 2019. All Rights Reserved
X. B. Zhai et al. (Eds.): MLICOM 2019, LNICST 294, pp. 222–234, 2019.
https://doi.org/10.1007/978-3-030-32388-2_19

With the continuous construction and deepening application of information technology in power supply enterprises, various businesses of power supply enterprises have been preliminarily integrated with information technology [4]. The number and types of business data in information systems are gradually increasing, and the need for data sharing is urgent. The data quality and data sharing utilization layer are not high [5]. First, the support degree of data for analysis and decision-making is low, and there are many sources and different statistical calibers for the same data. Second, the support degree of data for operation and management needs to be improved, the data quality is uneven, some data do not have business system support, lack of uniform norms, standards and clear data accountability; third, the number of front-line personnel. Data input is a huge workload, data duplicate input, business functions duplicate. Fourth, data quality control lags behind, management and control work is one-sided, there is no complete data quality control system and a comprehensive and effective data quality assurance mechanism, restricting the deep mining of data value. Therefore, it is necessary to focus on the enterprise data life cycle, closely integrate the requirements of the company to promote the innovation of management system and working mechanism, based on the current situation of the construction and application of information support system in operation monitoring center, draw lessons from the company data management experience, realize the whole process quality management of power supply enterprise data, consolidate the data base, improve the data quality, ensure the accuracy of data, which provides a strong guarantee for data integration and mining applications [6].

In order to solve the above problems, based on the full-service unified data center of power Grid Company, this paper puts forward the general framework of self-service power grid big data governance. In this paper, firstly, the related work of big data governance is reviewed; secondly, the architecture and characteristics of the grid company's full-service unified data center are analyzed; thirdly, the related requirements of self-service grid big data governance are analyzed; fourthly, the overall framework of self-service grid big data governance is proposed. The last part is the conclusion of this paper.

2 Related Works

In the theoretical field of data governance, many organizations have made pioneering contributions, especially ISO38500, DAMA, DGI, IBM DG Council, ISACA and Gartner [7]. Their main work is to analyze, summarize and refine data governance elements such as principles, scope and contributing factors, and to establish a self-contained data governance framework on this basis. ISO 38500 proposes an IT governance framework (including goals, principles and models) and considers that the framework is also applicable to the field of data governance [8]. In terms of objectives, ISO38500 considers that the goal of IT governance is to promote the efficient and rational use of IT by organizations. In terms of principles, ISO38500 defines six basic principles of IT governance: responsibilities, strategies, procurement, performance, conformity and personnel behavior. This principle describes the recommended behavior guiding decision-making. Each principle describes the measures to be taken, but does not explain how and what to do [9]. In terms of the model, ISO38500 believes that the leaders of an organization should focus on three core tasks: first, to assess the current and future IT utilization; second, to guide the policies and plans for the implementation of governance readiness; and third, to establish a cycle model of "evaluation, guidance and supervision" [10]. DAMA summarizes three main functions of data governance, including data governance, data architecture management, data development, data operation management, data security management, reference data and master data management, data warehouse and business intelligence management, document and content management, metadata management and data management, and puts data governance at the core [11]. Then it elaborates data governance in detail. Seven major environmental elements, namely goals and principles, activities, major deliverables, roles and responsibilities, technologies, practices and methods, have finally established the corresponding relationship between the ten functions and the seven major environmental elements. It is believed that the key point of data governance is to solve the matching between the ten functions and the seven major environmental elements. DAMA believes that data governance is the exercise of power and control over data asset management, including planning, monitoring and implementation. It also distinguishes between data governance and IT governance: IT governance targets IT investment, IT application portfolio and IT project portfolio, while data governance targets data; IT is like water pipe, data is like water in water pipe, water governance methods are obviously different from water pipe governance methods [12]. DGI believes that different IT governance should establish an independent data governance theory system. DGI summarizes ten key points of data governance from three levels of organization, rules and process, and proposes a DGI data governance framework. DGI data governance framework shows the logical relationship among ten basic components in the form of intuitive access paths, and forms a self-contained and complete system from method to implementation. Components are divided into three groups according to their functions: rules and collaborative work norms, personnel and organizational structure, and processes. Rules and collaborative work norms, i.e. establishing, coordinating and standardizing data governance rules (including policies, requirements, standards, responsibilities, controls and data definitions) to guide different departments to work together to formulate and implement rules of collaborative work norms [13]. It includes the following six components: mission and vision; objectives, measures of governance effectiveness, financial strategies; data rules and definitions; decision-making power; division of responsibilities and control. Personnel and organizational structure, that is, the organizational structure to formulate and implement data governance rules and norms. It includes the following three components: data stakeholders; data governance committee; and data managers. Processes, that is, the steps and processes that data governance should follow, should be formal, written, repeatable and recyclable [14]. It mainly includes the following contents: active, passive and ongoing data governance process. IBM Data Governance Committee puts forward a maturity model of data governance according to the characteristics of data. In the aspect of building a unified data governance hub, this paper puts forward an essential model of data governance, and considers that business objectives or results are the most critical proposition of data governance. In the factor model, there are several contributing factors that affect the achievement of business objectives, namely organizational structure and awareness, policy and data-related accountability; besides contributing factors, we must focus on the core elements and supporting elements of data governance [15]. Specifically, it includes data quality management, information life cycle management, information security and privacy, data architecture, classification and metadata, as well as auditing, logging and reporting. COBIT is a process-oriented information system audit and evaluation standard formulated by ISACA. It is an internationally recognized authoritative information technology management and control framework [16]. The current version has been updated to 5.0. COBIT 5 is a principle-based top-down framework that makes a strict distinction between governance and management. COBIT 5 puts forward five basic principles of data governance: meeting stakeholder needs, covering enterprises from end to end, adopting a single integration framework, introducing a comprehensive approach, and differentiating governance from management [17]. On the basis of this principle, COBIT 5 elaborates on relevant data governance theories, including stakeholders, contributing factors, scope, key areas of governance and management. The theory of data governance proposed by COBIT 5 is a principle-driven approach. It deduces the complete system of data governance through five basic principles, so that enterprises can establish an effective governance and management framework.

3   Full Service Unified Data Center of Power Grid Company

The full-service unified data center of Power Grid Company includes three parts: data management domain, data analysis domain and data processing domain. Figure 1 gives the architecture of full service unified data center.

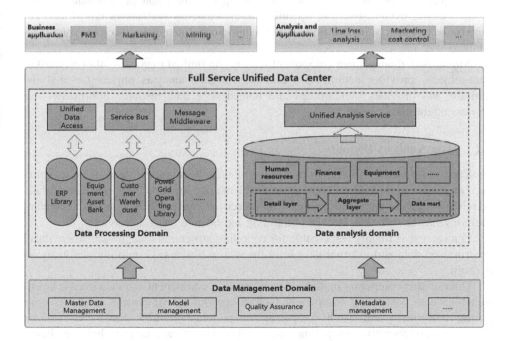

Fig. 1. Architecture of full service unified data center

3.1   Data Management Domain

Data management domain is the center of data model management and master data application in power Grid Company, and it is the key and guarantee to realize data standardization, security and correctness. The data management domain unifies the planning and control of the definition, storage and access of enterprise data in order to ensure the consistency, accuracy and reliability of enterprise-wide data. Data management domain mainly includes unified data model, enterprise-layer master data management system, data resource management component, and master data management component.

Unified data model is divided into two parts: enterprise information model (SG-CIM 3.0) and enterprise data warehouse model. Based on SG-CIM 2.0, the enterprise information model completes the design of core business objects in related subject domains. Based on the enterprise information model, the enterprise data warehouse model corresponds to the hierarchical structure of data analysis domain data warehouse, and completes the physical model design of data warehouse.

Enterprise-layer master data management system is used to sort out and identify business objects (such as organizations, personnel, projects, equipment, etc.) that are used and managed jointly by different professions, and clarify their definitions, attributes, source departments, maintenance methods, application processes and necessary technical implementation requirements.

Data Resource Management Component aims at realizing the unified management and control of the whole business data life cycle, realizing the whole management and control of model, the whole process of data account, the guarantee of data quality and the complete monitoring of data integration. It supports the whole process management of data model design, test and operation of all business systems in the processing domain, and supports the real-time online monitoring of data resources and flow in the analysis domain.

Master data management component realizes the unified management of all master data objects, provides authoritative and reliable data analysis objects for analysis domain, and provides standardized and unified core data resource information for processing domain.

3.2   Data Analysis Domain

Data analysis domain is the center of all kinds of data cleaning, conversion, aggregation and integration of power grid companies, which mainly supports the application of data acquisition, monitoring and analysis and decision-making. Data analysis domain includes data access, data storage computing and unified analysis services.

Data access is mainly responsible for collecting structured data, measurement data, unstructured data and external data from the source business system into the analysis domain.

Data storage computing includes data computing component and data storage layer, in which data computing component (stream computing component, memory computing component and batch computing component) provides distributed running engine and collaborative computing function. The data storage layer includes the basic data layer, the integration detail layer (SG-CIM), the slight summary layer and the data mart layer, in which the basic data layer includes the paste source historical area and the vertical historical area.

Unified analysis service provides unified data interface service, data mining service and self-service analysis service for all kinds of analysis applications. Data interface service component encapsulates different data storage types and computing requirements, realizes multi-table or view join and merge mechanism across libraries and different storage types, and realizes standardization and standardization of data service interface calls. Data mining service component supports data mining and trend prediction oriented to historical data, real-time discrimination and real-time analysis oriented to future prediction and Simulation in a service way. The self-service analysis component provides an intuitive and easy-to-use drag-and-drop interface. By choosing the tables related to the subject and the corresponding tables, charts, words and other presentation forms, setting layout, style and other information, it can realize the centralized, dynamic, real-time and interactive analysis and display of data information.

3.3 Data Analysis Domain

Data processing domain realizes the comprehensive integration and sharing of business data, and supports the construction of integrated business applications. Data processing domain realizes service integration architecture between systems through enterprise service bus and message middleware, realizes cross-departmental business collaboration and logical data sharing; constructs unified data access service, realizes unified access to different types of databases, provides flexible access to multiple data sources for business monitoring applications, and realizes unified data monitoring; follows the unified data model of the company and follows the unified data model of the company. Data architecture requirements, design business processing database, according to the main line of business reasonable division, deployment.

4 Demand Analysis of Big Data Governance in Power Grid

4.1 Deficiencies in Data Management of Power Grid Company

Data management domain is the center of data model management and master data application in power Grid Company, and it is the key and guarantee to realize data standardization, security and correctness. The data management domain unifies the planning and control of the definition, storage and access of enterprise data in order to ensure the consistency, accuracy and reliability of enterprise-wide data. Data management domain mainly includes unified data model, enterprise-layer master data management system, data resource management component, and master data management component.

According to the current situation of industry informatization development and the requirements of data governance in today's industry, power grid companies have the following shortcomings in data management at this stage:

(1) Data multi-head management, lack of organizations specializing in data management supervision and control. The construction and management functions of information systems are dispersed in various departments, which results in the decentralization of responsibilities and unclear powers and responsibilities of data management. Organizational departments pay attention to data from different perspectives. Lack of an organization to manage data from a global perspective makes it impossible to establish unified data management rules and standards, and the corresponding data management supervision measures cannot be implemented. The data assessment system of the organization has not yet been established, which cannot guarantee the effective implementation of data management standards and procedures.

(2) Decentralized multi-system construction, there is no standardized and unified provincial data standards and data models. In order to meet the rapidly changing market and social needs, organizations have gradually established their own information systems. Each Department produces, uses and manages data from its own standpoint, which makes the data dispersed in different departments and information systems. It lacks unified data planning, reliable data sources and data standards, resulting in data irregularity, inconsistency, redundancy and non-sharing. Problems arise, and it is difficult for organizations and departments to use consistent language to describe the understanding of data, resulting in inconsistent understanding.

(3) Lack of unified master data, the main information such as personnel between the core systems of organizations is not stored in an independent system, or maintained between systems through a unified business management process. Without the management of master data of power grid units, it is impossible to guarantee the consistency, integrity and controllability of master data in the whole business scope, resulting in the failure to guarantee the correctness of business data.

(4) Lack of a unified group data quality management process system. In the current situation, data quality management is mainly carried out separately by various organizations and departments; the mechanism of data quality communication between different departments and departments is not perfect; there is a lack of clear standards and standards for data quality control between different departments and departments; the randomness of data analysis is strong, and the business needs are unclear, which affects the data quality; the automatic data collection has not yet been fully realized, and the process of data processing is human-made. Previously, there are many problems in many departments, such as insufficient data quality management personnel, insufficient knowledge and experience, incomplete supervision methods, and lack of perfect data quality control process and system support ability.

(5) Data life cycle management is incomplete. At present, the norms and processes of data life cycle management for power grid companies are not perfect, which cannot identify expired and invalid data, and unstructured data is not included in the scope of data life cycle management; there is no information tool to support the query of data life cycle status, and metadata management is not effectively used.

4.2 Demand Analysis of Big Data Governance

In view of the problems existing in large data governance of power grid, this paper summarizes various governance scenarios and puts forward the following basic requirements for the framework of large data governance of power grid:

Firstly, the standard of large data for power grid should be established. Data standard is a set of standardization system which conforms to the reality of the group and covers the definition, operation and application of multi-layer data. The establishment of data standards is an important work in the informationization and digitization construction of group units. All kinds of data in the industry must be organized according to a unified standard in order to form a circulating and sharing information platform. The requirements for standards in big data governance can be divided into two categories: basic standards and applied standards. The former is mainly used to form a coordinate reference system for consistent understanding and unification of information among different systems, which is the basis of information collection, exchange and application, including data classification and coding, data dictionary and digital map standards; the latter is to provide certain standard specifications for all links involved in the platform function, so as to ensure the efficient collection and exchange of information, including data classification and coding, data dictionary and digital map standards. Metadata standards, data metadata standards for main entities, data classification and coding standards, data quality standards, and data processing process specifications (Fig. 2).

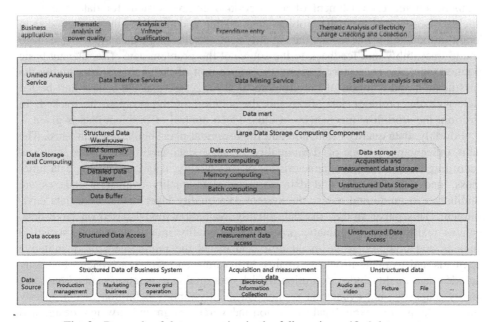

Fig. 2. Demands of data processing in the full service unified data center

Secondly, establish a total data quality management system. Low data quality will affect the application of data warehouse. Low data quality often results in the development of systems that are quite different from users expectations. Data quality is related to the success or failure of the construction of analytical information systems. At the same time, data resources are the strategic resources of the group units. Rational and effective use of correct data can guide the group units to make correct decisions and improve the comprehensive competitiveness of the province. The unreasonable use of incorrect data (i.e. poor data quality) can lead to the failure of decision-making, which can be said to be millions of millions and thousands of miles. Data quality management includes absolute data quality management and process quality management. Absolute quality is the authenticity, completeness and autonomy of data itself. Process quality refers to the quality of use, storage and transmission of data, and the quality of use of data refers to the correct use of data. If the correct data is used incorrectly, it is impossible to draw the correct conclusion. Data storage quality index data are safely stored in appropriate media. The so-called storage in an appropriate medium means that when data is needed, it can be taken out in time and conveniently. Data transmission quality refers to the efficiency and correctness of data in the process of transmission. In the whole life cycle of large data in power grid, a data quality control system is established, which runs through data acquisition, processing, fusion and application, to meet the data quality closed-loop management of "discovery-feedback-correction" of problem data. To provide quantitative automatic data quality evaluation and report for promoting data quality improvement and designing quality evaluation system.

Thirdly, the traceability mechanism of data governance should be established. Focusing on the establishment of a closed-loop control system for data quality to quickly discover and solve the problem data, mining and analyzing the problem data in depth, introducing the necessary data quality control fields in the data modeling stage to realize traceability and feedback to the source of the problem data. The relevant basic functions include: accurately locating the source unit of the problem data, giving the classification and solution of the problem. It is suggested that the source unit be fed back with the problem data sheet and the solution of the problem be tracked. In addition, the workflow mechanism of closed-loop control of problem data is given.

Fourthly, data quality evaluation and improvement plan should be established. The main influencing factors of data quality in large data environment are analyzed. According to the four key characteristics of data quality: data consistency, data timeliness, and data integrity and data accuracy, data quality evaluation indexes are established to guide and assess the system data quality layer under large data environment. This paper studies the data quality evaluation model based on large data, realizes real-time and automatic processing of quality index calculation, statistical analysis and comprehensive evaluation, and meets the requirement of quantitative diagnosis and evaluation of data quality in dynamic and real-time system. It mainly includes data quality index definition model, data quality evaluation method and data quality diagnosis and evaluation results. Quantitative index definition model, mainly studies data quality hierarchical evaluation index tree design, index weight design and . index score calculation; data quality evaluation method research, mainly through a certain data algorithm and calculation rules to establish evaluation model, realize the automatic calculation and analysis of index weight and index score, and generate diagnosis and evaluation results. Data administrators regularize data quality auditing, quality alteration processing, data quality assessment and evaluation, feedback to business systems, monitor the whole process from data source to data storage on the ground, solve problems in data quality, improve data quality, and form closed-loop data management.

Finally, the visualization of data governance is realized. The data stored in business system has the remarkable characteristics of wide coverage, large amount of data and long storage time. With the advancement of the practical process of business system, it is urgent for business system to provide a multi-dimensional, multi-form and visualized data display platform to facilitate data mining and statistical analysis of the platform. According to business analysis and data display requirements, multi-dimensional data view can be established. Managers can visually display and analyze large-scale data stored in business systems in multi-dimensional and diversified ways according to needs, and assist management to make more accurate decisions based on statistical analysis results. Combination of Visual Display Platform for Business System.

5 The Framework of Big Data Governance for Full Service Unified Data Center of Power Grid

According to the characteristics and scenario requirement analysis of large data governance in power grid, a data governance framework is proposed from the perspective of innovation of large data application in power grid. The whole governance framework is shown in the Fig. 3.

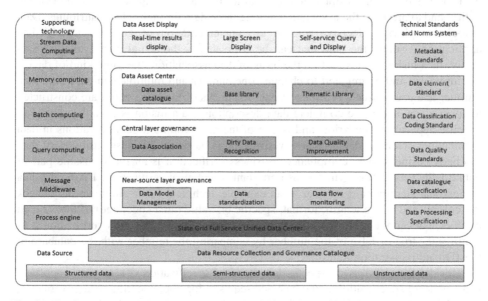

Fig. 3. The framework of big data governance for full service unified data center of power grid

The core idea of the proposed framework are near-source layer governance and central layer governance.

For near-source layer governance, first, in data modeling, master data and general data should be distinguished according to the degree of impact on business attributes, so as to meet the different requirements of data entities in business processes and data quality control. Master data refers to data that is critical to business impact, such as corporate registration information from industry, commerce, civil affairs and compilation; conversely, general data. At the same time, according to the impact of record attributes on data entity recognition, we should design weights for each attribute and distinguish between core and common attributes to meet the quality control requirements of deep data. Secondly, data standardization refers to format conversion, dictionary mapping and preliminary data specification of the collected source data (hereinafter referred to as source data) in accordance with metadata or metadata standard specifications. Thirdly, data verification is the core measure of data quality control. According to the existence of business relevance, it can be divided into technical verification and business verification. Among them, data technology checking refers to checking and checking data which does not involve business. That is to say, according to the data quality standard, using the data checking engine to check the quality of the source data such as format, range, repeatability, integrity and accuracy, so as to find and eliminate the problem data to the greatest extent and lay a solid foundation for the follow-up quality control. Fourthly, data quality assessment is the main output of source-affiliated governance, which is usually output in the form of data quality reports. Data quality report is composed of pre-defined quality evaluation indicators in the standard specification system, which can be used to feedback data governance stakeholders and trigger related business processes of data quality control.

For central layer governance, firstly, data association refers to the series of related data models based on business master data to form a holographic data portrait of the entity, and to preserve the association among these data through related attributes. Data association plays a decisive role in the implementation of government big data application. Usually the data that can be correlated is the actual data available. Secondly, data fusion means that on the basis of data association, the same kind of data is de-duplicated and aggregated to change "one number and multiple sources" into "one number and one source"; or different data fragments of the same entity are constructed to form a new and more complete data description. Data fusion is usually oriented to specific application scenarios, and is one of the most common data operations in data applications. Thirdly, data business verification is based on business attributes of data to check business logic compliance. Business verification is an indispensable part of data quality verification, which is as important as technical verification. Taking the data of personal identity card number as an example, technical verification can only check the compliance of the length, format, specific bit value (area code, age) of the ID card number, but cannot identify the true or false of the number; business verification is to confirm the true or false of the number by comparing the number with the database of the ID card registration authority.

Besides the above two aspects, data standard specification is also very important. Data standard specification is the basic prerequisite for implementing data governance, and plays a decisive role in the effectiveness of data governance. In short, there is no standard specification, no data governance; standard specification is incomplete, data governance is incomplete. For the big data of government affairs, the following norms need to be established and perfected in order to achieve good governance: first, metadata standards. It is necessary to establish metadata standards in an all-round way so as to cover the global data. Secondly, data element standard. It is necessary to establish data element standards selectively for main data entities. Third, data classification and coding standards. It is important to establish classification and coding standards for important data and to establish coding dictionary tables for basic data. Fourth, data catalogue specification. To the greatest extent possible, we should establish a unified directory specification for government data resources and standardize directory coding and operation to the greatest extent. Fifth, data quality standards. From the perspective of accuracy, compliance, consistency, repeatability, timeliness, integrity and other indicators, a comprehensive data quality standard should be established, and evaluation indicators and evaluation methods should be given. Sixth, data governance process specification. Processing is the guarantee of orderly governance. Data governance should be streamlined, corresponding process specifications should be established, and the layer of orderly governance should be improved by process specifications.

6 Conclusion

Based on the full-service unified data center of power Grid Company, this paper proposes a general frame-work of self-service power grid big data governance. In this paper, firstly, the related work of big data governance is reviewed; secondly, the architecture and characteristics of the grid company's full-service unified data center are analyzed; thirdly, the related requirements of self-service grid big data governance are analyzed; fourthly, the overall framework of self-service grid big data governance is proposed. Compared with other general big data governance framework, the proposed framework considers the specification of power grid as well as the features of self-service, making the framework more feasible.

Acknowledgments. This work was supported by the State Grid Corporation Science and Technology Project (Contract No.: SGLNXT00YJJS1800110).

References

1. Zaveri, A., Rula, A., Maurino, A., et al.: Quality assessment for linked data: a survey. Semant. Web **7**(1), 63–93 (2015)
2. Zhiqiang, W., Qinghai, Y.: Research on the quality and standardization of scientific data. Stan. Sci. **03**, 25–30 (2019)
3. Mohan, L., Jianzhong, L., Honghong, G.: Solution algorithm for data timeliness determination. J. Comput. Sci. **35**(11), 2348–2360 (2012)
4. Fan, W., Geerts, F.: Relative information completeness. ACM Trans. Database Syst. (TODS) **35**(4), 27 (2010)

5. Fan, W., Li, J., Ma, S., et al. Interaction between record matching and data repairing. In: Proceedings of the ACM SIGMOD International Conference on Management of Data, SIGMOD 2011, Athens, Greece, 12–16 June 2011. ACM (2011)

6. Fan, W., Ma, S., Tang, N., Yu, W.: Interaction between record matching and data repairing. J. Data Inf. Q. (JDIQ) **4**(4), 16 (2014)

7. Quercia, D., Hogan, B.: Proceedings of the Ninth International AAAI Conference on Web and Social Media, ICWSM 2015. AAAI Press (2015)

8. Ding, X., Wang, H., Zhang, X., et al.: Research on the relationship among various properties of data quality. J. Softw. **27**(7), 1626–1644 (2016)

9. Cheng, H., Feng, D., Shi, X., et al.: Data quality analysis and cleaning strategy for wireless sensor networks. EURASIP J. Wireless Commun. Netw. **2018**(1), 61 (2018)

10. Li, C., Liang, Yu., Yangyong, Z., et al.: Historical evolution and development trend of data quality. Comput. Sci. **45**(4), 1–10 (2018)

11. Saha, B., Srivastava, D.: Data quality: the other face of big data. In: IEEE International Conference on Data Engineering. IEEE (2014)

12. Wang, R.Y., Strong, D.M.: Beyond accuracy: what data quality means to data consumers. J. Manage. Inf. Syst. **12**(4), 5–33 (1996)

13. Sidi, F., Panahy, P.H.S., Affendey, L.S., et al.: Data quality: a survey of data quality dimensions. In: International Conference on Information Retrieval & Knowledge Management (2012)

14. Zhao, W., Li, C.: A review of the research on quality evaluation methods of associated data. Intell. Theory Pract., **39**(02), 134–138 + 128 (2016)

15. Liu, H.: Analysis of statistical data quality. In: International Joint Conference on Computational Sciences & Optimization. IEEE (2014)

16. Alpar, P., Winkelsträter, S.: Assessment of data quality in accounting data with association rules. Expert Syst. Appl. **41**(5), 2259–2268 (2014)

17. Song, C., Jing, W., Zeng, P., et al.: Energy consumption analysis of residential swimming pools for peak load shaving. Appl. Energy **220**, 176–191 (2018)

Data Cleaning Based on Multi-sensor Spatiotemporal Correlation

Baozhu Shao[1], Chunhe Song[2,3(✉)], Zhongfeng Wang[2,3], Zhexi Li[4], Shimao Yu[2,3], and Peng Zeng[2,3]

[1] Liaoning Electric Power Research Institute, State Grid Liaoning Electric Power Co., Ltd., Shenyang 110000, People's Republic of China
[2] Key Laboratory of Networked Control Systems, Shenyang Institute of Automation, Chinese Academy of Sciences, Shenyang 110016, People's Republic of China
songchunhe@sia.cn
[3] Institutes for Robotics and Intelligent Manufacturing, Chinese Academy of Sciences, Shenyang 110016, China
[4] Shenyang Power Supply Company, State Grid Liaoning Electric Power Co., Ltd., Shenyang 110000, People's Republic of China

Abstract. Sensor-based condition monitoring systems are becoming an important part of modern industry. However, the data collected from sensor nodes are usually unreliable and inaccurate. It is very critical to clean the sensor data before using them to detect actual events occurred in the physical world. Popular data cleaning methods, such as moving average and stacked denoise autoencoder, cannot meet the requirements of accuracy, energy efficiency or computation limitation in many sensor related applications. In this paper, we propose a data cleaning method based on multi-sensor spatiotemporal correlation. Specifically, we find out and repair the abnormal data according to the correlation of sensor data in adjacent time and adjacent space. Real data based simulation shows the effectiveness of our proposed method.

Keywords: Data cleaning · Spatiotemporal correlation · Sensor networks

1 Introduction

The development of modern network technology, especially the development of the Internet of Things (IoT), has made tremendous progress in industrial modernization. In particular, the sensor-based device condition monitoring system is becoming an important part of modern industry. In this kind of application, real time data mining of sensor data to promptly make intelligent decisions is essential [1–3]. However, the data collected from sensor nodes are usually unreliable and inaccurate due to the complex environments, hardware limitations, wireless interferences, etc., which further influence quality of raw data and aggregated results. Thus, it is extremely important to ensure the reliability and accuracy of sensor data before the decision-making process.

Many data cleaning approaches have been proposed, such as supervised neural network methods [5], unsupervised LOF algorithms [6–8], clustering algorithms [9, 10]

© ICST Institute for Computer Sciences, Social Informatics and Telecommunications Engineering 2019
Published by Springer Nature Switzerland AG 2019. All Rights Reserved
X. B. Zhai et al. (Eds.): MLICOM 2019, LNICST 294, pp. 235–243, 2019.
https://doi.org/10.1007/978-3-030-32388-2_20

and moving average [11]. Supervised algorithms usually require high computation capability and large storage space, which are not suitable for data cleaning of low-storage and low-power sensors. The unsupervised algorithms are designed to find a continuous period of abnormal data, which is not suitable to find the isolated abnormal point in the time series. Some time series based abnormal data detection algorithms also have high time and space complexity, which are not suitable for sensor network applications.

In many sensor-based applications, sensors are densely deployed and the sampling frequency of each sensor is high. The data of individual sensor usually have high temporal correlation, and the data of closed sensors usually have high spatial correlation. In this paper, we propose a multi-sensor based data cleaning approach based on the spatiotemporal correlation between sensor data, which can find and repair abnormal data efficiently. The time and space complexity of the proposed method are very low, so that the abnormal data can be found and repaired efficiently.

The remainder of this paper is organized as follows. In Sect. 2, we present the models and assumptions of this work. We analysis the problem and propose our algorithm in Sect. 3. Section 4 shows experimental results and analysis. Section 5 concludes this paper.

2   Models and Assumptions

We assume there are n sensors densely deployed in a surveillance region, each sensor reports the data in a small time-slot cycle and all sensors are time synchronous. In this case, the data reported from all sensors have temporal correlation and spatial correlation [12].

Let $x_{i,t}$ be a report from the sensor i at time t. Spatial correlation means that the data series of two sensors have similar trends if the two sensors are geographically closed to each other. For example, let $\{x_{1,t}, \ldots, x_{m,t}\}$ and $\{x_{1,s}, \ldots, x_{m,s}\}$ be normal data sets of m adjacent sensors at time t and s respectively. If the m adjacent sensors are closed enough, then there exists a parameter L and a small threshold σ, such that

$$L - \sigma \leq \{|x_{i,t} - x_{i,s}|\}_{1 \leq i \leq m} \leq L + \sigma. \tag{1}$$

Time correlation means that the data in a short period are usually similar with each other. For example, let $\{x_{m,t+1}, x_{m,t+2}, \ldots, x_{m,t+\Delta t}\}$ be a normal data set of the m-th sensor in Δt time slots. If Δt is small, then there exists a small threshold δ, such that

$$\max_{1 \leq i,j \leq \Delta t} \{|x_{m,i} - x_{m,j}|\} \leq \delta. \tag{2}$$

Sensors can produce abnormal data when working in unideal conditions. For example, high volatility, characterized by a sudden rise of variance in the data, can be caused by hardware failure or a weakening in battery supply. Single spikes, occasional unusually high or low readings occurred in a series of otherwise normal reading, can be caused by battery failure. Intense single spikes that occur with high frequency may indicate hardware malfunction [15].

Since the abnormal data is mainly generated by each sensor node itself, the abnormal data generated by different sensors have no correlation, thus we can detect the abnormal data according to the spatiotemporal correlation of the multiple sensors.

3 Problem Analysis and Algorithm Design

In this section, we discuss how to detect the abnormal data by spatiotemporal correlation and how to repair the abnormal data.

Let $X = \{X_1, X_2, \ldots, X_n\}$ be the collected data from n sensors in T time-slots, where $X_i = \{x_{i1}, x_{i2}, \ldots, x_{iT}\}^{\mathrm{T}}$ is the data set collected by sensor i and $\{\cdot\}^{\mathrm{T}}$ means the transpose of $\{\cdot\}$. The sequence of sensors is sorted according to the position of sensors, such that sensors with close serial numbers are also close to each other. Then temporal correlation refers to the relationship of the data in the column, while spatial correlation refers to the relationship of the data in the line.

Let

$$\Delta X = \{\Delta x_1, \Delta x_2, \ldots, \Delta x_{n-1}\},$$

where $\Delta x_i = \{\Delta x_{i1}, \Delta x_{i2}, \ldots, \Delta x_{iT}\}^{\mathrm{T}}$ and $\Delta x_{it} = |x_{i,t} - x_{i+1,t}|$. According to formula (1), if both $x_{i,t}$ and $x_{i+1,t}$ are normal data, then there exists a parameter L and a small threshold σ, such that $L - \sigma \leq \Delta x_{it} \leq L + \sigma$. Therefore, if Δx_{it} is not in the region $[L - \sigma, L + \sigma]$, then $x_{i,t}$ or $x_{i+1,t}$ may be abnormal data.

The parameter L is critical in this process. A general method to get L is to let it be the mean of Δx_i. However, when there are abnormal data, the average of Δx_i can be far away from the real gap between X_i and X_{i+1}. Then normal Δx_{it} may be not in $[L - \sigma, L + \sigma]$. To avoid this problem, we use the median of Δx_i instead of mean, since the abnormal data may cause large changes to the mean while have no impact to the median.

If $|x_{i,t} - x_{i+1,t}|$ is not in the region $[L - \sigma, L + \sigma]$, we need to determine which one of $x_{i,t}$ and $x_{i+1,t}$ is abnormal. According to formula (2), for adjacent timeslot t' of t, if $|x_{i,t} - x_{i,t'}|$ is bigger than the small threshold δ, $x_{i,t}$ may be abnormal data. However, if $x_{i,t'}$ is also abnormal, it will cause a false positive. To address this problem, we take a set of data with adjacent timeslots of t, say $x_{i,\Delta t}$, and compute the median $\overline{x_{i,\Delta t}}$ of $x_{i,\Delta t}$. Then if $|x_{i,t} - \overline{x_{i,\Delta t}}| > \delta$, we say $x_{i,t}$ is abnormal. When the abnormal data is detected, we can require the abnormal data by replacing the abnormal data with $\overline{x_{i,\Delta t}}$.

The pseudo code for the proposed method is shown in Algorithm 1. Firstly, the data set X of N sensors in T time slots are divided into several groups, where each group contains data set of N sensors in m time. Then the entire data set is divided into $num = \lceil T/m \rceil$ groups, and each group is a $m \times N$ matrix. For each $m \times N$ matrix, we calculate the differences between all adjacent columns to get the difference $m \times (N - 1)$ matrix D_k, and each D_k is a difference matrix of the X_k matrix. Secondly, for each column of D_k, we find its median L_{kj} and specify a threshold σ. For each matrix D_k, if

$|D_k[i][j] - L_{kj}| < \sigma$, the difference of $X_k[i,j]$ and $X_k[i,j+1]$ are normal, let $A_{ij} = 1$; if not, one of $X_k[i,j]$ and $X_k[i,j+1]$ are abnormal, let $A_{ij} = 0$. Thirdly, for the value of $A_{ij} = 1$, let $M_{ij} = \{X_k[i,j], X_k[i,j+1], \ldots, X_k[i,j+\lambda]\}$, and $m_{ij} = median(M_{ij})$. Compare $|X_k[i][j] - m_{ij}|$ with $|X_k[i+1][j] - m_{i+1,j}|$, if the former is greater than the latter, $X_k[i][j]$ is the abnormal value; otherwise, $X_k[i][j+1]$ is the abnormal value. Finally, for the data $X_k[i][j]$ judged to be abnormal values, the corresponding median m_{ij} is assigned to the value, and the repair is completed.

Algorithm 1 : Data cleaning algorithm

Input: data set $X = \{X_1, X_2, \ldots, X_n\}$, $X_i = \{x_{i1}, x_{i2}, \ldots, x_{iT}\}^{\mathrm{T}}$;Time series length of the matrix m; Threshold σ ; The length of the time series used to calculate the median λ

S1: Building matrix D ,let $D[i][j] = X[i][j+1] - X[i][j]$

S2: Let $num = \lceil T/m \rceil$, divide the matrix D into num small matrices $D_k, k = 1, 2, \ldots, num$. At the same time, the X matrix is re-divided into num matrices, and each D_k matrix is a difference matrix of the X_k matrix.

S3: **for** each matrix D_k , calculate the median L_{kj} of each column

    if $| D_k[i][j] - L_{kj} | < \sigma$,**return** $A[i][j] = 1$

S4: **for** each matrix D_k ,

    if $A[i][j] = 1$

    let $M_{ij} = \{X_k[i, j], X_k[i, j+1], \ldots, X_k[i, j+\lambda]\}$, $m_{ij} = median(M_{ij})$

    Compare $| X_k[i][j] - m_{ij} |$ with $| X_k[i+1][j] - m_{i+1, j} |$, if the former is greater than the latter, $X_k[i][j]$ is the abnormal value; otherwise, $X_k[i][j+1]$ is the abnormal value.

S5: For all the data $X_k[i][j]$ judged to be abnormal values, the corresponding median m_{ij} is assigned to the value, and the repair is completed.

We can see that the entire algorithm does not involve any complicated calculations, just some addition and subtraction of a matrix, so the time complexity of the algorithm is $O(n)$.

4   Experiment Analysis

We use the sensor data from Intel Labs to conduct experiments [14]. The data set contains temperature data collected by 53 sensors deployed at the Intel Berkeley Research Laboratory from February 28 to April 5, 2004. The sensor distribution is shown in Fig. 1. The sensor records data twice per second and collects time-stamped topology information every 31 s.

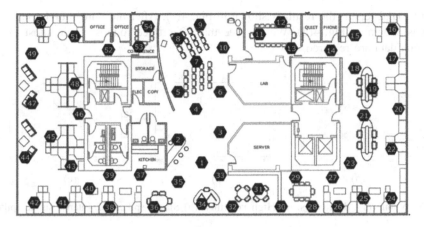

Fig. 1. The location of 54 sensors in the laboratory [14].

As shown in Fig. 2(a), from the normal data of 53 sensors in one day, we can see that they have similar trends. We take the sensor serial number as the x-axis and the temperature value as y-axis, and randomly take the data of 50 adjacent moments. As shown in Fig. 2(b), we can see that they have extremely similar trends. This shows that our algorithm based on spatiotemporal correlation is applicable. In the experiment, we let $m = 15$, $\sigma = 0.1$.

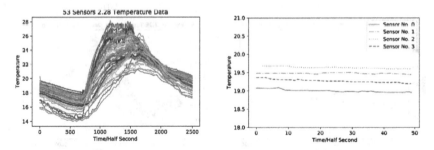

Fig. 2. Raw data of 53 sensors. (a) Spacial correlation (b) Temporal correlation

As discussed in Sect. 2, there are usually 3 types of abnormal data, as shown in Fig. 3. We add them to the raw data set as follows: 25% of data in 0–1000 time slots are replaced by the first type of abnormal data; 1% of data in 1000–2000 time slots are replaced by the second type of abnormal data; 20% of data in 2000–2500 time slots are replaced by the third type of abnormal data. The data set with abnormal data is shown in Fig. 4(a). After the first round repair, the result is shown in Fig. 4(b). After the second round repair, the result is shown in Fig. 4(c). After the third round repair, the result is shown in Fig. 4(d). We can see that after three rounds repair, most of the abnormal data are repaired.

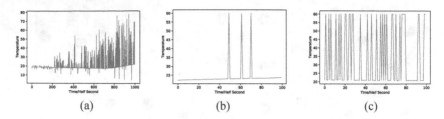

(a)   (b)   (c)

Fig. 3. 3 abnormal data types. (a) High volatility; (b) Single spikes; (c) Intense single spikes.

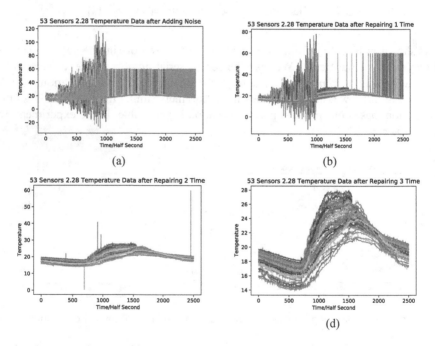

Fig. 4. The sensor data set with abnormal data and the three round repaired data. (a) The data set of 53 sensors after adding abnormal data; (b) The data set after the first round repair; (c) The data set after the second round repair; (d) The data set after the third round repair.

Figure 5 shows the raw data of the No. 1 sensor and the data after three repairs. We can see the repair effect of the algorithm more clearly.

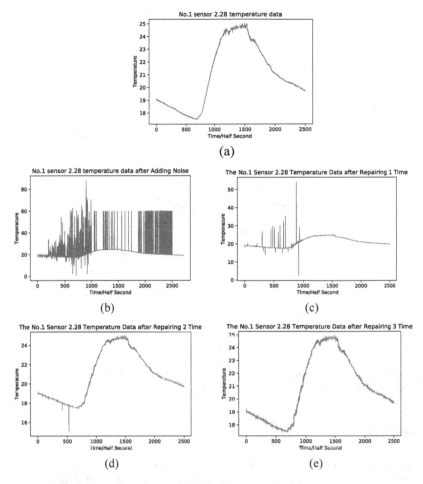

Fig. 5. The raw data of the No. 1 sensor and the data after three round repairs. (a) The raw sensor data; (b) Sensor data with abnormal data; (c) The sensor data after the first round repair; (d) The sensor data after the second round repair; (e) The sensor data after the third round repair.

We use the mean absolute error (MAE) to measure the accuracy of the algorithm. The smaller the MAE, the higher accuracy of the algorithm.

$$MAE = \frac{1}{T}\sum_{t=1}^{T}(\bar{x}_t - x_t), \qquad (2)$$

where x_t is the raw dataset data and $\bar{x}_t$ is the repaired dataset data.

We compare our method (MSC) with moving smoothing [16] and stacked denoise autoencoder (SDAE) [17]. The repair results of the three kinds of noise are shown in Fig. 6. we can see that our method always has the smallest MAE.

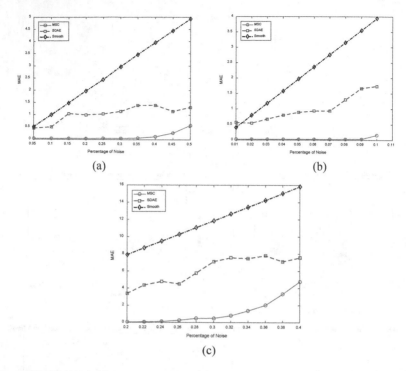

Fig. 6. (a) MAE with the first type of abnormal data; (b) MAE with the second type of abnormal data; (c) MAE with the third type of abnormal data.

5   Conclusion

This paper proposes a multi-sensor abnormal data detection method based on temporal and spatial correlation, which can indicate and repair the abnormal data according to the correlation of sensor data in adjacent time and adjacent space. We then conduct experiments with sensor data from Intel Labs to verify the effectiveness of our approach.

Acknowledgments. This work was supported by the State Grid Corporation Science and Technology Project (Contract No.: SG2NK00DWJS1800123).

References

1. Pan, S.K., Jiang, J.A., Chen, C.P.: Conductor temperature estimation using the hadoop mapreduce framework for smart grid applications. In: 2014 IEEE International Conference of High Performance Computing and Communications (2014)
2. Ganyun, L.V., Haozhong, C., Haibao, Z., Lixin, D.: Fault diagnosis of power transformer based on multi-layer SVM classifier. Electr. Power Syst. Res. **74**(1), 1–7 (2005)

3. Shi, W., Zhu, Y., Zhang, J., et al.: Improving power grid monitoring data quality: an efficient machine learning framework for missing data prediction. In: IEEE Computer Society, pp. 417–422 (2015)
4. Wang, Q., Kundur, D., Yuan, H., Liu, Y., Lu, J., Ma, Z.: Noise suppression of corona current measurement from HVdc transmission lines. IEEE Trans. Instrum. Meas. **65**(2), 264–275 (2016)
5. M. Yang and J. Ma.: Data completing of missing wind power data based on adaptive BP neural network. In:Proc. PMAPS pp. 1–6. Oct, Location (2016)
6. Breunig, M.M., Kriegel, H.P., Ng, R.T.: LOF: identifying density-based local outliers. In: ACM Sigmod International Conference on Management of Data, pp. 93–104 (2000)
7. Kriegel, H.P., Schubert, E., Zimek, A.: LoOP: local outlier probabilities, pp. 1649–1652 (2009)
8. Salehi, M., et al.: Fast memory efficient local outlier detection in data streams. In: IEEE Transactions on Knowledge and Data Engineering, pp. 1–1 (2016)
9. Christopher, T., Divya, M.T.: A comparative analysis of hierarchical and partitioning clustering algorithms for outlier detection in data streams. Int. J. Adv. Res. Comput. Commun. Eng. (2015)
10. Gurav, R.B., Rangdale, S.: Hybrid approach for outlier detection in high dimensional dataset. Int. J. Sci. Res. **3** (2014)
11. Chen, J., Li, W., Lau, A., Cao, J., Wang, K.: Automated load curve data cleansing in power systems. IEEE Trans. Smart Grid **1**(2), 213–221 (2010)
12. He, W., Qiao, P.L., Zhou, Z.J., et al.: A new belief-rule-based method for fault diagnosis of wireless sensor network. IEEE Access. **6**, 9404–9419 (2018)
13. Chen, P.Y., Yang, S., Mccann, J.A.: Distributed real-time anomaly detection in networked industrial sensing systems. IEEE Trans. Ind. Electr. **65**(6), 3832–3842 (2015)
14. Intel Lab Data. http://db.lcs.mit.edu/labdata/labdata.html
15. Ni, K., et al.: Sensor network data fault types. ACM Trans. Sens. Netw. **5**(3), 25:1–25:29 (2009)
16. Jeffery, S.R., Alonso, G., Franklin, M.J., Hong, W., Widom, J.: Declarative support for sensor data cleaning. In: Proceedings of PerCom (2006)
17. Dai, J., Song, H., Sheng, G., et al.: Cleaning method for status monitoring data of power equipment based on stacked denoising autoencoders. IEEE Access. **PP**(99):1 (2017)

Distributed Hierarchical Fault Diagnosis Based on Sparse Auto-Encoder and Random Forest

Tong Li[1], Chunhe Song[2,3]([⊠]), Yang Liu[1], Zhongfeng Wang[2,3],
Shimao Yu[2,3], and Shanting Su[4]

[1] Liaoning Electric Power Research Institute, State Grid Liaoning Electric
Power Co., Ltd., Shenyang 110000, People's Republic of China
[2] Key Laboratory of Networked Control Systems, Shenyang Institute
of Automation, Chinese Academy of Sciences, Shenyang 110016,
People's Republic of China
songchunhe@sia.cn
[3] Institutes for Robotics and Intelligent Manufacturing,
Chinese Academy of Sciences, Shenyang 110016, China
[4] Nanjing University of Aeronautics and Astronautics, Nanjing, China

Abstract. For the diagnosis of large-scale local devices, the traditional centralized fault diagnosis systems are becoming incompetent to meet the
requirement of real-time monitoring. This paper proposes the Distributed hierarchical Fault Diagnosis System (DFDS). Specifically, DFDS implements fault
monitoring by an improved Sparse Auto-Encoder (SAE) on the monitor layer,
classifies faults and identifies unknown faults by an improved random forest on
the classification layer, learns new knowledge and updates the system on the
decision layer. We apply DFDS in the laboratory data of Case Western Reserve
University to verify the efficiency of the proposed system. The experimental
results show that our method can accurately detect the fault and accurately
identify the fault type.

Keywords: Sparse auto-encoder · Distributed fault diagnosis · Fault
classification · Random forest

1 Introduction

Condition monitoring is essential for safe and reliable working operation of electric
power system such as transformer, GIS and High voltage circuit breaker. In recent
years, artificial intelligence (AI) technology has developed rapidly, and many AI based
methods have been developed to solve equipment failure problems such as neural
networks [1, 2], fault trees [3, 4], fuzzy theory [5, 6] and deep learning [7–9].

The traditional fault diagnosis method generally collects raw device information of
multiple local sensors and uploads them to the terminal device. The terminal device
extracts the original device signal characteristics and performs intelligent diagnosis.
The diagnostic complexity of this process is usually high and takes a lot of time. In
addition, each device has different faults and different fault handling methods. In this
case, the fault diagnosis system is required to identify the fault on each device to

© ICST Institute for Computer Sciences, Social Informatics and Telecommunications Engineering 2019
Published by Springer Nature Switzerland AG 2019. All Rights Reserved
X. B. Zhai et al. (Eds.): MLICOM 2019, LNICST 294, pp. 244–255, 2019.
https://doi.org/10.1007/978-3-030-32388-2_21

achieve the purpose of dynamic real-time monitoring. After the fault is identified, it can be processed in time. The traditional centralized fault diagnosis system cannot meet the above challenges.

This paper proposes a distributed artificial intelligence fault diagnosis system that is superior to the traditional centralized fault diagnosis system in large-scale equipment fault diagnosis. The proposed multi-level hierarchical fault diagnosis model is to monitor the original information in real time through the Sparse Auto-Encoder [16] (SAE) on the local monitoring layer (i.e., each device sensor), and report the fault signal for further processing. The improved random forest model is used in the fault classification layer to classify the detected faults and identify the unknown faults, which are uploaded to the decision-making layer for further processing. In summary, the contributions of this article are as follows:

(1) A novel distributed fault diagnosis framework and its implementation are proposed, which map multiple stages of device diagnosis to a distributed multi-level hierarchy.
(2) The fault monitoring model FM-SAE is embedded on the local device for large-scale real-time monitoring.
(3) Accurate classification of known faults and identification of unknown faults is achieved through an improved random forest model.

The rest of this paper is organized as follows. Section 2 outlines the architecture of the proposed distributed hierarchical fault diagnosis system. Section 3 introduces the implementation of the fault monitoring function of the model. Section 4 introduces the implementation of fault classification and update functions. Section 5 shows experimental results and analysis. Section 6 concludes this paper.

2 System Outline

In this section, we outline the architecture of the proposed Distributed hierarchical Fault Diagnosis System (DFDS) and describe how the system completes the process of device fault diagnosis through inter-level cooperation.

Equipment fault diagnosis is generally divided into a series of processes such as feature extraction, state detection, and fault classification. Due to the wide distribution of equipment, in order to provide timely fault monitoring for these devices, the primary layer of DFDS should be distributed on each device to reduce the complexity of the entire diagnostic process by making decisions directly on the original signal. Considering the diversity of equipment failures, if necessary, the secondary diagnostic layer subsystems can cooperate with each other and jointly diagnose, and the detected unknown faults should be reported to the superior diagnostic layer in time. Since the faults of each device are different, and the identified unknown faults are different, the third-level diagnostic layer should process the unknown faults in time to update the diagnostic knowledge of the secondary diagnostic layer subsystem, thereby improving the overall diagnostic level.

Based on the above starting point, the DFDS diagnostic system is divided into three layers: local monitoring layer, fault classification layer and decision-making layer.

Each of the three layers processes the respective tasks, and simultaneously communicates with each other to achieve the purpose of fault diagnosis. As shown in Fig. 1:

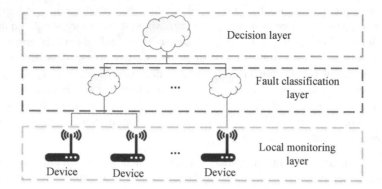

Fig. 1. The framework of DFDS.

In DFDS, The local monitoring layer is mainly responsible for detecting faults and reporting them to the fault classification layer in time. Directly process the original signal through the improved Fault Diagnosis Sparse Auto-Encoder (FM-SAE) model to determine if the device is faulty. Real-time monitoring of local devices is implemented without sending any information to the higher level diagnostic layer unless a fault signal is detected. For the detected fault signal, send it to the fault classification layer.

The fault classification layer is responsible for feature extraction of the received signals, classifying the faults and identifying unknown faults by improving the random forest. The fault classification layer may separately manage the local devices by multiple terminal devices, or may simultaneously manage multiple local devices by only one terminal device. They form multiple task nodes on the same level, they deal with problems independently of each other and are related to each other on the model, reducing the complexity of the diagnostic task.

The decision layer is responsible for the self-learning and updating of the entire system knowledge. By processing the unknown fault signal sent from the fault classification layer, learn new knowledge and update the system in real time.

DFDS completes the entire diagnostic process by implementing fault monitoring locally, classifying and updating at the terminal. Its various levels process their own tasks and coordinate with each other to achieve maximum fault diagnosis accuracy.

3   Fault Monitoring

This section describes the first phase of the model, the fault monitoring function, which is implemented by the local monitoring layer based on the improved sparse auto-encoder FM-SAE.

3.1   Theory of the Sparse Auto-Encoder Algorithm

The automatic encoder is a classic neural network whose purpose is to obtain the reduced-dimensional expression of the data $H = \{h_1, h_2, ..., h_m\}$ through training based on the input data set $X = \{x_1, x_2, ..., x_m\}$. This dimension-reduced feature is processed so that it can express the input better, and it has good performance in tasks such as classification monitoring [10–12]. The network structure of a single hidden layer AE is shown in Fig. 2, where the self-encoder is divided into two parts, the encoder and the decoder.

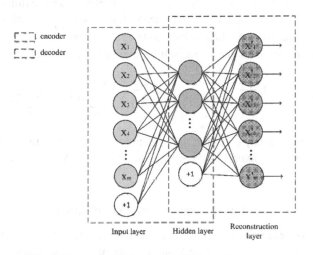

Fig. 2. A single hidden layer AE network structure.

Assume $a_i^{(l+1)}$ represents the activation value of the i-th neuron in the $(l + 1)$-th layer of the self-encoding neural network, then $a_i^{l+1} = f\left(z_i^{(l+1)}\right)$, $f(z)$ is the neuron activation function, z_i^{l+1} is the weighted sum of the input values of the i-th neuron in the $(l + 1)$-th layer, and its expression is:

$$z_i^{l+1} = \sum_{j=1}^{S_l} w_{ij}^{(l)} x_j + b_i^l, \tag{1}$$

where w_{ij}^l represents the weight coefficient connecting the j-th neuron of the l-th layer and the i-th neuron of the $(l + 1)$-th layer, $b_i^{(l)}$ represents the bias term of the $(i + 1)$-th neuron of the $(l + 1)$-th layer, S_l is the number of neurons in the l-th layer. The neuron activation function often uses the sigmoid function $f(z) = \frac{1}{1+e^{-z}}$ whose value range is [0, 1], or use the *tanh* function $f(z) = \frac{e^z-e^{-z}}{e^z+e^{-z}}$ whose value is [− 1, 1].

Adding a sparsity limit to the self-encoder, that is, at the same time, only some hidden layer nodes are 'active', thus obtaining a sparse self-encoder. Based on this, KL dispersion is introduced to measure the similarity between the average activation output of a hidden layer node and the set sparsity ρ:

$$KL(\rho\|\hat{\rho}_j) = \rho \log \frac{\rho}{\hat{\rho}_j} + (1 - \rho) \log \frac{1 - \rho}{1 - \hat{\rho}_j}, \tag{2}$$

where $\hat{\rho}_j = \frac{1}{m} \sum_{i=1}^{m} \left[a_j x^{(i)}\right]$, m is the number of training samples, $a_j x^{(i)}$ is the corresponding output of the j-th node of the hidden layer for i samples. In general we set the sparse factor $\rho = 0.05$ or 0.1. The larger the KL dispersion, the larger the difference between ρ and $\hat{\rho}_j$, and the KL dispersion equal to 0 means that the two are completely equal, that is, $\rho = \hat{\rho}_j$. Therefore, we can add KL dispersion as a regular term to the loss function to constrain the sparse rows of the entire self-encoder network:

$$J_{sparse}(W,b) = \frac{1}{m} \sum_{i=1}^{m} \frac{1}{2} \|x_i - \hat{x}_i\|^2 + \frac{\lambda}{2} \sum_{l=1}^{n_{l-1}} \sum_{i=1}^{S_l} \sum_{j=1}^{S_{l+1}} W_l^2 + \beta \sum_{j=1}^{S_2} KL(\rho\|\hat{\rho}_j), \tag{3}$$

where λ is the weight decay constant; n_l is the number of neural network layers; β is the coefficient that controls the unit of the sparse constraint, and S_2 is the number of hidden layer units.

3.2   The Implementation of Emerging New Classification

Sparse Auto-encoder automatically learns features from unlabeled data and gives better characterization than raw data. Based on this, we use sparse autoencoder to learn features from the original signal of the normal device and send the trained model to the local device. Then the device identifies the test sample according to the model. If the characteristics of the sample have a significant error compared to the characteristics of the normal signal, the sample is considered to be a fault signal and sent to the superior diagnostic layer.

Assume $X = \{(x_i, y_i)\}_{i=1}^{n}$, $x_i = \{t_{ij}\}_{j=1}^{c}$ is the training sample data set, where x_i represents the i-th training data, $y_i \in Y = \{1\}$ is the x_i corresponding label (note that only the normal device data is included in X), the x_i feature dimension is c, t_{ij} represents the j-th feature of the data x_i. $\hat{X} = \{(\hat{x}_i, y_i)\}_{i=1}^{n}$, $\hat{x}_i = \{h_{ij}\}_{j=1}^{v}$ is the SAE output data set of the training sample, where $\hat{x}_i$ represents the i-th output data, the $\hat{x}_i$ feature dimension is v, and h_{ij} represents the j-th feature of the data x_i; $X' = \{(x_i', y_i')\}_{i=1}^{m}$, $x_i' = \{t_{ij}'\}_{j=1}^{c}$ is the test sample data set, where x_i' represents the i-th test data, $y_i' \in Y = \{1, 2, \ldots, K\}(K > 1)$ is the corresponding label. Calculate the output feature center M_j of the normal class:

$$M_j = \frac{1}{n} \sum_{i}^{n} h_{ij} \tag{4}$$

The wave matrix D of the i-th data is constructed by calculating the Euclidean distance between h_{ij} and M_j:

$$d_{ij} = \left\| h_{ij} - M_j \right\| \tag{5}$$

Calculate the feature threshold matrix θ_j:

$$\theta_j = \frac{1}{n} \sum_{i}^{n} d_{ij} \tag{6}$$

$$\text{If } h'_{ij} - M_j > k\theta_j,\ y'_i \neq 1,\ else\ y'_i = 1$$

where k is the control threshold.

4 Fault Classification and Update Implementation

This section describes the model fault classification and update function. The fault classification of the model is responsible from the fault classification layer. This layer receives the fault data transmitted by the local monitoring layer. The data includes known faults and unknown faults. The fault classification layer is responsible for classifying known faults and identifying unknown faults. For the detected unknown faults, upload them to the decision-making layer, and the decision-making layer specifically identifies the unknown fault and makes an update decision.

4.1 Implementation of the Fault Classification Layer

Since many previous work showed that completely random trees have been successfully applied to the classification problem [13–15]. We improved the random forest model to implement the function of the fault classification layer.

Assume $X = \{(x_i, y_i)\}_{i=1}^{n}$ is the training sample data set, Where x_i represents the i-th training data, $y_i \in Y = \{1, 2, 3, \ldots, K\}$ is the corresponding label; $X' = \{(x'_i, y'_i)\}_{i=1}^{m}$ is the test sample data set, where x'_i represents the i-th test data, $y'_i \in Y = \{1, 2, \ldots, M\}(M > K)$ is the corresponding label; Randomly selecting a plurality of sample data from the training set X, and then randomly selecting one feature value of the data to divide the sample data into two subtrees, repeating the above two steps to continuously construct the child node until the number of data of the child node reaches the upper limit, then the construction of one tree is complete. Let $A = (x_1, x_2, x_3, \ldots, x_m)$ be the training instances that fall into the same leaf node, then build the ball O for set A, The center of A is defined as: $c = \frac{1}{m} \sum_{x \in A} x$, the radius of the ball O centered on c: $r = dist(c, e)$, where e is the farthest example of the distance c in A, and the $label(O)$ is the label that appears the most in set A. During testing, the test instances that fell into these balls were known fault, and the test instances that fell outside the ball were unknown fault.

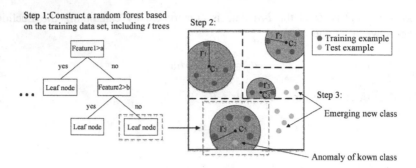

Fig. 3. The process of constructing and classifying a complete random tree.

Figure 3 shows the process of constructing and classifying a complete random tree:

Step1: Obtain a random forest model F according to the training data set X, which includes t random trees $\{f_1, f_2, f_3, \ldots, f_t\}$;

Step2: In each tree, build a ball O for an instance that falls into the same leaf node;

Step3: For test case x'_i, x'_i is defined in the category tag of the j-th tree as:

$$label(x'_i) = V_{\max}\left(\{f_j(x'_i)\}_{j=1}^t\right),$$

$$f_j(x'_i) = \begin{cases} label(O) & \text{if } x'_i \text{ falls in a spherical area } O \\ new & else \end{cases} \tag{7}$$

where $f_j(x'_i)$ represents the label class calculated by the j-th tree for the input data x'_i, which divides the x'_i into known or unknown classes. The function $V_{\max}\left(\{f_j(x'_i)\}_{j=1}^t\right)$ indicates that the label category with the highest frequency of occurrence calculated by all trees is output. If $label(x'_i) = new$, put the test instance into the buffer until the number of buffers reaches the upper limit and send it to the decision-making layer.

4.2   Decision-Making Layer Implementation

The unknown fault data uploaded by the fault classification layer may contain multiple unknown faults. The decision-making layer needs to detect it. If the data contains multiple unknown faults, correctly classify them, learn their characteristics and update the fault classification layer model.

For data set $S = \{x_i\}_{i=1}^n$ containing multiple unknown faults, we use the K-means clustering algorithm to cluster them. Since the K-means clustering algorithm requires the user to specify the number of clusters, the number of clusters that are too large or too small will make the data classification unreliable. Therefore, finding the optimal number of clusters is the key to achieving classification.

We use the Silhouette Coefficient to determine the number of clusters. The Silhouette Coefficient is a cluster validity index that combines the degree of agglomeration a_i and the degree of separation b_i, where b_i is the average distance of all other instances in the cluster to which the *i-th* instance belongs, and b_i is the average distance from the *i-th* instance to all instances in any cluster that does not contain the instance, then the Silhouette Coefficient of the *i-th* instance is $s_i = \frac{(b_i - a_i)}{\max(a_i, b_i)}$, the value is $[-1, 1]$, the larger the value, the better the clustering effect.

The specific classification processes are as follows:

(1) Determine the number of clusters as $N = 1 - \sigma\sqrt{n}$, n is the number of cluster data, σ is the control threshold.

(2) For the *N-th* cluster, calculate the contour coefficient of each data, and obtain $s(N) = \frac{1}{n}\sum_{i=1}^{n} s_i$, then the optimal number of clusters is *bestn* $= \arg\max(s(N))$.

(3) Output k-means clustering results according to *bestn*.

5 Experimental Results and Analysis

This paper uses the fan end bearing vibration data released by the Case Western Reserve University Bearing Experimental Center as the fault data for model verification. The data sampling frequency is 12 kHz. Six data types included in the data, which are the normal state, the inner ring fault F1, the rolling element fault F2, the central fault of the outer ring corresponding to the load zone F3, the central orthogonal fault of the outer ring corresponding load zone F4, and the center opposite fault of the outer ring corresponding load zone F5.

From the original signal, we collected 500 segments for each fault, each segment contains 1024 data points. Therefore each type of signal is represented by 500 data, and a total of 3000 data are considered for analysis.

The size of the original data in the high dimensional space is 3000×1024.

For the local detection layer, we used a subset of 70% normal data for training to obtain the FM-SAE diagnostic model. We will have 30% normal data set and F1 as test set 1; 30% normal data set, F1 and F2 as test set 2; 30% normal data set, F1, F2 and F3 as test set 3; 30% normal data set, F1, F2, F3 and F4 as test set 4; 30% normal data set, F1, F2, F3, F4 and F5 as test set 5. Figure 4 shows that after learning the characteristics of normal data, the FM-SAE separately characterizes the normal data and the fault data in the test set. Figure 4(a) (b) (c) show the fluctuations of three kinds of raw data, Fig. 4 (e) shows the normal data characteristic characterized by FM-SAE, and Fig. 4(f) (g) are the two fault data features characterized by FM-SAE. For a more intuitive display and normal data, the characteristics are shown in red. We can see that after learning the normal data characteristics, FM-SAE can easily distinguish it from other faults because their characteristics are very different.

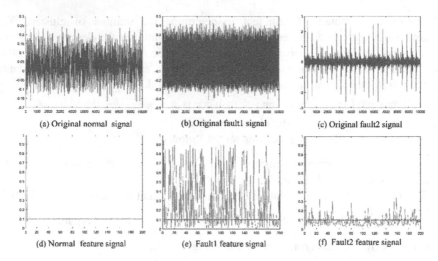

(a) Original normal signal   (b) Original fault1 signal   (c) Original fault2 signal

(d) Normal feature signal   (e) Fault1 feature signal   (f) Fault2 feature signal

Fig. 4. Characterize normal data and fault data characteristics.

The network structure definition of FM-SAE consists of two hidden layers whose hidden layers contain 500 and 200 nodes, respectively. Figure 5 shows the identification fault accuracy curve with two methods (SAE and FM-SAE for monitoring anomalies). For SAE, it needs to learn the characteristics of all the faults to be classified, and classify it on this basis, which is not feasible in practical use. In the case of an increase in the number of faults, we can see that the classification accuracy is significantly reduced, because it is wrongly classified fault. FM-SAE only needs to learn normal data characteristics, and the classification accuracy remains basically the same when the type of failure increases.

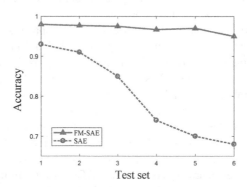

Fig. 5. Identification fault accuracy curve of two methods.

For the fault classification layer, we extract all the original fault data features, including the mean, standard deviation, peak, skewness, wave factor, crest factor and pulse factor, the feature data set size is 2500 × 6. Using 70% of F1, F2 fault characterization data for training to obtain a random forest model, leaving 30% of F1, F2 fault data and other fault data for testing. We will extract 70% F1, F2, F3 as the training set; extract the remaining 30% F1 as test set 1, remaining 30% F1 and all F4 as test set 2, remaining 30% F1 and all F4, F5 as test set 3, remaining 30% F1, F2 and all F4, F5 as test set 4, remaining 30% F1, F2, F3 and all F4, F5 as test set 4.

In order to verify the effectiveness of the improved random forest model classification in the fault classification layer, the effects of changing the number of trees and the number of fault types included in the unknown data set on the accuracy of fault classification detection are observed. During the experiment, other parameters are set unchanged. The experimental results are shown in Fig. 6. As shown in Fig. 6(a), the accuracy of the fault detection classification increases with the number of trees. When the number of trees exceeds 60, the accuracy of the fault detection classification increases slowly. From Fig. 6(b), in the case of five kinds of tests involving different types of faults, the fault classification accuracy rate is basically maintained above 92%.

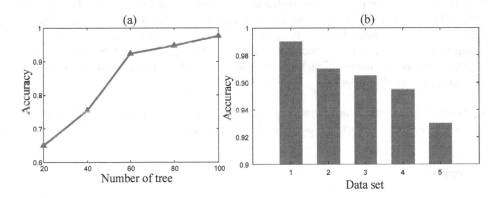

Fig. 6. Relationship between model parameter changes and fault classification accuracy.

For the decision-making layer, we use the three fault data sets F1, F2, and F3 to consider the case where N is equal to 1 to 20, cluster each N value and find the corresponding Silhouette Coefficient. Figure 7 shows the relationship between N and the Silhouette Coefficient. When the data is clustered into three categories, the Silhouette Coefficient is the highest.

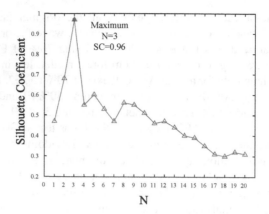

Fig. 7. The relationship between N and the Silhouette Coefficient.

6   Conclusion

In this paper, we propose a new distributed multi-level hierarchical fault diagnosis system based on SAE and random forest, called DFDS, for real-time monitoring of equipment. It can correctly classify faults and identify unknown faults while monitoring faults. Then, we verified the effectiveness of the system through experiments and evaluated the performance of each part to show the validity of the model. It provides new ideas for troubleshooting.

Acknowledgments. This work was supported by the State Grid Corporation Science and Technology Project (Contract No.: SG2NK00DWJS1800123).

References

1. Guoqian, J., Haibo, H., Jun, Y., et al.: Multiscale convolutional neural networks for fault diagnosis of wind turbine gearbox. IEEE Trans. Ind. Electr. **66**, 3196–3207 (2018)
2. Ince, T., et al.: Real-time motor fault detection by 1d convolutional neural networks. IEEE Trans. Ind. Electr. **63**, 7067–7075 (2016)
3. Tian, W.: Fault diagnosis of airborne equipment based on grey correlation fault tree identification method. In: World Congress on Intelligent Control & Automation IEEE (2008)
4. Yuliang, C., Tiejun, Z.: Research on the application of fuzzy fault tree analysis method in the machinery equipment fault diagnosis (2010)
5. Hong, G., Chen, X., Xue, X., et al.: Expert systems for fault diagnosis integrating neural network and fuzzy inference. In: International Conference on Information Technology (2011)
6. Lei, Z., et al.: Complex method of comprehensively evaluation and fault diagnosis in gun control system based on fuzzy reasoning. In: 11th International Conference on Electronic Measurement & Instruments. IEEE (2013)
7. Hu, Q., Zhang, R., Zhou, Y.: Transfer learning for short-term wind speed prediction with deep neural networks. Renewable Energy **85**, 83–95 (2016)

8. Chen, Z., Li, Z.: Research on fault diagnosis method of rotating machinery based on deep learning. In: 2017 Prognostics and System Health Management Conference (PHM-Harbin) (2017)
9. Xiuli, L., Xiaoli, X.: Fault diagnosis method of wind turbine gearbox based on deep belief network. Renewable Energy Res. (2017)
10. Qi, Y., Shen, C., Wang, D., et al.: Stacked sparse autoencoder-based deep network for fault diagnosis of rotating machinery. IEEE Access **5**, 15066–15079 (2017)
11. Chen, K., Hu, J., He, J.: Detection and classification of transmission line faults based on unsupervised feature learning and convolutional sparse autoencoder. IEEE Trans. Smart Grid **3**(9), 1748–1758 (2018)
12. Chen, Z., Li, W.: Multisensor feature fusion for bearing fault diagnosis using sparse autoencoder and deep belief network. IEEE Trans. Instrum. Measur. **66**, 1–10 (2017)
13. Yu, K., et al.: Classification with streaming features: an emerging-pattern mining ap-proach. ACM Trans. Knowl. Disc. Data **9**(4), 1–31 (2015)
14. Debarr, D., Ramanathan, V., Wechsler, H.: Phishing detection using traffic behavior, spectral clustering, and random forests. In: IEEE International Conference on Intelligence and Security Informatics IEEE (2013)
15. Zhang, M., Yian, L.: Signal sorting using teaching-learning-based optimization and random forest. In: 17th International Symposium on Distributed Computing and Applications for Business Engineering and Science (DCABES), IEEE Computer Society (2018)
16. Hinton, G.E., Salakhutdinov, R.R.: Reducing the dimensionality of data with neural networks. Science **313**(5786), 504–507 (2006)

A Data Quality Improvement Method Based on the Greedy Algorithm

Zhongfeng Wang[1,2], Yatong Fu[1,2], Chunhe Song[1,2(✉)], Weichun Ge[3],
Lin Qiao[3], and Hongyu Zhang[3]

[1] Key Laboratory of Networked Control Systems,
Shenyang Institute of Automation, Chinese Academy of Sciences,
Shenyang 110016, People's Republic of China
songchunhe@sia.cn
[2] Institutes for Robotics and Intelligent Manufacturing,
Chinese Academy of Sciences, Shenyang 110016, China
[3] State Grid Liaoning Electric Power Co., Ltd., Shenyang 110000,
People's Republic of China

Abstract. High-quality data is very important for data analysis and mining. Data quality can be indicated by many indicators, and some methods have been proposed for data quality improvement by improving one or more data quality indicators. However, there is few work to discuss the impact of the processing order of data quality indicators on the overall data quality. In this paper, first, some data quality indicators and their improvement methods are given; second, the impact of the processing order of data quality indicators on the overall data quality is discussed, and then a novel data quality improvement method based on the greedy algorithm is proposed. Experiments have been shown that the proposed method can improves the data quality while reducing the time and computational costs.

Keywords: Data quality · Improvement order · Greedy algorithm

1 Introduction

With the rapid development of Internet and information technology, data has become an important asset and competitive resource of enterprises. Almost all industries can benefit from data, but the problems of missing key fields, too much data noise and confused data classification in the original data make the quality of the original data too low. Low-quality data will directly affect the value of data analysis and mining. Data quality problems may occur in all stages of data acquisition and storage. How to effectively improve data quality has always been a difficult problem to solve. There are three main reasons. One is the lack of a standard definition of data quality. All walks of life have different understandings and needs for data quality. It is difficult to form a standardized and unified data quality standard. Secondly, it is difficult to determine data quality indicators. Data quality indicators are the process of quantifying data quality. Now the research on data quality indicators only focuses on a specific field, and there is no universal evaluation framework. Thirdly, data quality indicators are not independent,

X. B. Zhai et al. (Eds.): MLICOM 2019, LNICST 294, pp. 256–266, 2019.
https://doi.org/10.1007/978-3-030-32388-2_22

and the improvement of one data quality indicator may result in the reduction of another data quality indicator. How to determine an efficient data quality improvement strategy is a problem to be studied at present.

Data quality has already attracted extensive attention of researchers, and the research on data quality indicators is becoming more and more mature. However, the research on establishing efficient and reasonable data processing order based on data quality indicators is at an early stage. At present, the research on data quality indicators mainly focuses on the correlation between different indicators, but the correlation between indicators is the follow-up. However, it is difficult to prove the benefits of data processing. In determining the order of data processing, the current research mostly adopts traversal enumeration, which is a relatively inefficient method. In view of the current research situation, this paper first summarizes the commonly used indicators for data quality quantification and the methods used to improve each indicator; secondly, it analyses the impact of data quality improvement execution order on the overall data quality; finally, a greedy algorithm for data quality improvement is proposed, and an efficient and reasonable data processing order is determined. The validity of the data processing order is proved by simulation experiments.

The rest of this paper is organized as follows. Section 2 outlines the related works. Section 3 introduces data quality and data quality improvement methods. Section 4 analyzes the impact of the order on data quality improvement. Section 5 shows experimental results and analysis. Section 6 concludes this paper.

2   Related Works

In the field of data quality, Cai et al. have made a very detailed study of the history of data quality [1]. Researchers began to study data quality in the 1970s. At that time, although there was no knowledge system of data quality, they have found that poor quality data will have a negative impact on information systems. Saha and Srivastava point out that poor quality data are common in large databases and networks [2]. Poor quality data will have a serious impact on the results of data analysis. Data quality research was formally carried out in the 1990s, and data quality definition and measurement indicators began to be established. At present, data quality research is booming, data processing algorithms and frameworks continue to emerge, international organizations began to research and develop data quality standards. In terms of data quality indicators, [2–4] have conducted in-depth research on data quality dimensions. Wang et al. carried out extensive research work, investigated 118 kinds of data quality properties, summarized 20 kinds of commonly used data quality properties [2]. Sidi et al. analyzed 40 kinds of data quality properties in detail [3]. Zaveri et al. unified common terms of data quality, provided 18 data quality dimensions and 69 kinds of data quality measurement methods [4]. Wang et al. expounded the connotation of scientific data and data quality, studied the basic principles of data quality evaluation, analyzed the data quality structure, and put forward the scientific data quality evaluation index system based on basic level, criterion level and index level [5]. In [7], the problem of determining the timeliness of a set containing redundant records under a given time limit is studied, and an algorithm for solving the problem of determining the timeliness is proposed for the first time. [8] studies data integrity in detail. In data restoration, [9] studies record matching and data restoration, and points out that data quality indicators are not independent of each other. In [10], Fan et al. studied the new problems related to data cleaning, namely the interaction between record matching and data repair, and proved that data repair can effectively help identify matches and improve data quality. In [11], Gackowski et al. conducted a preliminary study on the establishment and validation of data quality indicators, and explored the logical relationship between data dimensions. [12–14] explores the correlation between different data quality indicators. Ding et al. proposed precise definitions and violation patterns of four data quality indicators, such as timeliness and accuracy [12]. Cheng et al. discussed the impact of the relationship between different data quality indicators, and determined an effective data cleaning strategy for data in wireless sensor networks [13]. Dominikus proposed improving data quality operations for multi-dimensional data quality assessment [14]. In [15], Helfert analyzed the dependence of data quality dimension, studied how to evaluate the overall quality of data by the total weighted dimension score, and examined the applicability of this method. [16] provides a wide range of technologies for evaluating and improving data quality, focusing on data quality assessment and improvement techniques. Zhao et al. comprehensively analyzed the content and method of quality evaluation of correlated data, providing reference for the construction of quality control and evaluation system [17]. In [18], Liu briefly analyzed the causes of some statistical dishonesty problems described in this paper, and proposed measures to improve the quality of statistical data. [19] uses association rules to evaluate data quality. Reza et al. found that most of the indicators developed so far do not take data weight into account, thus defining a new measurement standard based on data weight to further improve its data quality [20].

Table 1. Nomenclature

d_{ijt}	The j-th dimensional of the data d sampled from the i-th data source at the time t, where $i \in N$ and $j \in M$, and N and M are the numbers of data sources and the number of dimension of d
d_{ij}	The j-th dimensional of the data d sampled from the i-th data source over all time
d_{ijq1}, d_{ijq2}	Lower quantile and upper quartile of d_{ij}
$d_{ij\Delta q}$	Difference between d_{ijq1} and d_{ijq2}
Δt	Sampling interval
Δt_{mean}	Mean sampling interval
S	All data in the database

3   Data Quality and Data Quality Improvement

In this section, first, the precise definition of data quality model is given. Second, the methods used to improve each index are summarized. Finally, the impact of data quality improvement execution order on the overall data quality is analyzed, which lays the foundation for the next section of experimental simulation. For convenience, some nomenclatures used in this paper are given in Table 1.

3.1 Data Quality Indicators

Currently there are many data quality indicators, and in this paper, some most popular data quality indicators, including data integrity, data accuracy, data consistency, and data timeliness are used and analyzed.

Data integrity indicator $D_{integrity}$: is used to measure data integrity, including scale integrity, attribute integrity, content integrity and so on. Data integrity can be measured by data size, data volume, data coverage and so on. In order to simplify the data quality assessment model, in this paper, data integrity is defined as the degree of data missing. The following is the accurate definition of data integrity:

$$
s_{ijt} = \begin{cases} 1, d_{ijt} \neq None \\ 0, d_{ijt} = None \end{cases} \tag{1}
$$

$$
D_{integrity} = \frac{\sum\limits_{t \in T} \sum\limits_{j \in M} \sum\limits_{i \in N} s_{ijt} - S}{\sum\limits_{t \in T} \sum\limits_{j \in M} \sum\limits_{i \in N} s_{ijt}} \times 100\% \tag{2}
$$

Data accuracy indicator $D_{accuracy}$: is to measure the ability of data to accurately describe the physical world. Illegal values, invalid data types and low data accuracy can all be used to measure data accuracy. In order to simplify the data quality evaluation model, this paper defines data accuracy as the degree of data anomalies. The following is the precise definition of data accuracy:

$$
s_{ijt}^a = \begin{cases} 1, d_{ijt} \notin \left[d_{jq1} - 1.5 \times d_{j\Delta q}, d_{jq2} + 1.5 \times d_{j\Delta q} \right] \\ 0, d_{ijt} \in \left[d_{jq1} - 1.5 \times d_{j\Delta q}, d_{jq2} + 1.5 \times d_{j\Delta q} \right] \end{cases} \tag{3}
$$

$$
D_{accuracy} = \frac{\sum\limits_{t \in T} \sum\limits_{j \in M} \sum\limits_{i \in N} s_{ijt} - \sum\limits_{t \in T} \sum\limits_{j \in M} \sum\limits_{i \in N} s_{ijt}^a}{\sum\limits_{t \in T} \sum\limits_{j \in M} \sum\limits_{i \in N} s_{ijt}} \times 100\% \tag{4}
$$

Data consistency indicator $D_{consistency}$: is to measure the consistency of different data formats, contents and ranges of single or multiple data sources. It has been pointed out in [7] that data consistency includes conceptual consistency, format consistency, range consistency and time consistency. Different constraints are determined according to the data content. Data that violate the constraints are considered to have a consistency conflict. The more complex the constraints are, the more complex the consistency discrimination is. In order to simplify the data quality evaluation model, this paper only establishes a constraint condition: the sampled value range of the same node on the same attribute should be consistent. In this paper, data consistency is defined as the extent to which data violates constraints, using Eqs. (5) and (6):

$$s_{ijt}^c = \begin{cases} 1, d_{ijt} \notin \left[d_{ijq1} - 1.5 \times d_{ij\Delta q}, d_{ijq2} + 1.5 \times d_{ij\Delta q} \right] \\ 0, d_{ijt} \in \left[d_{ijq1} - 1.5 \times d_{ij\Delta q}, d_{ijq2} + 1.5 \times d_{ij\Delta q} \right] \end{cases} \tag{5}$$

$$D_{\text{consistency}} = \frac{\sum\limits_{t\in T}\sum\limits_{j\in M}\sum\limits_{i\in N} s_{ijt} - \sum\limits_{t\in T}\sum\limits_{j\in M}\sum\limits_{i\in N} s_{ijt}^c}{\sum\limits_{t\in T}\sum\limits_{j\in M}\sum\limits_{i\in N} s_{ijt}} \times 100\% \tag{6}$$

Data timeliness indicator $D_{\text{timeliness}}$: is to measure the freshness and availability of data. It refers to the time interval and efficiency of receiving, processing, transmitting and utilizing information from the information source. The shorter the time interval, the more timely information updates, the more time-sensitive data. In order to simplify the data quality assessment model, in this paper, data timeliness is defined as the degree of data update, using Eqs. (7) and (8):

$$s_{it}^t = \begin{cases} 1, \Delta t > 2 \times \Delta t_{mean} \\ 0, \Delta t \leq 2 \times \Delta t_{mean} \end{cases} \tag{7}$$

$$D_{\text{timeliness}} = \frac{\sum\limits_{i\in N}\sum\limits_{t\in T} s_{it} - \sum\limits_{i\in N}\sum\limits_{t\in T} s_{it}^t}{\sum\limits_{t\in T}\sum\limits_{i\in N} s_{it}} \times 100\% \tag{8}$$

According to the definition of data quality index above, the total quality of data is recorded as Q, the measure value of data quality index x is recorded as Q, and the weight of data quality index x is recorded as Q. Then the precise definition of data quality is defined as:

$$Q = \sum_{x\in X} \omega_x D_x \tag{9}$$

3.2   Data Quality Improvement Methods

According to the definitions of data integrity, data accuracy, data consistency, and data timeliness, there are many methods can be used to improve the data quality. In order to make the scheme proposed in this paper clear and comparable, following data quality indicators improvement methods are used:

The operation of improving data integrity $P_{\text{integrity}}$: for improving data integrity operation, there are mean interpolation, similar mean interpolation, modeling prediction, high-dimensional mapping, multiple interpolation and other methods. In this paper, the method of improving data integrity based on mean interpolation is used.

The operation of improving the accuracy of data $P_{accuracy}$: the abnormal data in data sets is the main reason for the low accuracy of data. The abnormal data can be identified by using data statistics technology and data visualization. The commonly used methods are box-dividing method, regression method, clustering method and so on. In order to improve the accuracy of data, this paper identifies the abnormal data and fills it with the mean value.

The operation of improving data consistency $P_{consistency}$: when data violates constraints, it is regarded as abnormal data, and the abnormal data is filled up according to constraints rules to improve data consistency.

The operation of improving data timeliness $P_{timeliness}$: judging the time items in the data set and deleting or filling the data with low timeliness.

4 Data Quality Improvement Based on the Greedy Algorithm

4.1 Analysis of the Impact of the Order on Data Quality Improvement

Before data processing, it is necessary to clarify the impact of the order of data quality improvement on the overall quality of data. Specifically, the following points need to be noted:

First, the improvement of a certain data quality indicator cannot ensure the improvement of the overall data quality. For example, suppose data consistency is denoted by $D_{consistency}$, and the total data quality is denoted by Q. After the data consistency operations, data consistency is $D'_{consistency}$ and the overall data quality is Q'. Although $D_{consistency} < D'_{consistency}$, Q' may be less than Q, that is to say, increasing individual data quality indicators does not always improve the overall data quality.

Second, individual data quality gains cannot be directly accumulated. For example, data integrity is $D_{integrity}$, data consistency is $D_{consistency}$, and the total data quality is denoted by Q. For a dataset, when carrying out the data integrity improvement operation $P_{integrity}$ individually, the resulted data quality is Q', and the data quality gains is $\Delta Q' = Q' - Q$; when carrying out the data integrity improvement operation $P_{consistency}$ individually, the resulted data quality is Q'', and the data quality gains is $\Delta Q'' = Q'' - Q$; when carrying out $P_{intergrity}$ and $P_{consistency}$ sequentially, the resulted data quality is Q''', and the data quality gains is $\Delta Q''' = Q''' - Q$; at this time, $\Delta Q''' \neq \Delta Q' + \Delta Q''$. In other words, data quality gains cannot be directly accumulated.

Third, different processing order of individual data quality indicators results in different overall data quality gains. For example, when carrying out $P_{integrity}$ and $P_{consistency}$ sequentially, the resulted data quality is Q, and the data quality gains is $\Delta Q' = Q' - Q$; when carrying out $P_{consistency}$ and $P_{integrity}$ sequentially, the resulted data quality is Q, and the data quality gains is $\Delta Q'' = Q'' - Q$; at this time, $\Delta Q' \neq \Delta Q''$. That is to say, different data processing order and different data quality gains.

Fourth, more data quality improvement operations cannot ensure better overall data quality gain. For example, data integrity is $D_{integrity}$, data consistency is $D_{consistency}$, and the total data quality is denoted by Q. For a dataset, when carrying out the data integrity improvement operation $P_{integrity}$ individually, the resulted data quality is Q', and the data quality gains is $\Delta Q' = Q' - Q$; when carrying out $P_{integrity}$ and $P_{consistency}$ sequentially, the resulted data quality is Q'', and the data quality gains is $\Delta Q'' = Q'' - Q$; at this time, $\Delta Q''$ is not always greater than Q'. That is to say, more data quality improvement operations cannot ensure better overall data quality gain.

4.2   The Proposed Method

Assuming that each data quality indicator corresponds to a data processing operation, and that each data processing operation is not reused. Suppose there are n data processing operations, then the total number of possible orders is:

$$O_n = \sum_{j=0}^{n} (\prod_{i=0}^{j} (n - i))$$

(10)

For example, when there are four data quality indicators, there will be 64 data processing orders to choose. When there are five data quality indicators, there will be 325 kinds of data. When the dimension of data quality index increases, the situation will become more complex. To find the optimal data processing strategy, it is necessary to traverse all data processing strategies. In order to save time and cost, it is a reasonable way to use greedy algorithm to determine the order of data processing.

The flowchart of the proposed method is shown in Fig. 1.

Suppose there are n data processing operations in the data operations set DO.

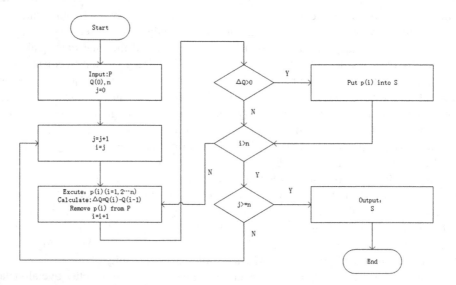

Fig. 1. The flowchart of the proposed method.

Step 1: select the i-th data processing operation P_i in DO, carry out data indicator improvement using P_i, suppose the resulted overall data quality is Q_i.

Step 2: calculate the data quality gain $\Delta Q = Q_i - Q_{i-1}$. If $\Delta Q > 0$, then put P_i into the operations set S_j . $i = i+1$, go to Step 1, until $i = n$.

Step 3: $j = j+1$, go to Step 1, until $j = n$.

5   Experimental Results and Analysis

5.1   The Experiment Data

The experiment data used in this paper is a random segment of data extracted from a substation database. The data records four attributes of network node Temperature, Absolute Pressure, Density and Moisture, totaling 1000 pieces of data. Some of the data are shown as follows (Table 2):

Table 2.   Some examples of data used in the experiment

Time	Temperature	Pressure	Density	Moisture
2000/1/2 15:40:54	19.39	0.408	0.409	18
2000/1/8 20:24:53	15.62	0.411	0.418	8.1
2000/1/13 10:46:28	9.42	0.402	0.419	12.8
2000/1/17 9:27:30	1.49	0.376	0.404	10.8
2000/1/20 18:35:13	21.13	0.402	0.4	20.8
2000/1/23 21:42:07	17.82	0.604	0.61	26.2

5.2   The Impact of Individual Data Quality Indicator Improvement on the Overall Data Quality

Table 3 gives the impact of data processing operations on the overall data quality.

Table 3.   The impact of data processing operations on the overall data quality

	$D_{integrity}$	$D_{consistency}$	$D_{accuracy}$	$D_{timeliness}$	Q
P_0	95.1%	85.4%	88.5%	77.5%	86.6%
$P_{integrity}$	100.0%	82.1	85.5%	77.5%	86.3%
$P_{consisency}$	83.6%	94.4%	87.8%	77.5%	85.8%
$P_{accuracy}$	86.1%	88.6%	93.7%	77.5%	86.5%
$P_{timeliness}$	95.1%	85.4%	88.5%	84.8%	88.4%

From the above table, it can be seen that the operation of data quality improvement corresponding to each data quality indicator will inevitably increase the value of the overall data quality. At the same time, the operation of one data quality indicator will also have a certain impact on other data quality indicators and affect the overall data quality.

5.3 Data Quality Improvement Using the Proposed Method

In this section, the proposed method is used for data quality improvement. To test the performance of the proposed method, certain operations are selected and ordered for comparison, as shown in Table 4, and results are shown in Fig. 2.

Table 4. Some pre-defined operations orders for comparison

Experiment 1	
Order	Detail
P_1	$P_{timeliness} \rightarrow P_{consistency}$
P_2	$P_{timeliness} \rightarrow P_{accuracy}$
P_3	$P_{integrity} \rightarrow P_{consistency}$
Experiment 2	
Order	Detail
P_1	$P_{timeliness} \rightarrow P_{integrity} \rightarrow P_{accuracy}$
P_2	$P_{consistency} \rightarrow P_{timeliness} \rightarrow P_{accuracy}$
P_3	$P_{integrity} \rightarrow P_{accuracy} \rightarrow P_{timeliness}$
Experiment 3	
Order	Detail
P_1	$P_{consistency} \rightarrow P_{accuracy} \rightarrow P_{integrity} \rightarrow P_{timeliness}$
P_2	$P_{consistency} \rightarrow P_{timeliness} \rightarrow P_{integrity} \rightarrow P_{accuracy}$
P_3	$P_{integrity} \rightarrow P_{accuracy} \rightarrow P_{timeliness} \rightarrow P_{consistency}$
Experiment 4	
Order	Detail
P_1	$P_{timeliness} \rightarrow P_{accuracy} \rightarrow P_{integrity} \rightarrow P_{consistency} \rightarrow P_{timeliness}$
P_2	$P_{timeliness} \rightarrow P_{accuracy} \rightarrow P_{integrity} \rightarrow P_{consistency} \rightarrow P_{accuracy}$
P_3	$P_{integrity} \rightarrow P_{consistency} \rightarrow P_{integrity} \rightarrow P_{consistency} \rightarrow P_{accuracy}$

From Fig. 2 it can be seen that in the first three groups of comparative experiments, the data quality gain of data processing strategy obtained by greedy algorithm is the largest. In the fourth group of experiments with repeated operations, only the data quality gain of the third path is slightly larger than that of the data processing strategy obtained by greedy algorithm. Therefore, the effectiveness of the proposed algorithm can be verified.

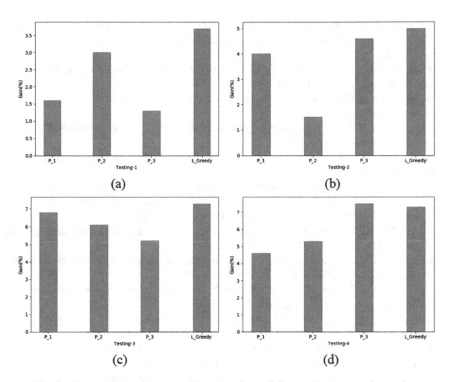

Fig. 2. Comparison of data quality gains from different data processing orders

6   Conclusion

This paper proposes a novel data quality improvement method based on the greedy algorithm. First, this paper establishes four data quality indicators, and gives the calculation formula of data quality. Second, a greedy algorithm is adapted for data quality improvement to find an efficient and reasonable data processing strategy. Finally, simulation experiments prove the correctness of the theorem and the validity of the data processing strategy.

Acknowledgments. This work was supported by the State Grid Corporation Science and Technology Project (Contract No.: SGLNXT00YJJS1800110).

References

1. Li, Cai, Yu, L., Zhu, Y., et al.: Historical evolution and development trend of data quality. Comput. Sci. **45**(4), 1–10 (2018)
2. Saha, B., Srivastava, D.: Data quality: the other face of big data. In: IEEE International Conference on Data Engineering. IEEE (2014)
3. Wang, R.Y., Strong, D.M.: Beyond accuracy: what data quality means to data consumers. J. Manag. Inf. Syst. **12**(4), 5–33 (1996)

4. Sidi, F., Panahy, P.H.S., Affendey, L.S., et al.: Data quality: a survey of data quality dimensions. In: International Conference on Information Retrieval & Knowledge Management (2012)
5. Zaveri, A., Rula, A., Maurino, A., et al.: Quality assessment for linked data: a survey. Semant. Web 7(1), 63–93 (2015)
6. Wang, Z., Yang, Q.: Research on the quality and standardization of scientific data. Stand. Sci. 03, 25–30 (2019)
7. Mohan, Li, Li, J., Gao, H.: Solution algorithm for data timeliness determination. J. Comput. Sci. 35(11), 2348–2360 (2012)
8. Fan, W., Geerts, F.: Relative information completeness. ACM Trans. Database Syst. (TODS) 35(4), 1–44 (2010)
9. Fan, W., Li, J., Ma, S., et al.: Interaction between record matching and data repairing. In: Proceedings of the ACM SIGMOD International Conference on Management of Data, SIGMOD 2011, 12–16 June 2011, Athens, Greece. ACM (2011)
10. Fan, W., Ma, S., Tang, N., Yu, W.: Interaction between record matching and data repairing. J. Data Inf. Qual. (JDIQ) 4(4), 16 (2014)
11. Quercia, D., Hogan, B.: Proceedings of the Ninth International AAAI Conference on Web and Social Media - ICWSM 2015. AAAI Press (2015)
12. Ding, X., Wang, H., Zhang, X., et al.: Research on the relationship among various properties of data quality. J. Softw. 27(7), 1626–1644 (2016)
13. Cheng, H., Feng, D., Shi, X., et al.: Data quality analysis and cleaning strategy for wireless sensor networks. Eurasip J. Wirel. Commun. Netw. 2018(1), 61 (2018)
14. Kleindienst, D.: The data quality improvement plan: deciding on choice and order of data quality improvements. Electron. Markets 27(4), 1–12 (2017)
15. Helfert, M., Foley, O., Ge, M., et al.: Limitations of Weighted Sum Measures for Information Quality (2009)
16. Batini, C., Cappiello, C., Francalanci, C., et al.: Methodologies for data quality assessment and improvement. ACM Comput. Surv. 41(3), 16 (2009)
17. Zhao, W., Li, C.: A review of the research on quality evaluation methods of associated data. Intell. Theory Practice 39(02), 134–138+128 (2016)
18. Liu, H.: Analysis of statistical data quality. In: International Joint Conference on Computational Sciences & Optimization. IEEE (2014)
19. Alpar, P., Winkelsträter, S.: Assessment of data quality accounting data with association rules. Expert Syst. Appl. 41(5), 2259–2268 (2014)
20. Vaziri, R., Mohsenzadeh, M., Habibi, J.: Measuring data quality with weighted metrics. Total Qual. Manag. Bus. Excellence 30(5–6), 708–720 (2019)

Research of Lightweight Encryption Algorithm Based on AES and Chaotic Sequences for Narrow-Band Internet of Things

Lianmin Shi[1,2(✉)], Yihuai Wang[2], Rongyuan Jia[2], Tao Peng[2], Jianwu Jiang[2], and Shilang Zhu[2]

[1] College of Information Technology, Suzhou Institute of Trade and Commerce, Suzhou, China
18915418296@163.com
[2] School of Computer Science and Technology, Soochow University, Suzhou, China

Abstract. Narrow-Band Internet of Things (NB-IoT), as a new LPWAN technology, has been applied in many fields, such as smart meter, smart parking, and so on. However, the security issues have become an important factor restricting rapid development of NB-IoT. A lightweight encryption algorithm based on AES and chaotic sequences (LCHAOSAES) is proposed to solve the data security in NB-IoT applications. Firstly, by reducing the number of AES (Advanced Encryption Standard) rounds and combining the three steps of 'SubBytes', 'ShiftRows' and 'MixColumns', time efficiency of LCHAOSAES is improved. Secondly, in order to make LCHAOSAES more secure, Logistic and Tent chaotic systems are adopted to generate dynamic keys for encryption. Finally, the remaining plaintext is encrypted by the keys, which are generated by Logistic and Tent chaotic systems, so that the length of the plaintext is equal to ciphertext. Theoretical analysis and field experiments performed in NB-IoT scenarios highlight significant performance when compared with, for instance, AES_128, LAES.

Keywords: NB-IoT · LCHAOSAES · AES · Chaotic sequences

1 Introduction

NB-IoT is a LPWAN technology based on cellular networks, which is proposed by the 3GPP in 2015, the series of standards was designated by the 3GPP in 2016 [1, 2]. Wide coverage, high capacity, flexible deployment, low power consumption and low cost are the most significant features of NB-IoT [3]. Nowadays, the ecological industry chain of NB-IoT has gradually matured. However, with the rapid development of NB-IoT applications, there will inevitably be many network security problems, such as, terminal nodes are counterfeited, the transmitted data is eavesdropped, and so on [4]. Therefore, according to the characteristics of NB-IoT, the research of security mechanisms can provide security for NB-IoT applications and promote the development of NB-IoT industry.

© ICST Institute for Computer Sciences, Social Informatics and Telecommunications Engineering 2019
Published by Springer Nature Switzerland AG 2019. All Rights Reserved
X. B. Zhai et al. (Eds.): MLICOM 2019, LNICST 294, pp. 267–280, 2019.
https://doi.org/10.1007/978-3-030-32388-2_23

Encryption technology is an effective way to protect network security. The storage, computing power and energy of NB-IoT nodes are usually limited. Therefore, the asymmetric encryption algorithms with large resources consumption are not suitable for NB-IoT applications, as a result, symmetric encryption algorithms with less computation are more suitable for resource-constrained NB-IoT nodes [5]. Highly simplified AES and other block ciphers have become the major research subjects in the field of NB-IoT security [6–9]. In [10], authors have reduced the rounds of AES and used the method of looking up tables to simplify the round function, accordingly, the time efficiency is improved. In [11], the efficiency is promoted by improving round function. Although the methods above have improved efficiency, they neglect the reduced security. In addition, NB-IoT is sensitive to the length of data transmitted, because the longer data not only consumes more energy, but also increases communication cost. AES is the block cipher, the length of ciphertext may be longer than that of plaintext. If AES is to be applied to NB-IoT, it needs to be optimized.

In summary, in order to solve the problem of data security in NB-IoT, according to the technical characteristics of NB-IoT, the advantages and disadvantages of AES in efficiency and security are analyzed, and a lightweight encryption algorithm called LCHAOSAES is proposed. The main ideas of LCHAOSAES are summarized as follows:

(1) Reduce the number of AES rounds to improve efficiency.
(2) Exchange the order of 'SubBytes' and 'ShiftRows', combine 'SubBytes', 'ShiftRows' and 'MixColumns', and design look-up tables.
(3) Provide different initial key for each round to form 'one-time pad' encryption system. These initial keys are chaotic sequences generated by Logistic and Tent chaotic systems.
(4) Encrypt the remaining bytes of the plaintext byte-by-byte to ensure that the length of plaintext is consistent with the length of ciphertext.

The remainder of this article is organized as follows. In Section 2 we review some simplified encryption algorithms based on AES. In Sect. 3 we briefly introduce the basic theory of AES and chaotic encryption algorithm. In Sect. 4 the LCHAOSAES is described in details. In Sect. 5 the encryption model of NB-IoT application is given. Security of the LCHAOSAES and data statistics are analyzed in Sect. 6. Finally, our work is been concluded in Sect. 7.

2   Related Work

Encryption technology is a kind of data security protection way commonly used in wireless networks. Classic encryption algorithms include: DES, AES, RC5, SM1, ECC, SM2, RSA, and so on. In [12], authors take DES, AES, SM1, SM2 and RSA as the research objectives, and compare them in three aspects: energy consumption, time efficiency and spatial efficiency. Experimental results show that the symmetric encryption algorithms such as DES, AES and SM1 are more suitable for wireless communication nodes. Comparing with DES and SM1, although AES is slightly larger than DES and SM1 in storage and time, its energy consumption is least. Therefore, AES is a suitable encryption algorithm for wireless communication nodes. Formerly, AES was mostly implemented by hardware, but this way would increase the burden on the hardware of nodes. In [13–16], Osvik and other researchers have used high-level programming language to quickly achieve AES, and adopted time efficiency and spatial efficiency to measure the pros and cons of AES.

There are many studies on simplified AES. For instance, in [17], Zhao et al. have combined the three steps of 'SubBytes', 'ShiftRows' and 'MixColumns' to replace the XOR operation. In [10], time efficiency of the algorithm has been improved by reducing the rounds. Although these methods promote the efficiency, they don't consider the security which have been reduced.

There are also many studies on enhancing the security of AES. In [18], binary number of the chaotic sequence has been used to replace the initial key of AES, but efficiency is not sufficient. In [19], Chen et al. have proposed a key generation based on two-dimensional logistic mapping to enhance the independence of sub-keys, but it lacks of considerations on efficiency. In [20], Yan et al. have proposed a complex chaotic sequence based on the dynamic key, and they use a double chaotic system to dynamically initialize the key for AES, but this method has made the efficiency of AES decrease a lot.

The improved algorithms based on standard AES could not meet actual requirement for data encryption of NB-IoT in efficiency and safety. As a result, a lightweight encryption algorithm (LCHAOSAES) based on AES and chaotic sequences for NB-IoT is proposed.

3 AES and Chaotic Encryption

3.1 AES

AES is a packet encryption algorithm based on symmetric keys, which is resistant to all known types of attacks other than violent attacks. Furthermore, AES is a symmetric-key block cipher that operates under different combinations of block and key sizes, e.g., 128, 192 or 256 bits [21]. Due to resource-constraint of NB-IoT nodes, we improve the 128-bit AES algorithm. The encryption process consists of four basic transformations: 'SubBytes', 'ShiftRows', 'MixColumns' and 'AddRoundkey'. Figure 1 outlines the steps of AES_128 encryption.

(1) 'SubBytes' is a nonlinear function with the role of confusion bytes, S-box can be used to improve operation speed.
(2) 'ShiftRows' is a linear function that shifts the lines.
(3) 'MixColumns' is a function that converts each byte into a linear combination of input bytes.
(4) 'AddRoundkey' is a simple XOR operation, and its sub-keys are calculated from the master key.

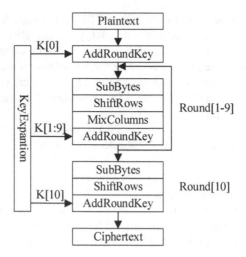

Fig. 1. Steps of AES_128 encryption

3.2   Chaotic Encryption

Chaotic encryption has been widely used in the field of information encryption with high computational speed, simple and real-time. In addition, chaos has many characteristics, such as nonperiodic, random, extremely sensitive to the initial state, easy to fork, and so on. Its model can be expressed as a nonlinear equation. The chaotic systems used in this paper are: Logistic and Tent mappings.

The one-dimensional Logistic equation is described as follows [22].

$$x_{n+1} = \mu x_n(1 - x_n) \tag{1}$$

where, x is a chaotic variable and $\mu \in (0,4]$ is a parameter that controls the chaotic equation. When $3.57 < \mu \leq 4$, the system exhibits a chaotic state and randomness of the sequence is better. When $\mu = 4$, the Logistic map has a great ductility and is very sensitive to initial value of the iteration, which is called the full-mapped chaotic state. Logistic chaotic sequences are similar to noise, and have high dependency on initial values and parameters. The same chaotic system will produce completely different chaotic sequence values even if it is disturbed by a small initial value or the number of iterations.

Tent mapping is a piecewise linear mapping system, the typical dynamic equation is described as follows.

$$y_{n+1} = \begin{cases} \lambda y_n, & 0 < y_n < 0.5 \\ \lambda(1 - y_n). & 0.5 < y_n < 1 \end{cases} \tag{2}$$

where, y is a chaotic variable and $\lambda \in (1.4, 2)$ is a parameter that controls the chaotic equation. Keep λ constant, any initial value $y0 \in (0, 1)$ can be iterated to get a definite numerical sequence. When $\lambda \in (1.4, 2)$, the system is in a chaotic state, and the value of λ is closer to 2, randomness of the chaotic sequence is better.

4   LCHAOSAES

In order to reduce the complexity of AES and improve the key security, we proposed LCHAOSAES, a lightweight encryption algorithm for NB-IoT applications.

4.1   Simplify AES

1. Reduce Number of Encrypted Rounds

In [10], Yao et al. have carried out an experiment of expanding key rounds with only 1-bit difference between each group of key seeds. Finally, the change rate in bits of each round key is obtained. The results show that the bit rate of change after 7 rounds is similar to that of 10. Consequently, setting the number of rounds to 7 is enough to resist known attacks. Based on the experimental result in [10], we take 7 as the number of encrypted rounds in LCHAOSAES.

2. Simplify Round Function

'MixColumns' involves multiplication on the finite field GF(28), computation of this magnitude are unbearable to NB-IoT nodes. Therefore, The LCHAOSAES exchanges 'SubBytes' with 'ShiftRows', and then replaces 'SubBytes', 'ShiftRows' and 'MixColumns' with method of looking up tables to improve efficiency.

During the first 6 rounds of LCHAOSAES, 'ShiftRows' does not actually operate on the input matrix, and only performs the row transform in the last round. R is the output of 'ShiftRows'. 'SubBytes' is represented by S(R), and the output is represented by B. 'MixColumns' takes B as input and C is its output.

'SubBytes' is described as follows.

$$B_{ij} = S(R_{ij}), \quad (0 \le i, j \le 3) \tag{3}$$

'MixColumns' is described as follows.

$$
\begin{bmatrix} C_{0j} \\ C_{1j} \\ C_{2j} \\ C_{3j} \end{bmatrix} =
\begin{bmatrix} 02\ 03\ 01\ 01 \\ 01\ 02\ 03\ 01 \\ 01\ 01\ 02\ 03 \\ 03\ 01\ 01\ 02 \end{bmatrix}
\begin{bmatrix} B_{0j} \\ B_{1j} \\ B_{2j} \\ B_{3j} \end{bmatrix}
$$

$$
= \begin{bmatrix} 02 \times B_{0j} \\ 01 \times B_{0j} \\ 01 \times B_{0j} \\ 03 \times B_{0j} \end{bmatrix}
\oplus
\begin{bmatrix} 03 \times B_{1j} \\ 02 \times B_{1j} \\ 01 \times B_{1j} \\ 01 \times B_{1j} \end{bmatrix}
\oplus
\begin{bmatrix} 01 \times B_{2j} \\ 03 \times B_{2j} \\ 02 \times B_{2j} \\ 01 \times B_{2j} \end{bmatrix}
\oplus
\begin{bmatrix} 01 \times B_{3j} \\ 01 \times B_{3j} \\ 03 \times B_{3j} \\ 02 \times B_{3j} \end{bmatrix}, \quad (0 \le j \le 3). \tag{4}
$$

According to (3) and (4), we get the following Eq. (5).

$$
\begin{bmatrix} C_{0j} \\ C_{1j} \\ C_{2j} \\ C_{3j} \end{bmatrix} = \begin{bmatrix} 02 \times S(R_{0j}) \\ 01 \times S(R_{0j}) \\ 01 \times S(R_{0j}) \\ 03 \times S(R_{0j}) \end{bmatrix} \oplus \begin{bmatrix} 03 \times S(R_{1j}) \\ 02 \times S(R_{1j}) \\ 01 \times S(R_{1j}) \\ 01 \times S(R_{1j}) \end{bmatrix} \oplus \begin{bmatrix} 01 \times S(R_{2j}) \\ 03 \times S(R_{2j}) \\ 02 \times S(R_{2j}) \\ 01 \times S(R_{2j}) \end{bmatrix} \oplus \begin{bmatrix} 01 \times S(R_{3j}) \\ 01 \times S(R_{3j}) \\ 03 \times S(R_{3j}) \\ 02 \times S(R_{3j}) \end{bmatrix}, \ (0 \leq j \leq 3).
$$

$$(5)$$

In conclusion, it is concluded that the 'ShiftRows', 'SubBytes' and 'MixColumns' of the 1–6 round can be replaced by 'SubBytes', if the three tables are stored in advance, such as S, 2*S and 3*S (* is represented as multiplication on GF(28)). Figure 2 outlines the various steps of encryption of LCHAOSAES.

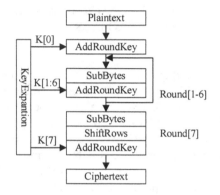

Fig. 2. Steps of LCHAOSAES encryption

4.2   Generate Chaotic Keys

One-dimensional chaotic system has some good characteristics, for instance, good initial sensitivity, pseudo-randomness and aperiodic. We use Logistic and Tent to construct a chaotic key generation system to generate chaotic sequences with high randomness and utilize these sequences to generate different initial keys for each AES plaintext packet. In this way, all plaintext blocks can be encrypted with different keys, which constitutes a 'one-time pad' encryption system.

LCHAOSAES requires that encryption and decryption use same parameters to create same chaotic system. And it generates the dynamic key through multiple iterations and encrypts plaintext block with the key.

The process of LCHAOSAES is described as follows.

1. Create chaotic systems with initialization parameters
   The key is passed through symmetric key encryption system. The key contains the control parameters μ and λ, the initial value x0 and y0, and the basic iteration

number N of Logistic and Tent maps to make encryption and decryption produce the same chaotic key generation system.

2. Block plaintext

   The plaintext is divided by 16 bytes, and the parameters m and n are calculated according to the length (length) of plaintext. m is described as the number of blocks, m = length/16. n represents the number of remaining bytes, n = length%16.

3. Generate chaotic sequences and compose the initial key

   Logistic N + m iterations and Tent N + n iterations to make the sequences sufficiently discrete, and correlate the number of iterations with the length of plaintext. A data block is encrypted at a time, Logistic and Tent are iterated 8 times to obtain 8 numbers. Then the first 4 digits are made up of the fractional part of each number and the integer is numbered on 256. The two sets of data are combined to form an initial key of 16 bytes.

4. Encrypt dynamically and handle the end of plaintext

   Encrypt the plaintext block by using the key generated in previous steps to obtain the ciphertext block. The remaining bytes of plaintext utilize XOR key to obtain ciphertext. This method of tail processing can greatly improve efficiency.

Finally, the m ciphertext blocks and n bytes of last ciphertext are combined to obtain the ciphertext, the length of ciphertext is equal to that of plaintext. Figures 3 and 4 depict the process of LCHAOSAES and a structure that uses a dynamic key for encryption, respectively.

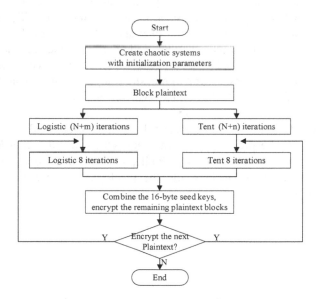

Fig. 3. The process of LCHAOSAES

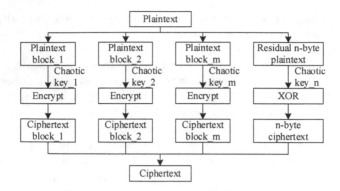

Fig. 4. Encryption structure using a dynamic key

5 The Encryption Model of NB-IoT Applications

5.1 NB-IoT Application Architecture

From perspective of technical science, NB-IoT application architecture can be abstracted as three components: UE (Ultimate-Equipment), MPO (Information Post Office) and HCI (Human-Computer Interaction System), as shown in Fig. 5. UE is an entity with hardware and software, which uses MCU as the core, with NB-IoT communication, data acquisition, control, computing and other functions, for instance, smart meters, etc. MPO is a data transmission system based on NB-IoT protocol, which is made up of operators' eNodeB, IoT controller and IoT Service Platform. HCI is able to achieve the specific application functions of the hardware and software systems, so that users can adopt laptops, mobile phones and other smart devices to achieve some intelligent applications, such as smart parking, smart logistics, and so on. In Fig. 5, the processes (1) and (2) represent the uplink data transmission, and processes (3) and (4) represent the downlink data transmission.

As can be seen from Fig. 5, Developers only need to design hardware and software of UE and HCI, and the problem about the data is transmitted within MPO will be resolved by the operators, such as China Mobile, Verizon and other operators. For the NB-IoT developers, they just need consider the development of hardware and software about UE and HCI.

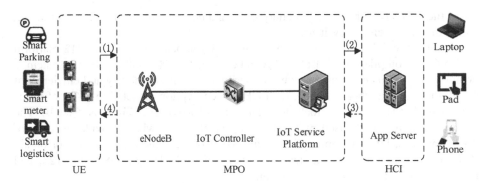

Fig. 5. NB-IoT application architecture

5.2 Encryption Model

In Fig. 5, data security may occur in any network communication process, such as processes (1), (2) (3), (4) and MPO. Each UE has a unique code IMEI (International Mobile Equipment Identity), it consists of 15-bit 'digital string'. We use IMEI to generate a fixed basic iteration number for each UE encryption key to reduce the difficulty of key management.

According to NB-IoT application architecture and IMEI, we propose the encryption model as shown in Fig. 6. When UE wants to send data to HCI, firstly, the last three digits of the IMEI are counted as number, and the number of basic LCHAOSAES iterations is set according to the number. If number < 100, then N = 100. Otherwise, N = number. After the key information is set, UE and HCI share the same key. UE encrypts the data using LCHAOSAES. The ciphertext is sent to HIC via MPO. Finally, HIC receives the ciphertext, decrypts it with the key, and gets the plaintext.

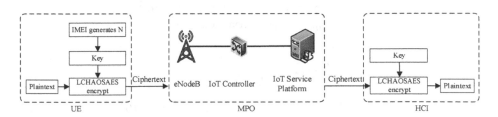

Fig. 6. Encryption model in NB-IoT applications

6 Experimental Evaluation

6.1 Experimental Environment

In this part, we will verify the security of LCHAOSAES by analysing key space and sensitivity, and compare the security with LAES and AES_128. Secondly, we will count the three algorithms used in encryption, and compare the results. The less time it takes, the higher efficiency it has.

In this paper, there are two experimental environments. One is VS2012 platform with VC ++ compiler, and 64-bit PC (clocked at 3.20 GHz) with operating system is Windows10. In this environment we will verify sensitivity of the key and efficiency of the algorithm. The other is the UE with NB-IoT encryption model. The MCU of UE is MKL36Z64VLH4, whose clock frequency is 48 MHz and Flash is 64 KB. The communication module used by the UE is Quectel BC95, which provides a series of AT commands. UE can communicate with MPO through these commands, or obtain IMEI of the module. We will test the efficiency of LCHAOSAES, AES_128, and LAES on the NB-IoT encryption model.

6.2 Security Analysis

1. Key space
   The size of key space affects the ability of encryption algorithm about resisting key search attacks. The LCHAOSAES key is controlled by five parameters, including the rounds of Logistic chaotic system and the initial value, the parameter and the initial value of Tent chaotic system, and the basic iteration number. Double type of data can be obtained after the decimal point of 15 significant figures. The size of each parameter space is shown in Table 1.

Table 1. The Size of parameter space

Parameter	Type	Range	Size
μ	Double	[3.57,4.0]	$K_\mu \approx 0.43 \times 10^{15}$
x_0	Double	(0,1)	$K_{x0} \approx 1 \times 10^{15}$
λ	Double	(1.4,2.0)	$K_\lambda \approx 0.6 \times 10^{15}$
y_0	Double	(0,1)	$K_{y0} \approx 1 \times 10^{15}$
N	Int	[100,1000)	$K_N \approx 900$

The size of key space of LCHAOSAES is:

$$K = K_\mu \times K_{x0} \times K_\lambda \times K_{y0} \times K_N \approx 2.32 \times 10^{62} \qquad (6)$$

In theory, key space sizes of AES_128 and LAES are 2128 ≈ 3.40 × 1038. Therefore, the size of key space of LCHAOSAES is much larger than that of AES_128 and LAES. The number of iterations of LCHAOSAES depends on the IMEI of UE and the length of plaintext, so its key space is uncertain, which further enhances the difficulty of using exhaustive method to crack the ciphertext information.

2. Sensitivity verification
   Sensitivity is a common index to measure the security of encryption algorithm [23], that is, the key satisfies the avalanche criterion. When the key changes slightly, half

of ciphertext bit changes. In order to verify sensitivity of AES_128, LAES, and LCHAOSAES, we conduct an experiment. In this experiment, we calculate the change rate of ciphertext obtained by encrypting the same plaintext with different algorithms, and the length of plaintext is 1000 bytes. The average results obtained in 20 experiments are shown in Fig. 7.

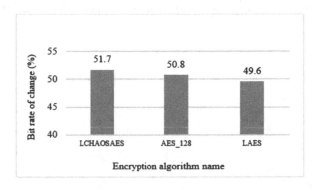

Fig. 7. The bit rate of change after encryption.

As can be seen from Fig. 7, the change bits rate of LCHAOSAES is the highest. This shows that LCHAOSAES is better in avalanche experiments. In the experiment, when the key changes slightly, the LCHAOSAES key changes to a small extent, resulting in a 51.7% change in the bit rate of ciphertext, and the avalanche of key is obvious. This proves that the sensitivity of LCHAOSAES key is superior to that of AES_128 and LAES, which means the higher security.

6.3   Algorithm Efficiency

The efficiency of algorithm is to evaluate the efficiency on each platform. The less time it takes for the algorithm, the higher efficiency it has. We use the C language to program AES_128, LAES proposed in [10] and LCHAOSAES. The operating system of 64-bit PC (clocked at 3.20 GHz) is Windows10 and the compiler is VS2012 platform VC ++. In the above experimental environment, 1000 bytes of text data were encrypted 50 times, and the average time consumed by each algorithm is shown in Table 2.

Table 2. Average time spent by each algorithm

Algorithm name	Average time (ms)
AES_128	2.271
LAES	1.245
LCHAOSAES	1.476

As can be seen from Table 2, AES_128 spent the most time in encryption, and LAES spend the least. Because LCHAOSAES improves efficiency while improving security, it is unavoidable that efficiency of LCHAOSAES is slightly lower than LAES, but it takes 35% less time than AES_128.

We transplanted the above three algorithms to our proposed encryption model. clock frequency of UE's MCU (MKL36Z64VLH4) is 48 MHz, flash size is 64 KB. The average time consumed by each algorithm to encrypt the data of different lengths is shown in Fig. 8.

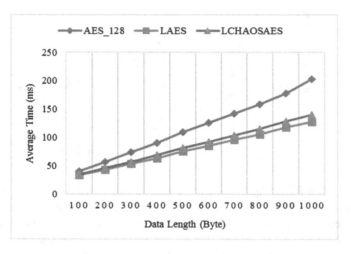

Fig. 8. Average time spent on data encryption for different lengths

Figure 8 shows that LCHAOSAES spent obviously less time than AES_128, slightly more than LAES. When the length of plaintext increases, AES_128 has a maximum growth rate, while time growth rate of LCHAOSAES and LAES are slightly smaller. Although LCHAOSAES is slightly less efficient than LAES, it is known from Table 2 that it is 35% more efficient than AES_128.

7   Conclusion

In order to solve the data security problem in NB-IoT applications, we proposed LCHAOSAES, a lightweight encryption algorithm based on AES and chaotic sequence. Furthermore, the encryption model is designed according to the NB-IoT application architecture. LCHAOSAES improves efficiency by reducing AES rounds and designing quick tables. In addition, it uses Logistic and Tent chaotic systems to generate complex chaotic sequences as encryption keys, and provides different keys for each round operation to improve the security and ensure that the length of ciphertext is the same as the plaintext. Through the theoretical analysis and experimental evaluation on the encryption model, we can see that the security of LCHAOSAES is obviously higher than that of AES_128 and LAES. Although the efficiency is slightly lower than

LAES, and 35% higher than AES_128. LCHAOSAES with high security and efficiency can be used as an encryption algorithm for NB-IoT applications.

In addition, the table designed to improve the efficiency of LCHAOSAES will take 1792 bytes of memory. Although the current MCU processor is enough to accommodate 1792 bytes, but we plan to solve this problem in the future work.

Acknowledgements. This work is supported in part by National Natural Science Foundation of China under Grant No. 61672370, 61672369 and 61872257, Natural Science Research Foundation of Jiangsu Higher Education Institutions under Grant No. 17KJB520037 and 17KJB520035, and CERNET Innovation Project under Grant No. NGII20170311.

References

1. 3GPP Revised Work Item: Narrowband IoT (NB-IoT), 3GPP RP-152284. 3GPP (2015)
2. Ericsson, Nokia, ZTE, NTT DOCOMO Inc: 3GPP RP-161248, Introduction of NB-IoT in 36.331. 3GPP TSG-RAN Meeting#72, Busan, South Korea, June 2016
3. 3GPP TR 23.720: Study on architecture enhancements for Cellular Internet of Things (Release 13). 3GPP (2016)
4. Ratasuk, R., Vejlgaard, B., Mangalvedhe, N., et al.: NB-IoT system for M2M communication. In: IEEE Wireless Communications and Networking Conference Workshops (WCNCW), pp. 1–5. IEEE, Doha (2016)
5. Lee, J., Kapitanova, K., Son, S.H.: The price of security in wireless sensor networks. Comput. Netw. **54**(17), 2967–2978 (2010)
6. Ben Othman, S., Trad, A., Youssef, H.: Performance evaluation of encryption algorithm for wireless sensor networks. In: International Conference on Information Technology & E-services, pp. 1–8. IEEE, Sousse (2012)
7. Chen, Q., Chen, Q., Min, Y., et al.: Design of encryption algorithm of data security for Wireless Sensor Network. In: International Conference on Electrical & Control Engineering, pp. 2983–2986. IEEE, Yichang (2011)
8. Msolli, A., Helali, A., Maaref, H.: Image encryption with the AES algorithm in wireless sensor network. In: International Conference on Advanced Technologies for Signal and Image Processing (ATSIP), pp. 41–45. IEEE, Monastir (2016)
9. Panda, M.: Data security in wireless sensor networks via AES algorithm. In: International Conference on Intelligent Systems & Control, pp. 1–5. IEEE, Coimbatore (2015)
10. Yao, Z., Ling, Y.E.: Encryption algorithms for wireless sensor networks based on AES. Comput. Eng. Des. **36**(3), 619–623 (2015)
11. Wei, G., Zhang, H.: The light-weight optimization of AES algorithm and its application in radio frequency identification tag. J. Wuhan Univ. **58**(6), 471–476 (2012)
12. Xi, Z., Li, L., Shi, G., Wang, S.: A comparative study of encryption algorithms in wireless sensor network. In: Zeng, Q.-A. (ed.) Wireless Communications, Networking and Applications. LNEE, vol. 348, pp. 1087–1097. Springer, New Delhi (2016). https://doi.org/10.1007/978-81-322-2580-5_99
13. Osvik, D.A., Bos, J.W., Stefan, D., et al.: Fast software AES encryption. In: Hong, S., Iwata, T. (eds.) FSE 2010. LNCS, vol. 6147, pp. 75–93. Springer, Heidelberg (2010). https://doi.org/10.1007/978-3-642-13858-4_5
14. Babu, T.R., Murthy, K.V.V.S., Sunil, G.: Implementation of AES algorithm on ARM. In: Proceedings of the ICWET 2011 International Conference & Workshop on Emerging Trends in Technology, pp. 1211–1213. ACM, Mumbai (2011)

15. Ahmed, W., Mahmood, H., Siddique, U.: The efficient implementation of S8 AES algorithm. Lect. Notes Eng. Comput. Sci. **2191**(1), 334–339 (2011)
16. Barnes, A., Fernando, R., Mettananda, K., et al.: Improving the throughput of the AES algorithm with multicore processors. In: International Conference on Industrial and Information Systems (ICIIS), pp. 1–6. IEEE, Chennai (2012)
17. Wong, M.M., Wong, M.L.D.: New lightweight AES S-box using LFSR. In: International Symposium on Intelligent Signal Processing & Communication Systems, pp. 115–120. IEEE, Kuching (2015)
18. Hong, C., Yi, C.: Research on AES algorithm based on CHAOS. J. Beijing Technol. Bus. Univ. **27**(5), 57–60 (2009)
19. Chen, D., Qing, D., Wang, D.: AES key expansion algorithm based on 2D logistic mapping. In: Fifth International Workshop on Chaos-fractals Theories & Applications, pp. 207–211. IEEE, Dalian (2012)
20. Wang, Y., Wang, J.: A new image encryption algorithm based on compound chaotic sequence. In: International Conference on Measurement, pp. 962–966. IEEE, Harbin (2012)
21. Muhaya, B.F.T.: Chaotic and AES cryptosystem for satellite imagery. Telecommun. Syst. **52**(2), 573–581 (2013)
22. He, C.G., Bao, S.D.: An encryption algorithm based on chaotic system for 3G security authentication. In: Youth Conference on Information, Computing and Telecommunications, pp. 351–354. IEEE, Beijing (2011)
23. Pradhan, C., Bisoi, A.K.: Chaotic variations of AES algorithm. Int. J. Chaos Control Model. Simul. **2**(2), 19–25 (2013)

Energy Efficiency Maximization for Green Cognitive Internet of Things with Energy Harvesting

Xin Liu[1(✉)], Xueyan Zhang[2], Weidang Lu[3], and Mudi Xiong[4]

[1] School of Information and Communication Engineering,
Dalian University of Technology, Dalian 116024, China
liuxinstar1984@dlut.edu.cn
[2] School of Civil Engineering,
Dalian University of Technology, Dalian 116024, China
xueyan@dlut.edu.cn
[3] College of Information Engineering,
Zhejiang University of Technology, Hangzhou 310014, China
luweid@zjut.edu.cn
[4] School of Information Science and Technology,
Dalian Maritime University, Dalian 116026, China
xiongmudi@dlmu.edu.cn

Abstract. In this paper, a green cognitive Internet of Things (CIoT) has been proposed to collect the radio frequency (RF) energy of primary user (PU) by using energy harvesting. The CIoT nodes are divided into two independent groups to perform spectrum sensing and energy harvesting simultaneously in the sensing slot. The energy efficiency of the CIoT is maximized by through jointly optimizing sensing time, number of sensing nodes and transmission power. The suboptimal solution to the optimization problem is achieved using a joint optimization algorithm based on alternating direction optimization. Simulation results have indicated that the optimal solution is existed and the green CIoT outperforms the traditional scheme.

Keywords: CIoT · Energy efficiency · Energy harvesting · Joint optimization

1 Introduction

Cognitive radio (CR) has been proposed to improve spectrum utilization by accessing the idle spectrum of a primary user (PU), providing that the normal communications of the PU cannot be disturbed [1]. In order to avoid causing any interference to the PU, the CR has to perform spectrum sensing before using an idle channel and access this channel only when detecting the absence of the PU [2]. Cooperative spectrum sensing exploiting sensing diversity gain is proposed as a high-performance spectrum sensing method, which allows multiple

X. B. Zhai et al. (Eds.): MLICOM 2019, LNICST 294, pp. 281–290, 2019.
https://doi.org/10.1007/978-3-030-32388-2_24

nodes to sense the PU collaboratively and gets a final decision by combining local sensing results of all the nodes with some fusion rules [3,4]. A sensing-throughput tradeoff scheme has been proposed to maximize the throughput of the CR by selecting an optimal sensing time [5].

Internet of things (IoT) has gotten more and more attentions with the development of social and economy, which connects everything through the internet and provides better quality of service (QoS) to users [6]. However, the IoT can only use some unlicensed spectrum that is competitively used by many communication equipments, such as WiFi, Bluetooth and WiMax etc. Thus, the inadequate spectrum resources have greatly limited the development of the IoT [7,8]. IoT combining with CR, namely cognitive IoT (CIoT), has been proposed to improve spectrum utilization of a IoT through using idle licensed spectrum. However, compared with the traditional IoTs, CIoT may consume more energy due to spectrum sensing [9]. Hence, it is an important to realize green CIoT.

Wireless energy harvesting has been investigated to realize green communications by collecting the radio frequency (RF) energy of ambient signal sources, which can convert RF energy to direct current (DC) voltage by deploying a rectifying circuit [10,11]. To guarantee enough transmission power, energy harvesting has been used in CR to collect the RF energy of a PU's signal following spectrum sensing [12]. In the previous literatures, resource optimizations are presented to maximize the transmission performance of the IoT, however, the energy efficiency optimization is not considered. In this paper, a green CIoT is proposed to decrease energy consumption using energy harvesting. The contributions of the paper are listed as follows

- A green CIoT is proposed to collect the RF energy of the PU's signal and the noise for compensating sensing energy consumption. The frame is divided into sensing slot and transmission slot, and the CIoT nodes are divided into two independent groups to perform spectrum sensing and energy harvesting simultaneously in the sensing slot.
- The maximization of energy efficiency by jointly optimizing sensing time, number of sensing nodes and transmission power is formulated as a multi-parameter non-convex optimization problem that is hard to be solved directly. A joint optimization algorithm has been proposed to achieve the suboptimal solution to the optimization problem.

2   System Model

Periodical spectrum sensing and transmission has been proposed to improve the spectrum efficiency of the CIoT, while avoiding producing any interference to the PU [13]. The frame structure of the CIoT is divided into sensing slot and transmission slot, and the transmission happens only when the PU has been detected in the sensing slot, as shown in Fig. 1.

However, compared with the traditional IoTs, the CIoT may consume more energy due to the energy consumption in spectrum sensing. Hence, a green CIoT is proposed to harvest the RF energy of the PU's signal to supplement energy consumption. In the sensing slot of the energy-efficient CIoT, a group of CIoT nodes detect the presence of the PU by cooperative spectrum sensing, while the other group of nodes collect the RF energy of the PU's signal using energy harvesting simultaneously, as shown in Fig. 2.

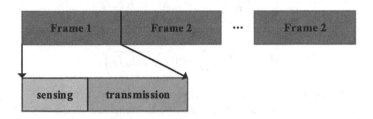

Fig. 1. Frame structure of CIoT.

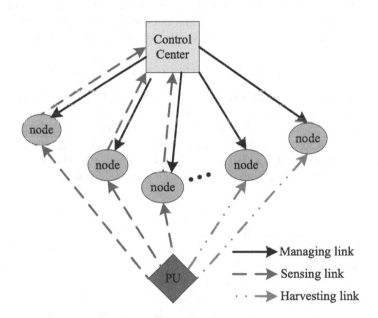

Fig. 2. Green CIoT structure.

We suppose that there are N nodes and one control center in the CIoT and K nodes are selected to perform cooperative spectrum sensing. In cooperative spectrum sensing, each node first senses the PU to get local detection information, and then all the detection information of K nodes are sent to the control center for combination [14]. The final decision is made at the control center by comparing the combined detection information to a threshold. The presence of the PU is decided if the combined detection value is above the preset threshold, otherwise, the absence of the PU is determined. False alarm probability and detection probability of cooperative spectrum sensing are respectively given as follows

$$P_d = Q\left(\left(\frac{\lambda}{\sigma_n^2} - \gamma - 1\right)\sqrt{\frac{Kt_s f_s}{(1+\gamma)^2}}\right) \tag{1}$$

$$P_f = Q\left(\left(\frac{\lambda}{\sigma_n^2} - 1\right)\sqrt{Kt_s f_s}\right) \tag{2}$$

where λ is detection threshold, σ_n^2 is noise power, γ is average PU's signal to noise ratio (PSNR), t_s is sensing time and f_s is sampling frequency.

P_f indicates the spectrum utilization of the CIoT, which should be decreased to improve the spectrum access probability of the CIoT; while P_d reflects the interference to the PU, whose should be increased to decrease the interference probability of the CIoT. As the primary task of the CIoT is to avoid causing harmful interference to the PU, the detection probability is often constrained as $P_d \geq P_d^{min}$, where P_d^{min} is the minimal detection probability satisfying the interference tolerance of the PU. Then the constraint of P_f is given by

$$P_f \geq Q\left(Q^{-1}(P_d^{min})(\gamma+1) + \gamma\sqrt{Kt_s f_s}\right) \tag{3}$$

The RF energy of wireless signals can be collected to convert to DC energy by a wireless system deploying an energy harvester with a rectifying circuit as the core device. The harvested energy is then stored in a rechargeable battery of the wireless system. In the CIoT, the remaining $N - K$ nodes are selected to harvest the RF energy of the PU's signal and the noise in the channel in the sensing slot. The harvested power of each node can be given by

$$p_h = u(1+\gamma)\sigma_n^2 \tag{4}$$

where u is energy-harvesting efficiency.

Assume that each sensing node reports its detection information to the control center in an independent time slot in case of transmission conflicts. The reporting time can be seen as cooperative sensing overhead, t_c, which is described as $t_c = K\tau$, where τ is the slot length. Thus, the total sensing slot length $T_s = t_s + t_c$. Supposing the frame time is T, the transmission time $T_d = T - T_s$. The CIoT can transmit data effectively only when the absence of the PU has been detected accurately in the probability of $(1 - P_f)P_0$ where P_0 is average idle probability of the PU. The average total throughput of the CIoT is given by

$$R = (T - t_s - K\tau)(1 - P_f)P_0 C \tag{5}$$

where C is transmission rate defined as follows

$$C = \sum_{n=1}^{N} \log\left(1 + \frac{p_i h_i^2}{\sigma_n^2}\right) \tag{6}$$

where p_i and h_i is transmission power and channel gain of node i, respectively.

The CIoT may consume energy during spectrum sensing and data transmission but save energy by energy harvesting. The total consumed sensing energy is given by $E_s = K p_s T_s$ where p_s is average sensing power in the sensing slot, the total consumed transmission energy is obtained by $E_d = p_t T_d$ where p_t is total power of N nodes, and the total harvested energy is given by $E_h = (N-K) p_h T_s$. Hence, the total consumed energy $E_c = E_s + E_d - E_h$. The energy efficiency of the CIoT, which is related with the parameters t_s, K and $\{p_i\}$, can be defined as follows

$$\eta\left(t_s, K, \{p_i\}\right) = \frac{R}{E_c} = \frac{(T - t_s - K\tau)(1 - P_f)P_0 \sum_{i=1}^{N} \log\left(1 + \frac{p_i h_i^2}{\sigma_n^2}\right)}{K p_s T_s + p_t T_d - (N - K)p_h T_s} \tag{7}$$

3 Model Optimization

In this paper, we try to maximize the energy efficiency of the CIoT by jointly optimizing sensing time, number of sensing nodes and transmission power, subject to the constraints of detection probability and transmission rate. The optimization problem is listed as follows

$$\max_{t_s, K, \{p_i\}} \quad \eta\left(t_s, K, \{p_i\}\right) \tag{8a}$$

$$\text{s.t.} \quad P_d \geq P_d^{min} \tag{8b}$$

$$C \geq C^{min} \tag{8c}$$

$$t_s + K\tau \leq T \tag{8d}$$

$$p_i \geq 0, i = 1, 2, ..., N \tag{8e}$$

$$1 \leq K \leq N, K \in Z \tag{8f}$$

where C^{min} is the minimal transmission rate. This is a multi-parameter non-convex optimization problem that is hard to be solved directly. In this paper, a suboptimal solving algorithm is proposed, which divides the optimization problem into two sub-optimization problems.

3.1 Power Optimization

From (7), η can be maximized with the minimal p_t, hence, an optimization problem to minimize p_t under the constraint of C is first given as follows

$$\min_{\{p_i\}} \; p_t = \sum_{i=1}^{N} p_i \tag{9a}$$

$$\text{s.t.} \; \sum_{i=1}^{N} \log\left(1 + \frac{p_i h_i^2}{\sigma_n^2}\right) \geq C^{min} \tag{9b}$$

$$p_i \geq 0, i = 1, 2, ..., N \tag{9c}$$

which can be solved by Lagrange optimization. The Lagrange function is given as follows

$$L\left(\lambda, \{p_i\}\right) = \sum_{i=1}^{N} p_i - \lambda \left(\sum_{n=1}^{N} \log\left(1 + \frac{p_i h_i^2}{\sigma_n^2}\right) - C^{min}\right) \tag{10}$$

where $\lambda > 0$ is Lagrange multiplier. The optimal power value p_i^* is achieved by letting $\frac{\partial L(\lambda, \{p_i\})}{p_i} = 0$ for $i = 1, 2, ..., N$. Noting that $p_i \geq 0$, p_i^* is calculated by

$$p_i^* = \left(\lambda - \frac{\sigma_n^2}{h_i^2}\right)^+ \tag{11}$$

where $(x)^+$ denotes the maximal value between x and 0.

3.2 Joint Optimization

After the optimal $\{p_i\}$ is achieved, t_s and K are jointly optimized. The optimization problem is formulated as follows

$$\max_{t_s, K} \; \eta\left(t_s, K\right) = \frac{(T - t_s - K\tau)(1 - P_f)P_0 C^{min}}{(Kp_s - (N - K)p_h)(t_s + K\tau) + p_t^*(T - t_s - K\tau)} \tag{12a}$$

$$\text{s.t.} \; P_d \geq P_d^{min} \tag{12b}$$

$$t_s + K\tau \leq T \tag{12c}$$

$$1 \leq K \leq N, K \in Z \tag{12d}$$

where $p_t^* = \sum_{i=1}^{N} p_i^*$. From (12), η improves with the decrease of P_f, hence, the maximal value of η can be achieved only when η equals its lower bound as shown in (3). The objective function η is rewritten as follows

$$\eta\left(t_s, K\right) = \frac{P_0 C^{min}(T - t_s - K\tau)\left(1 - Q\left(Q^{-1}(P_d^{min})(\gamma + 1) + \gamma\sqrt{Kt_s f_s}\right)\right)}{(Kp_s - (N - K)p_h)(t_s + K\tau) + p_t^*(T - t_s - K\tau)} \tag{13}$$

Firstly fixing K, we optimize t_s. Then let $\eta(t_s) = \frac{f_a(t_s)}{f_b(t_s)}$, where $f_a(t_s)$ and $f_b(t_s)$ are respectively given by

$$f_a(t_s) = P_0 C^{min}(T - t_s - K\tau)\left(1 - Q\left(Q^{-1}(P_d^{min})(\gamma + 1) + \gamma\sqrt{Kt_s f_s}\right)\right) \quad (14)$$

$$f_b(t_s) = (Kp_s - (N - K)p_h)(t_s + K\tau) + p_t^*(T - t_s - K\tau) \quad (15)$$

It has been proven that $f_a(t_s)$ is a convex function, meanwhile, $\eta_b(t_s)$ is a linear function. Hence, (12) can be solved by Dinkelbach's optimization that can solve convex-linear fractional optimization by an iterative procedure. An equivalent optimization function $F(\eta_l)$ is defined as follows

$$F(\eta^{(l)}) = f_a(t_s^{(l)}) - \eta^{(l)} f_b(t_s^{(l)}) \quad (16)$$

where l is iteration index. In each iteration, we try to maximize $F(\eta^{(l)})$. The optimal $\eta^{(l)} = \frac{f_a(t_s^{(l)})}{f_b(t_s^{(l)})}$ can be achieved when $F(\eta^{(l)})$ is convergent. The sensing time optimization algorithm is shown as Algorithm 1.

Algorithm 1. Sensing time optimization.

Input: $\eta^{(l)} = 0$ where $l = 1$, and the convergence accuracy δ;
1: **while** $F(\eta^{(l)}) > \delta$ **do**
2:     find the optimal solution to the optimization problem $t_s^{(l)} = arg\,max\left(f_a(t_s^{(l)}) - \eta^{(l)} f_b(t_s^{(l)})\right)$ using interior-point method;
3:     set $\eta^{(l+1)} = \frac{f_a(t_s^{(l)})}{f_b(t_s^{(l)})}$ and $l = l + 1$;
4: **end while**
Output: the optimal solution $t_s^* = t_s^{(l)}$.

Then with the optimal t_s^*, we continue to optimize K. Since K is an integer within $[0, N]$, it is not computational complexity to search optimal K^* using enumeration method, as follows

$$K^* = \arg\max_{1 \leq K \leq N} \eta\left(K|t_s = t_s^*\right) \quad (17)$$

Then we use ADO to achieve the joint optimal solution [15], through optimizing t_s and K alternatively until both of them are convergent. The joint optimization algorithm is described as Algorithm 2.

4   Simulations and Discussions

In the simulations, the frame time $T = 10\,\text{ms}$, the sampling frequency $f_s = 10\,\text{KHz}$, the number of nodes $N = 20$, the sensing power $p_s = 3\,\text{mW}$, the noise

Algorithm 2. Joint optimization algorithm.

Input: $t_s^{(l)} = 0$ and $K^{(l)} = 1$;

1: **while** t_s and K are not convergent or reaching the maximal iterations **do**
2:     fixing $K = K^{(l)}$, achieve optimal t_s^* using the Algorithm 1;
3:     set $t_s^{(l+1)} = t_s^*$;
4:     fixing $t_s = t_s^{(l+1)}$, achieve optimal K^* using enumeration method;
5:     set $K^{(l+1)} = K^*$ and $l = l + 1$;
6: **end while**

Output: the joint optimal solution $t_s^* = t_s^{(l)}$ and $K^* = K^{(l)}$.

---

power $\sigma_n^2 = 0.1\,\text{mW}$, the energy-harvesting efficiency $u = 50\%$, the idle probability $P_0 = 0.5$, the minimal transmission rate $C^{min} = 100\,\text{Kbps}$, and the average channel gain is $-5\,\text{dB}$.

Figure 3 shows energy efficiency η changing with sensing time t_s and number of sensing nodes K. It is seen that there is an optimal set of t_s and K that maximizes η. η first improves with the increase of t_s because of the improved spectrum access probability, and then decreases due to the increased energy consumption. Moreover, η has the similar trend with the increase of K, which first improves due to the increase of sensing performance but then decreases because of the increase of sensing overhead.

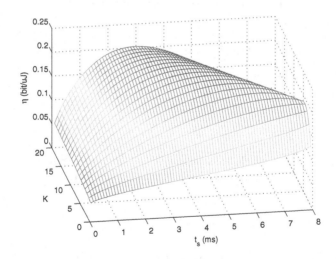

Fig. 3. Energy efficiency changing with sensing time and number of sensing nodes.

Figure 4 indicates throughput R changing with consumed energy E_c. It is seen that R first improves and then decreases as E_c increases, because the increase of E_c may improve the transmission performance but also increase the sensing overhead. Thus, there is tradeoff between transmission performance and

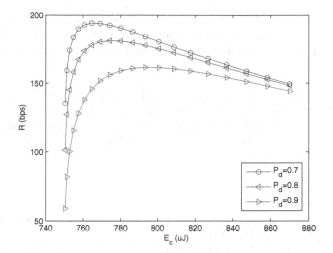

Fig. 4. Throughput changing with consumed energy.

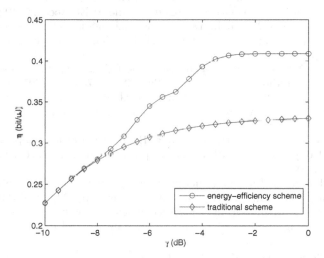

Fig. 5. Energy efficiency comparison.

energy consumption. Figure 5 compares energy efficiency of the proposed energy-efficient scheme and the traditional scheme. It shows that the proposed scheme can achieve larger energy efficiency as the PSNR increases.

5   Conclusions

In this paper, a green CIoT is proposed to harvest RF energy of the PU's signal to compensate sensing energy consumption. The energy efficiency of the green CIoT is maximized by jointly optimizing sensing time, number of sensing nodes and transmission power. From the simulations, there is an optimal set of sensing time and number of sensing nodes that maximizes the energy efficiency, and the green CIoT can achieve larger energy efficiency compared with the traditional CIoT.

Acknowledgements. This paper is supported by the National Natural Science Foundations of China under Grants 61601221 and 61871348, the Joint Foundation of the National Natural Science Foundations of China and the Civil Aviation of China under Grant U1833102, and the China Postdoctoral Science Foundations under Grants 2015M580425 and 2018T110496.

References

1. Mitola, J.: Cognitive radio for flexible mobile multimedia communications. Mob. Netw. Appl. **6**(5), 435–441 (2001)
2. Ghasemi, A., Sousa, E.S.: Spectrum sensing in cognitive radio networks: requirements, challenges and design trade-offs. IEEE Commun. Mag. **46**(4), 32–39 (2008)
3. Liu, X., Jia, M., Na, Z.: Multi-modal cooperative spectrum sensing based on dempster-shafer fusion in 5G-based cognitive radio. IEEE Access **6**, 199–208 (2018)
4. Lai, X., Fan, L., Lei, X., Li, J., Yang, N., Karagiannidis, G.K.: Distributed secure switch-and-stay combining over correlated fading channels. IEEE Trans. Inf. Forensics Secur. **pp**(99), 1–10 (2019)
5. Liu, X., Tan, X.: Optimization algorithm of periodical cooperative spectrum sensing in cognitive radio. Int. J. Commun. Syst. **27**(5), 705–720 (2014)
6. Liu, X., Jia, M., Zhang, X., Lu, W.: A novel multi-channel internet of things based on dynamic spectrum sharing in 5G communication. IEEE Internet Things J. **pp**(99), 1–9 (2018)
7. Chen, S., Xu, H., Liu, D., Hu, B., Wang, H.: A vision of IoT: applications, challenges, and opportunities with china perspective. IEEE Internet Things J. **1**(4), 349–359 (2014)
8. Liu, X., Zhang, X.: Rate and energy efficiency improvements for 5G-based IoT with simultaneous transfer. IEEE Internet Things J. **pp**(99), 1–10 (2018)
9. Liu, X., Li, F., Na, Z.: Optimal resource allocation in simultaneous cooperative spectrum sensing and energy harvesting for multichannel cognitive radio. IEEE Access **5**, 3801–3812 (2017)
10. Guo, J., Zhao, N., Yu, F.R., Liu, X., Leung, V.C.M.: Exploiting adversarial jamming signals for energy harvesting in interference networks. IEEE Trans. Wirel. Commun. **16**(2), 1267–1280 (2017)
11. Liu, L., Zhang, R., Chun, K.C.: Wireless information transfer with opportunistic energy harvesting. IEEE Trans. Wirel. Commun. **12**(1), 288–300 (2012)
12. Liu, X., Chen, K., Yan, J., Na, Z.: Optimal energy harvesting-based weighed cooperative spectrum sensing in cognitive radio network. Mob. Netw. Appl. **21**(6), 908–919 (2016)
13. Liu, X., Jia, M., Gu, X., Tan, X.: Optimal periodic cooperative spectrum sensing based on weight fusion in cognitive radio networks. Sensors **13**(4), 5251–5272 (2013)
14. Li, C., Zhou, W.: Enhanced secure transmission against intelligent attacks. IEEE Access **pp**(99), 1–6 (2019)
15. Stephen, B., Neal, P., Eric, C.: Distributed optimization and statistical learning via the alternating direction method of multipliers. Found. Trends Mach. Learn. **3**(1), 1–122 (2011)

Smart Internet of Things

A Smart Wearable Device for Preventing Indoor Electric Shock Hazards

Zaipeng Xie[1]([✉])[ID], Hanxiang Liu[1][ID], Junpeng Zhang[1][ID], Xiaorui Zhu[1][ID],
and Hongyu Lin[2][ID]

[1] Hohai University, Nanjing, China
zaipengxie@hhu.edu.cn
[2] Southeast University, Nanjing, China

Abstract. The emerging wearable IoT technology is evolving dramatically in recent years and resulted in a wide adoption in various applications. Electric shock hazard is one of the major indoor hazards for consumers who may fail to recognize potential electrical risks. This paper proposes a smart wearable IoT device with risk assessment algorithms for preventing indoor electrical shock hazards. This device consists of two hardware components: a receiver and a detector embedded in a power switch. The detector consists of a Wi-Fi module, a current sensor, a NFC module, and an Arduino mini module that communicates with a software routine monitoring the status of the power switch and its connected appliances. The receiver is a passive NFC tag that can be designed as an accessory or clothing that customers may wear. A risk assessment algorithm is proposed using a set of predefined inference rules. The software routine is developed to provide early warnings to customers where potential electrical shock risk level is high. This paper describes the implementation details as well as the algorithms. Experimental results are summarized and they demonstrate that the proposed smart wearable device can be effective in predicting electric shock hazards in an indoor environment.

Keywords: Wearable device · Smart device · IoT · Electric shock hazard · Risk analysis

1 Introduction

With the prevalence of appliances in modern families, indoor electric shock hazard has been reported [1] as one of the major causes of accidents in household. Electricity consumers could incur electric shock due to lack of experience and

Supported by the Innovative and Entrepreneurial Talent Program of Jiangsu Province (Grant No. 2016B17078) and partially supported by the National Key R&D Program of China (Grant No. 2016YFC0402710).

X. B. Zhai et al. (Eds.): MLICOM 2019, LNICST 294, pp. 293–304, 2019.
https://doi.org/10.1007/978-3-030-32388-2_25

failure of recognizing potential electric hazards. Recent research [2] revealed that power switch and appliance malfunction may cause electrical hazards, accounting for 40% of all electrical fatalities of year 2017 in China. The majority of these incidents were caused by direct contact with power lines, power outlets, appliances, and hand-carried conductive objects. Children and pets are especially vulnerable to electric shock hazards, because they are naturally inquisitive and can be tempted to approach and explore those areas. Hence, preventing indoor electric shock has become one of the primary issues for the household electrical safety.

Recent advances in the Internet of Things (IoT) technology has made smart IoT devices accessible to customers in vast industrial and household applications. For example, Kamilaris et al. [3] implemented a solution for a web-based energy-aware smart home framework that connects smart IoT devices to the Internet, where a star topology and a multi-hop topology was evaluated for apartments. Cloud-based IoT paradigm was proposed in [4] where all data from different IoT sensors can be gathered in the cloud platform that may provide a high reliability and scalability. IoT systems can bring a natural advantage for embedded applications to detect hazards. Lezama et. al. [5] developed an IoT system for AC series arc detection by inter-period correlations of current via embedded sensors. Mader et. al. [6] implemented hazard analysis framework for automotive IoT systems. IoT hardware for instrumentation and measurement [7] was widely adopted in several industrial applications [8] at CERN. Wearable devices [9] as one type of IoT devices are usually designed as accessories or clothing that people may wear. They are often expected to continuously collect and upload various data to improve the quality of life. Although small in size, wearable IoT devices often require reliable communication and reduced power consumption of the system. Many smart wearable IoT devices have emerged for the past several years in a variety of applications.

Smart wearable IoT technology can be effective in preventing indoor electric shock accidents and providing early warnings to customers. This paper explores a smart wearable IoT solution for preventing indoor electrical shock hazards that can provide modularity and economic viability. The proposed device consists of two hardware parts: the detector part is integrated in the power switch and it employs a Wi-Fi module, a current sensor, a Near Field Communication(NFC) module, and an Arduino mini [10] module that communicates with a software to monitor the status power switches and appliances; the receiver part is a passive device that can be worn by human or pets. Based on a set of predefined inference rules, a risk assessment algorithm is implemented and it is capable of evaluating the electric shock risk of power switches and appliances. The algorithm can be deployed on a local or cloud-based server and it will provide early warnings to the related personnel via portable devices. Potential electrical shock hazards are suggested based on the acquired data from the wearable devices. This paper presents the basic building hardware and software elements for delivering the infrastructure of the smart wearable device. Section 2 discusses system description that includes the hardware implementation and the risk assessment algorithm with he inference rules for risk analysis. Experimental results are demonstrated in Sect. 2.4 and final remarks are concluded in Sect. 3.

2   System Description

The proposed smart wearable IoT device consists of two hardware components: a detector and a receiver. A software is deployed on a local or cloud server to interact with the hardware. Figure 1 shows a diagram of the proposed system. The detector is integrated with a power switch where it contains a Wi-Fi module, a current sensor, a NFC module, and an Arduino mini module that communicates with a software routine to monitor the status of power consumption; the receiver is a passive device that can be designed as an accessory or clothing that people may wear. Based on a set of predefined inference rules, a risk assessment algorithm is implemented to evaluate the electric shock risk level of the power switches and appliances.

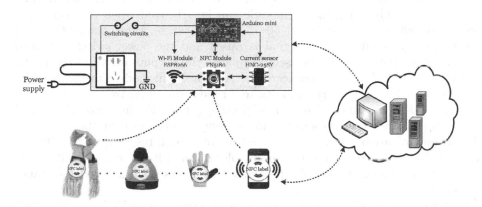

Fig. 1. Diagram of the proposed overall system.

2.1   Hardware Implementation

The designed hardware device has the following four major features: (1) to raise an alert when the wearable IoT device is detected within an effective range of the power switch that equipped with our detector; (2) to turn on and off the power switch automatically; (3) to monitor the average current of the power switch; (4) to connect with a wireless router and send/receive real-time data periodically. The system is required to be compact such that it can be fit into a typical electrical junction box. Hence, design consideration is required to implement the hardware in a compact size while achieving the aforementioned features.

Figure 2 shows the schematic of the proposed hardware. The proposed wearable hardware has a receiver component using a NFC tag and it does not require

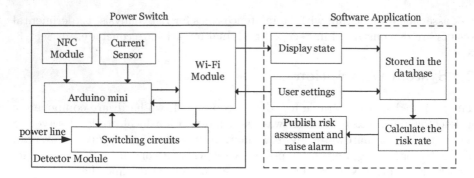

Fig. 2. Schematic of the proposed hardware implementation.

battery. The receiver can be designed as a clothing for human or a collar that a pet may wear. The proposed wearable hardware has a detector system that consists of a Wi-Fi module, a current sensor, a NFC reader module, and an Arduino mini module. The NFC reader module can be triggered when the receiver is within the effective range (about 50–75 cm of distance). When the NFC reader module is triggered, an alert signal is raised and the power switch is turned off simultaneously. The current sensor collects the output current of the power switch. The Wi-Fi module connects the Arduino mini module to the Internet and publish the real-time sensor data to a time series database.

The NFC module is implemented using a full NFC front-end IC (Model PN5180)[11] and it is responsible for sensing the distance of the NFC tag. The communication distance of PN5180 complies with the ISO/IEC 15693 and ISO/IEC 18000-3 communication protocols [12], and it can sense specific NFC tags within a range of about 50–75 cm, which makes it suitable as an distance sensor for our proposed system.

The current sensor is implemented using a multi-range Hall Current Sensor (model HNC-25SY) that has a high immunity to external interference. The main purpose of this sensor is to monitor the average AC current of the power switch and provides sensed data for the risk assessment algorithm.

The Wi-Fi module is implemented using the low-power Wi-Fi card (model ESP8266). The ESP8266 is an integrated microchip with a compact design that supports a variety of modes including softAP, station, softAP+station. The Wi-Fi module is connected to an ATmega168-based Arduino mini development board via a serial port and it provides a fast wireless data transfer rate.

The Arduino mini module [10] is a small micro-controller board based on the ATmega168 microprocessor. This module has 14 digital input and output pins, 6 analog inputs, an on-board resonator, and holes for mounting pin headers. This module has a compact size and easy to program. Its main role is to control the power switch and handle the transferring of sensor data and user instructions via the Wi-Fi module.

Figure 3 shows the control flow of the hardware system. When the system is turned on, the NFC module and the current sensor are initialized. If the Wi-Fi module has not been configured or the configuration information is incorrect, the system will transit to the configuration mode. After the Wi-Fi module is successfully configured and connected to the wireless network, the detector resumes the working mode. At the working mode, the Arduino mini module acquires the measured current data periodically. On receiving a user instruction, the Arduino mini module is interrupted and executes the user instruction. The NFC reader constantly monitors the existence of approaching NFC tag. It will produce a warning signal and shut down the power switch on detecting an wearable device that contains the NFC tag within its working range.

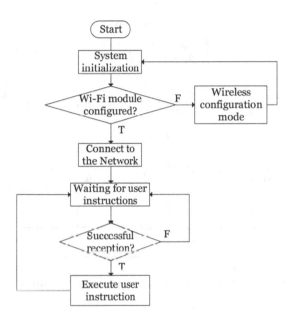

Fig. 3. The control flow of the hardware system.

2.2 Software Implementation

A software routine has been developed to allow users to view and configure the hardware at any time. The software routine can be run on a local or cloud-based server. The routine works as a finite state machine that transits between two states: the initialization state and the executing state. At the initialization state, it is required to configure the Wi-Fi module and pair the software routine with the hardware. On completion of the pairing, the software transits to the executing state, where the software is collecting data continuously on the server. The data includes the average current and the NFC alarm signal.

Figure 4 shows the flow chart of the software routine. The data captured on the software routine is interpreted for two purposes: (1) displaying the hardware

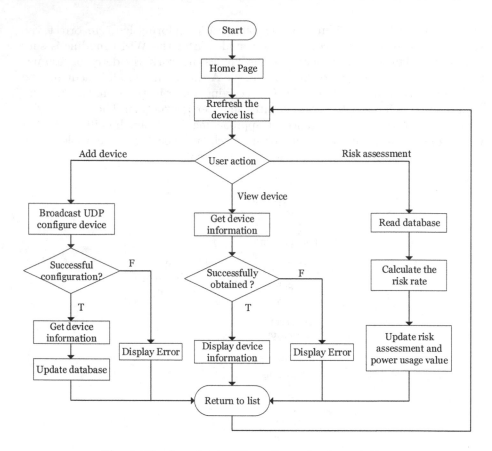

Fig. 4. The flow chart of the software implementation.

status; (2) calculating the risk factor of individual power switch. A risk assessment algorithm is implemented to assess an electric hazard risk using the historical data. At the same time, the user can perform operations such as switching on and off the switch, viewing historical data, and viewing the risk-level heatmap of all connected power switches.

2.3   The Risk Assessment Algorithm

The risk assessment algorithm is used for evaluating the level of the electric shock hazard at each device. A device is considered as a power switch containing the detector hardware. A heatmap is generated to describe each device's risk level based on collected data. The potential electric shock hazard is evaluated using the historical data and warning can be raised to assist preventing potential electric shock. This section describes the analysis model of the risk assessment algorithm. As shown in Fig. 5, the risk assessment algorithm has three input variables: the measured average current in Ampere, the number of NFC alarm events per time unit, and the age of the power switch. The output of the algorithm is the calculated risk level assessment.

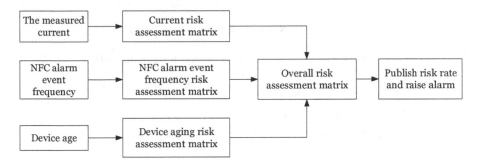

Fig. 5. Data flow of the risk assessment algorithm.

The Risk Assessment Matrix [14] is an effective method to evaluate potential risk in decision making systems by considering the category of risk rate against the category of severity. It employs a matrix to visualize potential risks in a qualitative way. The evaluated risks are generated using the input data and described in several risk levels. Four levels are adopted in our algorithm as Low I, Moderate II, High III, and Extreme IV. The Low I corresponds to a low risk and the power switch has no risk of electric shock. The potential electric shock hazard is small or negligible, the frequency of contact is close to zero. For this level of risk, no additional measures are required to reduce the risk. Moderate II corresponds to a moderately dangerous, slightly risky device that may cause a slight electric shock. The resulting hazard is moderate and may not occur as usual. For this level of risk, it is acceptable when the activity of children or pets is within the guardian's line of sight. High III corresponds to a high risk. Power switch at this level may cause an electric shock and great damage to the body. For this level of risk, strict prevention of customers from exploring such area is suggested. Extreme IV corresponds to a extremely high risk that may incur electric accidents and even life threats. For this level of risk, such device should be replaced and isolated from general contact, the area around the device should be isolated to children and pets.

The risk assessment for the average current is defined in Table 1 that determines the electrical shock risk level. When the current reaches [10, 30] mA through the human body, it will cause tender stimulus; a [30, 100] mA current will cause some pain on human body. While a [100, 250] mA current will cause a strong pain and possible cramp. When the current through the body exceeds 250 mA, the subject may incur severe damage to its tissue and even death. The risk level of the current is quantified to interpret electric shock hazards. Different current values correspond to different consequences, including A0, A1, A2, and

A3. The four levels can be summarized as given in Table 1. Here, level A0 has a quantization value of 1, level A1's quantization value is 10, and the quantization value of Level A2 and A3 are 100 and 1000 respectively.

Table 1. The Risk Matrix for the average current.

	Risk level	Average current (mA)	Risk quantization
A0	Low I	[10, 30]	1
A1	Moderate II	[30, 100]	10
A2	High III	[100, 250]	100
A3	Extreme IV	[250, +∞]	1000

The risk assessment for the number of NFC alarm events is also part of the overall risk analysis. Since the total number of NFC alarm event varies randomly in different scenarios. We propose using the NFC alarm event frequency, $\tilde{T}$, to assess its risk factor and it can be defined by the following equation

$$\tilde{T} = \frac{1}{N} \sum_{i=1}^{N} T_i \tag{1}$$

Here, the risk factor of the number of NFC alarm events can hereby be defined as the event frequency correspond to different NFC alarm risk levels, including E0, E1, E2, and E3. The four levels can be summarized as given in Table 2:

Table 2. The Risk Matrix for the NFC alarm events.

	Risk level	Event frequency	Risk quantization
E0	Low I	$[0, 0.5\tilde{T}]$	1
E1	Moderate II	$[0.5\tilde{T}, \tilde{T}]$	10
E2	High III	$[\tilde{T}, 1.5\tilde{T}]$	100
E3	Extreme IV	$[1.5\tilde{T}, +∞]$	1000

The risk assessment for the aging of electronic components is also one of the factors in the overall risk analysis. The aging of power switches can have a direct relationship with the electric shock hazard. The failure rate of electronics usually has a bathtub shape [13]: i.e., the risk level noticeably decreases due to early failures that could be caused by design faults or initial implementation defects. The risk level increases after a useful life span due to material fatigue and component aging. The bathtub shaped risk function is adopted in our algorithm as a piece-wise function with four segments. The risk assessment of the device aging is categorized into four risk levels, G0, G1, G2, and G3 as in Table 3.

Table 3. The Risk Matrix for the aging of electronics.

	Risk level	Age (years)	Risk quantization
G0	Low I	$[0, 0.5]$	10
G1	Moderate II	$[0.5, 1]$	1
G2	High III	$[1, 3]$	10
G3	Extreme IV	$[3, +\infty]$	100

The overall risk assessment for the proposed smart IoT wearable system is hence defined as a combination of the average current (A), the number of NFC alarm events (E), and the aging of electronic device (G) as given by Equation

$$V(I, \tilde{T}, age) - A(I) \cdot E(\tilde{T}) \cdot G(age) \tag{2}$$

where $V(I, \tilde{T}, age)$ is the overall risk assessment, I is the measured current of the particular power switch, and $\tilde{T}$ is the NFC alarm event frequency.

2.4 Experimental Results

The experiments were carried out in a $80\,\text{m}^2$ apartment building where a total of twenty power switches have been replaced by the proposed hardware. The NFC tag is worn by an adult who lives inside this apartment. Test procedures were constructed and executed to measure the reliability and effectiveness of the smart wearable IoT system. All experiments were conducted in an indoor environment to emulate the condition of a typical household scenario. The experiments lasted for about 18 months and for each set of experimental trials, the data are collected and stored in a local server.

Figure 6 shows the measured average current of three typical devices in 18 months. The figure shows that the measured average current varies each month. But the variation is relatively small, about 5% to 15%, in a year long aspect. However, the data reveal that the average current differs among devices and it may cause a varying level of electric shock hazard for different areas.

Figure 7 shows the number of NFC alarm events of three typical devices in 18 months. The number of NFC alarm events varies randomly from month to month. The data reveals that some devices can have frequent visits for several months. This may indicate that users visit those areas regularly and it may cause a high level of electric shock hazard near those devices. Customers can be suggested to pay extra attention to those areas and caution can be taken for individual devices.

Figure 8 shows the generated heatmap of all twenty devices in 18 months. The heatmap is an excellent visualization tool for the customers to understand potential hazards. In Fig. 8, the colorbar indicates potential hazard risk levels inside the house, where light blue means a relatively low risk level (Low I), yellow means a moderate risk level (Moderate II), green means a high risk level (High III), and red means an extreme situation where the probability of electric

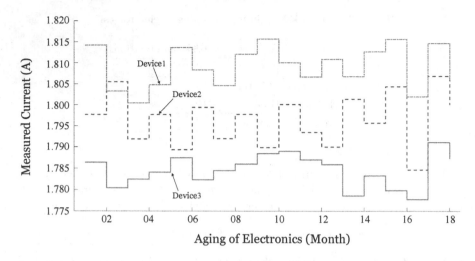

Fig. 6. The measured average current of three typical devices for 18 months.

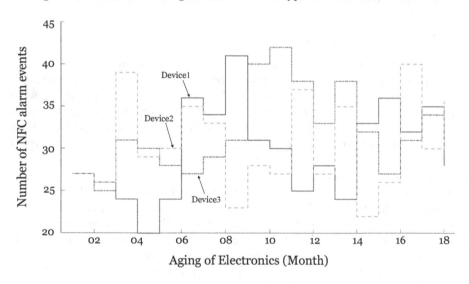

Fig. 7. The measured NFC alarm event of three typical devices for 18 months.

shock hazard can be very high (Extreme IV). The results reveal quite a lot of information about the potential electric shock hazards, for example, Device-2 shows a high risk level in the first two months and the hazard was prevented due to the isolation of those areas such that electric shock hazard can be prevented. Device-12 exhibits a repeating pattern of high risk levels and it could indicate that the user is visiting this area on a regular basis. Customers can, hence, take actions to prevent hazards just by viewing the heatmap. A fine-grained definition can be employed to manifests in a higher number of overall risk levels, which can potentially benefit in flexibility when highlighting the electric hazard. In summary, the experimental results demonstrated an example scenario where the proposed device can be effective in visualizing and estimating the risk factors of the corresponding area.

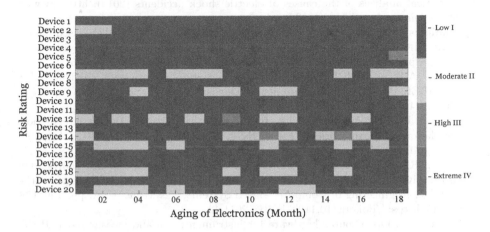

Fig. 8. The generated heat-map of all twenty devices for 18 months. (Color figure online)

3   Conclusions

This paper proposes a smart wearable IoT device that is capable of preventing indoor electric shock hazards. The overall hardware and software design details are described, and a recommended algorithm for assessing hazard risks is presented. The entire device utilizes an NFC module, a current sensor, a Wi-Fi module paired with an Arduino mini micro-controller to achieve the functionality. Customers can operate on the device through a software application where the sensor data, NFC signals, and the age of the equipment are used to evaluate the potential electric shock risk of each device. The risk assessment algorithm has been evaluated in an experimental test scenario for eighteen months; and the experimental results show that the proposed system can provide convenient and easy understandable visualization heatmaps to users. In summary, the proposed system is effective in preventing electric shock hazard and assisting parents and pet owners to protect their loved ones.

References

1. Gordon, L.B., et al.: A complete electrical shock hazard classification system and its application. IEEE Trans. Ind. Appl. **54**(6), 6554–6565 (2018). https://doi.org/10.1109/TIA.2018.2803768
2. Statistical analysis of the causes of electric shock accidents (2019). http://www.dgxue.com/anquan/jichu/1913.html
3. Kamilaris, A. et al.: HomeWeb: an application framework for Web-based smart homes. In: 18th International Conference on Telecommunications, Ayia Napa, Cyprus, pp. 134–139 (2011). https://doi.org/10.1109/CTS.2011.5898905
4. Biswas, A.R. et al.: IoT and cloud convergence: opportunities and challenges. In: 2014 IEEE World Forum on Internet of Things (WF-IoT), Seoul, Korea, pp. 375–376 (2014). https://doi.org/10.1109/WF-IoT.2014.6803194
5. Lezama, J., et al.: An embedded system for AC series arc detection by inter-period correlations of current. Electr. Power Syst. Res. **129**(1), 227–234 (2015). https://doi.org/10.1016/j.epsr.2015.08.005
6. Mader, R., et al.: A computer-aided approach to preliminary hazard analysis for automotive embedded systems. In: 18th IEEE International Conference and Workshops on Engineering of Computer-Based Systems, Las Vegas, USA, pp. 169–178 (2011). https://doi.org/10.1109/ECBS.2011.43
7. Harnett, C.: Open source hardware for instrumentation and measurement. IEEE Instrum. Meas. Mag. **14**(3), 34–38 (2011). https://doi.org/10.1109/MIM.2011.5773535
8. CERN Open Hardware Repository (2019). https://www.ohwr.org/projects/cernohl
9. Seneviratne, S., et al.: A survey of wearable devices and challenges. IEEE Commun. Surv. Tutor. **19**(4), 2573–2620 (2017). https://doi.org/10.1109/COMST.2017.2731979
10. Banzi, M., Shiloh, M.: Getting Started with Arduino: The Open Source Electronics Prototyping Platform. Maker Media Inc., Sebastopol (2014)
11. NXP Semiconductors.: PN5180 High-performance multiprotocol full NFC Forum-compliant frontend: Product data sheet, Rev. 3.2 (2017)
12. ISO/IEC 18000-3 (2019). https://www.iso.org/standard/53424.html
13. Bebbington, M., et al.: Useful periods for lifetime distributions with bathtub shaped hazard rate functions. IEEE Trans. Reliab. **55**(2), 245–251 (2006). https://doi.org/10.1109/TR.2001.874943
14. Yang, Q., et al.: A rough set approach for determining weights of decision makers in group decision making. PloS One **12**(2), e0172679 (2017). https://doi.org/10.1371/journal.pone.0172679

A VLP Approach Based
on a Single LED Lamp

Jing Chen[1]([⊠]), Jie Hao[1,2], Ran Wang[1,2], Ao Shen[1], and Ze Yu[1]

[1] College of Computer Science and Technology,
Nanjing University of Aeronautics and Astronautics, Nanjing, China
{cjcj81,haojie,wangran}@nuaa.edu.cn, 775458998@qq.com, 931624690@qq.com
[2] Collaborative Innovation Center of Novel Software Technology
and Industrialization, Nanjing, China

Abstract. Visible light positioning (VLP) has become a promising indoor localization approach as it can provide sub-meter localization. VLP usually requires no less than three LED lamps for angle-of-arrival (AoA) or received-signal-strength (RSS) based localization. However, it is hard to identify multiple LED lamps in some indoor environments, such as a long corridor or tunnel, which makes existing VLP useless. To address this problem, we propose a VLP approach using only a single LED lamp. In this approach, we utilize the inertial measurements to infer rotation angles and exploit visual projection geometry to calibrate rotation angles. The experiment results demonstrate the proposed VLP approach can achieve sub-meter positioning accuracy by using only one LED lamp.

Keywords: Indoor localization · Visible light communication · Visible light positioning · Smartphone camera

1 Introduction

Indoor localization has been a hot topic for decades for its massive applications. Although GPS technology can provide accurate positions outdoors, it's not a good choice for indoor localization because of the signal shielding of indoor buildings. Hence WiFi, RFID, UWB, iBeacon, infrared technique, ultrasound technique and so on have been applied for indoor localization. However, they all have inevitable drawbacks. For the WiFi positioning technology, it requires the deployment of WiFi modules in the surrounding environment and the accuracy will be degraded by the surrounding interference. As inertial navigation technology uses accelerometer and gyroscope to measure angle, direction, acceleration and etc., the accumulative error will increase with time. Thus, inertial navigation cannot be used independently due to the lack of self-correction. RFID performs poorly in anti-jamming ability, short operating distance and integration with the other technologies. Also the user security privacy protection and standardization of RFID is an issue to be solved too. Straight line of sight and short transmission

© ICST Institute for Computer Sciences, Social Informatics and Telecommunications Engineering 2019
Published by Springer Nature Switzerland AG 2019. All Rights Reserved
X. B. Zhai et al. (Eds.): MLICOM 2019, LNICST 294, pp. 305–312, 2019.
https://doi.org/10.1007/978-3-030-32388-2_26

Fig. 1. Only a single lamp can be captured by the light receiver (camera).

distance are two major drawbacks of infrared. Infrared positioning also needs to install receiving antennas in each region of interest, which is deployment expensive and it is easy to be disturbed by ambient light. At a relatively high cost, UWB can only achieve limited indoor coverage.

Recently, visible light positioning (VLP) has become a promising method for indoor localization. Along with LEDs are widespread available, people begin to use visible light emitted by the LED lamps as a means of green communication, indoor localization, etc. Generally, VLP mainly uses RSS based triangulation or AoA, which means no less than three LED lamps are required. However, as shown in Fig. 1 in some indoor environments including narrow corridors or tunnels, only one LED lamp can be captured by the light receiver. In such scenarios, RSS based triangulation and AoA are infeasible and VLP approach using only one (or two) LED lamp is required. In this paper, we propose a VLP approach using only a single LED lamp. The basic idea is utilizing the inertial measurements to infer rotation angles. Considering the high angle measurement error, we exploit visual projection geometry to calibrate rotation angles. The experimental results demonstrate the proposed VLP approach can achieve sub-meter positioning accuracy by using only one LED lamp.

2   Related Work

In this section, we review the literature on VLP using one LED lamp. We divide the literature into two classes, i.e., RSS based and AoA based VLP.

2.1   RSS Based VLP

Li et al. [4] explore how to achieve single LED based VLP with the user involvement. With the help of the guided hand motion and recorded inertial measurements, the light sensor can collect different RSS measurements for triangulation so that localization with one LED lamp is feasible. Xie et al. [7] use a similar method in which the light receiver needs to rotate to collect different RSS measurements. In addition, the authors design a receiver on which multi-face sensors are dedicated deployed [8]. In [1], a photodetector (PD) attached to a smartphone and a camera are used to measure RSS along with a magnetic field sensor is used to obtain incident light azimuth angle. However, the measurement error of the azimuth angle and the method using camera to measure RSS is not addressed.

2.2   AoA Based VLP

In [6], the authors design a receiver combining photodiodes (PDs) and apertures. With the apertures detecting the light emission direction, the receiver extracts AoA from the received signal by comparing the relative differences between the received signal strengths without awareness of the transmitted optical power. SmartLight [5] shifts all the design complexity to the LED lamp. It designs a LED lamp consisting of a LED array and a convex lens and exploits the light splitting properties of convex lens to localize the light receiver. The work of Zhang et al. [9] is the most similar to ours. It assumes the LED transmitter is circular and the geometric features of the LED image are computed to obtain the receiver's orientation and location relative to the reference LED. To address the symmetric feature of the circular LED lamp, a red point marker is added on the LED lamp for global rotation matrix calculation.

From the literature review, we can see that there is few work on VLP based on a single LED lamp. Most work requires dedicated transmitter/receiver design, i.e., non-commercial-off-the-shelf (non-COTS) light transmitters or receivers. In this paper, we present a single LED lamp based VLP using a COTS LED lamp as the transmitter and COTS smartphone as the receiver.

3   Localization

In an indoor environment, sparse LED lamps are mounted on the ceiling. For example, in a long lane, the LED lamps are deployed in a line with a long distance between neighboring LED lamps. In such cases, only one LED lamp can be captured by the camera held by the user or only the data transmitted from one LED lamp can be successfully decoded by the camera.

To achieve the single LED lamp based localization, the basic idea is combining the projection geometry and internal sensor measurements. While the inertial sensor measurements can be used to provide rotation angles for localization, they are not accurate enough and need to be calibrated. As well known, the projection geometry implies rich rotation information. For example, when shooting a circular LED lamp, the higher rotation angle along the horizontal axis, the flatter the ellipse on the image plane. Although we cannot derive the rotation angles directly

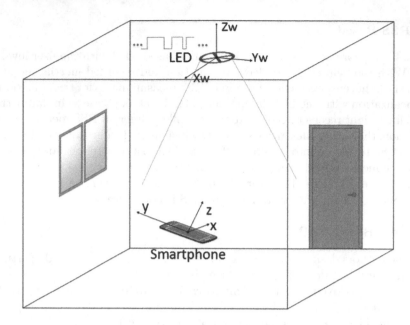

Fig. 2. System overview.

from the projection geometry, we can exploit the projection geometry to calibrate the inertial readings.

Figure 2 shows an application scenario of the proposed indoor VLP system using a single LED lamp. The circular LED lamps are mounted on the ceiling of the target indoor environment. Each LED lamp is assigned with a unique ID number which is stored in an ID-location database and broadcasts its ID number repeatedly by modulated light intensity (the readers may refer to [2] for a reliable LED-camera communication). The dimensions of the LED lamp (i.e. the radius) is also stored in the database. When a user holding a smartphone want to know his/her location, the smartphone will capture the LED lamp and record the inertial readings at the same time. The smartphone will firstly decode the ID information, process the projection geometry of the projected LED lamp, and then exploit this projection geometry to refine the inertial readings and finally derive the localization result.

3.1   Localization

A common circular LED lamp is used as the reference LED in our system, which is projected into an ellipse in the image plane. The LED lamp lies on the plane $z = 0$ and its world coordinate (the coordinate of the centre) is $O = (0, 0, 0)$. We need to derive the localization of the camera $P_c = [P_x, P_y, P_z]^T$. Each point on the LED lamp P projects to p by

$$p = KR(P - P_c),\tag{1}$$

where $K = diag\{f, f, 1\}$ is the camera calibration matrix which is calibrated in advance and f is the focal length, $p = [u, v, 1]^T$ is the image coordinate, P is a point in the world coordinate, and R is the rotation matrix as shown in (2),

$$R = R(\alpha, \beta, \gamma)$$
$$= \begin{bmatrix} 1 & 0 & 0 \\ 0 & \cos\gamma & -\sin\gamma \\ 0 & \sin\gamma & \cos\gamma \end{bmatrix} \begin{bmatrix} \cos\beta & 0 & \sin\beta \\ 0 & 1 & 0 \\ -\sin\beta & 0 & \cos\beta \end{bmatrix} \begin{bmatrix} \cos\alpha & -\sin\alpha & 0 \\ \sin\alpha & \cos\alpha & 0 \\ 0 & 0 & 1 \end{bmatrix}$$
$$= \begin{bmatrix} \cos\gamma\cos\beta & \cos\gamma\sin\beta\sin\alpha - \sin\gamma\cos\alpha & \cos\gamma\sin\beta\cos\alpha + \sin\gamma\sin\alpha \\ \sin\gamma\cos\beta & \sin\gamma\sin\beta\sin\alpha + \cos\gamma\cos\alpha & \sin\gamma\sin\beta\cos\alpha - \cos\gamma\sin\alpha \\ -\sin\beta & \cos\beta\sin\alpha & \cos\beta\cos\alpha \end{bmatrix} \quad (2)$$

Let $[X, Y, Z]^T = R(P - P_c)$, the projection can be re-written as

$$u = fX/Z \quad (3)$$
$$v = fY/Z. \quad (4)$$

If the dimension of LED lamp is significantly small compared with the distance of the camera and LED lamp and the LED lamp lies close to the optical axis, we can approximate perspective by weak perspective projection [10]. That is we can assume Z for every point P on the LED lamp is the same. Also under weak perspective projection, the major axis of the ellipse is always perpendicular to OE where E is the projected ellipse center [3] and there always exists a diameter which is perpendicular to OE in the circle. Thus the scale factor is a/r, where a is the major axis of the ellipse, r is the diameter of the circular LED lamp. Specifically, we have approximately

$$u = \frac{a}{r}X = fX/\bar{Z} \quad (5)$$
$$v = \frac{a}{r}Y = fY/\bar{Z}, \quad (6)$$

where $\bar{Z}$ is the average Z for all points on the LED lamp.

When we substitute O into (5)(6), we denote $[X_0, Y_0, Z_0]^T = R(O - P_c) = -RP_c$ and the projected $p_0 = [u_0, v_0]$ (i.e., the ellipse center). We can easily obtain $\bar{Z}$ as Z_0 and X_0, Y_0. Sequently, with the obtained $[X_0, Y_0, Z_0]^T$, we can derive P_c easily by $P_c = -R^{-1}[X_0, Y_0, Z_0]^T$. Now the problem unsolved is how to obtain the three rotation angles α, β, γ and further the rotation matrix R.

3.2 Angle Calculation

In this subsection, we describe how to obtain the three rotation angles. It is easy to obtain the pitch, roll, and azimuth angle which are denoted as α, β, γ, respectively from the IMU of the smartphone. However, we cannot directly use them for rotation matrix. As shown in [8], the pitch, roll angle has the measurement error of about $1°$–$2°$ while the error of azimuth angle is up to $26°$. The reason of the high error in the azimuth angle is the high noise in compass sensor. Therefore, we use the pitch and roll angle directly for rotation matrix but calibrate the azimuth angle by using projection geometry.

Firstly, we have

$$u' = u - u_0 = \frac{a}{r}(X - X_0),\tag{7}$$

$$v' = v - v_0 = \frac{a}{r}(Y - Y_0).\tag{8}$$

where $[X - X_0, Y - Y_0, Z - Z_0]^T = R(P - O) = RP$. As $p = [u, v, 1]^T$ is on the ellipse C_e, the point $p' = [u', v', 1]^T$ is on the conic of the same shape but with a translate. We denote the conic associated with p' as C'_e, and we have

$$p'^T C'_e p' = 0.\tag{9}$$

Under the perspective projection, we have

$$p' = KR(P - P_c) - KR(O - P_c) = KRP\tag{10}$$

Substituting (10) into (9), we can obtain

$$(KRP)^T C'_e (KRP) = P^T R^T K^T C'_e KRP = 0\tag{11}$$

Let $R^T K^T C'_e KR = [c_1, c_2, c_3; c_4, c_5, c_6; c_7, c_8, c_9]$ and $P = [x, y, 0]^T$ on the circular courteous of the LED lamp, for each $x^2 + y^2 = r^2$ we have

$$c_1 x^2 + c_5 y^2 + (c_2 + c_4)xy = 0.\tag{12}$$

Only $c_1 = 0$, $c_5 = 0$, $c_2 + c_4 = 0$ can meet (12) regardless the values of x, y.

As α, β have been obtained from IMU readings accurately, only γ is unknown. We can calculate γ from (12) by brute-force searching with initial value as the measured γ and searching radius 26°. During searching, we choose the solution that minimizes $c_1^2 + c_5^2 + (c_2 + c_4)^2$.

4   Evaluation

To evaluate the proposed VLP method, we build a testbed in which a circular LED lamp with a diameter of 21 cm is mounted on the ceiling. The LED lamp transmits its ID information at a frequency of 3 KHz repeatedly. As for the receiving end, the back faced camera of HUAWEI TRT-AL00A smartphone is used to decode the LED's ID information.

We divide the target area into grids of size 20 cm × 20 cm and let a volunteer holding a smartphone shoot the target LED lamp in each grid ten times with different rotation angles. The positioning results in Fig. 3 is the average errors of all localizations.

In Fig. 3, it is shown that the proposed positioning method in this paper achieves sub-meter positioning accuracy. All the positioning errors are below 16 cm and can be down to about 1.2 cm. Meanwhile, we also find that generally the higher the horizontal distance (thus the higher Euclidean distance) between the smartphone and the LED lamp, the higher the positioning error. When the smartphone is just below the LED lamp, we obtain the highest positioning accuracy, and the positioning error is as low as 1–2 cm. This result conforms with our intuitive understanding.

Figure 4 shows us more clearly how the VLP method performs in terms of Cumulative Distribution Function (CDF) of the localization errors. The errors achieved by ours are below 10 cm by the percentage of 90% and the average error is down to roughly 5 cm. In one word, our localization method that exploits the projection geometry to calibrate the rotation angles can achieve high localization accuracy.

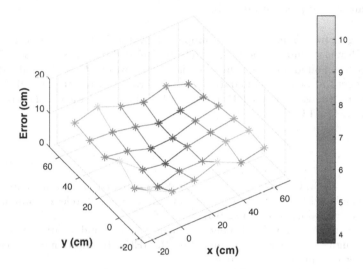

Fig. 3. Localization errors in each grid.

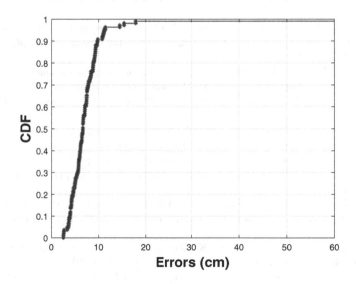

Fig. 4. CDF of the localization errors.

5   Conclusion

In this paper, we present an indoor positioning method with visible light communication based on a single LED lamp. We combine the multi-modal information collected by the camera and the IMU of the smartphone to compensate for the lack of information caused by a single LED lamp. Specifically, during the positioning process, we exploit the projection geometry to constrain the rotation angels of the smartphone. We build an experimental platform and evaluate the proposed VLP method. The results show that the errors achieved by ours are below 10 cm by the percentage of 90%.

Acknowledgments. This work was supported by the Natural Science Foundation of Jiangsu Province under Grant BK20160807, BK20160812, BK20170805, National Natural Science Foundation of China under Grant 61602242, 61701230, 61572253, China Postdoctoral Science Foundation Funded Project (Project No. 2017M611805, 2017M611806), Jiangsu Planned Projects for Postdoctoral Research Funds (Project No. 1701138B, 1701137A).

References

1. Hou, Y., Xue, Y., Chen, C., Xiao, S.: A RSS/AOA based indoor positioning system with a single led lamp. In: International Conference on Wireless Communications & Signal Processing, pp. 1–4 (2015)
2. Hao, J., Yang, Y., Luo, J.: Ceilingcast: energy efficient and location-bound broadcast through led-camera communication. In IEEE International Conference on Computer Communications (2016)
3. Li, L.F., Feng, Z.R., Peng, Q.K.: Detection and model analysis of circular feature for robot vision. In: International Conference on Machine Learning and Cybernetics (2004)
4. Li, L., Hu, P., Peng, C., Shen, G., Zhao, F.: Epsilon: a visible light based positioning system. In: Usenix Conference on Networked Systems Design and Implementation, pp. 331–343 (2014)
5. Liu, S., He, T.: Smartlight: light-weight 3d indoor localization using a single LED lamp. In Proceedings of the 15th ACM Conference on Embedded Network Sensor Systems, SenSys 2017, Delft, Netherlands, 06–08 November 2017, pp. 11:1–11:14 (2017)
6. Steendam, H.: A 3-d positioning algorithm for AOA-based VLP with an aperture-based receiver. IEEE J. Sel. Areas Commun. **36**(1), 23–33 (2018)
7. Xie, B., Gong, S., Tan, G.: LIPro: light-based indoor positioning with rotating handheld devices. Wireless Netw. **24**(1), 49–59 (2018). https://doi.org/10.1007/s11276-016-1312-1
8. Xie, B., Tan, G., Liu, Y., Mingming, L., Chen, K., He, T.: LIPS: a light intensity based positioning system for indoor environments. Acm Trans. Sensor Netw. **12**(4), 28 (2016)
9. Zhang, R., De Zhong, W., Qian, K., Zhang, S.: A single led positioning system based on circle projection. IEEE Photonics J. **9**(4), 1–9 (2017)
10. Zhang, Z.: Weak perspective projection. In: Ikeuchi, K. (ed.) Computer Vision. Springer, Boston (2014). https://doi.org/10.1007/978-0-387-31439-6_115

A Method of Calculating the Semantic Similarity Between English and Chinese Concepts

Jingwen Cao[1], Tiexin Wang[1,2(✉)], Wenxin Li[1], and Chuanqi Tao[1,2,3]

[1] College of Computer Science and Technology,
Nanjing University of Aeronautics and Astronautics, 29#, Jiangjun Road,
Jiangning District, Nanjing 211106, China
caojingwen1028@126.com, {tiexin.wang,
freedomtot}@nuaa.edu.cn, t-chuanqi@163.com
[2] Key Laboratory of Safety-Critical Software, Nanjing University of Aeronautics
and Astronautics, Ministry of Industry and Information Technology,
Nanjing, China
[3] State Key Laboratory for Novel Software Technology, Nanjing University,
Nanjing, People's Republic of China

Abstract. In the big data era, data and information processing is a common concern of diverse fields. To achieve the two keys "efficiency" and "intelligence" to the processing process, it's necessary to search, define and build the potential links among heterogeneous data. Focusing on this issue, this paper proposes a knowledge-driven method to calculate the semantic similarity between (bilingual English-Chinese) words. This method is built on the knowledge base "HowNet", which defines and maintains the "atom taxonomy tree" and the "semantic dictionary" - a network of knowledge system describing the relationships between word concepts and attributes of the concepts. Compared to other knowledge bases, HowNet pays more attention to the connections between words based on concepts. Besides, this method is more complete in the analysis of concepts and more convenient in calculation methods. The nonrelational database MongoDB is employed to improve the efficiency and fully use the rich knowledge maintained in HowNet. Considering both the structure of HowNet and characteristics of MongoDB, a certain number of equations are defined to calculate the semantic similarity.

Keywords: HowNet · MongoDB · Semantic similarity · Knowledge driven

1 Introduction

NLP (Natural Language Processing) is a science that integrates linguistics, computer science, and mathematics. The importance of a large-scale computer-available dictionary with rich information on NLP is obvious. In order to improve the efficiency of NLP technology, it is necessary to create large-scale knowledge resources, including machine-processable dictionaries [1].

© ICST Institute for Computer Sciences, Social Informatics and Telecommunications Engineering 2019
Published by Springer Nature Switzerland AG 2019. All Rights Reserved
X. B. Zhai et al. (Eds.): MLICOM 2019, LNICST 294, pp. 313–324, 2019.
https://doi.org/10.1007/978-3-030-32388-2_27

Currently, there are several existing large knowledge bases. Compared to other knowledge base, such as "WordNet" and "ConceptNet", "HowNet" emphasizes the relationships between concepts, the relationships between attributes and attributes of concepts.

Natural language uses words as basic units. Words can form sentences, and sentences form chapters. Therefore, the semantics of one text is synthesized by the semantics of all the sentences contained, and the semantics of one sentence is determined by the semantics of the words and certain grammars. As the basic unit of sentences and texts, the words have specific semantics and connotations. Semantic analysis is the fundamental problem of NLU (Natural Language Understanding), which has a wide range of applications in NLP, information retrieval, information filtering, information classification, and semantic mining.

In the big data era, the importance of semantic analysis is increasing. To accurately extract information, retrieve required information, tap potential information value, and provide intelligent knowledge services, semantic analysis for machine understanding is indispensable.

In order to detect the semantic similarity between the concepts of words (objects), this paper proposes a method named *SSDH (Semantic similarity detection based on HowNet)*. SSDH is built on the HowNet knowledge base. To improve the efficiency of SSDH, MongoDB is employed.

This paper is structured as follows. The second section presents the technology foundation of this paper (i.e., MongoDB and HowNet). The third section shows an overview of SSDH. The related work is illustrated in the fourth section. Finally, the fifth section draws a conclusion.

2   Pre-work

2.1   MongoDB

MongoDB is a product between a relational database and a non-relational database [2]. It is the most versatile and most relational database among non-relational databases.

MongoDB has two basic advantages in data storage and data query. First, the data structure it supports is very loose, which is similar to JSON's BSON format. So it can store more complex data types [3]. Second, it supports a very powerful query language with a similar syntax to the object-oriented query language. It realizes almost all the functions of relational database single-table query, and also supports indexing data [4].

MongoDB owns many fine features. Four of them are: (i) easy to store data of object types, (ii) dynamic query and full index, (iii) efficient binary data storage, and (iv) supporting Python, Java, C++ and many other languages.

MongoDB has been widely used, two main application scenarios are listed below.

- Real-time (website) data processing. MongoDB is ideal for real-time insertions, updates, and queries. It has the replication and high scalability required to store data in real time, making it ideal for databases consisting of tens or hundreds of servers.

- Cache. Due to its high performance, MongoDB is suitable as a caching layer for the information infrastructure. After the system is restarted, the persistent cache layer built by it can avoid overloading the underlying data source.

2.2   HowNet

HowNet is a bilingual (English-Chinese) knowledge base. It provides the knowledge to design real intelligent software. The total records in HowNet are more than 120,000, which are still expanding.

Considering HowNet, two concepts "atom" and "definition" needed to be explained firstly. **"Atom" is the smallest unit of meaning that cannot be divided**. The principle of choosing atoms is that the existing atoms must be able to describe all the concepts. **"Definition" is a concept normalized in HowNet, consisting of some atoms** [5].

As a common sense knowledge base, HowNet reveals the relationships between concepts, the relationships between attributes and attributes of concepts. The basic content is a networked organic knowledge system. *The semantic dictionary is the basic file of the HowNet base, composed of many records which contain the Chinese and English translations of words and the part of speech and definitions of words.* The semantic dictionary of HowNet is not simply copying English-Chinese dictionaries, the definition of each word is also based on the current popularity.

Figure 1 shows a combination of some records in HowNet semantic dictionary.

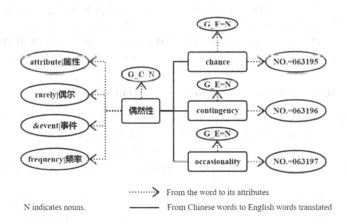

Fig. 1. An illustration of the HowNet semantic dictionary.

In Fig. 1, "*NO.=*" is followed by the serial number of the word in the dictionary. The "偶然性" in the middle of the figure is the Chinese interpretation of the word. And in English, its meaning is close to "accidentality". On the left is the definition of words made up of four atoms. The words after "*G_C =*" and "*G_E =*" are the attributes of Chinese words and the attributes of English words. In this example, they are all nouns. Due to cultural and language differences, Chinese words tend to correspond to more than one English word, such as "偶然性" to three English words "chance", "contingency", "occasionality".

Another basic file in the HowNet system is the atom taxonomy tree. Figure 2 shows an example (several layers) of the atom taxonomy tree. In this example, the closer the two atoms are (to the nearest common ancestor), the higher the similarity between the two atoms [6].

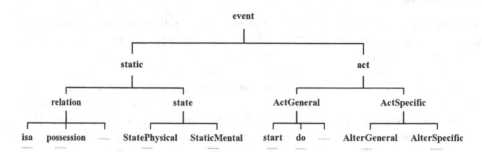

Fig. 2. An example of the atom taxonomy tree.

3 Main Work

In SSDH, the semantic similarity calculation is based on HowNet knowledge base. The data from HowNet needs to be processed and stored in MongoDB to be used.

The main work of this paper contains three parts: (i) processing HowNet data and storing it in MongoDB, (ii) querying the data stored in MongoDB for atom distance calculation and atom similarity calculation, (iii) comparing the atom similarity of each pair of definitions to calculate the semantic similarity between two words.

3.1 Processing HowNet Data and Store into MongoDB

Java is the main developing language of this work, and Eclipse is selected as the IDE. The detail of developing process of SSDH is out of the scope of this paper.

Since this work involves the usage of the atom taxonomy tree and semantic dictionary of HowNet, two collections in MongoDB were created to store these data: "atomtree" and "semanticdictionary".

MongoDB can store five kinds of tree structures: parent link structure, sub-link structure, ancestor queue structure, materialized path structure, and collection model. In this work, the "parent link structure" is employed.

MongoDB stores data as a document, and the data structure consists of key-value pairs. A MongoDB document is similar to a JSON object. Field values may contain other documents, arrays, and document arrays [7].

Figure 3 is a text file of the atom taxonomy tree stored in the parent node format. On each line, the serial number, the English name, the Chinese name of the atom, and the serial number of its parent node are listed sequentially.

```
1    0,event,事件,0
2    1,static,静态,0
3    2,relation,关系,1
4    3,isa,是非关系,2
5    4,be,是,3
6    5,become,成为,4
7    6,mean,指代,4
8    7,BeNot,非,3
9    8,possession,领属关系,2
10   9,own,有,8
11   10,obtain,得到,9
12   11,receive,收受,9
13   12,BelongTo,属于,8
```

Fig. 3. The text file of an atom taxonomy tree.

If an atom is the root node in a tree, serial number of its parent node will be its own serial number. After searching, these atoms form a total of nine trees. Taking the first line record as an example, the format stored in collection "atomtree" is as follows:

Document {{ID=0, EnglishName="event", ChineseName="事件", parent="0"}}

A record in a processed semantic dictionary consists of eight lines. As a document is stored in another collection, some definitions may not be currently used, but may be useful for future secondary development.

Take the number "2" as an example, the import process from HowNet to MongoDB is as follows.

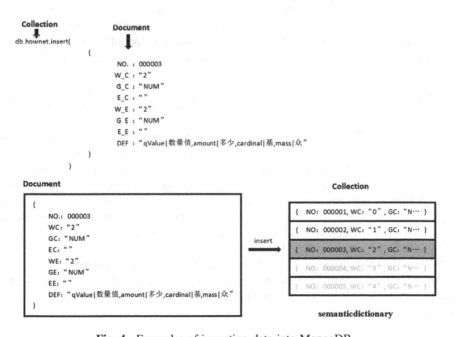

Fig. 4. Examples of importing data into MongoDB.

The format stored in collection "semanticdictionary" is presented below (Fig. 4).

Document {{NO=000003, WC=2, GC=NUM, EC=, WE=2, GE=NUM, EE=, DEF=qValue|数量值, amount|多少, cardinal|基, mass|众}}

After storing the data in MongoDB, the related key value is used for data indexing to select required documents for calculation.

Since each word has multiple attributes, this will increase the workload of the index, so two interfaces are created to provide arbitrary key value lookups for the documents in the two collections.

3.2 Calculating Atom Distance

HowNet defines and maintains the atom taxonomy tree, and the similarity of atom can be calculated by the relative distance on the atom taxonomy tree.

The nearest common ancestor of the two comparing atoms has to be located first. Then use the *upward recursive algorithm* to find the distance between the two atoms and the common ancestor, that is, the height difference between the layers, and add them to get the relative distance between the two atoms. If the two atoms are not on a tree, the default atom distance is 100.

Equation (1) is defined to calculate this.

$$AtomDistance(a, b) = Distance(a, com(a, b)) + Distance(b, com(a, b)) \qquad (1)$$

"*AtomDistance(a,b)*" is the distance between "atom a" and "atom b". "*com(a,b)*" is the nearest common ancestor to "atom a" and "atom b". "*Distance(a,com(a,b))*" is the distance between "atom a" and the nearest common ancestor (of the two atoms).

Then calculate the similarity between the two atoms by employing Eq. (2).

$$AtomSim(a, b) = (1 - \frac{AtomDistance(a, b)}{2 \times TreeHigh_i}) \times (\frac{TreeHigh_i}{TreeHigh_i + TreeHigh_i - Deep}) \qquad (2)$$

"*AtomSim(a,b)*" is the similarity between "atom a" and "atom b". "*TreeHigh_i*" is the height of the classification tree where the "atom a" and "atom b" are located. "*Deep*" is the depth of the root to the common ancestor (of "atom a" and "atom b").

For a branch node, the nodes of its first child are equidistant from all nodes of any other children in the same layer, and thus the longest distance of the two nodes can be roughly estimated to be twice the height of the tree. Different atom taxonomy trees have different "*TreeHigh(s)*", and it is necessary to determine which tree the atom is on and then find the corresponding "*TreeHigh(s)*".

Considering the usage of Eqs. (1) and (2), Table 1 shows a simple use case of comparing the atom distance and atom similarity between four pairs of words (i.e. male-female, male-young, Animal Human-human, royal-family). The testing results are also shown in Table 1.

Table 1. Experimental results on the similarity between two atom similarities.

No	Atom 1	Atom 2	Atom Distance	Atom Similarity
1	男|male	女|female	2	0.5
2	男|male	幼|young	4	0.2
3	动物|AnimalHuman	人|human	1	0.69
4	皇|royal	家|family	2	0.3

3.3　Computing Semantic Similarity

Since some Chinese words may correspond to multiple English words or have different meanings, it is necessary to compare all the definitions while calculating the similarity between two words. To find same definitions, Eq. (3) is defined.

$$comdef(A,B) = \{def|def \in DEF_A \wedge def \in DEF_B\} \tag{3}$$

"*comdef (A,B)*" is a collection of the same "*def(s)*". "*DEF_A*" is a collection storing all the definitions of word A, while "*def*" is one of the definitions of word A.

Then calculate the proportion of the same definition in all "*def(s)*", employing Eq. (4).

$$defRatio = \frac{|comdef|^2}{|DEF_A| \times |DEF_B|} \tag{4}$$

"*def Ratio*" is the same "*def*" rows account for the ratio in the "*DEF*" collection. "*|DEF_A|*" is the number of the "*def(s)*" in the "*DEF_A*" collection.

Some Chinese words correspond to different English words, but the definitions are the same, so there are cases where multiple definitions of a word are the same, and repeated definitions are counted as one in all calculations. If all the definitions of the two words are the same, then the similarity between the two words is judged to be 1, and the comparison is no longer continued.

$$WordSim(A,B) = 1 \tag{5}$$

"*WordSim(A,B)*" is the similarity between word A and word B.

Otherwise, the similarity between the two words needs to be continuously calculated, and the same definitions in the "def(s)" of the two definition items are respectively removed, only the definitions of the two words different are left, and then the similarity calculation of the atoms is performed for each pair of definitions of the two words.

First need to compare the first attribute of the two "def(s)", that is, whether the atoms are the same, if they are the same, let "*mainatom=1*", otherwise let "*mainatom=0*". And count the sum of the "*mainatom*" before Eq. (10).

$$allmainatom = \sum_{\substack{\forall def \,\in\, DEF_A \\ \forall def \,\in\, DEF_B}} mainatom \tag{6}$$

Then compare the remaining atoms, if a same atom exists in a pair of definitions setting to "def_{Ai}" and "def_{Bj}", put it into a collection "$Common(def_{Ai}, def_{Bj})$", and count the ratio of common atoms to all atoms in this pair of definitions.

$$sameatomRatio(def_{A_i}, def_{B_j}) = \frac{\left|Common\left(def_{A_i}, def_{B_j}\right)\right|^2}{(|def_{A_i}| - 1) \times (|def_{B_j}| - 1)} \tag{7}$$

"def_{Ai}" is the "i th" def in the collection "DEF_A". In each pair of "def(s)" between word A and word B, "$atomRatio$" is the common atoms account for the ratio of all atoms in the two "def" collections.

Sum the repetition rates of all common atoms as shown in Eq. (8) before Eq. (10).

$$allsameatom = \sum_{\substack{\forall def_A \,\in\, DEF_A \\ \forall def_B \,\in\, DEF_B}} \sum_{\forall atom \in Common(def_{A_i}, def_{B_j})} sameatomRatio(atom) \tag{8}$$

Then remove the same atoms in the two definitions, and sum the atom similarity between the remaining atoms and the sum is set to "$alldiffatomsim$" before Eq. (10).

$$alldiffatomism = \sum_{\substack{\forall def_{A_i} \,\in\, DEF_A \\ \forall def_{B_j} \,\in\, DEF_B}} \frac{(1 - sameatomRation(def_{A_i}, def_{B_j})) \sum AtomSim(a,b)}{(|def_{A_j}| - 1 - |comatom|) \times (|def_{B_j}| - 1 - |comatom|)}$$

$$\tag{9}$$

"a" belongs only to the remaining atoms in the collection "def_{Ai}" (not the intersection of "def_{Ai}" and collection "def_{Bj}").

Because there are many relationships in HowNet, such as component-total relationship (%), attribute-host relationship (&), material-finished relationship (?), incident event relationship (*), etc., these relationships will be reflected in adding the corresponding symbols "%", "&" etc. before atoms, and for these "$atom$"s, you need to compare them separately and compare the "$atom$"s with the same symbol. The comparison methods are the same as the above-mentioned same atoms processing methods and different atoms processing methods.

Finally define semantic similarity of two word.

$$WordSim(A, B) = defRatio$$

$$+ (1 - defRatio) \times \frac{\alpha \times allmainatom + \beta \times (allsameatom + alldiffatomsim)}{(|DEF_A| - |comdef|) \times (|DEF_B| - |comdef|)} \tag{10}$$

The parameters "α" and "β" do not only limit the similarity range between 0 and 1, but also set the importance of different levels of first atom and other atoms. "α" defaults to 0.6, "β" defaults to 0.4, but it can be changed as needed.

Table 2 shows the use case and testing results of applying the above equations. Four pairs of words are contained in this use case.

Table 2. Experimental result about semantic similarity calculation between two words.

No	Word 1	Word 2	Semantic Similarity
1	医生(doctor)	人(human)	0.30
2	男人(male)	女人(female)	0.76
3	男人(male)	girl	0.71
4	commute a sentence	reduce a penalty	1.0

4   Related Work

This section introduces a classical corpus called WordNet and makes a distinction between WordNet and HowNet, then presents some latest research works employing HowNet.

4.1   WordNet

WordNet [WordNet: a lexical database for English] [8] is an on-line lexical reference system whose design is inspired by current psycho linguistic theories of human lexical memory.

WordNet and HowNet [HowNet - a hybrid language and knowledge resource] [9] have the same semantic concepts, and both of them believe that semantics is the interpretation of the conceptual world in the human's brain. However, they have different methods to characterize the conceptual structures and the relationships. WordNet uses a different approach to express the semantics of verbs, nouns, adjectives, and adverbs with the interrelation between synonym and Synset. HowNet uses constructive conceptual representations to explain various relationships between concepts by using "Sememe".

In terms of relationship, "Sememe" can be regarded as a more economic expression of conceptual relations, and it can be used to explain conceptual relations. Therefore, the relationship between WordNet and HowNet can be regarded as a phenomenon and a corresponding interpretation, and use the "Sememe" in HowNet to make a general explanation of the semantic relationships in WordNet. In this way, the relationship between the two knowledge networks can be built.

4.2   Research Works Concerning HowNet

Semantic similarity detecting is one of the key technologies of natural language processing, which has been widely used in many fields such as information extraction and text classification. Certain of the research works about semantic similarity computation are based on HowNet.

In Ref. [10], Bai et al. presented an improved algorithm for detecting the semantic similarity based on HowNet. The method is built on the atom axonomy tree, and calculates the semantic similarity based on the atom distance. It considers the influence of the children's node density under the common parent node, and the similarity calculation between words of polysemy terms.

In Ref. [11], Zhu et al. proposed a word semantic similarity computation method based on the HowNet. They made full use of the semantic information of words in different knowledge networks to obtain a more accurate and reasonable similarity.

In Ref. [12], Nie et al. proposed a new semantic similarity detecting method based on HowNet. They consider the ordering of the weights of the "Sememe classes" and set a function to make the weights change moderately. Moreover, the authors proposed the element matching method for the similarity between two texts.

In Ref. [13], Zhang et al. proposed a word semantic similarity calculation method combining HowNet and search engine by making full use of rich network knowledge. They used double correlation detection algorithm and pointed mutual information method based on search engines to improve the match degree of the semantic description of the specific word and subjective cognition of vocabulary.

In Ref. [14], it presented a new depth & path-based semantic similarity method to improve the existing meaning-based approaches in HowNet. The authors construct a complete concept tree according to the concept definitions in HowNet and use the improved depth & path algorithm to compute the depth and path of concept in the concept tree.

A brief survey of related works proposed above is listed in Table 3. Two ways to improve the semantic similarity detecting algorithms: (i) an improved algorithm is often proposed according to the structure or the internal feature of the HowNet, for example [10, 12, 14], and (2) researchers introduce external information to optimize the algorithm. For example, other knowledge bases [11] or related information like search engine [13].

Table 3. A brief survey of the related work.

Research Works	Main contributions
Bai et al. [10]	Introduce the influence of sememe density; Reconsider the multi-meaning words
Zhu et al. [11]	Base on the HowNet CiLin; Propose a dynamic weighting strategy to calculate semantic similarity
Nie et al. [12]	Define a new semantic similarity; Propose an element matching method
Zhang et al. [13]	Combine HowNet and search engine algorithms
Guo et al. [14]	Construct a concept tree; Propose an improved depth & path algorithm

This paper introduces a novel method to measure the semantic similarity between two words. Different from existing research works, SSDH further supports to compare the semantic similarity between two paragraphs of text.

5   Conclusion

This paper proposes SSDH method, which is built on HowNet and implemented with MongoDB, to calculate the semantic similarity between words. Since HowNet is a bilingual knowledge base, SSDH supports language-cross (English - Chinese) semantic similarity detecting among concepts.

There are many potential relationships maintained in HowNet, such as the relevance of words. As mentioned above, HowNet is a networked organic knowledge system. In the HowNet knowledge system, in addition to the basic semantic relationship between words and words, there is also the relationship between possession, event implementer and event enforcer.

Based on these relationships, Knowledge Network can also detect word relevance. Figure 5 shows an example between word "community" and word "home-owner". Although they all have "#house" in their concept, their similarity is not high because the first attribute of "community" is "house" while the first attribute of "home-owner" is "human", and their relevance is high because the houses in the community are owned by the home-owners.

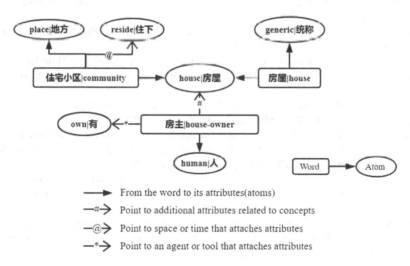

Fig. 5. The connection among "community", "house" and "house-owner".

The future research direction of SSDH will focus on word correlation detection to achieve more accurate requirements document analysis and a wider range of related content retrieval.

Acknowledgement. This work was supported by the "Fundamental Research Funds for the Central Universities Nos. 3082018NS2018057", the National Natural Science Foundation of China (61872182), the National Natural Science Foundation of China under Grant No.61402229 and No.61602267, the Open Fund of the State Key Laboratory for Novel Software Technology (KFKT2018B19) and the Open Fund of the Ministry Key Laboratory for Safety-Critical Software Development and Verification (1015-XCA1816401).

References

1. Banker, K.: MongoDB in Action. Manning Publications Co., Shelter Island (2011)
2. Brad, D.: The Definitive Guide to MongoDB: The Nosql Database for Cloud and Desktop Computing. Springer, Heidelberg (2010). https://doi.org/10.1007/978-1-4302-3052-6
3. Vohra, D.: Migrating mongodb (2015)
4. Boicea, A., Radulescu, F., Agapin, L.I.: MongoDB vs oracle – database comparison. In: Emerging Intelligent Data and Web Technologies (EIDWT), 2012 Third International Conference. IEEE (2012)
5. Dong, Z., Dong, Q.: HowNet - a hybrid language and knowledge resource. In: Natural Language Processing and Knowledge Engineering, 2003. Proceedings. 2003 International Conference. IEEE (2003)
6. Xu, Y., Fan, X.Z., Zhang, F.: Semantic relevancy computing based on hownet. J. Beijing Inst. Technol. **25**(5), 411–414 (2005)
7. Hows, D., Membrey, P., Plugge, E., Hawkins, T.: Installing mongodb. In: Definitive Guide to Mongodb, pp. 17–31 (2013). http://doi.org/10.1007/978-1-4302-5822-3_2
8. Miller, G.A.: Wordnet: a lexical database for English. Commun. Assoc. Comput. Mach. **38**(11), 39–41 (1995)
9. Diao, L., Yan, H., Fuxue, L.I., Xiumin, L.I., Lei, G.: An improved HowNet-based algorithm for semantic similarity computation (2017)
10. Bai, J., Bu, Y.: An improved algorithm for semantic similarity based on HowNet. In: 2018 2nd International Conference on Data Science and Business Analytics (ICDSBA), pp. 65–70 (2019)
11. Zhu, X.H., Ma, R.C., Sun, L., Chen, H.C.: Word semantic similarity computation based on HowNet and CiLin. J. Chin. Inf. Process. **30**(4), 29–36 (2016)
12. Nie, H., Zhou, J., Guo, Q., Huang, Z.: Improved semantic similarity method based on HowNet for text clustering. In: 2018 5th International Conference on Information Science and Control Engineering (ICISCE), pp. 266–269. IEEE (2018)
13. Zhang, S., Ouyang, C., Yang, X., Liu, Y., Liu, Z., et al.: Word semantic similarity computation based on integrating HowNet and search engines. J. Comput. Appl. **37**, 1056–1060 (2017)
14. Guo, X., Zhu, X., Li, F., Li, Q.: A new semantic similarity measurement based on HowNet concept tree. In: 2016 International Forum on Management, Education and Information Technology Application. Atlantis Press (2016)

A Bicycle-Borne Sensor Node for Monitoring Air Pollution Based on NB-IoT

Shu Shen[1,2], Caixia Lv[1], Xindi Xu[1], and Xiaoyu Liu[1(✉)]

[1] School of Computer Science, Nanjing University of Posts and Telecommunications,
Nanjing 210023, China
shens@njupt.edu.cn, m18734315011@163.com, XindiSindy@163.com,
1018041029@njupt.edu.cn
[2] Jiangsu High Technology Research Key Laboratory for Wireless Sensor Networks,
Nanjing 210023, China

Abstract. Nowadays, everybody knows that shared bicycles have become a new type of green transportation in the city. The impact on people's health caused by air pollutants exposed near roads has become a concern in recent years. This paper introduces a device which consists of a particulate detector, temperature and humidity sensor, micro-SD card, GPS receiver and the NB-IoT communication module. The device can be installed as a sensor node on a shared bike, and a mobile sensor network has been set up on a shared bike to monitor air quality throughout the city, which is of great significance for urban air quality testing.

Keywords: Air pollution · Environmental monitoring · NB-IoT ·
Shared bicycle

1 Introduction

1.1 Concepts

With the continuous progress of urbanization, intelligent transportation system has been popularized and developed in many cities. Intelligent transportation systems improve the mobility and safety of traffic and effectively reduce the environmental pollution [1]. In China, the shared bicycles has been developing rapidly since mid-2016. Since this way of travel is green, healthy and environmentally friendly, it has become an important tool for people. We can see it in many public fields, such as subway stations, bus stops, large shopping malls, residential neighborhoods and university campuses.

Narrowband Internet of Things (NB-IoT) is a new cellular technology introduced in 3GPP Release 13 for providing wide-area coverage for the Internet of Things (IoT). It is a new 3GPP radio-access technology in the sense that it is not fully backward compatible with existing 3GPP devices. However, it is

X. B. Zhai et al. (Eds.): MLICOM 2019, LNICST 294, pp. 325–332, 2019.
https://doi.org/10.1007/978-3-030-32388-2_28

designed to achieve excellent coexistence performance with legacy GSM, General Packet Radio Service (GPRS) and LTE technologies. NB-IoT requires 180 kHz minimum system bandwidth for both downlink and uplink, respectively [2].

1.2 Motivations

Due to the rapid growth of urban population, environmental pollution, traffic congestion, energy consumption and other problems. They are attracted the attention of all sectors of society, almost all cities of the country must face this problem [3]. With the development of intelligent transportation system in the city, shared bicycles as a new way of green travel play an increasingly important role. A survey report showed that 76.56% people used shared bicycles, and only a small number of people used public bicycles, mainly because the use of shared bicycles was more convenient and could be parked at any time [4]. The health issue of air pollutants near roads have become a concern in recent years, and shared bicycles has become an important part of urban transport. Therefore, the device can be installed as a sensor node on a shared bike, and a mobile sensor network has been established on the shared bicycles to monitor air quality throughout the city, which is of great significance for air quality inspection and management.

The rest of this paper is organized as follows. It is discussed related research in Sect. 2. Section 3 introduces the essential workflow and frame structure of the device. The test result and data collection are illustrated in Sect. 4. Section 5 has a prospect about NB-IoT. Section 6 concludes the paper.

2   Related Work

Liu et al. introduced the installation of similar nodes on public bicycles using the communication of Bluetooth [5]. Aguiari et al. also proposed the idea was used for electric bikes, based on WiFi transmission [6]. Compared with public bicycles, shared bicycles solve the problem of bicycle location restrictions. It is more suitable for the deployment of wireless sensor networks in the city by improving the diversity of environmental data collection. It also can realize the urban environment detection and management. In February 2017, ofo signed a partnership agreement about NB-IoT shared bicycles applications with China Telecom and Huawei, which will provide wireless network solutions including NB-IoT chips. The tripartite management said that the "Little Yellow Car" will be able to access the latest NB-IoT technology to provide users with a better use experience by China Telecom's wireless network in the future [7]. Due to the current combination of NB-IoT technology and shared bicycles have become a trend, this paper uses NB-IoT technology. The common means of communication are compared, as in Table 1 [8].

Considering the power consumption problem of GSM communication and GPRS positioning module and the large number of shared bicycles, we can see the advantages to use of NB-IoT technology [9].

Table 1. The Comparation of communication.

Subject	Bluetooth	WiFi	Zigbee	NB-IoT
Networking	Bluetooth-based Mesh gateway	Based wireless router	Based on Zigbee gateway	Based on the existing cellular network
Network deployment	Node	Node + router	Node + Gateway	Node
Transmission distance	10 m	A short distance (50 m)	Short range (10–100 m)	Long-range (up to a dozen kilometers, under normal circumstances 10 km above)
Access nodes	Theoretically about 60000	About 50	More than 60,00 theoretically 200 to 500	About 200,000
Battery life	Days	Hours	Theory about 2 years/AA batteries	Theory about 10 years/AA batteries
Cost		Modul about $7–8	Module about $1–2	$5–10 modules, the next target down to $1
Bands	2.4G	2.4G and 5G	unlicense band 2.4G	License band, band operators
Transfer speed	1M	2.4G: 1M–11M 5G: 1M–500M	Theory 250 kps, generally less than actual 100 kbps, limited low speed communication interface UART	Theoretical 160 kbps–250 Kbps, the actual generally less than 100 kbps, limited low speed communication interface UART
Network latency	Less than 1 S	Less than 1S	Less than 1 S	6–10 S

(1) Wide depth coverage: compared with GSM, NB-IoT can achieve more than a 20 db enhanced coverage. To a certain extent, it can effectively solve the problem that the shared bicycles cant be accurately positioned in the indoor, stairwell, basement and other deep coverage areas. Thus, use of NB-IoT technology can avoid the shared bicycle was private occupied and disorderly parked this problem. This can help the enterprise to carry out vehicle maintenance and other daily management.

(2) Oversized connection: In the rush hour, there are many shared cycles dense unlock to access network in the vicinity of the subway port and other business hotspot areas. The wireless access network capacity has put forward higher requirements. NB-IoT's low power consumption, massive connectivity capabilities can better meet the needs of user-intensive access.

(3) Ultra low power consumption: The protocol of the bicycles based on the NB-IoT modules is more simplified, and the centralization of the communication chips and modules are more higher. Besides, the power consumption will be significantly reduced compared with the original GSM modules.

3   Design Scheme

3.1   Frame Structure

The device consists of a particulate detector, a temperature and humidity sensor, a micro-SD card, a GPS receiver and the NB-IoT communication module, as shown in Fig. 1.

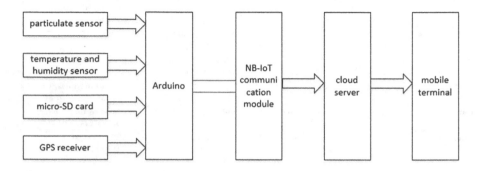

Fig. 1. Frame structure

3.2   Module Function

Particulate detector can be used to detect respirable particulate matter in the air. Temperature and humidity sensor can detect air temperature and humidity. A GPS receiver is for the acquisition of geographic information, and the micro-SD card can be stored data. These can be connected with Arduino, and through the NB-IoT communication module upload cloud server. Eventually, we can see the relevant data at the mobile terminal. If a bike is at rest, the geographical location remains the same and the environmental parameters fluctuate less. So GPS data can be uploaded once in a while, and the frequency of environmental acquisition can be reduced. When the bike is borrowed, the geographical location has been changing, then the GPS data upload frequency and the frequency of environmental collection should be improved.

Particulate Detector. PM 2.5/PM 10 laser sensor: It uses the laser scattering principle, so it can obtain the 0.3–10 μ suspended particulate matter concentration in the air. Using the imported laser and the photosensitive component, we can obtain the stable and reliable data. This detector has a fan in it and the output form is digital. Besides, it has a high integration.

Arduino Plartform. Arduino can sense the environment through a wide variety of sensors, feedback and influence the environment by controlling lights, motors and other devices. The microcontroller on the board can write programs through Arduino's programming language, and compile into binary files. Then the binary files are recorded in microcontrollers. The programming of Arduino is achieved through the Arduino programming language and the Arduino development environment [10].

SIM7000C Arduino NB-IoT/LTE/GPRS Expansion Board. SIM7000C Arduino NB-IOT/LTE/GPRS expansion board is a wireless communication module designed by DFRobot based on SIMCOM SIM7000C. This is the first product in China to introduce NB-IoT technology into the field of open source hardware. Whether for prototyping or for small batch production, the SIM7000C Arduino NB-IOT/LTE/GPRS expansion board is the best solution for low-power, low-latency, medium-throughput applications. In addition, SIM7000C GNSS Global Navigation Satellite System which supports GPS in the United States, GLONASS in Russia, Galileo in Europe, QZSS in Japan and Beidou navigation system developed independently by China. It is suitable for some IoT applications, such as remote control, mobile tracking, remote meter reading, and shared bicycles. SIM7000C NB-IOT/LTE/GPRS expansion board also supports ordinary SIM card and NB-IoT special card. It can be plugged into the ordinary SIM card for telephone calls, texting and other traditional GSM applications. It also can be plugged into NB-IoT dedicated card to use the NB-IoT Network for data transmission. In addition, the expansion board also provides BME280 environmental sensors, which can be developed as prototypes of the NB-IoT project to monitor temperature, humidity and air pressure values [11].

4 Data Presentation

We collect the data in 5 locations. And we record data every half an hour. Tables 2, 3, 4 and 5 presents the results of temperature, humidity, PM2.5, and PM10. We can see the numerical changes in all aspects.

Table 2. Temperature change (°C).

Time/h	Location 1	Location 2	Location 3	Location 4	Location 5
0	22.11	18.52	12.31	9.35	7.59
0.5	23.37	18.36	19.08	9.26	7.67
1	23.5	18.76	18.74	9.39	7.72
1.5	14.13	18.93	18.2	9.05	7.76
2	13.12	19.18	19.12	10.57	7.79

Table 3. Humidity change (%).

Time/h	Location 1	Location 2	Location 3	Location 4	Location 5
0	12.58	11.08	15.75	16.8	16.82
0.5	9.56	10.63	10.47	16.68	16.77
1	9.15	11.13	11.2	17.21	16.77
1.5	12.84	10.47	11.08	18.17	16.74
2	13.85	10.51	10.51	16.22	16.71

Table 4. PM2.5 change (ug/m^3).

Time/h	Location 1	Location 2	Location 3	Location 4	Location 5
0	9	22	19	7	2
0.5	10	23	19	7	2
1	8	23	19	8	2
1.5	6	21	21	8	3
2	6	21	22	22	2

Table 5. PM10 change (ug/m^3).

Time/h	Location 1	Location 2	Location 3	Location 4	Location 5
0	22	4	2	18	2
0.5	24	1	19	22	21
1	20	26	21	23	17
1.5	23	22	25	25	17
2	18	25	24	15	4

5   Prospect on NB-IoT

Cellular IoT is a low-power WAN IoT technology based on 2/3/4G technology, it mainly for large-scale IoT connection applications, and the design objectives are: low cost, low complexity, coverage enhancement, low power consumption, high capacity.

With the "Comprehensive promotion of mobile Internet of Things (NB-IoT) development notice" issued by the Ministry of Industry and Information of Industry in June 2017, NB-IoT technology has developed vigorously in China, the whole industry from chip, module, terminal to operator network, cloud computing platform, application and other fields have an all-round development. At present, China Telecom has completed a full network coverage of the NB-IoT network in China, China Mobile and Unicom will also improve the corresponding network construction in the near future, which makes China become the largest country in the global NB-IoT market [12].

The horn of the 5G era has begun. With the development of modern society, the 5G era is bound to come. 5G brings more than just faster network speed, but the intelligent interconnection of all things. Among them, NB-IoT is the prelude and foundation of 5G commercial, and it is the only way to realize the interconnection of everything in 5G, and it is also the best touchstone for 5G network operation capability in the future. Therefore, the evolution of NB-IoT is more important, such as support the multicast, continuous mobility, new power levels and so on. Only complete the NB-IoT infrastructure, 5G is possible to truly achieve [13]. Nowadays, NB-IoT has been used in many Internet of Things fields in China, for instance, smart water meters, intelligent parking and so on. With the continuous advancement of science and technology, we can see that the IoT industry will be get a great development, I believe that NB-IoT will play a key role.

6   Conclusion

This paper proposes a device, which consists of a particulate detector, temperature and humidity sensor, micro-SD card, GPS receiver and the NB-IoT communication module. The device can be installed as a sensor node on a shared bike, and a mobile sensor network has been set up on a shared bike to monitor air quality throughout the city. In the fourth part of this article, we present the collected data at intervals of half an hour. We can see that in a static environment, the difference of the data changes is small. Using this device will facilitate the detection that all parts of the city environment, in addition to, introduce the NB-IoT technology is better for this work. With the development of science and technology, I believe that NB-IoT technology will enter our life and become the key to connect all things.

Acknowledgment. The authors would like to thank the financial support by the National Science Foundation of P.R. China under Grant Nos. 61401221, 61572260, 61872196, China Postdoctoral Science Foundation under Grant No. 2016M601860, Postgraduate Research & Practice Innovation Program of Jiangsu Province under Grant Nos. SJKY19_0823,SJCX19_0240, NJUPT Teaching Reform Project under Grant No. JG00417JX74.

References

1. Lin, Y., Wang, P., Ma, M.: Intelligent transportation system (ITS): concept, challenge and opportunity. In: IEEE 3rd International Conference on Big Data Security on Cloud (big data security), pp. 167–172. IEEE(2017)
2. Wang, Y.P.E., Lin, X., Adhikary, A., et al.: A primer on 3GPP narrowband Internet of Things (NB-IoT). IEEE Commun. Mag. **55**(3), 117–123 (2016)
3. Shu, S., Zhao, Q.W., Li, J.S., et al.: The shared bicycle and its network internet of shared bicycle (IoSB). Sensors **18**(8), 1–24 (2018)

4. Zhang, J.Y., Sun, H., Li, P.F., Li, C.C.: The comprehensive benefit evaluation of take shared bicycles as connecting to public transit. In: International Conference on Sustainable Development on Energy and Environment Protection, vol. 86, pp. 1–6 (2017)
5. Liu, X., Li, B., Jiang, A., et al.: A bicycle-borne sensor for monitoring air pollution near roadways. In: IEEE International Conference on Consumer Electronics-Taiwan, pp. 166–167. IEEE(2015)
6. Aguiari, D., et al.: Designing a smart e-bike eco-system. In: IEEE Annual Consumer Communications & Networking Conference (CCNC), pp. 1–6. IEEE (2018)
7. Huang, H.F.: Telecommunications, ofo, Huawei join hands to explore NB-IoT shared bicycle "gold mine". In: Communication World, vol. 06, no. 46 (2017)
8. Comparison of NB-IoT / Lora / Zigbee / Wifi / Bluetooth wireless networking methods. https://blog.csdn.net/dwx1005526886/article/details/81915191. Accessed 25 Feb 2019
9. Huang, Y.H., Yang, G.: Editor-in-chief. In: Nb-iot IoT Technology Analysis and Case Details. Machinery Industry Press (2018)
10. Li, Z.: Arduino based environmental air monitoring system. In: Case Western Reserve University (2017)
11. SIM7000C Arduino NB-IOT/LTE/GPRS expansion board. http://wiki.dfrobot.com.cn/. Accessed 25 Feb 2019
12. Jin, J., Jiang, X., Wu, X., Hu, Z.M.: Analysis on the comparison and development of NB-IoT and EMTC technology. Inf. Commun. Technol. Policies **01**, 89–94 (2019)
13. NB-IoT is the only way to connect to the 5G of everything. http://www.qianjia.com/html/2017-07/. Accessed 25 Feb 2019

Power Beacons Deployment in Wireless Powered Communication with Truncated Poisson Cluster Process

Siyuan Zhou[✉], Jinhang Zhao, Guoping Tan, Xujie Li, and Qin Yan

College of Computer and Information, Hohai University, Nanjing, China
{siyuan.zhou,gptan,lixujie}@hhu.edu.cn,
yuyun555@126.com, yanqin@ieee.org

Abstract. Wireless powered communication (WPC) is able to provide the wireless devices (WDs) practically infinite energy for information transmission, by deploying multiple power beacons (PBs) as dedicated energy source. The performance of wireless energy transfer and wireless information transmission may significantly vary depending on the locations of the wireless nodes and the channels used for signal transmission. To enable efficient transmission and overcome the doubly-near-far problem in WPC, this paper proposes a PB deployment strategy where the distribution of PBs is subject to a truncated Poisson cluster process (PCP), and analytically investigates the performance of WPC in terms of the SNR outage probability. Specifically, we consider a harvest-then-transmit communication network, where WDs use RF harvested energy for the information transmission in each time block. The wireless energy transfer between WDs and PBs is achieved by either directed mode (WD is served by the closest PB) or isotropic mode (WD is served by multiple PBs). We first investigate the distribution of the distance between WD and an arbitrary PB in the associated cluster. Then, we derive a numerically computable form of the SNR outage probability for directed mode and a tight upper bound of the SNR outage probability for isotropic mode. Finally, numerical results verify the accuracy of the analytical results, present performance comparisons with varied network parameters, and reveal the advantages of the truncated PCP based PB deployment over the random PB deployment and the symmetric PB deployment.

Keywords: Wireless powered communication (WPC) · Power beacons (PBs) · Doubly-near-far problem · Poisson cluster process (PCP) · SNR outage probability

This work was supported in part by the National Natural Science Foundation of China (No. 61701168, 61832005, 61571303) and the Fundamental Research Funds for the Central Universities (No. 2019B15614).

X. B. Zhai et al. (Eds.): MLICOM 2019, LNICST 294, pp. 333–346, 2019.
https://doi.org/10.1007/978-3-030-32388-2_29

1 Introduction

Radio frequency (RF) energy harvesting is a potential and efficient approach to provide electricity for energy-constrained wireless devices (WDs) in the forthcoming 5G networks. By leveraging such solution, WDs are able to harvest energy from RF signals and convert it into electricity, without replacing or recharging batteries manually. Basically there are two main architectures to apply RF energy harvesting in wireless communication networks: simultaneous wireless information and power transfer (SWIPT), and wireless powered communication (WPC). In SWIPT scheme, WDs within long information transmission distance might not be able to collect energy from RF signals, due to the huge gap on the operational threshold level of the received signal strength between RF energy harvesting and wireless information transmission. WPC architecture is thus established by transferring energy signal to WDs from the dedicated power beacons (PBs) in the network [1,2]. In WPC network, a WD first harvests energy from PBs and then communicates with the access point (AP) using the stored energy. As such, the performance of WPC depends on the interactions between PBs, WDs, and AP.

1.1 Literature Study

The performance analysis of WPC starts from a landmark contribution [1], where WDs served by single PB is called *directed mode* and WDs served by multiple PBs simultaneously is called *isotropic mode*. Thus, a paradigm shift is initiated where the required energy can be transferred to WDs from PBs on request resulting in uninterrupted power supply. In WPC architecture, each time block is partitioned into two phases for energy harvesting between PBs and WD and information transmission between WD and AP. Without considering the transmit power constraint on the WD, the power of the received information signal at AP can be characterized by exploiting the product distribution of channel gains belonging to energy harvesting and information transmission channels, if the geometric location of all nodes are fixed and known. Within this derived closed-form distributions, the network performance is analyzed in [3,4].

In a large-scale WPC networks, the path-loss effect of the signal transmission becomes more crucial for both wireless energy transfer and wireless information transmission. Plenty of literature on performance of WPC has been carried out by assuming the locations of PBs, WDs, and AP to be deterministic. In practice, however, due to the distributed nature of the network and the mobility of terminals, their locations are usually dynamic. The ever-growing randomness and irregularity in the locations of nodes in WPC has led to a growing interest in the application of stochastic geometry for modeling a tractable network [2,5]. Considering the scenario where PBs are uniformly distributed, performance of energy harvesting and information transmission is evaluated by using a homogeneous Poisson Point Process (PPP) model [2]. In [6], a Poisson Cluster Process (PCP) is adopted to model the hotspot deployment of PBs when PBs are densely distributed and the performance of wireless powered backscatter communication is analyzed. By assuming the PB is located in the cluster center, the distribution of users around the PB is characterized by a truncated PCP model that creates a guard zone for preventing the singularity of the path-loss effect [7].

1.2 Motivations and Contributions

The doubly-near-far problem in WPC results from the fact that if both energy source and information receiver are collocated, a far-away WD is highly vulnerable to the SNR outage compared to a nearby WD. When multiple low-cost PBs can be distributed to overcome such problem, the performance of energy harvesting and information transmission highly depends on the deployment strategy of PBs [8]. An optimization approach of node deployment in WPC is exploited in [9] by jointly optimize the locations of PBs and APs. If AP is located in the center and the WDs are uniformly distributed, the analytical performance of WPC when PBs are uniformly scattered in each cluster (also known as Matern PCP) can be considered as a performance benchmark. A symmetric PB deployment is proposed to achieve the performance improvement in terms of the SNR outage zone in [10]. Since the far-away WDs exhibit both larger PDF of the distance to AP [11] and higher probability to suffer the SNR outage, it is apparently inefficient to place dense PBs closed to AP and more reasonable to correlate the distribution of PBs with that of WDs.

To this end, this paper develops a mathematical architecture of WPC based on a two-tier heterogeneous network (HetNet) model, characterizes the distribution of the transmission distance between WDs and PBs, presents the expressions of the SNR outage probability, and compares the performance of WPC under various PB deployment strategies. The key contributions of this work can be summarized as follows.

- The two-tier WPC HetNet with correlated WD and PB locations is developed. In particular, The WDs are distributed as a Matern PCP where the parent point process of the PCP stands for the distribution of APs. Using the same parent point process, PBs are located based on a truncated PCP model. The common parent point process of two different PCPs captures the coupling effect between the locations of WDs and PBs.
- The analytical performance of the proposed WPC network for both directed energy transfer mode and isotropic energy transfer mode is investigated. The distance distributions between a WD and an arbitrary PB is characterized in a piecewise fashion. Consequently, the SNR outage probability of a randomly distributed WD in directed energy transfer mode is given in a semi-closed form. The upper bound of the SNR outage probability in isotropic energy transfer mode is provided. The simplified expressions of the SNR outage probability in special cases are also presented.
- The improvement of the proposed truncated PCP based PB deployment is analyzed. The minimum SNR outage probability can be achieved by optimizing the radius of the hole in the truncated PCP. Numerical results validate the

analytical expressions, compare the proposed PB deployment with the random PB deployment and the symmetric PB deployment, and provide insights into the system design of the PB assisted WPC networks.

2   System Model

We consider a WPC network as depicted in Fig. 1, where WDs powered by surrounding PBs communicate with the associated APs. In this harvest-then-transmit WPC model, each time block is partitioned into two phases for wireless energy transfer (WET) and wireless information transmission (WIT). We assume the WDs are supercapacitor equipped and all energy harvested in one time block is used for the information uplink. WET can be achieved in two modes: *directed mode* where one PB is paired with the closed PB (as shown in cell 1 of Fig. 1), and *isotropic mode* where one PB receive energy signals from all intra-cluster PBs (as shown in cell 2 of Fig. 1).

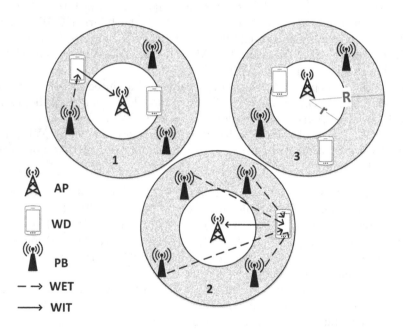

Fig. 1. A network model of PB assisted WPC communications.

2.1   Spatial Model

The clustering nature of the WDs is captured by assuming the WDs are randomly distributed as a Matern PCP. The PBs also exhibit clustering pattern and can be modeled by a truncated PCP. The correlation between PBs and WDs is captured by placing APs as the parent point process of two PCPs, modeling the geographical centers of hotspots. A similar HetNet model with two correlated PCPs is also presented in [12].

Specifically, we model the locations of APs as a homogeneous PPP $\mathbf{x} \in \Psi_a$. Since we aim to investigate the information uplink from WD to AP, the AP in the representative cluster is assumed to be located at the origin. Denoting Ψ_a as the common parent point process, the locations of WDs are characterized by a Matern PCP Ψ_s, and the layout of PBs are modeled by a truncated MCP Ψ_p. As shown in the Fig. 1, the PBs are randomly distributed in the shaded area. The radius of the hole in the truncated PCP (the lower bound of the offspring point distribution) is denoted by r and the cluster radius (the upper bound of the offspring point distribution) of two PCPs is represented by R, as illustrated in cell 3 of Fig. 1. The offspring point process of WDs with respect to the AP $\mathbf{x}$ is denoted by $\{\mathbf{y}_s\} \equiv B_s(\mathbf{x}, R)$, and similarly, the offspring point process of PBs with respect to the AP $\mathbf{x}$ is denoted by $\{\mathbf{y}_p\} \equiv B_p(\mathbf{x}, r, R)$. The number of WDs and PBs in each cluster is Poisson distributed with mean $\bar{m}_l, l \in \{s, p\}$.

As such, in each cluster, the PBs are uniformly distributed around the corresponding AP in the annulus area, with density

$$f_{\mathbf{Y}_p}(\mathbf{y}_p) = \frac{1}{\pi(R^2 - r^2)}, \ r \leq \| \mathbf{y}_p \| \leq R \tag{1}$$

where $\|\mathbf{y}_p\| = v$ is the distance of an arbitrary PB to the cluster center, and the PDF of v is expressed as

$$f_v(x) = \frac{2x}{(R^2 - r^2)}, \ r \leq x \leq R \tag{2}$$

Meanwhile, the WDs are uniformly distributed around the AP in the circular area with density $f_{\mathbf{Y}_s}(\mathbf{y}_s) = \frac{1}{\pi R^2}, \ 0 \leq \| \mathbf{y}_s \| \leq R$, and the PDF of the distance between an arbitrary WD to the cluster center is $\tilde{f}_v(x) = \frac{2x}{R^2}, \ 0 \leq x \leq R$.

2.2   Propagation Model

Assuming one transmission period is L seconds, in the first phase with length $\tau L, 0 < \tau < 1$, the WD harvests energy from PBs. Then, by using all stored energy, the WD sends the information to the AP in the rest of the time with length $(1 - \tau)L$. We assume WIT is influenced by Rayleigh fading and the path-loss effect, while WET is impaired by the path-loss effect without fading due to the relatively short distance of efficient WET [6]. The characterization of WET can be divided into two categories: directed mode and isotropic mode.

Directed Mode: In directed mode, the WD is paired with the nearest PB in the cluster. The associated PB is able to deliver energy signal to the WD by beamforming, while other non-associated PBs keep silent. By neglecting the effects of the noise, the received energy at the WD in each WET phase is written as

$$E_s = \tau L \mu P_p w d_c^{-\alpha} \tag{3}$$

where μ represents the energy conversion efficiency, P_p is the transmit power of PB, w stands for the antenna array gain, and d_c represents the distance between WD and the closed PB.

Isotropic Mode: In isotropic mode, all PBs in the cluster transmit energy signals in an omni-directional manner to all WDs in the WET phase. Thus the WD can receive energy signal from all PBs in the corresponding cluster. The received energy at the WD in each WET phase is expressed as

$$E_s = \tau L \mu \sum_{i \in B_p(\mathbf{x}, r, R)} P_p d_i^{-\alpha} \tag{4}$$

where d_i represents the distance between the WD and the i-th PB.

Depending on the amount of the harvested energy, the WDs transmit information signal to AP in the second phase with power P_s. Since the WD is equipped with super-capacitor, it is able to quickly store and release energy from dedicated energy sources. Without considering the transmit power limits, the energy for information transmission in one time period is less than or equal to the harvested energy in the first phase. The relationship between E_s and P_s is characterized as

$$P_s = \frac{E_s}{(1 - \tau)L} \tag{5}$$

Assuming the distance between the reference WD and the associated AP is v and the Rayleigh fading of the WIT channel is denoted by h_s, the SNR outage probability of WIT is expressed as the probability that the received SNR γ at AP is less than the SNR outage threshold γ_{th},

$$\mathcal{O} = \mathbb{P}(\gamma < \gamma_{th}) = \mathbb{P}\left(\frac{P_s h_s v^{-\alpha}}{N_0} < \gamma_{th} \right) \tag{6}$$

where N_0 represents the power of the thermal noise. Note that there is no intra-cluster interference since each WD transmits during its allocated time slot [10]. The influence of the inter-cell interference is also neglected and could be the extension of this work.

3   Distance Distribution

In order to analyze the performance of the proposed WPC model, it is crucial to characterize of the distance distribution between WDs and PBs. We consider a randomly selected WD is located in the origin and the distance between AP (cluster center) and the WD is v. The statistics of the distance d_R between the WD and an arbitrary PB in the cluster depends on the relationship between d_R, v, r and R, due to the fact that the distribution of PBs and WDs are two correlated PCPs. The conditional PDF of d_R can be derived in the following proposition.

Table 1. Conditional PDF of d_R with different parameters configuration.

$f_{d_R}(u\|v)$ when $r < \frac{R}{3}$	$v \in [0,r)$	$v \in [r, \frac{R-r}{2})$
	E1, $u \in (0, r-v]$	E2, $u \in (0, v-r]$
	E3, $u \in (r-v, r+v]$	E3, $u \in (v-r, v+r]$
	E2, $u \in (r+v, R-v]$	E2, $u \in (r+v, R-v]$
	E4, $u \in (R-v, R+v]$	E4, $u \in (R-v, R+v]$
	$v \in [\frac{R-r}{2}, \frac{R+r}{2})$	$v \in [\frac{R+r}{2}, R)$
	E2, $u \in (0, v-r]$	E2, $u \in (0, R-v]$
	E3, $u \in (v-r, R-v]$	E4, $u \in (R-v, v-r]$
	E5, $u \in (R-v, r+v]$	E5, $u \in (v-r, v+r]$
	E4, $u \in (r+v, R+v]$	E4, $u \in (v+r, R+v]$
$f_{d_R}(u\|v)$ when $r \geq \frac{R}{3}$	$v \in [0, \frac{R-r}{2})$	$v \in [\frac{R-r}{2}, r)$
	E1, $u \in (0, r-v]$	E1, $u \in (0, r-v]$
	E3, $u \in (r-v, r+v]$	E3, $u \in (r-v, R-v]$
	E2, $u \in (r+v, R-v]$	E5, $u \in (R-v, r+v]$
	E4, $u \in (R-v, R+v]$	E4, $u \in (r+v, R+v]$
	$v \in [r, \frac{R+r}{2})$	$v \in [\frac{R+r}{2}, R)$
	E2, $u \in (0, v-r]$	E2, $u \in (0, R-v]$
	E3, $u \in (v-r, R-v]$	E4, $u \in (R-v, v-r]$
	E5, $u \in (R-v, r+v]$	E5, $u \in (v-r, v+r]$
	E4, $u \in (r+v, R+v]$	E4, $u \in (v+r, R+v]$

Proposition 1. *In the proposed WPC model, the conditional PDF $f_{d_R}(u|v)$ of the distance between a WD and an arbitrary PB given the distance between the WD and AP is presented in a piecewise fashion for each specific configuration between u, v, r, and R, as shown in Table 1 at the top of the next page. The expressions of E1–E5 in Table 1 are written in (7)–(11).*

$$E1 = 0 \tag{7}$$

$$E2 = \frac{2u}{R^2 - r^2} \tag{8}$$

$$E3 = \frac{2u}{R^2 - r^2}\left(1 - \frac{1}{\pi}\arccos\left(\frac{v^2 + u^2 - r^2}{2uv}\right)\right) \tag{9}$$

$$E4 = \frac{2u}{\pi(R^2 - r^2)}\arccos\left(\frac{u^2 + v^2 - R^2}{2vu}\right) \tag{10}$$

$$E5 = \frac{2u}{\pi(R^2 - r^2)}\left(\arccos\left(\frac{u^2 + v^2 - R^2}{2vu}\right) - \arccos\left(\frac{v^2 + u^2 - r^2}{2uv}\right)\right) \tag{11}$$

Proof. The proof is given in Appendix.

Then, for each parameters configuration, the conditional CDF of d_R can be obtained by integrating $f_{d_R}(u|v)$, written as $F_{d_R}(u|v) = \int_0^u f_{d_R}(x|v)\,dx$. Hence, the conditional CDF of the distance between a WD and the closed PB is expressed as $F_{d_C}(u|v) = 1 - \exp(-\bar{m}_p F_{d_R}(u|v))$. The conditional PDF of d_C can be derived as,

$$f_{d_C}(u|v) = \bar{m}_p \exp(-\bar{m}_p F_{d_R}(u|v)) f_{d_R}(u|v) \tag{12}$$

4   Performance Analysis

We first derive the generalized form of the SNR outage probability for each energy transfer mode. Then, the simplified expressions in certain special cases are presented.

4.1   Directed Mode

In the directed mode, the statistics of the harvested energy depends on the distribution of the distance d_C. Assuming the channel gain and the locations of nodes keep unchanged during the transmission period L, the SNR outage probability at AP is written as

$$
\begin{aligned}
\mathcal{O}_d &= \mathbb{P}(\tau \mu P_p d_C^{-\alpha} < \gamma_0 N_0 v^\alpha g^{-1}(1-\tau)) \\
&= \mathbb{P}(g < \frac{\gamma_0 N_0 d_C^\alpha (1-\tau)}{\mu P_p v^{-\alpha} \tau}) \\
&= \mathbb{E}_{d_c, v}[1 - \exp(-C d_C^\alpha v^\alpha)]
\end{aligned}
\tag{13}
$$

where $C = \frac{\gamma_0 N_0 (1-\tau)}{\mu P_p \tau}$ and the last step follows from the exponential distribution of g. Since the PDF of d_C is a piecewise function depending on v, $\mathcal{O}_d$ can be computed by integrating over each interval, shown in the following proposition.

Proposition 2. *When WET is achieved in directed mode, the SNR outage probability can be expressed in a semi-analytical form as,*

$$\mathcal{O}_d = \int_0^R \mathbb{E}_{d_C}[1 - \exp(-C d_C^\alpha v^\alpha)] \frac{2v}{R^2}\,dv \tag{14}$$

where the conditional PDF of d_C is expressed in (12).

The computation of (12) can be adopted by resorting to Gauss-legendre quadrature. Due to the conditional PDF of d_C is a piecewise function, it is complicated to analytically express the SNR outage probability in the generalized case. However, when the location of WD is known and the distribution of PB is subject to a truncation-free PCP model, the SNR outage probability can be further simplified.

4.2   Isotropic Mode

In the isotropic mode, the WD is able to receive the energy signal from all PBs in the cluster. As such, different to the directed mode, the statistics of the harvested energy depends on the distribution of the distance d_R and the number of PBs. Assuming the channel gain and the locations of nodes keep unchanged during the transmission period L, the SNR outage probability at AP is written as

$$\mathcal{O}_i = \mathbb{P}(\tau \mu P_p \sum_i d_i^{-\alpha} < \gamma_0 N_0 v^\alpha g^{-1}(1-\tau))$$

$$\overset{(a)}{=} 1 - \mathbb{E}\Big[\exp\Big(-\frac{Cv^\alpha}{\sum_i d_i^{-\alpha}}\Big)\Big]$$

$$= 1 - \mathbb{E}_v\Big[\exp\Big(-Cv^\alpha \int_0^\infty \exp(-t\sum_i d_i^{-\alpha})\,\mathrm{d}t\Big)\Big]$$

$$\overset{(b)}{\leq} 1 - \mathbb{E}_v\Big[\exp\Big(-Cv^\alpha \int_0^\infty \mathbb{E}_{B_p(\mathbf{x},r,R)}\big[e^{-t\sum_i d_i^{-\alpha}}\big]\,\mathrm{d}t\Big)\Big]$$

where (a) is obtained by incorporating the exponential distribution of g and (b) follows from the Jensen inequality. The expectation with respect to all PBs belonging to $B_p(\mathbf{x}, r, R)$ in last equation can be derived due to the fact that the number of PBs per cluster is Poisson distributed [13],

$$\mathbb{E}_i\Big[\exp(-t\sum_i d_i^{-\alpha})\Big]$$

$$= \exp\Big(-\bar{m}_p \int_0^{R+v} (1 - e^{-tu^{-\alpha}}) f_{d_R}(u|v)\,\mathrm{d}u\Big) \tag{15}$$

As such, an upper bound of the SNR outage probability is expressed in next proposition.

Proposition 3. *When WET is achieved in isotropic mode, the upper bound of the SNR outage probability can be expressed in a semi-analytical form written as,*

$$\mathcal{O}_i^u = 1 - \int_0^R \exp\Big(-Cv^\alpha \int_0^\infty \exp\Big(-\bar{m}_p$$

$$\cdot(1 - \int_0^{R+v} e^{-tu^{-\alpha}} f_{d_R}(u|v)\,\mathrm{d}u)\Big)\,\mathrm{d}t\Big)\frac{2v}{R^2}\,\mathrm{d}v \tag{16}$$

Note that the integrals in the above expression can be accurately computed by resorting to Gauss quadrature.

4.3   Special Case: Fixed WD Location and Truncation-Free Distribution of PB

In the truncation-free PCP model with $r = 0$, the conditional PDF of d_R is simplified to the following expression,

$$\tilde{f}_{d_R}(u|v) = \begin{cases} \frac{2u}{R^2}, & 0 \leq u \leq R - v \\ \frac{2u}{\pi R^2} \arccos(\frac{u^2+v^2-R^2}{2vu}), & R - v \leq u \leq R + v \end{cases}$$

Note that the same expression of the conditional PDF in a different network layout is presented in [14]. The simplified expressions of the SNR outage probability in two energy transfer modes are provided in the following.

Directed Mode: In this case, the SNR outage probability with a fixed WD location v can be derived as

$$
\begin{aligned}
\tilde{\mathcal{O}}_d &= \mathbb{E}_{d_c}[1 - \exp(-Cd_C^\alpha v^\alpha)] \\
&= 1 - \int_0^{R-v} \exp(-Cv^\alpha u^\alpha) f_{d_C}(u|v) \, du \\
&\quad - \int_{R-v}^{R+v} \exp(-Cv^\alpha u^\alpha) f_{d_C}(u|v) \, du \\
&= 1 - \int_0^{(R-v)^2} \exp(-Cv^\alpha x^{\frac{\alpha}{2}} - \frac{\bar{m}_p}{R^2}x)\frac{\bar{m}_p}{R^2} \, dx \\
&\quad - \int_{R-v}^{R+v} \exp(-Cv^\alpha u^\alpha)\bar{m}_p\frac{2u}{\pi R^2}\arccos(\frac{u^2+v^2-R^2}{2vu}) \\
&\quad \cdot \exp\left[-\bar{m}_p\left(\frac{(R-v)^2}{R^2} + C_1(u)\right)\right] du
\end{aligned}
\tag{17}
$$

where $C_1(u) = \int_{R-v}^u \frac{2x}{\pi R^2}\arccos(\frac{x^2+v^2-R^2}{2vx}) \, dx$.

Isotropic Mode: When the path-loss factor $\alpha = 2$, the upper bound of SNR outage probability with a known WD location v can be simplified into

$$
\begin{aligned}
\tilde{\mathcal{O}}_i^u &= 1 - \exp\left(-Cv^2 \int_0^\infty \exp\left(-\bar{m}_p(1 - \frac{1}{R^2}\right.\right. \\
&\quad \cdot (t\mathrm{Ei}(\frac{-t}{(R-v)^2}) + e^{\frac{-t}{(R-v)^2}}(R-v)^2) - C_2(t)) \, dt\Big)
\end{aligned}
\tag{18}
$$

where $C_2(t) = \int_{R-v}^{R+v} e^{-tx^{-2}}\frac{2x}{\pi R^2}\arccos(\frac{x^2+v^2-R^2}{2vx}) \, dx$, and $\mathrm{Ei}(\cdot)$ denotes the exponential integral.

5   Numerical Results

In this section, we numerically investigate the performance of the proposed WPC network for different PB deployment strategies. The accuracy of the derived distribution of the distance between a WD and an arbitrary PB and the expressions of the SNR outage probability are verified by comparing them in the results with the Monte-Carlo simulations. In addition to our analytical results, the performance of the WPC network when PBs are randomly distributed or symmetrically located are also shown. A comparative performance analysis of the three considered deployments is conducted.

The cluster radius is taken as $R = 90\,\mathrm{m}$ and the path-loss factor is assumed as $\alpha = 3$. In the WET process, the average number of PBs in each cluster is set as $\bar{m}_p = 50$, which represent a scenario where PBs are densely distributed. The transmit power of PBs are identical as $P_p = 10\,\text{W}$, the energy conversion efficiency is set as $\mu = 0.8$, the proportion of time slot allocated for WET is $\tau = 0.6$, and the antenna array gain for directed mode is $w = 20$. In the WIT process, the thermal noise power is $N_0 = 10^{-9}\,\text{W}$, and the threshold of SNR outage is $\gamma_{th} = 5\,\text{dB}$.

The SNR outage probability of directed mode and isotropic mode is presented in Figs. 2 and 3, respectively. In both figures, the Monte Carlo results and the analytical results for the truncated PCP based PB deployment are shown in circle symbols and solid line, respectively. The results for the symmetric PB deployment are shown in dashed line, and the results for the random PB deployment are displayed in dotted line. It can be observed that with the increasing of the radius r of the hole in truncated PCP, the Monte Carlo results match the analytical expressions of the SNR outage probability well in directed WET mode, and the simulation results are tightly bounded by the proposed upper bound of the SNR outage probability in isotropic WET mode.

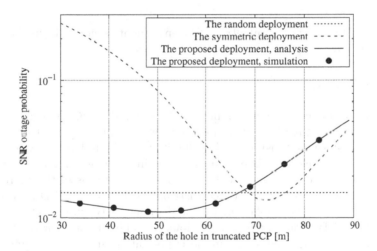

Fig. 2. The SNR outage probability versus r with different PB deployments in directed WET mode.

It is also observed that with the optimized value of r, the minimum of the SNR outage probability can be obtained for the truncated PCP based PB deployment in both energy transfer modes. Besides, in this scenario with dense PBs, the optimal placement of the PBs in a truncated PCP model outperforms both the random PB deployment and the symmetric PB deployment. The reason is that when WDs are randomly distributed in the cluster, the WDs located far away from the AP suffers severer outage probability than the nearby WDs due to the doubly-near-far problem. Thus it is necessary to deploy the PBs more densely in the area far away from the cluster center. Moreover, When PBs are

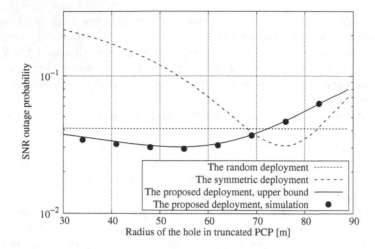

Fig. 3. The SNR outage probability versus r with different PB deployments in isotropic WET mode.

densely distributed, the symmetric PB deployment is not only inefficient but also impractical.

6   Conclusion

In order to improve the performance of PB-assisted WPC, a truncated PCP based PB deployment strategy is proposed in this paper. Based on the constructed harvest-then-transmit model, the PCP distributed WD is wireless powered by either one closed PB or multiple PBs in the cluster. The performance of such WPC network is analytically investigated in terms of the SNR outage probability. Specifically, the distance distribution between a WD and an arbitrary PB is first derived, followed by the distance distribution between a WD and the closed PB. Consequently, a semi-analytical expression for the SNR outage probability in directed WET mode is presented, and a tight upper bound of the SNR outage probability in isotropic WET mode is given. The simplified versions of the SNR outage probability in two WET modes are provided for special cases. Our analysis is validated by showing the excellent match between the results obtained through our exact expressions and those obtained via Monte Carlo simulations. The advantage of the proposed PB deployment is pointed out through comparison with the random PB deployment and the symmetric deployment. The derived results could provide valuable insights for designing the practical WPC systems.

Appendix

Let us denote the reference WD chosen uniformly at random in the representative cluster is located at origin. Without loss of generality, we assume the location of the AP in the cluster is denoted by $\mathbf{x}_o = (v, 0)$, and the region where PB can be distributed is represented by $A_p = B_p(\mathbf{x}_o, r, R)$ (the shaded regions in Fig. 4). The expression of the CDF of the distance d_R is

$$F_{d_R}(u|v) = \int_{B(o,u) \cap A_p} f_{\mathbf{Y}_p}(\mathbf{y}_p) \, d\mathbf{y}_p$$
$$= |B(o, u) \cap A_p| \frac{1}{\pi(R^2 - r^2)} \tag{19}$$

where $B(o, u)$ denotes the circle centered at origin with radius u (red circles in Fig. 4) and $|\varXi|$ represents the area covered by any generic region $\varXi \in \mathbb{R}^2$. The area of the joint region between A_p and $B(o, u)$ can be computed for different configurations between r, R, u, and v. As shown in Fig. 4, when $r \geq \frac{R}{3}$, with the increasing of v, four different configurations have to be considered and thus four varied piecewise function of $F_{d_R}(u|v)$ can be derived. The similar characterization can be carried out for $r < \frac{R}{3}$. Finally, the expressions of PDF of d_R is obtained by differentiating $F_{d_R}(u|v)$ with respect to u.

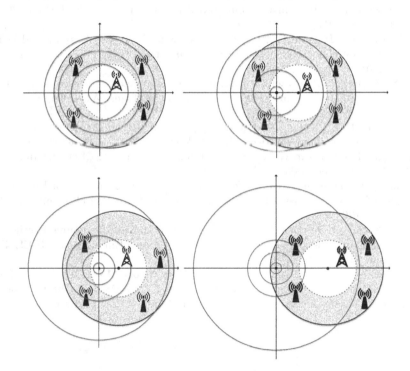

Fig. 4. Graphical illustration of the different parameters configuration in computation of the area of the joint region ($r \geq \frac{R}{3}$). (Color figure online)

References

1. Huang, K., Zhou, X.: Cutting last wires for mobile communication by microwave power transfer. IEEE Commun. Mag. **53**(6), 86–93 (2015)
2. Huang, K., Lau, V.K.N.: Enabling wireless power transfer in cellular networks: architecture, modeling and deployment. IEEE Trans. Wirel. Commun. **13**(2), 902–912 (2014)
3. Zhong, C., Chen, X., Zhang, Z., Karagiannidis, G.K.: Wireless powered communications: performance analysis and optimization. IEEE Trans. Commun. **63**(12), 5178–5190 (2015)
4. Huang, W., Chen, H., Li, Y., Vucetic, B.: On the performance of multi-antenna wireless-powered communications with energy beamforming. IEEE Trans. Veh. Technol. **65**(3), 1801–1808 (2015)
5. Lee, S., Zhang, R., Huang, K.: Opportunistic wireless energy harvesting in cognitive networks. IEEE Trans. Wirel. Commun. **12**(9), 4788–4799 (2013)
6. Han, K., Huang, K.: Wirelessly powered backscatter communication networks: modeling, coverage, and capacity. IEEE Trans. Wirel. Commun. **16**(4), 2548–2561 (2017)
7. Chen, L., Wang, W., Zhang, C.: Stochastic wireless powered communication networks with truncated cluster point process. IEEE Trans. Veh. Technol. **66**(12), 11286–11294 (2017)
8. Tabassum, H., Hossain, E., Ogundipe, A., Kim, D.I.: Wireless-powered cellular networks: key challenges and solution techniques. IEEE Commun. Mag. **53**(6), 63–71 (2015)
9. Bi, S., Zhang, R.: Placement optimization of energy and information access points in wireless powered communication networks. IEEE Trans. Wirel. Commun. **15**(3), 2351–2364 (2015)
10. Tabassum, H., Hossain, E.: On the deployment of energy sources in wireless-powered cellular networks. IEEE Trans. Commun. **63**(9), 3391–3404 (2015)
11. Haenggi, M.: On distances in uniformly random networks. IEEE Trans. Inf. Theory **51**(10), 3584–3586 (2005)
12. Afshang, M., Dhillon, H.: Poisson cluster process based analysis of Hetnets with correlated user and base station locations. IEEE Trans. Wirel. Commun. **17**(4), 2417–2431 (2018)
13. Hemachandra, K.T., Beaulieu, N.C.: Outage analysis of opportunistic scheduling in dual-hop multiuser relay networks in the presence of interference. IEEE Trans. Commun. **61**(5), 1786–1796 (2013)
14. Hayajneh, A.M., Zaidi, S.A.R., McLernon, D.C., Renzo, M.D., Ghogho, M.: Performance analysis of UAV enabled disaster recovery networks: a stochastic geometric framework based on cluster processes. IEEE Access **6**, 26215–26230 (2018)

Mobile Edge Computing-Enabled Resource Allocation for Ultra-Reliable and Low-Latency Communications

Yun Yu$^{(\boxtimes)}$, Siyuan Zhou, Xiaocan Lian, Guoping Tan, and Yingchi Mao

College of Computer and Information, Hohai University, Nanjing, China
`yuyun555@126.com, gptan@hhu.edu.cn`

Abstract. Mission critical services and applications with computation-intensive tasks require extremely low latency, while task offloading for mobile edge computing (MEC) incurs extra latency. In this work, the optimization of power consumption and delay are studied under ultra reliable and low latency (URLLC) framework in a multiuser MEC scenario. Delay and reliability are relying on users' task queue lengths, which is attested by probabilistic constraints. Different from the current literature, we consider a comprehensive system model taking into account the effects of bandwidth, computation capability, and transmit power. By introducing the approach of Lyapunov stochastic optimization, the problem is solved by splitting the multi-objective optimization problem into three single optimization problems. Performance analysis is conducted for the proposed algorithm, which illustrates that the tradeoff parameter indicates the tradeoff between power and delay. Simulation results are presented to validate the theoretical analysis of the impact of various parameters and demonstrate the effectiveness of the proposed approach.

Keywords: Mobile edge computing · Resource allocation · Probability constraints · Ultra reliable and low latency (URLLC) · Stochastic network optimization

1 Introduction

5G mobile network promotes extensive and deep integrations with vertical industry. The concept of Mobile Edge Computing (MEC) emerged and gradually evolved as one of the possible basic core structures of 5G. As a structure under 5G architecture, MEC adapts to dissimilar computing, caching and communication deployments in various scenarios [1–4]. Relying on the structure MEC, mobile network and Internet service achieve effective integration and further expand

This work was supported in part by the National Natural Science Foundation of China (No. 61701168, 61832005, 61571303) and the Fundamental Research Funds for the Central Universities (No. 2019B15614).

to other fields, like location service, advanced reality, Internet-of-Things, and computation assistant. Ultra reliable and low latency communication (URLLC) corresponds to services requiring low latency and high reliability, such as self-driving, industrial automation, etc.

MEC system is located between wired network and wireless access point and established by one or more MEC servers which are the core of the whole system. By offloading computation-intensive tasks to nearby MEC servers could significantly enhance the performance of user devices, including battery life and latency [5]. Applying MEC on URLLC needs emphasis on reducing latency and power consumption. Nevertheless, task offloading introduces extra latency, and its efficiency relying highly on channel conditions. Therefore, it is of value to consider bandwidth which is closely connected to channel conditions and wireless radio resources [6].

Resource allocation on MEC has attracted great attention. You *et al.* proposed a MECO system with multiple users to optimize energy consumption [7]. In [8], a joint allocation of computation and communication resources are studied in multi-user mobile cloud computing under power and latency constraints. Work of [9] focus on completion time minimization and compare two different access schemes. Furthermore, Liu *et al.* introduce stochastic network optimization on MEC system and establish a multi-user multi-server system to study the tradeoff between power and delay [10].

Nevertheless, [10] consider radio resource allocation and [11] considers violation constraints, channel condition on [11] is interference-related which makes it complicated to estimate transmission rate. Also, CPU cores are independent on servers with one-to-one correspondence to user devices on multi-user condition. In this case, queuing on servers can be simplified and better channel model should be felicitated.

In our work, seeking clarification of the relationship between power and delay indulges the optimization of our work. We consider an MEC system with multiple mobile devices in which computing tasks arrive on mobile devices in a random manner. Based on the Lyapunov optimization theory [12], the radio and computational resources are joint considered to make the power consumption minimize under the latency and reliability constraints. Pickands-Balkema-de Haan theorem of extreme value theory is used to descript the queue length which exceed the threshold. And the results show the trade-off between power consumption and latency of mobile devices.

The organization of this paper is characterized as follows. We describe a system model that satisfies the requirements of URLLC structure in Sect. 2, latency and reliability constraints are imposed in Sect. 3, and optimization problems are schemed and solved in Sect. 4. Simulation results are displayed in Sect. 5 with analysis, and we will conclude this paper in Sect. 6.

2 System Model

As shown in Fig. 1, a set U of UEs with local computation capacity is considered in our system. A single server with N CPU cores deals with the tasks offloaded by UEs in parallel. Tasks are emerged by UEs and part of them are offloaded to MEC server, meanwhile the UEs simultaneously process the rest of tasks locally. Therefore, queues exist at both users and server side. Channel access scheme is chosen as Frequency Division Multiple Access (FDMA), transmission rate is proportional to bandwidth. End-to-End delay includes transmission delay on offloading condition and computing delay. Resource allocation directed at URLLC works is reflected at computational resource allocation and power control, and constrained by power consumption and delay.

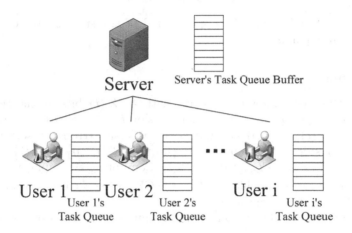

Fig. 1. System model

2.1 Queuing Model at User Side

Tasks arrive in stochastically and follow an arbitrary probability distribution. Task queue length is $Q_i(t)$ on time slot $t \in \{0, 1, 2, ...\}$ for the user $i \in U$. Task arrivals $A_i^u(t)$ meets Poisson task arrivals during time slot t with mean value γ in the unit of bits and are independent and identically distributed [12]. $B_i^u(t)$ is the task accomplishment in time slot t in the unit of bits, in which the local computation tasks $B_i^{u1}(t) = \tau \frac{f_i^u(t)}{L_i}$ and offloaded tasks $B_i^{u2}(t) = \tau R_i(t)$ are both considered, $B_i^u(t) = B_i^{u1}(t) + B_i^{u2}(t)$. L_i denotes the required CPU cycle frequency per bit, CPU cycle frequency is $f_i^u(t)$. The queue length on slot $t+1$ (in the unit of bits) evolves as $Q_i(t+1) = \max\{Q_i(t) - B_i^u(t), 0\} + A_i^u(t)$. The transmission rate at UE side for task offloading is

$$R_i(t) = \alpha_i(t) W \log_2 \left(1 + \frac{p_i(t) H_i(t)}{N_0 \alpha_i(t) W}\right). \tag{1}$$

W is total system bandwidth, N_0 is the power spectral density of the additive white Gaussian noise, and $\alpha_i(t)$ is a bandwidth allocation vector applying FDMA for user $i \in U$. $H_i(t)$ denotes the channel power gain from user $i \in U$ to the server with transmit power $p_i(t)$.

For local computational resource and transmit power allocation, we impose following constraints for each UE $i \in U$:

$$
\begin{cases}
\sum_{i \in U} \alpha_i(t) \leq 1 \\
\alpha_i(t) \geq 0 \\
0 \leq p_i(t) \leq p_i^{\max} \\
0 \leq f_i^u(t) \leq f_u^{\max}
\end{cases}
\tag{2}
$$

where $p_i^{\max}$ and $f_u^{\max}$ are the upper bound of transmission power and local computational capability.

2.2 Queuing Model at Server Side

We denote the task offloading queue length as $Z_i(t)$ bits at the server side on time slot t, the queue length at time slot $t + 1$ evolves as $Z_i(t + 1) = \max\{Z_i(t) - B_i^s(t), 0\} + A_i^s(t)$, $A_i^s(t)$ denotes task arrivals at server in time slot t at server side, $A_i^s(t) = \min\{\max\{Q_i(t) - B_i^{u1}(t), 0\}, \tau R_t(t)\}$. Therefore $Z_i(t+1) \leq \max\{Z_i(t) - B_i^s(t), 0\} + \tau R_t(t)$. Computing accomplishment in time slot t is $B_i^s(t) = \tau \frac{f_i^s(t)}{L_i}$ in which $f_i^s(t)$ is the CPU cycle frequency that allocated to each CPU core to serve user $i \in U$.

At the server side, the computational resource is allocated by constraints as follows:

$$
\begin{cases}
\sum_{i \in U} \mathbb{1} \cdot \{f_i^s(t) > 0\} \leq N \\
f_i^s(t) \in \{0, f_s^{\max}\}, i \in U
\end{cases}
\tag{3}
$$

where $\mathbb{1}\{\cdot\}$ is an indicator function, $f_s^{\max}$ is the upper bound of the computational capability at server side.

3   Latency and Reliability Constraints

According to Little's Law, the average queuing delay is proportional to the average queue length. However, relying only on the average queue length without considering queuing length probability distribution to evaluate latency and reliability lacks accuracy. Taking the statistic results of queue length and queuing delay into account could increase accuracy immensely. Furthermore, violation of the queue length and queuing delay constraints could decrease the reliability of computation tasks. For instance, offloaded tasks would be deleted if a finite-length queuing buffer is overloaded. So, we impose the queue length probability constraint:

$$
\lim_{T \to \infty} \frac{1}{T} \sum_{t=1}^{T} \Pr\left(Q_i(t) > d_i^u\right) \leq \varepsilon_i^u,
\tag{4}
$$

in which d_i^u is the queue length bound, ε_i^u is the tolerable violation probability and $\varepsilon_i^u \ll 1$.

According to Pickands-Balkema-de Haan theorem for exceedances over thresholds, when the threshold d_i^u is platitudinous high, the cumulative distribution function (CDF) of the excess part of the queue closely approaches generalized Pareto Distribution (GPD) [13].

Applying Pickands-Balkema-de Haan Theory to our problem, the expectation and variance of the conditional excess queue value on user side are $\frac{\sigma_u}{1-\xi_u}$ and $\frac{\sigma_u^2}{(1-\xi_u)^2(1-2\xi_u)}$, where σ_u is the scale parameter and ξ_u is the shape parameter. The mean value and the variance of the CDF would decline while the scale parameter and shape parameter are reduced. The threshold of the scale parameter and the shape parameter are given as $\sigma_u \le \sigma_u^{th}$ and $\xi_u \le \xi_u^{th}$.

Define the excess value of queue length of user $i \in U$ on time slot t is $X_i^u(t)\big|_{Q_i(t)>d_i^u} = Q_i(t) - d_i^u$, and $Y_i^u(t) = [X_i^u(t)]^2$.

Time averaged mean value of excess queue length $\overline{X_i^u}$ and its second moment $\overline{Y_i^u}$ are:

$$\overline{X_i^u} = \lim_{T\to\infty} \frac{1}{T} \sum_{t=1}^{T} \mathbb{E}[X_i^u(t)\,|Q_i(t) > d_i^u] \le \frac{\sigma_u^{th}}{1-\xi_u^{th}}, \tag{5}$$

$$\overline{Y_i^u} = \lim_{T\to\infty} \frac{1}{T} \sum_{t=1}^{T} \mathbb{E}[Y_i^u(t)\,|Q_i(t) > d_i^u] \le \frac{2(\sigma_u^{th})^2}{(1-\xi_u^{th})(1-2\xi_u^{th})}, \tag{6}$$

Likewise, the average queue length $Z_i(t)$ and average queuing delay on the server side are proportional to the average task offloading rate. The queuing delay probability constraint at server side is:

$$\lim_{T\to\infty} \frac{1}{T} \sum_{t=1}^{T} \Pr\left(\frac{Z_i(t)}{R_i(t-1)} > d_i^s\right) \le \varepsilon_i^s, \tag{7}$$

in which $\tilde{R}_i(t-1) = \frac{1}{t} \sum_{\omega=0}^{t-1} R_i(\omega)$, d_i^s denotes the queuing delay bound and ε_i^s denotes the tolerable violation probability at server side, $\varepsilon_i^s \ll 1$.

Define the excess queue length at server side for user $i \in U$ on time slot t as $X_i^s(t)\big|_{Z_i(t)>\tilde{R}_i(t-1)d_i^s} = Z_i(t) - \tilde{R}_i(t-1)d_i^s$, and $Y_i^s(t) = [X_i^s(t)]^2$. We have the expectation and variance of the conditional excess queue value on server side as $\frac{\sigma_s}{1-\xi_s}$ and $\frac{\sigma_s^2}{(1-\xi_s)^2(1-2\xi_s)}$, and $\sigma_s \le \sigma_s^{th}$, $\xi_s \le \xi_s^{th}$, where σ_s^{th} and ξ_s^{th} are the thresholds of scale and shape parameter at server side.

Thus, similar to the above, we have constraints as below:

$$\overline{X_i^s} = \lim_{T\to\infty} \frac{1}{T} \sum_{t=1}^{T} \mathbb{E}\left[X_i^s(t)\Big|Z_i(t) > \tilde{R}_i(t-1)d_i^s\right] \le \frac{\sigma_s^{th}}{1-\xi_s^{th}} \tag{8}$$

$$\overline{Y_i^s} = \lim_{T\to\infty} \frac{1}{T} \sum_{t=1}^{T} \mathbb{E}\left[Y_i^s(t)\Big|Z_i(t) > \tilde{R}_i(t-1)d_i^s\right] \le \frac{2(\sigma_s^{th})^2}{(1-\xi_s^{th})(1-2\xi_s^{th})} \tag{9}$$

At the user side, computational delay $f_i^u(t)$ and transmission delay $R_i(t)$ are inversely proportional. As users executing local computing tasks, allocating higher local CPU cycle frequency could partially reduce computational delay. For decreasing transmission delay, larger transmit power is needed instead. Therefore, queue length constraints from both user side and server side have already taken these two delays into account. On the other hand, UE's battery consumption would pay for higher computation capability and/or transmit power. Consequently, the tradeoff between power and delay is fatal. As for server side, the computational delay can be neglected, since a better CPU core with preferable computing capability is focusing on the one UE's offloaded task.

Teasing above factors, the end-to-end delay is composed by three components:

- Queuing delay from both user side and server side;
- Computing delay from both user side and server side;
- Transmission delay for users' task offloading.

4 Optimization Framework and Resource Allocation Scheme

Denoting the user side computational resource allocation as $\mathbf{f^u(t)} = \left(f_i^u(t), i \in U\right)$, transmit power allocation as $\mathbf{p(t)} = (p_i(t), i \in U)$, bandwidth resource allocation as $\alpha(\mathbf{t}) = (\alpha_i(t), i \in U)$, the server side computational resource allocation as $\mathbf{f^s(t)} = (f_i^s(t), i \in U)$. The power consumption is influenced by hardware architecture and CPU-cycle frequency $f_i^u(t)$, so we give out the local power consumption as $\kappa[f_i^u(t)]^3$, $P(t) = \sum\limits_{i \in U} \left(\kappa[f_i^u(t)]^3 + p_i(t)\right)$.

We formulate an optimization problem as follows:

$$\min_{\mathbf{f^u(t)}, \mathbf{p(t)}, \alpha(\mathbf{t}), \mathbf{f^s(t)}} \quad \lim_{T \to \infty} \frac{1}{T} \sum_{t=0}^{T-1} \mathbb{E}[P(t)]$$

$$\text{s.t.} \quad \text{(2) and (3) for resource allocation} \tag{10}$$
$$\text{(4) and (7) for queue length and delay}$$
$$\text{(5), (6), (8) and (9) for GDP}$$

4.1 Lyapunov Optimization

The constraints above are dedicated to make corresponding virtual queues and will be satisfied if the time averaged rate is stable. (11) shows the corresponding virtual queues, and $[\cdot]^+ = max\{\cdot, 0\}$.

$$Q_i^{(Q)}(t+1) = \left[Q_i^{(Q)}(t) + \mathbb{1} \cdot \{Q_i(t+1) > d_i^u\} - \varepsilon_i^u, 0\right]^+$$

$$Q_i^{(X)}(t+1) = \left[Q_i^{(X)}(t) + \left(X_i^u(t+1) - \frac{\sigma_u^{th}}{1-\xi_u^{th}}\right) \times \mathbb{1} \cdot \{Q_i(t+1) > d_i^u\}, 0\right]$$

$$Q_i^{(Y)}(t+1) = \left[Q_i^{(Y)}(t) + \left(Y_i^u(t+1) - \frac{2\left(\sigma_u^{th}\right)^2}{(1-\xi_u^{th})(1-2\xi_u^{th})}\right) \times \mathbb{1} \cdot \{Q_i(t+1) > d_i^u\}, 0\right]^+$$

$$Z_i^{(Z)}(t+1) = \left[Z_i^{(Z)}(t) + \mathbb{1} \cdot \left\{Z_i(t+1) > \tilde{R}_i(t)d_i^s\right\} - \varepsilon_i^s, 0\right]^+$$

$$Z_i^{(X)}(t+1) = \left[Z_i^{(X)}(t) + \left(X_i^s(t+1) - \frac{\sigma_s^{th}}{1-\xi_s^{th}}\right) \times \mathbb{1} \cdot \left\{Z_i(t+1) > \tilde{R}_i(t)d_i^s\right\}, 0\right]^+$$

$$Z_i^{(Y)}(t+1) = \left[Z_i^{(Y)}(t) + \left(Y_i^s(t+1) - \frac{2\left(\sigma_s^{th}\right)^2}{(1-\xi_s^{th})(1-2\xi_s^{th})}\right) \times \mathbb{1} \cdot \left\{Z_i(t+1) > \tilde{R}_i(t)d_i^s\right\}, 0\right]^+$$

$$(11)$$

Combining these virtual queues, we can get system queue vector $\mathbf{Q}(t) = \left(Q_i^{(Q)}(t), Q_i^{(X)}(t), Q_i^{(Y)}(t), Z_i^{(Z)}(t), Z_i^{(X)}(t), Z_i^{(Y)}(t), i \in U\right)$ and then have the Lyapunov function $L(\mathbf{Q}(t)) = \frac{1}{2} \sum_{i \in U} \left[\left(Q_i^{(Q)}(t)\right)^2 + \left(Q_i^{(X)}(t)\right)^2 + \left(Q_i^{(Y)}(t)\right)^2 + \left(Z_i^{(Z)}(t)\right)^2 + \left(Z_i^{(X)}(t)\right)^2 + \left(Z_i^{(Y)}(t)\right)^2\right]$ and conditional Lyapunov drift-plus-penalty for time slot t:

$$\mathbb{E}\left[\Delta L(t) + VP(t)|Q(t)\right]$$

$$\leq C + E\left[-\sum_{i \in U}\left[B_i^u(t)\left(Q_i^{(x)}(t)Q_i(t) + A_i^u(t) + 2Q_i^Y(t) \cdot (Q_i(t) + A_i^u(t))\right.\right.\right.$$

$$+ 2(Q_i(t) + A_i^u(t))^3\Big) + Q_i^{(Q)}(t)\Big] \times \mathbb{1} \cdot \left\{\max\left\{Q_i(t) - B_i^u(t), 0\right\} + A_i^u(t) > d_i^u\right\}$$

$$+ \sum_{i \in U}\left[\left(\tau R_i(t) - B_i^s(t)\right)\left(Z_i^{(X)}(t) + Z_i(t) + 2Z_i^Y(t)Z_i(t) + 2(Z_i(t))^3\right) + Z_i^{(Z)}(t)\right] \quad (12)$$

$$\times \mathbb{1} \cdot \left\{\max\left\{z_i(t) - B_i^s(t), 0\right\} + \tau R_i(t) > \tilde{R}_i(t)d_i^s\right\}$$

$$+ V\sum_{i \in U}\left(\kappa[f_i^u(t)]^3 + p_i(t)\right)\Big|Q(t)\right]$$

where $V \in (0, +\infty)$ is a non-negative Lyapunov tradeoff parameter in the unit of $bits^2/W$. According to Lyapunov Optimization Framework, the optimal solution of our problem P is the upper bound of (12).

Resolve this problem into three optimization problems in one time slot : CPU resources allocation at user side and server side, and transmission resource at user side.

4.2   CPU Computational Resource Allocation at User Side

Since the users are independent to each other, the optimal solution of CPU computational resource at user side can be obtained directly by resolving the above optimal problem.

Constraints at user side can be rewritten as:

$$\min_{0 \le f_i^u(t) \le f_u^{max}} \sum_{i \in U} V\kappa [f_i^u(t)]^3 - a_i(t)\tau f_i^u(t)/L_i \tag{13}$$

with $a_i(t) = Q_i^{(Q)}(t) + Q_i(t) + A_i^u(t) + (Q_i^{(X)}(t) + Q_i(t) + A_i^u(t) + 2Q_i^{(Y)}(t)$
$\times (Q_i(t) + A_i^u(t)) + 2(Q_i(t) + A_i^u(t))^3) \times \mathbb{1} \cdot \{Q_i(t) + A_i^u(t) > d_i^u\}$. Since users are independent to each other, $f_i^*(t) = \min\left\{\sqrt{\frac{a_i(t)\tau}{3V\kappa L_i}}, f_u^{max}\right\}$ is the answer after differentiation.

Algorithm 1. User side bandwidth allocation

1: Make accuracy parameter $\mu = 10^{-7}$, allow maximum iteration number $I_{max} = 200$.
2: Initialize $l = 0$, $\alpha_i(t) = 0$, $\widetilde{\lambda}_L = \lambda_L(t)$, $\widetilde{\lambda}_U = \lambda_U(t)$.
3: **while** $\left| \sum_{i \in U} \alpha_i(t) - 1 \right| \ge \mu$ and $l \le I_{max}$ **do**
4:      $\widetilde{\lambda} = \frac{1}{2}\left(\widetilde{\lambda}_L + \widetilde{\lambda}_U\right)$.
5:      $l = l + 1$.
6:      $\alpha_i(t) = max\left\{\mathcal{A}_i\left(\widetilde{\lambda}\right), 0\right\}$.
7:      **if** $\sum_{i \in U} \alpha_i(t) > 1$ **then**
8:          $\widetilde{\lambda}_L = \widetilde{\lambda}$.
9:      **else**
10:          $\widetilde{\lambda}_U = \widetilde{\lambda}$.
11:      **end if**
12: **end while**

4.3   Transmit Power and Bandwidth Allocation at User Side

$$\min_{\mathbf{p}(t), \alpha(t)} \sum_{i \in U} Vp_i(t) + (b_i(t) - a_i(t))\tau R_i(t) \tag{14}$$

with $b_i(t) = Z_i^{(Z)}(t) + Z_i(t) + \left(Z_i^{(X)}(t) + Z_i(t) + 2Z_i^{(Y)}(t) \cdot Z_i(t) + 2(Z_i(t))^3\right) \times \left\{Z_i(t) + \tau R_i(t) > \tilde{R}_i(t-1)d_i^s\right\}$.

For user set $U'(t) = \{i \,|\, i \in U, a_i(t) \le b_i(t)\}$, if $a_i(t) \le b_i(t)$, the optimal transmit power and bandwidth are $p_i^*(t) = 0$ and $\alpha_i^*(t) = 0$. Only if the quantity of local task buffer is larger than that on server side would the mobile device execute offloading. For $U^c(t) = U \backslash U'(t)$, apart from user $i \in U'(t)$, we consider solving transmit power and bandwidth allocation through alternating optimization. In each iteration, all numerical results are obtained in closed forms by Lagrangian Method. The alternating minimization process ensures the global optimal solution, which is literally termed as the Gaussian-Seidel Method.

– Transmit Power Allocation:

$$\min_{0 \leq p_i(t) \leq p_i^{\max}, i \in U^c(t)} V p_i(t) + (b_i(t) - a_i(t)) \tau R_i(t). \tag{15}$$

On condition that the transmission bandwidth is fixed, we can get $p_i^*(t) = \min \left\{ \alpha_i(t) W \max \left\{ \frac{\tau(a_i(t) - b_i(t))}{V \ln 2} - \frac{N_0}{H_i(t)}, 0 \right\}, p_i^{\max} \right\}$.

– Transmission Bandwidth Allocation:

$$\begin{aligned} \min_{0 \leq \alpha_i(t) \leq 1} & \sum_{i \in U} (b_i(t) - a_i(t)) \tau R_i(t) \\ & \sum_{i \in U} \alpha_i(t) \leq 1, i \in U^c(t) \\ & \alpha_i(t) > 0, i \in U^c(t) \end{aligned} \tag{16}$$

For a fixed transmit power, the Lagrangian method provides an efficient way to obtain optimal results: $\mathcal{L}(\alpha(t), \lambda(t)) = \sum_{i \in U^c(t)} (b_i(t) - a_i(t)) \tau \alpha_i(t) W \cdot$

$\log_2 \left(1 + \frac{p_i(t) H_i(t)}{N_0 \alpha_i(t) W} \right) + \lambda(t) \left(\sum_{i \in U^c(t)} \alpha_i(t) - 1 \right)$, $\lambda(t)$ is the Lagrange multiplier, $\alpha^*(t)$ and $\lambda^*(t)$ are the optimal results of this problem.

Applying the Karush-Kuhn-Tucker (KKT) conditions to our problem,

$$\begin{aligned} \frac{\partial \mathcal{L}(\alpha(t), \lambda(t))}{\partial \alpha_i(t)} \Big|_{\alpha_i(t) = \alpha_i^*(t)} \\ = \tau(b_i(t) - a_i(t)) \frac{dR_i(t)}{d\alpha_i(t)} + \lambda(t) = 0 \\ \sum_{i \in U^c(t)} \alpha_i^*(t) - 1 \leq 0 \\ \lambda^*(t) \geq 0 \\ \lambda^*(t) \left(\sum_{i \in U^c(t)} \alpha_i^*(t) - 1 \right) = 0 \end{aligned} \tag{17}$$

When $\lambda^*(t) > 0$, $\sum_{i \in U^c(t)} \alpha_i^*(t) - 1 = 0$; if $\lambda^*(t) = 0$, $\sum_{i \in U^c(t)} \alpha_i^*(t) - 1 \leq 0$. Also, if transmit power $p_i(t) = 0$, $\alpha_i(t) \triangleq 0$. $\frac{dR_i(t)}{d\alpha_i(t)}$ is inversely proportional to $\alpha_i(t)$, and $\lim_{\alpha_i(t) \to +\infty} \frac{dR_i(t)}{d\alpha_i(t)} = 0$, $\lim_{\alpha_i(t) \to 0+} \frac{dR_i(t)}{d\alpha_i(t)} = +\infty$. Apply bisection search over $[\lambda_L(t), \lambda_U(t)]$ for the optimal $\lambda^*(t)$.

$$\begin{cases} \lambda_L(t) = \max_{i \in U} \tau(a_i(t) - b_i(t)) \frac{dR_i(t)}{d\alpha_i(t)} \Big|_{\alpha_i(t) = 1} \\ \lambda_U(t) = \max_{i \in U} \tau(a_i(t) - b_i(t)) \frac{dR_i(t)}{d\alpha_i(t)} \Big|_{\alpha_i(t) \to 0} \end{cases} \tag{18}$$

Obtain $\alpha_i^*(t) = \max\{\mathcal{A}_i(\lambda^*(t)), 0\}$, in which $\mathcal{A}_i(\lambda^*(t))$ is the solution of $\tau(b_i(t) - a_i(t)) \frac{dR_i(t)}{d\alpha_i(t)} + \lambda^*(t) = 0$. Detail of the solution is particulized in Algorithm 1.

4.4 Server Side CPU Computational Resource Allocation

At the server side, computational resource allocation is measured by CPU cycle frequency which is solved as follows:

$$\max_{f_i^s(t)} \sum_{i \in U} b_i(t) \tau f_i^s(t)/L_i$$
$$\sum_{i \in U} \mathbb{1} \cdot \{f_i^s(t) > 0\} \leq N \tag{19}$$
$$f_i^s(t) \in \{0 f_s^{\max}\}, \forall i \in U.$$

Solution to (19) is elaborated in Algorithm 2.

Algorithm 2. Server side computational resource allocation

1: Initialize $k = 1$ and $U = U^c$.
2: **while** $k \leq N$ and $\widetilde{U} \neq \emptyset$ **do**
3:     $m^* = argmax_{i \in \widetilde{U}} \{b_i(t)/L_i\}$.
4:     $f_{i^*}(t) = f_j^{max}$.
5:     $k = k + 1$.
6:     $U^c = U^c \backslash U'$.
7: **end while**

---

5 Numerical Results

We consider an MEC system with 8 users and 1 server, the server is deployed with 8 CPU cores that can serve different users simultaneously. Maximum local computation capability is 10^9 cycle/s and maximum computation capability at server is 10^{10} cycle/s. Assuming the transmission frequency is 5.8 GHz with path loss $L = 60 + 20\log_{10}(5.8) + 24\log_{10} d(\text{dB})$. Users are evenly distributed near the base station. d is the distance between base station and users. We set the parameter $d_i^u = 4\tau\gamma(\text{bit})$, $\varepsilon_i^u = 0.01$, $\sigma_u^{th} = 4\tau\gamma(\text{bit})$, $\xi_u^{th} = 0.3$, $d_i^s = 20\,\text{s}$, $\varepsilon_i^s = 0.01$, $\sigma_s^{th} = 4\tau\widetilde{R}_i(\infty)(\text{bit})$, $\xi_s^{th} = 0.3$. Path loss increases with the transmission frequency, the coherence time is 40 ms. A single wireless channel experience Rayleigh fading with unit variance. Slot length $\tau = 40$ ms. Besides, $N_0 = -174\,\text{dBm/Hz}$, $W = 10\,\text{MHz}$, $\kappa = 10^{-27}\,\text{Watt s}^3/cycle^3$, $P_i^{max} = 20\,\text{dBm}$. We first show the convergence of optimal objective function in (14) in Fig. 2. As iteration time rises, the value of optimization objective function converge to the minimum, which proves the validation of the our optimal framework. V is the tradeoff factor (Lyapunov tradeoff parameter) that indicates the relationship between power consumption and latency in our work. Results in Fig. 3 show that, the power consumption at user side decreases as V increases, which means the optimization lays particular emphasis on task queue length with small V. On condition that $V = 0$, local power consumption is small because tasks are unnecessary to be offloaded to MEC server and there is no offloading power

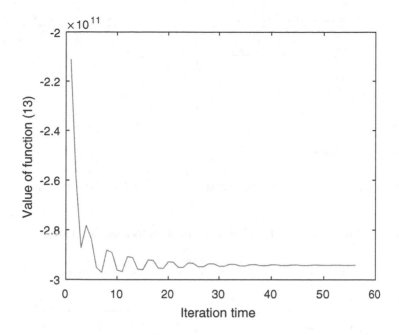

Fig. 2. Iteration convergence of objective function in constraint (14).

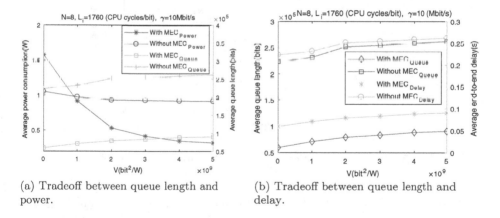

(a) Tradeoff between queue length and power.

(b) Tradeoff between queue length and delay.

Fig. 3. Tradeoff between a UE's average power consumption and task queue length.

consumption but the power consumption of local CPU computing. Main work of optimization at this moment reflects on the control of task queue length. To decrease the task queue length under the condition of having MEC server, users offload data to server with its local CPU still functioning, so the power consumption is high. With the increasement of V, optimization inclines to power consumption and the requirement of queue length abates, while the server could afford part of users' tasks, therefore transmission power is smaller comparing to

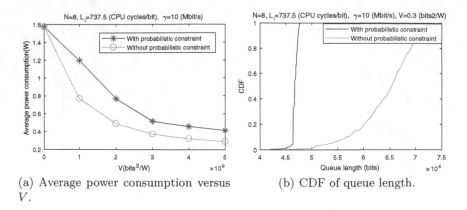

(a) Average power consumption versus V.

(b) CDF of queue length.

Fig. 4. Influence of probabilistic constraint on task queue length and V.

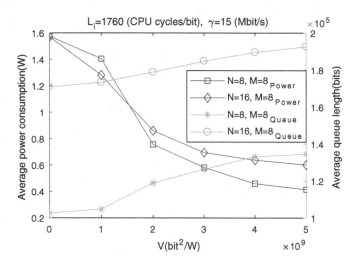

Fig. 5. Power consumption versus V with various numbers of UEs.

local process, and the benefit of using MEC server emerges. Task queue length of users and end-to-end delay are increasing as V increases. Local computing capability is limited and tasks come in continuously, therefore the local task queue length is always longer than that on server. Also, the optimizations on power consumption under both conditions emerge with increase of V and correspond sacrifice part of the queue length, which explains that queue length is getting longer as V increases. According to Little's Law, delay is proportional to queue length, and their variation trend converge gradually.

We consider the delay bound violation of task queue length in Fig. 4(a). Adding the probabilistic constraints of task queue length potentially constraint the delay of task queue and make performance of delay better. The CDF of task queue length in Fig. 4(b) demonstrates this theory. With these probabilistic constraints, the quantity of exceed task queue lengths suffer sharp decreases. And for reducing queuing delay, higher CPU cycle frequency and/or higher transmission power are/is required.

Furthermore, let's focus on quantity of users M and CPU core number of servers N in Fig. 5. For users who offload tasks on server, if $N < M$, computational resources can be allocated to each user and there is no extra delay; for $N > M$, with limited CPU cores, allocation of computational resource demand optimization which leads to additional waiting time.

6   Conclusion

In this work, we focus on MEC offloading structure under URLLC framework with multiple users and single server. Each UE could process local computation and offload tasks to servers and the tasks are piled up at both user and server side. The offloading rate is proportional to bandwidth with a coefficient, and the probability constraints claim restricts on task queue length. By applying Lyapunov optimization framework on our work, we transfer constraints into virtual queues and reform our constraints into three parts, different methods are applied to solve these optimization problems. We analyze the influence of the tradeoff factor and the probability constraints, discover that there is a tradeoff between delay and power consumption, and the performance of delay with an MEC server is better than no MEC situation. Quantity of UEs could increase delay if it is larger than server's CPU core number. Convergence of iteration and the CDF of task queue length shows the accuracy of optimization.

References

1. Andreev, S., et al.: Exploring synergy between communications, caching, and computing in 5G-grade deployments. IEEE Commun. Mag. **54**(8), 60–69 (2016)
2. Chiang, M., Ha, S., Chih-Lin, I., Risso, F., Zhang, T.: Clarifying fog computing and networking: 10 questions and answers. IEEE Commun. Mag. **55**(4), 18–20 (2017)
3. Mao, Y., You, C., Zhang, J., Huang, K., Letaief, K.B.: A survey on mobile edge computing: the communication perspective. IEEE Commun. Surv. Tutor. **19**(4), 2322–2358 (2017)
4. Elbamby, M.S., Bennis, M., Saad, W.: Proactive edge computing in latency-constrained fog networks. In: 2017 European Conference on Networks and Communications (EuCNC), Oulu, pp. 1–6 (2017)
5. Sardellitti, S., Barbarossa, S., Scutari, G.: Distributed mobile cloud computing: joint optimization of radio and computational resources. In: IEEE Globecom Workshops (GC Wkshps), Austin, TX, pp. 1505–1510 (2014)
6. Kwak, J., Kim, Y., Lee, J., Chong, S.: DREAM: dynamic resource and task allocation for energy minimization in mobile cloud systems. IEEE J. Sel. Areas Commun. **33**(12), 2510–2523 (2015)
7. You, C., Huang, K.: Multiuser resource allocation for mobile-edge computation offloading. In: IEEE Global Communications Conference (GLOBECOM), Washington, DC, pp. 1–6 (2016)

8. Barbarossa, S., Sardellitti, S., Di Lorenzo, P.: Joint allocation of computation and communication resources in multiuser mobile cloud computing. In: IEEE 14th Workshop on Signal Processing Advances in Wireless Communications (SPAWC), Darmstadt, pp. 26–30 (2013)
9. Le, H.Q., Al-Shatri, H., Klein, A.: Efficient resource allocation in mobile-edge computation offloading: completion time minimization. In: IEEE International Symposium on Information Theory (ISIT), Aachen, pp. 2513–2517 (2017)
10. Mao, Y., Zhang, J., Song, S.H., Letaief, K.B.: Power-delay tradeoff in multi-user mobile-edge computing systems. In: IEEE Global Communications Conference (GLOBECOM), Washington, DC, pp. 1–6 (2016)
11. Liu, C., Bennis, M., Poor, H.V.: Latency and reliability-aware task offloading and resource allocation for mobile edge computing. In: IEEE Globecom Workshops (GC Wkshps), Singapore, pp. 1–7 (2017)
12. Neely, M.J.: Stochastic Network Optimization with Application to Communication and Queueing Systems. Morgan and Claypool Publishers, San Rafael (2010)
13. Coles, S.: An Introduction to Statistical Modeling of Extreme Values. Springer, London (2001). https://doi.org/10.1007/978-1-4471-3675-0

A Bayesian Method for Link Prediction with Considering Path Information

Suyuan Zhang[1], Lunbo Li[1(✉)], Cunlai Pu[1], and Siyuan Zhou[2]

[1] School of Computer Science and Engineering,
Nanjing University of Science and Technology, Nanjing 210096, China
`lunboli@163.com`, `pucunlai@njust.edu.cn`
[2] College of Computer and Information, Hohai University, Nanjing 210098, China

Abstract. Predicting links among nodes in the network is an interesting and practical problem. Many link prediction methods based on local or global topology alone have been proposed. There is a need to combine these two types of methods to further improve the prediction performance. In line with this direction, we study the link prediction problem based on the Bayesian method and propose a new link prediction method, i.e., path-based Bayesian (PB) method. In this prediction method, we give the definition of clustering coefficients of paths and use it to quantify the contribution of paths to link generation. Then, we propose a new link prediction method by combining the clustering coefficient of paths and Bayesian theory. Simulation results on real-world networks show that our prediction method has higher prediction accuracy than the mainstream methods.

Keywords: Link prediction · Path information · Bayesian method · Structural similarity

1 Introduction

There are countless networks in real world, such as social networks, communication networks, and transportation networks [1]. However, the part of these networks that we can directly observe is usually incomplete. If we use scientific methods to detect the complete network structure, it will consume a lot of resources. Under this circumstance, link prediction is getting more and more attention, since its aim is to predict missing links based on incomplete information with low cost [2]. For example, in protein networks, link prediction method proposed in Ref. [3] is able to suppress the indirect interactions in proteins and further reveal unknown direct relations in the network. In social networks, link prediction methods help to explore the relations among individuals. Friend recommendation system is built on this basis. In recent year, a lot of link prediction methods have been proposed [4], but the prediction performance of these methods still have a large room to improve. So we did some research in this paper to get higher prediction accuracy.

© ICST Institute for Computer Sciences, Social Informatics and Telecommunications Engineering 2019
Published by Springer Nature Switzerland AG 2019. All Rights Reserved
X. B. Zhai et al. (Eds.): MLICOM 2019, LNICST 294, pp. 361–374, 2019.
https://doi.org/10.1007/978-3-030-32388-2_31

The common assumption of link prediction is that if two nodes are similar, they have some tendency to be connected. Existing link prediction studies fall into two categories. One of them considers structural similarity and further design prediction methods. Structural similarity is determined by the network topology. The other applies machine learning methods to link prediction problems. Machine learning methods quantify the similarity of nodes based on their attributes, such as job, gender, hobby, etc.

The structural similarity based methods use information of local, global, or semi-local topology to make predictions. Link prediction methods based on common neighbors, such as common neighbor (CN) index [5], Adamin-Adar (AA) index [6], and Resource Allocation (RA) index [7], rate node pairs with common neighbors shared by them. It is consistent with the fact that the more common friends people have, the more likely they are to be introduced as friends. Different similarity standards describe different interaction modes of nodes in the network. Link prediction methods based on paths, e.g., the Katz index [8], are convinced that paths promote link generation in networks and weights of paths of different lengths are different. Link prediction method based on random walk can help us analyze the flow of information when the network structure is too complicated. In order to predict the evolutionary trend of the overall structure of the network, a structural perturbation method [9] is proposed for link prediction. This method applies the perturbation method which is used to determine the structural consistency to predict missing links.

Machine learning based link prediction methods have wide coverage, including Bayesian method [10], Markov chain [11], deep learning [12], etc. These methods mainly determine whether links are going to be generated or not based on node attribute information. For the first time, Liu et al. [13] applied a naive Bayesian model to link prediction problem. This algorithm takes the posterior probability of the link generation as the score of the link. If more network information is added, such as the degree of common neighbors, the accuracy of the algorithm can be further improved. Deep learning method is capable of understanding complicated networks. Wang et al. [14] proposed a hierarchical Bayesian deep learning method, which comprehensively considers high-dimensional attribute information and link structure with hidden variables. This algorithm makes full use of information and improves prediction accuracy. Although machine learning based link prediction method obtains good prediction results and is able to handle the cold start problem, its learning process is sometimes too complicated to complete in a certain period of time. Besides, some real information is difficult to obtain in practice.

As mentioned before, one of the mainstream research directions for link prediction is to make full use of network topological information. However, existing topology-based link prediction algorithms still have room for further research. In the existing prediction methods, paths of the same length are generally considered to be equivalent, but even paths of the same length have different structure. So their contribution to the formation of links should be different. On the other hand, the relative importance of paths of different lengths should be determined by the actual network topology, but there is currently no acknowledged standard to determine the relative importance of paths of different lengths in link prediction. Existing methods use only local topology information or global topology information for link prediction. Few methods consider multiple types of information at the same time. The actual score of a node pair is not determined by a certain factor alone. It is affected by the local topology, the global topology, and the evolution trend of the network at the same time.

In order to solve these problems and obtain more accurate prediction results, this paper proposes a path-based Bayesian method for link prediction based on network topology. Specifically, in order to determine the contribution of a single path, a statistical method is used to generalize the clustering coefficient of nodes to the clustering coefficient of paths, and then use it to quantify the contribution of paths to link generation. On this basis, we use Bayesian theory to further revise the contribution of paths which makes the score of paths more reasonable. The sum of paths scores between nodes is proportional to the possibility of link generation. Experiments are carried out in the real network to test the performance of the algorithm. The main contributions of this paper are as follows:

- First, inspired by the clustering coefficient of nodes, this paper proposes the clustering coefficient of paths to quantify the ability of paths to facilitate links in networks. Through the statistics of local topological information around a path, we can get the clustering coefficient of paths. Only after that can we calculate the prior contribution of paths.
- Second, Bayesian method converts prior contribution into posteriori contribution. In the process of transformation, global topological information is introduced which makes the posteriori contribution more reasonable. By using Bayesian method in different dimensions, we can get the relative weights of different length paths in the network. Based on this idea, this paper proposes a path-based Bayesian method for link prediction.
- Third, we tested the proposed algorithm in several real networks with AUC and Precision indexes. Results of the experiments show that the proposed method performs better than traditional algorithms. Afterwards, the results of experiments and the causes are discussed in detail. The results of the experiments prove the availability of our algorithm.

The rest of this paper is organized as follows. In Sect. 2, we define the clustering coefficient of paths according to the actual topological structure of networks, so that it can be used to define the prior contribution of paths. In Sect. 3, we describe Bayesian theory and discuss its applicability in link prediction problems. In particular, we analyze why Bayesian theory can use global topological information to estimate the weights of paths of different lengths. Combining known information of current networks, we propose a path-based Bayesian method for link prediction and show the process of realizing this method in Sect. 4. Section 5 introduces the indexes which are going to be tested in the following experiments. Then, we show the results of link prediction methods in several real world networks. These results and their causes are discussed in Sect. 6. In the end, conclusion is made in Sect. 7.

2   Clustering Coefficient of Paths

Among the existing link prediction research, methods based on local information use little information and have limited prediction accuracy. On the other hand, methods based on global information are computationally complex. Methods based on paths guarantee prediction accuracy to a certain extent and are easy to calculate. Therefore, in a homogeneous network, it is reasonable to use a link prediction method based on paths.

In the design of link prediction algorithms, it is necessary to quantify the contribution of the paths to link generation. We use this contribution as a score for node pairs to predict links in the network. In order to get higher prediction accuracy, the score of each path needs to reflect its ability to facilitate links in the network. Inspired by the definition of the clustering coefficient of nodes [15], we define the clustering coefficient of paths (CCP) and use it to quantify the contribution of a single path. The clustering coefficient of the path is defined as the probability that the core of paths contributes to the link. As shown in the Fig. 1, in order to calculate the clustering coefficient of the path, we define the embedded path ω_{pq} of the path ω_{xy} as the core of the path ω_{xy}. In the case where the path length is 2, the node p coincides with the node q.

Fig. 1. Embedded path ω_{pq} is the core of path ω_{xy}.

In the case where a path of length k is known to exist, statistical methods are applied to calculate its contribution to facilitate a link between its source node and its destination node. At first, we assume that the number of links that were successfully contributed by the path, which is represented as N_L, and the number of links that were not successfully contributed, which is represented as N_U, are all 1. As shown in the Fig. 2, starting from the core of paths, the neighbor combinations of the core (x_i, y_j) is going to be detected. For each combination, if it is connected, the number of links which are successfully contributed by this path is increased by 1 and vice versa. The clustering coefficient of paths is the probability that the core of paths contributes to the link, which can be represented as

$$CCP = \frac{N_L}{N_L + N_U}. \tag{1}$$

Since one core serves multiple paths at the same time, the clustering coefficient of the path need to be further modified based on the path structure to quantify the contribution of a single path to the link generation. Inspired by the RA index, we use the degree of the nodes at both ends of the core to modify the clustering coefficient of the path. The greater the degree the nodes at both ends of the core have, the smaller contribution the path own. After modification, the prior contribution of a single path $P(A_1|\omega_k)$ is

$$P(A_1|\omega_k) = \frac{2}{k(p) + k(q)} * CCP, \tag{2}$$

where A_1 indicates that the link exists. ω_k represents a path of length k. $P(A_1|\omega_k)$ describes the possibility that a path of length k facilitate a link. $k(p)$ and $k(q)$ are degrees of node p and node q.

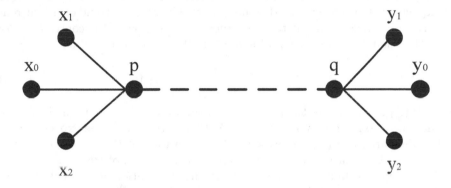

Fig. 2. (x_i, y_j) represents the neighbor combinations of the core of path.

3   Bayesian Method

After calculating the contribution of a single path, it is also necessary to use the network information to determine the relative weights of the paths of different lengths. The traditional link prediction method considers that the longer the path, the smaller the contribution it has. However, length of the path is not the only determinant. If path of a certain length appears more in the network, it means this kind of path plays important role in the network communication. As a result, its weight should be greater. To distinguish the importance of paths of different lengths, we use the Bayesian method. This method modifies the prior contribution $P(A_1|\omega_k)$ of paths with global topology information to obtain conditional probability $P(\omega_k|A_1)$, which is

$$P(\omega_k|A_1) = \frac{P(\omega_k)}{P(A_1)} * P(A_1|\omega_k), \tag{3}$$

where $P(A_1)$ indicates the existing probability of the link between target node pair (a,b). Since the node pairs which we want to predict are not connected, it is impossible to calculate the existing probability of link directly. We ignore the differences between links and take the probability of links appearing in the network as $P(A_1)$, i.e., $P(A_1) = N(A_1)/N_{max}(A_1)$. $N(A_1)$ represents the number of links which exist in the network. $N_{max}(A_1)$ represents the maximum number of links that may appear in the network. $P(\omega_k)$ represents the probability of a path of length k existing between two nodes. Similarly, it is processed in the same way as $P(A_1)$, i.e., $P(\omega_k) = N(\omega_k)/N_{max}(\omega_k)$. $N(\omega_k)$ represents the number of paths of length k which exist in the network. $N_{max}(\omega_k)$ represents the maximum number of paths of length k that may appear in the network. This method of processing data can effectively reduce the computational complexity.

At the same time, since the network rarely mutates, the existing probability of the path of length k in the network will fluctuate around its expected value $E(P(\omega_k))$ for a period of time. The more active the path of length k, the higher the expected value. The expected value reflects the evolution trend of the current network, so we need to use it to make another correction to the contribution of the path. The true contribution of a single path will be corrected as

$$P'(A_1|\omega_k) = \frac{E(P(A_1))}{E(P(\omega_k))} * P(\omega_k|A_1), \qquad (4)$$

where $P'(A_1|\omega_k)$ indicates the posterior contribution of a known path of length k to link generation between a node pair. $E(P(A_1))$ represents the expectation of $P(A_1)$. Similarly, $E(P(\omega_k))$ represents the expectation of $P(\omega_k)$. In the absence of additional information, we believe that the expectation of $P(\omega_k)$ is a ratio of the maximum possibility. At the same time, the expectation of paths of different lengths are assumed to be the same, i.e., $E(P(\omega_k)) = \lambda$. This parameter can be further calculated when more information is available for reference.

4   Our Method

In a network $G(V, E)$, V represents nodes in the network, and E represents relationships between nodes. The number of nodes in the network is represented by $|V| = N$, and the number of edges is $|E| = M$. If we only have a single-layer network, the expected number of paths of length 1 is the same as the number of links which actually exist, that is $E(P(A_1)) = P(A_1)$. In a single-layer network, we suppose that $E(P(\omega_k))$ is a fixed ratio of the maximum value of $P(\omega_k)$ at any k value. In this case, the posterior contribution of the path can be simplified as

$$P'(A_1|\omega_k) = \frac{P(\omega_k)}{*} P(A_1|\omega_k), \qquad (5)$$

where $P(\omega_k)$ indicates the existing possibility of paths of length k. The more active the path of this length is, the more important it is in the network. As a result, its weight should be greater. Paths of lengths 2 and 3 in the network are highly efficient in transmitting information due to their short length. These paths dominate the path algorithm, so we only need to calculate $P(\omega_2)$, and $P(\omega_3)$. We can know from previous discussion: $P(\omega_2) = N(\omega_2)/N_{max}(\omega_2)$, and $P(\omega_3) = N(\omega_3)/N_{max}(\omega_3)$. $N_{max}(\omega_2)$ represents the maximum number of paths of length 2 that may appear in the network, which is

$$N_{max}(\omega_2) = \begin{cases} M(M-1) & M \leq N \\ n_2 L_{2max} + 2m_2 n_2 + \dfrac{m_2(m_2-1)}{2} & M > N, \end{cases} \tag{6}$$

where L_{2max} means the max number of paths of length 2 that can be created by one node, so $L_{2max} = (N-1)(N-2)$. n_2 is the maximum number of the nodes in the network that connect to all other nodes. m_2 represents the number of edges remaining after n_2 nodes connect to all other nodes, $m_2 = M - n_2(N-1) + n_2(n_2-1)/2$. $N_{max}(\omega_3)$ represents the maximum number of paths of length 3 in the network, which is

$$N_{max}(\omega_3) = \frac{n_3(n_3-1)(n_3-2)(n_3-2)}{2}$$
$$- \frac{n_3(n_3-1)(n_3-2)}{3} \tag{7}$$
$$+ m_3(n_3-1)(n_3-2) + \frac{m_3(m_3-1)(2n_3-3)}{2},$$

where n_3 is the number of nodes that achieve full connectivity. m_3 represents the number of edges remaining after n_3 nodes achieve full connectivity, $m_3 = M - n_3(n_3-1)/2$.

After knowing the true contributions of all the paths that connect node pairs, the tendency to generate a link is represented by the sum of them. This is called as the path-based Bayesian (PB) method, which is given as

$$s_{xy}^{PB} = \sum_{k-1}^{L} \sum_{\omega_k \in O_{xy}} P'(A_1|\omega_k), \tag{8}$$

where s_{xy}^{PB} is the score of PB method. O_{xy} represents the set of all paths between node pair (x,y).

The way to calculate PB method is

I. We first divide the network adjacency matrix A into a training set A^T and a probe set A^R.

II. To calculate the contribution of a path of length k, we need to locate the core of this path, which is included in $(A^T)^{k-2}$.

III. When $k = 2$, the core of paths constitutes unit matrix I. Depending on the core of paths, we can calculate the prior contribution of each path of length 2, which is $C_2(i, i)$. When $k \geq 3$, for any node pairs $ij(i < j)$ in the upper triangular matrix, if there are cores between them, i.e., $(A^T)^{k-2} > 0$, we calculate its prior contribution, which is $C_k(i, j)$. Since the network is undirected, only the upper triangular matrix need to be calculated, i.e., $C_k(j, i) = C_k(i, j)$.

IV. At the beginning, $N_L(i, j) = 1$, $N_U(i, j) = 1$. In order to calculate $C_k(i, j)$, the first step is to go through all the combination of node i's neighbors $N(i)$ and node j's neighbors $N(j)$ to get the prior contribution $C_k(i, j)$. When $A^T(N(i), N(j)) > 0$, we add one to $N_L(i, j)$. We add one to $N_U(i, j)$ in other cases. The prior contribution is calculated according to Eq. 2.

V. After getting prior contribution of each path, $P(\omega_k)$, and $E(P(\omega_k))$, the posterior contribution of a path of length k can be obtained by the Eq. 5.

VI. We modify the value of length k and repeat step II to step V until the posterior contribution of all the paths that needs to be obtained is calculated.

VII. We need to traverse all the the node pairs ij without links in the network and calculate the posterior probability of the link generation between them. Since the network is undirected, only the upper triangular matrix needs to be calculated. The score of node pairs is the sum of the posterior contribution of all the paths between node pairs, which can be calculated according to the Eq. 8.

5   Evaluation Method

Like most studies, this paper uses AUC and Precision to evaluate prediction results of link prediction methods [16]. When calculating AUC [17], we repeatedly compare the score of a random edge that should be predicted with that of a random edge that should not be predicted. If the score of the edge that should be predicted is higher, we add 1 node. When the scores of both edges are equal, 0.5 nodes will be added. We repeat this experiment independently n times. If there are n' times that edge should be predicted has a higher score, and n'' times that both edges have same score, AUC can be calculated as

$$AUC = \frac{n' + 0.5 * n''}{n}. \tag{9}$$

If there are t edges in both the probe set and top T ranked edges, Precision [18] can be represented as

$$AUC = \frac{t}{T}. \tag{10}$$

Both of these indexes estimate the accuracy of the link prediction algorithm by predicting the probe set, but they have different perspectives on the prediction algorithm. AUC measures the performance of the algorithm as a whole, while Precision only considers the prediction accuracy of T top-ranked edges. In a network, if one of the two indexes has the same score, then the link prediction method that the other index performs better is more suitable for this network.

In order to compare the prediction effects of the algorithm, this paper introduces four traditional indexes and an index similar to the proposed algorithm, and then compares their prediction effects with the proposed algorithm. Besides, all of these indexes are based on the topology of the network.

The Common Neighbor (CN) index is one of the most important link prediction algorithms. This algorithm believes that more common neighbors are more likely to facilitate links between node pairs, that is

$$s_{xy}^{CN} = |R(x) \cap R(y)|, \tag{11}$$

where $R(x)$ represents the set of neighbors of node x. $|R(x) \cap R(y)|$ represents the number of common neighbors of the node pairs xy.

The contribution of the common neighbors to Adamin-Adar (AA) index is related to the degree of the common neighbors. It is proportional to the reciprocal of the log of the common neighbor degree, which is

$$s_{xy}^{AA} = \sum_{z \in R(x) \cap R(y)} \frac{1}{log k_z}, \tag{12}$$

where $z \in R(x) \cap R(y)$ means node z in the set of common neighbors of the node pairs xy. k_z refers to the degree of node z.

The difference between the Resource Allocation (RA) index and the AA indicator is that the RA index considers that the resources passing through the nodes are equally allocated, so the contribution of the common neighbors is inversely proportional to the degree of the common neighbors, which is

$$s_{xy}^{RA} = \sum_{z \in R(x) \cap R(y)} \frac{1}{k_z}, \tag{13}$$

The Katz index counts paths of the same length between pairs of nodes. Meanwhile, it assigns different weights to reflect the difference in the contribution of paths of different length to the formation of links between node pairs, which is

$$s_{xy}^{Katz} = \sum_{l=1}^{\infty} \alpha^l |path_{xy}^l|, \tag{14}$$

where α is a hyperparameter. l indicates the length of paths. It affects the weights of paths of different lengths as well. Generally speaking, it is meaningless to calculate a path that is too long, because the information in the network is often time-sensitive and almost no information will be transmitted through a long path. Therefore, the path with a length of 3 or 4 is generally counted at most.

Local Naive Bayes (LNB) index applies a machine learning model to link prediction problem based on local information. According to the Naive Bayesian model, the algorithm considers that the contribution of the common neighbors to the link generation between node pairs is the product of the posterior probabilities generated by the common neighbors, which is

$$P(A_1|R(x) \cap R(y)) = \frac{P(A_1)}{P(R(x) \cap R(y))} \prod_{z \in R(x) \cap R(y)} P(z|A_1), \tag{15}$$

$$P(A_0|R(x) \cap R(y)) = \frac{P(A_0)}{P(R(x) \cap R(y))} \prod_{z \in R(x) \cap R(y)} P(z|A_0), \qquad (16)$$

where $R(x) \cap R(y)$ represents all the common neighbors between node pairs xy, and z is one of the common neighbors. After normalization, we can get the final score s_{xy}^{LNB}, which is

$$s_{xy}^{LNB} = |R(x) \cap R(y)| log \frac{P(A_0)}{P(A_1)} + \sum_{z \in R(x) \cap R(y)} log \frac{P(A_1|z)}{P(A_0|z)}. \qquad (17)$$

If we further optimize this link prediction index by combining local information indexes, we can obtain LNB-CN, LNB-AA, and LNB-RA indexes. The formulas are as follows:

$$s_{xy}^{LNB-CN} = |R(x) \cap R(y)| log \frac{P(A_0)}{P(A_1)} + \sum_{z \in R(x) \cap R(y)} log \frac{P(A_1|z)}{P(A_0|z)}, \qquad (18)$$

$$s_{xy}^{LNB-AA} = \sum_{z \in R(x) \cap R(y)} \frac{1}{log k_z} (log \frac{P(A_0)}{P(A_1)} + log \frac{P(A_1|z)}{P(A_0|z)}), \qquad (19)$$

$$s_{xy}^{LNB-RA} = \sum_{z \in R(x) \cap R(y)} \frac{1}{k_z} (log \frac{P(A_0)}{P(A_1)} + log \frac{P(A_1|z)}{P(A_0|z)}). \qquad (20)$$

6   Experiments and Discussion

In order to test the prediction effect of the link prediction method in this paper, the prediction accuracy is tested in the food network (Florida [19], Everglades [20], StMarks [21]), the biological network (C. elegans [22]), the social network (email-Eu-core temporal network [23], Political blogs [24]), the protein-protein interaction network (Yeast [25]) and the power network (Power [26]). To simplify the problem, the experiment was conducted in the undirected and unweighted network. In the network, the weights of edges are ignored, and all

Table 1. Performance of different link prediction methods under Precision index.

Network	CN	AA	RA	Katz	LNB-CN	LNB-AA	LNB-RA	PB
Florida	0.070	0.075	0.072	0.288	0.088	0.089	0.088	**0.309**
C.elegans	0.100	0.102	0.103	0.123	0.107	0.108	0.101	**0.135**
Everglades	0.153	0.163	0.173	0.374	0.169	0.185	0.192	**0.400**
StMarks	0.131	0.148	0.157	0.224	0.177	0.174	0.171	**0.257**
email-Eu-core-temporal	0.198	0.225	0.259	0.168	0.218	0.248	**0.272**	0.221
Political blogs	0.166	0.176	0.146	0.183	0.168	0.165	0.161	**0.188**
Yeast	0.149	0.179	0.254	0.250	0.151	0.189	0.280	**0.341**
Power	0.045	0.024	0.021	**0.045**	0.042	0.025	0.028	0.040

edges are considered to be bidirectional. In addition, the existence of a self-loop is not allowed in the network. The experimental results are shown in the following table.

Table 1 shows the prediction results of different link prediction methods under the Precision index. The method we studied is the PB method in the rightmost column of the table. The bold font represents the link prediction method with the highest prediction accuracy in the network. From Table 1, we can see that PB method has a good prediction effect under Precision index. Only in the Email and Power networks, the prediction effect of PB method is not the best. The reason is that single layer network can not provide enough effective information in extreme cases. For example, in Power network, since the network is too sparse, the existing probability of different length paths is very low. PB method judges the relative weights of different length paths according to the probability of path occurrence. The relative weights of different length paths are misjudged, which results in the wrong estimation of the score between nodes and the decrease of the prediction accuracy of the PB method. On the other hand, the excellent performance of PB method in other networks shows that PB method can more accurately describe the relationship between node pairs on the premise that the network can provide enough information, making the node pairs that tend to generate connections rank ahead.

Table 2. Performance of different link prediction methods under AUC index.

Network	CN	AA	RA	Katz	LNB-CN	LNB-AA	LNB-RA	PB
Florida	0.610	0.612	0.614	0.811	0.692	0.696	0.697	**0.849**
C.elegans	0.846	0.861	0.862	0.845	0.856	0.862	0.862	**0.890**
Everglades	0.693	0.698	0.712	0.838	0.731	0.735	0.734	**0.877**
StMarks	0.658	0.670	0.679	0.717	0.721	0.723	0.715	**0.781**
email-Eu-core-temporal	0.943	0.946	0.949	0.925	0.945	0.948	**0.950**	0.947
Political blogs	0.919	0.919	0.920	0.930	0.919	0.920	0.922	**0.941**
Yeast	0.895	0.894	0.892	0.930	0.888	0.892	0.898	**0.939**
Power	0.586	0.586	0.584	**0.628**	0.587	0.592	0.585	0.604

Table 2 shows the prediction effect of different link prediction methods under AUC index. AUC calculates the mean value of prediction effect under different thresholds, which reflects the overall prediction effect of link prediction method. As we can see from Table 2, PB method has the highest prediction accuracy in Florida network, C. elegans network, Everglades network, StMarks network, Blogs network and Yeast network. This phenomenon shows that PB method can calculate the score of node pairs more reasonably, and ensure that the node pairs that should be predicted score higher than those that should not be predicted.

Tables 1 and 2 show that PB method in this paper has high prediction accuracy under Precision and AUC indices in single layer networks. The reason is that this method not only quantifies the contribution of the path by using the clustering coefficient of the path, but also modifies the contribution of the path by using the global topological information. Our method integrates local topo-logical information, global topological information and network evolution trend to predict links in the network which makes full use of topological information. The prediction effect is obviously better than that of traditional and similar indicators. In addition, for the reason that this algorithm does not need to deter-mine the hyperparameter through repeated experiments, it effectively reduces the redundant experimental process.

Compared with the LNB index, the PB method is more reasonable. Although both of them believe that the probability of link generation between nodes is related to the paths between nodes, the LNB index treats the paths which con-nect node pairs as a kind of restriction. This idea holds true in image problems, because the correlation between pixels is very strong, but it is not always the case in the network. In LNB index, contributions of paths are multiplied as the contribution to the formation of links. On the contrary, PB method is convinced that the sum of the contribution of each path between node pairs represents the possibility to generate a link, which is more in line with common sense. Moreover, the final score generated by LNB index is related to the number of links existing in the network, that is, the more links there are in the network, the easier it is to generate links. However, in real life, when the network tends to be saturated, its desire to generate links should be extremely low. Our PB algorithm assigns weights of paths according to the actual network topology. The weights of paths of different lengths is proportional to its importance in the network, so the weight of each path is arranged more reasonably in the proposed algorithm.

7   Conclusion

In summary, this paper proposes a path-based Bayesian method for link predic-tion. In this method, we define clustering coefficient of paths which quantifies the priori contribution of paths to link generation. Then, we use Bayesian method to transform the priori contribution to the posterior contribution which reflects the true contribution of the path. The path-based Bayesian algorithm performs well compared to existing link prediction methods. Compared with the link prediction methods based on local information, it applies more network information and achieves better prediction accuracy. Besides, it reduces redundant calculations which is used by traditional path-based link prediction algorithm to determine relative weights of paths of different lengths. Furthermore, this method only makes simple use of global topological information which gives it better robust-ness. Last but not least, our method only uses topological information, so the information source is more reliable.

Although this method has many advantages, it still has room for further study. The use of extra information which can reflect the evolution trend of the network can make the weights of paths of different length more accurate. In the future, we are looking forward to improve this approach in more informative networks, such as multilayer networks.

Acknowledgements. This work was supported in part by National Natural Science Foundation of China (No. 61872187, No. 61871444, No. 61773215) and Major Special Project of Core Electronic Devices, High-end Generic Chips and Basic Software (No. 2015ZX01041101).

References

1. Chen, S., Huang, W., Cattani, C., Altieri, G.: Traffic dynamics on complex networks: a survey. Math. Probl. Eng. **2012** (2012)
2. Taskar, B., Wong, M.-F., Abbeel, P., Koller, D.: Link prediction in relational data. In: Advances in Neural Information Processing Systems, pp. 659–666 (2004)
3. Barzel, B., Barabási, A.-L.: Network link prediction by global silencing of indirect correlations. Nat. Biotechnol. **31**(8), 720 (2013)
4. Lü, L., Zhou, T.: Link prediction in complex networks: a survey. Phys. A **390**(6), 1150–1170 (2011)
5. Lorrain, F., White, H.C.: Structural equivalence of individuals in social networks. J. Math. Sociol. **1**(1), 49–80 (1971)
6. Adamic, L.A., Adar, E.: Friends and neighbors on the web. Soc. Netw. **25**(3), 211–230 (2003)
7. Zhou, T., Lü, L., Zhang, Y.-C.: Predicting missing links via local information. Eur. Phys. J. B **71**(4), 623–630 (2009)
8. Katz, L.: A new status index derived from sociometric analysis. Psychometrika **18**(1), 39–43 (1953)
9. Lü, L., Pan, L., Zhou, T., Zhang, Y.-C., Stanley, H.E.: Toward link predictability of complex networks. Proc. Natl. Acad. Sci. **112**(8), 2325–2330 (2015)
10. Miller, K., Jordan, M.I., Griffiths, T.L.: Nonparametric latent feature models for link prediction. In: Advances in Neural Information Processing Systems, pp. 1276–1284 (2009)
11. Sarukkai, R.R.: Link prediction and path analysis using Markov chains. Comput. Netw. **33**(1–6), 377–386 (2000)
12. Al Hasan, M., Chaoji, V., Salem, S., Zaki, M.: Link prediction using supervised learning. In: SDM06: Workshop on Link Analysis, Counter-Terrorism and Security (2006)
13. Liu, Z., Zhang, Q.-M., Lü, L., Zhou, T.: Link prediction in complex networks: a local naïve Bayes model. EPL (Eur. Lett.) **96**(4), 48007 (2011)
14. Wang, H., Shi, X., Yeung, D.-Y.: Relational deep learning: a deep latent variable model for link prediction. In: Thirty-First AAAI Conference on Artificial Intelligence (2017)
15. Saramäki, J., Kivelä, M., Onnela, J.-P., Kaski, K., Kertesz, J.: Generalizations of the clustering coefficient to weighted complex networks. Phys. Rev. E **75**(2), 027105 (2007)
16. Yang, Y., Lichtenwalter, R.N., Chawla, N.V.: Evaluating link prediction methods. Knowl. Inf. Syst. **45**(3), 751–782 (2015)
17. Hanley, J.A., McNeil, B.J.: The meaning and use of the area under a receiver operating characteristic (ROC) curve. Radiology **143**(1), 29–36 (1982)
18. Herlocker, J.L., Konstan, J.A., Terveen, L.G., Riedl, J.T.: Evaluating collaborative filtering recommender systems. ACM Trans. Inf. Syst. (TOIS) **22**(1), 5–53 (2004)

19. Ulanowicz, R.E., Bondavalli, C., Egnotovich, M.S.: Network analysis of trophic dynamics in South Florida ecosystem, FY 97: the Florida Bay ecosystem. Annual Report to the United States Geological Service Biological Resources Division Ref. No. [UMCES] CBL, pp. 98–123 (1998)
20. Ulanowicz, R.E., Bondavalli, C., Heymans, J.J., Egnotovich, M.S.: Network analysis of trophic dynamics in South Florida ecosystem, FY 99: the graminoid ecosystem. Annual Report to the United States Geological Service Biological Resources Division Ref. No. [UMCES] CBL 00–0176, Chesapeake Biological Laboratory, University of Maryland (2000)
21. Baird, D., Luczkovich, J., Christian, R.R.: Assessment of spatial and temporal variability in ecosystem attributes of the St Marks national wildlife refuge, Apalachee Bay, Florida. Estuar. Coast. Shelf Sci. **47**(3), 329–349 (1998)
22. Stiernagle, T.: Maintenance of c. elegans. C. elegans **2**, 51–67 (1999)
23. Paranjape, A., Benson, A.R., Leskovec, J.: Proceedings of the Tenth ACM International Conference on Web Search and Data Mining, WSDM 2017 (2017)
24. Ackland, R., et al.: Mapping the us political blogosphere: are conservative bloggers more prominent? In: BlogTalk Downunder 2005 Conference, Sydney (2005)
25. Von Mering, C., et al.: Comparative assessment of large-scale data sets of protein-protein interactions. Nature **417**(6887), 399 (2002)
26. Watts, D.J., et al.: Nature (London) **393**, 440 (1998)

Identifying Sources of Random Walk-Based Epidemic Spreading in Networks

Bo Qin🆔 and Cunlai Pu$^{(\boxtimes)}$🆔

School of Computer Science and Engineering,
Nanjing University of Science and Technology, Nanjing 210094, China
pucunlai@njust.edu.cn

Abstract. Identifying the sources of epidemic spreading is of critical importance to epidemic control and network immunization. However, the task of source identification is very challenging, since in real situations the dynamics of the spreading process is usually not clear. In this paper, we formulate the multiple source epidemic spreading process as the multiple random walks, which is a theoretical model applicable to various spreading processes. Considering the different influence of distinct epidemic sources on the observed infection graph, we derive the maximum likelihood estimator of the multiple source identification problem. Simulation results on real-world networks and network models, such as the Price model and Erdös-Rényi (ER) model, demonstrate the efficiency of our estimator. Furthermore, we find that the efficiency of our estimator increases with the enhancement of network sparsity and heterogeneity.

Keywords: Source identification · Random walk · Maximum likelihood (ML) · Network heterogeneity

1 Introduction

Epidemic spreading is an universal process in nature and man-made systems, such as the spread of cyber viruses in communication networks, rumors in social networks and diseases in biological networks. Identifying the sources of these harmful spreading processes is of practical interest to researchers as well as system administrators for forensic purposes. In addition, early recognition of the epidemic sources helps to block the epidemic spreading promptly and eventually decrease the loss. Accurately identifying the sources of epidemic spreading is a very challenging task, since we usually have very limited information, such as the observed network structure and states of nodes. A more relaxed problem is to estimate the likelihood of nodes being the spreading sources based on the

Supported in part by National Natural Science Foundation of China (No. 61872187, No. 61871444, No. 61773215) and Major Special Project of Core Electronic Devices, Hign-end Generic Chips and Basic Software (No. 2015ZX01041101).

© ICST Institute for Computer Sciences, Social Informatics and Telecommunications Engineering 2019
Published by Springer Nature Switzerland AG 2019. All Rights Reserved
X. B. Zhai et al. (Eds.): MLICOM 2019, LNICST 294, pp. 375–386, 2019.
https://doi.org/10.1007/978-3-030-32388-2_32

maximum likelihood estimate (MLE) [1,2]. In recent years, many source identification methods for this problem have been proposed. A large portion of them is based on some sort of node centrality. For example, Shah et al. proposed the first algorithm of source identification according to the rumor centrality [3–5]. Later, Luo et al. extended the work of Shah to the case of multiple sources [6–8]. Zhu et al. presented a novel identification method based on the Jordan infection center [9,10]. By calculating the dynamical age of nodes in the infection graph, Fioriti et al. obtained that old nodes are more likely to be the infection sources than young nodes [11,12]. Moreover, Comin provided an identification algorithm based on the unbiased betweenness centrality [13], and then Zang extended this algorithm to the multiple source scenario [14].

In addition to the centrality-based methods, there are some other remarkable identification methods. For instance, Lokhov et al. gave the dynamic message-passing (DMP) algorithm to estimate the likelihood of every node [15]. Altarelli et al. proposed the belief propagation algorithm based on the factor graph to infer the origin of an epidemic [16]. Antulov-Fantulin et al. used the Monte-Carlo method to simulate the possible propagation process to conjecture the source [17]. Prakash et al. proposed the NetSleuth algorithm which transforms the source identification problem into an optimization problem that solves the minimum description length [18,19]. Most of these methods depend on some sort of approximation in the construction of maximum likelihood probability, and in most of the cases, they require either large computational complexity to find near-optimal solutions, or simplified heuristics to achieve suboptimal performance.

Random walk is a general process that can be used to describe many diffusion processes on networks. In particular, the spread of some viruses in reality can be modeled as random-walk diffusion, such as the spread of Bluetongue virus driven by the random movements of insect vectors and the cyber virus driven by the random transmission of information packets. Most recently, Abigail et al. proposed a single source identification algorithm by considering the random walk of virus [20]. Their calculation takes account all the possible spreading paths, while the previous work considers only the shortest paths or some high-probability paths. Their simulation results on the food supply network data demonstrated the efficiency of the algorithm.

Enlightened by Abigail's work, we investigate the case of multiple infection sources in networks. It is apparent that the source of an infected node can be anyone in the source set. Different source nodes have different possibilities to infected a node. Accordingly, in the calculation, we provide two ways to approximate this possibility. We further calculate the likelihood of a candidate set to be the source by considering all the possible infection paths from the set, and obtain our maximum likelihood estimator. The set of maximum likelihood is supposed to be the source.

To validate our estimator, we apply it to the complex network models, such as the ER and Price models, and some real-world networks. Source sets of two and three nodes are considered. The experimental results demonstrate the efficiency of our estimator. Furthermore, we observe that the efficiency of our estimator increases with the enhancement of network sparsity and heterogeneity.

2 Problem Formulation and Our Method

We consider the problem of identifying multiple infection sources. Previous work usually uses the susceptible-infected (SI) model to describe the virus spreading process. Differently, we consider the diffusion-based spread of virus. In particular, we assume that the spread of virus is based on multiple random walks (simultaneous random walks starting from multiple sources). In this section, we first present our diffusion model, and then derive the maximum likelihood estimator of our model.

2.1 Diffusion Model

Let $G(V, E)$ be a directed graph, where V and E represent the set of all nodes and the set of all edges, respectively. Assume that the set of terminal nodes, which have zero out-degree, is V_T, and the set of non-terminal nodes is V_N. We randomly select m (> 1) non-terminal nodes to be the infection sources, which form the source set $s^* = \{s_1, s_2, \ldots, s_m\}, \forall s_i \in V_N$. At the beginning, every infection source propagates one copy of the virus to one of its neighbor nodes. The movements of different virus copies are assumed to be independent and identical random walks. A node is infected if it has ever been visited by the virus; otherwise, it is healthy, while susceptible to the virus. We do not consider the recovery of infected nodes. At each time step, every infected node spreads one copy of virus to one of its neighbor nodes. After a period of time, we observe that the set of infected terminal nodes is $\Theta = \{o_1, o_2, \ldots, o_K\}, \forall o_k \in V_T$. Our aim is to estimate the source set s^* based on the set of infected terminal nodes Θ.

Since the movement of virus copy is a random walk process, i.e., Markov process, each neighbor of an infected node will receive the virus copy with equal probability. For instance, if the out-degree of the infected node i is k_i, then its neighbor node j receives the virus copy with probability $p_{ij} = 1/k_i$. Considering all node pairs, we have the one-step probability transition matrix P, of which the element is p_{ij}. We further partition matrix P into a 4×4 block matrix, which is as follows:

$$P = \begin{bmatrix} P_N & P_T \\ 0 & I_T \end{bmatrix},$$ (1)

where P_N is the $|V_N| \times |V_N|$ submatrix concerning the transition probabilities between non-terminal nodes, and P_T is the $|V_N| \times |V_T|$ submatrix, which consists of the transition probabilities from non-terminal nodes to terminal nodes. The submatrix I_T is an identity matrix of order $|V_T|$, since we assume that the self-transition probability of a terminal node is 1. Note that the transition probability from terminal node to non-terminal node is 0, which corresponds to the zero submatrix of P. According to the principle of Markov process, the n-step transition probability is the nth power of the one-step transition matrix. For instance, the n-step transition probability from node i to j is $\{P^n\}_{ij}$.

2.2   Multiple Source Estimator: Maximum Likelihood (ML)

In the source identification problem, the available information is the network G and the set of infected terminal nodes Θ. We utilize the maximum likelihood estimate to infer the set of infection sources, which is expressed as

$$\hat{s} = \arg\max_{s \in \Omega} P(\Theta | s^* = s), \tag{2}$$

where Ω represents the set of all possible combinations of m non-terminal nodes, and s is a candidate source set. Equation (2) implies that our target set is the one which maximizes the condition probability of the set of infected terminal nodes given the candidate source set.

To facilitate the calculation of $P(\Theta | s^* = s)$, we make the following denotations:

- γ_{so_k}: A path starting from an arbitrary node in set s to an infected terminal node o_k, $o_k \in \Theta$.
- Γ_{so_k}: The set of all paths starting from nodes in set s to the infected terminal node o_k, $\Gamma_{so_k} = \{\gamma_{so_k}\}$.
- π_s: A specific permutation of K paths, which start from nodes of set s to the K infected terminal nodes (one-one correspondence), $\pi_s = (\gamma_{so_1}, \ldots, \gamma_{so_K})$. Actually, π_s is an element of the Cartesian product of all $\{\Gamma_{so_k}\}_{o_k \in \Theta}$, i.e., $\pi_s \in \Gamma_{so_1} \times \cdots \times \Gamma_{so_K}$.
- Π_s: The set of all possible path permutations $\{\pi_s\}$, i.e., $\Pi_s = \{\pi_s\} = \Gamma_{so_1} \times \cdots \times \Gamma_{so_K} = \{(\gamma_{so_1}, \ldots, \gamma_{so_K}) : \gamma_{so_k} \in \Gamma_{so_k}\}$.

Similar to [20], we consider all possible spreading paths starting from the nodes of the given candidate source set. Each path permutation π_s has some probability to be the actual one. Thus, we have

$$
\begin{aligned}
P(\Theta | s^* = s) &= \sum_{\pi_s \in \Pi_s} P(\pi_s | s) \\
&= P(\Pi_s | s) \\
&= P(\Gamma_{so_1} \times \cdots \times \Gamma_{so_K} | s).
\end{aligned} \tag{3}
$$

Since we assume that the virus copies perform random walks independently, the infection of terminal nodes is also independent. Thus, we have

$$
\begin{aligned}
P(\Gamma_{so_1} \times \cdots \times \Gamma_{so_K} | s) &= P(\prod_{o_k \in \Theta} \Gamma_{so_k} | s) \\
&= \prod_{o_k \in \Theta} P(\Gamma_{so_k} | s),
\end{aligned} \tag{4}
$$

where $P(\Gamma_{so_k}|s)$ is equal to the sum of probabilities of all possible infection paths starting from set s to node o_k, $\sum_{\gamma_{so_k} \in \Gamma_{so_k}} P(\gamma_{so_k}|s)$. Combining (3) and (4), we can get [20]:

$$P(\Theta|s^* = s) = \prod_{o_k \in \Theta} P(\Gamma_{so_k}|s), \tag{5}$$

In order to calculate $P(\Gamma_{so_k}|s)$, we need to enumerate all possible paths. Although we use Γ_{so_k} to indicate all paths of source set s infecting o_k, actually o_k is infected by a certain node or several nodes in the collection s and the probability that different node in s infects o_k is different. So we have the following definition:

$$P(\Gamma_{so_k}|s) = \sum_{i=1}^{|s^*|} P(\Gamma_{s_i o_k}|s_i) P(s_i|s). \tag{6}$$

Therefore, $P(\Gamma_{so_k}|s)$ can be expressed as

$$P(\Gamma_{so_k}|s) = \sum_{i=1}^{|s^*|} \sum_{n=0}^{\infty} \sum_{l \in V_N} p_{s_i} p_{s_i l}^{(n)} p_{lo_k}, \tag{7}$$

where p_{s_i} represents the probability that among the $|s^*|$ source nodes, node s_i infects terminal node o_k. $p_{s_i l}^{(n)}$ denotes the probability that source node s_i infects non-terminal node l in exactly n steps, and it equals the value of the $(s_i, l)th$ element of matrix $(P_N)^n$. p_{lo_k} represents the probability that non-terminal node l infects terminal node o_k in exactly one step, and it is equivalent to the value of the $(s_i, l)th$ element of matrix P_T. The right side of Eq. (7) indicates that we consider all spreading paths from a node of the source set to a terminal node and the probability of the former to be the exact source node of the latter.

In Eq. (7), p_{s_i} is hard to obtain, and its value might be different for different nodes in set s. Here we propose two approximation methods of p_{s_i}. The first one is based on the transition probability matrix P. We assume that p_{s_i} is proportional to the sum of one-step transition probabilities to all the terminal nodes, which can be written as

$$p_{s_i} = \frac{\sum_{o_k \in \Theta} (p_{s_i o_k}^{(1)} + \varepsilon)}{\sum_{j=1}^{|s^*|} \sum_{o_k \in \Theta} (p_{s_j o_k}^{(1)} + \varepsilon)}, \tag{8}$$

where $p_{s_i o_k}^{(1)}$ represents the $(s_i, o_k)th$ element of matrix P. ε is a small positive number to ensure the denominator is non-zero. In non-sparse networks, this approximation method works well. However, in sparse network, many elements of the one-step transition matrix is zero, and in this case p_{s_i} will be equal for all the source nodes. This is contradictory to the assumption that each node in s might has different possibility to be the source.

To better quantify the possibility of a node to be the source, we propose another approximation method, which considers the mean first passage time

(FPT) [21] of a random walk. We assume that p_{s_i} is proportional to the reciprocal of the sum of FPT from s_i to all the terminal nodes, which is

$$p'_{s_i} = \frac{1/\sum_{o_k \in \Theta} t_{s_i o_k}}{\sum_{j=1}^{|s^*|} 1/\sum_{o_k \in \Theta} t_{s_j o_k}}, \tag{9}$$

where $t_{s_i o_k}$ is the FPT from node s_i to node o_k. The smaller $t_{s_i o_k}$, the more likely that s_i is the source. The pseudocode of FPT calculation is shown in Algorithm 1.

Algorithm 1. FPT Calculation

1: **Input:** directed graph $G(V, E)$, iteration times n, diffusion time t, source node s_i, target node o_k.
2: **for** $i := 1$ to n **do**
3:     **for** $j := 1$ to t **do**
4:         **for** each non-terminal node **do**
5:             **if** the node is infected **then**
6:                 Randomly select a neighbour node to infect.
7:             **End If**
8:             **if** node o_k is infected **then**
9:                 Record the current time as the FPT of this iteration, and cease this iteration.
10:            **End If**
11:        **End For**
12:    **End For**
13:    **if** there is no path between s_i and o_k **then**
14:        $t_{s_i o_k} := t$.
15:    **End If**
16: **End For**
17: Calculate the mean of all iteration results to get $t_{s_i o_k}$.
18: **Output:** $t_{s_i o_k}$.

Furthermore, we can get the matrix form of Eq. (7)

$$A = (\sum_{i=1}^{|s^*|} P_{w_i}) \sum_{n=0}^{\infty} P_N^n P_T, \tag{10}$$

where P_{w_i} is a $|C_{|V_N|}^{|s^*|}| \times |V_N|$ matrix. It is apparent that the quantity of rows in this matrix represents the quantity of possible combinations of all non-terminal nodes. Let $\bar{s}$ be a certain source node combination and $\bar{s}_i$ be the ith node in this combination. The $\bar{s}_i th$ element of each line of matrix P_{w_i} is $p_{\bar{s}_i}$ and the remaining elements are zero.

According to the summation formula of geometric series, we obtain

$$A = (\sum_{i=1}^{|s^*|} P_{w_i})(I - P_N)^{-1} P_T, \tag{11}$$

where $I - P_Q$ has an inverse matrix [22]. It should be noted that $\{A\}_{ij}$ represents the sum of probabilities of all possible infection paths from the ith source combination s to terminal node o_j. In other words, $\{A\}_{ij}$ is equivalent to $P(\Gamma_{so_j}|s)$. Combining (5) and (11), we can get

$$P(\Theta|s^* = s) = \prod_{o_k \in \Theta} \{(\sum_{i=1}^{|s^*|} P_{w_i})(I - P_N)^{-1} P_T\}_{so_k}. \tag{12}$$

Based on Eq. (12), we can obtain the likelihood of each candidate node combination. Combining (2) and (12), we finally obtain

$$\hat{s} = \underset{s \in \Omega}{\arg\max} \prod_{o_k \in \Theta} \{(\sum_{i=1}^{|s^*|} P_{w_i})(I - P_N)^{-1} P_T\}_{so_k}. \tag{13}$$

It worths mentioning that our solution considers all possible infection paths. In addition, due to the fact that we need to enumerate all possible node combinations, the time complexity of our solution is $O(n^{|s^*|+1})$.

3   Results

In this section, we evaluate the efficiency of our estimator. In the experiments, we only consider cases of two and three sources. We use complex network models such as the ER and Price models and some real-world networks, including the GD96_d network and the power-494-bus network. We test the efficiency of our estimator on different networks. In addition, we investigate how network heterogeneity and density impact efficiency of our estimator.

To quantify the efficiency of our estimator, we provide a metric, i.e., minimum error distance, which is given as follows:

$$\Delta = \sum_{i=1}^{|s^*|} d(\hat{s}_i, s_i^*),$$

where $d(\hat{s}_i, s_i^*)$ represents the shortest distance between each source node $\hat{s}_i$ in the prediction result and node s_i^* which is the closest node to $\hat{s}_i$ in the real sources set. In the experiments, we mainly check the distribution of Δ to evaluate our estimator.

3.1   Synthetic Networks

We do experiments on synthetic networks. First, we use the ER model to generate random networks. In this model, every node pair has the same connection probability. The pseudocode of ER model is shown in Algorithm 2, in which p_{ER} controls the density of the network. The larger p_{ER}, the denser network. We set network size $N = 500$, and then change the network density to investigate how

---

Algorithm 2. ER Network Generation Algorithm

1: **Input:** total number of nodes N, connection probability p_{ER}.
2: **Initialization:** $N := 500$ and $p_{ER} \in [0,1]$.
3: **for** each nodes pair (i , j) **do**
4:     Generate a random number $r \in [0,1]$.
5:     **if** $r < p_{ER}$ **then**
6:         Add an edge between node pairs (i , j).
7:     **End If**
8: **End For**
9: **Output:** $G(N, p_{ER})$.

---

the minimum error distance distribution change. The number of source nodes is 2. The first approximation method (Eq. (8)) is employed in our estimator with $\varepsilon = 0.0001$. We perform 1000 independent runs. In Fig. 1(a), we see that when $p_{ER} = 0.001$, the probability of $\Delta = 0$ is more than 0.5, which means the identification accuracy is more than half. However, when p_{ER} increases, the identification accuracy decreases accordingly.

Algorithm 3. Price Network Generation Algorithm

1: **Input:** strongly connected graph with m_0 nodes, total number of nodes N, priority connection probability p_{pri}, the number of added edges for each new node m.
2: **Initialization:** add the end nodes of all directed edges in the initial network to array $Array$, $m_0 := 5$ $N := 500$, $m := 3$ and $p_{pri} \in [0,1]$.
3: **for** $N - m_0$ remaining nodes **do**
4:     **for** $i{:=}i$ to m **do**
5:         Generate a random number $r \in [0,1]$.
6:         **if** $r < p_{pri}$ **then**
7:             Randomly select a node in $Array$ and make sure that newly selected m nodes are unique.
8:         **else**
9:             Randomly select a node that already exists in the network, and make sure that newly selected m nodes are unique.
10:         **End If**
11:     **End For**
12:     For each selected node, add a directed edge pointing to the newly added node, and add the selected m nodes to $Array$.
13: **End For**
14: **Output:** $G(N, p_{pri})$.

Then, we use the Price model to generate the scale-free networks with 500 nodes. The pseudocode of the Price model is given in Algorithm 3, in which the network heterogeneity is controlled by p_{pri}. The larger p_{pri}, the larger network heterogeneity. As shown in Algorithm 3, we slightly modify the Price model by reversing the direction of links, which is originally pointing from newly added

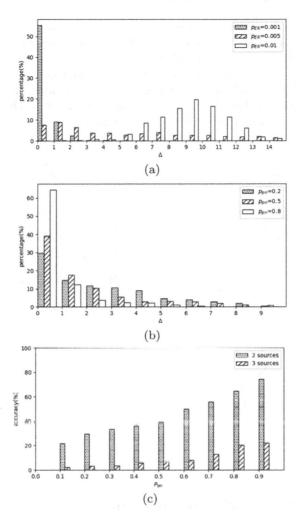

Fig. 1. (a) Distribution of minimum error distance for the ER network. (b) Distribution of minimum error distance for the Price network. (c) Accuracy of identification under different p_{pri} values in the Price network with 2 sources and 3 sources. p_{pri} reflects the heterogeneity of price network.

nodes to old nodes. This modification maintains the statistical property of the model, while lead to the emerge of terminal nodes, which are fit for our model setting, but do not exist in the original model. The number of source nodes is 2. The first approximation method (Eq. (8)) is employed in our estimator with $\varepsilon = 0.0001$. We perform 1000 independent runs and calculate the distribution of Δ for different network heterogeneity. In Fig. 1(b), we can see that $\Delta < 10$, and this indicates the source nodes identified based on our estimator are topologically very close to the real source nodes. Moreover, the larger p, the larger identification accuracy. For instance, when $p_{pri} = 0.8$, Δ is more than 0.6, while when $p_{pri} = 0.5$, Δ decreases to less than 0.4. This means that heterogeneous networks facilitate source identification.

Next, we increase the number of source nodes to 3. As shown in Fig. 1(c), we obtain the same conclusion as in Fig. 1(b) that the identification accuracy increases with network heterogeneity. Also, we can infer that the identification accuracy decreases when the number of source nodes increases.

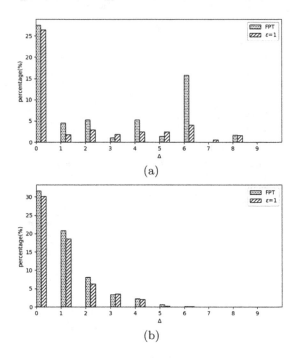

Fig. 2. (a) Distribution of minimum error distance for the GD96_d network. (b) Distribution of minimum error distance for the power-494-bus network.

3.2   Real-World Network

Finally, we do experiments on real-world networks including the GD96_d network [23] and the power-494-bus network [23]. The GD96_d network contains 180 nodes and 229 edges, and the power network has 494 nodes, 1381 edges. Based on these two networks, we compare the two approximation methods, Eqs. (8) and (9), to see which one is better when employing in our estimator. For the first approximation, we set $\varepsilon = 1$. For each network, 1000 independent runs are performed. The simulation result on GD96_d network is shown in Fig. 2(a). We can see that the identification accuracy of the FPT-based approximation is larger than the ε-based approximation. The distribution of minimum error distance of the former is more to the left than the latter, which means in general the error distance of FPT-based approximation is smaller than the ε-based approximation.

The initial power network dose not have any terminal nodes. Thus, we set all the nodes with only one out-edge as terminal nodes, and randomly choose two non-terminal nodes as the real infection sources. As shown in Fig. 2(b), we can also see that the FPT-based approximation is better than the ε-based approximation for our estimator in terms of identification accuracy and minimum error distance. The advantage of FPT-based approximation is that it can differentiate the impacts of different source nodes better than the ε-based approximation.

4   Conclusion

In summary, we propose a method to identify multiple sources of random walk-based epidemic spreading process. Our method is based on the maximum likelyhood estimate. When deriving the estimator, we consider the different possibilities of different source nodes infecting a terminal node and all possible spreading paths from a source node to a terminal node. We propose two approximation methods to quantifying the possibility of a certain source node in set s infecting terminal nodes, which are ε-based approximation and FPT-based approximation. We validate our method on model networks and real-world networks by investigating the distribution of minimum error distance. Experimental results show that the performance of our method increases with network heterogeneity, while decreases with network density. Moreover, the FPT-based approximation is better than the ε-based approximation. Since we enumerate all possible node combinations in the calculation, the time complexity of our identification method is $O(n^{|s^*|+1})$. In the future, we will develop fast algorithms to solve the multiple-source identification problem.

References

1. Brightwell, G., Winkler, P.: Counting linear extensions. Order 8(3), 225–242 (1991)
2. Valiant, L.G.: The complexity of enumeration and reliability problems. SIAM J. Comput. 8(3), 410–421 (1979)
3. Shah, D., Zaman, T.: Detecting sources of computer viruses in networks: theory and experiment. In: ACM SIGMETRICS Performance Evaluation Review, vol. 38, pp. 203–214. ACM (2010)
4. Shah, D., Zaman, T.: Rumors in a network: who's the culprit? IEEE Trans. Inf. Theory 57(8), 5163–5181 (2011)
5. Shah, D., Zaman, T.: Rumor centrality: a universal source detector. In: ACM SIGMETRICS Performance Evaluation Review, vol. 40, pp. 199–210. ACM (2012)
6. Luo, W., Tay, W.-P., Leng, M.: Identifying infection sources and regions in large networks. IEEE Trans. Signal Process. 61(11), 2850–2865 (2013)
7. Luo , W., Tay, W.P.: Identifying multiple infection sources in a network. In: 2012 Conference Record of the Forty Sixth Asilomar Conference on Signals, Systems and Computers (ASILOMAR), pp. 1483–1489. IEEE (2012)

8. Luo, W., Tay, W.P.: Identifying infection sources in large tree networks. In: 2012 9th Annual IEEE Communications Society Conference on Sensor, Mesh and Ad Hoc Communications and Networks (SECON), pp. 281–289. IEEE (2012)

9. Zhu, K., Ying, L.: Information source detection in the SIR model: a sample-path-based approach. IEEE/ACM Trans. Netw. (TON) **24**(1), 408–421 (2016)

10. Luo, W., Tay, W.P.: Estimating infection sources in a network with incomplete observations. In: 2013 IEEE Global Conference on Signal and Information Processing (GlobalSIP), pp. 301–304. IEEE (2013)

11. Restrepo, J.G., Ott, E., Hunt, B.R.: Characterizing the dynamical importance of network nodes and links. Phys. Rev. Lett. **97**(9), 094102 (2006)

12. Fioriti, V., Chinnici, M.: Predicting the sources of an outbreak with a spectral technique. arXiv preprint arXiv:1211.2333 (2012)

13. Comin, C.H., da Fontoura Costa, L.: Identifying the starting point of a spreading process in complex networks. Phys. Rev. E **84**(5), 056105 (2011)

14. Zang, W., Peng, Z., Zhou, C., Li, G.: Locating multiple sources in social networks under the SIR model: a divide-and-conquer approach. J. Comput. Sci. **10**, 278–287 (2015)

15. Lokhov, A.Y., Mézard, M., Ohta, H., Zdeborová, L.: Inferring the origin of an epidemic with a dynamic message-passing algorithm. Phys. Rev. E **90**(1), 012801 (2014)

16. Altarelli, F., Braunstein, A., et al.: Bayesian inference of epidemics on networks via belief propagation. Phys. Rev. Lett. **112**(11), 118701 (2014)

17. Antulov-Fantulin, N., Lančić, A., Šmuc, T., Štefančić, H., Šikić, M.: Identification of patient zero in static and temporal networks: robustness and limitations. Phys. Rev. Lett. **114**(24), 248701 (2015)

18. Prakash, B.A., Vreeken, J., Faloutsos, C.: Efficiently spotting the starting points of an epidemic in a large graph. Knowl. Inf. Syst. **38**(1), 35–59 (2014)

19. Prakash, B.A., Vreeken, J., Faloutsos, C.: Spotting culprits in epidemics: how many and which ones? In: 2012 IEEE 12th International Conference on Data Mining (ICDM), pp. 11–20. IEEE (2012)

20. Horn, A.L., Friedrich, H.: Locating the source of large-scale diffusion of foodborne contamination. arXiv preprint arXiv:1805.03137 (2018)

21. Wang, S.P., Pei, W.J.: First passage time of multiple Brownian particles on networks with applications. Phys. A **387**(18), 4699–4708 (2008)

22. Kemeny, J.G., Snell, J.L.: Finite Markov Chains: With a New Appendix "Generalization of a Fundamental Matrix". Springer, New York (1983)

23. Rossi, R.A., Ahmed, N.K.: The network data repository with interactive graph analytics and visualization. In: Proceedings of the Twenty-Ninth AAAI Conference on Artificial Intelligence (2015)

Design of Intelligent Lighting System for Office Workplace Based on ZigBee Technology

Shishun Liu, Rimiao Li, Ping Li$^{(\boxtimes)}$, and Kejian Hu

School of Information Science and Engineering, Dalian Polytechnic University,
Dalian 116034, China
liping@dlpu.edu.cn

Abstract. This design is a ZigBee-based intelligent office lighting system, which aims to optimize the current office space using traditional lighting mode. The system can collect the illumination in the office area in real-time, compensate the illumination environment in the office area, and fully utilize the technical features of LED lamps to be energy efficient. Each lighting node in the system can switch different lighting schemes according to different areas of the office, and meet different situational requirements in combination with actual conditions to realize intelligent and humanized office lighting.

Keywords: ZigBee · Intelligent lighting · Green lighting · Transparent transmission

1 Introduction

At present, whether at the national level or people's lives, and the word "intelligence" penetrates various fields of society. The efficient combination of high-efficiency and energy-saving lighting features of LED lighting technology and IoT technology has introduced a new concept of intelligent lighting. As an indispensable part of urban life, office lighting should be closer to "intelligent lighting". At present, the task of the lighting system is not only to provide a simple light environment for the office staff, but also to provide a suitable lighting environment for the office staff to have a good working experience and improve the working efficiency. The traditional lighting system mainly adopts manual control, even if some places use single-chip microcomputer to control the lighting equipment, but it is only a single point of control, and does not meet the design requirements of intelligent lighting [1]. This paper designs a ZigBee-based office intelligent lighting system. Use ZigBee technology to wirelessly network the lighting nodes in diverse areas of the office, and use the illuminance sensor to detect the lighting environment parameters of each area. Use smart phones or PCs to connect to WIFI to monitor numerous areas in real time, and real-time control of the lighting environment of office space to create an intelligent office lighting mode.

X. B. Zhai et al. (Eds.): MLICOM 2019, LNICST 294, pp. 387–394, 2019.
https://doi.org/10.1007/978-3-030-32388-2_33

2 Overall System Design

As showed in Fig. 1, the system is mainly divided into four parts, namely the control module, the system gateway, the drive module and the lighting node module. The system uses the CC2530f256 ZigBee chip as the core, and uses its technical advantages of a self-organizing network to form a typical ZigBee network. The light environment monitoring module in the control terminal can monitor the lighting conditions of each lighting area in real time and feed back to the coordinator in the ZigBee network to provide a suitable lighting environment for each office area [2]. The system adopts two control modes: an intelligent terminal and touch pad. It can use mobile phones, tablet computers and other devices to connect to WIFI to control the lamps through the system gateway, and can also use the touch pad to directly change the lighting state of the lamps using the ZigBee network. LED lighting technology is adopted in each lighting node to maximize the high-performance benefits of LED light source and create a high-quality office lighting environment. The intelligent terminal can connect to the ZigBee lighting terminal in the WIFI control system. The system reserves peripheral interface circuits for the corresponding sensors to detect more environmental parameters (such as temperature, humidity, smoke, etc.), making the system more workable.

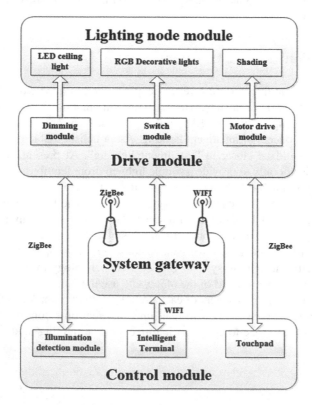

Fig. 1. System block diagram

3 System Hardware Circuit Design

3.1 ZigBee Core Board Design

The core of the system uses the CC2530f256 chip, which is fully consistent with the 8051 core, comes with an AD conversion circuit, and supports the IEEE 802.15.4 protocol. In the development of the ZigBee wireless sensor network, different sensor signal conditioning circuits are needed, but the circuit of the ZigBee communication part can be left unchanged, which greatly streamlines the design of the hardware circuit [3].

3.2 LED Dimming Mode Circuit Design

The LED dimming function of the system is expected to be completed by the CC2530 and the LED constant current driving PWM dimming module. The dimming node receives the optical environment parameters given by the coordinator, and issues a command to the PWM dimming module to adjust the brightness of the LED lamps. The light compensates for the natural light and maximizes the use of natural light to create a suitable office environment. The schematic diagram of the LED dimming node is illustrated in Fig. 2.

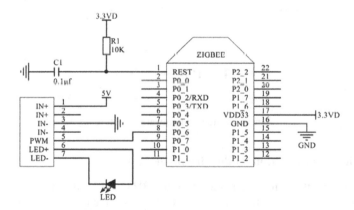

Fig. 2. Schematic diagram of PWM constant current dimming circuit

For a certain frequency of PWM dimming, the output current of the driver has a certain relationship with the duty cycle of the PWM signal. The calculation method is as shown in Eq. (1).

$$I_{o\_set} = \frac{DT}{T} I_{o\_norm} \tag{1}$$

Where I_{o_set} is the desired output current (mA), D is the duty cycle (%) of the PWM signal, T is the period (S) of the PWM signal, and I_{o_norm} is the rated output value (mA) of the driver.

After the terminal node receives different duty cycle values, the PWM control signal will be generated in the callback function, but since the illumination terminal node includes the optocoupler isolation relay drive, the frequency of the PWM signal is not suitable too high. In addition, the system further includes a touch panel controller for performing spot dimming according to the measured value returned by the illumination detection module to the coordinator.

3.3   System Gateway Node Hardware Designs

System gateway is mainly composed of CC2530ZigBee module and ESP8266WIFI module. The ZigBee module combines the sensor module, the controller module and the lighting node into a wireless sensor network. The WIFI module can enable the intelligent terminal to access the wireless router network, thereby achieving the goal of controlling each lighting node [4]. The WIFI module communicates with the ZigBee module through the serial port. The hardware structure of the gateway is given in Fig. 3.

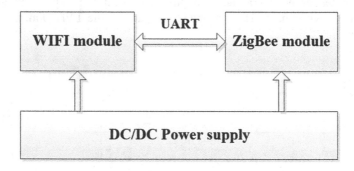

Fig. 3.   Gateway hardware structure

3.4   Illuminance Collection Node Circuit Designs

The illuminance collection node is based on the BH1750FVI illuminance sensor. The sensor does not require additional external plug-ins. It can directly determine the intensity of light in the environment, and send the collected illuminance information to the coordinator through the ZigBee module to compare the required areas. The optimum illuminance value, the coordinator sends control commands to each lighting node to adjust the LED luminaire to the most suitable brightness. The BH1750FVI illuminance sensor has a wide range of input light and can be utilized in most functional areas in the office. The schematic diagram of the illumination collection node is illustrated in Fig. 4.

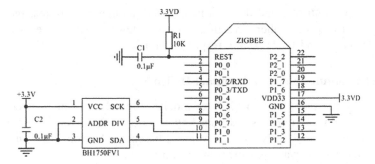

Fig. 4. Schematic diagram of the illumination acquisition node circuit

4 System Software Design

The software design of the system mainly relies on TI's z-stack protocol Stack and IAR integrated development environment.

4.1 Coordinator Node

The coordinator is the core of the wireless sensor network. Its main function is to manage the ZigBee network and communicate with the gateway. After entering the system, the coordinator node will first determine whether there is data to transmit, and then establish the data transmission network. After receiving the control instructions from the gateway, the coordinator will send commands to the lighting terminal to change the lighting state of the lamps. Normally, the coordinator node is in a dormant state. When there is data transmission, the clock signal will send a signal to wake it up. This working mode can effectively reduce power consumption and extend the service life of ZigBee nodes.

4.2 Router Node

According to the needs of the system, multiple routing nodes are set to increase the coverage area of the whole ZigBee network, forming a typical network topology and improving the reliability of the system. After power on and initialization, the routing nodes apply to join the network, search for signals, determine the data transmission path, package the data according to the ZigBee communication protocol, and send it to the next node.

4.3 Lighting Terminal Node

The software design of the lighting terminal node is divided into two parts: LED lamp driver design and sensor detection data transceiver program. At this time, the gateway creates a new device node in the virtual device list for the node, and the coordinator receives the signal sent by the lighting terminal, and then sends the variable value of the terminal device to the gateway [5]. At this time, the lighting terminal has established contact with the controller and the coordinator, and the lighting terminal receives the command sent by the controller through the system gateway, changes the working state of the LED lamps, and feeds back a response variable.

4.4   Host Computer Control Terminal Design

The host computer includes two kinds of mobile terminal and computer control terminal. The computer terminal is developed by using C# software under .Net platform, and the mobile terminal software is developed based on Android SDK in Java language. The control interface is shown in Figs. 5 and 6.

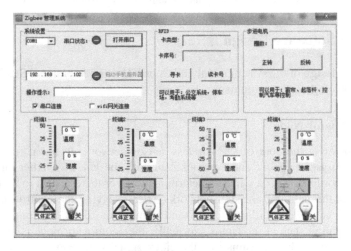

Fig. 5. Computer control interface

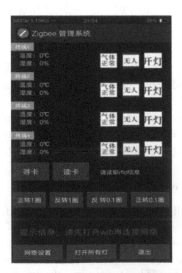

Fig. 6. Mobile phone control interface

5 System Debugging

As showed in Fig. 7, the office area of a nearby company is used as an experimental point. The office area is about 180 m^2. ZigBee nodes are arranged in each functional area to form a ZigBee-based intelligent lighting system. After the coordinator node is completed from the networking, it is determined that the ZigBee network covers the entire office area, and the serial port is used to connect the host computer with the coordinator and the terminal node, and the serial debugging assistant is used for data transmission and reception, the simulation system runs the communication process, and the test data transmission is performed [6].

A coordinator node is set in the central area of the office area, and each lighting area node is set to one lighting terminal node, and only three nodes having forwarding data tasks are set as router nodes, and the remaining nodes are all set as terminal nodes, so that reduce the cost of ZigBee chips and avoid unnecessary consumption. The lighting experiment was carried out by using a mobile phone, computer and touch pad respectively. The dimming of LED lamps was split into high brightness, medium bright, bright and soft four levels. RGB decorative lights were installed in the front desk and a conference room, and various scene modes were set. In the automatic mode, the coordinator receives the data feedback of the illumination detection node to automatically adjust the light of each functional area.

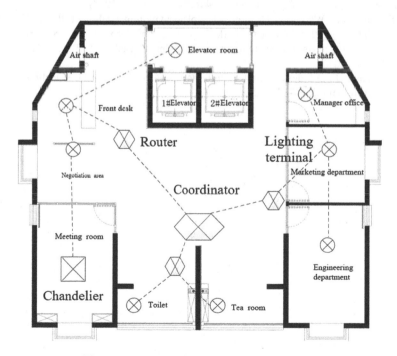

Fig. 7. Experimental point ZigBee node layout

6 Summary

The intelligent lighting system of the office based on ZigBee technology can monitor the lighting environment in each functional area of the office area in real time. The intelligent terminal is used to adjust the lighting mode to maximize the use of natural light to provide the most suitable office lighting environment for office workers in the area, to achieve "Green smart lighting". With the rapid development of intelligent control technology, LED intelligent lighting technology will also be improved, for the energy conservation and emission reduction initiatives proposed by the state, the intelligent and information roads inject huge energy [7].

References

1. Chen, Z., Zhang, J., Li, H.: Design of wireless intelligent lighting system based on ZigBee and WiFi. Comput. Meas. Control **24**(2), 228–231 (2016)
2. Wang, X.: Intelligent LED lighting control system based on ZigBee. Electr. Appl. **3**, 3–8 (2014)
3. Dai, R., Wang, H., Chai, G.: Design of intelligent illumination system based on ZigBee. Electron. World **8**, 186–187 (2018)
4. Zhan, J., Wu, L., Tang, Z.: Design and realization of the intelligent illuminating control system based on ZigBee. Power Electron. **41**(10), 25–26, 51 (2007)
5. Sun, H., Chen, W., Wang, N.: Design and implementation of intelligent illumination system based on ZigBee wireless sensor network. Mod. Electron. Tech. **40**(11), 183–186 (2017)
6. Su, Y.: An intelligent lighting system for office buildings based on ZigBee. J. Binzhou Univ. **33**(4), 74–77 (2017)
7. Wu, G., Zhang, J.: Wireless intelligent lighting system based on ZigBee technology. Mod. Electron. Tech. **31**(14), 67–69 (2008)

Machine Learning I

Active Sampling Based on MMD
for Model Adaptation

Qi Zhang[1,2], Donghai Guan[1,2(✉)], Weiwei Yuan[1,2], and Asad Masood Khattak[3]

[1] College of Computer Science and Technology,
Nanjing University of Aeronautics and Astronautics, Nanjing, China
{stonewell,dhguan,yuanweiwei}@nuaa.edu.cn
[2] Collaborative Innovation Center of Novel Software Technology and
Industrialization, Nanjing 210016, China
[3] College of Technological Innovation, Zayed University,
Dubai, United Arab Emirates
Asad.Khattak@zu.ac.ae

Abstract. In this paper, we demonstrate a method for transfer learning with minimal supervised information. Recently, researchers have proposed various algorithms to solve transfer learning problems, especially the unsupervised domain adaptation problem. They mainly focus on how to learn a good common representation and use it directly for downstream task. Unfortunately, they ignore the fact that this representation may not capture target-specific feature for target task well. In order to solve this problem, this paper attempts to capture target-specific feature by utilizing labeled data in target domain. Now it's a challenge that how to seek as little supervised information as possible to achieve good results. To overcome this challenge, we actively select instances for training and model adaptation based on MMD method. In this process, we try to label some valuable target data to capture target-specific feature and fine-tune the classifier networks. We choose a batch of data in target domain far from common representation space and having maximum entropy. The first requirement is helpful to learn a good representation for target domain and the second requirement tries to improve the classifier performance. Finally, we experiment with our method on several datasets which shows significant improvement and competitive advantage against common methods.

Keywords: Active sampling · Maximum mean discrepancy ·
Transfer learning · Characteristics · Uncertainty

1 Introduction

Recent years, deep learning have made great success in various applications across many fields. For example, there have been many CNN models such as AlexNet [12], GoogLeNet [21], ResNet [7] and so on, which have improved classification accuracy on images datasets. It's well known that training deep convolutional neural networks always need numerous labeled data. However, in many

© ICST Institute for Computer Sciences, Social Informatics and Telecommunications Engineering 2019
Published by Springer Nature Switzerland AG 2019. All Rights Reserved
X. B. Zhai et al. (Eds.): MLICOM 2019, LNICST 294, pp. 397–409, 2019.
https://doi.org/10.1007/978-3-030-32388-2_34

cases, there're not enough labelled data due to expensive cost and huge time consumption. There are two paradigms-transfer learning and active learning-which can effectively overcome that challenge.

Transfer learning or domain adaptation [16] tries to tackles this problem by transferring knowledge from a label-rich and similar domain (known as source domain) to a label-scarce domain (known as target domain). At present, researchers mainly devoted much attention to unsupervised domain adaptation assuming that there are sufficient labeled data in source domain and no labeled data in target domain. However, different domains have their own characteristics so that the model learned only from labeled source data can't generalize well to the target domain. It's easily to consider obtaining labeled target domain data to solve this problem. So, the following question is can we use as small amount of supervised information of target domain as possible while keeping the model's performance improving. That encourages us to combine transfer learning with active learning in CNN model.

Active learning [19] is one of effective paradigms to reduce the labeling cost. Its basic assumption is that different data has different amount of information. Therefore, people can query the most valuable instance to label and obtain considerable performance's improvement. Based on this idea, various criteria have been proposed to evaluate data's value. For instance [10], informativeness and representativeness are two frequently used criteria to choose data. [1, 2] proposed an method that select data based on marginal distribution matching. When it comes to transfer learning, we know that there must exist distribution shift. So, many traditional active learning methods can't adapt to such case well while distribution based sampling strategy will be a good choice. What's more, our classifiers are typical CNN models. Hence, researchers should consider both network architecture and datasets shift when designing strategy for selecting data. Recently, there are several works [3,24] to combine active learning and deep neural networks. However, their methods can not be adapted to transfer learning models well and thus may lead to waste of annotated data by learning from scratch.

In common transfer learning process, initially, we can use pre-trained model as a backbone and then use labeled source data and unlabeled target data to update the parameters of the model. These two steps are so called unsupervised domain adaptation. But it's well known that the insight behind transfer learning or unsupervised domain adaptation is we can learn the common parts from similar domains. So, if the target domain is not much similar to source domain, the learned common representation may be unsatisfactory for target task. To address this problem, we attempt to provide as little supervised information in target domain as possible to capture the good representation beneficial to target domain task. In this paper, we propose to a new method based on maximum mean discrepancy (MMD) [6,9], which can effectively select data based on distribution to train models. The intuition behind the method is that we can choose data in target domain most dissimilar to source domain to capture the distinctive information in target task.

Eventually, We perform experiments on several datasets. The results demonstrate that our approach can effectively learn distinctive representation for target task and significantly improve accuracy with lower labelling cost comparing with other method such as random sampling, entropy-based sampling and ADMA [11]. The main contribution of our paper are summarized as follows:

- We utilize MMD method which can identify data's distinctiveness for target task, and based on this we can choose the most valuable data for query.
- Our selecting strategy can adapt well to distribution shift scenario.
- We evaluate our approach on various datasets and achieve a satisfactory results.

The rest of this paper is organized as follows. In Sect. 2, we presents a brief review of related work. Section 3 introduces the background knowledge of MMD. Section 4 discusses the detailed components of our approach and the corresponding algorithm. Section 5 demonstrates the experimental results and the corresponding empirical analysis. Section 6 makes a conclusion of this paper.

2   Related Work

Domain adaptation is one of hot topics in transfer learning, especially unsupervised domain adaptation(UDA) which attracts many people's attention. Towards transfer learning paradigm, it aims to match distributions between source data and target data with smaller loss after feature transformation. To tackle this problem, the core is how to measure the difference or loss between source domain and target domain after feature transformation. There are about three ways to deal with it—discrepancy loss, reconstruction loss and adversarial loss. The first one [14,15,23] often utilize MMD criterion, MMD computes the norm of the difference between kernel mean embedding in two domains. The DDC method [23] shares common features in low level across different domains but adds adaptation layers in high level layers using MMD to minimize distance between two domains. The deep adaptation network (DAN) [14] uses MMD when task-specific layers embedded in a RKHS where the mean embedding of different domain distributions can be explicitly matched. But the method only considers the marginal distribution matching. To deal with this problem, joint adaptation networks (JAN) [15] was proposed to learn a transfer network by aligning joint distributions of multiple domain-specific layers across domains based on a joint MMD criterion. The second [5] proposed an auto-encoder based framework for domain adaptation by simultaneously minimizing the reconstruction loss of the auto-encoder and the classification error. The last [4,8,22] using adversarial method currently is the mainstream, which has chosen an adversarial loss to minimize domain distribution shift distance. In this method, the network adds a module discriminator that discriminates the learned representation coming from target data or source data. If the discriminator can't distinguish well, then we can admit that source domain and target domain are aligning. For instance, the

DANN [4] introduces a domain classifier with binary labels to distinguish the source domain from target domain to learn invariant representation.

Though there are have been extensive prior work on UDA, some researchers have noted that if we can learn the difference or distinctiveness for target task, then the performance will make a step forward. Prior mainstream domain adaptation approaches tied weights of source and target domain on the model. Such as DANN [4,20], source domain and target domain learned the feature representation through the same convolutional layers that means both of them learn the representation by the same way. In intuition, target domain dataset learning representation in such way may lose its distinctive information. To reform such network architecture, the ADDA [22] method designs a new adversarial training networks that source domain and target domain have their own mapping networks and share common label classifier. Through different convolutional layers, the extracted feature can maintain domain-specific information. [18] introduce a new approach that attempts to align distributions of source and target by utilizing the task-specific decision boundaries. It firstly maximizes the discrepancy between two classifiers' output to detect target samples far from the support of source, then feature generator learns to generate target features near the support to minimize the discrepancy. Such two methods above don't utilize any supervised information, so we can't be sure of the quality of learned representation. But the following tries to use as little supervised information as possible to achieve significant improvement in performance.

[11] proposed ADMA algorithm that iteratively selected data according to its distinctiveness and uncertainty. Its main contribution is introducing a novel criterion *distinctiveness* to measure the ability of an instance on improving the representation quality of the neural network for target task. ADMA aims to use a few labeled data to update the parameters of pre-trained model but in some extend, it doesn't care much about domain distribution shift. [1] is one of classical work about combining transfer learning and active learning, which selects data and adjusts weights simultaneously. But noticing that transfer learning based on endowing instance with weight is not the best method. What's more, the method is built on the shallow model which can not model for complex situation well. Our approach adopts part of this paper's basic idea and designs a novel criterion which can be used in deep CNN models.

3   Preliminary

3.1   Kernel Embedding of Probability Distributions

Given any positive definite kernel function $k : \mathcal{X} \times \mathcal{X} \rightarrow \mathcal{R}$, there exists a unique reproducing kernel Hilbert space(RKHS) $\mathcal{H}$ which is a function space. Let $f : \mathcal{X} \rightarrow \mathbb{R}$ where evaluation can be written as an inner product, specifically, $f(x) = <f, k(\cdot, x)>_{\mathcal{H}}$, for all $f \in \mathcal{H}, x \in \mathcal{X}$. Furthermore, if a probability distribution P was given, then its kernel mean embedding into $\mathcal{H}$ is defined as:

$$\mu_P \triangleq E_P[f(x)] = \int_{\mathcal{X}} f(x) \, dP(x)$$

Considering a dataset $X = x_1, \cdots, x_n$ drawn from P(x), then its empirical kernel mean embedding is

$$\widehat{\mu_P} = \frac{1}{n} \sum_{i=1}^{n} f(x_i)$$

3.2   Maximum Mean Discrepancy(MMD)

Given observations $X_s = \{x_1^s, \cdots, x_{n_s}^s\}$ and $X_t = \{x_1^t, \cdots, x_{n_t}^t\}$ drawn from distributions P(X) and Q(X) respectively. Maximum Mean Discrepancy(MMD) used as a test statistic in a two-sample test which rejects or accepts the null hypothesis $P = Q$. The basic idea behind MMD is that if two distributions are identical, all of the statistics are the same. We define the MMD and its empirical estimation as:

$$MMD[P,Q] = \sup_{f \in \mathcal{H}} \|E_{x^s \sim P}[f(x^s)] - E_{x^t \sim Q}[f(x^t)]\|_{\mathcal{H}}^2 \tag{1}$$

$$MMD[X_s, X_t] = \sup_{f \in \mathcal{H}} \|\frac{1}{n_s} \sum_{i=1}^{n_s} f(x_i) - \frac{1}{n_t} \sum_{j=1}^{n_t} f(x_j)\|_{\mathcal{H}}^2 \tag{2}$$

where $\mathcal{H}$ is an universal RKHS that is rich enough to distinguish two distributions. From the formula, we can see the MMD is defined as the squared distance between the mean embedding. [6] gave the theoretical result that $P = Q$ if and only if $MMD[P,Q] = 0$. Formula (2) is an unbiased estimate of formula (1). In practice, we can extend the formula (2) as the following result:

$$MMD[P,Q] = \frac{1}{n_s^2} \sum_{i=1}^{n_s} \sum_{j=1}^{n_s} k(x_i^s, x_j^s) + \frac{1}{n_t^2} \sum_{i=1}^{n_t} \sum_{j=1}^{n_t} k(x_i^t, x_j^t) - \frac{2}{n_s n_t} \sum_{i=1}^{n_s} \sum_{j=1}^{n_t} k(x_i^s, x_j^t)$$
$$\tag{3}$$

where k is a kernel function in $\mathcal{H}$.

4   The Proposed Approach and Criteria

Let $X^t = \{x_i^t\}_{i=1}^{n_t}$ denotes the unlabelled target domain with n_t instances and the model in iteration t will be denoted as $\mathcal{M}_t$. In this paper, we perform batch-mode active learning. At each iteration, we will select a small batch of instances (batchsize = b) $Q = \{x_i^t\}_{i=1}^{b}$ for querying their labels. We will use each batch of data to retrain the current model to update the parameters. To improve the neural network's performance with less cost, we must consider two points. First one is the instance's contribution for learning target-specific feature. Second point is the instance's contribution for learning classifier's distinctiveness.

Comparing with conventional methods of active learning strategy, we should consider distribution shift. In many UDA approaches, we can align the distributions between source domain and target domain transformed or mapped by neural networks. But it's worth noting that specific features for target task are ignored by many UDA algorithms. Furthermore, without relational labeled data, it's hard to capture the specific features. In order to be from good to better, we query as few instances as possible for labeling. In each iteration, we aim to select a small batch of data and we hope there exists vast difference between such selected instances and source domain instances. Because, the intuition tells us that vast difference may promote to learn specific features by such instances in target domain. MMD is a powerful tool to measure the distance between two different distributions. We can evaluate the instances' contribution to specific features by this tool. Simultaneously, the uncertainty of instance should is necessary to consider. Combining such two criteria, we can evaluate each batch of instances' value well. The following is concrete formula for such two criteria. For the sake of writing conveniently, the symbol x_i^s, x_j^t are not the original data in domains but the features extracted by convolutional layers.

4.1 Characteristics

To describe the instance's ability of learning target-specific feature representation, we introduce the *characteristics* as an index.

$$\| \frac{1}{n_s} \sum_{i=1}^{n_s} \phi(x_i^s) - \frac{1}{b} \sum_{j=1}^{n_t} \alpha_j \phi(x_j^t) \|_{\mathcal{H}}^2, \qquad \alpha_j \in \{0,1\}$$

This formula compute distance between a batch of b instances and source domain data. If we minimize the index that means we hope to find most similar instances to source domain data. It will be beneficial for learning the common representation. In this paper, we solve the problem that we have been learned a good common representation and aim to capture the specific features for target task. So, we can maximize *characteristics* to find instances in target domain dissimilar to source domain distribution. Actually, the maximal value is hard or impossible to find. In practical computation, we will use approximate point-wise computational method to find such b instances. The detailed explanation will be occurred in the next content.

4.2 Uncertainty

To combine with conventional active sampling strategy, we consider the uncertainty based method. Uncertainty is a commonly used criterion to evaluate how uncertain the prediction of the model for a given instance. In this paper, we adopt the maximum information entropy as our evaluation criterion. Of course, you can use any other methods such as margin-based or low-confidence approaches. Assume that there are $|\mathcal{Y}|$ classes for target task. Then the information entropy can be written as:

$$H(x) = -\sum_{i=1}^{|\mathcal{Y}|} p_i log(p_i)$$

where the p_i is the corresponding probability of class i.

4.3   Combination

Now combining such two criteria, we can get the following objective function:

$$\max_{\alpha} \quad \| \frac{1}{n_s} \sum_{i=1}^{n_s} \phi(x_i^s) - \frac{1}{b} \sum_{j=1}^{n_t} \alpha_j \phi(x_j^t) \|_{\mathcal{H}}^2 + \sum_{j=1}^{n_t} \alpha_j H(x_j^t)$$

$$\text{s.t.} \quad \sum_{i=1}^{n_t} \alpha_i = b \tag{4}$$

$$\alpha_i \in \{0,1\}$$

where $H(x_j^t)$ is the corresponding entropy of x_j^t towards the classifier. It's easy to extend the objective function as the following form:

$$\max_{\alpha} \quad \frac{1}{n_s^2} \sum_{i=1}^{n_s} \sum_{j=1}^{n_s} k(x_i^s, x_j^s) + \frac{1}{b^2} \sum_{i=1}^{n_t} \sum_{j=1}^{n_t} \alpha_i \alpha_j k(x_i^t, x_j^t)$$

$$- \frac{2}{n_s b} \sum_{i=1}^{n_s} \sum_{j=1}^{n_t} \alpha_j k(x_i^s, x_j^t) + \sum_{j=1}^{n_t} \alpha_j H(x_i^t) \tag{5}$$

$$\text{s.t.} \quad \sum_{i=1}^{n_t} \alpha_i = b$$

$$\alpha_i \in \{0,1\}$$

$\alpha = (\alpha_i, \cdots, \alpha_{n_t})^T$. Dropping the constant term, formula (5) can be rewritten as :

$$\max_{\alpha} \quad \frac{1}{b^2} \alpha^T K_{t,t}\, \alpha - \frac{2}{n_s b} \mathbb{1}_{n_s}^T K_{s,t} \alpha + H(X^t)^T \alpha$$

$$\text{s.t.} \quad \mathbb{1}_{n_t}^T \alpha_i = b \tag{6}$$

$$\alpha_i \in \{0,1\}$$

The formula (6) is similar to convex quadratic programming, unfortunately, it can't be sufficient for QP's conditions. The constraints make the problem be an integer programming problem. Furthermore, the key point is the objective function is expecting for a maximum value and $K_{t,t}$ is a positive matrix. So it's not a conventional convex optimization problem. And if we relax the constraint $\alpha_i \in \{0,1\}$ to be a linear inequation $\alpha_i \in [0,1]$, then the maximal value is impossible or reaches at boundary. To escape of this dilemma, we propose a approximate method to find a suboptimal solution. Looking back to the formula (5), the first term is a constant and the second term measures the similarity of data pairs in selected dataset Q, the next term measures the similarity of instances in Q with data in X^s and the last term evaluates the entropy. So towards instances in Q, if each of them is much similar with other data in Q and dissimilar with data in X^s simultaneously has a large information entropy then such batch of b instances are good enough to label. Actually, the second term's computation is unbearable because it has to compute $C_b^2 C_{n_t}^b$ of times. So, we can drop this term and consider the third term that means selecting b instances dissimilar with source domain data then we have a larger possibility to make function (5)'s value larger. So each data's *characteristics* in target domain can be reduced to:

$$characteristics(x_i^t) = -\sum_{i=1}^{n_s} k(x_i^s, x_j^t)$$

Actually, without considering the constant term, the definition is equal to:

$$\| \frac{1}{n_s} \sum_{i=1}^{n_s} \phi(x_i^s) - \phi(x_j^t) \|_{\mathcal{H}}^2$$

4.4   Practical Computation

We define each data's score as:

$$\mathcal{S}(x) = \lambda \cdot characteristics(x) + (1 - \lambda)uncertainty(x)$$

Here, we introduce a balanced factor λ which is relational with iterations. As discussed before, *characteristics* measures the ability of capturing specific features for target task and *uncertainty* measures the ability of improving the classifier's performance. At the start of iterations, the key point is adapting the feature extractor—convolutional layers and assures features extracted can be beneficial to target task. But with the progress of iterations, such feature extractor is good enough to extract features for target task. If the selected data is still to change the feature extractor then classifier' performance will be degraded. At this time, *uncertainty* need more attention. Hence, the dynamic trade-off is necessary.

Algorithm: AL_MMD

Input:
X^t: Unlabeled target dataset
$\mathcal{M}_t$: the model in iteration t
$\mathcal{M}_0$: the initial model trained by domain adaptation methods
Initialization:
Use DANN algorithm to get the initial model $\mathcal{M}_0$
While $t < iterations$:
    For each instance in $x \in X^t$
        compute $x's$ transformation after convolutional layers $x = conv(x)$
        compute $characteristics(x) = -\sum_{i=1}^{n_s} k(x_i^s, x)$
        compute $uncertainty(x) = -\sum_{i=1}^{|\mathcal{Y}|} p_i log(p_i)$
        compute $\mathcal{S}(x) = \lambda \cdot characteristics(x) + (1 - \lambda)uncertainty(x)$
    End For
Select top b largest $\mathcal{S}(x)$ in target domain for Q
Query such b instances' labels and remove Q from X^t
Fine-tune the model $\mathcal{M}_t$ with Q
End While

---

5   Experiments and Results

We perform our proposed approach on two popular image datasets comparing with maximum entropy strategy, random sampling strategy. Towards active learning, we know a good initial model $\mathcal{M}_0$ is necessary. Models trained by various UDA algorithms can be qualified for this task. In this paper, we choose DANN [4] to train our initial model. Based on it, we use AL_MMD to select instances with larger *characteristics* and *uncertainty* to fine-tune the initial model. The following are two different datasets and corresponding results.

5.1   Datasets

MNIST and MNIST-M. Our first experiment deals with the MNIST dataset [13] (as source domain). MNIST-M (as target domain) is a dataset that MNIST blends digits with color photos.

Office-31 [17] is a standard dataset for domain adaptation, which consists of 3 domains *Amazon*(A), *Webcam*(W), and *Dslr*(D). Each contains images from amazon.com, or office environment images taken with varying lighting and pose changes using a webcam or a dslr camera, respectively. And it includes 4652 images with 31 classes. In this dataset, we do two transfer experiments *Amazon* → *Dslr* and *Dslr* → *Webcam*.

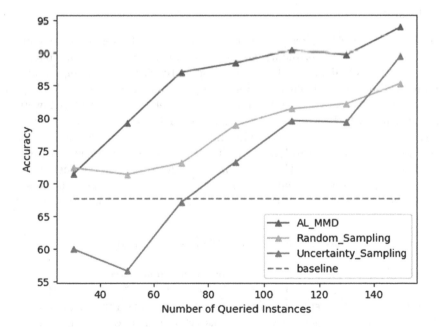

Fig. 1. Dslr → Webcam.

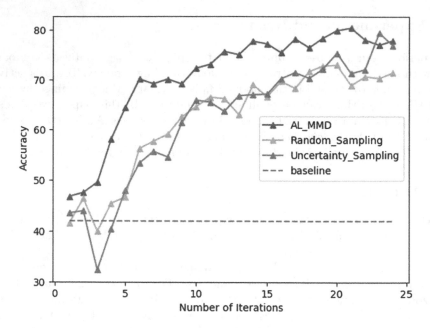

Fig. 2. MNIST → MNIST-M

5.2   Results

In MNIST → MNIST-M transfer experiment, we use LeNet as our backbone.
In Office-31 transfer experiment, we use pre-trained AlexNet as our backbone.
Then we use DANN algorithm to update weights to get initial model. Eventually,
we compare our method with random sampling and entropy-based sampling.
Table 1 and Fig. 1 were the results in MNIST dataset. Table 2 and Fig. 2 were the
results in Office-31. The results show that our methods have achieved superior
performance. From the figure, you will find that at the start of iterations, results
of entropy_sampling and random_sampling are so volatile. On the contrary, our
method is stable comparing these two methods. According to our method' idea,
we aim to learn good representation for target task so that we need less data
to modify the parameters. But towards another two methods, if the learned

Table 1. Accuracy on MNIST → MNIST_M(%)

Methods	Number of queried instances							
	20	50	80	110	140	170	200	230
AL_MMD	**47.600**	**64.400**	**70.100**	**73.066**	**77.714**	**78.177**	**79.920**	77.000
Random_sampling	46.400	46.720	59.120	66.480	68.960	68.320	72.960	70.320
Entropy_sampling	44.000	48.000	54.640	65.520	67.043	71.440	75.360	**79.440**

Table 2. Accuracy on Dslr $\rightarrow$ Webcam(%)

Methods	Number of queried instances						
	30	50	70	90	110	130	150
AL_MMD	71.446	**79.245**	**87.044**	**88.0427**	**90.440**	**89.685**	**93.962**
Random_sampling	**72.410**	71.404	73.123	78.867	81.425	82.180	85.283
Entropy_sampling	60.025	56.654	67.169	73.283	79.597	79.371	89.590

representations are not proper, the classifier needs more data to modify and the corresponding curve are much more volatile.

6   Conclusion and Future Work

In this paper, we design an active sampling strategy based on MMD to select valuable data in transfer learning process. We propose a new criterion *characteristics* to select data that can capture target-specific feature well. And the aforementioned experiments have shown our method's efficacy. Through this method, we can find MMD is a powerful tool. In the feature work, We can also filter the data in source domain similar to target domain at the beginning. It can effectively resist the impact of noisy data. What's more, we hope to seek for an efficient and scalable algorithm to extend our method to larger datasets.

Acknowledgements. This research was supported by Natural Science Foundation of China (Grant no. 61572252, 61672284). Meanwhile, this research work was supported by Zayed University Research Cluster Award \# R18038.

References

1. Chattopadhyay, R., Fan, W., Davidson, I., Panchanathan, S., Ye, J.: Joint transfer and batch-mode active learning. In: Proceedings of the 30th International Conference on Machine Learning, ICML 2013, 16–21 June 2013, Atlanta, GA, USA, pp. 253–261 (2013). http://jmlr.org/proceedings/papers/v28/chattopadhyay13.html
2. Chattopadhyay, R., Wang, Z., Fan, W., Davidson, I., Panchanathan, S., Ye, J.: Batch mode active sampling based on marginal probability distribution matching. TKDD **7**(3), 13:1–13:25 (2013). https://doi.org/10.1145/2513092.2513094
3. Gal, Y., Islam, R., Ghahramani, Z.: Deep Bayesian active learning with image data. In: Proceedings of the 34th International Conference on Machine Learning, ICML 2017, 6–11 August 2017, Sydney, NSW, Australia, pp. 1183–1192 (2017). http://proceedings.mlr.press/v70/gal17a.html
4. Ganin, Y., et al.: Domain-adversarial training of neural networks. J. Mach. Learn. Res. **17**(1), 2096–2030 (2016)
5. Ghifary, M., Kleijn, W.B., Zhang, M., Balduzzi, D., Li, W.: Deep reconstruction-classification networks for unsupervised domain adaptation. In: Leibe, B., Matas, J., Sebe, N., Welling, M. (eds.) ECCV 2016. LNCS, vol. 9908, pp. 597–613. Springer, Cham (2016). https://doi.org/10.1007/978-3-319-46493-0_36

6. Gretton, A., Borgwardt, K.M., Rasch, M.J., Schölkopf, B., Smola, A.J.: A kernel two-sample test. J. Mach. Learn. Res. **13**, 723–773 (2012). http://dl.acm.org/citation.cfm?id=2188410

7. He, K., Zhang, X., Ren, S., Sun, J.: Deep residual learning for image recognition. In: 2016 IEEE Conference on Computer Vision and Pattern Recognition, CVPR 2016, 27–30 June 2016, Las Vegas, NV, USA, pp. 770–778 (2016). https://doi.org/10.1109/CVPR.2016.90

8. Hoffman, J., et al.: CyCADA: cycle-consistent adversarial domain adaptation. In: Proceedings of the 35th International Conference on Machine Learning, ICML 2018, 10–15 July 2018, Stockholmsmässan, Stockholm, Sweden, pp. 1994–2003 (2018). http://proceedings.mlr.press/v80/hoffman18a.html

9. Huang, J., Smola, A.J., Gretton, A., Borgwardt, K.M., Schölkopf, B.: Correcting sample selection bias by unlabeled data. In: Advances in Neural Information Processing Systems 19, Proceedings of the Twentieth Annual Conference on Neural Information Processing Systems, 4–7 December 2006, Vancouver, British Columbia, Canada, pp. 601–608 (2006). http://papers.nips.cc/paper/3075-correcting-sample-selection-bias-by-unlabeled-data

10. Huang, S., Jin, R., Zhou, Z.: Active learning by querying informative and representative examples. IEEE Trans. Pattern Anal. Mach. Intell. **36**(10), 1936–1949 (2014). https://doi.org/10.1109/TPAMI.2014.2307881

11. Huang, S., Zhao, J., Liu, Z.: Cost-effective training of deep CNNs with active model adaptation. In: Proceedings of the 24th ACM SIGKDD International Conference on Knowledge Discovery & Data Mining, KDD 2018, 19–23 August 2018, London, UK, pp. 1580–1588 (2018). https://doi.org/10.1145/3219819.3220026

12. Krizhevsky, A., Sutskever, I., Hinton, G.E.: Imagenet classification with deep convolutional neural networks. Commun. ACM **60**(6), 84–90 (2017). https://doi.org/10.1145/3065386

13. LeCun, Y., Bottou, L., Bengio, Y., Haffner, P., et al.: Gradient-based learning applied to document recognition. Proc. IEEE **86**(11), 2278–2324 (1998)

14. Long, M., Cao, Y., Wang, J., Jordan, M.I.: Learning transferable features with deep adaptation networks. In: Proceedings of the 32nd International Conference on Machine Learning, ICML 2015, 6–11 July 2015, Lille, France, pp. 97–105 (2015). http://jmlr.org/proceedings/papers/v37/long15.html

15. Long, M., Zhu, H., Wang, J., Jordan, M.I.: Deep transfer learning with joint adaptation networks. In: Proceedings of the 34th International Conference on Machine Learning, ICML 2017, 6–11 August 2017, Sydney, NSW, Australia, pp. 2208–2217 (2017). http://proceedings.mlr.press/v70/long17a.html

16. Pan, S.J., Yang, Q.: A survey on transfer learning. IEEE Trans. Knowl. Data Eng. **22**(10), 1345–1359 (2010). https://doi.org/10.1109/TKDE.2009.191

17. Saenko, K., Kulis, B., Fritz, M., Darrell, T.: Adapting visual category models to new domains. In: Daniilidis, K., Maragos, P., Paragios, N. (eds.) ECCV 2010. LNCS, vol. 6314, pp. 213–226. Springer, Heidelberg (2010). https://doi.org/10.1007/978-3-642-15561-1_16

18. Saito, K., Watanabe, K., Ushiku, Y., Harada, T.: Maximum classifier discrepancy for unsupervised domain adaptation. In: 2018 IEEE Conference on Computer Vision and Pattern Recognition, CVPR 2018, 18–22 June 2018, Salt Lake City, UT, USA, pp. 3723–3732 (2018). https://doi.org/10.1109/CVPR.2018.00392, http://openaccess.thecvf.com/content_cvpr_2018/html/Saito_Maximum_Classifier_Discrepancy_CVPR_2018_paper.html

19. Settles, B.: Active Learning. Synthesis Lectures on Artificial Intelligence and Machine Learning. Morgan & Claypool Publishers (2012). https://doi.org/10. 2200/S00429ED1V01Y201207AIM018
20. Shu, Y., Cao, Z., Long, M., Wang, J.: Transferable curriculum for weakly-supervised domain adaptation (2019)
21. Szegedy, C., et al.: Going deeper with convolutions. CoRR abs/1409.4842 (2014). http://arxiv.org/abs/1409.4842
22. Tzeng, E., Hoffman, J., Saenko, K., Darrell, T.: Adversarial discriminative domain adaptation. In: 2017 IEEE Conference on Computer Vision and Pattern Recognition, CVPR 2017, 21–26 July 2017, Honolulu, HI, USA, pp. 2962–2971 (2017). https://doi.org/10.1109/CVPR.2017.316
23. Tzeng, E., Hoffman, J., Zhang, N., Saenko, K., Darrell, T.: Deep domain confusion: Maximizing for domain invariance. CoRR abs/1412.3474 (2014). http://arxiv.org/abs/1412.3474
24. Wang, K., Zhang, D., Li, Y., Zhang, R., Lin, L.: Cost-effective active learning for deep image classification. IEEE Trans. Circuits Syst. Video Techn. 27(12), 2591–2600 (2017). https://doi.org/10.1109/TCSVT.2016.2589879

Optimal Dwell Time for Frequency Hopping in a Stackelberg Game with a Smart Jammer

Long Yu[✉], Yonggang Zhu, and Yusheng Li

Sixty-third Research Institute, National University of Defense Technology,
Nanjing 210007, China
elong025@163.com

Abstract. Frequency hopping (FH) technique is usually used to anti-jamming communication. Frequency dwell time is an important parameter for FH communication. Short dwell time will reduce the communication efficiency due to frequency switching time, while long dwell time will increase the time to be jammed after the sensing of a smart jammer. The dwell time of the cognitive user and the sensing time of the jammer are interactive. We formulate the interactions between the user and the jammer as a Stackelberg game. The jammer first senses the user's operating frequency and then jams the user based on the sensing result. The user determines its dwell time according to the reward under the jamming. A tiered reinforcement learning algorithm is proposed to solve the game. The optimal dwell time of the user is given when the Stackelberg Equilibrium is achieved.

Keywords: Frequency hopping · Anti-jamming · Dwell time ·
Stackelberg game · Tiered reinforcement learning algorithm

1 Introduction

Wireless networks are suffering more and more security threats [1, 2]. Jamming attack is one of the vital threats where the jammer jams the communication process of the users by radiating high power signal. To cope with the jamming attack, various techniques have been proposed. Frequency hopping [3, 4] is one of the efficient anti-jamming techniques where the user's operating frequency hops from one to another with time slots. High-dimensional modulation [5–7], message driven methods [8, 9], M-ary orthogonal Walsh sequence keying modulation [10], families of sequences with good correlations [11], applied in the frequency hopping technique, have been researched in the previous works. However, these works have not considered the presence of the smart jammer with cognitive and reconfigurable abilities. In this paper, we focus on the anti-jamming strategy of FH system to cope with a smart jammer.

In [12, 13], a Stackelberg game was formulated, in which the players are a cognitive user and a smart jammer. Further, to solve the incomplete information problem in the game, an anti-jamming Bayesian Stackelberg game was proposed [14]. The optimal strategies based on duality optimization theory were derived. However, those works all based on the assumption that the jammer senses the user's power correctly. In practice

X. B. Zhai et al. (Eds.): MLICOM 2019, LNICST 294, pp. 410–418, 2019.
https://doi.org/10.1007/978-3-030-32388-2_35

scenario, the sensing results may be error, and the sensing performance is relevant with the sensing time, signal power, etc.

In this paper, we expect to get the optimal frequency dwell time of FH with consideration of the detection performance of a smart jammer. Frequency dwell time is an important parameter for FH communication. Short dwell time will reduce the communication efficiency due to the frequency switching time, while long dwell time will increase the time to be jammed after the sensing of the smart jammer. Sensing time is also a key parameter for the jammer. Short sensing time will decrease the sensing performance while long sensing time will shorten the jamming time. It is obvious that the dwell time of the user and the sensing time of the jammer are interactive. In this paper, we formulate the interaction as a Stackelberg game. The jammer first senses the user's operating frequency and then jams the user based on the sensing result. The user determines its dwell time according to the reward under the jamming. A tiered reinforcement learning algorithm is proposed to solve the game. The optimal dwell time of the user is obtained when the Stackelberg Equilibrium is achieved.

2 System Model

It consists of a user (a transmitter-receiver pair) and a jammer in the system. Both of the user and the jammer are equipped with a single radio and work with time slotted. The slot structure of the user and the jammer are shown in Fig. 1. The parameters for the user and the jammer are assumed to remain unchanged during a time slot.

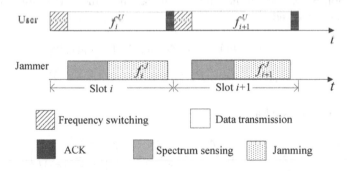

Fig. 1. Transmission structure of the user and the jammer.

The user hops from one frequency to another along with time slot to avoid jamming. The user's frequency f^U is selected from a frequency set $\mathcal{F}$ with $|\mathcal{F}| = M$. Denote Γ as the dwell time, which is the duration between two adjacent frequency switching points. Since transmission cannot be started immediately due to the settling time of radio frequency devices after tuning the frequency of the transceivers, a fixed frequency switching time t_c is considered in each time slot.

The jammer starts to transmit jamming signals after sensing at each time slot. This type of jammer is referred to as reactive jammer [2]. Since the user works with frequency hopping mode, the jammer's sensing objective is to detect which frequency the user operates on. The sensing time of the jammer is denoted as τ. Based on the sensing result the reactive jammer obtains the user's operating frequency estimation f^J. Then, the reactive jammer will jam the frequency f^J.

3 Problem Formulation

After sensing, the jammer gets results. One result is that the jammer correctly detects the user's frequency, that is, $f^J = f^U$. The user will be jammed after the jammer sensing. The immediate payoff u_0 of the user in this case is defined as:

$$u_0 = \frac{1}{\Gamma}[\tau C_0 + (\Gamma - t_c - \tau)C_1], \tag{1}$$

where C_0 and C_1 represent the channel capability without and with jamming, respectively. The other result is that the jammer detects the user's frequency incorrectly, that is, $f^J \neq f^U$. The user will not be jammed during the slot in this case. The immediate payoff u_1 of the user in this case is defined as:

$$u_1 = \frac{1}{\Gamma}[(\Gamma - t_c)C_0]. \tag{2}$$

Based on the two results the user gets an expected payoff. Define $P_d(\tau)$ as the correct detection probability of the jammer with sensing time τ. The utility function of the user can be expressed as:

$$u(\Gamma, \tau) = P_d(\tau)u_0 + (1 - P_d(\tau))u_1$$
$$= \frac{1}{\Gamma}((\Gamma - t_c)C_0 - P_d(\tau)(\Gamma - t_c - \tau)(C_0 - C_1)) \tag{3}$$

$P_d(\tau)$ can be expressed as:

$$P_d(\tau) = \sum_{m=0}^{M-1}(-1)^m \binom{M-1}{m}\frac{1}{m+1}\exp\left(\frac{-m}{2(m+1)}\frac{gP\tau}{\sigma^2 M}\right), \tag{4}$$

where P is the user's transmission power, g is the channel gain between the user and the jammer, and σ^2 is the noise power.

The user expects to maximize the utility. The optimization problem for the user can be expressed as:

$$\max_{\Gamma} u(\Gamma, \tau). \tag{5}$$

Opposite to the user, the jammer expects to decrease the user's payoff. The instant return of the jammer in the jth time slot is expressed as:

$$v(j) = \frac{1}{T}[(\beta(t_d + \tau) + (1 - \beta)(T - t_c))]C_0, \tag{6}$$

where β is the indication function. $\beta = 1$ represents that the jamming is successful, and $\beta = 0$ represents that the jamming is failed. The utility of the jammer is defined as:

$$v_J(\Gamma, \tau) = I - u(\Gamma, \tau), \tag{7}$$

where I is a constant value to grantee v positive. From the perspective of the user, the optimization problem can be expressed as:

$$\max_{\tau} v_J(\Gamma, \tau). \tag{8}$$

It can be seen that the optimization problems of the user and the jammer are mutually influential. Hence, the problem can be formulated as a game. Since the scenario is that jammer adjusts its own strategy after sensing the user, a Stackelberg game can be used. The user is set as leader and the jammer is set as follower. Mathematically, the Stackelberg game is expressed as $\mathcal{G} = \{\mathcal{N}, \mathcal{T}, \mathcal{S}, u, v\}$, where $\mathcal{N}$ denotes the player set including the user and the jammer, $\mathcal{T}$ and $\mathcal{S}$ represent the strategy space of the user and the jammer, respectively. In the game, the user selects the dwell time Γ from a discrete strategy space $\mathcal{T}$ in each time slot, where $\mathcal{T} \triangleq \{T_1, T_2, \ldots, T_W\}$, and T_i is the ith optional action in the space $\mathcal{T}$. The jammer selects its sensing time τ from its strategy space $\mathcal{S}$, where $\mathcal{S} \triangleq \{S_1, S_2, \ldots, S_L\}$, and S_i is the ith optional action in the space $\mathcal{S}$.

4 Tiered Reinforcement Learning Algorithm

In the game, since there is no information interaction between the user and the jammer, the two parties can only choose to optimize their own strategies based on the observation on the other's strategy. Because the two strategies are mutually influential, it is very suitable to solve the game using a tiered reinforcement learning algorithm.

The algorithm is performed with two layers, the upper layer and the lower layer. The upper layer subject is the user, and the lower layer subject is the jammer. First, the user selects an action. The jammer learns the optimal response policy under this action. Then, the user calculates the reward under the policy selected by the jammer and updates its own action accordingly. Again, the jammer learns and loops until both the user and the jammer learn the optimal response policy.

The user and jammer updates their policies with different time scales. The frame structure of the tiered reinforcement learning algorithm is shown in Fig. 2. The user updates the policy each epoch, and the jammer updates its policy in each time slot. $R(k)$ represents the number of time slots in the kth epoch. Since the epoch duration is greater than the slot duration, the user has plenty of time to coordinate the receiver and transmitter when the dwell time is changed.

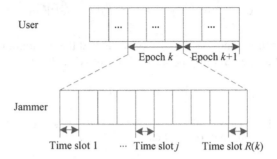

Fig. 2. The frame structure of the tiered reinforcement learning algorithm

In the tiered reinforcement learning procedure, both the user and the jammer expect an optimal long-term return, called an average cumulative reward. In the lower layer, the average cumulative reward vector of the jammer $\mathbf{Q}^J = (Q_1^J, Q_2^J, \ldots, Q_L^J)$, where Q_i^J is the average cumulative reward with the action S_i. When the jammer selects the action S_i, its average cumulative reward is updated as follows:

$$Q_i^J(j+1) = Q_i^J(j) + \frac{1}{\eta_i(j)}\left(v(j) - Q_i^J(j)\right), \qquad (9)$$

where $\eta_i(j)$ is the times that the action S_i is selected within j time slot, and $v(j)$ is the instant return of the jammer in the jth time slot.

The jammer selects its action according to the following rules:

$$\tau(j) = \begin{cases} \text{selected from } S \text{ randomly with uniform distribution,} & \text{with probability } \delta_J(j), \\ \arg\max_i Q_i^J(j), & \text{with probability } 1 - \delta_J(j). \end{cases}$$

$$(10)$$

where $\tau(j)$ is the action selected by the jammer during the jth time slot, and $\delta_J(j)$ is the temperature coefficient of the jammer during the jth slot. $\delta_J(j)$ is used to control the tradeoff between exploration and exploitation in the learning process.

In the upper layer, the average cumulative reward vector of the user is defined as $\mathbf{Q}^u$, where $\mathbf{Q}^u = (Q_1^u, Q_2^u, \ldots, Q_W^u)$. Q_i^u is the average cumulative reward with the action T_i. When the user selects the action T_i, its average cumulative reward is updated as:

$$Q_i^u(k+1) = Q_i^u(k) + \frac{1}{\kappa_i(k)}\left(\hat{u}_i(k) - Q_i^u(k)\right), \qquad (11)$$

where $\kappa_i(k)$ is the times that the action T_i is selected within k epochs, and $\hat{u}_i(k) = \sum_{j=1}^{R(k)} u(j)/R(k)$, represents the average reward of the user in the kth epoch with the strategy T_i.

The user's action is updated according to:

$$\Gamma(k) = \begin{cases} \text{selected from } T \text{ randomly with uniform distribution,} & \text{with probability } \delta_u(k), \\ \arg\max_i Q_i^u(k), & \text{with probability } 1 - \delta_u(k). \end{cases}$$

(12)

where $\Gamma(k)$ is the action selected by the user during the kth epoch, and $\delta_u(k)$ is the temperature coefficient of the user during the kth epoch.

The specific flow of the algorithm is shown in Algorithm 1.

Step 1: Initialization. Set $k=1$, $j=1$. Initialize the average cumulative reward vector $\mathbf{Q}^u$ and $\mathbf{Q}^J$.

Step 2: In the kth epoch, the user selects an action from the strategy set according to Equation (12).

Step 3: The learning process of the jammer.

 (1) In time slot j, the jammer selects its action from the strategy space according to Equation (10).

 (2) The jammer measures its instant return using Equation (6).

 (3) The jammer updates $\mathbf{Q}^J$ according to Equation (7).

 (4) Update $j = j+1$, go to (1), until $j = R(k)$.

Step 4: The user measures its average reward $\hat{u}(k)$ in the learning process of the jammer.

Step 5: The user updates $\mathbf{Q}^u$ according to (11).

Step 6: Update $k = k+1$. Set $j=1$. Go to Step 2, and until the stopping criterion holds.

---

5 Numerical Results

In this section, simulation results are presented. The strategy space of the user is set as $\{\frac{1}{1500}, \frac{1}{500}, \frac{1}{200}, \frac{1}{10}\}$, while the strategy space of the jammer is set as $\{m/1000, m = 1, 2, \ldots, 9\}$. Each epoch contains 1000 time slots. The channel gain between the user and the jammer is 10^{-3}. The frequency switching time t_c is set as 50 μs. The temperature coefficient of the user and the jammer are given as $0.5/1.01^k$ and $0.5/1.001^j$, respectively.

The convergence behavior of the user is given in Fig. 3. After learning, the selection probability of the user converges to a stationary mixed strategy. The convergence behavior of the jammer is given in Fig. 4 where the user's dwell time is 1/1500 s. It is seen that the selection probability of the jammer also converges to a stationary mixed strategy.

Figure 5 shows the optimal average cumulative reward of the user under different transmission power. It can be found that as the number of epoch increases, the average cumulative reward of the user at different transmission power converges to a steady value. When the user power is 0.01 W, the average cumulative reward of the user hardly changes as the number of epoch increases. This is because when the user's power is very low, the detection probability of the jammer is almost zero. At this time, the average utility of the user is almost independent of the jammer's sensing time, but only related to the user's dwell time. Since the user's frequency switching time is almost negligible compared to the user's dwell time, no matter which action is selected by the user, the utility is almost the same. When the user power is 10 W, the steady-state value of the user's average cumulative reward is reduced compared to that when the user power is 0.1 W and 1 W. This is because as the power of the user increases, the detection probability of the jammer increases, and the optimal sensing time decreases. This increases the jamming duration, which makes the user's average accumulative reward reduced. Therefore, in the presence of a smart jammer, an increase in user's power does not necessarily increase the user's utility, but may reduce it.

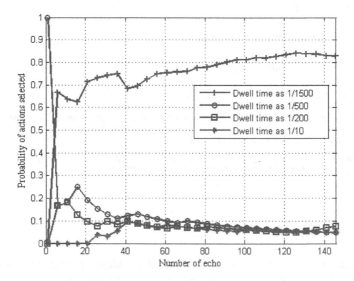

Fig. 3. The convergence behavior of the user.

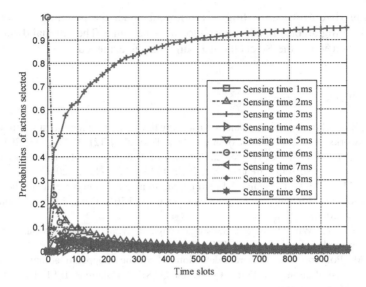

Fig. 4. The convergence behavior of the jammer.

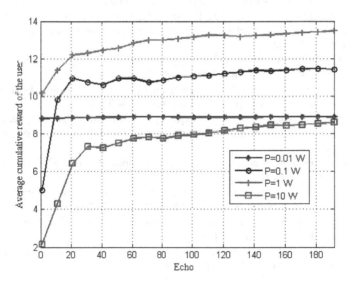

Fig. 5. Convergence process of the user's average cumulative reward under different transmission power.

6 Conclusions

In this paper, the interaction between the dwell time of the user and the sensing time of the jammer is formulated as a Stackelberg game. The jammer first senses the user's operating frequency and then jams the user based on the sensing result. The user determines its dwell time according to the reward under the jamming. A tiered reinforcement learning algorithm is proposed to solve the game. The optimal dwell time of the user is given when the Stackelberg Equilibrium is achieved.

References

1. Sharma, R.K., Rawat, D.B.: Advances on security threats and countermeasures for cognitive radio networks: a survey. IEEE Commun. Surv. Tutorials **17**(2), 1023–1043 (2015)
2. Zou, Y., Zhu, J., Wang, X., Hanzo, L.: A survey on wireless security: technical challenges, recent advances, and future trends. Proc. IEEE **104**(9), 1727–1765 (2016)
3. Hanawal, M.K., Abdel-Rahman, M.J., Krunz, M.: Joint adaptation of frequency hopping and transmission rate for anti-jamming wireless systems. IEEE Trans. Mob. Comput. **15**(9), 2247–2259 (2016)
4. Yu, L., Xu, Y., Wu, Q., et al.: Self-organizing hit avoidance in distributed frequency hopping multiple access networks. IEEE Access **5**, 26614–26622 (2017)
5. Simon, M., Polydoros, A.: Coherent detection of frequency-hopped quadrature modulations in the presence of jamming—Part I: QPSK and QASK modulations. IEEE Trans. Commun. **29**(11), 1644–1660 (1981)
6. Choi, K., Cheun, K.: Maximum throughput of FHSS multiple-access networks using MFSK modulation. IEEE Trans. Commun. **52**(3), 426–434 (2004)
7. Peng, K.-C., Huang, C.-H., Li, C.-J., Horng, T.-S.: High-performance frequency-hopping transmitters using two-point delta-sigma modulation. IEEE Trans. Microw. Theory Techn. **52**(11), 2529–2535 (2004)
8. Ling, Q., Li, T.: Message-driven frequency hopping: design and analysis. IEEE Trans. Wirel. Commun. **8**(4), 1773–1782 (2009)
9. Zhang, L., Wang, H., Li, T.: Anti-jamming message-driven frequency hopping—Part I: system design. IEEE Trans. Wirel. Commun. **12**(1), 70–79 (2013)
10. Cho, J., Kim, Y., Cheun, K.: A novel frequency-hopping spread spectrum multiple-access network using M-ary orthogonal Walsh sequence keying. IEEE Trans. Commun. **51**(11), 1885–1896 (2003)
11. Bao, J., Ji, L.: Frequency hopping sequences with optimal partial Hamming correlation. IEEE Trans. Inf. Theory **62**(6), 3768–3783 (2016)
12. Yang, D., et al.: Coping with a smart jammer in wireless networks: a Stackelberg game approach. IEEE Trans. Wirele. Commun. **12**(8), 4038–4047 (2013)
13. Xiao, L., et al.: Anti-jamming transmission stackelberg game with observation errors. IEEE Commun. Lett. **19**(6), 949–952 (2015)
14. Jia, L., et al.: Bayesian Stackelberg game for anti-jamming with incomplete information. IEEE Commun. Lett. **20**(10), 1991–1994 (2016)

An Active Noise Correction Graph Embedding Method Based on Active Learning for Graph Noisy Data

Zhiyuan Cui[1,2], Donghai Guan[1,2(✉)], Cong Li[1,2], Weiwei Guan[1,2],
and Asad Masood Khattak[3]

[1] College of Computer Science and Technology,
Nanjing University of Aeronautics and Astronautics, Nanjing, China
565508802@qq.com, {dhguan,yuanweiwei}@nuaa.edu.cn, 18851870127@163.com
[2] Collaborative Innovation Center of Novel Software Technology and
Industrialization, Nanjing 210016, China
[3] College of Technological Innovation, Zayed University,
Dubai, United Arab Emirates
Asad.Khattak@zu.ac.ae

Abstract. In various scenarios of the real world, there are various graph data. Most graph structures are confronted with the problems of complex structure and large consumption of memory space. Graph embedding is an effective method to overcome such challenges, which converts graph structure into a low-dimensional dense vector space. In the real world, label acquisition is expensive, and there may be noise in the data. Therefore, it is important to find valuable noise nodes as much as possible to improve the performance of downstream task. In this paper, we propose a novel active sampling strategy for graph noisy data named Active Noise Correction Graph Embedding method (ANCGE). Given the label budget, the proposed method aims to use semi-supervised graph embedding algorithm to find valuable mislabeled nodes. ANCGE measures the value of noise nodes according to their representativeness and influence on the graph. The experimental results on three open datasets demonstrate the effectiveness of our method and its stability under different noise rates.

Keywords: Graph embedding · Noisy label · Active correction · Active learning

1   Introduction

In various scenarios of the real world, there are various network structures that represent the relationship between objects. For example, social graphs in social media networks, citation maps in research fields [3]. In computer science, the network structure is represented as a graph structure containing nodes and edges. However, most graph structures have the characteristics of huge structure and large space overhead, so the computational task is very heavy.

X. B. Zhai et al. (Eds.): MLICOM 2019, LNICST 294, pp. 419–433, 2019.
https://doi.org/10.1007/978-3-030-32388-2_36

Graph embedding is an effective method to solve this problem. Graph embedding transforms graph structure information into low-dimensional dense real vector and maps it to a low-dimensional latent space. Moreover, graph embedding can maximumly preserve the structure information and attributes of the graph, which be used for input of existing machine learning algorithms. Through graph embedding, various applications such as node classification, node recommendation, and link prediction can be performed on the graph [2].

According to whether the graph nodes used for training include labels and whether they are completely included, the graph embedding algorithm can be divided into three categories: unsupervised, semi-supervised and supervised. In the real world, the acquisition of labels is expensive, and it is generally difficult to obtain labels for all nodes in the graph structure. In order to make use of the information of the node label without too much cost, a small number of node labels will be acquired in practice. Therefore, for a scenario where such a small number of nodes have labels and most of the nodes are unlabeled, a semi-supervised graph embedding algorithm [9,21] can be employed.

But in real-world scenarios, the label data in the graph structure is not always correct. There may be a certain amount of noise in the labeled graph data. Using these noisy node labels for training can affect the performance of graph embedding and classifiers, which in turn reduces the accuracy of node classification. Therefore, it is very important to solve the classifier degradation under noisy scenes in the node label [11]. However, using domain experts to modify all noise labels is not only time-consuming, but also economically expensive. Therefore, given the label budget, it is very important to select the nodes that need expert marking in the labeled nodes to maximally find the noise nodes that have the greatest impact on the graph structure and improve the performance of the node classification. Active learning [15] can solve this problem very well.

In this paper, we propose an active corrective graph embedding method (ANCGE) based on active learning for graph noisy data. Given the label budget, we use semi-supervised graph embedding algorithm to find more noise in labeled nodes by active learning. And when the active corrective graph embedding method chooses the noise nodes which need to be corrected, the noise nodes which have large amount of representativeness and great influence on the graph are selected as far as possible by considering the structure of the graph.

The specific details of our method are as follows: Firstly, the semi-supervised graph embedding algorithm GCN [9] is used to train and generate graph embedding from noisy labeled graph data. Secondly, graph embedding is used to detect noise in graph data, and the noise probability scores of all nodes in graph data are calculated. Given the label budget, the node most likely to be labeled incorrectly is selected. Thirdly, by calculating the graph centrality score [1] in the representative query criteria of active learning, we can find out the nodes with the greatest amount of information from the selected nodes with high probability of noise, and then give these nodes to the domain experts for correction. Finally, the active corrected nodes are added to the labeled node set, and then the training set is updated. The updated data is used to retrain the graph embedding, and then the node classifier is trained.

The above is a complete label correction and classifier training process, and then we iteratively proceed with the above steps. As the process progresses, graph embed-ding will produce more and more accurate node embedding, which will provide more information for the training of labeled nodes, and the performance of classifier will be improved very well.

The contributions of this paper are summarized as below:

- We propose an active corrective graph embedding method on graph noise data, which can effectively find and correct the noise in graph data, and then optimize the performance of graph embedding.
- We combine the noisy possibility with the graph centrality to find out the nodes which are not only noisy but also have great influence on the graph structure. In the case of a small number of label requests, the performance of the classifier can be improved as much as possible.

The rest of this paper is organized in the following way. Section 2 reviews the literature related to graph embedding, noise data learning and active learning. In Sect. 3, we describe the framework of the proposed active noise correction graph embedding algorithm, as well as the noise detection correction graph embedding algorithm (NDCGE) and active learning correction graph embedding algorithm (ALCGE). In Sect. 4, the experimental results are analyzed. Finally, we summarize the paper in Sect. 5.

2   Related Work

2.1   Graph Embedding

Graph embedding converts the graph data into a low dimensional space in which the graph structural information and graph properties are preserved.

Matrix factorization is an early algorithm for graph embedding. It based graph embedding represent graph property in the form of a matrix and factorize this matrix to obtain node embedding. There are several common algorithms of matrix factorization based graph embedding, such as LLE, Laplacian Eigenmaps and GraRep [5, 19].

After that, embedding techniques using random walks on graphs to obtain node embeddings have been proposed: DeepWalk [13] and node2vec [6] are two examples. Deepwalk is an online graph embedding algorithm based on local information of nodes. Given a network, it first generates random walks to get the sequence of nodes. DeepWalk regards each node as a word and the sequence of nodes as a sentence, and then uses Skip-Gram [10], a typical training word vector model, to train the embedding of nodes. Node2vec model is an extension of DeepWalk. By improving the random walk strategy of DeepWalk model, node2vec can generate higher quality sequence of nodes.

In addition, LINE [17] is also a network representation learning model for large-scale networks. LINE defines the first-order proximity and the second-order proximity between nodes in social networks. SDNE [20] introduces typical deep neural networks into graph embedding for the first time. It jointly optimizes the first-order proximity and second-order proximity, which solves the challenge of high nonlinearity.

But this method can be computationally expensive for large sparse graphs. Graph Convolutional Network (GCN) solves this problem by defining a convolution operator on graph. It is an extensible semi-supervised learning method based on graph structured data. And it has good classifier performance in node classification and other applications. So in this paper, we use GCN as a graph embedding framework.

2.2 Noisy Data Learning

In the real world, the acquired data will inevitably be affected by noise. There are many methods to deal with noise in the existing literature.

In the past, when researchers dealt with noise, one was to label an example with multiple non-expert labels. The EM algorithm of Dempster et al. [4] is a popular procedure for finding maximum likelihood estimates of parameters where the model depends on unobserved latent variables. EM algorithm is shown to provide a slow but sure way of obtaining maximum likelihood estimates of the parameters of interest. In another study in the field of natural language processing, Snow et al. [16] concluded that multiple inexpensive tags might be preferable to an expert.

In addition, in the literature [8,18], the method uses classifier prediction to detect noise. It trains the classifier with labeled noise data, and then deletes instances of error classification. However, this method deletes a large number of instances, which will reduce a lot of training data and degrade the performance of the classifier. How-ever, the above methods can't effectively find noise nodes in noisy graph data and make use of noise label.

Therefore, in our method, we can iteratively find the noise nodes from the graph data, and then correct the noise data. And we can train the classifier from the corrected data to improve the performance of the classifier.

2.3 Active Learning

Given the label budget, active learning can find those nodes with large amount of information to be corrected by experts, and then improve the performance of the classifier. According to the query strategy, active learning algorithms can be divided into three categories: the heterogeneity based, the performance based and the representativeness based [15].

There are three sub-categories of active learning based on heterogeneity. Uncertainty Sampling is probably the simplest and most commonly used query framework. In this framework, an active learner queries the instances about which it is least certain how to label. Another, more theoretically-motivated query selection framework is query-by-committee (QBC) algorithm. Each committee member needs to vote on the label being queried and then use the instance they most disagree as the most informative query. The last method is Expected Model Change. Its main idea is to label the most different instances from the current known models. If we know the label of the current model, it will bring the greatest change to the current model.

Performance-based active learning method includes two sub- categories. One method is expected error reduction and it uses the remaining unlabeled instances to estimate the expected future error of the model, and uses the smallest expected future error to query the instances. The other method is variance reduction and this method indirectly reduces generalization error by minimizing output variance.

The Representative-Based active learning method [7] can select representative unlabeled instances to query their labels. It can explore unknown areas of data and then avoid non-representativeness of query labels. So in our method, we use the representative query strategy to select nodes with large amount of information. And we evaluate the representativeness by calculating the center score of PageRank centrality [14] for each node.

3 Proposed Approach

In the first two sections of this chapter, we first propose two label correction algorithms: noise detection correction graph embedding algorithm and active learning correction graph embedding algorithm. In the third section, we integrate the two algorithms and propose an active noise correction graph embedding algorithm based on active learning. Next, we will introduce the details of three noise label correction algorithms.

3.1 Noise Detection Correction Graph Embedding Algorithm

Algorithm 1 gives the relevant input and specific flow of the noise detection correction graph embedding algorithm. The algorithm can effectively detect the noise nodes in the labeled graph data, and iteratively correct the most likely noise nodes. The performance of the classifier can be greatly improved by using the updated label set to relearn the classifier.

The details of the algorithm are as follows: Firstly, we input graph embedding $X = \{X_1, X_2, \ldots, X_n\}$ of noisy labeled graph data generated by GCN algorithm and label correction budget B given by the algorithm. The first step is to train a classifier based on graph embedding X. Then set up a node set C to store corrective labels.

For a graph dataset with k categories of labels, the conditional probabilities of each label are $P_1(y|x), P_2(y|x), \cdots, P_k(y|x)$. Conditional probability $P(y|x)$ is the probability that the label of a node is y when the graph embedding is X. For the calculation of conditional probability $P(y|x)$, we adopt one-against-one SVM multi-classification method.

So in the noise correction algorithm, the third step is to find the corresponding label y in the label matrix Y. By calculating the conditional probability

---

Algorithm 1. Noise Detection Correction Graph Embedding(NDCGE)

Input: Graph embedding X, label budget B

Output: Updated labeled set L and retrained classifier

1. Train a base-classifier on X
2. Set of nodes with corrective labels $C = \{\}$
3. Compute the possibility of Label y, $P(y|x)$
4. Compute node noise probability $1 - P(y|x)$
5. Generate an ordered set M of potentially mislabeled nodes, and $M \bigcap C = \{\}$
6. Generate M_n, the top n nodes from M for label correction
7. Generate the labels $y = \{y_1, y_2, \ldots, y_n\}$, and update Y
8. $C = C \cup M_n$
9. Retrain the classifier
10. While $M \neq \{\}$ and the number of C is less than B : Repeat steps 3–9

---

of the label y under embedding X_i generated by GCN algorithm, we can get the possibility that the label of the node v_i is y. We can calculate the noise probability of the node by formula $1 - P(y|x)$.

Then the fifth step is to generate a node set M sorted according to the noise possibility, and ensure that the intersection of M and C is empty. Then we select M_n, the top n nodes about the noise possibility from M for label correction. The seventh step of the algorithm is to generate the updated label set $y = \{y_1, y_2, \cdots, y_n\}$, and then update the label matrix Y of the label graph node set G_L. Next, update the node set C that used to store the corrective label and add M_n to C. Finally, retrain the classifier about graph embedding. When node set M is not empty or the number of node set C is less than label budget B, repeat steps 3–9 and iterate the algorithm until it stops.

Given the label budget, the noise detection correction algorithm can iteratively and effectively correct the noise in the graph data, and relearn the classifier according to the updated label to improve the performance of the classifier. However, the algorithm only considers the influence of noise nodes in the data set, and does not consider the structure of the graph data itself. The situation of graph nodes themselves is different, and the information and representation of each node are different. Therefore, in the next section, we propose an active learning correction graph embedding method based on active learning.

3.2   Active Learning Correction Graph Embedding Algorithm

Our algorithm inputs are not independent identically distributed data but connected graph structures. So we should consider edge-to-edge connections between nodes when using active learning strategies. Therefore, we adopt a representativeness-based AL query criteria [7]. We use graph centrality $\phi_{(centrality)}$ as a representativeness measurement. This method uses graph structure to measure the representativeness of nodes by calculating the graph centrality score of nodes. Graph centrality is first proposed in [12]. The existing graph centrality methods include classical methods and eigenvector-based methods. Because the eigenvector-based method is superior to other methods, we use PageRank centrality [14] to calculate graph centrality. Algorithm formula of PageRank is as follows:

$$x = (I - \alpha AD^{-1})^{-1}I = D(D - \alpha A)^{-1}I \tag{1}$$

Where A is the adjacency matrix of the graph and D is the diagonal matrix of the graph. There is a range of values for A, which is less than the reciprocal of the maximum eigenvalue of AD^{-1}. For undirected graphs, the value of α is 1, and for a directed graph, the value depends on the calculation. The calculation formula for the PageRank centrality of the candidate node v_i to be calculated is:

$$\phi_{centrality}(v_i) = \rho \sum_j A_{ij} \frac{\phi_{centrality}(v_j)}{\sum_k A_{jk}} + \frac{1 - \rho}{N} \tag{2}$$

where ρ is the damping parameter.

Algorithm 2. Active Learning Correction Graph Embedding(ALCGE)

Input: Graph embedding X, label budget B

Output: Updated labeled set L and retrained classifier

1. Train a base-classifier on X
2. Set of nodes with corrective labels $C = \{\}$
3. Compute the possibility of Label y, $P(y|x)$
4. Compute node noise probability $1 - P(y|x)$
5. Generate an ordered set M of node graph centrality, and $M \cap C = \{\}$
6. Generate M_m, the top m nodes from M for label correction
7. Generate the labels $y = \{y_1, y_2, \cdots, y_m\}$, and update Y
8. $C = C \cup M_m$
9. Retrain the classifier
10. While $M \neq \{\}$ and the number of C is less than B : Repeat steps 3–9

Algorithm 2 gives the relevant input and specific flow of the active learning correction graph embedding algorithm. Its steps are basically similar to those of Algorithm 1, except that steps 5–8. Then the fifth step is to generate a node set M sorted according to node graph centrality, and ensure that the intersection of M and C is empty. Then we select M_m, the top m nodes about the node graph centrality from M for label correction. The seventh step of the algorithm is to generate the updated label set $y = \{y_1, y_2, \cdots, y_m\}$, and then update the label matrix Y of the label graph node set G_L. Next, update the node set C that used to store the corrective label and add M_m to C.

Given the label budget, the active learning correction algorithm can iteratively and effectively correct the large amount of information and representative nodes in the graph data, and relearn the classifier according to the updated label to improve the performance of the classifier. However, contrary to Algorithm 1, Algorithm 2 only considers the structure of the data itself, and does not consider the noise problem in the graph data set. In the next section, we propose an active noise correction graph embedding method based on active learning by combining the advantages of the two algorithms.

3.3   Active Noise Correction Graph Embedding Framework

Algorithm 3 gives the relevant input and specific flow of the active noise correction graph embedding algorithm. It is the fusion of Algorithm 1 and Algorithm 2, and it is the same as step 1–6 of Algorithm 1.

Algorithm 3. Active Noise Correction Graph Embedding(ANCGE)

Input: Graph embedding X, label budget B

Output: Updated labeled set L and retrained classifier

1. Train a base-classifier on X
2. Set of nodes with corrective labels $C = \{\}$
3. Compute the possibility of Label $y, P(y|x)$
4. Compute node noise probability $1 - P(y|x)$
5. Generate an ordered set M of potentially mislabeled nodes, and $M \cap C = \{\}$
6. Generate M_n , the top n nodes from M for label correction
7. Generate an ordered set N_n of node graph centrality with n nodes
8. Generate N_m, the top m nodes from N_n for label correction, and $m < n$
9. Generate the labels $y = \{y_1, y_2, \cdots, y_m\}$, and update Y
10. $C = C \cup N_m$
11. Retrain the classifier
12. While $M \neq \{\}$ and the number of C is less than B : Repeat steps 3–11

Then the seventh step is to generate a node set N_n sorted according to the graph centrality of n nodes. Then we select N_m , the top m nodes about the node graph centrality from N_n for label correction. In addition, make sure that *mislessthann*. The ninth step of the algorithm is to generate the updated label set $y = \{y_1, y_2, \cdots, y_m\}$, and then update the label matrix Y of the label graph node set G_L. Next, update the node set C that used to store the corrective label and add N_m to C. Finally, retrain the classifier about graph embedding. When node set M is not empty or the number of node set C is less than label budget B, repeat steps 3–11 and iterate the algorithm until it stops.

Given the label budget, the active noise correction algorithm can iteratively and effectively correct the noise nodes of graph data, and select those noise nodes with large amount of information and great influence on graph. More-over, ANCGE can iteratively correct the selected nodes and relearn the classifier according to the updated labels to improve the performance of the classifier.

4   Experiments

The purpose of our design experiment is to: (1) prove the performance of our proposed active noise correction graph embedding model; (2) verify the stability of ANCGE model under different noise rates. We first introduce our experimental setup, and then analyze the experimental results.

4.1   Datasets

All experiments were conducted on three public citation network datasets, Cora, Citeseer and Pubmed [9]. Dataset statistics are summarized in Table 1. Each dataset contains a sparse bag-of-words feature vector of a document and a list of citation links between documents. Each document has a class label. And nodes are documents and edges are citation links. Label rate denotes the number of labeled nodes that are used for training divided by the total number of nodes in each dataset.

Table 1. Dataset statistics

Datasets	Nodes	Edges	Classes	Features	Label rate
Cora	2708	5429	7	1433	0.185
Citeseer	3327	4732	6	3703	0.150
Pubmed	19717	44338	3	500	0.025

4.2   Experimental Settings

For each dataset, we use 500 nodes for training, 500 nodes for validation and 1000 nodes for node classification testing. We randomly extract 500 nodes from non-training and non-testing nodes and use them as validation sets for all experiments to ensure the stability of performance in experiments.

For each data set, we set up 500 labeled nodes. The labeling rates of the three data sets are 0.185, 0.150 and 0.025. In addition, we use 10% label budget B, that is, which means B is 50 nodes. We divide label budget B into five groups, correcting 10 nodes each time, and iterate five times for each algorithm. In the experiment, we can simulate data sets in the real world by randomly modifying data labels and artificially increasing noise.

4.3   Evaluation Metrics

Node classification is a common task to evaluate the performance of graph embedding algorithms. Therefore, in this paper, we use node classification to verify the performance of the algorithm, and use the accuracy of node classification as an evaluation metrics.

4.4   Comparison of Label Correction Algorithm

In this section, we compare the advantages and disadvantages of three label correction methods and one random correction graph embedding method (RCGE) for node classification on three data sets. For each data set, the experiment set up 500 labeled nodes and 10% noise rate. The label budget is 50 nodes, which are iterated five times. The experimental results are shown in Figs. 1, 2 and 3. We use Random Label Correction Graph Embedding (RCGE) as the baseline. Given the label budget, it randomly selects the correct nodes from the data set each time, and iteratively corrects the nodes. The other steps are the same as those of other algorithms except the strategy of selecting nodes.

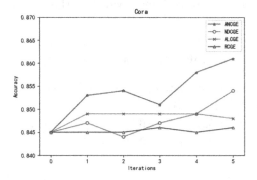

Fig. 1. Comparison of label correction algorithms on dataset Cora

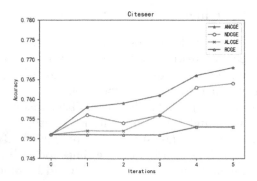

Fig. 2. Comparison of label correction algorithms on dataset Citeseer

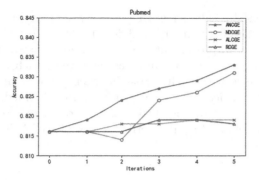

Fig. 3. Comparison of label correction algorithms on dataset Pubmed

Through three experimental results, we can draw the following conclusions: on the whole, with the increase of iteration times, the performance of classifier on each data set has been improved almost. For the three data sets, the performance is respectively improved by 1.6%, 1.7% and 1.7%. But in the process of iteration, the algorithm will fluctuate slightly. Sometimes performance degrades, but eventually performance improves. Specifically, RCGE and ALCGE are difficult to improve the performance of node classification. ALCGE is slightly better than RCGE. The reason for the poor performance of ALCGE is that it only considers the nodes which have great influence on the graph structure, and does not consider more noise selection. Compared with RCGE and ALCGE, NDCGE can effectively improve the performance of node classification. However, in data sets Cora and Pubmed, NDCGE is not as effective as ALCGE at the beginning of iteration. But after several iterations, NDCGE speeds up and surpasses ALCGE. However, the best performance is ANCGE, which is superior to all other algorithms in node classification performance on all data sets.

So it can be seen that active learning can't significantly improve the performance of classifiers, but it can bring positive impact and make NDCGE better. Therefore, in noisy data, priority of correcting is given to the node where the noise possibility is high. ANCGE, which combines active learning and noise detection, can effectively improve the performance of classifier. The above experimental results prove the effectiveness of ANCGE algorithm.

4.5   Stability of ANCGE Model

In this section, we compare the performance of ANCGE model on three data sets with different noise rates. For each data set, we respectively take 10%, 20% and 30% noise rates. In this experiment, 500 labeled nodes are set up. The label budget is 50 nodes, which are iterated five times. The experimental results are shown in Figs. 4, 5 and 6.

Three experimental results show that ANCGE can greatly improve the performance of node classification under different noise rates. For different data sets, the performance improvement range is different between different noise rates. Table 2 is the performance improvement rate of each data set after five iterations. As can be seen from the table, in general, the greater the noise rate, the greater the performance improvement. For dataset Pubmed, the performance improvement at 20% noise rate is better than the other two noise rates. Therefore, the above experimental results verify the stability of ANCGE model under different noise rates.

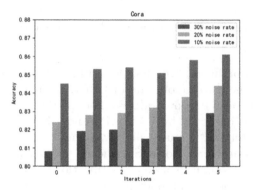

Fig. 4. Accuracy of ANCGE under different noise rates on dataset Cora

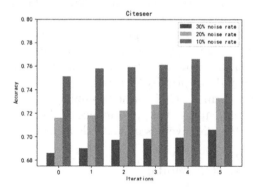

Fig. 5. Accuracy of ANCGE under different noise rates on dataset Citeseer

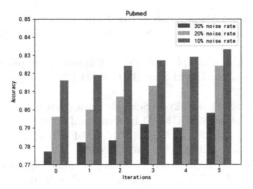

Fig. 6. Accuracy of ANCGE under different noise rates on dataset Pubmed

Table 2. Performance improvement rate of ANCGE

Noise rate	10%	20%	30%
Cora	1.6%	2.0	2.1%
Citeser	1.7%	1.7%	2.0%
Pubmed	1.7%	2.8%	2.1%

5 Conclusion

In this paper, we propose an active correction graph embedding method (ANCGE) based on active learning for image noise data. Given the label budget, it can improve the performance of the classifier by actively learning to find those noisy nodes with large amount of information and great influence on the graph. The experimental results on three open datasets demonstrate the effectiveness of our method and its stability under different noise rates.

Acknowledgements. This research was supported by Natural Science Foundation of China (Grant no. 61572252, 61672284). Meanwhile, this research work was supported by Zayed University Research Cluster Award \# R18038.

References

1. Bloch, F., Jackson, M.O., Tebaldi, P.: Centrality measures in networks. Available at SSRN 2749124 (2017)
2. Cai, H., Zheng, V.W., Chang, K.C.: A comprehensive survey of graph embedding: problems, techniques, and applications. IEEE Trans. Knowl. Data Eng. **30**(9), 1616–1637 (2018). https://doi.org/10.1109/TKDE.2018.2807452
3. Cai, H., Zheng, V.W., Chang, K.C.: Active learning for graph embedding. CoRR abs/1705.05085 (2017). http://arxiv.org/abs/1705.05085

4. Dawid, A.P., Skene, A.M.: Maximum likelihood estimation of observer error-rates using the EM algorithm. J. Roy. Stat. Soc.: Ser. C (Appl. Stat.) **28**(1), 20–28 (1979)
5. Goyal, P., Ferrara, E.: Graph embedding techniques, applications, and performance: a survey. Knowl.-Based Syst. **151**, 78–94 (2018). https://doi.org/10.1016/j.knosys.2018.03.022
6. Grover, A., Leskovec, J.: node2vec: Scalable feature learning for networks. In: Proceedings of the 22nd ACM SIGKDD International Conference on Knowledge Discovery and Data Mining, 13–17 August 2016, San Francisco, CA, USA, pp. 855–864 (2016). https://doi.org/10.1145/2939672.2939754
7. Huang, S., Jin, R., Zhou, Z.: Active learning by querying informative and representative examples. IEEE Trans. Pattern Anal. Mach. Intell. **36**(10), 1936–1949 (2014). https://doi.org/10.1109/TPAMI.2014.2307881
8. Jeatrakul, P., Wong, K.W., Fung, C.C.: Data cleaning for classification using misclassification analysis. JACIII **14**(3), 297–302 (2010). https://doi.org/10.20965/jaciii.2010.p0297
9. Kipf, T.N., Welling, M.: Semi-supervised classification with graph convolutional networks. In: 5th International Conference on Learning Representations, ICLR 2017, 24–26 April 2017, Toulon, France, Conference Track Proceedings (2017). https://openreview.net/forum?id=SJU4ayYgl
10. Mikolov, T., Chen, K., Corrado, G., Dean, J.: Efficient estimation of word representations in vector space. In: 1st International Conference on Learning Representations, ICLR 2013, 2–4 May 2013, Scottsdale, Arizona, USA, Workshop Track Proceedings (2013). http://arxiv.org/abs/1301.3781
11. Nallapati, R., Surdeanu, M., Manning, C.: Corractive learning: learning from noisy data through human interaction. In: IJCAI Workshop on Intelligence and Interaction. Citeseer (2009)
12. Newman, M.: Networks: An Introduction. Oxford University Press, Oxford (2010)
13. Perozzi, B., Al-Rfou, R., Skiena, S.: Deepwalk: online learning of social representations. In: The 20th ACM SIGKDD International Conference on Knowledge Discovery and Data Mining, KDD 2014, 24–27 August 2014, New York, NY, USA, pp. 701–710 (2014). https://doi.org/10.1145/2623330.2623732
14. Rodriguez, M.A.: Grammar-based random walkers in semantic networks. Knowl.-Based Syst. **21**(7), 727–739 (2008). https://doi.org/10.1016/j.knosys.2008.03.030
15. Settles, B.: Active learning literature survey. Technical report, University of Wisconsin-Madison, Department of Computer Sciences (2009)
16. Snow, R., O'Connor, B., Jurafsky, D., Ng, A.Y.: Cheap and fast–but is it good?: evaluating non-expert annotations for natural language tasks. In: Proceedings of the Conference on Empirical Methods in Natural Language Processing, pp. 254–263. Association for Computational Linguistics (2008)
17. Tang, J., Qu, M., Wang, M., Zhang, M., Yan, J., Mei, Q.: LINE: large-scale information network embedding. In: Proceedings of the 24th International Conference on World Wide Web, WWW 2015, 18–22 May 2015, Florence, Italy, pp. 1067–1077 (2015). https://doi.org/10.1145/2736277.2741093
18. Thongkam, J., Xu, G., Zhang, Y., Huang, F.: Support vector machine for outlier detection in breast cancer survivability prediction. In: Ishikawa, Y., et al. (eds.) APWeb 2008. LNCS, vol. 4977, pp. 99–109. Springer, Heidelberg (2008). https://doi.org/10.1007/978-3-540-89376-9_10
19. Tu, C., Yang, C., Liu, Z., Sun, M.: Network representation learning: an overview. SCIENTIA SINICA Informationis **47**(8), 980–996 (2017)

20. Wang, D., Cui, P., Zhu, W.: Structural deep network embedding. In: Proceedings of the 22nd ACM SIGKDD International Conference on Knowledge Discovery and Data Mining, 13–17 August 2016, San Francisco, CA, USA, pp. 1225–1234 (2016). https://doi.org/10.1145/2939672.2939753
21. Yang, Z., Cohen, W.W., Salakhutdinov, R.: Revisiting semi-supervised learning with graph embeddings. In: Proceedings of the 33nd International Conference on Machine Learning, ICML 2016, 19–24 June 2016, New York City, NY, USA, pp. 40–48 (2016). http://proceedings.mlr.press/v48/yanga16.html

Semi-supervised Learning via Adaptive Low-Rank Graph

Mingbo Zhao[1]([envelope]), Jiang Zhang[1], and Cuili Yang[2]

[1] Donghua University, Shanghai, People's Republic of China
mzhao4@dhu.edu.cn, jiangzhang_2016@163.com
[2] Beijing University of Technology, Beijing, People's Republic of China
clyang5@bjut.edu.cn

Abstract. Graph-based semi-supervised learning (SSL) is one of the most popular topics in the past decades. Most conventional graph-based SSL methods utilize two stage-approach to infer the class labels of the unlabeled data, i.e. it firstly constructs a graph for capturing the geometry of data manifold and then perform SSL for prediction. However, it suffers from three drawbacks: (1) the graph construction and SSL stages are separate. They do not share common information to enhance the performance of classification; (2) the graph construction and SSL should be scalable. However, most methods mainly focus on the improvement of classification accuracy but neglect the computational cost; (3) the graph should also be adaptive and robust to the parameters and datasets. However, this will usually increase computational cost making the efficiency cannot be guaranteed simultaneously. In this paper, we aim to handle the above issues. To achieve adaptiveness of SSL, we adopt a bilinear low-rank model for graph construction, where the coefficient matrix of the low-rank model is calculated through an adaptive and efficient procedure the corresponding constructed graph can capture the global structure of data manifold. Meriting from such a graph, we then propose a unified framework for scalable SSL, where we have involved the graph construction and SSL into a unified optimization problem. As a result, the discriminative information learned by SSL can be provided to improve the discriminative ability of graph construction, while the updated graph can further enhance the classification results of SSL. Simulation indicates that the proposed method can achieve better classification and clustering performance compared with other state-of-the-art graph-based SSL methods.

Keywords: Semi-supervised learning · Unsupervised learning · Spectral clustering · Adaptive low-rank model

1 Introduction

Due to the insufficiency of the labeled set, SSL, which incorporates a small number of labeled data and a large number of unlabeled data into learning, has

X. B. Zhai et al. (Eds.): MLICOM 2019, LNICST 294, pp. 434–443, 2019.
https://doi.org/10.1007/978-3-030-32388-2_37

attracted considerable attention in the artificial intelligence and pattern recognition area. Among different methods for SSL, graph-based SSL approaches, a kind of methods that model the data on a graph, have been extensive study during the past decades. The big advantage for these methods is that the graph can naturally characterize diverse types of the geometry of data manifold. According to the clustering and manifold assumptions, i.e., nearby samples (or samples of the same cluster or data manifold) share the same label [12,17,18], current graph-based SSL methods include Manifold Regularization (MR) [1], Gaussian Fields and Harmonic Functions (GFHF) [18], Learning with Local and Global Consistency (LLGC) [17], and Special Label Propagation (SLP) [10,11]. These methods usually model labeled and unlabeled data by a graph, and then calculate the graph Laplacian matrix to capture the geometrical structure of data manifold [3].

While most conventional graph-based SSL generally perform well in many real-world applications, a good graph-based SSL model should satisfy the following issues: (1) the graph construction should be adaptive and robust to the parameters and datasets. In the conventional graph-based SSL, the graph usually represents a kNN graph associated with weight on it. Many ways are proposed to define the graph weight which include Gaussian function [10,11,17,18], Locally Linear Reconstruction [13,14], Local Regression and Global Alignment [16] and Local Spline Regression [15]. A key limit for these methods is that the number of k needs to be carefully adjusted hence they are not adaptive. Fortunately, this drawback can be solved by the sparse or low-rank representation graph, where SR based graphs can model the data with good properties of adaptiveness, sparsity and high discriminating power, while LRR based graphs can characterize the global structure of data. However, the huge computational cost is needed in order to solve l_1 or trace-norm minimization problem for calculating the sparse or low-rank graph; (2) the graph construction and SSL strategy should also be efficient and scalable to large-scale data. As analyzed in [7,8], the computational cost for searching the k neighbors of data in conventional kNN graph is $O\left(kn^2\right)$. While those for calculating the weight matrix in the SR graph and LRR graph are $O\left(n^3\right)$. None of them is linear with the number of datasets.

To handle this problem, Liu et al. [7,8] have proposed an efficient anchor graph framework by exploring a set of anchors from data points, where it is first to establish a similarity matrix between data points and anchors, and then to construct the anchor graph for inferring the class labels of anchors instead of the whole data points. As a result, the computational cost can be reduced to be linear with n. Many variants of AGR have been proposed during the past few years. However, the similarity matrix in AGR and its variants are still not adaptive and need to be adjusted according to a different dataset. In other words, it is quite hard to guarantee the adaptiveness and scalability simultaneously; (3) the graph construction and SSL stages are separate. They do not share common information to enhance the performance of classification. In another word, the graph won't be updated once it is constructed. However, the estimated class labels will include some discriminative information and can further be utilized to update the graph. As a result, the class label inference can further be enhanced.

In this paper, we aim to solve the above problems by developing a new framework for scalable SSL. Specifically, in order to achieve adaptiveness for SSL, we adopt a bilinear low-rank model for graph construction, where the coefficient matrix of the model is calculated through an adaptive and efficient way. We thereby construct the graph based on such weight matrix following the basic concept of AGR. As a result, the adaptiveness and scalability can both be achieved. The corresponding graph can also capture the global structure of the data manifold. Meriting from such a graph, we then propose a unified framework for scalable SSL, where we have involved the graph construction and SSL into a unified optimization problem. As a result, the discriminative information learned by SSL can be provided to improve the discriminative ability of graph construction, while the updated graph can further enhance the classification results of SSL. Simulation indicates that the proposed method can achieve better classification results compared with other state-of-the-art graph-based SSL methods.

The main contributions of this paper are as follows:

(1) We have developed an adaptive bilinear low-rank model for graph construction. With the group sparsity and non-negative constraint, the low-rank value can be automatically determined, and the learned coefficient matrix S is non-negative and can characterize the global structure of data;

(2) We have developed a new graph-based SSL framework, in which the developed low-rank model and SLP are unified into a single optimization problem. In this way, the discriminative information learned by SLP can be provided to improve the discriminative ability of graph construction, while the updated graph can further enhance the classification results of SSL.

(3) We have developed an efficient iterative approach for optimization. Theoretical analysis has guaranteed the convergence and the computational cost is linear with the number of data points. Thereby, the solution is efficient and scalable to large-scale data;

The rest of this paper is organized as follows: In Sect. 1, we will provide some basic notations and reviews of related work; in Sect. 2, we will present the proposed bilinear low-rank model for graph construction. We then develop a unified framework for graph-based SSL. Extensive simulations are conducted in Sect. 3 and final conclusions are drawn in Sect. 4.

2   Adaptive Low-Rank Graph Regularization for Semi-supervised Learning

2.1   Graph Construction via Adaptive Low-Rank Model

Denote $X = [X_l, X_u] \in R^{d \times (l+u)}$ as the data matrix, in which d is the number of features, the first l and the remaining u data points in X form the labeled set X_l and unlabeled set X_u, respectively, $Y = [y_1, y_2, \ldots, y_{l+u}] \in R^{c \times (l+u)}$ is the original class labels of all data that satisfies: $y_{ij} = 1$, given x_j is within the ith class;

otherwise, $y_{ij} = 0$. Accordingly, denote $F = [f_1, f_2, \ldots, f_{l+u}] \in R^{c \times (l+u)}$ be the estimated class label matrix, where f_i is a column vector satisfying $0 \leq f_{ij} \leq 1$. The AGR has assumed each data point can be approximately reconstructed by its nearby anchors, i.e. $x_j = \sum_{i=1}^{m} a_i Z_{ij}$ or $X \approx AZ$. The coefficient Z_j for each x_j is then calculated by Kernel-defined weights or local reconstructed strategy one by one, i.e.

$$\min_Z \frac{1}{2} \|x_j - Az_j\|_F^2 \quad s.t.\ z_{ij} \geq 0, \ \sum_{i=1}^{m} z_{ij} = 1 \tag{1}$$

However, a key problem for the above strategies is Z is not adaptive since some key parameters (such as the number of anchors m) need to be carefully adjusted. Another problem is that Z cannot preserve the global structure of data manifold since each coefficient vector is only associated with nearby anchor data. On the other hand, the low-rank model can capture the global information as well as achieve data-adaptiveness. We thereby develop an adaptive low-rank model to calculate the weight matrix. Specifically, we first reformulate Eq. (1) as follows:

$$\min_{A,Z} \frac{1}{2} \|X - AZ - O\|_F^2 + \gamma \|O\|_1. \tag{2}$$

where we let $X = AZ + O$ and $O \in R^{d \times n}$ is the additive matrix measuring the corruption of X, $\|O\|_1$ is the sparse l_1-norm of O since we assume the corruptions usually affects some entries of X making O is sparse. In order to grasp the global structure of the whole data and achieve data-adaptiveness, we add a low-rank constraint on AZ, then Eq. (2) can be formulated as:

$$\min_{A,Z} \frac{1}{2} \|X - M - O\|_F^2 + \lambda \|M\|_* + \gamma \|O\|_1 \quad s.t.\ M = AZ. \tag{3}$$

where $\|M\|_*$ is the nuclear norm approximating the rank of M. In addition, as pointed in [], the nuclear norm M can be further reformulated as the penalty of bilinear factorizations, i.e.

$$\|M\|_* = \min_{A,Z} \frac{1}{2} \|A\|_F^2 + \frac{1}{2} \|Z\|_F^2 \quad s.t.\ AZ = M. \tag{4}$$

where M is optimized via the SVD of $M = U\Sigma V^T$ so that $A = U\Sigma^{1/2} \in R^{d \times q}$ and $Z = \Sigma^{1/2} V^T \in R^{q \times n}$, q is the low-rank value of M. Here, let $P = [A, Z^T]^T \in R^{q \times (d+n)}$ denote a joint matrix, we have:

$$\|P\|_F^2 = [A, Z^T]^T = \|A\|_F^2 + \|Z\|_F^2. \tag{5}$$

Obviously, the low-rank value is the number of anchors, i.e. $q = m$, then Eq. (5) can be roughly equivalent to the following problem by combining Eqs. (3), (4) and (5):

$$\min_{B,S,O} \frac{1}{2} \|X - AZ - O\|_F^2 + \frac{\lambda}{2} \|P\|_F^2 + \gamma \|O\|_1 \tag{6}$$

Note that optimizing $l_{2,1}$-norm term $\|P\|_{2,1}$ in Eq. (6) enable the columns of P sparse, i.e. some columns of P are non-zero while others are close to zero. Since each column of P, i.e. p_j, is formed by an anchor a_j and its corresponding coefficient z_j, setting the norm of p_j to zero means a_j is less important and can be neglected, while the p_j with non-zero value means the corresponding a_j is more important. As a result, the most important anchors a_j combined with its coefficient z_j can be selected when solving the optimization problem. Therefore, the optimal value of m can be adaptively selected.

After we obtain the weight matrix Z, we can construct the similarity matrix of graph [7,8] in a low-rank form as follows:

$$W_s = Z^T Z. \tag{7}$$

where the inner product is regarded as the adjacent weight between any pairwise x_i and x_j. In other words, if x_i and x_j share common anchors, their s_i and s_j will be similar making W_{ij}^s to be a large value; otherwise, W_{ij}^s will be close to 0, if x_i and x_j do not have any anchors. Hence W^s can also reflect the geometry of data manifold.

2.2   Problem Formulation

It should be noted the labeled information is very effective to improve the discriminative ability of the graph if one can involve limited label information into the graph construction. However, as shown above, the partial label information is not utilized in graph construction. On the other hand, the SLP is to propagate the class label information of labeled set to unlabeled set, where the class labels of unlabeled set can be predicted. This motivates us to consider utilizing the additional labeled information to improve the discriminant of affinity matrix. Motivated by this end, we develop an effective and scalable approach to solve the above problem, where we integrate the adaptive graph construction and SLP into a unified framework. As a result, the discriminative information can be involved to guide the graph construction, while the newly updated graph construction can further improve the classification results for SSL. In addition, both the graph construction and SSL share a unified objective function which can be simultaneously optimized in one step and to guarantee the overall optimum. Specifically, we give our model for SSL as follows:

$$\min_{B,S,O} \tfrac{1}{2} \left\| X - B^T S - O \right\|_F^2 + \tfrac{\beta}{2} \|P\|_{2,1} + \gamma \|O\|_1$$
$$+ \alpha \left(\tfrac{1}{2} Tr \left(F L_s F^T \right) + Tr \left(F - Y \right) U D_s (F - Y)^T \right) \tag{8}$$
$$s.t.\ B \geq 0,\ S \geq 0,\ O \geq 0,\ \forall j,\ \|s_j\|_0 \leq T_0$$

where L_s is the graph Laplacian matrix for W_s, $B \geq 0$, $S \geq 0$, $O \geq 0$ are the non-negative constraints for guaranteeing the non-negativity for $X = B^T S + O$.

2.3   Solution

We will develop an iterative approach to handle the problem of Eq. (8). It can be noted that $\|P\|_{2,1}$ can be written as $\|P\|_{2,1} = Tr \left(S^T G S \right) + Tr \left(B^T G B \right)$,

$G \in R^{q \times q}$ is a diagonal matrix satisfying:

$$
[G \leftarrow \begin{bmatrix} \frac{1}{2\|z_1\|_2} & & \\ & \ddots & \\ & & \frac{1}{2\|z_q\|_2} \end{bmatrix} \tag{9}
$$

where $\|p_i\|_2$ is the norm of the i-th column of P. We also denote $R \in R^{n \times n}$ as a sparse matrix with each element satisfying $R_{ij} = \|f_i - f_j\|_F^2$, so that the following equation holds:

$$
\begin{aligned}
Tr\left(FL_sF^T\right) &= \sum_{i,j=1}^{n} \|f_i - f_j\|_F^2 (W_s)_{ij} \\
&= \sum_{i,j=1}^{n} (R \odot W_s) = Tr\left(SRS^T\right)
\end{aligned} \tag{10}
$$

where $\odot$ is the pair-wise product and the third equation is satisfied as $\sum_{i,j=1}^{n} (R \odot W_s) = Tr(RW_s) = Tr\left(SRS^T\right)$. We then develop multiplicative updating rules by formulating the Lagrange function to the problem of Eq. (10) with non-negative constraints as follows:

$$
\begin{aligned}
\min_{B,S,O} \tfrac{1}{2} \|X - BS - O\|_F^2 + \tfrac{\beta}{2} Tr\left(S^TGS + B^TGB\right) \\
+ \alpha \left(Tr\left(FL_sF^T\right) + Tr\left(F - Y\right)UD_s(F - Y)^T\right) \\
+ \gamma Tr\left(E^TO\right) + Tr\left(\phi O\right) + Tr\left(\varphi B\right) + Tr\left(\psi S\right)
\end{aligned} \tag{11}
$$

where ϕ, φ and ψ are three Lagrange multipliers to constrain $O_{ij} \geq 0$, $B_{ij} \geq 0$ and $S_{ij} \geq 0$. Here, by setting the derivative w.r.t. B_{ij}, S_{ij} and O_{ij} to zero and utilizing the Karush-Kuhn-Tuckre (KKT) condition $\phi_{ij}O_{ij} = 0$, $\varphi_{ij}B_{ij} = 0$ and $\psi_{ij}S_{ij} = 0$, O_{ij}, B_{ij} and S_{ij}, can be updated as follows:

$$
O_{ij} \leftarrow O_{ij} \frac{(X - B^TS)_{ij}}{(O + \gamma E)_{ij}} \tag{12}
$$

$$
B_{ij} \leftarrow B_{ij} \frac{\left(S(X - O)^T\right)_{ij}}{(SS^TB + \beta GB)_{ij}} \tag{13}
$$

$$
S_{ij} \leftarrow S_{ij} \frac{(B(X - O))_{ij}}{(BB^TS + \beta GS + \alpha SR)_{ij}} \tag{14}
$$

It should be noted that the main computation for calculating the optimal solution F is to perform the inverse of $L_s + UD_s$, in which the complexity is $O\left(n^3\right)$. However, such computational complexity for F can be dramatical given the data is large-scale. Fortunately, by the form of $W_s = S^TS$, Eq. (14) can be rewritten as follows:

$$
\begin{aligned}
F &= YUD_s(L_s + UD_s)^{-1} \\
&= YU\left(I - S^TSD_s^{-1} + U\right)^{-1} \\
&= YI_\alpha\left(I - S^TSD_s^{-1}I_\beta\right)^{-1} \\
&= YI_\alpha\left(I + S^T\left(I_q + SI_\beta D_s^{-1}S^T\right)^{-1}SD_s^{-1}I_\beta\right)
\end{aligned} \tag{15}
$$

Following Eq. (15), we can observe that the computational complexity for performing the inverse of F reduces from $O\left(n^3\right)$ to $O\left(q^3\right)$. Given $q \ll n$, the calculation for F can be significantly speeded up by Eq. (15), which is good for dealing with large-scaled data.

3   Simulations

3.1   Dataset Description

We in this section conduct extensive simulations on three synthetic data as well as several real-world datasets to evaluate the effectiveness of the proposed method. In the synthetic dataset, we evaluate the proposed method based on two-swiss-roll and two-moon datasets, where each dataset has two classes and each class per dataset follows a two-swiss-roll and two-moon distribution. In real-world datasets, we illustrate the performance of the proposed method as well as compare with those of other state-of-the-art SSL methods based on six real-world datasets, which include Extended Yale-B dataset [2], COIL100 [9], ETH80 [6].

For each dataset, we randomly annotate 5%, 10%, 15% and 20% data from each class to form labeled set while the remaining data is selected as an unlabeled set and 20% data per class is selected as a test set.

3.2   Image Classification

We in this subsection evaluate our method for image classification and compare the results with other graph-based SSL methods, which include LGC, SLP, LNP, AGR, EMR and Manifold Regularization (MR). We also choose SVM as a baseline in our simulation. For the parameter k in LGC, SLP, LNP, AGR, EMR and MR to formulate the k neighborhood graph, we use five-fold cross-validation to determine the best value, where the candidates are were chosen from 6 to 20. For the parameter σ used in LGC, SLP EMR and MR as the Gaussian variance, we utilize the same approach in [4] to choose its best value. For LGC, LNP AGR, EMR and the proposed method, they need to determine the regularized parameter, and we set the candidates from $\left\{10^{-6}, 10^{-3}, 10^{-1}, 1, 10, 10^3, 10^6\right\}$ by using five-fold cross-validation.

The simulation results over 20 random splits with varied numbers of labeled data for different methods are shown in Table 1. We can have the following results:

(1) The classification accuracies become higher given the number of labeled data is increased. In detail, the accuracy of the proposed method is increased by approximately 15% given the labeled data varies from 5% to 20% in most cases. This can even be achieved by about 17% for the CASIA-HWDB dataset. This indicates that the labeled data actually be useful for image classification. In addition, we can also see that the accuracies will not change any more given sufficient labeled data;

(2) among all SSL methods, the proposed method can almost obtain the best results in all cases. For example, the proposed method can achieve 4%–7% superiority to LGC, SLP and LNP, in most cases. This improvement can even achieve 8% in the CASIA-HWDB dataset. In addition, AGR and EMR can obtain competitive accuracy to the proposed method in most cases. But the results of AGR and EMR are achieved by carefully adjusting the parameters, while the proposed method can adaptively calculate the weight matrix for constructing the graph;

(3) another observation is that similar to the unlabeled data, the accuracies of test data of the proposed method, LNP, AGR and MR increase given that the number of labeled data increases. Specifically, the accuracy of the test set will increase by approximately 10% given the number of labeled data increases from 5% to 20% for most cases. The accuracies of unlabeled data are better than those of test data. This can be natural due to the reason that the test data are not be used in training the method as unlabeled data.

Table 1. Classification accuracies of different datasets

Datasets	Methods	5% Training Labeled		10% Training Labeled		15% Training Labeled		20% Training Labeled	
		Unlabeled	Test	Unlabeled	Test	Unlabeled	Test	Unlabeled	Test
Yale-B [5]	SVM	53.1±1.1	52.7±1.0	68.8±2.0	67.7±0.6	75.2±1.1	73.7±1.3	80.0±1.8	78.8±1.2
	MR	59.0±1.2	58.5±1.3	70.3±1.1	69.4±0.5	76.4±1.3	74.9±1.5	80.7±1.3	79.0±1.1
	LGC	64.7±1.0		71.8±1.1		76.4±4.2		80.8±1.0	
	SLP	65.6±2.3		73.9±1.0		78.0±1.8		81.8±1.0	
	LNP	64.9±1.3	53.8±2.7	72.0±1.2	71.2±0.4	78.0±2.4	76.6±2.1	81.6±1.0	80.0±1.4
	AGR	66.6±1.5	65.8±1.3	74.3±1.2	72.2±0.4	78.1±1.5	77.3±1.7	83.0±1.2	80.0±4.5
	EMR	66.9±0.8		74.4±1.1		78.0±1.5		84.4±2.4	
	EAGR	69.9±0.4	67.2±1.0	75.7±1.1	74.0±3.3	79.4±1.0	78.3±1.1	86.3±2.5	82.8±2.4
	ALG	**69.9±0.4**	**67.2±1.0**	**75.7±1.1**	**74.0±3.3**	**79.4±1.0**	**78.3±1.1**	**80.3±2.5**	**82.8±2.4**
COIL100 [9]	SVM	83.6±0.9	83.2±0.8	88.5±0.8	86.6±0.8	91.8±0.8	91.4±0.7	95.3±0.8	94.5±1.6
	MR	83.7±1.0	83.4±0.9	89.0±0.9	87.3±0.9	92.1±0.8	91.6±0.9	95.3±0.7	94.7±1.3
	LGC	85.5±0.8		89.3±0.9		92.4±0.8		95.5±0.6	
	SLP	86.4±0.7		89.3±0.9		92.8±0.6		95.6±0.8	
	LNP	86.5±0.7	85.6±0.7	89.6±0.9	88.7±0.7	92.9±0.7	92.4±0.8	95.8±0.7	95.1±1.3
	AGR	86.5±0.6	85.8±0.9	90.9±0.9	88.8±0.8	93.3±0.6	92.7±0.9	95.8±0.7	95.3±1.4
	EMR	86.6±0.7		89.9±0.9		93.2±0.6		96.0±0.7	
	ALG	**87.0±0.6**	**86.7±1.0**	**91.8±0.9**	**89.7±0.8**	**94.7±0.6**	**93.2±0.8**	**97.0±0.6**	**95.6±0.9**
ETH80 [6]	SVM	61.1±1.3	59.4±0.3	71.1±1.9	70.2±2.0	75.9±1.5	75.3±3.1	78.9±2.0	77.9±2.5
	MR	62.3±0.8	60.0±0.2	71.7±2.0	71.0±2.7	76.2±1.0	75.3±2.8	78.9±1.9	78.3±2.5
	LGC	65.7±1.4		73.5±1.4		76.8±1.5		79.0±1.7	
	SLP	65.9±1.5		73.9±1.2		76.9±1.6		79.3±1.8	
	LNP	64.9±0.9	62.2±0.2	73.4±2.0	71.4±2.6	76.7±1.1	76.0±2.6	79.0±1.8	78.5±2.0
	AGR	66.4±1.6	65.1±0.2	75.0±1.7	72.2±2.2	76.9±1.7	76.1±2.5	79.6±2.0	78.9±1.9
	EMR	68.2±1.7		74.9±1.4		77.3±1.7		80.0±2.2	
	ALG	**69.4±1.9**	**67.2±0.1**	**74.0±1.3**	**74.2±2.2**	**77.5±1.9**	**77.3±1.8**	**79.8±2.2**	**79.0±2.2**

4   Conclusion

In this paper, we develop a graph-based semi-supervised learning framework for image classification and clustering. According to the theoretical analysis and simulation results, we can draw the following conclusions: (1) we have developed an adaptive bilinear low-rank model for graph construction. With the group sparsity and non-negative constraint, the low-rank value can be automatically determined, and the learned coefficient matrix S is non-negative and can grasp the global structure of whole data; (2) We have developed a new graph-based

SSL framework, in which the developed low-rank model and SLP are unified into a single optimization problem. In this way, the discriminative information learned by SLP can be provided to improve the discriminative ability of graph construction, while the updated graph can further enhance the classification results of SSL.

Acknowledgment. The work is supported by the National Natural Science Foundation of China (61601112). It is also supported by the Fundamental Research Funds for the Central Universities and DHU Distinguished Young Professor Program.

References

1. Belkin, M., Niyogi, P., Sindhwani, V.: Manifold regularization: a geometric framework for learning from labeled and unlabeled samples. J. Mach. Learn. Res. **7**, 2399–2434 (2006)
2. Georghiades, A.S., Belhumeur, P.N., Kriegman, D.J.: From few to many: illumination cone models for face recognition under variable lighting and pose. IEEE Trans. Pattern Anal. Mach. Intell. **23**(6), 643–660 (2001)
3. He, X., Yan, S., Hu, Y., Niyogi, P., Zhang, H.: Face recognition using Laplacian faces. IEEE Trans. Pattern Anal. Mach. Intell. **27**(3), 328–340 (2005)
4. Hou, C., Nie, F., Wang, F., Zhang, C., Wu, Y.: Semisupervised learning using negative labels. IEEE Trans. Neural Netw. **22**(3), 420–432 (2011)
5. Lee, K., Ho, J., Kriegman, D.: Acquiring linear subspaces for face recognition under variable lighting. IEEE Trans. Pattern Anal. Mach. Intell. **27**(5), 947–963 (2005)
6. Leibe, B., Schiele, B.: Analyzing appearance and contour based methods for object categorization. In: Proceedings of 2003 IEEE Computer Society Conference on Computer Vision and Pattern Recognition, vol. 2, p. II-409. IEEE (2003)
7. Liu, W., He, J., Chang, S.F.: Large graph construction for scalable semi-supervised learning. In: Proceedings of the 27th International Conference on Machine Learning (ICML-2010), pp. 679–686 (2010)
8. Liu, W., Wang, J., Chang, S.F.: Robust and scalable graph-based semisupervised learning. Proc. IEEE **100**(9), 2624–2638 (2012)
9. Nene, S.A., Nayar, S.K., Murase, H.: Columbia object image library (coil-100). Technical report, Technical Report CUCS-005-96, Columbia University (1996)
10. Nie, F., Xiang, S., Liu, Y., Zhang, C.: A general graph based semi-supervised learning with novel class discovery. Neural Comput. Appl. **19**(4), 549–555 (2010)
11. Nie, F., Xu, D., Li, X., Xiang, S.: Semisupervised dimensionality reduction and classification through virtual label regression. IEEE Trans. Syst. Man Cybern. Part B (Cybern.) **41**(3), 675–685 (2011)
12. Szummer, M., Jaakkola, T.: Patially labeled classification with Markov random walks. In: NIPS (2002)
13. Wang, F., Zhang, C.: Label propagation through linear neighborhoods. IEEE Trans. Knowl. Data Eng. **20**(1), 55–67 (2008)
14. Wang, J., Wang, F., Zhang, C., Shen, H.C., Quan, L.: Linear neighborhood propagation and its applications. IEEE Trans. Pattern Anal. Mach. Intell. **31**(9), 1600–1615 (2009)
15. Xiang, S., Nie, F., Zhang, C.: Semi-supervised classification via local spline regression. IEEE Trans. Pattern Anal. Mach. Intell. **32**(11), 2039–2053 (2010)

16. Yang, Y., Nie, F., Xu, D., Luo, J., Zhuang, Y., Pan, Y.: A multimedia retrieval framework based on semi-supervised ranking and relevance feedback. IEEE Trans. Pattern Anal. Mach. Intell. **34**(4), 723–742 (2012)
17. Zhou, D., Bousquet, O., Lal, T.N., Weston, J., Scholkopf, B.: Learning with local and global consistency. In: NIPS (2004)
18. Zhu, X., Ghahramani, Z., Lafferty, J.D.: Semi-supervised learning using gaussian fields and harmonic functions. In: ICML (2003)

Transaction Cost Analysis
via Label-Spreading Learning

Pangjing Wu[✉] and Xiaodong Li

College of Computer and Information, Hohai University, Nanjing, China
{pangjing.wu,xiaodong.li}@hhu.edu.cn

Abstract. When the investment institution analyzes the transaction cost of stock orders, it is costly to obtain the transaction cost of the stock orders by trading it. In contrast, many simulated trading orders cannot get the exact transaction cost. Due to the lack of enough labeled data, it is usually hard to use a supervised learner to estimate accurate transaction cost of stock orders. Label-spreading, a graph-based semi-supervised learner, can integrate a small number of labeled real orders and a large number of unlabeled simulated orders, and train a learner simultaneously. Using a RBF kernel, the learner constructs a graph structure through the spatial similarity measure between the transaction cost samples, and propagates the label through edges of graph in high-dimensional space. The results of experiments show that the label-spreading learner can make full use of the information of unlabeled data to improve classification of transaction cost.

Keywords: Label-spreading · Semi-supervised learning · Algorithm trading

1 Introduction

When investment institutions analyze the transaction cost of the stock orders, accurate data of transaction cost is required for investment institution to analyze the transaction cost. However, it is costly to obtain the transaction cost of stock orders by trading it. Besides, the large amount of simulated data generated by the stock trading simulator is simulated estimation, which lacks real value and cannot obtain the exact transaction cost of stock orders. Therefore, transaction cost data is not enough and accurate for investment institutions to analyze the order transaction cost by supervised learner.

This paper intends to provide the solution to the problem that when the transaction data of stock orders is scarce and hard to mark, the graph-based

This work was supported in part by the National Key R&D Program of China under Grant 2018YFC0407901, in part by the National Natural Science Foundation of China under Grant 61602149, and in part by the Fundamental Research Funds for the Central Universities under Grant 2019B15514.

semi-supervised learner can be applied to study transaction data of stock orders, which make full use of the readily available unlabeled data and generalize a well-performed classifier to predict transaction cost.

Semi-supervised learning can learn both labeled data and unlabeled data. Its basic principle is to improve the learning effect by using many unlabeled data to assist a few labeled data. As early as 1970s, some scholars tried to use the unlabeled samples to improve the performance of the classifier. Based on generative model theory, they proposed the first semi-supervised learning model and EM algorithm [4] to solve the model. Subsequently, in 1990s, Vapnik proposed TSVM [9] based on the idea that the decision boundary should keep the maximum distance from the labeled and unlabeled samples, which had a greater impact on the early semi-supervised learning model. And then, Blum and Mitchell proposed co-train model [2] from the perspective of learning-views. Limited to TSVM is a non-convex optimization problem and the assumptions of co-train are harsh, these methods have difficulties in practical applications, so people began to try other methods for semi-supervised learning. Based on the graph theory, scholars proposed a series of graph-based semi-supervised learners such as min-cut [1], local and global consistency theory [12], label propagation [13]. Compared with the earlier methods, most of the learners are convex, which means that the global optimal solution can be easily obtained. In addition, the calculation is based on matrix operations, which is efficient and easy to understand and implement. In recent years, graph-based semi-supervised learners have received extensive attention in research and application [3,5,7].

The rest of this paper will be organized as follows. Section 2 describe the dataset and select features and labels. We build the label-spreading model in Sect. 3 and predict the transaction cost label for the stock orders in Sect. 4. Section 4.2 analyzes the properties of the label-spreading learner further. And the conclusions will be presented in Sect. 5.

2   Data Sets of Stock Orders

The data sets used for the experiment is consisted of a transaction data set of real stock orders $L = \{(\boldsymbol{x}_1, y_1), \ldots, (\boldsymbol{x}_{|L|}, y_{|L|})\}$ and a transaction data set of simulation stock orders $U = \{\boldsymbol{x}_{|L|+1}, \ldots, \boldsymbol{x}_{|L|+|U|}\}$. L contains 93 items of transaction information, and U contains 3776. The data in L and U are derived from Charles River Advisors Ltd. [6]. For ease of calculation, let $l = |L|, u = |U|, n = l + u$.

2.1   Features Selection

As shown in Table 1, the transaction data sets of stock orders contain six trading features.

Since the deviation between the weighted price and average price can reflect the trading market of the order. The Intraday VWAP, TWAP and Full Day VWAP are the weighted prices of stocks. Therefore, we calculate the relative

Table 1. Features in transaction data sets of stock orders

Feature	Meaning
Average	Average transaction price per share
Liq. Consumption	Order volume accounts for the size of stock liquidity
Execution Time	The time elapsed from the start to the completion of execution
Intraday VWAP	Intraday volume weighted average price
TWAP	Time-weighted average price
Full day VWAP	Full day volume weighted average price

deviation between the three features and average price according to Eq. 1, which is used as the features for learning. Where features include Intraday VWAP, TWAP, Full day VWAP. Thus, the features for semi-supervised learning are $x = \{$Liq. Consumption, Execution Time, Δ Intraday VWAP, Δ TWAP, Δ Full day VWAP$\}$.

$$Features = \frac{Features - Average}{Average} \tag{1}$$

To eliminate the deviation generated by different dimensions and of unit each feature, this paper use the Z-score equation to standardize the data. Calculate the mean value $\bar{x}$ and the variance σ of the features in L. Then, according to Eq. 2, obtain the standardized features L_x of data set L and the standardized features U_x of data set U.

$$Z(x_i) = \frac{x_i - \bar{x}}{\sigma}, \ i = 1, \ldots, n. \tag{2}$$

2.2 Label of Transaction Cost

Intraday VWAP slippage is used in data set L to describe the transaction cost of stock orders, which indicates the deviation of Intraday VWAP between the trading algorithm transmit a buy or sell signal and actually completes the buy or sell.

For the buyer, intraday VWAP slippage greater than 0 means that the intraday VWAP when actually completes the buy transaction is lower than the trading algorithm transmit signal. Stock is bought at a lower than expected price, and the transaction cost decreases. On the contrary, the transaction cost increases when slippage is less than 0. The situation is reversed for the seller. Slippage greater than 0 means stock is sold at a lower than expected price, that the transaction cost increases. On the contrary, when slippage less than 0, the transaction cost decreases. In the data set mentioned above, we have changed the sign of slippage according to the direction of buying and selling. So that intraday VWAP slippage greater than 0 indicates the transaction cost of decreases, and less than 0 indicates the transaction cost increases.

Because the intraday VWAP slippage is the actual value, so the transaction cost label y needs to be initialized according Eq. 3 before classifying.

$$y = \begin{cases} 1, & Intraday\ VWAP\ Slippage \geq 0; \\ 0, & Intraday\ VWAP\ Slippage \leq 0; \\ -1, & Unlabeled. \end{cases} \quad (3)$$

3   Label-Spreading Learner

Based on L and U, we construct graph $G = (V, E)$. Where, $V = \{x_1, \ldots, x_n\}$ is consisted by x, and edge set is represented by the affinity matrix $\mathbf{W}$.

In the graph-based semi-supervised learner, the k-nearest neighbor (k-NN) kernel and the radial basis function (RBF) kernel are commonly used as graph kernel. In the graph using the k-NN kernel, the node only establishes the joint edge with its k neighbors, and only reflects the local relationship of each node. The affinity matrix $\mathbf{W}$ is a sparse matrix, and the calculation speed is relatively fast. In the graph of RBF kernel, the node establishes edge with all other nodes to form a complete graph, which fully reflects the global relationship of each node, but the defect is that the calculation speed is slow. In order to ensure that the semi-supervised learner has good generalization, this paper uses radial basis function as graph kernel. Substitutes $L \cup U$ into Eq. 4 to calculate affinity matrix $\mathbf{W}$ and construct graph structure. Where, let RBF parameter $\gamma - \frac{1}{2\sigma^2} = 1$ according to experiment.

$$(\mathbf{W})_{ij} = \begin{cases} \exp(\dfrac{-\|x_i - x_j\|_2^2}{2\sigma^2}), & i \neq j; \\ 0, & Otherwise. \end{cases} \quad (4)$$

We assume that in the complete graph $G = (V, E)$ constructed by $L \cup U$, a real-valued function $f : V \rightarrow R$ can be obtained by learning. So that f approaches the true label at the labeled nodes and has smoothness on entire graph. According to the study by Zhu et al. [14], adjacent nodes on the feature space should have similar labels, so the energy function of f is defined using the quadratic energy function. Where, f is the prediction of the transaction cost. The diagonal matrix $\mathbf{D} = diag\,(d_1, \ldots, d_n)$ whose element $d_i = \sum_{j=1}^{n} (\mathbf{W})_{ij}$ is the sum of the elements of the i-th row of affinity matrix $\mathbf{W}$.

$$E(f) = \frac{1}{2} \sum_{i=1}^{n} \sum_{j=1}^{n} (\mathbf{W}_{ij})(f(x_i) - f(x_j))^2 \quad (5)$$
$$= f^T (\mathbf{D} - \mathbf{W}) f.$$

By minimizing the energy function (Eq. 5), f can approaches the true label at the labeled nodes and has smoothness across the graph, i.e. $\forall x_i \in L$, $f(x_i) = y_i$, $\mathbf{\Delta} f = 0$, $\mathbf{\Delta} = \mathbf{D} - \mathbf{W}$. In order to minimize the energy function easily, we split affinity matrix $\mathbf{W}$ into 4 blocks after l-th row and column,

$$\mathbf{W} = \begin{bmatrix} \mathbf{W}_{ll} & \mathbf{W}_{lu} \\ \mathbf{W}_{ul} & \mathbf{W}_{uu} \end{bmatrix}, \mathbf{D} = \begin{bmatrix} \mathbf{D}_{ll} & \mathbf{0} \\ \mathbf{0} & \mathbf{D}_{uu} \end{bmatrix}. \quad (6)$$

The energy function (Eq. 5) can be expressed as

$$E(f) = \boldsymbol{f}_l^T(\mathbf{D}_{ll} - \mathbf{W}_{ll})\boldsymbol{f}_l - 2\boldsymbol{f}_u^T\mathbf{W}_{ul}\boldsymbol{f}_l + \boldsymbol{f}_u^T(\mathbf{D}_{uu} - \mathbf{W}_{uu})\boldsymbol{f}_u. \qquad (7)$$

Let

$$\mathbf{P} = \mathbf{D}^{-1}\mathbf{W} = \begin{bmatrix} \mathbf{D}_{ll}^{-1}\mathbf{W}_{ll} & \mathbf{D}_{ll}^{-1}\mathbf{W}_{lu} \\ \mathbf{D}_{uu}^{-1}\mathbf{W}_{ul} & \mathbf{D}_{uu}^{-1}\mathbf{W}_{uu} \end{bmatrix}, \qquad (8)$$

there is $\mathbf{P}_{uu} = \mathbf{D}_{uu}^{-1}\mathbf{W}_{uu}, \mathbf{P}_{ul} = \mathbf{D}_{uu}^{-1}\mathbf{W}_{ul}$. From $\frac{\partial E(f)}{\partial f_u} = 0$ can get

$$\begin{aligned} \boldsymbol{f}_u &= (\mathbf{D}_{uu} - \mathbf{W}_{uu})^{-1}\mathbf{W}_{ul}\boldsymbol{f}_l \\ &= (\mathbf{D}_{uu}(\mathbf{I} - \mathbf{D}_{uu}^{-1}\mathbf{W}_{uu}))^{-1}\mathbf{W}_{ul}\boldsymbol{f}_l \\ &= (\mathbf{I} - \mathbf{D}_{uu}^{-1}\mathbf{W}_{uu})^{-1}\mathbf{D}_{uu}^{-1}\mathbf{W}_{ul}\boldsymbol{f}_l \\ &= (\mathbf{I} - \mathbf{P}_{uu})^{-1}\mathbf{P}_{ul}\boldsymbol{f}_l \end{aligned} \qquad (9)$$

Then, according to the established graph structure, take the label information $\boldsymbol{f}_l = (y_1; y_2; , \ldots ; y_l)$ into Eq. 9, and the prediction result $\boldsymbol{f}_u$ of the unlabeled data can be obtained.

Furthermore, Zhou et al. [11] proposed a regularization framework equivalent to Eq. 9, i.e. label-spreading learner.

$$\min_{F} \frac{1}{2} \left(\sum_{i,j=1}^{l+u} (\mathbf{W})_{ij}^2 \left\| \frac{1}{\sqrt{d_i}}\mathbf{F}_i - \frac{1}{\sqrt{d_j}}\mathbf{F}_j \right\|^2 \right) + \mu \sum_{i=1}^{l} \|\mathbf{F}_i - \mathbf{Y}_i\|^2. \qquad (10)$$

The learner learns labels by minimizing the loss function with regularization characteristics, which is more robust to noise in most cases. Where, $\mathbf{F}$ is a non-negative label matrix. $\mathbf{Y}$ is the matrix with actual label of data set L. the regularization parameter $\mu = \frac{1-\alpha}{\alpha}, \alpha \in [0, 1]$ is clamping factor specified by user. The first item in Eq. 10 forces similar samples to have similar labels, and the second item forces the learning result to be as identical as possible to the real label on the labeled sample.

4   Experiments

4.1   Transaction Cost Classification

Let $\hat{y}$ be the transaction cost label predicted by the label-spreading learner. Because the actual transaction cost label y_U in U is unknown, the learning effect of the learner cannot be evaluated by comparing y_U and $\hat{y}_U$. So that, this paper compares the prediction labels of the test set $\hat{y}_{TE}$ and the actual label y_{TE} to evaluate the learning effect of the learner. 80 data are randomly extracted from L as the labeled part of training set L_{TR}, and the remaining 13 data are used as the test set L_{TE}.

In order to reduce the of influence of special case, we slack the limit of the label of labeled samples, making the clamping factor $\alpha = 0.1$ (i.e., the regularization parameter $\mu = 9$) in Eq. 10. Some labeled samples are allowed to be assigned incorrect labels, so that the labels in graph are smoother.

Take L_{TR} and U into the label-spreading learner (Eq. 10) to learn and predict the label $\hat{y}_{TE}$ of L_{TE}. Because the graph-based semi-supervised learning is transductive, the process of graph construction can only consider the training set $L_{TR} \bigcup U$ and cannot judge the position of the new sample in graph. Using label-spreading learner to predict the label of newly added test data L_{TE} is essentially added L_{TE} to the training set as an unlabeled sample, then reconstruct the graph and propagate label information on the graph to obtain the test set label $\hat{y}_{TE}$. Therefore, based on the above experimental ideas, we can simplify the process of graph construction. Set the label in L_{TE} to unlabeled state and participate in the construction of the graph structure with the training set $L_{TR} \bigcup U$. When the iteration of learner converges, $\hat{y}_{TE}$ is obtained, which saves the tedious calculation of reconstructing, and the experiment takes about 0.803s.

To avoid accidental errors, the experiment was repeated 100 times, and the mode of the transaction cost label $\left\{ \hat{y}_{TE}^{(i)} \middle|, i = 1, 2, \ldots, 100 \right\}$ predicted in 100 experiments was taken as the transaction cost prediction label $\hat{y}_{TE}$. The learning effect of the label-spreading is evaluated by calculating the f1-score value of $\hat{y}_{TE}$, which shown in Table 2.

Table 2. Label-spreading classification report

Label	Precision	Recall	F1-score
0	0.73	1.00	0.84
1	1.00	0.40	0.57
Weight average	0.83	0.77	0.74

From the experimental results, the weighted average f1-score reached 0.74, which means the label $\hat{y}_{TE}$ predicted by label-spreading for the test set L_{TE} is more consistent with the actual label y_{TE}. Because the stock market fluctuations have complex properties such as uncertainty, chaos, and abruptness, the internal mechanism relationship is very complicated [8]. Moreover, in practical applications, when the weighted average f1-score is greater than 0.5, the classifier can be considered to have a good learning effect. Therefore, it is feasible to use label-spreading to classify and predict the transaction cost of stock orders.

Among the results, the recall of the class 0 is 1, indicating that all transaction cost loss orders in L_{TE} have been correctly labeled, and the precision of the class 1 is 1, indicating all transaction cost data labeled as 1 in L_{TE} are classified correctly. This learner can effectively reduce the risk of loss of order transaction and be sensitive to loss risk when predict the transaction cost. It can correctly label all orders with rising transaction costs and ensure that the actual situation marked as a profit order sample is profitable.

4.2   Analysis

Graph Kernel. In label-spreading learner, the k-nearest neighbor kernel and the radial basis function kernel are commonly used as graph kernel. In Sect. 3, we use the RBF kernel of the graph to improve the learning effect of label-spreading learner. Compared with the complete graph based on the RBF kernel, the graph structure based on the k-NN kernel is sparse and has certain advantages in calculation speed. Below we will build a graph based on the k-NN neighbor kernel and analyze the prediction effect of the label-spreading based on k-NN kernel in the transaction cost prediction experiment.

We take the nearest neighbors $k = \{5, \ldots, 9\}$ and train label-spreading learner based on different k. To avoid accidental errors, the experiment was repeated 20 times. The average of results is shown in Table 3.

When $k = 8$, the label-spreading learner based on k-NN kernel has the best learning effect on transaction cost, and the f1-score is 0.47. However, the f1-score is only 63.5% of the learner based on RBF kernel, which means that the learning effect of label-spreading learner based on k-NN kernel is generally inferior to the learner based on RBF kernel. Although the calculation speed of the learner based on k-NN kernel is about 271.5% faster, from the perspective of guaranteeing investors income, the label-spreading learner should be based on RBF kernel when predicting the transaction cost of stock orders.

Table 3. Label-spreading classification report

k	Precision	Recall	F1-score	Time cost
5	0.36	0.54	0.43	0.216
6	0.36	0.54	0.43	0.217
7	0.36	0.54	0.43	0.217
8	0.38	0.62	0.47	0.218
9	0.36	0.54	0.43	0.219

Parameters of Label-Spreading Learning. The setting of parameters affects the learning effect and convergence speed of learner. In the label-spreading learner based on the RBF kernel, the parameters that need manually set are the clamping factor α and the RBF parameter γ. The effect of parameter changes on label-spreading learner is analyzed by changing one parameter and fixing the values of other parameters. The learning effect is measured by the weighted average f1-score of L_{TE}, and the convergence speed of learner is evaluated by the running time of code.

First, we fixed the RBF kernel parameters, let $\gamma = 1$, and analyze the influence of the change of the parameter α on the learner. Because $\alpha \in [0, 1]$ and usually take less than 0.1, the exponential function with base 10 is used to select the clamping factor α, i.e. let $\alpha = 10^a, a \in [-5, 0)$ and a set of α is obtained in steps of 0.25, i.e. $A = \{\alpha_i = 10^{-5+\frac{i}{4}} |, i = 0, \ldots, 20\}$. To avoid accidental errors, the experiment was repeated 10 times for each α_i. The average of results is shown in Fig. 1.

As shown in Fig. 1, The clamping factor has less effect on the prediction of the learner. When the clamping factor is in a reasonable range, i.e. $\alpha \in [10^{-5}, 10^{-1}]$, the prediction of label has no significant change, and the prediction performance of the learner is greatly reduced when α is close to 1. For the calculation speed of the learner, when $\alpha \in [10^{-5}, 10^{-1}]$, the time for training is roughly the same, and it increases dramatically when α is close to 1.

Then, let the $\alpha = 0.1$ to analyze the effect of changes in γ on the learner. Similarly, since the value of γ often in $[0, 1]$, so let $\gamma = 10^g$, $g \in [-2, 2]$. In a step of 0.2, get a set of RBF parameter $\varGamma = \{\gamma_i = 10^{-2+\frac{i}{5}} |, i = 0, \ldots, 20\}$. To avoid accidental errors, the experiment was repeated 10 times for each γ_i. The average of results is shown in Fig. 1.

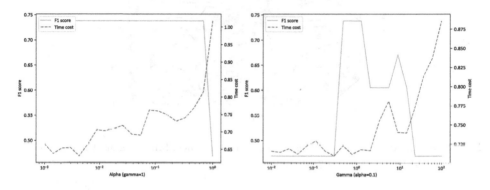

Fig. 1. Analysis of parameters of label-spreading learner.

Contrast with Supervised Learning. In theory, the information provided by unlabeled data can improve the learning effect [10]. In order to analyze the improvement of learning effect by unlabeled data in label-spreading, a typical supervised learning learner, support vector classifier (SVC), is selected for comparison, which is based on RBF kernel.

In data set L, the number of samples of class 0 is 61, and the number of samples of class 1 32. There is a large deviation in the number of samples of the two classes, which will cause SVC to make the decision boundary offset during classification and resulting in incorrect classification results. So that the class weight should be set to reduce the deviation. According to Eq. 11, class 0 weight is 0.34, and a class 1 weight is 0.56.

$$w_i = 1 - \frac{l_i}{l}, \ i \in \{0, 1\}. \tag{11}$$

In order to improve the learning effect of SVC, we use grid search with cross-validation to search for optimal parameters. Because the correlation between the transaction orders is not obvious, it is assumed in the cross-validation that each order is independently distributed. It can be known from the SVC principle that the penalty factor C and the RBF parameter γ are crucial to the learning effect. So, let $C = 10^c, c \in [0,3], step = 0.15$; $\gamma = 10^g, g \in [10^{-2}, 10^2], step = 0.25$. Perform a 10-fold cross-validation on the parameter grid consisting of C and γ to search for the optima parameter (C^*, γ^*). The cross-validation score is represented by the weighted average f1-score and show in Fig. 2.

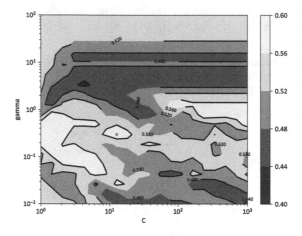

Fig. 2. Weighted f1-score on the grid of parameter space, blue dots are the parameters with the best score. (Color figure online)

According to the optimal parameter(C^*, γ^*), set SVC and train L_{TR}, then predict labels of L_{TE} to evaluate the learning effect of SVC. As Table 4 show, there is a large error in using SVC to predict transaction costs, and the weighted average f1-score is only 0.39. Moreover, the f1-score of class 1 is 0, which means in cannot predict the decline in transaction costs.

Table 4. SVC classification report

Label	Precision	Recall	F1-score
0	0.55	0.75	0.63
1	0.00	0.00	0.00
Weight average	0.34	0.46	0.39

Comparing the classification results of label-spreading and SVC in Table 5, it is obviously that the learning effect of label-spreading is significantly better than

SVC. Especially the label-spreading learner based on RBF kernel, the weighted average f1-Score is 89.7% more than SVC. It can be seen that a large number of easy-to-obtain simulated order data can improve the learning effect of predicting transaction cost.

Table 5. Comparison of learners

Learner	Precision	Recall	F1-score	Time cost
Label-spreading (RBF)	0.83	0.77	0.74	0.803
Label-spreading (knn)	0.38	0.62	0.47	0.219
SVC	0.34	0.46	0.39	2.272

5 Conclusions

This paper uses label-spreading algorithm to predict the transaction cost of stock orders. It can accurately classify the transaction costs of stock orders when the actual transaction data is scarce and difficult to label. The label-spreading learner integrate a small number of labeled real orders and a large number of unlabeled simulated orders, and train a learner simultaneously, thus the transaction cost classifier based on label-spreading has sufficient generalization performance. It can make full use of unlabeled data to improve the classifier and has a good learning effect on the transaction cost of stock orders, whose performance is far superior to the supervised classifier SVC.

The label-spreading model can construct a graph structure by k-NN kernel or RBF kernel. Compared with the RBF kernel, the graph built by k-NN kernel has a faster calculation speed, but the prediction effect is not good. In order to pursue the optimal prediction effect and ensure the return of investors, the label-spreading learner based on the RBF kernel should be used in analyzing and predicting the transaction cost of stock orders.

References

1. Blum, A., Chawla, S.: Learning from labeled and unlabeled data using graph min-cuts. In: Proceedings of the Eighteenth International Conference on Machine Learning (2001)
2. Blum, A., Mitchell, T.: Combining labeled and unlabeled data with co-training. In: Proceedings of the Conference on Computational Learning Theory (1998)
3. Bo, P., Lee, L.: A sentimental education: sentiment analysis using subjectivity summarization based on minimum cuts. In: Proceedings of the Association for Computational Linguistics (2004)
4. Dempster, A.P., Laird, N.M., Rubin, D.B.: Maximum likelihood from incomplete data via the EM algorithm. J. R. Stat. Soc. **39**(1), 1–38 (1977)

5. Goldberg, A., Zhu, X.B.T.: Graph-based semi-supervised learning for sentiment categorization. In: Workshop on Graph Based Methods for Natural Language Processing (2006)
6. Charles River Advisors Ltd. (2014). https://www.crd.com/
7. Niu, Z.Y., Ji, D.H., Tan, C.L.: Word sense disambiguation using label propagation based semi-supervised learning. In: Proceedings of the ACL (2005)
8. Sun, B.W.: Research on the complexity of stock market volatility. In: Complexity Problems-Proceedings of Ccast (2001)
9. Vapnik, V.N.: The Nature of Statistical Learning Theory. Springer, New York (1995). https://doi.org/10.1007/978-1-4757-2440-0
10. Zhang, C.G., Yan, Z.: Semi-Supervised Learning (2013)
11. Zhou, D., Bousquet, O., Lal, T.N., Weston, J.: Learning with local and global consistency. In: International Conference on Neural Information Processing Systems (2004)
12. Zhou, D., Bousquet, O., Lal, T.N., Weston, J., Olkopf, B.: Learning with local and global consistency. In: Advances in Neural Information Processing Systems (2003)
13. Zhu, X., Ghahramani, Z.: Learning from labeled and unlabeled data. Technical report, vol. 3175, no. 2004, pp. 237–244 (2002)
14. Zhu, X., Ghahramani, Z., Lafferty, J.: Semi-supervised learning using gaussian fields and harmonic functions. In: Proceedings of the 20th International Conference on Machine Learning (ICML), Washington, DC, pp. 912–919 (2003)

A Novel PCA-DBN Based Bearing Fault Diagnosis Approach

Jing Zhu[1,2,3](✉) and Tianzhen Hu[1]

[1] College of Automation Engineering, Nanjing University of Aeronautics
and Astronautics, Nanjing, China
[2] Key Laboratory of Navigation, Control and Health-Management Technologies
of Advanced Aerocraft (Nanjing University of Aeronautics and Astronautics),
Ministry of Industry and information Technology, Nanjing, China
[3] Jiangsu Key Laboratory of Internet of Things and Control Technologies
(Nanjing University of Aeronautics and Astronautics), Nanjing, China
drzhujing@nuaa.edu.cn

Abstract. This paper is concerned with fault diagnosis problem of a
widely used component in vast rotating machinery, rolling element bearing. We propose a novel intelligent fault diagnosis approach based on
principal component analysis (PCA) and deep belief network (DBN)
techniques. By adopting PCA technique, the dimension of raw bearing
vibration signals is reduced and the bearing fault features are extracted
in terms of primary eigenvalues and eigenvectors. Parts of the modified
samples are trained by DBN for fault classification and diagnosis and
the rest are tested to examine the algorithm. A distinctive feature of
this approach is that it requires no complex signal processing procedure
of bearing vibration signals. The experimental results demonstrate the
effectiveness of the PCA-DBN based fault diagnosis approach with a
more than 90% accuracy rate.

Keywords: PCA · DBN · Rolling element bearing · Fault diagnosis

1 Introduction

Rolling element bearings are widely used in numerous rotating machinery. As the
high precision requirement in practical applications, it is of significant importance to monitor bearing components and maintain them in good conditions.
Bearing component in general is likely to encounter impact, oscillation, frac-
ture, structure change and clearance chang, etc. For most cases, these failures
may degrade the component efficiency and lifetime, even lead to catastrophic
accidents, which pose great challenge to the implement of rotating machinery.

This research was supported in part by the National Natural Science Foundation of
China under Grant 61603179, in part by the China Postdoctoral Science Foundation
under Grant 2019T120427, and in part by the Fundamental Research Funds for the
Central Universities under Grant NJ20170005.

© ICST Institute for Computer Sciences, Social Informatics and Telecommunications Engineering 2019
Published by Springer Nature Switzerland AG 2019. All Rights Reserved
X. B. Zhai et al. (Eds.): MLICOM 2019, LNICST 294, pp. 455–464, 2019.
https://doi.org/10.1007/978-3-030-32388-2_39

With the development of fault diagnosis techniques, nevertheless, various bearing fault diagnosis schemes have been proposed over the last two decades (see [1,13,18], and the references therein). An overwhelming majority of the available results are obtained in virture of analyzing the vibration signal of bearings, where the vibration is measured by an accelerometer directly [12,17]. Sorts of advanced signal processing and parameter identification methods are utilized, such as short-time Fourier transform [4], wavelet time-scale decomposition [21], cumulant spectrum [8], to name a few. Among those achievements, it is worth noting that [10] proposed a wavelet-based feature extraction method based on minimum Shannon Entropy Criterion to extract statistical features from wavelet coefficients of raw vibration signals; [15] developed a new fault diagnosis scheme utilizing the wavelet transform to process vibration signals and using an adaptive neuro-fuzzy system to classify the fault data; [17] presented a localized bearing defects detection method based on wavelet transform; [24] classified bearing fault categories and identified the fault level by adopting the Hilbert-Huang transform. These results somehow shed light on the signal-processing based bearing fault diagnosis. Frankly speaking, however, the difficulty in processing the vibration signal arises from the complicate and unclear formulation of the involved dynamic model, especially the nonlinearity in vibration signals and the uncertainty in fault state information. It is hard to get a precise model representation either from time domain or frequency domain aspects, rendering a dilemma of extracting fault-related features from bearing vibration signals. Furthermore, with the increasing scale and complexity of industrial control systems, vibration signals are partial to be with high dimensions and numerous data, making it far more intricate to process bearing vibration signals [14].

To this end, we propose an intelligent fault diagnosis method in this paper to extract the fault features from raw vibration signals in spirit of PCA technique. PCA is a statistical procedure and widely used for dimensionality reduction [16]. The idea that applying PCA to deal with bearing fault diagnosis was first advocated in [11], where a PCA-based decision tree was introduced and proved to have better classification performance compared with normal decision tree. In [19] and [5], a PCA and support vector machine (SVM) fusion bearing fault feature extraction method was proposed. [9] applied spectral kurtosis and cross correlation techniques to extract bearing fault features and developed a health index using PCA and a semi-supervised k-nearest neighbor distance measure. In [25], PCA was used to get description features from the combination of energy spectrums and statistical feature and then a BP based neural network model is established for the diagnosis of rolling bearing faults. Our work reinforces these existing results and develop the intelligent fault diagnosis approach further. We propose a novel approach based on PCA method and DBN technique. We use PCA to reduce dimensions of raw vibration signals, extract bearing fault features, and then generate fault feature vectors. Parts of these fault feature vectors are then input into a DBN as the training set, while the rest are tested to examine the proposed algorithm.

The rest of the paper is organized as follows. In Sect. 2, we introduce the basic theories on PCA and DBN. Section 3 presents our results on PCA-DBN based bearing fault diagnosis approach. Experiments are carried out to show the effectiveness of the proposed algorithm. In the end, Sect. 4 concludes the whole paper.

2 Preliminary Theories of PCA and DBN

2.1 Dimensionality Reduction by PCA

PCA is a multi-variate statistical method that transforms a large number of possibly correlated variables into a smaller number of uncorrelated variables. It is widely used in dimensionality reduction algorithm to reduce signal dimension by the following steps:

- Step 1. Given a set of vibration signal $X \in R^{N \times M}$, in which each row vector in X refers to one measurement and each column vector in X to refers to a samples $x_i \in R^{N \times 1}, i = 1, ..., M$. Compute the average value vector of all the training sets, which is denoted by A

$$A = \frac{1}{M} \sum_{i=1}^{M} x_i \tag{1}$$

- Step 2. Compute the covariance matrix P

$$P = \frac{1}{M-1} \sum_{i=1}^{M} (x_i - A)(x_i - A)^T \tag{2}$$

It is worth noting that since $P \in R^{N \times N}$, there are N eigenvectors in P. Calculate the eigenvalue $\lambda_i, i = 1, ..., N$ and eigenvectors $v_i, i = 1, ..., N$ of the covariance matrix P.
- Step 3. Sequence the eigenvalues from big to small as $\lambda_1 \geqslant \lambda_2 \geqslant ... \geqslant \lambda_N$ along with the corresponding eigenvectors $v_i, i = 1, ..., N$. The cumulative contribution rate α is consequently calculated in terms of the first r principal components

$$\alpha = \sum_{i=1}^{r} \lambda_i / \sum_{i=1}^{N} \lambda_i \tag{3}$$

- Step 4. If $\alpha \geqslant 0.85$, construct a new matrix $E \in R^{N \times r}$ composed of eigenvectors $v_i, i = 1, ..., r$, i.e., $E = (v_1, v_2, ..., v_r)$. The new sample set X' can be obtained by mapping the raw data through matrix E

$$X' = E^T X \tag{4}$$

where $X' \in R^{r \times M}$.

As such, a modified bering vibration signal set is generated which has lower dimension compared with the original one but maintains the primary feature information at the mean time.

2.2   Feature Classification by DBN

As is known to all, DBN technique has been frequently used in face recognition and hyperspectral image classification [20,23]. It was applied for aircraft engine health diagnosis and electric power transformer health diagnosis as well [22]. In [3], DBN was directly adopted for bearing fault diagnosis using raw measured vibration signal. Upon this, we propose an intelligent bearing fault diagnosis approach by using DBN to train the modified samples (i.e. the dimensionally reduced vibration signals) obtained by PCA. This can be viewed as the key step to the proposed intelligent bearing fault diagnosis approach. In what follows, we shall illustrate the main strategy of DBN technique.

DBN is a probabilistic multi-layer neural network consist of a plurality of Restricted Boltzmann Machines (RBMs), which are constructed by connections of visible layers and hidden layers [7]. The visible units (denoted by v) and the hidden units (denoted by h) are symmetrically connected upon weights w_{ij}. There is no connection among units within the same layer [2]. In this paper, we consider a DBN model consist of two RBMs, where the structure is as shown in Fig. 1.

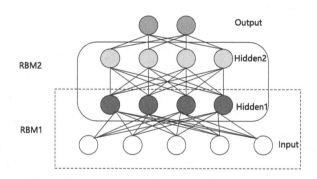

Fig. 1. Architecture of DBN

Define the energy function $E(v, h)$ of a RBM as

$$E(v, h; \theta) = -\sum_{i=1}^{n_v} a_i v_i - \sum_{j=1}^{n_h} b_j h_j - \sum_{i=1}^{n_v} \sum_{j=1}^{n_h} h_j w_{ij} v_i \tag{5}$$

where v_i and h_j are the states of visible units and hidden units respectively with a_i, b_j being corresponding biases. Let $\theta = \{w_{ij}, a_i, b_j\}$ refer to the parameter of RBM.

The joint probability of the visible units and hidden units is

$$P(v, h; \theta) = \frac{e^{-E(v,h;\theta)}}{Z(\theta)}, Z(\theta) = \sum_{v,h} e^{-E(v,h;\theta)} \tag{6}$$

where $Z(\theta)$ is the normalization factor. Besides, we have

$$P(h|v) = \frac{e^{-E(v,h)}}{\sum_{j=1}^{n_h} e^{-E(v,h)}} \tag{7}$$

$$P(v|h) = \frac{e^{-E(v,h)}}{\sum_{i=1}^{n_v} e^{-E(v,h)}} \tag{8}$$

Since that $v, h \in \{0, 1\}$ and there is no connection between the same layer, the probabilistic version of the neuron activation functions are derived as

$$P(h_j = 1|v) = \frac{P(h_j = 1|v)}{P(h_j = 1|v) + P(h_j = 0|v)} = sigmoid(b_j + \sum_{i=1}^{n_v} w_{ij} v_i) \tag{9}$$

$$P(v_i = 1|h) = \frac{P(v_i = 1|v)}{P(v_i = 1|v) + P(v_i = 0|v)} = sigmoid(a_i + \sum_{j=1}^{n_h} w_{ij} h_j) \tag{10}$$

The objective of training RBM is to increase the probability of input data $P(v)$ by following the parameters update laws

$$\Delta W_{ij} = \eta(< v_i h_j >_{data} - < v_i h_j >_{recon})$$
$$\Delta a_i = \eta(< v_i >_{data} - < v_i >_{recon}) \tag{11}$$
$$\Delta b_j = \eta(< h_j >_{data} - < h_j >_{recon})$$

where η is the learning rate, the notation of $< \cdot >_{data}$ refers to the expectation with respect to the distribution of observed data and $< \cdot >_{recon}$ refers to the expectation with respect to the distribution of reconstructions produced.

Due to the existence of normalization factor $Z(\theta)$, it is complex to calculate the joint probability distribution $P(v, h; \theta)$. In [6], a Contrastive Divergence (CD)-k solution was developed. It has been proved that $k = 1$ works well in practical applications. The CD-K algorithm is as shown in Algorithm 1.

3   Intelligent Bearing Fault Diagnosis Approach

The bearing fault diagnosis problem typically is regarded as a class of pattern classification problem, thus contains four main steps as data acquisition, feature extraction, feature selection and health condition identification. Our fault diagnosis scheme in this paper is carried out by following the procedure stated in Table 1. In the first place, we acquire bearing vibration signals. In the next, we define normal and fault types of the bearing component. Three types of fault

Algorithm 1. CD-k algorithm

Require: $k, S, RBM(W, a, b)$
Ensure: $\Delta W, \Delta a, \Delta b$
$\quad Initialize : \Delta W = 0, \Delta a = 0, \Delta b = 0$;
$\quad$ **for all** $v \in S$ **do**
$\qquad v^{(0)} := v$;
$\qquad$ **for** $t = 0, 1, \cdots, k - 1$ **do**
$\qquad\qquad h^t = sample\_h\_given\_v(v^{(t)}, RBM(W, a, b))$;
$\qquad\qquad v^{t+1} = sample\_v\_given\_h(v^{(t)}, RBM(W, a, b))$
$\qquad$ **end for**
$\qquad$ **for** $i = 1, 2, \cdots, n_h; j = 1, 2, \cdots, n_v$ **do**
$\qquad\qquad \Delta W_{j,i} = \delta W_{j,i} + [P(h_j = 1|v^{(0)})v_i^{(0)} - P(h_j = 1|v^{(k)})v_j^{(k)}]$;
$\qquad\qquad \Delta a_i = \Delta a_i + [v_i^{(0)} - v_i^{(k)}]$;
$\qquad\qquad \Delta b_j = \Delta b_j + [P(h_j = 1|v^{(0)}) - P(h_j = 1|v^{(k)})]$;
$\qquad$ **end for**
$\quad$ **end for**

---

categories are considered including inner race fault, outer race fault and ball fault with diameters ranging from 0.007, 0.014 to 0.021 in., which eventually leads up to 10 kinds of state conditions totally. Then we use PCA method to reduce the dimension of all the vibration signals and normalize the data within the range $[0, 1]$. In the followed step, the modified data are divided into two parts, training set and testing set. Then we initialize the parameters of DBN. The DBN is trained by training set and then examined by testing set. In the last, we analyze and obtain the final fault diagnosis result. We shall present our PCA-DBN based intelligent bearing fault diagnosis approach detailedly in the following paragraph.

Table 1. Procedure of our intelligent bearing fault diagnosis method

Step	Description
Step 1	Acquire bearing vibration data
Step 2	Define normal and fault types
Step 3	Apply PCA to reduce data dimension
Step 4	Divide data into training set and testing set
Step 5	Initial parameters of the DBN
Step 6	Train DBN by training set and diagnose on testing set
Step 7	Analyze and obtain the fault diagnosis result

3.1   Data Description and Reduction

We get the bearing vibration signals from Case Western Reserve University Bearing Data Center and use 2 hp reliance electric motor to conduct the experimental simulations, where the acceleration data are measured at locations near to and remote from motor bearings.

In most rotating machinery, the diameter of bering component ranges from 0.007 in. to 0.021 in. We consider three common sorts of bearings with diameter being 0.007, 0.014 and 0.021 in., respectively. At the meanwhile, three typical fault categories such as ball fault, inner race fault, outer race fault are concerned. Consequently, there are 10 state conditions in total including normal state, or in other words, 10 feature classifications in all. Parts of the time-domain response are as shown in Fig. 2. Obviously, it is hard to observe and classify these signal state features directly from their time-domain response. Alternatively, on the other hand, it is useful to collect all these points to extract feature by using the eigenvalues and eigenvectors of the generated fault feature matrix. To this effect, PCA technique is adopted to reduce the dimension of raw bearing vibration signals instead of common vibration signals processing.

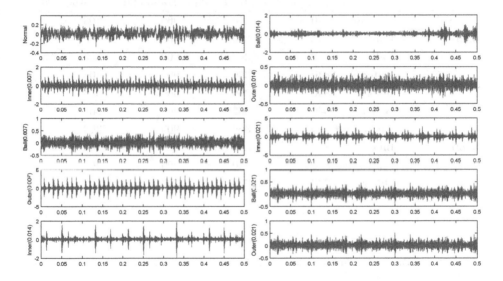

Fig. 2. Time-domain responses of different bearing vibrations signals

3.2   Experimental Results and Discussion

In this part, we use experimental results to examine the effectness of our proposed approach. The experiment data are collected at 12 kHz. All the datasets are collected upon four different loads as 0, 1, 2, 3 hp. Let the motor speed be close to 1800 rpm, and each sample contain 400 data points.

We consider four different situations. The dataset A and C are with 12000 original samples and the remaining dataset B and D are with 12120 original samples. In other words, we examine our fault diagnosis scheme under different sample sizes. On the other hand, we compare the DBN based and PCA-DBN based fault diagnosis schemes between the dataset with same sample size. The vibration signals in dataset A and B are directly input into DBN to diagnose the state condition and those data in dataset C and D are input into DBN after a PCA procedure. The four experimental dataset are described as in Table 2. From Table 2 we can conclude dataset A and B are with 400 dimension, and the dimension of dataset C and D is reduced from 400 to 123 since that the cumulate contribution rate of prior 123 dimension eigenvalues exceeds 95%. In what follows, we divide dataset A, B, C, D into two parts, training set and testing set, and normalize all the datasets into the range of [0, 1].

Table 2. Description of four experimental datasets

Fault diameter	Conditions	Dataset A and C		Dataset B and D	
		Training data	Testing data	Training data	Testing data
None	Normal	840	360	909	303
0.007	Inner	840	360	909	303
	Ball	840	360	909	303
	Outer	840	360	909	303
0.014	Inner	840	360	909	303
	Ball	840	360	909	303
	Outer	840	360	909	303
0.021	Inner	840	360	909	303
	Ball	840	360	909	303
	Outer	840	360	909	303

Table 3. Classification rate of four experimental datasets

Dataset	Training accuracy rate	Testing accuracy rate
Dataset A	85.96%	69.66%
Dataset B	88.38%	76.94%
Dataset C	94%	88.78%
Dataset D	99.6%	91.16%

The DBN model for Dataset A and B has a 400-300-100-10 structure, while that for Dataset C and D has a 123-100-100-10 sturcture. The learning rate of η of forward stacked RBM is set to 0.1. The momentum is set to 0.9 and the dropout is set to 0.1. The fault classification rates of four experimental datasets are as demonstrated in Table 3. From Table 3, we can see dataset C and D exhibit better accuracy rate than dataset A and B, which means the PCA-DBN based fault diagnosis scheme is better than the pure DBN based fault diagnosis scheme. In addition, dataset D shows the best accurate rate among all, indicating a larger number of sample contributes a better accurate rate. However, it is worth noting that PCA-DBN base intelligent bearing fault diagnosis approach hearing is not exempt from overfitting phenomena.

4 Conclusion

This paper presents a novel PCA-DBN based fault diagnosis approach for bearing component. We firstly utilize PCA technique to reduce samples dimensions, extract fault features, and then adopt DBN for fault classification and diagnosis. The effectiveness of the proposed intelligent bearing fault diagnosis approach is examined by experimental results. In addition, the PCA-DBN based fault diagnosis strategy can be applied into other large scale industrial fault diagnosis systems without manual feature selection.

References

1. Altmann, J., Mathew, J.: Multiple band-pass autoregressive demodulation for rolling-element bearing fault diagnosis. Mech. Syst. Signal Process. **15**(5), 963–977 (2001)
2. Chao, G., Yan, Y., Hong, P., Li, T., Jin, W.: Fault analysis of high speed train with DBN hierarchical ensemble. In: International Joint Conference on Neural Networks (2016)
3. Chen, Z., Zeng, X., Li, W., Liao, G.: Machine fault classification using deep belief network. In: Instrumentation & Measurement Technology Conference (2016)
4. Gao, H., Lin, L., Chen, X., Xu, G.: Feature extraction and recognition for rolling element bearing fault utilizing short-time Fourier transform and non-negative matrix factorization. Chin. J. Mech. Eng. **28**(1), 96–105 (2015)
5. Gu, Y., Cheng, Z., Zhu, F.: Rolling bearing fault feature fusion based on PCA and SVM. China Mech. Eng. **26**(20), 2278–2283 (2015)
6. Hinton, G.E.: Training Products of Experts by Minimizing Contrastive Divergence (2002)
7. Hinton, G.E.: A practical guide to training restricted Boltzmann machines. Momentum **9**(1), 926–947 (2010)
8. Huang, J.Y., Pan, H.X., Shi-Hua, B.I., Yang, X.W.: Bearing fault diagnosis based on higher-order cumulant spectrum. J. Gun Launch Control **2**, 56–59 (2007)
9. Jing, T., Morillo, C., Azarian, M.H., Pecht, M.: Motor bearing fault detection using spectral kurtosis based feature extraction and k-nearest neighbor distance analysis. IEEE Trans. Ind. Electron. **63**(3), 1793–1803 (2016)
10. Kankar, P.K., Sharma, S.C., Harsha, S.P.: Rolling element bearing fault diagnosis using wavelet transform. Neurocomputing **74**(10), 1638–1645 (2011)
11. Lee, H.-H., Nguyen, N.-T., Kwon, J.-M.: Bearing diagnosis using time-domain features and decision tree. In: Huang, D.-S., Heutte, L., Loog, M. (eds.) ICIC 2007. LNCS (LNAI), vol. 4682, pp. 952–960. Springer, Heidelberg (2007). https://doi.org/10.1007/978-3-540-74205-0_99

12. Li, B., Chow, M.Y., Tipsuwan, Y., Hung, J.C.: Neural-network-based motor rolling bearing fault diagnosis. IEEE Trans. Ind. Electron. **47**(5), 1060–1069 (2002)
13. Li, Y., Xu, M., Liang, X., Huang, W.: Application of bandwidth emd and adaptive multi-scale morphology analysis for incipient fault diagnosis of rolling bearings. IEEE Trans. Ind. Electron. **64**(8), 6506–6517 (2017)
14. Li, Z., Yan, X.: Study on data fusion of multi-dimensional sensors for health monitoring of rolling bearings. Insight: Non-Destr. Test. Cond. Monit. **55**(3), 147–151 (2013)
15. Lou, X., Loparo, K.A.: Bearing fault diagnosis based on wavelet transform and fuzzy inference. Mech. Syst. Signal Process. **18**(5), 1077–1095 (2004)
16. Mutelo, R.M., Woo, W.L., Dlay, S.S.: Two-dimensional reduction PCA: a novel approach for feature extraction, representation, and recognition. In: Electronic Imaging (2006)
17. Purushotham, V., Narayanan, S., Prasad, S.A.N.: Multi-fault diagnosis of rolling bearing elements using wavelet analysis and hidden Markov model based fault recognition. Ndt & E Int. **38**(8), 654–664 (2005)
18. Rai, A., Upadhyay, S.H.: A review on signal processing techniques utilized in the fault diagnosis of rolling element bearings. Tribol. Int. **96**, 289–306 (2016)
19. Shuang, L., Meng, L.: Bearing fault diagnosis based on PCA and SVM. In: International Conference on Mechatronics & Automation (2007)
20. Sun, K., Xin, Y., Yang, M.: The face recognition method based on CS-LBP and DBN. In: Joint International Information Technology, Mechanical and Electronic Engineering Conference (2017)
21. Tabrizi, A., Garibaldi, L., Fasana, A., Marchesiello, S.: Early damage detection of roller bearings using wavelet packet decomposition, ensemble empirical mode decomposition and support vector machine. Meccanica **50**(3), 865–874 (2015)
22. Tamilselvan, P., Wang, P.: Failure diagnosis using deep belief learning based health state classification. Reliab. Eng. Syst. Saf. **115**(7), 124–135 (2013)
23. Tong, G., Yong, L., Cao, L., Chen, J.: A DBN for hyperspectral remote sensing image classification. In: IEEE Conference on Industrial Electronics and Applications, pp. 2158–2297 (2017)
24. Wu, T.Y., Wang, C.C., Chung, Y.L.: The bearing fault diagnosis of rotating machinery by using Hilbert-Huang transform, pp. 6238–6241. IEEE (2011)
25. Xi, J., Han, Y., Su, R.: New fault diagnosis method for rolling bearing based on PCA. In: 25th Chinese Control and Decision Conference (2013)

A Visual Semantic Relations Detecting Method Based on WordNet

Wenxin Li[1], Tiexin Wang[1,2(✉)], Jingwen Cao[1], and Chuanqi Tao[1,2,3]

[1] College of Computer Science and Technology, Nanjing University
of Aeronautics and Astronautics, 29#, Jiangjun Road, Jiangning District,
211106 Nanjing, China
{freedomtot, tiexin.wang}@nuaa.edu.cn,
caojingwen1028@126.com, t-chuanqi@163.com
[2] Ministry Key Laboratory for Safety-Critical Software Development
and Verification, Nanjing University of Aeronautics and Astronautics,
Nanjing 211100, China
[3] State Key Laboratory for Novel Software Technology, Nanjing University,
Nanjing, People's Republic of China

Abstract. In order to implement automatic inference, this paper proposes a visual semantic-relations detecting method (VSRDM) based on WordNet. WordNet is an excellent relational dictionary, but it lacks deep semantic topology function because of its index-based text storage structure. As a graphical database, Neo4J provides visualization of its internal data. Since the abstract data structure in WordNet matches Neo4J's ternary storage structure, it is very suitable to map WordNet completely with Neo4J graph instance. This paper studies how to fully describe WordNet in Neo4J through a ternary structure. Neo4J stores the data as graphs (nodes and edges) and provides certain native graph algorithms to search the data. The speed of matching query between nodes is varying linearly with the number of nodes, so the efficiency of basic operation is guaranteed. With the help of Neo4J, VSRDM works as a semantic dictionary providing relationships matching, reasoning auxiliary and other functions.

Keywords: WordNet · Neo4J · Semantic relations · Knowledge-Driven

1 Introduction

In a server, when the CPU has a high load, skilled maintenance staff will initially locate the problem according to experience, and gradually deduce and troubleshoot. The staff conducts daily maintenance and troubleshooting based on each log that reports an error. How to use tools to automatically interpret or infer potential situations based on current states or conditions? Admittedly, using deep learning to train inferential models based on massive data is an effective mode, but how to make a reasonable judgment with limited data sets? WordNet is a tool that can help complete the above work. However, since WordNet is only a collection of structured data, a powerful processing engine is required to dig its potential.

© ICST Institute for Computer Sciences, Social Informatics and Telecommunications Engineering 2019
Published by Springer Nature Switzerland AG 2019. All Rights Reserved
X. B. Zhai et al. (Eds.): MLICOM 2019, LNICST 294, pp. 465–476, 2019.
https://doi.org/10.1007/978-3-030-32388-2_40

WordNet is an English dictionary based on cognitive linguistics designed by experts from Princeton University [1]. It has rich semantic relations, so it can be used as ontology and plays an important role in related fields.

However, most of the current applications built up on WordNet are purely semantic computing, which cannot give full play to the ability of WordNet as ontology. The native WordNet only provides functional interface and service as a dictionary. We urgently need a method to describe WordNet in a structured way and give full play to it as ontology.

Currently, Neo4J has been employed quite often in industry applications. For example, it has played a significant role in financial domain application [2], user map in social field and enterprise relationship map. The combination usage of Neo4J and WordNet will play a certain role as an easy-to-use ontology in an increasingly intelligent world.

In order to make full use of WordNet, this paper proposes a visual semantic relations detecting method based on WordNet. The mapping rules from WordNet to Neo4J are defined by analyzing the structure of the two. In addition, several simple application methods of WordNet powered by Neo4J are put forward to play a role of introducing jade. Figure 1 shows the overall structure of VSRDM.

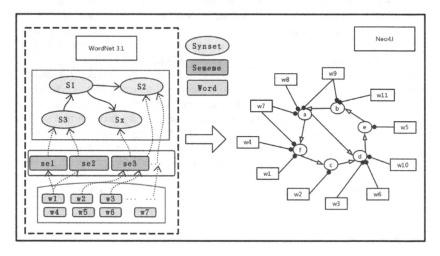

Fig. 1. The overall structure of VSRDM

The structure of this paper is as follows. The second section presents the technology foundation (i.e., WordNet and Neo4J). The third section analyzes the data structure of WordNet and shows the structure of the Neo4J database instance. VSRDM is implemented based on the analysis of these data structures. The fourth section shows a use case of VSRDM. Finally, the fifth section draws a conclusion.

2 Related Work

As a cognitive linguistics (English) dictionary, WordNet overcomes the problem of information organization in traditional dictionaries, it is suitable for semantic computing. Its core lies in extracting the semantic relationship between words, realizing the visualization through the concept of synonym set, and forming a semantic relationship network [3]. Each synonym set represents a basic semantic concept in which words are linked to each other in an indirect way. In WordNet, there are noun semantic network, verb semantic network, adjective semantic network and adverb semantic network [1].

At present, researches on WordNet are mainly concerning on semantic computation. In view of the present word similarity algorithm is widespread in the single source of information, the results of nonlinear on the high side, and the computing performance and efficiency of the inconsistent defect [4]. Based on the upper and lower relation diagram of WordNet synonym set, an algorithm is implemented which can calculate the similarity between English - English, Chinese - English and Chinese - Chinese words.

The affective dictionary constructed by HowNet is of high accuracy and availability in the construction of catering review affective dictionary. This proves that similar research can be done in WordNet [5].

WordNet is often used in the analysis of concatenation of multiple languages. In order to improve the adaptability of WordNet in different language environments, researchers in many countries carried out researches on how to add additional relevant clauses to increase the efficiency and accuracy of queries [6] (Table 1).

Table 1. Comparison of VSRDM and related studies.

	Semantic detection	Knowledge reasoning	Reasoning auxiliary	Knowledge graph construction
Research [7]	Y	–	–	–
Research [8]	–	Y	Y	–
Research [9]	Y	–	–	–
VSRDM	Y	–	Y	Y

Neo4J is a graph database specially used for network graph storage. It has higher mass data processing speed, more intuitive data, more flexible data storage and stable computing efficiency [10]. When the data volume and data association reach a certain degree, the traditional relational database becomes gradually weak, and Neo4J can deal with it stably.

Compared with the traditional SQL statement, the Cyper language used by Neo4J is more intuitive to express relationships. New data is stored as edges, nodes, edge attributes and node attributes without considering the structure of tables. Neo4J operates at a consistent speed thanks to its underlying graph storage structure and optimization algorithm based on graph data structure.

Many investigators study the embedded application of graph database by taking the graph of author collaboration in the field of education as an example to provide a fast and dynamic storage method. Research shows that graphic data is easy to use in database creation, query, update and other aspects, especially suitable for processing a large number of complex, dynamic, interconnection, low structured data, is an effective method to solve the social network, information visualization and other fields of mass related data storage [11].

3   An Overview of VSRDM

3.1   Preparation Work

WordNet Data Structure. WordNet enables to classify words by explanation, and a group of words with the same meaning is named as synset. WordNet provides a brief definition for each synset and records the semantic relationships between different synsets. There are four synonymic networks, namely, noun network, verb network, adjective network and adverb network.

The underlying data structure of WordNet consists of entry, sememe, and synonym sets, each of which has its own entry ID and is stored in specific text file. Each entry contains its dependent sememe ID, each sememe points to its dependent synonym set file, synonym set ID, and each synonym set entry contains its definition, usage, and relationship to other synonyms (Table 2).

Table 2. Synonym set relationships in WordNet.

Class	Core relationship
Noun	*Hyponymy/Merony/ComponentOf/Holonymy/Antonymy/Attribute/...*
Verb.	*Antonymy/Entailment/Cause/AlsoSee*
Adj.	*Similarity/Relational/AlsoSee/Attribute*
Adv.	*Antonymy/DerivedFrom*

Diagram Storage Structure of Neo4J. Neo4J stores user-defined nodes and relationships in a graph way, which can start from a certain nodes and find out the relationships between the initial and target nodes by taking advantage of the inter-node relationships with high efficiency.

The underlying storage way of Neo4J determines the capable direction. Figure 2 shows the case of supply chain management provided by Neo4J official website. Due to the large quantities and complicated types of factors involved in the supply chain, the analysis and decision-making of the supply chain is quite complicated. Therefore, it is quite significant to organize a clear overview and understanding of the whole supply chain. Neo4J enables to do us a favor to acquire a great understanding for supply chain management.

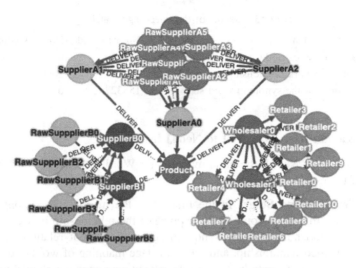

Fig. 2. Supply chain management [12].

3.2 Mapping Rule Definition

The mappings between WordNet and Neo4J can be realized based on the above analysis. The words and synonym sets are nodes, but they have different attributes of key-value pairs, such as lemma, WID (word's ID), sense attributes, the use of case examples, SID. Word related with synonym set, synonym set associated with synonym set ought to have connections, and these two kinds of connections also enable to possess various attributes, which respectively corresponds to the word and a synonym set.

While building the mappings, the difficulty exists in how to achieve a complete semantic mapping of heterogeneous data structure. This method applies the idea of three-segment mapping to achieve the semantic preservation of the mapping of WordNet dictionary to Neo4J database in a nearly complete approach.

The first step is matching synonym sets, in which all kinds of relational mappings between synonym aggregation points are not generated at the same time.

The second step is matching synonym set relational mappings. In this mapping process, breadth-first algorithm is used to traverse each synonym set associated with a specific relation based on the association set of each synonym set, and the connections between synonym aggregation points in the corresponding Neo4J is generated, and the related connection properties are filled in.

The third step is matching word mappings, in which all the words in WordNet are traversed and each word's sememe set is traversed, and the words are bound to the corresponding synonym set in fixed attribute connection based on the synonym set specified in the sememe (Table 3).

Table 3. Details of the three-stage matching.

	Processing content	No. new node	No. new connection
1st	Thesaurus network node	175979	0
2nd	Thesaurus network relationships	0	207016
3rd	The children of the synonym word set network	155327	0

3.3 Transaction from WordNet to Neo4J Instances

Due to the nature of Neo4J, the node mapping for WordNet must be implemented in the order of three-segment mapping.

Synonym Set Mapping Stage. In the first stage, the mapping of synonym sets is mainly to ensure that the second-stage mapping of the relationship between synonym sets and the establishment of the synonym aggregation point relationship will not generate a one-sided relationship, and the third-stage mapping of word nodes will not indicate null nodes. In this study, a WordNet parsing engine is maintained to generate Cyper statements for constructing synonym nodes. The general process is described by the following pseudo-code:

FOREACH(synset:ITERATOR)

CreateState+=createCyperOfSynset(synset)

Val STATE = CreateState

Neo4J_DRIVER.run(STATE)

In the first step, a fixed Synset type Synset is generated for each synonym assembly point, the name being determined by the Synset's corresponding lexical, and each synonym assembly point has the synonym set ID attribute, SID, and the description attribute Gloss. The generated Cyper statement is roughly as follows.

CREATE (a:Synset:[lexical1]{SID:[offset1],Gloss:[gloss1]})

+ CREATE (b:Synset:[lexical2]{SID:[offset2],Gloss:[gloss2]}) + ...

Synonym Set Semantic Relation Network Mapping Stage. In the second phase, the core of WordNet is implemented according to BFS: the mapping of semantic relation network between synonyms. During the construction of the Cyper statement by the interpretation engine, the MATCH and WHERE sub-statements are de-reprocessed, and the general process of generating the Cyper statement was described by the following pseudo-code.

FOREACH(subSynset:ITERATOR)

CreateState+=createCyperOfSubSynset(subSynset)

MatchState+=matchCyperOfSubSynset(subSynset)

WhereState+=whereCyperOfSubSynset(subSynset)

Val STATE = MatchState + WhereState + CreateState

Neo4J_DRIVER.run(STATE)

The second phase starts with each synonym marshalling point and traverses all the synonym marshalling points which have a direct semantic relationship with them. Each corresponds to a MATCH clause, a WHERE clause, and a CREATE clause. The connection between each generated synonym assembly point has various connection types according to the semantic relation, such as hyponymy, hypernymy, meronymy, component_of and so on. The generated Cyper statement is roughly as follows.

MATCH (s1:[lexcal_file_name]) , (s[offset1]:[lexxical_file_name1]) , ...

+ WHERE (s1.SID=[offset]) AND (s[offset1].SID=[offset1]) AND...

+ CREATE (s1)-[:[pointer1]]->(s[offset1]) + ...

Mapping Stage of Lexeme and Word Node. In the third stage, all words are traversed to generate corresponding word nodes, and word to synonym set binding is realized based on sememe. The explain engine will build MATCH and WHERE statements based on the SID of the synonym set pointed to in the sememe and generate CREATE statements that build the connections between the word and the synonym set. The general process of generating Cyper statements is described by the following pseudo-code.

FOREACH(synset:SENSE_LIST)

MatchState+=matchCyperOfSynset(synset)

WhereState+=whereCyperOfSynset(synset)

CreateState+=createCyperOfWordRelation(word,synset)

Val STATE = MatchState + WhereState + CreateState

Neo4J_DRIVER.run(STATE)

In the stage of building the word and synonym assembly point relationship, the creations of the word node and the related synonym set are resolved after the traversal of the sememe of the current word, where the connection type of the word to the synonym set is the fixed type word2synset. The Cyper statements built during the mapping process are roughly as follows.

MATCH (s[offset1]:Synset:[lexical1]) , (s[offset2]:Synset:[lexical2]) ...

+ WHERE (s[offset1].SID=[offset1]) AND (s[offset2].SID=[offset2]) ...

+ CREATE(word:Word{lamma:[lemma]})

+ CREATE (word)-[:word2synset]->(s[offset1]) + ...

3.4   Performance Optimization

Theoretically, the first stage and the third stage shall take the same time to create nodes. However, the reality is that, in the third stage, the word node creation takes two times higher than the first stage of the time-consuming. The reason is that Cyper statement need to find them (MATCH) if expect to link the two existing nodes.

While creating semantic relationships between a single word and multiple synonyms, the mapping node of each synonym set needs querying first. If multiple words are semantically related to the same synonym set, there will be too many synonyms in the current implementation to repeat the query process, which is also the reason for the huge time consumption gap between the third stage and the first stage. Similar problems were encountered in the second phase of creating semantic relationships for the same reason.

One approach to solving the problem of repeated query of nodes is to take advantages of DFS algorithm to create multiple relationships between multiple nodes in the same Cyper statement in a complete DFS recursive process, so as to reduce repeated query of the same node.

Another solution is that although the relationships between the three stages must be synchronous, any creation operation in each stage is thread-safe, that is, the creation of nodes and connections within each stage can be realized by multi-thread creation, thus improving the operation efficiency (Table 4).

Table 4. A comparison of matching processes.

Stage	Before optimization	After optimization
1st	1260 s	900 s
2nd	1800 s	1320 s
3rd	1400 s	1100 s

4   Functional Design

4.1   Maintain Native Dictionary Functionality

WordNet officially provides a web service, which supplies a complete dictionary function based on WordNet data and user inputs. In the mapped Neo4J entities, this capability is still maintained. Figure 3 is the web dictionary service provided by the official WordNet website.

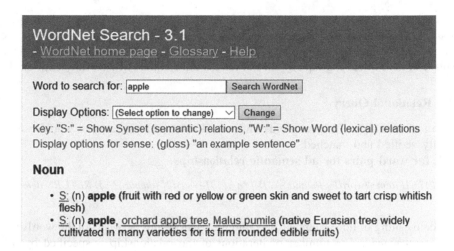

Fig. 3. Dictionary function [13]

4.2 Dictionary Functional Verification

Only use a single layer of semantic detection to query the nodes directly related to "apple" and compare it with the dictionary function provided by WordNet website. The Cyper statement is:

MATCH (n:Word)-[*1..2]-(k) WHERE n.lamma="apple" RETURN n,k

Based on this statement, it successfully found two synonym aggregation points directly connected with "apple", and the results can be displayed by JSON and visualization. The following Fig. 4 respectively shows the matching results of simulated dictionary query.

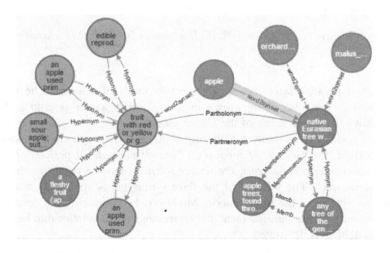

Fig. 4. Dictionary functionality based on Neo4J - "apple"

As shown in the figure, it successfully found two sets of synonyms of apple's direct semantic relationship by mapping the Neo4J instance, namely the junction of the noun_food type and the noun_planet type, and after comparing the JSON data and the result data of the webpage query, all the related information will be fully expressed.

4.3   Relational Query

In term of Neo4J, multi-level words and nested relationships between words can be visually verified and matched.

Look for word pairs for all semantic relationships.

MATCH item=(word1 { lamma :?...})-[*n...{...}]-(word2{ lamma :?...}) RETURN item

The meaning of this statement is to find the relationships between all the words i.e., *word1* and *word2*. The number of iterations of the relationship is specified by '*n*', which can be limited or determined.

Verify multilevel relationships of word pairs.

MATCH (word1)-[]->(synset1)-[]-...-[]<-(synsetn)-(word2)

The process of semantic detection is the analysis of the relationship between pairs of words. The analysis of the relationship between pairs of words generally sets the specified default value and has no other qualification conditions.

In order to implement a semi - automated generation of template - based Cyper statements, the implementation of relational - based semantic detection requires supplying a common interface to further extend the function of the method.

4.4   Relational Query Function Validation

To facilitate the description, it assumes that the following application example, using the Cyper statement:

MATCH (n:Word)-[*1..4]-(k:Word) WHERE n.lamma="spring" AND k.lamma="winter" RETURN n,k

In common sense, *winter* and *spring* are two kinds of seasons. The difference between them is that everything grows in spring while winter is cold and silent. Figure 5 shows the query result of the Cyper statement.

The blue node is the synonym gathering point, and each synonym set describes, from left to right, the *"season of recovery"*, *"one of the natural periods of the year divided by atmospheric conditions, the winter solstice, and the vernal equinox"*, and *"the coldest season"*. The relation of the three synonyms is apparently that the two nodes are the hyphen of the middle node. Moreover, by comparing the description of the synonym set with the familiar facts, the correctness of the relationship between the word pair matching is illustrated.

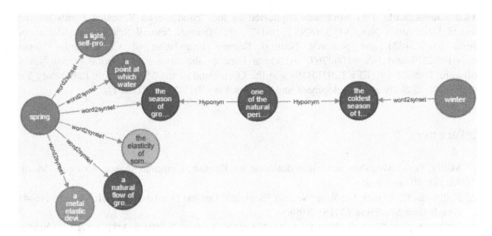

Fig. 5. Semantic relationship detection - "spring" and "winter". (Color figure online)

4.5 Reasoning Auxiliary

Regarding WordNet as ontology (semantic relation as the core and synonym set as the foundation), it has a clear description of semantic relation causality, hyponemical relation, inclusion relation, equivalence relation and so on. But also because of the natural structure of WordNet, the derivation of the complex and deep iterative semantic relations can only be detected by the traversal and judgment of relations. Fortunately, WordNet powered by Neo4J, provides the ability to truly network knowledge. The optimized graph algorithm in Neo4J can quickly and even visually show all the internal relations between things, and further realize the auxiliary functions of semantic reasoning.

5 Conclusion

This paper compares and analyzes the differences and connections between WordNet data structure and Neo4J graph instance storage structure, and describes a complete mapping scheme from WordNet to Neo4J graph instance. VSRDM is implemented and a use case of it is shown. Users can easily use VSRDM to achieve semantic relationships detection, semantic-based reasoning and knowledge graph construction.

However, the core of VSRDM, WordNet, has not been updated iteratively for a long time, so VSRDM cannot provide deep semantic analysis for vertical domains. On the other hand, the reasoning auxiliary function of VSRDM lacks automatic relation link extraction, and it is easy to have redundant relations in the process of relation inference. These problems require further study.

In the future, it is planned to expand the ontology adopted by VSRDM into domain-cross ontologies to further improve the ability of semantic relations detection of VSRDM.

Acknowledgement. This work was supported by the "Fundamental Research Funds for the Central Universities Nos. 3082018NS2018057", the National Natural Science Foundation of China (61872182), the National Natural Science Foundation of China under Grant No. 61402229 and No. 61602267, the Open Fund of the State Key Laboratory for Novel Software Technology (KFKT2018B19) and the Open Fund of the Ministry Key Laboratory for Safety-Critical Software Development and Verification (1015-XCA1816401).

References

1. Miller, G.A.: WordNet: a lexical database for English. Commun. Assoc. Comput. Mach. **38**(11), 39–41 (1995)
2. Fellbaum, C., Miller, G.: WordNet: an Electronic Lexical Database. In: Lal, M. (ed.) Neo4J Graph Data Modeling (2015). 1998
3. Fellbaum, C., Miller, G.: WordNet: An Electronic Lexical Database. MIT press, Cambridge (1998)
4. Kashyap, L., Joshi, S.R., Bhattacharyya, P.: Insights on Hindi WordNet coming from the IndoWordNet. In: Dash, N.S., Bhattacharyya, P., Pawar, J.D. (eds.) The WordNet in Indian Languages, pp. 19–44. Springer, Singapore (2017). https://doi.org/10.1007/978-981-10-1909-8_2
5. Rong, X.: word2vec parameter learning explained. In: Computer Science (2014)
6. Belalem, G., et al.: Arabic query expansion using WordNet and association rules. Int. J. Intell. Inf. Technol. 51–64 (2017)
7. Duong, T.H., Tran, M.Q., Nguyen, T.P.: Collaborative Vietnamese WordNet building using consensus quality. Vietnam J. Compu. Sci. **4**(2), 85–96 (2017). https://doi.org/10.1007/s40595-016-0077-x
8. Suchanek, F.M., Kasneci, G., Weikum, G.: Yago: a core of semantic knowledge. In: International Conference on World Wide Web (2007)
9. Pedersen, T., Patwardhan, S., Michelizzi, J.: WordNet: similarity - measuring the relatedness of concepts. In: National Conference on Artificial Intelligence AAAI Press (2004)
10. Drakopoulos, G., Gourgaris, P., Kanavos, A.: Graph communities in Neo4J. Evolving Syst. **6**, 1–11 (2018)
11. Lu, H., Hong, Z., Shi, M.: Analysis of film data based on Neo4J. In: IEEE/ACIS International Conference on Computer & Information Science (2017)
12. Neo4J Homepage. https://Neo4J.com. Accessed 05 Mar 2019
13. WordNet Homepage. https://WordNet.princeton.edu. Accessed 06 Mar 2019

Statement Generation Based on Big Data for Keyword Search

Qingqing Liu and Zhengyou Xia[✉]

College of Computer Science and Technology,
Nanjing University of Aeronautics and Astronautics, Nanjing 210016, China
zhengyou_xia@nuaa.edu.cn

Abstract. Natural language generation (NLG) is the process of automatically generating a high-quality natural language text through a planning process based on some key information. Regular NLG generates sentences by analyzing grammatical and semantics, generating rules, and then organizing elements based on rules and heuristics. However, sentences generated by such methods are too strict, poorly scalable and difficult to adapt to the changing language style of human beings nowadays. Our goal is to generate smooth, personal, multi-sentence text for end users. This paper introduces a new NLG system, which can generate distinctive statements, and discard the knowledge of semantics, syntax etc., which are required by the original rule-based generation statements. This system turns out to be simple and efficient. We obtain required corpus from the network, and then use the idea of the search engine to find sentences from a large amount of data that matches the meaning of the keyword provided by users. Such generated sentences are more consistent with people's daily life. Finally, we apply our system in the web commentary domain, evaluating our system based on three criteria. The result shows that our system works well in this field and can continue to deepen.

Keywords: NLG · Web crawler · Lucene structure

1 Introduction

Natural language processing includes natural language understanding and natural language generation. Natural language generation is a branch of artificial intelligence and computational linguistics. The corresponding language generation system is a computer model based on language information processing. Contrary to natural language analysis, it starts from the abstract concept level by selecting and executing certain semantics and grammar rules to generate text [1]. Natural language generation is the process of deliberately constructing a natural language text in order to meet specified communicative goals. Most of the previous statement generation is based on rules or statistics. For people's language tends to be more colloquial now, generator based on these algorithms are too rigid and can not express emotion, so it is difficult to generate statements that meet the public's requirements. So, after research, we introduced a simple, keyword-based statement generation system. The system requires a large amount of corpus resources, using the search mechanism, based on the keyword

© ICST Institute for Computer Sciences, Social Informatics and Telecommunications Engineering 2019
Published by Springer Nature Switzerland AG 2019. All Rights Reserved
X. B. Zhai et al. (Eds.): MLICOM 2019, LNICST 294, pp. 477–488, 2019.
https://doi.org/10.1007/978-3-030-32388-2_41

to perform a matching search in the corpus, and then feedback to the user's desired statement.

Review previous statement generation methods, usually use semantic grammar analysis. Through discovering the rules, generate some templates, and then use rules and some heuristic methods, putting words on the certain template's location to generate statements. There are also some better methods based on statistic like language model. In our network public opinion control, in the hope that the generated network reply content is in line with the spoken language of the Internet users, not stiff and with personal emotional colors. The statements generated by the previous methods are mechanical, without theme emotions, which can give people a clear feeling that it is a machine-generated statement that does not conform to the network terminology and our aesthetic orientation, so it is difficult to use it in some filed such as network public opinion control. Since the previous methods are difficult to fulfill our requirements for generated statements, in order to avoid generating mechanized statements, our idea is to use the Lucene framework and existing network statements to generate statements that conform to personal orientation.

In order to generate statements, we must first have corpus. We use web crawler technology to grab a large number of comments from popular websites such as Weibo and Zhihu. Then we build a keyword-based search mechanism using Lucene architecture. More details are illustrated in Sect. 3. After that, we conduct experiments to verify the effect of the system. Finally, we make a conclusion about our work, and based on that, we also make a plan for the future work.

2 Related Work

The generation of natural language requires some key information. Sometimes, the input is incomplete or inaccurate, which will affect the operation of the generator. In order to resist this problem, Knight and Hatzivassiloglou [2] suggested overcoming the knowledge acquisition bottleneck in generation by tapping the information inherent in textual corpora. Their experiments show that automatically acquired corpus-based knowledge greatly reduces the need for deep handcrafted knowledge. In their approach, lattice is used to instead a large number of phrases, which saving a lot of space. Although the lattice-based method is promising, it has some disadvantages. So Langkilde [3] presents a new statistical approach to sentence generation in which alternative phrases are represented as packed sets of trees, or forests, which are more compact than a grid. With the development of NLG, many scholars have proposed new NLG methods. Galanis and Androutsopoulos [4] present a natural language generation system—Naturalowl, which produces texts describing individuals or classes of owl ontologies in three steps: document planning, micro-planning, and surface realization. It can generate fluent and coherent multi-sentence texts for end-users, but Naturalowl was used mostly to describe cultural heritage objects. It has domain dependencies, so it has limited practicality. Samely, Cimiano et al. [5] develop a Natural Language Generation (NLG) system that converts RDF data into natural language text based on an ontology and an associated ontology lexicon. They apply this system to the field of cooking, and evaluating the fluency and sufficiency of this system, which works well.

Recently, Recurrent Neural Networks (RNNs) based approaches have shown promising performance in tackling the NLG problems. Mikolov [6] proposed a language model based on the recurrent neural network (RNNLM), which used for speech recognition. Zhang and Lapata [7] used RNN to create interesting Chinese poems; Wen et al. [8] recently proposed a recurrent neural network (RNN) for end-to-end learning generation based on Mikolov's RNNLM, then uses CNN and a backward RNNLM as rerankers to generate utterances. Because of the variety of human language styles, each NLG system has a targeted field. Here, we introduce a different statement generation system.

3 Automatic Generation of Statements Based on Keywords

We use web crawler technology to get comments from popular websites such as Weibo and Zhihu. Web crawler (also known as a Web spider) is a program that can autonomously collect web page content [9]. According to system structure and implementation technology, Web Crawler can be roughly divided into the following types: General Purpose Web Crawler, Focused Web Crawler, Incremental Web Crawler and Deep Web Crawler [10]. Based on our needs, we choose to use the simpler focused web crawler.

3.1 Focused Web Crawler

Focused Web Crawler, also known as Topical Crawler, is a web crawler that selectively crawls pages related to pre-defined topics. Compared with the general web crawler, the focus crawler only needs to crawl the page related to the theme, which greatly saves the hardware and network resources. The saved pages are also updated quickly due to the small number, and it also satisfies the needs of specific people for specific domain information [10].

Chen [11] improved the crawling strategy of the focused crawler system based on the Fish-Search algorithm and the Shark-Search algorithm. Although the accuracy of the crawling was slightly decreased, it could obtain a higher rate of discovery of the subject resources; Hailiang et al. [12] introduced a set of efficient crawler algorithm with less resources and customizable themes, which met the personalized needs of users; Zhang [13] combined the search engine supported by the web crawler and RSS information to learn from each other's strengths, and researched the RSS-based focused web crawler, which achieved good results in the university website group; Fang [14] and others used the link navigation technology based on the site page link structure to achieve efficient crawling of the topic information, and constructed a lightweight focused web crawler with low resource consumption, high data collection accuracy and control ability. A hybrid update mechanism is proposed to reduce the implementation complexity of incremental updates. Topic description, page filtering and link filtering are the focus of research on web crawlers. Compared with various types of improved focused web crawlers, we find that Fang Qiming et al.'s research is more suitable for crawling data in our research, so we study it as a reference for our crawling.

Since we crawled the data in order to reserve a large number of statements, did not need to analyze the data or for other uses. Therefore, we partially borrowed the ideas of the customizable focused web crawler for P2P search by Fang Qiming and others, and abandoned its theme customization features and other additional highlights. We make some simplifies on the basis of it, so that it can be more concise and efficient in our research. The general structural framework of our web crawling is shown in Fig. 1. Based on the consideration of the user's future use, we crawled the comment and grabbed the like number of the comment together. It turns out that the more comments' like number, the more influential of the comments. We have crawled 100,000 pieces of data from the Internet.

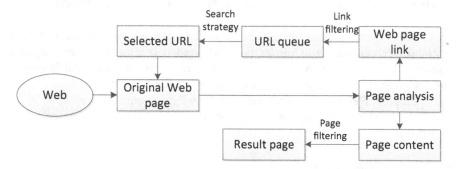

Fig. 1. The general system structure of the focused web crawler

3.2   Data Storage

When people express their opinions on Weibo, Zhihu and Tianya etc., they usually enhance their emotions by attaching some related expressions or pictures. When we crawl statements, these expressions and pictures are also being crawled, but their forms will be changed in this process. Irregular symbols will affect the normal expression of the statement. When the user uses it later, it will cause confusion. Therefore, when we grab the comment statement, we use the regularization expression to filter out these irregular expressions, only retain the text expression in the comment statement, and store it in the database. The specific process is shown in Fig. 2.

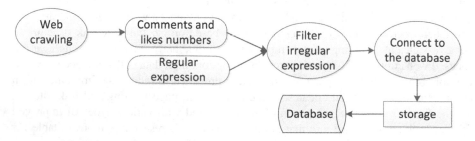

Fig. 2. Data filtering and storage

3.3   Search Framework Construction - The Use of Lucene

The search in this study is based on keyword search and borrowing the idea of search engine. For search engines, the most important thing is how to respond quickly and effectively to a large number of user retrieval needs. Therefore, when designing a search engine, the large amount of computation should be done as much as possible when the index is created. In the design of the search program, we should strive to improve the efficiency. Therefore, it is necessary to establish an efficient index library for documents. Lucene as an open source project, has triggered a huge response from the open source community since its inception. Programmers not only use it to build specific full-text search applications, but also integrate it into various system software to build Web applications, and even some commercial software use Lucene as the core of their internal full-text search subsystem.

Lucene [15] is a sub-project of the apache software foundation jakarta project. It has the characteristics of complete structure, clear hierarchy and good scalability, and provides relatively complete API documentation. At the same time, Lucene also has object-oriented and platform-independent—the core part of the system is encapsulated into an abstract class or interface. The specific platform implementation is designed as an abstract class or interface. It is a full-text retrieval engine architecture with low coupling, high efficiency and easy secondary development [16]. As an excellent full-text search engine architecture, Lucene adopts a highly optimized inverted index structure [17], which greatly improves the retrieval efficiency. Lucene implements full-text search in roughly two processes, index creation and index query. Figure 3 shows the entire search process.

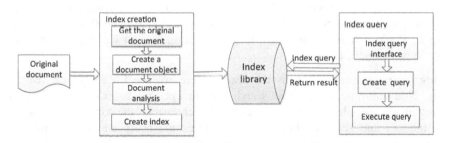

Fig. 3. Lucene full-text indexing process

Index Creation. *Get the Original Document.* The original document refers to the content to be indexed and searched, including web pages on the Internet, data in the database, files on the disk, and so on. Here, it refers to the data we crawled from the web page and saved in the database. We get the comment content and corresponding like number from the database as the original document.

Create Document Object. A document object represents a collection of fields. The domain of the document represents some metadata related to the document or the document. Based on our needs, we created two fields, which are stored separately and indexed as different domains of the document.

Document Analysis. After the original content is created as a document containing the domain, the content of the domain is parsed. Specifically, the text is split into a series of independent atomic elements called vocabulary units. Each vocabulary unit roughly corresponds to a "word" in the language. Because the language we want to parse is Chinese, and Lucene's own Chinese parser segmentation performance is not ideal, compare several different third-party Chinese word segmentation devices, taking into account the factors of the segmentation speed and the correct rate, we choose mmseg4j as our tokenizer.

Create Index. The traditional indexing method is find the content of the file according to the file and match the search keyword in the file content. This method is a sequential scanning method, data volume is large and search is slow. The inverted index structure creates an index that is indexed on the vocabulary unit, and the document is found by words. In order to achieve fast retrieval, Lucene uses an inverted index data structure. The specific steps to create an index are as follows: 1. Create an IndexWriter object.2. Create the document object. 3. Create a field object and add the field to the document object. 4. Write the document object to the index library using the indexwriter object. The index is created in this process. Index and document objects are written to the index library. 5. Close the IndexWriter object.

Index Query. *Index Query Interface.* The index query interface is an interface for the user to input keywords, complete the search and display the results.

Create Query. Before the user enters the keyword to perform the search, a query object need to be created. The query object can specify the document field and query keyword to be searched, and the query object generates a specific query syntax. There are two ways to create query object: use Query subclass provided by Lucene and use Query-Parser to parse the query expression. Since QueryParser can be flexibly combined, including Boolean logic expressions, fuzzy matching, etc., so we choose use Query-Parser to parse query expressions.

Execute Query. Lucene performs the search. Here we use Lucene's near real-time search. Near-real-time search can search the content that IndexWriter has not yet committed. The introduction of near real-time search enables the contents in the system to be indexed and searched faster, which reduces the overhead incurred when the system submits the index operation. Lucene implements near real-time search through the NRTManager class. Synchronization users after index update can get the latest index (IndexSearcher) in two ways: 1. Call the NRTManagerReopenThread object, which is responsible for tracking the changes of the index memory in real time, calling the maybeReopen method every time it changes, keep the latest index and open a new IndexSearcher object. IndexSearcher object which user need is NRTManager to obtain the SearcherManager object by calling the getSearcherManager method, then get the IndexSearcher object through the SearcherManager object and return it to user. After using it, call the release method of the SearcherManager to release the IndexSearcher object and close NRTManagerReopenThread; 2. Instead of using the NRTMan-agerReopenThread object, directly call NRTManager's maybeReopen method to get the latest IndexSearcher object to get the latest index. Here we use the second method.

4 Experiment

Natural language generation is domain dependent. NLG system invented by Sugiyama et al. [18] is oriented to the dialogue system, so the sentences they generate are used to simulate human dialogue, requiring sentences to be coherent and consistent with the topic of dialogue. Finally, they check their effectiveness by chatting with real users. The effect pursued by our system is to generate coherent sentences with personal opinions and emotional expressions and we made our experiment on the web comments filed. According to the needs of the field, we set three standards for the statements generated: smooth expression, clear theme and emotion. The following experiments are based on these three criteria to determine the effect of the generated statement. In order to better and more impartially evaluate the effectiveness of the system, we invited 7 netizens with online comment experience to participate in our experiment, based on there own inputs, making judgment on the three criteria of generation statements, and the opinion of the majority is taken as the final result.

4.1 Algorithm Evaluation

In the past, natural language generation was mostly based on rules and statistics. In order to verify the effectiveness of the proposed method, we performed a comparison experiment between different statement generation algorithms. Since our experimental field is web comments, the content format of the comment varies from person to person, and the syntax of each comment is different. The rule-based algorithm is not very good in our experiments, so we chose the statistics -based algorithms, two very popular language generation model—N-gram language model [19] and hidden Markov model.

N-Gram Language Model. N-gram is an algorithm based on statistical language models. The basic idea is to slide the contents of the text into a n-sized slide window, forming a sequence of n-length fragments of bytes. The occurrence frequency of all gram is counted and filtered according to the preset threshold to form a vector feature space of the text. Each gram in the list is a feature vector dimension. The model is based on the Markov assumption that in a piece of text, the appearance of the Nth word is only related to the first n-1 words, and is not related to any other words. Based on such a hypothesis, the probability of occurrence of each word in the text can be assessed, and the probability of the entire sentence is the product of the probability of each word.

Hidden Markov Model. The hidden Markov model is a statistical model for dealing with sequence problems. It describes a sequence of unobservable states randomly generated by a hidden Markov chain, and then randomly generating an observation from each state to produce an observed sequence. Hidden Markov model is a generation model that has been used by many scholars in natural language processing domain and has achieved good results.

Before the start of the experiment, some uncertain parameters of these two algorithms will affect the generation of the results. In order to carry out the experiment more efficiently, we select and determine the important parameters of the two models in advance. Since we only select parameters that perform better, in order to carry out more efficiently, we only extract 10,000 data from our corpus for experimentation of parameter selection. For the N-gram model, the value of n will greatly affect the generation results, so we have chosen different n values for experimentation. For the hidden markov model, we selected the number of hidden states as the important parameters for the experiment. The results of the two experiments are shown in Figs. 4 and 5.

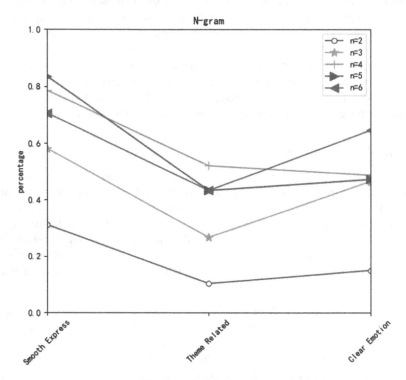

Fig. 4. Result for N-gram

Figures 4 and 5 show the experimental results of the two model parameter selections. For the N-gram model, we can see that when n is 5 the comprehensive effect is best, but in the experiment we find that the larger n is, the more repeated statements are generated, and when n is 5, more repeated statements are generated. But when n = 4, the repeated statements are relatively small and the model performs well on each standard, so we take n to 4 for the experiment. For the HMM model, we randomly took 5 numbers. The experimental results showed that the sentence coherence performed well, and other standards' performance were similar. After combining various aspects, we decided to set the number of hidden states to 10.

Table 1 is the result of our comparative experiment. It can be found that the 4-gram and HMM models perform well in the sentence coherence standard, but compared with the proposed algorithm, there is still a certain gap. Logically speaking, the statement we

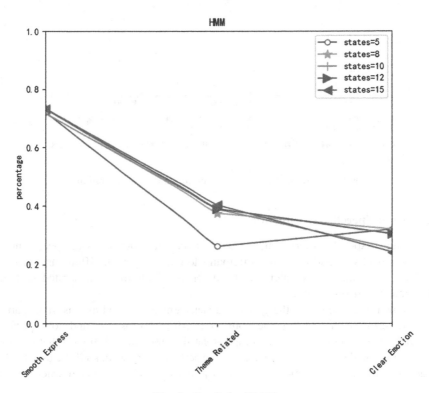

Fig. 5. Result for HMM

generated came from the reviewer, and the fluency should be better, but due to some network symbols and grammatical errors, our fluency did not reach 100%, but the effect is still very good. The performance of 4-gram and HMM model in terms of theme and emotion is not ideal, On the contrary, the model we presented is doing very well. Overall, our model performs well on all three standards. This means that our algorithm performs well in the generation of network statements, especially in capturing themes and expressing emotions. In order to more intuitively express the effects of our generator, we posted some sentences generated by our generator based on the keywords provided by the participants, as shown in Fig. 6.

Table 1. Comparison results of the three algorithms

Model	Smooth expression (%)	Theme related (%)	Clear emotion (%)
4-gram	70.73	39.02	36.10
HMM	72.50	38.33	33.33
Proposed	93.04	81.32	68.09

From the perspective of user usage, we also make experiments with the part-of-speech selection of keywords.

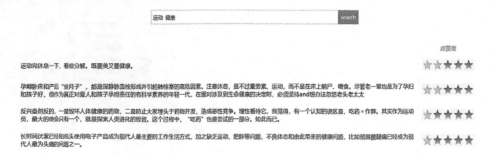

Fig. 6. Example for keyword-based statement generation

4.2　Part of Speech Experiment

For the part-of-speech experiment, we chose three important parts of speech: nouns, verbs and adjectives, and make 7 participants to randomly input 10 nouns, verbs and adjectives, then statistically calculate the different effects of the generated sentences with different part-of-speech.

As shown, the fluency of the generated statement is as good as it is in all parts of speech. In terms of the subject, the noun and verb performs well and noun performs better, if the user wants to generate a topic-related statement, we suggest that input is a noun. Finally, on the emotional side, adjective perform very well, so if the user tends to produce statements with some emotions, adjectives are recommended when entering

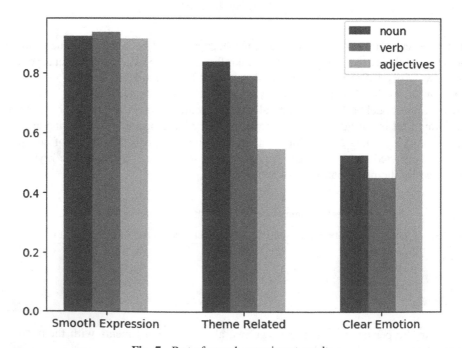

Fig. 7. Part of speech experiment results

keywords. But we can see form the figure, in general, nouns perform well in all aspects, so if the statements you want to generate cover a wider range, the noun is preferred (Fig. 7).

5 Conclusion and Future Work

We propose a keyword-based statement generation method that utilizes the idea of a search engine on big data. We uses the Lucene search framework to quickly generate a large number of statements related to keywords that user wants. Experiments show that sentences generated by our system are smooth, have clear themes and can express personal feelings, which is consistent with the effect of netizens' usual online reviews. At the same time, part-of-speech experiments show that users can get sentences that match individual inclinations by inputting keywords with different part of speech.

Although the statement generation of the system is simple and easy to use, but in our experiment, we also find that when the user uses the system to generate statements, statements that didn't match users' purpose will be generated, a lot of useless statements that are not related to the user's requirements are also generated. The reason for the phenomenon is that the corpus of the system is not perfect. The system relies heavily on the corpus, so the corpus is very important. And the content of the corpus needs to be updated continuously to generate statements that conform to the popular style, which is time consuming and labor intensive. So our future research will try to reduce the reliance on the corpus and generate statements in a more intelligent way.

References

1. Zhang, J., Chen, J.: Overview of natural language generation. Comput. Appl. Res. (08) (2006)
2. Knight, K., Hatzivassiloglou, V.: Two-level, many paths generation. In: Proceedings of ACL 1995 (1995)
3. Langkilde, I.: Forest-based statistical sentence generation. In: Proceedings of the 1st Annual Meeting of the North American Chapter of the Association for Computational Linguistics, Seattle, WA (2000)
4. Galanis, D., Androutsopoulos, I.: Generating multilingual descriptions from linguistically annotated OWL ontologies: the NaturalOWL system. In: Proceedings of 11th European Workshop on Natural Language Generation, pp. 143–146 (2007)
5. Cimiano, P., Nagel, D., Unger, C.: Exploiting ontology lexica for generating natural language texts from RDF data. In: Proceedings of 14th European Workshop on NLG, pp. 10–19 (2013)
6. Mikolov, T., Karafit, M., Burget, L., Cernocky, J., Khudanpur, S.: Recurrent neural network based language model. In: Proceedings on InterSpeech (2010)
7. Zhang, X., Lapata, M.: Chinese poetry generation with recurrent neural networks. In: Proceedings of the 2014 Conference on Empirical Methods in Natural Language Processing (EMNLP), pp. 670–680. Association for Computational Linguistics (2014)

8. Wen, T.-H., et al.: Stochastic language generation in dialogue using recurrent neural networks with convolutional sentence reranking. In: Proceedings of SIGdial. Association for Computational Linguistics (2015)
9. Chakrabarti, S., Van Den Berg, M., Dom, B.: Focused crawling: a new approach to topic specific web resource discovery. Comput. Netw. **31**(11), 1623–1640 (1999)
10. Sun, L., He, G., Wu, L.: Research on the Web Crawler. Comput. Knowl. Technol. (2010)
11. Chen, H.: Research and realization on focused crawler key technologies of vertical search engine. Master's thesis, Central China Normal University, Wuhan
12. Hailiang, Z., Li, S.: A customized focusing crawler. Electron. Technol. 51–54 (2009)
13. Zhang, R.: Research on RSS-based focused web crawler in college website group. Nanchang University (2012)
14. Fang, Q., Yang, G., Wu, Y.: Customized focused crawler for peer-to-peer Web search. J. Huazhong Univ. Sci. Technol. (Nat. Sci.) 153–157 (2007)
15. Hatcher, C.E., Gospodnetic, O., McCandless, M.: Lucene in Action, 2nd edn. Manning Publication, Stamford (2010)
16. Tang, H., He, Y., Xu, X.: Distributed parallel index based on Lucene. Comput. Technol. Dev. 123–126 (2011)
17. Liu, C., Guo, Q.: Analysis and research of web chinese retrieval system based Lucene, pp. 1051–1055. Computer Society (2009)
18. Sugiyama, H., Meguro, T., Higashinaka, R., Minami, Y.: Open-domain utterance generation for conversational dialogue systems using web-scale dependency structures. In: SIGDIAL, pp. 334–338 (2013)
19. Oh, A.H., Rudnicky, A.I.: Stochastic language generation for spoken dialogue systems. In: Proceedings of the 2000 ANLP/NAACL Workshop on Conversational systems, vol. 3, pp. 27–32. Association for Computational Linguistics (2000)

Machine Learning II

Batch Gradient Training Method with Smoothing l_0 Regularization for Echo State Networks

Zohaib Ahmad$^{(\boxtimes)}$, Kaizhe Nie, Junfei Qiao, and Cuili Yang

Faculty of Information Technology, Beijing University of Technology Beijing Key
Laboratory of Computational Intelligence and Intelligence System,
Beijing 100124, People's Republic of China
ahmedzohaib03@gmail.com, 1036685809@qq.com

Abstract. The echo state networks (ESNs) have been widely used
for time series prediction, due to their excellent learning performance
and fast convergence speed. However, the obtained output weight
of ESN by pseudoinverse is always ill-posed. In order to solve this
problem, the ESN with batch gradient method and smoothing ℓ_0
regularization (ESN-BGSL0) is studied. By introducing a smooth ℓ_0
regularizer into the traditional error function, some redundant output
weights of ESN-BGSL0 are driven to zeros and pruned. Two examples
are performed to illustrate the efficiency of the proposed algorithm in
terms of estimation accuracy and network compactness.

Keywords: Each state networks · Gradient method · ℓ_0
regularization · Sparsity

1 Introduction

Recently, the artificial neural networks are widely used to fit nonlinear dynamic
system with arbitrary precision [1]. The typical artificial neural networks include
radial basis function neural network (RBF) [2], echo state network (ESN) [3],
fuzzy neural network [4], hopfield network [5], and so on. Among these networks,
ESN have gained many attentions. As a kind of recursive artificial neural
network, the ESN is consisted of an input layer, a reservoir and an output
layer [6]. In the training process, only the output weights are trained. Hence,
the computational burden of ESN is less than other artificial neural networks.

The performance of an ESN is closely related with its reservoir size. If the
reservoir contains too many nodes, the training error may be small, but the
over-training problem also exists which leads to high computational complexity
and poor generalization performance. If the reservoir size is too small, the
ESN has to face the under-training problem. To optimize network size, many
algorithms have been proposed, among which the growing and pruning methods
are two main trends [7–12]. The growing ESN starts with a small network

© ICST Institute for Computer Sciences, Social Informatics and Telecommunications Engineering 2019
Published by Springer Nature Switzerland AG 2019. All Rights Reserved
X. B. Zhai et al. (Eds.): MLICOM 2019, LNICST 294, pp. 491–500, 2019.
https://doi.org/10.1007/978-3-030-32388-2_42

and adds reservoir nodes one-by-one or group-by-group in the network training process [8,9], this operation requires a long training time which results to heavy computational burden. On the other hand, the pruning method initializes with a large network and removes reservoir neurons or output weights in the learning process [10–12], the network performance can be increased by pruning the unnecessary neurons or weights. Hence, the pruning method is focused in this paper.

To generate sparse network architecture, the regularization methods are studied by adding the norm of weights into the corresponding objective function [13–20]. The commonly used regularization methods include the ℓ_2 regularization [16], ℓ_1 regularization [17,18], $\ell_{1/2}$ regularization [19] and ℓ_0 regularization [20]. As illustrated in [16], the ℓ_2 regularizer is able to control the risk of error amplification, but it is a biased estimation. The ℓ_1 regularization based algorithms could reduce network complexity. However, the ℓ_1 regularizer cannot satisfy the oracle property. Moreover, the $\ell_{1/2}$ regularization has the unbiasedness, sparsity and oracle properties. While, the $\ell_{1/2}$ regularization is not differentiable at the origin which causes oscillations in the training process. Furthermore, according to the regularization theory, the ℓ_0 regularizer is able to yield the most sparse solution among all the regularization based algorithms [20]. However, the ℓ_0 regularization is a NP-hard problem which is difficult to solve.

To optimize network size, the ESN with batch gradient method and smoothing ℓ_0 regularizer (ESN-BGSL0) is proposed in this paper. Since the ℓ_0 regularization penalty term is a NP-hard optimization problem, a continuous function is used to approximate the ℓ_0 regularizer. In ESN-BGSL0, only the output weights are updated by using the batch gradient method and smoothing ℓ_0 regularization, hence its computation complexity is greatly reduced than the traditional recurrent neural networks. Finally, two time series experiments are carried out to show the effectiveness of the proposed algorithm in terms of estimation accuracy and network sparsity.

The rest paper is organized as follows. The original ESN is introduced in Sect. 2. The proposed ESN-BGSL0 is described in Sect. 3. The experiments are done in Sect. 4. Finally, some conclusions are drawn in Sect. 5.

2   Preliminariies

The structure of an original ESN (OESN) without feedback connections is illustrated in Fig. 1. Without loss of generality, it is supposed that the OESN has n input nodes, N neurons and 1 output unit. For given L training samples $\{\mathbf{u}(k), t(k)\}_{k=1}^{L}$, where $\mathbf{u}(k) = [u_1(k), u_2(k), ..., u_n(k)]^T \in \mathbb{R}^n$ are inputs and $t(k)$ denote outputs, the echo states $\mathbf{x}(k) \in \mathbb{R}^N$ at the time step k is calculated as below:

$$\mathbf{x}(k) = \mathbf{g}(\mathbf{W}\mathbf{x}(k-1) + \mathbf{W}^{in}\mathbf{u}(k)) \tag{1}$$

where $\mathbf{g}(\cdot) = [g_1(\cdot), ..., g_N(\cdot)]^T$ are the activation functions of reservoir neurons, $\mathbf{W}^{in} \in \mathbb{R}^{N \times n}$ stands for the input weight and $\mathbf{W} \in \mathbb{R}^{N \times N}$ is the internal weight

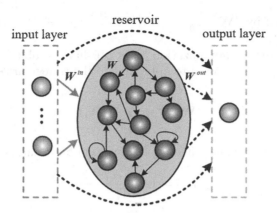

Fig. 1. The structure of the ESN without output feedback.

of reservoir, these two matrices are unchanged after initialization. Then, the OESN output $\mathbf{y}(k)$ at the step k is updated by the following equation:

$$y(k) = \mathbf{W}^{out}(k)\mathbf{x}(k) \tag{2}$$

where $\mathbf{W}^{out} = (W_1, W_2, ..., W_{N+n})^T \in \mathbb{R}^{n+N}$ is the output weight matrix, which is only updated during the learning process.

Now, suppose $\mathbf{X} = [\mathbf{x}(1), \mathbf{x}(2), ..., \mathbf{x}(L)]^T$ represent the internal state matrix and $\mathbf{T} = [\mathbf{t}(1), \mathbf{t}(2), ..., \mathbf{t}(L)]^T$ stand for the target output matrix, the output weights $\mathbf{W}^{out}$ can be computed by minimizing the mean square error as below:

$$\tilde{E}(\mathbf{W}^{out}) = \frac{1}{2} \left\| \mathbf{X}\mathbf{W}^{out} - \mathbf{T} \right\|_2^2 \tag{3}$$

where $\|\cdot\|_2$ denotes the ℓ_2 norm. The solution of $\mathbf{W}^{out}$ is commonly solved by using pseudoinverse [21]:

$$\mathbf{W}^{out} = (\mathbf{X}^T\mathbf{X})^{-1}\mathbf{X}^T\mathbf{T} \tag{4}$$

3   The Proposed ESN-BGSL0

Generally speaking, if the network size N is too large or the training data contains too much noise, the solution of Eq. (4) is likely to be ill-posed, which results in the poor prediction model. To solve this problem, the regularization method is introduced into ESN to prune network output weights and increase its estimation performance. By adding the ℓ_0 regularization item into Eq. (3), the conventional cost function is rewritten as below:

$$E(\mathbf{W}^{out}) = \tilde{E}(\mathbf{W}^{out}) + \lambda \left\| \mathbf{W}^{out} \right\|_0^0 \tag{5}$$

where λ is the regularization coefficient to balance the tradeoff between training accuracy and network compactness, $\left\| \mathbf{W}^{out} \right\|_0^0$ represents the ℓ_0 regularizer [22], which is calculated by $\left\|\mathbf{W}^{out}\right\|_0 = (|W_1|^0 + |W_2|^0 + \cdots + |W_{N+n}|^0)$ for $\mathbf{W}^{out} = (W_1, W_2 \cdots W_{N+n})^T$.

Since the ℓ_0 norm minimization is a NP-hard problem, the following continuous function $f(\cdot)$ is used to approximate the ℓ_0 regularizer,

$$f(\mathbf{W}^{out}) = \sum_{i=1}^{n+N} f(W_i) \tag{6}$$

where $f(W_i)$ is a continuous differentiable function on $\mathbb{R}$ and defined as below

$$f(W_i) = 1 - \frac{\varphi}{W_i^2 + \varphi^2} \tag{7}$$

where φ is set to a positive value. Based on Eqs. (6) and (7), the proposed cost function Eq. (5) can be rewritten as below

$$E(\mathbf{W}^{out}) = \tilde{E}(\mathbf{W}^{out}) + \lambda f(\mathbf{W}^{out}) \tag{8}$$

The gradient of the cost function Eq. (8) is given as

$$\frac{\partial E(\mathbf{W}^{out})}{\partial \mathbf{W}^{out}} = -\mathbf{X}^T(\mathbf{T} - \mathbf{X}\mathbf{W}^{out}) + \lambda \frac{\partial f(\mathbf{W}^{out})}{\partial \mathbf{W}^{out}} \tag{9}$$

with

$$\frac{\partial f(\mathbf{W}^{out})}{\partial \mathbf{W}^{out}} = \sum_{i=1}^{n+N} \frac{\partial f(W_i)}{\partial W_i} = \sum_{i=1}^{n+N} \frac{2\varphi W_i}{(W_i + \varphi^2)^2} \tag{10}$$

With an arbitrary initial value, the output weights can be iteratively updated by the batch gradient method,

$$\mathbf{W}^{out}(j+1) = \mathbf{W}^{out}(j) - \eta \frac{\partial E(\mathbf{W}^{out})}{\partial \mathbf{W}^{out}} \tag{11}$$

where $\eta > 0$ is the pre-defined learning rate and j is the updating iteration.

Based on above discussion, the operational process of the proposed ESN-BGSL0 can be summarized as below,

Step 1. Randomly generate an initial reservoir weight matrix $\mathbf{W}_0$ with predefined sparsity and reservoir size N, then update the matrix $\mathbf{W}_0$ as $\mathbf{W} = \alpha_{\mathbf{W}} \mathbf{W}_0 / \rho(\mathbf{W}_0)$, where $0 < \alpha_{\mathbf{W}} < 1$ and $\rho(\mathbf{W}_0)$ is the spectral radius of $\mathbf{W}_0$. Furthermore, initialize the input weight matrix $\mathbf{W}^{in}$.
Step 2. Drive the reservoir by input signals as shown in Eq. (2), collect the reservoir states to obtain the internal state matrix $\mathbf{X}$.
Step 3. Set $j = 0$, initial the output weights matrix $\mathbf{W}^{out}$.
Step 4. Increase $j = j+1$, With the predefined learning rate η, regularization coefficient λ and positive value φ, update the output weights matrix $\mathbf{W}^{out}(j)$ according to Eqs. (7) to (11).
Step 5. If j reaches to the predefined maximum iteration J, the algorithm stops; Otherwise, turn to Step 4.

4 Simulation Results and Discussion

In this section, the effectiveness of the proposed ESN-BGLS0 is evaluated by the root mean square error (RMSE) [2], which is defined as follows

$$RMSE = \sqrt{\sum_{k=1}^{L} \frac{(t(k) - y(k))^2}{L}} \tag{12}$$

where $t(k)$ and $y(k)$ denote the kth target and ESN outputs, respectively, L is the number of training sample. Moreover, the ESN-BGLS0 is tested on the Lorenz time series prediction and Mackey-Glass time series prediction problems.

4.1 Lorenz Time Series Prediction

As a chaotic dynamical time series, the Lorenz system is governed by the following equations [21]

$$\frac{dx}{di} = a(-x + y)$$

$$\frac{dy}{di} = bx - y - xz \tag{13}$$

$$\frac{dz}{di} = xy - cz$$

where the parameters are set as $a = 10$, $b = 28$ and $c = 8/3$. The Runge-Kutta method with step 0.01 is used to generate the Lorenz time series values. In each pair of training samples and test samples, $y(k - 3)$, $y(k - 2)$ and $y(k - 1)$ are used to predict $y(k)$. In addition, the initial reservoir size is set as 300. In this experiment, 2400 samples are generated, in which 1200 samples are used as the training dataset and the remaining values are treated as testing dataset.

To study the effectiveness of regularization coefficient λ on network performance, the training RMSE values and the resulted network size $\tilde{N}$ with different λ are illustrated in Table 1. It is noted that the learning rate is set as $\eta = 0.01$ and $\varphi = 0.05$. It is easily found that too large ($\lambda = 10$) or too small ($\lambda = 0$) regularization parameter cannot generate good prediction accuracy. While the proper value $\lambda = 1$ could obtain the sparse network topology $\tilde{N} = 24$ and good training RMSE value 0.0291. Therefore, the determination of regularization parameter is critical for ESN-BGLS0.

The evolving process of training RMSE and the number of non-zero output weights number versus algorithm iterations j are shown in Fig. 2(a) and (b), respectively. It is easily found that when j increases, the training RMSE decreases monotonically and tends to a constant value. Simultaneously, the network size is gradually reduced, which means that the batch gradient with smoothing ℓ_0 regularizer generates the spare network topology.

Table 1. Algorithm parameters for Lorenz time series prediction

λ	10	1	0.1	0.01	0
$\tilde{N}$	4	24	141	147	161
Training RMSE	0.1821	0.0291	0.0304	0.0313	0.0334
Testing RMSE	0.1878	0.0307	0.0327	0.0337	0.0361

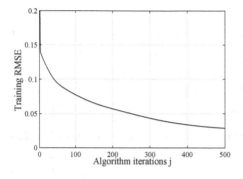 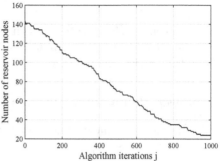

(a) The training RMSE values evolving process.　(b) The network size evolving process.

Fig. 2. The evolving process of training RMSE values and network size versus algorithm iterations j.

In the testing phase, the prediction results and testing errors of ESN-BGLS0 and OESN are illustrated in Fig. 3(a) and (b), respectively. It is easily found that the outputs of ESN-BGLS0 could fit to the targets well, also the testing error of ESN-BGLS0 is smaller than that of OESN. This observations imply that the better prediction performance is obtained by ESN-BGLS0 than OESN.

To proof of the effectiveness of ESN-BGLS0, its performance is compared with OESN and the ESN which is trained by the batch gradient (ESN-BG). The comparisons are showed in Table 2, including the training time (s), the training and testing RMSE values, the final network size $\tilde{N}$. From Table 2, it is easily found that the ESN-BGLS0 obtains the smallest training and testing RMSE values with the sparsest network topology among all the evaluated algorithms.

Table 2. Algorithm comparisons for Lorenz time series prediction

Approaches	$\tilde{N}$	Training time(s)	Training RMSE	Testing RMSE
ESN-BGSL0 ($\lambda = 1$)	3	157.217	0.0291	0.0307
ESN-BGSL0	161	150.494	0.0334	0.0361
OESN	300	1.257	0.0519	0.0554

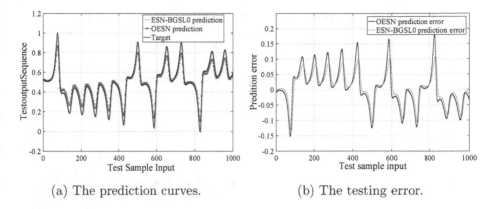

(a) The prediction curves.   (b) The testing error.

Fig. 3. The prediction and testing error of ESN-BGSL0 and OESN.

4.2 Mackey-Glass Time Series Prediction

The Mackey-Glass time series is derived by a time-delay differential system with the following form [23]

$$\frac{\mathrm{d}x}{\mathrm{d}t} = \beta x(t) + \frac{ax(t-\delta)}{1 + x(t-\delta)^{10}} \tag{14}$$

where the parameters are set as $\beta = 0$, $\alpha = 0.2$, and $\delta = 17$. The dataset is constructed by the second-order Runge-Kutta method with step size 0.1. In this experiment, 2400 samples are used, in which 1200 samples are used as training dataset and the remaining 1200 values are treated as test dataset.

The training RMSE values with different regularization parameters λ are listed in Table 3. Obviously, the too large or too small λ cannot generate good network compactness and training accuracy. To further study the effectiveness of the proposed ESN-BGSL0, the training RMSE values and the number of non-zero output weights versus batch gradient iterations j are shown in Fig. 4(a) and (b), respectively. It can be clearly seen that the training RMSE values is gradually reduced when j is increased. In addition, the complexity of the network is greatly simplified in the training process, which implies the network sparsity is improved.

To evaluate the estimation performance of ESN-BGSL0, the prediction outputs and prediction errors of ESN-BGSL0 and OESN are shown in Fig. 5(a) and (b), respectively. Obviously, the ESN-BGSL0 has smaller prediction error than that of OESN, thus the validity of ESN-BGSL0 is illustrated.

The performance comparisons between different algorithms are given in Table 4. It can be seen that the ESN-BGSL0 has the smallest training RMSE value (0.0346) and the best network size (18), this fact implies that the network estimation accuracy and network compactness have been greatly improved by using the smoothing ℓ_0 regularization penalty term.

Table 3. Algorithm parameters for Mackey-Glass time-series prediction

λ	3	0.3	0.03	0.003	0
$\tilde{N}$	4	18	133	139	148
Training RMSE	0.0463	0.0346	0.0350	0.0371	0.0383
Testing RMSE	0.0481	0.0349	0.0354	0.0384	0.0395

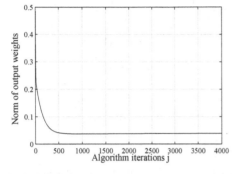 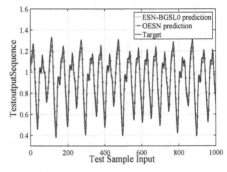

(a) The training RMSE values evolving (b) The network size evolving process.
process.

Fig. 4. The evolving process of training RMSE and network size versus algorithm iterations j.

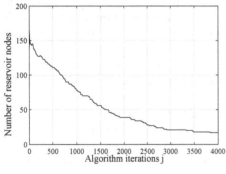 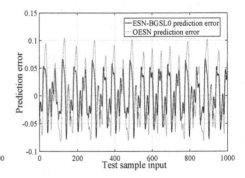

(a) The prediction curves.   (b) The testing error.

Fig. 5. The prediction and testing error of ESN-BGSL0 and OESN for Mackey-Glass time series prediction.

Table 4. Algorithm comparisons for Mackey-Glass time series prediction

Approaches	$\tilde{N}$	Training time(s)	Training RMSE	Testing RMSE
ESN-BGSL0 ($\lambda = 0.3$)	18	627.172	0.0346	0.0349
ESN-BGSL0	148	614.975	0.0383	0.0395
OESN	300	1.168	0.0503	0.0524

5   Conclusions

To solve the ill-posed problem is ESN, the batch gradient method and ℓ_0 regularization are combined together to train and prune ESN topology. In the proposed algorithm, the ℓ_0 norm of output weights are added into the objective function, which is solved by the batch gradient descent algorithm. As illustrated by the simulation results, the proposed ESN owns smaller network size and better prediction accuracy than OESN.

Acknowledgement. This work was supported by the National Natural Science Foundation of China under Grants 61603012, 61533002 and 61890930-5, the Beijing Municipal Education Commission Foundation under Grant KM201710005025, the Major Science and Technology Program for Water Pollution Control and Treatment of China (2018ZX07111005), the National Key Research and Development Project under Grants 2018YFC1900800-5.

References

1. Schäfer, A.M., Zimmermann, H.G.: Recurrent neural networks are universal approximators. In: Kollias, S.D., Stafylopatis, A., Duch, W., Oja, E. (eds.) ICANN 2006. LNCS, vol. 4131, pp. 632–640. Springer, Heidelberg (2006). https://doi.org/10.1007/11840817_66
2. Han, H.G., Chen, Q.L., Qiao, J.F.: An efficient self-organizing RBF neural network for water quality prediction. Neural Netw. Off. J. Int. Neural Netw. Soc. **24**(7), 717–725 (2011)
3. Jaeger, H.: Echo state network. Scholarpedia **2**(9), 1479–1482 (2007)
4. Hayashi, Y., Buckley, J.J., Czogala, E.: Fuzzy neural network with fuzzy signals and weights. Int. J. Intell. Syst. **8**(4), 527–537 (2010)
5. Song, B., Zhang, Y., Shu, Z., et al.: Stability analysis of Hopfield neural networks perturbed by Poisson noises. Neurocomputing **196**(C), 53–58 (2016)
6. Xue, Y., Yang, L., Haykin, S.: Decoupled echo state networks with lateral inhibition. Neural Netw. Off. J. Int. Neural Netw. Soc. **20**(3), 365–376 (2007)
7. Augasta, M.G., Kathirvalavakumar, T.: A novel pruning algorithm for optimizing feedforward neural network of classification problems. Neural Process. Lett. **34**(3), 241–258 (2011)
8. Fan-jun, L., Ying, L.: An approach to design growing echo state networks. In: Yin, H., et al. (eds.) IDEAL 2016. LNCS, vol. 9937, pp. 220–230. Springer, Cham (2016). https://doi.org/10.1007/978-3-319-46257-8_24
9. Qiao, J., Li, F., Han, H., et al.: Growing echo-state network with multiple subreservoirs. IEEE Trans. Neural Netw. Learn. Syst. **28**(2), 391–404 (2017)
10. Scardapane, S., Nocco, G., Comminiello, D., et al.: An effective criterion for pruning reservoir's connections in echo state networks. In: International Joint Conference on Neural Networks. IEEE (2015)
11. Scardapane, S., Comminiello, D., Scarpiniti, M., Uncini, A.: Significance-based pruning for reservoir's neurons in echo state networks. In: Bassis, S., Esposito, A., Morabito, F.C. (eds.) Advances in Neural Networks: Computational and Theoretical Issues. SIST, vol. 37, pp. 31–38. Springer, Cham (2015). https://doi.org/10.1007/978-3-319-18164-6_4

12. Li, D., Liu, F., Qiao, J., et al.: Structure optimization for echo state network based on contribution. Tsinghua Sci. Technol. **24**(01), 99–107 (2019)
13. Loone, S., Irwin, G.: Improving neural network training solutions using regularisation. Neurocomputing, **37**, 71–90
14. Setiono, R.: A penalty-function approach for pruning feedforward neural networks. Neural Comput. **9**, 185–204
15. Shao, H.M., Xu, D.P., Zheng, G.F., Liu, L.J.: Convergence of an online gradient method with inner-product penalty and adaptive momentum. Neurocomputing, **77**, 243–252
16. Dutoit, X., Schrauwen, B., Campenhout, J.V., et al.: Pruning and regularization in reservoir computing. Neurocomputing **72**(7–9), 1534–1546 (2009)
17. Han, M., Ren, W.-J., Xu, M.-L.: An improved echo state network via L1-norm regularization. Acta Automatica Sinica **40**(11), 2428–2435 (2014)
18. Scardapane, S., Panella, M., Comminiello, D., Hussian, A., Uncini, A.: Distributed reservoir computing with sparse readouts research frontier. IEEE Comput. **11**(4), 59–70 (2016)
19. Wu, W., Fan, Q., Zurada, J.M., et al.: Batch gradient method with smoothing $l_1/2$ regularization for training of feedforward neural networks. Neural Netw. Off. J. Int. Neural Netw. Soc. **50**(2), 72 (2013)
20. Louizos, C., Welling, M., Kingma, D.P.: Learning sparse neural networks through l_0 regularization (2018)
21. Yang, C., Qiao, J., Han, H., et al.: Design of polynomial echo state networks for time series prediction. Neurocomputing **290**, 148–160 (2018)
22. Zhang, H., Tang, Y., Liu, X.: Batch gradient training method with smoothing l_0 regularization for feedforward neural networks. Neural Comput. Appl. **26**(2), 383–390 (2015)
23. Yang, C., Qiao, J., Wang, L., et al.: Dynamical regularized echo state network for time series prediction. Neural Comput. Appl. (3–4), 1–14 (2018)

A Backward Learning Algorithm in Polynomial Echo State Networks

Cuili Yang[✉], Xinxin Zhu, and Junfei Qiao

Faculty of Information Technology,
Beijing University of Technology Beijing Key Laboratory
of Computational Intelligence and Intelligence System,
Beijing 100124, People's Republic of China
{clyang5,junfeiq}@bjut.edu.cn,
804340106@qq.com, 1205580412@qq.com

Abstract. Recently, the polynomial echo state network (PESN) has been proposed to incorporate the high order information of input features. However, there are some redundant inputs in PESN, which results in high computational cost. To solve this problem, a backward learning algorithm is designed for PESN, which is denoted as BL-PESN for short. The criterion for input features removing is designed to prune the insignificant input features one by one. The simulation results illustrate that the proposed approach has better prediction accuracy and less testing time than other ESNs.

Keywords: Polynomial echo state network · Subset selection · Backward learning algorithm

1 Introduction

Echo state network (ESN) has drawn great interest in the research field [1]. Compared with the traditional gradient based recurrent neural networks (RNNs), the ESN has faster convergence speed with better performance. The core structure of an ESN is the reservoir, which is consisted of a large number of recurrent connected neurons. In an ESN, the internal weights and input weights are randomly given, while the weights connecting the reservoir and the readouts are trained by the standard linear regression routines. Recently, the ESN has been adopted in different fields, such as time series prediction [2], the pattern extraction [3], speech recognition [4], and adaptive control [5].

Recently, many various ESN schemes have been explored, such as augmented complex ESNs [6], the minimum complexity ESN [7], the robust ESN [8]. However, in the above methods, the high order information of input features are not mentioned. To solve this problem, the polynomial ESN (PESN) was investigated [9] by employing the polynomial functions of complete input features into output weights. The experimental results showed that PESN performed better than traditional ESNs in terms of accuracy and testing speed.

© ICST Institute for Computer Sciences, Social Informatics and Telecommunications Engineering 2019
Published by Springer Nature Switzerland AG 2019. All Rights Reserved
X. B. Zhai et al. (Eds.): MLICOM 2019, LNICST 294, pp. 501–509, 2019.
https://doi.org/10.1007/978-3-030-32388-2_43

However, some redundant input features of PESN may be incorporated to construct the polynomial output weights, which not only increase the computational cost but also worse the testing accuracy. Thus, it is essential to prune the redundant features. To solve this problem, the forward and backward learning algorithms provide an effective way. The forward learning algorithms start with an empty model, then gradually add the term with the largest decrease in the cost function [10]. While the backward learning algorithms involve an over-sized network and delete the unnecessary term one by one [11]. Compared with backward learning algorithms, the forward learning algorithms are always sensitive to the initial conditions. Thus, the backward learning algorithm is focused in this paper. Recently, several backward learning algorithms have been developed for ESNs. For example, a pruning and regularization algorithm was proposed in [12] to prune the insignificant connection of the reservoir. Then, a sensitive iterative pruning algorithm was designed to remove the the least sensitive reservoir neurons.

In this paper, a backward learning algorithm is designed for polynomial ESN (BL-PESN) to remove the redundant input features. The BL-PESN is started with a p-order PESN in which the complete input features are chosen as output weights. Then, the redundant or insignificant features are pruned one by one until the required criterion is satisfied. Finally, some experiments are carried out to illustrate the effectiveness of the proposed method.

The rest of the paper is organized as follows. Section 2 describes the ESN and the PESN briefly. The criterion of pruning feature for BL-PESN is given in Sect. 3. In Sect. 4, three experiments are done. Section 5 concludes the paper.

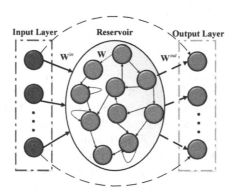

Fig. 1. The structure of the ESN without output feedback.

2   Preliminaries

In this section, the original ESN (OESN) and the PESN are briefly described, respectively.

2.1 OESN

The general structure of an ESN without output feedback is shown in Fig. 1. It is composed of n input units, m readouts and N recurrent connected neurons called the reservoir. $\mathbf{W}^{in}$ and $\mathbf{W}$ are the input weight matrix and reservoir weight matrix. The output weights $\mathbf{W}^{out}$ is trained by linear regression method. At the time step k, the vectors of input, output and internal state are denoted by $\mathbf{u}(k) = [u_1(k), u_2(k), ..., u_n(k)]^T$, $\mathbf{y}(k) = [y_1(k), y_2(k), ..., y_m(k)]^T$, and $\mathbf{x}(k) = [x_1(k), x_2(k), ..., x_N(k)]^T$, respectively. The internal state dynamic and the output equations of the ESN can be described as below

$$\mathbf{s}(k) = \mathbf{g}(\mathbf{W}\mathbf{s}(k-1) + \mathbf{W}^{in}\mathbf{u}(k)) \tag{1}$$

$$\mathbf{y}(k) = \mathbf{W}^{out}[\mathbf{s}(k)^T, \mathbf{u}(k)^T]^T = \mathbf{W}^{out}\mathbf{x}(k) \tag{2}$$

where $\mathbf{g}(\cdot)$ is the activation function and $\mathbf{x}(k) - [\mathbf{s}(k)^T, \mathbf{u}(k)^T]^T$ is the concatenation of the internal state $\mathbf{s}(k)$ and input vector $\mathbf{u}(k)$.

Denote $\mathbf{X} = [\mathbf{x}(1), \mathbf{x}(2), ..., \mathbf{x}(L)]$ as the internal state matrix, and the corresponding matrix of targets as $\mathbf{T} = [\mathbf{t}(1), \mathbf{t}(2), ..., \mathbf{t}(L)]$, with $\mathbf{t}(k) = [t_1(k), t_2(k), ..., t_m(k)]^T$. The least-squares estimation of $\mathbf{W}^{out}$ is calculated as

$$\mathbf{W}^{out} = \mathbf{T}\mathbf{X}^\dagger = \mathbf{T}\mathbf{X}^T(\mathbf{X}\mathbf{X}^T)^{-1} \tag{3}$$

where $\mathbf{X}^\dagger$ is the Moore-Penrose generalized inverse of $\mathbf{X}$.

2.2 PESN

In OESN, the high order information of the inputs is not considered. To solve this problems, the polynomial echo state network (PESN) is presented. In PESN, the p-order polynomial function of full input features is constructed as the output weights, which is expressed as below

$$\mathbf{w}_i(\mathbf{u}(k)) = \mathbf{w}_{i00} + \sum_{q=1}^{p}\sum_{j=1}^{n} \mathbf{w}_{ijq}^T u_j^q(k) = \mathbf{B}_i \mathbf{z}(k) \tag{4}$$

where $i = 1, ..., N+n$, p is the polynomial order. Define $M = np+1$, $\mathbf{z}(k) \in \mathbb{R}^M$ and $\mathbf{B}_i \in \mathbb{R}^{m \times M}$ are given by

$$\mathbf{z}(k) = [1, u_1(k), ..., u_n(k), u_1^p(k), ..., u_n^p(k)]^T \tag{5}$$

$$\mathbf{B}_i = [\mathbf{w}_{i00}, \mathbf{w}_{i11}, ..., \mathbf{w}_{in1}, ..., \mathbf{w}_{i1p}, ..., \mathbf{w}_{inp}] \tag{6}$$

Similar to Eq. (2), the output of the PESN at the time step k is described as

$$\mathbf{y}(k) = \mathbf{W}^{out}(\mathbf{u}(k))\mathbf{x}(k) \tag{7}$$

where $\mathbf{W}^{out}(\mathbf{u}(k))$ is generated as below

$$\begin{aligned}
\mathbf{W}^{out}(\mathbf{u}(k)) &= [\mathbf{w}_1(\mathbf{u}(k)), \mathbf{w}_2(\mathbf{u}(k)), ..., \mathbf{w}_{N+n}(\mathbf{u}(k))] \\
&= [\mathbf{B}_1 \mathbf{z}(k), \mathbf{B}_2 \mathbf{z}(k), .., \mathbf{B}_{N+n} \mathbf{z}(k)] \\
&= \mathbf{B}(\mathbf{I}_{N+n} \otimes \mathbf{z}(k))
\end{aligned} \tag{8}$$

where $\otimes$ is the Kronecker product, $\mathbf{I}_{N+n} \in \mathbb{R}^{(N+n)\times(N+n)}$ is an unit matrix, and the unknown parameter matrix $\mathbf{B} \in \mathbb{R}^{m\times M(N+n)}$ is shown as below

$$\mathbf{B} = [\mathbf{B}_1, ..., \mathbf{B}_{N+n}] \tag{9}$$

Substituting the Eq. (8) into Eq. (7), one obtains

$$\mathbf{y}(k) = \mathbf{B}\left(\mathbf{x}(k) \otimes \mathbf{z}(k)\right) \tag{10}$$

In this context, calculating the solution of $\mathbf{B}$ is equivalent to finding the least square solution of the following linear formula

$$J = \arg\min_{\mathbf{B}} \left\{ C \|\mathbf{B}\|_F^2 + \|\mathbf{B}\bar{\mathbf{X}} - \mathbf{T}\|_F^2 \right\} \tag{11}$$

where $\|\cdot\|_F$ denotes the Frobenius-norm, $C > 0$ is the ridge parameter, $\bar{\mathbf{X}} \in \mathbb{R}^{M(N+n)\times L}$, is given as

$$\bar{\mathbf{X}} = [\mathbf{x}(1) \otimes \mathbf{z}(1), \mathbf{x}(2) \otimes \mathbf{z}(2), ..., \mathbf{x}(L) \otimes \mathbf{z}(L)] \tag{12}$$

By setting $\frac{dJ}{d\mathbf{B}} = 0$, one gets

$$\hat{\mathbf{B}} = \mathbf{T}\bar{\mathbf{X}}^T \left(\bar{\mathbf{X}}\bar{\mathbf{X}}^T + C\mathbf{I}\right)^{-1} \tag{13}$$

3   The Proposed BS-PESN

In this paper, BL-PESN is proposed to prune the insignificant input features. In the following, the details of the proposed BL-PESN are presented.

Firstly, Eq. (5) can be reorganized as

$$\mathbf{z}(k) = [1, u_1(k), ..., u_1^P(k), ..., u_n(k), ..., u_n^p(k)]^T = [1, \mathbf{z}_i(k), ..., \mathbf{z}_n(k)]^T \tag{14}$$

where $\mathbf{z}_i(k) = [u_i(k), ..., u_i^P(k)]$, $i = 1, ..., n$. Following Eq. (12), $\bar{\mathbf{X}}$ is given as

$$
\begin{aligned}
\bar{\mathbf{X}} &= [\mathbf{x}(1) \otimes \mathbf{z}(1), \mathbf{x}(2) \otimes \mathbf{z}(2), ..., \mathbf{x}(L) \otimes \mathbf{z}(L)] \\
&= \begin{bmatrix} \mathbf{x}(1) & \mathbf{x}(2) & \cdots & \mathbf{x}(L) \\ \mathbf{x}(1) \otimes \mathbf{z}_1^T(1) & \mathbf{x}(2) \otimes \mathbf{z}_1^T(2) & \cdots & \mathbf{x}(L) \otimes \mathbf{z}_1^T(L) \\ \vdots & \vdots & \ddots & \vdots \\ \mathbf{x}(1) \otimes \mathbf{z}_n^T(1) & \mathbf{x}(2) \otimes \mathbf{z}_n^T(2) & \cdots & \mathbf{x}(L) \otimes \mathbf{z}_n^T(L) \end{bmatrix} = \begin{bmatrix} \bar{\mathbf{X}}_0 \\ \bar{\mathbf{X}}_1 \\ \vdots \\ \bar{\mathbf{X}}_n \end{bmatrix}
\end{aligned} \tag{15}
$$

where $\bar{\mathbf{X}}_0 = \mathbf{X}$, $\bar{\mathbf{X}}_i = \left[\mathbf{x}(1) \otimes \mathbf{z}_i^T(1), \mathbf{x}(2) \otimes \mathbf{z}_i^T(2), ..., \mathbf{x}(L) \otimes \mathbf{z}_i^T(L)\right]$. Correspondingly, the matrix $\mathbf{B}$ in Eq. (9) is rewritten as

$$\mathbf{B} = [\mathbf{B}_0, \mathbf{B}_1, ..., \mathbf{B}_n] \tag{16}$$

It can be determined that pruning the insignificant input features from PESN is equivalent to deleting $\bar{\mathbf{X}}_i$ from $\bar{\mathbf{X}}$. It has been proved that the cost function is gradually increased with an decreasing number of features. The smaller the increase value on the cost function incurred by pruning one feature is, the less important this feature is viewed to be. Hence, it can be justified which feature is insignificant from the increase value. Define a full index set $P = \{1, ..., n\}$, BL-PESN is initialized with $\bar{\mathbf{X}}_P = \bar{\mathbf{X}}$ in Eq. (15), and $l = 0$.

Assuming that BL-PESN is at the lth iteration. The cost function is described as below

$$\hat{J}^{(l)} = \min_{\mathbf{B}_P} \left\{ J^{(l)} = C \|\mathbf{B}_P\|_F^2 + \|\mathbf{B}_P \bar{\mathbf{X}}_P - \mathbf{T}\|_F^2 \right\} \tag{17}$$

If at the $(l + 1)$th iteration, the ith feature is pruned according to a certain criterion. Equation (17) becomes

$$\hat{J}^{(l+1)}_{-i} = \min_{\mathbf{B}_{P\setminus\{i\}}} \left\{ J^{(l+1)}_{-i} = C \|\mathbf{B}_{P\setminus\{i\}}\|_F^2 + \|\mathbf{B}_{P\setminus\{i\}} \bar{\mathbf{X}}_{P\setminus\{i\}} - \mathbf{T}\|_F^2 \right\} \tag{18}$$

Here, $\bar{\mathbf{X}}_P = \begin{bmatrix} \bar{\mathbf{X}}_{P\setminus\{i\}} \\ \bar{\mathbf{X}}_i \end{bmatrix}$, $\mathbf{B}_P = [\mathbf{B}_{P\setminus\{i\}}, \mathbf{B}_i]$. Equation (17) can be rewritten as

$$\begin{aligned} \hat{J}^{(q)} &= \arg\min_{\mathbf{B}_p} \left\{ J^{(q)} = C \|[\mathbf{B}_{P\setminus\{i\}}, \mathbf{B}_i]\|_F^2 + \left\|[\mathbf{B}_{P\setminus\{i\}}, \mathbf{B}_i] \begin{bmatrix} \bar{\mathbf{X}}_{P\setminus\{i\}} \\ \bar{\mathbf{X}}_i \end{bmatrix} - \mathbf{T} \right\|_F^2 \right\} \\ &= \arg\min_{\mathbf{B}_i} \left\{ \hat{J}^{(q+1)}_{-i} + \|\mathbf{B}_i \bar{\mathbf{X}}_i\|_F^2 + C \|\mathbf{B}_i\|_F^2 - 2tr\left(\left(\hat{\mathbf{B}}_{P\setminus\{i\}} \bar{\mathbf{X}}_{P\setminus\{i\}} - \mathbf{T}\right)^T \mathbf{B}_i \bar{\mathbf{X}}_i \right) \right\} \end{aligned} \tag{19}$$

where $tr(\cdot)$ represents the trace of square matrix.

By setting $\frac{d\hat{J}^{(q)}}{d\mathbf{B}_i} = 0$, one gets

$$\hat{\mathbf{B}}_i = \left(\hat{\mathbf{B}}_{P\setminus\{i\}} \bar{\mathbf{X}}_{P\setminus\{i\}} - \mathbf{T}\right) \bar{\mathbf{X}}_i^T \left(\bar{\mathbf{X}}_i \bar{\mathbf{X}}_i^T + C\mathbf{I}\right)^{-1} \tag{20}$$

Substituting (20) into (19) obtains

$$\hat{J}^{(q)} = \hat{J}^{(q+1)}_{-i} - tr\left(\left(\hat{\mathbf{B}}_{P\setminus\{i\}} \bar{\mathbf{X}}_{P\setminus\{i\}} - \mathbf{T}\right)^T \hat{\mathbf{B}}_i \bar{\mathbf{X}}_i \right) \tag{21}$$

Hence, when removing ith input feature at the $(q+1)$th iteration, the error value can be expressed as

$$\Delta_{-i} = \hat{J}^{(q+1)}_{-i} - \hat{J}^{(q)} = tr\left(\left(\hat{\mathbf{B}}_{P\setminus\{i\}} \bar{\mathbf{X}}_{P\setminus\{i\}} - \mathbf{T}\right)^T \hat{\mathbf{B}}_i \bar{\mathbf{X}}_i \right) \tag{22}$$

Define the criterion of pruning feature as

$$s = \arg\min_{i \in P} \left\{ \Delta_{-i} = tr\left(\left(\hat{\mathbf{B}}_{P\setminus\{i\}} \bar{\mathbf{X}}_{P\setminus\{i\}} - \mathbf{T}\right)^T \hat{\mathbf{B}}_i \bar{\mathbf{X}}_i \right) \right\} \tag{23}$$

According to Sherman-Morrison formula [14], we can calculate $\hat{\mathbf{B}}_{P\setminus\{i\}}$ in Eq. (23) with a fast speed.

Firstly, denote $(\bar{\mathbf{X}}_P \bar{\mathbf{X}}_P^T + C\mathbf{I})^{-1}$ by $\mathbf{D}^{(l)}$, $\mathbf{D}^{(l)}$ is decomposed in the block form as

$$\mathbf{D}^{(l)} = \begin{bmatrix} \mathbf{D}_{11} & \mathbf{D}_{12} & \mathbf{D}_{13} \\ \mathbf{D}_{12}^T & \mathbf{D}_{22} & \mathbf{D}_{32}^T \\ \mathbf{D}_{13}^T & \mathbf{D}_{32} & \mathbf{D}_{33} \end{bmatrix} \tag{24}$$

where $\begin{bmatrix} \mathbf{D}_{12}^T & \mathbf{D}_{22} & \mathbf{D}_{32}^T \end{bmatrix}$ is the corresponding row to the ith feature. Hence, when the ith feature is pruned at the $(l+1)$th iteration,

$$\mathbf{D}_{-i}^{(l+1)} = \begin{bmatrix} \mathbf{D}_{11} & \mathbf{D}_{13} \\ \mathbf{D}_{13}^T & \mathbf{D}_{33} \end{bmatrix} - \begin{bmatrix} \mathbf{D}_{12} \\ \mathbf{D}_{32} \end{bmatrix} \mathbf{D}_{22}^{-1} \begin{bmatrix} \mathbf{D}_{12}^T & \mathbf{D}_{32}^T \end{bmatrix} \tag{25}$$

Correspondingly, the output weights can be updated as below

$$\hat{\mathbf{B}}_{P\setminus\{i\}} = \mathbf{T}\mathbf{X}_{P\setminus\{i\}}^T \mathbf{D}_{-i}^{(l+1)} \tag{26}$$

3.1   The Flowchart of BL-PESN Algorithm

The complete process of BL-PESN is given as below

- Step 1. Input the training samples $\{(\mathbf{u}(k), \mathbf{t}(k))_{k=1}^L | \mathbf{u}(k) \in \mathbb{R}^n, \mathbf{t}(k) \in \mathbb{R}^m\}$, generate the matrices $\mathbf{W}^{in}$ and $\mathbf{W}$ randomly, define the reservoir state matrix $\mathbf{X} = [\mathbf{x}(1), \mathbf{x}(2), ..., \mathbf{x}(L)]$ and the target output matrix $\mathbf{T} = [\mathbf{t}(1), \mathbf{t}(2), ..., \mathbf{t}(L)]$.
- Step 2. Determine the matrices $\mathbf{z}^T(k)$ in Eq. (14) and $\bar{\mathbf{X}}$ in Eq. (15).
- Step 3. Choose the ridge parameter C, and decide the maximum algorithm iteration $n_{\max}(0 \leq n_{\max} \leq n)$. In the initialization, let $P = \{1, ..., n\}$, and $l = 0$. Set $\bar{\mathbf{X}}_P = \bar{\mathbf{X}}$, $\mathbf{D}^{(0)} = (\bar{\mathbf{X}}_P^T \bar{\mathbf{X}}_P + C\mathbf{I})^{-1}$, and calculate $\hat{\mathbf{B}}_P = \mathbf{T}\bar{\mathbf{X}}_P^T \mathbf{D}^{(0)}$.
- Step 4. Determine the index s in Eq. (23) and find $\bar{\mathbf{X}}_s$ from $\bar{\mathbf{X}}$.
- Step 5. Calculate $\hat{\mathbf{B}}_{P\setminus\{s\}}$ in Eq. (26). Meanwhile, let $P \leftarrow P\setminus\{s\}$, and $l \leftarrow l+1$.
- Step 6. If $l \geq n_{\max}$ is satisfied , go to Step 7; otherwise, turn to Step 4.
- Step 7. Choose the network with the most important set of input features.

4   Simulation Results and Discussion

In this section, the performance of the proposed BL-PESN is compared with the PESN and the OESN. The ridge parameter C is chosen from a wide range of candidates $\{2^{-20}, 2^{-19}, ..., 2^{19}, 2^{20}\}$ for each dataset. The characteristics of regression datasets and the nearly optimal parameter C are shown in Table 1.

To facilitate comparisons among different algorithms, the performance index root mean square error (RMSE) is defined by

$$\text{RMSE} = \sqrt{\sum_{k=1}^{L} (\mathbf{t}(k) - \mathbf{y}(k))^2 / L} \tag{27}$$

Table 1. Information of the regression benchmark problems

Datasets	#Training samples	#Testing samples	#Features	#Outputs	p	$log_2 C$
Boston housing	350	156	13	1	1	−1
					2	−3
Stocks domain	450	500	9	1	1	−7
					2	−5
Wine-white	2600	2298	11	1	1	−3
					2	−3

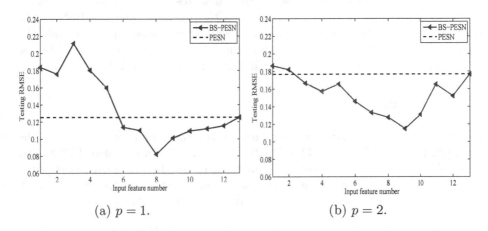

(a) $p = 1$.   (b) $p = 2$.

Fig. 2. Experimental results for Boston housing datasets. (Color figure online)

Table 2. Detailed experimented results of regression datasets.

Datasets	p	Algorithms	#nodes	#Feature	Training RMSE	Testing RMSE	Training time (s)	Testing time (s)
Boston housing	0	OESN	200	13	**0.0413**	0.1107	0.3769	0.3205
	1	PESN	72	13	0.0579	0.0751	1.2310	0.0995
		BS-PESN	72	8	0.0665	**0.0702**	4.8133	**0.0877**
	2	PESN	38	13	**0.0574**	0.0755	1.5312	0.0649
		BS-PESN	38	9	0.0582	0.0721	6.5818	**0.0641**
Stocks domain	0	OESN	250	9	0.0364	0.0828	0.2686	0.0608
	1	PESN	100	9	**0.0331**	0.0437	0.4525	0.3528
		BS-PESN	100	5	0.0422	0.0428	1.9434	**0.2641**
	2	PESN	53	9	0.0391	0.0411	0.4454	0.3378
		BS-PESN	53	6	0.0354	**0.0401**	3.2356	**0.3447**
Wine-white	0	OESN	500	11	**0.0946**	0.1513	0.3608	0.1012
	1	PESN	84	11	0.1083	0.1254	7.0332	5.6358
		BS-PESN	84	8	0.1169	0.1259	8.9192	**5.2360**
	2	PESN	45	11	**0.1013**	0.1545	10.7579	8.2422
		BS-PESN	45	6	0.1160	**0.1225**	11.3372	**7.2810**

where $\mathbf{y}(k)$ and $\mathbf{t}(k)$ are the estimated output and target output at time k. The smaller the RMSE value stands for better performance for each algorithm.

Figure 2 shows the experimental results for Boston housing. In each figure, there are two lines, in which the black dash line represents the PESN, and the blue solid line with triangle marks is represented as BL-PESN. For each blue line, there are always some marks below the dash line, which indicated that BS-PESN can obtain better performance than the PESN. Due to space limitation, the similar results of other regression experiments are omitted.

The comparisons between the proposed BL-PESN, PESN and OESN are shown in Table 2. The results are average over 30 independent runs. Obviously, the BL-PESN always needs fewer input features to construct the p-order polynomial function, thus it needs the less testing time than the PESN. The testing RMSE values of BL-PESN are always the smallest among all the compared methods, which means that the BL-PESN is able to improve the generalization by pruning some insignificant features from the PESN.

5   Conclusions

In this paper, a backward learning algorithm is designed for PESN to prune the insignificant input features. The BL-PESN begins with a complete PESN, and gradually prunes the insignificant input features one by one until the required criterion is satisfied. The simulation results show that the proposed BL-PESN has better prediction accuracy and training speed than other ESNs.

Acknowledgement. This work was supported by the National Natural Science Foundation of China under Grants 61603012, 61533002 and 61890930-5, the Beijing Municipal Education Commission Foundation under Grant KM201710005025, the Major Science and Technology Program for Water Pollution Control and Treatment of China (2018ZX07111005), the National Key Research and Development Project under Grants 2018YFC1900800-5.

References

1. Jaeger, H., Haas, H.: Harnessing nonlinearity: predicting chaotic systems and saving energy in wireless communication. Science **304**(5667), 78–80 (2004)
2. Shi, Z., Han, M.: Support vector echo-state machine for chaotic time-series prediction. IEEE Trans. Neural Netw. **18**, 359–372 (2007)
3. Levy, B., Attux, R., Zuben, F.: Self-organization and lateral interaction in echo state network reservoirs. Neurocomputing **138**, 297–309 (2014)
4. Skowronski, M., Harris, J.: Automatic speech recognition using a predictive echo state network classifier. Neural Netw. **20**, 414–423 (2007)
5. Han, S., Lee, J.: Fuzzy echo state neural networks and funnel dynamic surface control for prescribed performance of a nonlinear dynamic system. IEEE Trans. Indus. Elect. **61**(2), 1099–1112 (2014)
6. Xia, Y., Jelfs, B., Van Hulle, M., Príncipe, J., Mandic, D.: An augmented echo state network for nonlinear adaptive filtering of complex noncircular signals. IEEE Trans. Neural Netw. **22**(1), 74–83 (2011)
7. Rodan, A., Tino, P.: Minimum complexity echo state network. IEEE Trans. Neural Netw. **22**(1), 131–144 (2011)

8. Li, D., Han, M., Wang, J.: Chaotic time series prediction based on a novel ro bust echo state network. IEEE Trans. Neural Netw. Learn. Syst. **23**(5), 787–799 (2012)
9. Yang, C., Qiao, J., Han, H., Wang, L.: Design of polynomial echo state networks for time series prediction. Neurocomputing **290**, 148–160 (2018)
10. Miller, A.: Subset Selection in Regression. Chapman and Hall, London (2002)
11. Cotter, S., Kreutz-Delgado, K., Rao, B.: Backward sequential elimination for sparse vector subset selection. Sig. Process. **81**(9), 1849–1864 (2001)
12. Dutoit, X., Schrauwen, B., Campenhout, J., Stroobandt, D., Brussel, H., Nuttin, M.: Pruning and regularization in reservoir computing. Neurocomputing **72**(7–9), 1534–1546 (2009)
13. Liu, S., Trenkler, G., Hadamard, K.: Kronecker and other matrix products. Int. J. Inform. Syst. Sci. **4**(1), 160–177 (2008)
14. Zhang, X.: Matrix Analysis and Applications. Tsinghua University Press, Beijing (2004)

Using LSTM GRU and Hybrid Models for Streamflow Forecasting

Abdullahi Uwaisu Muhammad, Xiaodong Li[(⊠)], and Jun Feng

College of Computer and Information, Hohai University, Nanjing, China
uwaisabdullahi87@yahoo.com,
{xiaodong.li,fengjun}@hhu.edu.cn

Abstract. Forecasting streamflow discharge have economic impact as well as reducing the effects of floods in flood prone regimes by presenting early warning. To minimize it's effects in these regimes, a powerful class of machine learning algorithms called long short-term memory (LSTM) and gated recurrent units (GRU) models, which have become popular in time series forecasting, because they are explicitly designed to avoid the long-term dependency problems is applied. LSTM and GRU models have also demonstrated their capacity in sequence modelling, speech recognition and streamflow forecasting. In this paper we proposed a hybrid model for streamflow forecasting using 35 consecutive years Model Parameter Estimation Experiment (MOPEX) data set of ten basins having different basin characteristics from different climatic regions in United States. The proposed hybrid model's performance is compared to the conventional LSTM and GRU models. Our experiments on the 10 MOPEX's river basins demonstrate that, although the proposed hybrid model outperforms conventional LSTM with respect to streamflow forecasting, but the performance is almost same with GRU and is therefore highly recommended as an efficient and reliable approach in hydrological fields.

Keywords: LSTM · MOPEX · Recurrent neural networks · Streamflow forecasting

1 Introduction

Forecasting daily streamflow is one of the tools applied by water authorities to allocate scarce water resources among competitive users, as well as in flood prone regions where early warning can reduce the effects of flood. Floods are one of the most frequently occurring natural disasters which affect many regions of the world resulting in loss of lives and billions worth of properties especially in flood prone regions. Information at any stage of streams/rivers are very important in the analysis, design and construction of water resources projects such as reservoirs flow, dams, channels for flood controls and in streamflow forecasting. In deep learning algorithms, a model class of artificial neural networks which are inspired by biological nervous system called the LSTM are employed to solve the problems of vanishing gradient by controlling information flow using input, forget and output gates. Another default behaviour of an LSTM model is there ability in remembering past information for a long period of time.

X. B. Zhai et al. (Eds.): MLICOM 2019, LNICST 294, pp. 510–524, 2019.
https://doi.org/10.1007/978-3-030-32388-2_44

They also have the capability to process as well as for predicting time series data. Short or long term forecasting of streamflow events helps to optimize and plan for future expansion or reduction. Time series models are models that have its data collected at constant interval of time. These data are analyzed to determine the long-term trends so as to forecast the future or perform some other forms of analysis. Water resources planning are very sensitive in many regions around the globe, and as such it has to be managed in a very sustainable manner. The main purpose of this research is to proposed a hybrid model and compare with the conventional LSTM and GRU models for streamflow forecasting using 35 consecutive years daily streamflow data set from 10 MOPEX basins that have different basin characteristics from different climatic regions in United States.

More recently deep learning LSTM RNN have been applied in streamflow forecasting by [16] for rainfall-runoff modeling, in air pollution [10], compared a long short-term memory neural network extended (LSTME) model to other statistical-based models proving LSTME to be superior. For traffic speed prediction [11], provided an insightful information for transportation professionals to reduce congestion, improve traffic safety, route preplanning as well as rescheduling for the benefit of travellers, although they suggested adding multiple layers in the architecture which might enhance the learning capabilities of the neural networks. LSTM models are also applied for information retrieval and in gesture recognition [19], designed a model which exhibited good performance in sequence level classification, although the model faces the limitation of frame classification while executing gesture recognition. [1] presented an LSTM-based model that can jointly reason across multiple individuals to predict human trajectories in a scene. They suggest future research to extend multi-class settings sharing the same space, thus allowing jointly modeling of human-human and human-space interactions in the same framework.

In this study, whose main objectives is to propose a hybrid model while comparing it's relative performance with an LSTM and GRU models for streamflow forecasting using 10 MOPEX basins data set as a case study. MOPEX's basins contains historical hydrometeorlogical data and river basin characteristics from a range of climates throughout the world for long lead-streamflow forecasting. These models are applied on ten MOPEX's basins; Sandy river, Nezinscot river, Royal river, Saco river, Pemigewasset river, Quinebaug river, Ammonoosuc river, Housatonic river, Tenmile river, and Sacandaga river basins in United States. We also analysed streamflow discharge history for 35 consecutive years in the river basins and applied it to predict future streamflow. The overall performance of the models on the different climatic regimes are evaluated using root mean square error (RMSE) and mean absolute error (MAE). A very important event in water resources management that can affect flood control when designing various hydraulic structures such as dams is accurate streamflow forecast. Although there are many parameters affecting streamflow discharge such as amount of rainfall, the rate of snow pack and glacier melt due to temperature variations etc., the discharge serves only as the input to all the models in the present study.

The rest of the paper is organized as follows; Previous works related to the study of LSTM and GRU models are presented in Sect. 2. We described LSTM, GRU and our proposed hybrid models in details in Sect. 3. Conducting of our experiment including the study areas, methodology and the experimental results are presented in Sect. 4. Finally we conclude the paper and indicate some future work directions in Sect. 5.

2 Related Works

Numerous studies have presented the advantages and applications of recurrent neural network (RNN) including: [16] applies Streamflow Hydrology Estimate using Machine Learning (SHEM) for providing accurate and timely proxy streamflow data set for inoperative streamgages whose result's can be used by first responders and decision makers responding to flood events. [8] applies same data set to compare the relative performance of artificial neural networks and auto-regression models for river flow forecasting. The results proves that neural networks were able to produce better results than auto-regressive models.

Significant attention has been given lately to compare multiple climatic models for streamflow forecasting using hydrological data variables. [9] compares feedforward networks (FFNs) and RNNs models. The results proves RNNs to perform better than feedforward networks for both single step and multi-step ahead forecasting. [3] compares static and dynamic feedback neural network. From the results obtained the dynamic neural network generally produce better and are more stable in streamflow forecasting. [4] employed RNNs and were able to forecast the streamflow where meteorological and hydrological data is rarely available for advanced models.

[1] presented an LSTM-based model that can jointly reason across multiple individuals to predict human trajectories in a scene. They qualitatively prove that social-LSTM successfully predicts various non-linear behaviors arising from social interactions, such as a group of individuals moving together. [21] proposed a model to forecast off-line customer flow for over two thousand shops by considering both online and off-line periodic customer behaviors. The promising experimental results demonstrated that, the proposed approach is superior to the state-of-the-art algorithms such as lasso regression and gradient boosting regression tree. This indicated the wider applicability of the proposed forecast approach.

Another research conducted by [14] proves that, an ANNs model trained with pseudo-inverse rule was capable of performing prediction of combined sewer overflow depth with less than 0.05 error for prediction 5 times ahead for unseen data set. [24] applied Internet of Things (IoT) monitoring combined sewer overflow structures, and compares four different neural networks; multilayer perceptron (MLP), wavelet neural networks (WNN), gated recurrent unit (GRU) and LSTM. LSTM and GRU performed superior performance for multistep ahead prediction with GRU achieving quicker learning curves. [23] designed two different models per city for forecasting weather. The result proves that, LSTM can be considered a better alternative to the traditional methods.

Following the methodology of [11], who proposes a novel LSTM neural networks which is desirable for traffic prediction problem where future traffic condition is relevant to the previous events with long time span. They suggest adding multiple layers which might enhance the learning capability of the neural networks. [2] proposed a multi-step ahead reinforced real-time RNN. The proposed model achieves superior performance while improving the precision of multi-step ahead forecast when compared to two dynamic and one static neural networks. [13] proves that RNN LSTM gives satisfactory improvement with significance of 0.16 correlation and 0.68 in mean squared error over perfect prognosis statistical downscaling techniques.

[7] compares four different artificial intelligence models; ANNs, support vector regression (SVR), wavelet-ANN and wavelet-SVR. From the research conducted, non of the models outperformed the others in more than one watershed, suggesting that some models may be more suitable for certain types of data set. [17] applied timed lagged RNNs and the results out-performed general RNNs in predicting short term flood flow. [22] proposed a method for tweets classification which utilizes weakly-labeled tweets and can significantly improve the accuracy of tweets classification, although they did not include discrimination detection in multiple categories. [15] applied Levenberg Marquardt algorithm to develop an artificial neural network. The results prove's a relatively good agreement between predicted and observed values.

Research conducted by [12], demonstrated the advantages of LSTM model for analyzing the complex non-linear variations of traffic speeds as well as its promising prediction accuracy. [18] proposes a hybrid model of wavelet transform and LSTM. The hybrid model provided better results than the LSTM, Elman and Jordan recurrent neural networks. [10] compares spatio-temporal deep learning model, time delay neural network, auto regressive moving average, support vector regression, and traditional LSTM neural network models. The results demonstrated the long short-term memory neural network extended (LSTME) as superior to the other statistical-based models.

While [5] proposed a field-programmable gate array (FPGA) based accelerator for long short term memory recurrent neural networks, which optimizes both computational performance and communication requirements. The results of design achieves significant speedup over software implementations and it outperforms previous long short term memory recurrent neural network accelerators. [6] designed a model that integrates time delay and RNN. The results obtained proves it to predict better forecast than the statistical autoregressive-moving average with exogenous terms (ARMAX) model. [25] hybrid Ensemble Empirical Mode Composition (EEMD-LSTM) model performed better than the recurrent neural network, long short term memory, EMD-recurrent neural network, EMD-long short term memory and EEMD-recurrent neural network model for daily land surface temperature data series forecasting.

While [20] compares short and long term forecast. Results proves short term forecast can clearly improve real-time operation, however long term forecast still requires improvement in the forecast. From the previous researches conducted, it is clearly proven that promising results have been observed when applying LSTM and GRU models.

This paper presents a hybrid model for streamflow forecasting and compares it's relative performance with LSTM and GRU models using United States Geological Survey (USGS) National Water Information System (NWIS) data set. 35 consecutive years (35 water years) data set from 10 MOPEX river basins having different basins characteristic from different climatic regions were applied as a case study.

3 Modelling

In this study, we applied three artificial intelligence approaches for streamflow fore-casting. The first approach is the conventional LSTM model, followed by GRU model and we compares it with the hybrid model (LSTM and GRU). We applied LSTM and GRU models on streamflow data set because they are equipped with the forget and update gates respectively. These gates enables the artificial intelligence models to memorize long term dependencies of specific features from the input data without being erased as well as solving the problems of vanishing gradient. Although in LSTM model, the amount of memory content is controlled by the output gate, the reverse is the case in GRU as they have no full control over it memory content. Thirty five water years historical daily streamflow data set of 10 MOPEX basins in USA obtained from the United States Geological Survey (USGS) National Water Information System (NWIS) are applied as input to these artificial intelligence models.

3.1 LSTM Model

Daily streamflow discharge of each river basins over the period of thirty five con-secutive years (35 Water years) were applied on the LSTM model. To validate the effectiveness of the LSTM model. The historical data set were divided into two selected sub-groups, corresponding to 8:2 for training and testing respectively for each of the basins. The first step in the training section involves normalization of the data set between (0 and 1) using Min Max Scaler, which is a simple technique for fitting the data set in a pre-defined boundary. The second step is segmentation of the time series data input using sliding window to determine the prediction accuracy and it was set as 3. Finally we designed the LSTM model consisting of 5 LSTM blocks which is fully connected with epoch, batch size and verbose set as 31, 1 and 2 respectively. RMSE of the train score and test score as well as MAE were applied to evaluate the performance of the model at both training and testing phase respectively.

3.2 Hybrid Model

The proposed hybrid model in this paper is an integration of both LSTM and GRU models. This hybrid model is thought to exploit not only the characteristics and learning capabilities, but also the strength of both GRU and LSTM models, so as to produce a more accurate and reliable forecast on the streamflow data set. The pro-portion between train and test data sets is 8:2. To validate the effectiveness of the proposed hybrid model, the data set was first divided into two sets; training and testing data set, each of which contains several processes. The first step is the training section, as it involves normalization of the data set between (0 and 1) using Min Max Scaler which is a simple technique for fitting data in a pre-defined boundary. The second step is segmentation of the time series data input, using sliding window to determine the prediction accuracy and it was set as 3. The output of the LSTM model is fed into the GRU model in order to produce a single, final output as it's being concatenated and formed a fully-connected layer. The network is trained and tested with the hybrid model each of which are fully connected with epoch, batch size and verbose set as 31, 1 and 2 respectively. The configuration chosen for the hybrid model in this study is 1-2-1, namely; one input layer, two hidden layers with the first hidden layer having 5 LSTM neurons and the second hidden layer having 5 GRU neurons and an output layer, as this is the multi layer perceptron adopted throughout the study. RMSE of the training and testing data set as well as MAE were applied to evaluate the performance of the model at both training and testing phase respectively. The flowchart of the proposed hybrid model indicating the flow of data from the input to the output state consisting hybrid blocks with a fully connected hidden layer is presented below (Fig. 1).

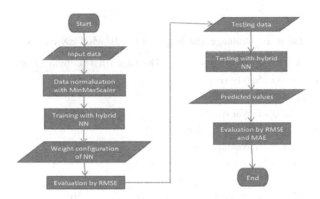

Fig. 1. Flowchart of hybrid model

4 Experiments

This section mainly describes the experimental setup in details including; the study area, the methodology applied in conducting the experiments and the experimental results.

4.1 Study Areas

The hydrological streamflow data set operated by USGS of 10 MOPEX river basins retrieved from the National Water Information System (NWIS, http://waterdata.usgs.gov/nwis, accessed March 2018) for thirty five consecutive years (35 water years) are applied in this study. Since continuous streamflow data are common to all the 10 studied basins and are therefore used for this study in calibrating, evaluating and testing the model. These 10 basins are chosen as study areas because they have minimal or no regulation streamflow. The rationale for choosing these time intervals pertained to the availability of data in each river basin, as each have atleast 50 years of continuous streamgage data records available. The study basins as represented in both geographic and climatic variability and they are; Sandy river, Saco river, Royal river, Quinebaug river, Sacandaga river, Ammonoosuc river, Pemigewasset river, Nezinscot river, Housatonic river and Tenmile river. Streamflow varies depending on the amount of rainfall, geology, rate of snow pack and glacier melt due to temperature variations, seasonal weather conditions, and land cover. Additional physical attributes of the basins were also described; mean areal precipitation (mm), climatic potential evaporation (mm), daily streamflow discharge (mm), daily maximum air temperature (Celsius), daily minimum air temperature (Celsius) by the USGS. The change of stage in a river results from variation of discharge. The gaging stations are established mainly for knowing the flow regime of the river. Details of the case study areas are summarized in the tables below (Tables 1, 2 and 3).

Table 1. Drainage and length of the 10 MOPEX basins.

Station ID	Station name	Drainage (m^2)	Length (mile)
01048000	Sandy river	516	56
01064500	Saco river	385	136
01060000	Royal river	141	39
01127000	Quinebaug river	850	69
01321000	Sacandaga river	491	64
01138000	Ammonoosuc river	850	55
01076500	Pemigewasset river	622	70
01055500	Nezinscot river	169	30
01197000	Housatonic river	1950	149
01200000	Tenmile river	203	8.6

Table 2. Location of the 10 MOPEX basins.

Station ID	Latitude	Longitude
01048000	44.71	−69.94
01064500	43.99	−71.09
01060000	43.79	−70.18
01127000	41.59	−71.99
01321000	43.31	−73.84
01138000	44.22	−71.91
01076500	43.75	−71.69
01055500	44.27	−70.23
01197000	42.23	−73.36
01200000	41.66	−73.53

Table 3. Streamflow discharge history of the 10 MOPEX basins.

Station ID	Max.	Avg.	Min.
01048000	2340(1996)	232	71(1993)
01064500	2470(1996)	297	125(1991)
01060000	11500(1977)	2500	1120(1957)
01127000	3890(1938)	810	73(1946)
01321000	32,000(1913)	12000	16(1913)
01138000	1030(1991)	74	30(2008)
01076500	3270(1996)	352	112(1919)
01055500	874(1996)	62	24.2(1985)
01197000	372(1938)	33	6.90(1962)
01200000	1980(1938)	84	12(1957)

4.2   Methodology

Daily streamflow discharge of each of the 10 MOPEX river basins for the period of thirty five consecutive years (35 Water years) was used in the study. The streamflow data set were obtained from the United States Geological Survey (USGS) National Water Information System (NWIS). It is thought that, the hybrid model to exploit not only the characteristics and learning capabilities but also the strength of both GRU and LSTM models so as to provide a more accurate and reliable forecast on the streamflow data set. The data set is divided into ten subsets of chosen size (35 water year) each. The subsets are first normalized between the range (0 to 1) using Minimum Maximum Scaler, for preserving zero entries in sparse data and including robustness to very small standard deviations of features. For model training and testing, the historical data set were divided into two selected groups, corresponding to 0.8 and 0.2 for training and testing respectively for each of the subset. The training data set were used for training the LSTM, GRU and hybrid models, followed by testing for evaluating the accuracy of the trained networks. The sliding window, which was designed to maximize the retention of the forecast sharpness for forecast systems associated with higher skills was set as 3. After testing the models on different neurons, a model consisting of 5 neurons each of LSTM, GRU and hybrid model respectively with fully connected hidden layer with batch size and verbose set as 1 and 2 respectively was adopted in this study.

In order to estimate the forecasting performance and evaluate the accuracy of the hybrid model. RMSE and MAE are applied on both the LSTM, GRU and hybrid models. The RMSE is basically applied to measure the differences between the predicted and true values of the model, while MAE measures accuracy for continuous variables without considering their directions. Both formulas were applied because they have a good performance to distribution error and could be used to measure the error rate of the models. The mathematical expressions of RMSE and MAE are presented respectively below:

$$RMSE = \sqrt{\frac{\sum (y - x)^2}{n}}$$

$$MAE = \frac{\sum |y - x|}{n}$$

Where y and x are the forecast and observed streamflow data set respectively, n is the total number of samples in each of the data set. The results of the hybrid models are compared with our reference LSTM and GRU models. Tables 4, 5 and 6 presents the statistical test results obtained from the calculated train score RMSE, test score RMSE and MAE of the LSTM, GRU and hybrid models, when the same data set of each basin are applied. The best model is normally the one having least values of MAE and RMSE.

4.3   Experimental Results

In this section, the selective results of all 10 testing phases of the river basins containing the observed and predicted values in the study are presented. The results and discussion are presented in details as shown below.

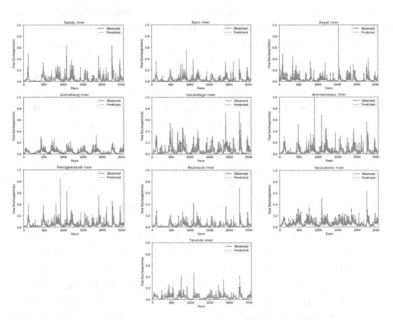

Fig. 2. Testing phase of the river basins using LSTM model.

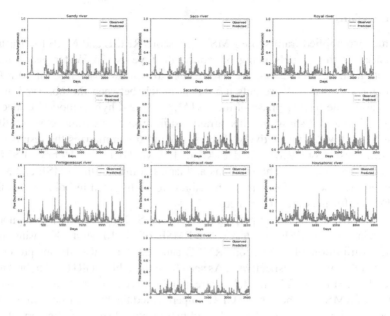

Fig. 3. Testing phase of the river basins using GRU model.

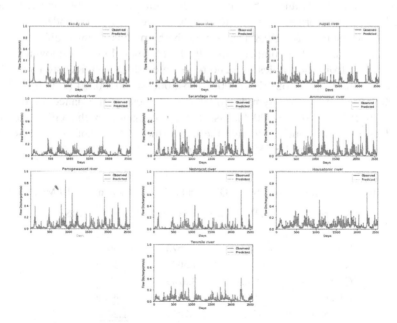

Fig. 4. Testing phase of the river basins using hybrid model.

4.4 Discussions

In this study we applied train score RMSE, test score RMSE and MAE to measure the performances of the models using 35 consecutive years (35 Water years) data set splitted into training and testing for forecasting streamflow discharge on 10 MOPEX basins. Figures 2, 3 and 4 presents the extent match between the observed and predicted values of the testing phase of the LSTM, GRU and hybrid models respectively. While Figs. 5, 6 and 7 shows the histogram distribution of the train score RMSE, test score RMSE and MAE respectively. Tables 4, 5 and 6 summarizes the results of train score RMSE, test score RMSE and MAE of LSTM, GRU and Hybrid (LSTM and GRU) models respectively. These graphs and tables compares the RMSE and MAE of the 3 models. The best performers on the tables are highlighted in bold font, while the second best performers are underlined.

The summarized forecasting performance of the LSTM, GRU and hybrid models in terms of train score RMSE and test score RMSE of all 10 MOPEX basins and the histogram distribution of train score RMSE and test score RMSE are presented in Tables 4, 5 and Figs. 5, 6 respectively. As seen from the tables, GRU and hybrid models performed better than LSTM model in streamflow forecasting because they have the least values of RMSE. Although the GRU outperformed the hybrid model in 6 of the 10 basins, but the performance of the GRU and hybrid model seems to be very close.

Table 6 presents the results of the calculated MAE, while Fig. 7 shows the plot of the histogram distribution of MAE of the 10 MOPEX basins when same data set are applied on LSTM, GRU and hybrid models. As seen from the table, the GRU model exhibited it's best performances in 6 MOPEX basins, while hybrid model exhibited it's best performances in 4 MOPEX basins with both models slightly different to each other, but never the less they outperformed the LSTM model in streamflow forecasting.

It is obvious from the Tables 4, 5 and 6 presented that, the GRU are most efficient for streamflow forecasting on 01048000, 01064500, 01060000, 01127000, 01321000, 01138000 basins with the hybrid model having best performance in 01076500, 01055500, 01197000, 01200000 basins. The performance of the GRU and hybrid models does not differ much, although the hybrid model have both the characteristics and properties of both the LSTM and GRU models.

Table 4. Train score RMSE of LSTM, GRU and hybrid models of the 10 MOPEX basins,

Rivers	LSTM RMSE	GRU RMSE	Hybrid RMSE
Sandy	4.9782	**1.5376**	<u>1.5393</u>
Saco	7.4384	**2.2672**	<u>2.3089</u>
Royal	5.4146	**1.5047**	<u>1.5122</u>
Quinebaug	3.7090	**0.6765**	<u>0.7797</u>
Sacandaga	4.1191	**1.2369**	<u>1.3485</u>
Ammonoosuc	3.8715	**1.2414**	<u>1.2488</u>
Pemigewasset	5.4605	<u>1.8866</u>	**1.8151**
Nezinscot	4.5402	<u>1.0741</u>	**1.0463**
Housatonic	3.2846	<u>0.8739</u>	**0.7079**
Tenmile	3.7099	<u>1.8853</u>	**0.9426**

Table 5. Test score RMSE of LSTM, GRU and hybrid models of the 10 MOPEX basins.

Rivers	LSTM RMSE	GRU RMSE	Hybrid RMSE
Sandy	5.8595	**1.8161**	1.8209
Saco	7.9457	**2.2349**	2.2530
Royal	6.1550	**2.0571**	2.0745
Quinebaug	3.8878	**0.6481**	0.7333
Sacandaga	4.8287	**1.4959**	1.5465
Ammonoosuc	4.2415	**1.5033**	1.5351
Pemigewasset	6.0844	2.1386	**2.0704**
Nezinscot	5.1345	1.2112	**1.2064**
Housatonic	3.5813	0.9273	**0.7877**
Tenmile	4.2478	1.8923	**0.9839**

Table 6. MAE of LSTM, GRU and hybrid models of the 10 MOPEX basins.

Rivers	LSTM MAE	GRU MAE	Hybrid MAE
Sandy	0.6454	**0.1193**	0.1196
Saco	0.8904	**0.2150**	0.2159
Royal	0.6494	**0.1647**	0.1657
Quinebaug	0.3367	**0.0325**	0.0349
Sacandaga	0.5647	**0.0943**	0.0977
Ammonoosuc	0.5685	**0.1400**	0.1425
Pemigewasset	0.7577	0.1954	**0.1906**
Nezinscot	0.4595	0.0556	**0.0554**
Housatonic	0.3975	0.0911	**0.0853**
Tenmile	0.3837	0.1014	**0.0510**

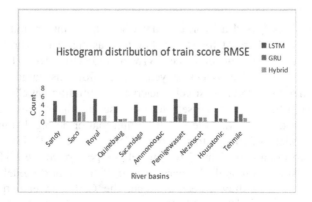

Fig. 5. Histogram on distribution of train score RMSE.

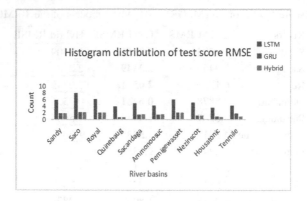

Fig. 6. Histogram on distribution of test score RMSE.

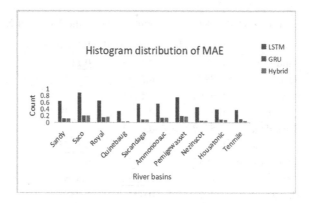

Fig. 7. Histogram on distribution of MAE.

5 Conclusion

In this research we proposed a hybrid model which is an integration of LSTM and GRU models while applying it for streamflow forecasting. The hybrid model's performance is compared with our reference LSTM and GRU models. These models are trained and tested with 35 consecutive years streamflow discharge data set of 10 MOPEX basins having different basin characteristics from different climatic regions in United States. MOPEX basins were selected because they have atleast 50 years continuous streamflow data set available that have minimal or no regulation. The performance of each model in terms of train score RMSE, test score RMSE and MAE are evaluated. The proposed hybrid and GRU models outperformed the LSTM model for streamflow forecasting. Although the performance of the hybrid model is almost the same with GRU in streamflow forecasting, but the GRU model outperformed the hybrid model slightly in 6 of the 10 MOPEX basins suggesting that some models may be more suitable for certain types of data sets.

Acknowledgement. This work was supported in part by the National Key R&D Program of China under Grant 2018YFC0407901, in part by the National Natural Science Foundation of China under Grant 61602149, and in part by the Fundamental Research Funds for the Central Universities under Grant 2019B15514.

References

1. Alahi, A., Goel, K., Ramanathan, V., Robicquet, A., Fei-Fei, L., Savarese, S.: Social LSTM: human trajectory prediction in crowded spaces. In: Proceedings of the IEEE Conference on Computer Vision and Pattern Recognition, pp. 961–971 (2016)
2. Chen, P.A., Chang, L.C., Chang, F.J.: Reinforced recurrent neural networks for multi-step-ahead flood forecasts. J. Hydrol. **497**, 71–79 (2013)
3. Chiang, Y.M., Chang, L.C., Chang, F.J.: Comparison of static-feedforward and dynamic-feedback neural networks for rainfall runoff modeling. J. Hydrol. **290**(3–4), 297–311 (2004)
4. Daniyal, H., et al.: Application of neural network for river flow forecasting. Int. J. Sci. Eng. **8**, 1365–1371 (2004)
5. Guan, Y., Yuan, Z., Sun, G., Cong, J.: FPGA-based accelerator for long short-term memory recurrent neural networks. In: 2017 22nd Asia and South Pacific Design Automation Conference (ASP-DAC), pp. 629–634. IEEE (2017)
6. Karamouz, M., Razavi, S., Araghinejad, S.: Long-lead seasonal rainfall forecasting using time-delay recurrent neural networks: a case study. Hydrol. Process. Int. J. **22**(2), 229–241 (2008)
7. Karran, D.J., Morin, E., Adamowski, J.: Multi-step streamflow forecasting using data-driven non-linear methods in contrasting climate regimes. J. Hydroinformatics **16**(3), 671–689 (2014)
8. Kisi, O.: Daily river flow forecasting using artificial neural networks and auto-regressive models. Turk. J. Eng. Environ. Sci. **29**(1), 9–20 (2005)
9. Kumar, D.N., Raju, K.S., Sathish, T.: River flow forecasting using recurrent neural networks. Water Resour. Manag. **18**(2), 143–161 (2004)
10. Li, X., et al.: Long short-term memory neural network for air pollutant concentration predictions: method development and evaluation. Environ. Pollut. **231**, 997–1004 (2017)
11. Ma, X., Tao, Z., Wang, Y., Yu, H., Wang, Y.: Long short-term memory neural network for traffic speed prediction using remote microwave sensor data. Transp. Res. Part C Emerg. Technol. **54**, 187–197 (2015)
12. Chen, M., Yu, G., Chen, P., Wang, Y.: Traffic congestion prediction based on long-short term memory neural network models. In: CICTP 2017: Transportation Reform and Change —Equity, Inclusiveness, Sharing, and Innovation, pp. 673–681 (2018)
13. Misra, S., Sarkar, S., Mitra, P.: Statistical downscaling of precipitation using long short-term memory recurrent neural networks. Theor. Appl. Climatol. **134**(3–4), 1179–1196 (2018)
14. Mounce, S.R., Shepherd, W., Sailor, G., Shucksmith, J., Saul, A.J.: Predicting combined sewer overflows chamber depth using artificial neural networks with rainfall radar data. Water Sci. Technol. **69**(6), 1326–1333 (2014)
15. Othman, F., Naseri, M.: Reservoir inflow forecasting using artificial neural network. Int. J. Phys. Sci. **6**(3), 434–440 (2011)
16. Petty, T.R., Dhingra, P.: Streamflow hydrology estimate using machine learning (SHEM). JAWRA J. Am. Water Resour. Assoc. **54**(1), 55–68 (2018)
17. Deshmukh, R.P., Ghatol, A.A.: Short term flood forecasting using general recurrent neural network modeling a comparative study. Int. J. Comput. Appl. **8**(12), 5–9 (2010)

18. Sugiartawan, P., Pulungan, R., Sari, A.K.: Prediction by a hybrid of wavelet transform and long-short-term-memory neural network. Int. J. Adv. Comput. Sci. Appl. **8**(2), 326–332 (2017)
19. Tsironi, E., Barros, P., Wermter, S.: Gesture recognition with a convolutional long short-term memory recurrent neural network. In: Proceedings of the European Symposium on Artificial Neural Networks Computational Intelligence and Machine Learning (ESANN), pp. 213–218 (2016)
20. Tucci, C.E., Collischonn, W., Clarke, R.T., Paz, A.R., Allasia, D.: Short-and long-term flow forecasting in the Rio Grande watershed (Brazil). Atmos. Sci. Lett. **9**(2), 53–56 (2008)
21. Yin, Z., Zhu, J., Zhang, X.: Forecast customer flow using long short-term memory networks. In: 2017 International Conference on Security, Pattern Analysis, and Cybernetics (SPAC), pp. 61–66. IEEE (2017)
22. Yuan, S., Wu, X., Xiang, Y.: Incorporating pre-training in long short-term memory networks for tweet classification. Social network analysis and mining. In: Proceedings of the IEEE 16th International Conference on Data Mining, pp. 1329–1334 (2018). https://doi.org/10.1109/icdm.2016.91
23. Zaytar, M.A., El Amrani, C.: Sequence to sequence weather forecasting with long short-term memory recurrent neural networks. Int. J. Comput. Appl. **143**(11), 7–11 (2016)
24. Zhang, D., Lindholm, G., Ratnaweera, H.: Use long short-term memory to enhance Internet of Things for combined sewer overflow monitoring. J. Hydrol. **556**, 409–418 (2018)
25. Zhang, X., Zhang, Q., Zhang, G., Nie, Z., Gui, Z., Que, H.: A novel hybrid data-driven model for daily land surface temperature forecasting using long short-term memory neural network based on ensemble empirical mode decomposition. Int. J. Environ. Res. Public Health **15**(5), 1032 (2018)

Backscatter-Aided Hybrid Data Offloading for Mobile Edge Computing via Deep Reinforcement Learning

Yutong Xie[1,2], Zhengzhuo Xu[3], Jing Xu[3], Shimin Gong[4(✉)] [ID], and Yi Wang[5,6]

[1] Shenzhen Institutes of Advanced Technology,
Chinese Academy of Sciences, Beijing, China
evnxie@foxmail.com
[2] University of Chinese Academy of Sciences, Beijing, China
[3] School of Electronic Information and Communications,
Huazhong University of Science and Technology, Wuhan, China
1157567638@qq.com, xujing@hust.edu.cn
[4] School of Intelligent Systems Engineering,
Sun Yat-sen University, Shenzhen, China
gong0012@e.ntu.edu.sg
[5] SUSTech Institute of Future Networks,
Southern University of Science and Technology, Shenzhen, China
wangy37@sustc.edu.cn
[6] Pengcheng Laboratory, Shenzhen, China

Abstract. Data offloading in mobile edge computing (MEC) allows the low power IoT devices in the edge to optionally offload power-consuming computation tasks to MEC servers. In this paper, we consider a novel backscatter-aided hybrid data offloading scheme to further reduce the power consumption in data transmission. In particular, each device has a dual-mode radio that can offload data via either the conventional active RF communications or the passive backscatter communications with extreme low power consumption. The flexibility in the radio mode switching makes it more complicated to design the optimal offloading strategy, especially in a dynamic network with time-varying workload and energy supply at each device. Hence, we propose the deep reinforcement learning (DRL) framework to handle huge state space under uncertain network state information. By a simple quantization scheme, we design the learning policy in the Double Deep Q-Network (DDQN) framework, which is shown to have better stability and convergence properties. The numerical results demonstrate that the proposed DRL approach can learn and

The authors would like to thank the anonymous reviewers for their valuable comments. This work is partially supported by an NSFC project grant (ref. no. 61872420), and the project of "PCL Future Regional Network Facilities for Large-scale Experiments and Applications (ref. no. PCL2018KP001)". The work of Shimin Gong was supported in part by National Science Foundation of China (NSFC) under Grant 61601449, 61503368, and the Shenzhen Talent Peacock Plan Program under Grant KQTD2015071715073798.

converge to the maximal energy efficiency compared with other baseline approaches.

Keywords: Deep reinforcement learning · Double DQN · Computation offloading · Backscatter communications

1   Introduction

Mobile edge computing (MEC) provides the IoT devices in the network edge with cloud-like computation capability at the easy-to-access and resource-rich MEC servers, which can be integrated with the wireless access points or small-cell base stations [11]. The edge devices (e.g., wireless sensor nodes) are allowed to offload sensing data and computation tasks (e.g., data compressing and encryption) to the MEC servers, and then the MEC servers return the processed data for fulfilling the application requests at the edge devices. Data offloading of IoT devices is conventionally achieved by wireless RF communications, which is inherently power consuming by using RF communication radios (referred to as the active radios) to generate RF carrier signals [6]. The high power consumption in active radios may not be affordable by low-power edge devices and hence prevents them from using the MEC servers. Hence, the edge devices have to optimally balance the use of precious energy supply, depending on the channel conditions, energy status, and the users' workloads.

Wireless backscatter is recently introduced as novel communication technology with extremely low power consumption. The backscatter radios operate in *passive* mode by modulating and reflecting the incident RF signal via load modulation [1]. The passive radios are featured with low power consumption and low data rate [8]. Whereas the active radios can transmit in a higher data rate by adapting the transmit power against the channel fading. Hence, we expect to achieve a radio diversity gain by switching data offloading in two radio modes, e.g., [5] and [14]. In this paper, we consider a hybrid data offloading scheme combining local computation, passive and active offloading in a wireless powered MEC scenario, which allows a more flexible control to balance the power consumption in computation and offloading. The critical problem is to determine the optimal time scheduling and workload allocation strategies in each computation scheme, taking into account the time-varying channel conditions, energy supply, workload dynamics, and various resource constraints [2].

Due to network dynamics and close couplings among different network entities, the optimization of MEC offloading strategy become very challenging as the dimensionality and complexity rapidly increase. It is further complicated by the interactions among multiple wireless users, base stations, and MEC servers [10]. For example, different wireless users may compete for resources (e.g., channel, and computation capacities) to fulfill individuals' computation workloads. To deal with those complexities, we propose the model-free DRL-based framework to learn the optimal MEC offloading strategy with uncertain network information. We observe that the MEC offloading decisions are generally continuous variables. By a simple quantization and encoding scheme, we turn the strategy space into a finite discrete set and then design the learning policy in the double deep Q-network (DDQN) framework to stabilize the learning process. Our numerical results verify that the proposed DDQN framework can achieve the maximum energy efficiency compared to other baseline approaches.

2   System Model

We consider a wireless edge network consisting of one hybrid access point (HAP) and N user devices that can sense and process data independently. To assist their data processing, the user edge devices can offload their sensing data to the HAP, which is co-located with an MEC server. The MEC server will return the processed data to the edge devices after the completion of computation workload. The system model is depicted in Fig. 1. We assume that the MEC server has enhanced computation capability and persistent power supply. Its computation and transmission of results can be performed instantly. Let $\mathcal{N} = \{1, 2, ..., N\}$ denote the set of all edge nodes and S_i denote the i-th edge node for $i \in \mathcal{N}$. Each node is equipped with single antenna capable of harvesting energy from the HAP. The complex uplink and downlink channels between HAP and node S_i are denoted by $h_i \in \mathcal{C}$ and $g_i \in \mathcal{C}$, respectively. Each S_i is allocated a time slot t_i for its data offloading and capable of energy harvesting in other time slots. The workload of each edge node S_i is given by L_i, which is defined as the number of data bits to be processed either locally or remotely at the MEC center. We assume that the workload of each device is generated at the beginning of each time slot, and it has to be processed before the end of data frame.

2.1   Hybrid Data Offloading Scheme

The data offloading from each edge node to the HAP or MEC server can be performed in either passive backscatter communications or the conventional active RF communications, depending on its energy profile and the channel conditions. The switch between passive and active mode can be achieved by tuning the load impedance, e.g., [7]. As each edge node has only one antenna, we assume that it can only transmit in one radio mode or harvest energy from the HAP. Each edge node can switch its radio mode according to this channel conditions and energy status. As such, we further divide each time slot t_j allocated to S_j into two sub-slots, as shown in Fig. 1(b). One sub-slot $t_{a,j}$ is used for data offloading in active mode and the other sub-slot $t_{p,j}$ is for backscatter communications. The active data offloading is powered by the energy harvested from the HAP over consecutive time slots. While the passive data offloading is powered by power-splitting (PS) scheme, i.e., a part of the incident RF signals, denoted by the PS ratio ρ_j, is harvested to power the operation of backscatter radio, and the other part $1 - \rho_j$ is modulated and instantly reflected back to the HAP. Besides data offloading, the data computation can be also performed locally at the edge devices. In this case, the computation can be parallel to data offloading, as shown in Fig. 1(b).

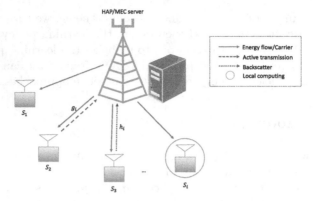

(a) System model of wireless power hybrid MEC offloading

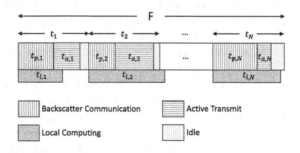

(b) Time allocation for hybrid MEC offloading

Fig. 1. Backscatter-aided hybrid MEC offloading scheme.

2.2 Workload Allocation

The workload generated in each time slot can be allocated among local computation, active and passive offloading. Note that different computation schemes have different processing capabilities and power consumption. Hence, the design of optimal MEC offloading scheme aims to divide the workload into three schemes, according to the dynamics in workload, channel conditions, and the energy supply of each edge device.

Active Offloading. Let $p_{a,i}$ denote the transmit power in active data offloading. The received signal at HAP is given by $y = \sqrt{p_{a,i}}h_i s(t) + \nu_d$, where $s(t)$ denotes the information with unit power and $\nu_d \sim \mathcal{CN}(0, \sigma^2)$ denotes the noise at the HAP. Then, the data rate in active mode can be denoted by

$$r_{a,i} = B \log_2 \left(1 + p_{a,i}|h_i|^2/\sigma^2\right), \tag{1}$$

where B denotes the bandwidth of active data transmission. The relationship between $p_{a,i}$ and $r_{a,i}$ is given by:

$$p_{a,i} = \beta(r_{a,i}) \triangleq \left(2^{r_{a,i}/B} - 1\right)\sigma^2/|h_i|^2. \tag{2}$$

Hence, the total power consumption in active mode is given by $\tilde{\beta}(r_{a,i}) \triangleq \beta(r_{a,i}) + p_{c,i}$, where $p_{c,i}$ denotes the constant power to excite the circuit.

Passive Offloading. For passive data offloading, the data rate can be viewed as a constant, i.e., $r_{p,i} = r_p$, which relates to the ambient symbol rate and the signal detection scheme at the receiver [8]. Typically the backscatter communications rate r_p is less than that of active RF communications. However, power consumption for backscatter communications can be significantly less than the active RF communications and sustainable via wireless energy harvesting. In particular, a part of the incident RF power can be harvested to power the circuit of backscatter radio [9]. This implies that the edge device prefers to use high rate RF communications when energy is sufficient, and turns to backscatter communications if energy becomes insufficient.

Local Computation. The edge device can also perform local computation in parallel with MEC offloading, similar to [11]. Let f_i denote the processor's computing speed (cycles per second) and $0 \leq t_{l,i} \leq F$ denote the time for local computation. Here F can be the total number time slots during one data frame. Then, the amount of information bits processed locally by the edge node is given by $f_i t_{l,i}/\phi$, where $\phi > 0$ denotes the number of cycles needed to process one bit of task data. The energy consumption of local computation is constrained by $k_i f_i^3 t_{l,i} \leq E_i$ [3], where k_i denotes the coefficient of computation energy efficiency. To maximize the data processing capability, each edge device should exhaust the harvested energy and perform computation throughout the data frame. Hence, we have $f_i^* = (\frac{E_i}{k_i F})^{\frac{1}{3}}$ and the local computation rate (in bits per second) is given by $r_{l,i} = \frac{f_i^* t_i^*}{\phi F}$.

3   Deep Reinforcement Learning Approach for MEC Offloading Optimization

3.1   Optimization of MEC Offloading

We aim to reduce the total energy cost and fulfill the computation workload of every edge node. To this end, we propose an optimization formulation to maximize the energy efficiency in MEC offloading, which is defined as the ratio between the total computation workload and the energy consumption:

$$R(\mathbf{t}) \triangleq \frac{\sum_{i \in N} L_i x_i}{\sum_{i \in N}[\tilde{\beta}(r_{a,i})t_{a,i} + p_{c,i}t_{p,i} + k_i f_i^3 t_{l,i}]}, \tag{3}$$

which depends on the time or workload allocation among different computation schemes. Here binary $x_i = \{0, 1\}$ denotes the outage event that happens when the workload is not finished within a time deadline or the energy supply is not sufficient. Once outage happens, e.g., $x_i = 0$, the computation becomes invalid and will not generate any useful information to the edge device. The hybrid offloading policy has to satisfy the resource constraints from at least two aspects:

Workload Completion. The edge user's workload generated in each time slot has to be completed before a fixed delay bound. The hybrid MEC offloading model provides three schemes to complete the workload, i.e., local computation, active and passive offloading. To cooperate with other edge nodes, we stipulate that each edge node has to complete active and passive offloading within a time slot, whereas local computing can be completed during different time slots but also within a time frame. Therefore, we have $t_{a,i} + t_{p,i} \leq F/N$, where F denotes the frame length and N denotes the total number slots. The combination of computation capabilities in three schemes have to fulfill the user's application requirement. That is, $l_{a,i} + l_{p,i} + l_{l,i} \geq L_i$, where $l_{c,i}$ for $c \in \{l, a, p\}$ denotes the workload of user S_i completed in different computation schemes, including local computation, active, and passive offloading. Typically we have $l_{c,i} = t_{c,i} r_{c,i}$. Note that the computation capability may vary in different schemes, which implies an optimal division of the user's workload to minimize the task outage probability.

Energy Budget. Without loss of generality, we assume that the battery of each node is initially fully charged with the maximum capacity $E_{\max}$. Different computation schemes also vary in their energy consumptions. In particular, local computation consumes power in CPU cycles, while active offloading consumes high power in RF communications. For simplicity, we omit the power consumption in wireless backscatter, which is much less than that of RF communications [12]. Hence, the total energy consumption of each edge node in one time slot is denoted by $k_i f_i^3 t_{l,i} + t_{a,i} \widetilde{\beta}(\frac{l_{a,i}}{t_{a,i}})$, corresponding to local computation and active offloading, respectively.

At the beginning of each data frame, the energy in battery is equal to the energy left in the previous time frame plus the energy collected in other time slots. As such, we define the energy dynamics in k-th data frame of i-th node as follows:

$$E_{k,i} = \min \left(E_{\max}, E_{k-1,i} + \eta \sum_{j \neq i} p_0 g_i^2 t_{p,j} \right), \quad (4)$$

where η denotes energy conversion efficiency and p_0 represents transmit power of HAP. Given the edge user's battery status, the transmission scheduling in two radio modes has to meet the energy budget constraint.

Problem Formulation. Till this point, we can formulate the optimization problem as follows:

$$\max_{\mathbf{t}} \ R(\mathbf{t}) \tag{5a}$$

$$s.t. \ t_{a,i} + t_{p,i} \leq F/N, \tag{5b}$$

$$l_{a,i} + l_{p,i} + l_{l,i} \geq L_i, \tag{5c}$$

$$t_{a,i}\widetilde{\beta}(\frac{l_{a,i}}{t_{a,i}}) + k_i f_i^3 t_i \leq E_{k,i}, \tag{5d}$$

$$\mathbf{t}_a \succeq 0, \mathbf{t}_p \succeq 0, \ and \ \mathbf{t}_l \succeq 0 \tag{5e}$$

where $\mathbf{t}_l \triangleq [t_{l,1}, t_{l,2}, \ldots, t_{l,N}]^T$, $\mathbf{t}_a \triangleq [t_{a,1}, t_{a,2}, \ldots, t_{a,N}]^T$, and $\mathbf{t}_p \triangleq [t_{p,1}, t_{p,2}, \ldots, t_{p,N}]^T$ denote the allocation of computation time in local computation, active, and passive offloading, respectively. The major difficulties of solving problem (5) are caused by the non-convex problem structure, and the couplings among multiple network entities in a dynamic environment. Hence, the conventional model-based optimization techniques become very inflexible and inefficient.

In the following, we resort to a model-free learning based approach. In particular, we integrate deep neural networks (DNNs) and the conventional reinforcement learning for autonomous decision making [13] with huge state space under dynamic network environment.

3.2 DRL Approach for Hybrid MEC Offloading

Relying on the success of DNNs, DRL is capable of solving high dimensional, non-convex, and even model-free network control problems, e.g., multiple access, transmission scheduling, and resource allocation in a dynamic network environment [10]. These are very difficult to handle by classical techniques such as convex optimization, dynamic and stochastic programming, due to the imprecise modeling, uncertain system dynamics, and huge state spaces. In this part, we propose the DRL approach to learn the optimal MEC offloading policy from past experience, without exact knowledge about the network conditions.

Double DQN Framework. Deep Q-Network (DQN) is a popular DRL approach that uses a set of DNNs to approximate the action value function $Q^\pi(s, a; \boldsymbol{\theta})$ in conventional reinforcement learning, given the state s and action a. Let $\boldsymbol{\theta}$ denote the vector of parameters of the multi-layer DNNs, which can be built with different structures, e.g., deep convolutional neural network (CNN) and recurrent neural network (RNN). An overview of DRL approaches and its applications in wireless networking can be found in the survey paper [10]. In general, DQN employs two key mechanisms, i.e., experience replay and target Q-network, to stabilize the learning process. The experience replay mechanism randomly selects a set of transition samples, i.e., mini-batch, from a replay memory of historical transition samples to train the DNN. This can break the correlations and ensure more efficient training by independent transition samples.

The training of DQN is performed by minimizing the loss function $L_i(\theta)$:

$$L_i(\boldsymbol{\theta}_i) = \mathbb{E}\left[(y_i - Q(s_i, a_i; \boldsymbol{\theta}_i))^2\right], \tag{6}$$

where y_i denotes the target Q-value and $Q(s_i, a_i; \boldsymbol{\theta}_i)$ is the output of DNN parameterized by $\boldsymbol{\theta}_i$. To stabilize Q-learning, the DQN algorithm uses a separate Q-network with the parameter θ' to generate the target values as $r + Q(s', a'; \theta')$. The target Q-network keeps θ' fixed between successive updates and only updates it by copying the value from θ every a few steps. This mechanism adds a time delay between the update to the online Q-network and the evaluation of the target value.

DQN usually results in overoptimistic estimation of Q-value as we introduce a positive bias by finding the maximum action value $\max_a Q(s_{i+1}, a; \boldsymbol{\theta}_i')$ in each decision epoch. The same transition data is used to decide the best action with the highest reward. To correct this, an extension of DQN, namely, Double DQN (DDQN), provides a better estimate by updating the action in the online network, and then using the target network to estimate the value function [4].

$$y_i^d = r_i + \gamma Q'(s_{i+1}, \arg\max_a Q(s_{i+1}, a; \boldsymbol{\theta}_i); \boldsymbol{\theta}_i'), \tag{7}$$

where γ is a discount factor. Note that the selection of action in (7) is still based on the online parameter $\boldsymbol{\theta}_i$, as illustrated in Fig. 2. However, the second parameter $\boldsymbol{\theta}_i'$ is used to evaluate the Q-value. Hence, the action is decoupled from the generation of target Q-value, which makes the training faster and more reliable.

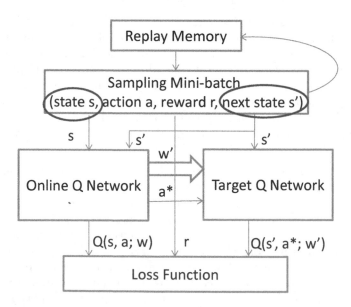

Fig. 2. Information flow of DDQN with DNN parameters **w** and **w'**.

DDQN for Hybrid MEC Offloading. We define the state space of i-th edge device as $\mathcal{S} = \{(\mathcal{W}, \mathcal{E}, \mathcal{C})\}$, where $w \in \mathcal{W} \triangleq \{0, 1, \ldots, W\}$ represents the workload of edge node at the beginning of each time frame, $e \in \mathcal{E} \triangleq \{0, 1, \ldots, E\}$, and $c \in \mathcal{C} \triangleq \{0, 1, \ldots, C\}$ represent the finite state energy status and channel conditions, respectively. At the k-th time frame, the system state $S_k \in \mathcal{S}$ consists of the channel conditions, the user's energy supply, and random workload. In particular, the channel from the HBS to each user can be modeled in a finite-state Markov chain. This leads to state transitions in the edge user's offloading rate and power consumption. It further affects the transmit performance in two radio modes. Due to the uncertainty in ambient environment, the harvested energy is random and following an unknown stochastic process. The power consumption also varies with the channel conditions. This implies a dynamic process of the edge user's battery status. The workload of each edge user is also uncertain due to the user's mobility and time-varying behaviors of upper layer applications. We assume that the workload can be divided flexibly and processed separately without affecting the integrity. The state transition function $P(S_{k+1}|S_k, a_k)$ represents the distribution of the next state S_{k+1} given the current state S_k and the offloading action a_k.

We define the action space of i-th edge node as $\mathcal{A} = \{a; a \in \{0, 1, 2\}\}$, where $a = 0, 1$, and 2 correspond to active offloading, passive offloading, and local computation, respectively. Given the dynamics of channel conditions, energy status, and workload, each user device will choose its action accordingly to maximize its reward function. Moreover, the action also needs to divide workload in different computation schemes. To avoid continuous action space, we equally divide each time slot into multiple sub-slots. In each sub-slot, the edge user follows the same DRL framework to optimize its offloading decision. By this quantization, we actually optimize the workload allocation among local computation, passive, and active offloading. To maximize the system performance, we define the reward function as the energy efficiency, i.e., the successfully completed workload per unit energy. It captures the immediate value at each time frame, which is given by $R(t) = \frac{L_i x_i}{\overline{\beta}(r_{a,i}) t_{a,i} + k_i f_i^3 t_{l,i}}$. If workload is completed successfully, e.g., $x_i = 1$, the reward value is a positive number that represents the throughput per unit of energy. Otherwise, the reward value is 0. This allows the DRL agent to constantly search for a better strategy to maximize the total energy efficiency. Algorithm 1 summarizes the DDQN approach for hybrid MEC offloading.

4 Numerical Evaluation

In this section, we evaluate the performance of the proposed DRL algorithm. A fixed transmit power at HAP is set to $p_0 = 100$ mW and the energy conversion efficiency is $\eta = 0.6$. We compare the performance of our hybrid data offloading scheme with the conventional active offloading and local computing scheme without the support for backscatter communications. Besides, greedy algorithm and random algorithm are compared as well. We assume flat block fading channels, i.e., the channel gains remain the same within one time frame and follow

---

Algorithm 1. DDQN Approach for Hybrid MEC offloading

Require: Initial workload, channel and energy conditions.
Ensure: Convergent hybrid MEC offloading strategy π^*.
  Initialize replay memory D, DNN parameters $\boldsymbol{\theta}$, $\boldsymbol{\theta}'$.
  for episode $k \leq 1, 2, ..., K$ **do**
    if $mod(k, 100) == 0$ **then**
      Change the initialization to the current best result.
    end if
    Choose a random probability number p.
    if $p < \varepsilon$ **then**
      $a^*(t) = \arg\max_a Q(s, a; \boldsymbol{\theta})$.
    else
      Choose $a(t)$ randomly.
    end if
    Execute action $a(t)$ and receive immediate reward $r(t)$.
    Observe next environment state s'.
    Store transition (s, a, r, s') in replay memory D.
    Sample random mini-batch of transitions from D.
    Calculate the target Q-value $y(t)$ from the target network,

$$y(t) = r(t) + \gamma \max Q'(s_{t+1}, \arg\max_a Q(s_{i+1}, a; \theta); \boldsymbol{\theta}').$$

    Update the parameters $\boldsymbol{\theta}$ of the online Q-network.
    Copy $\boldsymbol{\theta}$ to the target network for every K steps.
  end for

Table 1. Parameter settings in the DRL framework

Parameters	Value
Number of hidden layers	2
Fully connected neuron network size	64×64
Activation	ReLU
Optimizer	Adam
Learning rate α	0.01
Discount rate γ	0.9
ϵ-greedy	0.9
Mini-batch size	32
Experience replay memory size	2000
Target network update frequency	100

a finite-state Markov chain over consecutive time frames. The workload of each edge node is randomly generated in the range $[4, 32]$ kbits. We set the constant circuit power to $p_c = 1\,\mu\text{W}$ and the constant data rate in passive mode as $r_p = 5$ kbps. The noise power is set to $\sigma^2 = -70\,\text{dBm}$ and the bandwidth is given by $B = 400\,\text{kHz}$. Table 1 lists the parameter settings in our DRL framework.

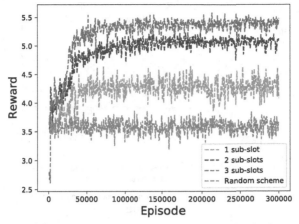

(a) Rewards with different number of sub-slots

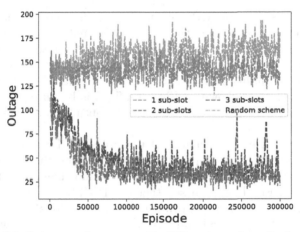

(b) Outage performance with different number of sub-slots

Fig. 3. Performance comparison with different number of sub-slots.

Figure 3 shows the average reward of 500 episodes with different sub-slots at individual edge node. We denote reward as the throughput of hybrid offloading or local computing per energy unit when the workload is fulfilled successfully. To account for workload allocation, we further divide each time slot into a number of sub-slots to realize dual-mode data offloading. When the number of sub-slots is 2, it means that the workload can be assigned to different offloading modes. Firstly, we observe that averaged reward is higher than that of the random scheme, when the number of sub-slot is set to one, which means that the edge user can only work in one mode for data offloading in one time slot. However, the outage performance in this case becomes worse than that of the random

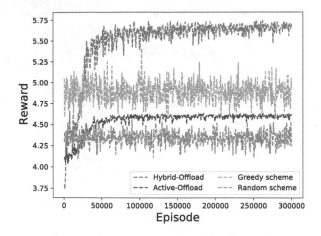

Fig. 4. Rewards in different algorithms.

scheme. The reason is that, the DRL agent may sacrifice outage performance to obtain a higher reward value when the edge user is unable to switch the radio's operating mode during MEC offloading. In Fig. 3(a), we also observe that the average reward grows significantly with the increase in the number of sub-slots, which allows more flexibility in workload allocation. Meanwhile, the number of outage events decreases as shown in Fig. 3(b). This is because, with more sub-slots, the partition of workload can be closer to optimal and thus achieve an improved performance.

We also compare the performance of the proposed DRL-based offloading algorithm with a few baseline approaches, which include the greedy and random algorithms, as well as the conventional active offloading algorithm without passive mode. From Fig. 4, we can see that the DRL-based algorithm achieve the best performance with highest reward. The conventional active offloading algorithm is inferior to the greedy algorithm slightly and much lower than the hybrid offloading algorithm in this set of parameters. This verifies that the hybrid offloading strategy has an significant performance improvement over the conventional offloading scheme, due to its flexibility in mode switch.

5   Conclusions

In this paper, we have proposed a deep reinforcement learning based hybrid offloading algorithm to maximize the energy efficiency in wireless powered MEC networks with hybrid data offloading. We first formulate the energy efficiency function as a non-convex optimization problem. To solve it, we have developed the DDQN-based algorithm to learn the near optimal offloading policy. The numerical results demonstrate that the proposed DRL solution can achieve better performance than the conventional methods.

References

1. Boyer, C., Roy, S.: Backscatter communication and RFID: coding, energy, and MIMO analysis. IEEE Trans. Commun. **62**(3), 770–785 (2014)
2. Chen, X., Zhang, H., Wu, C., Mao, S., Ji, Y., Bennis, M.: Optimized computation offloading performance in virtual edge computing systems via deep reinforcement learning. IEEE Internet Things J. (2019). https://doi.org/10.1109/JIOT.2018.2876279
3. Guo, S., Xiao, B., Yang, Y., Yang, Y.: Energy-efficient dynamic offloading and resource scheduling in mobile cloud computing. In: IEEE INFOCOM, pp. 1–9, April 2016
4. Van Hasselt, H., Guez, A., Silver, D.: Deep reinforcement learning with double Q-learning. In: Proceedings of AAAI Conference on Artificial Intelligence, pp. 2094–2100, February 2016
5. Hoang, D.T., Niyato, D., Wang, P., Kim, D.I., Han, Z.: Ambient backscatter: a new approach to improve network performance for RF-powered cognitive radio networks. IEEE Trans. Commun. **65**(9), 3659–3674 (2017)
6. Li, J., Xu, J., Gong, S., Huang, X., Wang, P.: Robust radio mode selection in wirelessly powered communications with uncertain channel information. In: Proceedings of IEEE GLOBECOM, December 2017
7. Li, J., Xu, J., Gong, S., Li, C., Niyato, D.: A game theoretic approach for backscatter-aided relay communications in hybrid radio networks. In: Proceedings of IEEE GLOBECOM, December 2018
8. Liu, V., Parks, A., Talla, V., Gollakota, S., Wetherall, D., Smith, J.R.: Ambient backscatter: wireless communication out of thin air. In: Proceedings of ACM SIGGOMM, New York, August 2013
9. Lu, X., Wang, P., Niyato, D., Kim, D.I., Han, Z.: Wireless networks with RF energy harvesting: a contemporary survey. IEEE Commun. Surv. Tutor. **17**(2), 757–789 (2015)
10. Luong, N.C., et al.: Applications of deep reinforcement learning in communications and networking: a survey. CoRR abs/1810.07862. http://arxiv.org/abs/1810.07862 (2018)
11. Mao, Y., You, C., Zhang, J., Huang, K., Letaief, K.B.: Mobile edge computing: Survey and research outlook. https://arxiv.org/abs/1701.01090v3
12. Niyato, D., Kim, D.I., Maso, M., Han, Z.: Wireless powered communication networks: research directions and technological approaches. IEEE Wirel. Commun. **PP**(99), 2–11 (2017)
13. Sutton, R.S., Barto, A.G.: Reinforcement Learning: An Introduction. MIT Press, Cambridge (1998)
14. Xu, L., Zhu, K., Wang, R., Gong, S.: Performance analysis of RF-powered cognitive radio networks with integrated ambient backscatter communications. Wirel. Commun. Mob. Comput. **2018**, 16 (2018)

An Efficient Federated Learning Scheme with Differential Privacy in Mobile Edge Computing

Jiale Zhang$^{(\boxtimes)}$, Junyu Wang, Yanchao Zhao, and Bing Chen

College of Computer Science and Technology,
Nanjing University of Aeronautics and Astronautics, Nanjing 211106, China
{jlzhang,wangjunyu,yczhao,cb_china}@nuaa.edu.cn

Abstract. In this paper, we consider a mobile edge computing (MEC) system that multiple users participate in the federated learning protocol by jointly training a deep neural network (DNN) with their private training datasets. The main challenges of applying federated learning to MEC are: (1) it incurs tremendous computational cost by carrying out the deep neural network training phase on the resource-constraint mobile edge devices; (2) existing literature demonstrates that the parameters of a DNN trained on a dataset can be exploited to partially reconstruct the training samples in original dataset. To address the aforementioned issues, we introduce an efficiently private federated learning scheme in mobile edge computing, named FedMEC, with model partition technique and differential privacy method in this work. The experimental results demonstrate that our proposed FedMEC scheme can achieve high model accuracy under different perturbation strengths.

Keywords: Federated learning · Mobile edge computing ·
Deep neural network · Differential privacy

1 Introduction

Nowadays the Internet of Things (IoT) devices, such as smartphones, cameras, and medical tools, have shown explosive growth and became nearly ubiquitous. As a distributed intelligent computation architecture, mobile edge computing [1] shows the powerful real-time and on-devices data processing capability, which achieved great success in numerous networking applications. Along with edge computing, on-device deep learning has turned into a universal and indispensable service [2], including recommendation systems, language translation, security surveillance, and health monitoring. However, such intelligent computation

Supported in part by the National Key Research and Development Program of China, under Grant 2017YFB0802303, in part by the National Natural Science Foundation of China, under Grant 61672283, and in part by the Postgraduate Research & Practice Innovation Program of Jiangsu Province under Grant KYCX18_0308.

X. B. Zhai et al. (Eds.): MLICOM 2019, LNICST 294, pp. 538–550, 2019.
https://doi.org/10.1007/978-3-030-32388-2_46

scenario rely on the users to outsource their sensitive data to the cloud in order to carry out deep learning services, which causes a number of privacy concerns and resources impacts for the smartphone users [3,4].

Federated learning [5,6] is a recent concept which enables training a deep learning model across thousands of participants in a collaborative manner. It allows the users locally train their model in a distributed manner, and upload its local model update, i.e., parameters of gradient and weight, instead of sharing their private data samples to the central server. Participants in federated learning act as the data provider to train a local deep model, and the server maintains a global model by averaging local model parameters (i.e., gradients) generated by randomly selected participants until it tends to convergence [7]. One biggest achievement for federated learning is the corresponding model average algorithm [8], which can benefit from a wide range of non-IID and unbalanced data distribution among diversity participants.

It seems that federated learning is a promising approach to provide on-device deep learning services on mobile edge computing architecture while protecting user-side data privacy. However, we notice that applying the federated learning approach to mobile edge computing environment would face two practical issues:

- It presents tremendous computational cost by carrying out the deep neural network training phase on the resource-constraint mobile edge devices, meaning that the mobile devices cannot afford such heavy computation processing required in federated learning approach [9–11];
- The parameters of a DNN trained on a dataset can still be exploited to partially reconstruction the training examples in that dataset, which means the conventional federated learning mechanism cannot provide strong privacy guarantee against malicious entities, such as edge and cloud servers [12,13].

To address the above problems, we propose an efficiently private federated learning scheme in mobile edge computing, named FedMEC, based on model partition technique and differential privacy method. The main contributions can be summarized as follows:

- We design a flexible framework which enabling federated learning in the mobile edge computing environment based on the model partitioned technique, reducing the computation overhead on the mobile devices. Specifically, the FedMEC framework partitions a deep neural network into two parts: the client-side DNN and edge-side DNN, so the most complex computations can be outsourced to the edge server.
- We also propose a differentially private data perturbation mechanism on the clients-side to prevent the privacy leakage from the local model parameters. In particular, the edge clients and edge server run the different portion of a deep neural network, and the updates from an edge device to the edge server is perturbed by Laplace noise to achieve differential privacy.

The rest of this paper are organized as follows. In Sect. 2, we briefly introduce the basic knowledge of federated learning and differential privacy. The system framework is presented in Sect. 3, and the construction of proposed FedMEC scheme is detailed in Sect. 4. Extensive experimental evaluation is conducted in Sect. 5. Finally, Sect. 6 gives the conclusion and future work.

2   Preliminaries

2.1   Federated Learning

Federated learning was firstly proposed by Google [8] which aims to build a distributed machine learning models based on massive distribution datasets across multiple devices. Compared to the conventional centralized training method, participants in the federated learning system can locally train a global model using their private data and upload the model update in form of gradients. Such a localized model training method presents significant advantages in privacy preserving because the clients do not need to share their private data to any third party.

During the federated learning, all the clients agree on a common learning objective and model structure. Assuming that m_t is a fraction of sampled participants who own the different private dataset. In a certain communication round t, each client downloads the global model parameters from the server, then the model is trained locally to generate the local model update $\Delta w_{t+1}^{(i)}$ using its own private dataset. Finally, each participant sends the resulting updates back to the server, where the updates are averaged by the central server to obtain a new joint global model:

$$w_{t+1}^{(global)} = w_t^{(global)} + \frac{1}{m_t} \sum_{i=1}^{m_t} \Delta w_{t+1}^{(i)}, \tag{1}$$

where $w_t^{(global)}$ indicates the global model at the t-th communication round, and $\Delta w_{t+1}^{(i)}$ denotes the local update from the i-th participant at communication round $t + 1$.

2.2   Differential Privacy

Differential privacy [14] provides a rigorous privacy guarantee for randomized algorithms on aggregated sensitive datasets. It is defined in terms of the data query on two adjacent databases $\mathcal{D}$ and $\mathcal{D}'$ where the query results are statistically similar, but differing in one data item. The formal definition of ϵ-differential privacy can be described as follow:

Definition 1 (ϵ-differential privacy)**:** *A randomized mechanism* $\mathcal{M} : \mathcal{D} \to \mathcal{R}$ *fulfills* ϵ-*differential privacy for certain non-negative number* ϵ, *iff for any adjacent input* $d \in \mathcal{D}$ *and* $d' \in \mathcal{D}'$, *and any output* $S \subseteq \mathcal{R}$, *it holds that*

$$Pr[\mathcal{M}(d \in \mathcal{D}) \in S] \le e^{\epsilon} \cdot Pr[\mathcal{M}(d' \in \mathcal{D}') \in S], \tag{2}$$

where ϵ is defined as the privacy budget, which measures the level of privacy guarantee of the randomized mechanism $\mathcal{M}$: the smaller ϵ, the stronger privacy guarantee.

3   System Framework

3.1   Federated Learning with MEC

In this section, we present a mobile edge computing structure for federated learning tasks as shown in Fig. 1. Assume a scenario where all the edge devices intend to obtain desired machine learning services from a cloud central server. At the same time, these users try to prevent the leakage of any private information to the cloud server by executing the federated learning protocol. In this situation, we consider a three-layer mobile edge computing framework that provides the perfect architecture supportive of federated learning protocol with multiple participants. Specifically, the entities involved in our framework including the edge devices, the edge servers, and a cloud central server.

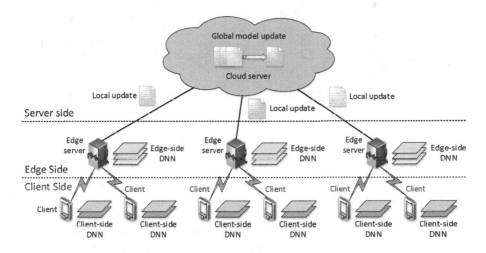

Fig. 1. Federated learning with mobile edge computing

Specifically, implementing the federated learning framework in mobile edge computing faced on two practical issues. Firstly, carrying out the DNN training phase on the mobile devices will definitely present incredible computational cost, while the terminals connected to the mobile edge computing system are usually resource-constraint devices. Secondly, we must consider the user's privacy contained in the outsourced data (or features) due to the edge server and cloud server may not be trusted. Thus, the main challenge of applying federated learning with mobile edge computing is how to design a valid scheme to reduce the computation overhead on edge devices without broke the federated learning mechanism, while protecting user-side data privacy contained in the original data.

3.2   Overview of FedMEC

To solve the aforementioned challenge, we consider to partition the neural network along the last layer of convolutional layers and all the intermediate results generated by the user-side DNN are hidden from the other entities. The effectiveness of the partition mechanism in DNN architecture lies in the loosely coupled property among multiple insider layers. That is, each hidden layer in DNN can be executed separately by taking the previous layer's output as its input.

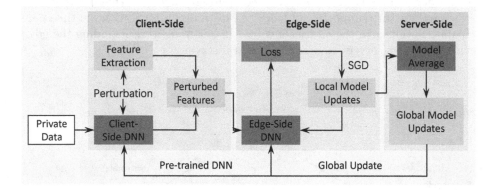

Fig. 2. Overview of proposed FedMEC framework

The overview of FedMEC is presented in Fig. 2. FedMEC relies on the mobile edge computing environment and divides the whole federated learning process into three parts: client-side part, edge-side part, and server-side part. The client-side neural network is assigned by the cloud serve whose network structure and parameters are frozen and the edge-side DNN is fine-turned, the biggest difference between our work and [9] is the iteratively model updates will be aggregated and averaged in the cloud server. In this situation, edge devices merely undertake the simple and lightweight feature extraction and perturbation.

In order to guarantee the performance of the frozen neural network in the client side, we use the public data which has the similar distribution with private data as the auxiliary information dataset to pretrain a deep neural network as an initialized global model in cloud side. Then the pretrained global neural network will be partitioned along the last layer of the convolution layer. Later, the well-trained convolution layer will send to each client for feature extraction. Based on our three-layer federated learning architecture with mobile edge computing, all the resource-hungry tasks are offloaded to the edge servers and cloud center while mobile edge devices merely undertake the simple feature extraction through a local neural network assigned by the cloud center. At last, for the privacy concerns, we perturb the results computed from the original data before being transmitted to the edge server to protect the privacy contained in the raw data.

4 Efficient Federated Learning with Differential Privacy

4.1 Deep Neural Network Partition

In the deep neural network partition strategy, we set the pivot on the last layer of the conversational layers and separate a large DNN into two parts: client-side DNN and edge-side DNN. Specifically, the client-side DNN forms the front portions of a DNN structure (i.e., convolution layers) which are deployed on edge devices to extract features from the raw data. Note that the client-side network is pretrained by the cloud server and the structure and parameters are frozen during the whole training phase in federated learning procedure. The edge-side DNN containing the remaining portions of the DNN network (i.e., dense layers) to update the model parameters by executing the forward and backward propagation procedures. The whole partition process on the deep neural network is illustrated in Fig. 3.

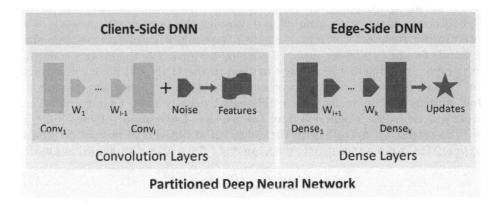

Fig. 3. Partition process on the deep neural network

Therefore, based on our DNN partition mechanism, the complex computation operations on the client side can be greatly reduced. As the experiment shown in [15], the partitioned mechanism can perform lightweight resource consumption when a part of the DNN is offloaded to the third party. In addition to resource and energy considerations, partitioning solutions are attractive to deep learning service providers, paving the way for federated learning applications on mobile edge devices.

4.2 Differentially Private Data Perturbation

Federated learning protocol is designed for providing basic privacy guarantee for each participants' raw data due to its local training property. However, a participant's sensitive data is still possibly leaked to the untrusted third parties, such as edge server and cloud server, even with a small portion of updated parameters (i.e., features and gradients). For examples, according to [12], the server in federated learning can easily launch the model inversion attack to obtain parts of training data distributions, and the gradient backward inference described in [13] also enables an adversary to get a fraction of private data from the participants' local updates. Therefore, it is necessary to design a practical preserving mechanism to protect the privacy of each participant against the untrusted third parties in federated learning.

Differential privacy [14] is a great solution to provide the rigorous privacy guarantee by adding deliberate perturb on the sensitive datasets. However, adding the perturb to the original data directly may lead to significant negative effects about learning performance. Thus, we can perturb the features generated by the convolutional layers of partitioned DNN, so as to preserve the privacy contained in the raw data. In this paper, we solve the aforementioned problem by considering a differentially private data perturbation mechanism which can protect the privacy information contained in the extracted features after executing the client-side DNN.

Following by the work from [9], we consider the deep neural network as a deterministic function $x_l = \mathcal{F}(x_r)$, where x_r represents the private raw data and x_l stands for the l-th layer output of a neural network. For the privacy concern, we applying the differential privacy method to the DNN and further construct our private federated learning protocol in mobile edge computing paradigm. One efficient way to realize the ϵ-differential privacy is to adding controlled Laplace noise which is sampled from the Laplace distribution with scale $\Delta\mathcal{F}/\epsilon$ into the output x_l. According to the definition of differential privacy described in Sect. 2.2, the global sensitivity for a query $f : \mathcal{D} \rightarrow \mathcal{R}$ can be defined as follow:

$$\Delta f = \max_{d \in D, d' \in D'} ||f(d) - f(d')|| \tag{3}$$

However, the biggest challenge here is that the global sensitivity $\Delta\mathcal{F}$ is difficult to quantification in the deep neural network. Directly adding the Laplace perturbations into the output features will destroy the utility of the representations for the future predictions.

To address this problem, we employ the nullification and norm bounding methods to enhance the availability of differential privacy in deep neural networks. Specifically, before a participant starting to extract the features from his sensitive raw data x_r using the pretrained client-side DNN, he firstly performs the nullification operation to masking the high sensitive data items as $x'_r = x_r \odot I_n$, where $\odot$ is the multiplication operation and I_n is the nullification matrix with the same dimensions as input sensitive raw data. Besides, the nullification matrix I_n is a random binary matrix (i.e., consisted of 0 and 1) and its structure is determined by a nullification rate μ, meaning that the number of zeros is the supremum of $Sup(n \cdot \mu)$. Apparently, μ has a significant impact on the prediction accuracy which will be discussed in Sect. 5.

After the nullification operation on the sensitive raw data, each participant needs to run the client-side DNN on x'_r to extract the features as $x_l = \mathcal{F}(x'_r)$.

Then, we consider the norm bounding method to enforce a certain global sensitivity as follow:

$$x'_l = x_l / \max(1, \frac{||x_l||_\infty}{B}) \tag{4}$$

where $||x_l||_\infty$ represents the infinite norm of the l-th layer outputs. This formula indicates that x'_l is upper bounded by S, meaning that the sensitivity of x_l can be preserved as long as $||x_l||_\infty \leq B$, whereas it will be scaled by B when $||x_l||_\infty > B$. According to [16], the scaling factor B usually be set as the median of $||x_l||_\infty$. The Laplace perturbation (scaled to B) now is added into the bounded features x'_l to further preserve the privacy as follow:

$$\tilde{x}_l = x'_l + Lap(B/\sigma I) \tag{5}$$

Note that the Laplace noise is added into the final output of the convolutional layers. Due to the same network structure for each client-side DNN, we use the same notation $\tilde{x}_l$ to represent the latest perturbed features for all participants.

4.3   Differentially Private Federated Learning

According to the standard federated learning protocol [8], after adding the Laplace perturbation on the features extracted from the client-side DNN, all the perturbed features will be fed to the edge-side DNN to further generate the local model update by running the SGD algorithm. For simplicity, we use $\tilde{x}_i$ to represent the i-th participant's update (i.e., participant i's perturbed features), where $i \in [1, n]$. The SGD mechanism is an optimization method to find the parameter w by minimizing the loss function $\mathcal{L}(w, \tilde{x}_i)$. In a certain communication round t, SGD algorithm first compute the gradient $g_t(\tilde{x}_i)$ for any input features $\tilde{x}_i$ as follow:

$$g_t^{(i)} = \nabla_{w_t} \mathcal{L}(w_t, \tilde{x}_i) \tag{6}$$

To achieving distributed computation capability, we adopt the distributed selective stochastic gradient descent (DSSGD) mechanism instead of the conventional SGD algorithm into the federated learning procedure. DSSGD splits the weight w_t and the gradient g_t into n parts, namely $w_t = (w_t^1, \cdots, w_t^n)$ and $g_t = (g_t^1, \cdots, g_t^n)$, so the local parameters update rule becomes as follow:

$$w_{t+1}^{(i)} = w_t^{(i)} - \eta \cdot g_t^{(i)} \tag{7}$$

Then the conventional SGD algorithm was executed to calculate the local model update as:

$$\Delta w_{t+1}^{(i)} = w_{t+1}^{(i)} - w_t^{(i)} \tag{8}$$

At last, each edge server sends the local model updates $\Delta w_{t+1}^{(i)}$ to the cloud server to further executing the federated average procedure:

$$w_{t+1}^{(global)} = w_t^{(global)} + \frac{1}{n} \sum_{i=1}^{n} \Delta w_{t+1}^{(i)}, \tag{9}$$

The whole federated learning procedure will be executed iteratively until the global model $w_t^{(global)}$ tends to convergence.

5   Experimental Evaluation

5.1   Dataset and Experiment Setup

Dataset: MNIST (Modified National Institute of Standards and Technology) is one of the popular benchmark datasets which is commonly used in training and testing of deep learning related research fields. The MNIST dataset contains 70000 handwritten grayscale digits images ranging from 0 to 9 (i.e., 10 classes). Each image is with the size of 28 × 28 pixels, and the whole MNIST dataset is divided into the 60000 training records and 10000 testing data records.

Experiment Setup: In order to estimate our proposed FedMEC algorithm, we run the federated learning protocol on an image classification task. We use the Convolutional Neural Network (CNN) based architecture to construct the classifier in our FedMEC system. The deep neural network structure for MNIST dataset consists of 3 convolutional layers and 2 dense layers. The kernel size of all three convolutional layers is 3 × 3 and the stride for these convolutional layers is set as 2. In particular, the activation functions applied in the neural network structure is LReLU. As aforementioned in Sect. 4, the perturbation strength (μ, b) are the main parameters in our FedMEC scheme, where μ is the nullification rate and b is the diversity of the Laplace mechanism. According to these two parameters, we test the effectiveness of our differentially private data perturbation method by applying the convolutional denoising autoencoder [17] under different perturbation strength. Then, we give a general experimental evaluation under the setting of $\mu = 10\%$ and $b = 3$ to demonstrate the accuracy of our FedMEC scheme. Furthermore, we also test the changes in accuracy when pre-assign different perturbation strengths to the edge clients.

5.2   Experimental Results

Effectiveness of Data Perturbation: To evaluate the effectiveness of our differentially private data perturbation mechanism, we adopt the convolutional denoising autoencoder under the settings of federated learning to visualize the noise and reconstruction, which the perturbation strength is represented by (μ, b). We train our model based on two perturbation strengths $(\mu = 1\%, b = 1)$ and $(\mu = 10\%, b = 5)$. Figure 4 shows the results of visualizing noise and reconstruction. The first row is the real samples from MNIST dataset and the second row shows the perturbed results under two perturbation strengths by using our differentially private data perturbation mechanism. The last row represents the reconstructed samples based on the convolution denoising autoencoder. According to the perturbation and reconstruction results, we can see that the perturbed digits can be reconstructed to a certain degree at the perturbation strengths of $(\mu = 1\%, b = 1)$ as shown in Fig. 4(a). However, as shown in Fig. 4(b), it is hard to reconstruct the original digital when the perturbation strength reaches $(\mu = 10\%, b = 5)$, even the perturbed data is public.

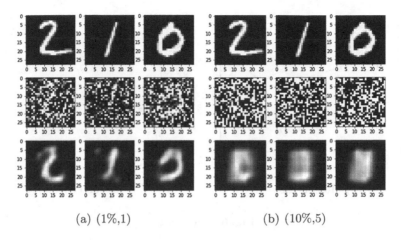

(a) (1%,1)   (b) (10%,5)

Fig. 4. Visualization of noise and reconstruction

Impact of Data Perturbation: As we know, federated learning allows each participant to training their data locally and only updating the parameters. In this situation, edge device users could change their perturbation strength before sending to the edge server. Thus, we estimate the impact of our differentially private data perturbation mechanism under different perturbation strength on the model accuracy, meaning that the client-side DNN will be trained by the pre-assigned perturbation strength. In our experiments, we set two scenarios that the numbers of edge clients n are 100 and 300, and the training is stopped when the communication round reaches 30 and 50 for 100 clients and 300 clients, respectively.

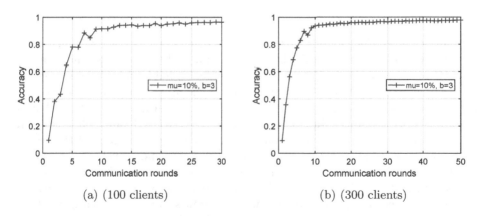

(a) (100 clients)   (b) (300 clients)

Fig. 5. Accuracy for $\mu = 10\%$ and $b = 3$.

The goal of our first group of experiments is to estimate the changes of accuracy under strength ($\mu = 10\%, b = 3$). From the results shown in Fig. 5,

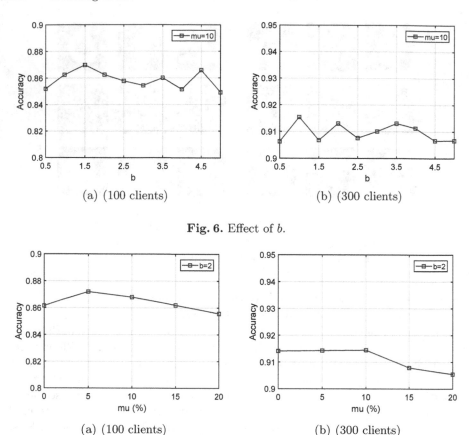

Fig. 6. Effect of b.

Fig. 7. Effect of μ.

we can see that the model can get high accuracy very quickly within several communication rounds in both 100 clients and 300 clients settings, meaning our FedMEC scheme works well in the settings of federated learning while providing sufficient privacy guarantees. We also design a group of experiments to evaluate the global model accuracy by changing one of the parameters in perturbation strength (μ, b), while keeping another parameter as a fixed value. Here, we consider the mean accuracy for each parameter setting by averaging all the results with 30 and 50 communication rounds for 100 clients and 300 clients. As shown in Figs. 6 and 7, our FedMEC scheme can perform more than 85% classification accuracy for all the parameter combinations. Besides, with the gradual increase of perturbation strength, the model accuracy tends to the decreasing trend due to the large perturbation on the features will bring a negative impact in the prediction stage. Despite this, the change range of classification accuracy is less than 5%, which shows the stability and validity of our FedMEC scheme.

6 Conclusion

In this work, we proposed the FedMEC framework which enables highly efficient federated learning service on the mobile edge computing environment. To reduce the computation complexity on the mobile edge devices, we designed a new framework based on the model partition technique to split a deep neural network into two parts, where the most part of heavy computation works can be offloaded to the edge server. Besides, we also presented a differentially private data perturbation mechanism to perturb the Laplacian random noises to the client-side features before uploading to the edge server. The extensive experimental results on a benchmark dataset demonstrated that our proposed FedMEC scheme can achieve high model accuracy while providing sufficient privacy guarantees.

Acknowledgment. This work was supported in part by the National Key Research and Development Program of China under Grant 2017YFB0802303, in part by the National Natural Science Foundation of China under Grant 61672283 and Grant 61602238, in part by the Natural Science Foundation of Jiangsu Province under Grant BK20160805, and in part by the Postgraduate Research & Practice Innovation Program of Jiangsu Province under Grant KYCX18_0308.

References

1. Mach, P., Becvar, Z.: Mobile edge computing: a survey on architecture and computation offloading. IEEE Commun. Surv. Tutor. **19**(3), 1628–1656 (2017)
2. Hesamifard, E., Takabi, H., Ghasemi, M., Wright, R.N.: Privacy-preserving machine learning as a service. In: Proceedings of 19th Privacy Enhancing Technologies Symposium, PETS, Barcelona, Spain, July 2018, pp. 123–142 (2018)
3. Zhang, Q., Yang, L.T., Chen, Z.: Privacy preserving deep computation model on cloud for big data feature learning. IEEE Trans. Comput. **65**(5), 1351–1362 (2016)
4. Zhang, J., Chen, B., Zhao, Y., Cheng, X., Hu, F.: Data security and privacy-preserving in edge computing paradigm: survey and open issues. IEEE Access **6**, 18209–18237 (2018)
5. Smith, V., Chiang, C.-K., Sanjabi, M., Talwalkar, A.S.: Federated multi-task learning. In: Proceedings of the 32nd Annual Conference on Neural Information Processing Systems, NIPS, Long Beach, CA, USA, December 2017, pp. 4427–4437 (2017)
6. Yang, Q., Liu, Y., Chen, T., Tong, Y.: Federated machine learning: concept and applications. ACM Trans. Intell. Syst. Technol. **10**(2), 1–19 (2019)
7. Shokri, R., Shmatikov, V.: Privacy-preserving deep learning. In: Proceedings of the 22nd ACM Conference on Computer and Communications Security, CCS, Denver, Colorado, USA, October 2008, pp. 1310–1321 (2015)
8. McMahan, H.B., Moore, E., Ramage, D., Hampson, S., Agüera y Arcas, B.: Communication-efficient learning of deep networks from decentralized data. In: Proceedings of the 20th International Conference on Artificial Intelligence and Statistics, AISTATS, Fort Lauderadale, Florida, USA, April 2017, pp. 1–10 (2017)

9. Wang, J., Zhang, J., Bao, W., Zhu, X., Cao, B., Yu, P.S.: Not just privacy: improving performance of private deep learning in mobile cloud. In: Proceedings of the 24th ACM SIGKDD International Conference on Knowledge Discovery and Data Mining, KDD, London, United Kingdom, August 2018, pp. 2407–2416 (2018)
10. Mao, Y., Yi, S., Li, Q., Feng, J., Xu, F., Zhong, S.: Learning from differentially private neural activations with edge computing. In: Proceedings of the 3rd IEEE/ACM Symposium on Edge Computing, SEC, Seattle, WA, USA, October 2018, pp. 90–102 (2018)
11. Osia, S.A., et al.: A hybrid deep learning architecture for privacy-preserving mobile analytics. ACM Trans. Knowl. Discov. Data $1(1)$, 1–21 (2018)
12. Fredrikson, F., Jha, S., Ristenpart, T.: Model inversion attacks that exploit confidence information and basic countermeasures. In: Proceedings of the 22th ACM Conference on Computer and Communications Security, CCS, Denver, Colorado, USA, October 2015, pp. 1322–1333 (2015)
13. Phong, L.T., Aono, Y., Hayashi, T., Wang, L., Moriai, S.: Privacy-preserving deep learning via additively homomorphic encryption. IEEE Trans. Inf. Forensics Secur. $\mathbf{13}(5)$, 1333–1345 (2018)
14. Dwork, C., Roth, A.: The algorithmic foundations of differential privacy. Found. Trends Theor. Comput. Sci. $\mathbf{9}(3)$, 211–407 (2014)
15. Lane, N.D., Georgiev, P.: Can deep learning revolutionize mobile sensing? In: Proceedings of the 16th International Workshop on Mobile Computing Systems and Applications, HotMobile, Santa Fe, New Mexico, USA, February 2015, pp. 117–122 (2015)
16. Abadi, M., et al.: Deep learning with differential privacy. In: Proceedings of the 23th ACM Conference on Computer and Communications Security, CCS, Vienna, Austria, October 2016, pp. 308–318 (2016)
17. Dong, C., Loy, C.C., He, K., Tang, X.: Image super-resolution using deep convolutional networks. IEEE Trans. Pattern Anal. Mach. Intell. $\mathbf{38}(2)$, 295–307 (2016)

Joint Power and Channel Selection for Anti-jamming Communications: A Reinforcement Learning Approach

Xufang Pei$^{(\boxtimes)}$, Ximing Wang, Lang Ruan, Luying Huang, Xingyue Yu, and Heyu Luan

College of Communications Engineering, Army Engineering University of PLA, Nanjing 210000, China
peixufang@163.com, lgdxwxm@sina.com, ruanlangjyy@163.com, 15931876710@163.com, fistaon@163.com, 13201677586@163.com

Abstract. In this paper, the decision-making problem for anti-jamming communications is studied. Most of the existing anti-jamming researches mainly focus on the single-domain anti-jamming such as power domain or frequency domain, which has limited performance facing strong jamming. Therefore, to effectively deal with some jamming attack, this paper proposes a multi-domain joint anti-jamming scheme, and considers the power domain and the frequency domain jointly. By modeling the anti-jamming process as a Markov decision process (MDP), reinforcement learning (RL) is adopted to solve the MDP. Then, the multi-domain joint anti-jamming algorithm is proposed to find the optimal decision-making strategy. Moreover, the proposed algorithm is verified to converge to an effective strategy. Simulation results show that the proposed algorithm has better throughput performance than the sensing-based random selection algorithm.

Keywords: Multi-domain anti-jamming ·
Markov decision process (MDP) · Reinforcement learning

1 Introduction

Owing to the open nature of radio, wireless communication is badly threaten by jamming attacks [1–3]. Recently, with the fast advancement of artificial intelligence technologies, jamming technologies have become increasingly intelligent. Due to low spectrum utilization and fixed transmission patterns, traditional anti-jamming technologies such as spread spectrum and frequency hopping technologies [4,5] can not be able to meet the increasing anti-jamming

This work was supported by the National Natural Science Foundation of China under Grant No. 61771488, No. 61671473 and No. 61631020, in part by the Natural Science Foundation for Distinguished Young Scholars of Jiangsu Province under Grant No. BK20160034.

X. B. Zhai et al. (Eds.): MLICOM 2019, LNICST 294, pp. 551–562, 2019.
https://doi.org/10.1007/978-3-030-32388-2_47

requirements. Intelligent anti-jamming technologies are required to enhance the jamming-resistance ability of wireless communication systems.

In the existing research works [6–9], game theory can well model the decision-making interaction process between players, and has been widely used in the field of wireless communication anti-jamming. For example, authors in [10,11] used the Stackelberg game to model the confrontational relationship between users and jammers, and obtained the anti-jamming decision by solving the equilibrium solution. Similarly, authors in [12,13] modeled the confrontational relationship through zero-sum game. However, all the above studies assume that both sides of the game (users and jammers) know each other's information, which is impractical in actual communication.

Reinforcement learning is an effective way to make real-time decision making in unknown environment [14–16]. Researchers have applied reinforcement learning to explore the optimal policy for dynamic spectrum access and anti-jamming problems. For instance, authors in [17] investigated the dynamic spectrum access problem in multi-user scenario. In [18], the dynamic spectrum anti-jamming problem in fading environment was studied. Considering the difference of channel transmission rate of actual channel, a reinforcement learning based channel selection scheme was proposed, which significantly improves the throughput performance of users compared with the random channel selection algorithm. In [14], authors proposed a modified Q-learning algorithm. When the cognitive agent learns the jamming mode of the jammer, it adopts a way of updating the Q value table in parallel, which improves the convergence speed of the algorithm. However, these studies mainly focus on solving the single-domain anti-jamming problems. It will fail when the power of the jamming is strong or the frequency band is very wide.

There are several studies that consider multi-domain anti-jamming. In [19], a multi-domain anti-jamming decision-making problem with unknown channel state was studied. Specifically, in the power domain, the user's transmit power was adjusted to confront the jamming. When the jamming was severe (the jamming power exceeds a certain threshold), the channel switching mode chose to avoid the jamming attack. However, this mechanism only considers switching between power domain and frequency domain, which has low energy efficiency. A joint optimization of power and frequency resources is in need.

Inspired by above studies, this paper studies the multi-domain joint anti-jamming problem. Modeling the anti-jamming decisions as MDP, our object is to maximize long-term cumulative throughput while considering transmission overhead. In order to find the optimal strategy, a multi-domain joint anti-jamming algorithm based on reinforcement learning is designed. In simulation results, the performance of the proposed algorithm is verified compared with the sensing-based random selection strategy algorithm.

The remainder of the paper is organized as follows. In Sect. 2, the system model and problem formulations are investigated. In Sect. 3, a Q-learning based multi-domain anti-jamming communication scheme is proposed. In Sect. 4, the simulations and analysis are given. In the end, the paper is concluded in Sect. 5.

2 System Model

2.1 System Model

As Fig. 1 shows, in the system model, there exist one user (containing a transmitter and a receiver) and a malicious jammer. The available channel set is assumed to be $\mathcal{M} = \{1, 2, \ldots, M_i\}$, i.e., there are M available channels with B bandwidth. The user's available power set is defined as $\mathcal{P} = \{1, 2, \ldots, P_i\}$, and the jamming power is defined as a constant J. The transmitter transmits data information to the receiver through data link. The receiver is responsible for running the intelligent decision-making algorithm and returns the decision information to the transmitter through the control link. The jammer transmits the jamming signal to block the normal communication of the user. In order to facilitate calculation and intelligent decision making, we divide the transmission time into several equal-length slot units, and the transmission slot set is defined as $\{1, 2, \ldots, K\}$. The user is assumed to access only one channel in each time slot.

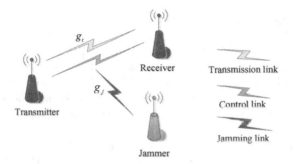

Fig. 1. System model.

Assuming that the channel has large-scale fading, the signal will have path loss during transmission. As shown in Fig. 1, g_t represents the link gain between user transmitter and receiver, Specifically, it can be defined as

$$g_t = (d_t)^{-\alpha} \varepsilon_t, \tag{1}$$

where d_t denotes the distance between the user transmitter and receiver, α represents the user's path fading factor, ε_t represents the user's instantaneous fading coefficient. Similarly, g_j represents the link gain from the jammer to the user receiver, which is specifically defined as:

$$g_j = (d_j)^{-\beta} \varepsilon_j, \tag{2}$$

where d_j denotes the distance from the jammer to the user receiver, β represents the path fading factor of the jammer, and ε_j represent the instantaneous fading coefficient of the jammer, both ε_t and ε_j obey the lognormal fading. Therefore, the user's signal-to-interference-plus-noise ratio can be denoted as follows:

$$SINR = \frac{g_t P(k)}{N_0 + g_j J \delta(f_t - f_j)}, \tag{3}$$

where $P(k)$ represents the transmission power selected by the user, N_0 represents the background noise power, J represents the power of jamming, f_t represents the channel of user signal, f_j represents the channel of jamming signal, and $\delta(\cdot)$ is the indication function. The indication function indicates the occupancy of the selected working channel of the user, and the specific definition is as follows:

$$\delta(f_t - f_j) = \begin{cases} 1, f_t = f_j, \\ 0, f_t \neq f_j. \end{cases} \tag{4}$$

That is, when $f_t = f_j$ indicates that the jamming is on the same channel as the user, the user collides with the jamming, otherwise the two are on different channels, that is, the user is not interfered.

2.2   Problem Modeling

In order to solve the problems mentioned above [20,21], user's anti-jamming decision process can be modeled as a Markov decision process (MDP). MDP is generally defined by a four-tuple, namely (S, A, O, R), whose core elements are defined as follows: S represents the state space, A represents the action space, O represents the state transition probability matrix, and R represents the reward value.

In the actual communication scenario, assuming that there are M_i available channel, the user has P_i power levels. Taking the $M_i = 5$, $P_i = 3$, and jamming modes to continuously apply the sweep jamming as an example, the jammer interferes with multiple channels simultaneously. The jamming variation pattern is shown in Fig. 2. In the figure, the yellow square denotes that the current channel is disturbed and the white square denotes that it is not disturbed. To define the k-th time slot user channel and power selection strategy as $a(k)$, the user's utility can be defined as:

$$U_k = \begin{cases} B \log_2(1 + SINR) - C_s P(k) + X, SINR \geq \Gamma \\ 0, \ otherwise \end{cases}, \tag{5}$$

where B represents the channel bandwidth and C_s represents the user unit power transmission cost. X represents a constant in case of the reward of the user being negative. Γ indicates the set threshold. If $SINR$ is higher than the given threshold Γ, the transmitted data packet can be successfully received. Otherwise, if $SINR$ is less than a given threshold Γ, the transmitted data packet fails to be received.

Under the jamming condition, the user starts to select the best transmission channel and transmission power according to its own strategy at each time

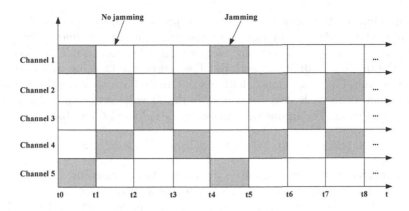

Fig. 2. Diagram of cross sweep jamming. (Color figure online)

slot. Under energy constraints, users must save transmission power to reduce transmission overhead while meeting minimum communication requirements. Therefore, the user's reward $R(k)$ is defined as:

$$R_k = U_k \frac{T_{\text{tran}}}{T_s}, \tag{6}$$

where T_s is the length of a time slot length, T_{tran} is the transmission time. The user's goal is to find the optimal policy to get the maximum cumulative rewards, which can be formulated as:

$$\pi^* = \arg\max_{\pi \in \Omega} E_\pi [\sum_{k=0}^{\infty} R(k)]. \tag{7}$$

This paper assumes that the jammer's strategy (jamming mode) remains unchanged. For the anti-jamming decision problem in such fixed jamming scenarios, the reinforcement learning method can be used to solve the MDP. Since reinforcement learning can learn the optimal strategy in the unknown environment without state transition probability, this paper uses Q-learning [22] algorithm to solve the power and channel selection optimization problem, it is one of the most widely used algorithms in reinforcement learning. Different from the definition of Q-learning action space in [18], this paper combines channel and power to make decision when selecting action, and proposes a Q-learning based multi-domain joint anti-jamming algorithm.

3   Q-learning Based Multi-domain Anti-jamming Communication Scheme

3.1   Algorithm Description

In the strategy selection process, considering the influence of power against jamming performance, this paper designs a multi-domain anti-jamming algorithm based on reinforcement learning to solve this problem. In the process of the user performing the reinforcement learning algorithm, the user evaluates the quality of different actions in each state by maintaining a Q values table. The Q value reflects the quality of different actions. The larger the Q value, the better the selected action. The algorithm calculates the immediate reward value obtained by taking action in each state, and update the Q values corresponding to each action in real time. The updating function of Q values [18] can be expressed as

$$Q_{k+1}(S_k, a_k) = Q_k(S_k, a_k) + \alpha(R_k + \gamma V_{k+1} - Q_k(S_k, a_k)), \qquad (8)$$

where α represents the learning step, γ represents the discount factor, that is, the importance of future returns to the current selection action, $\alpha, \gamma \in (0, 1]$, R_k represents the immediate return value of the current S_k state, and V_{k+1} is the maximum Q values of all strategies in the S_{k+1} state. After the agent selects and executes the action a_k, it reaches the S_{k+1} state in the $(k+1)$-th time slot. The calculation formula of V_{k+1} is as follows:

$$V_{k+1} = \max Q_k(S_{k+1}, \tilde{a}), \forall \tilde{a} \in \mathcal{M} \times \mathcal{P}, \qquad (9)$$

$\tilde{a}$ is an optional power and channel set under the state S_{k+1}. The update formula of the action selection probability vector $W(k) = (w_1(k), \ldots, w_c(k))$ denotes as [18]:

$$w_c(k+1) = \frac{\exp(\xi Q(S_k, c))}{\sum\limits_{c \in \mathcal{M} \times \mathcal{P}} \exp(\xi Q(S_k, c))}, \forall c \in \mathcal{M} \times \mathcal{P}, \qquad (10)$$

where ξ represents the Boltzmann coefficient constant, $w_c(k+1)$ denotes the probability that the $(k+1)$-th time slot selects the power and channel combination strategy as c.

3.2   Communication Process Description

As shown in Fig. 3, the user-jamming slot diagram in the anti-jamming decision process, wherein the length of the jamming slot is T_j, and the length of the user slot is T_s. The user's single time slot composition includes a transmission phase, a sensing phase, a learning phase, and an ACK feedback phase, and executed in this order.

- Transmission phase: The initial state of a given user is $S_0(f_t(0), f_j(0))$, and the user randomly selects a transmission power $P_t(0)$, that is, the user starts transmitting data on the given channel $f_t(0)$ with the power of the $P_t(0)$ at the 0-th slot, where $f_j(0)$ is obtained through wideband spectrum sensing. Simultaneously, the return value $R(0)$ of the current working channel $f_t(0)$ and transmission power $P_t(0)$ is calculated.
- Sensing phase: Detecting the occupancy of each channel in the current time slot through wideband spectrum sensing and obtaining the jamming channel $f_j(1)$;

- Learning phase: The reinforcement learning algorithm is executed to determine the transmission channel $f_t(1)$ and the transmission power $P_t(1)$ of the next time slot. Note that the Q-learning process time is ignored;
- ACK feedback phase: The selected policy (i.e., the working channel and transmission power of the next time slot) is fed back to the user transmitter through the control link, and the user status is updated to $S_1(f_t(1), f_j(1))$.

In the next $k - 1$ time slots, the user goes through the same process to update the working channel and transmission power through the reinforcement learning decision. In particular, the Q values table of the 0-th time slot is an all-zero matrix, and in the subsequent time slots, the user updates the Q values of the selected action in the current state by reinforcement learning. The user cyclically executes the process to continuously enhance the awareness of the environment, and finally achieves a state of stable optimal strategy in a complex dynamic environment. The flow of multi-domain joint anti-jamming algorithm based on reinforcement learning is shown in Algorithm 1.

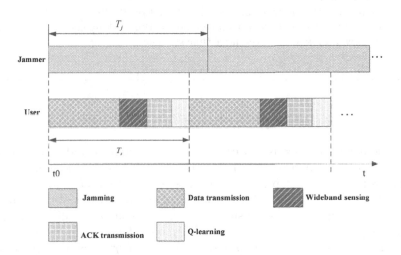

Fig. 3. Time slot structure.

4   Simulation Results and Discussions

This paper mainly studies how to choose the optimal strategy to effectively deal with jamming. The convergence performance of the algorithm is simulated and analyzed. In order to prove the validity of the proposed algorithm, this paper compares the proposed algorithm with the sensing-based random selection algorithm. The sensing-based random selection algorithm firstly implement wideband spectrum sensing at each time slot to obtain the location of the jamming, and then randomly selects one transmitting power and one channel for access. For

---

Algorithm 1. Q-learning based multi-domain joint anti-jamming algorithm.

1: **Initialization:** Set parameter α, γ, the total simulation time slot to K and the time index $k = 0$. Initialize Q values matrix $Q(S, a) = 0$. Set the initial state is represented as $S_0(f_t(0), f_j(0))$.

2: **While** $k < K$, do

3:    The user receives data information on the $f_t(k)$ channel with the power of $P_t(k)$, updates the state to $S_k(f_t(k), f_j(k))$, and calculates the $SINR$ of the $f_t(k)$ channel according to Equation (3), and compares whether the $SINR$ is greater than the set threshold;

4:        if $SINR > \Gamma$
$$R_k = U_k \frac{T_{tran}}{T_s}, \text{ where } U_k \text{ can be obtained from Equation (5),}$$

5:        else
$$R_k = 0.$$

6:        end

7:        The current jamming channel $f_j(k+1)$ is found by wideband spectrum sensing;

8:        The action selection probability vector $W(k)$ is updated according to Equation (10), and the action $a(k) = (f_t(k+1), P_t(k+1))$ of the next time slot is selected according to the $P(k)$;

9:        update the Q value table according to Equation (8);

10:        Return ACK to the user transmitter, adjust the working channel $f_t(k+1)$ and transmit power $P_t(k+1)$ of the next time slot user;

11:        $k = k + 1$

12: **End while**

---

both algorithms, the performance of the system under different parameters is analyzed.

Considering that there is a user (including transmitter and receiver) and a malicious jamming (interferer) in the wireless communication system, the jammer applies two cross-sweep jamming signals. The system has 4 available channels and 3 power levels. Considering the fading characteristics of the channel, a lognormal fading model is established to reflect the channel quality [17,23], and the channel gain can be expressed as e^Z. Among them, Z represents a Gaussian variable with a mean of zero and a variance of η^2. The lognormal fading model can generally be expressed as $\eta = 0.1 \log(10)\eta_{dB}$. Assuming that the user accesses only one channel in one time slot, the jamming can interfere with two channels at the same time. The algorithm simulation specific parameter settings are shown in Table 1, where the time slot parameter setting refers to [18], and the channel parameter setting refers to [17,23].

The Q values variation curve and the selection probability curve of each action in the state $S(f_t = 2, f_j = 1, 4)$ (i.e., the user transmits data on the transmission channel-2, the jamming signals are in channel-1 and channel-4) are shown in Fig. 4, Fig. 5. The simulation results show that the Q values of each action is 0 at the beginning of the reinforcement learning, and the probability of selecting each action is equal. With the enhancement of users' cognition of the environment, the Q values table maintained by users is constantly updated.

Table 1. Simulation parameter setting.

Parameters	Value
Number of channels	$M_i = 4$
Number of user power levels	$P_i = 3$
The user's transmission power set	$\mathcal{P}_t = \{2\,\mathrm{W},\ 4\,\mathrm{W},\ 6\,\mathrm{W}\}$
Jamming constant power	$\mathcal{P}_j = 3.5\,\mathrm{W}$
Channel noise power spectral density	$N0 = -135\,\mathrm{dB/Hz}$
Channel bandwidth	$B = 1\,\mathrm{MHz}$
The distance between the transmitter and the receiver	$d_t = 5\,\mathrm{km}$
The distance between the jammer and the receiver	$d_j = 25\,\mathrm{km}$
Jamming time slot length	$T_{jam} = 4\,\mathrm{ms}$
Data transmission time	$T_d = 2\,\mathrm{ms}$
ACK transmission time	$T_A = 0.3\,\mathrm{ms}$
Wideband sensing time	$T_W = 0.6\,\mathrm{ms}$
Transmission time slot length	$T_s = T_d + T_A + T_W = 2.9\,\mathrm{ms}$
Learning step	$\alpha = (0, 1]$
Discount factor	$\gamma = 0.8$
Boltzmann coefficient	$\xi = 5\text{--}20$

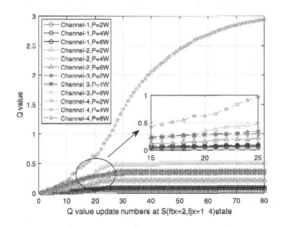

Fig. 4. Q value curves at $S(f_t = 2, f_j = 1, 4)$ state.

In the later stage of learning, the user selects the working channel-4 and the transmission power $2W$ with a probability close to 1.

In Fig. 6, we set the threshold $\Gamma = 3.8\,\mathrm{dB}$, the unit power transmission cost coefficient $C_s = 0.1$. We compared the system throughput performance of the multi-domain joint anti-jamming algorithm and the sensing-based random selection algorithm. In order to make the simulation results more clear, the throughput value of each time slot in the figure is calculated by averaging the throughput value of 50 consecutive time slots. The simulation results

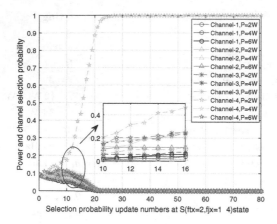

Fig. 5. Selection probability curves at $S(f_t = 2, f_j = 1, 4)$ state.

show that the throughput based on the sensing algorithm is about 0.5Mbps, while that the multi-domain joint anti-jamming algorithm based on Q-learning is about 0.88Mbps. Therefore, the proposed algorithm has better anti-jamming performance than the sensing-based random selection algorithm.

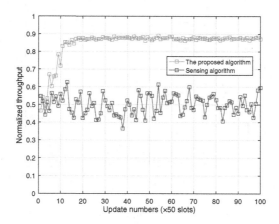

Fig. 6. Performance comparison of throughput for different algorithms.

5   Conclusions

Aiming at the problem of user's power and channel joint decision in jamming environment, the multi-domain anti-jamming decision process is modeled as a MDP. A Q-learning based multi-domain joint anti-jamming algorithm is proposed to execute decision-making. By the exploration and exploitation process of Q-learning, the algorithm can learn the jamming strategy based on the historical information. Simulation results show that the proposed algorithm can not only converge in the complex jamming environment, but also obtain the optimal power and channel selection in the continuous communication process. What's more, the throughput performance of the proposed algorithm is significantly improved compared with the sensing-based algorithm. On the basis of this paper, we will consider more complex jamming environment in the future research.

References

1. Zou, Y., Zhu, J., Wang, X., Hanzo, L.: A survey on wireless security: technical challenges, recent advances, and future trends. Proc. IEEE **104**(9), 1727–1765 (2016)
2. Sagduyu, Y.E., Berry, R.A., Ephremides, A.: Jamming games in wireless networks with incomplete information. IEEE Commun. Mag. **49**(8), 112–118 (2011)
3. Sharma, R.K., Rawat, D.B.: Advances on security threats and countermeasures for cognitive radio networks: a survey. IEEE Commun. Surv. Tutor. **17**(2), 1023–1043 (2015)
4. Pelechrinis, K., Iliofotou, M., Krishnamurthy, S.V.: Denial of service attacks in wireless networks: the case of jammers. IEEE Commun. Surv. Tutor. **13**(2), 245–257 (2011)
5. Worthen, A., Stark, W.: Interference mitigation in frequency-hopped spread-spectrum systems. In: 2000 IEEE Sixth International Symposium on Spread Spectrum Techniques and Applications, vol. 1, pp. 58–62 (2000)
6. Yu, L., Li, Y., Pan, C., Jia, L.: Anti-jamming power control game for data packets transmission. In: 2017 IEEE 17th International Conference on Communication Technology (ICCT), Chengdu, pp. 1255–1259 (2017)
7. Xiao, L., Chen, T., Liu, J., Dai, H.: Anti-jamming transmission stackelberg game with observation errors. IEEE Commun. Lett. **19**(6), 949–952 (2015)
8. Zhang, Y., et al.: A multi-leader one-follower stackelberg game approach for cooperative anti-jamming: no pains, no gains. IEEE Commun. Lett. **22**(8), 1680–1683 (2018)
9. Gao, Y., Xiao, Y., Wu, M., Xiao, M., Shao, J.: Game theory-based anti-jamming strategies for frequency hopping wireless communications. IEEE Trans. Wirel. Commun. **17**(8), 5314–5326 (2018)
10. Jia, L., Yao, F., Sun, Y., Xu, Y., Feng, S., Anpalagan, A.: A hierarchical learning solution for anti-jamming stackelberg game with discrete power strategies. IEEE Wirel. Commun. Lett. **6**(6), 818–821 (2017)
11. Xu, Y., Ren, G., Chen, J., Jia, L., Xu, Y.: Anti-jamming transmission in UAV communication networks: a Stackelberg game approach. In: 2017 IEEE/CIC International Conference on Communications in China (ICCC), Qingdao, pp. 1–6 (2017)
12. Chen, T., Liu, J., Xiao, L., Huang, L.: Anti-jamming transmissions with learning in heterogenous cognitive radio networks. In: 2015 IEEE Wireless Communications and Networking Conference Workshops (WCNCW), New Orleans, pp. 293–298 (2015)
13. Wang, B., Wu, Y., Liu, K.J.R., Clancy, T.C.: An anti-jamming stochastic game for cognitive radio networks. IEEE J. Sel. Areas Commun. **29**(4), 877–889 (2011)

14. Slimeni, F., Scheers, B., Chtourou, Z., Le Nir, V.: Jamming mitigation in cognitive radio networks using a modified Q-learning algorithm. In: 2015 International Conference on Military Communications and Information Systems (ICMCIS), Cracow, pp. 1–7 (2015)
15. Slimeni, F., Chtourou, Z., Schaeers, B., Nir, V.L., Attia, R.: Cooperative Q-learning based channel selection for cognitive radio. Wirel. Netw. **4**, 1–11 (2018)
16. Xu, N., Zhang, H., Xu, F., Wang, Z.: Q-learning based interference-aware channel handoff for partially observable cognitive radio ad hoc networks. Chin. J. Electron. **26**(4), 856–863 (2017)
17. Wu, Q., Xu, Y., Wang, J., Shen, L., Zheng, J., Anpalagan, A.: Distributed channel selection in time-varying radio environment: interference mitigation game with uncoupled stochastic learning. IEEE Trans. Veh. Technol. **62**(9), 4524–4538 (2013)
18. Kong, L., Xu, Y., Zhang, Y., et al.: A reinforcement learning approach for dynamic spectrum anti-jamming in fading environment. In: IEEE 18th International Conference on Communication Technology (ICCT), Chongqing, pp. 51–58 (2018)
19. Jia, L., Xu, Y., Sun, Y., Feng, S., Yu, L., Anpalagan, A.: A multi-domain anti-jamming defense scheme in heterogeneous wireless networks. IEEE Access **6**, 40177–40188 (2018)
20. Singh, S., Trivedi, A.: Anti-jamming in cognitive radio networks using reinforcement learning algorithms. In: 2012 Ninth International Conference on Wireless and Optical Communications Networks (WOCN), Indore, pp. 1–5 (2012)
21. Cavazos-Cadena, R., Fernandez-Gaucherand, E.: Markov decision processes with risk-sensitive criteria: dynamic programming operators and discounted stochastic games. In: Proceedings of the 40th IEEE Conference on Decision and Control, vol. 3, pp. 2110–2112 (2001)
22. Machuzak, S., Jayaweera, S.K.: Reinforcement learning based anti-jamming with wideband autonomous cognitive radios. In: 2016 IEEE/CIC International Conference on Communications in China (ICCC), Chengdu, pp. 1–5 (2016)
23. Stuber, G.: Principles of Mobile Communications. Kluwer Academic Publishers, Dordrecht (2001)

Motion Classification Based on sEMG Signals Using Deep Learning

Shu Shen[1,2], Kang Gu[1], Xinrong Chen[3,4(✉)], and Ruchuan Wang[1,2]

[1] School of Computer Science, Nanjing University of Posts and Telecommunications,
Nanjing 210023, China
{shens,1218043119,wangrc}@njupt.edu.cn
[2] Jiangsu High Technology Research Key Laboratory for Wireless Sensor Networks,
Nanjing 210023, China
[3] Academy for Engineering and Technology, Fudan University,
Shanghai 200433, China
chenxinrong@fudan.edu.cn
[4] Shanghai Key Laboratory of Medical Image Computing and Computer Assisted
Intervention, Shanghai 200032, China

Abstract. Nowadays, surface electromyography (sEMG) signal plays an important role in helping physically disabled people during daily life. The development of electronic information technology has also led to the emergence of low-cost, multi-channel, wearable sEMG signal acquisition devices. Therefore, this paper proposes a new motion recognition model based on deep learning to improve the accuracy of motion recognition of sEMG signals. The model uses architecture including 6 convolutional layers and 6 pooling layers which enables the Batch Normalization layer to enhance network performance and prevent overfitting. In the experiment, NinaPro DB5 data set was used for training and testing. The data set consists of sEMG signal data collected by the double Myo armbands which contains data of 52 movements for 10 subjects. The results show that the accuracy of about 90% can be achieved when using 52 sEMG signal data from every single subject or all subjects.

Keywords: Surface electromyogram signal · Deep learning · Wearable device · Motion recognition

1 Introduction

Human muscle is made up of many motor units, and as the muscles move, certain motion units are activated to produce bioelectrical signals. The superposition of bioelectrical signals produces myoelectric signal [1], which is reflected by sEMG signal. sEMG signal records the muscle activity from the skin surface and reflect the generation of myoelectric signals. Moreover, sEMG is a non-invasive method for collecting bioelectrical feedback signal. Therefore, sEMG signal is the critical technology used in motion recognition, which has been widely used in muscle

© ICST Institute for Computer Sciences, Social Informatics and Telecommunications Engineering 2019
Published by Springer Nature Switzerland AG 2019. All Rights Reserved
X. B. Zhai et al. (Eds.): MLICOM 2019, LNICST 294, pp. 563–572, 2019.
https://doi.org/10.1007/978-3-030-32388-2_48

feedback devices such as prosthetic control [2]. How to perform motion recognition based on the sEMG signal can be considered as a problem of pattern recognition. The motion recognition based on the sEMG signal is faced with several challenges and one of the most critical challenges is the original electromyography signals in each channel are non-stationary, non-linear, random and unpredictable. To solve the problem, deep learning methods for classification are proposed and have better accuracy and effectiveness [1].

Deep learning is a new technology in the area of machine learning. Its motivation is derived from the simulation and establishment of the neural network in human brain analysis and learning. Now, deep learning is one of the most popular techniques in image recognition, natural language processing, and speech recognition. At the same time, deep learning is a key technology used for data analysis, processing, and identification by various research teams. In this paper, a motion recognition model based on deep learning is proposed. The motion classification is carried out by the feature extraction of sEMG signals using multi-layer convolutional neural network. The model takes into account the valid information in the sEMG signal, which is usually ignored, and the performance of motion recognition is improved.

The rest of this paper is organized as follows. Section 2 discusses related research on this topic. Section 3 introduces the sEMG signal data set used in this experiment and the method of preprocessing the data. A motion recognition model using deep learning is proposed and the structure of the model is described in detail. The training and testing of the motion recognition model in Sect. 4 describes the experiment results. Section 5 summarizes the full text.

2   Related Work

Due to the development of non-invasive sEMG detection and machine learning, many researchers are committed to identifying human motion through sEMG signals. Many researchers have developed some methods for sEMG signal recognition based on time domain, frequency domain and time-frequency domain. At the same time, many researchers apply machine learning to sEMG recognition.

Pizzolato et al. [3] compared the six sEMG acquisition methods based on the NinaPro project and used SVM and Random Forests method to classify the characteristics of sEMG with a correct rate of 69%. Thakur et al. [4] presented a method which based on wavelet transform and support vector machine to classify the movements of human elbows. There are also some methods using feature extraction and machine learning which achieved good results [5–11]. Cote-Allard et al. [12] proposed a method with migration learning using convolutional neural networks to classify sEMG signals reducing the size of the training set required for model training. A parallel architecture deep convolutional network with five convolutional layers was proposed in [13], which realized the recognition of 17 kinds of actions, and the correct rate reached 82%. Zhou et al. [14] presented the method combining AdaBoost algorithm and BP neural network to identify 8 wrist movements and 12 finger movements. The sEMG signal was proposed to be imaged in [15] and identified using a deep learning method.

3 Motion Recognition

3.1 Frame

This study focused on sEMG signal data acquired by wearable armbands. Such devices are often portable and low power consumption. Although the accuracy is not very high, the cost is much lower than that of professional acquisition equipments. They are very suitable for people with physical disabilities to control prostheses. Figure 1 shows the frame of motion recognition using armbands, including acquisition of **sEMG signals, data preprocessing, signal feature extraction** and **motion classification.**

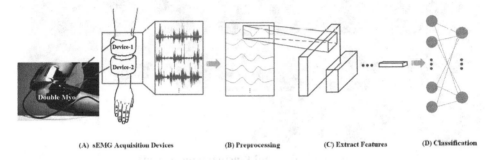

(A) sEMG Acquisition Devices   (B) Preprocessing   (C) Extract Features   (D) Classification

Fig. 1. Motion recognition frame

3.2 Data Set

NinaPro [16] is a project in progress to help research myoelectric prostheses in the hands with open data sets. It now contains seven databases related to the sEMG signal. The data set used in this paper is NinaPro DB5.

Acquisition Protocol. NinaPro DB5 contains a total of 52 motion data, all selected from manual taxonomy and manual robot literature. These actions are divided into three groups, named **Basic movement of the finger, Isometric, isotonic hand configurations and basic wrist movements, Grasping and functional movements.** A schematic representation of the actions from the NinaPro DB5 data set is shown in Fig. 2. During the acquisition of the sEMG signal, the subject is required to repeat the action. Each exercise is repeated for 5 s, then the rest is for 3 s. The NinaPro DB5 database contains a total of 6 repetitions of 52 different exercises (plus rest) performed by 10 intact subjects.

(A) Basic movement of the finger

(B) Isometric, isotonic hand configurations and basic wrist movements

(C) Grasping and functional movements

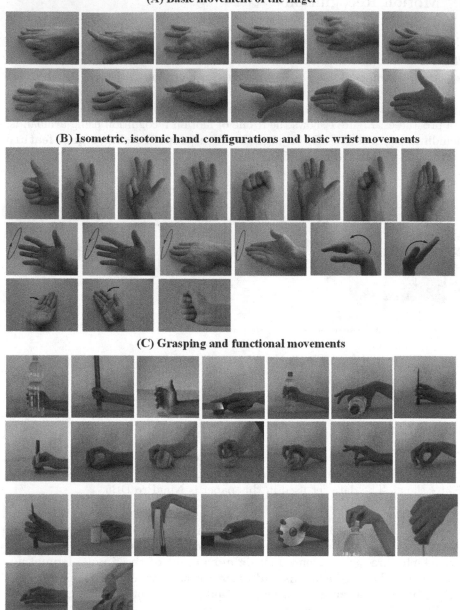

Fig. 2. The 52 movements in DB5

Acquisition Setup. The database has sEMG data for 10 subjects. Part (A) in Fig. 1 shows the acquisition device. Each subject wears two Myo armbands, one after the other, including 16 active single differential wireless electrodes while acquiring the sEMG signal. The top Myo arm strap is placed close to the elbow and the first sensor is placed on the tibial joint. The second Myo arm band is placed behind the first one, close to the hand, tilted 22.5° to provide an extended uniform muscle mapping. Each Myo armband samples the sEMG signal at the rate of 200 Hz.

Preprocessing. The data needs to be pre-processed before training. Because the data used in this paper is sampled at the frequency of 200 Hz and the sampling time for each action is 5 s, the data length of each channel is aligned to 1000. Firstly, data segmentation is performed according to the data labels in the DB5 database, and the sEMG signal data of each action is separated. Then, each channel has a data length greater than 1000 and is intermittently sampled, and less than 1000 is subjected to cubic interpolation. After the length normalization is performed, the amplitude of the data is normalized between 0 and 1. We use Eq. (1) to perform amplitude normalization.

$$A_n = \frac{A_r + 256.0}{512.0} \tag{1}$$

A_r is the original data of the sEMG signal, and A_n is the data after the amplitude is normalized.

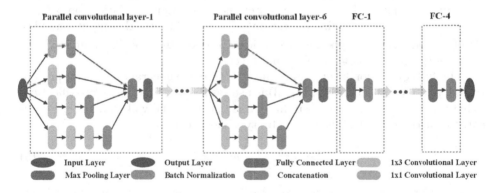

Fig. 3. Model

3.3   Recognition Model

The sEMG signal processed in this paper has 16 channel and each channel has 1000 data. Therefore, in order to complete the recognition of motion, we represent them by a matrix of 16×1000 and use the convolutional neural network to extract the features of the sEMG signal in order to complete the recognition of motion. The sEMG motion recognition model based on convolutional neural network proposed for us in Fig. 3. The input layer is 16×1000 sEMG signal data. Six parallel convolutional layer stacking structures are used to extract the features of the sEMG signal step by step. The high-dimensional features are then mapped to low dimensions using a 4-layer fully-connected network, which is then classified by the output layer. The parallel convolutional layer uses four types of individual convolutions for feature extracting. At the same time, batch standardization was added after each type of convolution. 1×1 and 1×3 size one-dimensional convolution kernels are used for feature extraction of single-channel data which reduces interference between channels and improves the performance of the model. The output of each layer of parallel convolutional layers is the Eq. (2).

$$
\begin{aligned}
y_1^{(i)} &= F_{BN}(\tanh(F_{conv}(x^{(i)}, [1,1]))) \\
y_2^{(i)} &= F_{BN}(\tanh(F_{conv}(x^{(i)}, [1,3]))) \\
y_3^{(i)} &= F_{BN}(\tanh(F_{conv}(F_{conv}(x^{(i)}, [1,3]), [1,3]))) \\
y_4^{(i)} &= F_{BN}(\tanh(F_{conv}(F_{conv}(F_{conv}(x^{(i)}, [1,3]), [1,3]), [1,3]))) \\
y_o^{(i)} &= Pool(concat(y_1^{(i)}, y_2^{(i)}, y_3^{(i)}, y_4^{(i)}), pool\_size)
\end{aligned}
\tag{2}
$$

Where $y_j^{(i)}, j = \{1,2,3,4\}$ is the jth type output of the sample i and $F_{conv}(x, [m, n])$ is the convolution operation of the sample x using the convolution kernel of size $[m, n]$. Tanh is the activation function used by the convolutional layer. $F_{BN}(x)$ is a batch normalization operation on sample x. $concat(x_1, x_2, \ldots)$ is the operation of connecting to the input samples. $Pool(x, pool\_size)$ is a pooling operation for pool_size size for sample x. $y_o^{(i)}$ is the output of parallel convolutional layer.

The full connection layer adopts the structure of a general multi-layer perceptron. Cross-entropy defined in Eq. (3) is used as the loss function of classification, Where $y^{(i)}$ represents the probability value that is actually class i, and $\hat{y}^{(i)}$ indicates that the prediction is a probability value of class i.

$$
Loss = -\sum_i y^{(i)} \log \hat{y}^{(i)}
\tag{3}
$$

Table 1 shows specific parameters of each layer about convolutional neural network designed proposed. The number of convolution kernel channels in the same layer is constant. We expound the number of specific channels of the convolution kernel in rows 2–7 of the table and the pooling size of each max pooling layer in row 8–13. The number of neurons about fully connected and output layers is in the remaining rows. Convolutional layer and the fully connected layer use tanh as the activation function. The output layer uses softmax as the activation function.

Table 1. Parameters of each layer about convolutional neural network proposed.

Name	Number	Parameter		Activation
Parallel convolutional layer	1	Each convolution kernel channel	4	tanh
	2		8	
	3		16	
	4		32	
	5		64	
	6		256	
Max Pooling layer	1	Pool size	[1, 5]	None
	2		[1, 5]	
	3		[1, 2]	
	4		[1, 2]	
	5		[1, 2]	
	6		[1, 5]	
FC layer	1	Units	2048	tanh
	2		1024	
	3		512	
	4		128	
Output layer	1		52	Softmax

Table 2. Test accuracy of the model proposed in the paper.

Subject number	Train set/Test set accuracy			Average accuracy
	(1, 2)(3, 4)/(5, 6)	(1, 2)(5, 6)/(3, 4)	(3, 4)(5, 6)/(1, 2)	
1	90.38%	93.27%	81.73%	88.64%
2	94.23%	95.19%	84.62%	91.35%
3	97.12%	99.04%	90.38%	95.51%
4	89.42%	93.27%	84.62%	89.10%
5	95.19%	95.19%	81.65%	90.68%
6	90.38%	97.12%	82.69%	90.06%
7	89.40%	93.27%	76.96%	86.54%
8	87.50%	92.31%	77.88%	85.90%
9	93.27%	99.04%	87.51%	93.27%
10	89.42%	93.26%	82.69%	88.46%
All subject	91.06%	93.26%	83.26%	89.45%

4   Simulation

Data of 10 subjects in NinaPro DB5 database is used to train and test the model designed in this paper. The data of 6 repetitions of each action in the DB5 database is divided into three groups of (1, 2), (3, 4), and (5, 6). Each test selects one of them as the test set and the rest as the training set. The average correct rate of three times is used as the final correct rate. The result of the tests on the data of each subject and all subjects is presented in Table 2. The test was confirmed to be 89.95% ± 2.78% on the data of each subject. The accuracy of testing on all subjects was 89.45%.

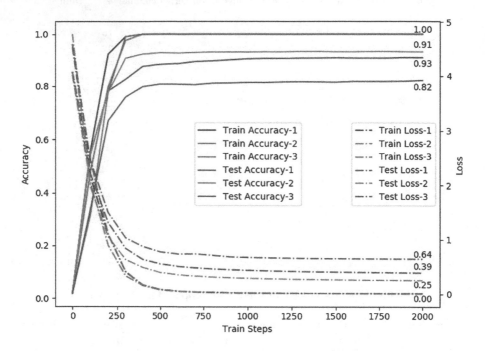

Fig. 4. Accuracy and loss in all subject

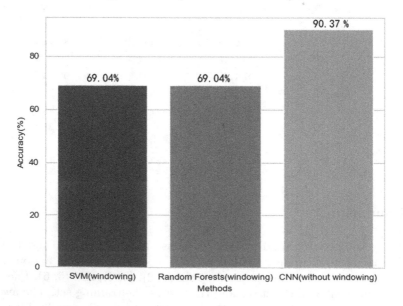

Fig. 5. Comparison

Figure 4 shows a plot of accuracy, error, and number of training steps was tested on the data of all subjects. We conducted a total of 2000 steps on the network and recorded the error and accuracy of the network on the training set and test set for each 100 steps. We also used the data of 41 movements in group B and group C to test the model and compare with the test accuracy of using SVM and Random Forests in [3]. Figure 5 shows the results of the comparison. However, windowing was performed when using SVM and Random Forests for sEMG signal recognition, and the work we did was not windowed. We will study the windowed signals in the next work.

5 Conclusion

This paper proposes a motion recognition model based on sEMG using deep learning. The model uses a multi-layer parallel convolutional neural network to extract features from sEMG signals. Compared with the traditional feature extraction method, it can extract more effective information and improve the accuracy of motion recognition. The NinaPro DB5 data set is used to train in the simulation section and the model is tested on 52 motion data from 10 subjects. The experiment results demonstrate the proposed method has a better performance than both the traditional SVM method and the Random Forests methods. In the future, because windowing has an effect on the performance of the recognition method, we will study the windowed signals in the next work.

Lab Environment. The CPU for the desktop used in the experiment was Intel(R) Core(TM) i7-7800X CPU @ 3.5 GHz (3504 MHz), and the GPU was NVIDIA TITAN Xp (12 GB). The software environment used in the experiment was Tensorflow gpu 1.12.

Acknowledgment. The authors would like to thank the financial support by the National Science Foundation of P.R. China under Grant Nos. 61401221, 61873131, 61872196, 61701168, 61572261, 61572260, China Postdoctoral Science Foundation under Grant No. 2016M601860, Postgraduate Research & Practice Innovation Program of Jiangsu Province under Grant Nos. SJCX19_0240, SJKY19_0823, NJUPT Teaching Reform Project under Grant No. JG00417JX74.

The authors are very grateful to the open source dataset provided by the NinaPro project team, which is an important prerequisite for the successful implementation of this paper. Furthermore, we would like to thank NVIDIA for supporting to this project. All of the experiments in this article worked smoothly on NVIDIA TITAN Xp.

References

1. Alam, R.U., Rhivu, S.R., Haque, M.: Improved gesture recognition using deep neural networks on sEMG. In: 2018 International Conference on Engineering, Applied Sciences, and Technology (ICEAST), pp. 1–4. IEEE (2018)

2. Sayin, F.S., Ozen, S., Baspinar, U.: Hand gesture recognition by using sEMG signals for human machine interaction applications. In: 2018 Signal Processing: Algorithms, Architectures, Arrangements, and Applications (SPA), pp. 27–30. IEEE (2018)

3. Pizzolato, S., Tagliapietra, L., Cognolato, M., Reggiani, M., Müller, H., Atzori, M.: Comparison of six electromyography acquisition setups on hand movement classification tasks. PLoS ONE **12**(10), e0186132 (2017)

4. Thakur, N., Mathew, L.: sEMG signal classification using ensemble learning classification approach and DWT. In: 2018 International Conference on Current Trends towards Converging Technologies (ICCTCT), pp. 1–4. IEEE (2018)

5. Atzori, M., et al.: Electromyography data for non-invasive naturally-controlled robotic hand prostheses. Sci. Data **1**, 140053 (2014)

6. Atzori, M., et al.: Characterization of a benchmark database for myoelectric movement classification. IEEE Trans. Neural Syst. Rehabil. Eng. **23**(1), 73–83 (2015)

7. Xue, Y., Ju, Z., Xiang, K.: Classification of dynamic in-hand manipulation based on SEMG and Kinect. In: 2018 Eighth International Conference on Information Science and Technology (ICIST), pp. 342–346. IEEE (2018)

8. Jose, N., Raj, R., Adithya, P., Sivanadan, K.: Classification of forearm movements from sEMG time domain features using machine learning algorithms. In: 2017 IEEE Region 10 Conference, TENCON 2017, pp. 1624–1628. IEEE (2017)

9. Zhengyi, L., Hui, Z., Dandan, Y., Shuiqing, X.: Multimodal deep learning network based hand ADLs tasks classification for prosthetics control. In: 2017 International Conference on Progress in Informatics and Computing (PIC), pp. 91–95. IEEE (2017)

10. Cene, V.H., dos Santos, R.R., Balbinot, A.: Using Antonyan Vardan transform and extreme learning machines for accurate sEMG signal classification. In: 2018 40th Annual International Conference of the IEEE Engineering in Medicine and Biology Society (EMBC), pp. 5224–5227. IEEE (2018)

11. Gijsberts, A., Atzori, M., Castellini, C., Müller, H., Caputo, B.: Movement error rate for evaluation of machine learning methods for sEMG-based hand movement classification. IEEE Trans. Neural Syst. Rehabil. Eng. **22**(4), 735–744 (2014)

12. Cote-Allard, U., Fall, C.L., Campeau-Lecours, A., Gosselin, C., Laviolette, F., Gosselin, B.: Transfer learning for sEMG hand gestures recognition using convolutional neural networks. In: 2017 IEEE International Conference on Systems, Man, and Cybernetics (SMC), pp. 1663–1668. IEEE (2017)

13. Xing, K., et al.: Hand gesture recognition based on deep learning method. In: 2018 IEEE Third International Conference on Data Science in Cyberspace (DSC), pp. 542–546. IEEE (2018)

14. Zhou, S., Yin, K., Liu, Z., Fei, F., Guo, J.: sEMG-based hand motion recognition by means of multi-class adaboost algorithm. In: 2017 IEEE International Conference on Robotics and Biomimetics (ROBIO), pp. 1056–1061. IEEE (2017)

15. Geng, W., Du, Y., Jin, W., Wei, W., Hu, Y., Li, J.: Gesture recognition by instantaneous surface EMG images. Sci. Rep. **6**, 36571 (2016)

16. The Ninapro Team: Ninaweb. http://ninapro.hevs.ch/. Accessed 25 Feb 2019

Realization of Transmission Control Protocol Based on µC/OS-II

Qianyuan Wang[✉] and Yujun Gao

Tongji University, No. 4800 Cao'an Highway, Shanghai 201804, China
wangqianyuan123@qq.com

Abstract. TCP/IP protocol suite plays an important role in computer network, in which TCP is a crucial protocol. To realize a general TCP on µC/OS, this paper adopts the embedded TCP/IP protocol stack called µC/IP as a basic version. The original TCP code in µC/IP will be modified to realize all functions defined in standard TCP. The modified TCP is integrated with standard IP, network interface protocol and tested on STM32F407 demoboard. The demoboard can communicate with computer, which proves the correctness of the modified TCP.

Keywords: TCP · µC/OS-II · Transmission reliability

1 Introduction

Operating system is important in embedded devices. µC/OS-II [1] is an operating system with open source code, compact structure and deprived real-time kernel. Therefore, most projects prefer to choose µC/OS-II as embedded operating system.

Embedded TCP/IP protocol stack is extensively adopted in embedded devices for communication. LwIP [2] and µC/IP [3] are two widely used embedded TCP/IP protocol stacks. It is difficult to separate TCP from LwIP. Whereas, it is very easy to separate TCP code from µC/IP which is designed for µC/OS-II. To realize a general separated TCP function, this paper selects µC/IP as embedded TCP/IP protocol stack. The TCP code in µC/IP does not contain all functions defined in the standard TCP. Therefore, this paper modifies the TCP code in µC/IP to realize a general TCP containing all functions.

The main work in this paper contains three parts. The first part is transplanting LwIP and µC/OS-II in the demoboard. The second part is modifying the existing TCP code in µC/IP and replacing the TCP in LwIP with the modified TCP. The final part is building a TCP client and a server task to test the modified TCP.

The rest of the paper will be organized as follows: In Sect. 2, µC/OS-II is introduced. In Sect. 3, the detailed implementation of TCP is explained. In Sect. 4, the testing results are given. In Sect. 5, we will conclude the paper.

X. B. Zhai et al. (Eds.): MLICOM 2019, LNICST 294, pp. 573–579, 2019.
https://doi.org/10.1007/978-3-030-32388-2_49

2 Brief Review of μC/OS-II

μC/OS-II is a real-time operating system. Because it takes up a small amount of space, it is very suitable for transplanting to embedded devices.

μC/OS-II provides many mechanisms to protect shared data and provide intertask communication [1]. Semaphore is an important mechanism. μC/OS-II's semaphores consists of two elements: a 16-bit unsigned integer used to hold the semaphore count, and a list of tasks waiting for the semaphore count to be greater than 0. Semaphore is used to protect shared data. If semaphore is not available, a task will need to be put to sleep until another task signals the semaphore. Therefore, shared data will be used by only one task.

3 The Implementation of TCP

TCP is a connection-oriented and reliable transport layer protocol [4, 5]. TCP operations include connection establishment, data transfer, and connection termination. A TCP connection is point-to-point and it consists of a server and a client. The process that initiates the connection establishment is called the client process. The process that passively waits for the connection to be established is called the server process.

The flowchart of the client and server is shown in Fig. 1. The client and the server bind the source port number and source IP address. Then, the client will connect with the server. After the connection is established, the client and the server can transmit and receive data. When the client and the server don't need to transmit or receive data, they will close the connection.

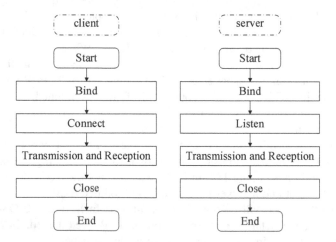

Fig. 1. The flowchart of client and server.

3.1   Connection Establishment

Connection establishment is called three-way handshake. The server and the client bind their own source port number and source IP address. Then the client sends a SYN segment to the server. After receiving the SYN segment sent by the client, the server will also send a SYNACK message to the client. Finally, the client will send an ACK segment to the server. The connection between the client and the server is established. Connection establishment sets initial parameters such as the sending sequence number and the receiving sequence number.

3.2   Data Transfer

A TCP connection provides a full-duplex service. Therefore, the server and the client need to establish their own transmitting and receiving buffers. A TCP connection provides a reliable data transfer service which ensures that data stream is in sequence and not duplicate. As illustrated in Fig. 2, there are four functions to transmit and receive data, namely tcpInput, tcpOutput, tcpRead and tcpWrite. The function called tcpRead is used to receive data from transport layer to application layer. The function called tcpWrite is used to send data from application layer to transport layer. The function called tcpInput is used to receive data from network layer to transport layer. The function called tcpOutput is used to send data from transport layer to network layer.

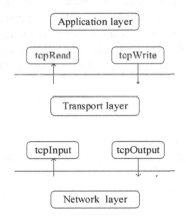

Fig. 2. Functions of data transmission.

As shown in Fig. 3, tcpInput receives and processes segments from network layer. Firstly, the received segment needs to be checked. If checked unsuccessfully, the segment will be discarded. If the segment is checked successfully, the keepalive timer will be reset. Then, data in the received segment will be extracted and saved in receiving buffers. When a new segment is received, out-of-order segments will be handled.

There are only two TCP congestion-control algorithms (slow start and congestion avoidance) in the TCP of µC/IP. By modifying the TCP code, another two TCP congestion-control algorithms (fast retransmit and fast recovery) are added.

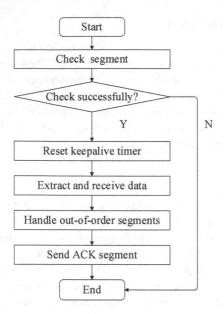

Fig. 3. The flowchart of tcpInput

As shown in Fig. 4, tcpOutput sends segments from transport layer to network layer. If the sending window is 0, the sender will open persistence timer to update the sending window. When the sending window is greater than 0, data will be extracted from the sending buffer to the segment. Then the TCP header of the segment will be filled. When the segment is sent, the retransmission timer will open.

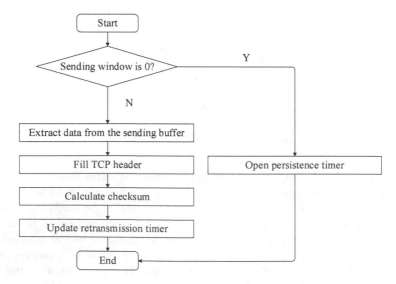

Fig. 4. The flowchart of tcpOutput

Data will be extracted from the receiving buffer to application layer by calling the function called tcpRead. The application process can choose the number of data that extracted from the receiving buffer.

Data will be put into sending buffer by calling the function called tcpWrite. The data will be sent by calling the function called tcpOutput.

3.3 Timer Management

There are mainly three timers (retransmission timer, persistence timer and keepalive timer) in a TCP connection.

To prevent the segments from being unacknowledged or lost, retransmission timer is established. If the segment that has been sent is not acknowledged within a certain period of time, the sender will resend the segment to the receiver. Therefore, the data stream will be in sequence and the transmission will be reliable.

When the sender's sending window is 0, the sender will open persistence timer to check whether the receiving window of the receiver is greater than 0. When the receiver' receiving window is greater than 0, the persistence timer will be closed.

The keepalive timer is used in the server. The keepalive timer is mainly to check whether the client is alive. When the client and the server don't transmit or receive data for a long time, the server will send a segment without data to check whether the client is closed.

The keepalive timer and the persistence timer are combined in the TCP of μC/IP. By modifying the TCP code of μC/IP, the keepalive timer and the persistence timer will work individually.

A timer task is established to process the timers in TCP. Firstly, an empty timer linked list is created. Then different timers are inserted into the timer linked list. The timer task will check whether the latest timer is timeout. When the timer is timeout, the related function will work and the timer will be deleted from the timer linked list.

3.4 Connection Termination

The client or the server can decide to close. Suppose that the client decides to close the connection. Firstly, the client sends a FIN segment to the server. After receiving the FIN segment, the server will send an ACK segment to the client. When the server also decides to close, it will send a FIN segment to the client. The client will send an ACK segment. Eventually, the connection between the client and the server is closed.

4 Testing Results

The hardware is STM32F407 demoboard. μC/OS-II is transplanted in demoboard. Standard IP and network interface protocol is integrated by LwIP. Finally, the modified TCP code is downloaded in demboard. The demoboard and the computer are connected via a network cable.

As shown in Fig. 5, TCP client is established in embedded device and TCP server is established in the computer. The computer's source IP address is 192.168.1.108 and the computer's port number is 8087. The embedded device's source IP address is 192.168.1.101 and the embedded device's source port number is 49154. The computer receives 750 bytes from the embedded device. It proves that the modified TCP can work with standard TCP.

Fig. 5. TCP client is the embedded device. TCP server is the computer.

As shown in Fig. 6, TCP client is established in the computer and TCP server is established in the embedded device. The computer's source IP address is

Fig. 6. TCP client is the computer. TCP server is the embedded device.

192.168.1.108 and the computer's source port number is 1922. The embedded device's source IP address is 192.168.1.101 and the embedded device's source port number is 49154. The computer receives 8 bytes from the embedded device.

5   Conclusions

This paper completes the transplantation of TCP in embedded devices. Tested by net assistant, the modified TCP communicates successfully with standard TCP. Many parameters can be reconfigured according to users' requirements in the modified TCP code. Therefore, the modified TCP is a general TCP and easy to change and use for users.

Acknowledgment. This work is supported by the National Natural Science Foundation of China under Grant No. U1733114, the Fundamental Research Funds for the Central Universities, and Shanghai Rising-star Program under Grant No. 19QA1409100.

References

1. Labrosse, J.: MicroC/OS-II: The Real-Time Kernel, 2nd ed, pp. 153–178. CMP Books (2002)
2. Dunkels, A.: Design and implementation of the lwIP TCP/IP stack, pp. 1–3. Swedish Institute of Computer Science (2001)
3. http://ucip.sourceforge.net
4. Kurose, J.F., Ross, K.W.: Computer Networking: A Top-Down Approach, 6th edn, pp. 230–285. Addison-Wesley, Boston (2001)
5. Stevens, W.R.: TCP/IP Illustrated (Vol. 1): The Protocols, 2nd edn, pp. 575–803. Addison-Wesley, Boston (2012)

Applications of Machine Learning I

Applications and Machine Learning

Knowledge Graph Embedding Based on Hyperplane and Quantitative Credibility

Shuo Chen[1], Lin Qiao[1], Biqi Liu[1], Jue Bo[1], Yuanning Cui[2(✉)], and Jing Li[2]

[1] State Grid Liaoning Electric Power Supply Co, LTD., Shenyang 110004, Liaoning, China
[2] College of Computer Science and Technology, Nanjing University of Aeronautics and Astronautics, Nanjing 210016, Jiangsu, China
yuanningcui@163.com

Abstract. Knowledge representation learning is one of the research hotspots in the field of knowledge graph in recent years. How to improve the training algorithm of knowledge representation model and improve the accuracy of knowledge graph knowledge completion prediction is the main research goal in this field. Applying more implicit semantic information to model training is the primary means of improving accuracy. The traditional method does not consider the change of knowledge validity with time. So for this problem, we study the distribution law of quantitative changes of knowledge, design the model to simulate the quantitative changes of knowledge, put forward the concept of quantitative credibility, and apply it to the training algorithm of the model, and put forward A new learning method of knowledge representation QCHyTE. We compare the trained model with the best-recognized algorithms, and the results show that our improved algorithm greatly improves the prediction accuracy of the model.

Keywords: Knowledge graph · Time aware · Representation learning · Link Prediction

1 Introduction

The study of knowledge graphs has made great progress in recent years. Knowledge graph is a generalized formal description framework of semantic knowledge. It uses nodes to represent semantic symbols and edges to represent semantic relations between symbols. The common way is to store entities in the real world in the form of structured triples. And the relationship between entities. The way in which knowledge is expressed determines its expressive power and the complexity of semantic computing. The numerical representation method of the trigram's expression form knowledge graph has strong expressive ability, but it is difficult to use computer to do semantic calculation. It means that learning is a numerical representation method, which improves the semantic graph semantic calculation validness.

© ICST Institute for Computer Sciences, Social Informatics and Telecommunications Engineering 2019
Published by Springer Nature Switzerland AG 2019. All Rights Reserved
X. B. Zhai et al. (Eds.): MLICOM 2019, LNICST 294, pp. 583–594, 2019.
https://doi.org/10.1007/978-3-030-32388-2_50

Representation learning is one of the hot topics of knowledge graph research. It uses discrete symbols (entities, attributes, relationships, values, etc.) in the knowledge graph to represent continuous semantic values. This representation can reflect the semantic information of entities and relationships. Efficient computation of entities, relationships, and their complex semantic associations. At present, the knowledge graph indicates that there are two main categories of learning: one is the representation learning method based on tensor decomposition, and the most representative ones are RASCAL [1], DistMult [2], HoIT [3] and TuckER [4]. The idea of this type of method is to use tensor to represent the knowledge in the knowledge graph, and to complete the knowledge based on tensor decomposition, and achieved good results. The other type is translation-based representation learning methods, the most representative of which are TransE [5], TransH [6], TransR [7], TransD [8] and so on. They treat the relationship in the triple as a translation vector from the head to the tail. The goal of the training is to make the translation of the head entity vector through the relation vector close to the vector of the tail entity. The advantage of the tensor decomposition based method is that the information of the entire knowledge graph is integrated in the process of encoding entities and relationships. Its disadvantage is that the tensor is large for the Large Scale knowledge graph, and the decomposition process is computationally intensive; The translation-based model overcomes the problem of low learning efficiency can quickly complete representation learning in a large-scale knowledge graph. The disadvantage is that only a part of the information in the knowledge graph can be learned, and the expression power is not as good as the method based on tensor decomposition.

Time information is used in knowledge graph embedded learning, which is a new research direction in recent years. Most models assume that the knowledge graph exists in the same space-time condition, which is obviously not true. For example, Trump is the president of the United States. This fact was established in 2018 and was not established in 2014. Therefore, time information is an important implicit semantic information of the knowledge graph. Jiang [9] and others used the temporal information for the first time in the knowledge graph embedded learning, and achieved good results. Dasgupta [10] used the TransH [6] method to use time information as the main measure to distinguish one-to-many relationship, and proposed the HyTE [10] model. Their work graphs entities and relationships through temporal information to the temporal hyperplane and then computes the energy function. This method creatively embeds temporal information directly into the hyperplane space. Their experimental results show that the HyTE [10] model has better prediction effects than TransE [5], TransH [6], t-TransE [9] and HoIE [3].

From TransE to HyTE, it can be found from the development of the translation model that it is helpful to include more implicit semantic information in the model to improve the knowledge completion effect. But the more information that is not included, the better. Generally speaking, the more semantic information is included in the model, the more parameters need to be trained. The more parameters that need to be trained, the longer it takes to train the model. So the model needs to find a balance between expressiveness and efficiency.

We found that for datasets with time stamps, the duration of most relationships satisfies certain rules. For example, the relationship of GraduatedFrom, the valid duration is mostly from three years to six years, but a small part is from one years to two years or from seven years to ten years. We believe that this law is a priori knowledge, and the HyTE model cannot learn this knowledge duration the learning process. So we studied the law of the law of the quantitative change of knowledge, modeled the quantitative change, and used it to improve the model training algorithm.

The main contributions of our method includes:

(1) We propose the concept of quantitative credibility of knowledge. The concept of knowledge quantitative credibility is put forward, and its calculation formula is proposed by quantitative change modeling for meta-facts.
(2) An improved model training algorithm is proposed. The QCHyTE model was proposed by improving the HyTE model with quantitative credibility.
(3) Our experimental results demonstrate the validness of our approach. Design comparison experiments demonstrate the impact of our improvements on the accuracy of model predictions and analyze the causes of the impact.

2 Background

Before introducing the method of this paper, we will introduce TransE and TransH, and then introduce the temporal perception model HyTE in detail, because our method is based on the temporal perception model HyTE, and TransE and TransH are the basis of HyTE.

2.1 Knowledge Graph

The knowledge graph stores the entities in the real world and the relationships between the entities in the form of structured triples, expressed as $G = \{\varepsilon, R, \delta\}$, where $\varepsilon = \{e_1, e_2, \ldots, e_{|\varepsilon|}\}$ Representing a set of entities, $R = \{r_1, r_2, \ldots r_{|R|}\}$ represents a set of relationships, and $\delta \in R \times \varepsilon \times \varepsilon$ represents a set of triples in the knowledge graph.

2.2 TransE

TransE [5] uses a low-dimensional vector to represent each entity and relationship in the entity and relationship set of the knowledge graph, and uses the triples in the triple set as training samples. h, r, t in a triple (h, r, t) represent the head entity, relationship, and tail entity, respectively. TransE regards the relation vector as the translation vector from the head entity to the tail entity. For the two entity vectors $e_h, e_r \in R^n$, the difference between $e_h + e_r$ and e_t is used to score the translation effect. Its evaluation function can be expressed as: $f(h, r, t) = ||e_h + e_r - e_t||_{l_1/l_2}$. Where $||.||_{l_1/l_2}$ is l_1 norm or l_2-norm.

2.3 TransH

TransE has a poor predictive effect on one-to-many and many-to-one relationships. TransH [6] for this problem, each of the relations in the set R is represented by a hyperplane, and the unit normal vector of the hyperplane is denoted as w_r. Before the evaluation function is calculated, the head and tail entities are graphped to the relational hyperplane. The evaluation function of the TransH model can be expressed as:

$$f_r(h, r, t) = ||(e_h - w_r^T e_h w_r) + d_r - (e_t - w_r^t e_t w_r)||_2^2 \tag{1}$$

d_r represents the corresponding relationship between the pair of entities. For the same relationship, there can be multiple d_r, so TransH can better represent one-to-many, many-to-one, and many-to-many relationships than TransE.

2.4   HyTE

In some large knowledge graph, some meta facts are time stamped. These meta-facts can be structurally represented as $(h, r, t, [\tau_s, \tau_e])$, and $[\tau_s, \tau_e]$ represents the valid time of this triple.

The HyTE [10] model is a model designed on the basis of TransE [5] and inspired by TransH [6]. For these meta-facts containing event markers, Dasgupta et al. think that time is the main factor in their relationship between one-to-many and many-to-one. They use a hyperplane for each time, and the normal vector of hyperplane is recorded as w_t. Before calculating the evaluation function, the head and tail entities and relationship vectors are graphped to the temporal hyperplane, and then the evaluation function is calculated. The evaluation function of HyTE is:

$$f_\tau(h, r, t) = ||P_\tau(e_h) + P_\tau(e_r) - P_\tau(e_t)||_{l_{1/2}} \tag{2}$$

where $P_\tau(e_h) = e_h - w_\tau^T e_h w_\tau$, $P_\tau(e_t) = e_t - w_\tau^T e_t w_\tau$ and $P_\tau(e_r) = e_r - w_\tau^T e_r w_\tau$.

Where $P_\tau(?)$ represents the vector on the temporal hyperplane obtained by projecting the head entity, tail entity or relationship vector onto the time Label τ.

The main contribution of HyTE is that it splits the triple valid time into time labels, then uses the normal vector of the time hyperplane as the training parameter, and trains the entity with the relationship vector. The advantage of this is that the valid time information is subtly included in the model, so its prediction of the temporal perception of the knowledge graph is better than TransE and TransH.

3   Proposed Method: QCHyTE

Qualitative changes of events are caused by quantitative changes. The quantitative process of similar events is similar, and the time from the beginning to the qualitative change is also similar. Inspired by this rule, we modeled the quantitative process of similar events in the knowledge graph by studying the duration of events. QCHyTE is proposed by applying the learned rule of event quantity change to the improvement of knowledge representation model.

3.1 Quantitative Change Modeling

In general, a fact triple in a knowledge graph that contains a time stamp is subject to the process of invalid → valid → invalid in the time dimension. HyTE believes this process is abrupt. In other words, they believe that the establishment of knowledge at a certain point in time is a binary problem, not 0 or 1.

This is obviously contrary to our perception. A life from birth to death, an event from start to finish, is a gradual change, from quantitative change to qualitative change. So we believe that not all relationships are mutated, they undergo some random quantitative changes before they produce a qualitative change. We think this is the reason why many facts validly last for a certain distribution.

We extracted data from two relationships in the Wikidata dataset. The duration of their statistics is shown in the left part of Fig. 1. Their distribution satisfies the density function that is concentrated on a certain value and whose distribution pattern is close to the Gaussian distribution. In addition, some relationships occur instantaneously and end, and their start time and end time are the same. As shown in the right part of Fig. 1 below.

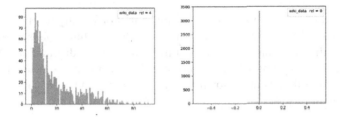

Fig. 1. The distribution of persistent relationships and transient relationship

Firstly, we divide the relationship into two categories according to the duration of the event, one is a persistent relationship, and the second is a transient relationship. The duration distribution of the relationships shown in Fig. 1 is the subject of our main study.

Persistent Relationships. A persistent relationship is a relationship in which the relationship is valid for a certain period of time, such as LiveIn and WorkFor. Since this type of relationship is not zero, we can think of it as a process of quantitative change.

We propose the quantitative credibility (QC) to represent the probability of an event, which represents the degree of credibility of the meta facts in the knowledge graph that persists at a certain point in time. It has been observed that the beginning and end of an event often satisfy the Gaussian distribution, so we use the difference between the two Gaussian distribution functions to simulate the distribution of QC (Fig. 3).

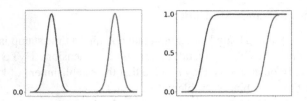

Fig. 2. The PDF and CDF of the start and end of the valid duration

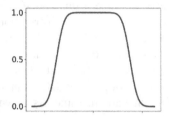

Fig. 3. The curve of quantitative credibility

As shown in Fig. 2, we use two Gaussian distribution density functions to simulate the probability that the event starts and ends near the two time points τs and τe. The two graphs are the distribution functions of the two Gaussian distributions. We use the distribution function starting with the valid time. The distribution function at the end of the deduction valid time is also shown in Fig. 2. Therefore the calculation function of quantitative credibility is:

$$QC(\tau_s, \tau_e, \tau_p) = \int_{-\infty}^{\tau_p} \frac{1}{\sigma\sqrt{2\pi}} e - \frac{(y-\tau_s)^2}{2\sigma^2} dy - \int_{-\infty}^{\tau_p} \frac{1}{\sigma\sqrt{2\pi}} e - \frac{(y-\tau_e)^2}{2\sigma^2} dy \quad (3)$$

In this way, we have well simulated the quantitative credibility of a triple in the knowledge graph in the time dimension, which provides the basis for us to use quantitative change credibility for knowledge embedded representation.

Transient Relationship. The transient relationship means that this relationship occurs at a certain time and does not persist, such as WasBornIn and DeadIn. Since this type of relationship has a duration of 0, we can think of it as a process of mutation. Its quantitative credibility is 1 at the valid time point and 0 at the invalid time point.

3.2   Model Training Based on Quantitative Credibility

In the HyTE model, the distribution of the triples in the knowledge graph in the time dimension is regarded as binary. They thought that the QC at all time points between the τs and τe of the triples is 1. Since HyTE is also a kind of model based on the energy function, the quantitative change credibility represents the distribution of energy in some ways. However, the objective fact is that the stability at these points in time is different. We observe that the credibility at the intermediate time point of the event establishment period is higher than the edge time point. So we tried to add QC to the scoring function and use this implicit information for KG Embedding duration training.

Both TransE and models based on it use a training strategy that uses negative sampling to speed up training. The QC of positive and negative samples will be calculated differently. The QC of a positive sample typically experiences a change from 0 to almost 1 then to 0 in the time dimension. The negative sample is an unknown random triple, which is not in the correct triple. It is generally considered to be invalid in any time plane duration the training process, so the QC of the negative sample is 1. QC can be expressed as:

$$QC(\tau_s, \tau_e, \tau_p, \mathbf{r}) = \begin{cases} \int_{-\infty}^{\tau_p} \frac{1}{\sigma\sqrt{2\pi}} e^{-\frac{(y-\tau_s)^2}{2\sigma^2}} - \frac{1}{\sigma\sqrt{2\pi}} e^{-\frac{(y-\tau_e)^2}{2\sigma^2}} dy + q, & triple \in \mathcal{D}^+ \ and \ r \in R_p \\ 1, & triple \in \mathcal{D}^- \ or \ r \notin R_p \end{cases}$$

(4)

τ_p in the formula represents the current time point, the value of the positive sample QC is in $(0, 1)$, and the QC of the negative sample is 1. Since our QC does not consider the data outside the marked valid period in the knowledge graph, therefore, the training evaluation function of the positive sample is actually reduced. If such QC is directly applied to the instructional training, the role of the positive sample in training will be reduced. So for a positive sample, we add q on the basis of QC, the purpose is to correct the QC of the positive sample to maintain the balance between the positive and negative samples.

QCHyTE, like HyTE, is a time-driven model. As with the HyTE model, our model graphs the evaluation function to the time plane as well. We use time to express it in a hyperplane. For T time points, we represent the normal vectors of T different time hyperplanes. The evaluation function we propose can be expressed as:

$$f_T(h, r, t, \tau_s, \tau_e, \tau_p) = QC(\tau_s, \tau_e, \tau_p, \mathbf{r})||(e_h + e_r - e_t) - \omega_\tau^T(e_h + e_r - e_t)\omega_\tau||_{l_{1/2}} \quad (5)$$

Compared with HyTE, QCHyTE does not have more parameters, so when calculating the loss function, it can be calculated by the following function:

$$L = \sum_{\tau \in [T]} \sum_{x \in \mathcal{D}_\tau^+} \sum_{y \in \mathcal{D}_\tau^-} \max(0, f_\tau(x) - f_\tau(y) + \gamma) \quad (6)$$

Where D_τ^+ represents a set of valid triples at each time point τ, and a negative sample is collected on the basis of the valid triples to obtain a set D_τ^- of negative samples. The method of taking a negative sample is a negative sampling method that does not count time:

$$\mathcal{D}^- = \{(h', r, t, \tau)|h' \in \xi, (h', r, t) \notin \mathcal{D}^+\} \cup \{(h, r, t', \tau)|t' \in \xi, (h, r, t') \notin \mathcal{D}^+\} \quad (7)$$

4   Experimental Results

In this part, we will test our model through experiments. We evaluate the model with the effect and accuracy of Link Prediction, which is a common evaluation method in the KG Embedding field. Then we compare the experimental results with the current advanced methods and analyze the reasons for this result.

4.1   Datasets

WikiData and YAGO are two large knowledge graphs, and most of the KG Embedding method experiments use these two datasets. YAGO11k and Wikidata12k are tense-aware knowledge graph datasets composed of meta-facts containing event marker information from these two datasets. The meta facts in YAGO11k are stored in the form (#factID, occurSince, ts), (#factID, occurUntil, te), which is extracted from the fact that the YAGO data set contains time stamps, which contains 20.5k triples, 10623 entities and 10 frequent relationships. Similar to YAGO11k, Wikidata12k is extracted from the Wikidata dataset and contains 24 frequent relationships, 40k triples, and 12.5k entities. This is the two data sets used in HyTE.

In order to better prove the validity of the model training algorithm proposed in this paper, we further extract the data according to the persistence and relational type of the data set relationship, and extract 15525 pieces of data containing the continuous relationship in the triple from the YAGO data set, and then the facts. The entities and relationships contained in the data are extracted to form a new continuous relational data set YGP10K. Sampling the same extraction method for Wikidata data, we have (Table 1).

Table 1. Dataset

Dataset	#R	#E	#Train	#Test	#Valid
Wikidata12K	24	12554	32497	4062	4062
YAGO11K	10	10623	16408	2051	2046

4.2   Details

Evaluation Indicators. In order to accurately evaluate our model approach, we used a general evaluation index for the TransE-based model. For each triple that needs to be tested, we remove the head and tail entities separately, and then replace them with all the entities in the dataset. After graphping to the time hyperplane, we use the evaluation function to score and sort all the entity evaluation results. The average ranking of the correct entities in all entities (Mean Rank) is used as an evaluation indicator, and then the percentage of the top ten data of all entities in the correct entity (Hit@10) is counted as an evaluation criterion. Similarly, the relationship vector in the triple is deleted, then replaced by all the relationships in the dataset, and scored using the evaluation function. The average ranking of the correct relationship in all entities (Mean Rank) is used as an evaluation indicator, and then the percentage of the data with the correct relationship among the first in all relationships (Hit@1) is used as an evaluation index.

Baseline Settings. The first method is TransE, which is the most classic method based on the translation model. It does not consider time stamp information, uses a triple set as a training set, and outputs a vector for each entity and each relationship. HoIE is a KG representation learning method. Its prediction effect is state-of-the-art. It is also a method that does not consider time stamping. TransH is a method based on TransE. It is the first time to apply hyperplane to knowledge representation learning. The HyTE method is also inspired by this. t-TransE is also a translation-based model that applies time information to knowledge representation learning for the first time, but this method does not have direct training in time learning. HyTE is an improved model method based on TransE and TransH. It considers time as the main factor in generating one-to-many and many-to-one relationships. Our method is based on HyTE. QCHyTE is our proposed method. We add the distribution of events in time as prior knowledge to the training. For the specific introduction, please see Sect. 3.

We used the baseline method to test on our dataset. The learning process of TransE, TransH and HoIE did not use time information. The learning process of t-TransE, HyTE and QCHyTE used time information. We set the appropriate parameters for these algorithms.

Parameter Setting. For all methods, we keep b = 10k on both datasets, the value of the embedded dimension is chosen in {64, 128, 256}, the boundary is chosen in {1, 2, 5, 10}, the learning rate is {0.01, Selected from 0.001, 0.0001}, the adjustment factor is selected in {0.3, 0.4, 0.5, 0.6, 0.7}. In the course of the experiment, we observed a dimension of 128, a boundary of 10, a learning rate of 0.0001, an adjustment factor of 0.6, and an evaluation model using the 1 paradigm to obtain the best model.

4.3   Results and Analysis

Entity Prediction. On the two datasets we prepared, we made the predictions of the head and tail entities respectively. The indicators tested were the Mean Rank and Hits@10 (%) of the correct head and tail entities. Comparing our experimental results with the experimental results of the baseline method, the results are as follows (Table 2).

Table 2. Results of entity prediction

Dataset	Wikidata12K				YAGO11K			
Metric	Mean rank		Hits@10 (%)		Mean rank		Hits@10 (%)	
	Tail	Head	Tail	Head	Tail	Head	Tail	Head
HoIE [3]	734	808	25.0	12.3	1828	1953	29.4	13.7
TransE [5]	520	740	11.0	6.0	504	2020	4.4	1.2
TransH [6]	423	648	23.7	11.8	354	1808	5.8	1.5
t-TransE [9]	283	413	24.5	14.5	292	1692	6.2	1.3
HyTE [10]	179	237	41.6	25.0	**107**	1069	38.4	16.0
QCHyTE	**111**	**175**	**61.3**	**38.1**	115	**783**	**39.6**	**20.4**

On the Wikidata12K dataset, our method has achieved very good results, and each evaluation index has been significantly improved compared with the baseline method. On the YAGO11K, except for the MR of the tail, which is worse than the HyTE, other prediction effect indicators are Got an improvement. We analyzed the data of YAGO11K and Wikidata12K and found that the distribution of events is more regular in Wikidata12K. There are a large number of transient triples in the YAGO11K dataset, and there are a large number of missing values, and the duration of the relationship is relatively short. This is the reason why tail prediction is worse. We further compared the results of HyTE and QCHyTE predictions for tail and found that even if MR increases, QCHyTE has an improved prediction of 46% of the data, and 38% of the data predicts a decrease, and the prediction results are good. Triples tend to be better, and the test triples, which were poorly predicted, will be even worse. This is also the reason why Hit@10 (%) does not fall back when MR increases. Below we provide a comparison of the predicted results of several HyTE and QCHyTE tail entities (Table 3).

Table 3. Comparation of entity prediction between HyTE and QCHyTE

Test quadruples	HyTE_tail_pred	QCHyTE_tail_pred
James_Baker, isAffiliatedTo,?, [1970,####]	Republican_Party_(United_States), Democratic_Party_(United_States), Unionist_Party_(United_States), Independent_politician	Democratic_Party_(United_States), Republican_Party_(United_States), Unionist_Party_(United_States), Walsall_F.C.
Esperanza_Baur, isMarriedTo,?[1946-1954]	Esperanza_Baur, Josephine_Wayne, John_Wayne,	Esperanza_Baur, John_Wayne, Josephine_Wayne,
Edith_Baumann_ (politician), isAffiliatedTo,? [1946-1973]	Communist_Party_of_Germany, Socialist_Unity_Party_of_Germany, Social_Democratic_Party_of_Germany, Bulgarian_Communist_Party	Socialist_Unity_Party_of_Germany, Communist_Party_of_Germany, Nazi_Party, Oxford

Relation Prediction. On the two datasets we prepared, we made a prediction of the relationship. The indicators tested were Mean Rank and Hits@1 (%) of the correct relationship vector. Comparing our experimental results with the experimental results of the baseline method, the results are as follows (Table 4).

Table 4. Results of relation prediction

Dataset	Wikidata12K		YAGO11K	
Metric	Mean rank	Hits@1 (%)	Mean rank	Hits@1 (%)
HolE [3]	2.23	83.96	2.57	69.3
TransE [5]	1.35	88.4	1.7	78.4
TransH [6]	1.4	88.1	1.53	76.1
t-TransE [9]	1.97	74.2	1.66	75.5
HyTE [10]	1.13	92.6	1.23	81.2
QCHyTE	**1.10**	**94.2**	**1.14**	**86.1**

For the prediction of relationships, our method improves the accuracy of the prediction. We analyze the test triples with improved prediction results. The results are shown in the following Table 5.

Table 5. Comparison of relation prediction between HyTE and QCHyTE

Test quadruples	HyTE_rel_pred	QCHyTE_rel_pred
Norman_Borlaug, ?, University_of_Minnesota, [1937-1942]	isMarriedTo, graduatedFrom	graduatedFrom, wasBornIn
Francisco_Gallardo,?, Puskás_Akadémia_FC,[2013-2014]	isMarriedTo, playsFor	playsFor, isMarriedTo
Konstantinos_Tsatsos,?, Independent_politician, [1967-1974]	isMarriedTo, isAffiliatedTo	isAffiliatedTo, isMarriedTo
Donovan_Leitch_(actor),?, London,[1946-1967]	diedIn, wasBornIn	wasBornIn, diedIn
Kate_O'Mara,?, Leicester,[1939-1939]	isMarriedTo, wasBornIn	wasBornIn, diedIn

5 Conclusions

In order to add the distribution law of the quantitative change for of the meta-facts to KG Embedding, we proposed QCHyTE. We study the distribution of meta-facts in time and propose the credibility of QC quantitative change. This is semantic information implicit in the time dimension, and we apply it as a priori knowledge to KG Embedding. Through experiments, we compared the prediction effects of QCHyTE and BaseLine methods and verified the validness of QCHyTE. Then compared with the training time of HyTE, it proves that the training efficiency of QCHyTE has also been improved. In the course of the experiment, we found that the time stamp of the knowledge graph has many rules that can be applied to training, such as the periodicity of duration, which is the direction of our future work. In addition, knowledge representation learning is also an important basis for knowledge fusion and text extraction. How to use the time-sensing knowledge representation learning for knowledge fusion and text extraction is also worth studying.

Acknowledgement. The research was supported by the State Grid Liaoning Electric Power Supply CO., LTD, and we are grateful for the financial support for the "Key Technology and Application Research of the Self-Service Grid Big Data Governance (SGLNXT00YJJ S1800110)".

References

1. Nickel, M., Tresp, V., Kriegel, H.-P.: A three-way model for collective learning on multi-relational data. In: Proceedings of the 28th International Conference on Machine Learning, ICML 2011, pp. 809–816. Omnipress (2011)
2. Yang, B., Yih, W.-T., He, X., Gao, J., Deng, L.: Embedding entities and relations for learning and inference in knowledge bases. arXiv preprint arXiv:1412.6575 (2014)

3. Nickel, M., Rosasco, L., Poggio, T.: Holographic embeddings of knowledge graphs. In: Proceedings of the Thirtieth AAAI Conference on Artificial Intelligence, AAAI 2016, pp. 1955–1961. AAAI Press (2016)
4. Balažević, I., Allen, C., Hospedales, T.M.: TuckER: tensor factorization for knowledge graph completion (2019)
5. Bordes, A., Usunier, N., Garcia-Duran, A., Weston, J., Yakhnenko, O.: Translating embeddings for modeling multirelational data. In: Burges, C.J.C., Bottou, L., Welling, M., Ghahramani, Z., Weinberger, K.Q. (eds.) Advances in Neural Information Processing Systems, vol. 26, pp. 2787–2795. Curran Associates, Inc. (2013)
6. Wang, Z., Zhang, J., Feng, J., Chen, Z.: Knowledge graph embedding by translating on hyperplanes. In: Proceedings of the Twenty Eighth AAAI Conference on Artificial Intelligence, AAAI 2014, pp. 1112–1119. AAAI Press (2014)
7. Lin, Y., Liu, Z., Sun, M., Liu, Y., Zhu, X.: Learning entity and relation embeddings for knowledge graph completion. In: Proceedings of the Twenty-Ninth AAAI Conference on Artificial Intelligence, AAAI 2015, pp. 2181–2187. AAAI Press (2015)
8. Ji, G., He, S., Xu, L., Liu, K., Zhao, J.: Knowledge graph embedding via dynamic graphping matrix. In: Proceedings of the 53rd Annual Meeting of the Association for Computational Linguistics and the 7th International Joint Conference on Natural Language Processing (Volume 1: Long Papers), vol. 1, pp. 687–696 (2015)
9. Jiang, T., et al.: Encoding temporal information for time-aware link prediction. In: Proceedings of the 2016 Conference on Empirical Methods in Natural Language Processing, pp. 2350–2354. Association for Computational Linguistics (2016)
10. Dasgupta, S.S., Ray, S.N., Talukdar, P.: HyTE: hyperplane-based temporally aware knowledge graph embedding, pp. 2001–2011 (2018). D18-1225

Artificial Intelligence Approaches for Urban Water Demand Forecasting: A Review

Abdullahi Uwaisu Muhammad, Xiaodong Li[(⊠)], and Jun Feng

College of Computer and Information, Hohai University, Nanjing, China
uwaisabdullahi87@yahoo.com,
{xiaodong.li,fengjun}@hhu.edu.cn

Abstract. In various research fields such as medicine, science, marketing, engineering and military. Artificial intelligence approaches have been applied, mainly due to their powerful reasoning capability, flexibility, modeling and forecasting capacity. In this paper, an attempt to review urban water demand forecasting using various artificial intelligence based approaches such as fuzzy logic systems, support vector machines, extreme learning machines, ANN and an ARIMA as well as hybrid models which consist of an integration of two or more artificial intelligence approaches are applied. The paper illustrates how the different artificial intelligence approaches plays a vital role in urban water demand forecasting while recommending some future research directions.

Keywords: ANN · ARIMA · Forecasting · Water demand

1 Introduction

With rapid increase in world population, per capital income, industrialization and the impacts of global warmings due to climate change on the world [112, 111]. Forecasting of urban water demand will play a vital role in the planning, distribution and management of scarce water resources among competitive users [92]. A hybrid wavelet artificial neural network (WANN) was compared to three AI approaches; conventional sediment rating curve, MLR and ANN. The results illustrated WANN as the most accurate model for suspended sediment load forecasting. Research conducted by [26] proposed a particle swarm optimization (PSO) model while comparing it's relative performance with ANN to forecasting the level of water in river channel. The results illustrate it to serve as a method that is very reliable and efficient in training artificial neural network. Using four different time scales [45], presented a dynamic neural network (DNN) for forecasting urban water demand. The proposed DNN proves to be the most efficient in water demand prediction than ARIMA and ANN feed forward backward propagation with forecasting accuracy best in hourly model.

For water demand prediction [100], applied genetic expression programming (GEP) and SVM. Results obtained proves GEP to be very sensitive in classification of the data, genetic operators with optimal lag time, although the support vector machines models slightly outperformed the GEP models. [61] assess computational intelligence tools based on there ability to effectively support simulation of the social-economic parameters of the complete water resource systems. They as well proposes a specific

X. B. Zhai et al. (Eds.): MLICOM 2019, LNICST 294, pp. 595–622, 2019.
https://doi.org/10.1007/978-3-030-32388-2_51

research agenda as a road map for both hydro informatics and adaptive water management. [2] conducted a research by comparing time series analysis and MLR to ANN for peak water demand in summer days in Ottawa Canada. The ANN proved to perform best in prediction of peak summer water demand than the reference models. Being an arid country with harsh climate conditions [60], suggest the government to enhance and implement new policies and strategies that will assist in management of scarce water resources. For proper and efficient and reliable usage of water resources, the government should also be involved in the following activities; water treatment and reuse management, water loss management, public awareness, reducing subsidy policy, incentive pricing as well as inclusion in participation of private sector.

Research conducted by [50] compares a series of predictive models using hourly data set water demand that were obtained from water pumping stations in eastern Spain. The results identify the SVR as the best model followed by MARS, PPR and random forest. As [10] conducted a comparative survey and applied multiplicative season algorithm (MSA) and discrete wavelet transform (DWT) as an alternative data processing techniques. The output of the multiplicative season algorithm and discrete wavelet transform are applied as an input to multi linear perceptron to develop a combined model and compared it with stand alone multi linear perceptron. The results demonstrate that the combined MSA-MLP was found to perform the best through out the prediction lead time. They suggest further research to be taken for short term water demand while taking into consideration weather data and other socioeconomic factors as inputs variables. [96] in there research proves the heuristic model as the best in performance, however integration of 2 or different types of artificial intelligent models helps to improve the precision and accuracy by minimizing error to 15.96%. While [91] reviewed forecasting models for the previous 5 decades and proposed a novel technique that can model the system to reflect the relationship between water demand and macro economic environment. This was practically implemented by applying the research under a recent alternative fluctuation of economic boom as well as down town environment.

A novel technique that can estimate the total amount of dissolve solids, turbidity and electrical conductivity was proposed and applied in Johor river [81]. The model proves to have a greater effect in simulating and forecasting with an absolute error of 10% for streams, lakes, dams and rivers. In another study [88], designed and implemented an intelligent decision support system (IDSS) using hourly water demand data set for water demand management. The AI technique forecasting improves the performance when compared to reference conventional learning models, although they suggest a method for integrating the system to a multi agent system for further research. Research by [40] proposed water demand forecasting model by applying Markov chain, and compared the relative performance of homogeneous and non homogeneous Markov chain (HMC) models with ANN and naive models. The HMC model proves to be distinctly more efficient than the others. The authors suggest estimation of the proposed model's performance to other reference forecasting models using deterministic and probabilistic real life cases. While [48] presents an incremental ELM (IELM) designed to operate based on the principles ELM. The results proves the kernel based IELM to perform best than other online sequential ELM and LS-SVM with enormous data.

An analysis of new technique ANN, regression and time series analysis was conducted by [57] to determine which of the networks is best. The output results obtained establishes the suitability and superiority of the new technique of ANN over the referenced models. The performance of gradient powell-Beale ANN, MLR, resilient back propagation ANN and Levenberg Marquardt ANN using 3 different types of data set; temperature, precipitation and water consumption for six consecutive years was analyzed [6]. The Levenberg Marquardt ANN proves to be more precise, reliable and efficient than the bench mark models. [46] applied WANN and predicted ground water level for the next one year using genetic expression programming. The advantages of monitoring the ground water resources was suggested for future studies. The authors also suggested predicted water budget to be considered for further research on environmental planning. To address water demand forecasting for real time operation [84], applied multi layer perceptron back propagation ANN, dynamic neural networks [DNN], ANN hybrid and DNN Hybrid. The DNN hybrid performed the best with MAE 3.3 L/s and 2.8 L/s for train and test data set respectively for forecasting for the next one hour and 3.1 L/s and 3.0 L/s for train and test data set respectively for the subsequent 24 h respectively.

The rest of the paper is organized as follows; Sects. 2 to 7 provides the basics review and current research trends in urban water demand forecasting using various artificial intelligence approaches i.e. fuzzy logic systems, support vector machines, extreme learning machines, artificial neural networks, ARIMA model and a combination of various hybrid models respectively. Section 8 presents the discussions of the artificial intelligence in details based on the evaluation criteria, scaling pattern applied and input variables. In Sect. 9 we presents the limitations and recommend future research direction. Finally conclusion are discussed in Sect. 10.

2 Fuzzy Logic Systems

Fuzzy logic systems can be defined as formal method of reasoning to approximate reasoning. The process normally involves complexity and uncertainty generally appearing in different forms. The concept applied by a fuzzy logic system is considering the states of the system in the form of subset that are defined by the three special words; I.e. "big", "medium" and "low" etc. A suitable representation of both simple and complex physical systems can be used in fuzzy rule base [10]. Three main components that made up the architecture of a fuzzy logic system are the fuzzifier, fuzzy database and the defuzzifier. The fuzzifier assist's in converting the data set from scalars to vectors before executing it within the fuzzy database, the defuzzifier transforms the vectors obtained from the fuzzifier into the real data set. The fuzzy network models are divided into 2 sections; (i) the fuzzy rule base (ii) fuzzy inference system (FIS). The fuzzy rule base are defined by the conditional (IF-THEN) statements while the FIS is further subdivided into 3 main categories depending on the nature of inference operation of the conditional statement which are: Mamdani's system, Sugeno's system and Tsukamoto's system [8]. The membership function of a fuzzy logic enables the model to characterized the antecedents and consequents. They can be illustrated by four commonly used shapes; triangular, trapezoidal, sigmoid and gaussian shapes. These shapes assist in illustrating a clear direction on how the grades varies along the vertical-axis of the models [9].

Fuzzy sets enables the reduction of enormous data set to precise, quantitative and fewer variables which will be utilized by fuzzy logic systems. They also deals with human reasoning as well as analyzing uncertainties in the model. These models needs the least observations than most of the other forecasting models. Incomplete data set can be utilized to generate the predicted output results, although the output results obtained by the fuzzy logic system is not always accepted [42]. [10] conducted a research on fuzzy logic approach for the purpose of making predictions of water consumption in Istanbul city of Turkey. The results obtained proves an overall prediction relative error of less than 10%. A decision support system (DSS) that can be applied for identifying the following process; water reuse potentials, variables for observation of the reclamation of water level using fuzzy logic systems was developed by [9]. From the results obtained, water reuse potential is highly related to water exploitation index, drought, density of the population, waste water treatment and water demand. Considering city plans, nearness to cultural sites, medical facilities, education and transport systems for house pricing in Turkey [63], applied fuzzy logic systems. The results proves fuzzy logic to be able to predict house sale prices for different cities in the world.

By identifying many factors directly or indirectly related to pipe leakage potentials [54], proposes a novel fuzzy based algorithm for forecasting leakages in piped water distribution system for urban cities. The proposed model first implemented for water distribution in Thailand assists water stakeholders to prioritize there rehabilitation strategies of pipe water distribution system while establishing an effective, reliable and efficient method for water leakage control. While research conducted by [55], will have a important impact by assisting water stakeholders in controlling leakages in pipe distribution system within a minimum time after its occurred. This research will also help in prioritizing the management of leakages in pipe distribution systems. By applying fuzzy logic approach for the analysis of electricity energy demand in hydrophos electric power stations [56], reveals the method to be very effective, efficient and reliable. The step by step processes involved in the development of a prototype spatial decision support system (SDSS) was described and conducted by [72]. The output results obtained proves the model's application to compliment engineers in urban water management application while integrating it to users characteristics and site constraints.

3 Support Vector Machines

Support vector machines can be defined as a statistical modeling tool that can be applied for the analysis of both regression and classifications problems. These learning theory do not normally have a special characteristics or structure. The trained data sets are normally judged by there contribution, as such very few section of the trained data contribute to the final model's performance [36]. SVMs minimized the upper bond of the generalized error while regressing functions by utilizing a high set of its linear function [85]. Support vector regression (SVR) are very essential components employed for utilizing support vector machines. They involves mapping the input space s to the high dimensional space Q(s) in an approach that is non linear [80]. The process involves inserting the kernel function so as to avoid another dimension, this enables it to make possible for the model to analyze regression problems. The variables which are the data set applied are the input data plays a vital role as support on the training model [101]. The equation is illustrated below.

$$Y(x) = wK(x) + c \tag{1}$$

Y(x) represents output response variable, w is the weight vector, K is the kernel function that transforms the support vector in high dimensions, x is the input parameters and c is the bias. The performance of support vector regression depends on setting a regularization and kernel function constants that are excellent. The later assist in changing the dimensions of the input space, thus enabling it execute the regression analysis with high confidence level [36].

In terms of measurement of accurate stream flow and reservoir inflow [68], applied ANN, ARIMA and SVM. The results demonstrate the distinct capability and advantage of SVM in forecasting hydrological data set composed of linear and non linear characteristics. Research titled "Water demand prediction using ANN and support vector machines" by [80], compares two artificial intelligence models for water demand prediction. The results proves ANN to perform significantly better than SVM. A multi-scale relevance vector regression model which is applied for prediction of urban water demand to 2 real water works in Chongqing China was proposed by [15]. The results proves the hybrid model forecast on urban water demand to be more precise and accurate using 3 evaluations criteria; CoC, MAPE and NRMSE. [101] for assessing the usage of phase space reconstruction in there research prior to designing of model's input data set, designed a support vector machine for prediction urban water demand. The final results obtained, proves optimized lag time of the input data set assist in enhancing the accuracy and effectiveness the model. [25] proposed a water demand forecasting model and adopt a 2 stages learning procedure that operates based on time series data set clustering with SVR. The model which is applied at both aggregated level and individual consumption level proves to be very reliable and efficient on individual data set, due to it's ability to makes the final results more statistically accurate.

4 Extreme Learning Machines

[52] Proposed a state of art of a simple learning AI algorithm for a feed forward neural network. These algorithm obtained a better generalization performance and are faster than conventional learning algorithms, because they have a greater ability to store regression problems efficiently within a short modelling time, while showing better predictive performances [33, 75]. Extreme learning machine secure the name because the proposed algorithm tend to reach the least in training error, while obtaining the smallest forms of weight as well as best in generalization, they also execute programs faster than conventional learning algorithms [1, 51, 110]. Research conducted by [104]

compared the output results of an ANN and a recently developed ELM for prediction of urban water demand. These models are integrated with wavelet transform (W) or bootstrap (B), ELM, WELM, BELM, ANN, ANNW, ANNB while applying water demand and climate data set from three cities in Canada. The results obtained illustrated the importance superiority of wavelet transformation, due to its ability to improves the accuracy and efficiency of the models. The capability of an extreme learning machine model for estimating streamflow discharge in urban region of Australia was compared with the bench mark ANN models by [32]. Based on there findings, ELM with selected input data set has a good capability for estimating streamflow discharge and they also performs better than ANN model. They suggest the extreme learning model based model to be employed for analyzing the various processes in hydrological stations; such as river flows discharge for efficient and effective usage of water in agricultural lands, developing early warning strategies for drought and flood. [79] performed investigations on the potentials of MLR, ELM, SVR and ANN for short term urban water demand forecasting. Results justifies the superiority performance of ELM, due to its ability to improve in accuracy and precision of urban water demand forecast over the referenced models. They suggest further recommendations to include investigation which models will be more suitable for forecasting long term water demand values in other cities which have different climate characteristics while demanding the applications of ELM in forecasting streamflow discharge, ground water level and rainfall prediction.

A meta ELM which operates in 2 stages was proposed by [65]. The analysis and experimental results provided by the some of the bench mark ELM and ensemble models proves the proposed hybrid ELM model as more effective and efficient than the reference models. The authors suggest further research to include subset resampling selections and meta extreme learning machine model with heterogeneous extreme learning machines. In order to determine the structure of single hidden layer feedforward NN for regression problems [49], proposed an efficient model on error minimized ELM and particle swarm optimization. Experiments results illustrated the proposed model to achieve best generalization and performance with few hidden layer nodes than the reference ELM. They suggest future research work to include the steps involved in solving the problems, as well as applications of the proposed hybrid model for complex classification problems. [113] seven different artificial generated and nine real data sets are applied to estimate the accuracy of the fast incremental ELM models for classifying data streams with traditional algorithms. The proposed method proves to be simplest in structure, and also acquires a higher and more accurate results with least time consumption. The authors suggest to include in there future research to include the procedure of selecting a bridge parameter while ensuring accuracy, speed and stability. [116] proposed a novel approach that integrates the wavelet analysis, kernel extreme learning machines on self adaptive particle swarm optimization (PSO) and an ARMA so as to enhance forecasting performance while applying each of the model's characteristics. The performance of the proposed hybrid model proves it to produce the best performance as its produces more accurate, better generality and practicibility than single models.

5 Artificial Neural Networks

õA data processing, modelling and forecasting techniques that are motivated by the learning steps that takes place in nervous system of the human brain system composed of 3 sections; input, hidden and output layers are called artificial neural networks. These artificial intelligence models can also be applied for the of adaptation of an arbitrary and unknown equations with a degree of precision and accuracy [8, 99]. ANN can also be applied in forecasting future values of possible multivariate time series data set based on past values, and it can be described as a network model of with processing nodes which are interconnected in a specific order thereby assisting it to perform numerical calculations [6, 39, 82]. Without any physical involvement ANN, have the capacity and the means to learn behaviours from examples between the inputs and outputs layers a term referred to as generalization ability. It also has superior characteristics to be able to extract the various patterns obtained between the input and output variables without the need for an explanations [21, 120]. In order to determine the house prices in Turkey [99], compares the relative forecasting ability between hedonic regression and ANN. The study illustrated the ANN as the best alternative for prediction of houses prices.

To address water demand forecasting for real time operation [18, 23] applied ANN in residential water end use forecasting while [84], applied multiple layer perceptron back propagation ANN, dynamic neural networks [DNN], ANN hybrid and DNN Hybrid. The DNN hybrid performed the best with MAE 3.3 L/s and 2.8 L/s for training and testing data set respectively for forecasting for the next one hour and 3.1 L/s and 3.0 L/s for training and testing data set respectively for subsequent 24 h respectively. For modelling, control of water quality and drinking treatment process of water, [20] illustrated the performance of ANN as its captures the non linear characteristics of the process where the micro-scale interactions are not properly understood thereby pro viding the water treatment plant operators alternatives to scale experiments having the best process operating characteristics. [38] investigated the best fit input structure for predicting water consumption using a series of ANN networks. A new technology to forecast household water demand in China which provides an efficient and reliable method to formulate domestic water demand in urban area was proposed by [70]. The authors suggest for time extrapolation, multi variant method as well as forecasted information on population, income and water prices to be included in future studies.

By merging the output wavelet transform to ANN for crude oil price prediction using 2 main crude oil prices, [102] estimated the relative performance of the hybrid model to regular ANN. In both cases wavelet transform ANN illustrated crude oil prices more efficient and reliable forecast than a single ANN model [62]. A multiple layer feedforward neural network model was presented by [62], for forecasting spot price crude oil prices direction in short duration for three days ahead by finding optimal artificial neural network model structure. The output generated illustrated a very comprehensive crude oil price which is dynamic in nature, this will assist stakeholder and individuals in understanding risk management. By analyzing the learning steps of (back propagation, BFGS, conjugate gradient algorithm) and genetic algorithm [93], compared the relative performance of a single ANN for water demand prediction. Genetic algorithm outperformed the reference models with respect to forecasting.

6 ARIMA Models

The auto regressive integrated moving average (ARIMA) also referred as Box-Jenkin model, is one of the most applied artificial intelligent approaches that are also applicable in analysis and forecasting of time series data set. This is because the model have the ability and is capable of identifying complex patterns while analyzing and forecasting in time series data set [5, 109]. These models transforms the time series data sets into stationary forms by differencing process. For data set to be stationary, it's statistical process most be constant over a period of time [31]. Because it does not assume previous knowledge of any underlying models or relationship as in some methods, the use of ARIMA is uncertain as it depends essentially on past informations obtained from the data set as well as previous error for prediction [7, 85]. The ARIMA equation is normally represented by (p, d, q), where p represents the frequency of auto regressive terms, d is defined as the frequency of non seasonal differences while q represents the lagged forecast errors in the output prediction equation. There are three steps involved in an analyzing ARIMA model are identification, parameters estimation and prediction.

A model which combines wavelet transform, ARIMA and ANN to predict electricity demand and price simultaneously was proposed by [109]. The outputs obtained demonstrated the superiority of hybrid model due to its ability to provide a relevant improvement in water demand and price forecasting accurately when it is compared to other approaches that applied a single framework. [7] compares the forecasting ability of ARIMA and ANN using stock exchange data set. The output results obtained reveals the superiority of ANN over the ARIMA model. [85] proposes a hybrid neural network model that exploits the strengths of SVM and ARIMA models for stock price prediction. The results proves a combination of 2 good models does not necessary produce the best performance. By coupling wavelet transform and ANN [4], compares the relative performance of a proposed model to ARIMA and ANN for ground water level forecasting. The outcome proves wavelet transform ANN as potential and very useful for ground water level forecasting. While [89], applied ARIMA in identifying the relationship in urban water demand and weather variables.

7 Hybrid Models

A combination of two or more models give rise to a hybrid models. Since most of the historical time series data presented in this review paper employs the hybrid models, therefore a thorough review of the various combination of hybrid models are presented below.

7.1   Wavelet ANN (WANN)

One of the most common applied hybrid models is WANN. A mathematical equations that is capable of producing representation of the data set and their relationship, so that the data set can be analyzed is termed as wavelet transform. They also helps in analyzing, removing of unwanted noise from signals as well as in the compression of images. The data sets is broken down by the transformation into its wavelet that is a scale and shifted version of the mother wavelet. They also solves some of the disadvantages of fourier series analysis through capturing important information about the decomposition stages. Two main types of wavelet transforms are; the discrete and continuous wavelet transform (DWT), (CWT).

Wavelet transform also helps by capturing the various characteristics of the target data set while detecting localized information in a non stationary data set. WANN uses as input, data sets which are obtained from discrete or continuous wavelet transform on the original data set. The results of the wavelet decomposition serves as the input for WANN [2, 5, 19, 24, 46, 92, 102, 121]. A pictorial diagram illustrating a hybrid wavelet is represented in Fig. 1 below.

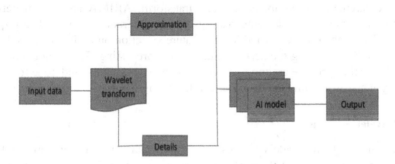

Fig. 1. A pictorial diagram of the hybrid wavelet model for artificial intelligent forecasting [83].

7.2   Adaptive Neuro Fuzzy Inference Systems (ANFIS)

A integration of artificial neural networks and fuzzy inference system is termed as ANFIS. For searching fuzzy rules so for that they can performs well on a given program, these models uses feed forward neural networks (FFNN). ANFIS models have an excellent capacity in categorization, training and production. They posses superiority thus allowing it to bring fuzzy rules learned from the data as well as in making rule base adaptive from numerical data. The results obtained from the ANNs serves as an input of the fuzzy inference system in this model [13, 14, 19, 37, 108, 119]. A hybrid model that consist of an integration of ANN and fuzzy linear regression, which are applied for urban water demand was presented by [14]. The model has shown its superiority over the conventional regression approach. It also proves to be robust against inconsistency and have a higher dimensionality and co-linearity for summer and winter days.

[37] investigated the relative performance of ANN and ANFIS models for predicting ground water level in Iran using 9 years data set. The results proves that, by executing different structures of ANFIS models have the best accuracy by having least number of errors, especially when it applied trapezoidal function and the hybrid methods. [108] presents a methodology to forecast consumers demand of water supply using 6 different models of ANFIS system while considering number of membership functions and the duration. The output result uncovered, the performance of ANFIS significantly improve with increase in input parameters.

7.3   ARIMA+SVM

[85] proposed a hybrid model which is composed of an integration of ARIMA an SVM models. The hybrid model captures both the characteristics and capabilities in the domains of the ARIMA and SVM. It can also model linear and non linear characteristics with overall enhanced prediction.

7.4   Wavelet+ARIMA+Neural Networks

In there research [109], combined wavelet transform, ARIMA and neural networks model for capturing the underlying patterns of the different networks. The proposed hybrid model algorithm is executed for the feature selection on each wavelet sub series data set with the NN using the best candidature for forecasting. The authors proves the proposed model to provide an improvement in both water demand and price forecasting accurately when it is compared to other models using a single AI model approach.

7.5   Wavelet SVM/R

The wavelet SVM are models that uses as input data set that were obtained from wavelet transform. Some of the advantages of wavelet transform are assisting in denoising, compression and decomposition of the data set. Thus the separation of some features in wavelet transform helps to exploit the underline patterns of original data set. All data set applied to SVM for forecasting proves the best performance when compared to other models ANN, SVM, WAMM, WSVM [36, 121]. Comprehensive comparison and discussion of WSVM, WANN, ANN and SVM by [121], proved that, wavelet preprocessed improves the forecasting capability and efficiency of the models. The WSVM provided more precised and reliable groundwater depth prediction with WANN close in some single coefficient.

7.6   SVR+Adaptive Fourier

In order to improve the prediction of SVR [23], built on top of the support vector regression model a fourier series. The output of the fourier series serves as an input to support vector regression thus helping the hybrid model to better adjust the maximum and minimum water demand peaks and captures part of the data set that the support vector gression cannot be able to reproduce. The proposed model proves to be an important tool for water utilities due to its ability to allow operators to program reliable manoeuvre so as to minimize the use of water and energy.

7.7 ANN+Time Series Model

The hybrid model presented in this subsection consist of ANN and time series model. For enhancement of ANN and fourier series, the output results of ANN obtained is feed into the time series model. The authors proved that, combining ANN with time series produces the best output compared to the individual usage of ANN and time series models [12].

7.8 Wavelet+Multiple Linear Regression

Multiple linear regression was applied to model the linear characteristics and relationship between dependent and independent variables. [36] applied the output of the wavelet transform as the input of the multiple linear regression. While [36], applied hybrid WNNs, wavelet linear regression (WLR), WSVR and compared with MLR, support vector regression and time delay neural networks for ground water level simulation for 2 wells in Iran. The study reveals wavelet improving the training of the neural network.

7.9 Wavelet+ANFIS

To improve the accuracy of there model, [19] applied wavelet pre processed data were used as input to ANFIS model. The data set that were decomposed were executed individually in the ANFIS model. By integrating the decomposed wavelet to ANFIS, the output results of the WANFIS were obtained. [19] compares the performance of ANN, ANFIS, WANN, WANFIS models for forecasting salinity in river basin using 28 years data set for conducting the practicals on the artificial intelligence models. The hybrid WANN and WANFIS models outperformed the reference models in predicting water salinity indicating the advantages of wavelet transforms.

7.10 Bootstrap NNs+Wavelet Bootstrap NNs

A data driven process that can simulate the multiple realization process from a given data set of a process is defined as bootstrap [105]. In bootstrap NNs the output results obtained from the bootstrap is applied as the input to the AI model. Thus enabling the model to obtain better results than NNs, due to it's ability to enhance the capability of the bootstrap. The bootstrap NN reduce the uncertainty of forecast and the performance of the forecasted confidence band are more accurate and reliable.

7.11 WBNNs

The model takes both the advantages of the capabilities of the of bootstrap re sampling and wavelet transformation techniques to form a single model. [105, 106] proposed a hybrid WBNN for prediction of water demand. The relative performance of the hybrid model is compared with ARIMA, ARIMAX, conventional neural networks, WNNs, bootstrap NNs and simple naive persistence index model. Results obtained demonstrated the hybrid wavelet bootstrap NN and wavelet analysis NN produce more accurate results. The bootstrap NN reduce the uncertainty of forecast and the performance of the forecasted confidence band are more accurate and reliable.

[12] compared time series networks, time series general regression NNs and general regression NNs for domestic water demand using data set obtained by meteorologist. The results proved that, temperature as the most important meteorological factor while rainfall as the least for training the model. Also time series general regression neural network produced the best results when they are compared to a individual time series and ANN models.

TSM = time series model, WTBM = wavelet transform base models, MAPE = Mean absolute percentage error, CoC = coefficient of correlation, CoE = coefficient of efficiency, CoD = coefficient of determination, MAE = mean absolute error, RMSE = root mean square error, AARE = average absolute relative error, RBF = radial basis function, RPE = relative percentage error, CoV = Coefficient of variation, ELM = extreme learning machines, GRNN = generalized regression neural network, WSVR = wavelet support vector regression, SVM = support vector machine, MLR = multiple linear regression, NSE = Nash sutcliffe efficiency, AAE = average absolute error, WANN = wavelet artificial neural network, ARE = average relative error, LR = linear regression, FFNN = feedforward neural network, GA = genetic algorithm, LSSVR = least square support vector regression, WLSSVR = wavelet least square support vector regression, WBANN = wavelet bootstrap artificial neural network, GNP = gross national product, WLR = wavelet linear regression, FNN = fuzzy neural network, WMLR = wavelet multiple linear regression, GP = genetic programming, SVR = support vector regression, DANN = dynamic artificial neural network, KPLS = kernel partial least square, WT = wavelet transform, PLS = partial least square, FTDNN = focused time delay neural network, HP = Hodrick prescott filter, VC OS-ELM = variable complexity online sequential extreme learning machines, SDARE = standard deviation of the absolute relative error, SSE = sum of square error, MGM = multiple step gradient method, VsSVR = variable structure support vector regression, MSRVR = multi scale relevance vector regression, DWT = discrete wavelet transform, NLR = non linear regression, WANN = wavelet artificial neural network, IoA = index of agreement, BoM = bank of models, OLS = ordinary least square regression model, MSE = mean square error, RCGA = real coded genetic algorithm, SOGA = structure optimization genetic algorithm, RCGA = real coded genetic algorithm, SOGA = structure optimization genetic algorithm, FCM = fuzzy cognitive maps, NRMSE = normalized root mean square error, WANN = wavelet artificial neural network, GRNN = general regression neural network, RF = random forest, WBNN = wavelet bootstrap neural network, WANN = wavelet neural network, GP = genetic programming, PDP = percentage deviation in peak, WELM = wavelet ELM ANFIS = adaptive neuro fuzzy inference system, BNN = bootstrap neural network.

8 Discussion

Due to artificial intelligence ability to improve the efficiency and effectiveness of the modelling process, the input layer is considered as the most important layer of a neural network. A very important factor in water price prediction is selection of input data sets. The process which is normally done depends on the knowledge of the artificial intelligence model and availability of data. The frequency of some common input variables applied in the reviewed article is illustrated in Fig. 2. As it can be seen, due to difficulty of acquiring some input data such as water quality, humidity and pressure due to lack of sensors and other privacy concern. Input data sets for instance water demand, precipitation, temperature and population figures are the most frequently applied input variables in water demand forecasting.

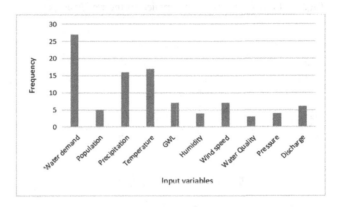

Fig. 2. Frequency of the input variables applied in the reviewed papers.

The time scale represents the sampling interval of sensors applied for the purpose of taking reading of various articles reviewed. The scaling pattern on the input variables applied in urban water demand forecasting are mainly divided into hourly, daily, weekly, monthly and annually. The most common applied time scale according to Fig. 3 is daily followed by monthly then hourly with the least being annual. The daily scale pattern is mostly applied due to the fact that it provides a more comprehensive information on urban water demand forecasting while the annual scaling have the least frequency due to its nature to focus on short term prediction.

Evaluation metrics are performed for the estimation of efficiency and effectiveness of the different artificial intelligence models. According to [29], evaluation is normally conducted with respect to closeness of fit and in most of the cases with respect to observations recorded. It is defined as a method of quantitative assessment, it defines what is to be measured as well as providing the process that are to be used to perform such operations. The frequency of the different standard evaluation criteria are performed as illustrated in Fig. 4. The most common ones are RMSE, MAPE, MAE, CoC, CoE, NSE and MSE.

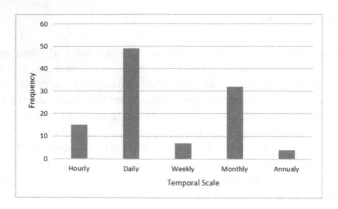

Fig. 3. Frequency of scaling applied in the reviewed papers.

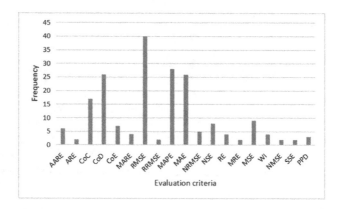

Fig. 4. Frequency evaluation criteria applied in the reviewed papers.

Although various studies have indicate increase in urban water demand due to factors such as global climate change, rapid urbanization, population growth and industrialization among others. This results to an increase in environmental concern for future generations, but the condition will not continue to rise forever due to environmental public awareness, economic recession of some nations as well as industrial saturation. Table 1. summarizes the various artificial intelligence of some selected articles, including authors, artificial intelligence approaches, location, input variables, evaluation criteria and temporal scale.

Table 1. Details of AI reviewed papers including authors, AI approaches, location, input variables, evaluation criteria and temporal scale.

Authors	AI approaches	Location	Input variables	Evaluation criteria	Temporal scale
[2]	ANN	Canada	Climate variables, water demand, population	AARE, Max ARE, CoD	Daily
[3]	Continuous wavelet transform	Canada	Water demand, precipitation, temperature	Fourier and cross spectral analysis	Daily
[4]	ANN, WANN and ARIMA	Canada	Precipitation, temperature and GWL	RMSE, CoE, CoD	Monthly
[5]	WANN, ARIMA, ANN and MLR	Canada	Water demand, precipitation, temperature	RMSE, CoD, RRMSE, Efficiency index	Daily
[6]	Multi variate regression and ANN	Cyprus	Water demand, temperature and rainfall	Max ARE, AARE, RMSE, CoD	Weekly
[9]	Fuzzy logic	Various cities	Water demand, population	Drought and water exploitation index	Monthly
[10]	Season algorithm, WTBM	Turkey	Water demand	RMSE, CoE	Monthly
[11]	Fuzzy logic	Turkey	Water demand	Average RPE, ARMSE	Monthly
[14]	Fuzzy linear regression, ANN	Iran	Water demand, climate	MAPE	Daily
[15]	MSRVR, FFNN, GRNN	China	Water demand	MAPE, CoC, NRMSE	Daily
[16]	SVR, VsSVR	China	Water demand	MAPE, RMSE, MAE	Daily
[17]	MLR, adaptive heuristic and transfer noise model	Netherland	Water demand, temperature	Relative error, MAPE, NSE	Daily
[19]	ANN, WANN, ANFIS, WANFIS	Iran	Water quality parameters	CoD, NSE, TS, NRMSE	Monthly
[20]	ANN	Canada	Water quality	MAE	Daily
[22]	LR, MLR, ARIMA, ANN	Canada	Water demand, temperature, precipitation	AARE, Max ARE, CoD	Weekly

(continued)

Table 1. (*continued*)

Authors	AI approaches	Location	Input variables	Evaluation criteria	Temporal scale
[23]	SVR+fourier time series	Brazil	Water demand, wind, precipitation	RMSE, MAE	Hourly
[25]	SVM	Italy	Water consumption	MAPE	Daily, hourly
[26]	ANN	China	Water level	RMSE, mean relative error, CoE	Daily
[27]	ARIMA, MLR	USA	Water demand, population, precipitation, temperature	Ordinary least square regression	Daily, monthly
[28]	GA, RBF, SVM	China	Water demand	MAPE	Daily
[30]	ANN, FFNN, MLP, RBF	Nil	Hypothetical	MSE, CoD, MAE, CoE, mean square relative error	Daily, monthly
[32]	ANN, ELM	Australia	Precipitation, temperature	MAE, CoD, NSE, Willmotts index	Monthly
[34]	WELM, WANN, ELM, LSSVR, WLSSVR, ANN, wavelet decomposition	Australia	Precipitation	RMSE, NSE, MAE, Willmotts index, PDP, CoC	Monthly
[35]	MLR	Zimbabwe	Population, rainfall, GDP	CoV	Monthly
[36]	ANN, MLR, WLR, WANN, SVR, WSVR	Iran	Ground water level	NSE, RMSE	Monthly
[37]	ANN, ANFIS	Iran	Precipitation, irrigation return, flow pumping rate	RMSE, CoD, MAE	Monthly
[38]	ANN FFNN, GRNN, cascade correlation NN	Turkey	Water consumption	AARE, NRMSE	Monthly
[41]	Base and season use model, auto regression model	Australia	Water demand, temperature, rainfall	Standard error, CoD	Daily
[44]	DANN, k-nearest neighbour model, FTDNN	Iran	Water demand	SSE, MSE	Daily, monthly, weekly

(*continued*)

Table 1. (*continued*)

Authors	AI approaches	Location	Input variables	Evaluation criteria	Temporal scale
[45]	ARIMA, DANN, ANN	USA	Water demand, weather variables	MAPE	Hourly, daily, weekly
[46]	WT-ANN, WT-GP	Iran	Water level	RMSE, NSE, MAE	Monthly
[47]	ANN, fuzzy model tree technique	India	Water level, water demand, discharge	CoC, RMSE	Daily
[53]	ARMA, WT-KPLS-ARMA, WT-PLS-ARMA KPLS	China	Water demand for industrial, domestic and agriculture	MAPE	Annual
[57]	ANN	India	Water demand, temperature, rainfall	MARE, AARE, TS	Weekly
[58]	LS SVM	China	Temperature, precipitation, discharge	MSE, MRE	Hourly
[59]	ARIMA, ARIMA+e smoothing	Sri Lanka	Water demand, population	CoC, CoD, RMSE, NSE	Hourly
[64]	FNN, MLR, MLR+MLR, HP-MLR+FNN, HP-FNN+FNN	China	Population, temperature, water demand, greenery coverage, GDP	Relative error	Annual
[66]	OS-ELM, OS-MLR	Canada	Discharge, wind speed, GWL, temperature, precipitation, humidity	MAE, RMSE, NSE	Daily, monthly annual
[67]	OS-ELM, VC-OS-ELM		Discharge, wind speed, GWL, temperature, precipitation, humidity, snow depth	MAE, RMSE, NSE	Daily, monthly annual
[68]	SVM, ANN, ARIMA	China	Streamflow discharge	RMSE, CoC	Monthly
[69]	ANFIS, fuzzy theory	China	Water demand for industrial and commercial operations, weather, population	Fuzzy rules	Hourly
[71]	ANN, ANFIS	India	Discharge	CoC, RMSE, NSE	Monthly

(*continued*)

Table 1. (*continued*)

Authors	AI approaches	Location	Input variables	Evaluation criteria	Temporal scale
[73]	ANN, WANN	India	Discharge, rainfall, temperature,	NSE, RMSE, MAE, PPD	Daily
[74]	ANFIS, multi variate analysis	Greece	Temperature, rainfall, wind speed, water demand, tourist	RMSE, MSE, MAE, MAPE, mean error	Daily
[76]	ANN	Iran	Temperature, precipitation, humidity, pressure, wind speed, population	MAPE	Daily
[77]	MLR, DWT, MLT+DWT	USA	Humidity, water demand, temperature, rainfall, wind speed	CoD, RMSE, MAPE	Daily, monthly
[78]	Constant rate model	UAE	Water demand, population, temperature, precipitation	SDARE, AARE	Daily, monthly
[79]	MLR, SVR, ANN, ELM	Canada	Rainfall, temperature, water demand	RMSE, CoD	Daily
[80]	ANN, SVM	South Africa	Water demand, population	Support vector genius, artificial neural genius	Daily
[81]	ANN	Malaysia	Water quality	SSE, MAPE	Daily
[84]	ANN, DNN, ANN-H, DNN-H, H = hybrid	Brazil	Water supply, temperature, humidity	MAE, pearson coefficient	Hourly
[86]	SOGA, RCGA, FCM, FCM +SOGA+ANN	Greece	Temperature, tourist arrivals, rainfall, water demand	MAE	Daily
[87]	FCM, RCGA, MGM	Greece	Temperature, tourist arrivals, rainfall, water demand, wind speed	MAPE, RMSE, MAE, MSE	Daily
[88]	ANN	Spain	Water demand	MAPE	Hourly
[90]	MLR, ANN, exponential smoothing, ARIMA	Spain	Water demand, temperature, precipitation, humidity, sunshine duration, wind speed	CoD, CoE, average relative variance, percentage standard error of prediction	Daily
[92]	ANN, MLR, WANN, conventional	USA	Suspended sediment load, river discharge	CoD, MAE	Daily

(*continued*)

Table 1. (*continued*)

Authors	AI approaches	Location	Input variables	Evaluation criteria	Temporal scale
	sediment rating curve				
[93]	ANN, Naive, BoM, QMMP +kNN, Holt winters GA	Spain	Water demand	RMSE, MSE, MAPE, MAE	Hourly
[94]	WTGA NN, GA optimised ANN	India	Discharge	RMSE, NSE, discrepancy ratio	Daily
[95]	ARIMA, LR, naive, ANN, Holt winters, RCGA FCM	Poland	Water demand, temperature, precipitation	MAPE	Daily
[96]	ARIMA, parallel adaptive weighting strategy and heuristic	Portugal	Water demand	MAPE, CoC	Hourly
[97]	SVM, ANN, NLR, ELM	Canada	Pipe attributes	CoC, CoE, IoA, RMSE	Annual
[98]	WANN, MLR, ANN, WMLR	India	Discharge	NSE, MAE, CoD, RMSE	Daily
[100]	GP, SVM	Canada	Water demand, population, temperature, wind speed, humidity, precipitation	RMSE, CoD, MAE	Monthly
[101]	SVM	Canada	Water demand, precipitation, temperature	CoD, RMSE	Monthly
[103]	ANN, adaptive sugeno fuzzy, ANFIS	Iran	Water demand, temperature, precipitation, sunshine duration, dew point, wind speed, pressure	CoC, MSE, NMSE, MAPE	Daily
[104]	ELM, ANN, WELM, WANN, BANN, BELM	Canada	Temperature, water demand, precipitation	MAE, PDP, CoD, RMSE	Daily
[105]	ARIMA, ARIMAX, BNN, NN, naive persistence	Canada	Water demand, temperature	RMSE, MAE, percentage deviation in peak,	Daily, weekly, monthly

(*continued*)

Table 1. (*continued*)

Authors	AI approaches	Location	Input variables	Evaluation criteria	Temporal scale
	index, WBNN, WNN			precipitation, CoD	
[107]	ANN, DNN, ELM, RF, MLR, Gaussian process regression	EU	Temperature, humidity, wind direction and speed	RMSE, R-squared, MSE, MAE	Hourly, daily
[108]	ANFIS	India	Water demand	RMSE, MAPE, CoC	Daily
[114]	System dynamics	China	Water demand, population, economic development	Relative error	Daily
[115]	ARIMA	Turkey	Industrial, agricultural, commercial water demand, pipe lines, dams	MAPE	Daily, Monthly
[117]	ELM, GRNN, SVR	Iraq	Discharge	Willmotts index, RMSE, MAE, NSE, CoC	Monthly
[118]	MR, NLR	Turkey	Water bill, temperature, humidity, rainfall, global solar radiation, pressure, water demand, sunshine duration	MAPE, CoC	Monthly

9   Recommendations for Future

From a thorough review of over 100 most recent and cited research articles from high impact journals. We state some limitations as well as suggest some future recommendations as follows:

- Some basic information on each of the artificial intelligence approaches presented in this study on urban water demand management are not provided in detail. The main reason is due to the fact that, the articles reviewed does not provide the overall picture of each of the models due to it been limited between 2008 to 2018. But we have tried to be as comprehensive as possible, while giving good applications that demonstrated the usefulness and applications of each model as solutions to urban water demand forecasting.
- We suggest future research to include the effects of climate variables such as pressure, humidity, temperature as well as water demand and population and

incorporate these data while taking there advantages to determine there relationship at multiple scales.

- Rather than focusing on error based evaluation criteria in evaluating the artificial based approaches. We suggest future research to apply evaluation based criteria based on non error based to measure the performance of the models.
- We also suggest the hybridization of novel artificial neural network model with other non expert systems for urban water demand prediction.
- The analysis of the advantages and disadvantages of each accuracy assessment to the nature of forecasting urban water demand problems can be an interesting area for future research works [43].

10 Conclusion

Recent research on urban water demand forecasting applied by different artificial intelligence approaches such as artificial neural network, ARIMA, extreme learning machines, fuzzy logic systems, support vector machines and an integration of two or more artificial intelligence approaches such as WBNN, ANFIS, WANFIS, WSVR, WMLR, ARIMA + SVM, SVR + adaptive fourier, ANN + times series model, Wavelet + ARIMA + NNs and BNNs + WBNNs from 2000 to 2018 are presented. More focus have been presented to wavelet transform, due to it's ability to assist in denoising while decomposing, manipulating and analyzing signals at different frequency bands and resolutions. Wavelet transform also helps to improve the efficiency and reliability of the AI model. The reviewed papers proves that, there is no single artificial intelligence or hybrid model that seems to be the overall best in performance for urban water demand forecasting.

The research also provided an analysis on over 100 most recent and cited research articles from high impact journals while providing guidance to researchers, academicians, households and water utility managers on urban water demand management. The reviewed papers affirmed that, urban water demand forecasting can be of positive impact for capital investment, revenue collection analysis and generation as well as market management for future generations. The paper also proves that artificial intelligence can successfully be applied for urban water demand forecasting while presenting some future research directions.

Acknowledgement. This work was supported in part by the National Key R&D Program of China under Grant 2018YFC0407901, in part by the National Natural Science Foundation of China under Grant 61602149, and in part by the Fundamental Research Funds for the Central Universities under Grant 2019B15514.

References

1. Acharya, N., Shrivastava, N.A., Panigrahi, B.K., Mohanty, U.C.: Development of an artificial neural network based multi-model ensemble to estimate the northeast monsoon rainfall over south peninsular India: an application of extreme learning machine. Clim. Dyn. **43**(5–6), 1303–1310 (2014)
2. Adamowski, J.F.: Peak daily water demand forecast modeling using artificial neural networks. J. Water Resour. Plann. Manag. **134**(2), 119–128 (2008)
3. Adamowski, J., Adamowski, K., Prokoph, A.: A spectral analysis based methodology to detect climatological influences on daily urban water demand. Math. Geosci. **45**(1), 49–68 (2013)
4. Adamowski, J., Chan, H.F.: A wavelet neural network conjunction model for groundwater level forecasting. J. Hydrol. **407**(1–4), 28–40 (2011)
5. Adamowski, J., Fung Chan, H., Prasher, S.O., Ozga-Zielinski, B., Sliusarieva, A.: Comparison of multiple linear and nonlinear regression, autoregressive integrated moving average, artificial neural network, and wavelet artificial neural network methods for urban water demand forecasting in Montreal, Canada. Water Resour. Res. **48**(1), 1–14 (2012)
6. Adamowski, J., Karapataki, C.: Comparison of multivariate regression and artificial neural networks for peak urban water-demand forecasting: evaluation of different ANN learning algorithms. J. Hydrol. Eng. **15**(10), 729–743 (2010)
7. Adebiyi, A.A., Adewumi, A.O., Ayo, C.K.: Comparison of ARIMA and artificial neural networks models for stock price prediction. J. Appl. Math. **2014**, 7 (2014)
8. Afan, H.A., El-shafie, A., Mohtar, W.H.M.W., Yaseen, Z.M.: Past, present and prospect of an Artificial Intelligence (AI) based model for sediment transport prediction. J. Hydrol. **541**, 902–913 (2016)
9. Almeida, G., Vieira, J., Marques, A.S., Kiperstok, A., Cardoso, A.: Estimating the potential water reuse based on fuzzy reasoning. J. Environ. Manag. **128**, 883–892 (2013)
10. Altunkaynak, A., Nigussie, T.A.: Monthly water consumption prediction using season algorithm and wavelet transform–based models. J. Water Resour. Plann. Manag. **143**(6), 04017011 (2017)
11. Altunkaynak, A., Ozger, M., Cakmakci, M.: Water consumption prediction of Istanbul city by using fuzzy logic approach. Water Resour. Manag. **19**(5), 641–654 (2005)
12. Al-Zahrani, M.A., Abo-Monasar, A.: Urban residential water demand prediction based on artificial neural networks and time series models. Water Resour. Manag. **29**(10), 3651–3662 (2015)
13. Ashrafi, M., Chua, L.H.C., Quek, C., Qin, X.: A fully-online Neuro-Fuzzy model for flow forecasting in basins with limited data. J. Hydrol. **545**, 424–435 (2017)
14. Azadeh, A., Neshat, N., Hamidipour, H.: Hybrid fuzzy regression–artificial neural network for improvement of short-term water consumption estimation and forecasting in uncertain and complex environments: case of a large metropolitan city. J. Water Resour. Plann. Manag. **138**(1), 71–75 (2011)
15. Bai, Y., Wang, P., Li, C., Xie, J., Wang, Y.: A multi-scale relevance vector regression approach for daily urban water demand forecasting. J. Hydrol. **517**, 236–245 (2014)
16. Bai, Y., Wang, P., Li, C., Xie, J., Wang, Y.: Dynamic forecast of daily urban water consumption using a variable-structure support vector regression model. J. Water Resour. Plann. Manag. **141**(3), 04014058 (2014)
17. Bakker, M., Van Duist, H., Van Schagen, K., Vreeburg, J., Rietveld, L.: Improving the performance of water demand forecasting models by using weather input. Proc. Eng. **70**, 93–102 (2014)

18. Bakker, M., Vreeburg, J.H.G., Van Schagen, K.M., Rietveld, L.C.: A fully adaptive forecasting model for short-term drinking water demand. Environ. Model. Softw. **48**, 141–151 (2013)

19. Barzegar, R., Adamowski, J., Moghaddam, A.A.: Application of wavelet-artificial intelligence hybrid models for water quality prediction: a case study in Aji-Chay River, Iran. Stoch. Environ. Res. Risk Assess. **30**(7), 1797–1819 (2016)

20. Baxter, C.W., Zhang, Q., Stanley, S.J., Shariff, R., Tupas, R.R., Stark, H.L.: Drinking water quality and treatment: the use of artificial neural networks. Can. J. Civ. Eng. **28**(S1), 26–35 (2001)

21. Bennett, C., Stewart, R.A., Beal, C.D.: ANN-based residential water end-use demand forecasting model. Expert Syst. Appl. **40**(4), 1014–1023 (2013)

22. Bougadis, J., Adamowski, K., Diduch, R.: Short-term municipal water demand forecasting. Hydrol. Process.: Int. J. **19**(1), 137–148 (2005)

23. Brentan, B.M., Luvizotto Jr., E., Herrera, M., Izquierdo, J., Perez-Garcia, R.: Hybrid regression model for near real-time urban water demand forecasting. J. Comput. Appl. Math. **309**, 532–541 (2017)

24. Campisi-Pinto, S., Adamowski, J., Oron, G.: Forecasting urban water demand via wavelet-denoising and neural network models. Case study: city of Syracuse, Italy. Water Resour. Manag. **26**(12), 3539–3558 (2012)

25. Candelieri, A., Soldi, D., Archetti, F.: Short-term forecasting of hourly water consumption by using automatic metering readers data. Proc. Eng. **119**, 844–853 (2015)

26. Chau, K.W.: Particle swarm optimization training algorithm for ANNs in stage prediction of Shing Mun River. J. Hydrol. **329**(3–4), 363–367 (2006)

27. Chang, H., Praskievicz, S., Parandvash, H.: Sensitivity of urban water consumption to weather and climate variability at multiple temporal scales: the case of Portland, Oregon. Int. J. Geospat. Environ. Res. **1**(1), 7 (2014)

28. Chen, X.: Prediction of urban water demand based on GA-SVM. In: 2009 ETP International Conference on Future Computer and Communication, pp. 285–288. IEEE, June 2009

29. Dawson, C.W., Abrahart, R.J., See, L.M.: HydroTest: a web-based toolbox of evaluation metrics for the standardised assessment of hydrological forecasts. Environ. Model. Softw. **22**(7), 1034–1052 (2007)

30. Dawson, C.W., Wilby, R.L.: Hydrological modelling using artificial neural networks. Prog. Phys. Geogr. **25**(1), 80–108 (2001)

31. Deb, C., Zhang, F., Yang, J., Lee, S.E., Shah, K.W.: A review on time series forecasting techniques for building energy consumption. Renew. Sustain. Energy Rev. **74**, 902–924 (2017)

32. Deo, R.C., Sahin, M.: An extreme learning machine model for the simulation of monthly mean streamflow water level in eastern Queensland. Environ. Monit. Assess. **188**(2), 90 (2016)

33. Deo, R.C., Sahin, M.: Application of the extreme learning machine algorithm for the prediction of monthly Effective Drought Index in eastern Australia. Atmos. Res. **153**, 512–525 (2015)

34. Deo, R.C., Tiwari, M.K., Adamowski, J.F., Quilty, J.M.: Forecasting effective drought index using a wavelet extreme learning machine (W-ELM) model. Stoch. Env. Res. Risk Assess. **31**(5), 1211–1240 (2017)

35. Dube, E., Van der Zaag, P.: Analysing water use patterns for demand management: the case of the city of Masvingo, Zimbabwe. Phys. Chem. Earth Parts A/B/C **28**(20–27), 805–815 (2003)

36. Ebrahimi, H., Rajaee, T.: Simulation of groundwater level variations using wavelet combined with neural network, linear regression and support vector machine. Global Planet. Change **148**, 181–191 (2017)

37. Emamgholizadeh, S., Moslemi, K., Karami, G.: Prediction the groundwater level of bastam plain (Iran) by artificial neural network (ANN) and adaptive neuro-fuzzy inference system (ANFIS). Water Resour. Manag. **28**(15), 5433–5446 (2014)

38. Firat, M., Turan, M.E., Yurdusev, M.A.: Comparative analysis of neural network techniques for predicting water consumption time series. J. Hydrol. **384**(1–2), 46–51 (2010)

39. Firat, M., Yurdusev, M.A., Turan, M.E.: Evaluation of artificial neural network techniques for municipal water consumption modeling. Water Resour. Manag. **23**(4), 617–632 (2009)

40. Gagliardi, F., Alvisi, S., Kapelan, Z., Franchini, M.: A probabilistic short-term water demand forecasting model based on the Markov Chain. Water **9**(7), 507 (2017)

41. Gato, S., Jayasuriya, N., Roberts, P.: Forecasting residential water demand: case study. J. Water Resour. Plann. Manag. **133**(4), 309–319 (2007)

42. Ghalehkhondabi, I., Ardjmand, E., Weckman, G.R., Young, W.A.: An overview of energy demand forecasting methods published in 2005–2015. Energy Syst. **8**(2), 411–447 (2017)

43. Ghalehkhondabi, I., Ardjmand, E., Young, W.A., Weckman, G.R.: Water demand forecasting: review of soft computing methods. Environ. Monit. Assess. **189**(7), 313 (2017)

44. Ghiassi, M., Fa'al, F., Abrishamchi, A.: Large metropolitan water demand forecasting using DAN2, FTDNN, and KNN models: a case study of the city of Tehran, Iran. Urban Water J. **14**(6), 655–659 (2017)

45. Ghiassi, M., Zimbra, D.K., Saidane, H.: Urban water demand forecasting with a dynamic artificial neural network model. J. Water Resour. Plann. Manag. **134**(2), 138–146 (2008)

46. Gorgij, A.D., Kisi, O., Moghaddam, A.A.: Groundwater budget forecasting, using hybrid wavelet-ANN-GP modelling: a case study of Azarshahr Plain, East Azerbaijan, Iran. Hydrol. Res. **48**(2), 455–467 (2017)

47. Goyal, M.K., Ojha, C.S.P., Singh, R.D., Swamee, P.K., Nema, R.K.: Application of ANN, fuzzy logic and decision tree algorithms for the development of reservoir operating rules. Water Resour. Manag. **27**(3), 911–925 (2013)

48. Guo, L., Hao, J.H., Liu, M.: An incremental extreme learning machine for online sequential learning problems. Neurocomputing **128**, 50–58 (2014)

49. Han, F., Zhao, M.R., Zhang, J.M., Ling, Q.H.: An improved incremental constructive single-hidden-layer feedforward networks for extreme learning machine based on particle swarm optimization. Neurocomputing **228**, 133–142 (2017)

50. Herrera, M., Torgo, L., Izquierdo, J., Perez-Garcia, R.: Predictive models for forecasting hourly urban water demand. J. Hydrol. **387**(1–2), 141–150 (2010)

51. Huang, G.B., Zhu, Q.Y., Siew, C.K.: Extreme learning machine: theory and applications. Neurocomputing **70**(1–3), 489–501 (2006)

52. Huang, G.B., Zhu, Q.Y., Siew, C.K.: Extreme learning machine: a new learning scheme of feedforward neural networks. In: Proceedings of the 2004 IEEE International Joint Conference on Neural Networks, vol. 2, pp. 985–990. IEEE (2004)

53. Huang, L., Zhang, C., Peng, Y., Zhou, H.: Application of a combination model based on wavelet transform and KPLS-ARMA for urban annual water demand forecasting. J. Water Resour. Plann. Manag. **140**(8), 04014013 (2013)

54. Islam, M.S., et al.: Evaluating leakage potential in water distribution systems: a fuzzy-based methodology. J. Water Supply: Res. Technol.-AQUA **61**(4), 240–252 (2012)

55. Islam, M.S., Sadiq, R., Rodriguez, M.J., Francisque, A., Najjaran, H., Hoorfar, M.: Leakage detection and location in water distribution systems using a fuzzy-based methodology. Urban Water J. **8**(6), 351–365 (2011)

56. Istrate, M., Grigoras, G.: Energy consumption estimation in water distribution systems using fuzzy techniques. Environ. Eng. Manag. J. **9**(2), 249–256 (2010)
57. Jain, A., Varshney, A.K., Joshi, U.C.: Short-term water demand forecast modelling at IIT Kanpur using artificial neural networks. Water Resour. Manag. **15**(5), 299–321 (2001)
58. Ji, G., Wang, J., Ge, Y., Liu, H.: Urban water demand forecasting by LS-SVM with tuning based on elitist teaching-learning-based optimization. In: The 26th Chinese Control and Decision Conference, CCDC 2014, pp. 3997–4002. IEEE, May 2014
59. Kang, H.S., Kim, H., Lee, J., Lee, I., Kwak, B.Y., Im, H.: Optimization of pumping schedule based on water demand forecasting using a combined model of autoregressive integrated moving average and exponential smoothing. Water Sci. Technol.: Water Supply **15**(1), 188–195 (2015)
60. Khajeh, M.: Water conservation in Kuwait: a fuzzy analysis approach (2010)
61. Koutiva, I., Makropoulos, C.: Towards adaptive water resources management: simulating the complete socio-technical system through computational intelligence. In: 12th International Conference on Environmental Science and Technology (CEST 2011), Rhodes, Greece, September 2011
62. Kulkarni, S., Haidar, I.: Forecasting model for crude oil price using artificial neural networks and commodity futures prices. arXiv preprint arXiv:0906.4838 (2009)
63. Kusan, H., Aytekin, O., Ozdemir, I.: The use of fuzzy logic in predicting house selling price. Expert Syst. Appl. **37**(3), 1808–1813 (2010)
64. Li, W., Huicheng, Z.: Urban water demand forecasting based on HP filter and fuzzy neural network. J. Hydroinform. **12**(2), 172–184 (2010)
65. Liao, S., Feng, C.: Meta-ELM: ELM with ELM hidden nodes. Neurocomputing **128**, 81–87 (2014)
66. Lima, A.R., Cannon, A.J., Hsieh, W.W.: Forecasting daily streamflow using online sequential extreme learning machines. J. Hydrol. **537**, 431–443 (2016)
67. Lima, A.R., Hsieh, W.W., Cannon, A.J.: Variable complexity online sequential extreme learning machine, with applications to streamflow prediction. J. Hydrol. **555**, 983–994 (2017)
68. Lin, J.Y., Cheng, C.T., Chau, K.W.: Using support vector machines for long-term discharge prediction. Hydrol. Sci. J. **51**(4), 599–612 (2006)
69. Liu, H., Deng, T., Zhang, H.: Research on forecasting method of urban water demand based on fuzzy theory. In: 2009 Sixth International Conference on Fuzzy Systems and Knowledge Discovery, vol. 6, pp. 389–395. IEEE, August 2009
70. Liu, J., Savenije, H.H., Xu, J.: Forecast of water demand in Weinan City in China using WDF-ANN model. Phys. Chem. Earth Parts A/B/C **28**(4–5), 219–224 (2003)
71. Lohani, A.K., Kumar, R., Singh, R.D.: Hydrological time series modeling: a comparison between adaptive neuro-fuzzy, neural network and autoregressive techniques. J. Hydrol. **442**, 23–35 (2012)
72. Makropoulos, C.K., Butler, D., Maksimovic, C.: Fuzzy logic spatial decision support system for urban water management. J. Water Resour. Plann. Manag. **129**(1), 69–77 (2003)
73. Makwana, J.J., Tiwari, M.K.: Intermittent streamflow forecasting and extreme event modelling using wavelet based artificial neural networks. Water Resour. Manag. **28**(13), 4857–4873 (2014)
74. Mellios, N., Kofinas, D., Papageorgiou, E., Laspidou, C.: A multivariate analysis of the daily water demand of Skiathos Island, Greece, implementing the artificial neuro-fuzzy inference system (ANFIS). In: E-Proceedings of the 36th IAHR World Congress, vol. 28, pp. 1–8, June 2015

75. Miche, Y., Bas, P., Jutten, C., Simula, O., Lendasse, A.: A methodology for building regression models using extreme learning machine: OP-ELM. In: ESANN, pp. 247–252, April 2008
76. Mohammadzadeh, A., Mahdipour, N., Mohammadzadeh, A., Ghadamyari, M.: Comparison of forecasting the cost of water using statistical and neural network methods: case study of Isfahan municipality. Afr. J. Bus. Manag. 6(8), 3001–3013 (2012)
77. Mohammed, J.R., Ibrahim, H.M.: Hybrid wavelet artificial neural network model for municipal water demand forecasting. ARPN J. Eng. Appl. Sci. 7(8), 1047–1065 (2012)
78. Mohamed, M.M., Al-Mualla, A.A.: Water demand forecasting in Umm Al-Quwain using the constant rate model. Desalination 259(1–3), 161–168 (2010)
79. Mouatadid, S., Adamowski, J.: Using extreme learning machines for short-term urban water demand forecasting. Urban Water J. 14(6), 630–638 (2017)
80. Msiza, I.S., Nelwamondo, F.V., Marwala, T.: Water demand prediction using artificial neural networks and support vector regression (2008)
81. Najah, A., Elshafie, A., Karim, O.A., Jaffar, O.: Prediction of Johor River water quality parameters using artificial neural networks. Eur. J. Sci. Res. 28(3), 422–435 (2009)
82. Nguyen, K.A., Stewart, R.A., Zhang, H., Sahin, O., Siriwardene, N.: Re-engineering traditional urban water management practices with smart metering and informatics. Environ. Model. Softw. 101, 256–267 (2018)
83. Nourani, V., Baghanam, A.H., Adamowski, J., Kisi, O.: Applications of hybrid wavelet–artificial intelligence models in hydrology: a review. J. Hydrol. 514, 358–377 (2014)
84. Odan, F.K., Reis, L.F.R.: Hybrid water demand forecasting model associating artificial neural network with Fourier series. J. Water Resour. Plann. Manag. 138(3), 245–256 (2012)
85. Pai, P.F., Lin, C.S.: A hybrid ARIMA and support vector machines model in stock price forecasting. Omega 33(6), 497–505 (2005)
86. Papageorgiou, E.I., Poczeta, K., Laspidou, C.: Hybrid model for water demand prediction based on fuzzy cognitive maps and artificial neural networks. In: 2016 IEEE International Conference on Fuzzy Systems (FUZZ-IEEE), pp. 1523–1530. IEEE (2016)
87. Papageorgiou, E.I., Poczeta, K., Laspidou, C.: Application of fuzzy cognitive maps to water demand prediction. In: 2015 IEEE International Conference on Fuzzy Systems (FUZZ-IEEE), pp. 1–8. IEEE (2015)
88. Ponte, B., De la Fuente, D., Parreño, J., Pino, R.: Intelligent decision support system for real-time water demand management. Int. J. Comput. Intell. Syst. 9(1), 168–183 (2016)
89. Praskievicz, S., Chang, H.: Identifying the relationships between urban water consumption and weather variables in Seoul, Korea. Phys. Geogr. 30(4), 324–337 (2009)
90. Pulido-Calvo, I., Roldán, J., López-Luque, R., Gutiérrez-Estrada, J.C.: Demand forecasting for irrigation water distribution systems. J. Irrig. Drainage Eng. 129(6), 422–431 (2003)
91. Qi, C., Chang, N.B.: System dynamics modeling for municipal water demand estimation in an urban region under uncertain economic impacts. J. Environ. Manag. 92(6), 1628–1641 (2011)
92. Rajaee, T.: Wavelet and ANN combination model for prediction of daily suspended sediment load in rivers. Sci. Total Environ. 409(15), 2917–2928 (2011)
93. Rangel, H.R., Puig, V., Farias, R.L., Flores, J.J.: Short-term demand forecast using a bank of neural network models trained using genetic algorithms for the optimal management of drinking water networks. J. Hydroinform. 19(1), 1–16 (2017)
94. Sahay, R.R., Srivastava, A.: Predicting monsoon floods in rivers embedding wavelet transform, genetic algorithm and neural network. Water Resour. Manag. 28(2), 301–317 (2014)

95. Salmeron, J.L., Froelich, W., Papageorgiou, E.I.: Application of fuzzy cognitive maps to the forecasting of daily water demand. In: Proceedings of 2015 ITISE (2015)
96. Sardinha-Lourenco, A., Andrade-Campos, A., Antunes, A., Oliveira, M.S.: Increased performance in the short-term water demand forecasting through the use of a parallel adaptive weighting strategy. J. Hydrol. **558**, 392–404 (2018)
97. Sattar, A.M., Ertuğrul, Ö.F., Gharabaghi, B., McBean, E.A., Cao, J.: Extreme learning machine model for water network management. Neural Comput. Appl. **31**(1), 157–169 (2019)
98. Sehgal, V., Tiwari, M.K., Chatterjee, C.: Wavelet bootstrap multiple linear regression based hybrid modeling for daily river discharge forecasting. Water Resour. Manag. **28**(10), 2793–2811 (2014)
99. Selim, H.: Determinants of house prices in Turkey: Hedonic regression versus artificial neural network. Expert Syst. Appl. **36**(2), 2843–2852 (2009)
100. Shabani, S., Yousefi, P., Adamowski, J., Naser, G.: Intelligent soft computing models in water demand forecasting. In: Water Stress in Plants. InTech (2016)
101. Shabani, S., Yousefi, P., Naser, G.: Support vector machines in urban water demand forecasting using phase space reconstruction. Proc. Eng. **186**, 537–543 (2017)
102. Shabri, A., Samsudin, R.: Daily crude oil price forecasting using hybridizing wavelet and artificial neural network model. Math. Probl. Eng. **2014**, 10 (2014)
103. Tabesh, M., Dini, M.: Fuzzy and neuro-fuzzy models for short-term water demand forecasting in Tehran. Iran. J. Sci. Technol. **33**(B1), 61 (2009)
104. Tiwari, M., Adamowski, J., Adamowski, K.: Water demand forecasting using extreme learning machines. J. Water Land Dev. **28**(1), 37–52 (2016)
105. Tiwari, M.K., Adamowski, J.: Urban water demand forecasting and uncertainty assessment using ensemble wavelet-bootstrap-neural network models. Water Resour. Res. **49**(10), 6486–6507 (2013)
106. Tiwari, M.K., Adamowski, J.F.: Medium-term urban water demand forecasting with limited data using an ensemble wavelet–bootstrap machine-learning approach. J. Water Resour. Plann. Manag. **141**(2), 04014053 (2014)
107. Vijai, P., Sivakumar, P.B.: Performance comparison of techniques for water demand forecasting. Proc. Comput. Sci. **143**, 258–266 (2018)
108. Vijayalaksmi, D.P., Babu, K.J.: Water supply system demand forecasting using adaptive neuro-fuzzy inference system. Aquat. Proc. **4**, 950–956 (2015)
109. Voronin, S., Partanen, J.: Forecasting electricity price and demand using a hybrid approach based on wavelet transform, ARIMA and neural networks. Int. J. Energy Res. **38**(5), 626–637 (2014)
110. Wang, D., Wei, S., Luo, H., Yue, C., Grunder, O.: A novel hybrid model for air quality index forecasting based on two-phase decomposition technique and modified extreme learning machine. Sci. Total Environ. **580**, 719–733 (2017)
111. Wang, X.J., et al.: Potential impact of climate change on future water demand in Yulin city, Northwest China. Mitig. Adapt. Strat. Glob. Change **20**(1), 1–19 (2015)
112. Wang, X.J., et al.: Adaptation to climate change impacts on water demand. Mitig. Adapt. Strat. Glob. Change **21**(1), 81–99 (2016)
113. Xu, S., Wang, J.: A fast incremental extreme learning machine algorithm for data streams classification. Expert Syst. Appl. **65**, 332–344 (2016)
114. Yadav, B., Ch, S., Mathur, S., Adamowski, J.: Discharge forecasting using an online sequential extreme learning machine (OS-ELM) model: a case study in Neckar River, Germany. Measurement **92**, 433–445 (2016)

115. Yalcintas, M., Bulu, M., Kucukvar, M., Samadi, H.: A framework for sustainable urban water management through demand and supply forecasting: the case of Istanbul. Sustainability 7(8), 11050–11067 (2015)
116. Yang, Z., Ce, L., Lian, L.: Electricity price forecasting by a hybrid model, combining wavelet transform, ARMA and kernel-based extreme learning machine methods. Appl. Energy 190, 291–305 (2017)
117. Yaseen, Z.M., et al.: Stream-flow forecasting using extreme learning machines: a case study in a semi-arid region in Iraq. J. Hydrol. 542, 603–614 (2016)
118. Yasar, A., Bilgili, M., Simsek, E.: Water demand forecasting based on stepwise multiple nonlinear regression analysis. Arab. J. Sci. Eng. 37(8), 2333–2341 (2012)
119. Yurdusev, M.A., Firat, M.: Adaptive neuro fuzzy inference system approach for municipal water consumption modeling: an application to Izmir, Turkey. J. Hydrol. 365(3–4), 225–234 (2009)
120. Zhou, S.L., McMahon, T.A., Walton, A., Lewis, J.: Forecasting operational demand for an urban water supply zone. J. Hydrol. 259(1–4), 189–202 (2002)
121. Zhou, T., Wang, F., Yang, Z.: Comparative analysis of ANN and SVM models combined with wavelet preprocess for groundwater depth prediction. Water 9(10), 781 (2017)

Cyberbullying Detection with BiRNN and Attention Mechanism

Anman Zhang[1]([✉]), Bohan Li[1,2,3], Shuo Wan[1], and Kai Wang[1]

[1] College of Computer Science and Technology,
Nanjing University of Aeronautics and Astronautics, Nanjing, China
{zhanganman,bhli}@nuaa.edu.cn
[2] Collaborative Innovation Center of Novel Software Technology and
Industrialization, Nanjing, China
[3] Jiangsu Easymap Geographic Information Technology Corp., Ltd., Nanjing, China

Abstract. While the social network has brought a lot of conveniences to our lives, it has also caused a series of severe problems, which include cyberbullying. Cyberbullying is an aggressive and intentional act carried out by a group or an individual to attack a victim on the Internet. Most of the existing works related to cyberbullying detection focus on making use of swearwords to classify text or images with short titles. Although previous methods such as SVM and logistic regression show some advantages in the accuracy of detection, few of them capture the semantic information of non-swearwords which could also make big difference to the final results. In this paper, we propose to use BiRNN and attention mechanism to identify bullies. BiRNN is used to integrate the contextual information, and the attention model reflects the weight of different words for classification. Meanwhile, we convert the severity calculated by the attention layer to the level of cyberbullying. Experiments conducted on three real-world text datasets show that our proposed method outperforms the state-of-art algorithms on text classification and identification effect.

Keywords: Attention model · Cyberbullying detection · Text classification · Social network

1 Introduction

An increasing number of people are suffering from cyberbullying in social network, especially adolescents. Cyberbullying is defined as "an aggressive and

This work is supported by National Natural Science Foundation of China (61728204, 61672284), Key laboratory of high security system software development and verification technology, ministry of industry and information technology (NJ2018014), Youth science and technology innovation fund (NT2018028), Foundation of state key laboratory of smart grid protection and operation control (national defense pre-research field), Jiangsu university advantageous discipline construction support project.

© ICST Institute for Computer Sciences, Social Informatics and Telecommunications Engineering 2019
Published by Springer Nature Switzerland AG 2019. All Rights Reserved
X. B. Zhai et al. (Eds.): MLICOM 2019, LNICST 294, pp. 623–635, 2019.
https://doi.org/10.1007/978-3-030-32388-2_52

intentional act carried out by a group or an individual repeatedly and continuously against victims through digital devices" [1]. In 2016, a study on 5,700 middle school and high school students aged 12–17 in the United States showed that 33.8% of them have long been cyberbullied [2]. Girls are more likely than boys to be disturbed by such problem. Meanwhile, another analysis on the prevalence of cyberbullying in Chinese college students [3] demonstrated that 39.18% of 781 subjects are involved in cyberbullying. Cyberbullying has been a widespread problem and could cause potential psychological harm to people.

Solving cyberbullying has received enormous attention in recent years. Some previous work based on dictionary matching counts the frequency of characteristic words as the evidence for text classification. Such methods depend on artificially designed features, so they cannot capture the contextual information, and the level of cyberbullying is difficult to be measured. Afterwards, some work starts to focus on text representation obtained by deep learning frameworks. Rosa et al. [4] reviewed related methods such as CNN, a hybrid CNN-LSTM and a mixed CNN-LSTM-DNN for cyberbullying detection. Cheng et al. [5] designed a hierarchical attention network to aggregate words into session vectors layer by layer.

Compared with them, we use BiRNN to identify various cyberbullying instances by analyzing social messages on the Internet, and then measure the severity of them. To summarize, we make the following contributions:

(1) We propose a novel model that incorporates attention into BiRNN to classify all the text into two types. One type contains cyberbullying content, while the other does not contain. Visualized attention values on the test set assist to select cyberbullying topics with high attention value for detection.
(2) According to weights of the attention layer, we assume that the influence of other roles like defenders is negligible, and mainly identify bullies who play the leading role in the cyberbullying event.
(3) We measure the severity of cyberbullying with attention values on three datasets. Experimental results demonstrate the identification accuracy and the severity level.

Table 1 lists all the notations and descriptions. The rest of this paper is organized as follows. Section 2 briefly overviews the related work. Section 3 introduces the two stages involved in the research process. The first stage focuses on text classification with BiRNN and Attention Model, and in the second stage we identify bullies and measure the degree of cyberbullying. Experiments are carried out in Sect. 4 to verify the effectiveness of our method. Conclusion is drawn in Sect. 5.

2   Related Work

Most of the existing methods related to cyberbullying detection could be divided into four categories: content-based, sentiment-based, user-based and network-based.

Table 1. Notations and descriptions.

Notations	Descriptions
S_i	The sentence i
w_{in}	The word vector n of the sentence i
W	A word vector matrix
$\overrightarrow{h_{in}}$	The hidden state in the bidirectional recurrent neural network corresponding to the word vector w_{in}
s_{in}	A scoring function based on the degree of correlation between $\overrightarrow{h_{in}}$ and final types
W_a	The weight of attention mechanism
b_a	The bias of attention mechanism
a_{in}	The attention value corresponding to the word vector w_{in}
C	The context information
b_{att}	The average attention value of the bully
$asst_{i,att}$	The average attention value of the assistant i
p_b	The number of posts written by the bully
p_{asst_i}	The number of posts written by the assistant i

Content-Based. Rafiq et al. [6] argued that profanity is not the only feature for cyberbullying detection. The classifier should be supplemented by other indicators such as the profile of user, media session, and comment features. Then Nahar et al. [7] took other features such as pronouns into consideration for further cyberbullying detection. Specially, on the MySpace platform, Dadvar et al. [8] classified the corpus by gender and trained SVM as the classifier. TFIDF is a way to measure the frequency of foul words used by men and women. Another content-driven detection [9] explored the relationship between text and visual content concerning cyberbullying. Methods in this paper are related to deep learning and unsupervised clustering.

Sentiment-Based. Sentiment analysis is closely related to pronoun usage and TFIDF. Nahar et al. [10] used Probabilistic Latent Semantic Analysis (PLSA) to analyze labeled bullying posts which include potential sentiment features, then the most influential people, i.e., victims and predators are detected and ranked. Xu et al. [11] leveraged Twitter Streaming API to identify "bully traces" and concluded eight roles played by people referenced within the tweets, which include bully, victim, bystander, assistant, defender, reporter, accuser, and reinforcer. In their follow-up work, they tried to find emotions expressed in tweets by training a SVM classifier using distant labeled data from Wikipedia.

User-Based. Compared with content-based and sentiment-based features, user-based features tend to be ignored. Recently, some efforts have been made to add user-related features into cyberbullying systems, such as gender, age, and race. Nahar et al. [12] used a multi-agent system to deal with streaming data from multiple social network sources. Under the circumstance of insufficient labelled data, they could still detect cyberbullying automatically. Chen et al. [13] observed users' conversation history and writing styles in order to form Lexical Syntactic Framework (LSF) and gave an offensiveness score for users.

Network-Based. Within the field of cyberbullying detection, researchers also pay more attention to network data such as number of friends, uploads and likes. To improve the effect of detection, Dadvar et al. [14,15] used number of uploads, membership duration, comments, and subscriptions as features, while the ego network was used by NaliniPriya and Asswini [16] to obtain temporal changes in the relationship among users, which are valuable in the process of detection. Online social network topology structure was referred in the paper of Chelmis et al. [17].

Various techniques have been applied to identify cyberbullying incidents automatically based on those mentioned features above, and most of them adopt supervised learning techniques which were first used by Yin et al. [18]. Potha and Maragoudakis [19] modeled data via three feature representation formats: BoW, weights allocation with SVM, and feature space simplification with SVD. Squicciarini et al. [20] used a C4.5 Decision Tree classifier based on content, personal features, and social network features to identify bullies.

However, deep learning methods are rarely mentioned although it has gained popularity in recent years. In contrast, our method is a combination of content-based features and sentiment-based features. It is superior to traditional methods in accuracy and displays the detection effect visually. Besides, bullies can be detected, and the cyberbullying degree can be measured.

3   Attention Detection Model

Attention is intuitively how much people pay attention to what they are interested in. The aim of constructing the attention detection model is summarized as two points. One is to train the classification model, the other is to measure the cyberbullying. The core part of the proposed method is the attention layer, where we calculate the average attention of every post and user to identify and measure the bullies.

3.1   Problem Description

Definition 1 *(Attention Detection). Assume that there is a topic T under which m users $(u_1, u_2, \ldots, u_m)$ send posts. Users in this topic include the bully, assistants and others whose posts are not related to the cyberbullying. The posts sent by each user are regarded as $post_i$, $i = 1, 2, \ldots, n$. Attention detection is aimed at measuring different effect of each word in $post_i$ of m users for classification, thus determining whether the cyberbullying is occurring.*

As shown in Fig. 1, the research framework is divided into two stages. The first stage is meant to classify all the text into two types, i.e. positive and negative.

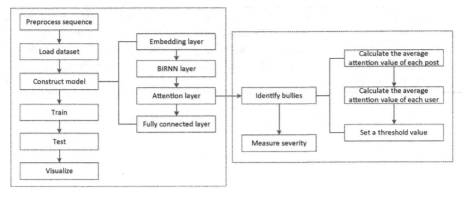

Construction and training of classification model   Identify and measure cyberbullying

Fig. 1. The research framework.

The negative type includes cyberbullying information, while the positive type contains non-cyberbullying information or few statements defending the victim. The second stage is meant to identify bullies who make offensive remarks about others and measure the severity of cyberbullying.

3.2 Attention Detection Based on BiRNN

During the process of constructing classification model, we use a model which combines Bidirectional Recurrent Neural Network (BiRNN) with Attention Model (AM). The BiRNN is designed to bind RNN that moves from the beginning of the sequence and RNN that starts at the end of the sequence, namely the forward layer and the backward layer respectively. It tends to average the accumulated output vectors of each time, assuming that each input word contributes equally to the text representation. While some words should own much greater weights, in particular sensitive words. Therefore, we incorporate attention model into BiRNN to classify text.

To illustrate it, Fig. 2 shows part of conversation in one topic and the symbol '+' separates different posts. The shades of color vary due to the difference in the attention value assigned to each word. It is understandable that the color of some signal words like 'stalker', 'faggotry' and 'homosexual' is much darker. However, the color of other non-swearwords also changes more or less. If these words are extracted separately, they seem to have nothing to do with cyberbullying. When we put them together in the context, their meanings are changed.

3.3 Text Classification

The process of text classification is the prerequisite to identify bullies and calculate the degree of cyberbullying. As shown in Fig. 3, it includes four steps:

> post your question in the hs thread trust me you'll get a lot of answers lolz + don't carry faggotry over. + so i now feel like a child molestor this is kinda fun. + eaaasy there stalker + exactly! + faggotry? is that a utensil used for homosexual pancakes? + so by exactly you mean spit then awesome. + + they're for layering on the batter. + can you get em on ebay or only on matthew stewart's site?

Fig. 2. One example concerning cyberbullying. (Color figure online)

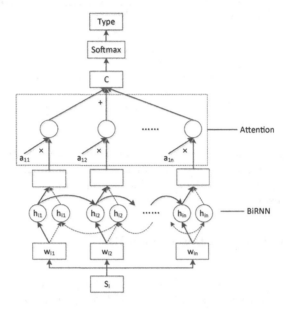

Fig. 3. Text classification process with BiRNN and attention model.

(1) The sentence S_i is divided into words, and each word is translated into the word vector sequence $w_{i1}, w_{i2}, \ldots, w_{in}$. Each sentence corresponds to a matrix $W = (w_{i1}, w_{i2}, \ldots, w_{in})$.

(2) In the BiRNN layer, each word is seen as a time node. The word vector is the input feature of each unit. The output vector of each time step is regarded as a contribution made by the corresponding input to the current task in the context. The forward and backward layers are composed of bidirectional characteristics. Each unit has state characteristics $\overrightarrow{h_{in}}$ and output characteristics after calculation. Output characteristics of each unit are used to calculate the weighted average of the attention layer.

(3) Formula (1) is a scoring function based on the degree of correlation between $\overrightarrow{h_{in}}$ and the final type. The more relevant, the greater s_{in} is. Here W_a and b_a are the weight and bias of attention.

$$s_{in} = tanh\left(W_a \overrightarrow{h_{in}} + b_a\right) \tag{1}$$

For all s_{in}, the final attention value a_{in} is obtained by a softmax function. The word context vector u_w is initialized randomly and learned jointly during the training process.

$$a_{in} = \frac{e^{s_{in}^T u_w}}{\sum_n e^{s_{ik}^T u_w}} \qquad (2)$$

The context information $c(1 \leq x \leq)$ for text classification is represented as Formula (3).

$$\begin{cases} h_{i1} * a_{11} + h_{i2} * a_{12} + \ldots + h_{in} * a_{1n} = c_1, \\ h_{i1} * a_{21} + h_{i2} * a_{22} + \ldots + h_{in} * a_{2n} = c_2 \end{cases} \qquad (3)$$

(4) We use the fully connected layer and the softmax function to output the probability of each type. Whether the text belongs to cyberbullying is dependent on these probabilities.

3.4   Cyberbullying Identification and Measurement

The second stage is to detect bullies who send aggressive posts and evaluate the severity of cyberbullying. Rather than count the frequency of swearwords, we compute the average attention value of all users in each topic containing cyberbullying information to set a threshold. As shown in Algorithm 1, threshold reflects the average level of attack.

Among all users whose average weight is above the threshold, the user with the highest value is the dominant bully, and the others can be regarded as assistants promoting this terrible event. Algorithm 2 illustrates the process of identifying the bully and assistants. Then, to calculate the severity of each topic that contains the bullying content, i.e. the level of attack, we regard attention values b_{att} and $asst_{i,att}$ pointing to cyberbullying type as the degree of attack. The number of posts written by per person is considered as a weight.

$$severity = \frac{b_{att} \times p_b + \sum (asst_{i,att} \times p_{asst_i})}{p_b + \sum p_{asst_i}} \qquad (4)$$

In Formula (4), b and $asst_i$ represent the bully and assistants in one topic. There is only one bully and there are many assistants. p_b and p_{asst_i} are the number of posts from the bully and each assistant.

4   Experiment

4.1   Dataset Collection

We conduct experiments on three datasets of the social network: Formspring, Twitter, and MySpace. Formspring is a question and answer platform launched in 2009. Twitter provides the microblogging service that allows users to update messages within 140 characters. MySpace is a social website, which provides

---

Algorithm 1. Threshold setting in the cyberbullying topic

Input: the post j of the user i, $post[i][j]$; the attention value j of the user i, $attention[i][j]$; the number of the bully and assistants, N; the attention value of the word, a

Output: threshold

```
 1: p_b ← 0, p_{asst_i} ← 0, i ← 0, j ← 0, count ← 0, sum ← 0
 2: for i < N do
 3:     for word in post[i][j] do
 4:         sum ← sum + a
 5:         count++
 6:     end for
 7:     attention[i][j] ← sum/count
 8:     i++
 9: end for
10:
11: i ← 0, j ← 0, count ← 0, sum ← 0
12: for i < N do
13:     if attention[i][j] exists then
14:         sum ← sum + attention[i][j]
15:         count++
16:         j++
17:     else
18:         ave[i] ← sum/count
19:         i++, j ← 0, count ← 0, sum ← 0
20:     end if
21: end for
22:
23: i ← 0, sum ← 0
24: for i < N do
25:     sum ← sum + ave[i]
26:     threshold ← sum/N
27: end for
28: return threshold
```

---

global users with an interactive platform integrating social networking, personal information sharing, instant messaging, and other functions.

Formspring[1]. This dataset contains 40,952 posts from 50 ids in Formspring. Each post is crowdsourced to three workers of Amazon Mechanical Turk (AMT) for labeling the cyberbullying content with 'Yes' or 'No'. About 3,469 posts are regarded as the bullying type by at least one worker and 37,349 posts are deemed non-cyberbullying. The rest of the data is not given a definitive judgment.

Twitter[2]. This dataset is collected from Twitter stream API. It has 7,321 tweets consisting of 2,102 'y' posts and 5,219 'n' posts. All the data has been labeled by experienced annotators for cyberbullying research.

---

[1] http://www.chatcoder.com/drupal/DataDownload.

[2] http://research.cs.wisc.edu/bullying/data.html.

Algorithm 2. Identify the bully and assistants

Input: N, $ave[i]$, p_b, p_{asst_i}, threshold
Output: b_{att}, $asst_{t,att}$

1: $i \leftarrow 0$, $j \leftarrow i+1$
2: $max \leftarrow ave[i]$
3: **for** $j < N$ **do**
4:    **if** $max < ave[j]$ **then**
5:       $max \leftarrow ave[j]$
6:    **end if**
7:    j++
8: **end for**
9:
10: $b_{att} \leftarrow max$
11: **for** $i < N$ **do**
12:    **if** $ave[i] == max$ **then**
13:       continue
14:    **else if** $ave[i] > threshold$ **then**
15:       $asst_{i,att} \leftarrow ave[i]$
16:    **end if**
17:    i++
18: **end for**
19: **return** b_{att}, $asst_{i,att}$

MySpace (See footnote 1). There are 381,557 posts that belong to 16,345 topics in the extended dataset. Firstly, we save swear words, bad words and curse words from a website called Swear Word List & Curse Filter[3]. Some Internet slang[4] and British slang[5] consisting of slang and acronyms that include foul words are also selected. Then we match these words with contents of all the posts to label each post automatically. If a post contains the bullying content, it is labelled as '1', otherwise it is labelled as '0'. Among all the topics, there are 10,629 labels for '1' and 5,716 labels for '0'.

4.2 Results and Analyses

In the process of training, we vary the learning rate to compare experimental results and seek the best parameter. Figure 4 demonstrates the parameter tuning on MySpace dataset. The x-coordinate represents iteration times, and the y-coordinate represents the accuracy and the cross entropy loss respectively. The overall trend of accuracy is on the rise and the loss is declining. It is obvious that the accuracy and loss reach a balance when the learning rate is set to $1e-3$. Parameter adjustments on other datasets are similar.

To verify the effectiveness of the proposed model on the test set, we set the iteration times of the experiment to 20 and repeat the experiment for 5 times.

---

[3] https://www.noswearing.com/dictionary.
[4] https://www.noslang.com/dictionary.
[5] https://www.translatebritish.com/dictionary.

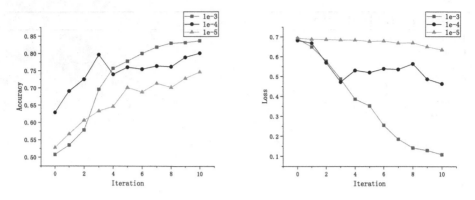

Fig. 4. Changes in accuracy and loss of test set varying the learning rate.

The average value of all indicators are taken as the final results. We take SVM, Logistic Regression, and CNN referred before as baseline algorithms. The effectiveness of these algorithms is evaluated from three aspects: accuracy, precision, and recall. As shown in Fig. 5, our method outperforms benchmark methods on all datasets. The traditional classification methods of artificial feature extraction such as SVM and Logistic Regression are inferior to the deep learning like CNN. Although our model is slightly better than CNN, we exploit the attention mechanism to detect the cyberbullying.

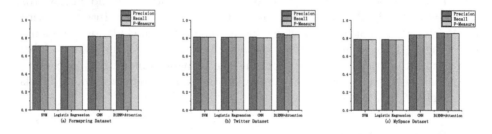

Fig. 5. Comparison between BiRNN+Attention and three advanced algorithms.

Taking MySpace as an example, Fig. 6 visualizes the impact of each word on the final classification. This topic is about 'Weed or Alcohol' and it contains 50 posts. The number of all words in these posts are nearly 1000. We mark several words with high weights in the following figure. Some insulting words like 'fuck', 'stalker' and 'faggotry' have higher weights, while some emotional words like 'lol' also deserve to be paid attention to. That is why we introduce attention mechanism into the process of identification, instead of depending on the number of swearwords. According to the distribution of attention value, the scope of identifying the bully can be reduced. Text with high and dense attention values calls for the special attention. It is most likely to be posted by the bully.

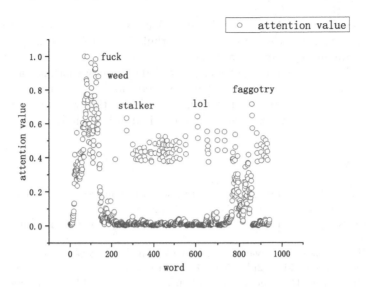

Fig. 6. The attention value of all words in one cyberbullying topic

With a preliminary analysis of attention values, we try to identify the bully and assistants. The first thing that we need to do is determining the threshold. We compute the average attention value of all users who belong to files marked as cyberbullying. Next, by Formula (4), the severity of cyberbullying can be measured. Table 2 shows the results of bully detection and severity measure. We select 1,000 posts labeled as cyberbullying from three test sets respectively. Finally, we convert the probabilities of the severity into the corresponding level from 1 to 9. It can be seen that the bullying problem in Twitter is more serious than other two platforms. It makes sense because Twitter is intuitively the most popular social platform of them. In addition, the more posts a bully sends, the worse the problem tends to be.

Table 2. Bully detection and severity measure.

Dataset	Posts	Bully	p_b	Threshold	Severity	Level
Formspring	1,000	joie***esu	22	0.48	0.5715	5
Twitter	1,000	31***104	56	0.66	0.7887	7
MySpace	1,000	$MS_1$3***63	8	0.23	0.3119	3

5   Conclusion and Future Work

In this paper, we study the problem of cyberbullying text detection and severity measure. We propose a model that takes advantage of BiRNN and Attention

Model to classify text. Weights of the attention layer are further used to identify the bully and measure the severity of cyberbullying. Visualized attention value assists in reducing the detection range of bullying text, and remarkable words are expected to be saved for building a knowledge base. Experimental results on three different datasets show that the proposed model is effective. Considering the many-to-many relationship between bully and victim, we will try to find the cyberbullying community instead of one dominated bully in our future work.

References

1. Smith, P.K.: Cyberbullying: its nature and impact in secondary school pupils. J. Child Psychol. Psychiatry **49**(4), 376–385 (2008)
2. Cyberbullying Data. https://cyberbullying.org/2016-cyberbullying-data. Accessed 26 Nov 2016
3. Zhu, H.: Analysis on prevalence of cyberbullying in college students in China. J. Jilin Univ. (Med. Ed.) **42**(3), 605–611 (2016)
4. Rosa, H., Matos, D., Ribeiro, R., Coheur, L., Carvalho, J.P.: A "Deeper" look at detecting cyberbullying in social networks. In: 2018 International Joint Conference on Neural Networks (IJCNN), pp. 1–8. IEEE, Rio (2018)
5. Cheng, L., Guo, R., Silva, Y., Hall, D., Liu, H.: Hierarchical attention networks for cyberbullying detection on the Instagram social network. In: SIAM International Conference on Data Mining. SDM, Calgary (2019)
6. Rafiq, R.I., Hosseinmardi, H., Han, R., Lv, Q., Mishra, S., Mattson, S.A.: Careful what you share in six seconds: detecting cyberbullying instances in Vine. In: Proceedings of the 2015 IEEE/ACM International Conference on Advances in Social Networks Analysis and Mining, pp. 617–622. ACM, Paris (2015)
7. Nahar, V.: An effective approach for cyberbullying detection. Commun. Inf. Sci. Manag. Eng. **3**(5), 238 (2013)
8. Dadvar, M., De Jong, F.: Cyberbullying detection: a step toward a safer internet yard. In: Proceedings of the 21st International Conference on World Wide Web, pp. 121–126. ACM, Lyon (2012)
9. Zhong, H., et al.: Content-driven detection of cyberbullying on the Instagram social network. In: Proceedings of the 25th International Joint Conference on Artificial Intelligence, pp. 3952–3958. AAAI, New York (2016)
10. Nahar, V., Unankard, S., Li, X., Pang, C.: Sentiment analysis for effective detection of cyber bullying. In: Sheng, Q.Z., Wang, G., Jensen, C.S., Xu, G. (eds.) APWeb 2012. LNCS, vol. 7235, pp. 767–774. Springer, Heidelberg (2012). https://doi.org/10.1007/978-3-642-29253-8_75
11. Xu, J.M., Jun, K.S., Zhu, X., Bellmore, A.: Learning from bullying traces in social media. In: Proceedings of the 2012 Conference of the North American Chapter of the Association for Computational Linguistics: Human Language Technologies, pp. 656–666. Association for Computational Linguistics, Montreal (2012)
12. Nahar, V.: Detecting cyberbullying in social networks using multi-agent system. Web Intell. Agent Syst.: Int. J. **12**(4), 375–388 (2014)
13. Chen, Y., Zhou, Y., Zhu, S., Xu, H.: Detecting offensive language in social media to protect adolescent online safety. In: 2012 International Conference on Privacy, Security, Risk and Trust and 2012 International Conference on Social Computing, pp. 71–80. IEEE, Amsterdam (2012)

14. Dadvar, M., Trieschnigg, R.B., de Jong, F.M.: Expert knowledge for automatic detection of bullies in social networks. In: 25th Benelux Conference on Artificial Intelligence, BNAIC 2013, pp. 57–64. Delft University of Technology, TU Delft (2013)
15. Dadvar, M., Trieschnigg, D., de Jong, F.: Experts and machines against bullies: a hybrid approach to detect cyberbullies. In: Sokolova, M., van Beek, P. (eds.) AI 2014. LNCS, vol. 8436, pp. 275–281. Springer, Cham (2014). https://doi.org/10.1007/978-3-319-06483-3_25
16. Salawu, S.: Approaches to automated detection of cyberbullying: a survey. IEEE Trans. Affect. Comput. (2017). https://doi.org/10.1109/TAFFC.2017.2761757
17. Chelmis, C., Zois, D.S., Yao, M.: Mining patterns of cyberbullying on Twitter. In: 2017 IEEE International Conference on Data Mining Workshops (ICDMW), pp. 126–133. IEEE, New Orleans (2017)
18. Yin, D., Xue, Z., Hong, L., Davison, B.D., Kontostathis, A., Edwards, L.: Detection of harassment on Web 2.0. In: Proceedings of the Content Analysis in the WEB, vol. 2, pp. 1–7. CAW2.0, Madrid (2009)
19. Potha, N., Maragoudakis, M.: Cyberbullying detection using time series modeling. In: 2014 IEEE International Conference on Data Mining Workshop, pp. 373–382. IEEE, Shenzhen (2014)
20. Squicciarini, A., Rajtmajer, S., Liu, Y., Griffin, C.: Identification and characterization of cyberbullying dynamics in an online social network. In: Proceedings of the 2015 IEEE/ACM International Conference on Advances in Social Networks Analysis and Mining, pp. 280–285. ACM, Paris (2015)

Sewage Treatment Control Method Based on Genetic-SOFNN

Zhuang Yang$^{(\boxtimes)}$, Cuili Yang, and Junfei Qiao

Faculty of Information Technology, Beijing Key Laboratory of Computational Intelligence and Intelligent System, Beijing University of Technology, Beijing 100124, People's Republic of China
892836748@qq.com, {clyang5,junfeiq}@bjut.edu.cn

Abstract. In the sewage treatment process, the dissolved oxygen concentration is a very important control target, but it is difficult to be controlled. To solve this problem, a self-organizing fuzzy neural network controller based on genetic ideas (G-SOFNN) is proposed. In the controller structure reduction process, the deleted neuron information is merged with the remaining neurons to reduce the interference set. During the controller structure increasing phase, the information of new neurons is initialized to avoid overlapping of information. Then, the controller parameters are trained by the projection algorithm to improve the control precision. Experiments illustrate that the proposed method can accurately control the concentration of dissolved oxygen in the sewage treatment process.

Keywords: Sewage treatment · Fuzzy neural network · Tracking control · Projection gradient learning

1 Introduction

Water pollution is one of the most serious urban environmental problems. In treating urban sewage, the activated sludge process is the most commonly used method, whose principle is to react microorganisms and organic substances in activated sludge to oxidize and decompose organic matter. While due to the complex nonlinear dynamics of the wastewater treatment process, it is very difficult to control the process [1].

In the sewage treatment process, the dissolved oxygen concentration is an important control target [2,3], since the value of the dissolved oxygen affects the activity of the microorganisms in the activated sludge. Recently, the traditional PID control method can not achieve the required control accuracy [4,5]. Therefore, some experts use the neural network as the intelligent controller to improve the control precision. For example, Han et al. implemented intelligent predictive control to improve the control accuracy of dissolved oxygen concentration [7]. Spall et al. used dynamic performance indicators to adjust the structure of the neural network, and accurately controlled the return flow of sewage [8].

© ICST Institute for Computer Sciences, Social Informatics and Telecommunications Engineering 2019
Published by Springer Nature Switzerland AG 2019. All Rights Reserved
X. B. Zhai et al. (Eds.): MLICOM 2019, LNICST 294, pp. 636–644, 2019.
https://doi.org/10.1007/978-3-030-32388-2_53

Qiao et al. designed the fuzzy neural network (FNN) structure as the controller to control the dissolved oxygen concentration [9].

The structure of the FNN plays a vital role in the process of solving the control problems. Therefore, experts have proposed their own methods for the adjustment of neural network structure [10,11]. Wu et al. proposed a FNN structure adjustment method based on the pre-rule extraction, which was verified in the classification problem [12]. Xu et al. adjusted the structure of the FNN network by incorporating the importance of neurons and the intensity of activation, and achieved good results in wastewater treatment [13]. But there are some problems in these methods: Firstly, in the process of structural deletion, these methods cannot guarantee the uselessness of the information contained in the deleted neuron and rule. Secondly, in the increasing phase, the added neuron and rule should ensure its information be different from original information.

Based on above problems, this paper combines the idea of genetic inheritance into the network structure adjustment process. In the structural deletion phase, the depleted neurons are merged with the remaining neurons, and the information is preserved while the structure is reduced. In the increasing phase, the new neurons are combined with mutation operators for parameter initialization to reduce the coincidence of information. Finally, through the projection algorithm to train parameters of the network, which can avoid falling into local optimum. Simulation results show that the sewage treatment controller can accurately track the dissolved oxygen concentration.

The sections of the article are arranged as follows: Sect. 2 introduces the control variables in the sewage treatment process and the structural composition of the fuzzy controller. Section 3 introduces the process of combining genetic ideas into self-organizing fuzzy controller. Section 4 proves the control effect of the proposed method by the experiments with BSM1. Section 5 is the conclusion.

2   FNN Controller Method for Sewage Treatment

The activated sludge process is the most widely used sewage treatment method, in which a series of microbial biochemical reactions occur in the aeration tank. The BSM1 model is a wastewater treatment imitation benchmark model jointly developed by the International Water Association and the European Union's Science and Technology Cooperation Organization [14,15]. The overall layout of the BSM1 model is shown in Fig. 1.

In the BSM1 model, the controller realizes the tracking control of the dissolved oxygen concentration in the fifth zone by controlling the oxygen transfer coefficient of the fifth unit. Therefore, the output of the controller is the amount of change in the oxygen transfer coefficient of the fifth zone, which is transferred to the BSM1 to complete the control of the dissolved oxygen concentration.

By incorporating the nonlinear dynamic characteristics and large time lag in the sewage treatment process, the overall controller design is shown in Fig. 2, and the controller used in this paper is based on fuzzy neural network. The input can be expressed as $\dot{x} = (e, de/dt)$, where e is the error between the set value and the true value, de/dt is the amount of error change.

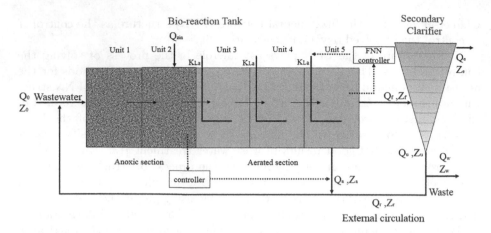

Fig. 1. BSM1 model of FNN dissolved controller for oxygen concentration.

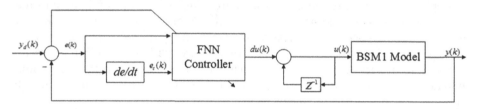

Fig. 2. The model of controller.

The fuzzy neural network structures are shown in the Fig. 3, which are mainly divided into input layer, membership layer, fuzzy rule layer, normalization layer and output layer. The input and output relationships with each layer are as follows:

The membership layer can be expressed as:

$$\mu_n^m = exp\frac{-(x_n - c_n^m)^2}{\delta_m^2} \tag{1}$$

In Eq. (1), μ_n^m indicates the output of this layer of neurons, x_n represents input, c_n^m represents the center, and δ_m represents the width.

The fuzzy rule layer can be expressed as:

$$b_m = \prod_{j=1}^{m} \omega_{nm}\mu_n^m \tag{2}$$

where b_m represents the output of the layer, ω_{nm} represents the connection weight of the membership layer and the fuzzy rule layer.

The normalization layer can be expressed as:

$$a_m = \frac{b_m}{\sum_{j=1}^{m} b_m} \tag{3}$$

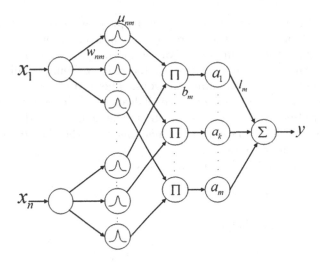

Fig. 3. The structure of FNN.

Finally, the output layer can be expressed as:

$$y = \sum_{j=1}^{m} l_m a_m \qquad (4)$$

where l_m represents the connection weight of the normalization layer and output layer.

The structure of FNN is fuzzied by Gaussian functions. The characteristics of the input data are extracted at the fuzzy rule layer. The final output layer is used to implement defuzzification and sharpening.

3 G-SOFNN Adjustment Method

To change the structure of fuzzy neural networks, many experts have proposed some structure adjustment methods [9–13,16,17]. The most widely used method is to increase or decrease the network structure by calculating the intensity of fuzzy rules or neurons. However, the network deletion threshold (I_{cth}) and increase threshold (I_{dth}) are depended on human experience. In the deletion phase, the uselessness of the information contained in neurons and rules cannot be guaranteed. While in the increasing phase, the added neurons and rules should also have great difference between its information and the original, to avoid overlapping information. Therefore, this paper proposes a self-organizing fuzzy neural network by incorporating the genetic operators (G-SOFNN).

3.1 Deletion Phase

In the genetic algorithm, the genetic variation in biology is cited, thus good results are obtained in the optimization algorithm. In this paper, the idea of genetic variation will also be introduced in the proposed structural algorithm. In the neuron reduction phase, the neuron reduction is based on the comparison of the threshold with the minimum activation intensity. According to the genetic inheritance methods, the information of the deleted neuron will be added as part of the gene to the remaining neurons. There are two steps during this period: Firstly, calculate the shortest euclidean distance between each neuron and the depleted neurons by Eq. (5) to obtain the neurons. And then, according to Eqs. (6)–(8), the information of the neurons with the shortest distance and the new parameters are obtained.

Euclidean distance is calculated as below:

$$d(x, y) = \sqrt{(x_1 - y_1)^2 + \cdots + (x_n - y_n)^2} \tag{5}$$

Center is updated as below:

$$C_{new} = I_{cth} \cdot C_k + (1 - I_{cth}) \cdot C_d \tag{6}$$

Weight is updated as below:

$$w_{new} = I_{cth} \cdot w_k + (1 - I_{cth}) \cdot w_d \tag{7}$$

Width is updated as below:

$$\delta_{new} = I_{cth} \cdot \delta_k + (1 - I_{cth}) \cdot \delta_d \tag{8}$$

where C_d, w_d, and δ_d represent the center, width, and weight of the deleted neurons, respectively, C_k, w_k, and δ_k represent the center, width, and weight of the fused neurons, respectively.

3.2   Increasing Phase

In the increasing phase, if the maximum value of all neuron activation intensities is less than the set growth threshold, it indicates that the current rules cannot effectively cover the new data, and it is necessary to increase the neurons to meet the requirements of the current control environment. However, the new data (center, weight, width) initialization process of the added neurons need to be differentiated from the original neurons, so that the added neurons can cover the information of the new data as much as possible. Therefore, the maximum activation intensity of neurons should be maximized variation when new neurons are generated.

In this period, we defined the mutation operator according to I_{cth} and I_{gth}, as shown in Eq. (9). Then, the center, width and weight of the new neuron are calculated according to the mutation operator, as shown in Eqs. (10)–(12).

The mutation operator is calculated as below:

$$\eta = \frac{I_{cth}}{I_{cth} + I_{gth}} \tag{9}$$

The new center is calculated as below:

$$C_{new} = \eta \cdot (C_1 + \cdots + C_k) \tag{10}$$

The new weight is calculated as below:

$$w_{new} = \eta \cdot (w_1 + \cdots + w_k) \tag{11}$$

The new width is calculated as below:

$$\delta_{new} = \eta \cdot (\delta_1 + \cdots + \delta_k) \tag{12}$$

where I_{cth} represents deletion threshold, I_{gth} represents increase threshold, C_k, w_k and δ_k represent the center, weight and width of the k-th existing neuron, respectively.

3.3 Learning Algorithm

In the network parameter adjustment process, the gradient projection is used. The method can avoid the solution in the parameter adjustment process. The adjustment process of the weight is as shown in Eq. (13).

$$w_i = \begin{cases} l_{rw} \cdot e \times b_m & if(\|w_i^2\| < h)or(\|w_i^2\| = h \ and \ b_m w_i \ge 0) \\ \dfrac{-l_{rw} \cdot e \times b_m + l_{rw} \cdot e \times b_m w_i^T}{\|w_i^2\|} & if(\|w_i^2\| = h_w \ and \ b_m w_i < 0) \end{cases} \tag{13}$$

The l_{rw} in the formula represents the learning rate, e is input error, b_m represents the output of the fuzzy rule layer, and h_w represents associated parameter bounds.

The update formula for the *center* and *width* is based on the gradient descent, the adjustment process is as follows:

$$c_t = c_{t-1} + \eta \frac{\omega_i}{\delta_i^2} \sum_{j=1}^{n} \beta_i e_i \phi_i(x_j)(x_j - c_i) \tag{14}$$

$$\delta_t = \delta_{t-1} + \eta \frac{\omega_i}{\delta_i^3} \sum_{j=1}^{n} \beta_i e_i \phi_i(x_j) \|x_j - c_i\|^2 \tag{15}$$

where η_i is the learning rate, β_i is the forgetting factor, e_i is the error signal between the network output and the real value, and $\phi_i(x_j)$ is the output of the first hidden node to x_j.

4 Experiments

In order to verify the proposed method, we designed the following experiment: Firstly, the method proposed in the paper controls the dissolved oxygen in BSM1 under dry weather (dissolved oxygen concentration set value $2 \, mg \cdot l^{-1}$) will be compared with PID controller and SOFNN controller. The results of the comparison are shown in the Fig. 4. At the same time, we also show the changes of the fuzzy neural network controller structure of G-SOFNN under three different weathers in Fig. 5.

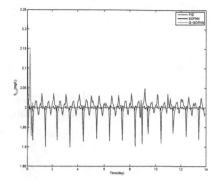

Fig. 4. Control comparison of DO.   **Fig. 5.** Rule change process.

According to Fig. 4, it takes a period of time to adapt the environment to the fuzzy neural network. In the period when PID and SOFNN and G-SOFNN are stable, it is obvious that the tracking effect of the PID controller is the worst, and the SOFNN controller is slightly better, G-SOFNN has the higher precision and ability to track dissolved oxygen concentration.

It can be seen from the Fig. 5 that under different weather conditions, the G-SOFNN method can adapt the current sewage environment in a short time. Although there is a process of change in the middle, the structure of the controller can be quickly adjusted to steady state, which also shows the stronger adaptive ability of the controller.

Then, we compared three indicators including integral absolute error (IAE), intergral square error (ISE) and maximum error (Dev^{max}) in rain weather and storm weather as shown in Table 1. The calculation process of the three indicators are as shown in Eqs. (16)–(18), respectively.

$$IAE = 1\frac{1}{t_f - t_0} \int_{t_0}^{t_f} |e_i| \, dt \tag{16}$$

$$ISE = 1\frac{1}{t_f - t_0} \int_{t_0}^{t_f} e_i^2 dt \tag{17}$$

$$Dev^{max} = max|e_i(t)| \tag{18}$$

where e_i refers to the difference between the dissolved oxygen concentration tracking set value and the actual value in BSM1, and $e_i(t)$ represents the systematic error value at time t.

Table 1. The control performance comparison under different weathers condition.

Methods	Rain weather			Storm weather		
	IAE	ISE	Dev^{max}	IAE	ISE	Dev^{max}
PID	4.536	0.153	0.099	4.848	0.181	0.095
SOFNN	0.858	0.005	0.018	0.984	0.012	0.092
G-SOFNN	0.156	0.003	0.008	0.453	0.031	0.016

The results of three algorithms are given in the Table 1. It is obvious that our algorithm obtains the best control effect compared to other algorithms. Also, the performance of the G-SOFNN algorithm is optimal in the comparison algorithm, which prove the effectiveness of genetic variation based methods.

5   Conclusions

In order to accurately track the dissolved oxygen concentration in the sewage environment, a self-organizing fuzzy neural network control method based on genetic operation is designed in this paper. First of all, in the deletion process of FNN, the genetics of the depleted neurons are genetically inherited. Furthermore, projection algorithm is used to train the FNN parameters online to prevent the network from falling into optimum and improves control accuracy. Moreover, through the tracking experiment of dissolved oxygen concentration in BSM1, it is proved that the proposed method can achieve high-precision control effect.

Acknowledgement. This work was supported by the National Natural Science Foundation of China under Grants 61603012, 61533002 and 61890930-5, the Beijing Municipal Education Commission Foundation under Grant KM201710005025, the Major Science and Technology Program for Water Pollution Control and Treatment of China (2018ZX07111005), the National Key Research and Development Project under Grants 2018YFC1900800-5.

References

1. Wang, H.M., Ren, Z.J.: Bioelectrochemical metal recovery from wastewater: a review. Water Res. **66**, 219–232 (2014)
2. Han, G.T., Qiao, J.F., Han, H.G.: Wastewater treatment control method based on recurrent fuzzy neural network. CIESC J. **67**, 954–959 (2016)
3. Shen, W., Chen, X., Pons, M.N., et al.: Model predictive control for wastewater treatment process with feedforward compensation. Chem. Eng. J. **155**(1), 161–174 (2009)
4. Samsudin, S.I., Rahmat, M.F., Wahab, N.A., et al.: Improvement of activated sludge process using enhanced nonlinear PI controller. Arab. J. Sci. Eng. **8**(39), 6575–6586 (2014)

5. Ye, H.T., Li, Z.Q., Luo, W.G.: Dissolved oxygen control of the activated sludge wastewater treatment process using adaptive fuzzy PID control. In: Control Conference, pp. 7510–7513 (2013)
6. Liu, X., Yu, W.: Research of dissolved oxygen concentration control strategy based on the fuzzy self-tuning PID parameter. In: IEEE Conference on Control and Decision, Chongqing, China, pp. 5928–5932 (2017)
7. Han, H.G., Qiao, J.F.: Nonlinear model-predictive control for industrial processes: an application to wastewater treatment process. IEEE Trans. Ind. Electron. **61**(4), 1970–1980 (2013)
8. Spall, J.C., Cristion, J.A.: A neural network controller for systems with unmodeled dynamics with applications to wastewater treatment. IEEE Trans. Syst. Man Cybern. **27**(3), 369–375 (1997)
9. Qiao, J.F., Wei, Z., Han, H.G.: Self-organizing fuzzy control for dissolved oxygen concentration using fuzzy neural network1. J. Intell. Fuzzy Syst. **30**(6), 3411–3422 (2016)
10. Wai, R.J., Muthusamy, R.: Design of fuzzy-neural-network-inherited backstepping control for robot manipulator including actuator dynamics. IEEE Trans. Fuzzy Syst. **22**(4), 709–722 (2014)
11. Qiao, J.F., Wang, H.D.: Structure self-organizing algorithm for fuzzy neural networks and its applications. Control Theory Appl. **25**(4), 703–707 (2008)
12. Wu, Y.H., Chen, X.: Fast learning algorithm of small multi-input fuzzy neural network structure. J. Fudan Univ. (Nat. Sci.) **25**(4), 56–60 (2005)
13. Xu, J.C., Yang, C.L., Qiao, J.F., et al.: Dissolved oxygen concentration control method based on self-organizing fuzzy neural network. CAAI Trans. Intell. Syst. **13**(6), 45–52 (2018)
14. Francisco, M., Vega, P., Revollar, S.: Model predictive control of BSM1 benchmark of wastewater treatment process: a tuning procedure. In: Decision & Control & European Control Conference (2012)
15. Shen, W., Chen, X., Corriou, J.P.: Application of model predictive control to the BSM1 benchmark of wastewater treatment process. Comput. Chem. Eng. **32**(12), 2849–2856 (2008)
16. Pires, O.C., Palma, C., Costa, J.C., et al.: Knowledge-based fuzzy system for diagnosis and control of an integrated biological wastewater treatment process. Water Sci. Technol. **53**(4–5), 313–320 (2006)
17. Kai, Z., Dong, X., Wang, D.: Intelligent vibration control of piezo-electric truss structure using GA-based fuzzy neural network. In: World Congress on Intelligent Control & Automation, vol. 20, no. 1, pp. 5136–5139 (2010)

Latent Flow Patterns Discovery by Dockless Bike Trajectory Data for Demand Analysis

Chao Ling, JingJing Gu$^{(\boxtimes)}$, and Ming Sun

College of Computer Science and Technology,
Nanjing University of Aeronautics and Astronautics, Nanjing, China
{lingchao,gujingjing}@nuaa.edu.cn, 15651648110@163.com

Abstract. The dockless shared bikes flourish as a new concept in recent years. It allows users to find bikes anywhere via a GPS-based mobile application, and flexible cycling and parking the bikes in the same way. From the bike trajectory data produced by Users, we can extract bike flow patterns for better urban planning and Point-of-Interest (POI) recommendation. In this paper, through conducting the spatio-temporal representations of bike activity acquired from bike trajectory logs, we first design a graph clustering model With sparsity constraints that combine time information to explore potential patterns of bike flow. Next, by comparing historical trajectory logs and POI information with the flow patterns, we dig out several typical categories of bike flow patterns, which can give suggestions for further urban planning and POI recommendation. Further, our experiments via Mobike trajectory data demonstrate the effectiveness of bike flow pattern discovery.

Keywords: Shared bikes · DNN · Graph clustering

1 Introduction

The dockless shared bikes have been receiving much attention in recent years, which change the way that people travel from motor ones to non-motor ones. Mobike[1], one of the largest bike sharing companies in the world, leads the development of bike-sharing industry and meets users' needs for more convenient short-distance travel [14]. It allows users to find, pick up and drop off their bikes anywhere through mobile applications. According to statistics from shared bikes, the orders exceed 50 million every day. What's more, we can easily analyze the temporal and spatial correlations through the trajectory data generated by the use of shared bikes, which could contribute to infer the users' preference for POI in a different time and space environments in further research. For example, riding destination could be different, such as subway stations, companies or supermarkets, and the duration of the trajectory could also change at the same

---

[1] https://mobike.com.

X. B. Zhai et al. (Eds.): MLICOM 2019, LNICST 294, pp. 645–658, 2019.
https://doi.org/10.1007/978-3-030-32388-2_54

time. Therefore, exploring the latent flow patterns of shared bikes is significant to urban construction, POI recommendation, and demand analysis.

In this paper, we propose a method for extracting latent flow patterns of shared bikes trajectory data. It is still a challenging task due to the following reasons. First, the riding flow of shared bikes changes over time in a day. Figure 1 shows the geographical distribution of riding destinations at the peak and normal time respectively. Second, bike flow can also be influenced by weather, temperature, and population. Finally, the riding flow is locally-invariant and sparse, because of the short riding distance and high mobility. Previous approaches [8, 15] fail to consider these factors. Therefore, how to utilize the characteristics and effectively extract the patterns of bike flow remains an open problem.

(a) The destinations in the normal (b) The destinations in the peak time
time

Fig. 1. The geographical distributions at different time

To solve the problems mentioned above, we study a large set of Mobike users' spatio-temporal trajectory in Shanghai to obtain patterns of bike flow. First, we divide the whole city into small region grids and identify the primary locations by users' activities, using a density-based algorithm named *bike ordering points to identify the clustering structure* (Bike-OPTICS). Differing from traditional road segmentation and equal-size grids, this method can effectively avoid achieving undeveloped or inaccessible areas. Second, to further explore the bike usage demand in different regions, we develop a graph auto-encoder by non-linear embedding the original graphics [9]. In addition, we model the spatio-temporal interactions between region pairs with a sparsity constraint, which characterizes the locally-invariant sparse of bike flow. Finally, we run the k-means algorithm to obtain clustering result, for identifying the latent travel patterns for urban planning and Point-of-Interest (POI) demands of visitors.

Overall, the main contributions of our work are summarized as follows.

- We propose a new density-based clustering method to merge the neighboring region grids with high flow together. Based on the result of cluster analysis, we find the type attribute of each cluster.

- A deep neural network (DNN) of stacking auto-encoder with sparsity constraints is presented to identify the latent travel patterns and POI demands of visitors.
- Some suggestions about urban planning and bike migration are given through large-scale data analysis in the real world.

2   Related Work

Recently, because of the flourishing of location technology services (LTS) [4,7] and the advantage of shared bikes trajectories in improving the quality of human life, researchers are encouraged to use bike trajectory as data sources in large-scale urban user mobility studies. In the literature, existing works on bike sharing systems mainly studied the problems of further expansion of the station [11], shared bikes traffic prediction [6] and rebalance scheduling [10,12]. For example, Bao et al. [3] proposed a data-driven approach to develop bike lane construction plans based on large-scale real-world bike trajectory data. Ai et al. [1] developed a convolutional long-term memory network (conv-LSTM) method to predict the short-term spatio-temporal distribution of bikes, which reduced the space dependence and time dependence of bikes. However, these methods are not able to directly applied to dockless ones and only considered the distribution of bikes and traffic forecasts. Moreover, few studies have focused on further analysis and exploration of bike traffic patterns.

There has already been lots of research looking at extracting latent patterns [8,15]. Zhou et al. [16] proposed a topic-based model to discover latent patterns of urban cultural interactions. Gao et al. [13] discovered human lifestyle by creating a topic model from their digital footprints and social links. Ziyatdinov et al. [9] proposed a pattern extraction method for multi-view data using spectral clustering algorithm.

Currently, some studies prove that the topic model is more effective for discovering potential movement patterns [16]. However, for bike research, problems do exist with this model. First, urban data is quite sensitive to time, and these temporal flow patterns in shared bikes can hardly be captured by topic models [14]. Second, there is no corresponding assessment measure in the topic model for shared bikes flow pattern analysis. Finally, bike flow data is a graph structure, which increases the difficulty of data disposal course. Thus, we exploit a graph auto-encoder with sparsity constraints to identify the latent travel patterns, which could better reflect the structure of the graph and the spatial interaction between the pairs of regions.

3   Problem Formulation

In this study, we use two sets of real-world data collected from Mobike, including bike trajectory logs and urban POI data. Specifically, the bike trajectory logs contain the use of records from bike users in Shanghai. Table 1 shows an example of the trajectory logs. Each record consists of a bike label, pick-up time and drop-off time, and the corresponding origin and destination with detailed GPS coordinates. Besides, most of the locations can be linked to a specific POI.

Table 1. An example of the trajectory logs

Bike ID	Pick-up time	Drop-off time	Trip origin	Trip destination
8621525316	1517511153	1517511619	121.45,31.20	121.43,31.22
8621633865	1517501153	1517501779	121.44,31.21	121.43,31.22
8621399390	1517511233	1517521779	121.43,31.25	121.43,31.24
8621399332	1516521133	1517123779	121.37,31.21	121.40,31.25
8621399312	1517521133	1517523779	121.40,31.21	121.42,31.25

This paper has two tasks. Specifically, (1) region partition and flow matrix construction, and (2) flow pattern extraction. In the first task, we aim to discover the integrated urban areas with high flow density and construct a flow matrix for the trajectory logs based on the travel flow information extracted from shared bikes. The ultimate goal of the second task is to extract flow patterns, by which we can perform urban planning and POI recommendations.

The investigation framework of our work is presented in Fig. 2. We firstly conduct the data preprocessing, and divide the urban area into small area grids. Secondly, by extracting the travel flows in these grids, we construct a flow matrix. Next, the similarity matrix of the flow matrix is constructed based on the similarity measurement. Finally, stacking auto-encoder is applied to the original graphics. This model can learn users' spatial-temporal preferences by studying their behaviors during the process of cycling, which can supply the travel demand analysis and targeted POI recommendation with strong supports.

4   Methodology

4.1   Region Partition and Flow Matrix Construction

The dockless shared bikes are different from the traditional station-based bikes due to their flexibility. The former doesn't need to be parked and locked at the designated places, which presents a challenge to the research. Therefore, constructing flow adjacency matrix is not easy. However, we find that the riders often come together automatically, when they have similar destinations. Inspired by this observation, we decide to cluster bike parking points into regions. Through the clustering results, we can make the flow adjacency matrix.

In this work, we find that the OPTICS algorithm [2] is a suitable approach for our problem of region partition. This method requires two parameters as input: the maximum radius *eps* for searching, and the least number of points *minpts* to form a cluster. The parking positions of bikes vary greatly, which needs to set the bike maximum radius carefully. With this limitation in mind, as Algorithm 1

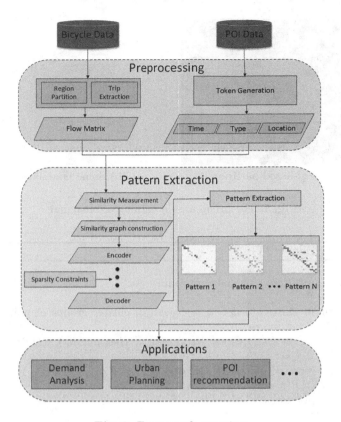

Fig. 2. Framework overview

shows, we propose a modified version named Bike-OPTICS that defines different reachable distances for different areas. In Bike-OPTICS, we collect all drop-off positions. In the procedure of clustering, the areas where bikes are densely distributed should be given higher weights. We define the maximum radius as:

$$MR = eps - \epsilon * \frac{getNeighbors(p, eps)}{N}, \tag{1}$$

where ϵ is set to be a small constant such as 0.01. Generally, the urban areas are split into small grids at first, as shown in Fig. 3(a). Then we start clustering using one of the grids, which is never categorized into existing clusters. Next, the rest grids which are reachable to the current grid to these new clusters are added. This process is repeated until all the grids are clustered, and no new cluster is created.

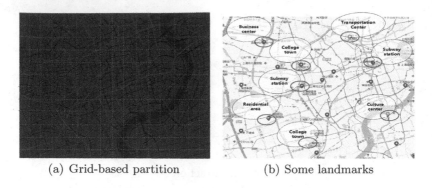

(a) Grid-based partition   (b) Some landmarks

Fig. 3. The urban area notations of Shanghai

Algorithm 1. Bike-OPTICS

Input:
    $DB = [...(p_i, location)...]$, maximum radius eps.
Output:
    center point of clusters $order = [c_1, c_2, ...c_n]$, cluster groups of points $c_{points} = [L_1^*, L_2^*...L_n^*]$, $L_i^* = [p_1, p_2...p_n]$
1: initialize $Order = list(), Se = list(), RD = list(maxdis), RD(0) = 0, MR = list(...MR_i...)$;
2: **for** each unprocessed point p of DB **do**
3:     $MR \leftarrow getMR(p, eps)$;
4:     mark p as processed;
5:     $Order \leftarrow p$;
6:     update RD;
7:     $Se \leftarrow getNeighbors(p, MR)$;
8:     **for** each unprocessed q in Se **do**
9:         $MR \leftarrow getMR(q, eps)$;
10:        marked q as processed;
11:        $Order \leftarrow q$;
12:        update RD;
13:        $Se \leftarrow getNeighbors(q, MR)$;
14:    **end for**
15: **end for**
16: **for** each p in DB **do**
17:    compute Reachable Distance to each point c_i in Order;
18:    **if** Reachable Distance $< MR_i$ **then**
19:        $L_i \leftarrow p$;
20:    **end if**
21: **end for**

Our algorithm is similar but different from the classic Density-Based Spatial Clustering of Applications with Noise (DBSCAN) algorithm [5]. In the DBSCAN algorithm, a radius and a threshold should be defined beforehand, but for Bike-OPTICS algorithm, it generates an augmented cluster ordering for cluster analysis, rather than clustered results explicitly. It reflects all the results from density-based clustering in any parameters setting. In other words, clustering based on any radius and any threshold can be derived from this ordering. For the sake of demonstration, we draw some landmarks in Fig. 3(b).

With the partitioned regions, we can construct flow matrix and flow tensor. After partitioning the entire city, a bike flow matrix that records flow between any two regions in the same time segment can be constructed. Given a whole city divided into M regions, the flow matrix is defined as $F^t = \{f^t_{ij}\} \in R^{M \times M}\}$, where f^t_{ij} denotes the number of rides from the ith region to the jth region in the t time fragment.

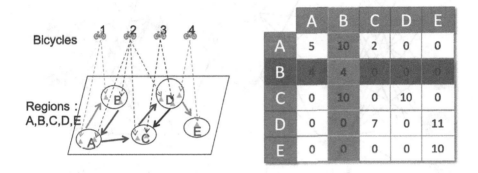

Fig. 4. A example of bike flow matrices construction

Figure 4 shows an example of the bike flow matrix structure. The x-value and y-value represent the starting region and the ending region of one bike trajectory respectively, and each matrix cell represents the bike flow between the two regions in a time slice. Particularly, we can also get the total pick-up flow or drop-off flow of region i (f^p_i and f^d_i) by calculating the sum of the corresponding column or a row. We have N flow matrices through which we build flow tensors $\mathscr{F} = \{F^{t_1}, F^{t_2}, \ldots, F^{t_N}\}$. In addition, we set the flow matrix interval as one hour.

4.2 Flow Pattern Extraction

In this section, we present a new graph clustering model based on the auto-encoder with sparsity constraints for extraction latent flow pattern. Due to the property of the bike trajectory data, the structure of the flow matrix is non-Euclidean, which does not have translation invariance. The traditional cluster methods cannot extract its internal structure very well. Therefore, we apply the deep learning method of graph clustering. Moreover, we add the sparsity constraints due to the local invariance of the bike flow.

We use an auto-encoder based on graph clustering model, which is a key component of a deep neural network. Figure 5 shows the main architecture of the auto-encoder. In order to rectify the problem of overfitting, we integrate the dropout layer into the DNN model.

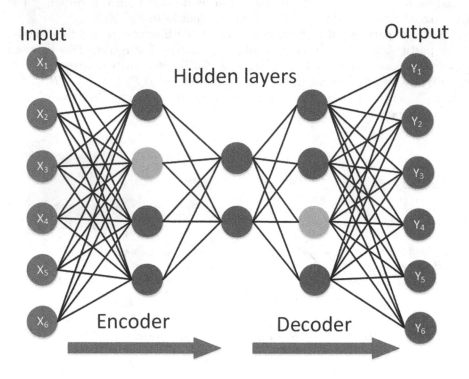

Fig. 5. DNN architecture

As stated in the previous section, an n-node graph G can be represented by its similarity matrix S. We use the Radial Basis Function (RBF) function to define the similarity matrix, which is widely used in the field of the similarity matrix:

$$S_{ij} = \exp(-\frac{\|F^i - F^j\|_2^2}{2\sigma^2}) \tag{2}$$

Next, we normalize the training set in the DNN and use the output features of the deepest layer as the graph embedding. Finally, we utilize the k-means algorithm for producing the final clustering result of graph embedding.

Algorithm 2. Clustering with sparse GraphEncoder

Input:
  Graph G, flow tensor $\mathscr{F}$, similarity matrix S, degree matrix D, DNN layer numbers ℓ, Dropout layer parameter p

Output:
  Clustering result.
1: initialization $a^0 = D^{-1}S$
2: **for** $i = 0$ to ℓ **do**
3:     Build a DNN architecture with input $a^{(i)}$;
4:     Multiply by the Dropout layer $r^{(l)}, a^{(i)} = r^{(i)} * a^{(i)}$;
5:     Train the DNN by optimizing (7) with sub-gradient method, Obtain the hidden layer activations $h^{(i)}$;
6:     Let $a^{(i+1)} = h^{(i)}$;
7: **end for**
8: Run k-means on $a^\ell \in R^{n \times n^{(\ell)}}$;

Specifically, for a DNN model with L layers, the output of a hidden layer can be described as:

$$r^{(l)} \sim Bernoulli(p), \tag{3}$$

$$\tilde{y}^{(l)} = r^{(l)} * y^{(l)}, \tag{4}$$

$$z^{(l+1)} = w^{(l+1)}\tilde{y}^{(l)} + b^{(l+1)}, \tag{5}$$

$$y^{(l+1)} = f(z^{(l+1)}). \tag{6}$$

where $l = 1 \dots L$, $a^0 = D^{-1}S$ is the input layer with feature vector x. w^l and b^l denote the DNN weight matrix and bias of the l-th hidden layer. $f(\cdot)$ represents the non-linear activation function of the hidden layer and the output layer, such as ReLu function:

$$ReLu(z) = max(0, z) \tag{7}$$

and tanh function:

$$\tanh(z) = \frac{e^z - e^{-z}}{e^z + e^{-z}} \tag{8}$$

Here, D is the diagonal matrix with the node degrees in the corresponding diagonal elements, and Q is the normalized Laplacian matrix. Due to the property of the Laplacian matrix, Q is symmetric. Then, the optimization goal is to minimize the reconstruction error between the original data x and the reconstructed data y.

$$\arg\min_{\theta \in \Theta} -\frac{1}{n} \sum_{i=1}^{n} [x \ln y - (1 - x) \ln(1 - y)]. \tag{9}$$

We also impose the sparsity constraints to the activation in the hidden layer, the loss function is:

$$Loss(\theta) = -\frac{1}{n} \sum_{i=1}^{n} [x \ln y - (1 - x) \ln(1 - y)] + \beta \|\hat{a}\|_1, \tag{10}$$

where β controls the weight of the sparsity penalty, and $\hat{a} = \frac{1}{n}\sum_{j=1}^{n} h_j$ is the average of the hidden layer activations.

For the Eq. 7, we can use back-propagation for training. Since the l_1-norm is non-differentiable and cannot be solved with the traditional gradient descent, we use the sub-gradient method to solve it.

Using the output of the hidden layer as the input to the next layer, we use the intermediate output of the encoder as a new representation of graph and run k-means on it to get the clustering results.

5   Evaluation

In this section, we first introduce the settings of the experiment including dataset, baseline algorithms and evaluation criteria that we use in the course of the experiment. Then we show the experimental results and give an in-depth analysis, which proves the superiority of our algorithm.

5.1   Experiment Settings

Dataset. The dataset we used covers $177, 357, 367$ riding records, generated by $389, 703$ shared bikes ranging from December 2017 to July 2018 in Shanghai city. Each record consists of a bike label, the pick-up time and drop-off time, as well as the corresponding origin and destination with detailed GPS coordinates.

Evaluation Criteria. Davis-Bolding Index (DBI), also known as the classification suitability index, is the sum of the average distance $avg(C)$ between the two clusters C_i and C_j divided by the distance between their center points u. The smaller the DBI, the better the clustering effect. Let $C = \{C_1, C_2, \dots, C_k\}$,

$$avg(C) = \frac{2}{|C|(|C| - 1)} \sum_{1 \le i < j \le |C|} dist(x_i, x_j), \tag{11}$$

$$u = \frac{1}{|C|} \sum_{1 \le i \le |C|} x_i, \tag{12}$$

$$DBI = \frac{1}{k} \sum_{i=1}^{k} \max_{i \ne j} (\frac{avg(C_i) + avg(C_j)}{dist(u_i, u_j)}). \tag{13}$$

Baselines. We use the following methods as baseline algorithms.

(1) Spectral Clustering. Spectral clustering is an algorithm that evolves from the graph theory and has been widely used in clustering. Compared with the traditional k-means algorithm, spectral clustering is more adaptable to our data distribution, and has better clustering results.
(2) K-means. In order to verify the validity of our method, we perform the k-means algorithm on the original graph structure.

5.2   Experimental Results

We selected two different hot spot regions to display our experimental results. At first, we performed the Bike-OPTICS algorithm using different parameters on these regions.

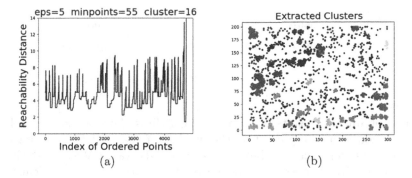

Fig. 6. Region partition in Grand Theatre

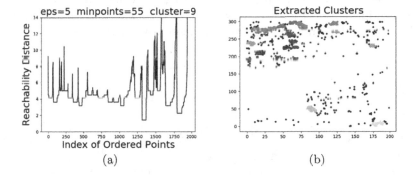

Fig. 7. Region partition in Grand Theatre

Figure 6 shows the results of the Bike-OPTICS algorithm in different regions. We choose Shanghai Grand Theatre and Shanghai World Expo Hall as center respectively, and take their surrounding areas within 2000 m radius as research regions. From Figs. 6 and 7, we can see that the two regions are divided into different numbers of clusters in Figs. 6(a) and 7(a). And in Figs. 6(b) and 7(b), every valley represents a cluster. Among them, purple represents noise which does not form any clustering. The Shanghai Grand Theatre locates at the center of Shanghai and the bikes distribute densely there, which results in more clusters. In contrast, the Expo Park is located in the suburbs of Shanghai, the bike distribution is very scattered and cannot form effective clusters.

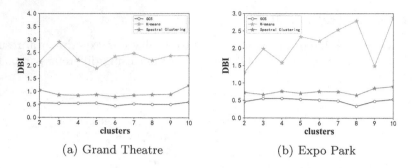

(a) Grand Theatre   (b) Expo Park

Fig. 8. Clustering results

The experimental results of the three algorithms above are shown in Fig. 8, with a horizontal axis representing the number of the predefined clusters, and the vertical axis representing the corresponding DBI value. We can see that: (i) Graph cluster with sparse constraint (GCS) outperforms the spectral clustering, which indicates that graph clustering with sparse constraint helps to improve the effectiveness of clustering. (ii) K-means can't handle graph structure very well, as the DBI value of k-means is much higher than spectral clustering and GCS. (iii) Different regions have different clustering results. In Fig. 8(a), GCS has the lowest DBI value when cluster number is 6, while it has the lowest DBI when clustering is 9 in Fig. 8(b), possibly because Expo Park is located in the suburbs of Shanghai and the activities are more diverse there.

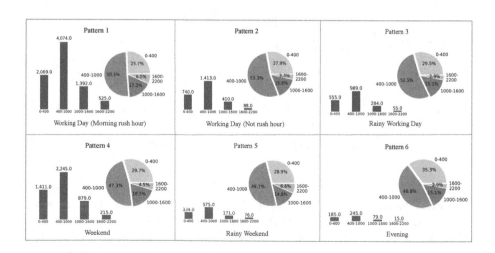

Fig. 9. Region partition in Grand Theatre

To further evaluate the performance of the model we proposed, we visualize and analyze the experimental results in another way. As shown in Fig. 9, our method has obtained six bike flow patterns including working day (morning rush hour), rainy working day and weekend, etc, regarding Shanghai Grand Theatre area as a study area. This proves that our method is effective for extracting bike flow patterns.

6   Conclusion

In this paper, we introduced a new method on bike flow patterns analysis through the bike trajectories data and POI data. At first, we divided urban Shanghai into small grid areas, and then proposed a density-based clustering method for merging neighboring grid areas into a cluster. With the clustering results, we constructed the bike flow matrix, which recorded flow between any two regions in the same time segment. To further explore the users' behavior patterns, we developed a graph clustering model with sparsity constraints. Finally, we estimated the performance of the model based on the large-scale real-world data collected from Mobike in Shanghai. The experimental results show that the method we proposed can effectively extract the bike flow pattern. In future work, we will apply the presented method to the demand analysis, POI recommendation, and other tasks.

References

1. Ai, Y., et al.: A deep learning approach on short-term spatiotemporal distribution forecasting of dockless bike-sharing system. Neural Comput. Appl. **31**, 1–13 (2018)
2. Ankerst, M., Dreunig, M., Kriegel, H., Ng, R., Sander, J.: Ordering points to identify the clustering structure. In: Proceedings of ACM SIGMOD, vol. 99 (2008)
3. Bao, J., He, T., Ruan, S., Li, Y., Zheng, Y.: Planning bike lanes based on sharing-bikes' trajectories, pp. 1377–1386 (2017)
4. Bauer, S., Noulas, A., Seaghdha, D.O., Clark, S., Mascolo, C.: Talking places: modelling and analysing linguistic content in foursquare, pp. 348–357 (2012)
5. Ester, M., Kriegel, H.P., Xu, X.: A density-based algorithm for discovering clusters a density-based algorithm for discovering clusters in large spatial databases with noise (1996)
6. Gast, N., Massonnet, G., Reijsbergen, D., Tribastone, M.: Probabilistic forecasts of bike-sharing systems for journey planning, pp. 703–712 (2015)
7. Hasan, S., Ukkusuri, S.V.: Urban activity pattern classification using topic models from online geo-location data. Transp. Res. Part C-Emerg. Technol. **44**, 363–381 (2014)
8. Hong, L., Zheng, Y., Yung, D., Shang, J., Zou, L.: Detecting urban black holes based on human mobility data. In: Proceedings of the 23rd SIGSPATIAL International Conference on Advances in Geographic Information Systems, p. 35. ACM (2015)
9. Kanaanizquierdo, S., Ziyatdinov, A., Pereralluna, A.: Multiview and multifeature spectral clustering using common eigenvectors. Pattern Recogn. Lett. **102**, 30–36 (2018)
10. Liu, J., Sun, L., Chen, W., Xiong, H.: Rebalancing bike sharing systems: a multi-source data smart optimization, pp. 1005–1014 (2016)

11. Liu, Z., Shen, Y., Zhu, Y.: Where will dockless shared bikes be stacked?:—parking hotspots detection in a new city. In: Proceedings of the 24th ACM SIGKDD International Conference on Knowledge Discovery & Data Mining, pp. 566–575. ACM (2018)
12. Pan, L., Cai, Q., Fang, Z., Tang, P., Huang, L.: Rebalancing dockless bike sharing systems. CoRR abs/1802.04592 (2018). http://arxiv.org/abs/1802.04592
13. Tian, F., Gao, B., Cui, Q., Chen, E., Liu, T.: Learning deep representations for graph clustering, pp. 1293–1299 (2014)
14. Yang, Z., Hu, J., Shu, Y., Cheng, P., Chen, J., Moscibroda, T.: Mobility modeling and prediction in bike-sharing systems, pp. 165–178 (2016)
15. Yuan, N.J., Zheng, Y., Xie, X., Wang, Y., Zheng, K., Xiong, H.: Discovering urban functional zones using latent activity trajectories. IEEE Trans. Knowl. Data Eng. **27**(3), 712–725 (2015)
16. Zhou, X., Noulas, A., Mascolo, C., Zhao, Z.: Discovering latent patterns of urban cultural interactions in WeChat for modern city planning. In: Knowledge Discovery and Data Mining, pp. 1069–1078 (2018)

Travel Time Estimation and Urban Key Routes Analysis Based on Call Detail Records Data: A Case Study of Guangzhou City

Weimin Mai[1,2], Shaohang Xie[1,2], and Xiang Chen[1,2]([✉])

[1] School of Electronics and Information Technology, Sun Yat-sen University,
Guangzhou 510006, China
chenxiang@mail.sysu.edu.cn
[2] Key Lab of EDA, Research Institute of Tsinghua University in Shenzhen (RITS),
Shenzhen 518075, China

Abstract. Nowadays, the study of urban traffic characteristics has become a major part of city management. With the popularization of the mobile communication network, the call detail records(CDR) have become important resources for the study of urban traffic, containing abundant temporal and spatial information of urban population. To excavate the traffic characteristics of Guangzhou city, this paper focuses on two aspects: travel time estimation and the analysis of key routes in urban area. First, we propose a method of estimating urban travel time based on traffic zones division using the traffic semantic attributes. According to the features of users flow extracted from CDR, we determine the traffic semantic attributes of the areas covered by base stations. With these semantic attributes, we cluster the cell areas into several traffic zones using a K-means method with a weighting dissimilarity measure. Then travel time between different positions in Guangzhou is estimated using the key locations of traffic zones, with an accuracy of 67%. Furthermore, we depict the key routes of Guangzhou city utilizing a DBSCAN method with the users' trajectories extracted from the CDR data. The results of obtained routes are validated by actual traffic conditions and provide some extra discoveries. Our works illustrate the effectiveness of CDR data in urban traffic and provide ideas for further research.

Keywords: Travel time estimation · Urban key routes · Call detail records

1 Introduction

The management of transportation has become a fundamental part in building a smart city. Traditional measurement of traffic conditions relies on on-road sensors. However, for most of cities, such real-time sensor systems are not sufficient

© ICST Institute for Computer Sciences, Social Informatics and Telecommunications Engineering 2019
Published by Springer Nature Switzerland AG 2019. All Rights Reserved
X. B. Zhai et al. (Eds.): MLICOM 2019, LNICST 294, pp. 659–676, 2019.
https://doi.org/10.1007/978-3-030-32388-2_55

due to their limited coverage and expensive cost. The quantity of mobile users is increasing that even in a small city there are huge numbers of mobile phone users. By 2013, mobile phone penetration rates have reached 128% and 89% in developed and developing countries, respectively [23]. CDR data in mobile cellular network contains abundant spatial and temporal information of urban populations since users in CDR data can be regarded as samples among the whole population of the city and the locations in CDR can be regarded as the samples of complete and continuous trajectories. The cost of collecting and storing CDR data is much lower than building an on-road sensor system, which motivates us to explore the generalizable methods of extracting traffic features based on CDR data.

Studies in many traffic aspects have been conducted using CDR data such as traffic flow estimation [4,12,28], mobility pattern analysis [5,8], daily trajectories analysis [18,19]. In this paper, we will mainly focus on utilizing CDR data to excavate traffic characteristics of urban area from two aspects: travel time estimation and the analysis of urban key routes. Both the knowledge of travel time between different locations of the city and the understanding of key routes bring us effective ways to find and settle the problems of urban congestion, providing strategies on planning urban roads. The awareness of commuting time can also guide urban residents on some daily services such as navigation and route selection. In addition, advertising and commercial site selection can be more targeted along these hot routes.

In this paper, Our contributions consist of two aspects:

- First, we propose a method of estimating urban travel time based on traffic zones division using the traffic semantic attributes. We associate the traffic time estimation with traffic zones, taking advantages of the inter-zone and intra-zone traffic characteristics. However, instead of dividing traffic zones with geographic information only, we introduce traffic semantic attributes obtained from features of users flow extracted from CDR into the process of traffic zone division, which makes the traffic zones more consistent with traffic ground true. Thus the estimation of travel time can be more convincing.
- Secondly, we apply a DBSCAN method to discover the key routes of Guangzhou city with the users' trajectories extracted from the CDR data. The obtained routes are validated by actual traffic conditions.

The rest of the paper is organized as follows. In Sect. 2, we take an overview of the study area and the data we use, and describe the process of data preprocessing. In Sect. 3, we determine the peak/off-peak hours of the city, which serve as the target periods of the following work. In Sect. 4, we explain how to estimate the travel time with traffic zones dividing method based on traffic semantic attributes and then evaluate the accuracies of the results. In Sect. 5, the key routes of the city are generated and analyzed according to actual traffic conditions. In Sect. 6 we will make a conclusion to the whole paper.

2 Data Description and Preprocessing

2.1 CDR Data

In this study, CDR of 3 weeks in May 2018 in Guangzhou are used, including Connection Management(CM) and Mobility Management(MM) records. The privacy-related information such as IMSI and cell-phone number have been encrypted and mapped into some certain strings corresponding to the original records.

Data cleaning is conducted because records in the original data may miss information in some fields and not all fields are useful for traffic study. The most important information of traffic analysis mainly includes three aspects: person, time and place. Therefore, we omit some fields other than IMSI, time and base station location and delete those records with missing fields. Then all remaining records are reformatted as shown in Table 1.

Table 1. Reformatted CDR

User ID	Time	Cell ID	Longitude, Latitude
001	2018-05-17 23:14:50	14	(113.2896, 23.0303)
002	2018-05-18 00:16:59	20	(113.2880, 23.0199)
...	...	...	...

The field *Time* is the middle instant of the duration of a record, representing when this record occurs. Note that we cannot know the exact location of a user when he generates a record, but can only estimate his location roughly through the location of the base station he accesses. The coverage radius of a base station in dense areas ranges from tens of meters to hundreds of meters, while the coverage radius in suburban areas can be several kilometers.

2.2 Study Area

The study was conducted in Guangzhou, a megacity in China with area more than 7,000 square kilometers and a population over 10 million.

If the whole city is considered into the study, some traffic characteristics tend to be covered by the average effect of the surrounding counties. Besides, traffic flow of a mega city may differ a lot between weekdays and weekends. Therefore, we only consider records of weekdays and limit the study area to downtown area of Guangzhou which contains 2225 base stations.

2.3 Data Preprocessing

The total number of valid reformatted records is about 1.57 billion. Since our purpose is to study the traffic characteristics such as travel time and key routes, we should first extract the OD (origin-destination) records that reflecting the users' location changing and the corresponding time from the CDR data. We group the reformatted records by *UserID* and sort them in ascending order according to *Time*. An OD record is generated from two adjacent ordered CDRs with the same user but different locations, which is shown in Table 2.

Table 2. OD records

User ID	Origin location	Destination location	Occurrence time	Duration (min)
033	(113.5054, 23.0655)	(113.5251, 23.0674)	2018-05-21 17:57:31	31
...	...	...	...	...

In Table 2, *OccurrenceTime* is the middle instant of the *Time* of two adjacent ordered CDRs, which is used to describe which period the OD records belong to. *Duration* means the difference of the *Time* of adjacent ordered CDRs.

Not all the OD records obtained above can reflect traffic characteristics because of the noise. On the one hand, duration or travel speed of some OD records deviate from the actual urban traffic conditions seriously. For example, *Duration* in an OD record can be several hours but travel time between the furthest two positions in a city cannot be more than 130 min. Such a record can only indicate that the user has moved but can provide little valuable information of the actual travel time. On the other hand, although a user did not take a travel, his positions may switch repeatedly among several adjacent base stations when the signal received by the user were at a low level. OD records generated from these conditions are useless to the study of urban traffic, so they are filtered out by the steps listed below:

- Delete the OD records whose *Duration*s are shorter than 5 min or longer than 130 min in consideration of the size of Guangzhou.
- Delete the OD records whose speeds are less than 5 km/h or more than 90 km/h in consideration of the traffic speed defined by the ratio of the linear distance between two positions to the duration.
- Delete the OD records generated by a user who switching repeatedly among several base stations.

About 280 million valid OD records are obtained after the above steps, which will become the basis of the following sections.

3   Determine Peak/Off-Peak Hours

Traffic characteristics vary at different slots in a day. The study on travel time and key routes is more valuable when we focus on specific periods instead of the whole day. Thus, in this section, we first determine the peak and off-peak hours of the city based on OD records.

An index proposed in [10] is adopted. A day is divided into 24 hour-slots, for each $slot_i$, a ratio is calculated as follows:

$$ratio_i = \frac{count\,(min)}{t_{ci}}. \tag{1}$$

t_{ci} is the total number of ODs in $slot_i$, while min_i corresponds to the ODs whose $Duration$ are almost the shortest among the ODs with the same $OriginLocation$ and $DestinationLocation$. The ratio should be smaller in peak hours than in off-peak hours. The results of the each slot arranged in ascending order are shown in Table 3.

Table 3. OD conditions in each hour-slot

slot	count (min)	t_{ci}	$ratio_i$
8	2123878	17826920	11.914%
18	2297994	18782738	12.235%
7	1664880	13433255	12.394%
17	2276326	18251610	12.472%
19	1845927	14795896	12.476%
12	1910879	15294000	12.494%
13	1822975	14498632	12.573%
9	2136199	16787798	12.725%
11	2013125	15644336	12.868%
20	1701205	13209582	12.879%
16	2127293	16494872	12.897%
6	790046	6076080	13.003%
14	1988096	15247447	13.039%
10	2055462	15763727	13.039%
15	2038210	15525905	13.128%
21	1626446	12379002	13.139%
22	1392017	10354612	13.443%
1	535763	3855155	13.897%
0	704587	5060986	13.922%
23	1009759	723423	13.958%
5	451215	3157483	14.290%
2	444051	3079807	14.418%
3	409281	2822401	14.501%
4	405517	2709823	14.965%

From the ratios of all hour-slots, we can conclude three peak periods of the city, which are consistent with our daily knowledge. Morning peak is defined as slot7-slot9, noon peak is defined as slot11-slot13 and evening peak is defined as slot17-slot19. The off-peak hours mainly lie in early morning.

4   Urban Travel Time Estimation

Traffic patterns vary from region to region. Based on the inter-features and intra-features of two different traffic zones, a method of estimating travel time was proposed in [10]. However, the method they used to divide traffic zones focused mainly on geographical proximity but ignored the information on traffic. In this section, we will introduce a method to estimate travel time based on traffic zones division with traffic semantic attributes.

4.1   Traffic Zones Division

To estimate the travel time, we should divide the traffic zones in advance. A traffic zone can be regarded as the combination of a group of cell-areas covered by adjacent base stations. The main idea of dividing the traffic zones is to extract the traffic features of the cell-areas and then partition the cell-areas into different clusters using these features. Dong et al. [7] proposed a method to cluster cell-areas according to the semantic attributes of the base stations, which is adopted in our work.

First, we idealize the coverage of the base stations, considering that they do not overlap with each other. Then, the coverage area of a base station can be represented by its corresponding Voronoi polygon [9], and a traffic zone is composed of several adjacent polygons. Part of the Voronoi plot is shown in the Fig. 1. The polygons of solid line are the areas covered by the base stations and the blue dots in the polygon represent the position of the base stations.

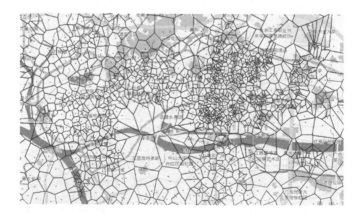

Fig. 1. Voronoi polygons division (Color figure online)

As mentioned above, we need to extract the traffic semantic attributes of cell-areas as one of the characteristics before dividing the traffic zones. This attribute is used to describe the main function of a cell-area in urban traffic networks. Traffic features such as real-time volume(V_t), hourly inflow(V_i), hourly outflow(V_o), hourly increment flow(V_{inc}), peak and valley values are considered when we use K-means methods to cluster all cell-areas into two categories of traffic semantics: working-entertainment areas and residential areas [7]. A 104-dimension feature vector $x_i = \left(x_i^1, x_i^2, \cdots, x_i^{104}\right)$ is constructed for every cell-area, the meaning of each dimension of the vector is described in the Table 4.

Table 4. Vector to determine traffic semantic attributes

Demension	Description
$\left(x_i^1, x_i^2, \cdots, x_i^{24}\right)$	Slot V_t, generated according to the total number of different users in a cell-area of each slot
$\left(x_i^{25}, x_i^{26}, \cdots, x_i^{48}\right)$	Slot V_i, generated according to the number of incoming users in a cell-area of each slot
$\left(x_i^{49}, x_i^{50}, \cdots, x_i^{72}\right)$	Slot V_o, generated according to the number of outgoing users in a cell-area of each slot
$\left(x_i^{73}, x_i^{74}, \cdots, x_i^{96}\right)$	Slot V_{inc}, generated according to the increment number of users in a cell-area of each slot, calculated from $V_{inc} = V_i - V_o$, a negative result is valid
$\left(x_i^{97}, x_i^{98}, \cdots, x_i^{104}\right)$	Peak values and valley values of the four kinds of features above

Results of two kinds of attributes are shown in Fig. 2. The base stations of the first attribute occupy a high proportion in Central Business District and other typical working-entertainment areas like Pazhou Exhibition Area, Baiyun Mountain Tourist Area and Beijing Road Business Area. Therefore, the base stations in the first cluster are tagged with working-entertainment zone attribute. By contrast, the distribution of base stations in the second cluster is not as concentrated as that of the first cluster. However, their proportion in typical residential areas like Liwan District and Baiyun District is relatively high so the base stations in the second cluster are tagged with residential attribute. These semantic attributes of cell-areas will be used as a dimension in feature vector when merging the cell-areas into traffic zones.

We believe that a traffic zone can be formed by connecting the adjacent cell-areas. Therefore, for traffic zones division, the most important factors that influence the results are geographical latitude and longitude, that is, the closer the cell-areas are, the more likely they are divided into the same zone. However, it is obviously unreasonable to only rely on the geographical latitude and longitude information, since this may ignore some information that matches with the actual traffic conditions. If a group of cell-areas is mostly of residential attribute while another group is mostly of entertainment attribute, it is more appropriate to divide them into different traffic zones. When the traffic attributes are taken into

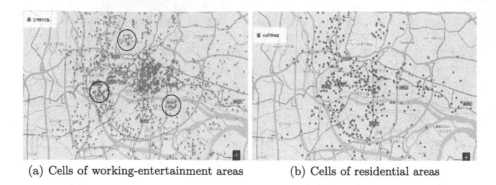

(a) Cells of working-entertainment areas   (b) Cells of residential areas

Fig. 2. Traffic semantic attributes

consideration, the boundary of traffic zones can be more diversified to match the more complex actual traffic conditions.

Using geographical longitude and latitude, traffic semantic attributes and the difference of average V_{inc} between morning peak and evening peak, we construct a 4-dimension feature vector for each cell area, where the traffic semantic attribute is either 0 or 1 (0 means the working-entertainment area and 1 represents the residential area). Then a K-means clustering method with a weighting dissimilarity measure [7] was applied to acquire traffic zones.

The K-means method needs to define the number of traffic zones to be divided in advance. Different values of K will lead to different division results. As for a medium or large city, it is generally divided into 50–100 traffic zones [26]. Since we only study on the downtown area of Guangzhou, the number of traffic zones is reduced to 20–60. However, method in [7] does not explain how to evaluate the clustering results to find the appropriate parameters. When evaluating whether a result is effective to estimate the travel time, the primary consideration is whether both the numbers of OD records within and between traffic zones are appropriate. A ratio described in [10] is chosen to determine the proper number K of traffic zones, which is explained by Eq. (2). The smaller the ratio is, the more appropriate the division result is.

$$Ratio = \frac{count(intraTravel) + count\,(invalidInterTravel)}{count\,(totalTravel)}. \tag{2}$$

As shown in Fig. 3, the base stations are regarded as points on a two-dimensional plane. Suppose $Z1$ and $Z2$ are two traffic zones, lines with red tags are $interTravels$ while lines with blue tags are $intraTravels$. If the number of the $interTravels$ between two zones is less than a threshold value, then all these $interTravels$ are called $invalidInterTravels$.

The ratio results are shown in Fig. 4. Finally, $K = 37$ is chosen as the parameter of K-means algorithm and the city is divided into 37 traffic zones as shown in Fig. 5. For each traffic zone, a major junction within it is selected as the key

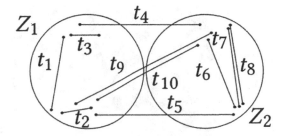

Fig. 3. *InterTravel* and *intraTravel* [10] (Color figure online)

location of this zone. The blue markers represent the original clustering centroids and the red car-shape markers are the selected key location.

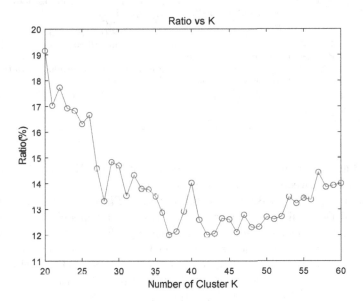

Fig. 4. Ratio of different K

4.2 Travel Time Estimation

By the steps above, we have divided the Guangzhou City into several traffic zones with traffic key locations. Now we apply the travel time estimation algorithm using key locations [10] to estimate the travel time between two positions in the city. The algorithm is explained in Algorithm 1.

Tables 5 and 6 show the $interTime_{avg}$ in morning peak and evening peak. Due to space limitation, we select only the first 13 zones to display. Some cells

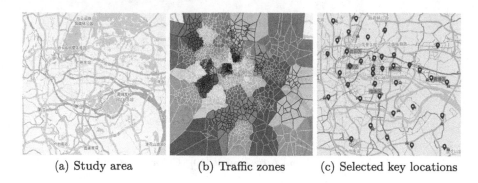

(a) Study area   (b) Traffic zones   (c) Selected key locations

Fig. 5. Results of traffic zones division (Color figure online)

Algorithm 1. Travel time estimation using key locations

1: Calculating $time(C_i, C_j)$ for each $interTravel$ with origin $P_i \in Z_i$ and destination $P_j \in Z_j$, where C_i and C_j are the key locations of Z_i and Z_j respectively:

$$time(C_i, C_j) = time(P_i, P_j) \times \frac{Dist(C_i, C_j)}{partialDist(P_i, P_j) + shortestDist(P_i, C_iC_j) + shortestDist(P_j, C_iC_j)}$$

2: For each pair of distinct combination of C_i and C_j, averaging all corresponding $time(C_i, C_j)$ obtained above to get $interTime_{avg}(Z_i, Z_j)$;

3: Calculate $intraSpeed_{avg}(Z_i)$ of each zone Z_i using $intraTravel$ corresponding to that zone;

4: Estimating travel time between any two positions $P_i \in Z_i$ and $P_j \in Z_j$:

$$time_{est}(P_i, P_j) = \frac{shortestDist(P_i, C_iC_j)}{intraSpeed_{avg}(Z_i)} + interTime_{avg}(Z_i, Z_j) \times \frac{partialDist(P_i, P_j)}{dist(C_i, C_j)} + \frac{shortestDist(P_i, C_iC_j)}{intraSpeed_{avg}(Z_i)}$$

---

are marked as "/", which denotes there are no sufficient OD records to estimate the travel time between the corresponding zones.

As can be seen from Tables 5 and 6, most $interTime_{avg}$ between two certain zones differ little in different peaks. However, for some specific zones, there are obvious differences between morning and evening peak. For example, it takes only 23 min in the morning peak hours while about 57.6 min in the evening to travel from Zone3 (lies in the center of the city) to Zone19 (lies in the northwest of the city). This result is consistent with the actual traffic conditions in Guangzhou that during the evening peak hours, the roads from the center of the city to Baiyun District are seriously congested due to the people returning home from work.

Table 7 shows the $intraSpeed_{avg}$ of the traffic zones. We can see that $intraSpeed_{avg}$ is relatively stable in each zone during different peaks.

To evaluate the effectiveness of this method in our study, we estimate the travel time of 30000 location pairs generated randomly in our study area, and then compare the results with the estimation in AMAP API. When the time deviation is less than 20%, the estimation of travel time is regarded to be accurate. The final accuracy of our method is about 67%. Inaccurate estimations occur mainly in the conditions that the two positions of the pair are very close to each other(travel time is less than 7 min) or they lie in two remote zones (travel time is more than 90 min).

Table 5. *interTime* of morning Peak. Unit: minute

	0	1	2	3	4	5	6	7	8	9	10	11	12
0	/	26.4	23.7	25.2	21	47.9	/	/	36.7	17	/	41.6	/
1	19.1	/	25.4	26.6	16.7	30.7	/	34.9	21.7	18.2	25.2	22.9	19.1
2	/	27.4	/	31.4	24.8	43.3	29.3	31.3	26.1	23.9	25.1	26.8	/
3	60.5	33.5	34.9	/	36.1	30.6	89.8	33.3	32.3	27.6	34.1	36.8	60.5
4	31.8	16.3	22.8	28.3	/	32	/	26.5	25	19	26.9	18.6	31.8
5	49.5	37.1	37.8	31.4	36.5	/	37.4	56.2	23.6	21.9	48.2	30.7	49.5
6	/	31.4	33.1	52	/	/	/	19.6	/	/	35.1	/	/
7	/	30.5	29.1	28.4	26.9	52.3	20.5	/	24.4	/	25.1	53.8	/
8	14.9	26.2	30.1	24.5	28.3	22.5	/	24	/	18	46.1	27.9	14.9
9	18.2	20.2	23.6	22.9	16.8	39.1	/	25.7	27.5	/	/	26	18.2
10	/	24.4	21.8	29.4	24.8	36.5	30.8	44.9	32.3	30.8	/	30.7	/
11	36.7	23.7	23.5	34.4	21	32.8	/	55.5	26.8	19.5	30.1	/	36.7
12	/	26.4	23.7	25.2	21	47.9	/	/	36.7	17	/	41.6	/

Table 6. *interTime* of evening Peak. Unit: minute

	0	1	2	3	4	5	6	7	8	9	10	11	12
0	/	52.5	/	25.2	20.3	45.4	/	/	35.8	16.8	/	46	/
1	14.7	/	26.1	35.7	16.7	32.7	/	32.9	22	19.7	25.7	23.7	31.7
2	23	27.1	/	34.6	23.7	45.1	31	31.9	26.1	24.7	24.3	26.7	14.9
3	55.1	38.4	36.9	/	42.6	29.7	90.6	38.1	36.4	23.7	35.2	46.5	37.3
4	33.1	16.1	22.8	34.8	/	33.1	/	50.9	24.7	23.4	27.3	19.2	26.1
5	/	32.6	41.6	33.2	33.3	/	/	60.6	21.9	20.1	46.7	30.3	30.8
6	/	30.3	30.8	50.2	/	/	/	22.7	/	/	32.1	/	15.1
7	52.1	35.7	29.2	29.9	26.1	49.8	18.8	/	27	27.7	27.6	50.9	27.3
8	29.1	24.8	30.9	30.2	24.3	24.1	/	24.2	/	20.2	41.7	27.8	20.8
9	18.9	19.2	19.5	30.3	19.1	31.3	/	/	26.9	/	/	15.9	22.4
10	37.6	24.8	25	27.3	27.2	42.3	38	56.3	36.5	37.1	/	32.9	25.9
11	35	22.8	23.6	40.6	19.8	33.5	/	71.5	27.3	22.7	30	/	33.6
12	/	27.6	12.9	34.1	21.7	43.1	/	27.9	19.7	21.4	25.8	38.9	/

Table 7. *interSpeed* of morning Peak and evening Peak. Unit: m/minute

Zones ID	0	1	2	3	4	5	6	7	8	9	10	11	12
Morn	348	327	362	435	353	375	437	407	354	399	461	388	322
Eve	334	327	364	411	359	369	423	408	358	404	450	390	316

Thus, it can be seen that OD information extracted from CDR data can reflect the information of travel time between traffic zones to some extent. Dividing traffic zones based on traffic semantics is a relatively helpful method for travel time estimation.

5   Urban Key Routes Analysis

In the previous section, we study the travel time estimation of Guangzhou city, revealing the characteristics in aspect of traffic zones. In this section, we focus on characteristics of another aspect: the key routes of the city.

With OD records, we can generate a trajectory for each user. The general idea of finding the key routes is to group the mobile phone users' trajectories into several clusters according to their similarity, and then from each cluster we can obtain a common route. Users' trajectories extracted from the CDR data are composed of a series of base stations' locations where the user stayed, which means these trajectories are of coarse granularity. Since the trajectories differ in length and time interval, it is difficult to cluster the trajectories according to Euclidean distance or cosine similarity.

To settle these problems, we use a DBSCAN method with length of common sub-track [16] as distance metric, which is more robust to trajectory noise and able to deal with clusters of any shape. The similarity of two trajectories Tr_i, Tr_j is defined as the ratio of their longest common subsequence [6] Tr_{ij}^{LCS} to the length of the shorter trajectory. See Algorithm 2 for details.

Algorithm 2. Obtaining urban key routes with DBSCAN method

1: **Step 1**: Calculating the distance matrix D of all trajectories.

2: $sim(Tr_i, Tr_j) = \begin{cases} 0, & min(L(Tr_i), L(Tr_j)) < \delta \\ \frac{L(Tr_{ij}^{LCS})}{min(L(Tr_i), L(Tr_j))}, & min(L(Tr_i), L(Tr_j)) \geq \delta \end{cases}$

3: $D_{i,j} = 1 - sim(Tr_i, Tr_j)$

4: D is stored by sparsed matrix.

5: **Step 2**: Trajectories clustering.

6: Using distance matrix D, cluster all trajectories into a set of clusters C with DBSCAN method.

7: $C = \{C_1, C_2, \cdots, C_m, \cdots\}$ where $C_m = \{Tr_1, Tr_2, \cdots, Tr_n, \cdots\}$

8: **Step 3**: Trajectories merging.

9: **for** $C_m \in C$ **do**

10:    $Tr_{repre}^m = Union(Tr_{ij}^{LCS}), Tr_i, Tr_j \in C_m$

11: **end for**

The representative trajectories of all clusters obtained above indicate the key routes of the city. Taking the evening peak hours defined in Sect. 3 as an example, we use OD records of one day, grouping them by users and ordering them chronologically to from users' trajectories.

Among all trajectories in this period, some contain more than 50 points while more than 90% trajectories contain no more than 11 points. In order to simplify the following task, we sample 11 points randomly on those trajectories with length more than 11. After the process mentioned above, we obtain 803,909 trajectories in total. The density of non-one values of the distance matrix is about 0.1%.

The parameters of DBSCAN algorithm are MinPts $= 1000$ and eps $= 0.5$, which lead to the results of 11 clusters. Clustering results of all trajectories clusters are shown in Table 8.

Table 8. Trajectories number of the clusters

Cluster ID	Number of trajectories
1	133740
2	3578
3	2176
4	1816
5	3335
6	3002
7	1356
8	1846
9	3631
10	2710
11	1356
Noise trajectory	645363
Full trajectory	803909

To generate smooth representative routes, we do not merge all Tr^{LCS} of a cluster into a trajectory. Instead, for each cluster, we count the number of each Tr^{LCS} and arrange them in ascending order. Only the Tr^{LCS} whose number is greater than 90% of the largest number of the cluster will be merge. The key routes in the downtown area of Guangzhou are shown in Fig. 6.

As can be seen from Table 8, in all trajectories clusters, the largest one consists of more than 0.13 million trajectories while the other ten clusters are relatively small. The key route of the first cluster is merged by many paths from Yuexiu District to Liwan District.

We can see that most of the key routes (Route 3, 5, 6, 8, 9, 10, 11) pass through the CBD area(west part of Tianhe District and east part of Yuexiu district) of Guangzhou. These routes correspond to North Guangzhou Avenue, Tiyuxi Road, Tianhe Road and several nearby roads in actual traffic networks. In the actual traffic network, each of the roads mentioned above has a high traffic flow. These roads locate near the most prosperous business areas, linking the regions of office buildings and the biggest shopping mall of Guangzhou city.

Fig. 6. Key routes of Guangzhou in evening peak

The traffic of the key routes mainly flows from the center of the city to the periphery of the city such as Baiyun District(in the northwest of the city) and Huangpu District(in the east of the city). This is a typical phenomenon of a metropolis. Most of the citizens in Guangzhou come from other cities and many of them tend to choose their house in the areas like Baiyun District, Panyu District and Huangpu District because of the price. In the evening peak, the car flows of driving home cause the roads scaterring from the center to suburb busy.

Three key routes (Route 1, Route 2, Route 8) locate closely in Liwan District in the west of the city, showing that these regions are crowded. When it comes to the traffic ground truth, these regions are the old town of Guangzhou, where there are several relatively narrow roads owning to the limitations of previous urban planning. It is worth mentioning that one of the key routes (Route 3) flows towards the city center from a periphery area in the southeast of the city. We find that the starting point of this route lies in Guangzhou Higher Education Mega Center, where most of the people working there live outside this area since it is mainly used for education. At evening peaks, a great quantity of students go to the city center of entertainment, which also contributes to this distinctive key route.

The discoveries mentioned above validate the key routes obtained from CDR data and can serve as a reference for urban roads planning. The results also demonstrate the applicability of mobile CDR data in the field of urban traffic.

6   Related Work

Researches Based on CDR: Ubiquitous mobile phones and the massive records they generate present new opportunities to excavate the spatial and temporal information of urban areas, which motivates many researchers to conduct studies on multiple aspects about cities with call detail records. For instance, Blumenstock et al. [2], Smith-Clarke et al. [20] and Frias-Martinez et al. [21] study the strategies for predicting economic levels of urban regions respectively. Moreover, Blumenstock et al. [3] also analysis the socioeconomic status of individuals combining CDRs with other survey ground truth. A bunch of works aim to localize the residential areas of the CDR users [9] with the or explore the periodic patterns on different scales [13,22,24]. Human location and mobility have become the major research fields with a lot of works such as [1,15]. Recently, owing to the limitations of data granularity, more and more studies take advantages of mobile traffic data gradually. Different from the research mentioned above, however, we mainly focus on estimating the traffic characteristics.

Traffic Time Estimation: Traffic time estimation and its application are traditional issues in the research field of transportation. Most of these studies are based on data of road networks. [14] designs a travel time model that separates trip travel times into link travel times and intersection delays. A fixed point approach is proposed in [17] to estimate travel time with simultaneous path inference. [25] introduces a good method to estimate time combining the temporal and historical contexts learned from different trajectories. [10] shows a good example to analyze travel time with OD information extracted from CDRs, associating the travels with traffic regions. Our work draw lessons from the idea of analyzing time according to traffic zones and take advantages of CDR data.

Urban Region Division: Many studies have worked on divide the urban areas into different regions to discover what functions they provide to the whole cities, which benefit the urban planning a lot. [29] proposes a topic-model-based method to divide urban regions, setting a precedent for combining POI data and human mobility in this field. Some other works such as Dong et al. [7] and Xu et al. [27] employ clustering-based algorithms to classify regions into several groups automatically. The regional semantics of these above-mentioned works may differ since they focus on different aspects of urban features.

Urban Trajectories Analysis: As for the analysis towards urban trajectories, Schlaich et al. [18] develop a method to generate trajectories of mobile phone users using the location-updating sequences and compare them with actual road networks. Hoteit et al. [11] put forward an idea of utilizing interpolation methods to estimate travel trajectories and find the positions of hotspots.

7   Conclusion

In this paper, based on the CDR data, we introduce traffic semantic attributes into the process of traffic zones division before estimating the travel time between any two positions of the city, making the inter-zone and intra-zone charateristics more consistent with actual traffic conditions. The accuracy of our proposing travel time estimating method can achieve 67%. This method provides ideas for estimating the travel time in urban area in a low-cost way. Furthermore, making use of the individual trajectories extracted from the CDR data, we analyze the key routes in Guangzhou city using a DBSCAN trajectories clustering method. These routes can be validated by the actual conditions of the city, providing some new discoveries and visual references for the planning of urban roads and further study on urban traffic. Both of these two aspects of urban traffic study highlight the value of CDR data in urban traffic and provide ideas for further research.

Acknowledgement. The work is supported in part by NSFC (No. U1711263), Science, Technology and Innovation Commission of Shenzhen Municipality (No. JCYJ20170816151823313), States Key Project of Research and Development Plan (No. 2017YFE0121300-6) and MOE-CMCC Joint Research Fund of China (MCM20160101).

References

1. Becker, R., et al.: Human mobility characterization from cellular network data. Commun. ACM **56**(1), 74–82 (2013)
2. Blumenstock, J., Cadamuro, G., On, R.: Predicting poverty and wealth from mobile phone metadata. Science **350**(6264), 1073–1076 (2015)
3. Blumenstock, J., Eagle, N.: Mobile divides: gender, socioeconomic status, and mobile phone use in Rwanda. In: Proceedings of the 4th ACM/IEEE International Conference on Information and Communication Technologies and Development, p. 6. ACM (2010)
4. Caceres, N., Romero, L.M., Benitez, F.G., Castillo, J.M.D.: Traffic flow estimation models using cellular phone data. IEEE Trans. Intell. Transp. Syst. **13**(3), 1430–1441 (2012)
5. Calabrese, F., Diao, M., Lorenzo, G.D., Ferreira, J., Ratti, C.: Understanding individual mobility patterns from urban sensing data: a mobile phone trace example. Transp. Res. Part C **26**(1), 301–313 (2013)
6. Cormen, T.H., Leiserson, C.E., Rivest, R.L., Stein, C.: Introduction to Algorithms, 3nd edn, pp. 390–396. The MIT Press, Cambridge (2009)
7. Dong, H., et al.: Traffic zone division based on big data from mobile phone base stations. Transp. Res. Part C **58**, 278–291 (2015)
8. Frias-Martinez, V., Soguero, C., Frias-Martinez, E.: Estimation of urban commuting patterns using cellphone network data. In: Proceedings of the ACM SIGKDD International Workshop on Urban Computing, UrbComp 2012, pp. 9–16. ACM, New York (2012). https://doi.org/10.1145/2346496.2346499. http://doi.acm.org/10.1145/2346496.2346499
9. Frias-Martinez, V., Virseda, J., Rubio, A., Frias-Martinez, E.: Towards large scale technology impact analyses: automatic residential localization from mobile phone-call data. In: Proceedings of the 4th ACM/IEEE International Conference on Information and Communication Technologies and Development, p. 11. ACM (2010)
10. Hasan, M.M., Ali, M.E.: Estimating travel time of Dhaka city from mobile phone call detail records. In: International Conference on Information and Communication Technologies and Development (2017)

11. Hoteit, S., Secci, S., Sobolevsky, S., Ratti, C., Pujolle, G.: Estimating human trajectories and hotspots through mobile phone data. Comput. Netw. **64**, 296–307 (2014)
12. Järv, O., Ahas, R., Saluveer, E., Derudder, B., Witlox, F.: Mobile phones in a traffic flow: a geographical perspective to evening rush hour traffic analysis using call detail records. PLoS ONE **7**(11), e49171–e49171 (2012)
13. Järv, O., Ahas, R., Witlox, F.: Understanding monthly variability in human activity spaces: a twelve-month study using mobile phone call detail records. Transp. Res. Part C: Emerg. Technol. **38**, 122–135 (2014)
14. Jenelius, E., Koutsopoulos, H.N.: Travel time estimation for urban road networks using low frequency probe vehicle data. Transp. Res. Part B: Methodol. **53**, 64–81 (2013)
15. Palchykov, V., Mitrović, M., Jo, H.H., Saramäki, J., Pan, R.K.: Inferring human mobility using communication patterns. Sci. Rep. **4**, 6174 (2014)
16. Qin, S., Zuo, Y., Wang, Y., Xuan, S., Dong, H.: Travel trajectories analysis based on call detail record data. In: Control and Decision Conference (2017)
17. Rahmani, M., Koutsopoulos, H.N., Jenelius, E.: Travel time estimation from sparse floating car data with consistent path inference: a fixed point approach. Transp. Res. Part C: Emerg. Technol. **85**, 628–643 (2017)
18. Schlaich, J., Otterstätter, T., Friedrich, M., et al.: Generating trajectories from mobile phone data. In: Proceedings of the 89th Annual Meeting Compendium of Papers, Transportation Research Board of the National Academies (2010)
19. Sevtsuk, A., Ratti, C.: Does urban mobility have a daily routine? Learning from the aggregate data of mobile networks. J. Urban Technol. **17**(1), 41–60 (2010)
20. Smith-Clarke, C., Mashhadi, A., Capra, L.: Poverty on the cheap: estimating poverty maps using aggregated mobile communication networks. In: Proceedings of the SIGCHI Conference on Human Factors in Computing Systems, pp. 511–520. ACM (2014)
21. Soto, V., Frias-Martinez, V., Virseda, J., Frias-Martinez, E.: Prediction of socioeconomic levels using cell phone records. In: Konstan, J.A., Conejo, R., Marzo, J.L., Oliver, N. (eds.) UMAP 2011. LNCS, vol. 6787, pp. 377–388. Springer, Heidelberg (2011). https://doi.org/10.1007/978-3-642-22362-4_35
22. Trasarti, R., et al.: Discovering urban and country dynamics from mobile phone data with spatial correlation patterns. Telecommun. Policy **39**(3–4), 347–362 (2015)
23. ITU: International Telecommunication Union (2013). https://www.itu.int/en/ITU-D/Statistics/Documents/facts/ICTFactsFigures2013-e.pdf. Accessed 4 Mar 2019
24. Vieira, M.R., Frías-Martínez, E., Bakalov, P., Frías-Martínez, V., Tsotras, V.J.: Querying spatio-temporal patterns in mobile phone-call databases. In: 2010 Eleventh International Conference on Mobile Data Management, pp. 239–248. IEEE (2010)
25. Wang, Y., Zheng, Y., Xue, Y.: Travel time estimation of a path using sparse trajectories. In: Proceedings of the 20th ACM SIGKDD International Conference on Knowledge Discovery and Data Mining, pp. 25–34. ACM (2014)
26. Xiao-Dan, L.I., Yang, X.G.: Study on traffic zone division based on spatial clustering analysis. Comput. Eng. Appl. **45**(5), 19–22 (2009)
27. Xu, F., Li, Y., Wang, H., Zhang, P., Jin, D.: Understanding mobile traffic patterns of large scale cellular towers in urban environment. IEEE/ACM Trans. Netw. (TON) **25**(2), 1147–1161 (2017)

28. Yi, H., Edara, P., Sun, C.: Traffic flow forecasting for urban work zones. IEEE Trans. Intell. Transp. Syst. **16**(4), 1761–1770 (2015)
29. Yuan, J., Zheng, Y., Xie, X.: Discovering regions of different functions in a city using human mobility and POIs. In: Proceedings of the 18th ACM SIGKDD International Conference on Knowledge Discovery and Data Mining, pp. 186–194. ACM (2012)

Task Allocation in Multi-agent Systems Using Many-objective Evolutionary Algorithm NSGA-III

Jing Zhou[1,2(✉)], Xiaozhe Zhao[1], Dongdong Zhao[3], and Zhong Lin[2]

[1] Faculty of Management and Economics, Dalian University of Technology,
Dalian, China
zj_0562@163.com
[2] Operation Software and Simulation Institute, Dalian Naval Academy,
Dalian, China
[3] School of Computer Science and Technology,
Wuhan University of Technology, Wuhan, China

Abstract. Task allocation is an important issue in multi-agent systems, and finding the optimal solution of task allocation has been demonstrated to be an NP-hard problem. In many scenarios, agents are equipped with not only communication resources but also computing resources, so that tasks can be allocated and executed more efficiently in a distributed and parallel manner. Presently, many methods have been proposed for distributed task allocation in multi-agent systems. Most of them are either based on complete/full search or local search, and the former usually can find the optimal solutions but requires high computational cost and communication cost; the latter is usually more efficient but could not guarantee the solution quality. Evolutionary algorithm (EA) is a promising optimization algorithm which could be more efficient than the full search algorithms and might have better search ability than the local search algorithms, but it is rarely applied to distributed task allocation in multi-agent systems. In this paper, we propose a distributed task allocation method based on EA. We choose the many-objective EA called NSGA-III to optimize four objectives (i.e., maximizing the number of successfully allocated and executed tasks, maximizing the gain by executing tasks, minimizing the resource cost, and minimizing the time cost) simultaneously. Experimental results show the effectiveness of the proposed method, and compared with the full search strategy, the proposed method could solve task allocation problems with more agents and tasks.

Keywords: Multi-agent system · Task allocation · Evolutionary algorithm

1 Introduction

Along with the rapid development of Internet of Things (IoTs) and wireless communication techniques, multi-agent systems are increasingly employed in industry and military fields. In multi-agent systems, there are usually a number of devices (e.g., robots and unmanned aerial vehicles) that can execute specified tasks automatically and intelligently.

© ICST Institute for Computer Sciences, Social Informatics and Telecommunications Engineering 2019
Published by Springer Nature Switzerland AG 2019. All Rights Reserved
X. B. Zhai et al. (Eds.): MLICOM 2019, LNICST 294, pp. 677–692, 2019.
https://doi.org/10.1007/978-3-030-32388-2_56

Task allocation is one of the most important issues in multi-agent systems, and it directly influences the system effectiveness. However, it has been demonstrated that finding the optimal solutions of task allocation in multi-agent systems would be an NP-hard problem [1]. Several objectives need to be optimized in the problem, e.g., maximizing the number of tasks that can be successfully allocated and executed by the agents, maximizing the benefits achieved by executing tasks, minimizing the resources cost during the task execution and minimizing the time cost. In many scenarios, agents are equipped with both communication resources and computing resources, and they can cooperate with a control centre in a distributed/decentralized manner to search for the optimal solutions of task allocation more efficiently.

Presently, many methods have been proposed for distributed task allocation in multi-agent systems, and they can be mainly divided into two classes depending on while they are based on the complete/full search strategy or local search strategy [2]. The methods based on the full search strategy, e.g., [3–7], can usually find the optimal task allocation solutions but they require a large amount of computational cost and communication cost, and it will become unbearable in large-scale systems (e.g., the number of agents or tasks is larger than 200). The methods based on the local search strategy, e.g., [8–11], are usually more efficient and require less communication cost, but they cannot guarantee the quality of obtained solutions, and they would only find few solutions that are local optimal and biased towards one objective. In some scenarios, if multiple objectives should be optimized simultaneously, the utility of these algorithms would decrease significantly. Therefore, it is meaningful to find some new methods for task allocation in multi-agent systems.

Evolutionary Algorithm (EA) is a promising algorithm for optimization [12], and it has been applied to many areas, e.g., Satisfaction Problem [13], Vehicle Routing Problem [14], Dynamic Shortest Path Problem [15], and Optimal Antenna Design Problem [16]. It is demonstrated that EA could be more efficient than the full search strategy and exhibits a better global search ability and could find better solutions than the local search strategy. Moreover, in the situation that multiple objectives are required to be optimized, EA could find more nondominated solutions than the local search strategy, and it enables the capacity of EA to account for diverse requirements. However, it is rarely applied to distributed task allocation in multi-agent systems. Therefore, in this paper, we propose a distributed task allocation method based on EA. We mainly consider four objectives, and we use a many-objective EA called NSGA-III [17] because traditional multi-objective EAs might only perform well on the optimization problems with 2 or 3 objectives. Specifically, the first objective we consider is to maximize the number of tasks that can be successfully allocated and executed by agents; the second objective is to maximize the benefits gained by executing tasks; the third objective is to minimize the resource cost by executing tasks; the last objective is to minimize the maximal time cost required among all agents to finish the tasks. Note that, most of existing works only consider one or two objectives, and these four objectives are rarely optimized simultaneously. To allocate the tasks in the distributed manner, we combine NSGA-III with the Master-Slave model [18], which is a typical distributed computation model.

The rest of this paper is organized as follows. Section 2 presents the preliminary knowledge of this work; Sect. 3 shows the proposed method; Sect. 4 gives the experimental results and discussion; Sect. 5 concludes the whole work.

2 Preliminaries

In this Section, we introduce the formal description of the task allocation problem in multi-agent systems and describe the Master-Slave model.

2.1 Task Allocation Problem

Task allocation involves different factors and constraints in different scenarios [2, 19, 20], and we extract some common elements to describe the problem we will solve. Specifically, we have:

(1) **Agents:** $A = \{a_1...a_m\}$, where m is number of agents. The locations of agents are: $L_A = \{l_{a1}...l_{am}\}$, where l_{ai} ($i = 1...m$) denotes the location of the agent a_i. The amount of resources equipped by agents is: $R = \{r_1...r_m\}$, where r_i ($i = 1...m$) is the amount of resources equipped by the agent a_i.

(2) **Tasks:** $V = \{v_1...v_n\}$, where n is the number of tasks. The locations of tasks are: $L_V = \{l_{v1}...l_{vn}\}$, where l_{vi} ($i = 1...n$) denotes the location of the task v_i. We suppose each task has an executing time limitation and we define it by the earliest start time and the latest start time of execution, i.e., $T_V = \{[low_1, up_1]...[low_n, up_n]\}$. That means a valid execution of the task v_i should start at the time between low_i and up_i. The time cost by executing the tasks is $Timecost = \{timecost_1... timecost_n\}$, where $timecost_i$ ($i = 1...n$) is the time cost by executing the task v_i. The resource cost by executing tasks is $Rescost = \{rescost_1...rescost_n\}$, where $rescost_i$ ($i - 1...n$) is the resource cost by executing the task v_i. The amount of benefits gained by executing tasks is $Gain = \{gain_1...gain_n\}$, where $gain_i$ ($i = 1...n$) is the amount of benefits achieved by executing the task v_i.

(3) **Task allocation:** $P = \{\pi_1...\pi_n\}$, where π_i ($i = 1...n$) denotes the allocating of task v_i, e.g., $\pi_1 = v_1 \rightarrow a_3$ means the task v_1 is allocated to the agent a_3 for execution, and for simplicity, we directly denote it as $\pi_1 = a_3$. If a task v_j is not allocated to any agents, we denote it as $\pi_j = Null$. Similar to [19], we assume that one task can be finished by one agent individually.

(4) **Agent execution:** $Q = \{q_1...q_m\}$, where q_i ($i = 1...m$) denotes a sequence of tasks will be executed by the agent a_i, e.g., $q_1 = v_1v_3v_5$ means q_1 will execute v_1, v_3 and v_5, respectively. Similar to [6, 19, 21], we suppose each agent can only execute one task at a point in time.

(5) **Objectives:** Different applications demand different optimization objectives, and in this work, we choose the following four widely studied objectives:

  (1) Maximizing the number of tasks that can be successfully allocated and executed by agents:

$$f_1 = maximize_{\forall P} \sum_{i=1}^{n} \{\pi_i \neq Null\} \qquad (1)$$

  where the notation $\{\pi_i \neq Null\}$ returns 1 if the predicate is true; otherwise it returns 0.

(2) Maximizing the benefits gained by executing tasks:

$$f_2 = maximize_{\forall P} \sum_{i=1}^{n} \{\pi_i \neq Null\} \times gain_i \tag{2}$$

(3) Minimizing the resource cost by executing tasks:

$$f_3 = minimize_{\forall Q} \sum_{i=1}^{m} \left(travel\_cost\left(l_{ai}, l_{vq_{i1}}\right) \right.$$
$$\left. + \sum_{j=2}^{|q_i|} travel\_cost\left(l_{vq_{i(j-1)}}, l_{vq_{ij}}\right) + \sum_{j=1}^{|q_i|} rescost_{q_{ij}} \right) \tag{3}$$

where the notation $|q_i|$ denotes the length of the sequence q_i, and $travel\_cost(l_x, l_y)$ is the resource cost by the agent for travelling from location l_x to location l_y.

(4) Minimizing the maximal time cost by executing tasks among all agents:

$$f_4 = minimize_{\forall Q} max_{i=1}^{m} Tcost(q_i, |q_i|) \tag{4}$$

where $Tcost(q_i, |q_i|)$ is the time cost by a_i for executing the $|q_i|$ tasks in q_i, and for $j = 2...|q_i|$:

$$Tcost(q_i, j) = max\left\{ Tcost(q_i, j-1) + travel\_time\left(l_{vq_{i(j-1)}}, l_{vq_{ij}}\right), low_{q_{ij}} \right\}$$
$$+ timecost_{q_{ij}}$$

and $Tcost(q_i, 1) = travel\_time\left(l_{ai}, l_{vq_{i1}}\right) + timecost_{q_{i1}}$ and $travel\_time(l_x, l_y)$ is the time cost by the agent for travelling from location l_x to l_y. We suppose that if an agent arrives the location of a task before its earliest start time, it will wait at that location.

(6) **Constraints:** There are usually several constraints in the task allocation problem, and we mainly consider the time constraint, the resource constraint and the function constraint

(1) *Time constraint*: An agent a_i ($1 \leq i \leq m$) can execute a task v_j successfully only if a_i arrives the location of the task and start the execution in the time interval $[low_j, up_j]$, and for the execution sequence q_i of a_i we have: For $j = 2...|q_i|$:

$$g_{ij}^T = arrival\_time(q_i, j)$$
$$= Tcost(q_i, j-1) + travel\_time\left(l_{vq_{i(j-1)}}, l_{vq_{ij}}\right) \leq up_{q_{ij}} \tag{5}$$

and $g_{i1}^T = arrival\_time(q_i, 1) = travel\_time\left(l_{ai}, l_{vq_{i1}}\right) \leq up_{q_{i1}}$.

(2) *Resource constraint*: An agent a_i ($1 \leq i \leq m$) can execute a task successfully only if the current resources loading on a_i are sufficient for travelling to the task and executing it, and for the execution sequence q_i of a_i we have: For $j = 1...|q_i|$:

$$g_{ij}^R = \text{resource\_cost}(q_i, j)$$

$$= travel\_cost\left(l_{ai}, l_{vq_{i1}}\right) + \sum_{k=2}^{j} travel\_cost\left(l_{vq_{i(k-1)}}, l_{vq_{ik}}\right) \qquad (6)$$

$$+ \sum_{k=1}^{j} rescost_{q_{ik}} \leq r_i$$

(3) *Function constraint*: In real-world applications, different kinds of agents may have different functions/abilities, and they can only execute the tasks fitting their functions. Specifically, we have:

(a) At the view of agents: for $i = 1...m$,

$$g_i^{FA} = \{v_{i_1}, \ldots, v_{i_b}\} :\rightarrow a_i \qquad (7)$$

This constraint describes that, according to the function of the agent a_i, it is able to execute the b tasks $v_{i_1}, \ldots, v_{i_b}$.

(b) At the view of tasks: for $j = 1...n$,

$$g_j^{FT} = v_j :\rightarrow \{a_{j_1}, \ldots, a_{j_c}\} \qquad (8)$$

This constraint describes that, according to the requirements of the task v_j on the agent functions, it can be allocated to any agent in $\{a_{j_1}, \ldots, a_{j_c}\}$ for execution.

2.2 Master-Slave Model

In this paper, we use a widely used distributed model for EA called Master-Slave [18] for task allocation. An example of the Master-Slave model is shown in Fig. 1. It contains one master and multiple slaves. The master has high computational and communication abilities and is responsible for the evolving process of EA, e.g., it conducts the population initialization, crossover operation, mutation operation, selection operation and iteration. The slaves are mainly responsible for evaluating individuals.

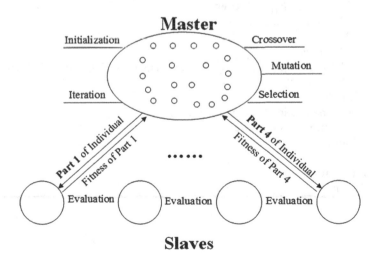

Fig. 1. The Master-Slave model for EA

The Master-Slave model is quite suitable for the scenarios that contain a control centre and a number of agents, where the control centre has high computational and communication abilities and is responsible for publishing tasks, sending orders to agents and allocating tasks to agents, and thus it corresponds to the master node. The agents are responsible for performing tasks and collecting the dynamic environment around the tasks. The effectiveness of a task allocation should be evaluated by agents because some data (e.g., the time cost, resource cost and current location) about the tasks could only be captured by agents and these data might change with the environment in some situation. In this paper, we assume that an agent could evaluate the part of solutions involves the tasks allocated to it, so each individual should be sent to multiple agents for a complete evaluation.

3   Distributed Task Allocation Based on NSGA-III

We present the distributed task allocation method based on the many-objective EA NSGA-III in this section.

Algorithm 1: NSGA-III [17]

Input: population size N, maximal iteration times $MaxIterN$, and the set of reference points Ref

Output: pareto set

1:     $i \leftarrow 1$
2:     Randomly initialize the popution P_i with N individuals, and evaluate the individuals
3:     **While** $i \leq MaxIterN$ **do**
4:         Perform the crossover, mutation operations on P_i to obtain offspring Q_i
5:         Evaluate all the individuals in Q_i
6:         Conduct nondominated sorting on $P_i \cup Q_i$ based on the objective values, and obtain the nondominated layers $F_1 \dots F_H$
7:         Find the h s.t., $|F_1 \cup \dots \cup F_{h-1}| < N \leq |F_1 \cup \dots \cup F_h|$
8:         **If** $|F_1 + \dots + F_h| = N$ **then**
9:             $P_{i+1} \downarrow F_1 \cup \dots \cup F_h$
10:        **Else**
11:            $P_{i+1} \downarrow F_1 \cup \dots \cup F_{h-1}$
12:            Select $N - |F_1 \cup \dots \cup F_{h-1}|$ individuals from F_h based on Ref, and add them into P_{i+1}
13:        **End if**
14:        **If** the population is convergent **then**
15:            Return F_1 as the pareto set
16:        **End if**
17:        $i \leftarrow i+1$
18:    **End while**
19:    Return F_1

3.1 Framework

NSGA-III [17] is improved from NSGA-II [22], which is a prominent multi-objective EA and has good performance on the optimization problems with 2 or 3 objectives. NSGA-III is proposed for solving the problems with more than 3 objectives. The procedure of the NSGA-III is shown in Algorithm 1. Specifically, (1) NSGA-III randomly initializes the population with N individuals, and evaluates them; (2) NSGA-III performs the crossover and mutation operation to generate offspring; (3) NSGA-III evaluates all individuals in both parent and offspring populations; (4) NSGA-III conducts nondominated sorting on the parent and offspring populations, and obtains H layers $F_1...F_H$ of nondominated fronts; (5) NSGA-III finds out the former h layers of nondominated fronts subject to $|F_1 \cup ... \cup F_{h-1}| < N \leq |F_1 \cup ... \cup F_h|$. (6) NSGA-III constructs the next generation of population: if $|F_1 \cup ... \cup F_h| = N$, then selects the individuals in the former h layers as the next population; otherwise, selects $N - |F_1 \cup ... \cup F_{h-1}|$ individuals using the reference points from the layer F_h and combines these individuals with the individuals in the former $h - 1$ layers to obtain the next population; (7) NSGA-III carries out the steps 2–6 until the population is convergent or the terminating condition (reach the maximal iteration times) is satisfied.

To find the optimal task allocation in multi-agent systems, we combine the NSGA-III algorithm with the Master-Slave model. As the control centre usually has high computational and communication abilities, it will play the role of master. The agents usually have limited computational and communication abilities, so they will play the role of slaves. In real-world applications, the cost of executing a task could only be captured by the agent that monitors the task, and the cost might change over the time. Moreover, sometimes, the environment might also change, e.g., some agents are broken, some new agents are available, or some new tasks appear. Therefore, it is more reasonable to distribute the evaluation of individuals to agents. Furthermore, we suppose that each agent can only evaluate the part of individuals that contains tasks which it can monitor and execute. This assumption is more practical, and the agents will spend less communication cost and computation cost.

Specifically, at the control centre C (Master) side:

1. C randomly initializes the population P_1, and makes the individuals distributed uniformly.
2. C divides each individual in P_i into m parts, and sends each part of the individuals to the corresponding agent for evaluation.
3. C collects the evaluation results from agents.
4. C performs the crossover, mutation operations on P_i to obtain offspring Q_i.
5. C sends each part of the individuals in Q_i to the corresponding agent for evaluation.
6. C collects the evaluation results from agents.
7. C conducts nondominated sorting on $P_i \cup Q_i$, computes nondominated layers, performs the selection operation based on reference points, and obtains the next generation of population (i.e., P_{i+1}).
8. C iteratively conducts steps 4–7 until the population is convergent or reaches the maximal iteration times.

At the agent (slave) side, each agent will receive a part of individuals sent from C, and it will evaluate the part and send back the evaluation results, i.e., the objective values. If the environment changes, the agent is also responsible for collecting the changed information and report to the control centre, and the control centre might request the re-evaluation of the population.

According to the procedure conducted by the control centre, the communication complexity at each iteration is $O(m \times |P|)$ because each individual will be divided into m parts and these m parts will be sent to m agents, respectively. Note that agents are usually much less than the tasks. For the worst case, i.e., the evolutionary process ends with the maximal iteration times, the total communication complexity of the proposed method is $O(m \times |P| \times maxIterN)$.

3.2   Chromosome Encoding, Crossover and Mutation

In EA, the individuals are represented as chromosomes, and the encoding of chromosomes influence the effectiveness of EA directly. In our work, to comprehensively contain the factors that affect the objective values, we encode a chromosome as: $x = x_1...x_m$, where x_i is a sequence of the indexes of tasks. Specifically, assume a_i is able to execute tasks $v_{i_1}, ..., v_{i_b}$ according to the function constraint, then x_i is a permutation of $i_1...i_b$, and it denotes the order that a_i would execute the tasks $v_{i_1}, ..., v_{i_b}$. For example, if there are 6 tasks and 2 agents, $x = 1\ 3\ 6\ 2\ 4\ 5$ and both a_1 and a_2 are able to execute 3 tasks, then x represents that a_1 would execute the tasks v_1, v_3 and v_6, respectively and a_2 would execute the tasks v_2, v_4 and v_5, respectively (Note that whether the agents can really execute these tasks successfully depends on the constraints are satisfied or not). By this encoding, all of the chromosomes have the same length when the function constraint is given, and the function constraint is always satisfied during the evolution. The initialization of individuals/chromosomes in the step 2 of Algorithm 1 could be quite easy. For example, we can initialize x_i of each individual as a random permutation of $i_1...i_b$. The time constraint and resource constraint will be blended in objective evaluation.

Based on the chromosome structure, we can use classic crossover and mutation strategies directly. For crossover, a split point s is first randomly chosen, and two individuals x, y exchange their parts according to s. After crossover, two new individuals x' and y' will be generated, and we have $x' = y_1...y_s x_{s+1}...x_m$ and $y' = x_1...x_s y_{s+1}...y_m$. For mutation, we set a parameter mr to control the mutation probability, if x_i is chosen to mutate according the probability, then we will randomly generate a permutation of $i_1...i_b$ to replace the current value of x_i. The selection operation remains the same with the original NSGA-III, please refer to [17] for details.

3.3   Evaluation

The evaluation process determines the search direction of EA, so it is important to design it carefully. In our work, we transform the four objectives in Sect. 2 into the "minimize" form and blend the constraints in objectives for evaluation. Specifically, when evaluating an individual x, we have:

(1) The first objective value of x could be calculated by:

$$f_1(x) = 1.0 - \frac{\sum_{i=1}^{m} e1(x_i)}{n} \qquad (9)$$

where $x_i = i_1 \ldots i_b$ and $e1(x_i)$ is calculated by:

$$e1(x_i) = \sum_{w=1}^{b} h(i_w)$$

where $h(i_w) = \begin{cases} 0 & \begin{array}{l} \textit{if } v_{i_w} \textit{ has been allocated,} \\ \textit{or arrival\_time}\left(x_i^E + i_w, \left|x_i^E\right| + 1\right) > up_{i_w}, \\ \textit{or resource\_cost}\left(x_i^E + i_w, \left|x_i^E\right| + 1\right) > r_i \end{array} \\ 1 & \textit{otherwise} \end{cases}$ and it judges whether

v_{i_w} can be added to the current execution sequence of a_i, x_i^E (it is the empty set at the beginning) is the current execution sequence of a_i, and $x_i^E + i_w$ denotes adding i_w to x_i^E.

(2) The second objective value of x could be calculated by:

$$f_2(x) = 1.0 - \frac{\sum_{i=1}^{m} e2(x_i)}{\sum_{i=1}^{n} gain_i} \qquad (10)$$

where $e2(x_i) = \sum_{w=1}^{b} h(i_w) \times gain_{i_w}$.

(3) The third objective value of x could be calculated by:

$$f_3(x) = \sum_{i=1}^{m} \frac{e3(x_i)}{m \times max\_t} \qquad (11)$$

where max_r is the maximal amount of the resources equipped by agents, $e3(x_i) = \sum_{w=1}^{k} h(i_w) \times (travel\_cost(l_{last}, l_{vi_w}) + rescost_{i_w})$, and l_{last} is the position of the last task allocated to a_i (l_{last} is the position of a_i when $w = 1$).

(4) The fourth objective value of x could be calculated by:

$$f_4(x) = max_{i=1}^{m} \frac{e4(x_i)}{m \times max\_t} \qquad (12)$$

where max_t is the maximal time that a task could be finished, and $e4(x_i) = \sum_{w=1}^{k} h(i_w) \times (travel\_time(l_{last}, l_{vi_w}) + timecost_{i_w})$.

It is worth to mention that, not all of the tasks encoded in a chromosome could be successfully allocated to agents, and the order that agents execute tasks is implied in chromosomes. The time constraint and resource constraint are blended in by the function $h()$. By the above transformation, we can easily evaluate an individual by inputting it into the four functions in (9)–(12).

4   Experiments and Discussion

In this section, we present experimental results to show the effectiveness of the proposed method, and we compare it with a typical full search strategy.

We first randomly generate the data about agents and tasks. Specifically, we vary the number of agents (i.e., m) from 10 to 250 and the number of tasks (i.e., n) from 10 to 1000 (n is 4 times to m by default). All agents are initially equipped with the same amount of resources, i.e., $r_i = 500$ for $i = 1...m$. They are set to be able to execute 5 tasks (i.e. $|q_i| = 5$), and these tasks are randomly distributed to agents to construct the function constraints. We denote the positions of agents and tasks by 2-dimensional points (x, y), and the range of x and y is [0, 100]. We randomly generate the positions of all agents and tasks. The earliest start time low_i ($i = 1...n$) of the task v_i is randomly generated in [0, 100], and the latest start time up_i is randomly generated in $[low_i, 150]$. To ensure an agent could execute multiple tasks, the time cost by executing a task is randomly generated in [1, 10], and the resource cost is randomly generated in [0, 100]. The benefits gained by executing a task is randomly generated as a double value in [0, 1]. For simplicity, we assume that both the time cost and resource cost by travelling are positively proportional to the distance.

After generating the test data, we implement our method on the source code of NSGA-III provided by prof. Chiang [23]. We set the maximal iteration times of NSGA-III as 1000 by default. The crossover rate is set to be 1.0, which means crossover operation is certainly performed once two parents are chosen. The mutation rate is set to be 1/(the length of chromosome), which means x_i ($i = 1...m$) will be mutated with this probability once the individual x is chosen.

4.1   Varying Problem Scale

To investigate the performance of the proposed method on different scales of problems, we choose three parameter settings: (1) $m = 10$, $n = 40$; (2) $m = 50$, $n = 200$; (3) $m = 250$, $n = 1000$. After generating the agents and tasks, we use the proposed method to solve the three problems, and the results are shown in Tables 1, 2 and 3.

For the case $m = 10$ and $n = 40$, if two groups of results are close to each other (the differences between their values for the first three objectives are less than 0.02), we only present one of them. Finally, we obtain 24 groups of nondominated results, and the results are correct to three decimal places. It is shown that the minimal values of f_1, f_2, f_3, f_4 are 0.350, 0.316, 0.226, 0.703, respectively, and the proposed method can finish at most 65% of the 40 tasks.

For the case $m = 50$ and $n = 200$, we filter the results in the same way, and finally we obtain 13 groups of nondominated results. It is shown that the minimal values of f_1, f_2, f_3, f_4 are 0.465, 0.417, 0.259, 0.776, respectively, and the proposed method can finish at most 54.5% of the 200 tasks.

For the case $m = 250$ and $n = 1000$, we also filter the results but use the difference threshold 0.01, and finally we only obtain 7 groups of nondominated results. It is shown that the minimal values of f_1, f_2, f_3, f_4 are 0.532, 0.482, 0.254, 0.850, respectively, and the proposed method can finish at most 46.8% of the 1000 tasks.

Table 1. The results of the proposed method when $m = 10$ and $n = 40$

f_1	f_2	f_3	f_4
0.350	0.330	0.386	0.775
0.375	0.377	0.364	0.897
0.400	0.316	0.356	0.775
0.400	0.387	0.352	0.771
0.425	0.333	0.351	0.775
0.425	0.400	0.341	0.703
0.450	0.407	0.330	0.703
0.450	0.447	0.321	0.736
0.475	0.354	0.319	0.775
0.475	0.400	0.306	0.897
0.500	0.403	0.309	0.703
0.500	0.437	0.297	0.736
0.500	0.501	0.282	0.897
0.500	0.521	0.276	0.771
0.525	0.461	0.280	0.707
0.525	0.496	0.282	0.703
0.525	0.502	0.262	0.897
0.550	0.506	0.265	0.736
0.550	0.532	0.260	0.897
0.550	0.558	0.248	0.746
0.575	0.546	0.256	0.707
0.575	0.568	0.241	0.897
0.575	0.588	0.234	0.746
0.600	0.624	0.226	0.746

Table 2. The results of the proposed method when $m = 50$ and $n = 200$

f_1	f_2	f_3	f_4
0.465	0.417	0.358	0.847
0.475	0.453	0.338	0.837
0.490	0.493	0.320	0.804
0.500	0.457	0.317	0.956
0.505	0.427	0.331	0.956
0.525	0.451	0.321	0.847
0.530	0.484	0.303	0.956
0.530	0.520	0.301	0.778
0.550	0.487	0.298	0.956
0.555	0.563	0.279	0.776
0.565	0.516	0.277	0.956
0.575	0.541	0.267	0.847
0.585	0.593	0.259	0.776

By comparing the three experiments, we find that the solutions found by the proposed method have worse minimal objective values on f_1, f_2, f_4 when m and n increase, and the three objectives might be more difficult to optimize in this case. But the optimization of f_3 seems have no obvious relationship with the increase of m and n. Moreover, we find that the diversity of solutions found by the proposed method decreases with the increase of m and n as less results have been filtered out.

Table 3. The results of the proposed method when $m = 250$ and $n = 1000$

f_1	f_2	f_3	f_4
0.532	0.482	0.293	0.931
0.544	0.501	0.286	0.882
0.555	0.506	0.277	0.892
0.561	0.518	0.275	0.850
0.573	0.529	0.266	0.860
0.578	0.540	0.259	0.931
0.591	0.556	0.254	0.850

Table 4. Results for $n/m = 1$

f_1	f_2	f_3	f_4
0.100	0.019	0.101	0.864
0.100	0.019	0.109	0.784
0.100	0.019	0.115	0.836
0.100	0.019	0.124	0.755
0.200	0.046	0.077	0.784
0.200	0.046	0.083	0.644

Table 5. Results for $n/m = 3$

f_1	f_2	f_3	f_4
0.133	0.163	0.367	0.901
0.167	0.143	0.361	0.901
0.167	0.211	0.341	0.901
0.200	0.157	0.363	0.861
0.200	0.197	0.332	0.764
0.200	0.265	0.312	0.856
0.233	0.156	0.342	0.901
0.233	0.246	0.313	0.675
0.233	0.311	0.288	0.856
0.267	0.180	0.338	0.861
0.267	0.210	0.313	0.732
0.267	0.249	0.308	0.675
0.267	0.290	0.282	0.764
0.267	0.359	0.278	0.856
0.300	0.191	0.333	0.861
0.300	0.259	0.293	0.675
0.300	0.304	0.271	0.675
0.333	0.280	0.275	0.901
0.333	0.318	0.255	0.901
0.367	0.233	0.290	0.901
0.367	0.278	0.268	0.697
0.367	0.362	0.240	0.901
0.367	0.400	0.226	0.675
0.367	0.442	0.220	0.675
0.400	0.288	0.261	0.697
0.400	0.338	0.244	0.697
0.400	0.444	0.217	0.675
0.433	0.301	0.245	0.901
0.433	0.351	0.247	0.656
0.433	0.423	0.203	0.901
0.467	0.361	0.242	0.656

Table 6. Results for $n/m = 5$

f_1	f_2	f_3	f_4
0.560	0.608	0.358	0.768
0.580	0.608	0.323	0.877
0.600	0.604	0.330	0.876
0.600	0.616	0.309	0.768
0.600	0.645	0.301	0.768
0.620	0.623	0.323	0.756
0.620	0.627	0.298	0.768
0.620	0.651	0.280	0.756
0.620	0.661	0.260	0.877
0.640	0.640	0.260	0.756
0.640	0.665	0.240	0.877
0.660	0.623	0.269	0.876
0.660	0.672	0.260	0.748
0.660	0.692	0.221	0.877
0.680	0.683	0.214	0.675
0.680	0.718	0.203	0.675
0.700	0.674	0.235	0.675
0.720	0.685	0.208	0.756
0.740	0.718	0.180	0.675
0.760	0.734	0.175	0.675

4.2 Varying n/m

In this section, we conduct three experiments to show the influence of the ratio n/m on the performance of the proposed method. In these experiments, m (i.e., the number of agents) is set to 10.

In the first experiment, we set n as 10 and n/m is 1, and the results are shown in Table 4. We filter the results using the difference threshold 0.005, and only 6 groups of data are obtained. The minimal values of f_1, f_2, f_3, f_4 are 0.1, 0.019, 0.077, and 0.644, respectively. The agents can finish at most 90% of the 10 tasks.

In the second experiment, we set n as 30 and n/m is 3, and the results are shown in Table 5. We filter the results using the difference threshold 0.02, and 31 groups of data are obtained. The minimal values of f_1, f_2, f_3, f_4 are 0.133, 0.143, 0.203, and 0.655, respectively. The agents can finish at most 86.7% of the 30 tasks.

In the third experiment, we set n as 50 and n/m is 5, and the results are shown in Table 6. We filter the results using the difference threshold 0.02, and 20 groups of data are obtained. The minimal values of f_1, f_2, f_3, f_4 are 0.560, 0.604, 0.175, and 0.675, respectively. The agents can finish at most 44% of the 50 tasks.

By comparing the results from the three experiments, we find that the objectives f_1 and f_2 seem more difficult to optimize when n/m increases, but no obvious rules about the optimization of f_3 and f_4 has been found.

4.3 Comparison

In this section, we compare the proposed method with the full search strategy, which simply enumerates every possible task allocation solution and records the best ones. As there are so many optimal solutions that we cannot present them one by one in this paper, so we only present those results that are better and closest to the results of the proposed method. We choose 5 parameter settings, i.e., (1) $m = 5$, $n = 5$; (2) $m = 5$, $n = 10$; (3) $m = 5$, $n = 20$; (4) $m = 10$, $n = 10$; (5) $m = 10$, $n = 20$. The results are shown in Tables 7, 8 and 9, and we do not present the comparison results for ($m = 5$, $n = 20$) and ($m = 10$, $n = 20$) because the full search strategy did not finish execution in 1 h (while the proposed method finished in 5 min). The results of the proposed method are filtered using the difference threshold 0.02 for $m = 5$ and 0.005 for $m = 10$.

Table 7. The results of the proposed method and the full search strategy when $m = 5$ and $n = 5$

Proposed method				Full search			
f_1	f_2	f_3	f_4	f_1	f_2	f_3	f_4
0.000	0.000	0.180	0.656	0.000	0.000	**0.159**	0.656

Table 8. The results of the proposed method and the full search strategy when $m = 5$ and $n = 10$

Proposed method				Full search			
f_1	f_2	f_3	f_4	f_1	f_2	f_3	f_4
0.300	0.355	0.243	0.753	0.300	0.355	**0.231**	0.753
0.300	0.355	0.265	0.715	0.300	0.355	0.265	0.715
0.400	0.415	0.227	0.638	0.400	0.415	0.227	0.638

Table 9. The results of the proposed method and full search strategy when $m = 10$ and $n = 10$

Proposed method				Full search			
f_1	f_2	f_3	f_4	f_1	f_2	f_3	f_4
0.100	0.019	0.101	0.864	0.100	0.019	**0.085**	**0.644**
0.100	0.019	0.109	0.784	0.100	0.019	**0.085**	**0.644**
0.100	0.019	0.115	0.836	0.100	0.019	**0.085**	**0.644**
0.100	0.019	0.124	0.755	0.100	0.019	**0.085**	**0.644**
0.200	0.046	0.077	0.784	0.200	0.046	**0.064**	**0.644**
0.200	0.046	0.083	0.644	0.200	0.046	**0.064**	0.644

By comparing the results of the proposed method with the full search strategy, we find that the proposed method could find solutions that are close to the global optimal solutions found by the full search strategy. For $m = 5$ and $n = 5$, the difference between the solution of the proposed method and the corresponding optimal solution found by the full search strategy is 0.021. For $m = 5$ and $n = 10$, the average difference between the solutions of the proposed method and the corresponding optimal solutions found by the full search strategy is 0.004, the maximal difference is 0.012, and the minimal difference is 0. For $m = 10$ and $n = 10$, the average difference between the solutions of the proposed method and the corresponding optimal solutions found by the full search strategy is 0.139, the maximal difference is 0.221, and the minimal difference is 0.019. Though, the full search strategy can find the best results but it can only solve small problems, and it could not be used when n or m is not less than 20. On the contrast, the proposed method could solve the problems even with $m \geq 250$ and $n \geq 1000$, so it would have better utility on solving large problems.

5   Conclusions

In this paper, we propose a distributed method for task allocation based on NSGA-III. Specifically, NSGA-III is combined with the Master-Slave model, which is a classical distributed model for EA. The control centre in multi-agent systems plays the master rule, and the agents play the slave rule. Experimental results show that, the proposed method could be used for searching optimal task allocation solutions even when the number of agents (i.e., m) is not less than 250 and the number of tasks (i.e., n) is not less than 1000, while the full search strategy is only effective when $m < 20$ or $n < 20$. It demonstrates that the proposed method would have better utility on solving large problems.

In future work, we attempt to combine NSGA-III with other distributed models, e.g., the Island-cellular hybrid model. We will also try to solve the task allocation problems with ordering constraints.

Acknowledgments. This work was partially supported by the National Natural Science Foundation of China (Grant No. 71701208).

References

1. Korsah, G.A., Stentz, A., Dias, M.B.: A comprehensive taxonomy for multi-robot task allocation. Int. J. Robot. Res. **32**(12), 1495–1512 (2013)
2. Nunes, E., Manner, M., Mitiche, H., Gini, M.: A taxonomy for task allocation problems with temporal and ordering constraints. Robot. Auton. Syst. **90**, 55–70 (2017)
3. JayModi, P., Shen, W., Tambe, M., Yokoo, M.: ADOPT: asynchronous distributed constraint optimization with quality guarantees. Artif. Intell. **161**(1), 149–180 (2005)
4. Petcu, A., Faltings, B.: DPOP: a scalable method for multiagent constraint optimization. In: Proceedings of the 19th International Joint Conference on Artificial Intelligence (IJCAI 2005), Acapulco, Mexico, pp. 266–271 (2005)
5. Mailler, R., Lesser, V.: Solving distributed constraint optimization problems using cooperative mediation. In: Proceedings of the 3rd International Joint Conference on Autonomous Agents and Multiagent Systems (AAMAS 2004), pp. 438–445 (2004)
6. Macarthur, K.S., Stranders, R., Ramchurn, S., Jennings, N.: A distributed anytime algorithm for dynamic task allocation in multi-agent systems. In: Twenty-Fifth AAAI Conference on Artificial Intelligence, pp. 701–706 (2011)
7. Xie, B., Chen, J., Shen, L.: Cooperation algorithms in multi-agent systems for dynamic task allocation: a brief overview. In: 2018 37th Chinese Control Conference (CCC), pp. 6776–6781 (2018)
8. Fitzpatrick, S., Meetrens, L.: Distributed Sensor Networks: A Multi-agent Perspective. Kluwer Academic, Dordrecht (2003)
9. Chapman, A.C., Micillo, R.A., Kota, R., Jenning, N.R.: Decentralised dynamic task allocation: a practical game-theoretic approach. In: Proceedings of 8th International Conference on Autonomous Agents and Multiagent Systems (AAMAS 2009), pp. 1–8 (2009)
10. Fitzpatrick, S., Meertens, L.: Distributed coordination through anarchic optimization. In: Lesser, V., Ortiz, C.L., Tambe, M. (eds.) Distributed Sensor Networks: A Multiagent Perspective. MASA, vol. 9, pp. 257–295. Springer, Boston (2003). https://doi.org/10.1007/978-1-4615-0363-7_11
11. Yedidsion, H., Zivan, R., Farinelli, A.: Applying max-sum to teams of mobile sensing agents. Eng. Appl. Artif. Intell. **71**, 87–99 (2018)
12. Zhang, Q., Li, H.: MOEA/D: a multiobjective evolutionary algorithm based on decomposition. IEEE Trans. Evol. Comput. **11**(6), 712–731 (2007)
13. Gottlieb, J., Marchiori, E., Rossi, C.: Evolutionary algorithms for the satisfiability problem. Evol. Comput. **10**(1), 35–50 (2002)

14. Yi, R., Luo, W., Bu, C., Lin, X.: A hybrid genetic algorithm for vehicle routing problems with dynamic requests. In: Proceedings of the 2017 IEEE Symposium Series on Computational Intelligence (IEEE SSCI 2017), Honolulu, Hawaii, USA, pp. 1–8 (2017)

15. Zhu, X., Luo, W., Zhu, T.: An improved genetic algorithm for dynamic shortest path problems. In: Proceedings of the 2014 IEEE Congress on Evolutionary Computation, Beijing, China, 6–11 July, pp. 2093–2100 (2014)

16. Hu, C., Zeng, S., Jiang, Y., Sun, Y., Jiang, Y., Gao, S.: A robust technique without additional computational cost in evolutionary antenna optimization. IEEE Trans. Antennas Propag. **67**(04), 1–10 (2019)

17. Deb, K., Jain, H.: An evolutionary many-objective optimization algorithm using reference-point-based nondominated sorting approach, Part I: solving problems with box constraints. IEEE Trans. Evol. Comput. **18**(4), 577–601 (2014)

18. Gong, Y., Chen, W., Zhan, Z., et al.: Distributed evolutionary algorithms and their models: a survey of the state-of-the-art. Appl. Soft Comput. **34**, 286–300 (2015)

19. Scerri, P., Farinelli, A., Okamoto, S., Tambe, M.: Allocating tasks in extreme teams. In: Proceedings of the Fourth International Joint Conference on Autonomous Agents and Multiagent Systems, pp. 727–734 (2005)

20. Gini, M.: Multi-robot allocation of tasks with temporal and ordering constraints. In: Thirty-First AAAI Conference on Artificial Intelligence, pp. 4863–4869 (2017)

21. Ramchurn, S.D., Polukarov, M., Farinelli, A., Truong, C., Jennings, N.R.: Coalition formation with spatial and temporal constraints. In: Proceedings of the 9th International Conference on Autonomous Agents and Multiagent Systems, pp. 1181–1188 (2010)

22. Deb, K., Agrawal, S., Pratap, A., Meyarivan, T.: A fast elitist non-dominated sorting genetic algorithm for multi-objective optimization: NSGA-II. In: Schoenauer, M., et al. (eds.) PPSN 2000. LNCS, vol. 1917, pp. 849–858. Springer, Heidelberg (2000). https://doi.org/10.1007/3-540-45356-3_83

23. Chiang, T.-C.: nsga3cpp: a C++ implementation of NSGA-III. https://web.ntnu.edu.tw/~tcchiang/publications/nsga3cpp/nsga3cpp.htm?tdsourcetag=s_pcqq_aiomsg. Accessed 28 Feb 2019

Applications of Machine Learning II

Robustness Analysis on Natural Language Processing Based AI Q&A Robots

Chengxiang Yuan[1], Mingfu Xue[1($\boxtimes$)], Lingling Zhang[1], and Heyi Wu[2]

[1] College of Computer Science and Technology,
Nanjing University of Aeronautics and Astronautics,
Nanjing, China
{yuancx,mingfu.xue}@nuaa.edu.cn, bluezhll@126.com
[2] School of Cyber Science and Engineering,
Southeast University, Nanjing, China
why1988seu@126.com

Abstract. Recently, the natural language processing (NLP) based intelligent question and answering (Q&A) robots have been used in a wide range of applications, such as smart assistant, smart customer service, government business. However, the robustness and security issues of these NLP based artificial intelligence (AI) Q&A robots have not been studied yet. In this paper, we analyze the robustness problems in current Q&A robots, which include four aspects: (1) semantic slot settings are incomplete; (2) sensitive words are not filtered efficiently and completely; (3) Q&A robots return the search results directly; (4) unsatisfactory matching algorithms and inappropriate matching threshold settings. Then, we design and implement two types of evaluation tests, bad language and user's typos, to evaluate the robustness of several state-of-the-art Q&A robots. Experiment results show that these common inputs (bad language and user's typos) can successfully make these Q&A robots malfunction, denial of service, or speaking dirty words. Besides, we also propose possible countermeasures to enhance the robustness of these Q&A robots. To the best of the authors' knowledge, this is the first work on analyzing the robustness and security problems of intelligent Q&A robots. This work can hopefully help provide guidelines to design robust and secure Q&A robots.

Keywords: AI security · Question and answer robots · Robustness · Natural language processing

This work is supported by the National Natural Science Foundation of China (No. 61602241), the Natural Science Foundation of Jiangsu Province (No. BK20150758), the CCF-Venustech Hongyan Research Plan (No. CCFVenustechRP2016005), the CCF-NSFocus Kunpeng Foundation (No. CCF-NSFocus2017003), and the Fundamental Research Funds for the Central Universities (No. NS2016096).

© ICST Institute for Computer Sciences, Social Informatics and Telecommunications Engineering 2019
Published by Springer Nature Switzerland AG 2019. All Rights Reserved
X. B. Zhai et al. (Eds.): MLICOM 2019, LNICST 294, pp. 695–711, 2019.
https://doi.org/10.1007/978-3-030-32388-2_57

1   Introduction

In recent years, artificial intelligence (AI) techniques achieved major break-throughs and have been used ubiquitously. A representative application of AI is the natural language processing (NLP) techniques based intelligent question and answering (Q&A) robots, which are widely used in general application areas, professional business, and government applications.

Traditionally, people can search various information from a search engine, e.g., Google, Baidu. The search engine will return a ranked list of related web documents according to the user's input. The user cannot get the answers they want quickly and accurately from a large number of search results. Unlike the information retrieval system, the task of an intelligent Q&A robot is to give the user a precise and concise answer in several interactions with the user. Generally, the Q&A robots have the following two features: (1) users can query the Q&A robots in natural language; (2) the Q&A robot directly returns the answer that the user needs (rather than a ranked list of relevant documents). Recently, many companies have developed their own Q&A robots, which have made great progress in human-computer interaction, such as Google assistant [1], Cortana [2], Siri [3], Alexa [4], Watson [5], DuerOS [6], Ali Xiaomi [7], JD Instant Messaging Intelligence [8]. On the other hand, many government agencies have also provided Q&A robots for public business, e.g., 12306 (Q&A robots of Chinese railway system), tax bureau.

However, the robustness of these NLP based AI Q&A robots has not been studied yet in the literature. In this paper, first, we review the working principles of current Q&A robots. Then, we analyze the robustness problems of current intelligent Q&A robots, which include four aspects: (1) the semantic slots settings are incomplete; (2) it is difficult for Q&A robots to filter all the sensitive words in both the user's questions and the returned answers; (3) some Q&A robots directly return the results from a search engine; (4) unsatisfactory matching algorithms or inappropriate matching thresholds. Then, we design and implement two types of evaluation tests, bad language and user's typos, on several state-of-the-art Q&A robots. These common inputs (bad language and typos) can successfully make the Q&A robots malfunction, denial of service (DoS), or speaking dirty words. These consequences are disastrous to the Q&A robots, which will face a recall or withdraw from the market. Experiment results show that the semantic slots of the tested Q&A robots are incomplete, and the Q&A robots do not consider the contextual information in the multi-round interactions with the user. For sensitive words filtering, current Q&A robots still do not have an effective solution. The matching degree between the answer given by the Q&A robot and the user's question is unsatisfactory, and the accuracy of the answers needs to be improved. In addition, we propose several possible countermeasures for these robust problems of the intelligent Q&A robots.

2 Working Principles of AI Q&A Robots

Generally, there are three kinds of working principles used by current AI Q&A robots, using the knowledge base (KB), using information retrieval (IR), and using guiding questions. We will describe these three types of working principles in Sects. 2.1, 2.2, and 2.3, respectively. In Sect. 2.4, we will summarize and present the most complete working principle of state-of-the-art AI Q&A robots, which is a combination of the above three mechanisms.

2.1 Knowledge Base Based Q&A Robots

The process of knowledge base (KB) based Q&A robots is shown in Fig. 1. After semantic parsing of the input questions, a standard structured query languages will be generated which will be searched directly in the KB. Then, it returns the answer to the user. There are several large-scale knowledge bases, such as DBpedia [9], Freebase [10], and YAGO [11], which store a large amount of valuable information in the form of Resource Description Framework (RDF) triples [12]. The key of KB based Q&A robots is to transform users' natural language questions into standard structured query formats.

Fig. 1. The process of KB-based Q&A robots.

The early Q&A robot is a natural language interface to database (NLIDB) that allows the user to query and access information from a database in natural language questions [13]. However, this method can only be used in domain-specific applications, while in open-domain question answering, the database will be extremely complex. In order to solve this problem, semantic parser is used to analyze the user's natural language questions. Semantic parsing includes four steps [14]: paraphrase extraction, mapping to formal meaning representation, semantic combination, data retrieval from the knowledge base. There are many semantic parsing methods [15–18]. In [15], Zettlemoyer *et al.* use a learning algorithm to map natural language sentences to a lambda calculus encoding of their semantics. Zelle *et al.* [16] use shift-reduce derivations to map sentences into database queries. Wang *et al.* [17] exploit statistical machine translation techniques to generate logical forms. Lu *et al.* [18] construct a generative model based on a hybrid tree whose nodes contain natural language words and meaning representation tokens.

Traditional semantic parsers require annotated logical forms as supervision and have only a few logical predicates [14]. Therefore, semantic understanding methods based on deep learning have been proposed recently. Yih *et al.* [19] first decompose each question into an entity mention and a relation pattern. Then, they use convolutional neural network models to measure the similarity between entity mentions and entities, and the similarity between relation patterns and relations in the KB. Yih *et al.* [20] use an entity linking system and deep convolutional neural network for question answering.

2.2 Information Retrieval Based Q&A Robots

Information retrieval (IR) based Q&A robots search for unstructured text documents and reorganize them into answers. These unstructured text documents, which are obtained from the web page using search engines, may contain the answer of the questions. Figure 2 presents the framework of a IR based Q&A robot, which includes three steps: question processing, passage retrieval and answer processing [21]. The question processing module consists of query formulation and answer type detection. The query formulation extracts one or more keywords from natural language questions. The answer type detection mainly extracts key information from the question and further explains the question in order to predict the answer type [14]. The passage retrieval module uses these keywords to retrieve the information from the web and obtain relevant documents that potentially contain the answer [14]. The relevant documents are ranked according to the matching degree of the question. Then, passages that contain potential answers are extracted and ranked. The answer processing module determines the type of the answer, and selects the most appropriate answer from the candidate answers by using a answer extraction algorithm. Pattern matching and N-gram tiling are two typical algorithms for extracting answers [14]. For example, Ravichandran *et al.* [22] develop a method to automatically learn patterns which can be used to find answers. [23] and [24] exploit the N-gram tiling method to extract answer.

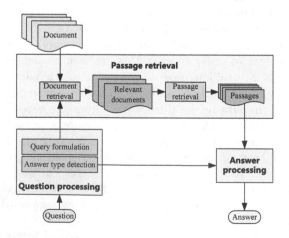

Fig. 2. The framework of IR-based Q&A robots [21].

2.3 Using Guiding Questions

When a Q&A robot can only understand a part of the question or consider the question to be ambiguous, it can further ask the user some guiding questions. These guiding questions can help the Q&A robot understand the user's intentions and return a more accurate answer. For example, suppose we want to query the 12306 Q&A robot for the train information from Shanghai to Beijing. If the Q&A robot does not use the guiding questions, it will return all the train information from Shanghai to Beijing. On the contrary, if the Q&A robot applies the guiding question technique, it can ask the user what time period of the trains the user wants to query. In this way, the returned result will be more accurate.

2.4 The Complete Working Principle of the State-of-the-art AI Q&A Robots

In this section, we will summarize and present the most complete working principle of the state-of-the-art AI Q&A robots, which is a combination of the above three mechanisms, as shown in Fig. 3. The Q&A robot first searches for similar questions from a question and answer database. The question and answer database contains a large number of questions and corresponding answers. The Q&A robot needs to perform text segmentation on the user's question. Keywords are extracted from the word segments, which are represented as a vector. The vector is used to match the answer in the Q&A database. The Q&A robot ranks the answers according to the matching degree, and returns the top k answers to the user. For example, if there are 4000 questions and 4000 corresponding answers in a Q&A database, the vector is used to match the keywords of 4000 questions, and the top 3 or top 5 answers are returned to the user. If the match

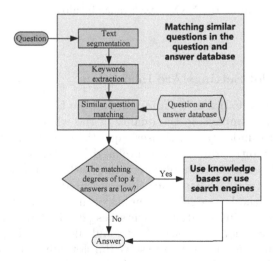

Fig. 3. The complete working principle of the state-of-the-art Q&A robots.

degrees between the user's question and the top k answers are very low, the Q&A robot will use other methods, e.g., using knowledge bases, using search engines, or using guiding questions, to further determine the answer.

3   Robustness Problems of Current Q&A Robots

Although there have been many studies on techniques used by the Q&A robots in the literature, there are still many robustness problems in the practical Q&A robots. For example, the news reported that the intelligent Q&A robot XXX1 insulted a user [25], as shown in Fig. 4. Robustness/security problems in Q&A robots will lead to serious consequences. We analyze the robustness problems of current Q&A robots in the following subsections.

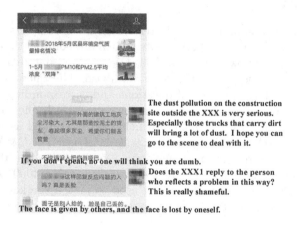

Fig. 4. News: the XXX1 Q&A robot insulted a user [25].

3.1   Semantic Slot Settings Are Incomplete

The slot filling process extracts key information from the user's questions, which has a very important impact on the quality of the whole question and answer system. In order to understand the user's questions correctly, the Q&A robot needs to use a semantic frame that contains different slots, and fills the key information in the semantic slots by interacting with the user.

Many semantic template-based methods are used in early slot filling techniques. In these method, recognition templates are constructed manually and used to extract the key information of sentences [26]. However, the construction of templates requires a lot of manual efforts, and the scope of application of the template is limited. A major method to solve the slot filling problem is to employ the sequence labeling model [27]. This method uses the sequence labeling model to mark the label for each word of a sentence, and generates the final slot filling result based on these labels. Recently, researches achieve better performance in slot filling by using recurrent neural network, such as [28,29]. However, there are still many problems in slot filling of the practical Q&A robots. Their semantic slots settings are incomplete, and the performance of many slot filling methods is unsatisfactory. Besides, in the multi-round interactions with the user, it can't effectively translate the user's initial intentions into explicit instructions.

3.2 Sensitive Words Are Not Filtered Effectively and Completely

In many cases, there are sensitive words in the questions that users enter into the Q&A robot, such as foul words, violent words, sensitive political words. The Q&A robot will directly use these sensitive words to search for answers in the knowledge base or in the Internet, and reply related results that are also likely to have these sensitive words to the user. This could be a disaster. However, many Q&A robots do not filter or cannot effectively filter sensitive words entered by the user. The reasons include the following two aspects. On the one hand, due to the variety of sensitive words, the number of sensitive words is extremely large, while the Q&A robot lacks a complete database of sensitive words. On the other hand, when detecting sensitive words, normal words may be incorrectly identified as sensitive words.

In addition, there also may be sensitive words in the process of extracting and generating the answers. Since the answers are typically obtained from the Internet, if the system cannot correctly identify those sensitive words, the answers returned to the user may contain these sensitive words, which will lead to a bad user experience.

3.3 Return the Search Results Directly

In general, after the Q&A robot obtains relevant documents that contain potential answers from the Internet, the Q&A robot needs to rank these relevant documents according to the matching degree of the question [14]. Some Q&A robots use a single feature to match and rank these relevant documents, while others rank these relevant documents by combining different features. However, we found that many Q&A robots on the market do not have this process. These Q&A robots directly return the results obtained from the search engine to the user, which results in a low matching degree between the answer and the question. Therefore, these answers are always unable to meet the users' needs.

3.4 Unsatisfactory Matching Algorithms and Inappropriate Matching Threshold Settings

In the process of matching the answers to the question, a predefined threshold is used to remove documents with low relevance to the question, and those documents that are highly correlated with the question are reserved [21]. However, the matching degrees between all the relevant documents and the question may be lower than the predefined threshold. In this case, the answer processing module cannot extract an answer to the question. Most current Q&A robots have two solutions to this issue. One solution is to tell the user directly that the question cannot be answered. Another solution is to extract the answer from the previously ranked documents and return it to the user. However, both these two solutions are unsatisfactory. The first solution will give users a bad user experience. The second solution will give users an irrelevant answer to the question.

Similarly, Q&A robots will also have this problem when ranking passages. Although numerous features are used to rank passages, these features may still be not good enough. The candidate answers may be inappropriate answers.

4   Bad Language Experiments

We design and implement five bad language tests in different ways to evaluate current Q&A robots. It is shown that most of the Q&A robots have more than one robustness problems. Note that, in order to protect the privacy and interests of these platforms, the names of these Q&A robots will be hidden in this paper, and replaced by numbers XXX2–XXX6 (XXX1 has been illustrated in Sect. 3). We also want to apologize for using some rude words to induce the system errors in the experiments.

4.1   Evaluation on the XXX2 Q&A Robot

As shown in Fig. 5, in the conversation with the XXX2 Q&A robot, we want to inquire the operation information of train No. G7097. Firstly, we only input the train number to the Q&A robot. The robot cannot query information about train No. G7097. At that time, the G7097 was a train that suddenly stop running due to irresistible factors, such as weather. Then, we ask the Q&A robot when does the train start running again. Because the Q&A robot lacks information of the train, it does not answer directly. To further understand the user's question, the robot asks the user to enter the train number. It also provides a list of other frequently asked questions to the user. We enter the train number again. The robot still cannot query information about the train. This experiment shows that, the XXX2 Q&A robot does not adopt slot filling technique and the guiding question technique. Its ability to understand the user's questions is unsatisfactory. Besides, the Q&A robot also does not consider the contextual information in the multi-round interactions with the user. Compared with the usual human customer service, the performance of this Q&A robot system is unsatisfactory.

4.2   Evaluation on the XXX3 Q&A Robot

Figure 6 shows our tests on the XXX3 Q&A robot. We input the sensitive word "shit" to the Q&A robot. Unexpectedly, the Q&A robot returns a sensitive sentence "Where to go shit" to the user without filtering them at all. Then, we input the sensitive sentence "You are a dog eating shit". The Q&A robot

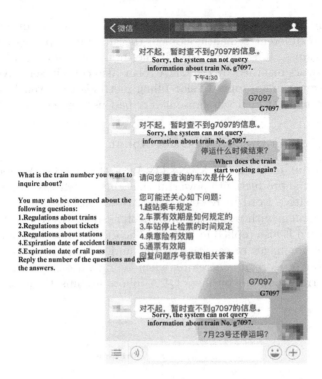

Fig. 5. Evaluation on the XXX2 Q&A robot.

Fig. 6. Evaluation on the XXX3 Q&A robot

answers "I am not a dog. You eat shit." The Q&A robot incorrectly fills the "shit dog" into different semantic slots in the slot filling process, resulting in very serious results. It is shown that if the input question contains sensitive words, the answers returned by the Q&A robot also contain sensitive words. To make things worse, inappropriate slot filling methods can even lead the Q&A robot to insult users, which will cause a very bad user experience.

4.3   Evaluation on the XXX4 Q&A Robot

Figure 7 shows our tests on the XXX4 Q&A robot. This Q&A robot is a very mature commercial product with powerful functions, which has been widely used. We input a sensitive word in Korean "You are an asshole". The robot replies "What's the problem with you in the process of 'asshole' (in Korean)?", in which the sensitive word is also replied in Korean. The Q&A robot does not filter other forms or other languages of sensitive words, and directly returns the sensitive word to the user in Korean. Therefore, when facing various sensitive words, the solutions of current popular business Q&A robots are unsatisfactory.

Fig. 7. Evaluation on the XXX4 Q&A robot.

4.4   Evaluation on the XXX5 Q&A Robot

Figure 8 shows our tests on the XXX5 Q&A robot, which includes three rounds. In the first round, as shown in Fig. 8(a), we enter an sensitive sentence "You are an asshole" into the Q&A robot in a different language. Like the XXX3 Q&A robot, the Q&A robot also does not filter the sensitive words and returns the translation of this sentence in Chinese to the user directly. Additionally, the Q&A robot replies a length of voice to the user. It is shown that this Q&A robot doesn't filter sensitive words and directly uses the translation results on the Internet. It also doesn't process the search results but returns it to the user directly.

After that, the developers of the XXX5 Q&A robot have fixed the problem of sensitive words. In our second round of experiment, as shown in Fig. 8(b), we enter the same sensitive sentence in different languages. The Q&A robot replies "Dear, I am glad to talk to you. If you have any questions, I am glad to help you.", "Little AI is thinking. Mom said that the child who likes to think will be more clever.", and a length of voice. Then, we input the same sensitive sentence again. The robot replies four periods, a length of voice, and "Hello, welcome to follow this account", and another piece of voice. Obviously, there is no correlation between the answers returned by the Q&A robot and the input questions. In this round, the Q&A robot filters the sensitive words but use results with inappropriate matching algorithms or low matching thresholds.

In the third round of experiment, as shown in Fig. 8(c), we still enter the same sensitive sentence in different languages. In this time, the system stops the service to the user, which shows "System error, please try again later".

This experiment illustrates that some Q&A robots return the search results directly, don't filter the sensitive words, and use unsatisfactory matching algorithms or inappropriate matching thresholds.

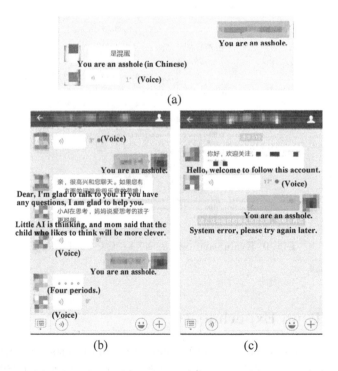

Fig. 8. Three rounds of tests on the XXX5 Q&A robot: (a) The first round; (b) The second round; (c) The third round.

4.5   Evaluation on the XXX6 Q&A Robot

As shown in Fig. 9, we test the XXX6 Q&A robot. This Q&A robot is also a mature commercial version, which has been widely used. We input "You are an asshole" in different languages one after another. The Q&A robot replies "What are you not satisfied with?", "How to bind your cell phone to your account? How to logout your account?", "Sorry, I am still learning. I can't understand your question right now. I can provide you with the following services.", respectively. There are no sensitive words in the answers returned by this Q&A robot. This Q&A robot also asks the users guiding questions to help it understand the user's intentions. However, it gives different answers each time, and all these answers are irrelevant to the question.

After several rounds of conversation with the user, the Q&A robot still does not understand the user's question, and it gives up answering this question. Therefore, this Q&A robot, although has sensitive words filtering and uses guiding questions, it still has the following problems: use unsatisfactory matching algorithms; replies irrelevant answers to the user; and gives up answering the question when failed several times.

Fig. 9. Evaluation on the XXX6 Q&A robot.

5   User's Typo Experiments

When a user interacts with a Q&A robot, the input questions are likely to contain some typos. A tiny typo may cause the Q&A robot to misunderstand the question and thus unable to answer the question correctly. In this section, we evaluate the robustness of Q&A robots when facing tiny typos.

5.1 Experimental Setup

Datasets: Three Q&A datasets, WebQuestionsSP [30], CuratedTREC [31] and WikiMovies-10k [32] are used to evaluate the accuracy and robustness of Q&A robots. The WebQuestionsSP dataset contains semantic parses for the questions from the WebQuestions dataset. The CuratedTREC dataset is collected from TREC1999, TREC2000, TREC2001 and TREC2002 data. The WikiMovies-10k dataset contains questions related to movies. The number of questions contained in the three datasets are 4737, 2180 and 10000, respectively.

Target Q&A Robots: In the experiment, two state-of-the-art Q&A robots, Siri [3] and Zo [33], are used as the target Q&A robots. Siri is a virtual assistant designed by Apple, which provides a user interface to answer questions. Users can ask Siri questions in natural language to obtain answers. Similarly, Zo is an intelligent chatting robot developed by Microsoft. Users can chat with Zo or ask Zo questions. In the experiment, we use the question and answer functions of Siri and Zo to evaluate their robustness.

5.2 Experimental Results of User's Typos

First, we evaluate the accuracy of Siri and Zo answering the original questions in the three Q&A datasets. The accuracy of Siri and Zo answering questions is shown in Table 1. For the questions in the three datasets, both Siri and Zo can only correctly answer a small number of the questions. This shows that the accuracy of current Q&A robot in answering questions is still low.

Table 1. The accuracy of Siri and Zo answering questions on the three Q&A datasets.

Target Q&A robot	WebQuestionSP	CuratedTREC	WikiMovies-10k
Siri	20.61%	22.68%	10.57%
Zo	26.24%	35.23%	13.72%

Since it is meaningless to generate typos with those original questions that the Q&A robot cannot answer, only the questions in the three datasets that the Q&A robot can answer correctly are selected to form new datasets. After that, we slightly modify these questions that the Q&A robot can answer correctly to generate questions with tiny typos. We use two methods to modify the original questions: (1) randomly replace one or more letters in a word; (2) replace the words in the original question with words that are spelled similarly. These generated questions with typos are used to evaluate the robustness of the Q&A robots. Table 2 presents three examples of questions with typos and the corresponding answers returned by the target Q&A robots, where the underlined letters represent the difference between the modified question and the original question. Although the target Q&A robots can correctly answer the original questions, they cannot give the correct answer when facing the questions with tiny typos. Moreover, the answer to the modified question is very different from the original answer. Table 3 shows the accuracy of Siri and Zo answering questions on the three modified Q&A datasets. It is shown that the typos in the questions will significantly reduce the accuracy of the Q&A robot answering questions. Compared with Zo, Siri is less robust to these typos in the questions. For many questions that contain typos, Siri cannot return correct answers. Obviously, the robustness of current Q&A robots needs to be further improved.

Table 2. Three examples of questions with typos and the corresponding answers returned by the target Q&A robots.

1	Original question	What is the density of gold?
	Modified question	What is the destiny of gold?
	Original answer	19.3 grams per cubic centimeter
	Siri answer	I didn't find anything for "What is the destiny of gold?"
	Zo answer	The gold with the power
2	Original question	Who does allen iverson play for now 2010?
	Modified question	Who does allen iverson pray for now 2010?
	Original answer	Philadelphia 76ers
	Siri answer	Allen Iverson played for the Denver Nuggets, Detroit Pistons, Memphis Grizzlies and Philadelphia 76ers in the NBA between 1996 and 2009
	Zo answer	One is definitely good for Allen Iverson
3	Original question	What did ryan dunn died from?
	Modified question	What did ryan dunn diked from?
	Original answer	Traffic collision
	Siri answer	The result is searched from the web
	Zo answer	Woops, sorry having trouble reading that...

Table 3. The accuracy of Siri and Zo answering questions on three modified Q&A datasets, where only the questions in the three datasets that the Q&A robot can answer correctly are retained and be used to generate questions with typos.

Target Q&A robot	WebQuestionSP	CuratedTREC	WikiMovies-10k
Siri	36.57%	42.62%	35.33%
Zo	73.66%	68.89%	69.21%

6 Proposed Countermeasures and Challenges

6.1 Use Explainable Machine Learning Models

When developers use machine learning to analyze the semantics of a question, they should try to choose or develop explainable models, e.g., linear models, decision trees. In this way, when the answer of the Q&A robot is wrong, they can modify the model accordingly. If they use complex nonlinear model, such as Deep Neural Networks, they cannot tell the details of the model or explain the generation process of the results. Once the Q&A robot makes mistakes, it is difficult to find out the reasons of these errors, and these problems cannot be fixed.

6.2 Rule-Based Filtering

Developers can manually create rules based on the characteristics of sensitive words. According to these rules, the Q&A robot detects and filters sensitive words in the user's questions and output answers. However, the performance of filtering sensitive words of this method is poor. There are a large number of and various kinds of sensitive words, just like a 'word games'. It is extremely difficult to define complete rules. Once the sensitive words are slightly changed, the filtering rules will probably fail. On the other hand, sometimes some normal words are misidentified as sensitive words by these rules.

6.3 Fuzzy Matching

Developers can also generate a dictionary of sensitive words to fuzzy match the user's questions. However, the efficiency of this method is low. Like the rule-based filtering method, this method may also fail when facing various kinds of sensitive words and their variants. Therefore, current Q&A robots do not have an effective way to filter sensitive words.

6.4 Spell Checking

A spell checking module is needed for the Q&A robots. If the Q&A robot cannot obtain the correct answer after searching in the knowledge base and related documents, the Q&A robot should use the spell checking module to check the question for typos. If there are typos in the question entered by the user, the Q&A robot corrects the typos in the question and confirms it to the user. Then, the Q&A robot can search the answer based on the revised correct question.

7 Conclusion

In this paper, we present four robustness (security) issues of current NLP based AI Q&A robots, which will lead to serious consequences to the Q&A robots. We design and implement two types of tests, which simulated two types of common inputs, bad language and user's typos, to evaluate state-of-the-art Q&A robots. Experiment results show that these common inputs can successfully make these Q&A robots malfunction, DoS, or speaking dirty words. Besides, we propose possible countermeasures to these robustness problems. However, our analysis show that there are no satisfactory solutions currently, which requires further joint efforts by both researchers and industry engineers.

References

1. Google assistant. https://assistant.google.com
2. Microsoft Cortana personal assistant. https://www.microsoft.com/en-us/cortana
3. Apple Siri personal assistant. https://www.apple.com/ios/siri
4. Amazon Alexa. http://alexa.amazon.com
5. IBM Watson. http://www.ibm.com/watson
6. Baidu DuerOS. https://dueros.baidu.com
7. Alibaba Ali Xiaomi. http://www.alixiaomi.com
8. JD Instant Messaging Intelligence. http://open.jimi.jd.com
9. Auer, S., Bizer, C., Kobilarov, G., Lehmann, J., Cyganiak, R., Ives, Z.: DBpedia: a nucleus for a web of open data. In: Aberer, K., et al. (eds.) ASWC/ISWC -2007. LNCS, vol. 4825, pp. 722–735. Springer, Heidelberg (2007). https://doi.org/10.1007/978-3-540-76298-0_52
10. Bollacker, K., Evans, C., Paritosh, P., Sturge, T., Taylor, J.: Freebase: a collaboratively created graph database for structuring human knowledge. In: Proceedings of the ACM SIGMOD International Conference on Management of Data, pp. 1247–1250 (2008)
11. Suchanek, F.M., Kasneci, G., Weikum, G.: YAGO: a core of semantic knowledge. In: Proceedings of the 16th International Conference on World Wide Web, pp. 697–706 (2007)
12. West, R., Gabrilovich, E., Murphy, K., Sun, S., Gupta, R., Lin, D.: Knowledge base completion via search-based question answering. In: Proceedings of the 23rd International Conference on World Wide Web, pp. 515–526 (2014)
13. Androutsopoulos, I., Ritchie, G.D., Thanisch, P.: Natural language interfaces to databases-an introduction. Nat. Lang. Eng. 1(1), 29–81 (1995)
14. Liu, X., Long, F.: A survey of multi-modal question answering systems for robotics. In: Proceedings of the 2nd International Conference on Advanced Robotics and Mechatronics (ICARM), pp. 189–194 (2017)
15. Zettlemoyer, L.S., Collins, M.: Learning to map sentences to logical form: structured classification with probabilistic categorial grammars. arXiv preprint arXiv:1207.1420 (2012)
16. Zelle, J.M., Mooney, R.J.: Learning to parse database queries using inductive logic programming. In: Proceedings of the National Conference on Artificial Intelligence, pp. 1050–1055 (1996)
17. Wong, Y.W., Mooney, R.: Learning synchronous grammars for semantic parsing with lambda calculus. In: Proceedings of the 45th Annual Meeting of the Association of Computational Linguistics, pp. 960–967 (2007)
18. Lu, W., Ng, H.T., Lee, W.S., Zettlemoyer, L.S.: A generative model for parsing natural language to meaning representations. In: Proceedings of the Conference on Empirical Methods in Natural Language Processing, pp. 783–792 (2008)
19. Yih, W.T., He, X., Meek, C.: Semantic parsing for single-relation question answering. In: Proceedings of the 52nd Annual Meeting of the Association for Computational Linguistics, pp. 643–648 (2014)
20. Yih, W.T., Chang, M.W., He, X., Gao, J.: Semantic parsing via staged query graph generation: question answering with knowledge base. In: Proceedings of the 53rd Annual Meeting of the Association for Computational Linguistics and the 7th International Joint Conference on Natural Language Processing, pp. 1321–1331 (2015)
21. Jurafsky, D.: Speech & Language Processing. Pearson Education India (2000)

22. Ravichandran, D., Hovy, E.: Learning surface text patterns for a question answering system. In: Proceedings of the 40th Annual Meeting of the Association for Computational Linguistics, pp. 41–47 (2002)

23. Brill, E., Dumais, S., Banko, M.: An analysis of the AskMSR question-answering system. In: Proceedings of the ACL Conference on Empirical Methods in Natural Language Processing, pp. 257–264 (2002)

24. Lin, J.: An exploration of the principles underlying redundancy-based factoid question answering. ACM Trans. Inf. Syst. (TOIS) **25**(2), 6 (2007)

25. Zigong environmental protection bureau insulted a reporter. http://baijiahao.baidu.com/s?id=1603776993370451221

26. Wang, Y., Deng, L., Acero, A.: Semantic frame-based spoken language understanding. In: Spoken Language Understanding: Systems for Extracting Semantic Information from Speech, pp. 41–91 (2011)

27. Li, P., et al.: Dataset and neural recurrent sequence labeling model for open-domain factoid question answering. arXiv preprint arXiv:1607.06275 (2016)

28. Mesnil, G., et al.: Using recurrent neural networks for slot filling in spoken language understanding. IEEE/ACM Trans. Audio Speech Lang. Process. **23**(3), 530–539 (2014)

29. Liu, B., Lane, I.: Recurrent neural network structured output prediction for spoken language understanding. In: Proceedings of the NIPS Workshop on Machine Learning for Spoken Language Understanding and Interactions, pp. 1–7 (2015)

30. Yih, W.T., Richardson, M., Meek, C., Chang, M.W., Suh, J.: The value of semantic parse labeling for knowledge base question answering. In: Proceedings of the 54th Annual Meeting of the Association for Computational Linguistics, vol. 2, pp. 201–206 (2016)

31. Baudiš, P., Šedivý, J.: Modeling of the question answering task in the YodaQA system. In: Mothe, J., et al. (eds.) CLEF 2015. LNCS, vol. 9283, pp. 222–228. Springer, Cham (2015). https://doi.org/10.1007/078_3_319_24027_5_20

32. Miller, A., Fisch, A., Dodge, J., Karimi, A.H., Bordes, A., Weston, J.: Key-value memory networks for directly reading documents. In: Proceedings of the 2016 Conference on Empirical Methods in Natural Language Processing, pp. 1400–1409 (2016)

33. Zo. https://www.zo.ai

BMI-Matching: Map-Matching with Bearing Meta-information

DaWei Wang and JingJing Gu[✉]

College of Computer Science and Technology,
Nanjing University of Aeronautics and Astronautics, Nanjing, China
wangdawei673@163.com, gujingjing@nuaa.edu.cn

Abstract. Map-matching is a fundamental pre-processing step for many applications which aligns a trajectory represented by a sequence of sampling points with the city road network on a digital map. With the help of GPS-embedded devices, a lot of GPS trajectories can be collected. However, the raw positions captured by GPS devices usually can not reflect the real positions because of physical constraints such as GPS signals blocked by buildings. And low-sampling-rate data is another challenge for map-matching. Although many approaches have been proposed to solve these problems, unfortunately, most of them only consider the position of the object or the topology structures of the road network. So it becomes significant to accurately match GPS trajectories to road network. We propose a method called BMI-matching (map-matching with bearing meta-information) which not only considers the two factors above but also focuses on the moving object bearing. Based on bearing, we can calculate the direction similarity between moving object and road segments to determine selecting which road segment is appropriate. We conduct experiments on real dataset and compare our method with two state-of-the-art algorithms. The results show that our approach gets better performance on matching accuracy.

Keywords: Map-matching · HMM · R-tree

1 Introduction

In recent years, with the advance of diverse location-acquisition technologies, mining object trajectories have attracted lots of researcher's attention. Map-matching deals with the problem of matching a series of GPS points to the city roads on a digital map. It is fairly useful for many applications, such as understanding urban mobility [8], discovering critical nodes in road network [19], popular routes finding [17], exploring the Urban Region-of-Interest [16] and travel plan recommendation [9]. Nevertheless, the raw position data collected by GPS devices may not report the real position of moving objects. Noisy data and low sampling rate data [14] are usually the big challenges for map-matching problem. The positions measured by GPS devices are not accurate. Especially when vehicle enters a tunnel or an urban canyon, the GPS is experiencing particularly high

© ICST Institute for Computer Sciences, Social Informatics and Telecommunications Engineering 2019
Published by Springer Nature Switzerland AG 2019. All Rights Reserved
X. B. Zhai et al. (Eds.): MLICOM 2019, LNICST 294, pp. 712–727, 2019.
https://doi.org/10.1007/978-3-030-32388-2_58

noise. GPS error can be described as a two dimensional Gaussian distribution. In Fig. 1, if we regard the sampling position as the origin, the distribution of real position is an ellipse or a circle, which depends on the variance and expectation of each dimensionality and correlation coefficient of two dimensionalities. The height represents the possibility of the real position. High noise means the real position is far away from the sampling point and makes map-matching more difficult. Low sampling rate may lead to the uncertainty of an object's moving track. Let us consider two sampling points p_1, p_2. If the sampling time interval is t and the object moving speed is v, the moving distance between these two points is $l = v * t$. In Fig. 2, p_1, p_2 are two foci of the ellipse, and $l_1 = l_2 = l$ are two paths where object may travel. Generally, if the sampling rate is low (large t), the number of possible paths will be large, which means huge uncertainty of track between these two points.

And we perform an analysis on the taxi trajectory dataset collected in Shanghai, China. The taxis often report their positions to the dispatching center with low sampling rates for saving energy and communication cost. The sampling rates usually vary from a few seconds to minutes. Owing to kinds of factors (sensor failure, transmission error, etc.), the location reported by devices may be noisy. As shown in Fig. 3, the sampling time interval in our data exceeds 2 min. In Fig. 4, the green lines represent road network, and the trajectory is represented by yellow points. Obviously, the trajectory misses many sampling points. It will be challenging to match these data on road network.

A number of approaches have been proposed for map-matching problem. Some conventional map-matching methods employ local or incremental algorithms [4] to map current or neighboring positions. But it may fail for low sampling rate data. A few methods match the trajectory exploiting global relationship to deal with the low sampling rate data [7,17]. But they can not perform well on complex environments such as thick road network. Although other methods for low-sampling-rate data [10,11] and noisy data [11] perform well, they need particular conditions such as complete information of road network which may not be available in practice.

Overall, in this paper, we make three contributions summarized as follows.

- We propose a method called BMI-matching which considers the bearing of the moving object besides the location of object and the topology structures of the road network. Based on moving object bearing, we can compare the direction similarity between moving object and road segments.
- In the complex road network, it is hard to query the candidate segments in a short time. We exploit spatial access method R-tree to accelerate the search process. Calculating shortest path is computationally high. We compute shortest paths covering hotspots in advance and save as an index table.
- We conduct experiments on real dataset and compare our algorithm with two state-of-the-art algorithms of ST-Matching [10] and HMM-Matching [11] in matching accuracy. The results show that the our algorithm gets better performance on accuracy.

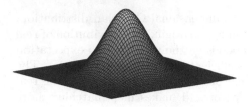

Fig. 1. Illustration of noisy data

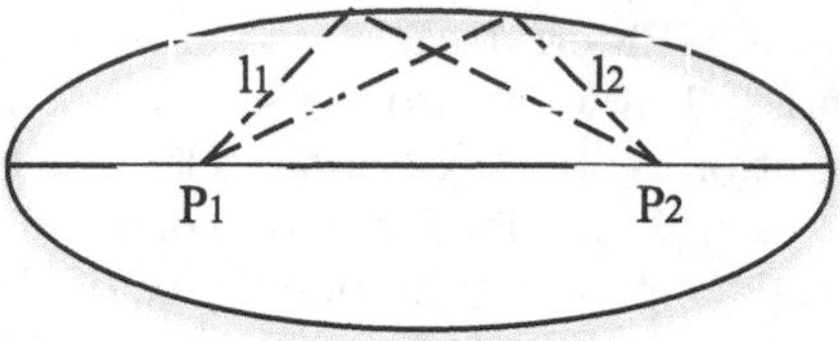

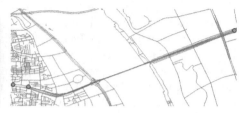

Fig. 2. Illustration of low sampling rate data

timestamp	lon	lat	speed	bearing
2015-04-01 05:41:01	121.583485	31.258670	18.600000	239.000000
2015-04-01 05:43:07	121.577143	31.258700	29.000000	257.000000
2015-04-01 05:45:13	121.562670	31.249288	60.299999	238.000000
2015-04-01 05:47:33	121.556897	31.245947	2.700000	236.000000
2015-04-01 05:49:33	121.540155	31.238440	0.000000	250.000000
2015-04-01 05:51:43	121.533490	31.236247	37.599998	249.000000
2015-04-01 05:54:43	121.518283	31.231423	26.500000	250.000000
2015-04-01 05:57:40	121.491698	31.223893	58.099998	284.000000
2015-04-01 05:59:41	121.477500	31.222400	0.000000	332.000000
2015-04-01 06:01:46	121.473377	31.225573	23.799999	160.000000

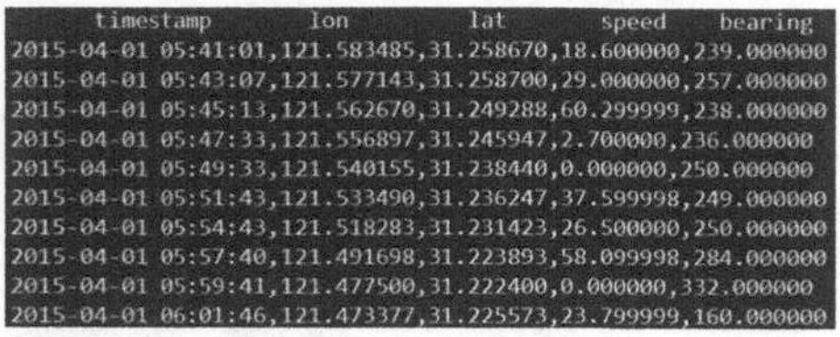

Fig. 3. The form of taxi data

Fig. 4. A trajectory visualized on digital map (Color figure online)

2 Related Work

Researchers pay more attention on mining moving objects trajectories to understand resident mobility, discover the functionality of different regions in a city [16] and construct the smart city. The fundamental step of all these applications is map-matching. A number of map-matching algorithms have been developed using different techniques. There are two approaches to classify map-matching methods, based on additional information used, or the range of sampling points considered in a trajectory.

According to the range of sampling points, map-matching algorithms can be classified into two groups: local/incremental and global methods. Some conventional map-matching methods employ local or incremental algorithms [4] to map current or neighboring positions. These approaches are fast in computation and work well when sampling frequency is very high. However, their performance is susceptible to the decrease of sampling frequency. Global algorithms aim to match an entire trajectory with a road network. Usually global methods are more accurate than local methods, but it may take long time and is often applied to offline tasks.

From the perspective of additional information used, map-matching algorithms can be classified into four categories: geometric, topological, probabilistic and advanced techniques. For geometric algorithms, they exploit the geometric information of the road network by only considering the shape of the links [2,4], such as matching a GPS point to the nearest road segment. A topological method for map-matching pays attention to the connectivity of the roads. The method proposed in [20] aims to find a minimum weight path based on edit distance. Method proposed in [1] utilizes the Fréchet distance to measure the fit between a GPS sequence and candidate road segment sequence. Probabilistic methods consider various error sources associated with the navigation sensor and the road network data quality [13]. Other advanced algorithms use Kalman filter [12], fuzzy logic [15], or the application of Hidden Markov Model [11]. Some variants of HMM based algorithm have been proposed in [10,21]. The ST-Matching algorithm proposed in [10] combines spatial analysis and temporal analysis which is based on the speed constraint of the road. However, the speed constraint of the road is the maximum speed, and moving objects have different travel speeds at different time of the day. Our algorithm is inspired by the HMM algorithm and considers the bearing of the moving objects.

3   Preliminary Knowledge

In this section, we will give some basic definitions.

Definition 1. *A **sampling point**(p) is a tuple denoted as <lon, lat, speed, bearing, timestamp>, which stands for the longitude, latitude, speed, moving direction of object and generation time of p.*

For representing the bearing, a basis and a positive direction are needed. We define the north as the basis and the clockwise as the positive direction. The bearing is the angle between the basis and the moving direction. As shown in Fig. 5, Y-axis denotes the basis and the moving direction of sampling point p_t is d, so the bearing can be represented as the angle θ ($\theta \in [0, 2\pi]$).

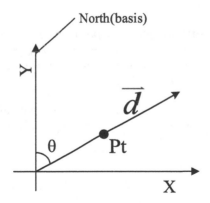

Fig. 5. The bearing of sampling point p at time t

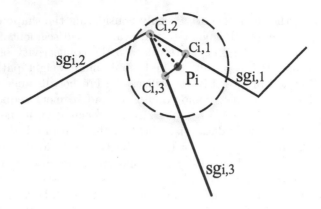

Fig. 6. Candidate segments and segment projection points (Color figure online)

Definition 2. *A **GPS trajectory**(tr) is a series of sampling points with the time interval between any consecutive sampling points not exceeding a certain threshold ΔT. $tr = \{p_1, p_2, ..., p_n\}$, where p_1 is the start point and p_n is the end point.*

Definition 3. *A **segment**(sg) is a directed edge with two terminal points(sg.sp, sg.ep) on road network, where sg.sp is the start point and sg.ep is the end point. Each segment also has two attributes of ID(sg.ID) and length(sg.l) .*

Definition 4. *A **road network** is a directed graph $G(V, E)$, where V is a set of nodes representing the intersections and terminal points of the road segments, and E is a set of directed edges representing road segments.*

Definition 5. *A **route**(r) is a set of segments. $r = \{sg_1, sg_2, ..., sg_n\}$, where $r.sp = sg_1.sp$ and $r.ep = sg_n.ep$*

Definition 6. *A **segment projection point**($c_{i,j}$) of a sampling point(p_i) on the segment($sg_{i,j}$) is a point such that $c_{i,j} = arg\ min_{\forall k_m \in sg_{i,j}}\ dist(p_i, k_m)$, where k_m is any point on $sg_{i,j}$ and $dist(p_i, k_m)$ is the distance between the sampling point and the point in segment.*

As shown in Fig. 6, red point and green points represent sampling point and segment projection points respectively, and segments $sg_{i,1}, sg_{i,2}, sg_{i,3}$ are candidate segments within radius R.

4   Framework

With the preliminary knowledge above, our improved algorithm is presented in this section. The application logic of our method is demonstrated in Fig. 7.

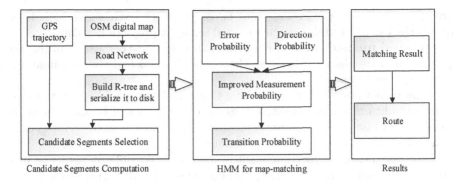

Fig. 7. System overview

HMM for map-matching: a hidden Markov model can be considered a generalization of a mixture model where the hidden variables, which control the mixture component to be selected for each observation, are related through a Markov process rather than independent of each other. As shown in Fig. 8, the observations are time sequence data and each observation may involve many possible states. there is a transition probability(tra_pro) between states and a measurement probability(mea_pro) between observation and state. Hidden Markov models are especially known for their application in temporal pattern recognition such as speech recognition, machine translation, gene prediction and so on.

As illustrated in Fig. 9, there is a trajectory marked with a sequence of sampling points $p_1, p_2, ..., p_n$ called observations and each point has a list of candidate road segments $sg_1, sg_2, ..., sg_m$ called states. The goal of HMM algorithm in map-matching problem is to find an optimal path in many feasible paths by picking one road segment for each sampling point.

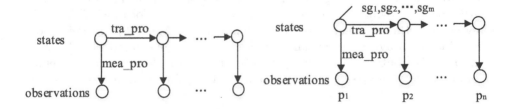

Fig. 8. HMM model   **Fig. 9.** HMM for map-matching

Candidate Segments Selection: first, this component accepts a GPS trajectory as an input. Then, it retrieves all candidate segments within radius R and adjusts the number of candidate segments according to N for each sampling point. Next, segment projection point is computed on each segment. It finally outputs the list of candidate segments and segment projection points.

Improved measurement probability: it considers the bearing of the moving object and the distance between the sampling point and the coordinate segment projection point.

Transition probability: we assume that the driver would follow the shortest path to obtain maximum interest. Some transitions will be more likely and vice versa. For instance, different segments with the same way ID or much closed to each other have high transition probability.

Matching result: this component evaluates all possible routes using probability information and gives the optimal route for the GPS trajectory.

5   Algorithm Details

In this section, we show our BMI-matching algorithm in details.

Candidate Segments Selection: given a GPS trajectory $tr = \{p_1, p_2, ..., p_n\}$, we retrieve all candidate segments of each sampling point p_i within radius R. Then we compute the segment projection point on each segment. Sometimes the city road network may be large and complicated, so it is hard to retrieve all candidate segments of each sampling point in a short time. To speed up the algorithm,we can use spatial access methods R-tree [5]. Because there are enough candidate segments within radius R, we set another parameter, number of candidate segments N, to reduce the execution time.

As shown in Fig. 6, the sampling point p_i has three candidate segments $sg_{i,1}, sg_{i,2}$ and $sg_{i,3}$. Projection point is computed simultaneously. The geometry projection point of p_i onto segment $sg_{i,2}$ is beyond endpoints, and we choose the nearest point $c_{i,2}$ as the projection point. Algorithm 1 shows the detailed procedure.

Improved measurement probability: in improved measurement probability, we make full use of geometric information of the road network and the bearing of the moving object. For map-matching, given a location of the sampling point p_t, there is an error (GPS error) probability $N(p_t|sg_i)$ and a direction probability $D(p_t|sg_i)$ for each candidate segment sg_i. We can model GPS error as normal distribution $N(\mu, \delta^2)$ based on previous work [3]. Formally, we define error probability $N(p_t|sg_i)$ of the sampling point p_t for the candidate segment sg_i as

$$N(p_t|sg_i) = \frac{1}{\delta\sqrt{2\pi}} e^{-\frac{(x_t^i - \mu)^2}{2\delta^2}} \tag{1}$$

where x_t^i is the distance between p_t and segment projection point $c_{t,i}$ on segment $sg_{t,i}$. We can easily determine the road segment when comparing the direction of moving object to the direction of road segment. We define the direction probability $D(p_t|sg_i)$ of the sampling point p_t for the segment sg_i as

$$D(p_t|sg_i) = log(1 + exp(-a))$$
$$a = min(\ |diff(\Theta_{p_t}, \Theta_{sg_i})|,\ 2\pi - |diff(\Theta_{p_t}, \Theta_{sg_i})|\ )$$

where Θ_{p_t} and Θ_{sg_i} are the bearing of moving object at time t and road segment sg_i respectively, and $diff(\Theta_{p_t}, \Theta_{sg_i})$ is the difference of bearing between them. With the error probability $N(p_t|sg_i)$ and direction probability $D(p_t|sg_i)$, we define the improved measurement probability of the sampling point p_t for the segment sg_i as

$$I(p_t|sg_i) = N * D \tag{2}$$

Algorithm 1. Candidate segments Selection

Pre-processing: build the R-tree of the city road network and serialize it to disk.

Input: road network $G < V, E >$, GPS trajectory tr, radius R, number of candidate segments N

Output: list of candidate segments SG and segment projection points C

1: **for** each point p_i in tr **do**
2:     retrieve the all candidate segments as a list SG_i in G within R
3:     **if** $len(SG_i) > N$ **then**
4:         select N segments $sg_{i,n}$ from SG_i.
5:         compute projection point in each segments as a list $c_{i,n}$.
6:         $SG.append(sg_{i,n})$
7:         $C.append(c_{i,n})$
8:     **if** $0 < len(SGi) < N$ **then**
9:         compute projection point in each segments as a list C_i.
10:        $SG.append(SG_i)$
11:        $C.append(C_i)$
12: **return** SG,C

Initial state probability: for map-matching, initial state probablity π gives the probability of the vehicle's first road segment over all segments. With the definition of improved measurement probability, we describe the initial state probability as the first improved measurement probability:

$$\pi_i = I(z_1|sg_i) = N(z_1|sg_i) * D(z_1|sg_i) \tag{3}$$

In practice, it is less possible to match the sampling point into the road segment which is far from it. So, we set to zero any error probability from a road segment that is more than radius R away from the sampling point.

Transition probability: given two sampling point p_t and p_{t+1}, transition probability is the probability of a vehicle driving between two candidate road segments at these two times. We assume that the driver would follow the shortest path to obtain maximum interest. The route distance will be computed by method of shortest path. Thus, the transitions whose great circle distance is about the route distance between two sampling points may be more possible. As shown in Fig. 10, there are four segments sg_1, sg_2, sg_3 and sg_4 and two sampling points p_t and p_{t+1}. $c_{t,1}$, $c_{t,2}$ and $c_{t+1,1}$ are projection points of the sampling point p_t and p_{t+1} respectively. Red dashed line represents the great circle distance between p_t and p_{t+1} denoted as $greatCD$. Green line and orange line represent the route distance denoted as $route1$ and $route2$ respectively. $greatCD$ is much closer to $route2$ rather than $route1$. In other words, the true path is $route2$. We define the transition probability as

$$p(sg_{t+1}|sg_t) = e^{-d_t}$$
$$d_t = |greatCircleDis(p_t, p_{t+1}) - routeDis(c_{t,i}, c_{t+1,j})|$$

where sg_t and sg_{t+1} are the candidate segments of the sampling point p_t and p_{t+1} at these two times respectively. The route distance can be calculated by shortest path methods such as Dijkstra, A* and so on, but all of them are computationally high. In practice, we compute some shortest paths covering hotspots in advance and save it to file as an index table. We can check the shortest paths file when needed.

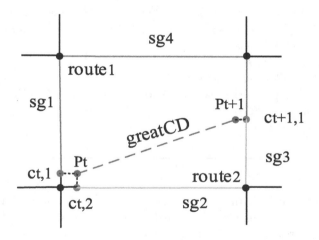

Fig. 10. Transition probability (Color figure online)

Matching result: with improved measurement probability, initial state probability and transition probability, we can compute the optimal path using the Viterbi algorithm. The Viterbi algorithm is a dynamic programming algorithm to maximize the product of the improved measurement probability and the transition probability for finding the most likely sequence of hidden states.

6   Experiment

In this section, we present the experimental evaluation and verify that our algorithm can achieve high accuracy. First we show the experimental setting, including the dataset and some parameters. Next we introduce two evaluation criteria. Then we compare our algorithm with two algorithms of the HMM-Matching proposed by Newson et al. [11] and ST-Matching proposed by Lou et al. [10].

6.1   Experimental Setting

Dataset

Road Network: we use Shanghai road network which can be obtained by OpenStreetMap (OSM). OSM is a collaborative project to create a free editable map of the world [6,18]. As depicted in Fig. 11, the road network(highway) of ShangHai includes 694,572 vertices and 887,153 road segments.

Fig. 11. A part of road network in Shanghai

Taxi Trajectory Data: we collect 13,636 taxis' trajectories for one month in Shanghai. We also select eight trajectories which cover not only downtown area but also suburban area as groundtruth.

Parameters

In our algorithm, there are some parameters that need to be set, including the search radius R in candidate segments selection, expectation μ and standard deviation δ in error probability. And we will turn these parameters according to the evaluation criteria defined next. We also compare our algorithm with HMM-Matching and ST-Matching as two baselines. For these two baseline algorithms, we use the empirical settings $\mu_b = 0, \delta_b = 25, \beta_b = 0.16$ as suggested in [10,11].

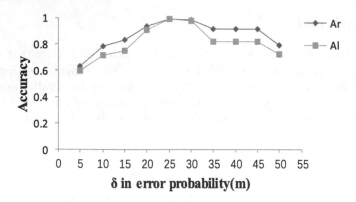

Fig. 12. The effect of δ in error probability

Evaluation Criteria

Our algorithm is evaluated both in terms of running time and matching accuracy. The actual program execution time is the measurement for running time. The matching accuracy is measured by two criteria A_r, A_l, computed by following equations:

$$A_r = \frac{number\ of\ correctly\ matched\ road\ segments}{number\ of\ all\ road\ segments\ of\ a\ test\ trajectory}$$

$$A_l = \frac{\Sigma\ length\ of\ correctly\ matched\ road\ segments}{length\ of\ a\ test\ trajectory}$$

6.2   Experimental Results

Error Probability Parameters μ, δ

GPS error follows the zero-mean Gaussian, so we set $\mu = 0$. We fix the other parameters by assigning the search radius R as 200 meters and number of candidate segments N as 50 and tuning δ.

As shown in Fig. 12, A_r and A_l increase with δ increasing when δ is smaller than 25 m. Ar and Al decrease with δ increasing when δ is large than 25 m. A small value of δ means we have more confidence in GPS device and the candidate segments nearby the sampling points will be selected as the matched segments in a high probability. However, when δ is large the effect of error probability will be diminished. The results of the experiment demonstrate that zero-mean normal distribution with the standard deviation of 25 m is suitable for our algorithm.

Running Time Evaluation

To test the actual program execution time of our algorithm, we select 6 trajectories with different lengths (number of sampling points) which cover different regions.

As depicted in Fig. 13, the execution time will increase with the number of sampling points increasing generally, but there are not much differences between the fifth and sixth trajectory in terms of running time. We find the road network around the sixth trajectory is not complicated when visualizing it on the digital map, which means the number of candidate segments for some sampling points are small. So the running time depends on not only the length of the trajectory but also the number of candidate segments.

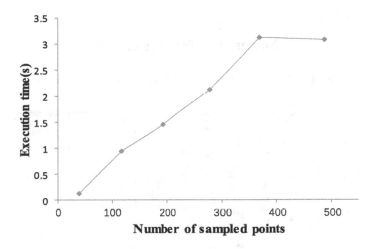

Fig. 13. The execution time with different number of sampling points

Number of Candidate Segments N and Search Radius R

We set search radius $R = 50$, because the δ in error probability is 25 m. Search radius R and number of candidate segments N determine the candidate segments and projection points. When N is small the accuracy will decrease, and a large N may lead to high program running time. So an appropriate value of N is required.

As shown in Fig. 14, A_r and A_l increase with N increasing when N is smaller than 5. A_r and A_l become steady when N exceeds 5. And we set $N = 5$ to get better performance on accuracy without much time cost.

Matching Result Comparison

We select eight groundtruth trajectories and compare our algorithm with HMM-Matching and ST-Matching based on two criteria A_r and A_l. In Figs. 15 and 16, we can find our algorithm gets higher accuracy compared to HMM-Matching and ST-Matching both on A_r and A_l.

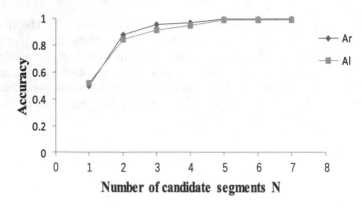

Fig. 14. The effect of number of candidate segments N

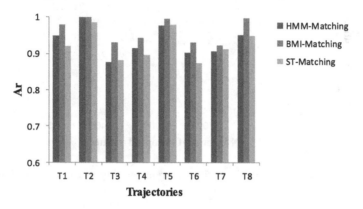

Fig. 15. The comparison on A_r

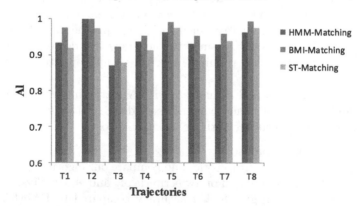

Fig. 16. The comparison on A_l

Our algorithm works well in some cases compared with the HMM-Matching algorithm and we don't need to tune parameters in transition probability. As

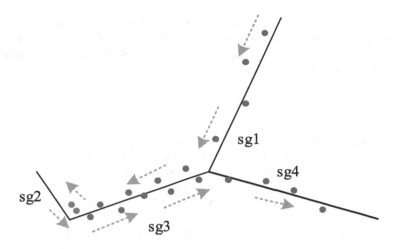

Fig. 17. Case1 (Color figure online)

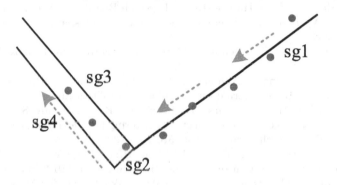

Fig. 18. Case2 (Color figure online)

depicted in Fig. 17, there are four road segments sg_1, sg_2, sg_3, sg_4. Blue arrows represent the direction of moving object. The true path is $sg_1 \longrightarrow sy_2 \longrightarrow sg_3 \longrightarrow sg_4$. The bearing of green points and raod segment sg_2 are similar, so we believe matching green points into $sg2$ is appropriate. But the HMM-Matching algorithm will match them into sg_3 instead of sg_2, which is not correct. In other words, the HMM-Matching algorithm will make errors in a short turn sometimes. In Fig. 18, the distance between last two red points and sg_3 or sg_4 is same, hence matching the green point into segment correctly becomes crucial. Because the green point is near to sg_3, HMM-Matching algorithm matchs it into sg_3 without considering the bearing.

7   Conclusion

In this paper, we introduce a BMI-Matching algorithm. We make full use of the position and bearing of moving objects and the topological structures of road network. We conduct experiments with a real dataset and perform the comparisons between our method and two algorithms of ST-Matching and HMM-Matching. The results show our method performs better than those algorithms in terms of A_r and A_l.

References

1. Brakatsoulas, S., Pfoser, D., Salas, R., Wenk, C.: On map-matching vehicle tracking data. In: International Conference on Very Large Data Bases (2005)
2. Chen, D., Driemel, A., Guibas, L.J., Nguyen, A., Wenk, C.: Approximate map matching with respect to the Fréchet distance. In: 2011 Proceedings of the Thirteenth Workshop on Algorithm Engineering and Experiments (ALENEX), pp. 75–83. SIAM (2011)
3. Diggelen, F.V.: GNSS accuracy: lies, damn lies, and statistics. Gps World, January 2007
4. Greenfeld, J.S.: Matching GPS observations to locations on a digital map. In: 81th Annual Meeting of the Transportation Research Board, vol. 1, pp. 164–173 (2002)
5. Guttman, A.: R-trees: a dynamic index structure for spatial searching, vol. 14. ACM (1984)
6. Haklay, M., Weber, P.: OpenStreetMap: user-generated street maps. IEEE Perv. Comput. **7**(4), 12–18 (2008)
7. Kai, Z., Yu, Z., Xing, X., Zhou, X.: Reducing uncertainty of low-sampling-rate trajectories. In: IEEE International Conference on Data Engineering (2012)
8. Kumar, D., Wu, H., Rajasegarar, S., Leckie, C., Krishnaswamy, S., Palaniswami, M.: Fast and scalable big data trajectory clustering for understanding urban mobility. IEEE Trans. Intell. Transp. Syst. **99**, 1–14 (2018)
9. Liu, H., Li, T., Hu, R., Fu, Y., Gu, J., Xiong, H.: Joint representation learning for multi-modal transportation recommendation. In: AAAI (2019, to appear)
10. Lou, Y., Zhang, C., Zheng, Y., Xie, X., Wang, W., Huang, Y.: Map-matching for low-sampling-rate GPS trajectories. In: Proceedings of the 17th ACM SIGSPATIAL International Conference on Advances in Geographic Information Systems, pp. 352–361. ACM (2009)
11. Newson, P., Krumm, J.: Hidden Markov map matching through noise and sparseness. In: ACM Sigspatial International Conference on Advances in Geographic Information Systems (2009)
12. Obradovic, D., Lenz, H., Schupfner, M.: Fusion of map and sensor data in a modern car navigation system. J. VLSI Sig. Process. Syst. Sig. Image Video Technol. **45**(1–2), 111–122 (2006)
13. Ochieng, W.Y., Quddus, M.A., Noland, R.B.: Map-matching in complex urban road networks (2003)
14. Pfoser, D., Jensen, C.S.: Capturing the uncertainty of moving-object representations. In: Güting, R.H., Papadias, D., Lochovsky, F. (eds.) SSD 1999. LNCS, vol. 1651, pp. 111–131. Springer, Heidelberg (1999). https://doi.org/10.1007/3-540-48482-5_9
15. Quddus, M.A., Noland, R.B., Ochieng, W.Y.: A high accuracy fuzzy logic based map matching algorithm for road transport. J. Intell. Transp. Syst. **10**(3), 103–115 (2006)

16. Sun, Y., Zhu, H., Zhuang, F., Gu, J., He, Q.: Exploring the urban region-of-interest through the analysis of online map search queries. In: Proceedings of the 24th ACM SIGKDD International Conference on Knowledge Discovery & Data Mining, pp. 2269–2278. ACM (2018)
17. Wei, L.Y., Zheng, Y., Peng, W.C.: Constructing popular routes from uncertain trajectories. In: Proceedings of the 18th ACM SIGKDD International Conference on Knowledge Discovery and Data Mining, pp. 195–203. ACM (2012)
18. Wikipedia: OpenStreetMap. https://en.wikipedia.org/wiki/OpenStreetMap. Accessed 18 Feb 2019
19. Xu, M., Wu, J., Liu, M., Xiao, Y., Wang, H., Hu, D.: Discovery of critical nodes in road networks through mining from vehicle trajectories. IEEE Trans. Intell. Transp. Syst. **20**, 583–593 (2018)
20. Yin, H., Wolfson, O.: A weight-based map matching method in moving objects databases. In: Proceedings of 16th International Conference on Scientific and Statistical Database Management, pp. 437–438. IEEE (2004)
21. Yuan, J., Zheng, Y., Zhang, C., Xie, X., Sun, G.Z.: An interactive-voting based map matching algorithm. In: Proceedings of the 2010 Eleventh International Conference on Mobile Data Management, pp. 43–52. IEEE Computer Society (2010)

Using Speech Emotion Recognition to Preclude Campus Bullying

Jianting Guo[✉] and Haiyan Yu

Harbin Institute of Technology at Weihai, Weihai, Shangdong, China
guojianting0616@163.com

Abstract. Campus bullying could have extremely adverse impact on pupils, leading to physical harm, mental disease, or even ultra behaviour like suicide. Hence, an accurate and efficient anti-bullying approach is badly needed. A campus bullying detection system based on speech emotion recognition is proposed in this paper to distinguish bullying situations from non-bullying situations. Initially, a Finland emotional speech database is divided into two parts, namely training-data and testing-data, from which MFCC (Mel Frequency Cepstrum Coefficient) parameters are garnered. Subsequently, ReliefF feature selection algorithm is applied to select the useful features to form a matrix. Then its dimensions is diminished with PCA (Principle Component Analysis) algorithm. Finally, KNN (K-Nearest Neighbor) algorithm is utilized to train the model. The final simulations show a recognition rate of 80.25%, verifying that this model is able to provide a useful tool for bullying detection.

Keywords: MFCC · PCA · KNN · Speech emotion recognition · Campus bullying

1 Introduction

It rarely surprises us that campus bullying has been a universal topic for the incredibly baneful effort it could bring to adolescence. However, most current anti-bullying approaches are either primitive (e.g. security patrol, surveillance cameras) or sketchy (e.g. ICE BlackBox). The main problem for the former is paucity of immediacy, while the latter requires behaviours which could be detected by the bullies. Although recently technics using movement sensors have been attached to this field. For example, Ye et al. [1] proposed a instance-based physical violence detection algorithm to prevent physical bullying, a great many bullying behaviours still manage to escape the detection.

The reason is simple. Neglecting the variety of bullying forms, most of these methodologies focus on physical bullying. Nevertheless, according to Olweus et al. [2], bullying action could be carried out by physical contact, by words and by other ways. Thus those speech bullying actions without any form of physical contact could easily escape most detections. Given the contemporary situation, this paper proposes a mechanism based on speech emotion recognition to

X. B. Zhai et al. (Eds.): MLICOM 2019, LNICST 294, pp. 728–734, 2019.
https://doi.org/10.1007/978-3-030-32388-2_59

discover the emotions contained by speeches under both bullying situation and non-bullying situation and distinguish them from each other. Every smart phone with a microphone should be able to use this mechanism.

Additionally, Salmivalli *et al.* [3] claimed that apart from victims and bullies, other roles like outsiders are also involved in a bullying situation. Some of those outsiders could be too scared to stop the bullying or call for help. With this speech emotion recognition mechanism, they would be able to report the bullying situation without infuriating the bullies, which will furnish us with another immediate anti-bullying method.

The paper is constructed as follows: Sect. 2 gives out some previous researches on speech emotion recognition. The emotion-recognising-based bullying detection algorithm is proposed in Sect. 3. Section 4 shows the simulation results, while Sect. 5 draws conclusions.

2 Previous Research on Speech Emotion Recognition

Recently, emotion recognition in speech has been an extremely voguish field, attracting tremendous amounts of researchers to modify this technique. Thanks for the researches done by the previous researchers, a variety of classifiers using different speech features (e.g. frequency, energy, speaking rate...) and different databases (e.g. Berlin Emotional Database, BelFast Database...) appear one after another. Some of those classifiers are capable of distinguish 5–7 kinds of human emotion. Although in this paper our ultimate goal is to differentiate bullying situation and non-bullying situation, which means the ability to specify every kind of emotion is not necessary, it is still helpful to review a couple of spectacular classifiers.

Some of the commonest classifiers for speech emotion recognition are SVM (Support Vector Machine), HMM (Hidden Markov Model), K Star and so on. Iliou *et al.* [4] extracted features like pitch, energy and MFCCs (mel-frequency cepstral coefficients) and attached K Star classifier to distinguish 7 different emotions based on these features. Their final accuracy in speaker-independent framework reached 74%. Petrushin [5], however, ultilised neural network recogniser to classify 5 dissimilar emotion at distinct rate. His classifier's recognition ability (namely the accuracy) fluctuates depending on different emotions (e.g. 70–80%-anger, 35–55%-fear), which is very similar to humans' own capability of distinguishing emotions. To obtain a relatively high accuracy and specific recognition ability, these classifiers inevitably have a high sophistication. Besides, they also consume more hardware resources.

Since our purpose is to distinguish bullying situation and non-bullying situation based on emotion recognition, which does not demand for high specification, we will attempt to diminish the complexity with less features and less labels. Bicocchi *et al.* [6] pointed out that KNN algorithm could achieve a similar recognition accuracy with much less calculation, therefore, this paper will focus on KNN classifier.

3 Bullying Detection Algorithm Based on Speech Emotion Recognition

The database that we use contains voices from different campus scenarios performed by a school of Finnish students. These voices could be divided into 6 kinds—bullying voice, normal conversation, clap hands, laugh, cry and voice that shows fear. Given that we aim at distinguishing bullying and non-bullying situation, we categorize these different voices into two groups (e.g bulling situation: bullying voice, cry, voice that shows fear, non-bullying situation: normal conversation, clap hands, laugh.), after which we can get a training set and a testing set each containing approximately same number of emotional voices from both situations (training set: 42 voices from bulling situation and 41 voices from non-bullying situation. testing set: 41 voices from bullying situation and 41 voices from non-bullying situation). Similar quantity of training voices from both sides could efficiently prevent the classifier from having a bias towards one side.

According to Kim *et al.* [7], MFCC (Mel Frequency Cepstral Coefficient) is the most commonly used feature in distinguishing speeches, emotions, speakers and so on. Hence, the speech feature extraction in this paper will mainly focus on MFCC.

Initially, to improve the resolution of high-frequency part of the voice signal, we use first order FIR filter to do pre-emphasis to the signal's spectrum. The function of the first order FIR filter is:

$$H(z) = 1 - 0.9375z^{-1}. \tag{1}$$

Figure 1 shows the spectrum of a voice signal before pre-emphasis, while Fig. 2 demonstrates the spectrum of the same voice signal after pre-emphasis. As illustrated in the figures, the interval between two peaks in the spectrum after pre-emphasis is more obvious than that in the spectrum before pre-emphasis, which shows a relatively higher resolution.

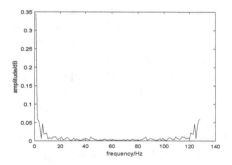

Fig. 1. Spectrum before pre-emphasis.

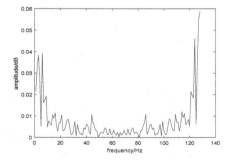

Fig. 2. Spectrum after pre-emphasis.

Subsequently, for the reason that voice signal is thought to be steady in 10 ms to 30 ms, we separate frame of all these voice signals with a Hamming window showed as following:

$$W(n, a) = (1 - a) - cos[2\pi * n/(N - 1)]. \tag{2}$$

where $a = 0.46$ and $N = 512$. To avoid data lost, the frame increment is set to be 256 which is half the length of Hamming window. Then MFCC parameters of every frame are calculated, after which first and second order differential MFCC parameters will also be reckoned. After the extraction of MFCC parameters, we calculate the arithmetic means of MFCCs and use them to form a matrix containing enormous characters of these voice signals. The formula used to compute the mean of MFCCs is:

$$x_{ave} = (x_1 + x_2 + ... + x_n)/n. \tag{3}$$

Considering that dealing with such an avalanche of features is sophisticated and unnecessary, we need to designate the useful ones from them. Thus, ReliefF feature selection algorithm is used to select features which is useful for the classifier. The ranks and weights of every feature is computed and only those features whose weight is greater than zero are kept while others are neglected. After the feature selection progress is done, 22 features are remained for each of the 83 samples in training set and 81 samples in testing set. Although the number of features is relatively small, they could still cost a lot of resources and be unnecessary. Consequently, PCA (Principle Component Analysis) is attached to diminish the dimension of features. The remaining 22 features of 83 elements in training set are used to form a matrix X with 83 rows and 22 columns. Then we do zero-mean to every row of matrix X, after which the covariance matrix C of X is calculated. Next, we find the eigenvalues of the covariance matrix C and the corresponding eigenvector r. Finally, the feature vectors are arranged in a matrix from top to bottom according to the corresponding feature value, and the first k rows are formed into a matrix P, which is the data after dimension reduction to k dimensions. The error and the percentage of information those features could deliver are computed using variances of features. We deem that keeping the features that could display 95% of primitive information would be adequate in this situation. Table 1 illustrates the relationship between the number of features and percentage of information they can deliver.

Table 1. Relationship between the number of features and the percentage of information they can deliver

The number of features	1	2	3	4	5	6	7
The percentage of information	47.45%	66.43%	79.50%	88.17%	93.76%	97.96%	99.09%

As can be seen from the table above, 6 features will be able to include 97.96% of the whole information in a signal voice. However, in order to make the classifier more accurate, we decide to keep 7 features, which could display 99.09% of all the information. Finally, we choose the KNN (K Nearest Neighbour) classifier to do the classification job due to its high accuracy and low complexity.

4 Classification and Analysis

According to Witten *et al.* [8], the class of testing set is predicted based on the nearest training instance in an instance-based learning situation. The KNN classifier we use in this article is also an instance-based classifier. Therefore, its classification result is mainly decided by how many kinds of labels the training set have and how many neighbours we set. Given that our mission is to distinguish two situations—bullying situation and non-bullying situation, we give 1 and 2 as two labels to the training set.

- 1 represents non-bullying situation.
- 2 represents bullying situation.

As for the value of K, we tried an array of different numbers and their corresponding accuracy with testing set varies. The accuracy calculation process is as follows.

Set $CTS(ClassifiedTestingSet)$ to be a vector that contains the classification result of testing set and $RTS(RealTestingSet)$ to be a vector containing the real value of testing set. In both vectors, 1 stands for non-bullying situation while 2 represents bullying situation. Considering that the two vectors have the same dimension, we can get their difference as:

$$D = CTS - RTS. \tag{4}$$

Set x to be the number of zeros in the D (Difference) vector, and y to be the length of the D vector. Then we have the formula for calculating the accuracy:

$$Accuracy = x/y. \tag{5}$$

Table 2 demonstrates some representative K values and their corresponding accuracy.

Table 2. Several representative K values and their corresponding accuracy

K	5	11	17	23	25	27
Accuracy	70.37%	76.54%	79.01%	79.01%	80.25%	79.01%

An increasing trend could be witnessed in accuracy with the rising of K value and the accuracy reaches its peak (80.25%) when K is 25, after which it begins to drop. So we set the ideal K value to be 25. The final accuracy is analogous to some of the recent speech emotion recognition algorithm. For example, Likitha *et al.* [9] also chose MFCC as the extracted feature in their paper and reached an efficiency of 80% for happy, sad and anger emotions. Nevertheless with ReliefF feature selection algorithm and PCA (Principle Component Analysis) algorithm which are not used in their algorithm, our method is able to gain a similar accuracy with less characters and less calculations.

Among all the incorrect classifications, most of them are from non-bullying situation, which means the classifier has a spectacular ability to detect bullying situation but its rate of misclassifying non-bullying situation is slightly high. The reason is not sophisticated. Bullying situation often includes shouting, crying, threatening and other fierce voices which are not commonly heard in normal situation. Their high specificity and low diversity make them relatively strong features, while normal situation often contains enormous different speech emotion—happy, excited, disappointed and so on, which makes features of normal situation weaker. Besides, some special situations in non-bullying situation like intense controversy contain some features that are very similar to features of bullying situation. Therefore, the classifier could sometimes mistake non-bullying situation for bullying situation.

5 Conclusion and Discussion

Campus bullying is universally acknowledged to be deleterious to students and most existing anti-bullying methods tend to focus on physical bullying and victims. In this paper, a instance-based speech emotion recognition algorithm is proposed to make great use of bystanders and detect language bullying which is easily neglected.

The database used in this paper consists of voice signals from different campus situations performed by a group of Finnish students. By analysing these voice signals, MFCC (Mel Frequency Cepstrum Coefficient) is extracted, after which ReliefF feature selection algorithm is attached to diminish the dimension of feature vector to 7 for reducing complexity. Then a two-label training set with approximately same number of factors from both bullying situation and non-bullying situation is used to train the KNN classifier and the classifier successfully reaches an accuracy of 80.25% with the testing sample. Considering the relatively high recognition accuracy, this approach can be attached to smart phones with microphones to detect and report campus bullying efficiently.

Aiming at developing a resource-friendly bullying detection mechanism, this paper utilizes only a limited number of features extracted from voice signals and 2 labels, which leads to a slightly high misclassification rate in non-bullying situation. In the future work, the author will focus on improving the specificity of classification using more emotional features in voice signals like pitch which is a character containing enormous information about emotional status.

References

1. Ye, L., Ferdinando, H., Seppanen, T., et al.: An instance-based physical violence detection algorithm for school bullying prevention. In: 2015 International Wireless Communications and Mobile Computing Conference (IWCMC). IEEE (2015)
2. Olweus, D.: Bullying At School: What We Know and What We Can Do. Wiley-Blackwell, New York (1993)

3. Salmivalli, C., Lagerspetz, K., Bjorkqvist, K., et al.: Bullying as a group process: particiant roles and their relations to social status within the group. Aggressive Behav. **1996**(22), 1–15 (2016)
4. Iliou, T., Paschalidis, G.: Using an automated speech emotion recognition technique to explore the impact of bullying on pupils social life. In: 2011 15th Panhellenic Conference on Informatics, Kastonia, pp. 18–22 (2011)
5. Petrushin, V.: Emotion recognition in speech signal: experimental study, development, and application. In: Proceedings of Sixth International Conference on Spoken Language Processing (ICSLP 2000), ISCA, vol. 2, pp. 222–225, October 2000
6. Bicocchi, N., Mamei, M., Zambonelli, F.: Detecting activities from body-worn accelerometers via instance-based algorithms. Pervasive Mobile Comput. J. **6**, 482–495 (2010)
7. Kim, S., Georgiou, P.G., Lee, S., Narayanan, S.: Real-time emotion detection system using speech: multi-modal fusion of different timescale features. In: IEEE 9th Workshop on Multimedia Signal Processing, Crete 2007, pp. 48–51 (2007)
8. Witten, I.H., Frank, E., Hall, M.A., et al.: Data mining: practical machine learning tools and techniques. ACM Sigmod Record **31**(1), 76–77 (2011)
9. Likitha, M.S., Gupta, S.R.R., Hasitha, K., Raju, A.U.: Speech based human emotion recognition using MFCC. In: 2017 International Conference on Wireless Communications, Signal Processing and Networking (WiSPNET), Chennai, pp. 2257–2260 (2017)

Optimal Control of Navigation Systems with Time Delays Using Neural Networks

Jing Zhu[1,2,3](✉) and Yijing Hou[1]

[1] College of Automation Engineering,
Nanjing University of Aeronautics and Astronautics,
Nanjing, China
drzhujing@nuaa.edu.cn
[2] Key Laboratory of Navigation, Control and Health-Management Technologies
of Advanced Aerocraft (Nanjing University of Aeronautics and Astronautics),
Ministry of Industry and Information Technology, Nanjing, China
[3] Jiangsu Key Laboratory of Internet of Things and Control Technologies
(Nanjing University of Aeronautics and Astronautics), Nanjing, China

Abstract. In this paper, an online adaptive dynamic programming (ADP) scheme is proposed to achieve the optimal regulation control of navigation control systems subject to time delays with input constraints. The optimal control strategy is developed in virtue of Lyapunov theories and neural networks (NNs) techniques. From a robust control perspective, we investigate the stability on navigation time delay systems concerning input constraints by means of linear matrix inequalities (LMIs) and set up the optimal control policy, on which basis that a novel NN-based approach is proposed. A single NN is used to estimate the performance function, the constrained control and consequently the optimal control policy with the weights online tuned. Finally, numerical examples are demonstrated to illustrate our results.

Keywords: Online ADP · Optimal control · Time delay · Neural network · Nonlinear control · Navigation control system

1 Introduction

It is not exaggerated to say that the history of navigation control systems is a reflection of the history of human civilization. Many scientific discoveries and technological inventions are developed by the need of navigation control, such as meteorology [5], Kalman filter method [9], satellite technology [12], micro-electromechanical technology [27], to name a few, which greatly promote the development of navigation control technology. Navigation control algorithm is a typical adaptive method, which can be effectively applied in the intelligent environment. In [20], optimal control of an UAV

This research was supported in part by the National Natural Science Foundation of China under Grant 61603179, in part by the China Postdoctoral Science Foundation under Grant 2016M601805, and in part by the Fundamental Research Funds for the Central Universities under Grant NJ20170005.

X. B. Zhai et al. (Eds.): MLICOM 2019, LNICST 294, pp. 735–747, 2019.
https://doi.org/10.1007/978-3-030-32388-2_60

autonomous navigation system was developed by using only on-board visual and internal sensing information. [8] introduces a navigation planning algorithm for a robot which is capable of autonomous navigation in a structured, partially known and dynamic environment. [23] develops a nonlinear optimal control method to solve the autonomous navigation of a truck and trailer system. Although various technologies have been widely developed in navigation control case by case, the fundamental issue on the robustness and control has been seldom studied.

Nowadays, optimal control theory has gained lots of progress with the development of robust control theories and numerical methods (see [6, 24, 26, 29], and the references therein). On one hand, the optimal control of linear systems has been well investigated and numerous results are readily applicable, such as maximum principle [1], dynamic programming [13], and convex optimization [4], to name a few. On the other hand, the optimal control of nonlinear systems mainly relies on the solution of Hamilton-Jacobi-Bellman (HJB) equation [22], which is difficult to solve analytically. For few special nonlinear systems, analytical solutions such as state dependent Riccati equation approach [21], alternative frozen Riccati equation method [15], etc., have been derived. A majority of current results on nonlinear optimal control, nevertheless, are carried out resorting to approximation linearization theory. In [14], an iterative ADP algorithm was adopted to deal with the optimal control of nonlinear system with time-delay, rendering a series of remarkable developments on optimal control of nonlinear systems.

In addition, the predominating studies of optimal control are investigated without considering actuator limitation. As for the navigation control systems, however, neglecting such constraint may cause undesirable transient response and even system instability [7, 30]. In the recent work [28] and [25], the optimal control method is proposed for linear system with saturation actuator, while in [26] and [19], an iterative heuristic dynamic programming (HDP) algorithm was introduced to solve the optimal control for a class of nonlinear discrete system with control constraints. The optimal control results refer to nonlinear navigation control time-delay systems with control constraints still remain relatively minor. As a consequence, it is of fundamental significance to study the optimal control of navigation control systems with control constraints.

In this paper, we consider the nonlinear optimal control of navigation control time delay systems with input constraints based on ADP algorithm. The navigation parameters, namely position, velocity, and attitude, is framed into a nonlinear state-space model on the basis of [2]. Large mathematical tools in robust control and optimal control theories are thus readily available. To achieve the optimal control goal, the appropriate performance index function under given constraints is constructed. A non-quadratic index function is adopted to measure the constrained control input, and consequently an approximate NN is introduced to estimate the performance function and calculate the optimal control at the same time. Other than using two NNs as most work does, we propose a novel NN-based optimal control strategy by using only one NN. The tuning weights estimation errors of NN is proved to convergent to zero, thus indicating the approximated NN-based optimal control policy for the navigation control system with time delays actually converges to the real optimal control policy. It is worth noting that the stability of the closed-loop navigation control system subject to time delays is guaranteed according to the Lyapunov stability theory. Numerical examples show the effectiveness of the proposed method.

This paper is organized as followed. In Sect. 2, we formulate the optimal control problem of nonlinear time-delay systems with control constraints. In Sect. 3, we present the optimal control solution is obtained by NN. Section 4 presents two illustrative examples and Sect. 5 concludes the paper.

2 Problem Formulation

In this paper, $\mathbb{R}$, $\mathbb{R}^n$, $\mathbb{R}^n_+$, $\mathbb{R}^{l \times p}$ refer to the space of real numbers, n-dimensional real vectors, n-dimensional of positive real vectors, and $1 \times p$-dimensional real vectors, respectively. For any real matrix and real function, $(\cdot)^T$ denotes its transpose. If A is a Hermitian matrix, let $\lambda(A)$ denote its largest eigenvalue. The expression $A \geq 0$ means A is non-negative definite, and $A > 0$ means it is positive definite. Let $\|x(t)\|$ denote the Euclidean norm of x(t), which is defined as

$$\|x(t)\| = \sqrt{x^t(t)x(t)}$$

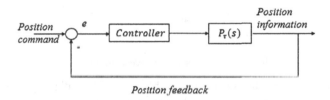

Fig. 1. A subsystem of navigation control systems.

Navigation control systems usually consist of several subsystems, the framework is as shown in Fig. 1. Based on [2] and [23], the state space expression of the navigation control system is derived upon kinetics equations, and can be further represented by the following nonlinear model

$$\dot{x}(t) = Ax(t - \tau) + f(t, x(t), x(t - \sigma)u(t)) \tag{1}$$

where $f(t, x(t), x(t - \sigma)) \in \mathbb{R}^{n \times n}$ is the nonlinear process model and satisfies Lipschitz continuous with $f(t, 0, 0) = 0$. $x(t), \in \mathbb{R}^n$ is the system state vector and $u(t)$ *is* the input vector, consisting of navigation parameters. τ and σ are constant but unknown time delays. Assume that A is a positive definite constant real matrix with appropriate dimension. To achieve high accuracy of attitude error, we use the second-order divided difference filter (DDF2) proposed in [2]. The objective in this paper is to find the constrained optimal control signal $u^*(t)$ that drives the system states to zero as well as to minimize the following performance index function of the system state.

$$J(x(t), u(t)) = \int_t^\infty L(x(s), u(s))ds \tag{2}$$

where

$$L(x(s), u(s)) = x^T(s)Qx(s) + U(u_t) \tag{3}$$

and Q is symmetric and positive definite and $U(u_t)$ is a quadratic and positive definite function without control constraints. Concerning the control constraint, we adopt the following function [21]

$$U(u_t) = 2\int_0^u \beta^{-T}\left(\overline{U}^{-1}v\right)\overline{U}Rdv \tag{4}$$

where $v, R \in \mathbb{R}^n$ is positive definite, and

$$\beta^{-1}(u_t) = \left[\varphi^{-1}(u_{1t}), \varphi^{-1}(u_{2t}), \cdots \varphi^{-1}(u_{mt})\right]^{-T}$$

$\varphi^{-1}(\cdot)$ refers to the inverse of $\varphi(\cdot)$, $\beta^{-1}(\cdot) = (\beta^{-1})^T$. $\varphi(\cdot)$ is a bounded monotonic odd function with

$$|\varphi(\cdot)| < 1$$

and

$$|\varphi'(\cdot)| < \mu, \ \mu \text{ is a positive constant}$$

In this paper, we choose $\varphi(\cdot) = \tanh(\cdot)$, and $R = \text{diag}(\gamma_1, \gamma_2, \cdots \gamma_m)$, with $\gamma_i > 0, i = 1, 2, \cdots m$ to simplify the subsequent analysis.

The Hamilton function is given as

$$H(x, u, t) = L(x(t), u(t)) + \nabla J^T(x)(Ax + fu) \tag{5}$$

with $\nabla J(x) = \frac{\partial J}{\partial x}$ referring to the partial derivative of the performance index function. Obviously, based on the Bellman's principle of optimal control theory [10], the optimal performance index function $J^*(x(t), u(t))$ satisfies the following HJB equation

$$J^*(x(t), u(t)) = \min\left\{\int_t^\infty x^T Qx + 2\int_0^u \beta^{-T}\left(\overline{U}^{-1}v\right)\overline{U}Rdv\right\} \tag{6}$$

It can be solved d by taking partial differential of $J^*(x(t), u(t))$ with respect to $u(t)$.

$$\frac{\partial J^*(x(t), u(t))}{\partial u(t)} = 2\tanh^{-1}\left(\overline{U}u\right)\overline{U}R + f^T\frac{\partial J}{\partial x} = 0 \tag{7}$$

Hence, the optimal input is obtained as

$$u^*(t) = -\overline{U}\tanh\left(\frac{1}{2}\left(\overline{U}R\right)^{-1}f^T\frac{\partial J^*}{\partial x}\right) \tag{8}$$

Consequently, the system (1) becomes the following when the optimal control is achieved.

$$\dot{x}(t) = Ax(t-\tau) - f(t, x(t), x(t-\sigma)\overline{U}\tanh\left(\frac{1}{2}\left(\overline{U}R\right)^{-1}f^T\frac{\partial J^*}{\partial x}\right) \tag{9}$$

By employing the so-called model transformation [18], the original system (1) can be rewritten as

$$\frac{d}{dt}\left(x(t) + A\int_{t-\tau}^{t}x(u)du\right) = Ax(t) + f(t, x(t), x(x-\sigma))u(t) \tag{10}$$

Moreover, system (10) can be further equivalent to

$$\frac{d}{dt}\left(x(t) + A\int_{t-\tau}^{t}x(u)du\right) = Ax(t) + F(t, x(t), x(x-\sigma)) \tag{11}$$

where $F(\cdot)$ denotes a nonlinear function of $x(t)$ with

$$F(x, x(t), x(t-\sigma)) = -f(t, x(t), x(t-\sigma)U\tanh(\frac{1}{2}\left(\overline{U}R\right)^{-1}f^T\frac{\partial J^*}{\partial x}$$

In what follows, we shall examine the stability of (9) when the optimal control law is achieved. To this end, the following assumption is required.

Assumption 1. *The nonlinear function $F(t, x, y)$ satisfies*

$$||F(t, x, y) - F(t, x_1, y_1)|| \leq \alpha||x - x_1||^2 + \beta||y - y_1||^2, \tag{12}$$

where $t, x, y, x_1, y_1 \in \mathbb{R}^n$ and α, β are some positive scalar.

In virtue of the famous contraction mapping theorem [3], we can conclude that the original nonlinear navigation control system (1) has unique equilibrium if the following in equation satisfies

$$\sqrt{\alpha + \beta}||A^{-1}|| \leq 1. \tag{13}$$

3   Main Results

3.1   Stability Analysis on Nonlinear Time Delay Systems

In this section, drawing upon Lyapunov stability theory, we present sufficient stability condition for navigation control time delay systems in terms of LMIs. The following theorem is derived.

Theorem 1. *The navigation control system* (1) *subject to input constraint* (8) *is asymptotically stable if for some positive real scalar* α, β, η_1 *and* η_2, *there exists a real matrix* $P = P^T > 0$ *such that the following LMIs hold*

$$\Phi < 0, \tag{14}$$

where

$$\Phi = Q_1 + \tau Q_2 + Q_3$$

$$Q_1 = PA + A^T P + \eta_1^{-1} P^2 + \alpha(\eta_1 + \tau \eta_2)I + \tau A^T PA$$

$$Q_2 = A^T PA + \eta_2^{-1} A^T P^2 A, Q_3 = \beta(\eta_1 + \tau \eta_2)I$$

and I *is the identity matrix with appropriate dimension.*

Proof: Construct the Lyapunov-Krasovskii functional $V(t)$ as

$$V(t) = \psi_1(t) + \psi_2(t),$$

where

$$\psi_1(t) = \left(x(t) + A \int_{t-\tau}^t x(u)du \right)^T P \left(x(t) + A \int_{t-\tau}^t x(u)du \right),$$

and

$$\psi_2(t) = \int_{t-\tau}^t \int_s^t x^T(u)Q_2 x(u)duds + \int_{t-\sigma}^t x^T(u)Q_3 x(u)du$$

In light of model transformation and Eq. (11), we are led to

$$\dot{\psi}_1(t) = 2\left(x(t) + A \int_{t-\tau}^t x(u)du \right)^T P(Ax(t) + F(t, x(t), x(t-\sigma)))$$

which is further bounded by

$$\dot{\psi}_1(t) \le x^T(t)Q_1 x(t) + \int_{t-\tau}^t x^T(u)Q_2 x(u)du + x^T(t-\sigma)Q_3 x(t-\sigma),$$

In the similar manner of [16], the time derivati ve of $V_2(t)$ is computed as

$$\dot{\psi}_2(t) = x^T(t)(\tau Q_2 + Q_3)x(t) - \int_{t-\tau}^t x^T(u)Q_2 x(u)du - x^T(t-\sigma)Q_3 x(t-\sigma),$$

Consequently, it yields to

$$\dot{V}(t) \le x^T(t)\Phi x(t)$$

According to Lyapunov stability theories, $\dot{V}(t)$ is negative definite if Φ is negative definite. As such, the nonlinear time-delay system with input constraint is stable if condition (14) satisfies. This completes the proof.   ■

3.2 NN-Based Online ADP Algorithm

In the following section, we shall develop the NN-based optimal control scheme with the aid of online ADP technique. As mentioned previously, most of past literatures use two NNs to approximate the performance function and optimal control input respectively so as to achieve the so-called optimal control goal. In this paper, however, we propose a novel NN-based optimal control strategy for navigation control systems by utilizing merely single NN other than two NNs, thus largely simplifies the whole structure and decreases the running time. In addition, the performance index function and optimal input arc tuned at the same time.

Let $W_c \in \mathbb{R}^{l \times p}$ refer to the ideal weight matrix of NN, $\phi_c(x)$ refer to the activation function and $\varepsilon_c(x)$ the approximation error. It is necessary to make the following assumption.

Assumption 2. *(a) The approximation error of NN has positive upper bound as* $\|\varepsilon_c\| \leq \varepsilon_{cM}$;
   (b) The residual error ε_H has a positive upper bounded as $\|\varepsilon_H\| \leq \varepsilon_{HM}$;
   (c) The activation function of the NN has a positive lower and upper bound as $\phi_m \leq \|\phi_c\| \leq \phi_M$.
Upon above assumption, the performance index function J(x) is nearly approximated by

$$J(x) = W_x^T \phi_c(x) + \varepsilon_c(x) \tag{15}$$

Be reminiscent of (5) and (15), we obtain the following equation

$$H(x(t), u(t), W_c) = W_c^T \nabla \phi_c(x) \dot{x} + x^T Q x + 2 \int_0^u \tanh(\frac{1}{2}(\overline{U}v)^{-1} \overline{U} R dv + \nabla \varepsilon_c(x) \dot{x} \tag{16}$$

where $\nabla \phi_c(x)$ is the partial derivative of $\phi_c(x)$ with respect to x. That is, $\nabla \phi_c(x) = \partial \phi_c / \partial x$. $\nabla \varepsilon_c(x)$ is the partial derivative of $\varepsilon_c(x)$. Thus, the Hamilton function is alternatively expressed by

$$W_c^T \nabla \phi_c(x) \dot{x} + x^T Q x + 2 \int_0^u \tanh(\frac{1}{2}(\overline{U}v)^{-1} \overline{U} R dv = -\nabla \varepsilon_c(x) \dot{x} = e_H \tag{17}$$

where e_H is the residual error caused by NN approximation. Let $\widehat{W}_c \in \mathbb{R}^{l \times p}$ refer to the real weight matrix of NN. Then the estimation of performance index function is

$$\hat{J}(x) = \widehat{W}_c^T \phi_c(x) \tag{18}$$

As a result, the gradient of $\hat{J}(x)$ is computed by

$$\nabla \hat{J}(x) = (\nabla \phi_c(x))^T \widehat{W}_c \tag{19}$$

Meanwhile, the corresponding Hamilton function can be expressed as

$$H\left(x(t), u(t), \widehat{W}_c\right) = W_c^T \nabla \phi_c(x)\dot{x} + x^T Q x + 2 \int_0^u \tanh(\frac{1}{2} \left(\overline{U}v\right)^{-1} \overline{U}R dv = e_c$$

Let $\tilde{W}_c$ refer to weight estimation error

$$\tilde{W}_c = W_c - \widehat{W}_c$$

We define the objective function $E_c(t)$ by

$$E_c(t) = \frac{1}{2} e_c^2 \tag{20}$$

We seek to find the optimal weight update law such that $E_c(t)$ is minimized. The gradient of objective function with respect to the NN weight estimate is given by

$$\frac{\partial E}{\partial \widehat{W}_c} = e_c \frac{\partial e_c}{\partial \widehat{W}_c} = e_c(\dot{x})^T (\nabla \phi_c)^T \tag{21}$$

On the basis of back propagation (BP) neural network algorithm [32], the weight update law of NN is derived as

$$\dot{\widehat{W}}_c = -\xi \frac{\partial e_c}{\partial \widehat{W}_c} = e_c(\dot{x})^T (\nabla \phi_c)^T \tag{22}$$

With the learning rate $\xi > 0$. As such, the ideal optimal control can be approximated achieved as

$$\hat{u}^*(t) = -\overline{U} \tanh\left(\frac{1}{2} \left(\overline{U}R\right)^{-1} f^T (\nabla \phi_c)^T W_c\right) \tag{23}$$

Theorem 2. *Consider nonlinear nagivation control system* (1) *with input constraint* (8). *Assume the weight update law of NN is given by* (22) *and the control signal* (23) *is applied to the nominal system* (1). *Then the system state $x(t)$ and the NN estimation errors $\widehat{W}_c$ are uniformly ultimately bounded (UUB) respectively.*

The proof herein shares the similarity as the proof in Theorem 1, thus is omitted [11, 17, 31].

4 Examples

In this section, we illustrate our results by two numerical examples.

Example 1. Consider the following second-order navigation control system

$$\dot{x}(t) = \begin{bmatrix} -2 & 1 \\ 1 & -1 \end{bmatrix} x(t - \tau) + \begin{bmatrix} sinx_2(t - \sigma) \\ sinx_1(t - \sigma) \end{bmatrix} u(t) \tag{24}$$

with initial state $x(0) = \begin{bmatrix} 2 & 1 \end{bmatrix}^T$.

We first examine the stability condition. As suggested in Theorem 1, the nominal system (24) is asymptotically stable if $\tau \leq 0.5$ with σ being arbitrarily large. From Fig. 2 (a)–(b) we can see the state response of the system (24) converges to zero when there is no delay and $\tau = \sigma = 0.5$, where the state response of the delay free system converges to 0 after 7 s, slightly shorter than that of the latter system. In contrast, from Fig. 3 we can see the nominal plant becomes unstable when $\tau = 0.7$.

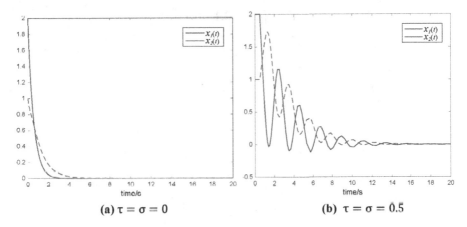

(a) $\tau = \sigma = 0$ (b) $\tau = \sigma = 0.5$

Fig. 2. State response of system (24).

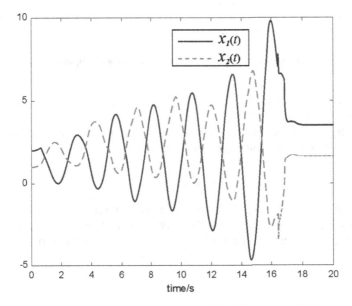

Fig. 3. State response of system (24) with $\tau = \sigma = 0.7$.

Example 2. Specifically, we examine the NN-based optimal control law for the case $\tau = \sigma = 0.5$. We consider the system (24) with input constraints

$$|u(t)| \leq \overline{U} = 0.1 \tag{25}$$

The optimal control objective is to drive the system state $x(t)$ to zero quickly as well as to minimize the performance function. By selecting $Q = R = 1$, the activation function of NN is equal to

$$\phi_c(x) = \begin{bmatrix} x_1^2 & x_1x_2 & x_2^2 \end{bmatrix}^T$$

Assume the initial weights are

$$W_c = \begin{bmatrix} 0.1 & 0.1 & 0.1 \end{bmatrix}^T$$

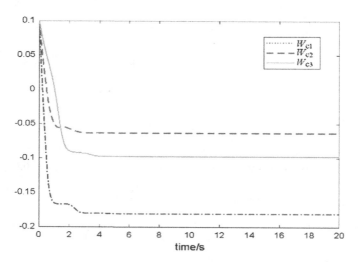

Fig. 4. Trajectories of NN weights for system (24) with input constraint (25)

Let the learning rate of NN be $\xi = 0.5$. The convergent trajectories of NN weights are shown in Fig. 4.

Besides, the optimally controlled signals for system (24) without control constraint, with input constraint (25), and with input constraint

$$|u(t)| \leq \overline{U} = 0.2 \tag{26}$$

are respectively drawn in Fig. 5, from which we can see that for the circumstance without constraint, control signal u varies within a relatively large range, while the proposed scheme regulates the input signal effectively for both cases of input constraint (25) and (26).

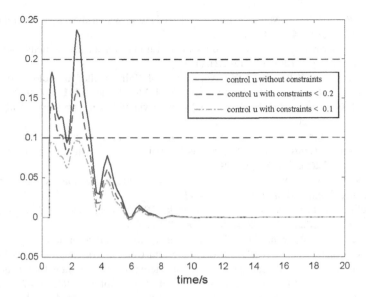

Fig. 5. Unconstrained and constrained control signals.

5 Conclusion

In this paper we propose a novel NN-based optimal control policy for navigation control systems subject to time delay. Optimal control strategy is proposed under the consideration of control constraints by applying a non-quadratic performance function. We investigate the stability on nonlinear time delay systems in terms of LMIs in the first. Afterwards, a novel NN-based optimal control policy is introduced to approximate the optimal cost function and obtain the optimal constrained control signal using only one NN. Finally, Numerical simulation shows the effectiveness of our results.

References

1. Abdellaoui, B.: Maximum principle and dynamic programming approaches of the optimal control of partially observed diffusions. Stochast. Int. J. Probab. Stoch. Process. **9**(3), 169–222 (1983)
2. Ali, J., Mirza, M.: Initial orientation of inertial navigation system realized through nonlinear modeling and filtering. Measurement **44**(5), 793–801 (2011)
3. Angelov, V.G.: A converse to a contraction mapping theorem in uniform spaces. Nonlin. Anal. **12**(10), 989–996 (1988)
4. Ben-Tal, A., Nemirovski, A.: Robust convex optimization. Math. Oper. Res. **23**(4), 769–805 (1998)
5. Bisiaux, M., Cox, M.E., Forrester, D.A., et al.: Possible improvements in meteorology for aircraft navigation. J. Navig. **36**(1), 10 (1983)
6. Branicky, M.S., Borkar, V.S., Mitter, S.K.: A unified framework for hybrid control: model and optimal control theory. IEEE Trans. Autom. Control **43**(1), 31–45 (2002)

7. Bruce, J.R., Veloso, M.M.: Safe multirobot navigation within dynamics constraints. Proc. IEEE **94**(7), 1398–1411 (2006)
8. Causse, O., Crowley, J.L.: Navigation with constraints for an autonomous mobile robot. Robot. Auton. Syst. **12**(3–4), 213–221 (1994)
9. Chen, Y., Zhang, X.J., Xue, Y.Y.: Application of Kalman filter technology to integrated INS/DR navigation system for land vehicle. Appl. Mech. Mater. **411–414**, 912–916 (2013)
10. Crespo, L.G., Sun, J.: Stochastic optimal control via Bellman's principle. Automatica **39** (12), 2109–2114 (2003)
11. Dierks, T., Thumati, B., Jagannathan, S.: Optimal control of unknown affine nonlinear discrete-time systems using offline-trained neural networks with proof of convergence. Neural Netw. **22**(5), 851–860 (2009)
12. Gounley, R., White, R., Gai, E.: Autonomous satellite navigation by stellar refraction. J. Guidance Control Dyn. **7**(2), 129–134 (1984)
13. Himmelberg, C.J., Parthasarathy, T., Vanvleck, F.S.: Optimal plans for dynamic programming problems. Math. Oper. Res. **1**(4), 390–394 (1976)
14. Huang, Y., Ling, X., Wang, D.: Adapted dynamic programming for nonlinear systems with saturated actuator and time-delay. J. Central South Univ. **44**(5), 1881–1887 (2013)
15. Huang, Y., Lu, W.: Nonlinear optimal control: alternatives to Hamilton-Jacobi equation. In: Proceedings of the IEEE Conference on Decision & Control, pp. 3942–3947 (1996)
16. Li, C., Huang, T.: On the stability of nonlinear systems with leakage delay. J. Franklin Inst. **346**(4), 366–377 (2009)
17. Liu, D., Yang, X., Wang, D.: Reinforcement-learning-based robust controller design for continuous-time uncertain nonlinear systems subject to input constraints. IEEE Trans. Cybern. **45**(7), 1372–1385 (2015)
18. Li, X., Gao, H.: A new model transformation of discrete-time systems with time-varying delay and its application to stability analysis. IEEE Trans. Autom. Control **56**(9), 2172–2178 (2011)
19. Luo, Y., Zhang, H.: Approximate optimal control for a class of nonlinear discrete-time systems with saturating actuators. Progress Nat. Sci. **18**(8), 1023–1029 (2008)
20. Mac, T.T., Copot, C., Keyser, R.D., et al.: The development of an autonomous navigation system with optimal control of an UAV in partly unknown indoor environment. Mechatronics **49**, 187–196 (2018)
21. Manousiouthakis, V., Chmielewski, D.J.: On constrained infinite-time nonlinear optimal control. Chem. Eng. Sci. **57**(1), 105–114 (2002)
22. Pasik-Duncan, B., Duncan, T.: Stochastic controls: hamiltonian systems and HJB equations. IEEE Trans. Autom. Control **46**(11), 1846 (1999)
23. Rigatos G.: Nonlinear optimal control for autonomous navigation of a truck and trailer system. In: 18th International Conference on Advanced Robotics, Hong Kong, China, pp. 505–510 (2017)
24. Ross, I.M., Karpenko, M.: A review of pseudo spectral optimal control: from theory to flight. Ann. Rev. Control **36**(2), 182–197 (2012)
25. Saberi, A., Lin, Z., Teel, A.R.: Control of linear systems with saturating actuators. IEEE Trans. Autom. Control **41**(3), 368–378 (1996)
26. Schwartz, A., Polak, E.: Consistent approximations for optimal control problems based on Runge-Kutta integration. SIAM J. Control Optim. **34**(4), 1235–1269 (1996)
27. Shen, S.C., Huang, H.J., Wang, Y.J.: Design and evaluation of a micro-electromechanical systems inertial navigation system for underwater vehicle. J. Comput. Theor. Nanosci. **18**(1), 16–24 (2012)
28. Sussmann, H.J., Sontag, E.D., Yang, Y.: A general result on the stabilization of linear systems using bounded controls. IEEE Trans. Autom. Control **39**(12), 2411–2425 (2002)

29. Tsai, M., Gu, D.: Robust and optimal control. Automatica **33**(11), 2095 (1997)
30. Yang, Y., Gao, W., Zhang, X.: Robust Kalman filtering with constraints: a case study for integrated navigation. J. Geodesy **84**(6), 373–381 (2010)
31. Zhang, M., Lu, Z.: Lyapunov-based analyse of weights' convergence on backpropagation neural networks algorithm. Mini-micro Syst. **25**(1), 93–95 (2004)
32. Zheng, H., Tuo, X., Peng, S.: Determination of gamma point source efficiency based on a backpropagation neural network. Nuclear Sci. Tech. **29**(5), 61 (2018)

Multi-spectral Palmprint Recognition with Deep Multi-view Representation Learning

Xiangyu Xu[1,2], Nuoya Xu[1], Huijie Li[1], and Qi Zhu[1,2(✉)]

[1] College of Computer Science and Technology,
Nanjing University of Aeronautics and Astronautics, Nanjing 211106, China
zhuqi@nuaa.edu.cn
[2] Collaborative Innovation Center of Novel Software Technology
and Industrialization, Nanjing 210093, China

Abstract. With the widespread application of biometrics in identification systems, palmprint recognition technology, as an emerging biometric technology, has received more and more attention in recent years. Palmprint recognition mainly focuses on image acquisition, preprocessing, feature selection and image matching. Feature extraction and matching are usually the most essential processes in palmprint recognition, and most of the research is based on feature selection and image matching, and many researchers use rich knowledge in machine learning and computer vision to solve these problems. In this paper, we propose a deep multi-view representation learning based multi-spectral palmprint fusion method, which uses deep neural networks to extract feature representation of multi-spectral palmprint images for palmprint classification. In this manner, the unique features of different spectral palmprint images can be used to learn a view-invariant representation of each palmprint. By using view-invariant representation, we can get better palmprint recognition performance than single modality. Experiments are performed on PolyU palmprint data set to validate the effectiveness of the proposed method.

Keywords: Person identification · Biometrics · Feature extraction · Multi-view learning · Palmprint recognition · Deep learning

1 Introduction

In realistic applications, palmprint as one of the important biological characteristics of the human body, has the characteristics of unique features, high stability, good safety and easy collection [1–3]. It is widely applied in biometric identification [4–6]. Compared to other biometric traits, such as fingerprint images, palmprint images have more rich features for individual recognition. Most palmprint recognition algorithms are based on the holistic and feature. Due to the wide application of image acquisition technology under multi-spectral, complementary information between different spectra can be well applied to classification, such as red, green, and other channels. According to a previous study of Zhang et al. [7], due to skin tissue's different ability to transmit light of different wavelengths, multi-spectral imaging technology can be applied to palmprint information collection, which can obtain more detailed feature information

X. B. Zhai et al. (Eds.): MLICOM 2019, LNICST 294, pp. 748–758, 2019.
https://doi.org/10.1007/978-3-030-32388-2_61

under different cortical layers. Multi-spectral palmprint recognition utilizes information obtained from different spectral wavelengths for personal identification. Since the vein is key part of the palmprint, multi-spectral features are necessary to improve the accuracy and robustness of palmprint recognition [8–12].

In many problems, we have to face multiple "views" of training data while most of the models can only handle two views [13]. The views here can also be multiple modalities, such as text and image, text and video, different spectral of image or different languages of text. As with this type of problem, multi-spectral palmprint recognition has also attracted people's attention. In this paper, we will focus on the difficulty in multi-spectral palmprint fusion classification.

Multi-spectral palmprint has aroused people's attention, many of them are focus on seeking a common space of two spectral [14, 15], it can also be treated as a multi-view representation problem, multi-view techniques learn a representation of data that captures the sources of variation common to all views [13]. Canonical correlation analysis [16] is also widely used in this field, which attempted to learn a projection of each view to maximize the correlation of the two views, the difference between the two views can be eliminated, and the public representation of the two views is obtained. As a classical common space learning method, CCA uses linear projection to learn a new subspace. However, the kernel function have successes in subspace learning [17], an improve method KCCA uses kernel function instead of linear method and makes better results. Now, deep learning is popular, Andrew et al. [18] propose deep CCA which greatly improved the performance of the original CCA with neural network. All of the existing methods are limited between two modalities (spectrums), to handle more than two views, many multi-view canonical correlation analysis method has been proposed [19, 20]. Like Deep Hyperalignment [21], we propose a DNN based multi-view representation learning method that use multiple networks for each modality to eliminate the difference between spectral.

In this paper the contributions are as follow. We apply deep neural networks to multi-spectral palmprint recognition problems, and the proposed method can process multiple modalities rather than two simultaneously. Using the information complementarity between different modalities, a discriminant feature representation can be generated. The proposed multi-modality palmprint recognition method has a good improvement compared to the single-mode palmprint recognition method.

2 Related Work

Canonical correlation analysis [16] has good performance in multi-view representation learning and its improvement to the nonlinear and multiple views, which will be described in this section.

2.1 Canonical Correlation Analysis (CCA)

Canonical correlation analysis (CCA) is a classic method that finds two linear projections that make two random vectors maximally correlated and is a fundamental multi-view learning technique. Given two input views, $X_1 \in \mathbb{R}^{d_1}$ and $X_2 \in \mathbb{R}^{d_2}$, with covariance matrices, $\sum_{11}$ and $\sum_{22}$, respectively, and cross-covariance matrix $\sum_{12}$, the objective function is to maximize the correlation between them:

$$\left(u_1^*, u_2^*\right) = \text{argmax}_{u_1 \in \mathbb{R}^{d_1}, u_2 \in \mathbb{R}^{d_2}} \, corr\left(u_1^T X_1, u_2^T X_2\right)$$

$$= \text{argmax}_{u_1 \in \mathbb{R}^{d_1}, u_2 \in \mathbb{R}^{d_2}} \frac{u_1^T \sum_{12} u_2}{\sqrt{u_1^T \sum_{11} u_1 u_2^T \sum_{22} u_2}} \tag{1}$$

2.2 Deep Canonical Correlation Analysis (DCCA)

In [18], deep canonical correlation analysis has been proposed, it is an extension of CCA that addresses the first limitation by finding maximally linearly correlated of two vectors with two non-linear transformations. By passing two input views through multiple fully connected layers with activation function and performing CCA on the output layer, linear projection is transformed into nonlinear. Let us use $f_1(X_1)$ and $f_2(X_2)$ to represent the result of network output layer. The weights of the network, W_1 and W_2, are trained through standard backpropagation to maximize the CCA objective:

$$\left(u_1^*, u_2^*, W_1^*, W_2^*\right) = \text{argmax} corr_{u_1, u_2}\left(u_1^T f_1(X_1), u_2^T f_2(X_2)\right) \tag{2}$$

2.3 DNN Feature Learning in Palmprint Recognition

In [23], Zhao et al. proposed the use of deep belief networks to deal with palmprint recognition problems and achieved good performance. First, the training data is used for top-down network training, and then the model parameters are adjusted to obtain more robust performance. Finally, the test sample can obtain the predicted label information by optimizing the parameters of the network.

As deep learning becomes more and more powerful, deep neural networks are increasingly used in extracting features [24]. Unlike other linear methods, the complexity of deep networks can extract deeper features of the sample space. Many multi-view methods based on deep learning have been proposed. [22], some approaches of them use neural networks with an objective similar to that of CCA to get a unified representation of all of the views under the assumption that the two views can share a common space.

3 The Proposed Algorithm

The proposed multi-view representation learning method is shown in Fig. 1. Multiple networks are federated to learn their respective nonlinear mappings to project corresponding views into a common space. All views of a sample are mapped into the new space, in which the distances are as close as possible. Moreover, the GCCA objectives are applied independently to the output layer, making the new representation discriminative. GCCA is another extension of CCA, which addresses the limitation on the number of views of the data. The same sample of different views will be highly correlated in the new subspace learned by the network.

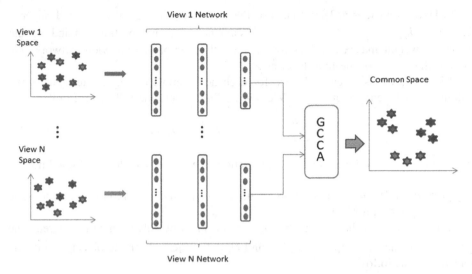

Fig. 1. The schematic of our proposed method for N views. Deep neural networks are jointly learned for each view, and GCCA uses its output for subspace learning. In the new space, all the views are maximally correlated. (The instance of same class is the same color) (Color figure online)

Multiple deep neural networks can learn common data representations from multiple views to eliminate differences of view. The network structure of our model refers to the DCCA network architecture which is simple full-connection layer architecture, and in the nonlinear part we use the sigmoid activation function. We train multiple nonlinear projections by updating the parameters of multiple networks by backpropagation to optimize the objective function, and then we use GCCA analysis to find the projection of each view, and use these projections as the fully connected layer of the last layer of the network. After training, Multi-view samples are nonlinearly mapped from high-dimensional space to a common low-dimensional space and then classified using sample features in low-dimensional space.

In order to learn the view-invariant representation from each view, we trained a network for each view. It is worth noting that the parameters and structure of the network of each perspective can be different from each other. This is specifically adjusted according to different problems. In the competition for multi-spectral palmprints, we have adopted the same network structure.

To this problem, the training set is denoted as $\mathcal{X} = \{ (x_1^i, \ldots, x_V^i) | x_1^i \in X_1, \ldots, x_V^i \in X_N, 1 \leq i \leq N \}$, where $(x_1^i, \ldots, x_v^i)$ is a training data with V views and dimension is d. We try to find V nonlinear view-invariant transforms $f_v(x; \theta_v): X_v \to Z_v$ that map the given data of multiple views to the common space Z_v. θ_v is the parameters of the v-th network.

In order to train a more robust classifier with discriminative representation, we need to make the same instance is close from different views using:

$$\min_U \sum_{i=1}^{V} \sum_{j=i+1}^{V} \left\| U_i^T Z_i - U_j^T Z_j \right\|_F^2 \text{ s.t. } U_i^T (Z_i Z_i^T) U_i = I , i = 1 : V \qquad (3)$$

From the model, nonlinear map of each view can be learned to maximize the correlation between the same samples across views. The network of v-th view consists of K_j layers, and k is at least four. For the v-th view, the output of the k-th layer is $h_k^v = s\left(W_k^v h_{k-1}^v + b_k^v\right)$, where $s : \mathbb{R} \rightarrow \mathbb{R}'$ is a nonlinear activation function and W_k^v and b_k^v is the weight matrix and bias matrix for k-th layer of the v-th view network. We denote the output of the final layer as Z_v.

Since Eq. (3) is calculated once for each new sample during the test phase, the calculation efficiency is not high. We rewrite Eq. (3) into the following form:

$$\min_{G,U} \sum_{i=1}^{V} \left\| G - U_i^T Z_i \right\|_F^2 \text{ s.t. } G^T G = I \tag{4}$$

where $G \in \mathbb{R}^{r \times N}$ is the result of the projection of each view under ideal conditions.

Optimization: We utilize stochastic gradient descent (SGD) with mini-batches to solve this optimization problem.

It can be shown that the solution can be obtained by solving a certain eigenvalue problem. Define $C_{ii} = Z_i Z_i^T \in \mathbb{R}^{c_d^i \times c_d^i}$, and $U_i = C_{ii}^{-1} Z_i G^T$. Then the objective function can rewrite as follows:

$$\sum_{i=1}^{V} \left\| G - U_i^T Z_i \right\|_F^2 = \sum_{i=1}^{V} \left\| G - G Z_i^T C_{ii}^{-1} Z_i \right\|_F^2 \tag{5}$$

Since we define $M = \sum_{i=1}^{V} P_i$, $P_i = Z_i^T C_{ii}^{-1} Z_i$, and the rows of G are the top r eigenvectors of M. Formula (5) can be rewritted as follow:

$$Jr - \text{Tr}\left(GMG^T\right) \tag{6}$$

We can write the rank-1 decomposition of M as $\sum_{k=1}^{N} \lambda_k g_k g_k^T$. So g_k is the kth column of G, and the rows of Q are the N eigenvectors of M, then $QQ^T = I_N$.

$$\sum_{k=1}^{N} \lambda_k g_k g_k^T = \sum_{K=1}^{N} M g_k g_k^T = MGG^T = M \tag{7}$$

since the matrix product $G g_k = \hat{e}_k$,

$$GMG^T = \sum_{K=1}^{N} \lambda_k G g_k (G g_k)^T = \sum_{k=1}^{r} \lambda_k \hat{e}_k \hat{e}_k^T \tag{8}$$

So, we can write the objective as

$$Jr - \sum_{i=1}^{r} \lambda_i(M) \tag{9}$$

We denote the sum of eigenvalues $\sum_{i=1}^{r} \lambda_i(M)$ by L, by the chain rule, and using the fact that $\frac{\partial L}{\partial M} = G^T G$.

$$\frac{\partial L}{\partial (Z_i)_{ab}} = \sum_{c,d=1}^{N} \frac{\partial L}{\partial M_{cd}} \frac{\partial M_{cd}}{\partial (Z_i)_{ab}} \tag{10}$$

Since $M = \sum_{i=1}^{J} P_j$, $\frac{\partial M}{\partial Z_i} = \frac{\partial P_i}{\partial Z_i}$.

$$(P_i)_{cd} = \sum_{k,l=1}^{c_k^j} (Z_i)_{kc} \left(C_{ii}^{-1}\right)_{kl} (Z_i)_{ld} \tag{11}$$

In summary, Eq. (10) can be calculated as follows:

$$\frac{\partial L}{\partial (Z_i)_{ab}} = \sum_{c,d=1}^{N} \left(G^T G\right)_{cd} (I_N - P_i)_{cb} \left(C_{ii}^{-1} Z_i\right)_{ad} + \sum_{c,d=1}^{N} \left(G^T G\right)_{cd} (I_N - P_i)_{db} \left(C_{ii}^{-1} Z_i\right)_{ac} \tag{12}$$

After simplification we get the following results:

$$\frac{\partial L}{\partial (Z_i)_{ab}} = 2 \left[C_{ii}^{-1} Z_i G^T G (I_N - P_i)\right]_{ab} \tag{13}$$

Therefore, since $U_i = C_{ii}^{-1} Z_i G^T$, the gradient of the objective function as follows:

$$\frac{\partial L}{\partial Z_i} = 2 C_{ii}^{-1} Z_i G^T G (I_N - P_i) = 2 U_i G - 2 U_i U_i^T Z_i \tag{14}$$

Algorithm 1 illustrates the execution process of the proposed method.

Algorithm 1. Deep Multi-View Representation Learning

Input: multi-view data: $X_1, X_2, \ldots, X_J$,

        number of iterations T, learning rate η

Output: $Z_1, Z_2, \ldots, Z_J$

1: Initialize neural network parameter $\theta_1, \theta_2, \ldots, \theta_J$

2: **for** iteration $t = 1, 2, \ldots, T$ **do**

3:     **for** each view $j = 1, 2 \ldots, J$ **do**

4:         $Z_j \leftarrow$ forward pass of X_j with network parameter θ_j

5:         mean-center Z_j

6:     **end for**

7:     $U_1, \ldots, U_J, G \leftarrow gcca(Z_1, \ldots, Z_J)$

8:     **for** each modality $j = 1, 2 \ldots, J$ **do**

9:         $\partial F / \partial Z_j \leftarrow U_j U_j^T Z_j - U_j G$

10:       $\nabla \theta_j \leftarrow$ backprop($\partial F / \partial Z_j, \theta_j$)

11:       $\theta_j \leftarrow \theta_j - \eta \nabla \theta_j$

12:     **end for**

13: **end for**

14: **for** each modality $j = 1, 2 \ldots, J$ **do**

15:     $Z_j \leftarrow$ forward pass of X_j with weights W_j

16:     mean-center Z_j

17: **end for**

18: $U_1, \ldots, U_J, G \leftarrow gcca(Z_1, \ldots, Z_J)$

19: **for** each modality $j = 1, 2 \ldots, J$ **do**

20:     $Z_j \leftarrow U_j^T Z_j$

21: **end for**

---

4 Experiment

4.1 Palmprint Database

In this paper the database we used to verify the proposed method is the PolyU multispectral palmprint Database. The multispectral palmprint images of the database were
collected from 250 volunteers, they are between the ages of 20 and 60, and the ratio of
male to female is about four to one. The samples were collected twice, each time
collecting 6 samples, and the two collections were separated by 9 days. Therefore, each
person collects a total of 24 palm pictures including the left and right hands. The multi-
spectral palmprint dataset is acquired under the red, green, blue, and near infrared
(NIR) illuminations. In total, the database contains 6,000 images from 500 different
palms for each illumination. We can treat each illumination as a view of sample, and
more unique representation of palmprint image can be obtained. In Fig. 2, we show
four typical regions of interested (ROI) images from different illuminations of the
PolyU database. In the experiment, the six images of each palm are divided into the
training sets and the other six are divided into testing sets.

Fig. 2. Four palmprint samples selected from the PolyU _Red, PolyU _Green, PolyU _Blue,
and PolyU _NIR palmprint databases.

4.2 Single Modality Palmprint Identification

The accuracy of the four spectral palmprints on the three baseline methods is listed in
Table 1. Support Vector Machine is a classic supervised learning method with associated learning algorithms that analyzes data used for classification and regression
analysis. k-nearest neighbors algorithm (k-NN) is a non-parametric method used for
classification and regression. The idea of k-NN is that if the k samples most similar to a
certain sample belong to a certain category in the feature space, the samples also
belongs to this category. Deep belief network (DBN) is a classical deep neural network
to be further trained with supervision to perform classification.

Table 1. Accuracy (%) of four spectral palmprints on baseline methods.

	SVM	k-NN	DBN
Red	92.93	96.86	71.63
NIR	89.76	95.56	63.4
Green	92.23	95.83	68.43
Blue	93.06	96.76	69.5

4.3   Multi-modality Palmprint Identification

In multi-modality palmprint verification experiments, we combined the four modality palmprint data in a total of five combinations: BDI, BGR, BIR, GIR, and BGIR. Randomly select six images of each palm as training data, and the remaining images as test data. In order to verify the effectiveness of our method, we chose some state-of-the-art methods as comparative methods including PCA, LDA, competitive code, LOBP, half orientation, MCCA, MKI, MvDA. Principal component analysis (PCA) and linear discriminant analysis (LDA) are the popular dimensionality reduction methods, the former one is supervised and the latter is unsupervised. Competitive coding extracts information from the palm line using Gabor filters, then use the matching algorithm to match the two sets of codes [25]. Local Orientation Binary Pattern (LOBP) method mainly captures the direction relationship information between the center point and the neighboring point, and then filters the local information into the final global information [26]. Half-orientation extraction method defines a bank of "Half-Gabor" filters for palmprint matching [27]. The three methods abovementioned are popular palmprint recognition method based on coding. Multi-view CCA(MCCA) [19] is an expansion of Linear CCA, it can handle multi-view problems. Multi-kernel learning method (MKL) is a common multi-view model, which use multiple kernel function to find the projection to high kernel space. Multi-view discriminant analysis (MvDA) jointly learns multiple view-specific linear projections to project multiple views into a common subspace. The recognition results are presented in Table 2.

Table 2.   ACC (%) of different methods on PolyU palmprint databases.

Methods	PCA	LDA	Competitive code	LOBP	Half orientation	MCCA	MKI	MvDA	Ours
BGI	96.67	95.23	96.60	98.89	96.74	94.36	97.33	98.12	**99.45**
BGR	97.76	97.40	96.67	98.89	96.79	95.61	98.40	97.00	**99.63**
BIR	98.40	97.10	96.47	98.91	96.38	96.90	97.83	99.00	**99.42**
GIR	98.40	96.96	96.41	98.91	96.44	97.10	98.40	95.40	**99.37**
BGIR	98.40	98.46	96.58	98.90	96.68	96.29	98.40	96.97	**99.65**

The receiver operating characteristic (ROC) curve is adopted to further evaluate the effectiveness of the proposed method, which is a graph of genuine accept rate (GAR) versus false accepted rate (FAR) on all possible decision thresholds. Figure 3 is the ROC curves of the proposed method and three popular methods.

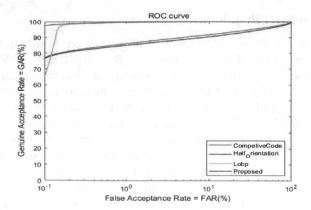

Fig. 3. The ROC curve of the proposed and other comparison method.

In addition, the equal error rate (EER), which is the point of false accept rate when it equals to false reject rate, is calculated as the basis of the evaluation. The EERs obtained using different methods are listed in Table 3.

Table 3. EERS of different methods.

Methods	Competitive code	LOBP	Half orientation	Proposed
BGI	0.0832	0.0780	0.0882	0.0712
BGR	0.0869	0.0750	0.1019	0.0722
BIR	0.0832	0.0790	0.0920	0.0753
GIR	0.0816	0.0800	0.0928	0.0736
BGIR	0.0922	0.0700	0.0893	0.0612

5 Conclusion

In this paper, we combine the unique characteristics of images under different illumination to solve the problem of multi-spectral palmprint recognition. We use deep neural networks to convert multispectral palmprint data into a common space where the distance of the same type of palmprint data is as small as possible. In the new space obtained, the palmprint can be better classified. A series of experimental results on polyU's multi-spectral palmprint dataset show that our proposed method has good performance on multi-spectral palmprint recognition. In the future work, we will optimize the efficiency and architecture of the model and explore the potential of this method in other palmprint recognition problems.

Acknowledgments. This work was supported in part by National Natural Science Foundation of China (Nos. 61501230, 61732006, 61876082 and 81771444), National Science and Technology Major Project (No. 2018ZX10201002), and the Fundamental Research Funds for the Central Universities No. NJ2019010.

References

1. Zheng, Q., Kumar, A., Pan, G.: Suspecting less and doing better: new insights on palmprint identification for faster and more accurate matching. IEEE Trans. Inf. Forensics Secur. **2**(5), 633–641 (2015)
2. Chakraborty, S., Bhattacharya, I., Chatterjee, A.: A palmprint based biometric authentication system using dual tree complex wavelet transform. Measurement **46**(10), 4179–4188 (2013)
3. Fei, L., Lu, G., Jia, W., Teng, S., Zhang, D.: Feature extraction methods for palmprint recognition: a survey and evaluation. IEEE Trans. Syst. Man Cybern.: Syst. **49**(2), 346–363 (2018)
4. Zhang, D.: Automated Biometrics: Technologies and Systems. Springer, New York (2013)
5. Jain, A., Ross, A., Prabhakar, S.: An introduction to biometric recognition. IEEE Trans. Circuits Syst. Video Technol. **14**(1), 4–20 (2004)
6. Chen, F., Huang, X., Zhou, J.: Hierarchical minutiae matching for fingerprint and palmprint identification. IEEE Trans. Image Process. **22**(12), 4964–4971 (2013)
7. Zhang, D., Kong, W., You, J., Wong, M.: Online palmprint identification. IEEE Trans. Pattern Anal. Mach. Intell. **25**(9), 1041–1050 (2003)
8. Han, D., Guo, Z., Zhang, D.: Multispectral palmprint recognition using wavelet-based image fusion. In: 9th International Conference on Signal Processing, pp. 2074–2077. IEEE (2008)
9. Hong, D., Liu, W., Su, J., Pan, Z., Wang, G.: A novel hierarchical approach for multispectral palmprint recognition. Neurocomputing **151**, 511–521 (2015)
10. Guo, Z., Zhang, L., Zhang, D.: Feature band selection for multispectral palmprint recognition. In: 20th International Conference on Pattern Recognition, pp. 1136–1139. IEEE (2010)
11. Hao, Y., Sun, Z., Tan, T., Ren, C.: Multispectral palm image fusion for accurate contact-free palmprint recognition. In: 15th IEEE International Conference on Image Processing, pp. 281–284. IEEE (2008)
12. Kisku, D., Rattani, A., Gupta, P., Sing, J., Hwang, C.: Human identity verification using multispectral palmprint fusion. J. Signal Inf. Process. 3(2), 263 (2012)
13. Kan, M., Shan, S., Zhang, H., Lao, S., Chen, X.: Multi-view discriminant analysis. IEEE Trans. Pattern Anal. Mach. Intell. **38**(1), 188–194 (2015)
14. Yang, X., Sun, D.: Feature-level fusion of palmprint and palm vein base on canonical correlation analysis. In: 13th International Conference on Signal Processing (ICSP), pp. 1353–1356. IEEE (2010)
15. Li, M., Xie, W., Shen, L.: Fusing 3D gabor and block-wise spatial features for hyperspectral palmprint recognition. In: Zhou, J., et al. (eds.) CCBR 2017. LNCS, vol. 10568, pp. 361–369. Springer, Cham (2017). https://doi.org/10.1007/978-3-319-69923-3_39
16. Thompson, B.: Canonical correlation analysis. In: Encyclopedia of Statistics in Behavioral Science (2016)
17. Akaho, S.: A kernel method for canonical correlation analysis. arXiv preprint (2006)
18. Andrew, G., Arora, R., Bilmes, J., Livescu, K.: Deep canonical correlation analysis. In: International conference on machine learning, pp. 1247–1255 (2010)
19. Rupnik, J., Shawe-Taylor, J.: Multi-view canonical correlation analysis. In: Conference on Data Mining and Data Warehouses (SiKDD) (2010)
20. Benton, A., Khayrallah, H., Gujral, B., Reisinger, D., Zhang, S., Arora, R.: Deep generalized canonical correlation analysis. arXiv preprint arXiv:1702.02519 (2017)
21. Yousefnezhad, M., Zhang, D.: Deep hyperalignment. In: Advances in Neural Information Processing Systems, pp. 1604–1612 (2017)

22. Wang, W., Arora, R., Livescu, K., Bilmes, J.: On deep multi-view representation learning. In: International Conference on Machine Learning, pp. 1083–1092 (2015)
23. Xin, Z., Xin, P., Xiaoling, L., Xiaojing, G.: Palmprint recognition based on deep learning. In: IET (2015)
24. Minaee, S., Wang, Y: Palmprint recognition using deep scattering convolutional network. arXiv preprint arXiv:1603.09027 (2016)
25. Kong, A., Zhang, D.: Competitive coding scheme for palmprint verification. In: Proceedings of the 17th International Conference on Pattern Recognition, pp. 520–523. IEEE (2010)
26. Fei, L., Xu, Y., Teng, S., Zhang, W., Tang, W., Fang, X.: Local orientation binary pattern with use for palmprint recognition. In: Zhou, J., et al. (eds.) CCBR 2017. LNCS, vol. 10568, pp. 213–220. Springer, Cham (2017). https://doi.org/10.1007/978-3-319-69923-3_23
27. Fei, L., Xu, Y., Zhang, D.: Half-orientation extraction of palmprint features. Pattern Recogn. Lett. **69**, 35–41 (2016)

Reinforcement Learning for HEVC Screen Content Intra Coding on Heterogeneous Mobile Devices

Yuanyuan Xu[✉] and Quanping Zeng

Hohai University, Nanjing 211100, China
yuanyuan_xu@hhu.edu.cn

Abstract. Intra coding of HEVC screen content coding has to evaluate HEVC intra coding modes and additional modes for screen contents, which poses a challenge for coding such a content on mobile devices. Furthermore, the heterogeneous mobile devices have varying complexity requirements. In this paper, a flexible screen content intra coding scheme is proposed, which can trade between encoding complexity and rate-distortion performance degradation via reinforcement learning (RL). Through the design of states, actions, and more importantly, the reward function for RL, the proposed scheme can learn a flexible coding policy offline. Experimental results show the effectiveness of the proposed scheme.

Keywords: Screen content coding · Coding mode decision · Reinforcement learning

1 Introduction

New applications, such as virtual desktop, wireless displays, cloud gaming, and massive online courses, generate an increasing demand in screen sharing between mobile devices. Compared with traditional camera captured videos, screen content videos have a substantial amount of computer generated graphics and text. Several distinguished properties, such as repeated patterns, irregular motions, limited colors, are presented in screen content videos. These properties motivate the screen content coding extension (SCC) of High Efficiency Video Coding (HEVC) standard [10,13]. New coding tools such as intra-block copy (IBC) and palette (PLT) mode are developed in HEVC-SCC, which make screen content intra coding more complex than that in the computationally intensive HEVC. Coding of such contents poses a great challenge for mobile devices with varying limited computation capabilities.

Supported by National Natural Science Foundation of China under Grant No. 61801167 and Natural Science Foundation of Jiangsu Province of China under Grant No. BK20160874.

X. B. Zhai et al. (Eds.): MLICOM 2019, LNICST 294, pp. 759–768, 2019.
https://doi.org/10.1007/978-3-030-32388-2_62

To address the complexity issue of screen content intra coding, fast intra prediction methods have been proposed in the literature [3,4,7–9,14]. In [8], coding units (CUs) are classified into natural content ones and screen content ones based on the statistical information, where early termination of splitting operations are performed accordingly. In [9], neighboring luminance gradient information and coding bits are exploited to perform early skipping of depth decision and mode prediction. Besides exploiting observed statistical information, machine learning techniques can be utilized to design fast screen content coding schemes. In [3], texture information of current CU and sub-CUs is utilized by neural network to guide coding unit (CU) partition, while decision trees are used to determine whether a CU is a natural image block or a screen content block, needs partitioning or not, and selects directional or non-directional modes in [4]. In [14], two classifiers are designed to determined whether the current CU is split into sub-CUs and whether SCC modes or traditional intra modes are performed for the unsplit CU, where texture information of current CU, coding information of current and neighboring CUs are used as features. In [7], dynamic and static information of current CU is utilized by decision trees to check either IBC or PLT mode for screen content blocks.

In these existing works, the amount of complexity reduction is fixed for a given screen content video, which cannot accommodate varying requirements of heterogeneous mobile devices with different computing capabilities, e.g., mobile phones, wireless head mounted displays (HMDs). In this paper, we propose a flexible screen content intra coding scheme which can adjust between encoding complexity reduction and rate-distortion performance degradation via reinforcement learning (RL). RL tries to learn a policy which maximizes the total rewards depending on inter-correlated decisions. It has been used in video coding for video encoder control [5], rate control [6] and unit split decision [2]. As far as we know, none of the existing works on screen content coding uses RL. The flexible screen content intra coding which selectively searches through different modes according to the capability of device is modeled as a RL problem. Motivated by the work in [5], the trade-off between complexity and rate-distortion performance of screen content intra coding is represented by a reward function in RL.

The rest of the paper is organized as follows. In Sect. 2, we provide preliminary information of screen content intra coding. The proposed flexible reinforcement learning based screen content intra coding scheme is presented in Sect. 3. Section 4 shows the experimental results, while Sect. 5 concludes the paper.

2   Preliminary

Prior to the HEVC, the H.264/MPEG-4 AVC standard [12] supports nine Intra_4 × 4, four Intra_16 × 16 and I_PCM prediction modes for traditional 16 × 16 luma samples. The coding structure of the HEVC is more complicated than that in H.264/MPEG-4 AVC. In the HEVC [11], variable-size coding tree units (CTUs) are supported, where the size of luma coding tree blocks (CTBs) may be equal to 16 × 16, 32 × 32, and 64 × 64. Each CTB can be used as a coding block

(CB) or further split into multiple CBs recursively using the quadtree syntax until a minimum allowed luma CB size is reached. The prediction block (PB) for intrapicture prediction is the same as the CB, except CBs with the smallest size which can be further split into four PBs. For the transform blocks (TBs), a luma CB can be further partitioned into multiple square TBs recursively, where the maximum depth of the residual quadtree is constrained and indicated in sequence parameter set (SPS). Figure 1 shows an example of CTB partition using the quadtree syntax. For each CB, 33 different directional modes, a planar prediction and a DC prediction mode are defined for intrapicture prediction, where the neighboring TBs are used to form the reconstruction signal.

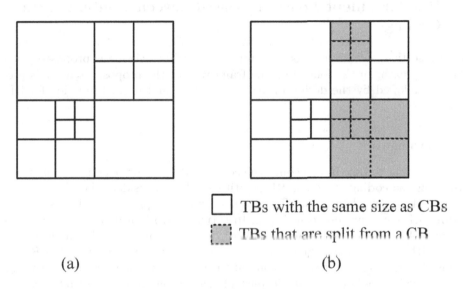

☐ TBs with the same size as CBs

▨ TBs that are split from a CB

(a)   (b)

Fig. 1. An example of coding tree block partition using the quadtree syntax (a) Code blocks. (b) Transform blocks.

Besides the above-mentioned coding framework of HEVC, the SCC extension of HEVC introduces new coding tools, including IBC and PLT modes. IBC is a new coding mode for CUs with repeated patterns, which uses similar reconstructed blocks in the same picture as a prediction signal. PLT mode is designed for blocks with limited colors, which lists all the color values and sends an index of color for each sample instead of coding each sample. For each CU, mode decision of intra coding is determined by exhaustive search, and it is implemented in the HEVC-SCC reference software as follow [7]. The IBC predictor is performed first which uses a few options of block vector (BV) from most recently coded CUs and neighboring CUs in the IBC mode. Then the intra coding modes of HEVC are evaluated, followed by examining IBC merge and skip mode. The IBC merge and skip mode is similar as those for interpicture prediction. Only a skip flag and the merge index are sent in the skip mode, while the merge mode allows residual coding. If the IBC skip mode is not the best mode so far, the IBC search is conducted. At last, the PLT mode is evaluated. Among all those modes, the coding mode with the smallest cost, $D + \lambda R$, is selected, where R, D, and λ are the coding bits, the distortion, and a Lagrange multiplier, respectively. To further complicate the intra coding procedure, the final partition of CTU into CUs is determined by evaluating all the possible partitions and choosing the one with the smallest cost. For each partition, intra coding modes for all of its CUs have to be decided as mentioned above. Machine learning methods can be used to develop fast intra coding scheme.

3   Reinforcement Learning Based Screen Content Intra Coding

In this section, a flexible screen content intra coding scheme is proposed using a RL approach. In the following, the framework of the proposed scheme is presented, followed by the design of feature selection and reward function for RL.

3.1   Framework

Since we want to take into account the cost of coding mode selection errors when applying the coding strategy, RL is utilized which considers the classification error in the reward function. The framework of the proposed RL based intra coding scheme is presented in Fig. 2. In this framework, a mobile device passes a trade-off coefficient between rate-distortion performance and complexity, μ, to the RL module. For a given μ, a coding policy is learned offline via RL by using the training set of screen content videos. The mobile device can use the learned coding policy as a static part of the coding to speed its intra coding mode decision procedure. Depending on the requirements of the mobile devices, different adjustment factors μ can be used in the RL module to make a flexible trade-off between coding efficiency and complexity. A mobile device with less computational resources passes a larger value of μ, while a smaller μ is associated with abundant computational resources. A learnt coding policy can be used for all the mobile devices with the same type.

3.2   Coding Policy Learning via RL

The proposed fast scheme tries to learn a coding policy that reduces the number of evaluated coding modes according to observed information of a CB. This coding policy is learned through RL module. In the RL module, the learning agent interacts with the learning environment (coding using screen content videos training set) repeatedly. The intra coding process can be seen as a series of coding decision episodes that repeatedly evaluating selected intra coding modes. At a time point t, the learning agent selects an action from the set of available actions (evaluating selected coding modes) to act on the learning environment

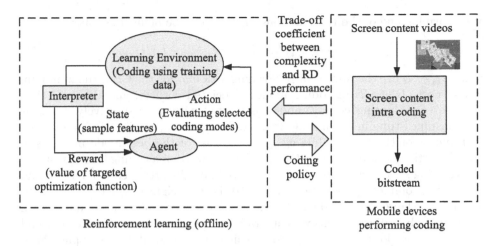

Fig. 2. Framework of the proposed reinforcement learning based intra coding scheme.

based on the environmental state information (sample features) s_t. After the action is executed, the interpreter feeds back information about the new state $s_{(t+1)}$ of the environment and reward $r_{(t+1)}$ (value of targeted optimization function) associated with the performed action. In the following, we will present the design of features, actions, and reward function in the RL module.

About the actions in the RL, all the coding modes associated with HEVC-SCC are roughly divided into three categories, which are HEVC coding modes, IBC mode, and PLT mode. Correspondingly, three actions are allowed for coding mode evaluations, which correspond to evaluating the HEVC intra mode, IBC mode, and PLT mode, respectively. Note that the IBC mode includes its predictor mode, merge and skip mode, and IBC search mode. Although only three actions are defined in this paper, the proposed work can be extended to the case with more actions.

About the feature design, we uses statistical information of a CB according to the allowed actions. For screen content coding, CBs with limited number of colors and the coding unit with sharp boundaries are usually coded with the PLT mode. The area of screen contents where the hue is discontinuous is usually encoded using IBC or palette mode. A uniform region usually uses an intra coding mode. Therefore, the following features of a CB are used: variance, the number of colors, the largest number of pixels with the same value, the maximum run length of pixel values horizontally, and the maximum run length of pixel values vertically.

The trade-off between rate-distortion performance and coding complexity of intra coding is achieved by designing a reward function for RL. The goal of RL is to maximize the expected reward in the future real coding process. The learning algorithm of this scheme estimates the reward through experiments on a set of N training samples $\sum_i r_i$, where r_i is the reward for CB i. The reward of performing one of the three actions for CB i can be defined as follows

$$r_i = -(c_i - c_{i,min})/c_{i,min} + \mu(t_{i,sum} - t_i)/t_{i,sum}, \tag{1}$$

where r_i, c_i, t_i are the reward of performing action a_i for the CB i, the minimum coding cost $(D + \lambda R)$ of coding modes associated with a_i, and the total time expense of evaluating coding modes associated with a_i, respectively. $t_{i,sum}$ is the consumed time in evaluating all of traditional intra modes, IBC mode, and PLT mode for the CB i, while $c_{i,min}$ is the cost of the best mode in terms of rate-distortion performance for the CB i. The reward of a coding strategy on the i-th training sample consists of two parts: the rate-distortion cost reduction and the coding complexity reduction. μ ($\mu > 0$) is the weight of the encoding complexity. The larger the weight is, the more the encoder limits the computational complexity. By adjusting this weight, trade-off between the coding efficiency and complexity can be flexibly adjusted to suit the needs of different applications. For, example, smartphone-based HMD devices should use a larger weight than computer-based HMD devices.

3.3 Coding Policy Learning Algorithm

With the above design of features, actions, and reward function, we use Q-learning to learning coding policy. Due to the aim of RL is to speed intra coding of screen content, a simple ternary classifier is used to represent the relationship between the value of features and selected action. The input layer consist of 6 nodes, while the output layer consists of 3 nodes. The three outputs correspond to three allowed actions. The classifier is configured by θ. The coding policy learning via RL can be summarized in Algorithm 1.

Algorithm 1. coding policy learning via RL

1: Initialize the classifier parameter θ
2: Initialize the learning parameter $\gamma = 0.9$
3: **for** samples $i = 0 \rightarrow N - 1$ **do**
4:     Calculate the values of features, s_i
5:     Choose the action with the maximum value $a_i = argmax_{a_i} Q(s_i, a_i; \theta)$
6:     Execute action a_i, observe the reward r_i
7:     Update θ with the new $Q'(s_i, a_i; \theta) = Q(s_i, a_i; \theta) + \gamma(r_i - Q(s_i, a_i; \theta))$
8:     Decrease γ
9: **end for**

After the coding policy, i.e., fixed parameter θ for classifier, is learned, it is sent to the mobile device and implemented as static part for coding on such a device. During the intra coding procedure on a mobile device, only the coding modes associated with the following action for each CU are evaluated.

$$a_i = argmax_{a_i} Q(s_i, a_i; \theta) \tag{2}$$

4   Experimental Results

The experimental results are obtained implementing the proposed method in the HEVC-SCC reference software HM-16.18 SCM 8.7. The all intra (AI) configuration is used. The coding performance is compared with the anchor that exhaustively searches through all the coding options in SCM 8.7. The video sequences used for coding policy learning are listed in Table 1, where TGM, M, and CC represent text and graphics with motion, mixed content, and camera-captured content, respectively.

Table 1. Training video sequences

Resolution	Sequence name	Category
1920×1080	sc_FlyingGraphics_1920 × 1080_60_8bit	TGM
1280×720	sc_Programming_1280 × 720_60_8bit	TGM
1280×720	sc_SlideEditing_1280 × 720_30_8bit_420	TGM
832×480	BasketballDrillText_832 × 480_50	M
1280×720	KristenAndSara_1280 × 720_60	CC
416×240	BlowingBubbles_416 × 240_50	CC

In the RL module, the training data for neural network are obtained in coding training video sequences using HM-16.18 with SCM 8.7. Specifically, for each CB, the rate distortion costs and the consumed time measured in microseconds are collected for the cases of performing IBC predictor, HEVC intra, IBC merge and skip, IBC search, and PLT modes. Note that the time complexity of IBC mode is the sum of those performing IBC predictor, IBC merge and skip, and IBC search, while the rate-distortion cost of IBC mode is the minimum cost associated with the above options. A subset using the a cropped window on the first frame of these sequences are used as training data. 8000 training samples are generated and randomized. The coefficients are learned using varying training steps with $\mu = 0.5$.

Table 2. Test video sequences

Resolution	Sequence name	Category
1920×1080	sc_desktop_1920 × 1080_60_8bit	TGM
1920×1080	MissionControlCllip3_1920 × 1080_60p_8b444	M
1280×720	sc_web_browsing_1280 × 720_30_8bit_420_r1	TGM
1280×720	sc_SlideShow_1280 × 720_20_8bit	TGM
1920×1080	Kimono1_1_1920 × 1080_24_10bits	CC

After the coding policies are learned, they are implemented in the intra coding of testing video sequences as listed in Table 2. Performance of the proposed scheme is compared with the benchmark of HM-16.18 SCM 8.7 for testing video sequences. Bjøntegaard delta rate (BD-rate) [1] is used to measure the rate-distortion performance degradation, in terms of the percentage of bitrate saving (negative values) or increasing (positive values). The coding complexity is measured by the percentage of encoding time saving. The comparison results using different video sequences are listed in Table 3. Among the screen content video sequences, the performance of the proposed scheme is better for the "WebBrowsing" than the other sequences, because most of training sequence are 4:2:0 sequences whose color format is the same as the one for "WebBrowsing" sequence. In our experiment, we also found that mode selection among traditional Intra modes, IBC mode, and PLT mode hardly affects the rate-distortion performance of camera captured sequences. Therefore, the camera captured "Kimino" sequence achieves almost 31% reduction in encoding time with only a slight BD-rate increase of 0.1%. The coding time comparison with varying QP values is shown in Table 4. It can be seen from the table that the proposed scheme can achieve up to 31.5% savings in coding complexity reduction for a fixed QP value. Performance of the proposed scheme gets better as the value of QP gets smaller.

Table 3. Coding performance compared with HM-16.18 SCM 8.7

Sequence	BD-rate	Encoding time
Desktop	12.1%	−17.7%
MissionControlClip3	10.1%	−19.0%
WebBrowsing	2.8%	−18.8%
SlideShow	14.1%	−7.0%
Kimino	0.1%	−31.0%
Average	7.8%	−18.7%

Table 4. Coding time comparison with HM-16.18 SCM 8.7 using varying QP

QP	Encoding time
37	−12.9%
32	−16.1%
27	−21.6%
22	−31.5%
Average	−20.5%

5   Conclusion

In this paper, a flexible screen content intra coding scheme is proposed to address the varying complexity requirements of heterogeneous mobile devices. In this scheme, a coding policy can be learned for a targeted type of devices through RL offline. The trade-off between encoding complexity and rate-distortion performance degradation is controlled by designing a reward function for RL. The learned coding policy is then utilized as a static part of coding at mobile devices to speed the intra coding of screen contents. The effectiveness of the proposed scheme is verified by the experimental results.

References

1. Bjøntegaard, G.: Calculation of average PSNR differences between RD-curves. In: Proceedings of the ITU-T Video Coding Experts Group (VCEG) Thirteenth Meeting, January 2001
2. Chung, C.H., Peng, W.H., Hu, J.H.: HEVC/H.265 coding unit split decision using deep reinforcement learning. In: Proceedings of 2017 IEEE International Symposium on Intelligent Signal Processing and Communication Systems (ISPACS), pp. 570–575 (2017)
3. Duanmu, F., Ma, Z., Wang, Y.: Fast CU partition decision using machine learning for screen content compression. In: Proceedings of 2015 IEEE International Conference on Image Processing (ICIP), pp. 4972–4976, September 2015
4. Duanmu, F., Ma, Z., Wang, Y.: Fast mode and partition decision using machine learning for intra-frame coding in HEVC screen content coding extension. IEEE J. Emerg. Sel. Topics Circuits Syst. **6**(4), 517–531 (2016)
5. Helle, P., Schwarz, H., Wiegand, T., Müller, K.R.: Reinforcement learning for video encoder control in HEVC. In: Proceedings of 2017 IEEE International Conference on Systems, Signals and Image Processing (IWSSIP), pp. 1–5 (2017)
6. Hu, J.H., Peng, W.H., Chung, C.H.: Reinforcement learning for HEVC/H.265 intra-frame rate control. In: Proceedings of 2018 IEEE International Symposium on Circuits and Systems (ISCAS), pp. 1–5 (2018)
7. Kuang, W., Chan, Y., Tsang, S., Siu, W.: Machine learning based fast intra mode decision for HEVC screen content coding via decision trees. IEEE Trans. Circuits Syst. Video Technol. 1 (2019, early access)
8. Lei, J., Li, D., Pan, Z., Sun, Z., Kwong, S., Hou, C.: Fast intra prediction based on content property analysis for low complexity HEVC-based screen content coding. IEEE Trans. Broadcast. **63**(1), 48–58 (2017)
9. Lu, Y., Liu, H., Lin, Y., Shen, L., Yin, H.: Efficient coding mode and partition decision for screen content intra coding. Sig. Process. Image Commun. **68**, 249–257 (2018)
10. Peng, W.H., et al.: Overview of screen content video coding: technologies, standards, and beyond. IEEE J. Emerg. Sel. Topics Circuits Syst. **6**(4), 393–408 (2016)
11. Sullivan, G.J., Ohm, J., Han, W., Wiegand, T.: Overview of the high efficiency video coding (HEVC) standard. IEEE Trans. Circuits Syst. Video Technol. **22**(12), 1649–1668 (2012)
12. Wiegand, T., Sullivan, G.J., Bjontegaard, G., Luthra, A.: Overview of the H.264/AVC video coding standard. IEEE Trans. Circuits Syst. Video Technol. **13**(7), 560–576 (2003)

13. Xu, J., Joshi, R., Cohen, R.A.: Overview of the emerging HEVC screen content coding extension. IEEE Trans. Circuits Syst. Video Technol. **26**(1), 50–62 (2016)
14. Yang, H., Shen, L., An, P.: Efficient screen content intra coding based on statistical learning. Sig. Process. Image Commun. **62**, 74–81 (2018)

An Accelerated PSO Based Self-organizing RBF Neural Network for Nonlinear System Identification and Modeling

Zohaib Ahmad[(✉)], Cuili Yang, and Junfei Qiao

Faculty of Information Technology, Beijing Key Laboratory of Computational
Intelligence and Intelligent System, Beijing University of Technology,
Beijing 100124, China
ahmedzohaib03@gmail.com,
{clyang5,junfeiq}@bjut.edu.cn

Abstract. In this paper, an accelerated particle swarm optimization (APSO) based radial basis function neural network (RBFNN) is designed for nonlinear system modeling. In APSO-RBFNN, the center, width of hidden neurons, weights of output layer and network size are optimized by using the APSO method. Two nonlinear system modeling experiments are used to illustrate the effectiveness of the proposed method. The simulation results show that the proposed method has obtained good performance in terms of network size and estimation accuracy.

Keywords: Accelerated particle swarm optimization · Radial basis function · Nonlinear system modeling

1 Introduction

Due to the simple topological structure and rapid training speed, the radial basis function neural networks (RBFNNs) have been widely used in many applications, such as the nonlinear system estimation [1], information processing [2], pattern recognition [3], and so on. For a RBF neural network, its performance is closely related with network architecture, thus how to determine the optimal network parameters and network size is very important.

If the network parameters are selected in a random manner, the network satisfactory performance cannot be achieved. To solve this problem, many different learning algorithms are designed to adjust network parameters. As the most commonly used method, the back propagation (BP) has been used to adjust RBFNN parameters [3]. However, the BP method always results in degraded global search experience and is easily trapped into local optimal [3]. Compared with BP method, the recursive least squares (RLS) methods can result in a more optimum convergence rate and improved network performance [4]. However, the application of RLS always needs the complicated mathematical expression and high computing resources.

The network size is also closely related with network performance of RBFNN. Hence, it is important to optimize the size of RBFNN to improve network performance. For example, the adaptive growing and pruning algorithm [5] is applied to construct the

X. B. Zhai et al. (Eds.): MLICOM 2019, LNICST 294, pp. 769–777, 2019.
https://doi.org/10.1007/978-3-030-32388-2_63

recurrent neural network, and the neurons are added or removed to improve network performance. Then, the forward and backward selection methods are used for the self-organizing RBFNN [6], in which the network size and parameters are optimized simultaneously.

Recently, the evolutionary algorithms (EA) are widely used to improve network performance. There have existed many EA algorithms, such as the differential evolution (DE), simulated annealing (SA), artificial immune algorithm (IA), particle swarm optimization (PSO), ant colony algorithm (AC), and genetic algorithm (GA). Among these algorithms, the PSO offers quick convergence rate and good global searching ability. However, the traditional PSO always suffer from weak solution diversity and premature convergence for highly nonlinear optimization problem. To solve this problem, the accelerated PSO (APSO) [7] is proposed which has shown superiority in terms of algorithm convergence speed and solution accuracy.

Based on above discussion, in this paper, the APSO is proposed to optimize network parameters and network size of RBFNN. Then, the developed network is compared with some existing methods. The simulation results show that the proposed method is efficient in terms of estimation accuracy and network compactness.

The rest of paper has been presented as follows: In Sect. 2, the RBFNN is discussed. Section 3 overviews the PSO and APSO. In Sect. 4, the simulation results have been depicted. Finally, the conclusion is presented in Sect. 5.

2   RBF Neural Network Model

The RBFNN contains three layers, including the input layer, hidden layer and output layer. The basic illustration of a RBFNN is presented in Fig. 1.

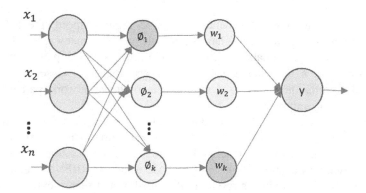

Fig. 1. The RBFNN network illustration

The output of RBFNN, $y(t)$, is specified by the given equation:

$$y(t) = \sum_{l=1}^{K} w_l(t)\phi_l(t); l = 1, 2, 3, \ldots, K \tag{1}$$

Where $w_l(t)$ is the weight of output at the time step t, l is the hidden neuron with $l = 1, 2, 3, \ldots, K$, $\phi_l(t)$ is the lth hidden neuron output as below:

$$\phi_l(t) = e^{\|x(t) - \mu_l(t)\| / \sigma_l^2(t)} \tag{2}$$

where $x(t) = [x_1(t), x_2(t), \ldots, x_n(t)]^{\mathrm{T}}$ are inputs of the RBFNN, n is the nodes number of input layer; $\mu_l(t)$ indicates the center vector of the lth hidden neuron; $\|x(t) - \mu_l(t)\|$ is the Euclidean distance among $x(t)$ and $\mu_l(t)$; $\sigma_l(t)$ is the radius or width of the lth hidden neuron. The network parameters, including width, center of hidden neurons, output weights and network size are adjusted in the training phase by using the training samples.

3   The Proposed APSO-RBFNN

3.1   Overview of PSO

In the traditional PSO [7], the swam is defined as a set $S = \{s_1, s_2, \ldots, s_N\}^{\mathrm{T}}$ of N particles. Each particle $s_i(k)$ at the iteration k is assigned a position vector, which is represented as below,

$$s_i(k) = [s_{i,1}(k), s_{i,2}(k), \ldots, s_{i,D}(k)] \tag{3}$$

where $i = 1, 2, \ldots, N$, and D stands for the search space dimension. Moreover, each particle has a velocity $v_i(k)$ which is denoted by:

$$v_i(k) = [v_{i,1}(k), v_{i,2}(k), v_{i,3}(k), \ldots, v_{i,D}(k)] \tag{4}$$

In order to allow each particle visit all the searching space, the velocity of each particle is updated according to its gained memory. Now, let us define $p_i(k)$ as the best previous position of the ith particle, which is denoted as $p_i(k) = [p_{i,1}(k), p_{i,2}(k), \ldots, p_{i,D}(k)]$. Then, the best position found by the whole swarm is recorded as $g_{best}(t) = [g_{best,1}(k), g_{best,2}(k), \ldots, g_{best,D}(k)]$.

At each iteration k, the velocity of each particle is updated as:

$$v_i(k+1) = \omega v_i(k) + c_1 r_1 (p_{best}(k) - s_i(k)) + c_2 r_2 (g_{best}(k) - s_i(k)) \tag{5}$$

where ω is the weight of inertia; r_1 and r_2 are random values derived from the interval [0,1], which are used to maintain the algorithm diversity; c_1 and c_2 are acceleration constants, which are used to push the swarm towards the local and global best position. Finally, the position of each particle is updated as below:

$$s_i(k+1) = v_i(k+1) + s_i(k) \tag{6}$$

3.2 Overview of APSO

Based on the traditional PSO, the accelerated particle swarm optimization (APSO) is proposed [7]. In traditional PSO, the particle best position p_i and the global best position g_{best} are used to update the velocity as shown in Eq. (6). While in the APSO, only the global best position g_{best} are used. Consequently, the particle's velocity in APSO is updated as below:

$$v_i(k+1) = v_i(k) + \alpha q + \beta(g_{best} - s_i(k)) \tag{7}$$

where q is a random number chosen from the range [0,1]. Generally, the parameter α is chosen from the range [0.1D, 0.5D], and β can be chosen from the range [0.1, 0.7]. Moreover, the position of each particle is simply calculated as below:

$$s_i(k+1) = (1 - \beta)s_i(k) + \beta g_{best} + \alpha q \tag{8}$$

As illustrated in [7], compared with traditional PSO, the APSO has shown good performance in terms of algorithm convergence and diversity.

3.3 Design Process of the Proposed APSO-RBFNN

In this paper, the APSO is used to optimize network parameters of RBFNN, the proposed method is denoted as APSO-RBFNN. In APSO-RBFNN, the network parameters, including width μ_l and center σ_l of hidden neurons, output weights w_l and network size are optimized by the APSO. The operation procedures of APSO-RBFNN are given as follows:

Step 1: Set the original iteration as $k = 0$. Randomly initialize the position s_i and velocity v_i of each particle i.
Step 2: Evaluate the fitness function for each particle i. Among all the particles, find g_{best} with the best fitness value.
Step 3: Calculate the positions and velocities of all particles according to Eqs. (7) and (8).
Step 4: Start the next generation $k = k + 1$ and go to Step 2. This process is repeated until the maximum iteration is reached.

4 Simulation Results

In the simulation part, the root-mean square error (RMSE) is used to test the network performance, it is also treated as the objective function of APSO. The mathematical function of RMSE is given as follows:

$$E_i(k) = \sqrt{\frac{1}{L}\sum\nolimits_{t=1}^{L} \left(y_d(t) - \hat{y}(t)^2\right)} \tag{9}$$

where, y_d is the desired output, L represents data samples length and $\hat{y}$ is the network's estimated output. The smaller the RMSE value, the better the neural network estimation performance. To demonstrate efficiency of the designed APSO- RBFNN, two non-linear system modeling experiments are illustrated.

4.1 The Mackey-Glass Time-Series Estimation

As a classical benchmark task for non-linear system modeling, the Mackey-Glass time-series are generated as below [5] (Fig. 2):

$$x(t+1) = (1-a)x(t) + \frac{bx(t-\tau)}{1+x^{10}(t-\tau)} \tag{10}$$

where the parameters are set as a = 0.1, b = 0.2, τ = 17, and the initial condition is $x(0) = 0$. In this experiment, 1000 samples are set as the training set, the first 500 data are discarded to reduce the influence of initial condition. The samples with $t = 1001$ to 1500 are set as the testing set. The simulation results of the proposed APSO-RBFNN are shown in Figs. 3, 4 and 5. In Fig. 3, the comparisons between the estimated outputs and target are shown. In Fig. 4, the evolution process of the hidden neurons is illustrated. While in Fig. 5, the testing RMSE curve is displayed. From Figs. 3, 4 and 5, it can be concluded that the proposed APSO-RBFNN has obtained good estimation result.

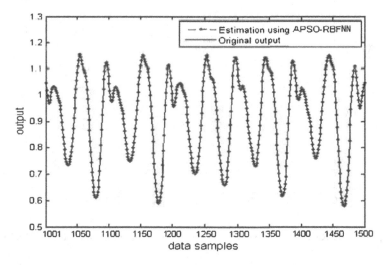

Fig. 2. The testing results of APSO-RBFNN for Mackey-Glass time series

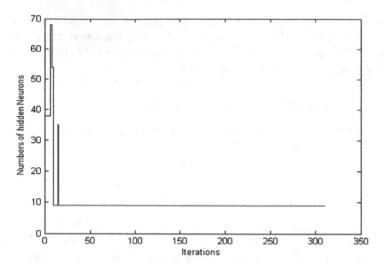

Fig. 3. The evolution of neurons versus iterations for APSO-RBFNN

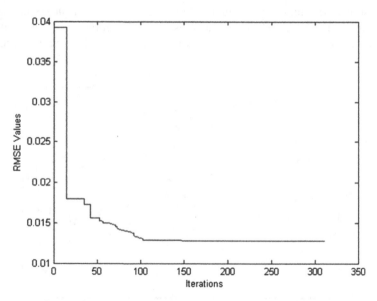

Fig. 4. The RMSE value evolving process versus iterations for APSO-RBFNN

In order to test the effectiveness of the proposed APSO-RBFNN, its performance is compared with other two methods, i.e., the PSO-RBFNN in which the network parameters are optimized by PSO, the DE-RBFNN whose network parameters are optimized by differential algorithm (DE). As shown in Table 1, the APSO-RBFNN owns the optimal compact network (10 hidden neurons), the lowest training RMSE of 0.0107 and the lowest testing RMSE of 0.0127.

Table 1. Performance of various methods for Mackey-Glass time-series estimation

Algorithm	RMSE (training)	RMSE (testing)	No. of hidden neurons
APSO-RBFNN	0.0107	0.0127	10
PSO-RBFNN	0.0256	0.0208	12
DE-RBFNN	0.0192	0.0189	13

4.2 Lorenz Time-Series Prediction

The Lorenz time-series prediction is another benchmark to evaluate the nonlinear system modeling performance for neural networks. Its differential equations are presented as below:

$$\begin{aligned} \frac{dx}{dt} &= \sigma(y - x), \\ \frac{dy}{dt} &= rx - y - xz, \\ \frac{dz}{dt} &= xy - bz \end{aligned} \tag{11}$$

where $\sigma = 10, b = 8/3, r = 28$, the initial conditions for each variable are set as $x(0) = y(0) = z(0) = 0.1$. A total of 5000 data samples are generated, the data samples with $t = 1$ to 3000 are set as the training set and the remaining part is set as the testing set. In the training set, the first 1000 samples are discarded.

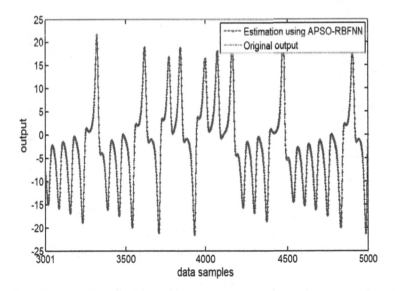

Fig. 5. The testing results of APSO-RBFNN for Lorenz time series prediction

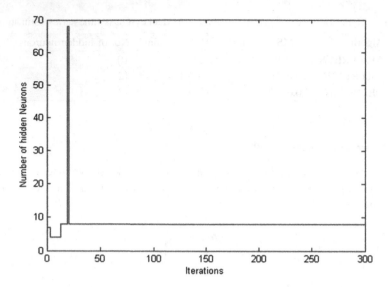

Fig. 6. The network size evolution process versus iterations for APSO-RBFNN

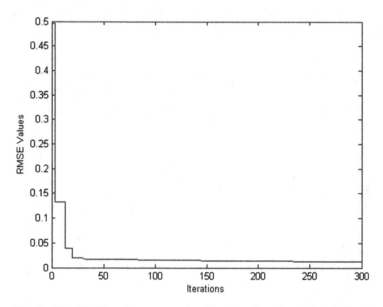

Fig. 7. The RMSE values versus algorithm iterations for APSO-RBFNN

The estimation results on the testing set of APSO-RBFNN are shown in Fig. 5, the evolving process of the network size is illustrated in Fig. 6, and the RMSE values versus algorithm iterations are given in Fig. 7. Furthermore, the performance of the proposed APSO-RBFNN is compared with PSO-RBFNN and DE-RBFNN. The comparison details are given in Table 2, it is easily found that the designed APSO-RBFNN has better training and testing RMSE as well as network size than the other two methods.

Table 2. Performance of various methods for Lorenz time series estimation

Algorithm	RMSE (training)	RMSE (testing)	No. of hidden neurons
APSO-RBFNN	0.0131	0.0126	8
PSO-RBFNN	0.2132	0.2677	9
DE-RBFNN	0.1900	0.2017	10

5 Conclusion

To solve the nonlinear system modeling problem, an accelerated particle swarm optimization (APSO) based radial basis function neural network (RBFNN) is proposed, which is denoted as APSO-RBFNN. In APSO-RBFNN, the center, width of hidden neurons, output weights and network size are optimized by using the APSO method. As shown in the simulation results, the proposed APSO-RBFNN outperforms other existing method in terms of network compactness and estimation accuracy.

Acknowledgement. This work was supported by the National Natural Science Foundation of China under Grants 61603012, 61533002 and 61890930-5, the Beijing Municipal Education Commission Foundation under Grant KM201710005025, the Major Science and Technology Program for Water Pollution Control and Treatment of China (2018ZX07111005), the National Key Research and Development Project under Grants 2018YFC1900800-5.

References

1. Jian, Y.E., Lindong, G.E., et al.: An application of improved RBF neural network in modulation recognition. Acta Automatica Sinica 33(6), 652–654 (2007)
2. Chen, S., Wolfgang, A., Harris, C.J., et al.: Symmetric RBF classifier for nonlinear detection in multiple antenna aided systems. IEEE Trans. Neural Netw. 19(5), 737 745 (2008)
3. Xu, Z., Zhang, R., Jing, W.: When does online BP training converge? IEEE Trans. Neural Netw. 20(10), 1529–1539 (2009)
4. Chen, B., Zhao, S., Zhu, P., Príncipe, J.C.: Quantized kernel recursive least squares algorithm. IEEE Trans. Neural Netw. Learn. Syst. 24(9), 1484–1491 (2013)
5. Han, H.G., Zhang, S., Qiao, J.F.: An adaptive growing and pruning algorithm for designing recurrent neural network. Neurocomputing 242, 51–62 (2017)
6. Qiao, J.F., Han, H.G.: Identification and modeling of nonlinear dynamical systems using a novel self-organizing RBF-based approach. Automatica 48(8), 1729–1734 (2012)
7. Guedria, N.B.: Improved accelerated PSO algorithm for mechanical engineering optimization problems. Appl. Soft Comput. 40(40), 455–467 (2016)

Non-negative Matrix Factorization with Community Kernel for Dynamic Community Detection

Saisai Liu and Zhengyou Xia[✉]

College of Computer Science and Technology,
Nanjing University of Aeronautics and Astronautics, Nanjing 210016, China
zhengyou_xia@nuaa.edu.cn

Abstract. Finding community structures from user data has become a hot topic in network analysis. However, there are rarely effective algorithms about the dynamic community detection. To recalculate the whole previous nodes and deal with excessive calculation is used to solve the problem of dynamically adding community nodes in the previous researches. In this paper, we propose an incremental community detection algorithm without recalculating the whole previous nodes using the incremental non-negative matrix factorization (INMF). In this algorithm, community kernel nodes with the largest node degree and adjacent triangle ratio is selected to calculate the data feature matrix, then the complexity of the calculations is largely simplified by reducing the dimension of the data feature matrix. We also propose a strategy to solve the problem of ensuring the feature space dimension and community number of NMF. We discuss our method with several previous ones on real data, and the results show that our method is effective and accurate in find potential communities.

Keywords: Community detection · Community kernel · Data mining · INMF · NMF

1 Introduction

Many systems take the form of networks. A complex network is composed of a large number of nodes and intricate relationships between them [1, 2]. Most networks seem to share a number of distinctive statistical properties, such as the small world effect, network transitivity, community structure, and so on. A community is a subset of these nodes. The connections are frequent in the same community and sparse between different communities [1, 3–5].

Non-negative matrix factorization (NMF) reduces the matrix dimension by factorizing a Non-negative data feature matrix into two matrices [6]. All the factor matrices are restricted to be Non-negative. The factorization can also make the characteristics of the data more obvious, which is conducive to extract data features. There are some application problems of NMF. One is the high computational complexity [6]. Another problem is the difficulty of determining the feature space dimension.

© ICST Institute for Computer Sciences, Social Informatics and Telecommunications Engineering 2019
Published by Springer Nature Switzerland AG 2019. All Rights Reserved
X. B. Zhai et al. (Eds.): MLICOM 2019, LNICST 294, pp. 778–792, 2019.
https://doi.org/10.1007/978-3-030-32388-2_64

In this paper, we proposed a incremental Non-negative matrix factorization algorithm with community kernel (CK-INMF) for dynamic community detection. The method can effectively solve above problems by using the community kernels to reduce the dimension of the data feature matrix and avoid the discussion of dimensions by clustering.

Most of the existing community detection algorithms are about static community. During the execution process of those algorithms, new nodes cannot be dynamically added. Dynamic community detection requires the ability to dynamically add some nodes. In most algorithms, adding new nodes requires to abandon the existing result of previous nodes and recalculate from the very beginning of the algorithm. It increases the computational cost.

CK-INMF (our method) expanses the current nodes feature matrix dimension and calculate the result base on the previous factorization. It offered an effective dynamic community strategy.

The remainder of the paper is organized as follows. Section 2 introduces the related work. We explain our CK-INMF model in Sect. 3. Then simulation experiments are carried out in Sect. 4. Finally, a concise conclusion is given in Sect. 5.

2 Related Work

Community detection has become a research hot spot in recent years, and more scholars have devoted to the research of community detection algorithm. In 2003, Newman first proposed the concept of modularity Q in community detection and achieved the effect of community division by optimizing the value of Q [7]. At present, common community detection algorithms can be divided into some categories, including graph-based segmentation, objective function optimization, clustering heuristic method, and so on [8–11]. The usual community detection studying belongs to the field of unsupervised learning. In recent years, scholars have paid attention to apply the Non-negative matrix factorization (NMF) to the community detection for its successful application in unsupervised learning.

NMF is a matrix decomposition strategy, first proposed by Paatero and Tapper [12]. NMF is an efficient clustering tool for small data sets. The NMFIB (Non-negative matrix factorization with iterative bipartition) proposed by He can obtain more statistically significant GO (geneontology) in the protein interaction network [12]. The BNMF (Bayesian Non-negative matrix factorization) model proposed by Rsorakis can obtain a more accurate community structure comparing with traditional hierarchical and spectral clustering methods [13].

Our algorithm CK-INMF is an improvement of algorithms based on NMF. Current NMF community detection algorithms usually adopt method of factorize a Non-negative data feature matrix $V = (v_1, v_2, ..., v_n)$ into the product of the feature space basis matrix W, the encoding matrix H, and $V_{mn} \approx W_{ms}H_{sn}$ shown in Fig. 1.

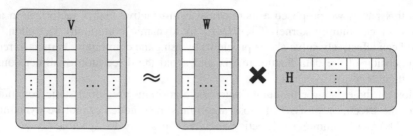

Fig. 1. NMF factorization formula V ≈ WH

Each column of the data feature matrix V represents a different node, and each column in V corresponds to one specific column of the encoding matrix H. s represents the new feature space dimension and the number of communities.

The goal of the NMF is to minimize the reconstruction error between the matrix V and WH. The objective function F is given by (1).

$$F(W, H) = \frac{1}{2}\|V - WH\|^2 = \frac{1}{2}\sum_{i=1}^{m}\sum_{j=1}^{n}(V_{ij} - (WH)_{ij})^2 \tag{1}$$

To optimize the problem of (1), iterative multiplicative (2), (3) can be used to update W and H during calculation.

$$W_{i\mu} \leftarrow W_{i\mu}\frac{(VH^T)_{i\mu}}{(WHH^T)_{i\mu}} \tag{2}$$

$$H_{\mu j} \leftarrow H_{\mu j}\frac{(W^T V)_{\mu j}}{(W^T WH)_{\mu j}} \tag{3}$$

$$\text{s.t. } i = 1, \ldots, m; j = 1, \ldots, n; \mu = 1, \ldots, s$$

According to the encoding matrix H, we can get the detected communities. h_{ij} reflects the extent of i_{th} node belonging to the j_{th} community. Let $h_{ik} = \max\{h_{i1}, h_{i2}, \ldots, h_{is}\}$. If the i_{th} node is divided into the only k_{th} community, the non-overlapping communities can be got; if the i_{th} node is divided into several communities, overlapping communities can be got.

There are some problems of current NMF community detection algorithms, as following:

(1) Most algorithms adopts the adjacency matrix as the data feature matrix V, and the high dimensional V increase the computational complexity.
(2) The new feature space dimension s has a great impact on the performance of community detection. But it is difficult to decide the precise value of s.
(3) When apply NMF to the dynamic community, it should recalculate the whole matrices. The cost is huge.

To deal with these problems, we propose the CK-NMF algorithm.

3 Our Algorithm CK-INMF: Community Detection Algorithm Model Based on INMF and Community Kernel

To dynamically add nodes, reduce the computational complexity and solve the problem of determining the feature space dimension during factorization, we suppose the CK-INMF algorithm. In CK-INMF, we use the INMF expanded NMF to detect the dynamical community. In this section, we would give the detail description of our CK-INMF algorithm. INMF is often used to the online blind source separation [9] and image and video processing [14]. Here we apply INMF to achieve the dynamic community detection. CK-INMF would adopt community kernel nodes to reduce the dimension of data feature matrix V. We cluster the preliminary detected communities to get the final detection, solving the problem of deciding the value of parameter s.

3.1 Detecting the Community Kernel Nodes and Reducing the Dimension of Feature Matrix

In CK-NMF algorithm, the initial Matrix Vmn is assigned based on the community kernel. Therefore, the first step of our algorithm is to find the community kernel. The community kernel is a set of nodes with greater influence than the other nodes in a network [15]. We believe that nodes with big degree and structure shown in Fig. 2 are more likely to become community kernel nodes. Figure 2(a) is an triangle structure. Node v1 own more influence than others and is one of the community kernel nodes in Fig. 2(b). So we measure the influence of one node by the degree of it and the ratio of the triangles that can be formed with its adjacent nodes.

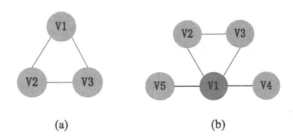

(a)   (b)

Fig. 2. Triangle structure in networks

The community kernel set includes m most influential nodes. CK-INMF adopts the matrix V_{mn} instead of V_{nn} and m $\ll$ n. So the computation complexity of the whole algorithm is greatly reduced. We select m nodes with the highest kernel weights. The weight formulation is (4):

$$w_i = r\left(\frac{den(i)}{maxDen}\right) + (1-r)\left(\frac{2triangle(i)}{den(i)(den(i)-1)}\right) \tag{4}$$

$$\text{s.t. } den(i) = \sum_j A_{ij} \quad maxDen = max\{den(1), den(2), \ldots, den(n)\}$$

$$triangle(i) = \sum_{j,h} a_{ij}\, a_{ih}\, a_{jh}$$

The detail description of community kernel detection is shown below.

---

1. **Algorithm1 Community kernel detection algorithm**

---

2. **Input**: Graph G=(V,E), size of kernel m

3. **Output**: A set of community kernel $K = (k_2, k_1, ..., k_m)$

4. $K \leftarrow \phi$

5. calculate the kernel weight of all nodes by (4)

6: all nodes are ordered in a descending influence sequence and stored in queue D

7: store the selected nodes during every cycle in queue stepK

8: /* Find m community kernel nodes */

9: **While** |K|<m **do**

10:                     **While** (|K|+|stepK|)<m **do**
            $stepK \leftarrow \phi$
11:

12:     /*store the selected nodes during this cycle in stepK*/

13:     obtain the front v from queue (D-K-stepK);

14:     **if** $\neg \exists edge(v, k_i), \forall k_i \in stepK$ **then**

15:         assign v as the kernel node: $stepK \leftarrow \{v\}$

16:     K=K+stepK

17:return community kernels $K = (k_1, k_2, ..., k_m)$

In CK-INMF, we adopt adjacency matrix A_{nn} of the network as V, but we would use the community kernel to reduce the dimension of $A = \{a_1^T, a_2^T, ..., a_n^T\}$. We delete the redundant rows $a_r = \{r \notin K, K = \{k_1, k_2, ..., k_m\}$ from A, and get matrix V, as shown in Fig. 3.

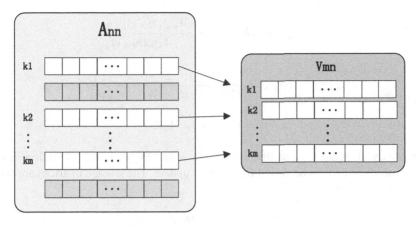

Fig. 3. Calculate matrix V according to adjacent matrix A

3.2   Dynamically Adding New Nodes

In some cases, we need to add some new nodes to the existing network. The goal of INMF equations are to update the matrices W and H while new nodes are added to the existing network. There is no need to recalculate the previous nodes by INMF. During this process, V and H will be added some new columns and W would be updated.

Let W_k and H_k represent the decomposition matrices obtained from the initial k nodes ($k \geq 2 m$), then the objective function of Non-negative matrix factorization can be expressed as (5).

$$F_k = \|V - WH\|^2 = \sum_{i=1}^{m} \sum_{j=1}^{k} (V_{ij} - (W_k H_k)_{ij})^2 \tag{5}$$

When the V_{k+1} nodes is added, both W and H are changed and the reconstructed objective function can be expressed as (6).

$$
\begin{aligned}
F_{k+1} &= \|V' - W_{k+1}H_{k+1}\|^2 = \sum_{i=1}^{m} \sum_{j=1}^{k+1} (V_{ij} - (W_{k+1}H_{k+1})_{ij})^2 \\
&= \sum_{i=1}^{m} \sum_{j=1}^{k} (V_{ij} - (W_{k+1}H_{k+1})_{ij})^2 + \sum_{i=1}^{m} ((v_{k+1})_i - (W_{k+1}H_{k+1})_i)^2 \\
&\cong F_k + f_{k+1}
\end{aligned}
\tag{6}
$$

From above, we can find that when the sample increases, the new objective function is the sum of the objective function F_k and increment f_{k+1}. In this way, the objective function F can be updated based on newly added sample without recalculating.

With the INMF in incremental learning, the variables of the objective function are the column and the base matrix. Using the gradient descent method, the iteration rules are as (7), (8).

$$(h_{k+1})_\mu \leftarrow (h_{k+1})_\mu \frac{(W_{k+1}^T v_{k+1})_\mu}{(W_{k+1}^T W_{k+1} h_{k+1})_\mu} \tag{7}$$

$$(W_{k+1})_{i\mu} \leftarrow (W_{k+1})_{i\mu} \frac{(V_{k+1} H_{k+1}^T + v_{k+1} h_{k+1}^T)_{i\mu}}{(W_{k+1} H_k H_k^T + W_{k+1} h_{k+1} h_{k+1}^T)_{i\mu}} \tag{8}$$

$$s.t.\ \mu = 1,\ldots,n;\ i = 1,\ldots,s$$

Besides saving the current iterative values h and W after every iteration, history information also needs to be stored for the next update. The storage matrices are shown in (9), (10).

$$A = V_{k+1} H_{k+1}^T = V_k H_k^T + v_{k+1} h_{k+1}^T \tag{9}$$

$$B = H_{k+1} H_{k+1}^T = H_k H_k^T + h_{k+1} h_{k+1}^T \tag{10}$$

From the iterative equations, we can infer that the storage matrices could reduce the amount of calculation during every iteration.

The process of adding new nodes is shown in Fig. 4.

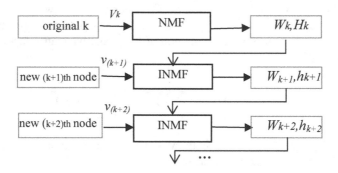

Fig. 4. The process of CK-INMF adding new nodes

3.3   Community Detecting Based on Encoding Matrix H

The factorization result is $V_{mn} \approx W_{ms} H_{sn}$. In current NMF non-overlapping community detection, let $h_{ik} = \max\{h_{i1}, h_{i2}, \ldots, h_{is}\}$ and the i_{th} node is mapped to the only k_{th} community. The s represent the community number, but sometimes we do not know the community number. So we need to search the value by a lot of test. But it is hard to decide the precise value of the community number. In CK-INMF, we propose a strategy to solve it by select a integer as s, which is larger than the ideal community number, then cluster the s communities into smaller amount communities according to modularity Q. During the clustering process, we calculate the ΔQ of each pair of communities. The we cluster the two communities which produce the biggest ΔQ, and calculate the ΔQ of new community with others and continue to compare ΔQ. Because of $s \ll n$, the strategy is effective. Figure 5 gives the description of the process of community detecting.

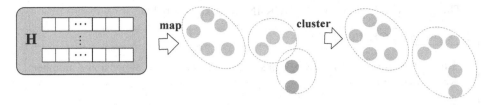

Fig. 5. Detecting communities based on encoding matrix H

3.4 CK-INMF Algorithm Pseudo-code Description

Figure 6 shows the CK-INMF algorithm framework.

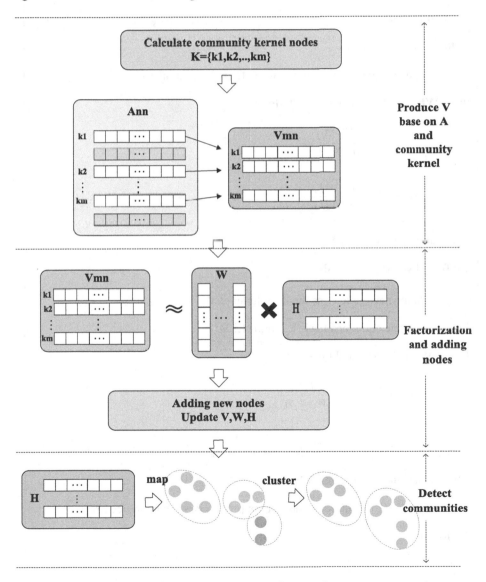

Fig. 6. The CK-INMF framework

The pseudo-code description of CK-INMF is shown below.

---

1. Algorithm2 CK-INMF

---

2. **Input**: Graph G=(V,E), new nodes set V_{new}, feature space dimension s, number of kernel nodes m

3. **Output**: A set of community $C=(c_1,c_2,...,c_r)$

4. $K \leftarrow \phi \quad C \leftarrow \phi \quad F=1$

5: calculate the community kernel $K=(k_1,k_2,...,k_m)$ based on algorithm1

6: calculate the feature matrix V_{mn}

7: **for** all $v_i \in V$ (i>1) **do**

8:     /* update equations iteratively for i=1,..,m;j=1,...,n,u=1,...,s */

9:     **While** F>10^{-3} and times<200 **do**

10:     $W_{i\mu} \leftarrow W_{i\mu} \dfrac{(VH^T)_{i\mu}}{(WHH^T)_{i\mu}}$

11:     $H_{\mu j} \leftarrow H_{\mu j} \dfrac{(W^T V)_{\mu j}}{(W^T WH)_{\mu j}}$

12: /* adding new nodes */

13: **for** all $v_k \in V_{new}$ (k>1) **do**

14:     add the new node v_k as the k_{th} column of V

15:     /* update equations for i=1,...,m;u=1,...,s*/

16:     **While** f_k>10^{-4} and times<200 **do**

17:     $(h_k)_{\mu} \leftarrow (h_k)_{\mu} \dfrac{(W_k^T v_k)_{\mu}}{(W_k^T W_k h_k)_{\mu}}$

18:     $(W_{k+1})_{i\mu} \leftarrow (W_{k+1})_{i\mu} \dfrac{(V_k H_k^T + v_{k+1} h_{k+1}^T)_{i\mu}}{(W_{k+1} H_k H_k^T + W_{k+1} h_{k+1} h_{k+1}^T)_{i\mu}}$

19:     calculate the matrices A,B

20: /*According to H, divide nodes into m preliminary communities P*/

21: **for** all $v_k \in V$ **do**

22:    add v_k to P_{index}, $P_{index}(index = rowNumberOf \max\{H_{1k}, H_{2k}, \cdots, H_{sk}\})$

23:/* cluster the m communities P according to modularity Q*/

24: **for** all $i,j \in n$ **do**

25:    **if** $q=Q(P_i)+Q(Pj)-Q(P_i+P_j)>0$ **do**

26:        add(i,j,q) into Qqueue

27: **While** Qqueue!=null **do**

28:    sort Qqueue from most to least based on q

29:    delete the first Qqueue to(i,j,q)

30:    delete all element of Qqueue including i and j

31:    merge P_i and P_j to P_k and calculate q with existing communities

32:    add new q into Qqueue

33: return the existing communities $C=(c_1,c_2,\cdots,c_r)$

4   Experimental Result and Analysis

In order to verify the feasibility of our proposed algorithm, we analyze the parameters of r and m by real-world networks dataset. We also compare CK-INMF with other related algorithms by real-world networks dataset. CK-INMF is implemented in python (Python 2.7) language, and the program runs as window 10 operating system, 2.00 GHZ, 8 GB memory.

4.1   Experiment Data and Evaluation Standard

In order to analysis the performances of CK-INMF, three real networks are selected for experiment. The real networks include the classic Zachary's Karate Club Network [16], the dolphin social network [17] and the college football network [18]. The Zachary's Karate Club Network owns a number of 34 nodes and 78 edges. The dolphin social network is a community of 62 nodes and 159 edges. The college football network consists of 115 nodes and 616 edges.

Here we adopt modularity (Q) and normalized mutual information(NMI) as evaluation standards to measure the effectiveness of CK-INMF partitioning result. The larger the values are, the better the results is.

Suppose graph G = (V, E) with N nodes, edges set E, community detection C = [c_1, c_2, .., c_r]:

The modularity Q is defined as follows:

$$Q = \frac{1}{2|E|} \sum_{ij} \left(\left(A_{ij} - \frac{k_i k_j}{2|E|} \right) \times \delta(c(i), c(j)) \right)$$

$$s.t. \, k_i = \sum_j A_{ij} \, \delta(c(i), c(j)) = \begin{cases} 0, & c(i)! = c(j) \\ 1, & c(i) = c(j) \end{cases}$$

Given a standard community detection result S = [s_1, s_2, ..., s_r]
The NMI is defined as follows:

$$MI(X, Y) = \sum_{i=1}^{|S|} \sum_{j=1}^{|C|} P(i,j) \log \left(\frac{P(i,j)}{P(i)P'(j)} \right)$$

$$s.t. \, P(i,j) = \frac{|S_i \cap C_j)}{N}; P(i) = \frac{|S_i|}{N}; P'(j) = \frac{|C_j|}{N}$$

$$NMI(S, C) = \frac{2MI(S, C)}{H(S) + H(C)}$$

$$s.t. \, H(S) = -\sum_{i=1}^{|S|} P(i) \log(P(i)); H(C) = -\sum_{j=1}^{|C|} P'(j) \log(P'(j));$$

4.2   Parameter Analysis of CK-INMF

The performances of CK-INMF are based on the selection of r. The results are shown in Fig. 7. The performance of the experiences change by the value of r. We can adjust the value of based on Q. We usually take the value of r which can maximize the value of Q.

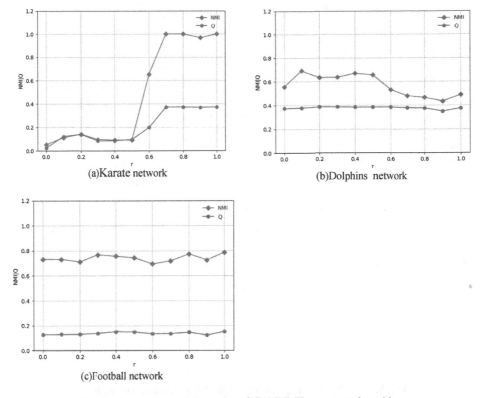

(a)Karate network

(b)Dolphins network

(c)Football network

Fig. 7. The NMI and Q results of CK-INMF on networks with r

The performances of CK-INMF are based on the selection of m. The obtained results are shown in Fig. 8. It tells us that we can select m between 0.3–0.5 of the ratio of m to e, to balance the performance and cost.

4.3   Comparison of CK-INMF with Other Related Algorithms

We compared CK-INMF with NMF_{KL} [3], BNMF [19], $BNMTF_{LSE}$ [20], $sBNMTF_{LSE}$ [20], SNMF [21]. The results are shown in Table 1. From it we can conclude that our algorithm is great predominant than others on Karate network, and need to improve on Dolphins and Football networks.

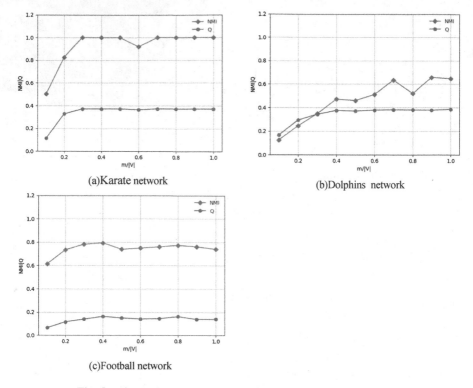

(a)Karate network

(b)Dolphins network

(c)Football network

Fig. 8. The NMI and Q results of CK-INMF on networks with m

Table 1. NMI of the community detection algorithms on real networks

Algorithm	Karate	Dolphins	Football
CK-INMF	0.996	0.634	0.794
NMF_{KL}	0.437	0.775	0.891
BNMF	0.603	0.831	0.878
$BNMTF_{LSE}$	0.553	0.590	0.891
$sBNMTF_{LSE}$	0.545	0.045	0.462
SNMF	0.983	0.872	0.902

5   Conclusion

We propose an CK-INMF incremental community detection algorithm. It gives a dynamic community detection model of achieving adding nodes without recalculating the whole existing nodes, which could save a lot of time coat. The algorithm firstly selects the m community kernel nodes with the largest node degree and adjacent triangle ratio, then calculates the feature matrix according to the m nodes. Comparing with the other NMF algorithms which directly use the complete adjacency matrix, the calculation complexity is largely simplified by reducing the dimension of the matrix.

By clustering the factorization encoding matrix, the problem of judging the dimension of feature space and the community number is solved. The performance of our algorithm on several real networks shows it is effective and useful. However, the parameter combination selected cannot play the best effect, and it is remained to future work to come up with a better way to balance the combination performance of parameters.

Acknowledgment. This paper is supported by National Natural Science Foundation of China (71871109).

References

1. Bu, Z., Zhang, C., Xia, Z., Wang, J.: A fast parallel modularity optimization algorithm (FPMQA) for community detection in online social network. Knowl.-Based Syst. **50**(Complete), 246–259 (2013)
2. Lancichinetti, A., Fortunato, S., Radicchi, F.: Benchmark graphs for testing community detection algorithms. Phys. Rev. E Stat. Nonlin. Soft Matter Phys. **78**(4 Pt 2), 046110 (2008)
3. Lee, D.D., Seung, H.S.: Learning the parts of objects by non-negative matrix factorization. Nature **401**(6755), 788–791 (1999)
4. Li, H.J., Bu, Z., Li, A., Liu, Z., Yong, S.: Fast and accurate mining the community structure: integrating center locating and membership optimization. IEEE Trans. Knowl. Data Eng. **28**(9), 2349–2362 (2016)
5. Zhan, B., Wu, Z., Jie, C., Jiang, Y.: Local community mining on distributed and dynamic networks from a multiagent perspective. IEEE Trans. Cybern. **46**(4), 986–999 (2017)
6. Zhan, B., Xia, Z., Wang, J., Zhang, C.: A last updating evolution model for online social networks. Phys. A Stat. Mech. Appl. **392**(9), 2240–2247 (2013)
7. Newman, M.E.: Fast algorithm for detecting community structure in networks. Phys. Rev. E Stat. Nonlin. Soft Matter Phys. **69**(6 Pt 2), 066133 (2004)
8. Bucak, S.S., Gunsel, B.: Incremental subspace learning via non-negative matrix factorization. Pattern Recognit. **42**(5), 788–797 (2009)
9. Guoxu, Z., Zuyuan, Y., Shengli, X., Jun-Mei, Y.: Online blind source separation using incremental nonnegative matrix factorization with volume constraint. IEEE Trans. Neural Netw. **22**(4), 550–560 (2011)
10. Adamic, L.A.: The political blogosphere and the 2004 u.s. election: Divided they blog. In: International Workshop on Link Discovery (2005)
11. Andrea, L., Santo, F., Filippo, R.: Benchmark graphs for testing community detection algorithms. Phys. Rev. E: Stat., Nonlin. Soft Matter Phys. **78**(4 Pt 2), 046110 (2008)
12. Paatero, P., Tapper, U.: Positive matrix factorization: a non-negative factor model with optimal utilization of error estimates of data values. Environmetrics **5**(2), 111–126 (2010)
13. Dongxiao, H., Di, J., Carlos, B., Dayou, L.: Link community detection using generative model and nonnegative matrix factorization. PLoS ONE **9**(1), e86899 (2014)
14. Bucak, S.S., Gunsel, B.: Incremental clustering via nonnegative matrix factorization. In: International Conference on Pattern Recognition (2012)
15. Zhen, L., Zheng, X., Nan, X., Chen, D.: CK-LPA: efficient community detection algorithm based on label propagation with community kernel. Phys. A Stat. Mech. Appl. **416**(C), 386–399 (2014)
16. Wayne, Zachary: An information flow model for conflict and fission in small groups. J. Anthropol. Res. **33**(4), 452–473 (1977)

17. Lusseau, D., Schneider, K., Boisseau, O.J., Haase, P., Slooten, E., Dawson, S.M.: The bottlenose dolphin community of doubtful sound features a large proportion of long-lasting associations. Behav. Ecol. Sociobiol. **54**(4), 396–405 (2003)
18. Girvan, M., Newman, M.E.J.: Community structure in social and biological networks. Proc. Natl. Acad. Sci. U.S.A. **99**, 7256–7821 (2002)
19. Ioannis, P., Stephen, R., Mark, E., Ben, S.: Overlapping community detection using bayesian non-negative matrix factorization. Phys. Rev. E Stat. Nonlin. Soft Matter Phys. **83**(2), 066114 (2011)
20. Yu, Z., Yeung, D.Y.: Overlapping community detection via bounded nonnegative matrix tri-factorization. In: ACM SIGKDD International Conference on Knowledge Discovery & Data Mining (2012)
21. Fei, W., Ding, C.: Community discovery using nonnegative matrix factorization. Data Min. Knowl. Discovery **22**(3), 493–521 (2011)

Author Index

Printed in the United States
By Bookmasters